PHOTOGRAPHIC PRINTING

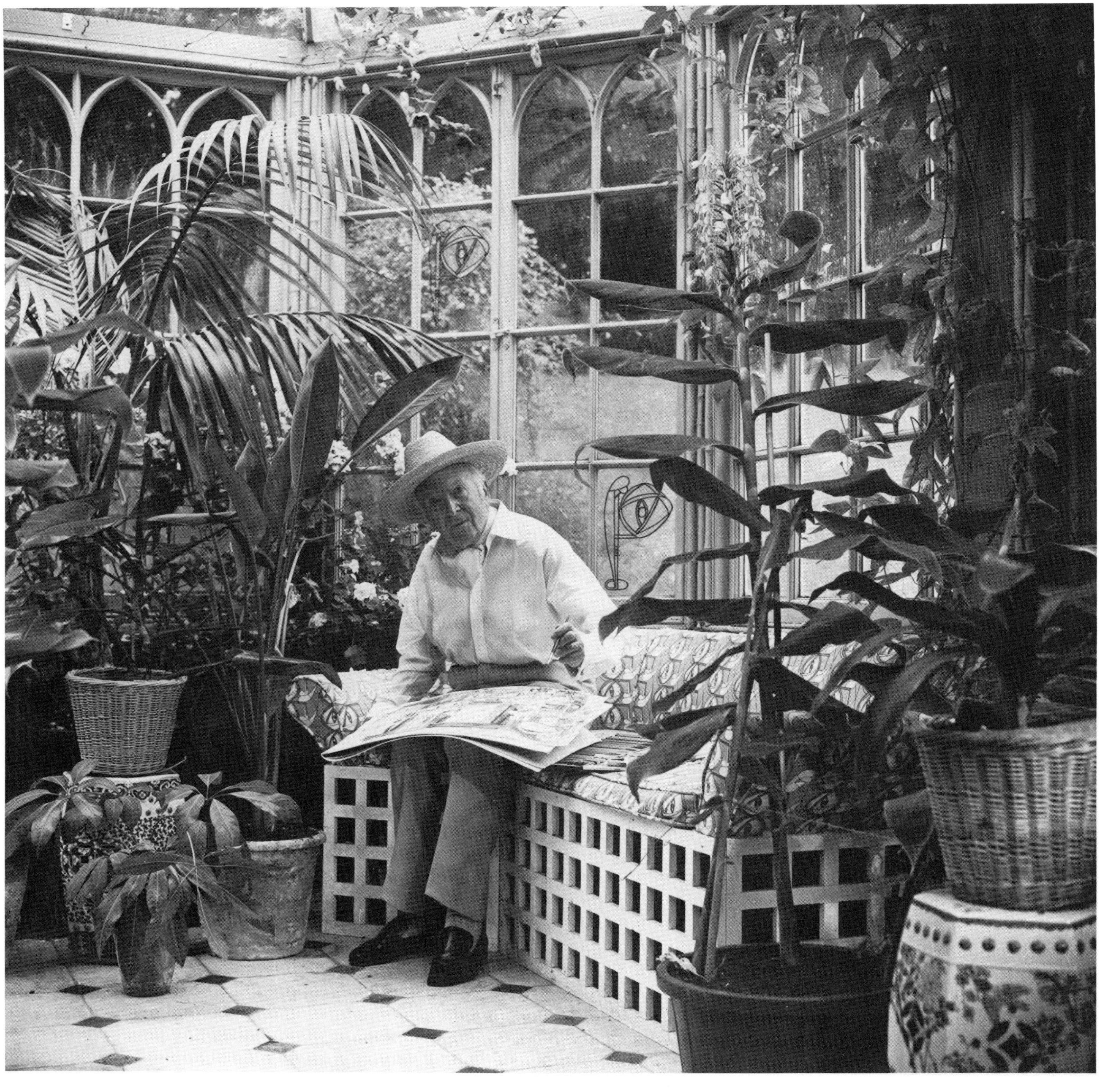

Cecil Beaton Lee Higham. One of the last pictures of Cecil Beaton.

PHOTOGRAPHIC PRINTING

GENE NOCON

Virgin

This edition first published in 1993 by Virgin Books,
an imprint of Virgin Publishing Ltd,
338 Ladbroke Grove, London W10 5AH
First published in Great Britain in 1987 by Planet Books

A catalogue record for this title is available from the
British Library.
ISBN 0-86369-653-8
Concept by John Stidolph
Editor: Sue Bilton
Assistant: Charles Jacoby
Design by Slapstick Design
Cover design by Slatter-Anderson
Typeset by BWS Graphics
Printed and bound in Great Britain by BPCC Hazells Ltd

Contents

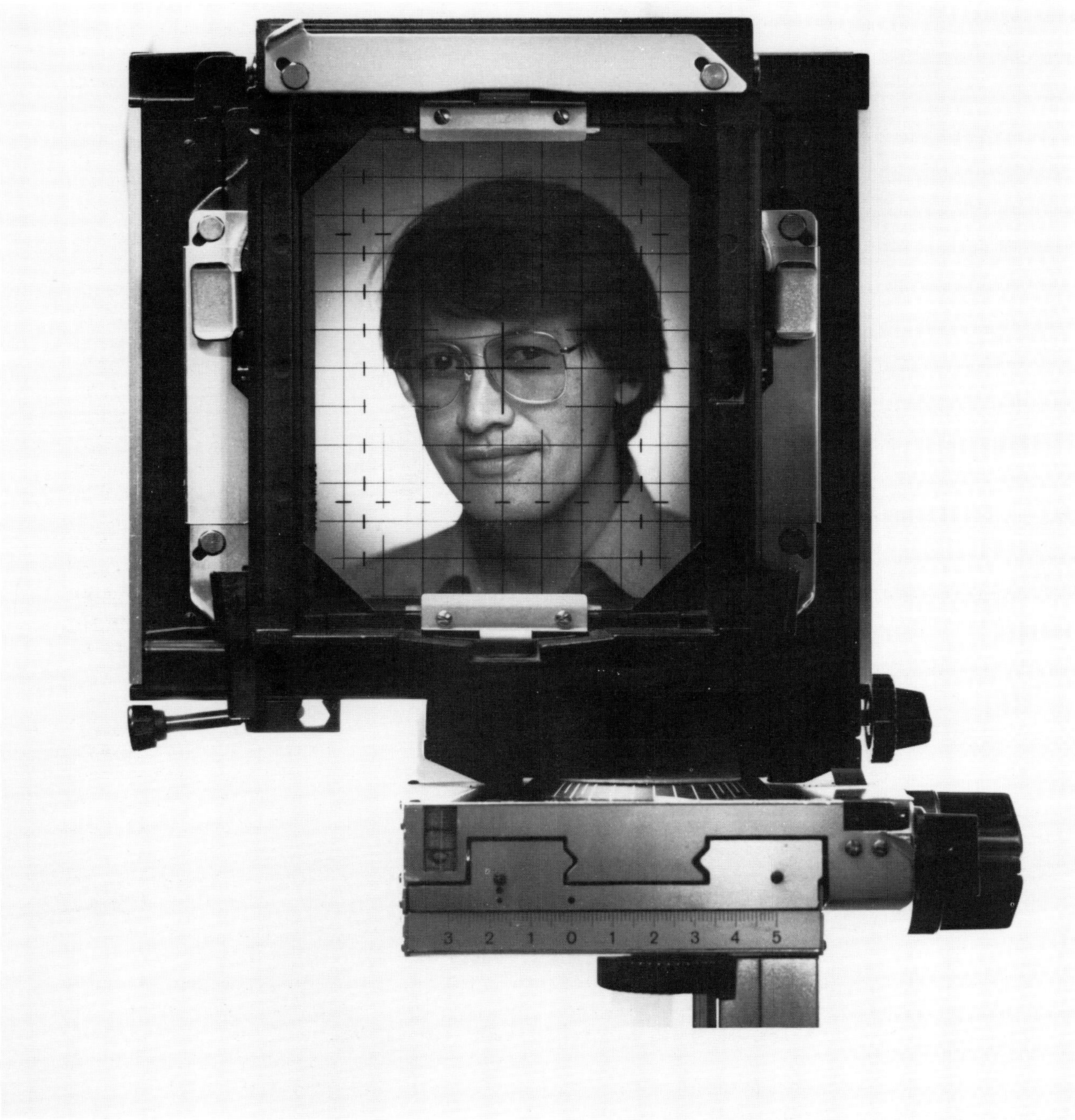

Gene Nocon by Nick Read.

Introduction

I have spent the better part of my working life as a professional photographic printer. During this time I have worked for hundreds of professional photographers, printing tens of thousands of photographs. The skills I have learned as a printer from this experience are the subject of this book.

I have had to refer to previously published material just to see what thoughts and ideas other people have had on printing. In this book, however, I present only my own methods and techniques. I have tried to explain the reasons for my methods to give you an understanding of the photographic principles involved. These explanations are based on what I know about the nature of photography, experimentation, and experience. I hope that an understanding of these principles will invite further experimentation on your part and allow you to go beyond the advice given here.

This book is about making a black-and-white print of exhibition quality. Apart from a short discussion on the technique of selective toning I have not entered into the methods one could employ to 'paint' one's prints. Hand-colouring, multiple-image printing, solarization, posterization, line or graphic printing – these are subjects of which I have no experience. Nor have I ever needed them in my professional capacity.

One book to which I have had to refer again and again is *Roget's Thesaurus*. It has become my inspiration for writing, just as I hope this book will become yours for printing. Writing is as difficult for me as printing may be for you.

In the Introduction to the Thesaurus is this statement by Peter Mark Roget: 'Communication of our thoughts ... constitutes a peculiar art, which, like other arts, cannot be acquired in any perfection but by long and continued practice'.

The techniques of photographic printing do not come naturally. It is only through practice that you will gain any degree of skill. You must, however, apply method and not simply trial and error.

Up till now, however, trial and error has been, for some reason, the nature of black-and-white photographic printing. Whereas those who work in the colour medium have been prepared to adapt to take account of the new technology, black-and-white printers have for the most part stuck rigidly to their time-honoured methods. With so much sophisticated equipment used for taking pictures it is incredible that the end product, the black-and-white print, should be produced in such a haphazard manner.

It has seemed to have no recognized method. Those of you with some experience in the darkroom will be aware of this when you try and produce a print. For the most part it is merely a matter of exposing the photosensitive paper and developing the print. If the result is too light, or too dark, another print is attempted by simply adjusting the exposure. How much more or less exposure is left to trial and error.

Now, however, there is a system for black-and-white printing, introduced in this book as the F/Stop Method of Printing. It is an easy and simple method of printing that requires nothing more than discipline to use. It can be used in any darkroom, no matter how modest or elaborate the equipment.

Again with reference to Roget's Introduction: 'It is to those who are thus painfully groping their way and struggling with the difficulties of composition, that this Work professes to hold out a helping hand'. Substitute the word printing for composition: this is the purpose of this book.

□

It was only ten years ago that circumstances made it possible for me to set up as a professional photographic printer. In that relatively short time I have been fortunate to print for a number of very experienced and knowledgeable photographers. Their patient and constructive criticism has been my education. It has been my honour to be associated with them and including their photographs in this book is my way of thanking them for the experience.

Thanks as well to my 'production crew': John Stidolph who instigated this book, Summer who loaned me her Walkman, Olivia for not using my word processor too often to type her name, and Liz for her encouragement and support.

Gene Nocon

CHAPTER ONE

CHAPTER ONE
The Darkroom

I remember my first darkroom. It was the bathroom in an apartment I shared with friends. The equipment and chemicals could only be set up very late at night, then had to be put away after each printing session. The late night activity minimized the inconvenience caused by my monopoly of the bathroom. But it was actually the best time to do any printing because the windows did not have to be blacked out and, in fact, could remain open for ventilation.

Photography was only a hobby then. I was a student and had use of the school darkroom during classes. The bathroom/darkroom was just for fun. I had neither the money nor the need to fit out the darkroom with other than the most basic of items.

The most essential piece of equipment was the enlarger. I bought it from another student who had no need of it. It came with an enlarging lens which I replaced later with a more respectable piece of glass. The light spread of the enlarger was a bit uneven, but it did not matter. With my pictures I could not tell whether this was a problem. I only wanted the convenience of my own darkroom, and the enlarger did not cost that much anyway.

A safelight fixture, a printing easel and a set of developing trays were the only other pieces that had to be purchased. The 'photographic' label on a product invariably added a premium to the price. So I made do with items like empty plastic bleach bottles to store my chemical solutions instead of 'photographic' storage containers.

I did not think there was much need for a timer. It all seemed haphazard anyway, so I simply counted elephants, 'elephant-1, elephant-2, etc.' and used a switch on the enlarger to turn the lamp on and off for making my exposures.

The bathroom counter became my bench for the enlarger. I cut a sheet of plywood to fit over the bathtub and then covered it with plastic to use as the worktop for the developing trays. A large plastic washbowl in the bath with a piece of rubber hose attached to the water tap served as my print-washer. The safelight replaced the light fixture on the bathroom ceiling.

I tried using a telephone book as a print-blotter for the fibre-based prints (RC papers were not available then) but the ink made marks on my prints. I even tried to glaze prints by pressing wet prints against the bathroom mirror. The 'mirror glazing' was only slightly successful. More often than not it resulted in my having to scrape photographic emulsion off the mirror surface when the print eventually dried.

I eventually updated all this equipment as my interest and expertise grew. This description of my early days is only to illustrate the point that a darkroom need not be elaborate nor equipped with expensive equipment to enable you to practise and enjoy printing photographs.

Since then I have gained a certain amount of experience working as a professional photographic printer and have had the opportunity to use and assess a variety of darkroom equipment. My own ideas and thoughts about darkrooms and darkroom equipment and the important features that should be considered in each are outlined in this opening chapter.

THE ENLARGER

This is the major piece of equipment. An even distribution of light is important – there should be no obvious 'hot-spot' of light. But even the most sophisticated enlargers will have light 'fall-off' at the corners. This must be expected. Light from the enlarger lens to the corner areas has a greater distance to travel than to the centre of the format area. The intensity of light will therefore appear to fall off. Using a 50mm enlarger lens to project a full 35mm format the corners have a light fall-off of ¼ f/stop.

Do not worry about the fall-off. The camera suffers the same problem. With the camera lens focused on infinity the light fall-off is ¼ f/stop in the corners of the negative. When this negative is projected through the enlarger the light loss in the corners of the negative is balanced by the light loss of the enlarger to produce an even distribution of light.

Make sure that the negative carrier is properly aligned and absolutely parallel to the baseboard and easel. Otherwise you will find it very difficult to keep the entire print area focused without having

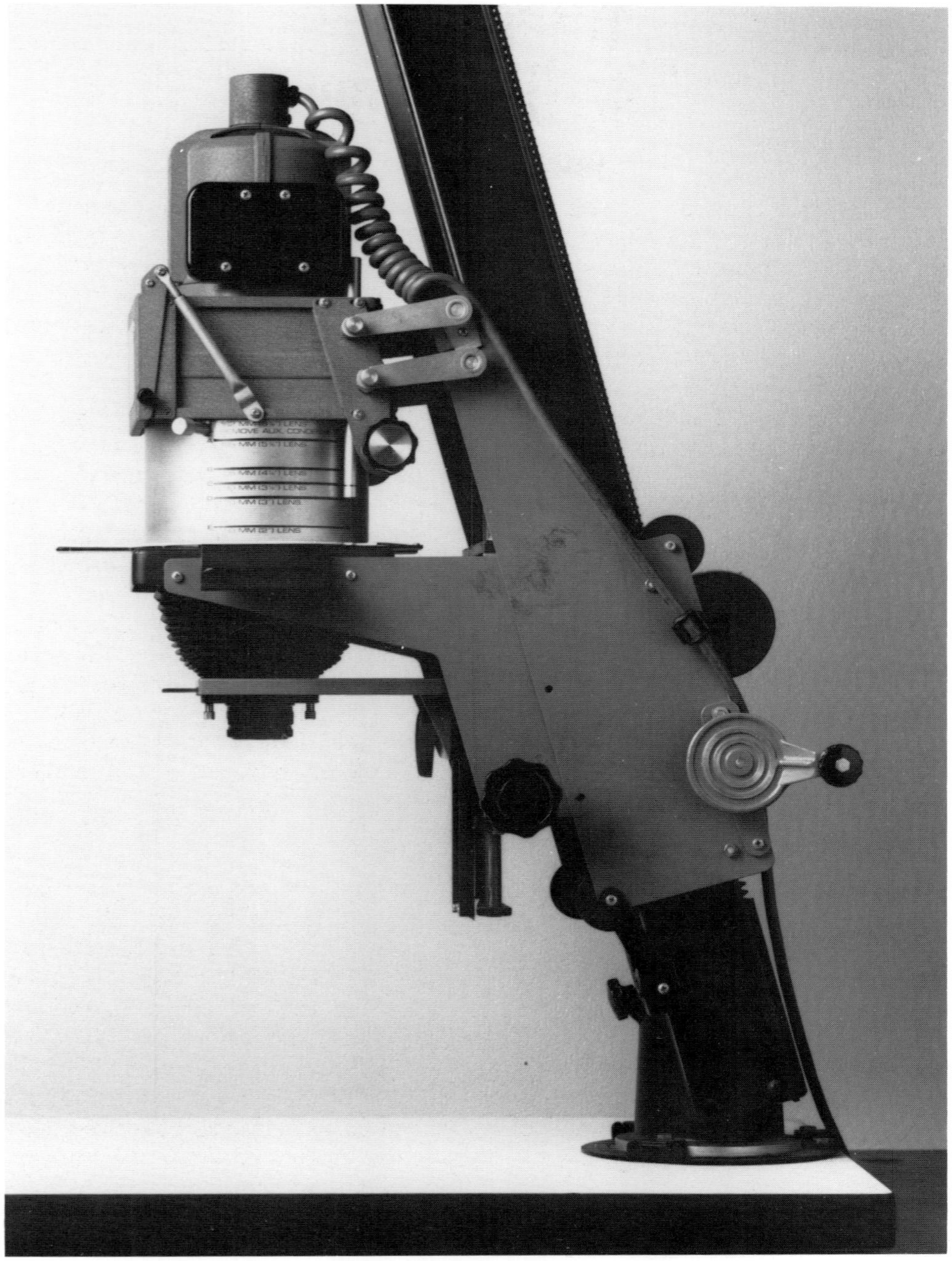

Condenser enlarger.

to stop the lens down considerably. The negative carrier panel must be able to hold the negative securely on all edges, particularly the end of a strip of negatives.

The clear edge of the negative can be used to print 'black borders'. The aperture dimension of the negative panel has to be slightly larger than the image area of the negative to allow this area of the negative to expose through. You may need to file out the negative carrier to enlarge the hole. After filing make sure that there are no rough edges or burrs which could scratch the negative. Sandwich and pull through a piece of tissue between the negative panels and check to see if any rough edges tear the tissue.

If you use glass negative carriers anti-Newton glass is essential to prevent 'Newton rings'. These rings are caused by light bouncing between two highly reflective surfaces and creating interference patterns. The interference produces the rings seen on the print. Anti-Newton glass has a very fine texture on the surface to reduce the reflection.

Some enlargers do look flimsy but provided the enlarger is not moved, attacked with a hammer, or in the vicinity of a passing train while you are making an exposure, vibrations should not be a problem.

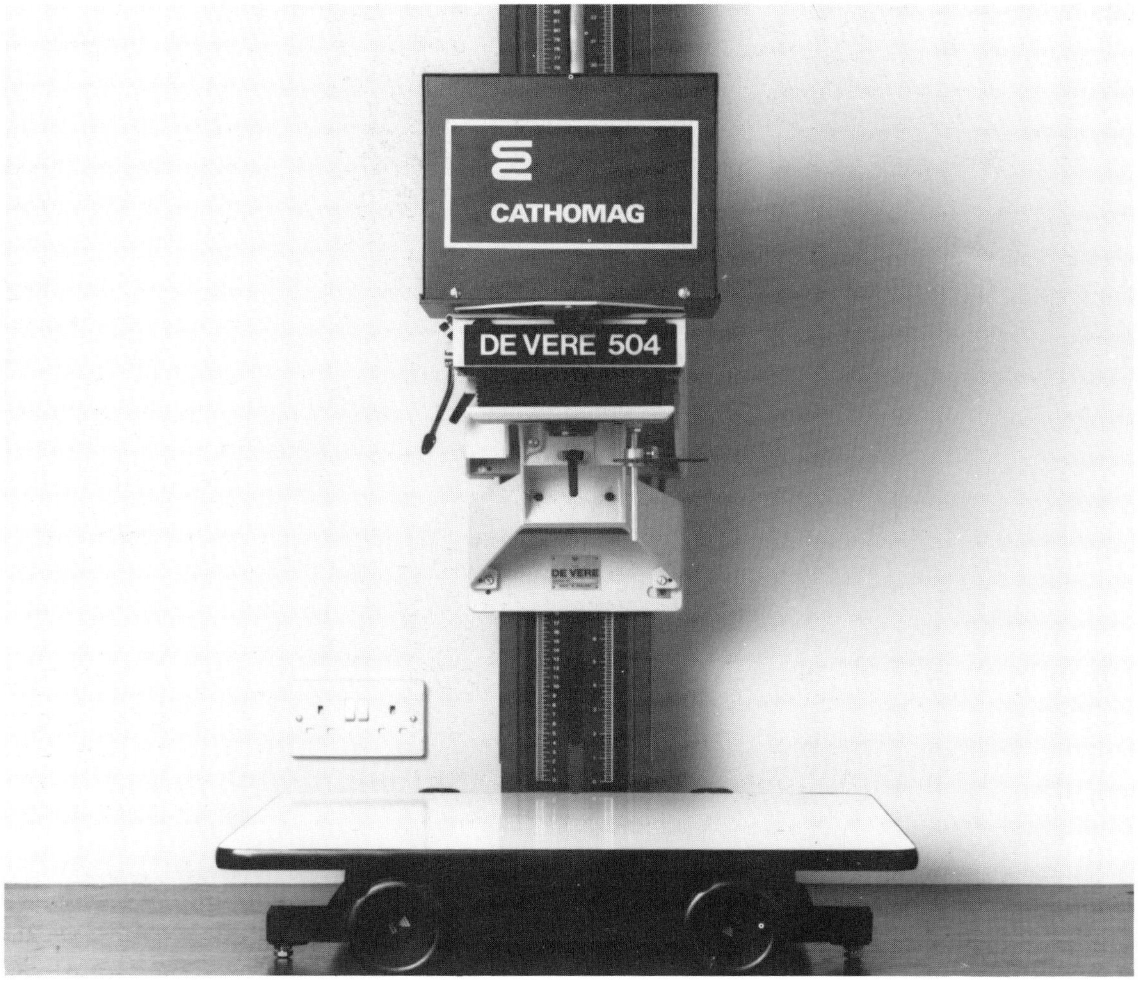

Cold cathode enlarger.

Three types of enlargers are generally available: CONDENSER, COLD CATHODE, and POINT SOURCE.

The Condenser is the type in most common use. This type of enlarger has a set of condenser lenses which concentrates and focuses the light through the negative panel and onto the baseboard. The light source is usually an opal Edison bulb, but lately there seem to be a number of manufacturers using tungsten halogen bulbs.

In the case of condenser enlargers with Edison bulbs (incandescent), the light is switched on and off virtually instantly. With tungsten halogen light sources, on the other hand, the light when switched on is slow to get to full intensity; when it is switched off it is slow to die. I personally see no advantage in using tungsten halogen lamps. Using a tungsten halogen lamp, with its on/off switching delay, makes worthless the precision of an enlarger timer. To overcome this problem you have to leave on the tungsten halogen lamp and use the safelight filter under the lens to 'switch' the exposure on and off.

The Cold Cathode Lamp source provides a

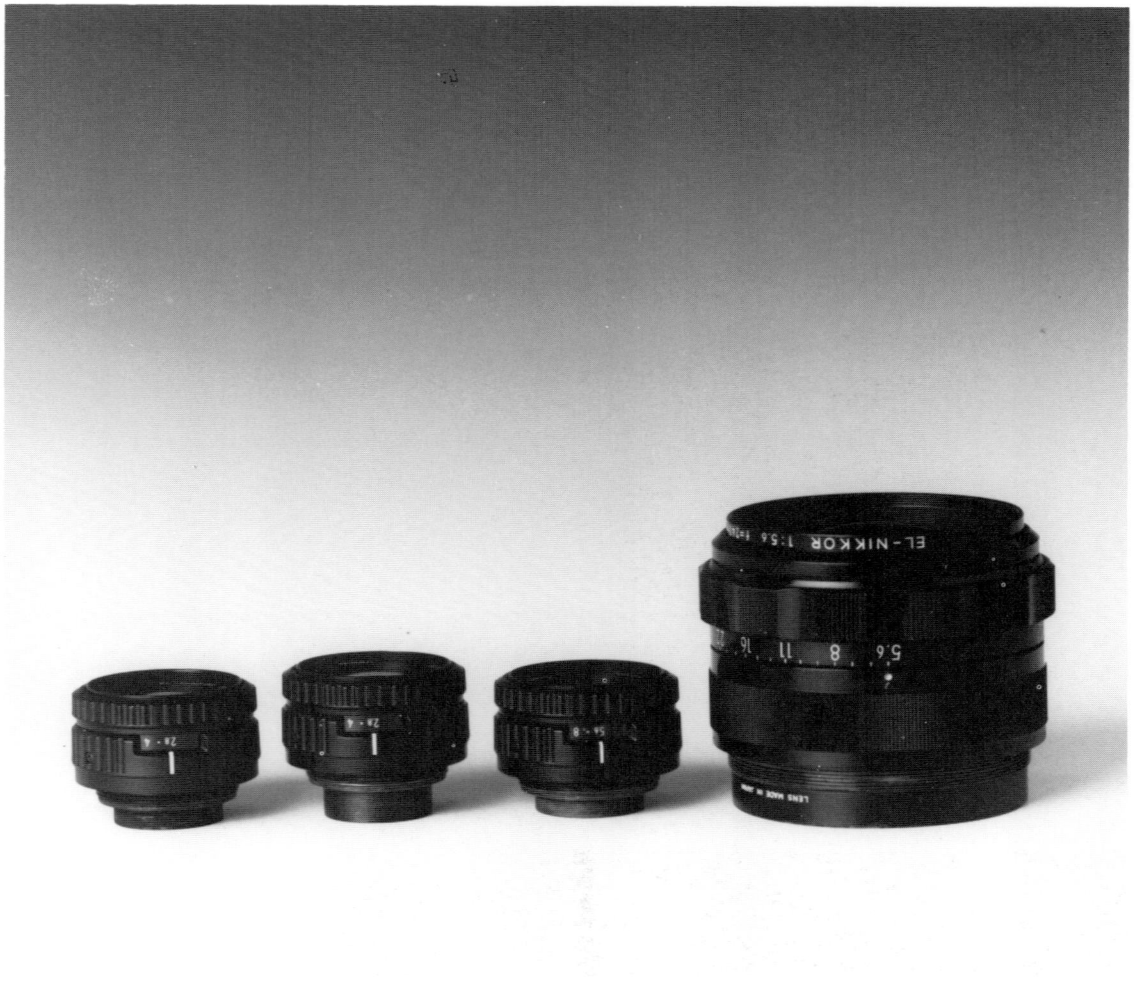

Enlarging lenses. I use a lens with a longer focal length whenever possible, for maximum sharpness throughout the image area.

large area of ambient light from the lamp head covering the entire area of the negative. Because of the cold nature of this light (blue), the effective speed and sensitivity of the paper are faster than with the condenser, and a softer contrast print is produced. Also, because of the diffused light, scratches and dust marks do not appear so pronounced on the print. There is not, however, any difference in the sharpness of the image. When comparisons are made with a print from a condenser the apparent sharpness of the latter can only be attributed to the higher contrast.

Photographic paper is sensitive to the blue spectral range of light. This explains the shorter exposure times of the cold cathode enlargers, though the actual intensity appears lower than a condenser. To a certain extent I can achieve the same degree of print contrast with a condenser enlarger as with a cold cathode enlarger, using the same grade of paper in each case, by simply placing a blue colour-correction filter on top of the enlarger lens.

The Point Source is a beast of an enlarger. My point source enlarger was developed for micro-films – it provides optimum sharpness. The light source is a miniature tungsten/halogen lamp, virtually a point – hence the name. This lamp is on the end of a spindle which is adjusted up or down to focus and distribute the light according to the size of enlargement and format required. EXPOSURE IS MADE WITH THE ENLARGING LENS AT WIDE OPEN APERTURE. The intensity of light is controlled with a rheostat which alters the voltage going through the lamp. Controlling the intensity in this way changes the colour temperature of the light. This colour temperature in turn alters the contrast.

If you only have a single camera system, for instance all 35mm negative formats, there is very little point in buying an enlarger capable of printing different formats. The extra money should contribute towards the best enlarging lens you can afford.

ENLARGING LENS

This is the most important piece of equipment. The print can only be as sharp as the lens is capable of producing. Printing from a less than high quality lens defeats the quality of the lenses used to take the picture.

Although the recommended focal length of the enlarger lens for 35mm format negatives has always been 50mm, I use one slightly longer – a 63mm. I find that the 50mm lens tends to spread the image too wide, which makes the edges and corners of the print appear soft and out of focus. In addition, given the projected light angle of 42 degrees with the 50mm enlarging lens, the light loss in the corners is very nearly $-\frac{1}{4}$ f/stop. The 63mm lens has a projection angle of 34 degrees with a light loss of $-\frac{1}{8}$ f/stop in the corners. Before the 63mm I preferred to use an 80mm lens for 35mm negative formats when the enlargement size was not too great. For $2\frac{1}{4}$ inch square (6 × 6cm) formats the 80mm lens is used. For up to 6 × 9cm the 105mm focal length is used. 4 × 5 inch formats need the 150mm focal length.

A faster lens, an f/2.8 rather than an f/4, permits shorter exposure times and provides a brighter image for focusing.

THE TIMER

Controlled and consistent printing can only be achieved with accurate measurement of exposure time. There has been very little discussion about this area of printing but the exposure time is one of the most crucial elements to consider and understand about photography.

It is important, therefore, to use an accurate timing device designed to control the exposure time.

I have invented, and I use, a photographic timer which incorporates the method of printing discussed in this book. It *automatically* provides the exposure times equal to the exposures expressed in units and fractions of f/stops.

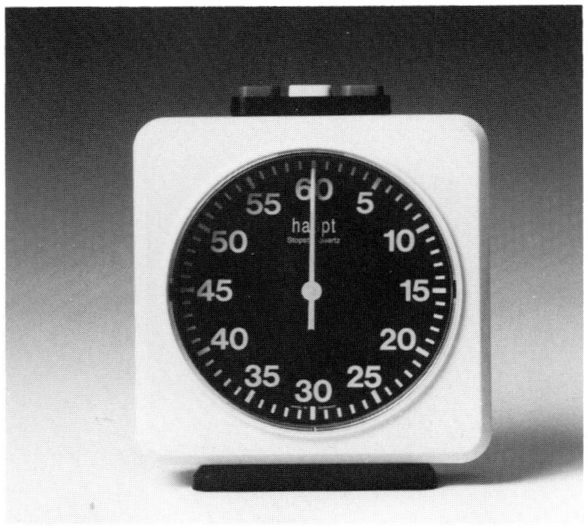

Sweep second timer.

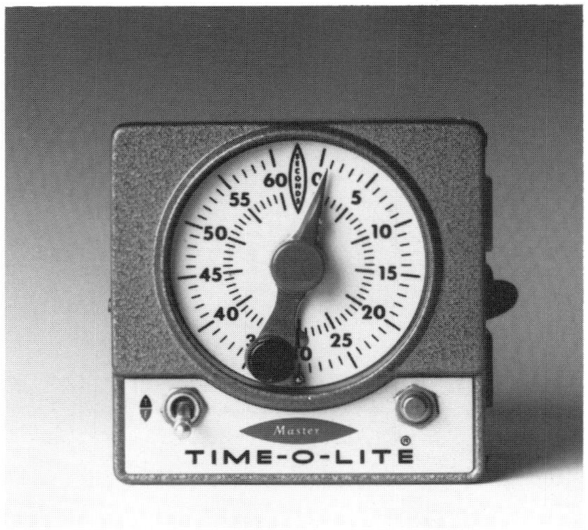

Count-down timer.

The darkroom timers that are generally available today are merely clocks that have switching devices to turn the enlarger lamp on and off. Not much relevance to photography is incorporated in their design.

The design of enlarger timers continues to encourage exposure strictly in terms of time. But exposure expressed in units of time is a hit-and-miss affair. Adding 2 seconds more, for example, onto an initial exposure of 2 seconds has a greater effect on the actual photographic result than the same 2 seconds added onto 20 seconds. The idea that exposure is a simple matter of increasing or reducing the exposure time has evolved from the days when taking pictures consisted of taking the lens cap off the lens. The duration of exposure consisted of counting 'thousand-one, thousand-two, thousand-three', then replacing the cap. This same haphazard technique is employed today by countless printers and at best 'helped' only by the automation of an enlarger timer.

Photographic exposure is a progressive process. The timing should therefore be progressive rather than involving the type of timers that can be seen to 'count down': 10, 9, 8, 7, etc., to 0. When clocks were initially introduced the mechanism perhaps necessitated the counting down. But today electronics make it possible to design purpose-built clocks which measure exposure by counting up.

The Nocon Photographic Timer has been designed for the specific purpose of expressing the duration of exposure in units of f/stops.

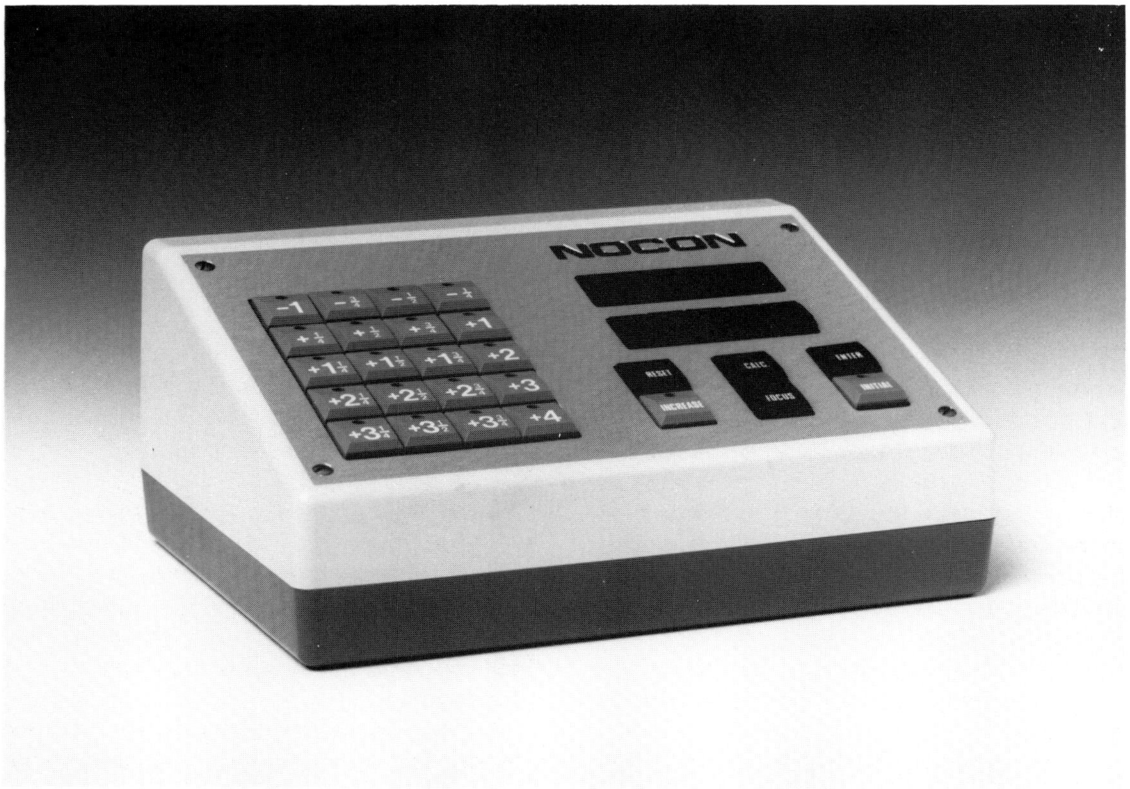

Nocon timer.

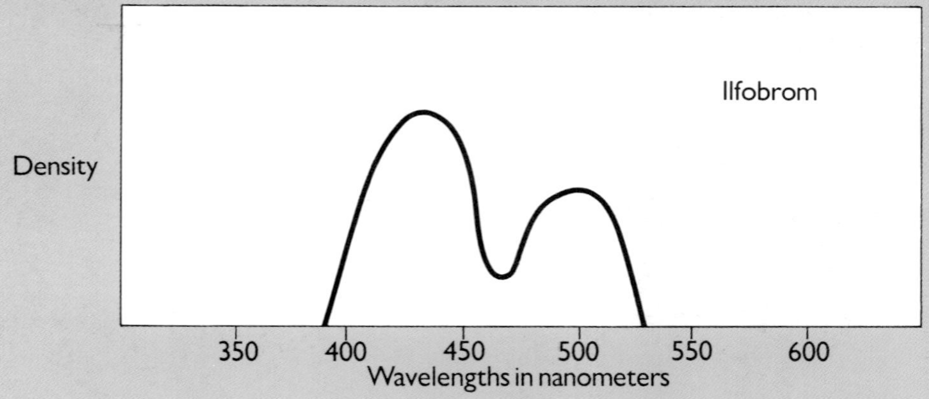

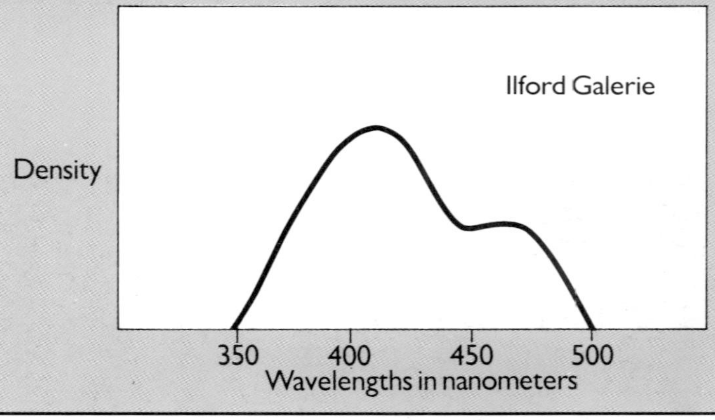

These spectrograms show the sensitivity to tungsten light of Ilford Galerie and Ilfobrom

Wavelengths of light (nm):

420 Violet
460 Blue
500 Blue-green
530 Green
560 Yellow-green
590 Yellow
620 Orange
660 Red
730 Dark red

Information courtesy of Ilford UK Ltd

GRAIN FOCUSER

I have a grain focuser capable of focusing not only on the centre of the projected image but on the edges and corners as well. It came supplied with a blue filter. The manufacturer claims the blue filter is to enhance the contrast to better focus on the grain. That is true to a certain extent. But it actually serves a more important purpose – the blue filter allows you to see what the photographic paper is capable of recording. Paper, as discussed earlier, is sensitive to the blue spectrum of light – it does not see red (hence red safelights).

Condenser enlargers with tungsten light sources project an image which, when visually focused, may not in fact be focused for the spectral sensitivity of the paper. The blue filter held over the grain focuser allows you to focus on what the paper actually 'sees' and records.

Stopping down the enlarging lens does not help. In much the same way, when you use infra-red film in the camera you actually have to shift the focus to the mark indicated on the lens. Stopping down the lens is not sufficient to bring the image into focus. There is a popular belief that focusing on a sheet of photographic paper placed on the baseboard will give you a more accurate result because it compensates for the thickness of the print. This is nonsense. Save your paper.

With point source enlargers, reducing the intensity of the light will shift the colour temperature of the light towards the red. Unless you use a grain focuser with a blue filter, you cannot focus the image.

The slightly blue colour of most silver-based films helps offset the redness of the tungsten light. But chromogenic films or colour negatives, with their inherent red base, will never print sharp if focused without this blue filter. Tungsten light, plus the red of the chromogenic or colour negative, projects a virtually red image onto your paper. Notice as well the long exposure time.

If, however, the results of your printing chromogenic negatives are satisfactory, the chances are that you are using a cold cathode enlarger. The cold cathode blue light negates the reddishness of the chromogenic or colour negative film.

It is important that the grain is in focus. Even an out-of-focus picture looks sharper when the grain is seen to be focused.

The grain focuser I use is the Omega Micro-grain Focuser. A blue filter attachment was supplied with it. But because it effectively cut down the light intensity when focusing and because I had no idea of its actual purpose I ignored using it.

It was the introduction of Ilford's XP1 chromogenic film that made me much more aware of grain sharpness. When I tried to print from a chromogenic negative I found that I could not produce a sharp print. It was always just slightly out of focus, even though I focused with the grain focuser. I could not find any fault with my equipment – the conventional film negatives produced sharper images. It was a problem which I, then, could not understand.

It was some time later that I had to use a blue felt-tip pen to mark the dimensions of a print on my print easel. I accidentally got some of the blue ink on the slanting edge of the easel and thought nothing more of it. I noticed, however, that the prints I made afterwards all had a slight fog mark along the top edge of the print. I could not understand what was causing it. Then I noticed that the fog mark followed the pattern of the blue mark on the easel. It became apparent that light hitting the blue mark on the easel reflected onto the paper to cause the fogging. Wiping it off resolved the problem.

But this started me thinking. We accept that photographic paper is not sensitive to the safelight colour. But to what colour light is it then most sensitive? My experience with the blue felt pen and the technical data available on photographic papers confirmed that the paper is, in fact, most sensitive to the blue spectral range of light.

I began experimenting with the blue-filter attachment on the grain focuser. When the blue filter was used there was a slight focus shift. Without the aid of the grain focuser the picture actually looked out of focus. But when a print was produced it was pin sharp! I then tried printing from a chromogenic film, focusing with the blue filter on top of the grain focuser, and that too became pin sharp.

There is an old adage in photography: if the print does not look sharp – it isn't! Use a grain focuser with a blue filter.

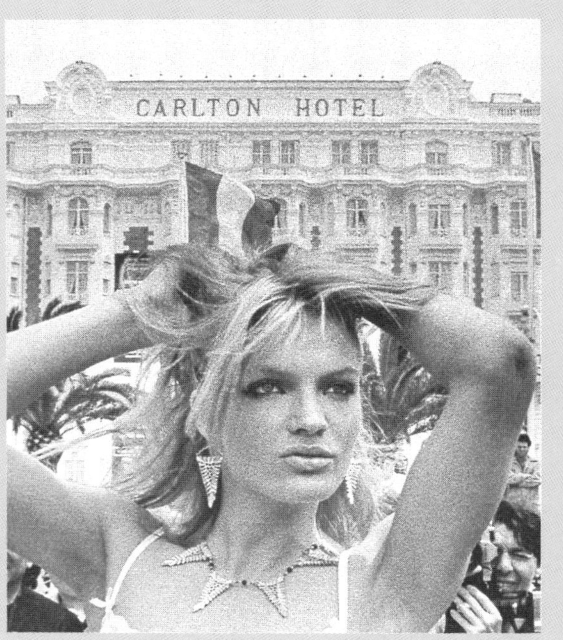

Using the blue filter on the Omega Micro-grain focuser at this enlargement the grain can be seen to be pin sharp on the print. The image projected onto the easel will actually appear out of focus after focusing with the blue filter, but the print produced will be sharply focused.

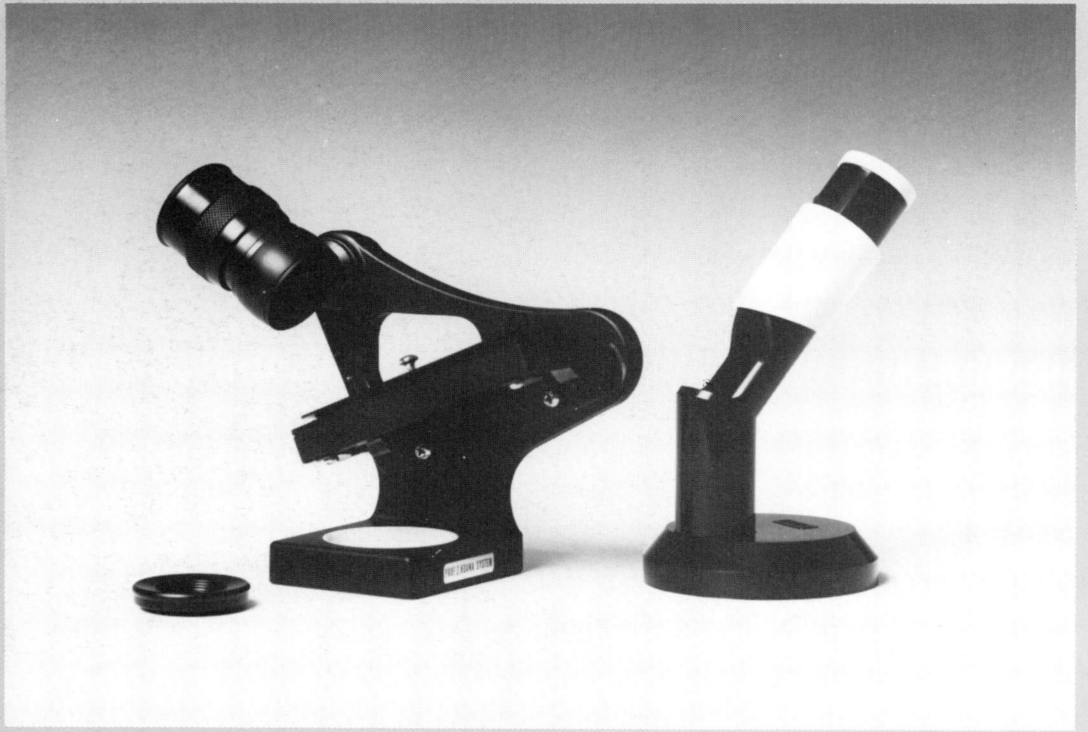

Optimum sharpness can only be achieved when the grain is focused. The Omega Micro-grain focuser, on the left, is supplied with a blue filter which fits over the eyepiece. This grain focuser tilts to enable checking the focus on the very edge and corners of the negative image. The Paterson grain focuser, on the right, is inexpensive and works nearly as well as its more expensive counterpart, but focusing is limited at or near the centre of the projected image.

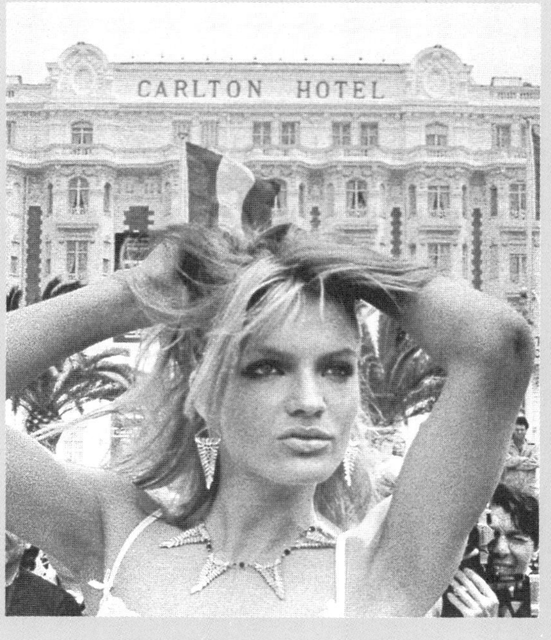

Without the blue filter on the grain focuser the image appeared to be in focus. The resulting print, however, is out of focus.

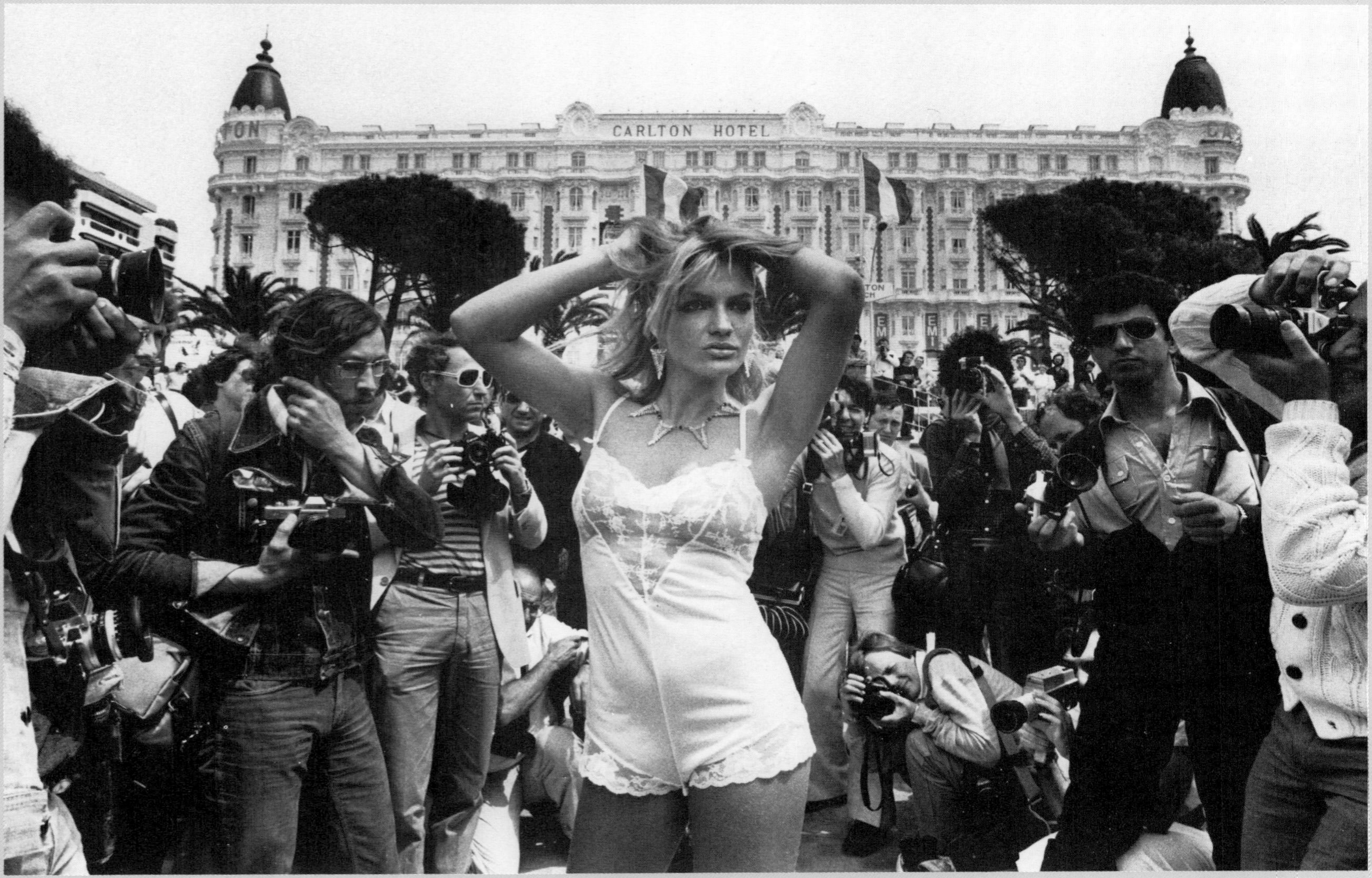

Cannes Benjamin Lee.

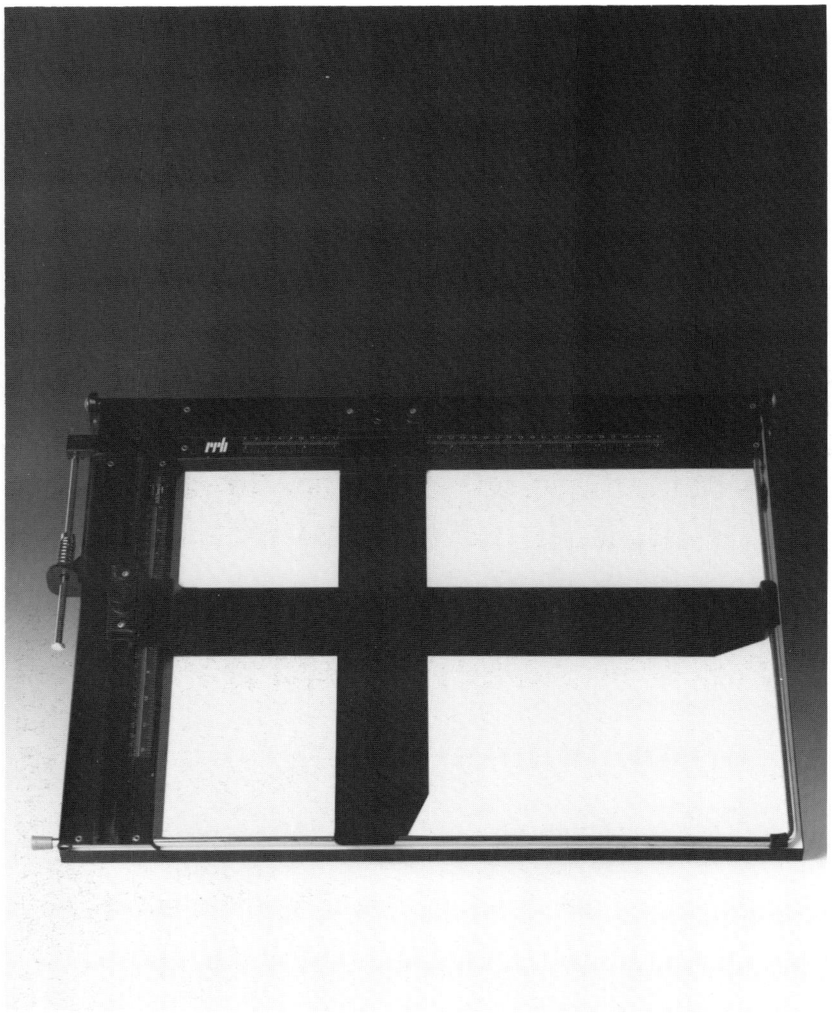

R R Beard print easel.

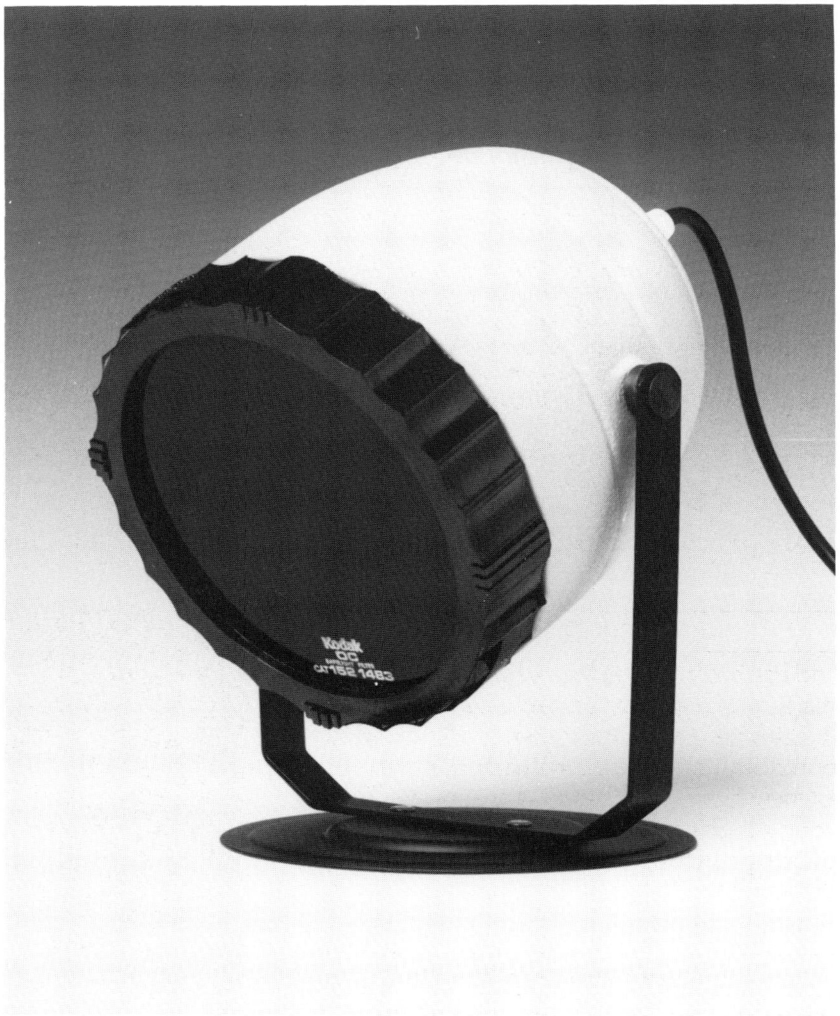

Kodak beehive safelight.

EASELS

A print easel with adjustable masking frames to crop and provide different print dimensions is recommended. Fixed-frame easels limit your print format.

The masking frames should be absolutely true and at right angles to one another.

The easel should be heavy with non-slip pads to prevent it from moving when the frame is adjusted or when the paper is inserted.

DEVELOPING TRAYS

You will need a minimum of three. One for the developer, one for the stop bath, and one for the fixer. They should be one size larger than the paper size you intend to use. This allows free circulation of the chemicals and paper and makes it unnecessary to bend up the edges or corners of the print when picking it up out of the solution.

SAFELIGHTS

Use the safelight recommended by the paper manufacturer. The safelight should be suspended directly over the developer tray. Placing it in the centre of the room will only cast your shadow over the print you are watching develop. Placing the safelight near the enlarger serves no purpose. The light may be so bright that you have to turn it off before you can see the image projected onto your easel.

The speed with which resin-coated paper (RC) can be processed, washed, and dried, is useful when I do print runs. It saves a considerable amount of time and effort, particularly at the washing and drying stage. Fast drying is accomplished with a RC hot air print dryer.

I also use it for making contact sheets (Chapter Three). The arguments for or against RC papers really depend on your particular needs. Most of my prints are used for commercial purposes, in advertising and publishing, and they often need retouching so that the use of fibre-based papers is necessary. Retouchers prefer fibre-based papers. For exhibition work, as well, I traditionally use the fibre-based papers.

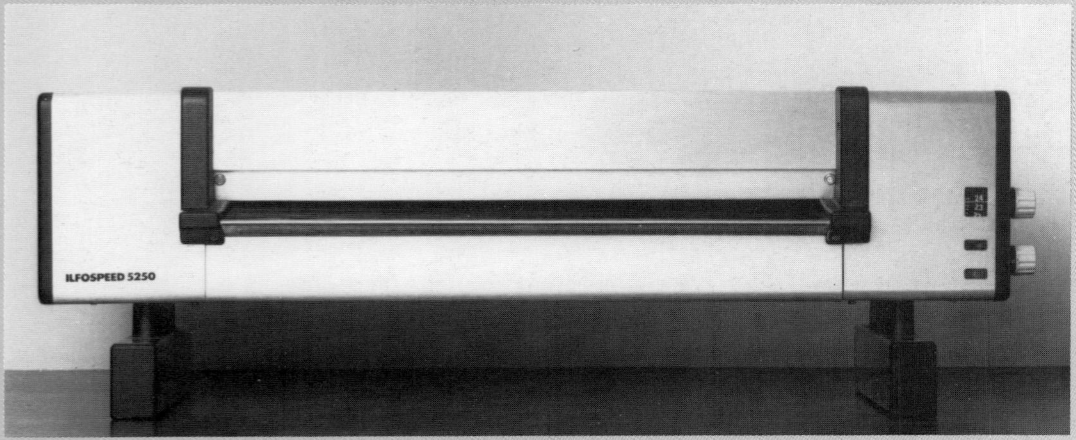

Ilford Ilfospeed (RC print dryer).

GLOVES/TONGS

I do not recommend the use of tongs. These can mark and scratch the soft emulsion of the paper. It is also very difficult to handle and pick up large prints with them. I use instead ordinary rubber kitchen gloves for handling the prints. Putting your gloved hand in the developer gives a feeling of being involved in the process. Tongs feel a bit detached.

PRINT-WASHER

Water flowing freely through and around the prints is essential for effective washing of chemicals from the print. Kodak supply an autosiphoning device and this is attached to a water supply and held in place onto a large washbowl or deep print tray.

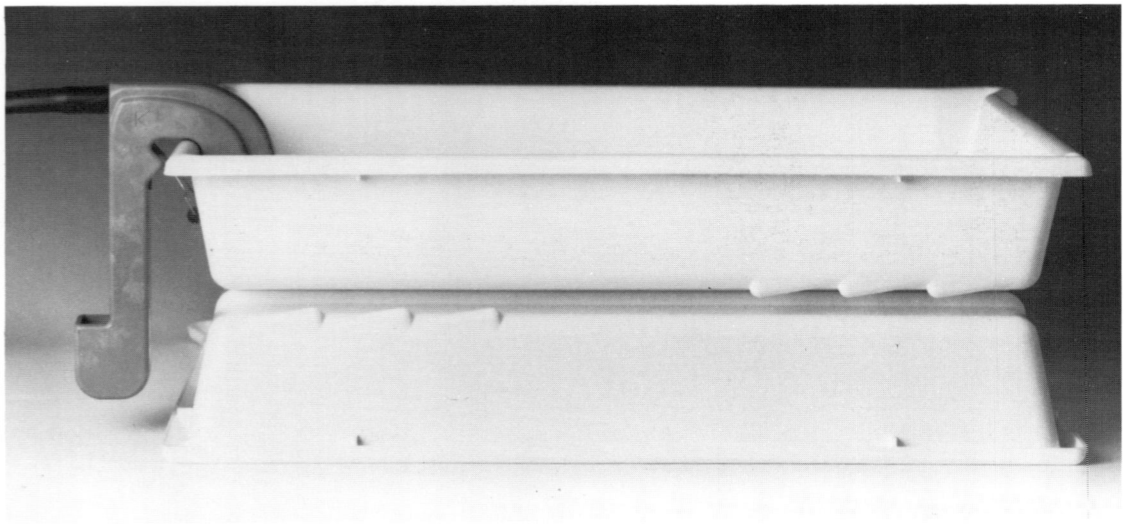

Kodak Autosyphon set up with developing trays for washing prints.

PHOTOGRAPHIC PAPER

Use whatever you like. Most brands of paper are contrast-graded, 1, 2, 3, and 4, and claim to have the same paper speed. This means the same exposure can be given to any one of these grades and the print density should be the same. You will find that the harder grade is often 1 f/stop slower, so it will need twice the amount of exposure to achieve the same density as the softer grades of paper.

I have recently rediscovered the advantages of multigrade paper. The different contrasts can be achieved simply by using the multigrade filters. Ilford Multigrade has a contrast range from 0 through to 5 in ½ contrast grade increments. The ½ grade increments have a distinct advantage over the fixed grades of paper because they enable you to match the negative to a particular grade of paper. Multigrade also makes it possible to change contrasts on a single print.

My renewed interest in multigrade is because it is now available on fibre-based paper. Its initial introduction was limited to the resin-coated papers.

Recent improvements made in multigrade paper have resulted in a constant paper speed throughout the contrast range, with the exception of the hardest grades, which, much like the fixed-grade papers, are 1 f/stop slower. The current multigrade papers are more sensitive than the conventional fixed-grade papers.

There are basically two kinds of paper available: BROMIDE and CHLORO-BROMIDE. The visible difference is that chloro-bromide is a warmer tone than bromide papers. The choice is personal.

CHEMICALS

There are no magic brews. Commercially-available chemicals should be used as recommended by the manufacturers.

I find the chloro-bromide papers to be too warm-toned when used with warm-tone paper developers. I favour the results produced by neutral or cold-tone developers.

PROCESSING EQUIPMENT

Choice of either plastic or stainless steel developing tanks and spirals depends on how much film you use and plan to develop. I use stainless steel in my lab because of the volume of work. Stainless steel tanks and processing spirals are expensive in comparison to plastic. But in the long term the best stainless steel is far more economical. The heavy-gauge spirals I bought ten years ago are still being used in my lab. Avoid the cheaper, flimsy stainless steel spirals. These go out of shape very easily and become absolutely useless – they become impossible to load.

You will need a 'changing bag' if you have no access to a completely darkened room. The least expensive but vital piece of equipment you will need is a bottle opener. This is to pry off the ends of the 35mm film cassettes. To remove excess water from processed film you will need a film squeegee.

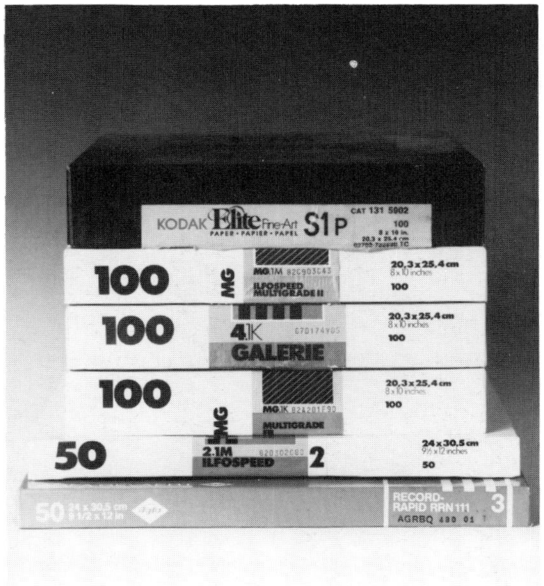

Photographic papers.

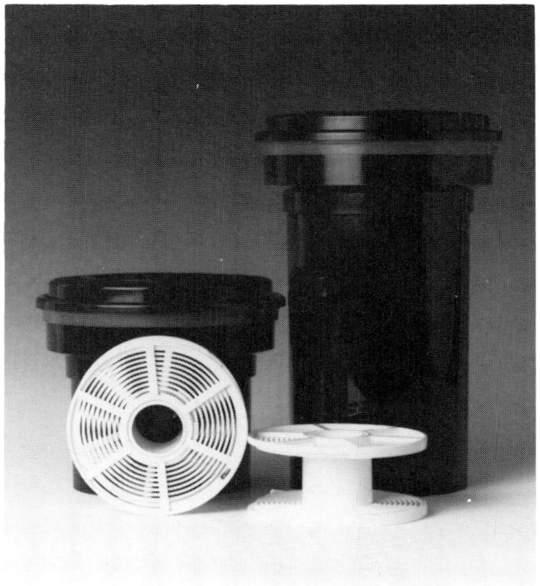

Paterson film spirals and tanks.

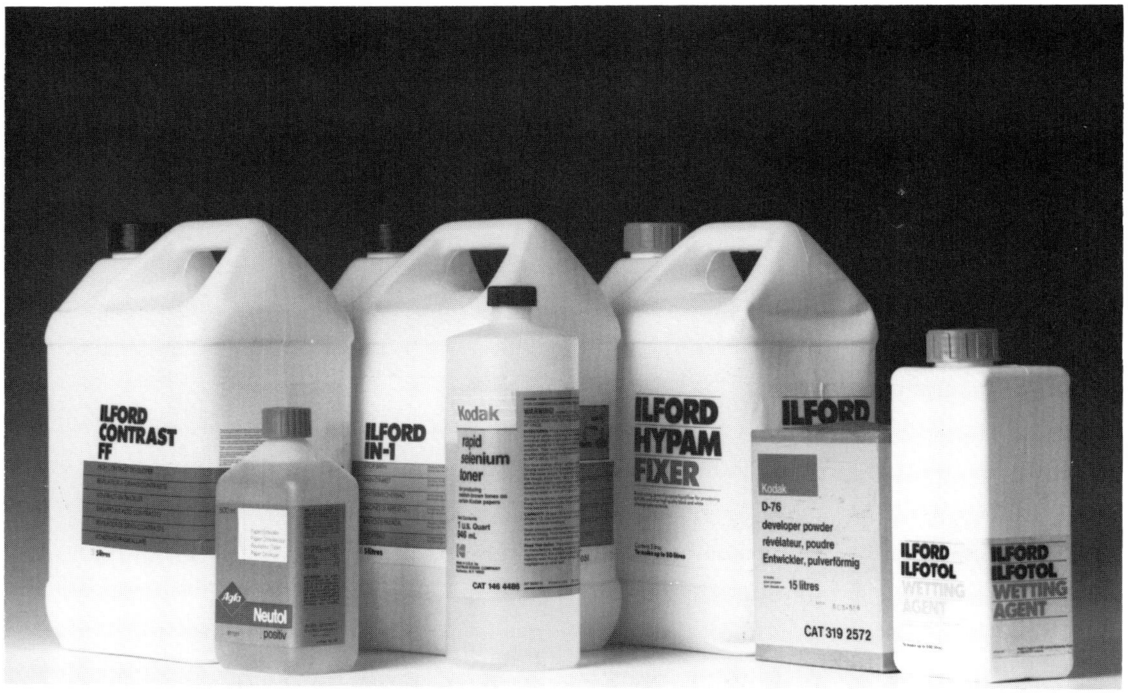

Photographic chemicals.

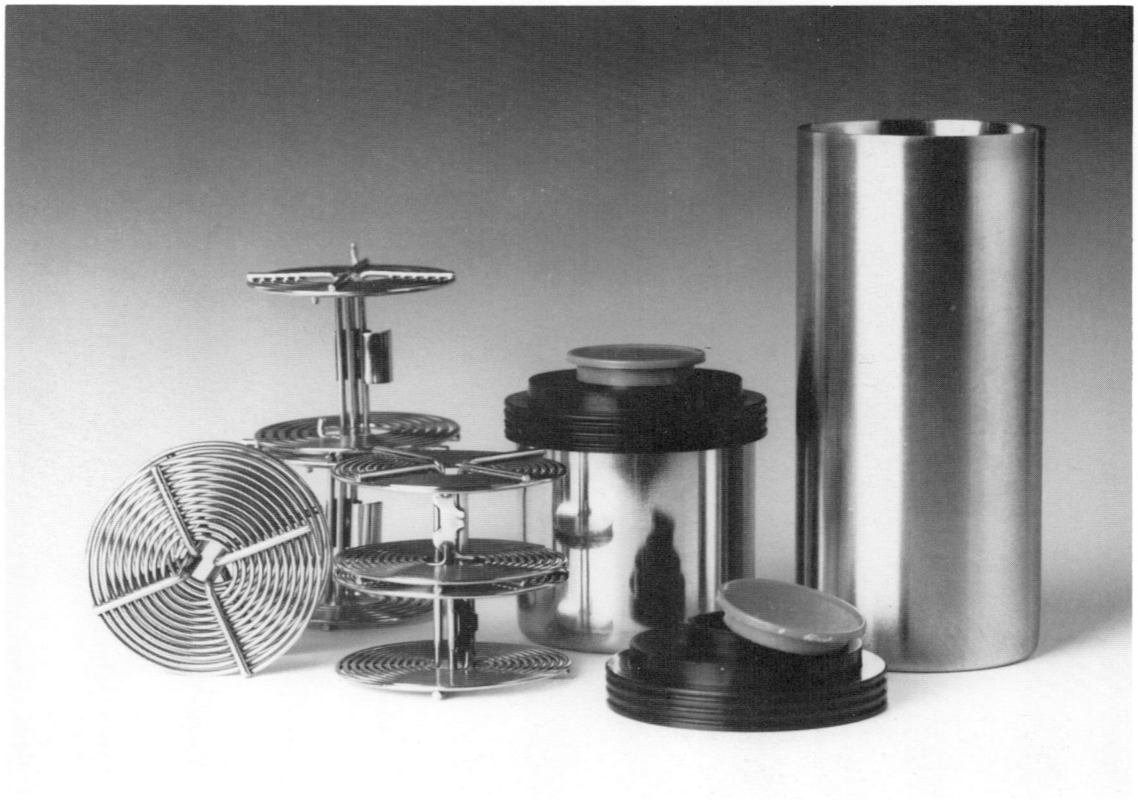

Kindermann tanks, Hewes stainless steel spirals.

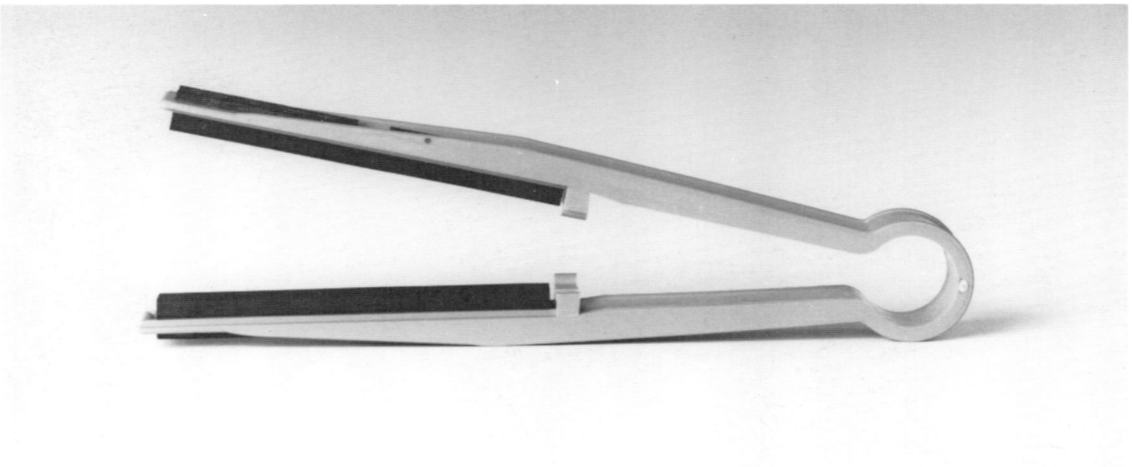

Kindermann film squeegee.

□

If your darkroom is not a permanent fixture then you have to make allowances for the temporary state of affairs. Black tape may be used to cover any holes leaking light into the room. A bath towel rolled up and placed at the bottom of the door will prevent light from coming through. Windows will have to be covered up, but if, like me with my first darkroom, you arrange to do your printing at night, this may not be necessary.

If facilities for a more permanent darkroom are available then some advice can be given to make it more comfortable and efficient:

Paint the walls the same colour as the safelight. This makes the darkroom appear brighter and any stray white light reflecting off these coloured walls bounces off 'safe'.

Designate one side or area as 'dry'. This area is for the enlarger, timer, photographic paper, and other items which must remain dry. At no time must there be anything on this side or area that is wet. Avoid all liquids in this area, including coffee cups or beverages! These, in the dark, can only invite disaster.

The 'wet' side or area is for your chemicals, developing trays, and wash-sink. A simple inspection lamp over the fixer tray that can be readily turned on makes it convenient for viewing prints. All electrical switches on this 'wet' side must be overhead toggle switches with a pull string. Keep a towel nearby on the wet side to dry your hands.

If possible install an extractor fan. Some substances, such as selenium toner, are highly toxic and require proper ventilation.

Keep the size of the darkroom to a minimum. The size should be adequate for you to have room to move about, but not so large as to mean constant trekking back and forth from the dry to the wet side. The walking will only tire you.

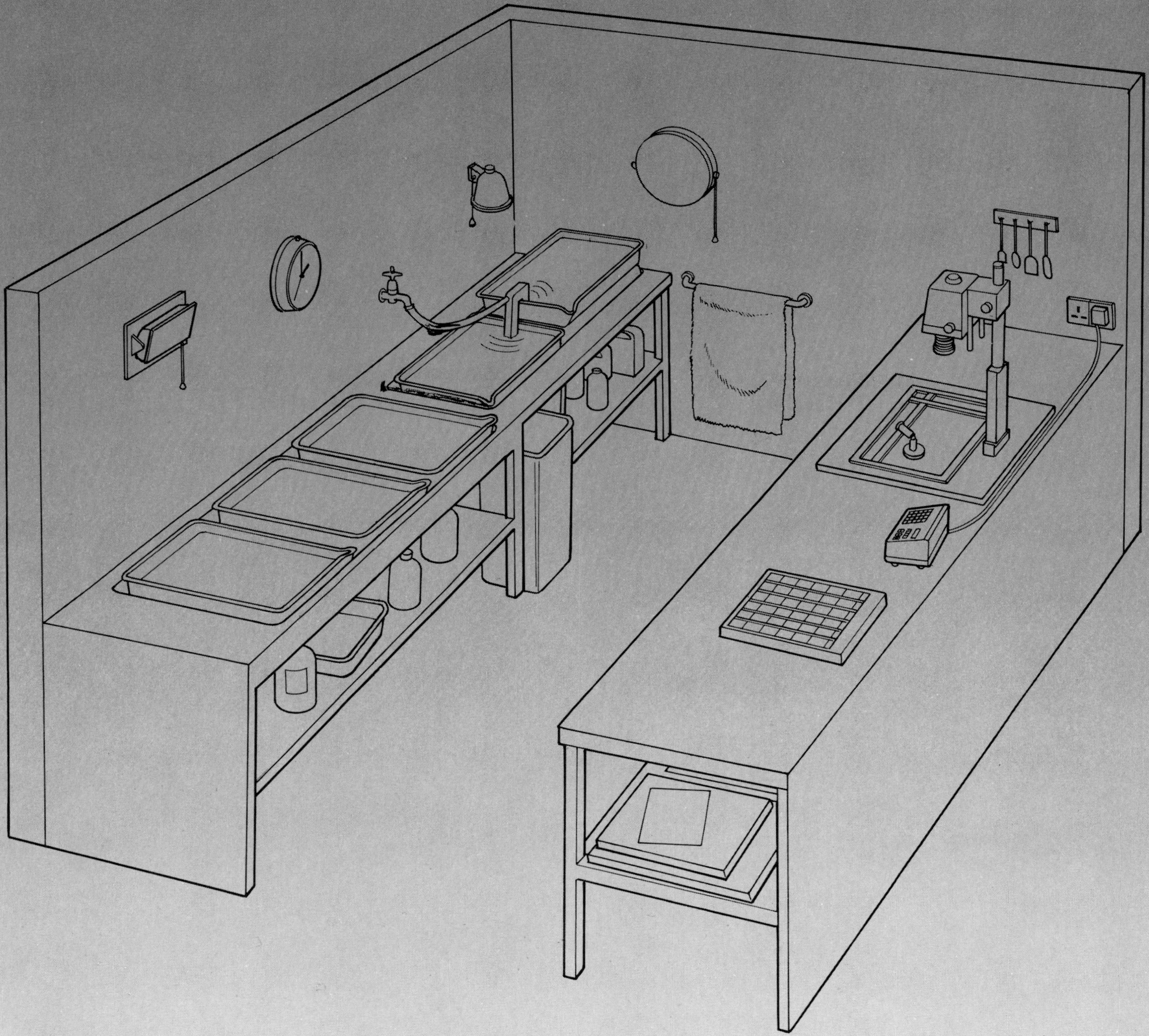

Layout of darkroom. The less cluttered the darkroom, the more effectively you can work. Keep it neat and tidy. Put away everything you don't need and make a habit of returning those items you use to their designated places. This makes it easy for you to find things without groping about in the dark.

CHAPTER TWO

CHAPTER TWO

Photographic Exposure

The negative is more than just a vehicle for the photographic image. It represents all that a print can be. The quality of the negative, in other words the exposure, is a vital factor in the production and success of the finished print.

So before we go into the darkroom we must first understand a few things about the negative and photographic exposure. This is a subject that I find confuses many photographers, amateur and professional.

It seems hardly necessary to think about exposure using today's photographic equipment. Nearly every 35mm camera and some larger formats feature a built-in light-metering system requiring little more than matching needles, or an LED (Light Emitting Diode), to determine exposure. The more modern cameras determine exposure automatically; some even automatically set the film's ASA. Cameras without a built-in exposure system require only the ability to read an external or hand-held light meter to determine the 'correct' exposure. This would appear to be the extent to which exposure is understood – reading light meters.

Certainly modern photographic equipment has made it much easier to take pictures. But total dependence on such equipment and the mere mechanics of using it have caused some confusion and misconceptions about exposure. The basic understanding of exposure is often neglected altogether.

Many photographers show this concern and uneasiness about negative exposure by 'bracketing' their exposures, doing 'clip tests' on their film, and going through the process of determining their 'personal ASA'.

The problems which we have, or might encounter, with exposure are attributable to the light meter and we have to recognize its limitations to understand the problems.

There are two types of exposure meter: INCIDENT and REFLECTION.

An incident light meter measures the intensity of light actually *falling on* the subject. A reflection light meter measures the intensity of light *reflecting off* the subject.

The through-the-lens exposure system in cameras is a reflection light meter. Most external or hand-held exposure meters can be used either as incident or reflection light meters.

Incident meters are characterized by an opaque sphere or cone covering the light-sensing probe. The probe is unobstructed for reflection light meters. On most light meters this sphere is attached or slides into position directly above the light probe which allows it to be used either as a reflected or as an incident meter.

The difference between the two types of metering is in the way the light is measured.

Incident metering measures the intensity of light actually falling on the subject. It is not affected by the

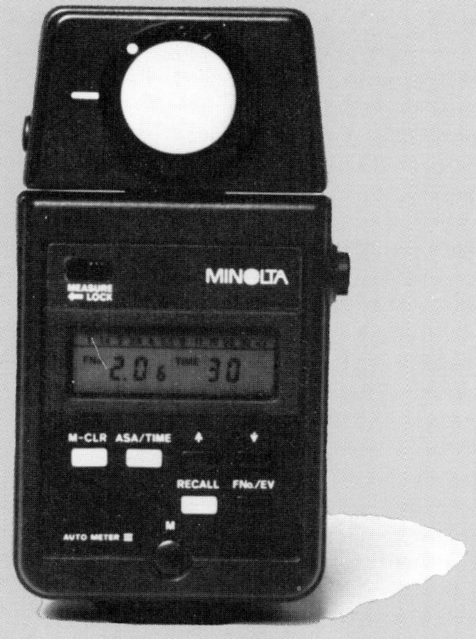

Incident light meter.

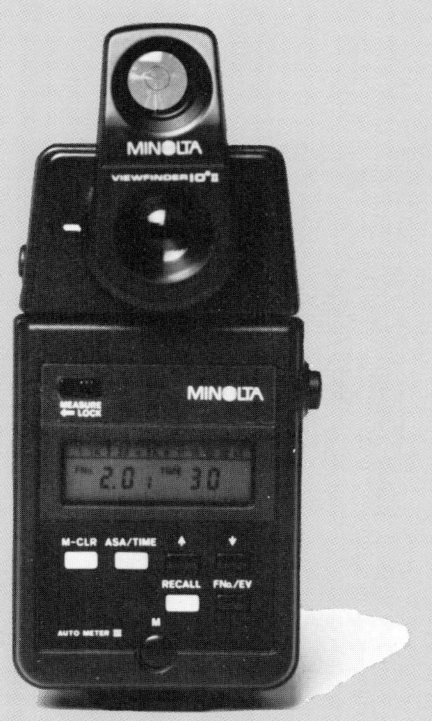

Reflection light meter.

absorptive or reflective light characteristics of the subject being photographed. Exposure is determined by placing the light meter in the subject area with the sphere *facing* the camera. The sphere itself represents the subject and as such is the true measure of the light *falling on* the actual subject. This would appear to be the best way to determine the exposure. But in situations where the contrast range is high the incident meter reading could underexpose the shadow areas. (This will be discussed in the next chapter on exposure/development.)

A reflection light meter measures the intensity of light reflecting off the subject. The light meter, without the cone or sphere, is pointed towards the subject. Unlike incident metering the exposure determined is affected by the reflective quality of the subject and therefore could lead to exposure misinterpretation. This is discussed further in this chapter.

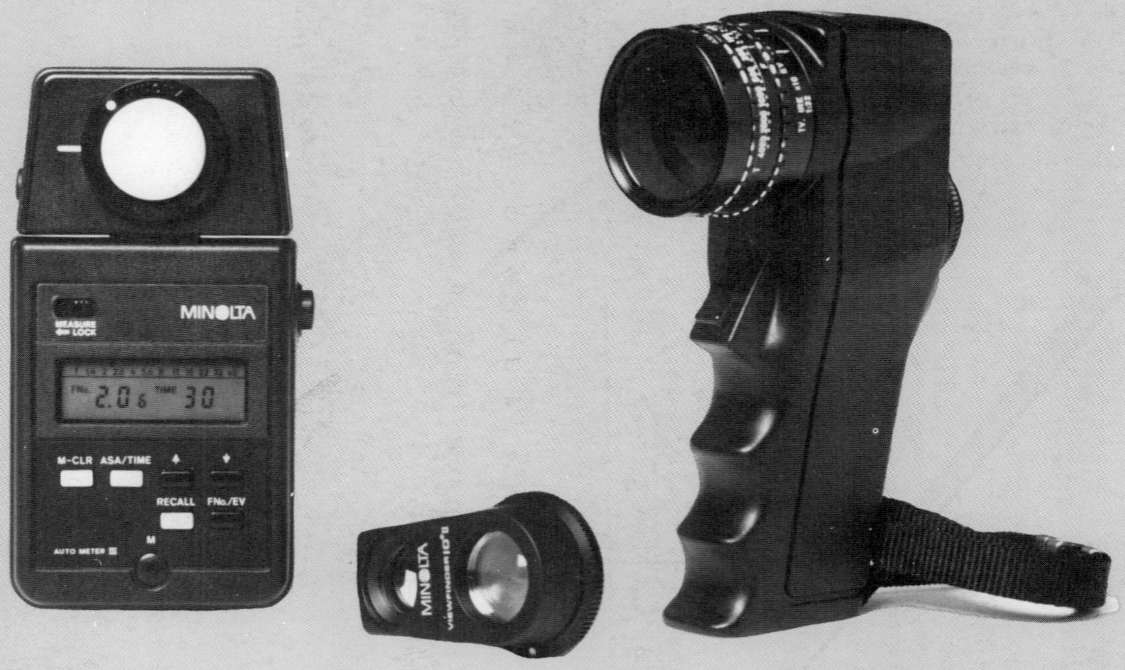

Light meter with reflection attachment.

A spot meter is a reflection exposure meter with a very narrow field of view – usually a 1° acceptance angle.

The exposure meter can measure only the intensity of light. This intensity is 'translated' into the combination of camera aperture and shutter speed that records the intensity of the subject-matter, however bright or dull, as mid-grey. THE THE EXPOSURE METER CANNOT MEASURE THE SUBJECTIVE BRIGHTNESS (i.e. the brightness of the original image). IT IS THE NEGATIVE EXPOSURE WHICH REPRESENTS THE BRIGHTNESS AND TONAL VALUES OF THE ORIGINAL SCENE.

A 'thin' negative of little exposure density, no shadow detail, and only a mid-range of tones will produce a dark and low-key print; whereas a negative of considerable exposure density will lend itself to a much brighter interpretation.

But a negative showing little density does not necessarily mean underexposure; nor does a negative with greater density mean overexposure. The 'thin' negative could represent a dark subject, in which case the exposure is correct. And if the dense negative represents a bright subject, then that exposure too is correct.

'Correct' exposure can then be defined as the negative that readily produces a finished print consistent with the brightness and range of tones of the photographed subject.

This in turn defines an underexposed negative as one whose results are dark and grey when, in fact, the actual scene is bright. A bright snow scene, for example, that appears thin on the negative can be considered underexposed. This can be corrected to a certain extent in the printing, but the desired result is not as easy to achieve nor is it as effective as printing from a negative with the correct exposure.

An overexposed negative, on the other hand, is one whose density level and range of tones is unlike the subject it represents. This particular negative would require a massive amount of print exposure, patience and skill to produce decent results.

We can expect satisfactory results in the majority of photographic situations. The problems and confusion occur when the brightness and tonal values are limited.

We can demonstrate this with the following experiment.

Frames 13a/14, 14a/15 and 15a/16 are, respectively, the exposures as seen by a through-the-lens exposure meter of a white, a grey, and a black card. Each individual card was 'seen' by the exposure meter as grey.

Frame 16a/17 is the result of increasing the exposure +2 f/stops to correctly expose for white. For 17a/18 the exposure remained unchanged to render the grey card grey. For 18a/19 the exposure was reduced to correctly expose the black card as black.

Frame 20a/21 is the exposure for a grey card with the lens set on infinity focus. Using the same exposure setting, but shifting the lens to its closest focus, frame 21a/22 is the result. The same exposure setting produced two different densities of exposure. This is due to the change in the lens extension. Frame 22a/23 is the exposure corrected for the lens extension-light loss at close focus.

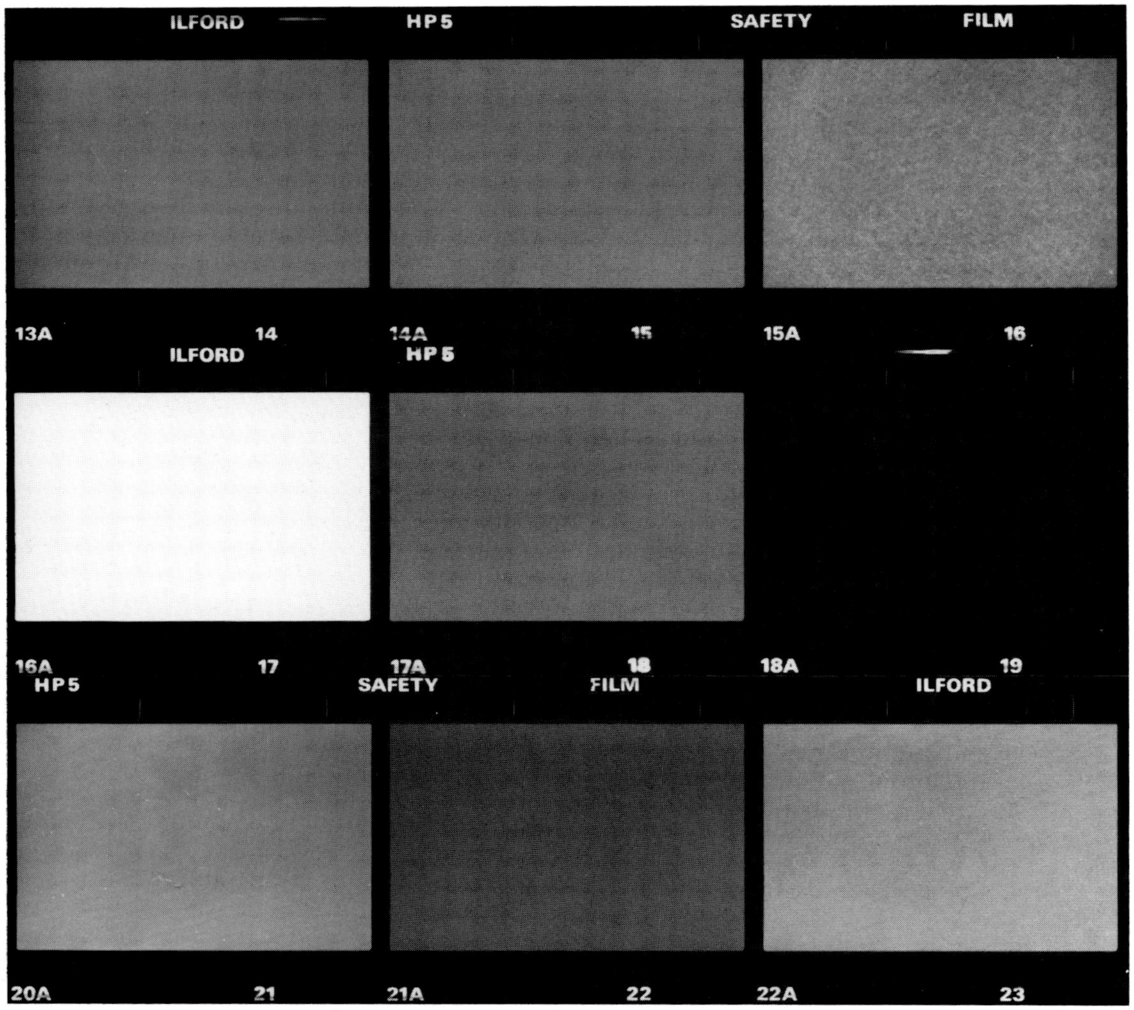

If we try and take pictures of three different shades of paper – white, grey, and black – and photograph each one individually, using reflection light-meter readings, the individually exposed negatives will result in the same exposure density. The light meter cannot differentiate between the individual values of tone – it can only provide the exposure to record each one as mid-grey.

The light meter's mid-grey reading will need correcting to expose the white paper as white. My own experience has been to correct the light-meter reading by increasing the exposure +2 f/stops. If, for instance, the light meter indicates an exposure of 1/60 at f/16 – which would render the paper as mid-grey – the correct exposure to render it white is 1/60 at f/8. (The same exposure correction could be made by increasing the exposure time to 1/15 with the aperture remaining at f/16.)

The grey paper will require no change to the indicated exposure because the light meter correctly exposes it as mid-grey.

To obtain the correct exposure for the black paper the indicated exposure will need to be reduced −2 f/stops. If the light meter indicates an exposure of 1/60 at f/4 – which would render the paper grey – the exposure to render it black is 1/60 at f/8. (Again the correction could also be made by reducing the exposure time to 1/250 with the aperture remaining at f/4.)

Automatic exposure cameras will compensate for the changes to the aperture (or shutter) when you try to correct the metered exposure. Increasing the aperture, for instance, to render white paper as white will cause the automatic metering system to adjust the shutter speed to expose the paper as mid-grey. In this case use the exposure compensation-facility dial, which is usually above the ASA setting dial, and marked −2, −1, 0, +1, +2, with smaller markings in-between. Set the dial on +2 when photographing the white paper, 0 for the grey, and −2 for the black paper.

If the automatic camera has no compensation facility the ASA setting must be used to make the corrections. If the film is rated at 400 ASA reducing this value by half to 200 effectively increases the exposure +1 f/stop. Reducing this again by half to 100 will increase the exposure +2 f/stops. Conversely, doubling the ASA to 800 will reduce the exposure −1 f/stop. Doubling this again to 1600 will reduce it −2 f/stops.

□

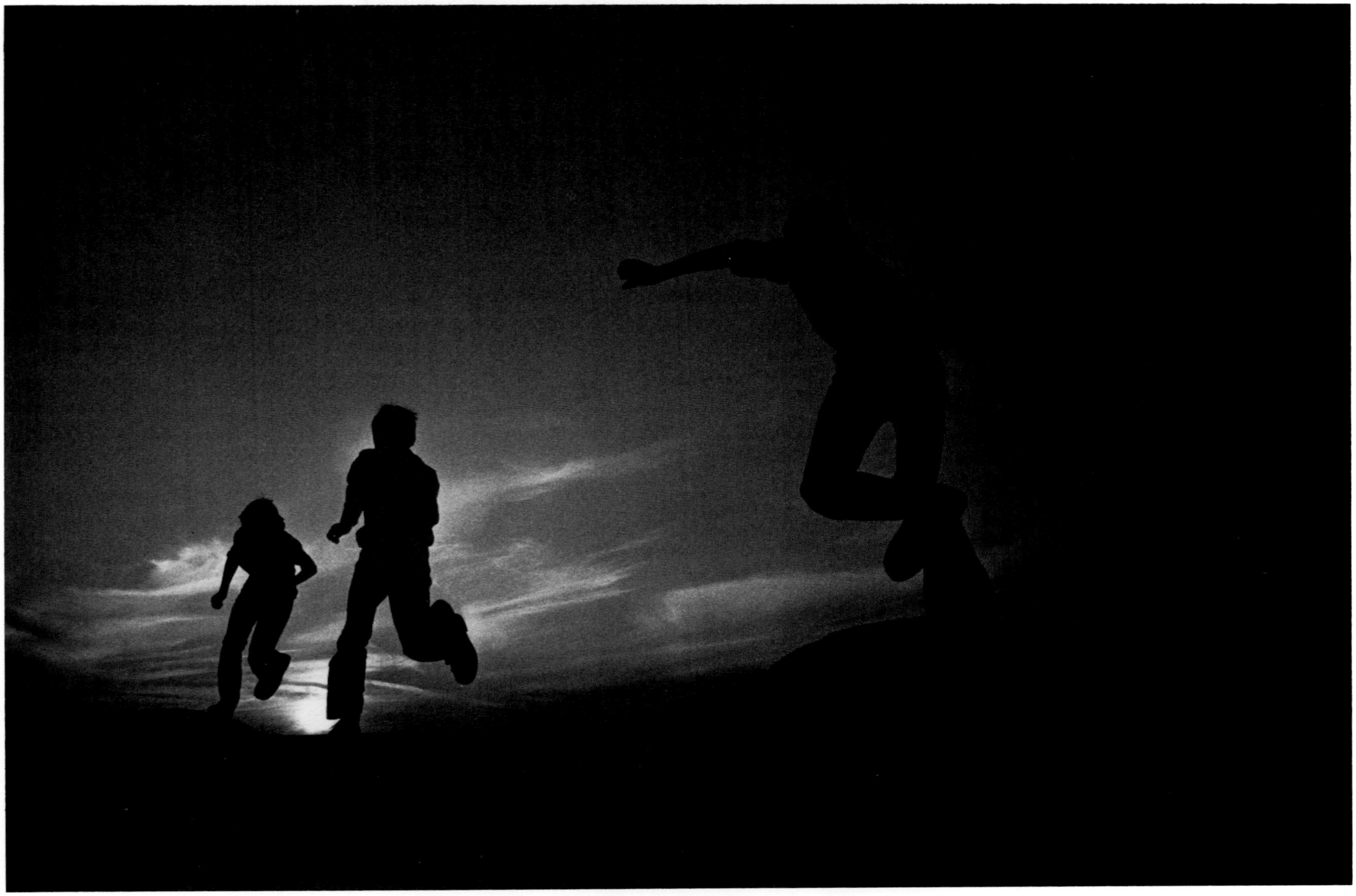

Running for the Sun Régis Bossu. This is the result of printing from a 'thin' negative. The exposure was deliberately made thin to produce this dramatic effect.

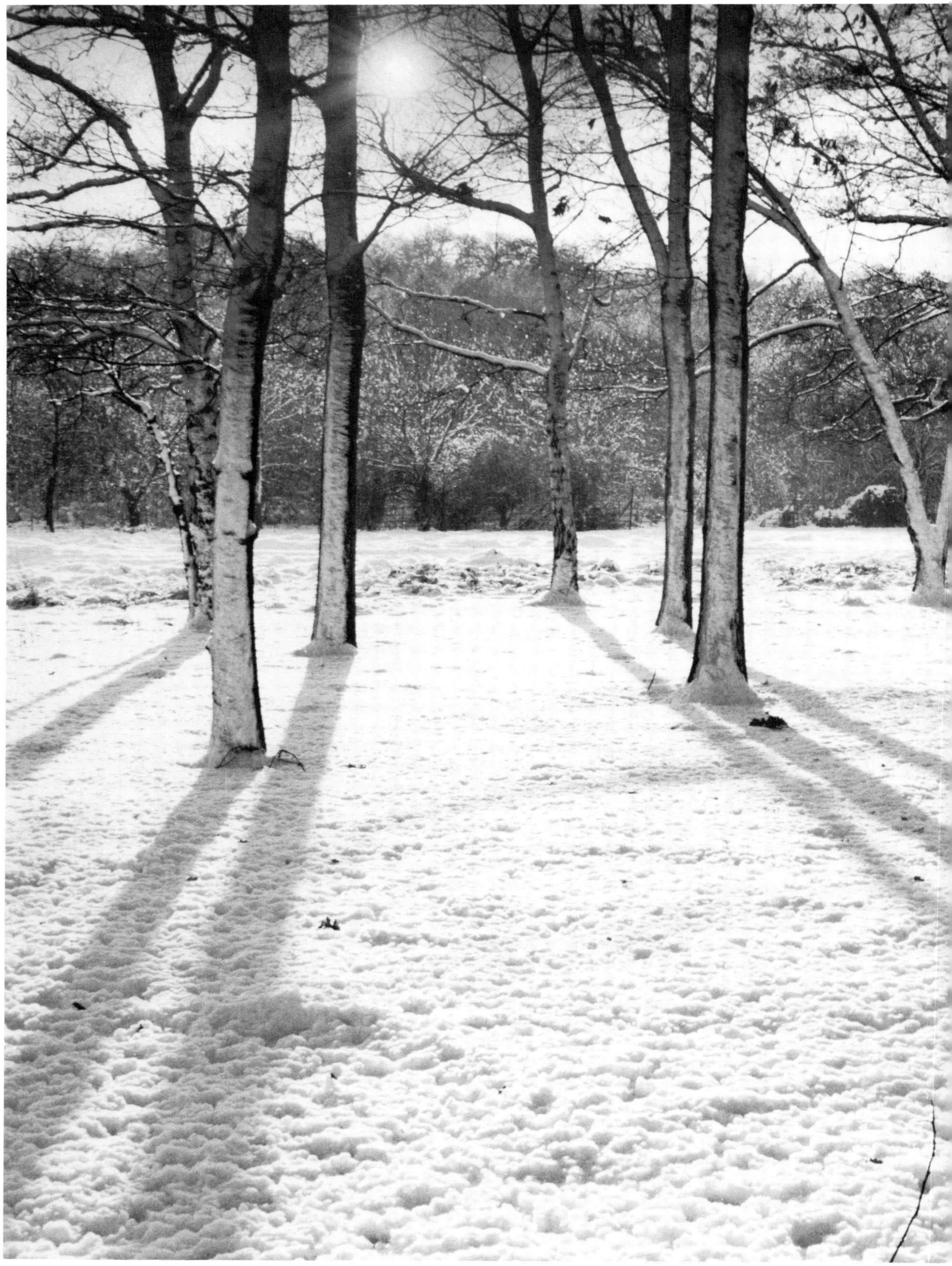

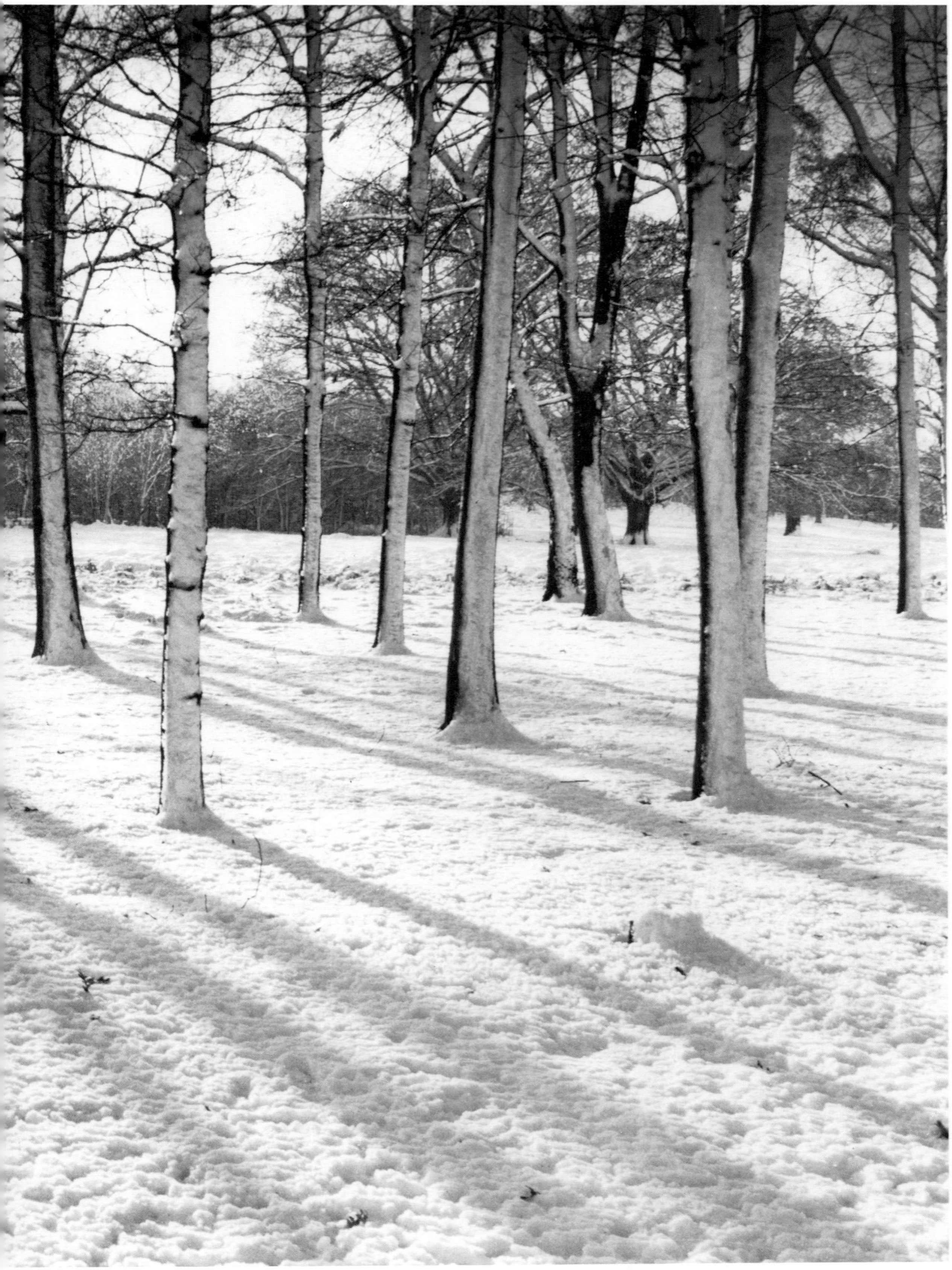

Richmond Park Lee Higham. To expose correctly for snow the film must be rated at ¼ its normal ASA. This increases the film exposure by +2 f/stops and thus conveys the brightness of the snow.

House on the Hill Tony White. The bright sky has been darkened for effect.

Seagull HRH The Prince Andrew. Rating the film at ½ its normal ASA increases the exposure + 1 f/stop to expose correctly for a bright sky.

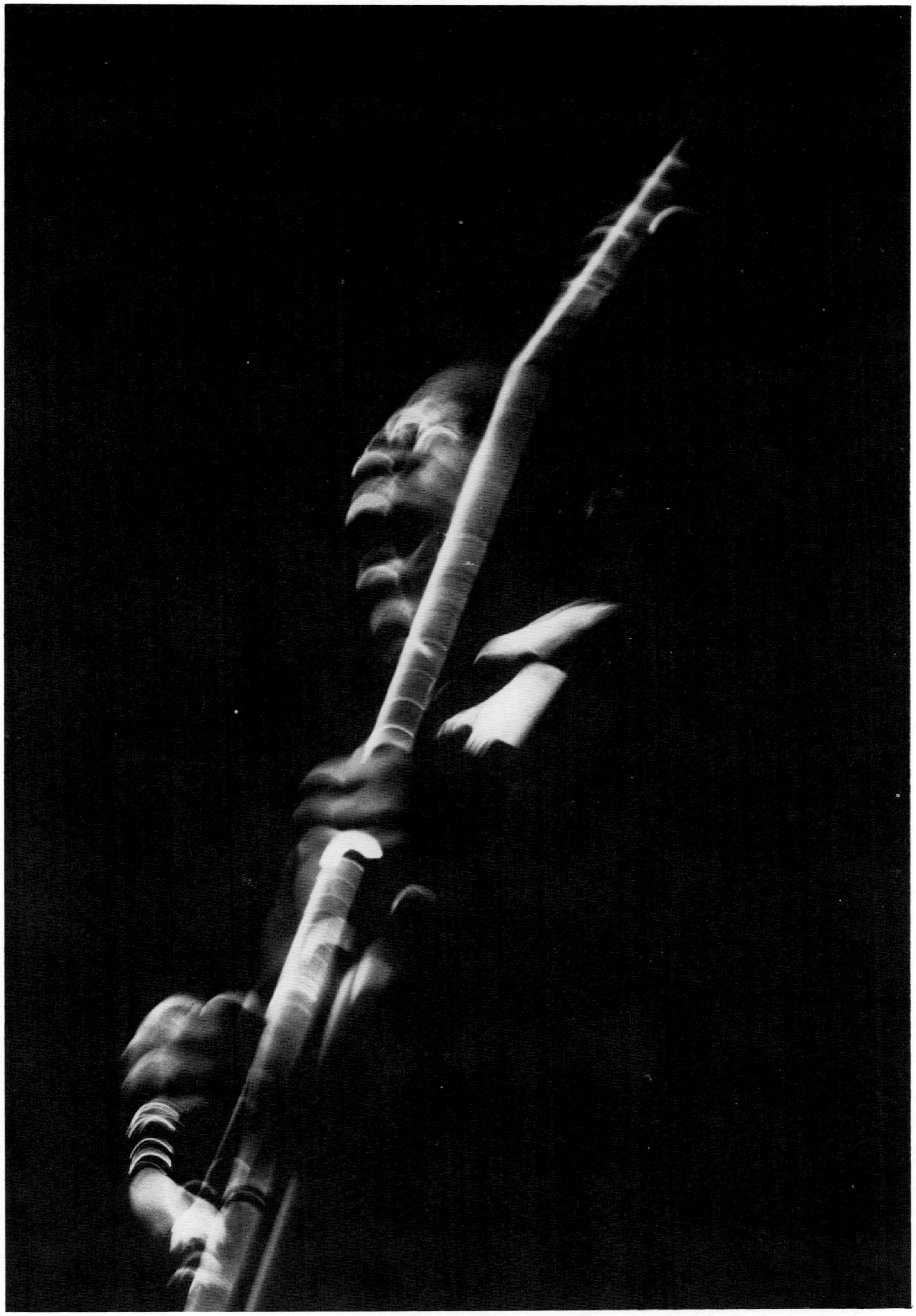

B B King Linda McCartney. Rating the film at four times its normal ASA reduces the exposure −2 f/stops to expose the dominant dark area as black. An exposure at the normal ASA would have rendered the dark stage as grey; it would also have increased the highlight density, making it difficult to print and see any detail.

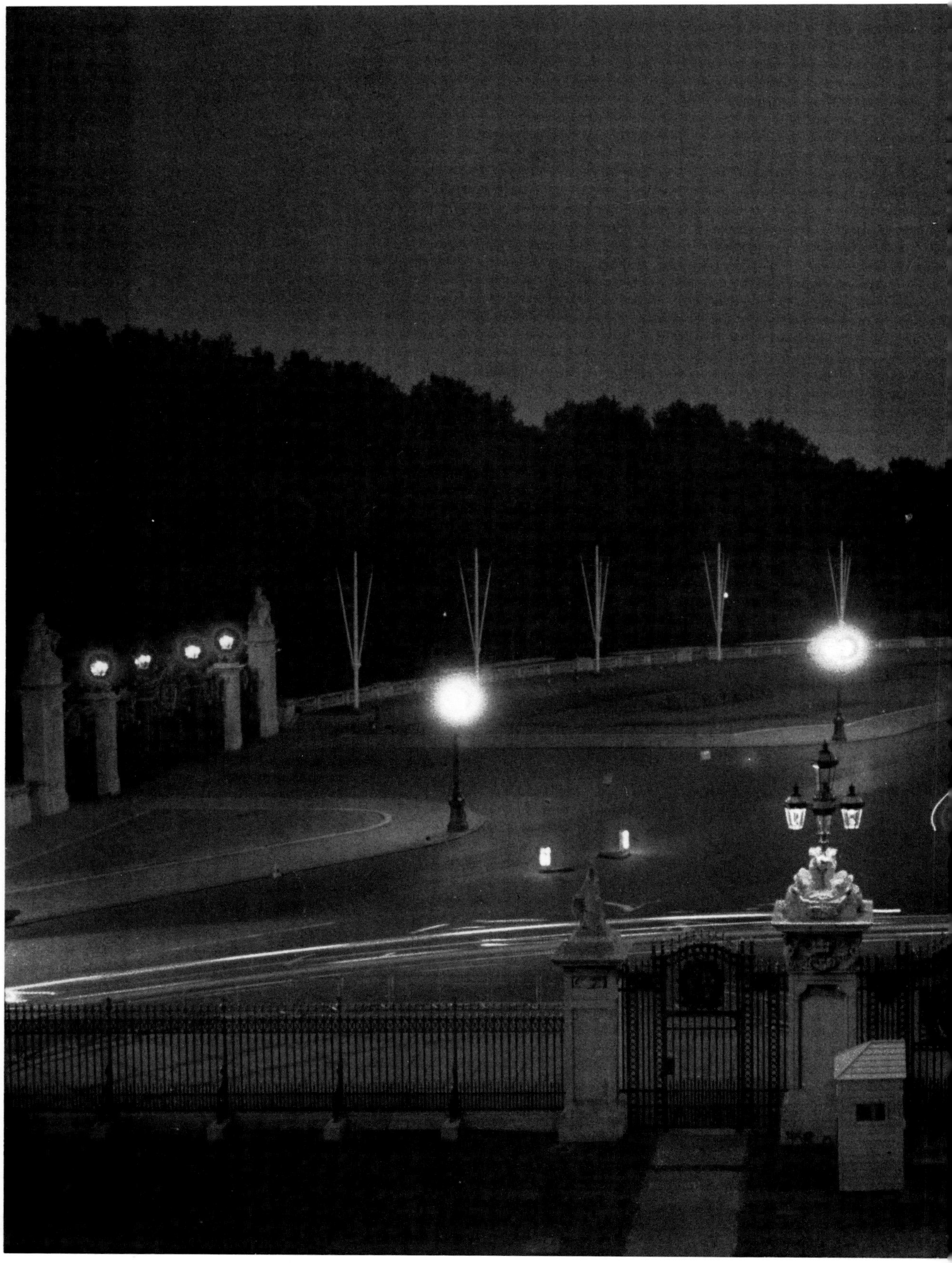

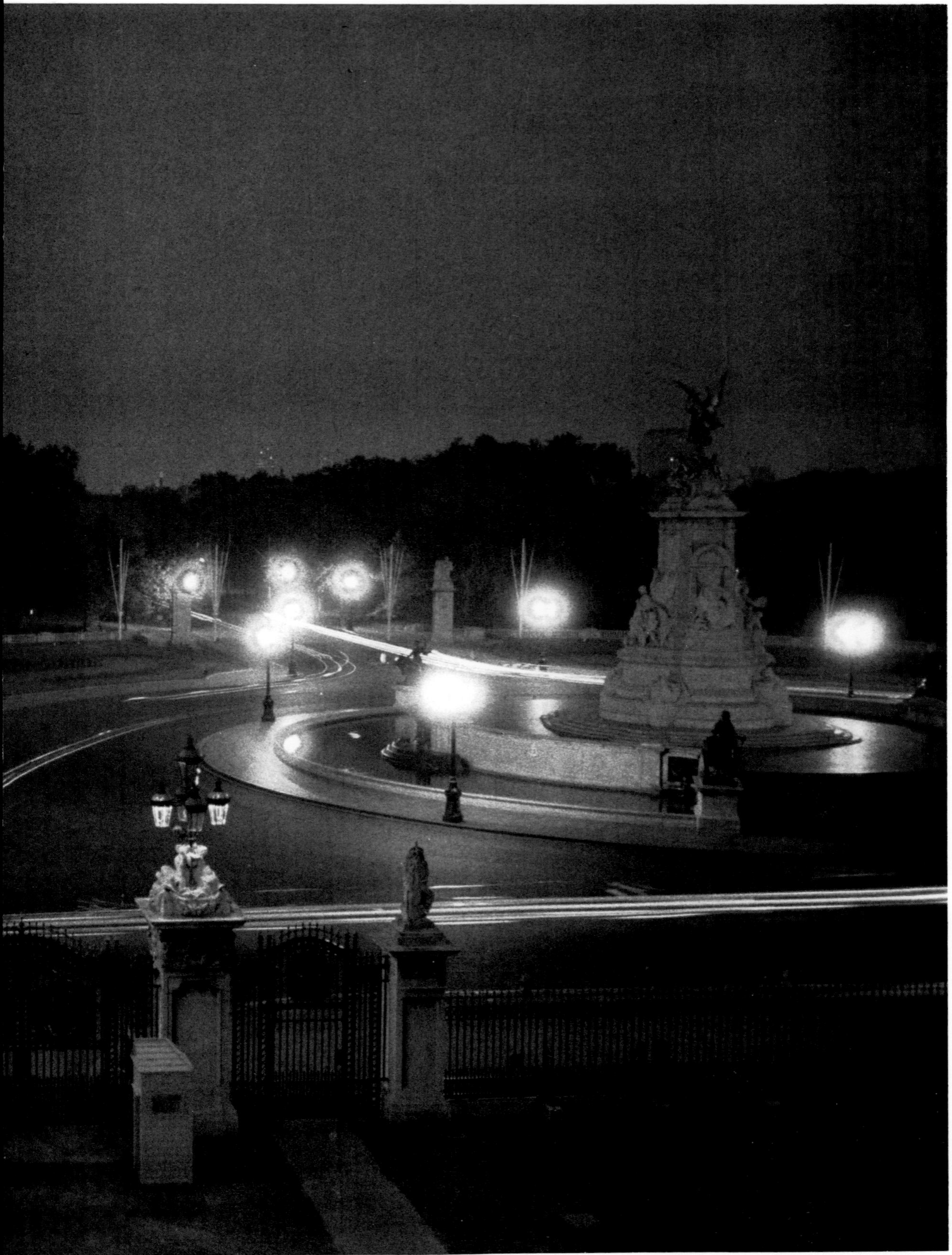

Buckingham Palace HRH The Prince Andrew. The thinnest negative of a bracket of exposures taken at night produced this result. Rating the film at the normal ASA when taking pictures at night will provide a set of exposures that will convey the impression of a grey day. Rate the film at four times its normal ASA (thus reducing the exposure −2 f/stops) to render night as night.

Apart from the demonstration on page 26, you will probably not be faced with photographing different shades of paper. But as with the sheets of paper there are situations where the dominant tone will require correction of the metered exposure. Take a winter snow scene, for example: the brightness of the scene can be correctly recorded by increasing the indicated exposure +2 f/stops.

Where the brightness is constant it is more convenient to set the compensation dial or the ASA rating to take account of the exposure correction, instead of continually correcting after each light reading. For example, 400 ASA film would have to be rated at 100 to be exposed correctly for the snow landscape.

A bright summer day would require an exposure correction of 1 f/stop. This would be equal to rating the film at 200 ASA. Only on a particularly dull and grey day would I ever rate the film at its grey ASA of 400.

Perhaps now you can begin to understand why your negatives generally appear a bit thin (underexposed) when photographing in bright daylight or why your photographs of winter snow scenes appear dull and grey.

Where the scene is predominantly dark the light meter again can only interpret and read the subject as grey. Therefore reduce the metered exposure 2 f/stops to photograph night as night. This 2 f/stops is equivalent to rating 400 ASA film at 1600 ASA.

Rating the film at 1600 ASA does *not* increase the sensitivity of the film! This is a misconception of some photographers who take pictures in low-light situations. The purpose of rating the film at 1600 is to make the exposure correction for the darkness.

The physical act of changing the ASA dial does nothing to increase the sensitivity of the film. If the photograph could not be taken with the film rated at 400 ASA, what logic is there in thinking that the image can be recorded when the exposure is reduced a further 2 f/stops?

The ASA (American Standards Association) number assigned by the film manufacturers designates the film's light sensitivity. The higher the ASA number, the greater the sensitivity of the film.

FOCUS DISTANCE – LIGHT LOSS

F/STOP LOSS:	¼	⅓	½	⅔	¾	1	1 ¼	1 ⅓	1 ½
LENS			Distance in Feet/[Metres]						
Nikkor 50mm f/1.4	**3**	**2.2**	**1.4**	—	—	—	—	—	—
	[.9	.66	.44	—	—	—	—	—	—]
Micro-Nikkor 55mm f/2.8	**3.3**	**2.5**	**1.6**	**1.25**	**1.2**	**1**	**10.5″**	**10″**	**9.9″**
	[1	.75	.5	.38	.37	.3	.27	.26	.25]
Nikkor 85mm f/1.4	**7.2**	**5.5**	**3.6**	—	—	—	—	—	—
	[2.1	1.7	1.1	—	—	—	—	—	—]
Nikkor 105mm f/1.8	**10.4**	**7.8**	**5.2**	**3.9**	**3.5**	—	—	—	—
	[3.2	2.4	1.6	1.2	1.1	—	—	—	—]
Nikkor 105mm f/2.5	**10.5**	**7.9**	**5.3**	**3.9**	**3.5**	—	—	—	—
	[3.2	2.4	1.6	1.2	1.1	—	—	—	—]
Nikkor 135mm f/3.5	**13.2**	**10**	**6.7**	**5**	**4.4**	—	—	—	—
	[4	3	2	1.5	1.3	—	—	—	—]
Hasselblad 80mm f/2.8 CF Planar	**3.5**	**2.7**	—	—	—	—	—	—	—
	[1.1	.8	—	—	—	—	—	—	—]
Hasselblad 80mm f/2.8 C Planar	**3.8**	**2.9**	—	—	—	—	—	—	—
	[1.2	.9	—	—	—	—	—	—	—]
Hasselblad 120mm f/4 CF Makro Planar	**7**	**5.3**	**3.5**	**2.6**	—	—	—	—	—
	[2.1	1.6	1.1	.8	—	—	—	—	—]
Hasselblad 150mm f/4 CF Sonnar	**10.8**	**8.2**	**5.5**	**4.1**	—	—	—	—	—
	[3.3	2.5	1.7	1.25	—	—	—	—	—]
Hasselblad 150mm f/4 C Sonnar	**10.5**	**8**	**5.3**	**4.3**	—	—	—	—	—
	[3.2	2.4	1.6	1.3	—	—	—	—	—]
Hasselblad 250mm f/5.6 CF Sonnar	**22**	**17**	**11.4**	**8.5**	—	—	—	—	—
	[6.7	5.2	3.5	2.6	—	—	—	—	—]

I calculated these focus distance-light loss values using the distance from the film plane to the black element, not the 'Nodal Point', of the lens. Wide angle lenses lose only ¼ f/stop when the lens is fully extended at the closest focus.

FOCUS DISTANCE – LIGHT LOSS

F/STOP LOSS:		¼	⅓	½	⅔	¾	1	1¼	1⅓	1½	
LENS		Distance in Feet/[Metres]									
Hasselblad 80mm		**3**	—	—	—	—	—	—	—	—	
f/2.8 CF Planar	[	.9	—	—	—	—	—	—	—	—	]
Hasselblad 80mm		**3**	—	—	—	—	—	—	—	—	
f/2.8 C Planar	[	.9	—	—	—	—	—	—	—	—	]
Hasselblad 120mm		**4.6**	**3.8**	**2.8**	—	—	—	—	—	—	
f/4 CF Makro Planar	[	1.4	1.15	.85	—	—	—	—	—	—	]
Hasselblad 150mm		**7.2**	**5.7**	**4.3**	—	—	—	—	—	—	
f/4 CF Sonnar	[	2.2	1.75	1.3	—	—	—	—	—	—	]
Hasselblad 150mm		**7.5**	**5.9**	**4.6**	—	—	—	—	—	—	
f/4 C Sonnar	[	2.3	1.8	1.4	—	—	—	—	—	—	]
Hasselblad 250mm		**15.4**	**12.5**	**8.5**	—	—	—	—	—	—	
f/5.6 CF Sonnar	[	4.7	3.8	2.6	—	—	—	—	—	—	]

Information courtesy of Hasselblad, Sweden.

Just before submitting my final draft for this book Hasselblad sent me this set of values for the light loss at close distances. These values were derived by measuring the illuminance at the film plane, eliminating the approximate measurement of the lens movement and the mathematical calculations which I had to use for determining the light loss. This, perhaps, explains any discrepancies. The difference, however, at most is only ⅙ f/stop.

The light loss is a continuous process and it is therefore advisable to compensate for interim distances between those given in the table, bearing in mind that it is better to overexpose slightly than to underexpose. At the minimum focus distance I have indicated the compensation for the nearest value of light loss.

This sensitivity is fixed. The ASA value is that setting which, when used, will render and record the image as mid-grey. The manufacturers, believe it or not, have got it right.

THE ASA NUMBER ASSIGNED TO THE FILM BY THE MANUFACTURER IS CORRECT *ONLY* WHEN THE CAMERA LENS IS FOCUSED ON INFINITY.

This is because the back lens element is closest to the film plane when the lens is focused on infinity. At other than infinity the lens barrel is further away from the film plane. Light therefore has to travel a greater distance with the subsequent loss of intensity.

A through-the-lens metering system will take this light loss into account. But an external or hand-held exposure meter is oblivious to this movement of the lens away from the film plane.

You can see this for yourself by taking a camera lens and watching the back elements move away from the film plane as you adjust the focus from infinity. To demonstrate how this affects exposure find an evenly-lit wall or point the camera up towards the sky and with the lens focused on infinity determine the precise exposure. Now adjust the lens to its minimum focus without changing the exposure. The camera's built-in meter will show a loss of light requiring a change in the exposure setting.

In a studio it is unlikely that the lens will be used focused on infinity. It is more the case that the lens, especially if it is a telephoto, will be focused on the minimum focus distance. Depending on the focal length of the lens, the difference in exposure between the lens focused on infinity and focused on the minimum distance is as much as ½ to 1 f/stop. For example, a Hasselblad 80mm lens loses ⅓ f/stop when focused on minimum distance, the 150mm lens loses ⅔ f/stop, and the 120mm lens loses ⅔ f/stop.

This light loss is significant! It has to be recognized and allowed for otherwise the actual exposure will not be as expected.

This is why professional photographers working in the studio, using a hand-held light meter, rate their film differently from the ASA recommended by the manufacturers. Using, for example, the 150mm lens they have to increase their exposures by, you guessed it, ⅔ f/stop. The 125 ASA film is rated at 80. This is the exposure correction for ⅔ f/stop.

If you ask professionals why they rate the film this way the answer is usually that experience tells them to do so. But now you know the real reason.

For those of you who insist on determining your 'personal ASA', this light loss through focusing must be considered. Otherwise the whole exercise becomes a waste of time. Using a Nikkor 135mm lens, you might, for instance, have determined your personal ASA to be 250 (instead of 400) when in the studio focused on a grey card at 5 feet (1.524 metres). When you have the focus on infinity that ASA will be wrong.

One other bit of information. When the camera lens is focused on infinity its back element is as close as it can get to the film plane. If the lens is also stopped down to its minimum aperture, light is

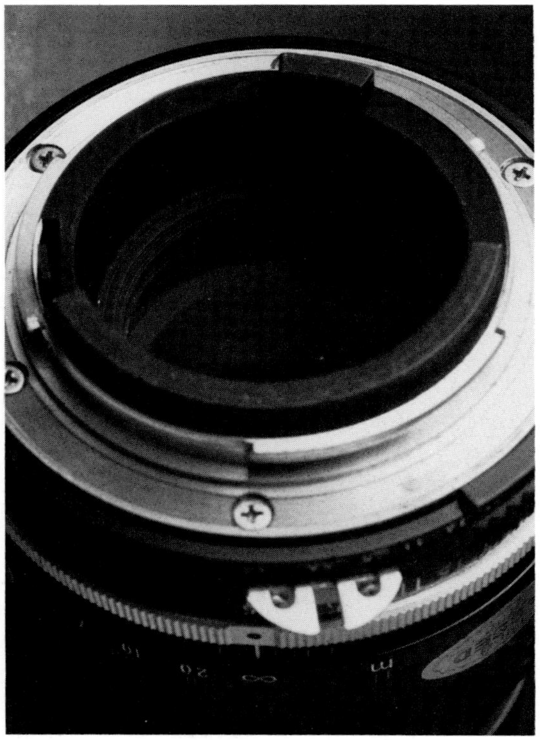

Lens focused at infinity.

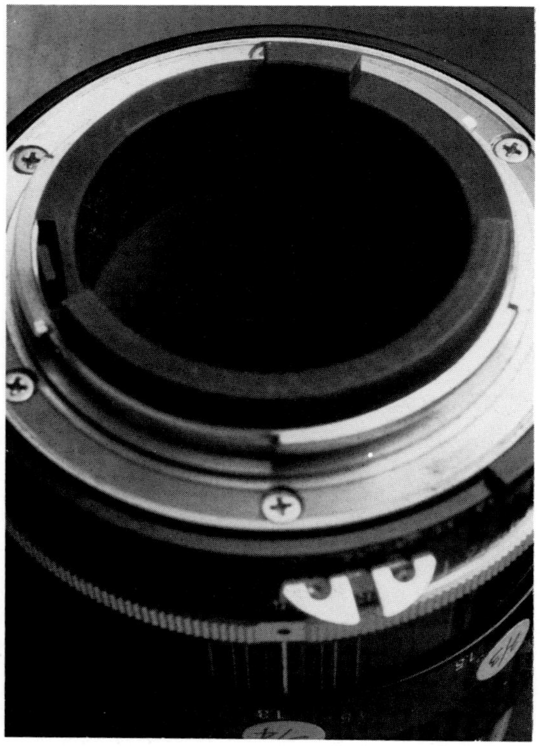

Lens focused close up.

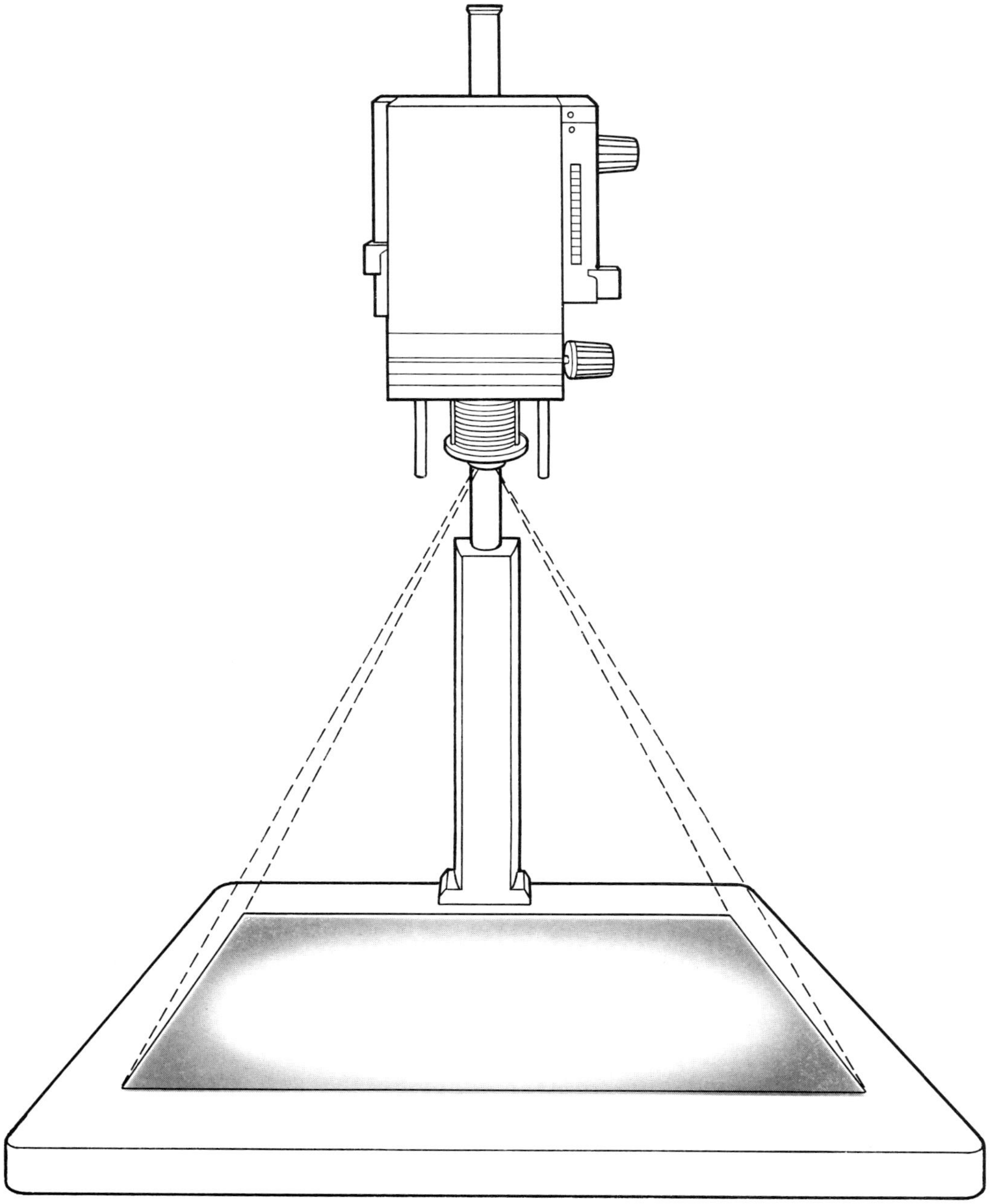

The light projected from the enlarger lens has to travel further to the corners and edges of the format area than to the centre. The intensity will thus be seen to diminish at the perimeter.

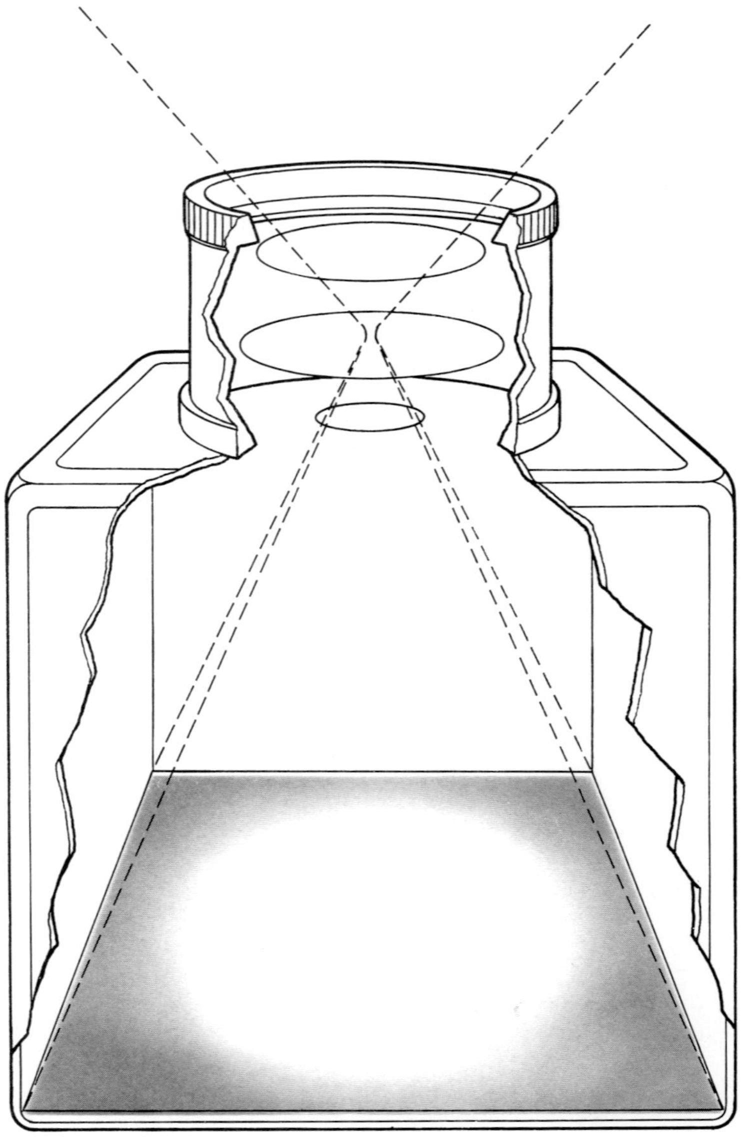

In the camera, again, the light has to travel further to the corners and edges of the film format area and diminishes in intensity. This is more pronounced when the lens is focused at infinity (the lens is closer to the film plane at that focus) and at the minimum aperture.

coming through virtually a pinhole. From that 'point' light has to travel further to the corners of the negative than it does to the centre. In doing so the light intensity will be greater in the centre of the negative and will fall off in proportion to the distance it has to travel from the centre. The image will be its darkest in the corners of the negative. A straight contact print made from such a negative will reveal this darkening or vignetting effect.

But, as we learned in the previous chapter, the light projected from an enlarger also has to travel further to the corners of the print area. Where the negative vignetting is not too great this loss of light from the enlarger compensates for the thinning-out of the density. But it is not always a perfect match. If your negatives consistently show this vignetting effect try using a wider aperture to avoid the pinhole effect and compensate by using a faster shutter speed.

Such vignetting can also be seen when copying an evenly-lit subject. This too can be attributed to the use of too small an aperture, even though the focus is not on infinity. Using a wider aperture avoids this pinhole effect and provides a better distribution of light throughout the negative area.

I therefore question the school of thought that encourages the use of the minimum aperture for landscape and pictorial photography.

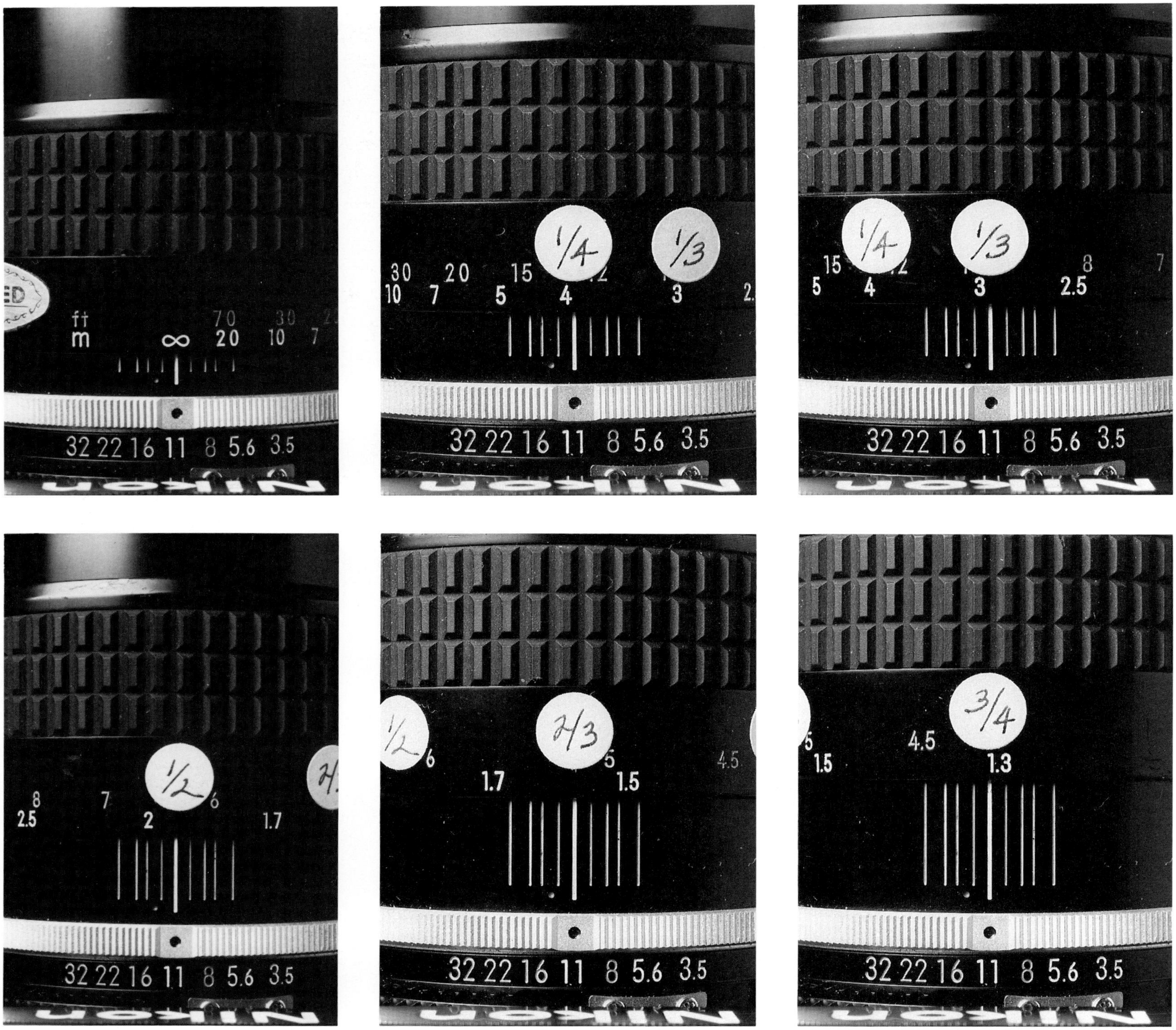

Markings on the lens to indicate exposure compensation for focusing distance.

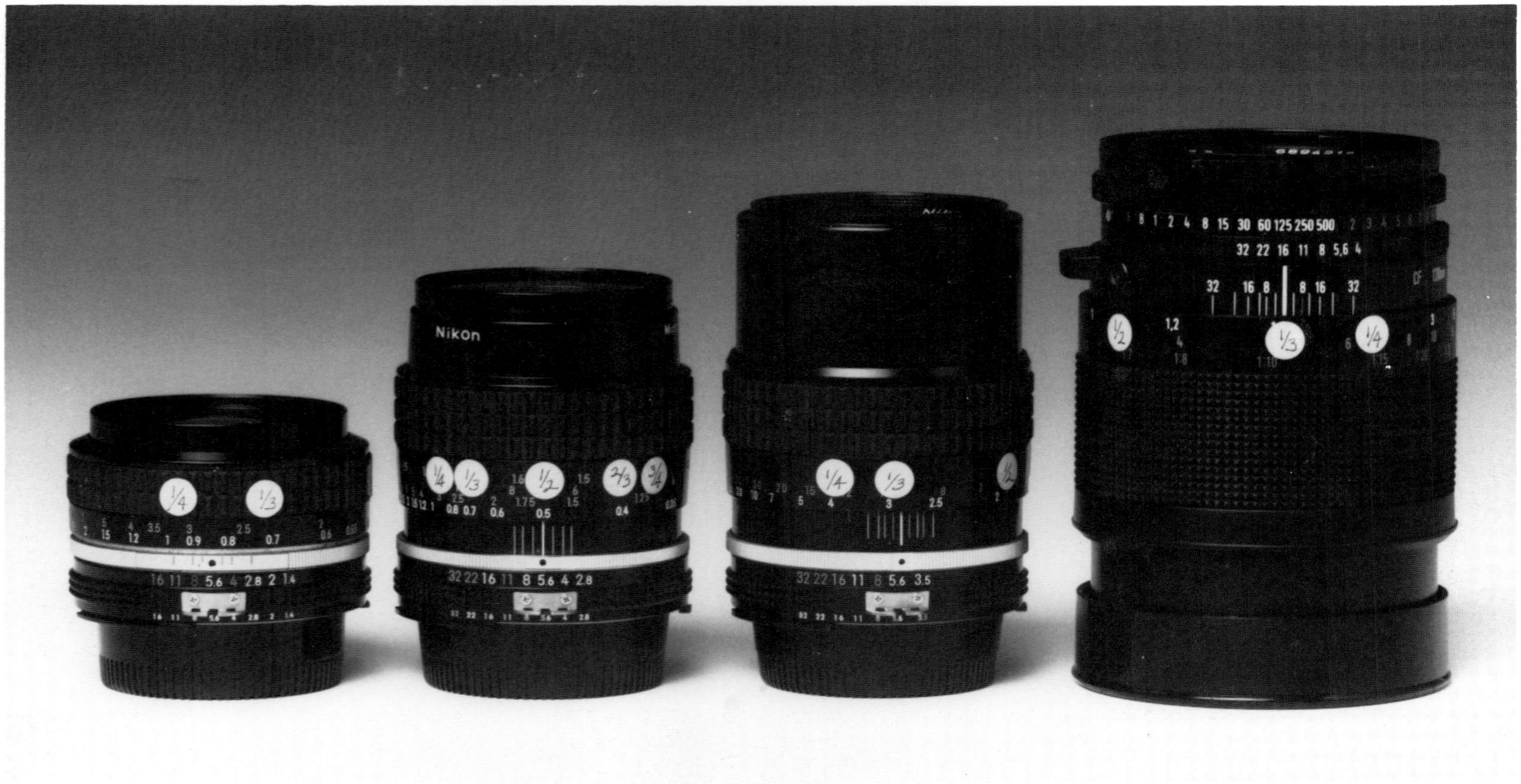

Camera lenses with light loss markings.

It would be useful if camera or lens manufacturers would indicate on the focusing barrel the effective light loss when focused on a certain distance. I have actually done this on my camera lenses by measuring the extension of the lens elements from the film plane and calculating the light loss when the lens is focused on that distance. On the lens barrel I have stuck a sticky label on the distance scale where the light loss occurs.

On the distance scale of the Hasselblad 150mm C Sonnar lens, for example, at the 10.5 feet (3.201 metres) position I have placed a sticky label indicating a light loss of ¼ f/stop, at 8 feet (2.439 metres) a light loss of ⅓ f/stop, at 5.3 feet (1.620 metres) a light loss of ½ f/stop, and at minimum focus distance of 4.3 feet (1.311 metres) a light loss of ⅔ f/stop.

Although a through-the-lens metering system exists on my 35mm cameras, which will compensate for the barrel extension, I have indicated as well the light loss at the appropriate focusing distance on my lenses. This allows me to make the appropriate exposure compensation when using a hand-held or external light meter, as when working with electronic flash in a studio.

These exposure markings on the focusing barrel indicate the exposure compensation that must be made to correct for the lens extension when focused other than on infinity. I may, for example, take a landscape picture and be focused on infinity. If it were a grey day and I were using a 400 ASA film the ASA setting on my hand-held meter would remain at 400. But if I wanted to take a picture of someone in the foreground and had to focus on him, say 8 feet (2.439 metres) away, this, on the Hasselblad 150mm lens, would indicate and require an exposure compensation of ⅓ f/stop. I would have to correct the exposure by increasing the aperture + ⅓ f/stop.

Now suppose I wanted to take that individual's portrait, in the same setting and the same light, and had to focus at minimum distance. The marking on the lens barrel, focused at that distance of 4.3 feet (1.311 metres), would indicate an exposure compensation of + ⅔ f/stop. To correct for the lens extension I would have to increase the light meter's exposure reading by increasing the exposure + ⅔ f/stop.

It sounds complicated, but this is the nature of the beast. If your interest is simply holiday snapping and sending your film away to be processed and developed, then this book is not for you. But photography, for those of you who really are seriously interested, is much more than happy snapping. It requires a conscious effort. Part of the satisfaction is in understanding and knowing how to use the tools.

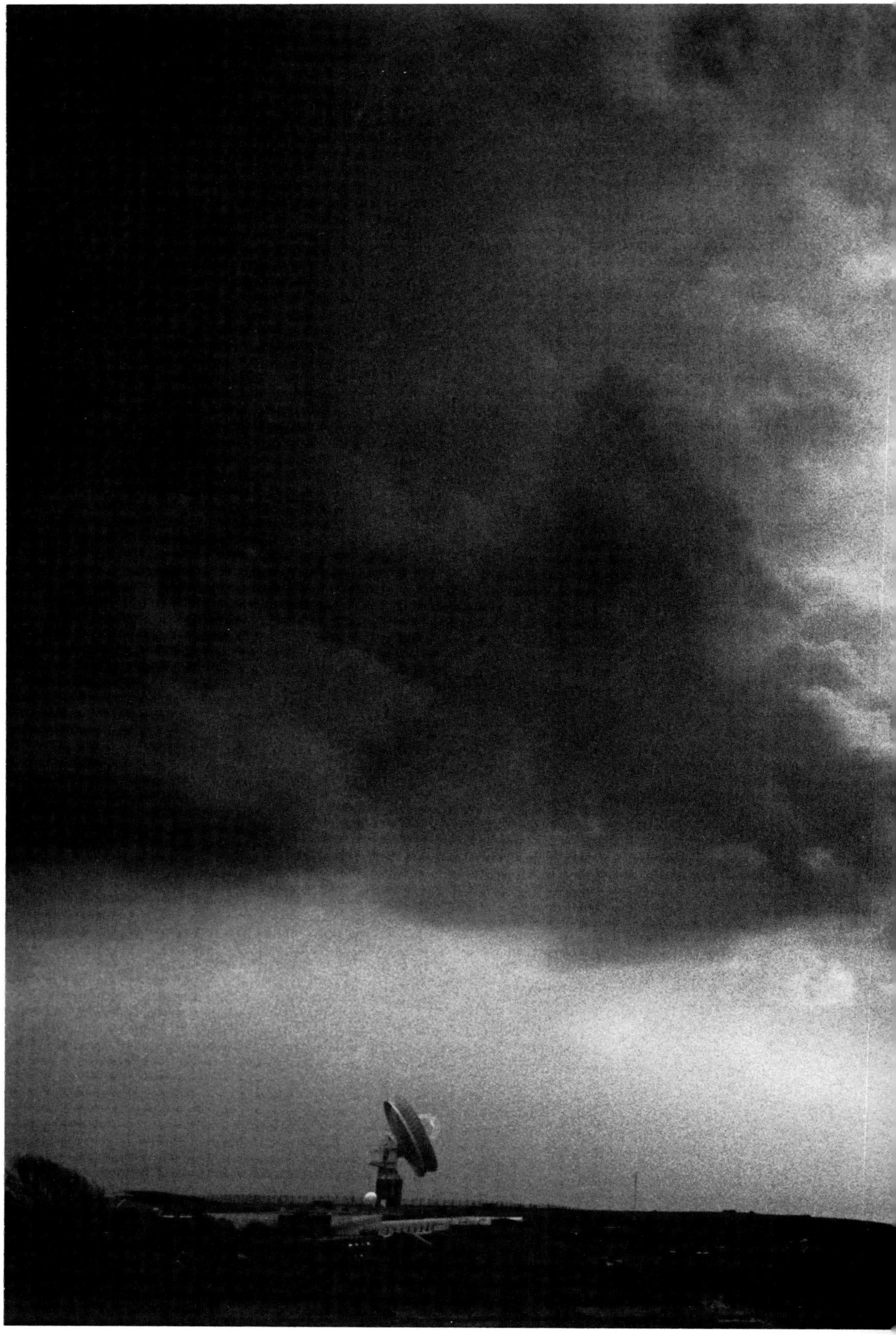

Anybody There? Dr Tim Rudman, FRPS. Exposure with lens focused at infinity – there is no exposure-light loss compensation. The photograph has been printed with image reversed. Our natural inclination to look left to right, he felt, made the picture 'read' better printed this way. I agree. Apart from cropping, dodging, burning-in and toning, reversing the image is another means of enhancing the print.

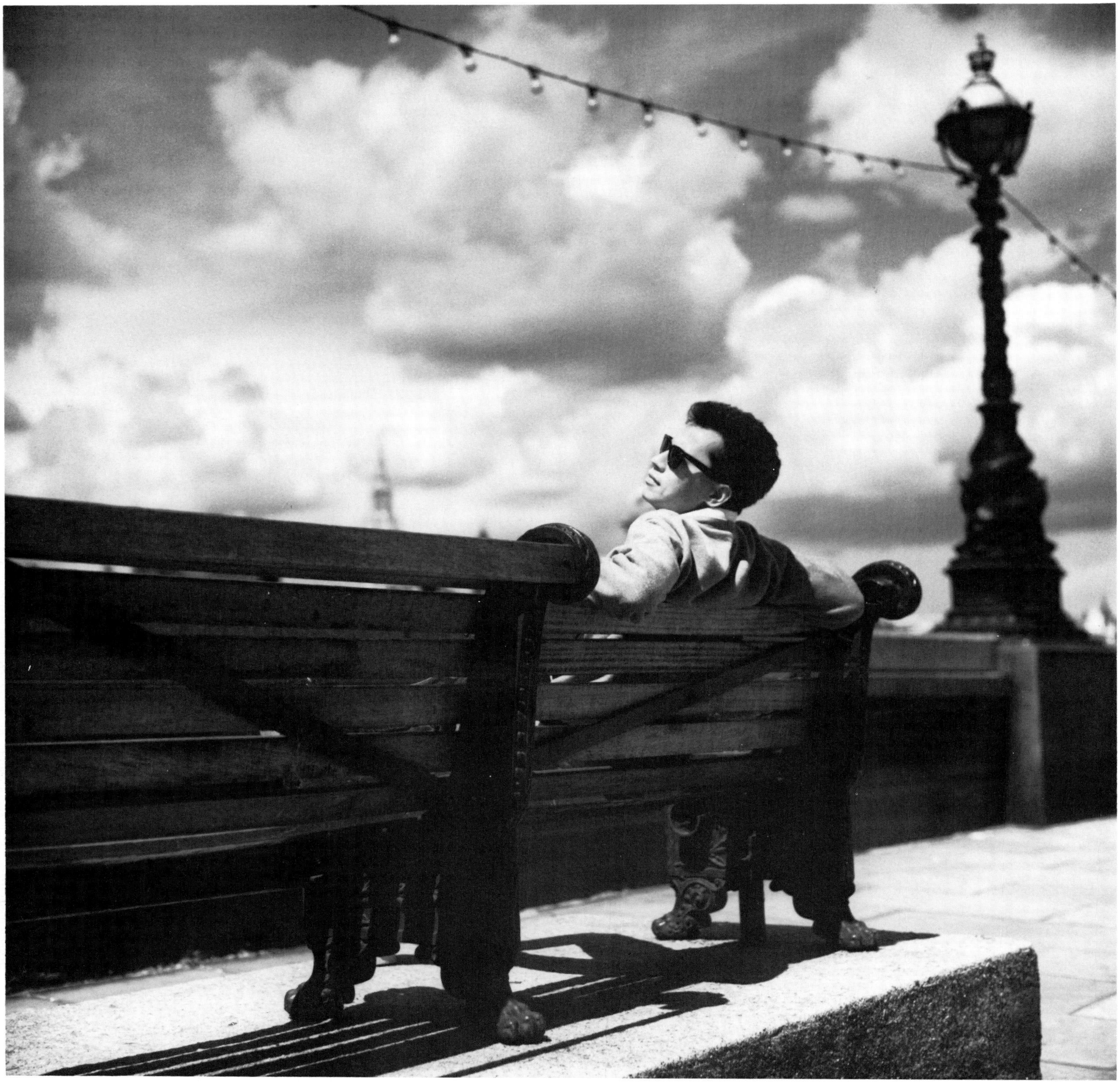

Rick Tony White. Exposure is increased to compensate for the light loss at close distances.

CHAPTER THREE

CHAPTER THREE
Film Processing

The most difficult part of processing film is loading the reels or spirals with the film. The actual processing is just a sequence of pouring chemicals in and out of the developing tanks. Provided the film has been properly loaded, the chemicals used in the right sequence, the correct temperature maintained, and the film agitated during the process, the results should be absolutely fine.

DEVELOPING FILM

There are not too many 'secrets' I can pass on. It really is very straightforward.

The exposed roll of film has to be handled and developed in total darkness. For small quantities of film I use 'daylight' developing tanks and processing spirals.

The film first has to be loaded onto spirals: the plastic ones are self-threading and easy to load; the stainless steel ones require a bit of practice to learn to load properly. Use a spare roll of film and practise loading with the light on. Then try it in the dark. Once you get used to the stainless steel spirals they become very easy and very fast to use.

The reels are then placed in the processing tank. After sealing the lid on the unit, the light can be switched on.

The chemicals can now be poured through the 'light-tight' opening on the tank lid.

DEVELOPING

With regard to specific developers, again I have no magic brew. I use what the film manufacturers recommend for developing their film. I follow as well the manufacturers' recommended time/temperature data for processing the film. I suggest you do the same.

The change in ASA does not change the normal processing time for the film. The processing time remains as if the film were rated at its normal ASA. A single roll of 400 ASA film could have been rated at 1600, at 800, at 400, at 200, and at 100 ASA to correctly expose a rock concert, a sunset, a grey card, a bright day, and a snow scene. This film would be processed normally.

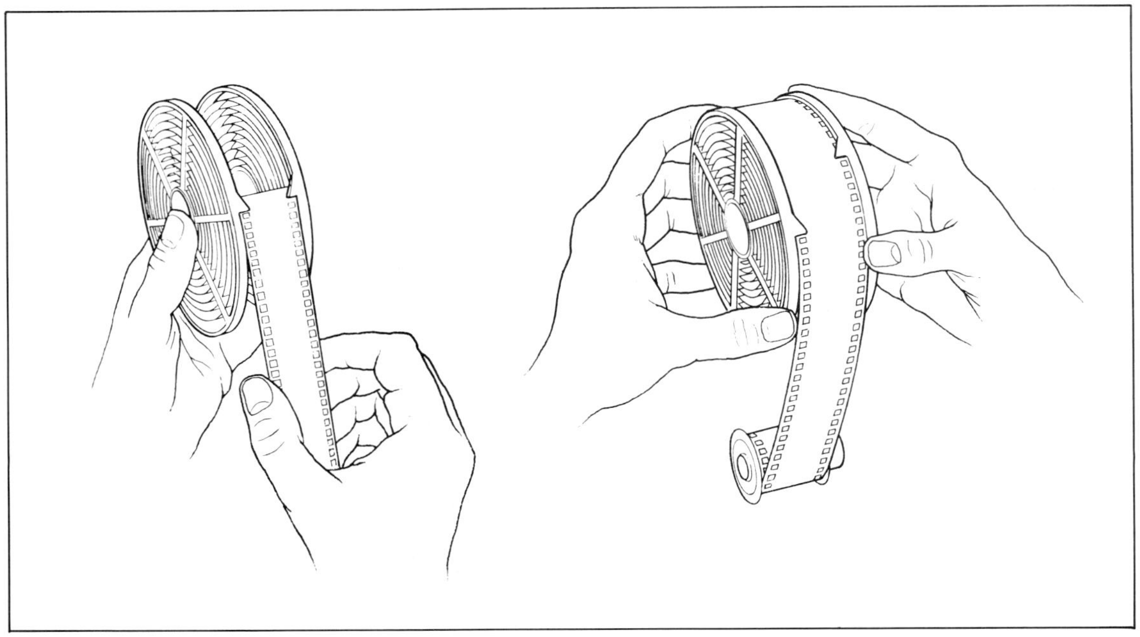

Paterson spirals. The spirals must be absolutely dry to load the film. Twist the spirals back and forth for the self-loading operation.

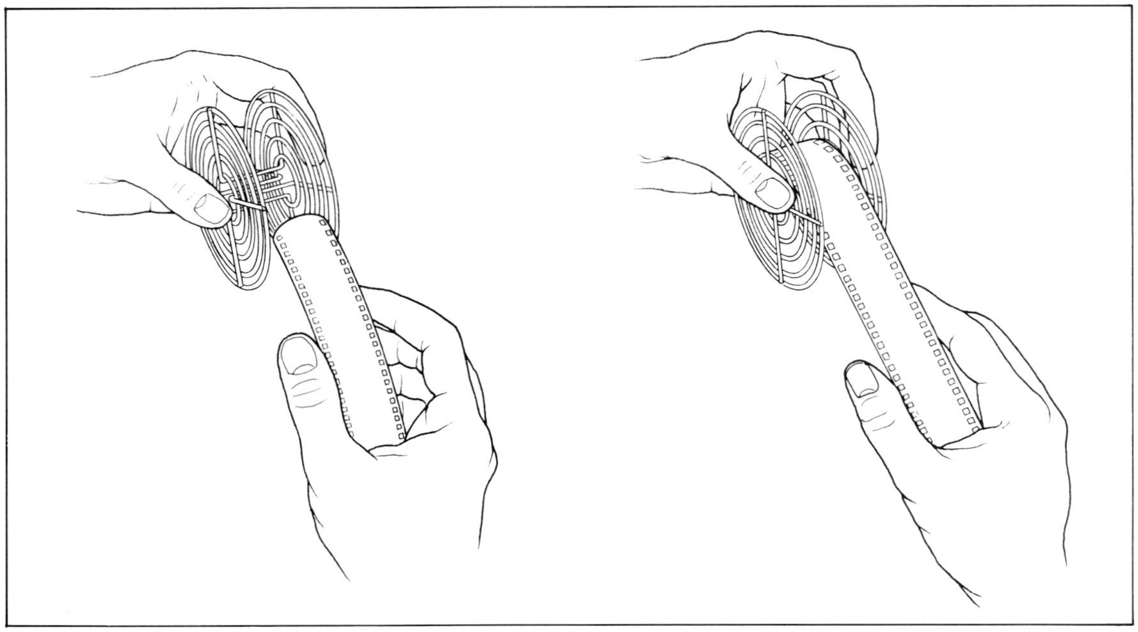

Stainless steel spirals. Simply rotate the spirals to load the film.

When I worked for a newspaper in Germany I was assigned to photograph a concert performance by a group called 'The Osmonds'. Earlier during the day, at a press call, I had used up half a roll of film photographing another group outdoors. I rated the film at 400 ASA to shoot in daylight.

Instead of putting in a new roll I wanted to use up the other half of the film already in the camera, and at the concert 'up-rated' the same roll to 1600. I shot a couple more rolls of the concert with the ASA at 1600.

The two rolls of film completely rated at 1600 were push processed by increasing their development time. But the one roll which had been rated half at 400, half at 1600, I decided to process for normal as I already had two rolls of the concert and it was the only roll with the other group. So the one roll was processed for the daylight shots – I thought I would have nothing of the concert.

After processing I was surprised to discover that the concert shots were not only beautifully exposed, but less contrasty and they printed up much better than the negatives that had been pushed.

Those of you who photograph at rock concerts and rate 400 ASA film at 1600 ASA are, in fact, correctly exposing for the dark stage. The mistake is made when the development time is extended to 'push process' the roll of film. Your highlight areas will be overdeveloped! There is no need to push process.

And the same applies to 400 ASA film correctly rated at 200 for photographs taken on a bright day. The film is processed for the manufacturers' recommended time.

There are cases where the film has to be 'pulled' or 'pushed'. But this is done to reduce or increase the film contrast, not to increase the film's sensitivity.

PUSH AND PULL PROCESSING

Push processing involves using a higher energy developer, or developing the film for a longer period of time. In practice, rather than changing developers, I extend the development time. This increased development time builds up the highlight density. Push processing effectively increases the contrast.

Reducing the development time or pull processing reduces the contrast of the negative.

Film sensitivity is generally recognized to have a latitude of about 5 f/stops. This means that the range where we can record detail in the shadow areas of the negative as well as detail in the highlight areas spans only 5 f/stops – a light ratio of 1:32. But a bright sunny day will reveal that the range between the shadow and the bright sky is anywhere up to 12 f/stops – a light ratio of 1:4096. The film must somehow compress this wide range. If we simply take an overall exposure meter reading and use the exposure thus determined we might lose all the detail in the shadow areas. If we then process the film normally we might lose the detail in the highlights because of the high build-up of density.

There is a basic relationship in photography which defines the relationship of exposure and development:
EXPOSE FOR SHADOWS, DEVELOP FOR HIGHLIGHTS

EXPOSE FOR SHADOWS

Photographic exposure and development is easier to understand if we make an analogy with tape recorders and sound recording. It is impossible to amplify and play back sounds that are not recorded. The same can be said for film exposure. What is not photographically recorded cannot be brought out in the processing.

Setting the exposure is much like setting the recording level on a tape recorder. The sound range can be seen with the softest sounds just causing the needle or LEDs (Light Emitting Diodes) to flicker. The loudest noise will send the needle or LEDs to, and often beyond, the maximum level of recording. The idea behind adjusting the recording level is to try to balance the two extremes and record every possible nuance of sound so that the softest to the loudest sound is recorded as faithfully as possible.

But unlike sound recording we do not have the facility to see, or perhaps test, our photographic recording before actually taking the picture. Professional photographers, leaving nothing to chance, will, however, test their exposures by shooting Polaroids. This allows them to make any basic changes before actually committing the exposure onto film. For most of us this is a luxury which we have to do without.

Remember, the light meter, set at the manufacturers' ASA rating, will determine the exposure only for mid-grey. A reflection light meter reading (which is the metering system in most cameras) of the shadow area will expose that area for mid-grey. But we know this to be the shadow area of the picture. Hence we have to reduce the exposure to *render* and expose the shadow areas as the darkest part of the picture.

To *expose for the shadows* reduce the exposure determined by the light meter of that area by −2 f/stops. For example, if the shadow reading happened to be 1/60 at f/4 the overall exposure for the entire picture should be 1/60 at f/8 or the equivalent exposure combination (1/250 at f/4, or 1/125 at f/5.6, etc). This −2 f/stop reduction for the shadow area is the minimum exposure that will ensure the shadow details being recorded. It becomes the minimum exposure in that 5 f/stop film latitude.

Exposing for the shadows guarantees the shadow exposure.

But what, you may ask, happens to the bright areas? The bright areas of the picture might very well be overexposed. The saving grace is that the film has yet to be processed!

DEVELOP FOR HIGHLIGHTS

You might be lucky and find (using your light meter) that the actual light ratio of the scene is within the 5 f/stop range of film. For instance, if the shadow area were seen by the light meter as 1/60 at f/4, and if the highlight reading (not the sun, of course) were 1/60 at f/16 – this is within the 5 f/stop range of the film.

Then, having exposed the film at 1/60 at f/8, the normal processing would result in a 'perfect' negative.

One f/stop difference, say a 4 or 6 f/stop light range, can easily be rectified when printing, by printing on a harder or softer contrast grade of paper. This is usually the case for most photographic situations. But beyond this you might need to process the film to compress or expand the contrast on the negative to get better results when printing.

Exposure and development work hand in hand. The exposure for shadows is to ensure that all the detail in the darkest area of the picture is recorded. Developing controls the density of the highlight areas.

Developing the film changes the silver halides that have been exposed to light into opaque silver. This development is consistent with the amount of silver halides exposed to light, and proceeds at an even rate throughout the film emulsion. The shadow areas, which have had the least exposure, after a period of development will have been completely processed and *will not* develop further. The highlight areas, however, having had more exposure will continue to build up in density for as long as the film is being developed. This highlight density is directly related to the developing time. Reducing the development time will reduce the build-up of the highlight density and therefore the overall contrast of the negative. Extending the development time will increase the density and likewise the contrast.

Provided the exposure has been made for the shadows and we have determined that the actual scene exceeds the film latitude we can then reduce the development time to provide a negative with a full range of tones.

How much to reduce the development time depends on the film, the developer and, of course, the contrast range of the actual scene. In my experience the minimum 'dev time', even for the most extreme need to reduce the contrast, must not be less than half the normal process time. The film needs this amount of time to adequately develop the shadow area. In practice the most satisfactory results are achieved when the film is processed for the normal time divided by the factor of 1.4. If, for example, the normal time is 10 minutes, dividing by 1.4 will give a time of 7 minutes.

I cannot be very precise about the development time to reduce the contrast. There are far too many variables in far too many individual cases to provide an absolute answer. I can only provide you with a set of development times that will offer some guidance (see the end of this section). You will need to experiment, but now at least you know the principle involved in controlling negative contrast.

But what of situations where the subject-matter is flat and the tonal range of the negative in need of extending? The same rule applies: EXPOSE FOR SHADOWS, DEVELOP FOR HIGHLIGHTS.

Again, determine the exposure for the shadows. Then extend the development time to increase the contrast range. Use the factor of 1.4 again, but this time multiply it by the normal development time. Instead of a normal 10 minutes, for instance, the extended or 'push' time is 14 minutes. If your initial experience proves this not enough, multiply 14 again by 1.4 for a development time of 20 minutes. If the results indicate perhaps development times in-between these values use the factor of 1.09.

To give some guidance I have calculated the 'pull' or 'push' development times against some generally-used normal development times:

DEVELOPMENT TIMES

PULL	6	5.5	4.5	4
	7	6.5	5	4.5
	8.5	7.5	6	5.5
NORMAL	**10**	**9**	**7**	**6.5**
PUSH	12	11	8.5	8
	14	13	10	9
	17	15	12	11
	20	18	14	13

AGITATION

Proper agitation of 35mm and 120 format films in the small tanks consists of inversion of the tank. This movement and flow of solution ensures even development. The first minute of development is with continuous agitation, after which the agitation is for 5 seconds every 30 seconds.

For larger quantities of film I use 15-litre tanks of chemicals and process totally in the dark. A processing basket enables me to process up to thirty rolls of 35mm film or eighteen rolls of 120 film at the same time. The basket is designed to hold six columns of reels stacked on top of one another. An unloaded 35mm reel is placed at the bottom of each stack to provide a better flow of solution through the film.

4 × 5 inch (10.2 × 12.7cm) and 8 × 10 inch (20.3 × 25.4cm) film has to be processed in the 15-litre deep tanks using film hangers and a processing frame. Agitation is even more important, because of the larger surface area of the film, but inversion is obviously impossible and the current design of the frame does not help. The frame is designed so that the film hangers hang straight down. When the frame is immersed in the tank the whole device cuts through the solution like a knife through water. There is very little movement or flow of solution past the film surface. This results in an uneven and patchy development.

Of course there is an answer to the problem. Place the film hangers so that they are slightly angled in the processing frame. When the frame is immersed in the solution the film angle causes the solution to push against the film surface rather than just sweeping by. This creates a tremendous amount of movement and agitation and assures the even development of sheet film.

The temperature is important. Any temperature variations will alter the development time, so try and maintain a constant temperature throughout the process. With the small tanks use a temperature water bath if you need to. Check the accuracy of your thermometer. I tested a number of thermometers and found a discrepancy of temperature readings for the same solution. There was as much as 5 degrees difference between the readings.

Stop and fix the film according to the manufacturers' instructions.

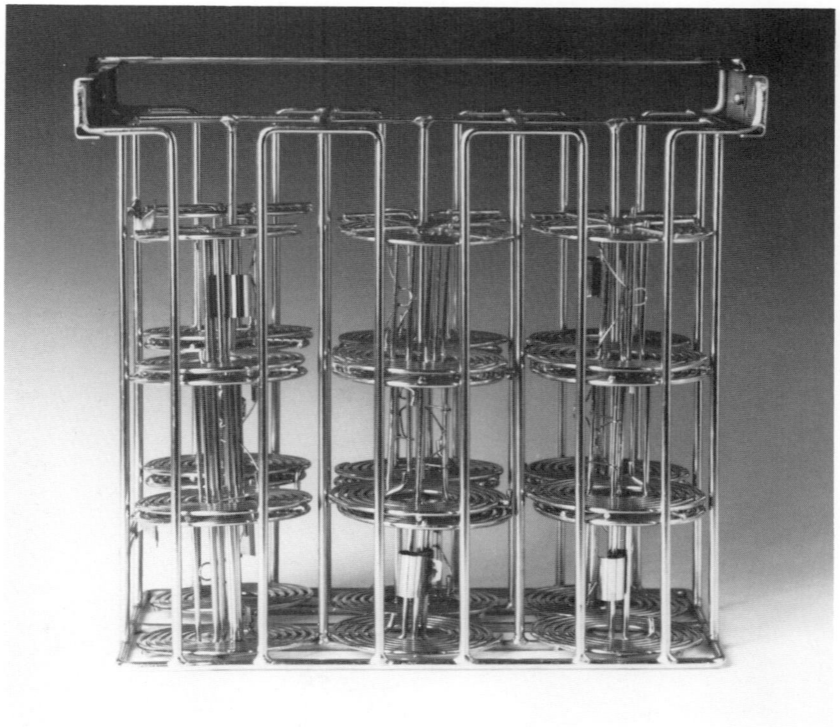

Hewes processing basket.

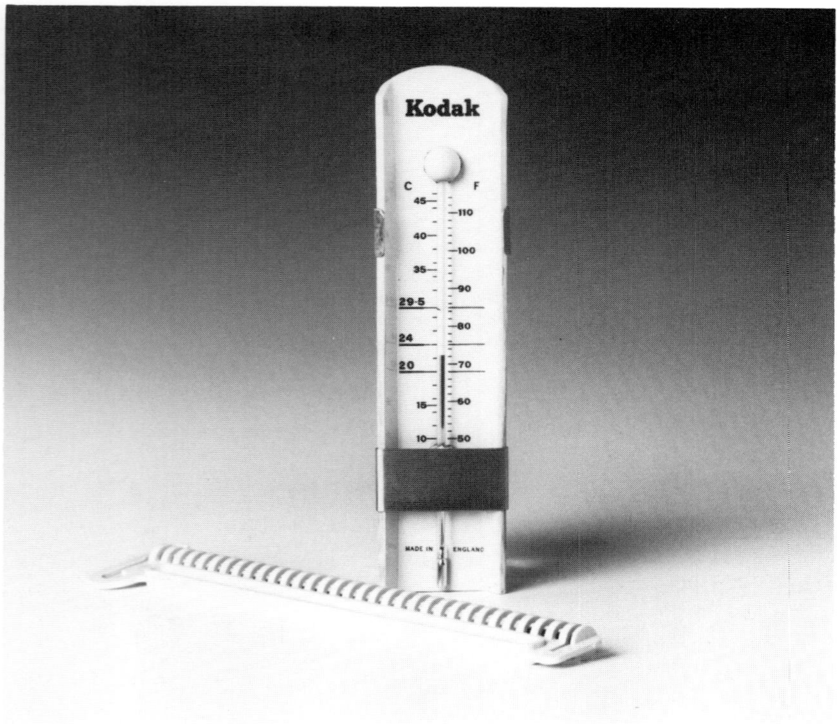

Paterson and Kodak thermometers.

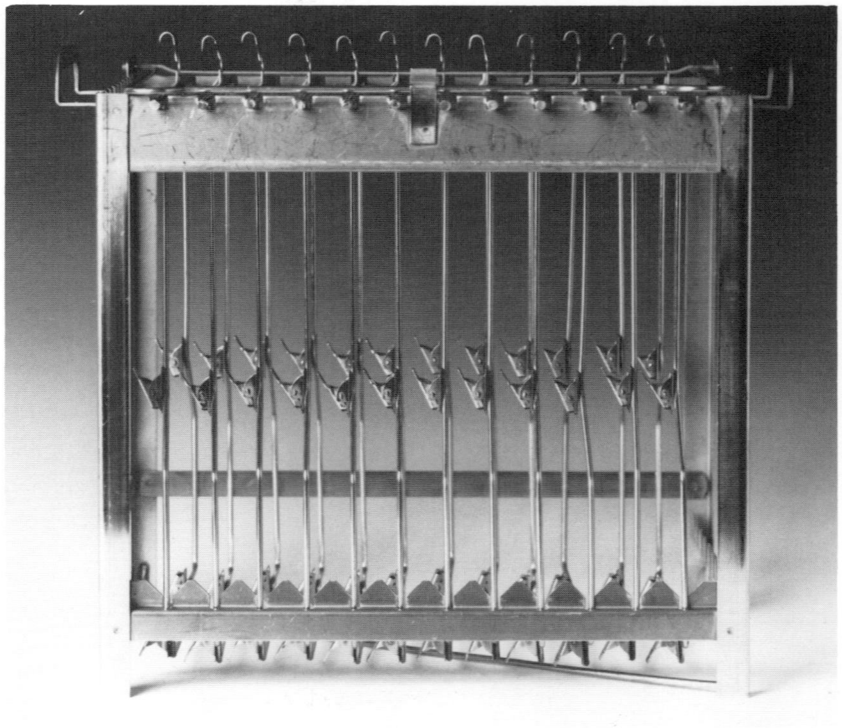

Kodak sheet film holder with processing frame. The standard method of hanging the film holder straight down.

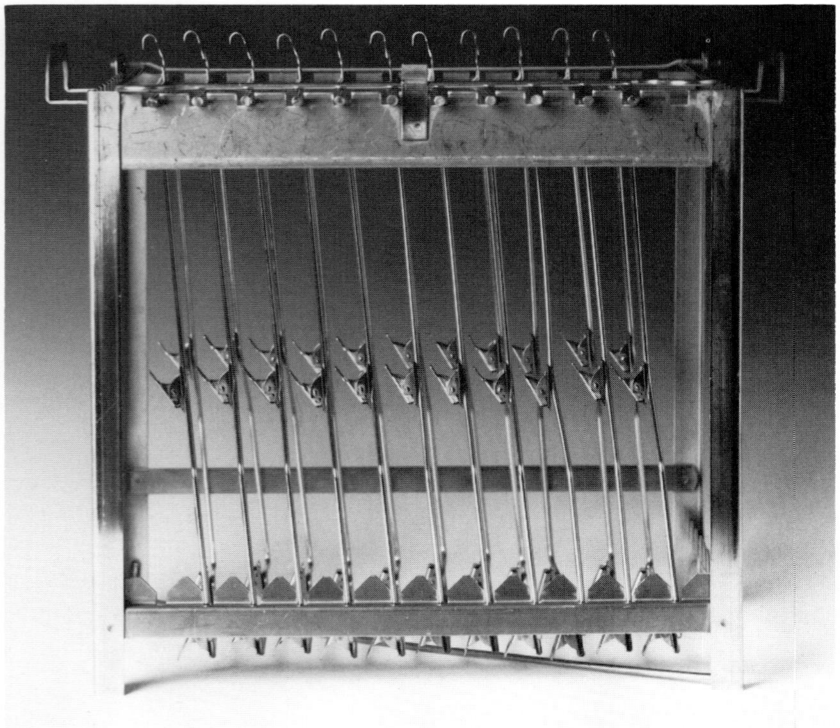

The film holders here are angled, allowing better agitation.

I had to put this exposure/development to the test when I helped Linda McCartney with a picture inside a barn. It was absolutely pitch black inside, with only the light coming through the barn doors providing illumination. A spot meter reading was taken of the darkest part of the barn where we wanted detail. I think the exposure was something like 2 seconds at f/4. To expose for the shadows this exposure was reduced by −2 f/stops, thus making the overall exposure 2 seconds at f/8.

We were using a 10 × 8 inch plate camera. We wanted to get as much depth of field as possible and so had to stop down to the minimum aperture of f/45. The equivalent exposure of 2 seconds at f/8 was 1 minute at f/45. (I was not too worried about reciprocity failure.) This exposure time did not cause me much concern as the camera was on a tripod. What did worry me was the 12 f/stop exposure difference between the shadow areas within the barn and the bit of land that could be seen through the barn doors.

We took two shots, both at the same exposure: one for testing, the other to make any adjustments.

My normal dev time for 10 × 8 inch (25.4 × 20.3cm) sheet film is 10 minutes. In order to compress the extreme exposure difference of the barn picture I reduced the dev time to 5 minutes with constant agitation. The results surprised even me. The negative was easily printable on a grade 1 paper. Had it been processed for normal the highlights would have been impossible to burn-in in the printing. Had it not been exposed for the shadows no detail would have been on the negative and it would certainly not have been revealed in printing.

The exposure/development technique is more applicable to sheet film than it is to 35mm or roll film. Shooting two sheets of film allows you to test one, make any necessary changes in the development, and process the second sheet should you need to. You could shoot an entire roll of film on the same subject and 'clip-test' a portion of it. In the dark cut a length of exposed film and use this for testing. Make sure the rest of the film is safely back in a film cassette or rolled back onto its spool and covered with the light-tight backing material.

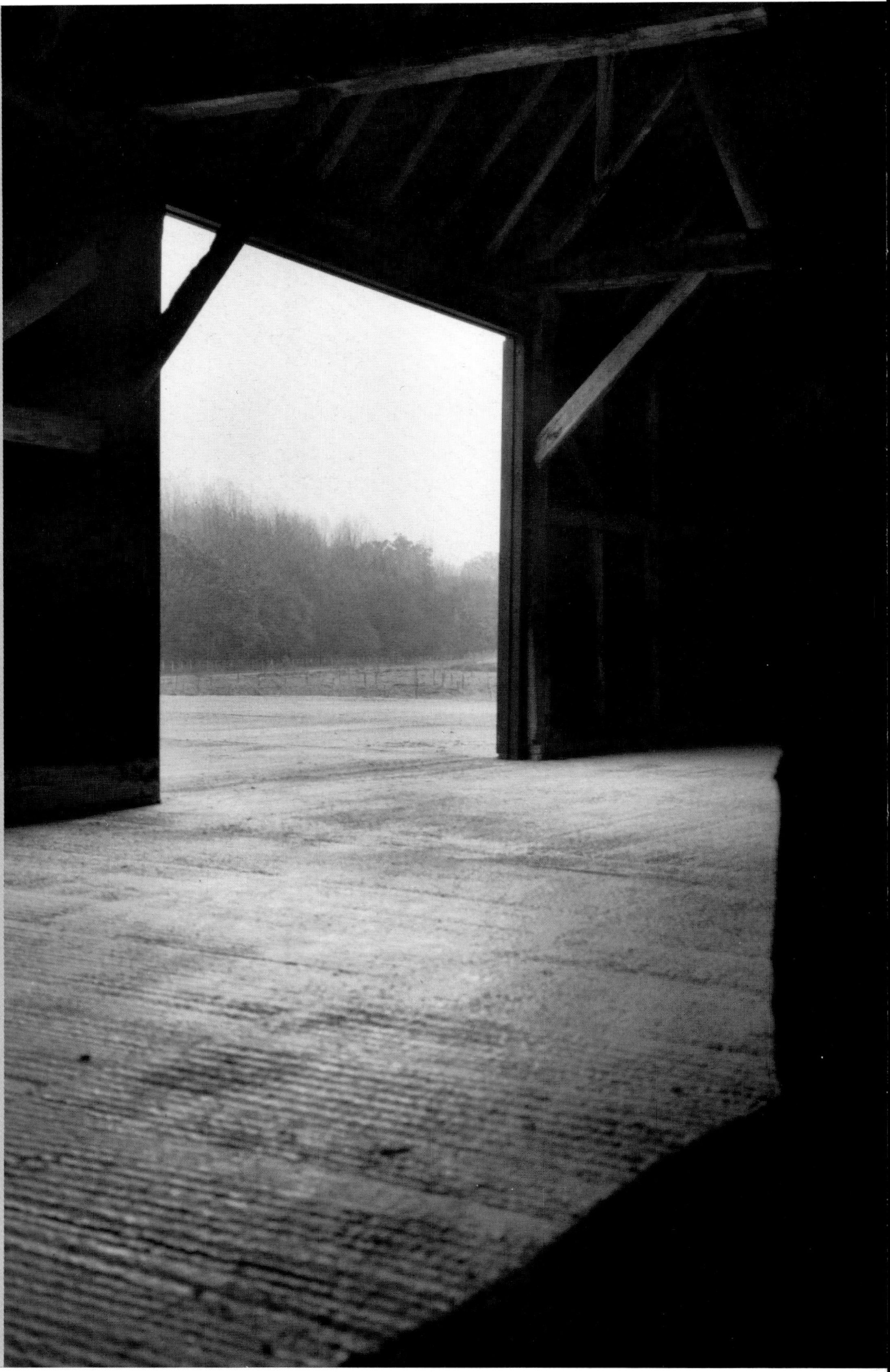

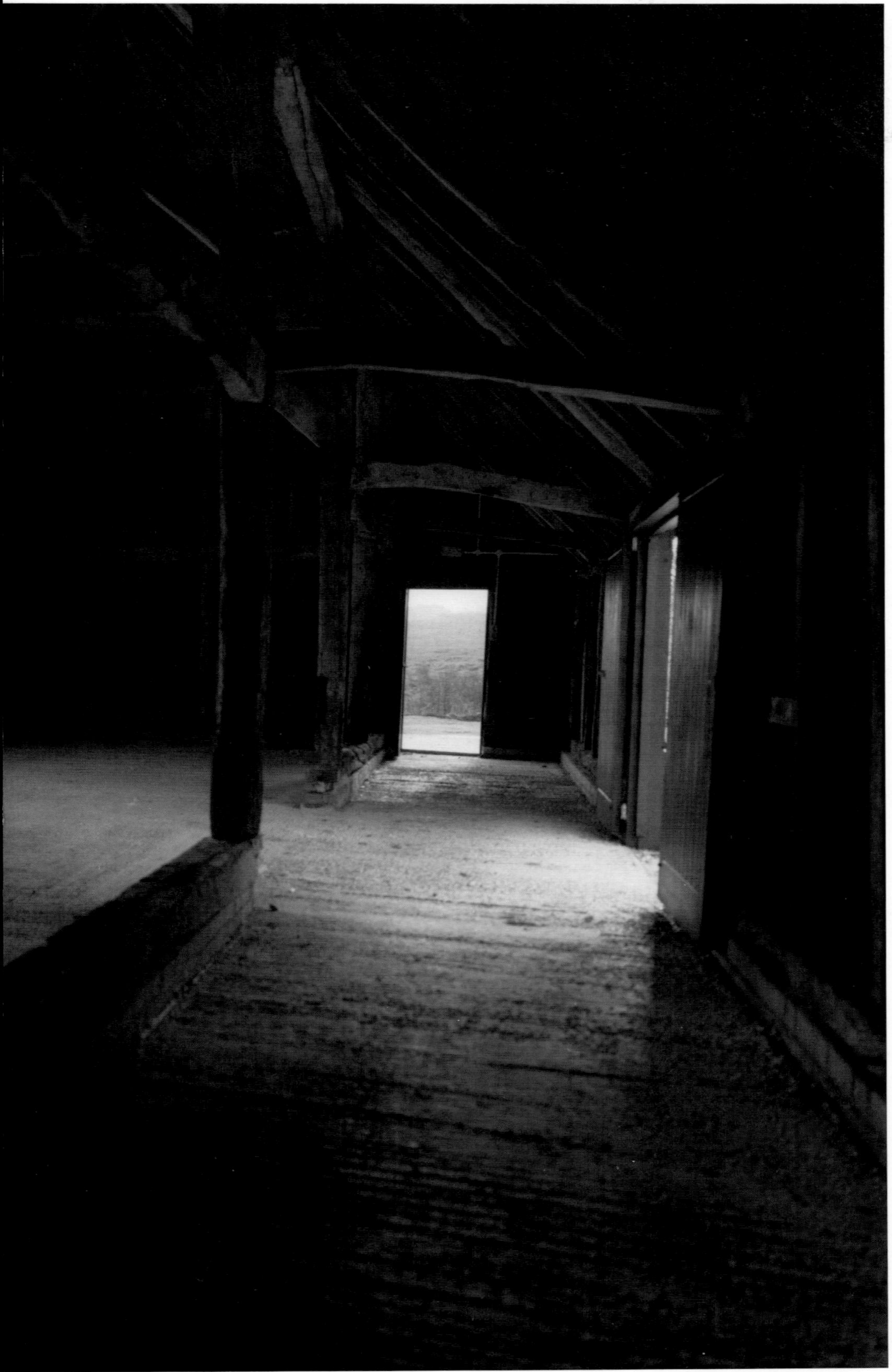

Before the Harvest Linda McCartney.
A spot meter was used to determine the exposure for the shadows. A highlight reading was taken as well to determine the contrast range as a guide for the developing time.

My main concern about filing and storing negatives in envelopes is whether the emulsion surface is in contact with the envelope itself. Inserting or drawing out the negative from sleeve-type containers creates a potentially hazardous situation where any grit on the negative or envelope will cause a scratch on the negative. Even the surface of the sleeve in contact with the emulsion side of the negative can scratch the film.

I store my negatives and those of my clients in an oversize glassine envelope. The strips of negatives of one entire roll of film are placed on top of one another and the stacked negatives inserted in the envelope. The only negative in danger of being scratched is the one at the bottom of the stack in direct sliding contact with the envelope.

In my working capacity I use the oversize glassine envelopes normally used for storing 2¼ inch square (6 × 6cm) negatives. But the best way to store negatives is to wrap the stacked strips in a sheet of light-weight paper like 'onion skin'. This totally eliminates the problems of scratching caused by sliding the negatives in and out of sleeves.

STOP BATH

A weak solution of acetic acid is used to 'stop' the development of the film. It neutralizes the alkalinity of the developing solution prior to the actual 'fixing' of the film. It helps to prolong the working life of the fixer.

FIXER

The fixer is a solution of sodium thiosulphate which removes the silver halides which have not been converted into metallic silver. This fixes the image.

Acid hardener is required in film fixer to 'harden' the soft emulsion against scratches.

WASHING AND DRYING

After fixing, the film must now be washed and dried. The reason for agitating the film is not only to circulate fresh developer but also to ensure against air bubbles clinging 'permanently' to the film. The air bubble prevents the area it occupies from developing. This applies to washing as well. Make sure that you agitate the film occasionally in the wash to get rid of the dreaded clinging bubbles.

Be particularly careful with the bubbles created with using film 'wetting agents'. Squeegee the film directly after using the wetting solution. This soapy substance leaves bubble impressions on the emulsion if the film is left to drain too long after using.

Hang up the film to dry in a dust-free environment. Use wooden clothes-pegs to weight down the ends. In my amateur days I would process my film at night and hang the film in the bathroom. It would be perfectly dry the next morning. The ideal way, in fact, is to dry the film at room temperature. This, in my experience, is less likely to produce drying marks.

The force-drying of film in a heated drying-cabinet is necessary in my professional capacity. The film must not be disturbed while drying. Opening the cabinet doors will cause a sudden drop in temperature which will create drying marks from any water or dampness still on the film.

When drying film sheets in their hangers unclip the top-most and bottom-most corners of the film as it hangs at an angle. Before hanging to dry, blow out the water remaining in the clips. The corners where the film is attached to the frame are always the last to dry. Getting rid of the excess water helps dry the film faster and eliminates the danger of water running down the film after the main area has dried.

NUMBERING

After drying I suggest cutting 35mm film in strips of six frames each, the 2¼ inch square (6 × 6cm) format in strips of four frames. Store these in negative glassine envelopes.

I use a draughtsman's inking pen to write either the date or our 'job' number on the end of the roll of film. This is our 'file number' for that roll of film. When the film is 'contacted' the number appears white on a black background.

If you choose to use the date to file your negatives do so in the following manner: year/month/date. For example:

88/11/05, which represents film processed or taken on 5 November 1988.

More than one roll of film processed or taken that day

88/11/05-1
88/11/05-2
88/11/05-3 etc.

This number filing is in sequence. If it is written as 05/11/88, the film processed the following day would be 06/11/88, which is not consecutive and will become confusing.

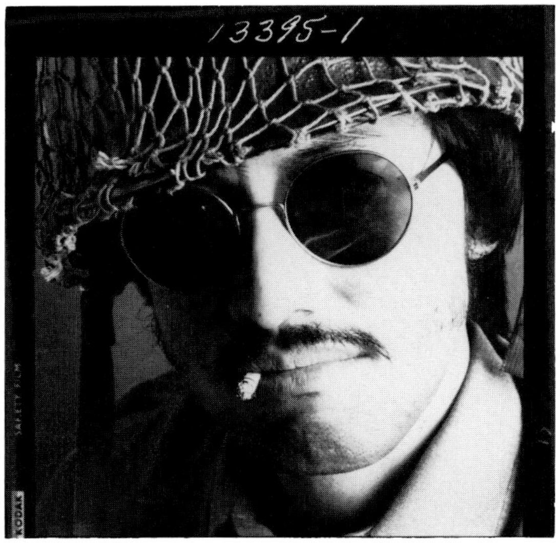

I write on the negative with a Rotring pen. When contacted the number serves as the negative file number.

CONTACTING

Set up the enlarger for 'contacting' by switching the lamp on and raising the lamp to provide sufficient light coverage of approximately 12 × 12 inches (30.5 × 30.5cm) on the baseboard. Focus the light by focusing the edge of the negative carrier. You may have to readjust the height of the enlarger.

Stop down 2 f/stops from the maximum aperture. Turn off the lamp.

The 'contact proofer' need only be a piece of foam and a clean sheet of glass. Use the piece of foam on the baseboard and lay a sheet of photographic paper on top. Take the negatives and place them 'emulsion to emulsion' on the paper. Sandwich the whole thing with the sheet of glass.

Now do a test strip, if you like (Chapter Four), to determine the best overall exposure for the whole series of negatives.

The contact sheet is used for reference. After processing, washing and drying, keep it filed with the negatives.

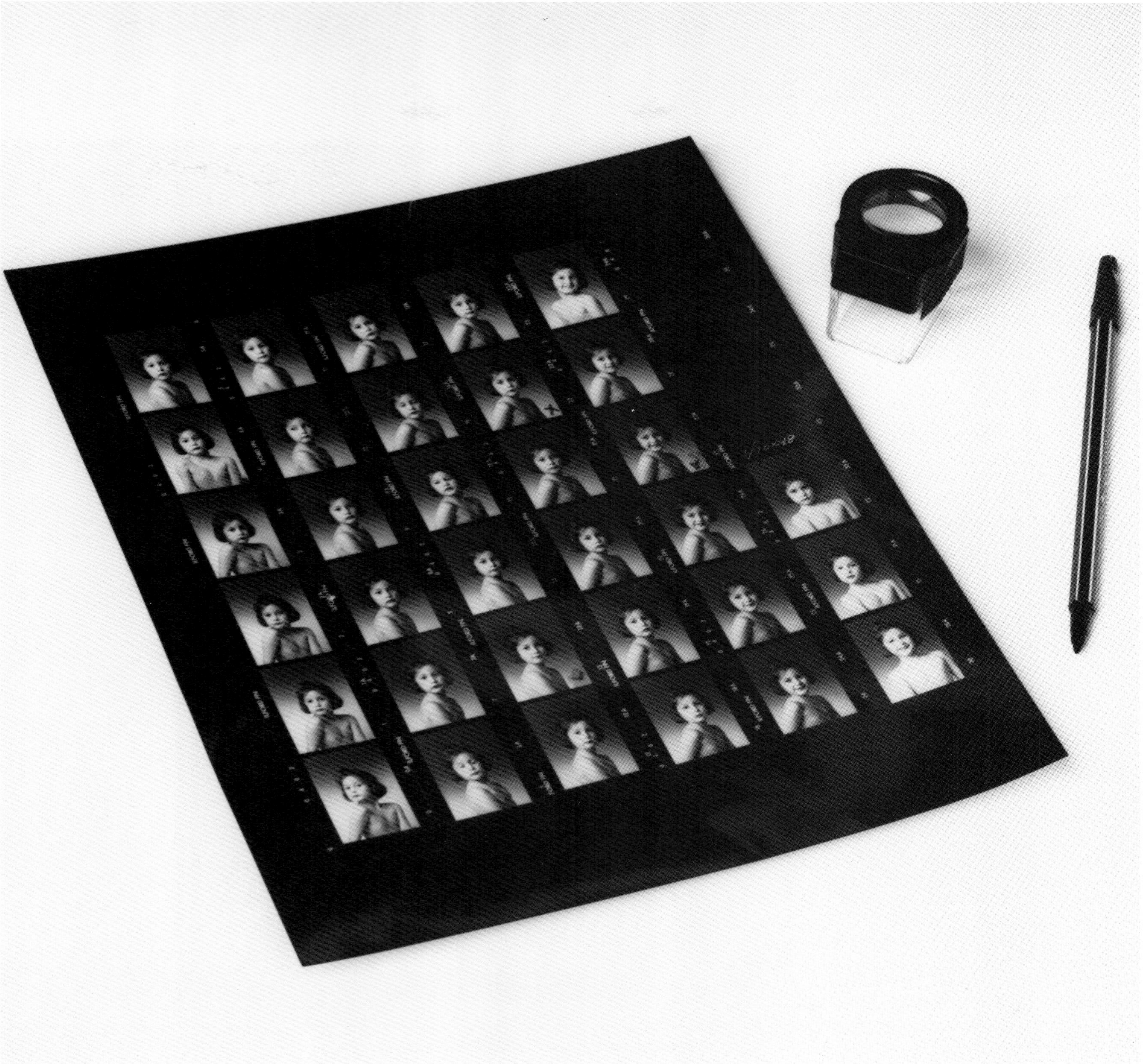

Contact sheet.

Paterson contact printer.

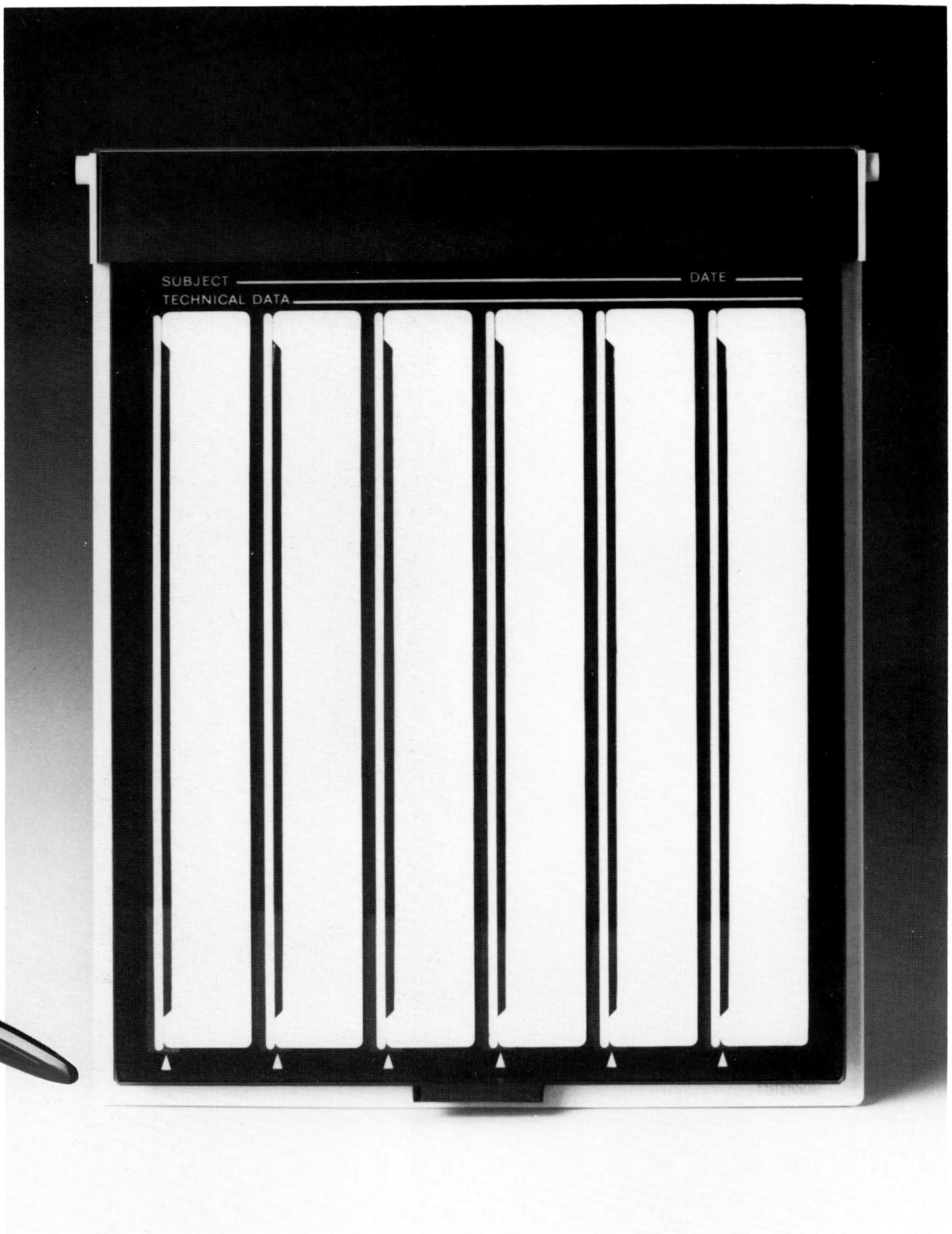

Lupes and magnifying glass.

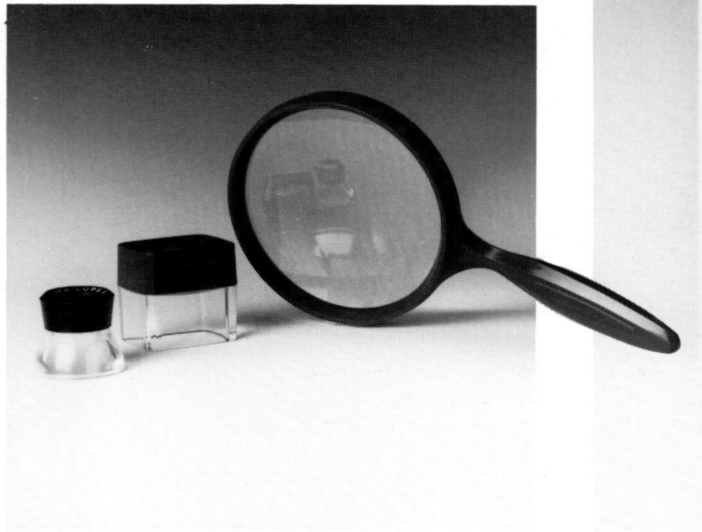

I use contacts only for reference. My inspiration for printing comes from looking at a negative. The contact sheet tends to stifle my creative instincts by showing me only what is there. The negative gives me inspiration because it shows me the potential. But that comes with experience. A negative is, to me, like a piece of lumber. I can look at it and see the possibilities for making a fine piece of furniture or merely use it for shelving. But if that lumber is already in a finished form this might inhibit other creative ideas.

The contact, however, is essential with facial expressions. With portraits a little gimmick to please the subject involves contacting with the negatives reversed. Let your customer make his or her choice from the reversed image. This mirror image is the way the subject sees himself or herself. Once the choice is made, print the negative the right way around. The mirror image is the face that pleases the subject – printing it the right way around is the public face he or she wants others to see.

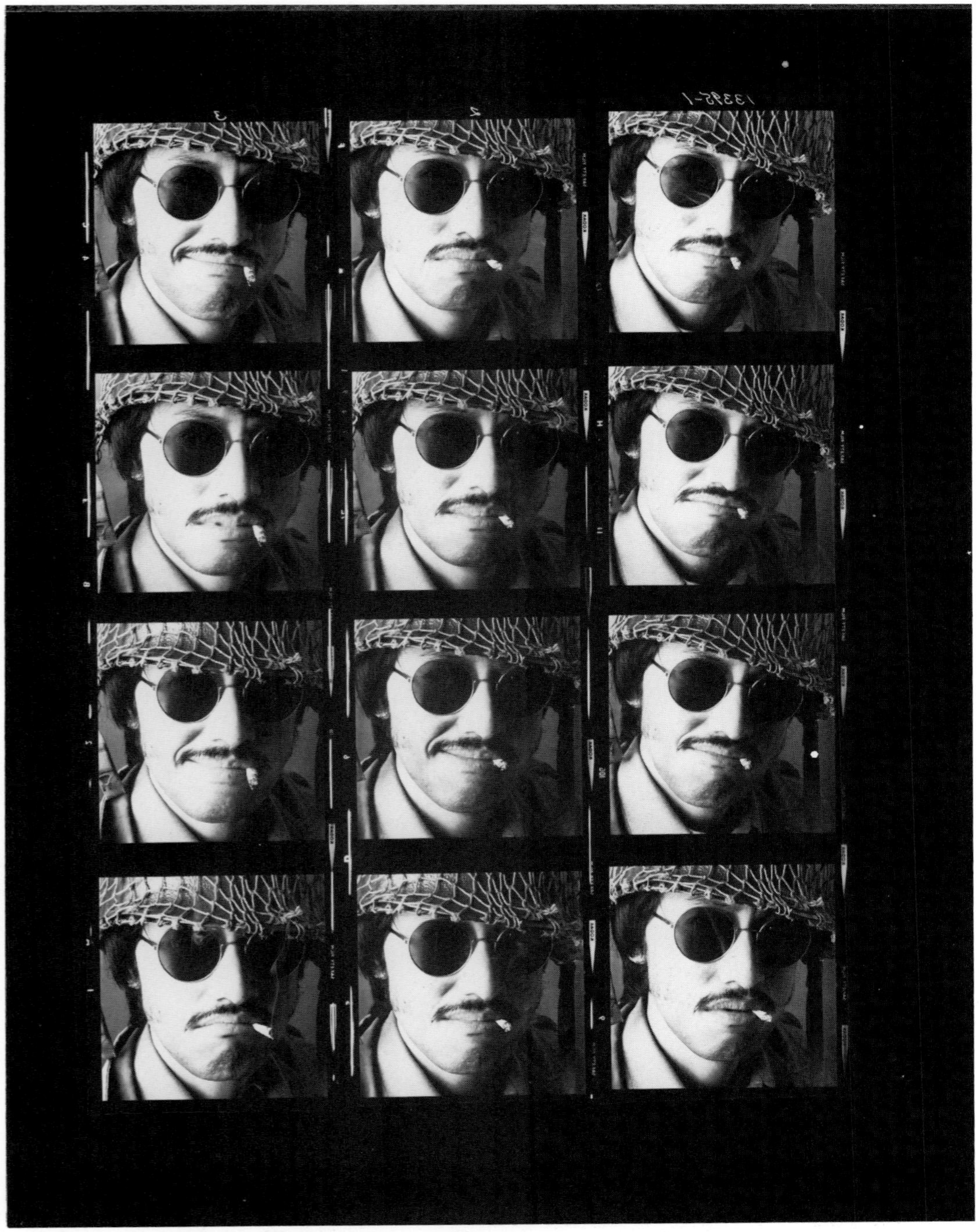

Just a little gimmick. For portraits the negatives are contact-printed in reverse. The mirror image helps your subject make his or her choice. The finished print, however, is made the right way round, thus portraying the subject as he or she is seen by others.

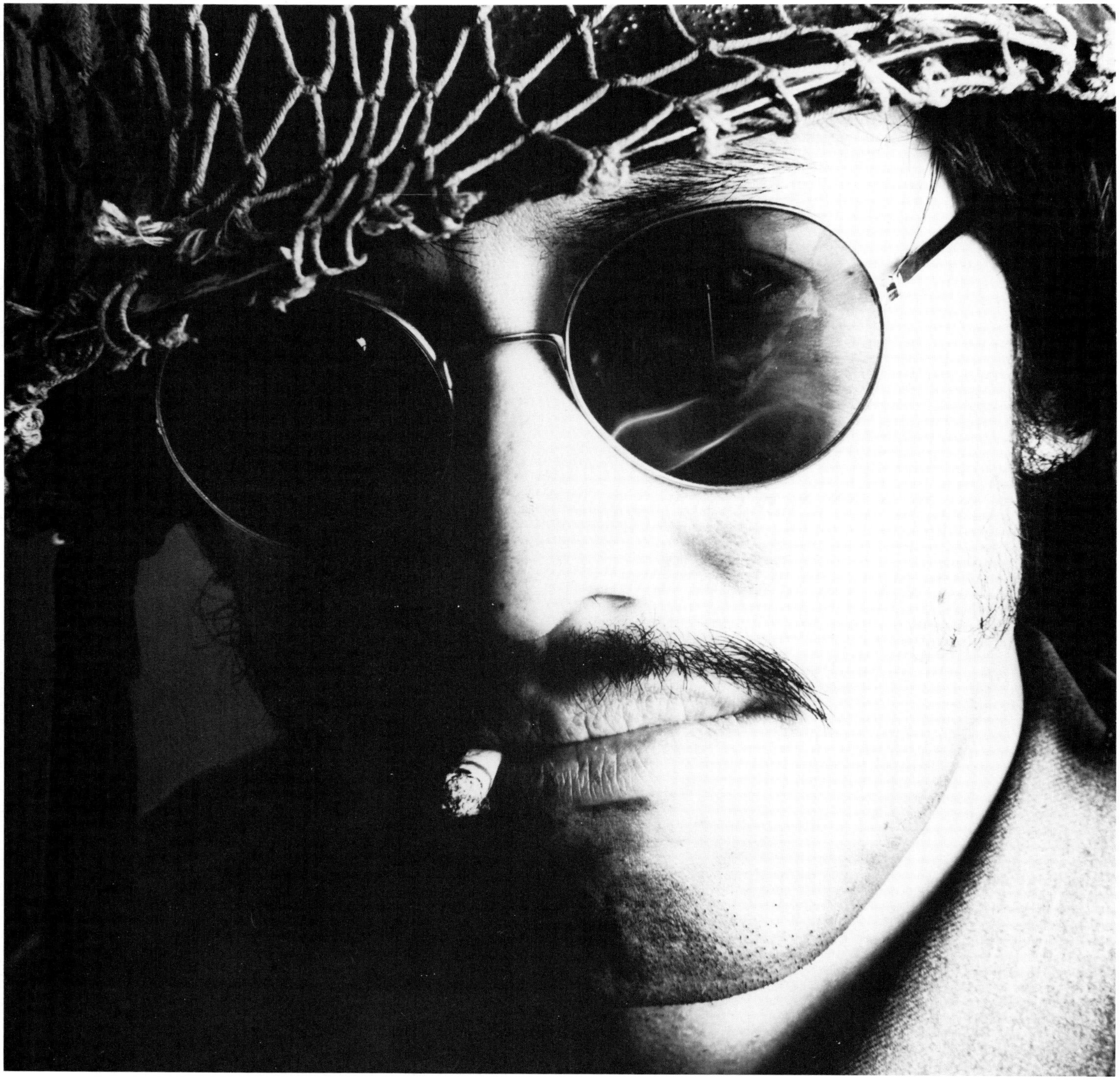

Sunglasses Jonathan Trapman.

CHAPTER FOUR

CHAPTER FOUR

The F/Stop Method of Printing and Basic Exposure

Every technique or method of photographic printing I have ever seen uses units of time to designate print exposure. The print will be shown to have been given a 'basic' exposure time of, for example, '10 seconds'. Areas that have had to be given more or less exposure are also assigned a time such as +2 seconds to 'burn-in' the hands and face, +10 seconds for the background, and, say, −5 seconds to hold back or 'dodge' the shadow areas.

Where the picture is printed to a specific enlargement, using specific paper, specific lens aperture, specific intensity of the enlarger lamp, a specific enlarger, a specific developer, then and only then do these specific times apply.

But what happens to these exposure times if there is any change to any one of these and many more variables?

What if that picture is nothing like yours? How would those specific times apply to your work? What have you learned about printing?

The same confusion would exist if a photographer changed the exposure by designating the change in units of time. Suppose, for example, he changed the exposure to 1/250 of a second. What would be the actual change in photographic exposure?

To answer, some information about his previous exposure time would be required. If it were 1/500 to begin with, he would be increasing the EXPOSURE (as opposed to 'exposure time') by +1 f/stop. But had his earlier exposure time been 1/30 – this change to 1/250 would mean reducing the EXPOSURE −3 f/stops.

If you have not skipped reading Chapter Two on photographic exposure you will have come to some basic understanding of how photographers designate exposure. It is NOT in units of time! Photographic 'exposure' can only be designated in *relative* values of 'f/stops'. 'Exposure time' is only a measure of duration. Time, I must stress, is NOT a unit of photographic exposure.

THE F/STOP IS THE UNIT OF PHOTOGRAPHIC EXPOSURE.

□

When we take pictures we readily refer to exposure in 'f/stops'. Changes to the exposure are usually made by adjusting the lens aperture. Rarely do we fiddle with the shutter or exposure-time setting.

So why did we start using units of time to express print exposure? How did we come to accept the arbitrary values of time to designate exposure? Simply for the convenience!

In the darkroom the controls available for adjusting the exposure, like those on the camera, are the lens aperture and the exposure time. But in a darkroom environment it is easier to adjust the exposure time than it is to adjust the enlarging lens aperture. This is why exposure has been referred to in terms of 'add on a couple of seconds'.

The F/Stop Method of Printing uses time as well, but only to measure duration of exposure. The system is similar to taking pictures: the exposure changes are designated in f/stops, but instead of changing the aperture the equivalent exposure time is used.

The F/Stop Method of Printing uses a fixed set of exposure times that represent increments of photographic exposure.

THEORY AND BACKGROUND

Notice the exposure times on the shutter speed control on your camera: 1/1000, 1/500, 1/250, 1/125, 1/60, 1/30, 1/15, 1/8, 1/4, 1/2, 1, 2, 4, 8 seconds.

These shutter speeds, or exposure times, represent values of exposure equal to individual aperture changes of (+) or (−) one photographic unit f/stop.

By adjusting the shutter speed you can effect changes in exposure, as if the lens aperture had been used. With the aperture fixed, changing the exposure time from 1/60 to 1/30 would be equal to increasing the aperture lens +1 f/stop. On the other hand, changing the exposure time to 1/125 would reduce the exposure −1 f/stop.

DOUBLING THE EXPOSURE TIME INCREASES EXPOSURE +1 F/STOP; HALVING THE TIME REDUCES IT −1 F/STOP.

This basic relationship is used to provide a set of exposure times for printing.

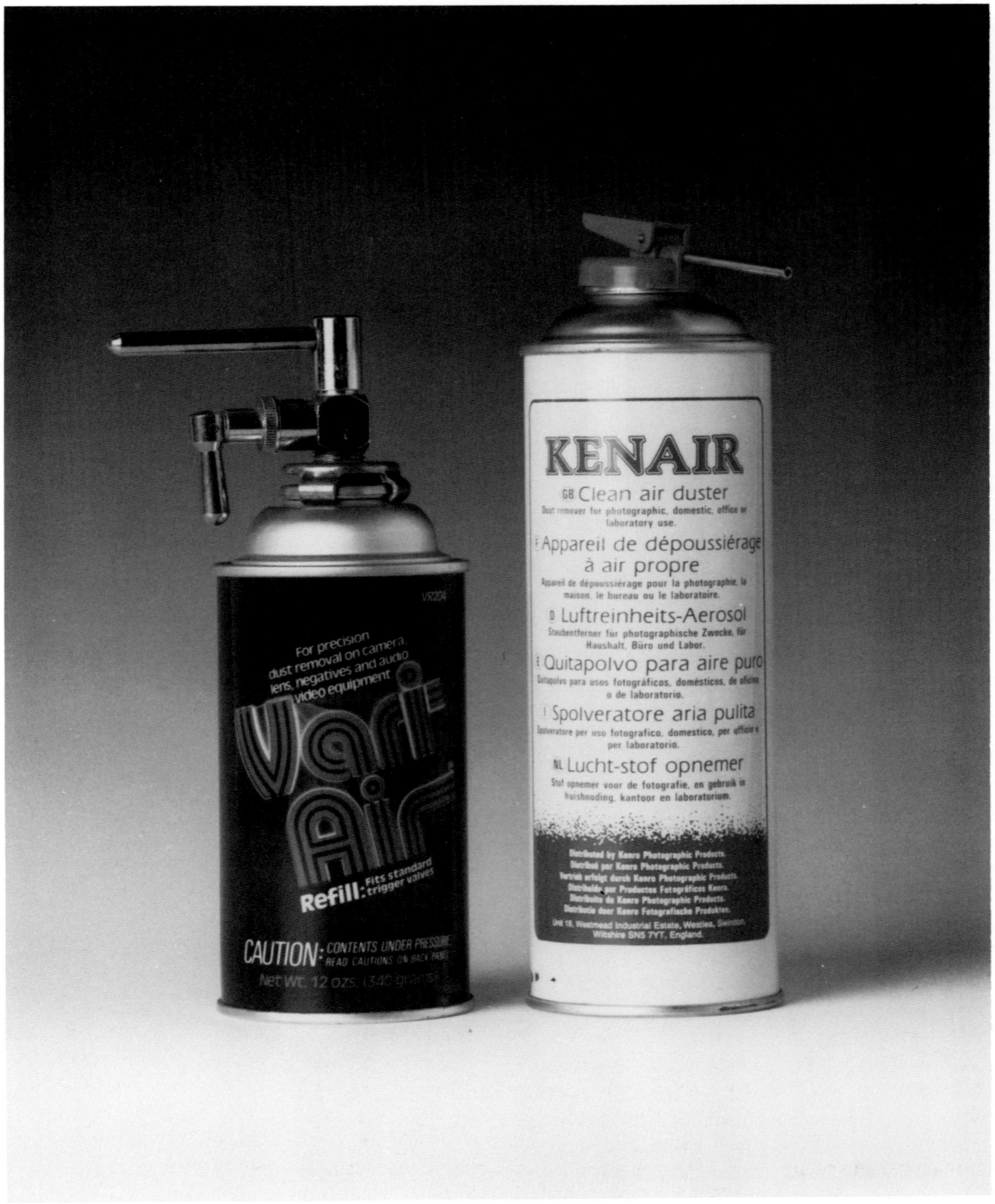

Containers of compressed air for blowing dust off negatives. Keep the container upright when using, otherwise the liquid will spray out.

If we start with an exposure time of 5 seconds and progressively double it the times are: 5, 10, 20, 40, 80 and 160 seconds. These individual exposure times represent intervals of whole f/stops. But these whole-unit intervals of exposure for printing are too great an exposure increment. Finer adjustments are needed.

On the camera, because the shutter speeds are fixed, fractional adjustments to exposure are made using the aperture.

In the darkroom, to effect finer changes of exposure when printing, smaller intervals of exposure time are needed. The progressions of 5, 10, 20, 40, 80, 160, can be subdivided into intermediate values of ¼ f/stop intervals for the F/Stop Method of Printing:
5, 5.9, 7.1, 8.4, *10*, 11.9, 14.1 16.8, *20*, 23.8, 28.3, 33.6, *40*, 47.6, 56.6, 67.3, *80*, 95.2, 113.2, 134.6, *160*.

(How these values are derived is explained in Chapter Twelve.)

For convenience these exposure times are presented in the following table form:

F/STOP EXPOSURE TIME

5	10	20	40	80
5.9	11.9	23.8	47.6	95.2
7.1	14.1	28.3	56.6	113.2
8.4	16.8	33.6	67.3	134.6

These individual exposure times are comparable to the shutter speeds on the camera: 1/1000, 1/500, 1/250, 1/125, 1/60, 1/30, etc. The print exposure times, however, represent the exposures in ¼ f/stop increments. Thus +¼ f/stop more than 10 seconds, for example, is 11.9 seconds; whilst −½ f/stop less than 20 is 14.1.

Using these fixed values avoids the confusion of just guessing how much more, or less, time to use. To add on, say, 2 seconds, may or may not make any difference to the initial exposure. If the exposure time had been 2 seconds to start with, adding 2 seconds more is a +1 f/stop increase and would show an appreciable change to the print. But the same 2 seconds added on to 40 seconds would do very little. Think, as well, of the results of reducing the exposure by 2 seconds in each of these examples!

DETERMINING THE BASIC EXPOSURE TIME FOR A PRINT

The basic exposure is the one single, overall exposure that provides the best possible print without any 'dodging' or 'burning-in' exposure modifications.

The following instructions and information are to guide you through the process of determining this exposure:

1. Prepare the DEVELOPER, STOP and FIX solutions as recommended by the chemical manufacturer.

The commercially-available chemicals are all I use – I have no magic brew. Kodak, Ilford, Agfa, and those others who manufacture photographic materials know more about chemicals than all of us put together! Mix your own chemicals if you must for economic reasons.

2. Clean the negative with brush and/or compressed air.

Check to see if any dust is still clinging to the film by holding it under the enlarger with the lamp on and holding it at an angle to the light. I refer to dust spots on the print as 'white grain'.

Fingerprints or other marks on the *non-emulsion* side of the negative that cannot be removed with either brush or compressed air need a bit more effort. My technique is to breathe on the non-emulsion side so as to leave a thin film of vapour. I then place this on a clean sheet of paper or negative bag and using a clean handkerchief or tissue paper immediately wipe the vapour off. This should rid the film of the marks as well. Failing this I use a bit of 'nose grease'. Rub the side of your nose with your forefinger. This natural oil is then rubbed on the offending marks and usually eliminates the problem. The oil is removed by breathing on the film and wiping it off. I use this natural oil as well to help eliminate scratches on the negative. Gently rub the oil in the direction of the scratches.

3. Place the negative in the carrier and ensure that the film is firmly held around its edges. Any side of the negative not held in place will be difficult, if not impossible, to focus.

4. Switch on the enlarger lamp, open up the lens to its widest aperture, size-up and focus the image. The enlargement size is entirely up to you. The F/Stop Method of Printing takes into account all the variables in printing. There is no need to specify the enlargement, intensity of light, focal length of lens, temperature of solutions, paper speed, and all the other variables in individual darkrooms.

5. Use a grain focuser to focus the film grain. The use of a blue filter will enable focusing for the sharpest image as explained in Chapter 1: Grain Focuser.

6. 'Stop down' the enlarging lens. The main purpose of this is to control the intensity of light, but it also provides *depth of focus*. Stopping down creates the depth of focus on the negative film plane to allow for any curvature or buckling of the film. I usually stop down 2 f/stops.

If you use glassless negative carriers allow sufficient time for the enlarger lamp to heat up and 'pop' the negative in position. The negative will remain stable in this position as long as the lamp is on. If you focus and then turn off the lamp for any appreciable length of time, the lamp head will cool and the chances are the negative will 'pop' back out of focus. This will produce an out-of-focus print irrespective of its having been pre-focused.

To minimize the heat loss between the time you finish focusing and actually start the exposure, leave the lamp on and use the red safe filter directly under the lens. Just before you make the exposure turn off the lamp, swing the red filter away, then start the exposure.

If you do not use a darkroom timer with the facility to switch the enlarger on and off, I would suggest using the safe filter as the on/off 'switch'. Leave the lamp on and swing the filter away to start, then swing it back to stop exposure.

7. Place a sheet of photographic paper in the easel. The emulsion side of the negative faces the emulsion side of the paper. Think 'emulsion to emulsion' if confused about which side of the negative to expose through or which side of the paper to expose on.

The contrast grade of paper will depend on your negative. I suggest that you use the normal grade 2 to begin with. The only way to learn which grade to use is to make a print. If the result appears 'flat' use a harder grade. If the range of tones is too 'hard' use a softer grade. The correct contrast grade will come with experience.

EXPOSING THE TEST STRIP

It is important that you should adhere to the following instructions exactly. It is surprising how many people do not make a proper test strip.

1. Expose the entire sheet of paper first for 5 seconds. Now *cover* ¼ of the paper with a large piece of card and expose for a further 5 seconds. Now move the card and *cover* ½ the paper area and expose for 10 seconds. Finally *cover* ¾ of the paper and expose this last bit for 20 seconds. The paper will now have been exposed for 5, 10, 20 and 40 seconds. These are exposure test strips in f/stop intervals!

2. Process the exposed sheet for the manufacturers' recommended time. 'Stop' and 'fix' the print. Stop the print from developing further by placing it in a tray of weak acetic acid solution. Use of a stop bath will help prevent the print from staining. Years ago I used only a tray of running water, thinking that a stop bath was unnecessary. It was only after many stained prints that I realized the value of using a stop bath. The direct interaction of developer and fixer causes the discolouration of the print.

Make sure that the print is agitated in the tray of fixer. Do not just leave it resting in the solution. Agitation in the fixer is just as important as agitation in the developer. The idea is to provide a fresh flow of fixer solution over the print to remove the unexposed silver halides. Follow the manufacturers' recommended time for fixing, and the working capacity of the solution. Do not prolong the fixing time as this will tend to bleach the image. The print, as well, will absorb more of the chemicals and require a longer washing time.

Now examine the results in normal viewing light. This print should show a range of exposure strips spanning a range of 4 f/stops.

If the image is very faint or if the result is much too dark 'open up' or 'stop down' the enlarging lens accordingly 2 aperture f/stops and make another set of 5, 10, 20, 40 seconds exposure strips.

One very important point: keep the developing time constant. Normal room temperature should maintain a constant temperature of the chemical solutions. In a later chapter I will describe how, to a certain extent, you can control the contrast of the print by adjusting the development time.

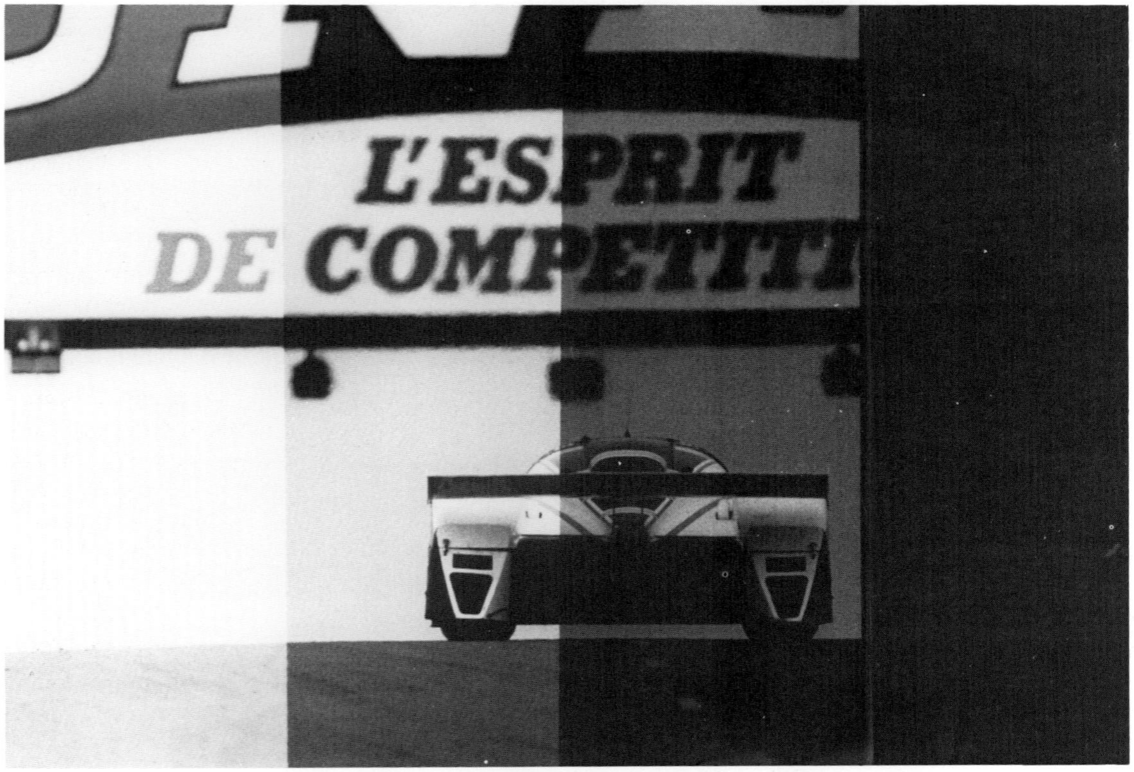

A test strip with exposures of 5, 10, 20, and 40 seconds. The exposure strips are at intervals of 1 f/stop. Remember to COVER, not uncover the image while making the exposures, otherwise you will have exposure strips of 40, 35, 30 and 20 seconds, which are not in f/stop increments so the result will serve no purpose.

The 10-second exposure is too light, the 20-second exposure too dark. Using the F/STOP EXPOSURE TIME Table the exposure time between these two values is 14.1 seconds.

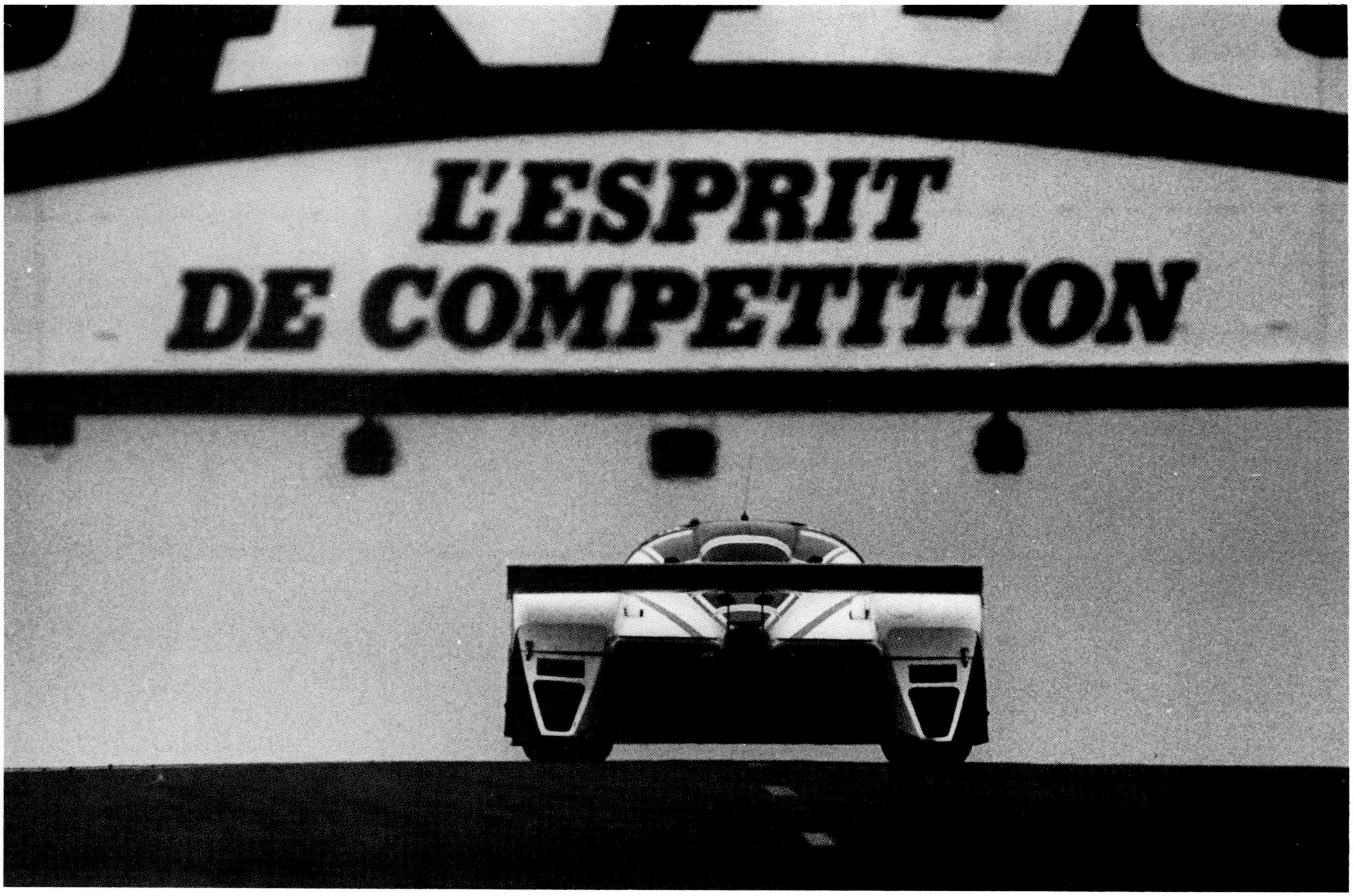

The exposure made for 14.1 seconds. It is just too dark for my liking. – ¼ f/stop less might prove better (an exposure time of 11.9 seconds).

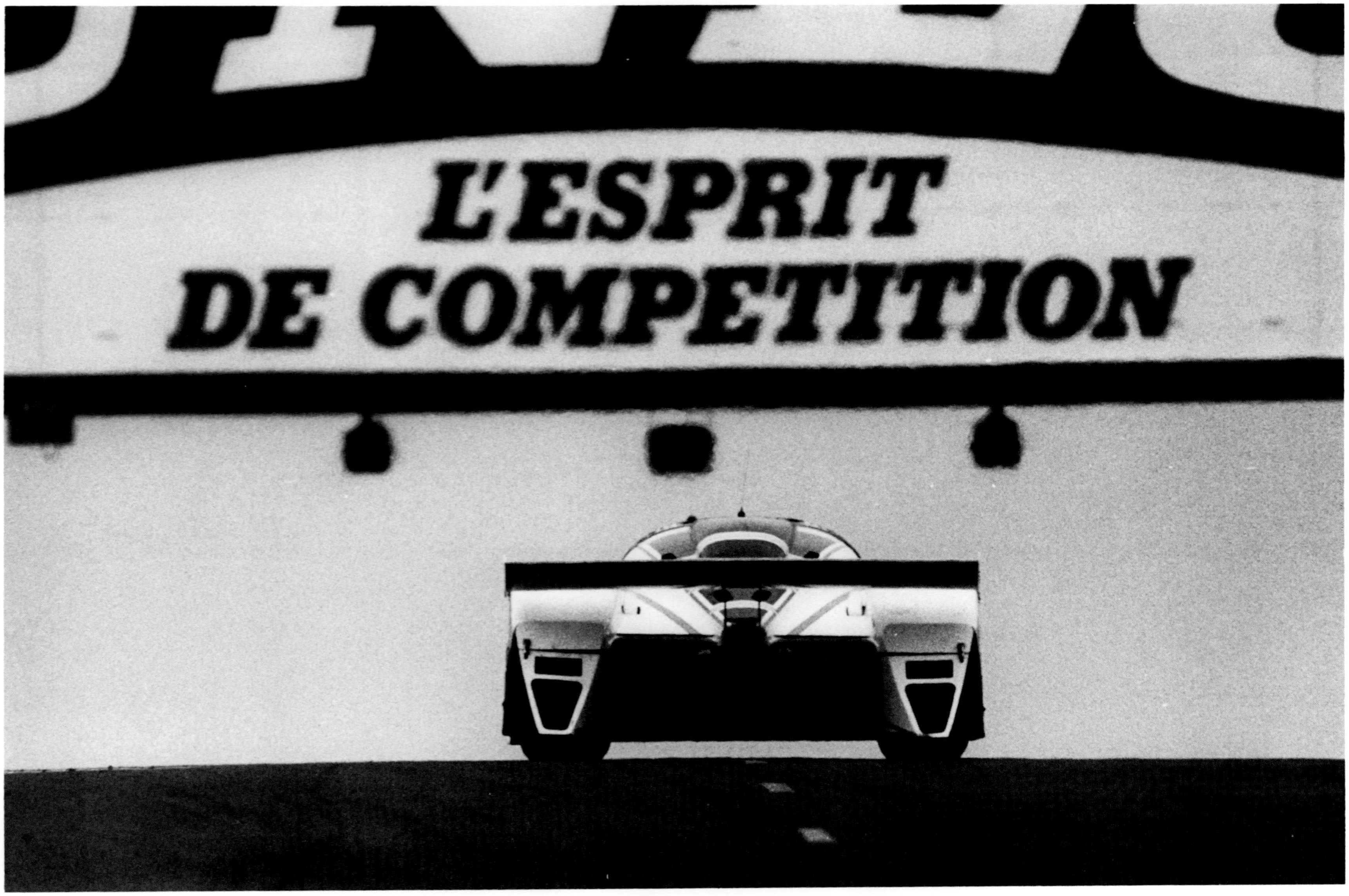

The print exposed for 11.0 seconds. No dodging or burning-in is necessary.

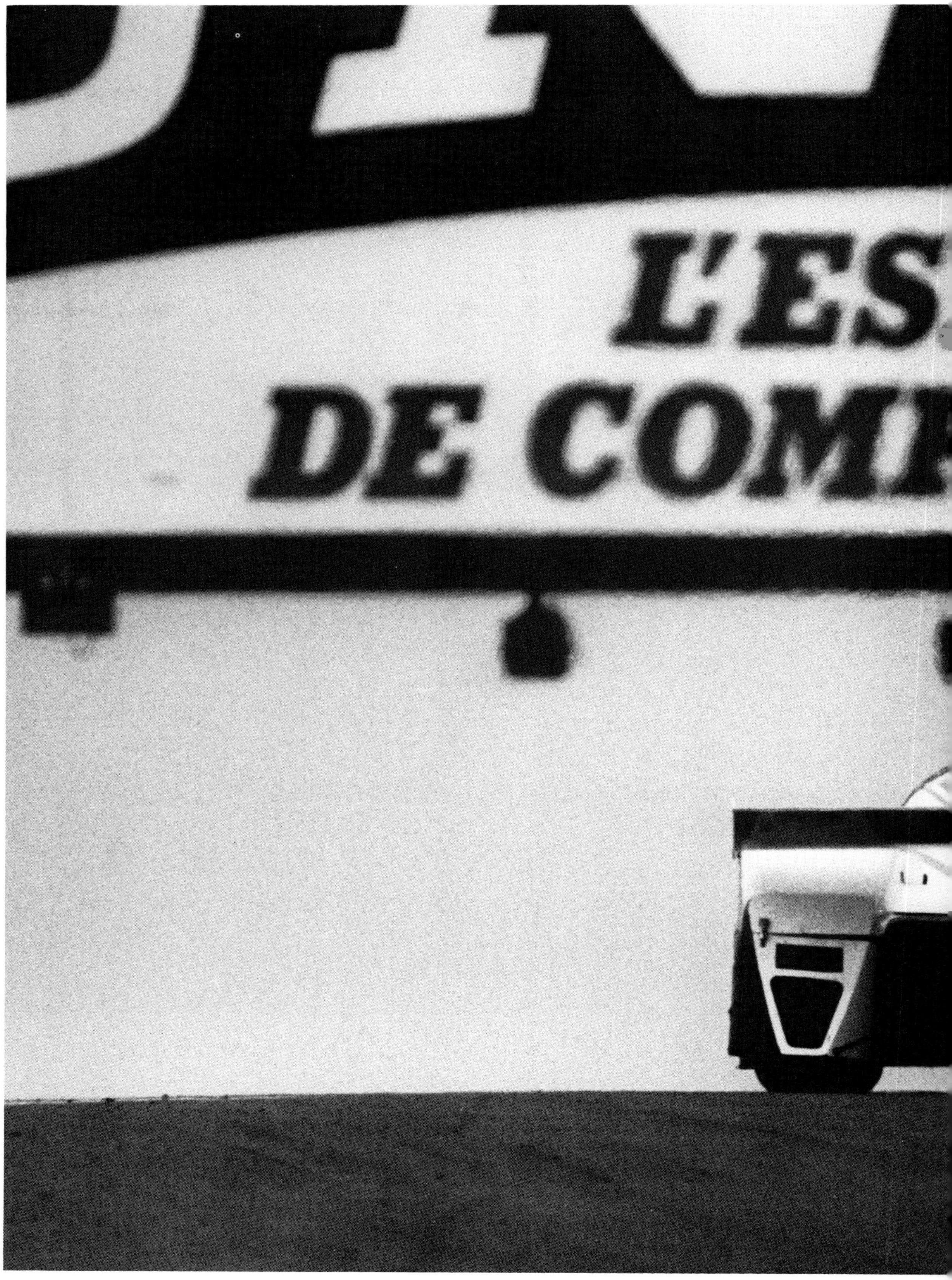
L'ES
DE COM

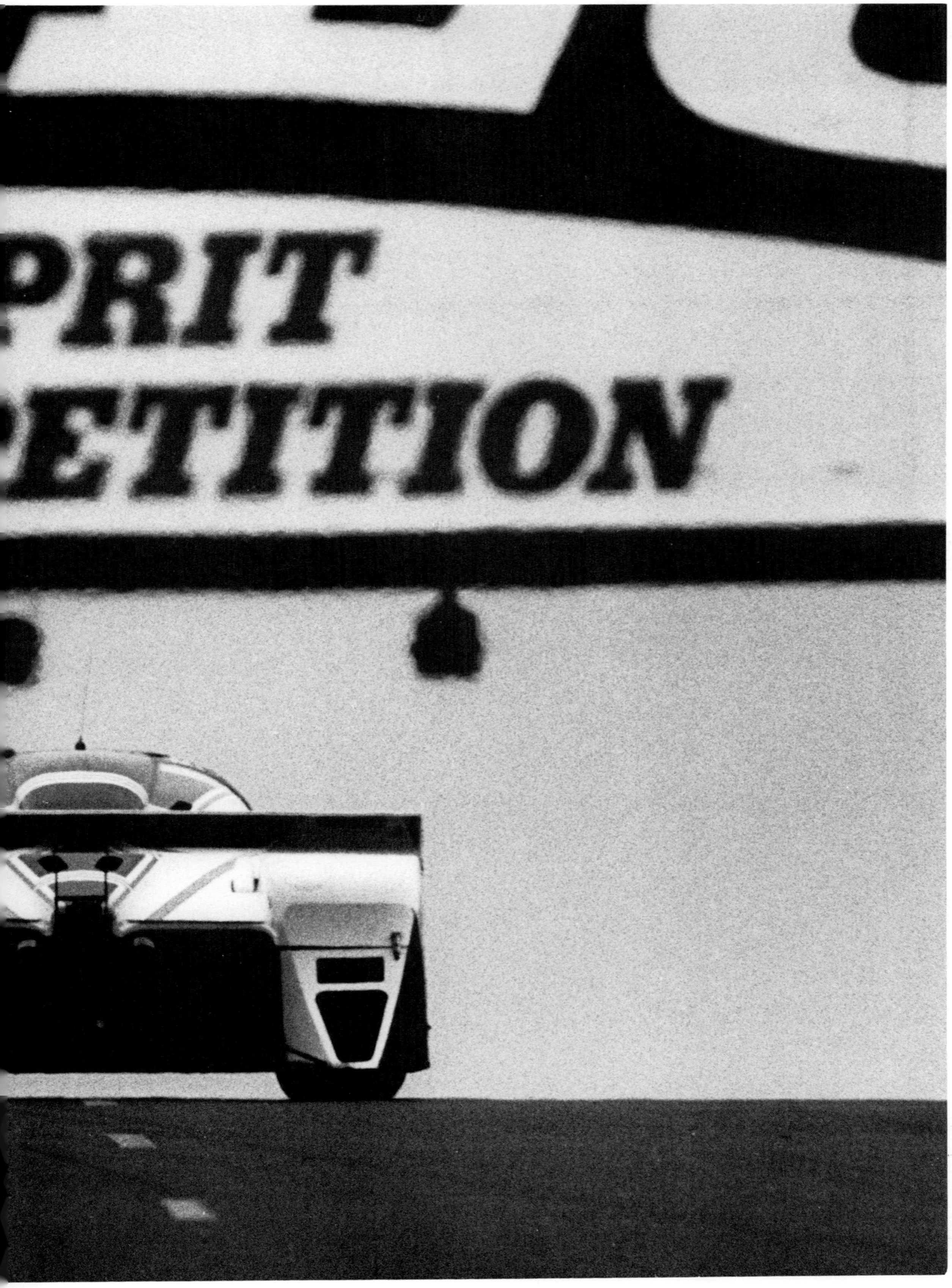

Spirit of Competition Malcolm Bryan.

THE BASIC EXPOSURE				
F/STOP EXPOSURE TIME				
5	10	20	40	80
5.9	11.9	23.8	47.6	95.2
7.1	14.1	28.3	56.6	113.2
8.4	16.8	33.6	67.3	134.6

1. Choose what appears to be the best exposure from the test strips. If it looks as if it is a value in-between the strips use the F/STOP EXPOSURE TIME Table to find the intermediate exposure time. If, for instance, the exposure is somewhere between the 10 and 20 seconds then use the exposure time in-between. This is 14.1 seconds. Expose and process the print. Remember to process it for the same time as the test strips.
2. Examine the print. If it needs further refinement refer again to the F/STOP EXPOSURE TIME Table. If it needs to be lighter simply use the time which represents a value of exposure $-\frac{1}{4}$ f/stop less than that previously tried. If it needs to be darker use the exposure representing $+\frac{1}{4}$ f/stop more.

How will you know if the BASIC EXPOSURE print is right?

Photography is the study of light. The print, for me, must have this study, this feeling of light. There had to be light to take the picture. The print should thus reflect the existence of light.

Finally. The F/Stop Method requires strict discipline. The method may seem objective, perhaps lacking artistic temperament and flair, but the discipline it stresses is very much a part of any artistic endeavour. Creativity is a conscious effort.

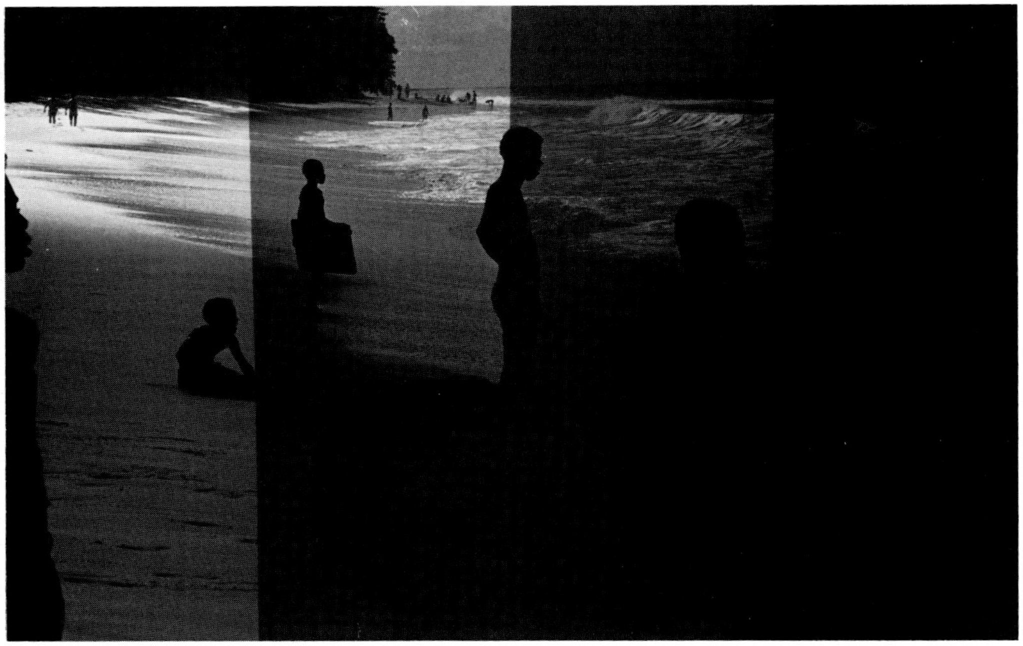

This set of test strips proved to be too dark. The detail in the shadow, if there is any, cannot be seen.

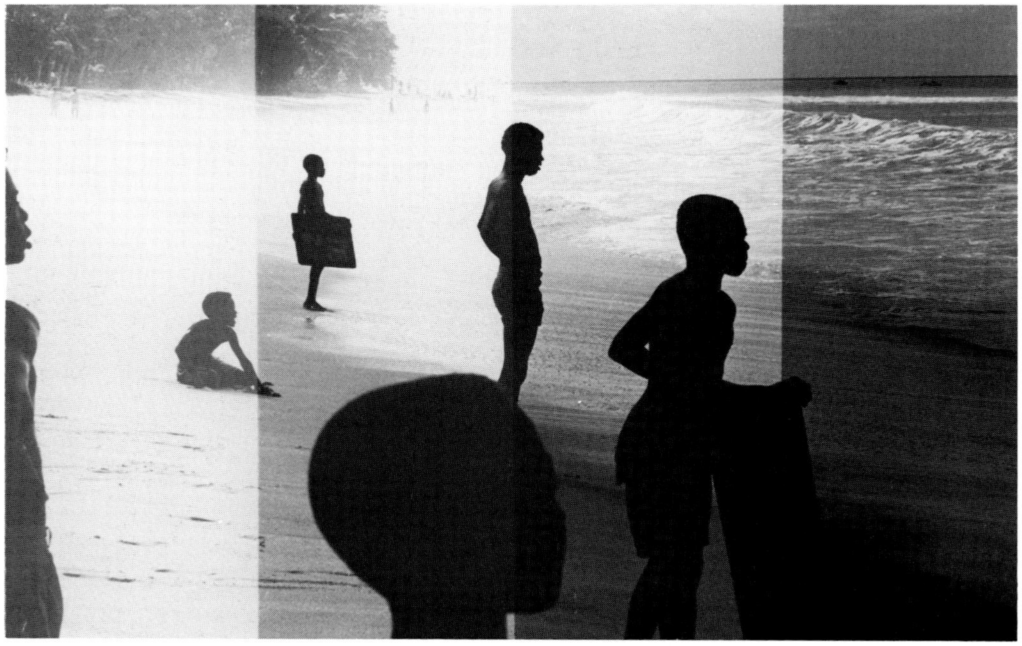

The lens was stopped down to produce this series of test strips. The last two exposures here represent the first two exposures of the first test strip. The detail that can be seen in the boys lends nothing to the picture overall, so I decided to use the third strip as my basic exposure. This would have been 20 seconds, but to reduce the exposure time I *opened up* the enlarger lens 2 f/stops, back to the original setting, thereby reducing the basic exposure time to 5 seconds.

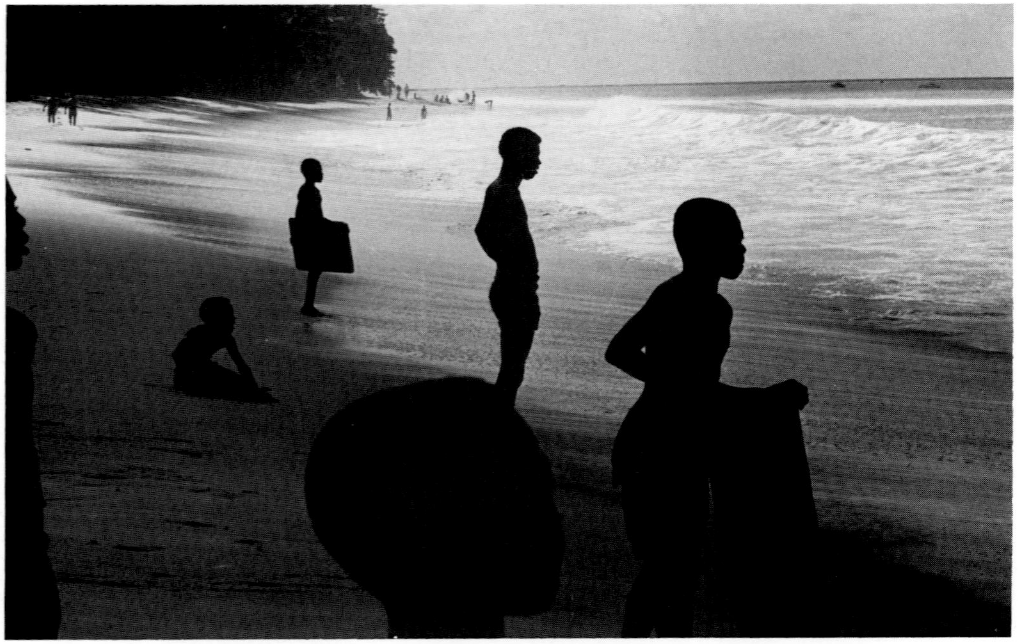

The basic exposure print, exposed for 5 seconds. The sky appears too light and to me is distracting.

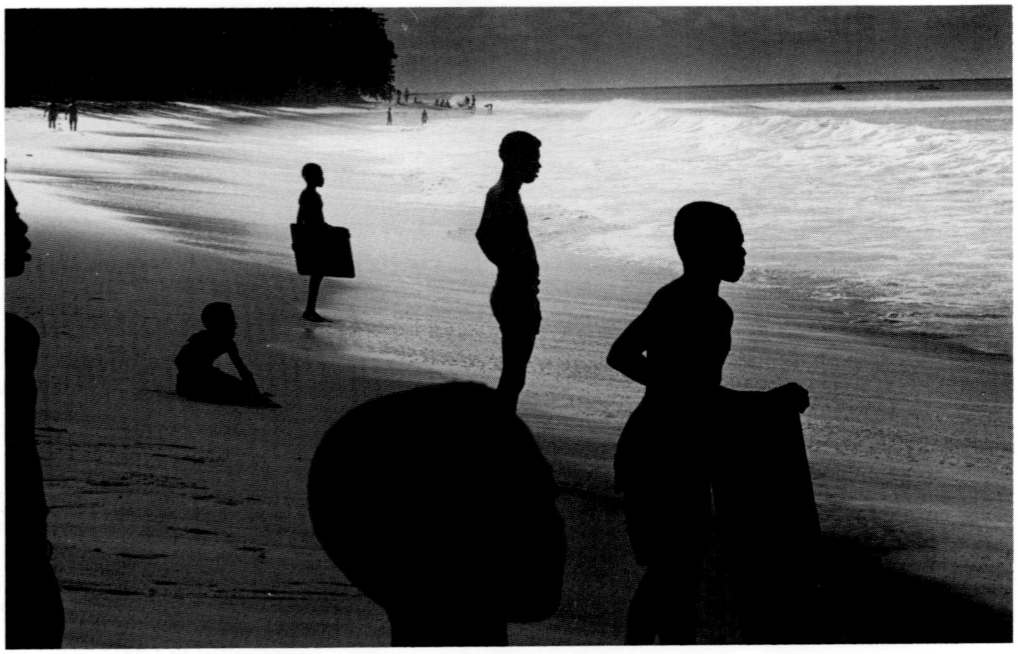

Here the right side of the sky has been burned-in + 1 f/stop (10 seconds) and blended in the centre for + 1 ½ f/stops (14.1 seconds). Notice, however, that the horizon is not level.

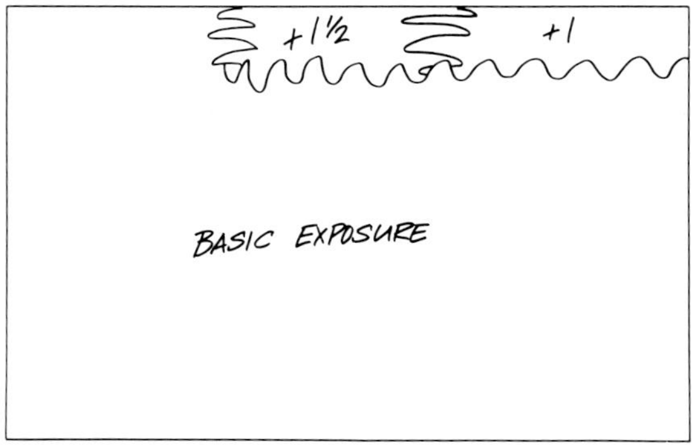

Final printing template.

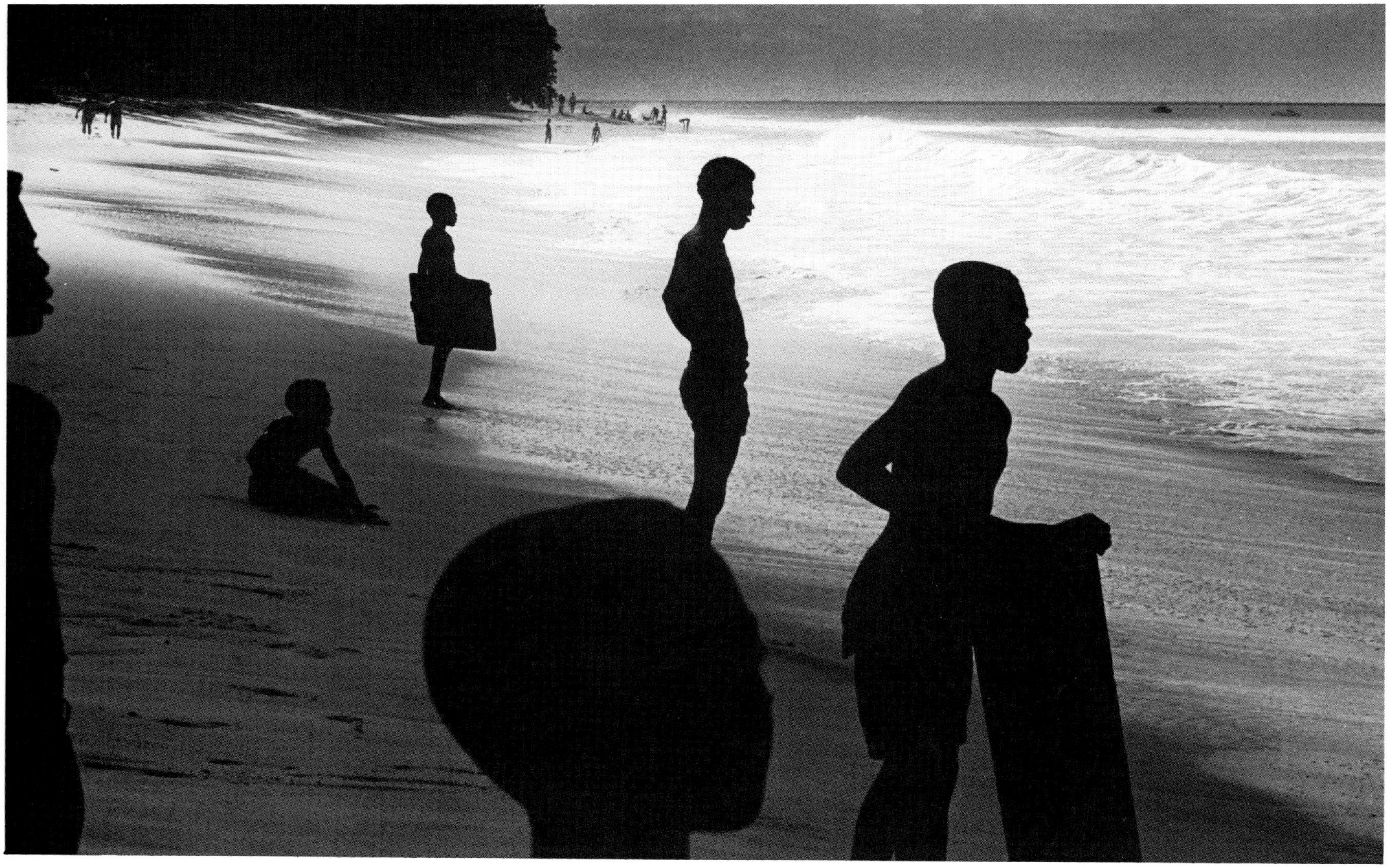

Boys on the Beach Linda McCartney.

CHAPTER FIVE

CHAPTER FIVE

Dodging and Burning-in Exposure Modifications

In the previous chapter the F/STOP EXPOSURE TIME Table was used to determine the *basic exposure* of a print. The basic exposure may be all that is needed to produce a satisfactory print. In which case that is all there is to printing.

'Dodging' or 'burning-in' selected areas of the picture is a personal choice. Whether to lighten or darken specific areas of the picture depends on the desired effect. I dodge and burn-in to ensure that both shadow and highlight details are visible on the print. The details may be lost in the shadow areas unless the exposure in that area is reduced – this requires dodging. An area of the print may be so pale as to need burning-in – needing more exposure.

This chapter explains the use of F/STOP EXPOSURE TIME for dodging and burning-in.

After determining the basic exposure time, use the print produced and make your own assessment of which areas of the picture could be enhanced by dodging or burning-in. Are the highlight areas nothing more than the base white of the paper? Think of the print as a piece of canvas – no area of the print should actually be the base white of the paper other than the highlight itself. If details can be seen in the dense area of the negative they should also be seen on the print.

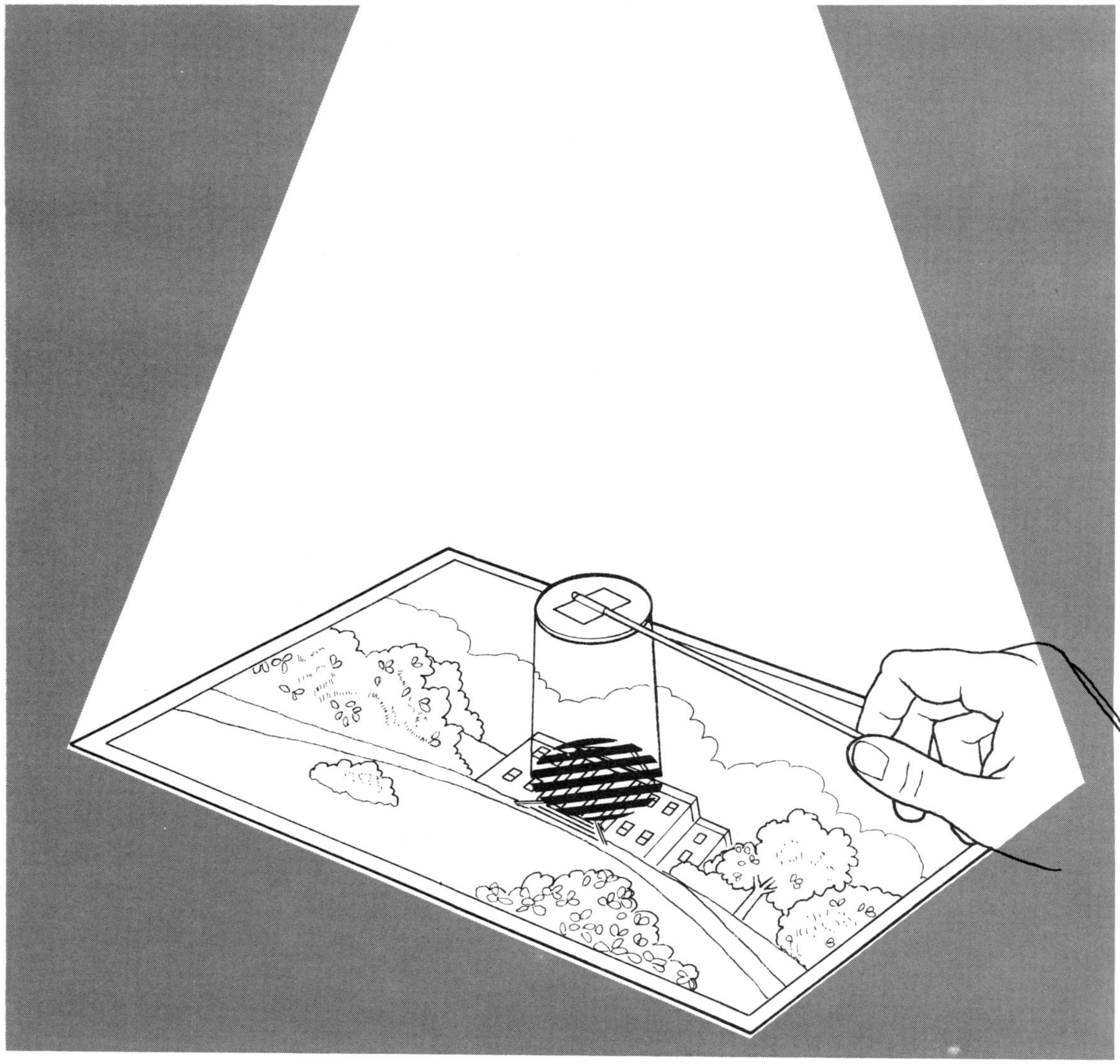

Right. The dodging tool being used to hold back the exposure.

Dodging tools.

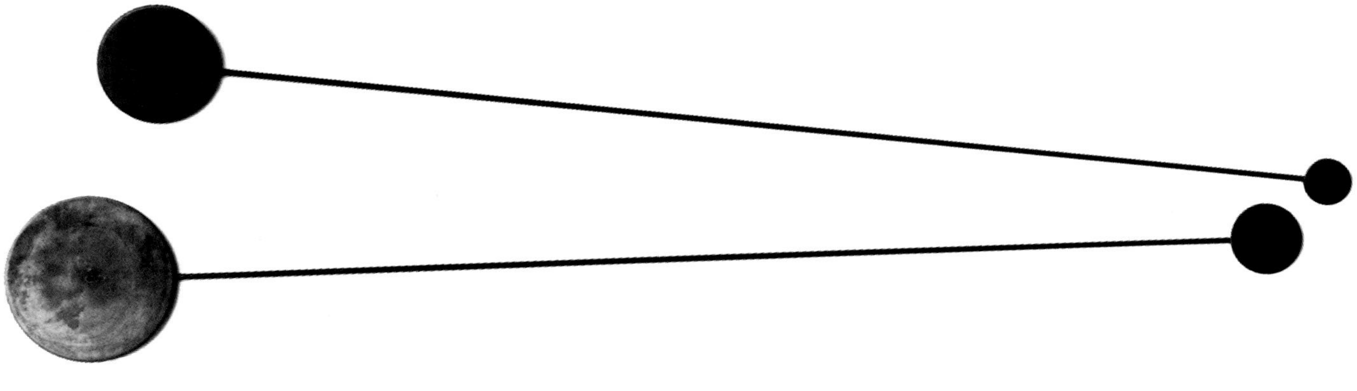

Unless the shadow or dark area of the photograph really is a deep black abyss, you should be able to see details in the shadow and dark areas of the picture. Remember, photography is the study of light.

If you can see detail in the negative you should be able to see it in the print – providing *you* want to see the detail.

Decide which areas need dodging or burning-in and assign the exposure needed to each of these areas in terms of *f/stops*. You may decide, for instance, that the basic exposure for a landscape picture requires −½ f/stop less exposure in the shadows and the sky area needs a +1 f/stop increase to bring out the clouds.

F/STOP EXPOSURE TIME

5	10	20	40	80
5.9	11.9	23.8	47.6	95.2
7.1	14.1	28.3	56.6	113.2
8.4	16.8	33.6	67.3	134.6

Refer to the F/STOP EXPOSURE TIME Table to find the equivalent exposure time for these designated areas. For instance, if the basic print exposure was 14.1 seconds then the shadow area (−½ f/stop) should only be exposed for 10 seconds. The +1 f/stop would have to be exposed for a total of 28.3 seconds. Another area may need burning-in +½ f/stop. This will need a total exposure of 20 seconds.

It's as simple as that.

TOOLS

My dodging tools consist of a set of bicycle spokes with a round piece of black card taped to one end. I use three different-size cards on each. One about ½ inch (1.3cm) in diameter, one 1 inch (2.5cm) in diameter, one 2 inches (5cm) in diameter.

For burning-in I simply use my hands and put them together to form any size aperture where the thumb and forefinger meet. I find this more convenient than having to cut holes out of pieces of card.

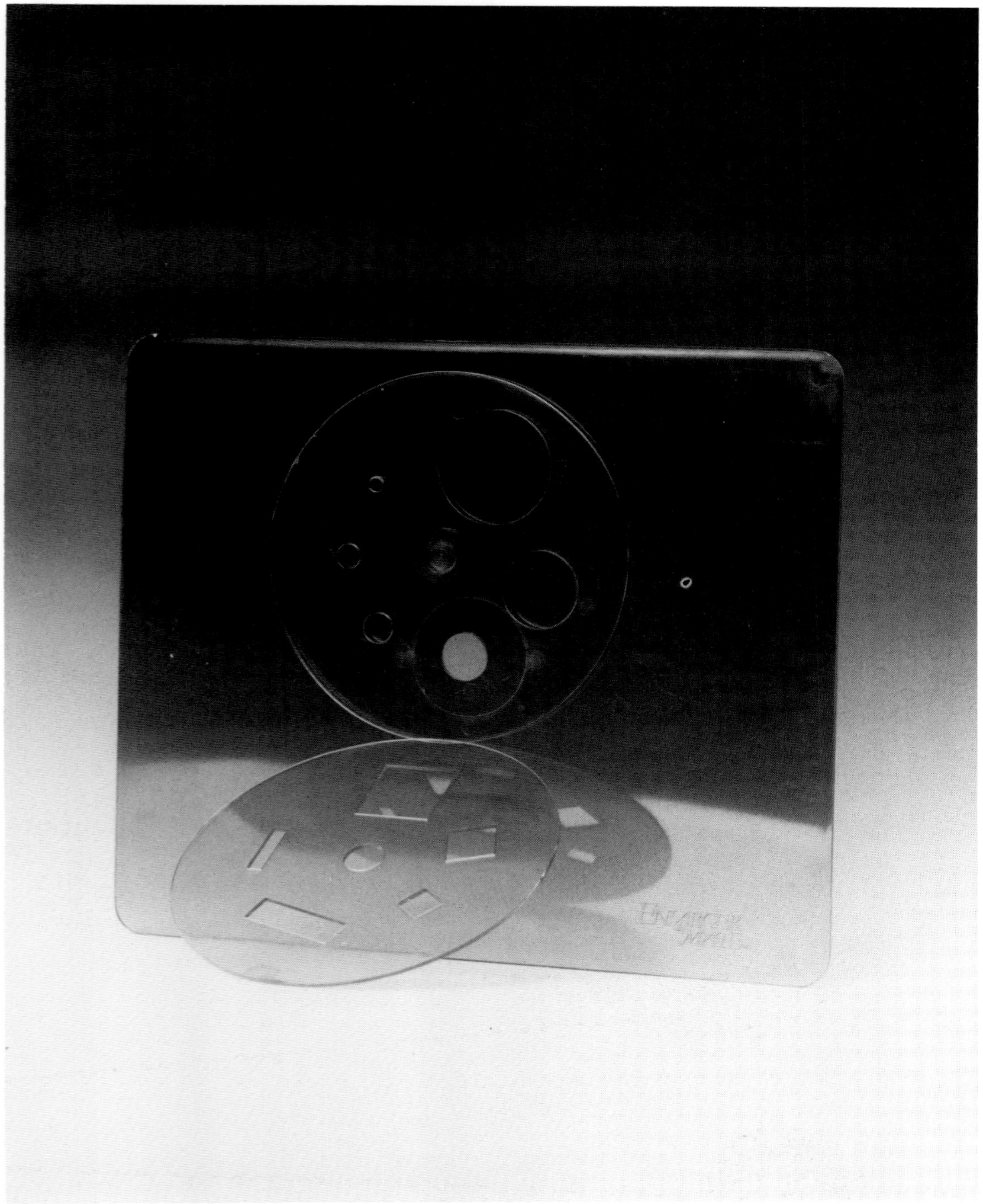

Burning-in tools.

DODGING

I do not recommend dodging back an area for more than − 1 f/stop. I find dodging any more than this creates too grey and weak an image – it *looks* underexposed.

Keep the number of areas to be dodged to a minimum – it is easier to burn-in. If you have quite a number of areas that have to be dodged I suggest your basic exposure time be brought down to the exposure value designated for the dodge area. For example, if a print has a number of areas needing − ½ f/stop dodging, find the exposure on the F/STOP EXPOSURE TIME Table corresponding to the − ½ f/stop value of exposure and use this as the basic exposure. Then burn-in what was previously the basic exposure area for + ½.

Method

Set your timer to expose for the basic exposure time. Have the appropriate dodging tool ready, be it the bicycle spoke, your hands or a piece of card, depending on the size of the area to be dodged. During the exposure the selected area is to be held back for the time difference between the value of the basic exposure and the dodge value. For instance, if the basic exposure time is 14.1 seconds and the area designated for dodging is to be held back for − ½ f/stop (exposure of 10 seconds), hold back that area for 4.1 seconds during the exposure for the basic time.

Another method would be to set the timer for the dodge area (i.e. 10 seconds). When this exposure has been completed, hold the dodge area back and add on the difference to expose the rest of the print for the basic exposure time (i.e. 14.1 seconds).

Constantly move the dodging tool by pivoting it around the area being dodged to avoid showing the line of the bicycle spoke. Don't try to cover the dodge area precisely – let some exposure spill over as the dodging should look feathered with soft edges. The dodging should not look obvious.

The test strip was for 5, 10, 20 and 40 seconds. Notice that I chose to make the strips get progressively darker moving towards the area of the sun. This was to see how much exposure would be needed to burn-in that area.

Using the 5 seconds as the basic exposure.

Using 5 seconds exposure for the foreground with +3 f/stops burning-in (40 seconds) for the sky. The left side is much too dark.

This is the second attempt. The left side of the sky has been burned-in for +1½ f/stops (14.1 seconds). The left side of the picture looks too patchy.

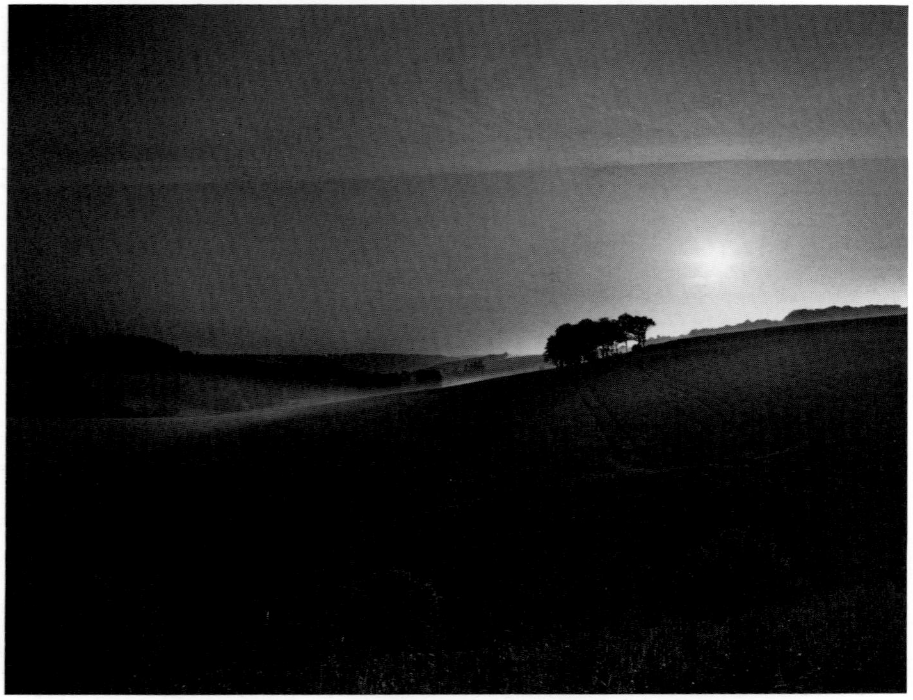

This is the third attempt. The left side has been burned-in for 2 f/stops (20 seconds). This looks better, but the burning-in just below the trees looks too obvious.

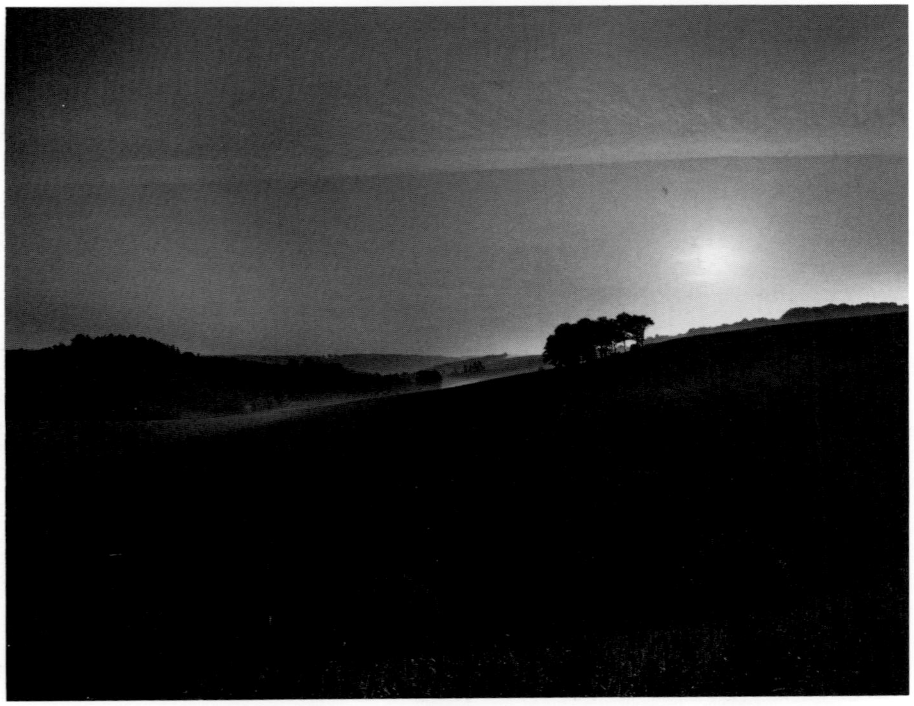

The final version. But I decided to crop the bottom of the picture.

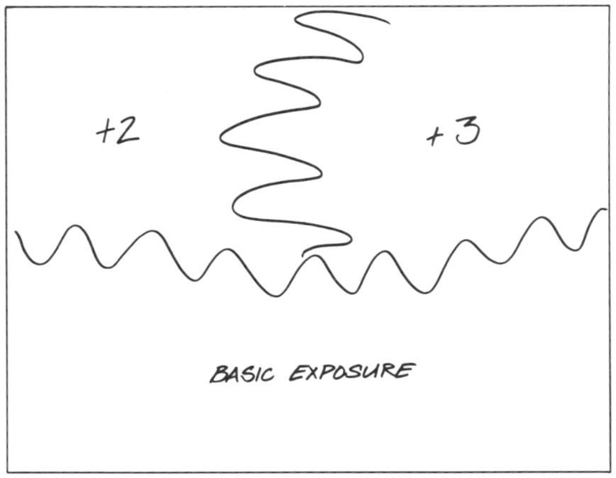

Final printing template.

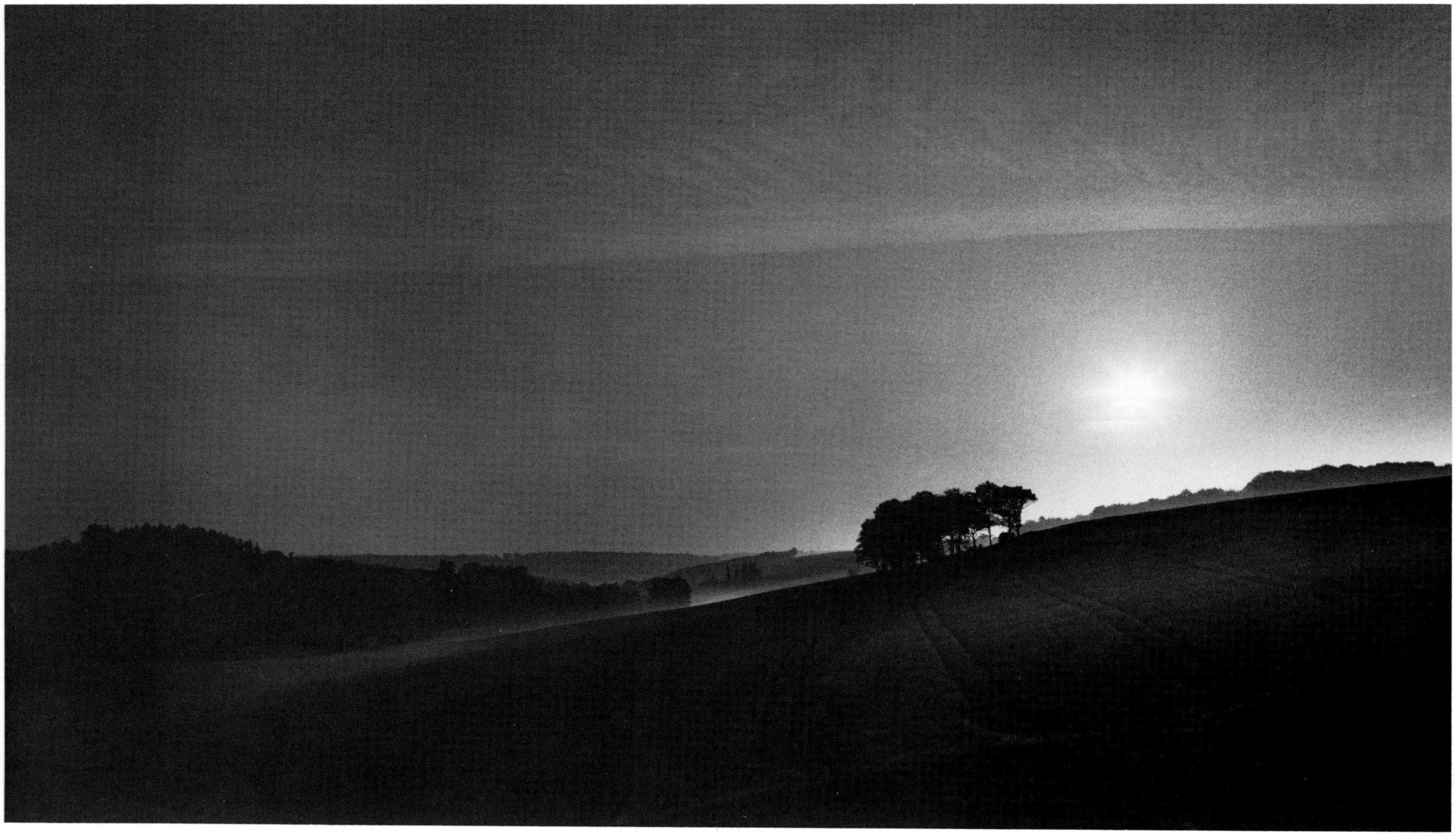

Bucks Morning Steve Smith, ARPS.

BURNING-IN

After dodging and arriving at the basic exposure, you can now start to provide the additional exposure time to areas of the print requiring more exposure. Assess these values in f/stops and provide the exposure time as designated with the F/STOP EXPOSURE TIME Table.

Method

There are two ways of doing this:

a) Set the clock for the time difference between the basic exposure and the time designated for burning-in. For example, to burn-in +½ f/stop with the basic exposure of 14.1 seconds the area to burn-in would require a further 5.9 seconds to make a total exposure time of 20 seconds (+½ f/stop more than 14.1). Another area may need to be burned-in say +1¼ f/stops to 33.6 seconds. This will require a further exposure time of 19.5 seconds.

b) With a sweep second timer and after making the basic exposure, reset and start the clock at '0'. Wait until the clock reaches the basic exposure time, then start to expose for the burning-in time assigned to the area. Repeat this procedure for any other areas to be burned-in.

As with dodging, don't worry about burning-in the area precisely. Let the light spill over. Like dodging, burning-in should not be obvious. A good black-and-white print should not look 'printed'.

□

There is no way of knowing what the results of dodging or burning-in may be until the print is actually produced. Whether or not the dodging or burning-in is effective and sufficient can only be visually assessed when the print is actually made.

A record of the printing instructions can be kept as a 'template' for future use. Using the F/Stop Method of Printing and the F/STOP EXPOSURE TIME Table, once the basic exposure time is determined the exposure modifications, designated in f/stops, remain the same.

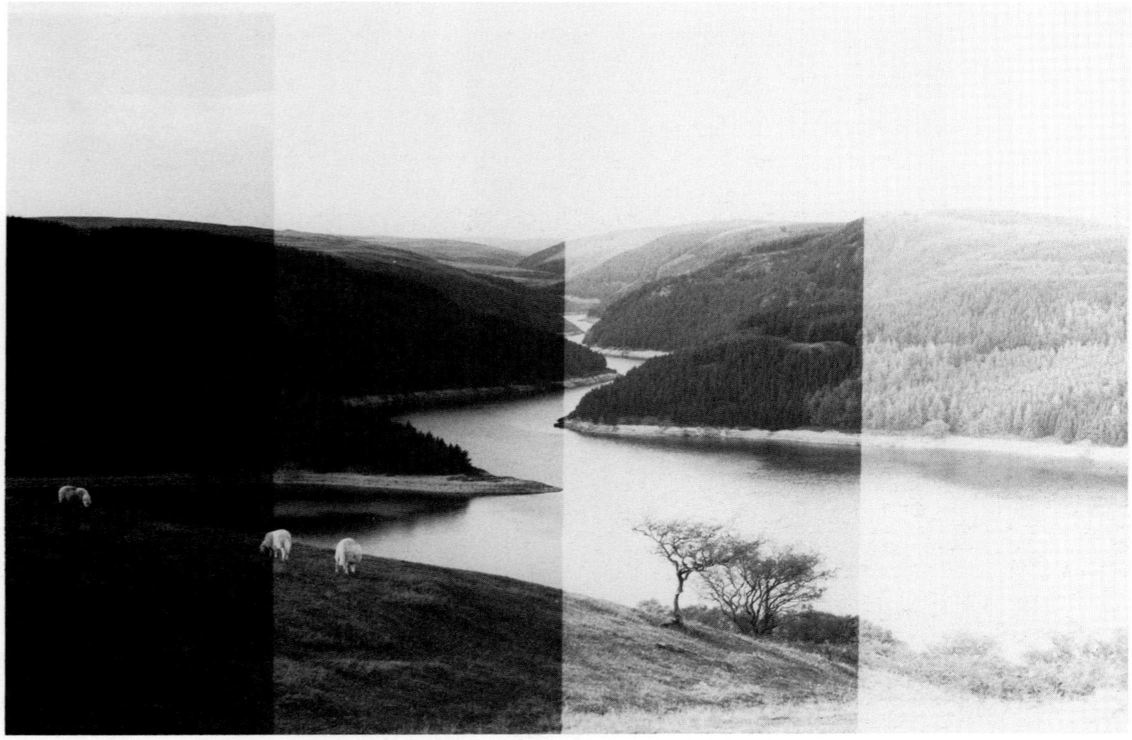

The first test strip produced a series of exposures which did not give any indication as to how dark the sky could be burned-in.

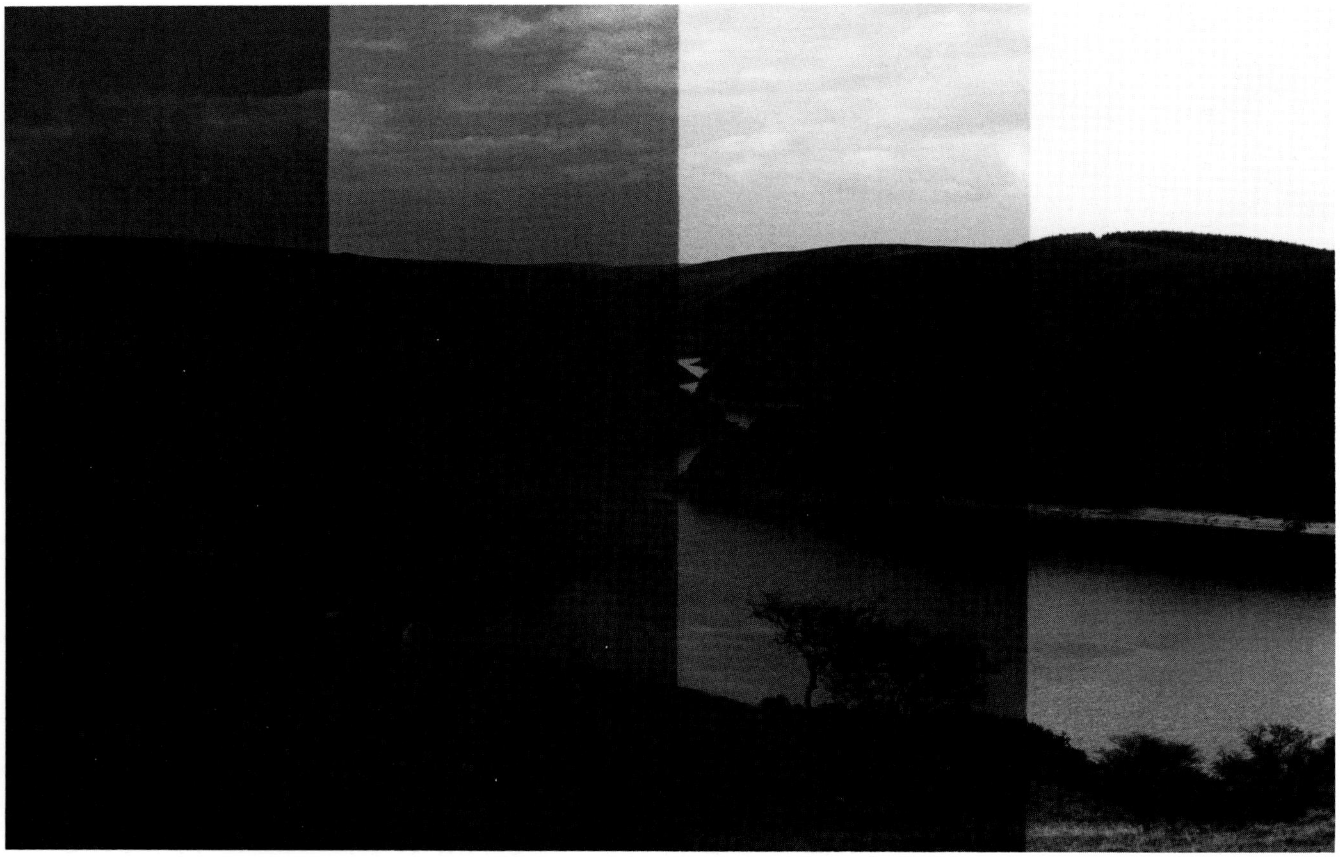

This second set of exposures was made by opening the enlarger aperture 2 f/stops. Notice that the last two exposure strips of the first test strip are represented by the first two exposure strips of this one.

Using the test strip, the 5-second strip looks much too dark. On the other hand, the 10-second strip is much too dark. I decided to try a basic exposure of ¼ f/stop more than 5 (5.9 seconds). Using the test strip as a guide, I decided to have the sky halfway between the 20-second and the 40-second exposures (28.3 seconds). This represents a +2¼ f/stop added onto 5.9 seconds.

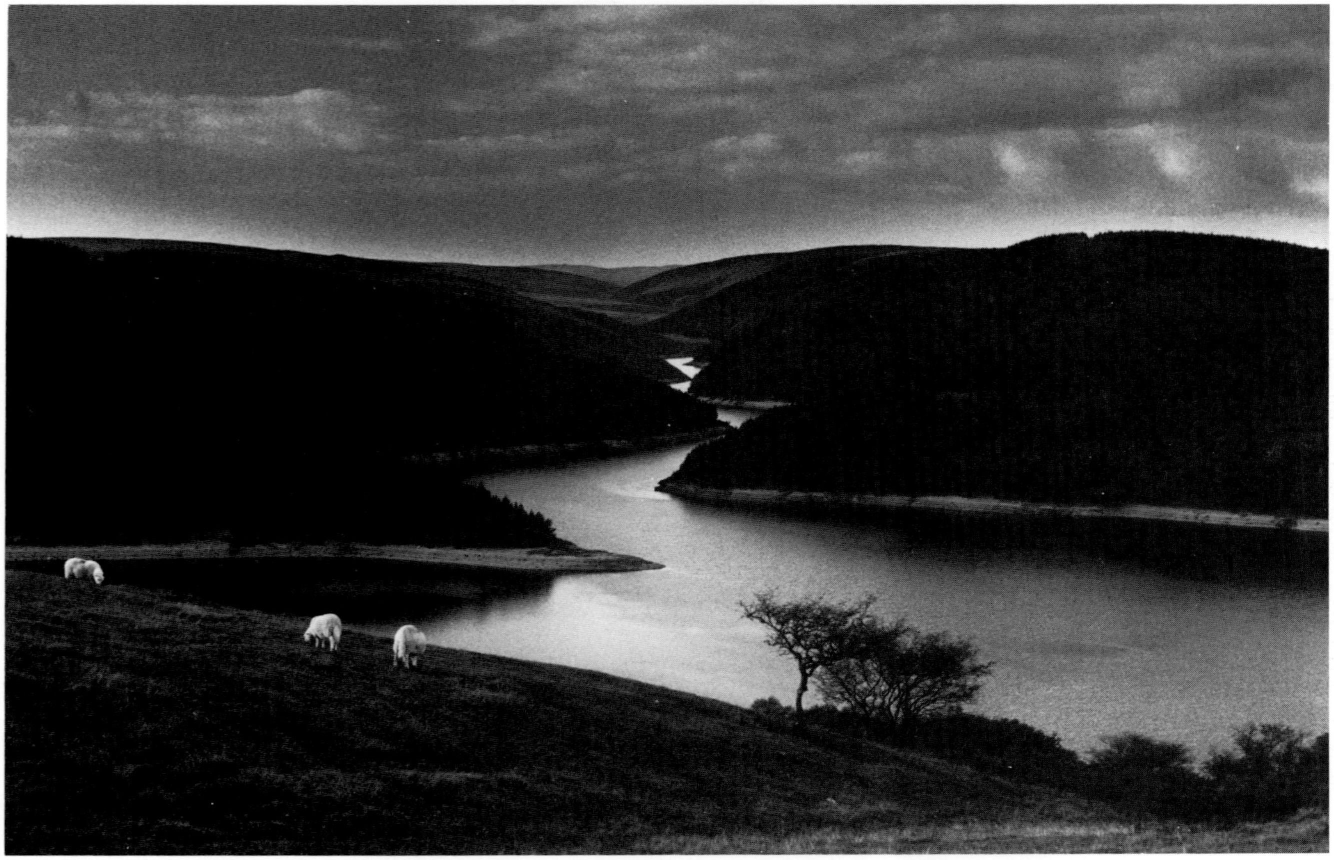

Not only does the print look too dark but it also appears to need more contrast.

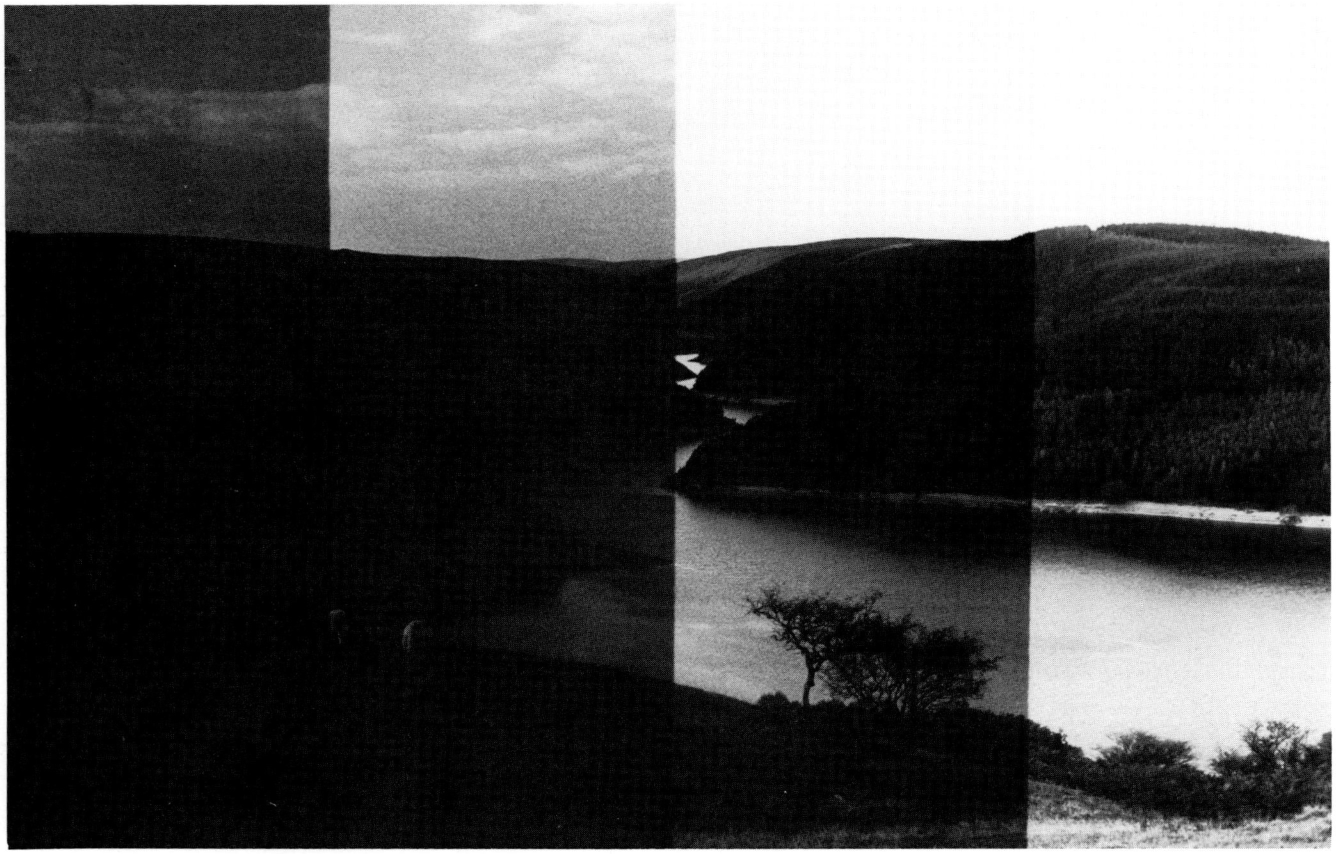

Another test strip, this time on a harder grade of paper. Note the contrast difference between this series of exposures and the last set on the softer grade of paper. Using this set of exposures, the 5 seconds is too light, the 10 seconds is too dark. Again I decided to try the exposure for + ¼ f/stop more than 5 (5.9 seconds). The sky looks dramatic at 40 seconds but would be too dark above the mountains themselves. The 20 seconds is too light for the top of the picture, but near the mountain range looks okay. So just above the mountains I decided to expose for 20 seconds, then to continue to expose the top half for 4 seconds. The 20 and 40 seconds represent + 1 ¾ and + 2¾ f/stops more than the basic exposure of 5.9 seconds.

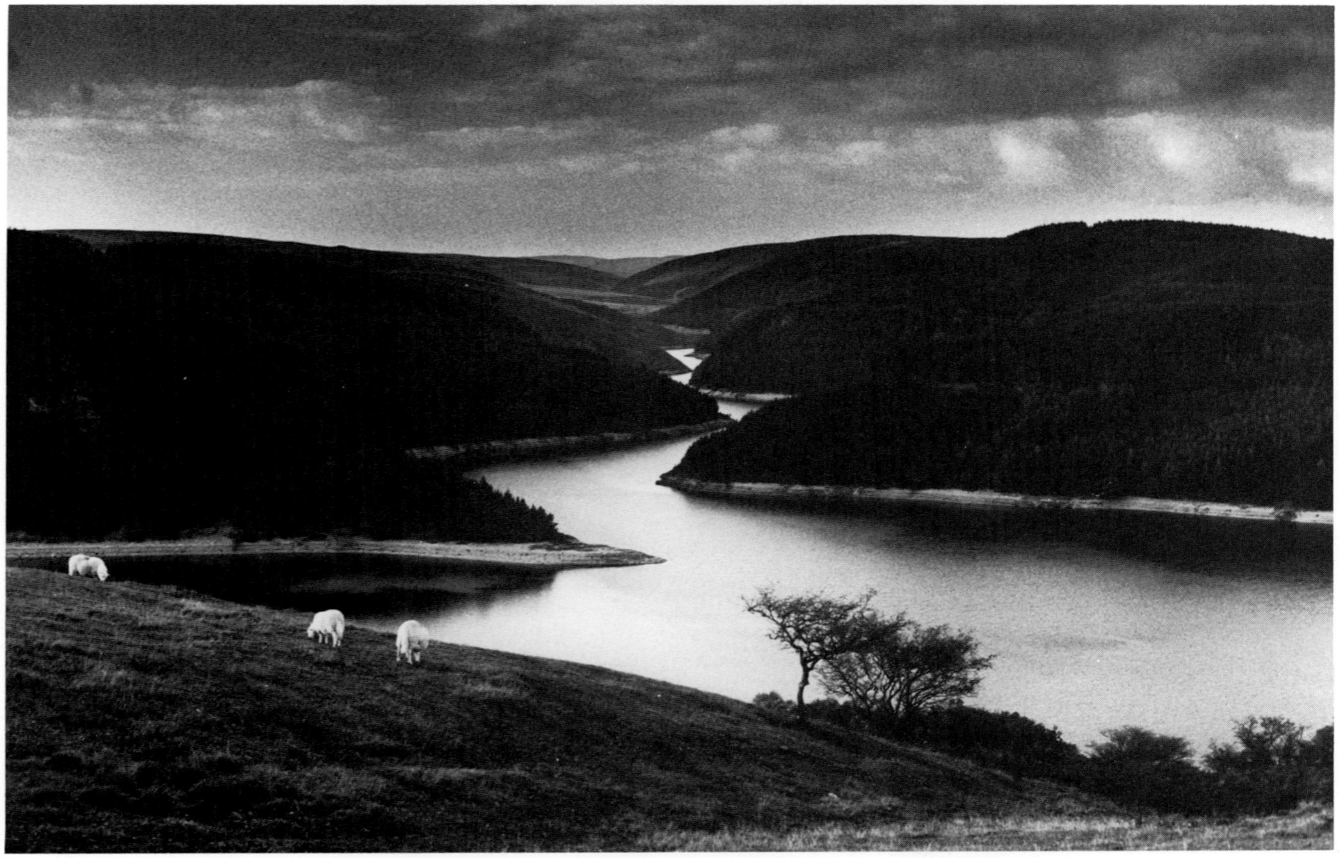

Not too bad, but the mountains on the left are too dark. So I decided to lighten that by − ¼ f/stop (5 seconds). For the final print I decided also to burn-in the foreground just in front of the sheep for + 1 f/stop (11.9 seconds).

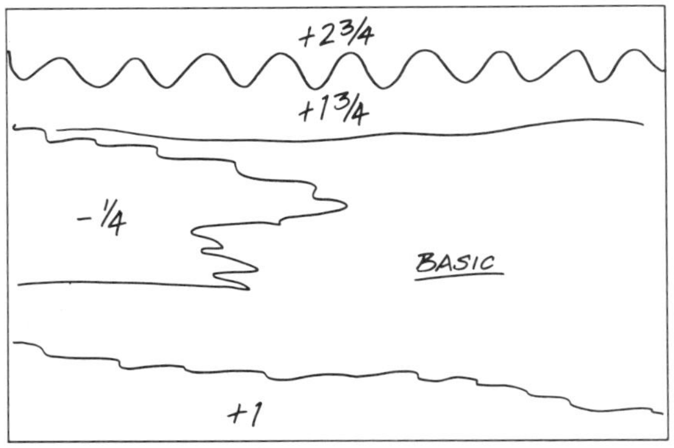

Final printing template.

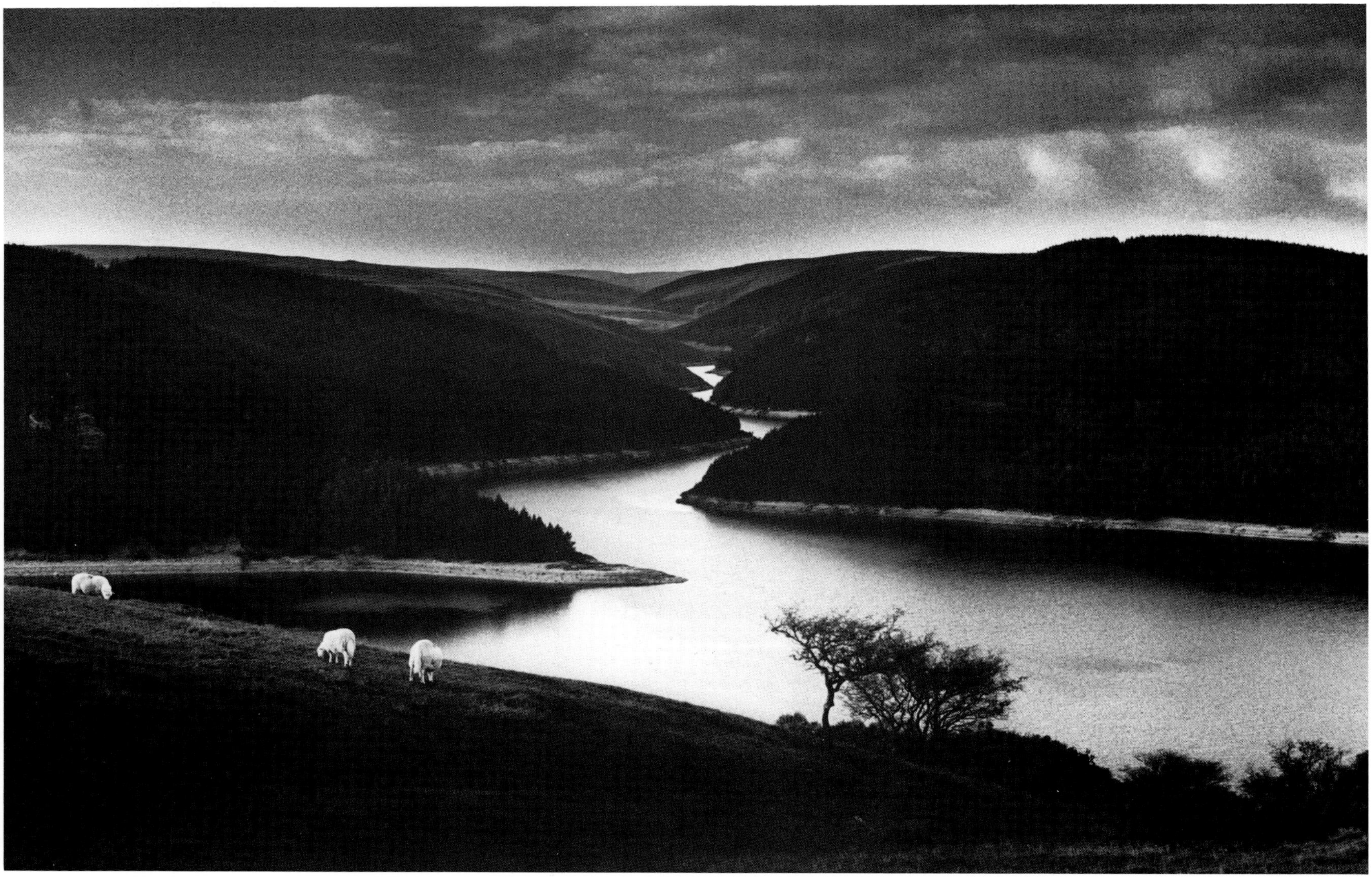

Wales Maria Teresa Silva.

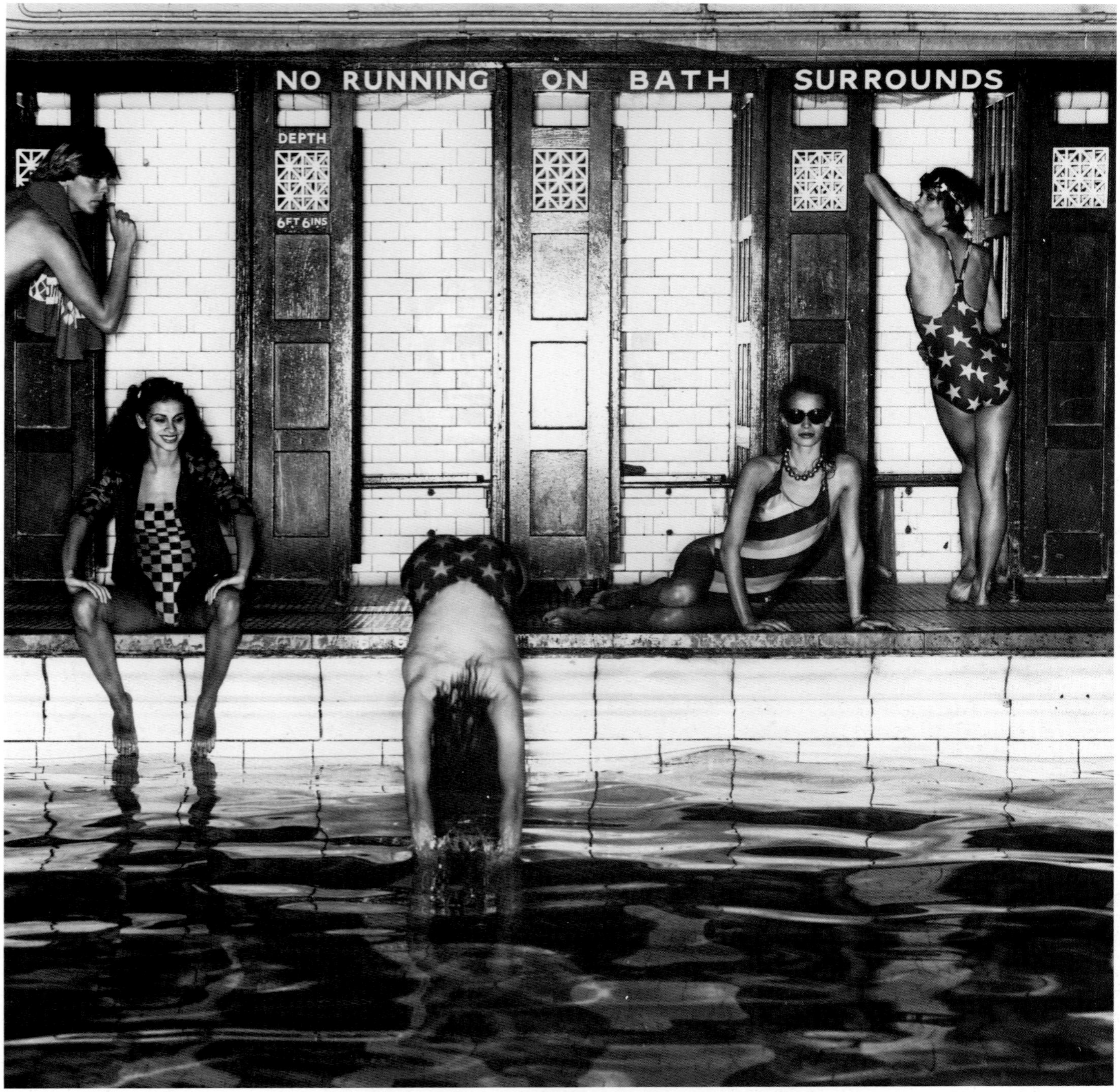

The Pool Jonathan Trapman. The tremendous range of tones in this picture requires a careful choice of contrast grade of paper. Too hard and the detail in the blacks and in the highlights would be lost; too soft and the print would look flat.

West Wycombe HRH The Prince Andrew. The bright sky had to be burned-in gradually to contain the tree line. The foreground was also darkened to give it contrast.

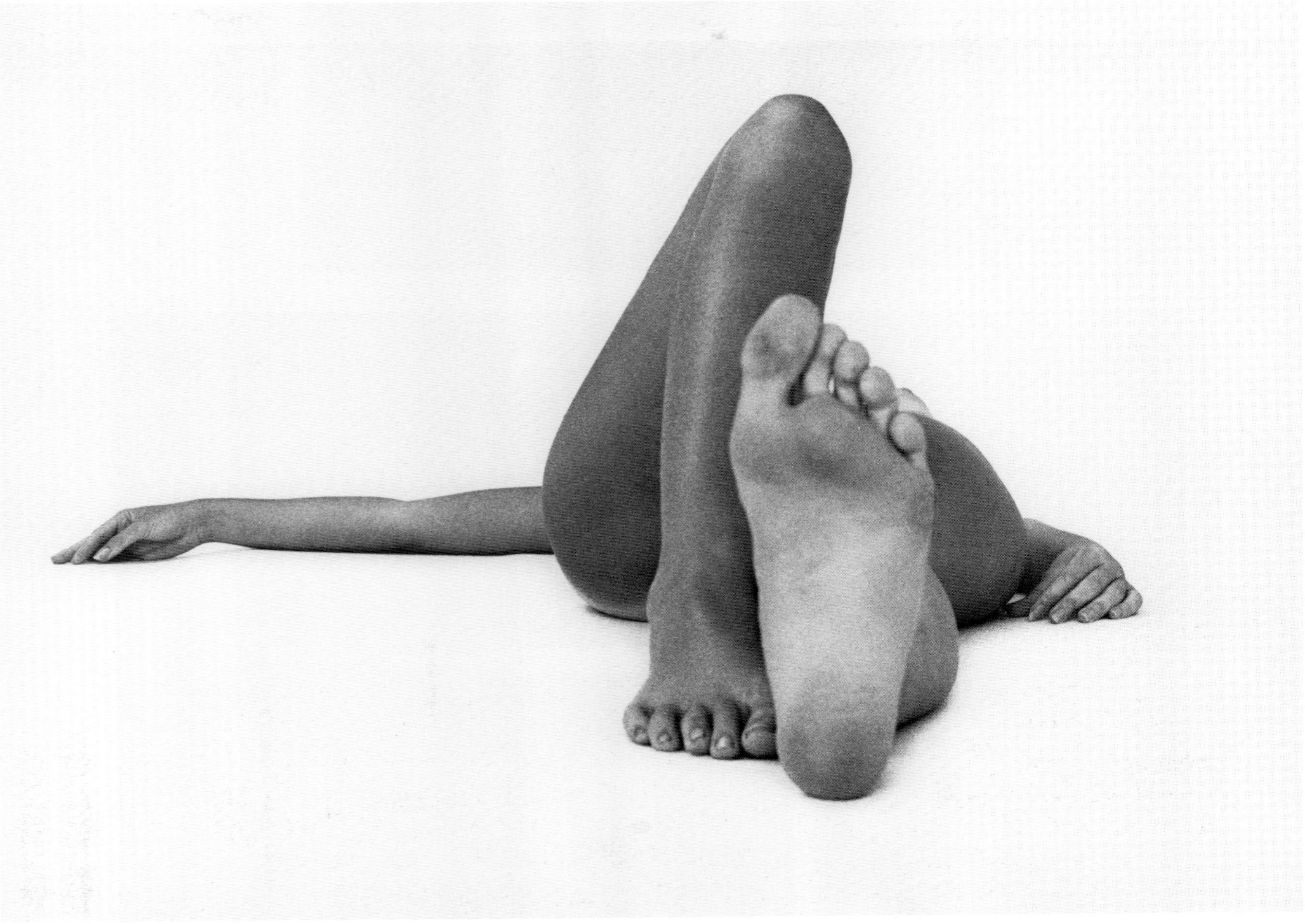

Barefoot Gene Nocon. An unusual view of the female form, 'barefoot' all over. Photographed against a seamless white background, the printing is 'straight' as per the negative. The Californian suntan provides all the contrast necessary.

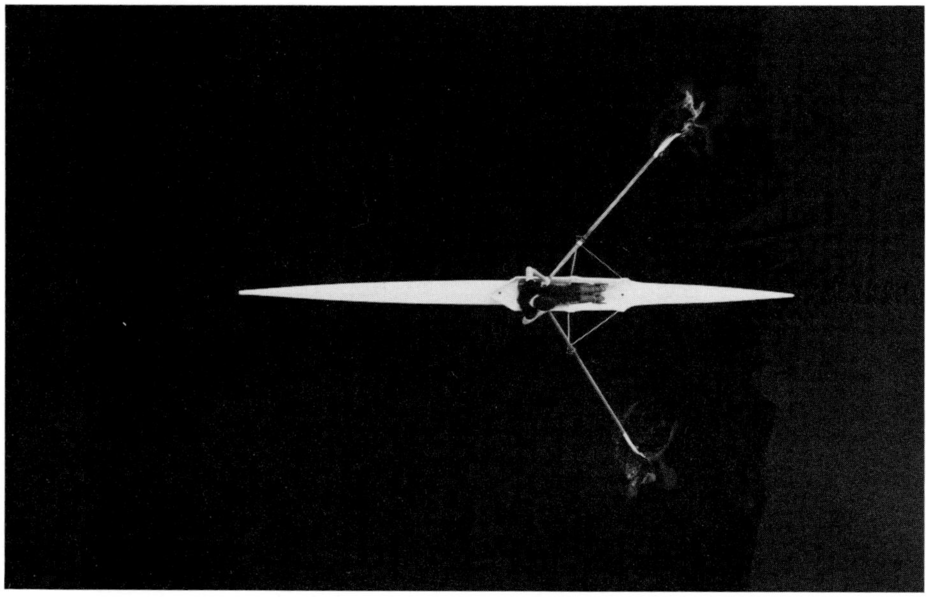

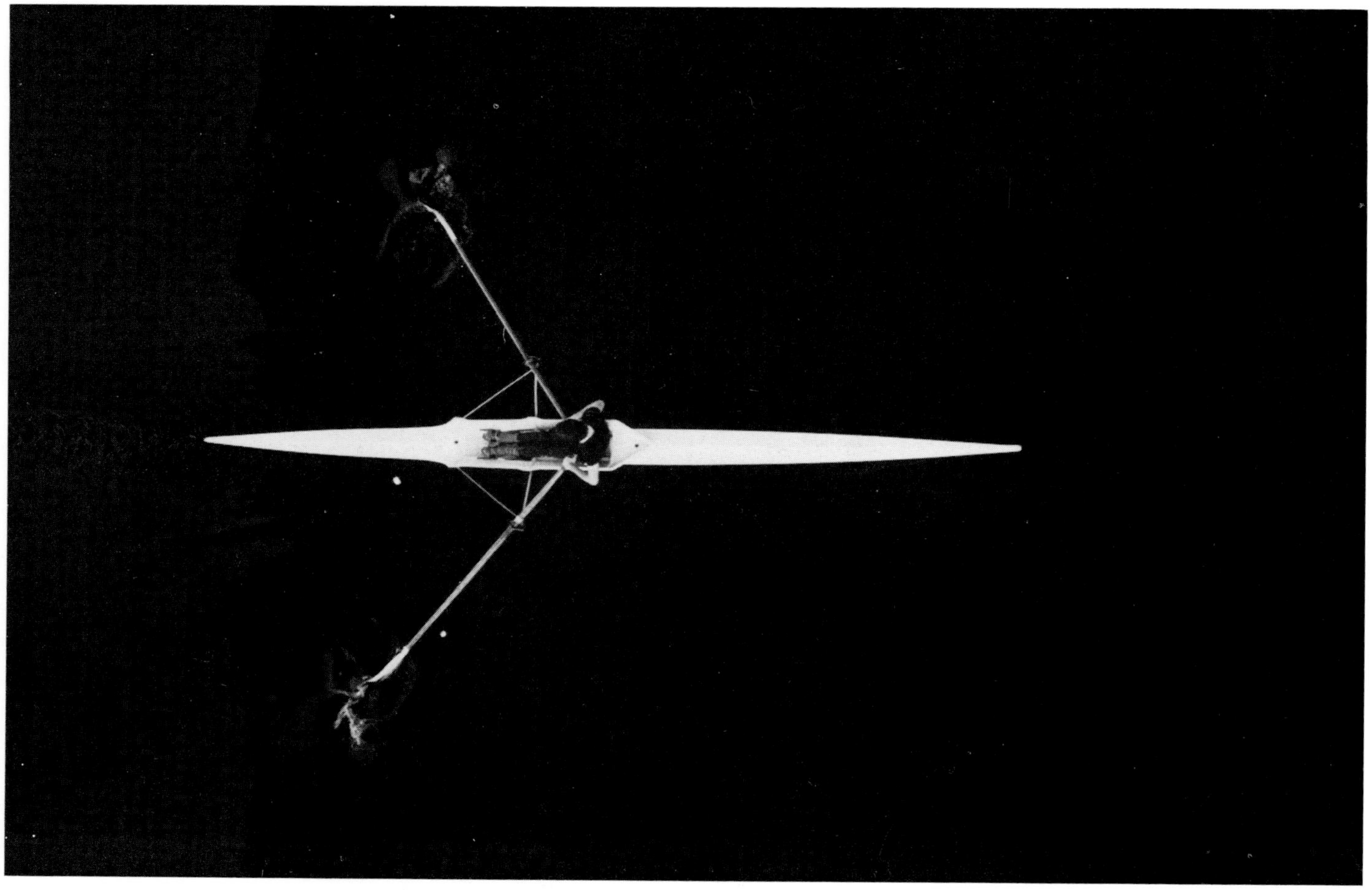

Sculling Régis Bossu. This picture, which has been reversed, can be seen to 'read' left to right. Compare this with the smaller image reproduced right to left.

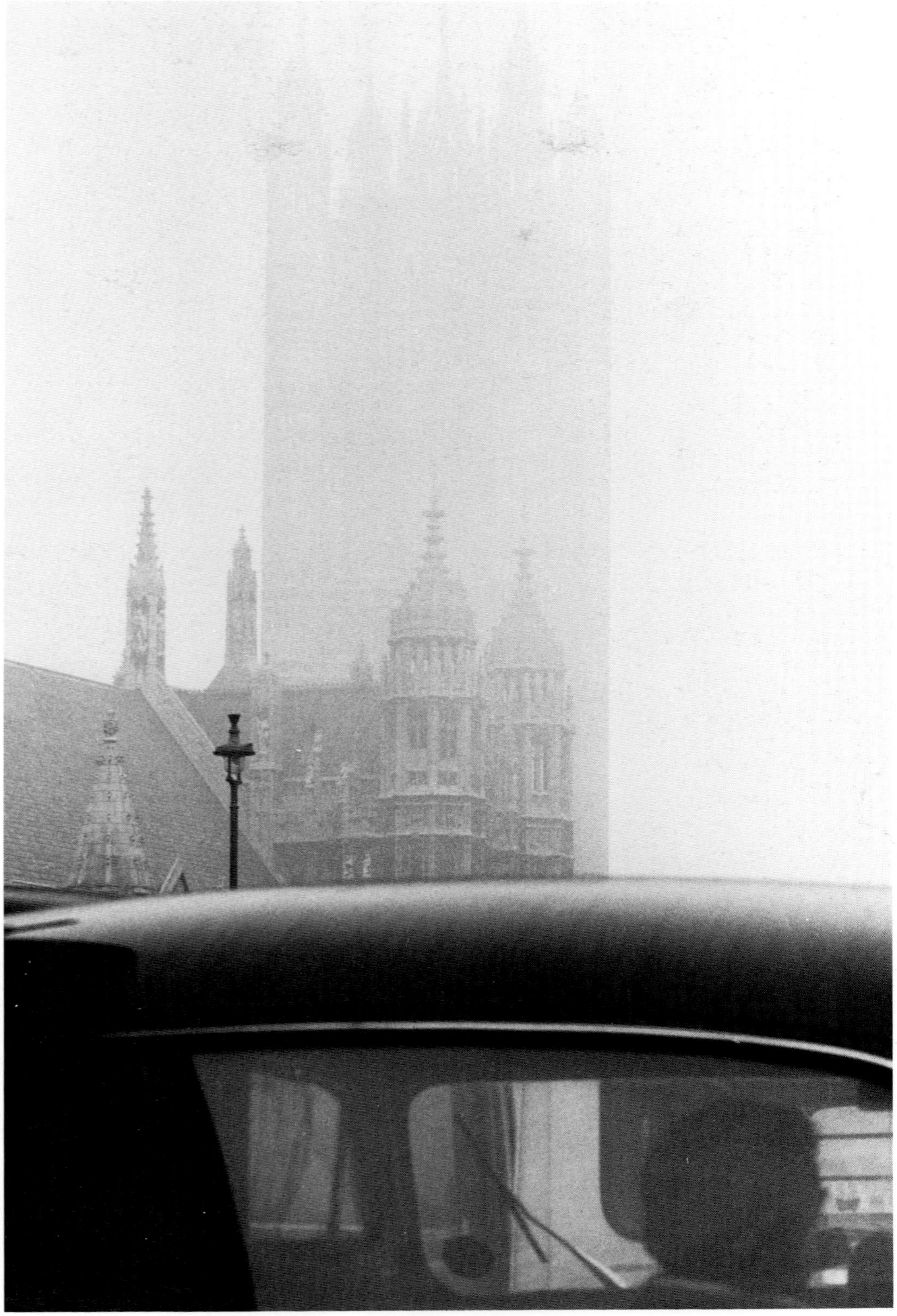

Lords' Tower Malcolm Cleaves. One of a collection of photographs taken by a London taxi driver for the *Personal Points of View* exhibition. Each of the photographs had a taxi or part of a taxi as the theme.

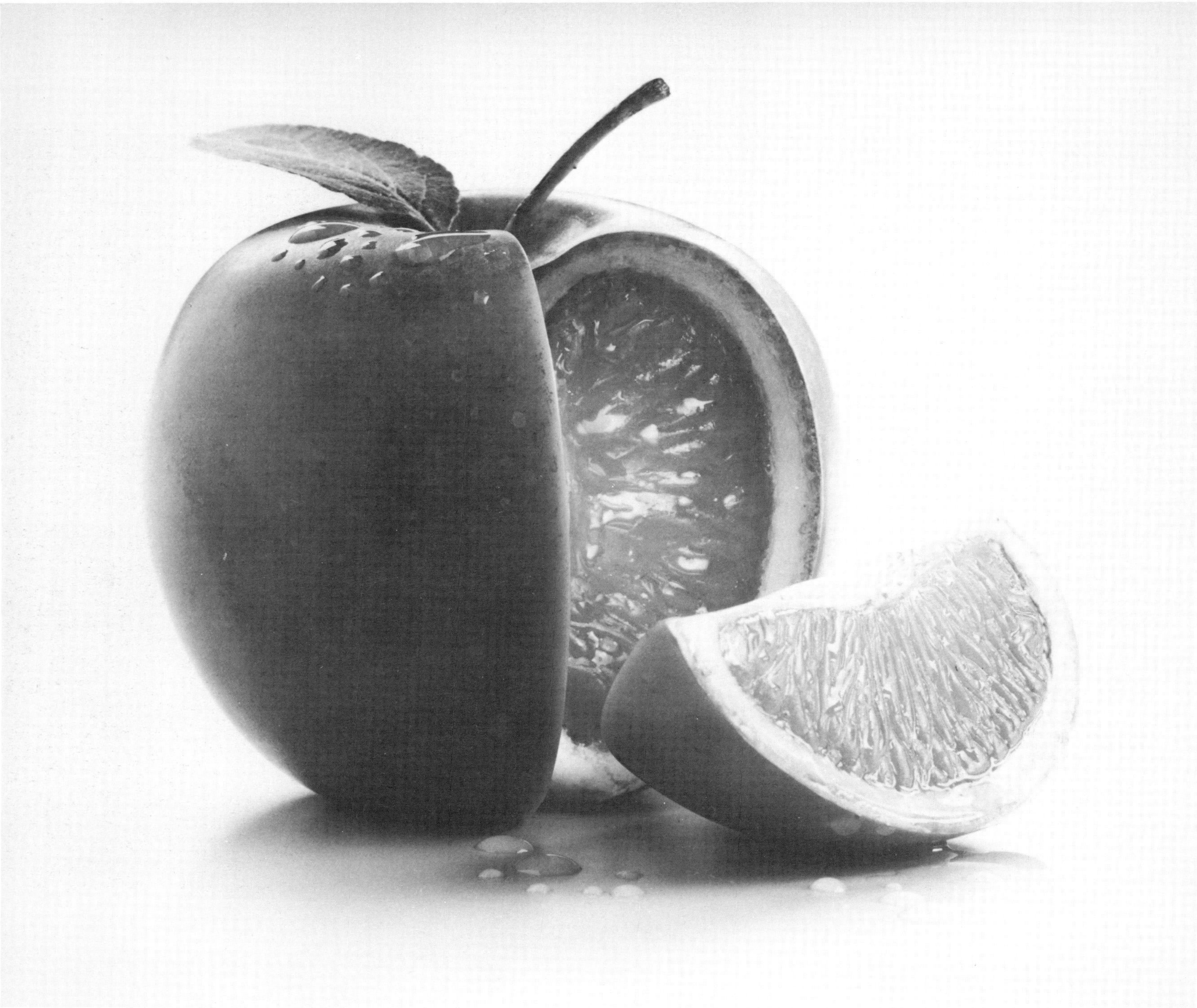

Bananas John Rawlings. A straightforward print ensuring only that the highlight detail on the right-hand side of the slice is evident. No trick printing is involved – just the handiwork of a professional photographer.

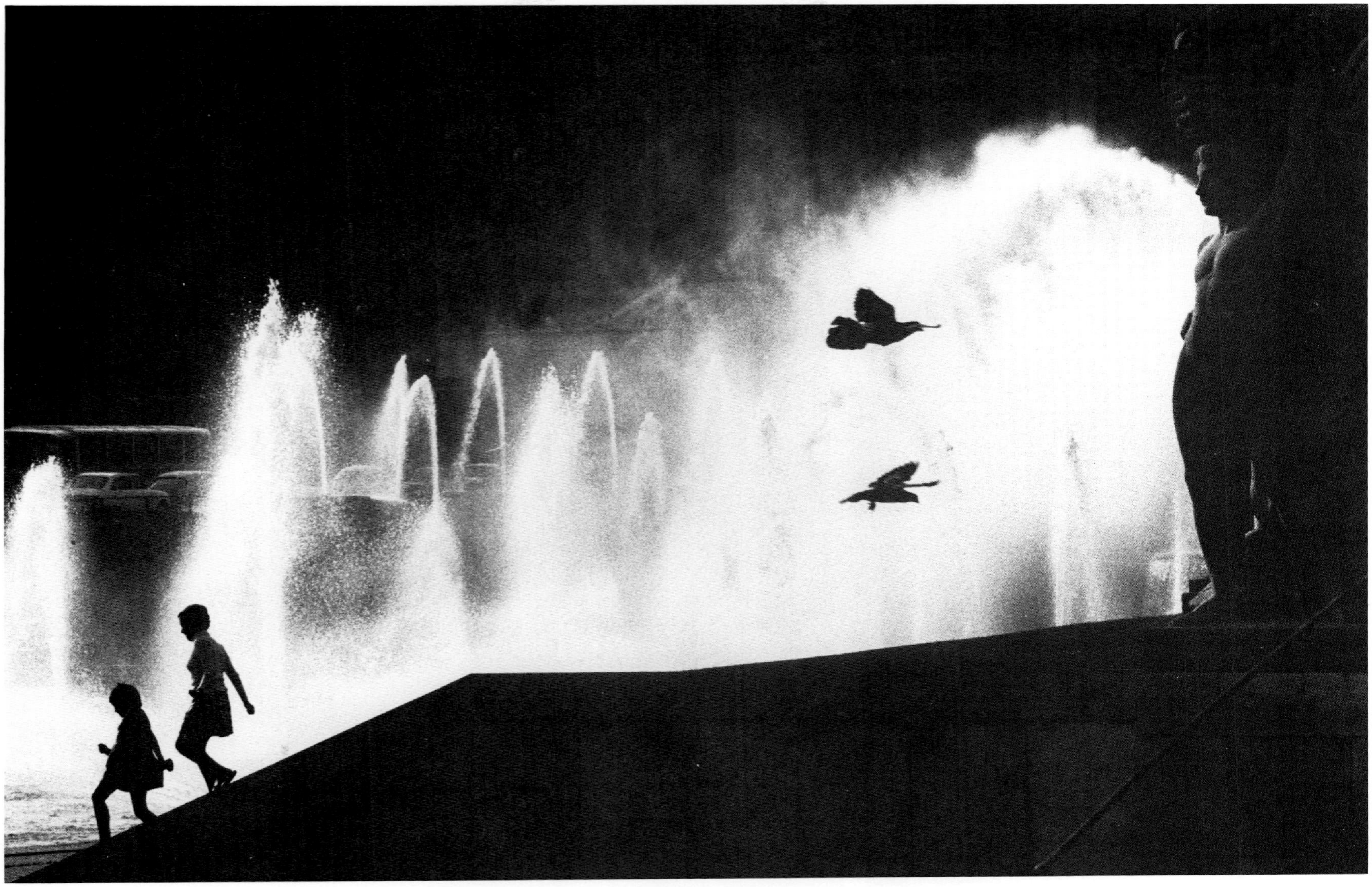

The Fountain Régis Bossu. Darkening the area above the fountain emphasizes the brightness of the water and appeal of this picture.

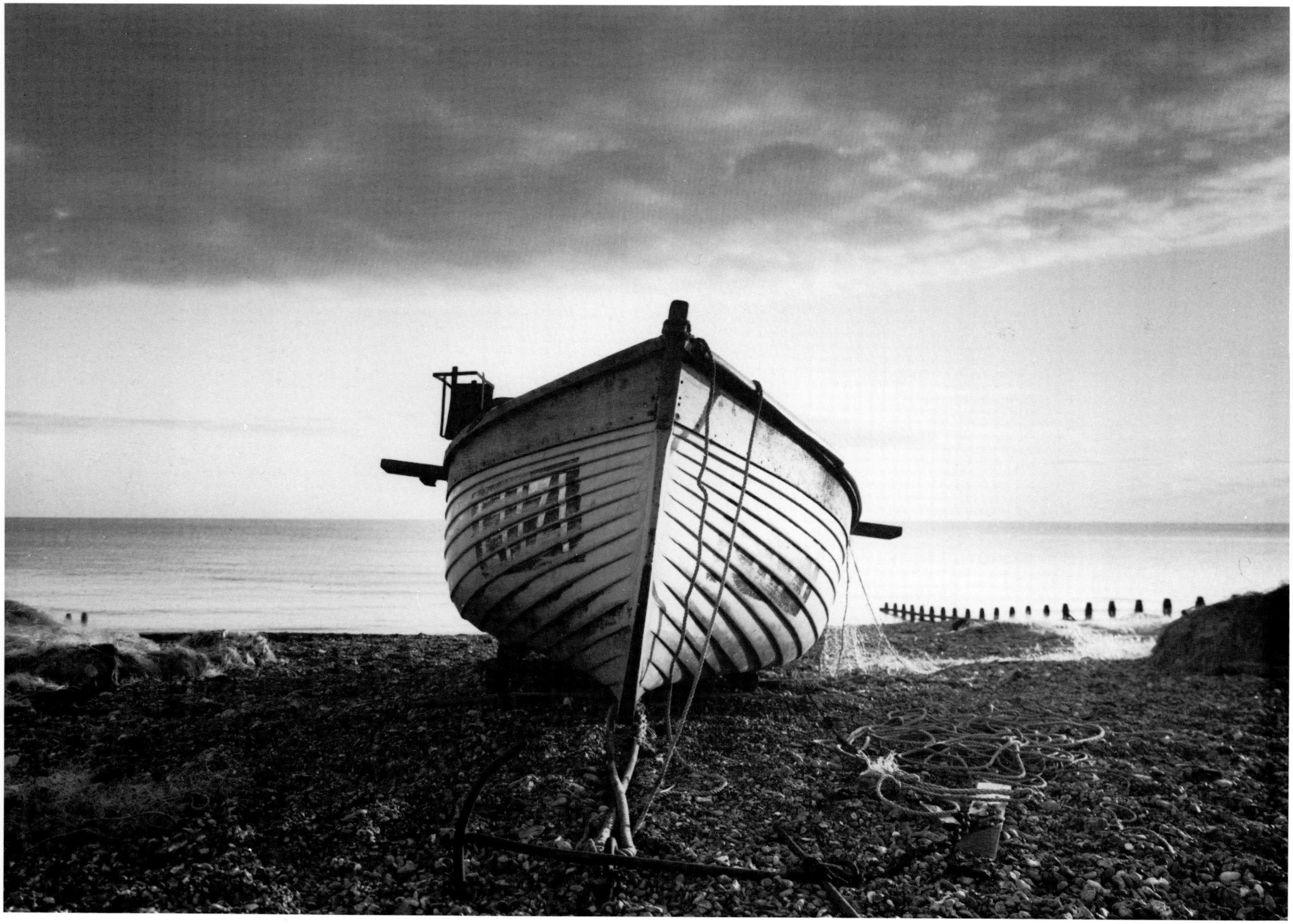

Boat on the Beach Tony White. Printing down the sky enhances the clouds, whilst darkening the foreground gives the shingle a feeling of depth.

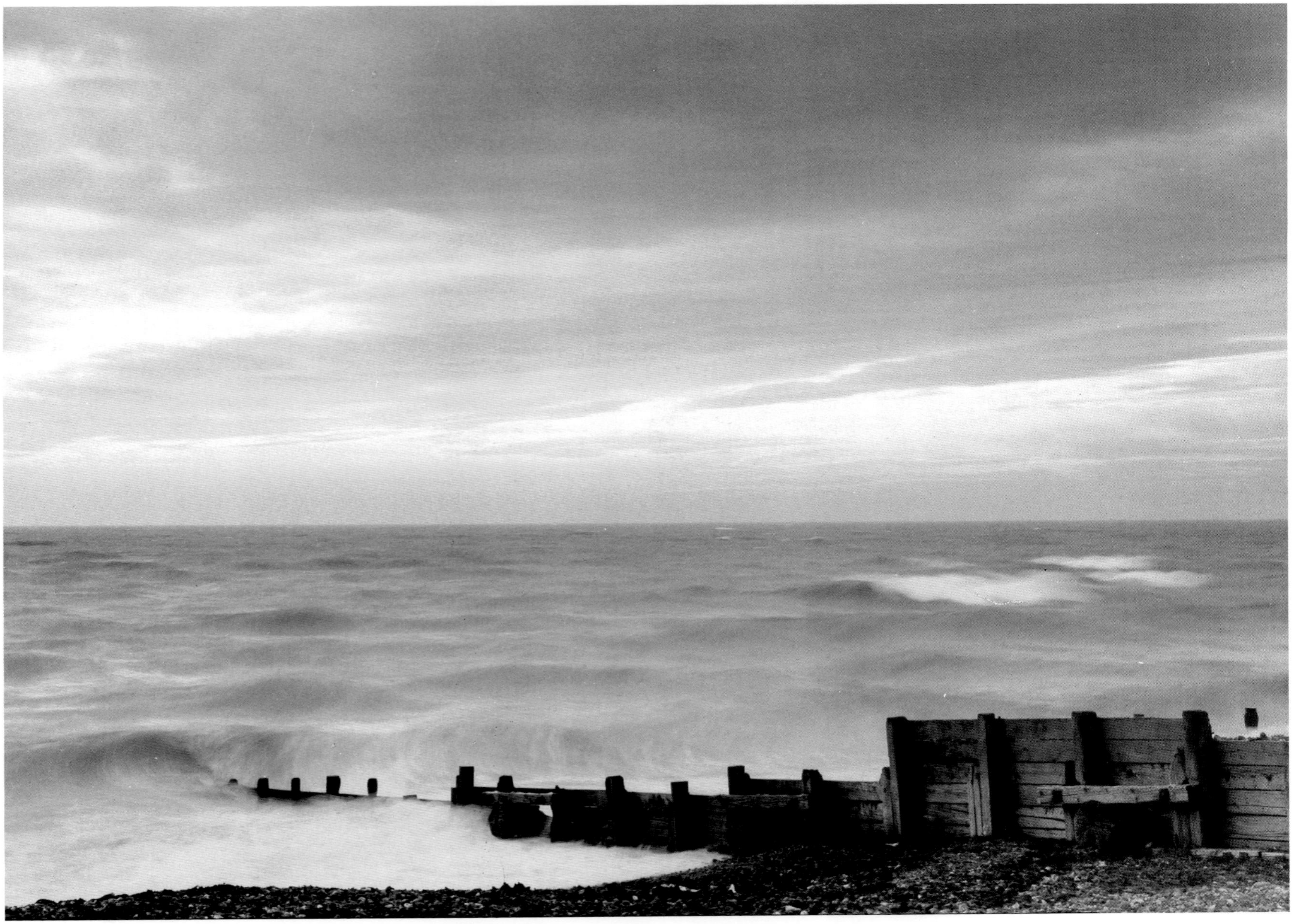

Breakwater Tony White. The sky and the horizon line were darkened and the picture was judiciously cropped to keep the horizontal emphasis at the same time as pointing the foreshore.

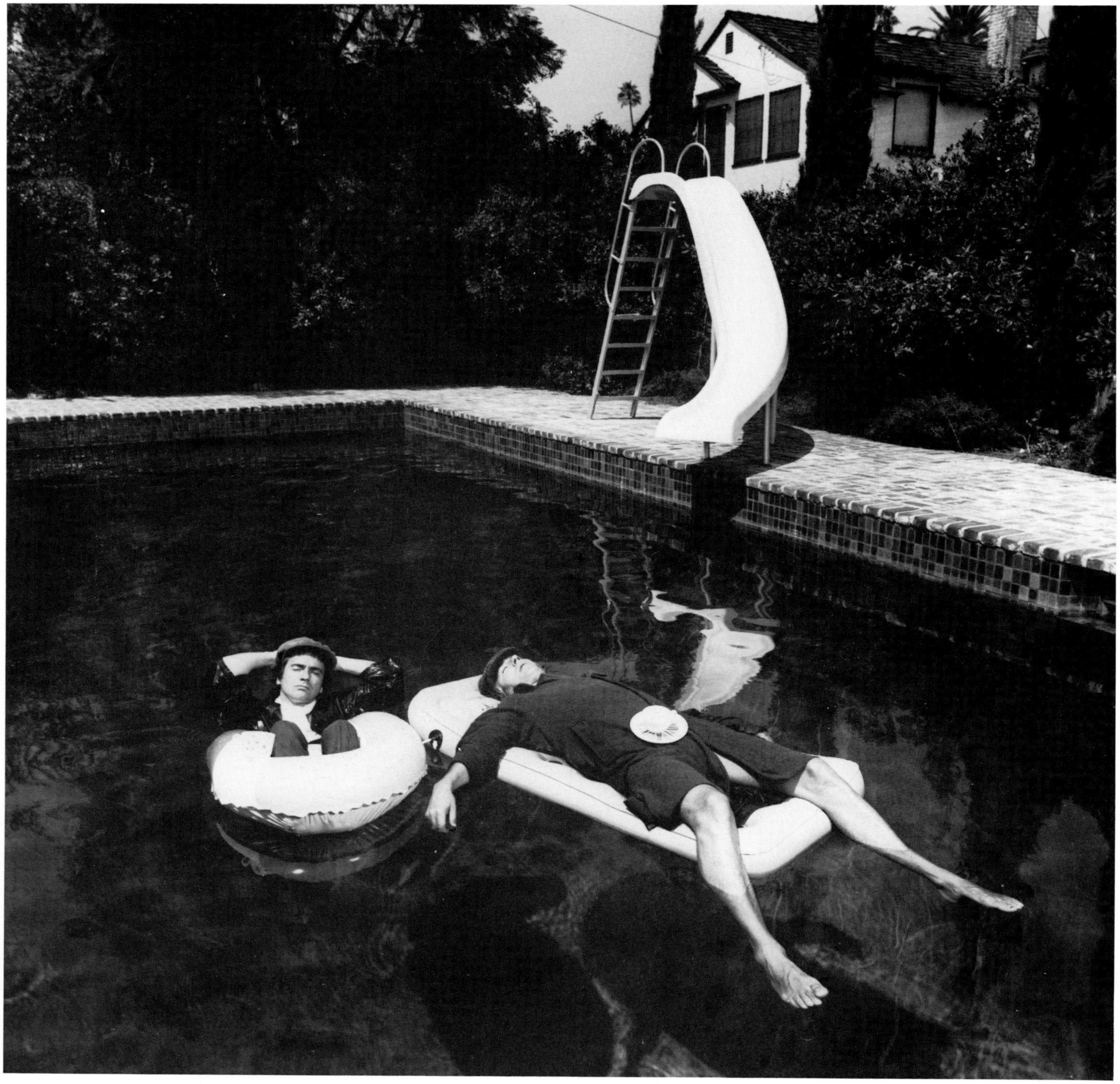

Peter Cooke and Dudley Moore Terry O'Neill. The detail has been retained by dodging the bushes. The slide and inflatables have been burned-in to retain the highlight details.

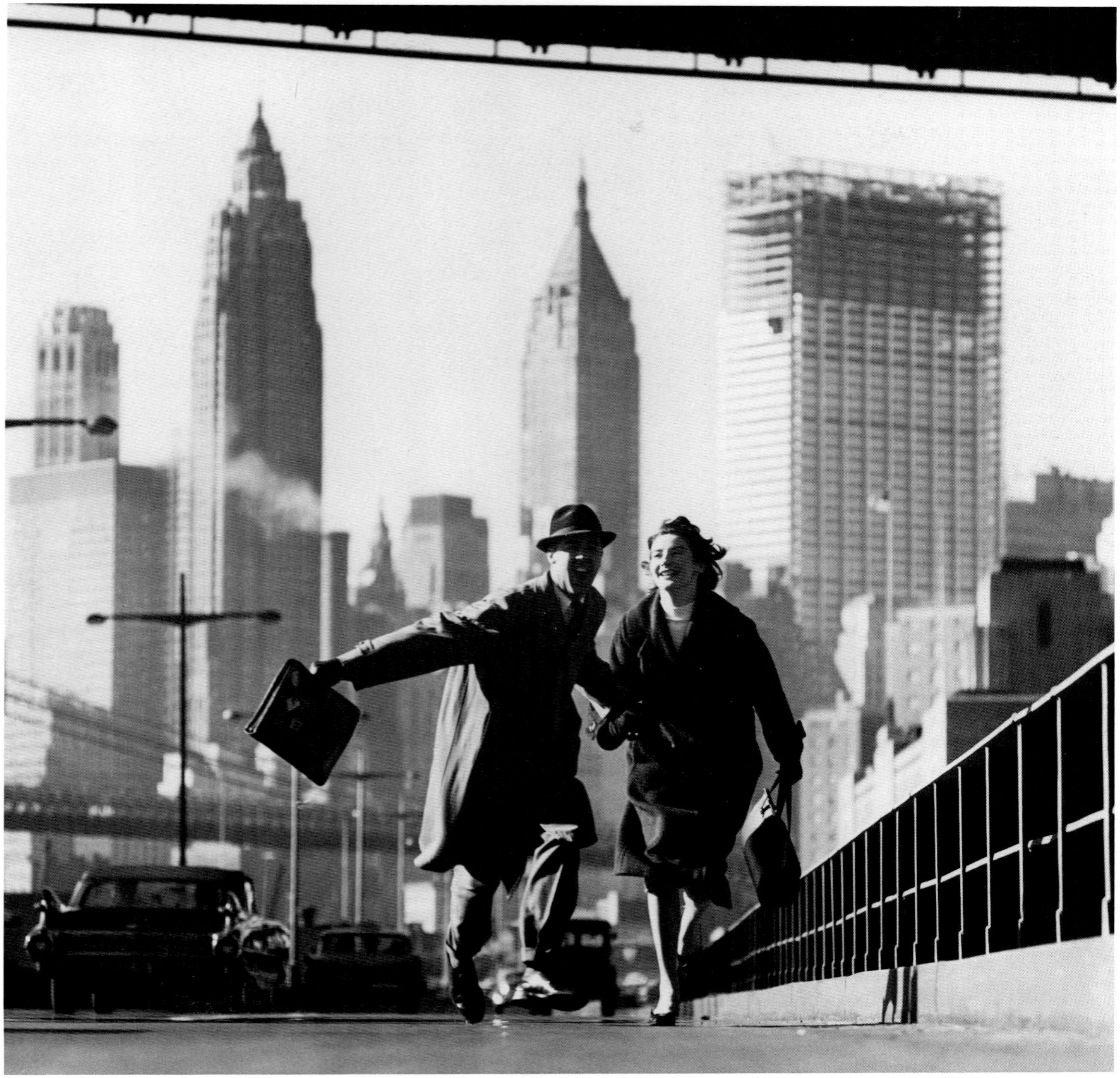

New York, New York. Norman Parkinson, CBE. The top of the bridge was included in the print to contain the picture. Note the pointing at the top left corner.

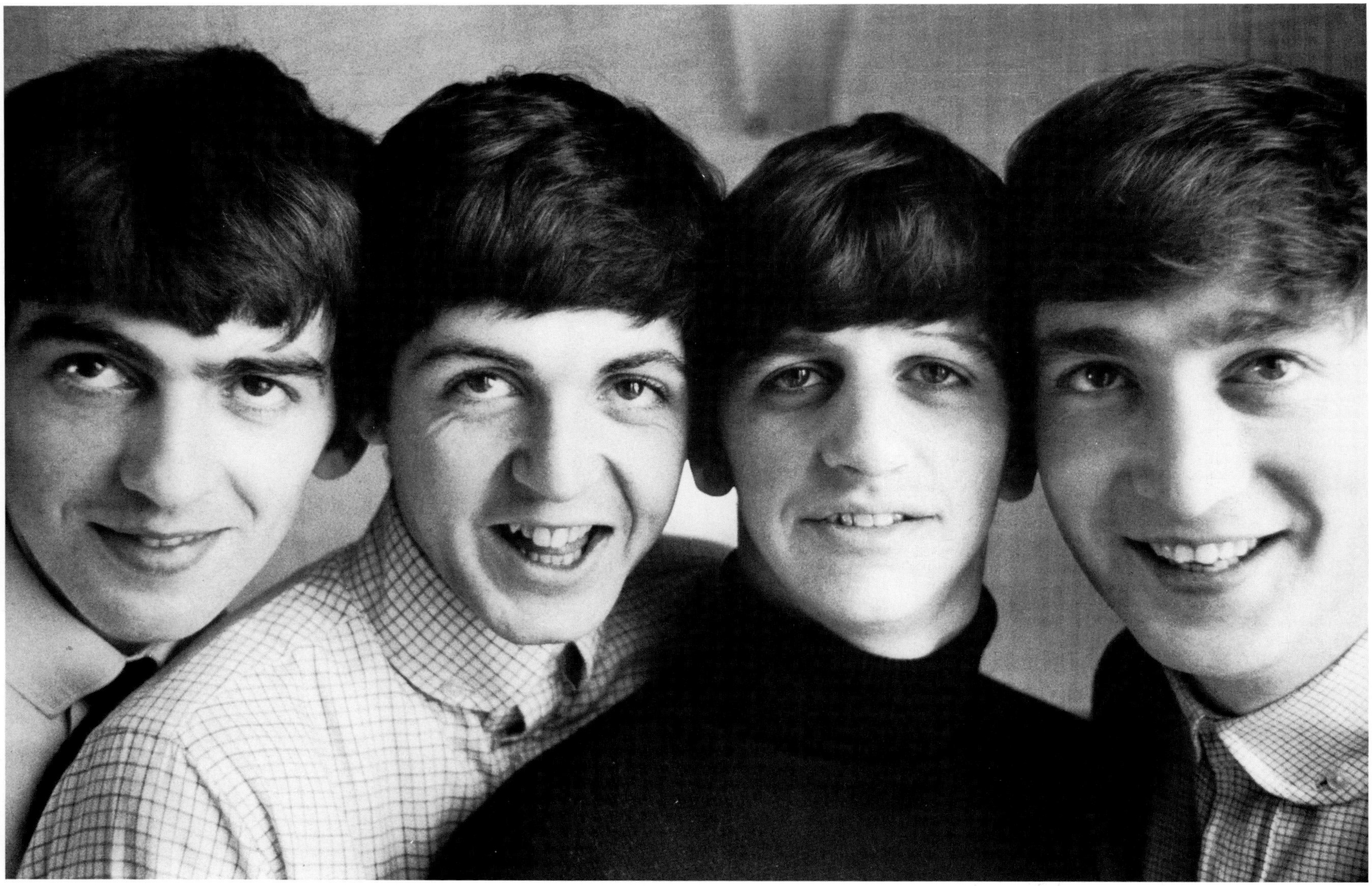

The Beatles 1964 Norman Parkinson, CBE. One of the first pictures I printed for Mr Parkinson. Printing on a contrast grade 2 produced a print which was too soft; on a grade 3 the print was too hard. Flashing a grade 3 provided the required range of tones and contrast.

CHAPTER SIX

CHAPTER SIX
Contrast Control

Before the availability of graded-contrast photographic papers, photographers or their printers could only increase or decrease the print contrast by applying the same techniques that were used to control film contrast.

Today the print contrast can be controlled by simply using a different grade of paper. The techniques used in the past have been abandoned with the availability of graded papers and multi-grade papers which employ filters to change contrast. Though graded papers provide the ease and simplicity of changing contrast, the techniques in the past can be used to provide even greater contrast control.

CONTRAST GRADES OF PAPER

Photographic paper is available in different contrast grades of 1, 2, 3, 4, and in some cases 5. Grade 2 is considered the 'normal' contrast. Grade 1 represents a 'soft' contrast while 3, 4, and 5 progressively get 'harder'.

There is no hard and fast rule about which grade of paper to use for a particular negative. That decision depends on personal taste and use of the photograph. My prints for reproduction, for example, are different from those for exhibitions or client presentations. Reproduction prints are softer for retouching and camera copying.

When in doubt or confused about which grade to use, try the print on grade 2 to see what it looks like on 'normal' paper. It is best to start with a soft print before doing a harder version. Printing the hard version first will make the following soft print appear softer than it really is.

The previous chapters describing the F/STOP EXPOSURE TIME method of printing stressed maintaining a standard development time. By changing this development time and using the F/STOP EXPOSURE TIME method I can now describe how to get the in-between contrast grades.

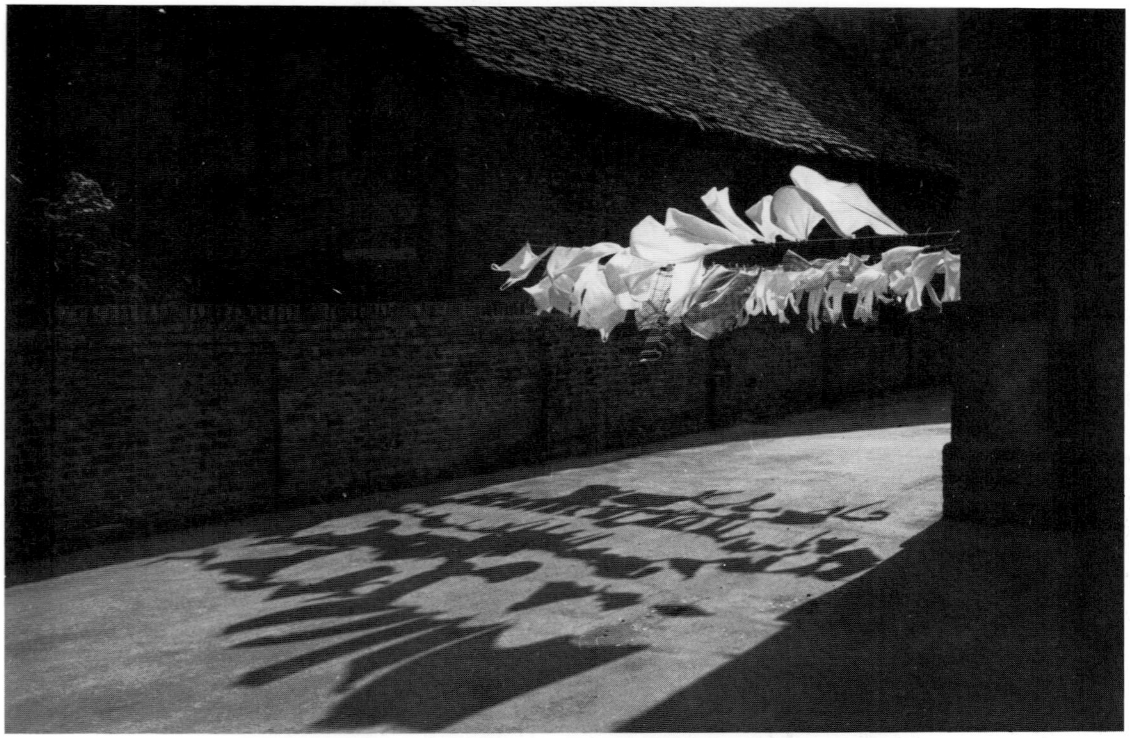

Grade 0

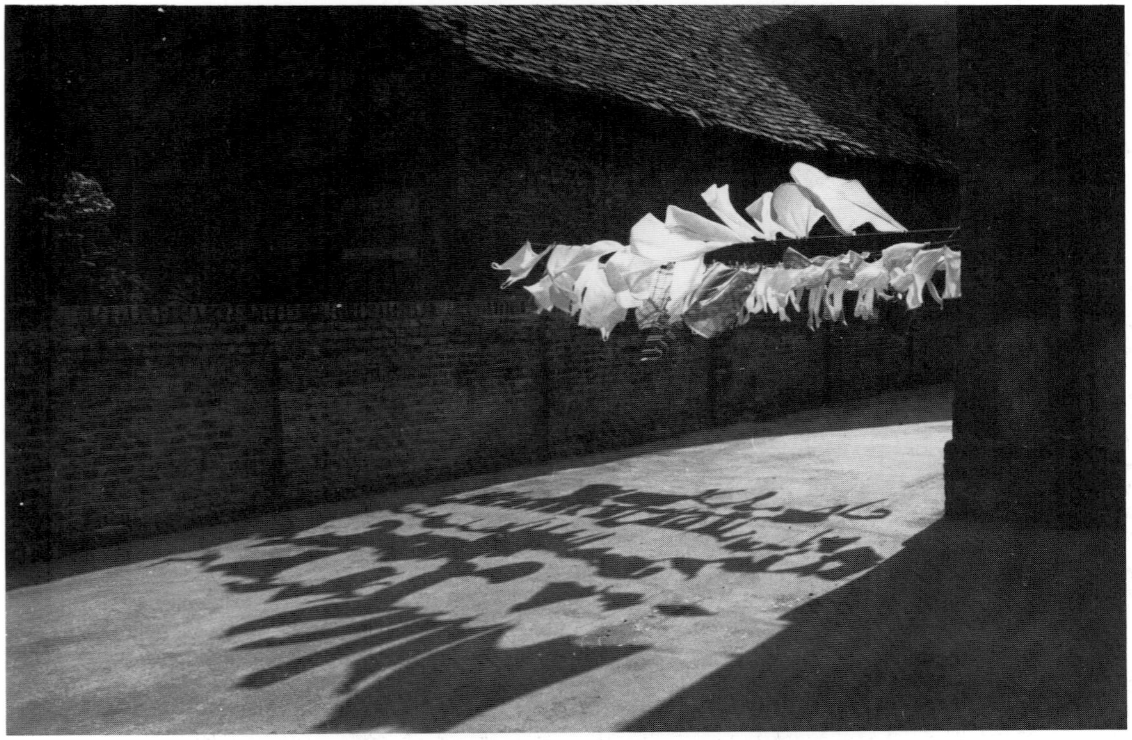

Grade 1

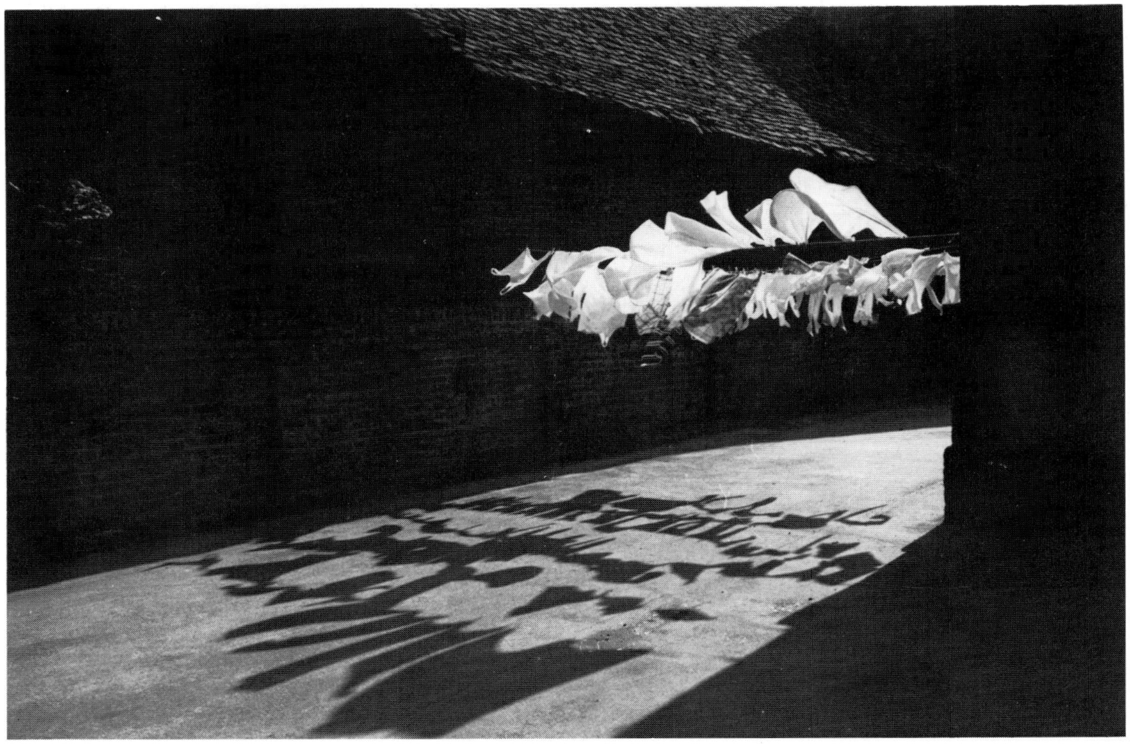

Grade 2

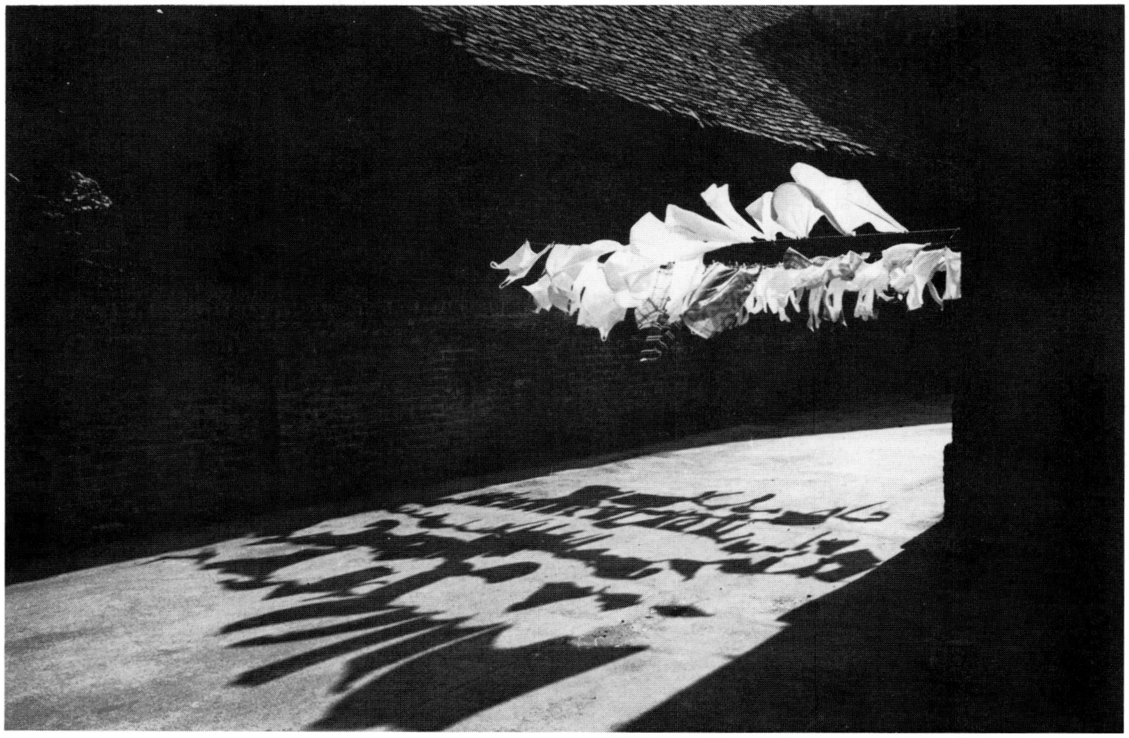

Grade 3

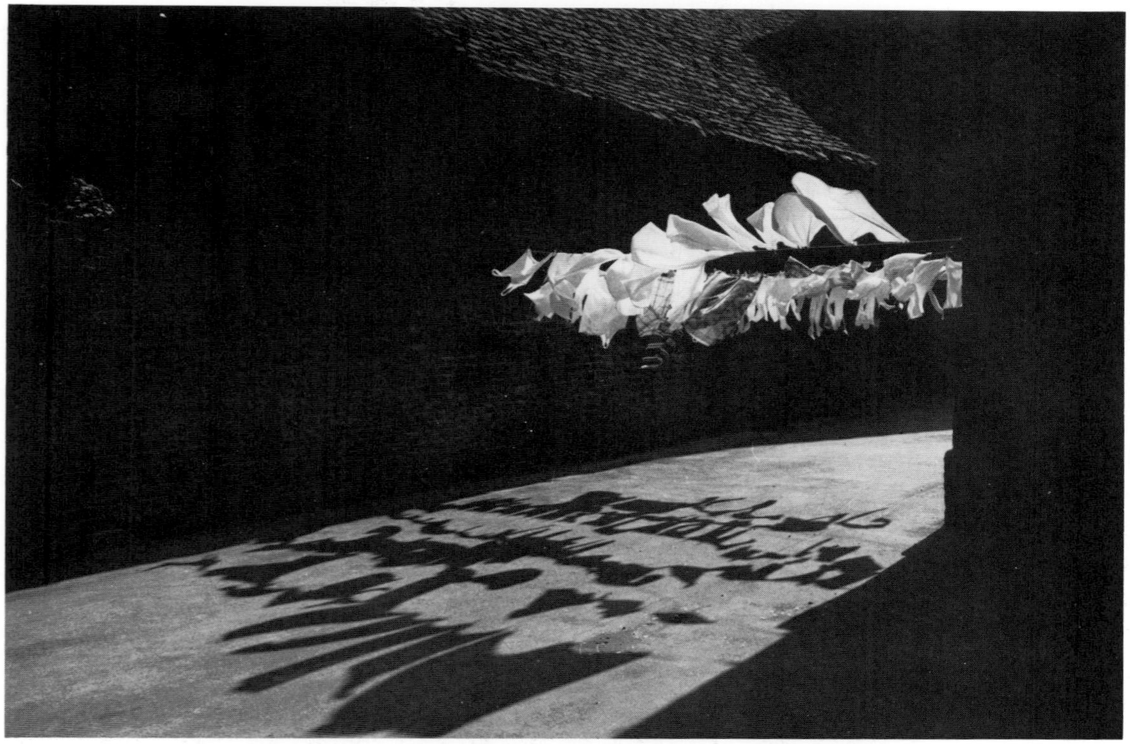

Grade 4

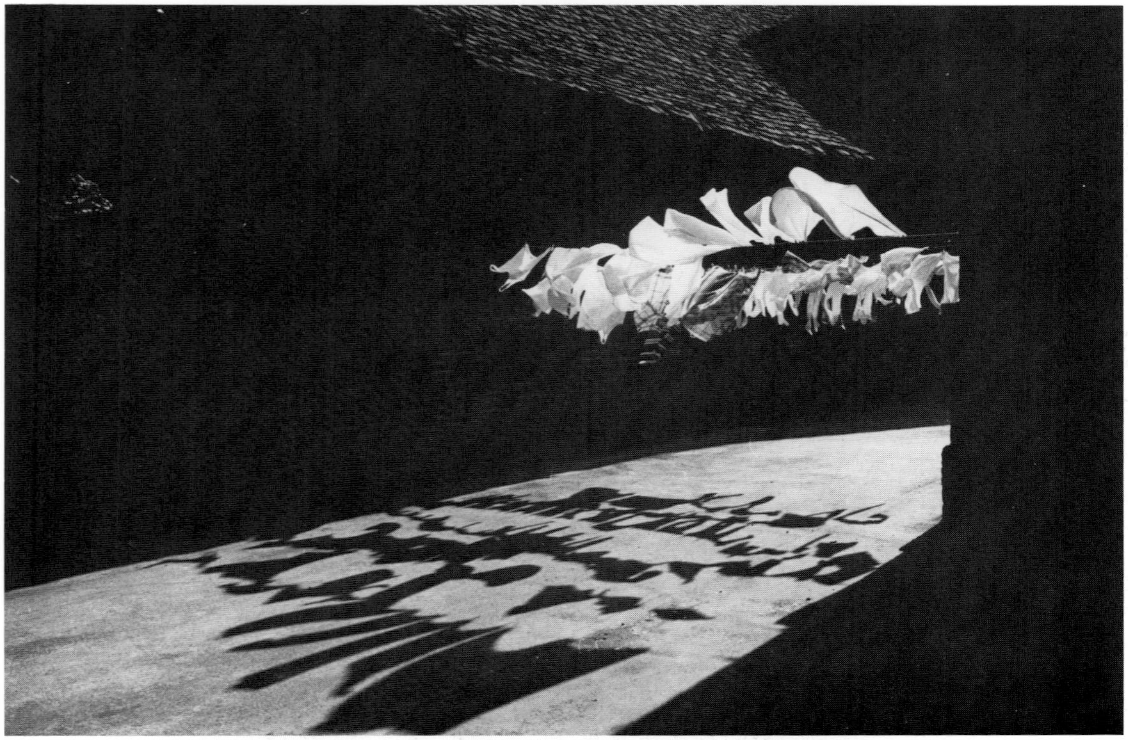

Grade 5

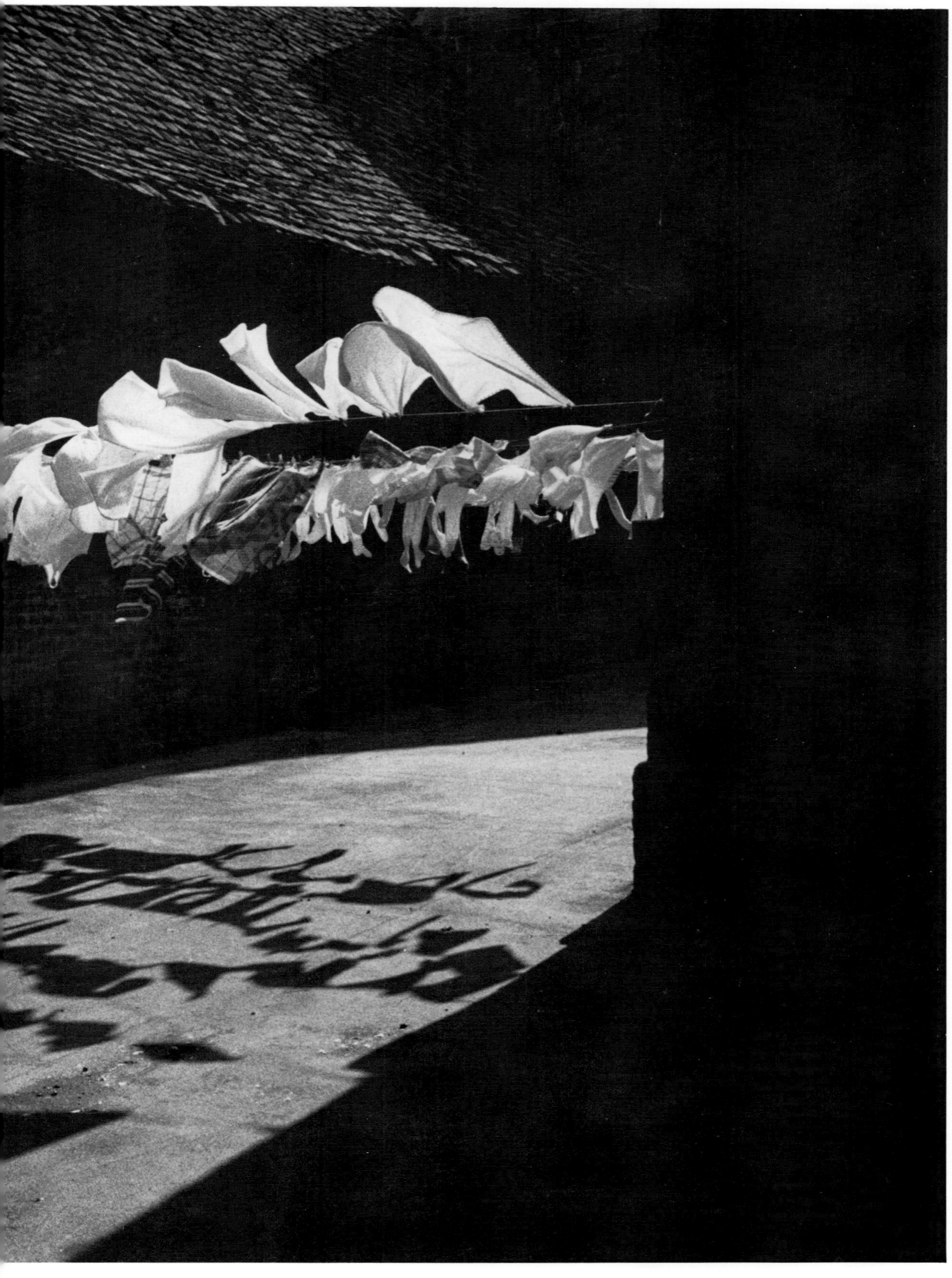

Washing Régis Bossu.

EXPOSURE/DEVELOPMENT

The technique to soften or harden the contrast of any one of the standard grades of paper is based on the relationship of the exposure and the development of photographic material: UNDEREXPOSE AND OVERDEVELOP TO INCREASE CONTRAST; OVEREXPOSE AND UNDERDEVELOP TO DECREASE CONTRAST.

This technique creates a grade in-between the contrast grades of fixed grade fibre-based papers. Multigrade users have the facility for a ½ grade by simply using the appropriate filter.

This technique can be used when, for example, the print appears soft on grade 2, and on grade 3 the print is too hard. To increase the contrast of grade 2 decrease the exposure by −¼ f/stop and increase the development time by a factor of 1.4. Using the harder grade of 3, increasing the overall exposure by +¼ f/stop and decreasing the development time by a factor of 0.7 will decrease the contrast.

My 'standard' development time is 2 minutes. The 'increase development' is 2 minutes 50 seconds. The 'decrease development' time is 1 minute 25 seconds.* If the standard time were 3 minutes, increased development time would be 4 minutes 15 seconds; decreased development would be 2 minutes 10 seconds.*

Underexposing the softer grade of paper makes it possible to increase the development time so the print does not merely get darker. The increased development provides the contrast by making the blacks blacker, and allows development of the highlight areas. Overexposing the harder grade of paper ensures the development of the highlight detail when the print is 'pulled' at the

**Rounded to the nearest 5 seconds*

The combination of exposure and development controls print contast.
Underexposure in each case was ¼ f/stop less than the 'normal' exposure time: overexposure was ¼ f/stop more than normal. The normal development time was for 2 minutes. Underdevelopment time was for 1 minute 25 seconds; overdevelopment time was 2 minutes 50 seconds.

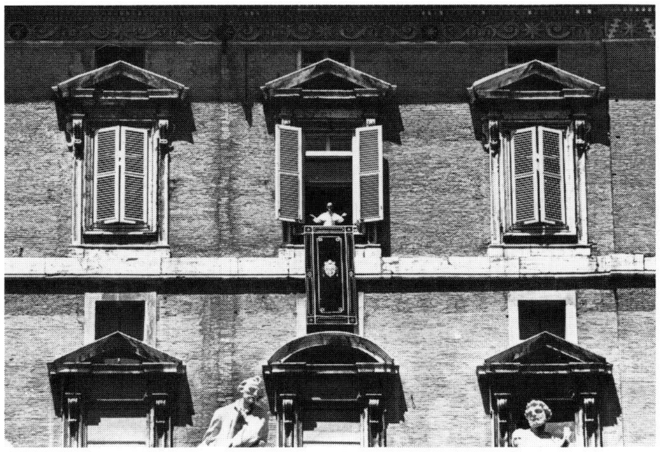

Underexposure, underdevelopment.

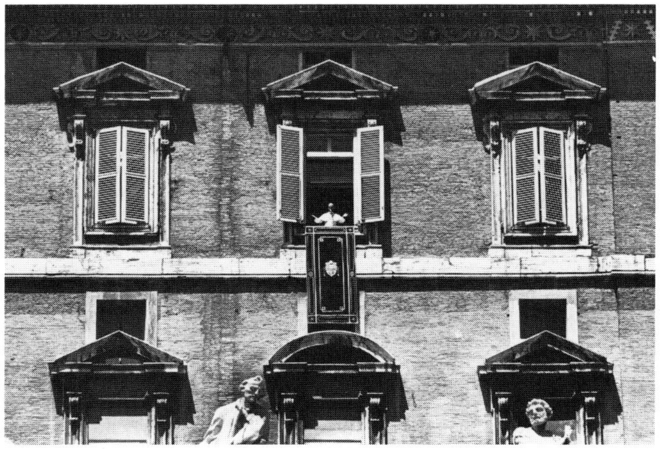

Underexposure, normal development.

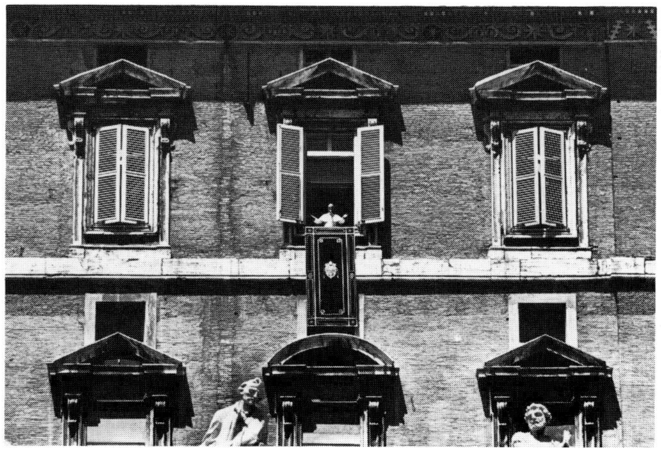

Underexposure, overdevelopment.

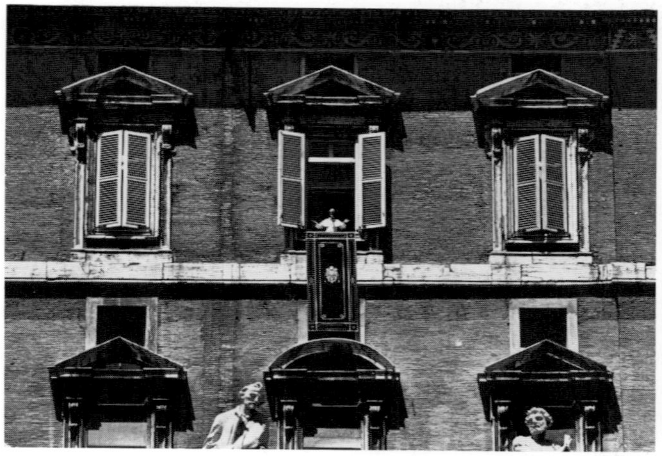

Normal exposure, underdevelopment.

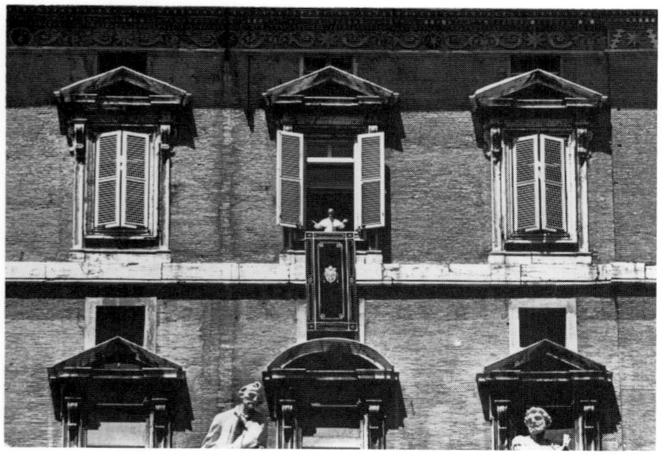

Overexposure, underdevelopment.

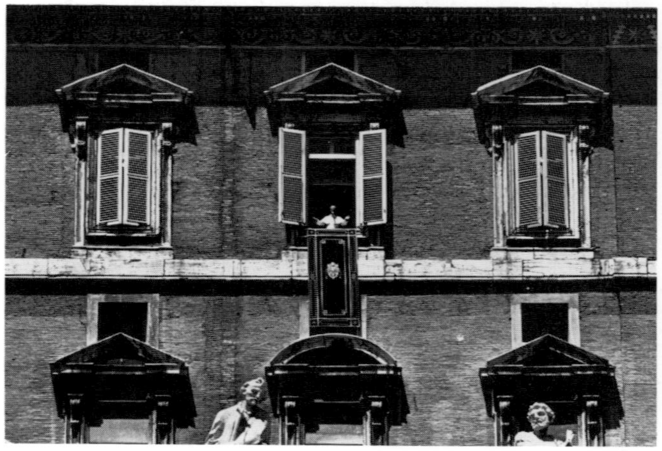

Normal exposure, normal development.

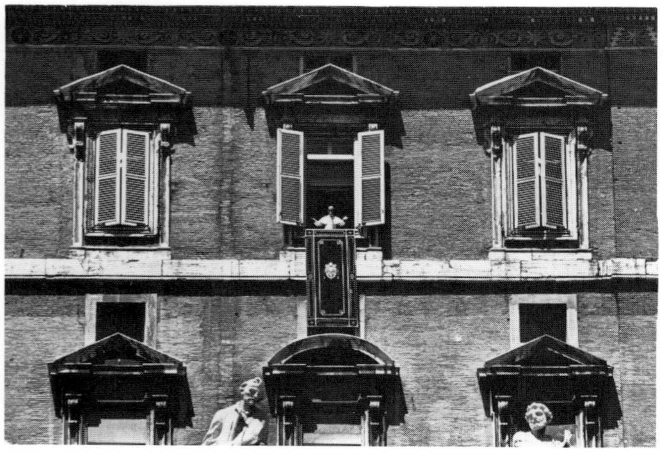

Overexposure, normal development.

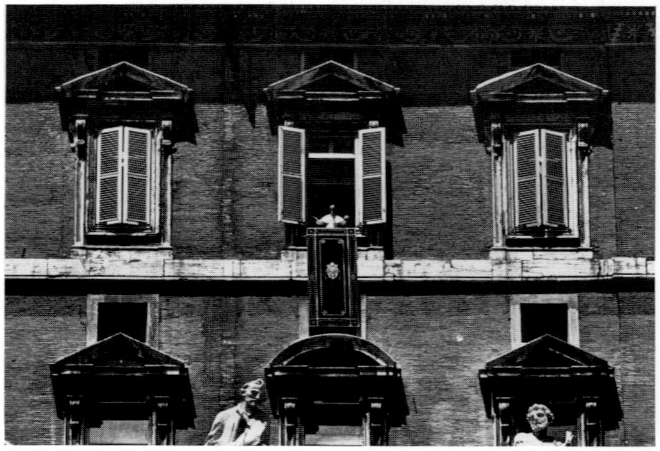

Normal exposure, overdevelopment.

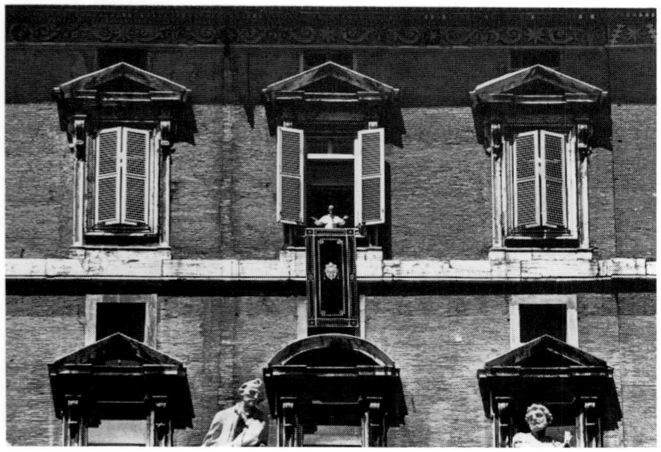

Overexposure, overdevelopment.

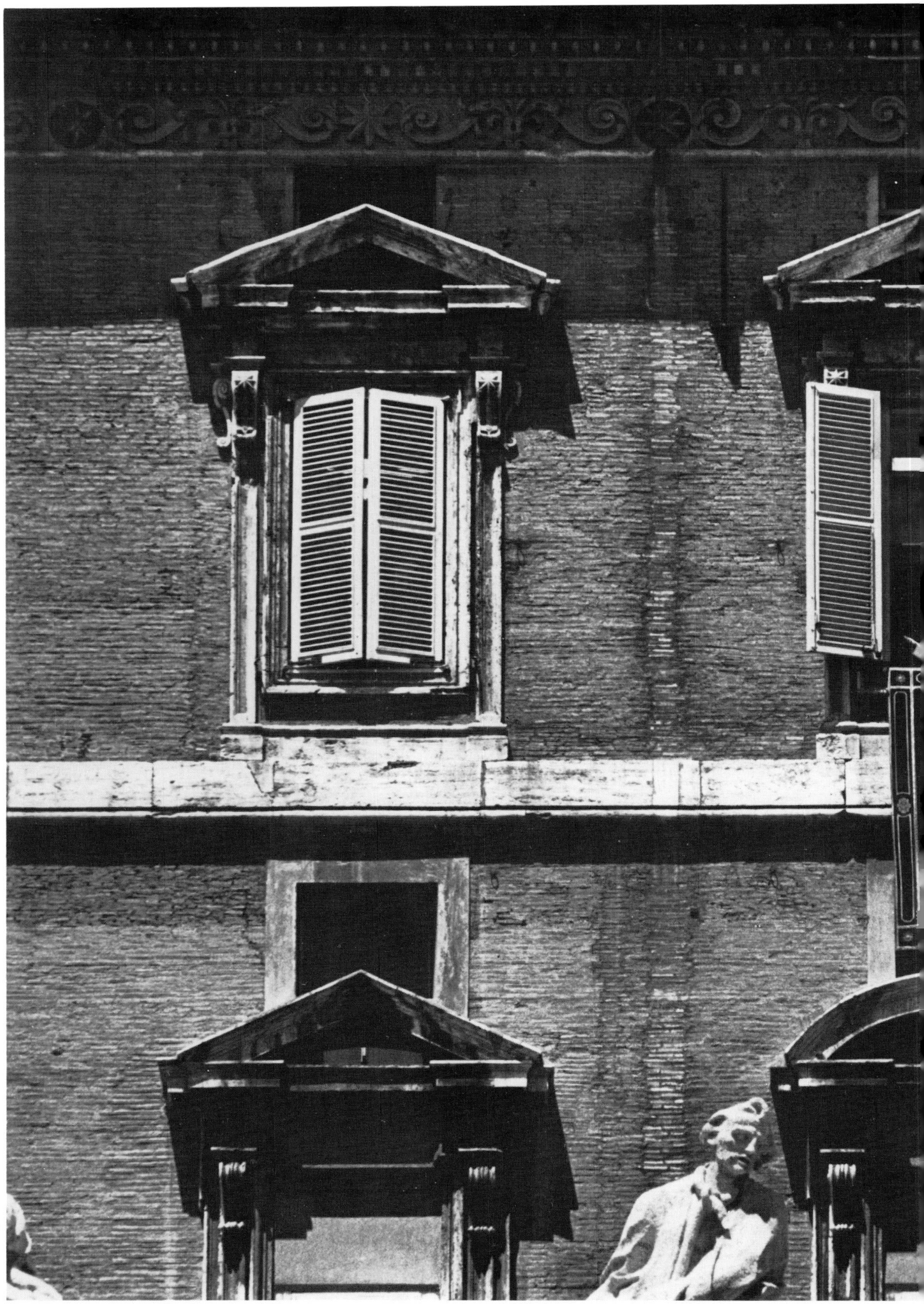

shortened development time. Overexposing ensures that the black is retained.

If no change were made to the exposure time on the softer grade of paper, and the print were simply left to develop for the increased development time, the result would only be a dark print. And if no increase were made to the exposure on the harder grade of paper, and the print were pulled at the decreased development time, the print would look flat with no blacks and the highlight would be lost.

To illustrate this technique let us take a print which we have determined to have a basic exposure of 10 seconds. On a grade 2 paper the print is soft, and on grade 3 a little hard. The decision whether to increase the contrast of grade 2 or to decrease the contrast of grade 3 paper depends on the degree of hardness or softness required. Say it needs to be only slightly softer than the grade 3 print. In this case, increase the exposure on grade 3 paper by +¼ f/stop and then develop the print for the reduced development time. On the other hand, should the print need to be only slightly harder than on grade 2 you should print on the same grade 2 but reduce the exposure by −¼ f/stop. Develop this print for the increased development time.

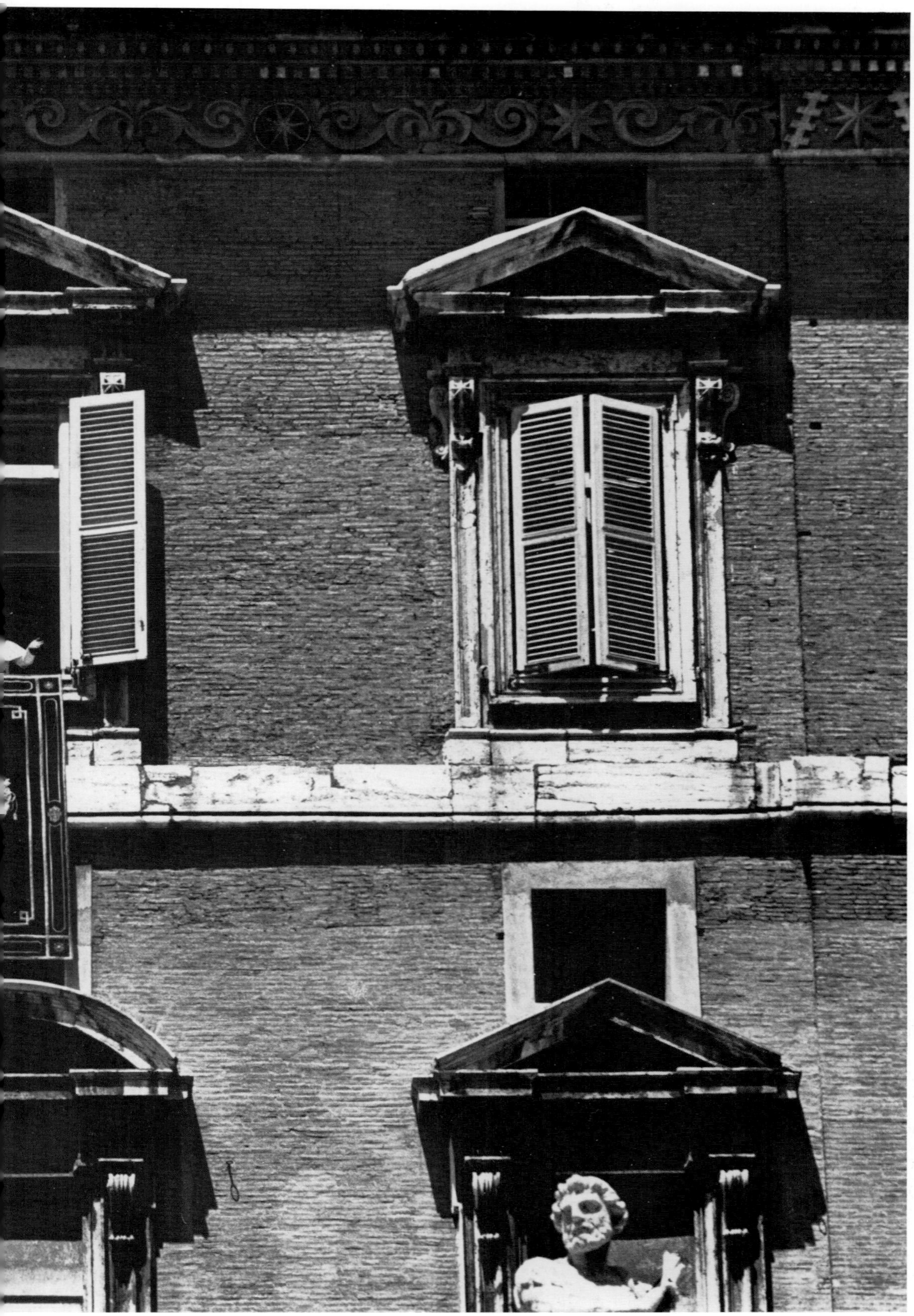

The Pope Gene Nocon.

FLASHING

Flashing is a technique allowing far greater control of print contrast. The method involves pre-exposing the paper to a 'flash' of light before exposing for the print. This provides the facility only to reduce, not increase, the contrast.

This flash exposure time is determined by first making a series of test strips on a sheet of photographic paper to find the 'threshold value' of exposure. The threshold level is the value of exposure that just begins to affect the paper and produce a discernible tone. A certain level of exposure is needed before any tone can be visibly detected. Up to that point the paper remains base white. For those of you who are more technically oriented, the characteristic curve of photographic material shows the density starting at an exposure value beyond 0. In other words, the characteristic curve does *not* start at 0 density, 0 exposure. The value of exposure between 0 and the start of the curve is the threshold value (see Chapter Twelve).

Determining the Threshold Value

Using only the negative carrier, raise the enlarger lamp as high as it will go. Switch the lamp on and focus the aperture edge of the negative carrier onto the baseboard. This ensures focusing on a 'clean' area free from any dust. Stop down the enlarger lens to its minimum aperture. Switch the lamp off. Now place an entire sheet of paper on the baseboard directly under the lamp and proceed to make a series of exposure strips.

Initially expose the entire sheet for 2 seconds. Proceed as if making a test strip as described in Chapter Four. *Cover* a strip of the paper with a large piece of card and continue to make exposures adding first 0.5 seconds, cover and expose for another 0.5 seconds, another 0.5 seconds, then 0.7, then 0.8, 0.9, 1.2, 1.3, 1.6, 1.9, 2.2, 2.7, and the final strip for 3.2 seconds. Cumulatively these strips will then have been exposed for 2, 2.5, 3, 3.5, 4.2, 5, 5.9, 7.1, 8.4, 10, 11.9, 14.1, 16.8, and 20 seconds.

Develop the exposed sheet for your standard time. Examine the results. There should be a series of exposures in ¼ f/stop increments. If you can see absolutely nothing, open up the enlarging lens 2 f/stops and repeat the exercise.

Test strip for finding the threshold value.

Find the strip that is *just* visible. This strip represents the *threshold value* of exposure. Count back from the darkest strip (20 seconds exposure) and match this to the corresponding exposure time.

MAX FLASH

The exposure strip adjacent to the threshold level that CANNOT be seen is 'MAX FLASH'. Count back and determine the corresponding exposure time for Max Flash. Keep a record of this exposure time as well as the height of the enlarger and the lens and aperture used. This can be used for future reference. Provided you know the relative speed of the paper, you need never again do an exposure test strip to determine the threshold value and Max Flash.

As you may have guessed, Max Flash is the *maximum flash* time for this paper. This provides maximum softening or 'de-grading' of the paper being used. Flashing for more than this value will only fog the paper. The exposure difference between the Max Flash value and the threshold value keeps the paper white.

Take it, for example, that the threshold value had been determined to be 5.9 seconds. Adjacent to that is the Max Flash value of 5 seconds. 5 seconds of flash will provide the greatest degree of softening the contrast. At 0 flash (no flash) the paper retains its designated contrast. Varying the flash time anywhere between 0 and Max Flash provides a considerable degree of control over the contrast. The closer the flash time to Max Flash, the softer the print can be made.

Flashing makes the paper more sensitive and for this reason the overall print exposure has to be reduced −¼ f/stop. Because the paper has become more sensitive the highlight areas are more likely to show detail, and because the overall exposure is decreased the shadow detail will be more in evidence.

Method

1. Having established the Max Flash time, flash a sheet of paper for this exposure time. Remember, you can only de-grade the paper – reduce its contrast. Hence if the print appears too soft on

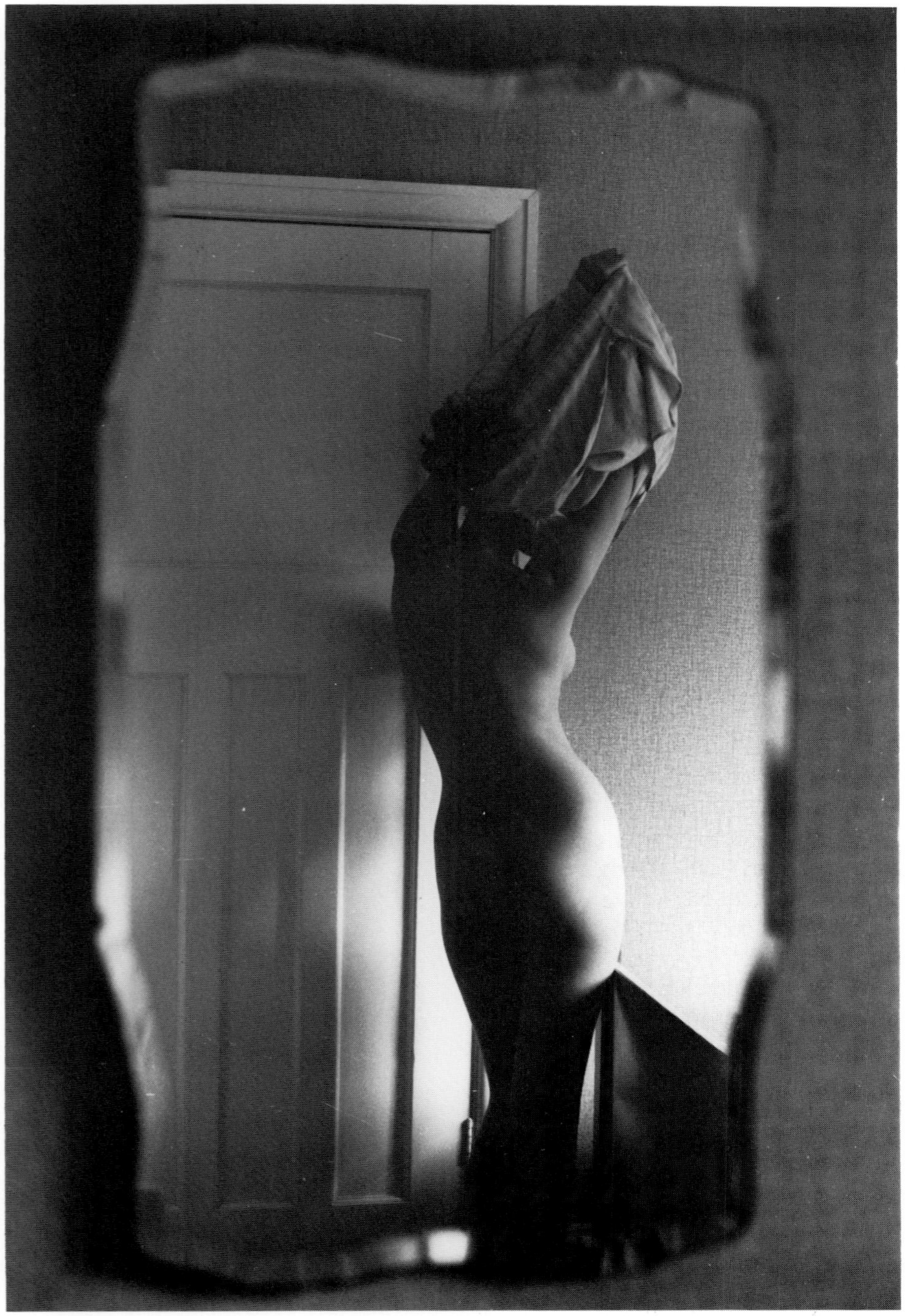

Printed on grade 3 paper this print lacks contrast.

grade 2 but too hard on grade 3, you have to flash the grade 3. It's easier to flash if you have two enlargers. One for printing, one for flashing. Otherwise flashing necessitates setting up the enlarger to flash before inserting the negative for printing.

2. Reduce the basic exposure of the print by — ¼ f/stop to compensate for the increased sensitivity of the flashed paper. The dodging and burning-in exposure times subsequently are reduced — ¼ f/stop as well. Use the F/STOP EXPOSURE TIME Table for these corresponding exposure times.

F/STOP EXPOSURE TIME

5	10	20	40	80
5.9	11.9	23.8	47.6	95.2
7.1	14.1	28.3	56.6	113.2
8.4	16.8	33.6	67.3	134.6

3. Examine the results. If the print is now too soft try printing with the flash time reduced — 1 f/stop. If the flash time was 5 seconds, for instance, and the print now appears too soft, try a flash time of 2.5 seconds. Reducing the flash time 'increases' the contrast.

I have noticed that any amount of flashing increases the sensitivity of the paper. Whether the flash time is 1 second or Max Flash, the overall exposure has to be reduced — ¼ f/stop.

This flashing technique requires a bit more preparation than the simple matter of changing the grade of paper. You need only, however, determine the threshold level once. And once the Max Flash value has been established it is just a matter of setting up the enlarger to flash.

Flashing is a technique which up till now has been largely guesswork and trial and error. It is a technique I use for all my printing. Besides providing me with virtually every contrast grade, the increased sensitivity provides a much wider range of tones for optimum quality prints.

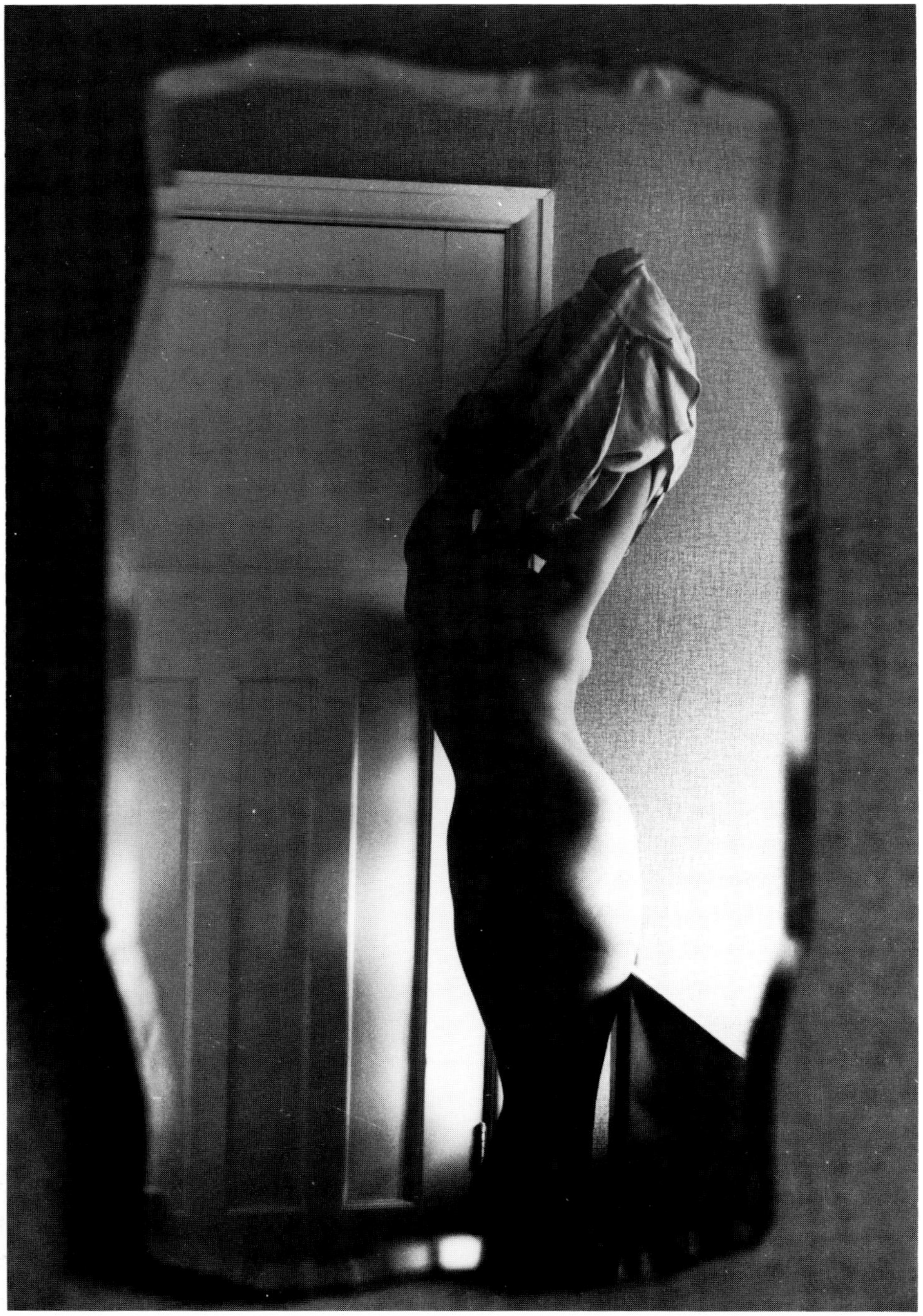

On grade 4 the print has slightly too much contrast and lacks both shadow and highlight detail.

MULTIGRADE PAPERS

I have started using fibre-based multigrade papers. I tried multigrade papers some years ago, but found they needed extraordinarily long exposure times. The paper speed varied, as well, which meant having to determine the basic exposure with each change in contrast.

All these problems have now been resolved. I find multigrade has a faster paper speed than the graded papers and, except for the hardest grades, this speed is *consistent* throughout the contrast range.

Multigrade papers certainly have made it much easier to control contrast – so easy, in fact, that there is really not much I can add about the techniques of using them – simply use the filters to change contrast.

But one interesting technique is worth mentioning. Multigrade allows you to print with variable contrast on one print. Some of the negatives I have to print require a very hard contrast to separate the tones in the thin shadow areas, as well as a softer grade to reveal the dense highlight features.

Before multigrade I had to Max Flash a grade 4. But careful burning-in of the highlight areas was still necessary. Any light spilling over from burning-in would darken the surrounding area. Because I was using a hard grade of paper this darkening was very pronounced.

Using multigrade resolves this problem. Start with the hardest contrast filter for the basic exposure to separate the tones in the shadow area, then burn-in the dense highlight areas using a softer contrast filter. The advantage of this is that the burn-in spill using the soft filter does not produce the same degree of darkening as the harder contrast.

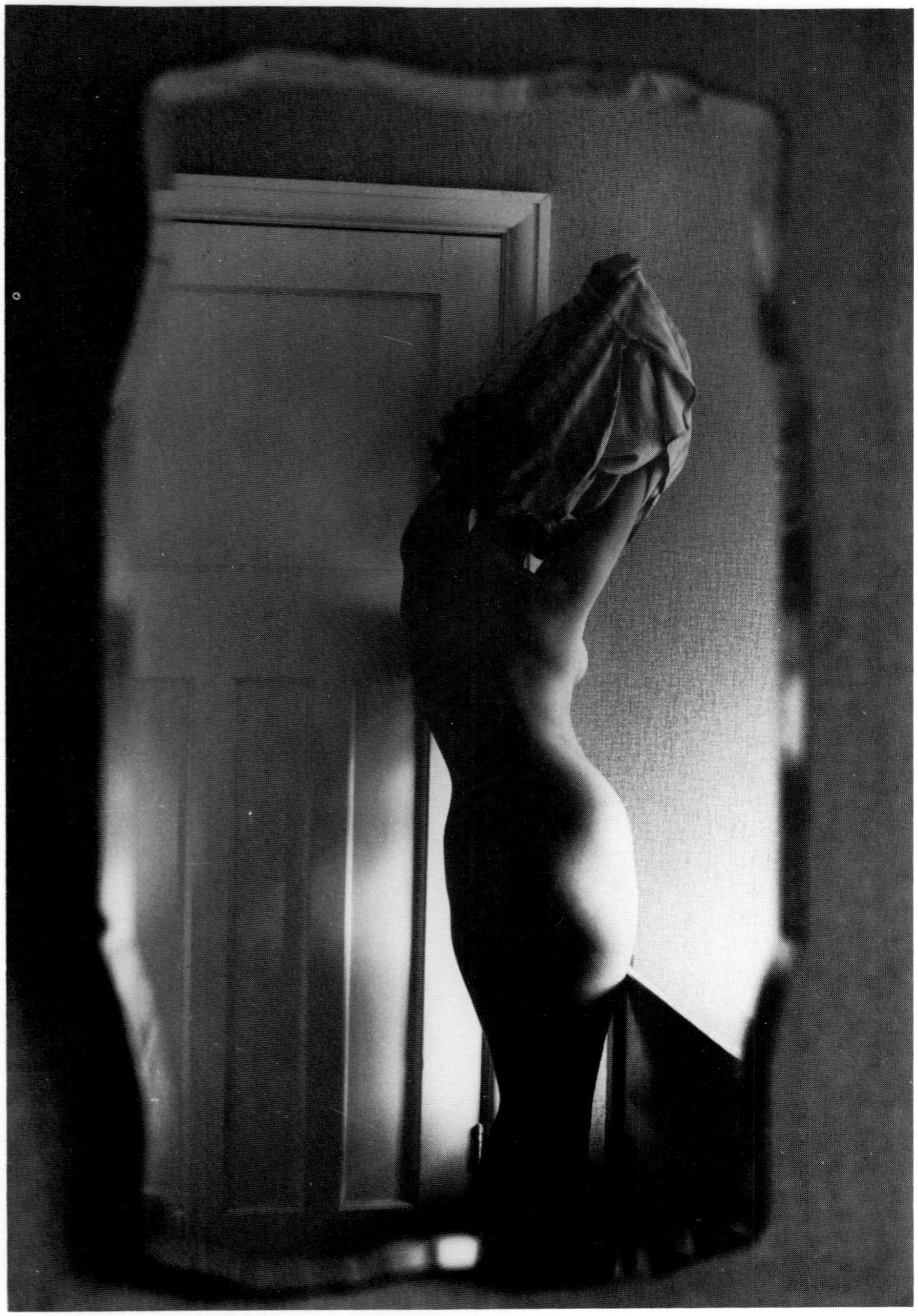

Flashing grade 4 paper 'de-grades' the paper to a contrast grade between 3 and 4. Highlight and shadow detail is revealed whilst retaining contrast.

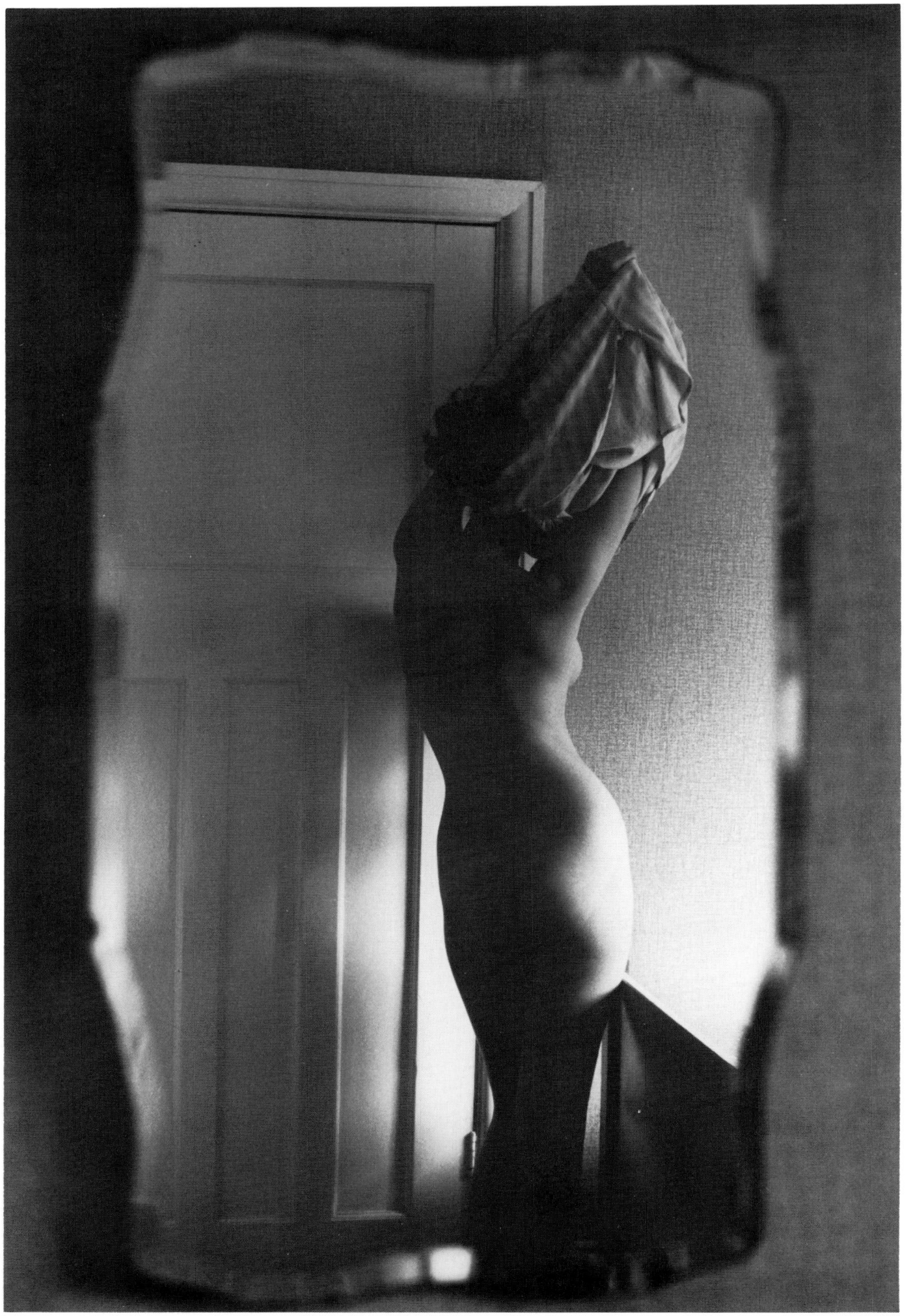

Mirror Image Clare Park.

CHAPTER SEVEN

CHAPTER SEVEN
Toning Prints and Special Effects

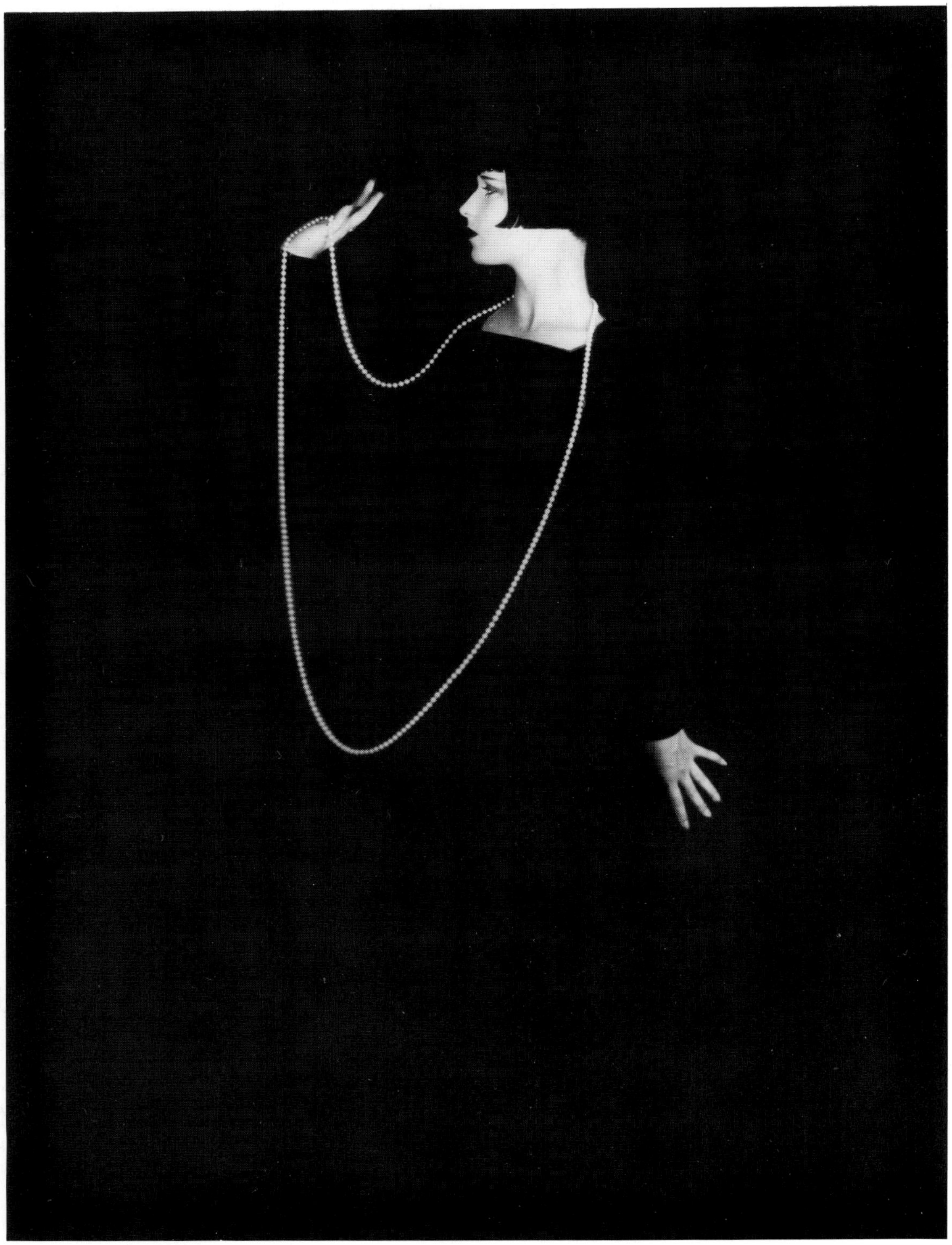

Black and white need not always be black and white. The different brand-makes and kinds of paper produce distinguishable variations in the colour of the print. Agfa Record Rapid has a warm-tone image. Kodak Elite paper is a cold tone. Ilford Galerie and Multigrade FB produce a more neutral tone not unlike the colour of slate. But apart from its natural tone, a print can be made a different 'colour' by chemical means.

My own reasons for toning pictures have nothing to do with the archival value toning contributes to the print. I choose to tone prints because certain pictures lend themselves to toning.

Louise Brooks Eugene R Richee, courtesy of John Kobal. Bromide print, using Ilford Galerie for a neutral tone.

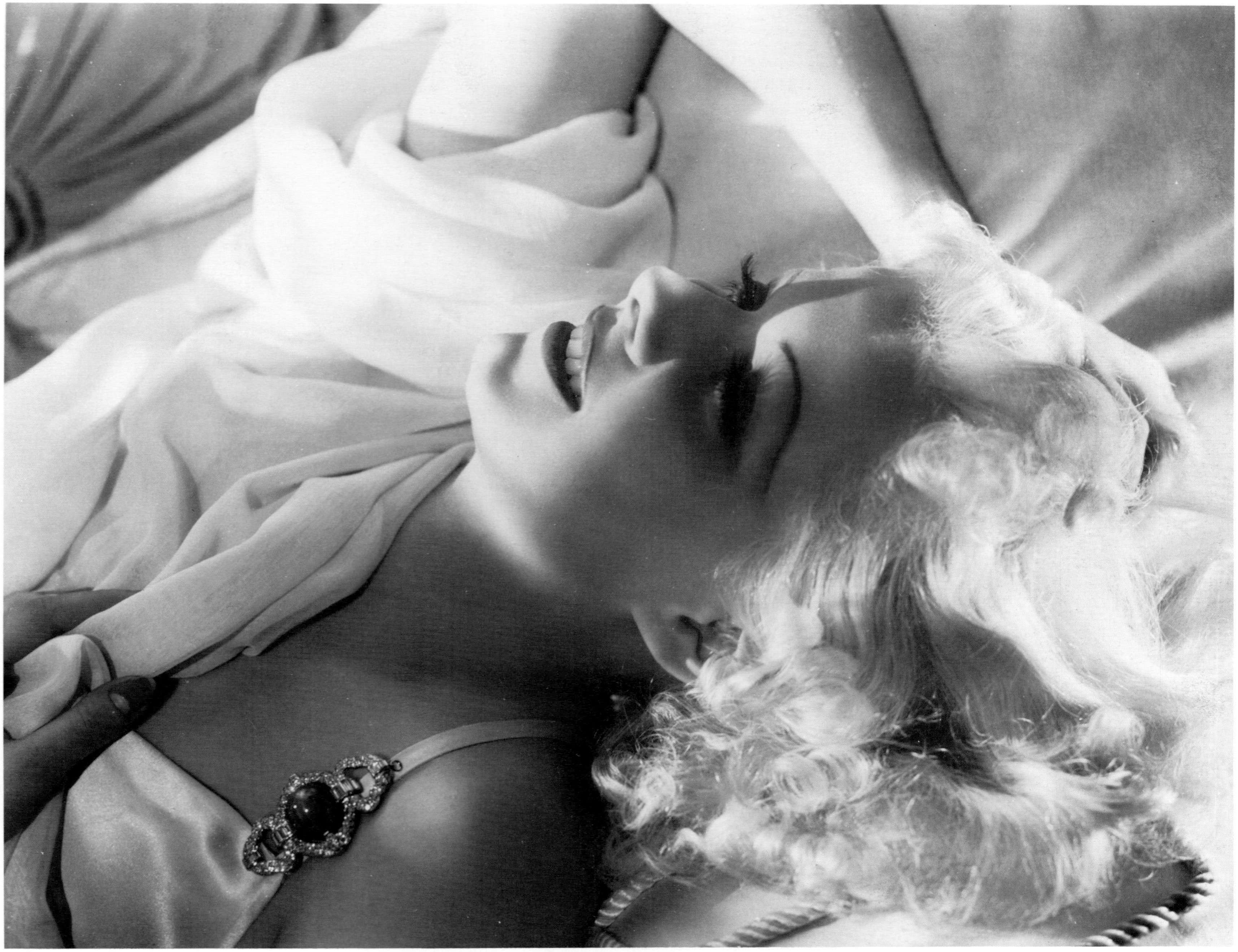

Jean Harlow George Hurrell, courtesy of John Kobal. Chloro-bromide print, using Agfa Record for a warm-tone image.

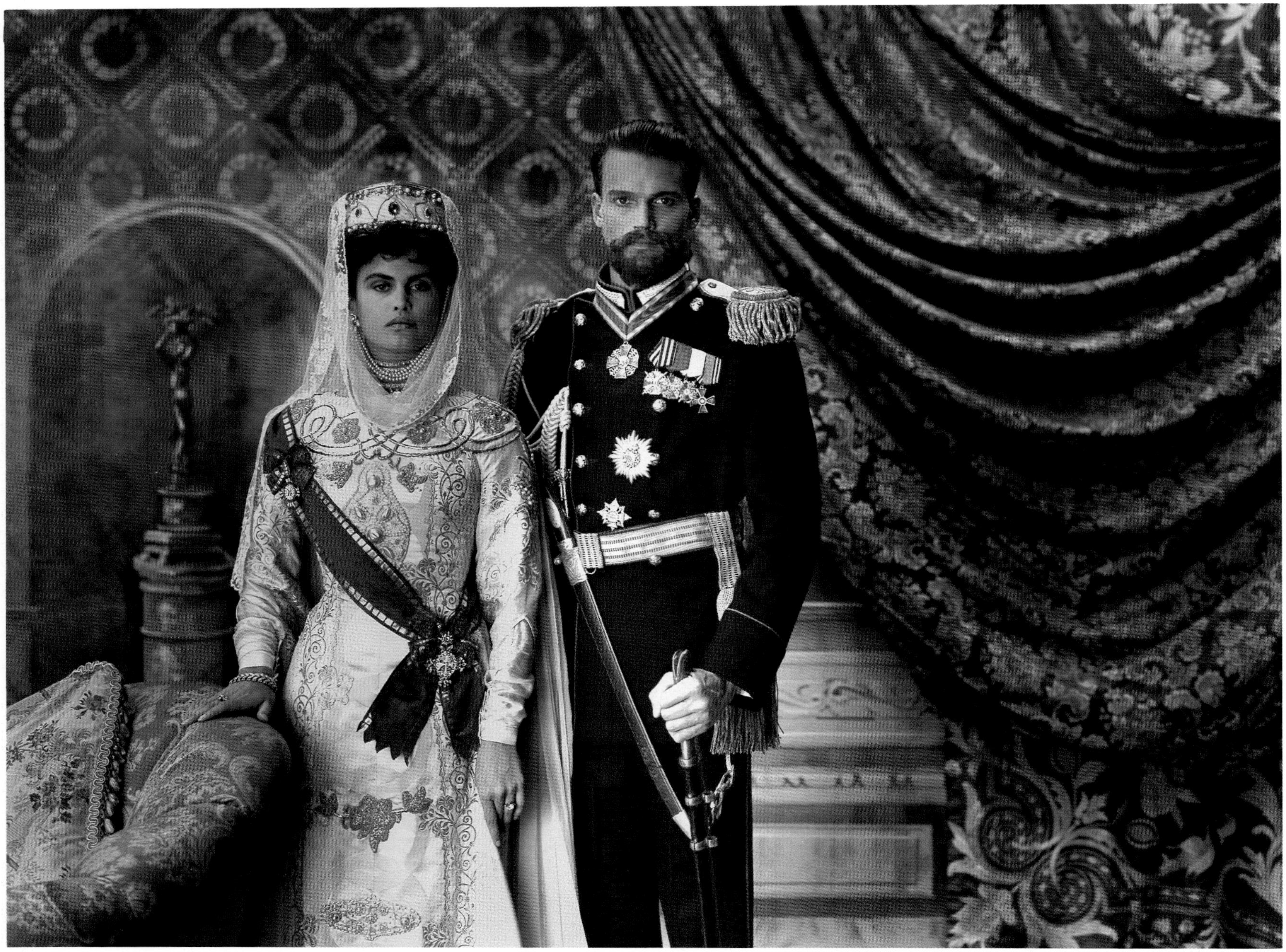

Photograph for Vladivar Vodka by Robert Dowling. Sepia and selenium toned bromide print.

SEPIA TONING

I make two prints of a photograph which I think might look better toned. One is printed as the black-and-white version and the other is printed for toning. Because sepia toning requires bleaching, the print designated for toning is printed darker by +½ f/stop. This is printed darker to retain the highlight details when the print is bleached and subsequently toned. I make no changes to the contrast paper used to make that print. The finished sepia-toned print will by its very nature be flatter than the untoned one. That is part of its appeal.

Develop, fix and wash the print to be toned in the same way as the print to be left as black and white. The black-and-white version can be left in the wash or dried.

The print to be toned is bleached in the following solution:

Bleach
1 tablespoon (approximately) of potassium ferricyanide
1 tablespoon (approximately) of potassium bromide
1 litre of water at room temperature

Immerse the print in a tray of this bleach solution until the darkest tones are pale in colour. The image will not disappear altogether. Completion will be reached when no further change can be seen. Now wash the print in a tray of running water until the yellow colouring of the bleach is removed from the print.

The bleached print can now be toned in the sepia toner. I do not, however, like the colour of 'sepia' and instead modify the toner with a small quantity of paper developer to give it a cooler 'woody' look. The toning solution consists of:

Sepia Toner
1 tablespoon (approximately) of sodium sulphide (flake)
1 litre of water at room temperature
¼ cup (approximately) of stock paper developer

This solution gives off an offensive odour and I recommend adequate ventilation to remove the smell. If no other toning is to be done in the immediate future I suggest the toner be discarded

Sepia toning reduces the contrast of the print. To offset this I use a very weak solution of Farmer's Reducer to 'clean-up' just the highlight areas. This bleaches the lightest part of the print so that when the print is eventually toned the toner has no effect on these bleached areas. The whites will look clean. Otherwise the toner will also affect the highlights and make these areas look dull, subsequently making the print appear flat and the highlights look dirty.

Farmer's Reducer is used before the bleaching stage for sepia toning.

FARMER'S REDUCER

¼ teaspoon (approximately) potassium ferricyanide
1 teaspoon (approximately) stock liquid concentrate fixer
1 litre of water at room temperature
Use this solution in a tray.

After fixing the black-and-white print, wash the print for about 10 minutes. Then place it in the tray of Farmer's Reducer. Watch the highlight areas. Just when you begin to notice some change in the brightness of the highlight area, remove the print and put it in the wash. Wash the print to remove the yellow solution, then put the print back in the fix. This stops any further bleaching action of the Farmer's Reducer. Wash the print now for the normal time and proceed with the instructions for bleaching and toning as discussed in this chapter.

Sepia toning has a different effect on different papers. The examples shown here were printed on Ilford Multigrade FB. On Kodak Elite the sepia colour is colder; on Agfa Record Rapid the sepia colour is much warmer.

I have read that a softer grade of paper produces a warmer tone than a hard grade of paper. But in fact you do not really have much choice in this matter as the grade you have to print on is determined by the negative you have to print (see Chapter Four).

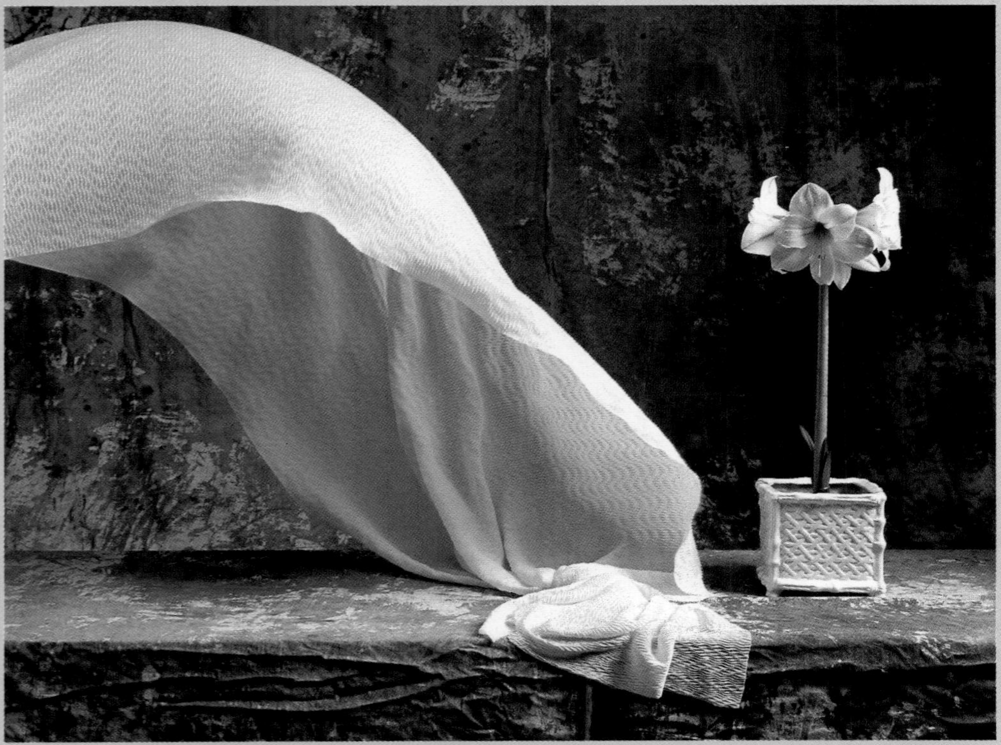

Amaryllis Julian Easten. Sepia-toned bromide print.

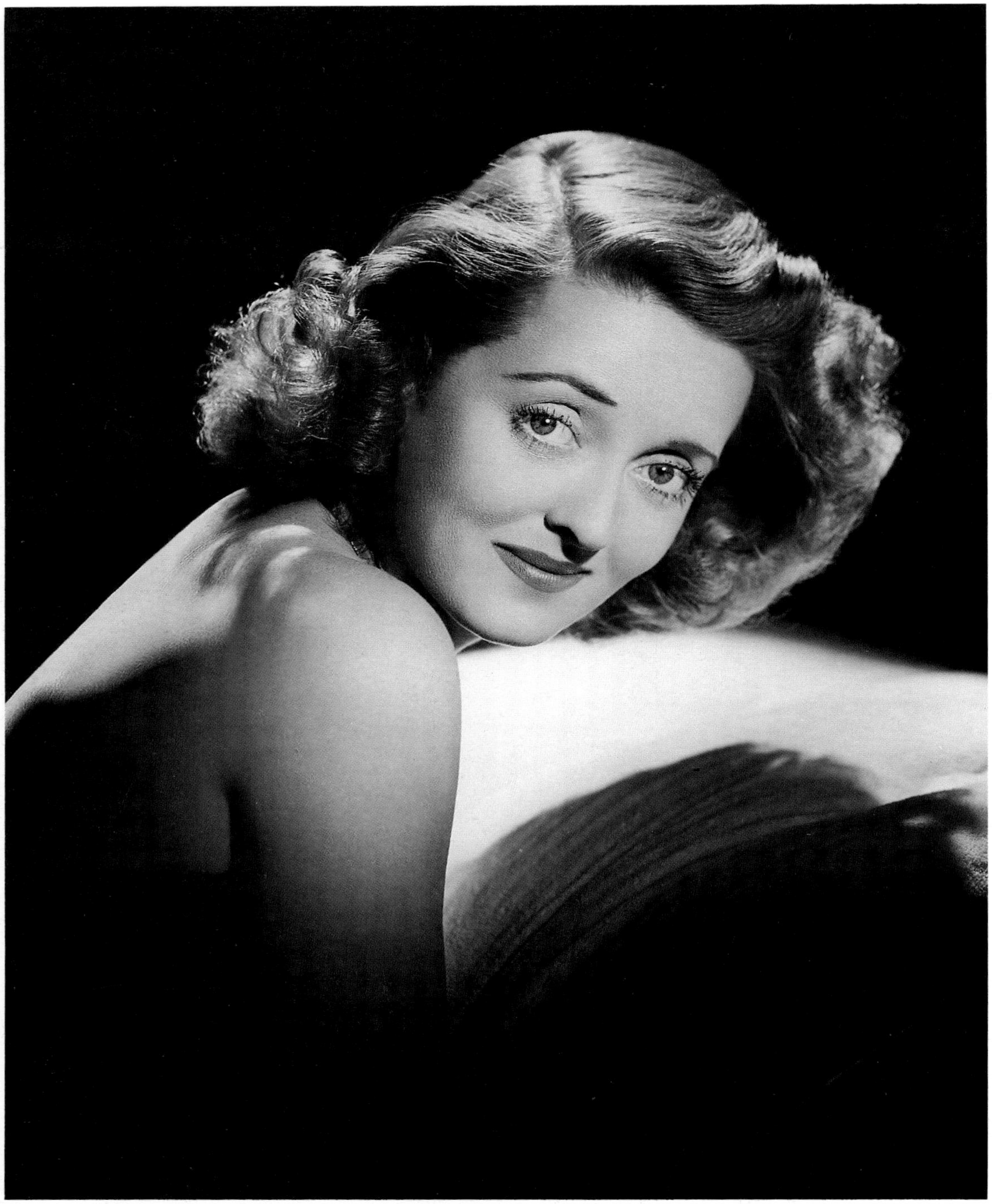

Bette Davis George Hurrell, courtesy of John Kobal. Selenium toned chloro-bromide print.

after use as its effectiveness is very short-lived. Avoid any contact with the fixer solution. The chemical reaction of the sulphide with fixer causes the formation of hydrogen sulphide gas which is the cause of the smell.

After toning wash the print for about half an hour before drying.

Various effects can be achieved depending on the degree of bleaching. Rather than bleaching to completion I often bleach just so the lightest part of the image is affected. The dark areas of the print retain their blackness. The toned effect of the partially bleached print is different to one where the print is totally bleached.

Whether the toned print is better than the black-and-white version is only a matter of opinion.

SELENIUM TONING

Kodak Rapid Selenium Toner is a highly toxic concentrate used diluted for toning. Selenium toning is recommended for archival purposes, but again I use it only for aesthetic reasons.

The actual effect selenium has on the print depends on the paper. On chloro-bromide papers such as Agfa's Record Rapid, selenium toner changes the dark tones a reddish colour. The effect of selenium toning on Ilford's Galerie and Multigrade FB is to increase the density of the blacks (making them blacker) and to bleach slightly the highlight areas. This effectively increases the contrast of the print; also the neutral colour changes to one of colder tones.

Kodak's Elite paper needs to be selenium toned if the print is to be heat-dried. Heat-drying will de-grade the black. Selenium toning Elite paper minimizes the de-grading effect. The purpose of the thickness or 'Premium Weight' of paper is to keep the print flat when it is air-dried.

The Kodak selenium toner is a concentrate. My dilution is 1:10 with the working solution at room temperature.

Prints to be selenium toned need to be thoroughly washed. The prints are then placed directly into a tray of selenium solution and visually assessed for the degree of toning desired – the longer in the toner the greater the toned effect.

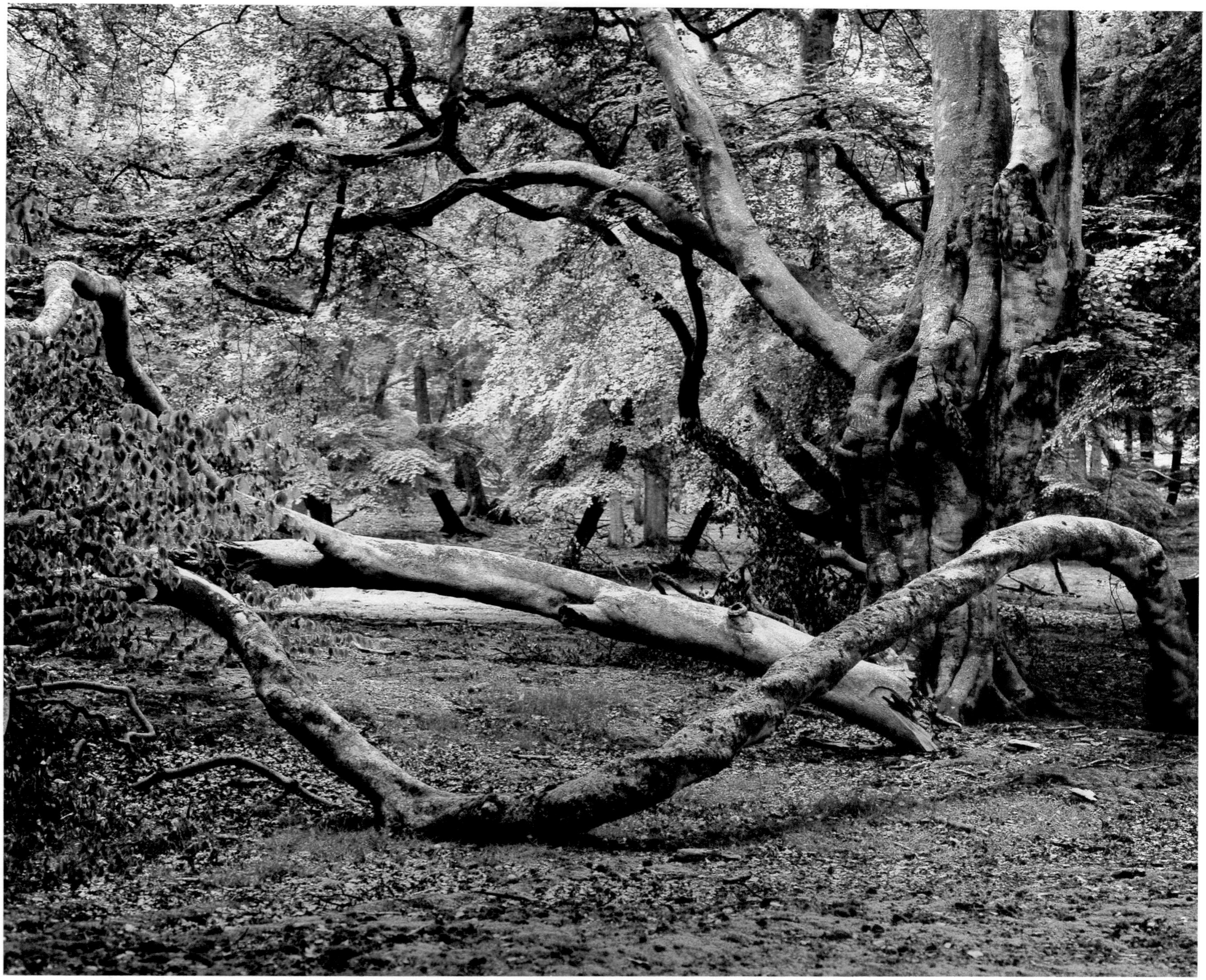

New Forest 1986 John Stathatos. Selenium toned bromide print.

The toning continues after the print has been removed from the toner, so anticipate the final effect. I recommend having a print nearby to compare the change in colour.

Using the 1:10 dilution I tone Galerie and Multigrade for one minute only. The print is then placed in a tray of fresh running water. The toning continues in the water sufficiently to increase the density (blackness) without losing the highlight detail.

Agfa's Record Rapid needs a considerably longer time in the selenium solution. The effect can be seen to warm the tones even more and continues to do so the longer the print is left in the solution. Your personal taste dictates this length of time.

An effect known as split-toning can be achieved with Record Rapid by using the selenium in its concentrate form. The dark areas turn red; the mid-tones split to shades of red and grey. Again the length of time in the concentrate depends on the desired effect.

Selenium toner is a highly toxic chemical so be sure to use it in a well-ventilated area. Use rubber gloves to protect your hands.

Selenium's strength is such that it breaks the surface emulsion of the print. This can be seen in what appear to be surface blemishes on the print, particularly on the Ilford papers. After washing, immerse the print in a tray of solution consisting of 1 litre of water and about ¼ cup of hardener for about a minute. This 'hardens' and smoothes out the emulsion surface and the blemishes. Wash the print thoroughly before drying.

SELECTIVE TONING

Some photographs lend themselves to localized toning.

This is done by applying a masking medium or painting a rubber compound such as 'Cow Gum' onto a dried print. Carefully mask or paint the area of the print which is to remain black and white. Then place the print in a tray of solution of bleach used for sepia toning. After bleaching, place the print in the toner. After toning, wash the print and peel or rub off the rubber compound. Wash and dry the print as normal.

REDEVELOPING

Another technique I employ to change the tone of the print is to bleach a print as if I were going to sepia it. But instead of using sepia toner I redevelop the print in the print developer. This produces a colder tone on Ilford and Kodak papers when redeveloped for the same amount of time as the normal print development period. If you take the print out sooner the effect is slightly bronze. After redevelopment, fix and wash the print as normal.

As with sepia toning, the print to be redeveloped has to be slightly darker than normal because of the bleaching effect on the highlight areas.

The toning of a print is another tool which can be used to produce a more interesting and striking print. There are other commercially-available toning kits which provide a variety of toning colours. In any skill the more tools available the greater the scope for personal creativity.

TEXTURED SCREENS

There are commercially prepared textured screens which are sandwiched with the negative to produce a pattern on the print. I have not used these, but have seen the results. Used judiciously they can be very effective.

I use instead a sheet of non-reflective glass to create a grain pattern on the print. The glass is laid on top of the paper and exposure is made through it.

Exposure has to be increased +½ f/stop because the glass reflects some of the light. The glass also reduces the contrast, so you will need to use a harder grade of paper to compensate.

The effect of the non-reflective glass is to introduce a slightly grainy pattern on the print. It works particularly well on misty landscapes.

Another way of achieving grain is to use Kodak RE 2475 Recording Film. This film was developed for low-light surveillance photography and, as such, can be rated as high as 6400 for low-light conditions. Bearing in mind its original purpose, I suspect the process times recommended are to achieve a higher degree of contrast to enable a better separation of tones in the low-light conditions.

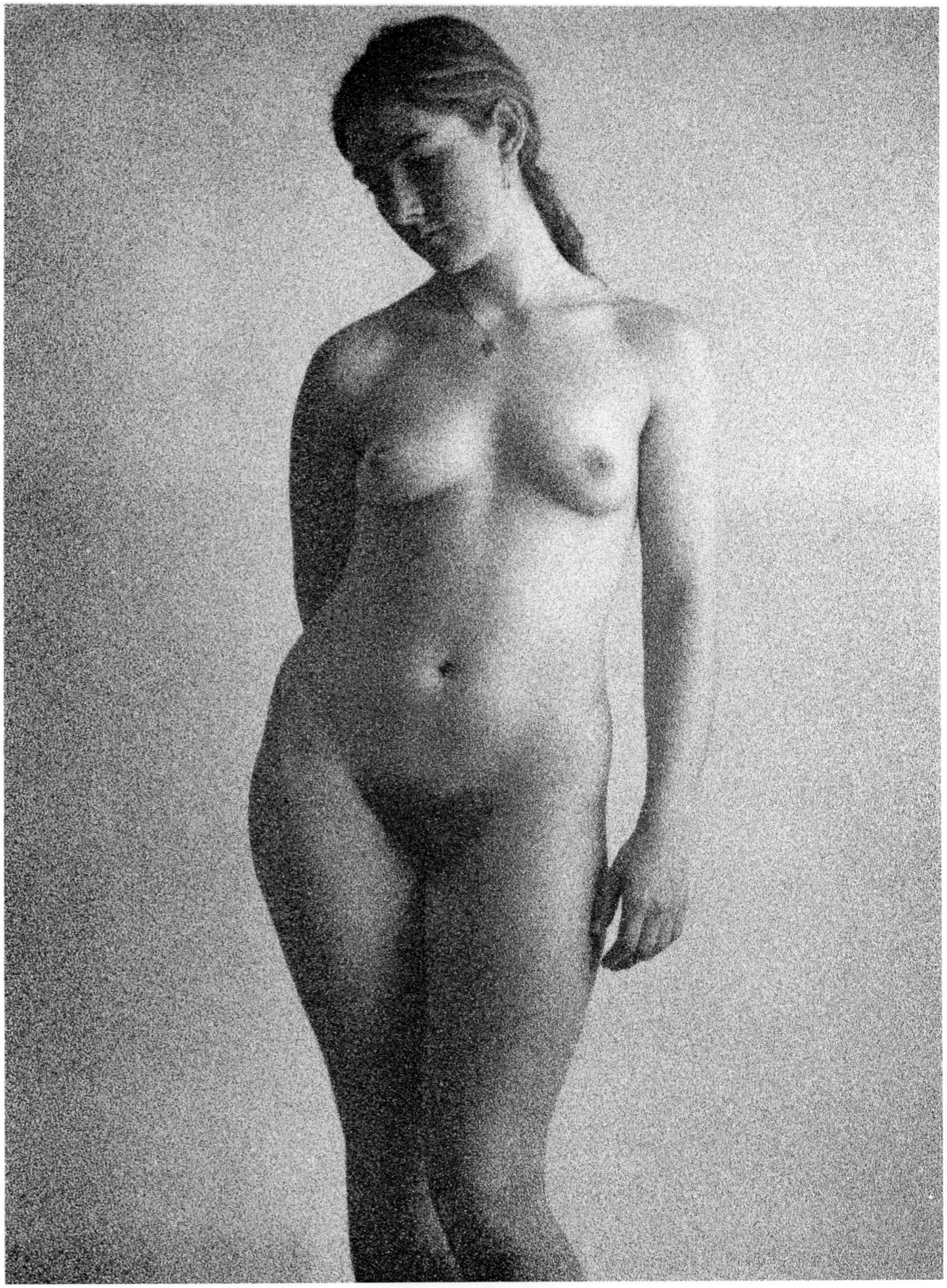

Statement – Legacy of Lillie Langtry John Marks, FRSA. Photographed with Kodak 2475 Recording Film for the grainy effect and printed on Kodak Kodalith LP paper (see Chapter Eight) for the very warm tones.

The back cover of this book is an example of how selective toning can add to the effectiveness of the print. The idea was simply to bring out and emphasize the black tyre.

I suppose selective toning could be considered a bit gimmicky. But no more so than hand-colouring or using textured screens. Used wisely it can add to the appeal of the picture.

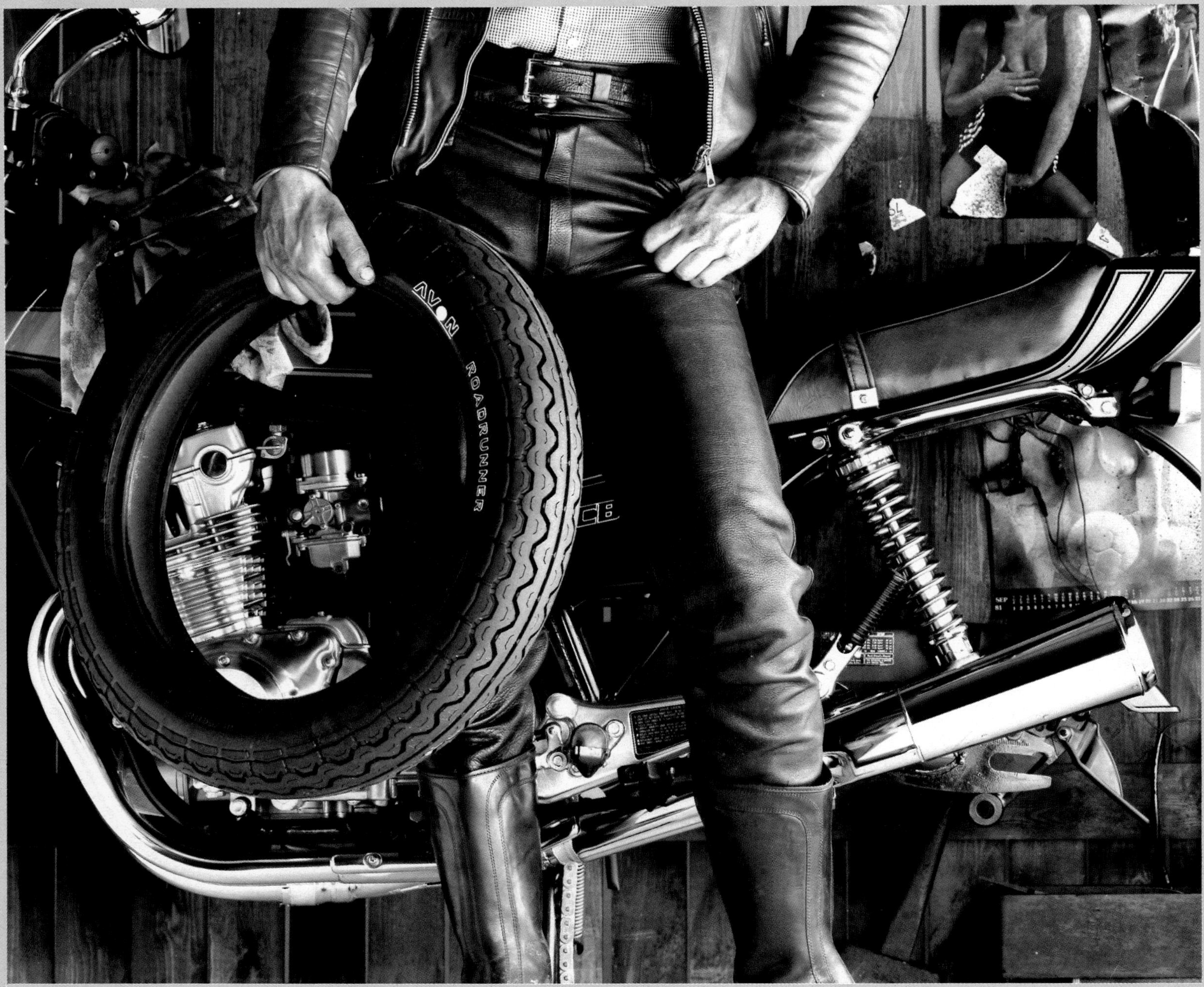

Black Tyre Ed Pritchard. Selective sepia toning on bromide paper.

But when RE 2475 is used in daylight or in a normal lighting situation the recommended time creates too high a film contrast. I therefore suggest that the normal processing time be reduced to lower the film contrast when shooting in normal lighting conditions.

HIGH-KEY AND LOW-KEY

High-key denotes the type of picture where the tonal values are basically from mid-grey to highlight white. There is the minimum amount of black, but where present it serves to enhance the lighter high-key values of the print.

The negative exposure is the key factor in the successful production of a high-key print. The negative must be exposed for high-key, i.e. it must be a dense negative.

It is possible to print high-key from normally exposed negatives by simply printing lighter. But the picture looks as if it has been printed too light. The sign of printing too light is the weak density of the shadow areas.

Snow and misty landscapes are ideal examples of high-key pictures. A correctly exposed negative of such a subject will print up effortlessly as high-key. This is why correct negative exposure is essential.

High-key portraits must be photographed with the minimum of shadows on the face and preferably with a white background and white, otherwise pale, clothing.

If you use an *incident* light meter in the studio remember to compensate for the lens extension because of the close-up focus. After adjusting the exposure for the extension, increase the exposure +1 f/stop. This will increase the exposure density of the negative enabling you to print the picture high-key without much effort. The film is processed for normal.

With a *reflection* light meter, position a white card or sheet of white paper where your subject is or will be. Again remember to compensate for the lens extension if you are using a hand-held light meter. If you are using the lens metering system in your camera this extension is automatically taken into account. Make sure, however, when taking an exposure reading with the camera, that the area being read by the camera is all white, and that the focus distance remains roughly the same as the focus distance for your subject.

Remember that the exposure reading of the white card or paper is 'seen' by the light meter as mid-grey. You must therefore increase the exposure by +2 f/stops to correctly expose this white paper as white. Now increase this exposure by a further +1 f/stop to produce a high-key negative. Process the film for normal.

When printing high-key negatives you may need to use a soft grade of paper to produce a minimum of contrast. Do not attempt to print down the highlights in a high-key portrait. The very nature of high-key prints is the light tonal values. A slight bleaching in Farmer's Reducer will clean up the whites and enhance the high-key quality of the picture.

Low-key prints are seen to have an overall dark and moody quality with tones spanning from mid-grey to the dark shadows.

I don't recall ever deliberately making such a print. I have never printed a picture with the intention of making it low-key.

Pictures that I have printed that might be

Once a year, for Christmas, I try and coax my two daughters to sit for their portraits to send to family and friends in our Christmas cards. The pictures are shot as high-key.

When I print them I vignette the picture by holding back any print exposure to their bodies – thus showing only their faces. The results are as shown here.

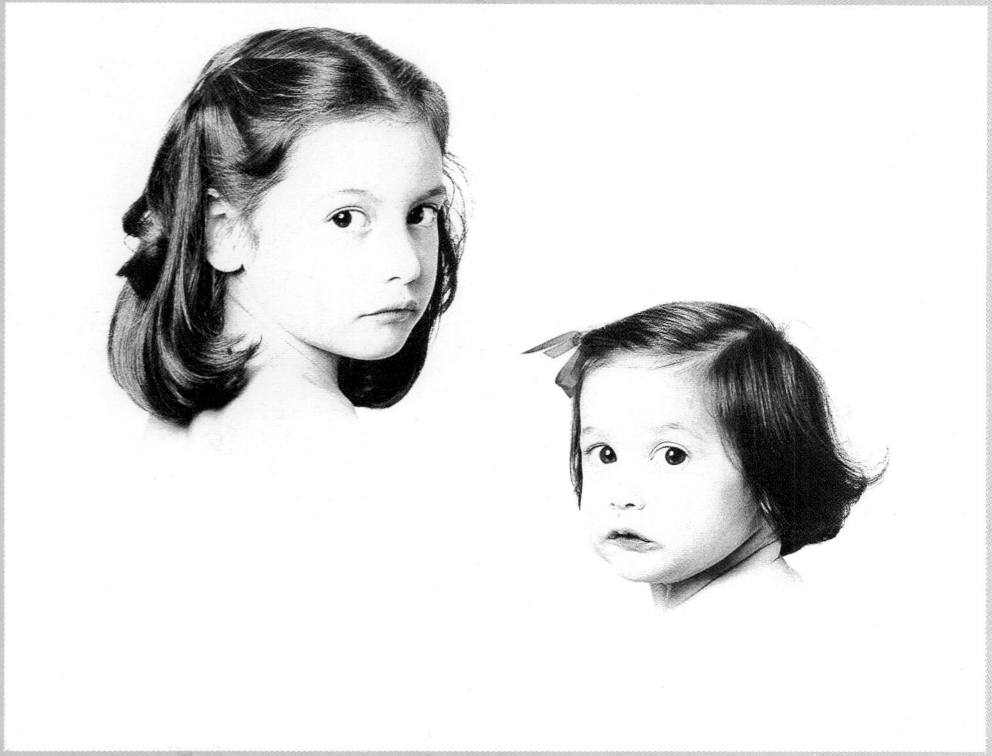

Summer and Olivia Gene Nocon. High-key print using Ilford IRP 110.

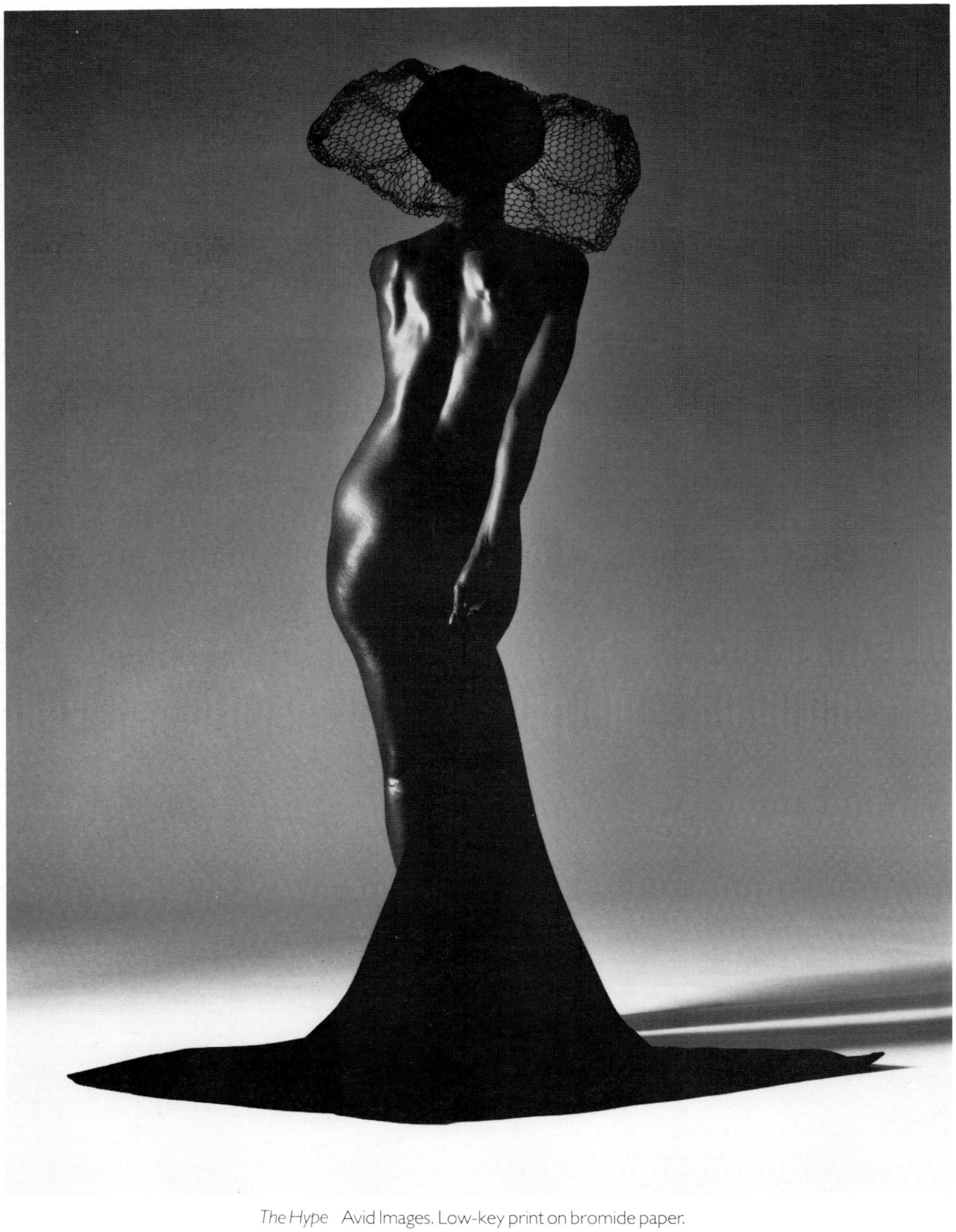

The Hype Avid Images. Low-key print on bromide paper.

considered 'low-key' could only be landscapes where the sky is burned-in dramatically. This burning-in is to enhance, where it exists, the light passing through the clouds.

A reflection light meter, and preferably a selective 'spot' metering one, should be used and the highlight read. Use this exposure. This reading exposes the highlight as mid-grey, which for the definition of low-key pictures represents the maximum tonal value. Forget about any shadow detail. These areas will, in all probability, be completely black. Just to give the negative a little more contrast push process film + ½ f/stop. This is the development time (see Development Times, Chapter Three) one step beyond the 'normal' time.

Do not print so dark as to lose what highlights may be in the picture. Like black tones on a high-key print, the highlight in the low-key print enhances the darkness and drama of the picture.

Low-key portraits are characterized by the overall dark mood of the picture. I personally do not use black as the background and instead use grey.

Exposure should be as determined by the light meter with the compensation to correct for the light loss. With an incident light meter use the exposure thus determined. With a reflection light meter use a grey card to determine the exposure. Make no changes to the exposure, other than to correct for the focus distance. Process the film for normal.

The reason for using a grey background, instead of black, is so that the person stands out of the background. Black hair, for instance, would only merge into the black background. Using grey, you can burn-in and darken the background just above the head, but still have a slight 'halo' separation between the head and background material.

CHAPTER EIGHT

CHAPTER EIGHT
Lith Printing

In 1980 I won the title of Ilford Printer of the Year with a picture printed on paper not normally recognized or used for printing photographs. The print was on lithographic paper used for phototypesetting. The 'lith' paper was Ilford IRP 110. I had also been able to achieve the same effect with Kodak Kodalith LP, but this had been discontinued at that time.

Unfortunately Ilford IRP 110, like Kodak 'lith', is no longer in production. But similar papers are still available, such as Agfa L 720 RC Litex Paper. If you should have any of these 'lith' papers or something similar this chapter will provide you with some guidance for its use.

The techniques you have learned so far, particularly those of Chapter Five on contrast control, will provide considerable help and understanding in the printing on lith paper.

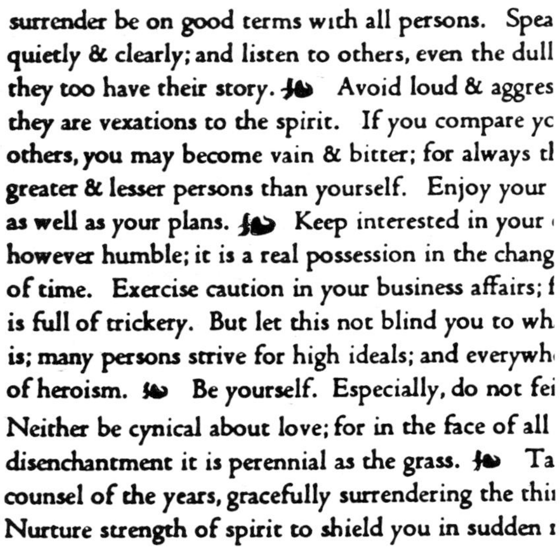
surrender be on good terms with all persons. Spea
quietly & clearly; and listen to others, even the dull
they too have their story. Avoid loud & aggres
they are vexations to the spirit. If you compare yc
others, you may become vain & bitter; for always tl
greater & lesser persons than yourself. Enjoy your
as well as your plans. Keep interested in your
however humble; it is a real possession in the chang
of time. Exercise caution in your business affairs; f
is full of trickery. But let this not blind you to wh
is; many persons strive for high ideals; and everywh
of heroism. Be yourself. Especially, do not fei
Neither be cynical about love; for in the face of all
disenchantment it is perennial as the grass. Ta
counsel of the years, gracefully surrendering the thi
Nurture strength of spirit to shield you in sudden

Lithographic paper is normally used for typesetting black on white with no mid-tones.

LITH PAPER

I have used three makes of lith paper: Kodak Kodalith LP, Ilford IRP 110, and Agfa L720 RC Litex. I continue to print on these papers only when my clients bring in their own. Other makes of lith papers may not be available in photographic shops but in graphic art suppliers.

I can only imagine that the papers available long before the convenience of graded-contrast papers and multigrade had the same characteristics as film. Like film the tonal range and contrast could only be controlled in the exposure and development.

Lith paper is similar to film. Its normal application, however, is to produce absolutely black tones against a white background – there are no mid-tones. Hence its use for phototypesetting.

Just as an experiment I tried using lith paper to print a full-tonal-range negative to produce a high contrast print. It was during the experiments that I noticed that after a certain period of time in lith developer, detail and various tones of the negative would suddenly appear and just as quickly disappear turning solid black.

I tried to time the development so that as these tones and detail appeared I would snatch the print out of the developer and try to stop further development. It was hit and miss and I wasted quite a lot of paper trying to catch the print just at the right moment.

I first tried slowing down the process by using a colder developer temperature but the results were patchy and inconsistent. Then it dawned on me that the whole process could be slowed down by simply diluting the lith developer.

LITH DEVELOPER

I use Kodak Kodalith Developer, but there are lith developers made by other manufacturers. Lith developer comes in two packages marked A and B. In liquid form the normal working solution is 1 part A, 1 part B, and 9 parts water. This mixture is used for producing prints and negatives with no mid-tones.

To produce lith prints the mixture is made up of 1 part A, 1 part B, and 40 parts water. This dilution stretches the development time. This enables the slow and even development of the tones and contrast of the print. Try to maintain a fairly constant temperature.

The stop bath and the fixer are as for normal printing papers.

EXPOSING/DEVELOPING

Print exposure is at least 2 f/stops more than normal photographic paper. This is to ensure exposure of the highlights. The shadow detail is controlled with development. There is little need for burning-in or dodging.

Make a series of exposure strips (see Chapter Four) to give you some idea of the exposure time.

Development is important. The print must go in the solution as smoothly and evenly as possible. My method is to hold one end of the print just at the surface of the developer and to pull the entire sheet through the developer. Keep the print face up. Once in the developer leave it there – do not pick it up out of the solution, but rock it in its tray. When the image starts to appear, carefully watch the development and the moment you think the image is right pull the print out and put it into the stop bath. Note the development time. It should be anywhere between 1½ and 3 minutes. Fix the print.

There is no fixed development time. Lith printing is very much like exposing and developing photographic film: expose for shadows; develop for highlights. But as applied to lith printing the expression becomes: EXPOSE FOR THE HIGHLIGHT; DEVELOP FOR THE SHADOW. Do not be afraid to 'overexpose' lith paper. You must provide enough exposure to ensure the highlight details printing up. Developing controls the contrast and shadow density.

Let us say the development time for the test strips was for 2 minutes. Had the development time been shorter the test strips would have appeared flatter and more likely to show the detail in the shadow areas. If the development time were longer this would have increased the contrast at the expense of losing the shadow detail which would have turned black.

The test strip is only a guide for the exposure/development. It will give you some idea about how much exposure is required and whether to increase or decrease the contrast.

Say, for example, the test strips are of exposure times of 10, 20, 40, and 80 seconds and the development time had been 2 minutes. If the 20-second strip developed for 2 minutes appears

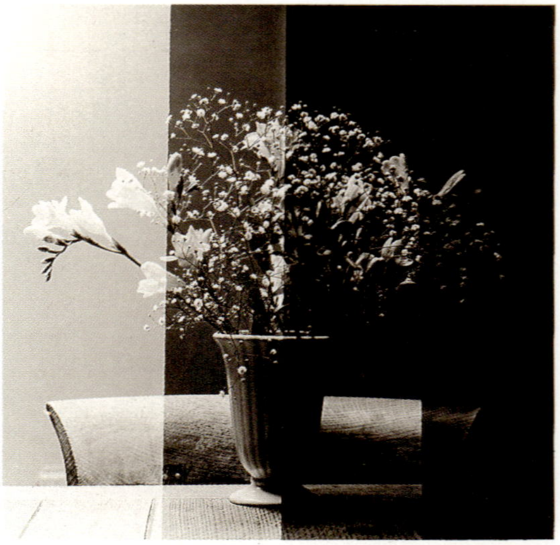

Test strip with exposures for 10, 20, 40 and 80 seconds on Ilford IRP 110 developed for 2 minutes in Kodak Kodalith developer. After the first minute I could see the mid-tone values I wanted in the 40-second exposure strip. The 2-minute development only darkened it.

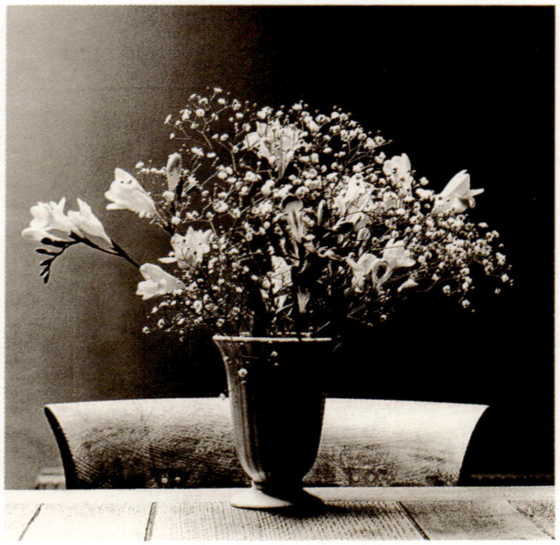

Underexposure, overdevelopment: 10 seconds exposure time, developed for 2 minutes 50 seconds.

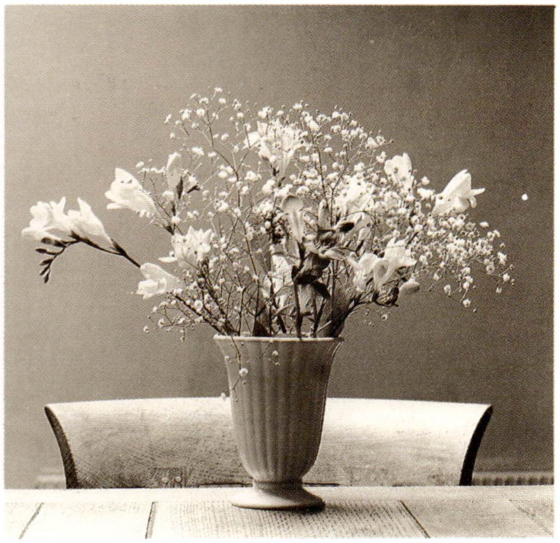

This is the print exposed for 40 seconds developed for 1 minute 25 seconds. There was slightly too much contrast, so another print was tried, using + ½ f/stop more exposure (56.6 seconds) and developing for 1 minute. The resulting print was then selenium toned for the final version.

to be the best of the lot, but just a bit too flat, try a print by *reducing* the exposure − ½ f/stop (see the F/STOP EXPOSURE TIME Table) and *increase* the development time beyond 2 minutes. If that particular strip was just slightly too contrasty *increase* the exposure + ½ f/stop and *reduce* the development time.

TO INCREASE CONTRAST
UNDEREXPOSE AND OVERDEVELOP
TO DECREASE CONTRAST
OVEREXPOSE AND UNDERDEVELOP

F/STOP EXPOSURE TIME

5	10	20	40	80
5.9	11.9	23.8	47.6	95.2
7.1	14.1	28.3	56.6	113.2
8.4	16.8	33.6	67.3	134.6

You will find that the fixer will bleach and lighten the print. You will need, therefore, to develop the lith print just beyond the time where the image looks right. With experience you will learn how much longer to keep the print in the developer to get the tones and contrast you want.

Do not leave the lith prints too long in the fixer. You will notice when you switch on an inspection lamp that the paper is a yellow colour. Most of this is bleached away in the fixer. But I personally do not like the colour. This yellow cast can be eliminated by using a very diluted solution of ferricyanide. Mix up a solution in a processing tray. After fixing, wash the lith print for about 10 minutes in running water. Then put the lith print in the ferricyanide solution. This must be done in the light so you can see the yellow just disappear. Do not keep the print in much longer or the highlight detail will bleach away. Wash the prints in running water and dry as you would normal paper. Ilford and Agfa lith papers are resin-coated. Hang these prints up to dry.

You can change the colour of the image by toning the print in Kodak selenium toner. Be careful when you use this stuff. Follow the instructions on the bottle and wear gloves.

The selenium toner is effective only on Ilford IRP 110. If you have other makes of lith paper you may want to experiment. After washing immerse the print in the selenium toner. Watch the results. You will see the dark and mid-grey areas turning a deep red-grey colour. You can stop at this stage by pulling it out of the toner and washing the print. This is a 'split-tone' print.

It might seem pointless to discuss lith printing techniques when the paper is no longer available, but to this day I still have individual photographers coming in with old boxes of lith paper which I use for printing their pictures. If you have a box of 'lith' lying around now you know how to use it. It does produce the most beautiful prints!

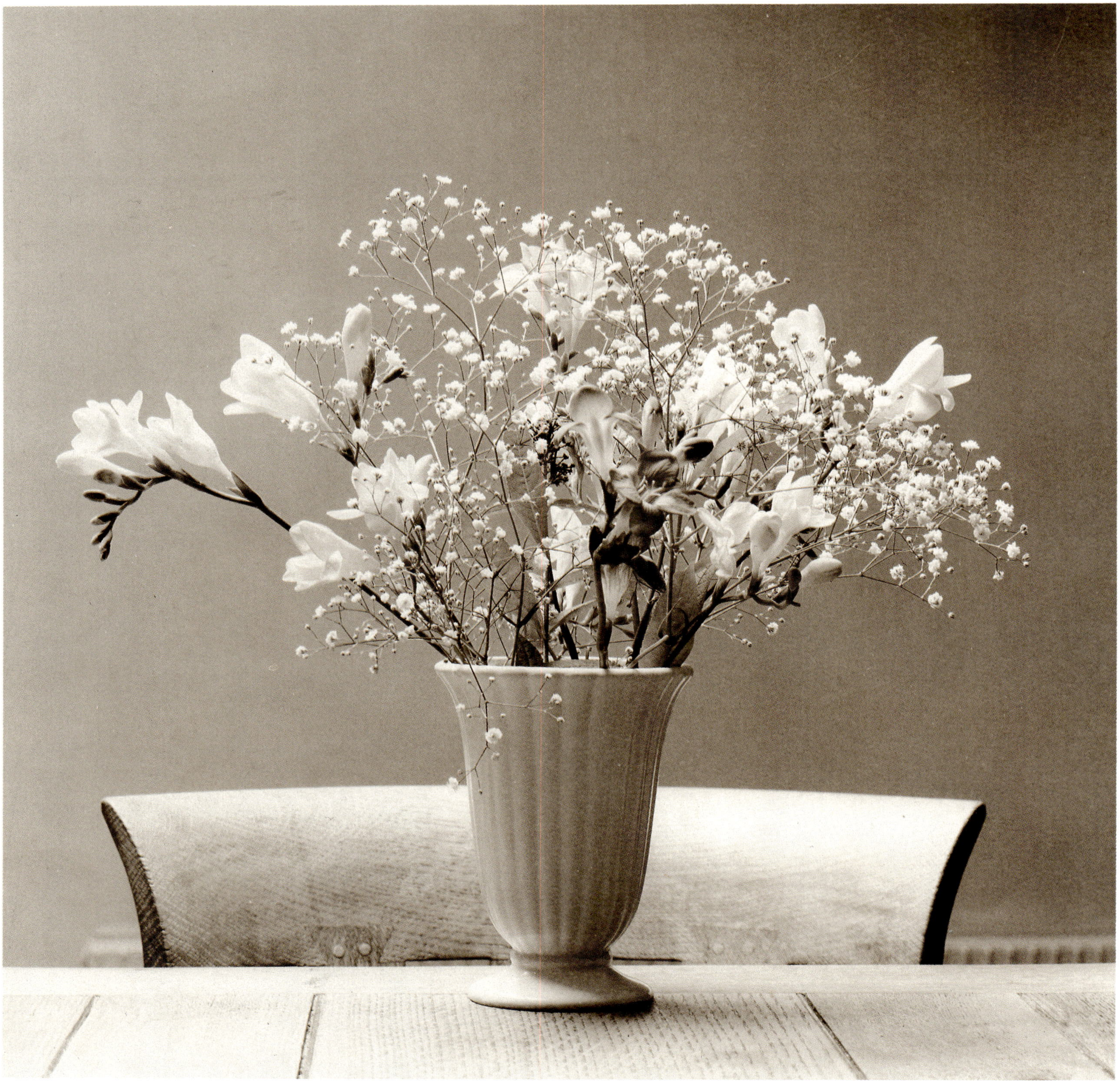

Birthday Flowers Gene Nocon. Printed on Ilford IRP 110 and selenium toned.

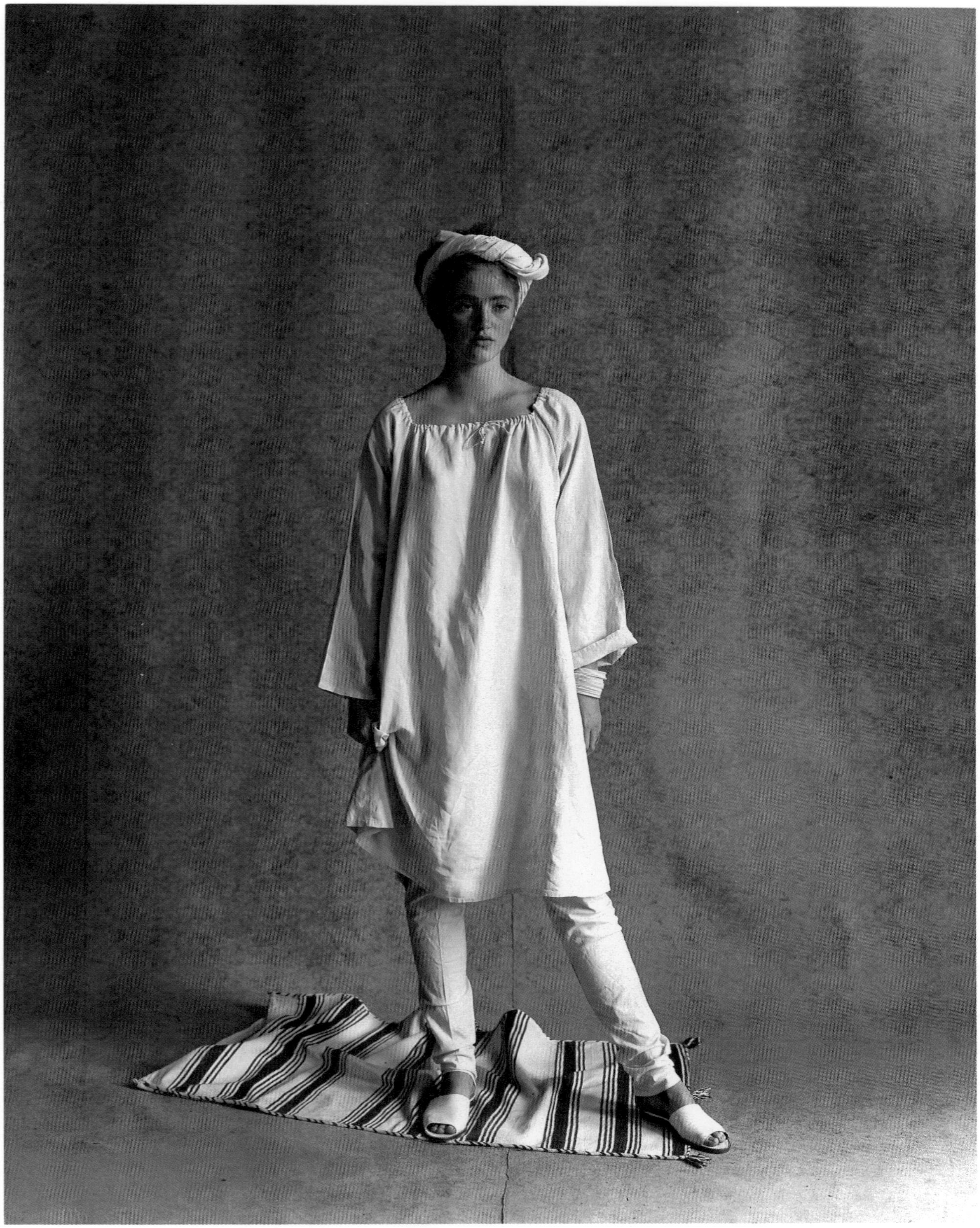

Picture for English *Vogue* by Barry Lategan. Printed on Ilford IRP 110 paper and selenium split-toned.

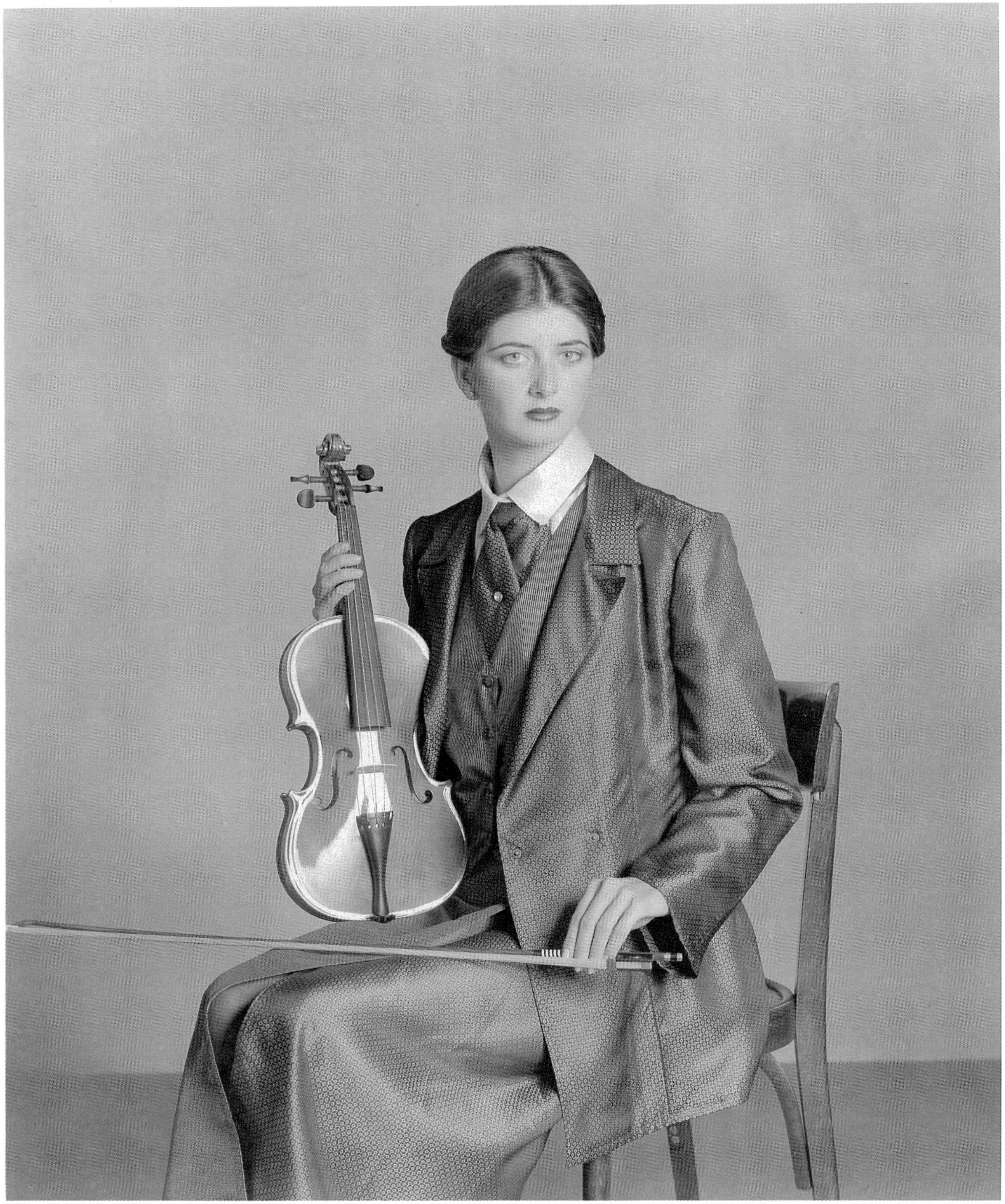

Picture for *Vogue Italia* by Barry Lategan. Printed on Kodak Kodalith LP paper and selenium toned.

CHAPTER NINE

CHAPTER NINE

Enlarging or Reducing Prints

The F/Stop Method of Printing has an advantage over any other method in that it allows you to keep a record of the printing instructions by simply designating the areas of the print that have been dodged or burned-in in f/stops. This is all you need to record to repeat and duplicate the print at a later date.

There is no need to remember the other variables such as the aperture f/stop, the size of the print, the concentration and temperature of the developer, etc. The test strip takes all these variables into account in determining the basic exposure. The dodging or burning-in instructions *expressed in f/stops* remains the same.

The basic exposure for a picture printed today, for example, may be 10 seconds and the background burned-in, say +½ f/stop (14.1 seconds). This same picture printed at some later date might have a different base exposure time, for instance 20 seconds, but the background would still need burning-in +½ f/stop (28.3 seconds).

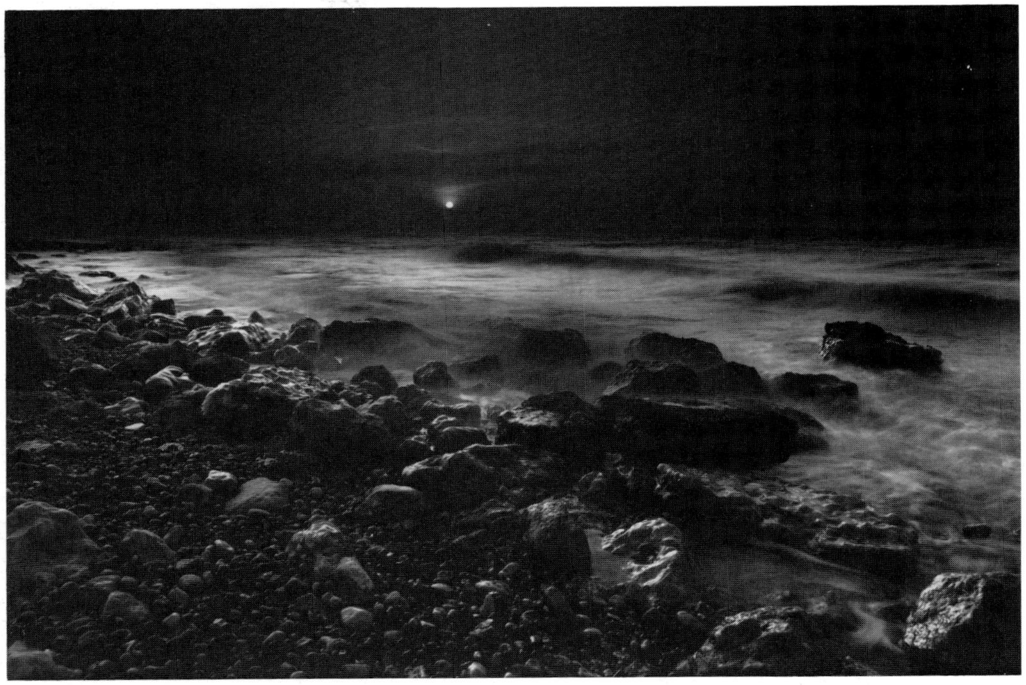

Instead of wasting large sheets of paper to determine the basic exposure and the dodging and burning-in modifications I use 8 × 10 inch (20.3 × 25.4cm) paper to determine these values. This is the print as an 8 × 10 inch (20.3 × 25.4cm) with the dodging and burning-in modifications approved by the photographer. The basic exposure time (T1) was 5 seconds for the image length (L1) of 9½ inches (24.1cm).

ENLARGING OR REDUCING IMAGE SIZE

The following formula can be used to calculate the basic exposure time for different enlargements of the same negative:

$$T2 = (L2/L1)^2 \times T1$$

where:

L1 = measured length of original size
L2 = length of new size
T1 = basic time of original print
and T2 = calculated basic time of new size

For example, if a print 9 inches wide had a basic exposure time of 10 seconds, enlarging this print to 15 inches, the basic exposure time can be determined:

T1 = 10 seconds, L1 = 9 inches, L2 = 15 inches

$$T2 = (L2/L1)^2 \times T1$$
$$= (15/9)^2 \times 10$$
$$= (1.667)^2 \times 10$$
$$= 2.778 \times 10$$

T2 = 27.78, rounding this to 27.8 seconds.

Thus the print enlarged from 9 to 15 inches needs as its basic exposure a time of 27.8 seconds.

F/STOP EXPOSURE TIME

5	10	20	40	80
5.9	11.9	23.8	47.6	95.2
7.1	14.1	28.3	56.6	113.2
8.4	16.8	33.6	67.3	134.6

Looking at the F/STOP EXPOSURE TIME Table this is near enough to 28.3 seconds to be used as the basic exposure time. (The exposure difference between 27.8 seconds and 28.3 is only 1/50 f/stop).

The dodging and burning-in expressed in f/stops for the larger print is the same as that on the small print. If the basic exposure time for the larger print is too long you can open up the enlarging lens 1 f/stop and use the time −1 f/stop less in the F/STOP EXPOSURE TIME Table.

The same batch of paper must be used for making the different-size prints. I have found that the paper speed varies between different batches by as much as ½ f/stop.

The same contrast grade of paper is used, as

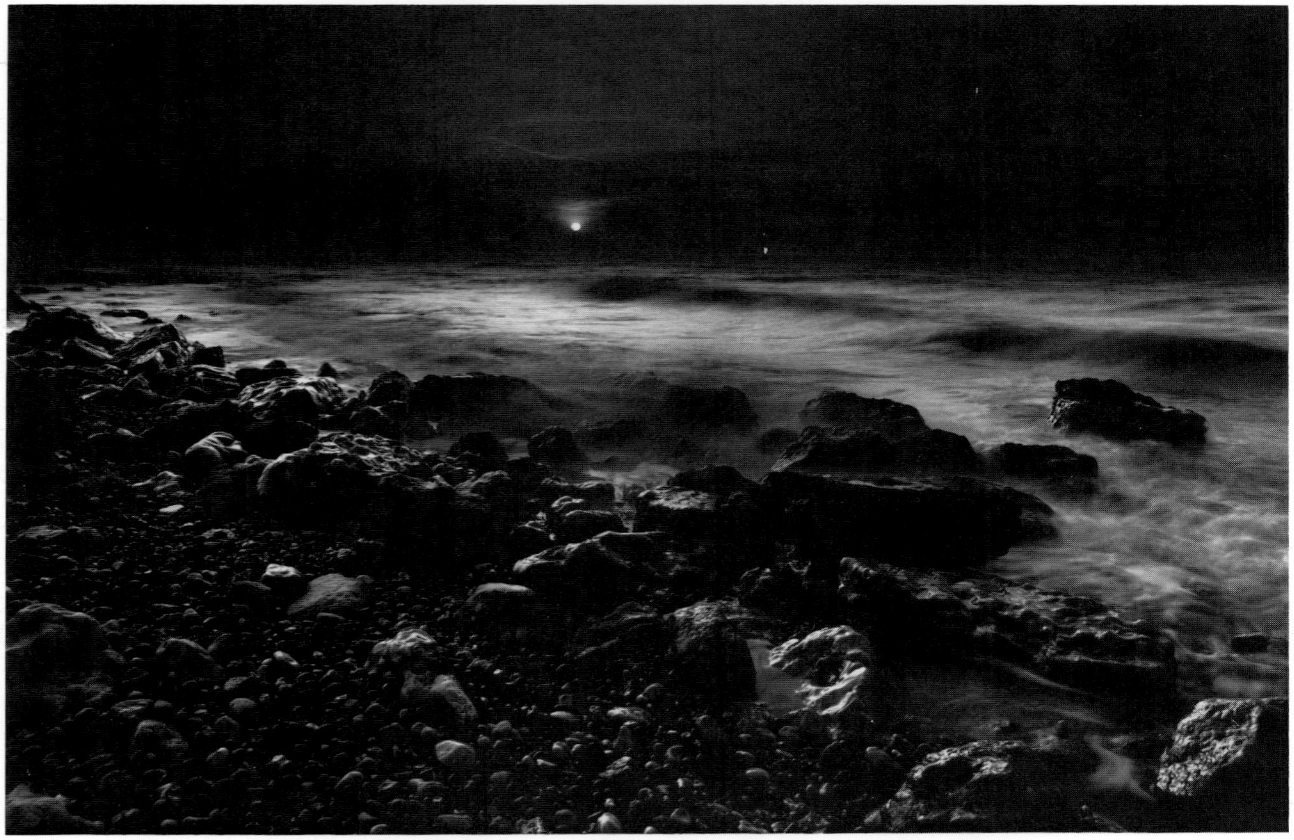

Enlarging the image now to (L2) 12 inches (30.5cm) and using the enlargement formula given this chapter, the basic exposure time (T2) was calculated as 8 seconds. This is near enough to 1/16 f/stop for 8.4 seconds on the F/STOP EXPOSURE TIME Table to be used as the basic exposure time for the 12 inch (30.5cm) enlargement. The dodging and burning-in modifications expressed in f/stops remain the same, although the actual times change.

well, throughout the range of enlargements. If you use a grade 2 to make an 8 × 10 inch (20.3 × 25.4cm) print you will require a grade 2 for making a bigger (or smaller) print.

This formula enables you to make small 'test' prints with all the necessary dodging and burning-in before attempting to produce a much larger print. For exhibitions I make 8 × 10 inch (20.3 × 25.4cm) prints for my client's approval before actually producing the final print. This saves a lot of time and certainly materials.

One assignment I had was to print a series of prints of the same negative with the image size progressively getting smaller.

One of my clients had taken a picture of a mainframe computer shot in perspective. It was the only one available, but in reality it represented just one of a bank of seven computers working side by side. The agency needed seven different-sized prints of the one computer which they could then cut out and paste together to create an impression of the seven working together.

Using the formula in this chapter it was a simple matter to determine the different exposure times.

BACKGROUND AND THEORY

The formula above is based on the inverse square law of light. This is best understood with the analogy of a spoonful of jam spread on a single piece of toast. That same amount of jam over four pieces of toast produces a thinner 'density' – there is only a quarter as much as on a single piece of toast. To equal the original 'spread' the jam will have to be increased fourfold.

The amount of light spreading on to an 8 × 10 inch (20.3 × 25.4cm) area is likewise diminished to

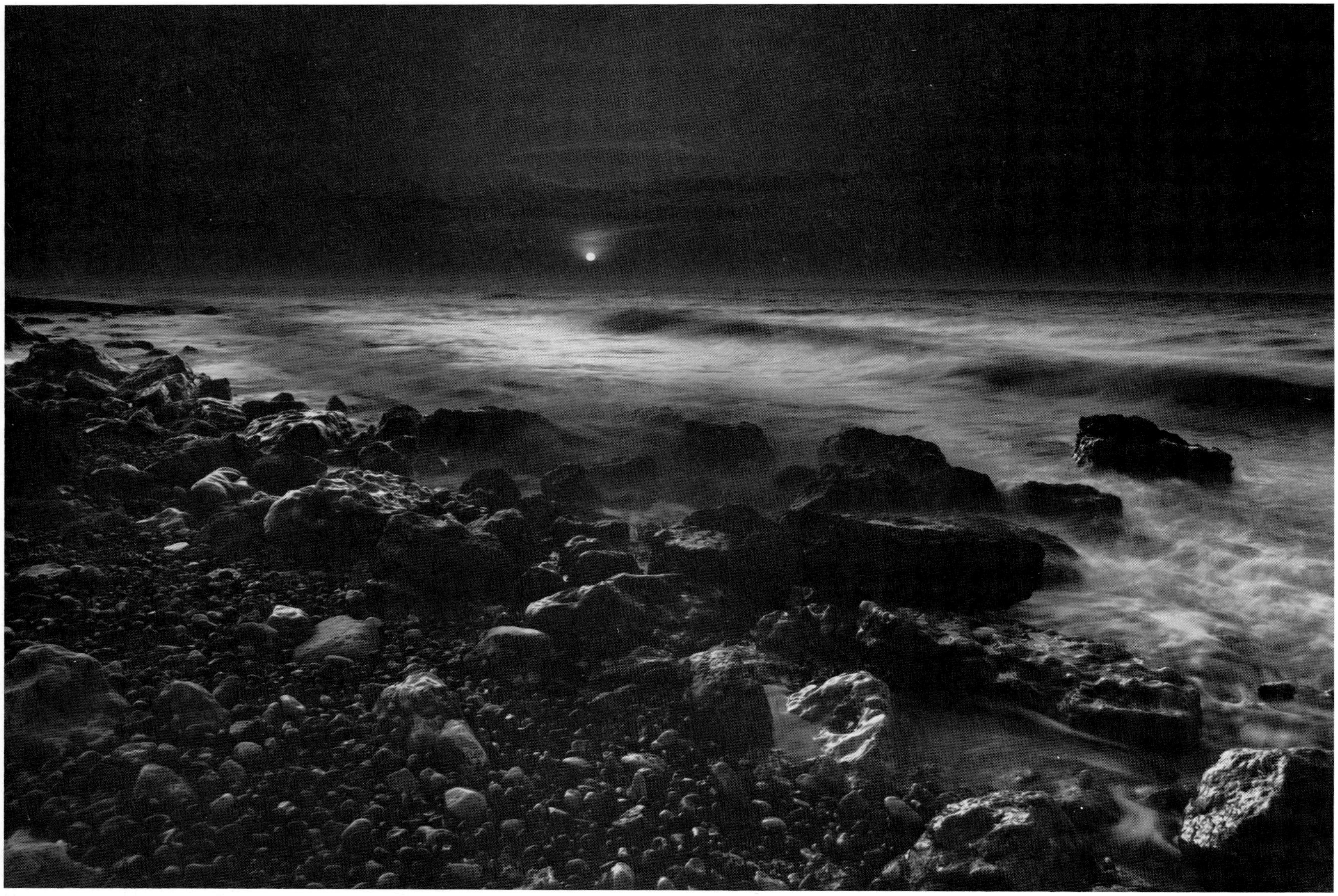

Beachscape Ken Niven.

Enlarging the print to 16 inches (40.6cm), the basic exposure time was calculated as 14.2 seconds. Using the F/STOP EXPOSURE TIME Table take 14.1 seconds as the basic exposure time (there is only 1/100 f/stop difference between these two values). Again the dodging and burning-in modifications expressed in f/stops remain the same. The final print is reproduced above.

a quarter of the density when spread on to a 16 × 20 inch (40.6 × 50.8cm) area. We will need, as with the toast, four times the original exposure to accommodate the area. This is done by increasing the exposure time by a multiple of four.

To derive the general formula we compare the image area to the exposure time:

$$\frac{A1}{T1} = \frac{A2}{T2}$$

where A1 and A2 represents the image area of two different-size enlargements. And T1 and T2 are the respective exposure times.

If this were a square format the length of one side would need only be squared to find the area. So using L1 to represent a side of A1, its area would equal $(L1)^2$; and $(L2)^2$ would be the area for A2.

$$\frac{A1}{T1} = \frac{A2}{T2}$$

can now be written as:

$$\frac{(L1)^2}{T1} = \frac{(L2)^2}{T2}$$

This can be rewritten:

$$T2 = (L2/L1)^2 \times T1$$

CHAPTER TEN

CHAPTER TEN

Print Presentation

There are as many ways to print and present a picture as there are sheets of photographic paper. Positioning of the image, cropping, 'black borders', printing dark and heavy or light and airy: all these contribute to the effect and success of the finished print.

ENLARGEMENT AND IMAGE POSITION

When I first started printing I printed everything to fit the format of the paper. At that time I had a fixed 8 × 10 inch (20.3 × 25.4cm) easel. This provided ¼ inch (6mm) borders so that all my prints were 7½ × 9½ inch (19.1 × 24.2cm) images on the paper. I even marked and pencilled onto the focusing screen of my 35mm camera this particular format. I saw and tried to photograph everything as an 8 × 10 inch (20.3 × 25.4cm) for the sake of filling the entire sheet of paper. I must have thought that leaving any unexposed area of the print was a waste of good photographic paper! The size of paper should only dictate the maximum image size.

Now I am inclined to print the whole of the 35mm negative as a 6 × 9 inch (15.2 × 22.9cm) image centred evenly on the sides but with a wider border on the bottom than on the top of the picture. This makes the picture appear balanced – if it were evenly spaced on the top and bottom the picture would look bottom-heavy.

I rarely print to fill the area of the paper. On 16 × 20 inch (40.6 × 50.8cm) paper I print a 35mm negative with a maximum image size of 12 × 18 inches (30.5 × 45.7cm). For a horizontal image this means a 1 inch (2.5cm) border on both sides, 1¾ inches (4.4cm) for the top border, leaving 2¼ inches (5.7cm) for the bottom. The vertical image will dictate 2 inches (5cm) for the sides. Because the image is so large, the top and bottom borders are left equal at 1 inch (2.5cm) each.

But I like big borders. The extra white around the actual image makes the picture stand out and makes it look brighter. It might appear a bit extravagant, but a 35mm negative printed 8 × 12 inches (20.3 × 30.5cm) on a 16 × 20 inch (40.6 × 50.8cm) paper (with the appropriate borders) looks very grand. This smaller print size for 35mm negatives also minimizes the grain.

The print using the whole of an 8 × 10 (20.3 × 25.4cm) piece of paper.

This is the entire negative image printed on 8 × 10 inch (20.3 × 25.4cm) paper.

Blenheim Gene Nocon.

BLACK BORDERS

The 'black border' is a simple but effective means of embellishing the print. The black border is created by exposing the clear area around the negative image – the rebate area. It can only be done if the aperture of the negative carrier is slightly larger than the negative format.

Some enlargers have negative carriers with a slightly bigger aperture to enable printing black borders. If yours does not, the negative aperture will need careful filing to enlarge the opening. There is no need to file all four sides. File only the edges that correspond to the bottom and right side of the aperture when the carrier is in place and the lamp is switched on. After filing, finish the rough edges with a very fine emery cloth to ensure against any pieces or fragments of metal that could scratch or gouge the negative when pulled through. Test this by pulling a sheet of ordinary writing paper through the negative carrier.

When printing the black border keep the width of this exposed rebate area to a minimum. This is to avoid any flaring on the print which can be caused when the light passing through this clear rebate area strikes the bevelled edges of some print easels. This flare can be seen as a darkening of the edges of the image area.

Adjust the blades on the easel to crop and finish the edge of the rebate borders. This leaves a clean black border around the image. Some photographers choose to print the whole of the negative showing the rough aperture edges of the negative carrier.

Negative carrier with black-border facility.

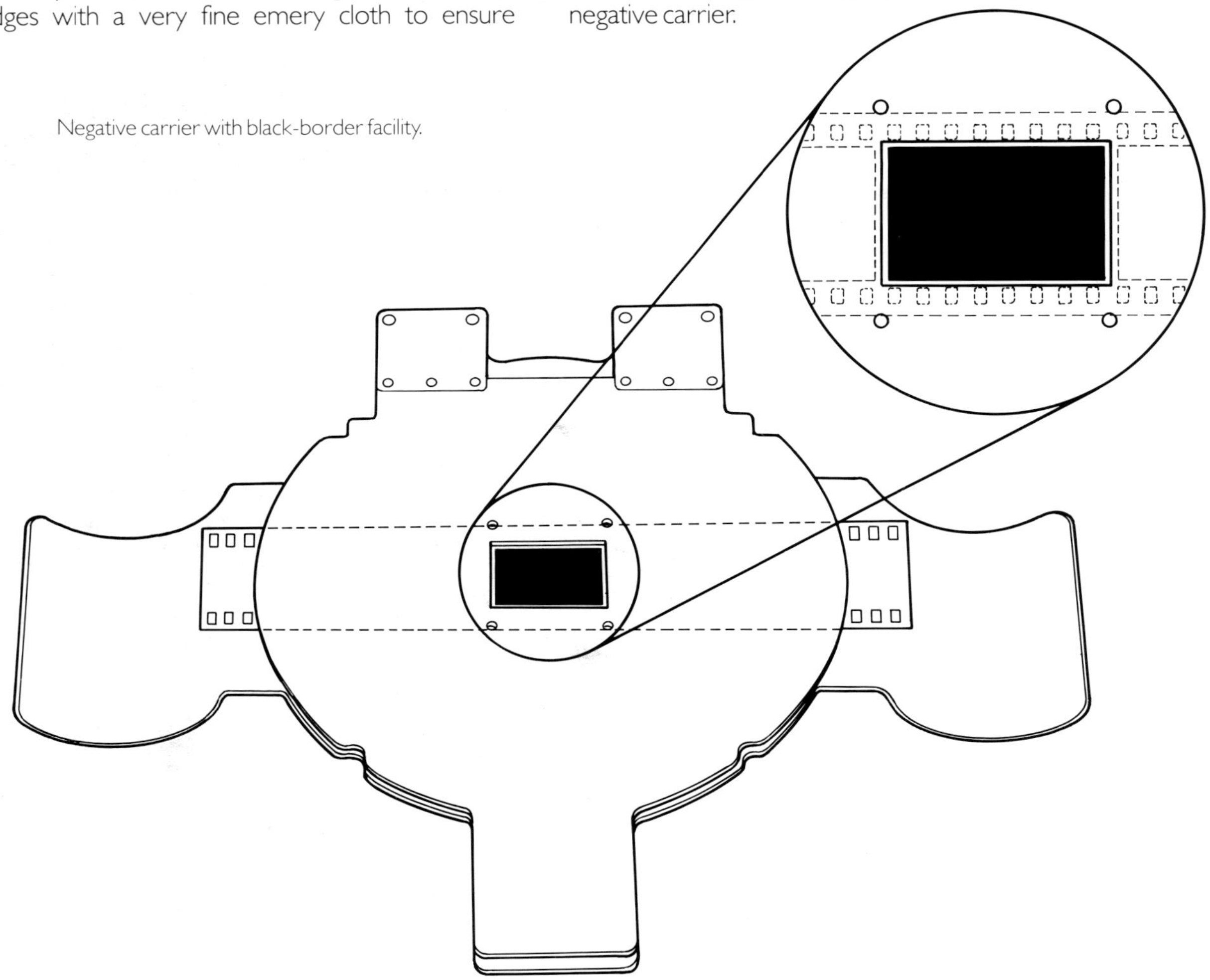

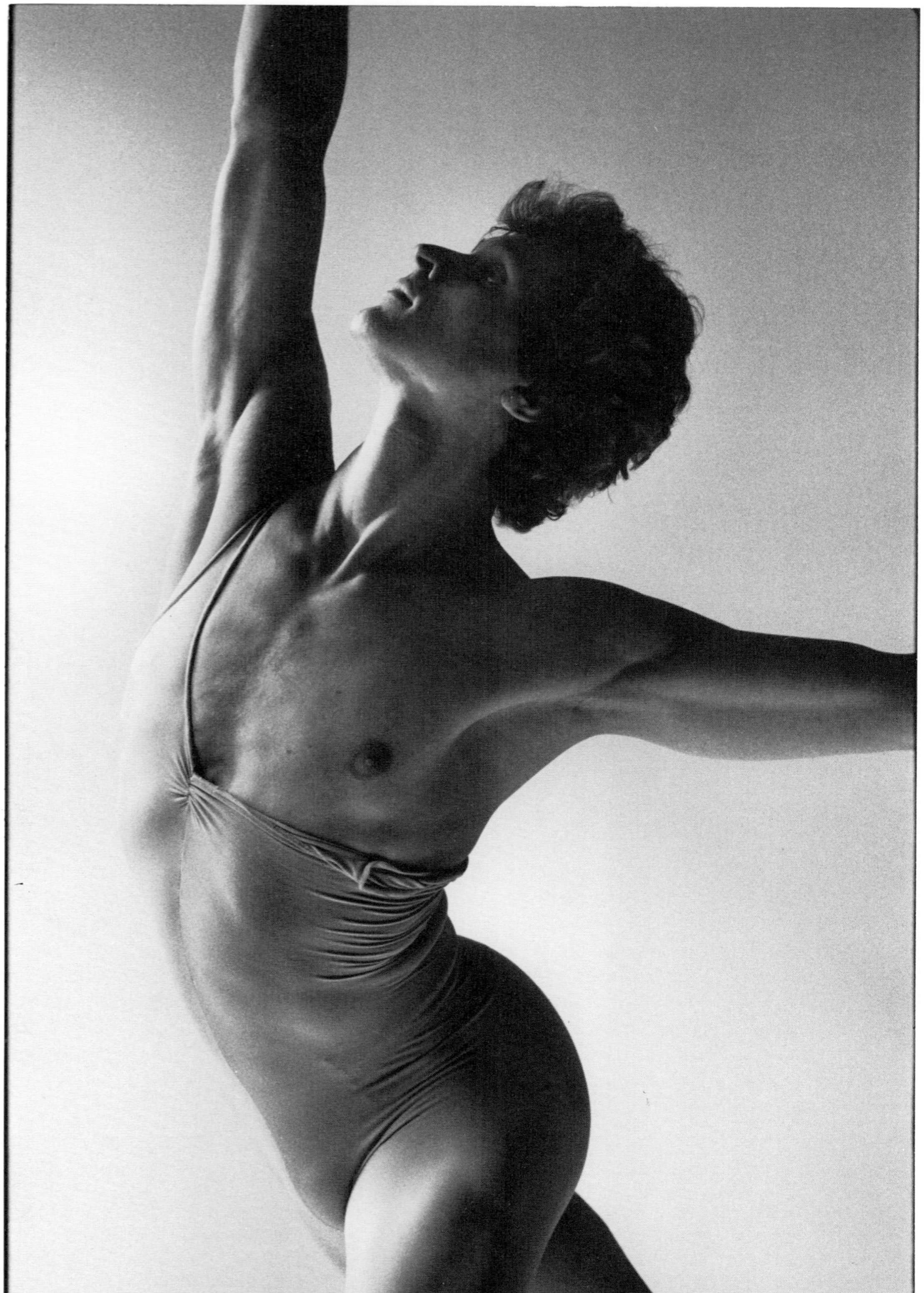

Peter Schaufuss Clare Park. Printing the rebate area around the image as a black border is a personal choice.

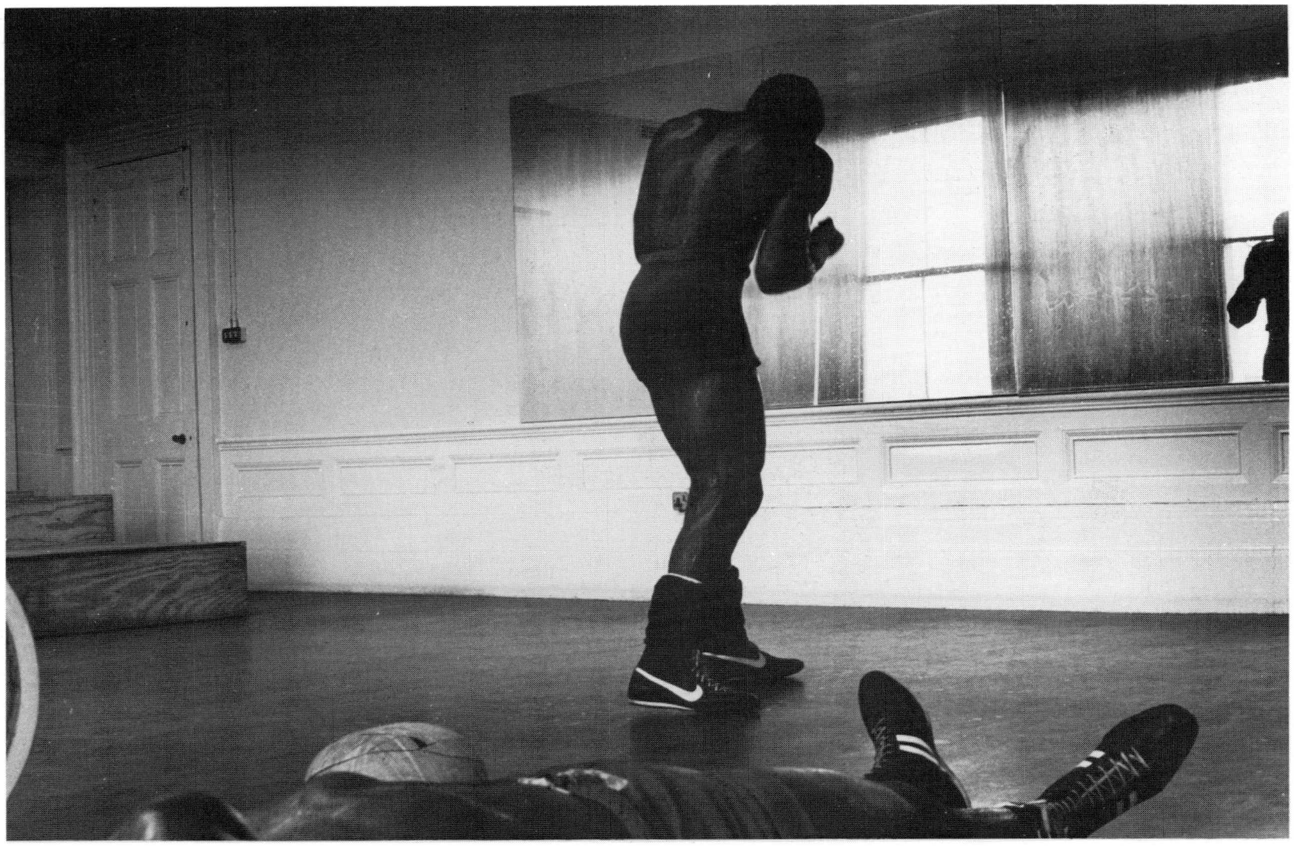

The entire image shows a training room. The cropped version tells a different story. Which to convey is your choice.

CROPPING AND COMPOSITION

Cropping

I generally do very little cropping, respecting the total image seen by the photographer. This is particularly true with 35mm formats. To me, the spontaneity that can be captured with a 35mm camera is its appeal. I crop mainly to eliminate areas of the image that I cannot modify through burning-in or dodging. There are times, as well, when the horizon line is not level. In which case, adjusting the easel will necessitate cropping slightly.

Composition

All I can say about this subject is that there are no rules. Composition is part of artistic temperament. If you follow rules this tends to eliminate your own personal judgment. What makes your pictures unique depends on you, your artistry – not the rules of others. Photography, aside from the purpose of simply recording, provides tremendous scope for personal creativity.

But, having said that, I have my own set of 'rules' which you might like to use in your own printing.

I saw an exhibition of portraits which included paintings as well as photographs. I do not like to make comparisons about paintings and photographs because they are two different forms of art. But the actual physical dimensions of the paintings, at least in this exhibition, were so great that they had to be measured in feet whereas those of the photographs were measurable in inches.

I mention this physical comparison only to present my thoughts about the size of prints. Photographs that are printed large only become bill posters; they cease to be photographs.

There is a curiosity factor in the appeal of photographs. They entice you to look into the picture. And for this reason I like them small. Not necessarily the size of postcards, but of a size that allows you to hold them at arm's length and see the entire picture. There is really no point in printing something so big that you have to stand back to see what is there.

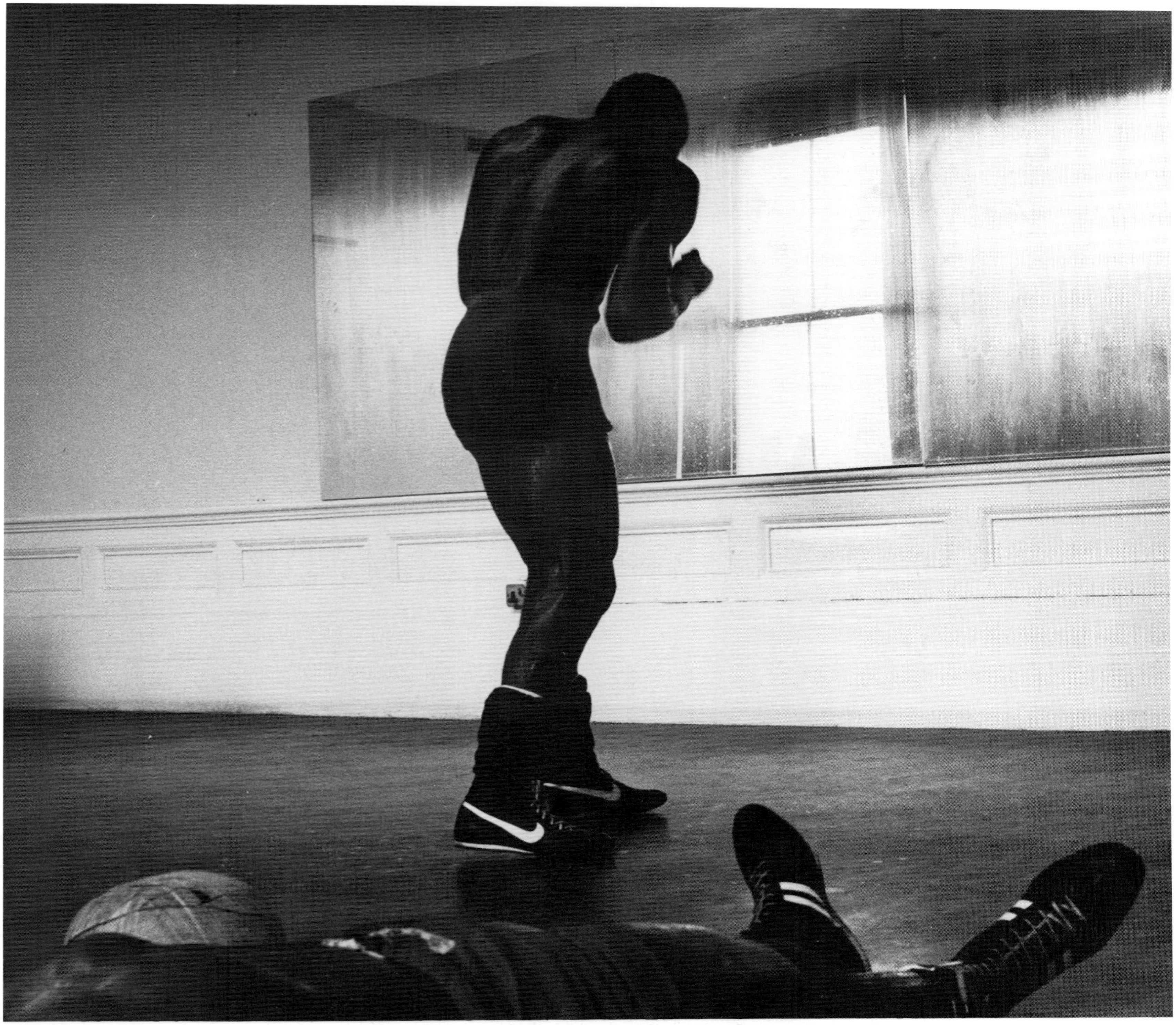

Bruno Robert Keen.

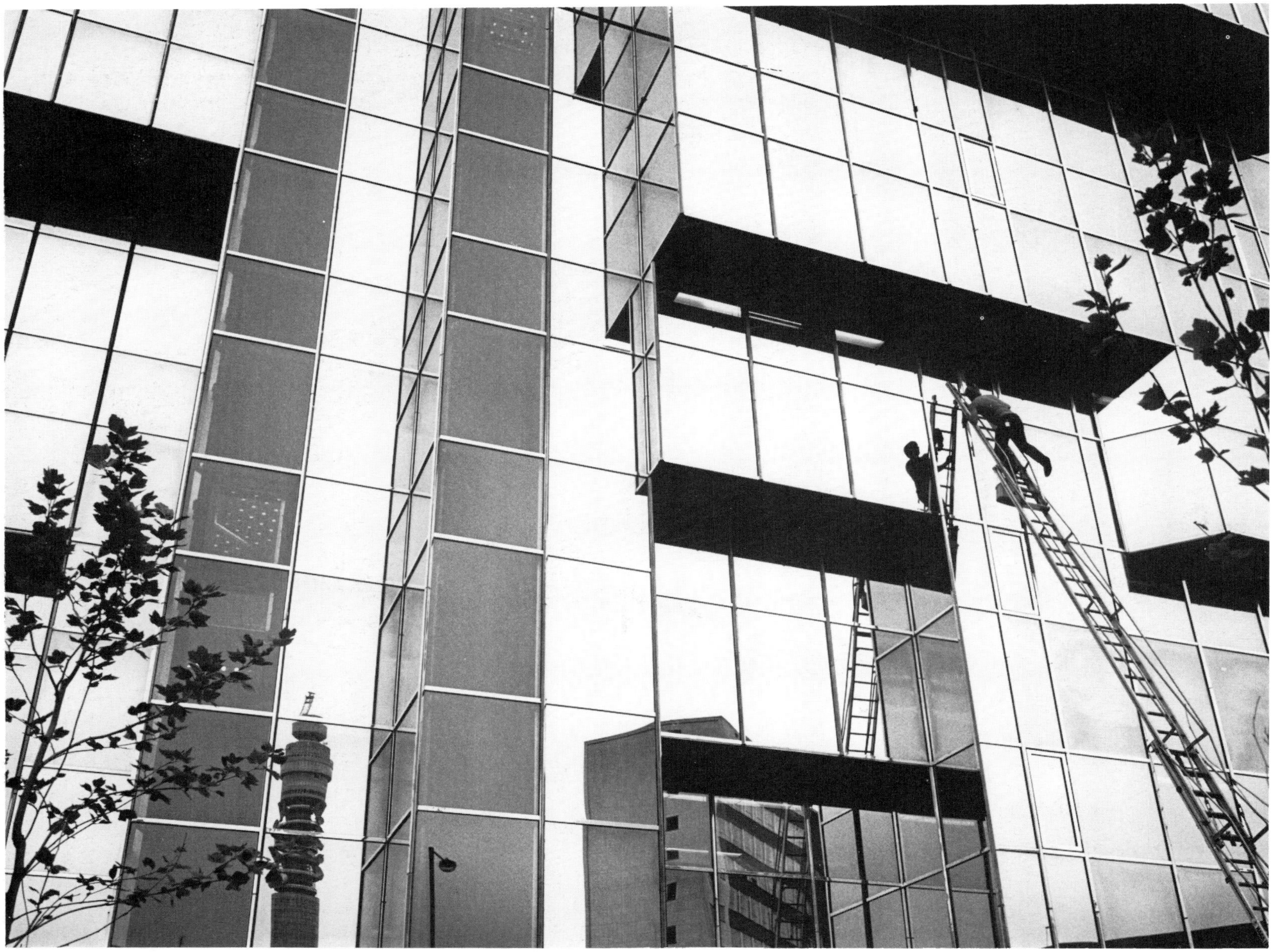

Cropping and 'pointing' this picture reduces the impact of the entire image reproduced in the large illustration.

Pointing Often a picture will have a diagonal line, such as the base of a wall, the flap of a coat, the disappearing perspective of a street, which can be cropped so that it meets the corner of the image area. I call this 'pointing'. It seems, and is, a conscious effort of composition.

Verticals Unless you use a view camera which will enable you to correct for converging verticals, you will find that pictures taken of buildings or anything with dominant vertical lines will show the convergence of lines. I have never thought this detrimental to the picture. Like selective focusing, this is, in fact, one of the unique features of photographs. Just think, painters do not, but could, I suppose, paint out of focus. Nor, except perhaps in illustrations, do they paint verticals converging. Yet converging vertical lines can prove to be very dramatic in photographs.

When printing such photographs, the most central line should be vertical, with the lines to the left and right of it falling towards it.

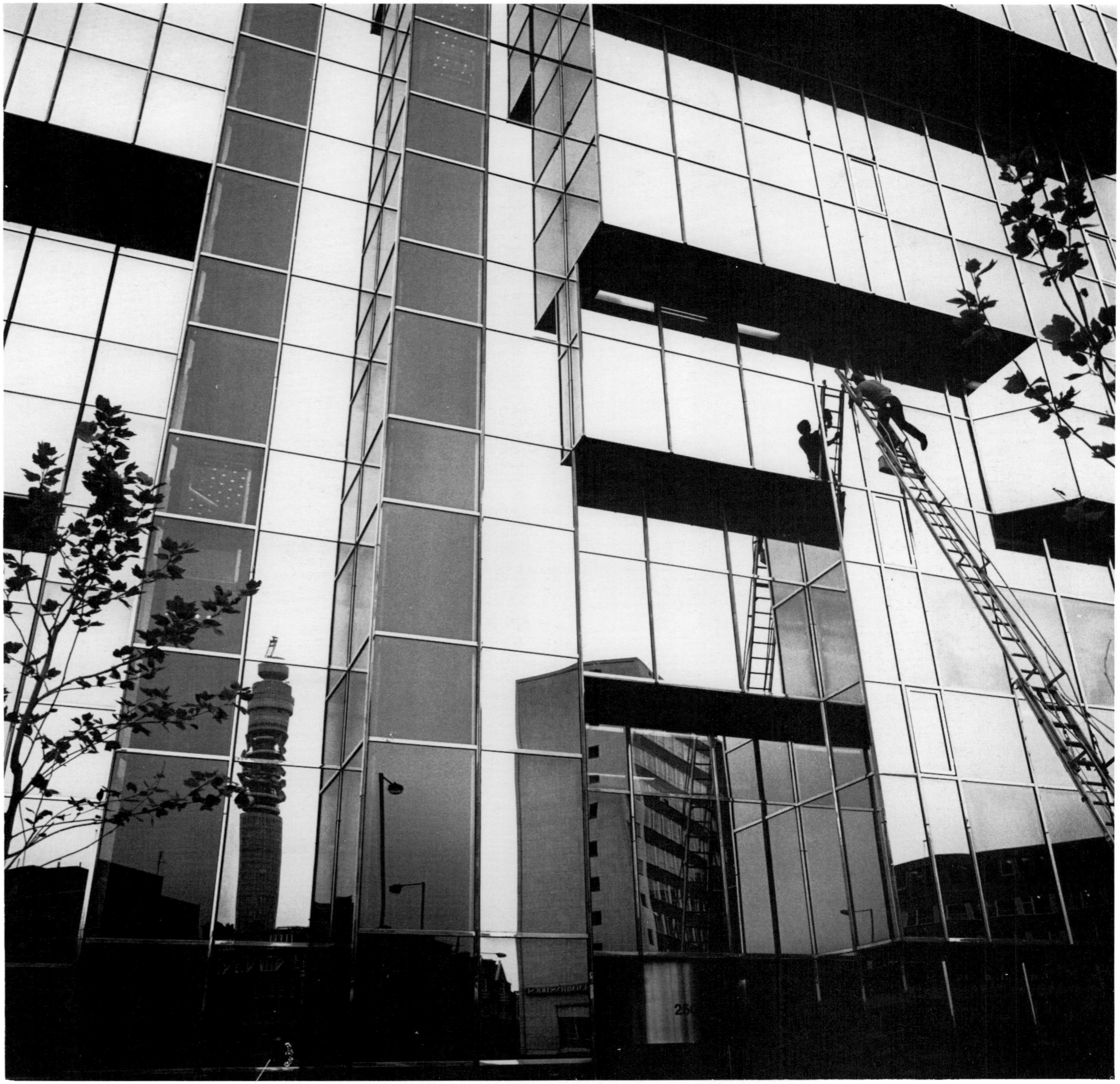

When I'm Cleaning Windows Ken Keen, ARPS.

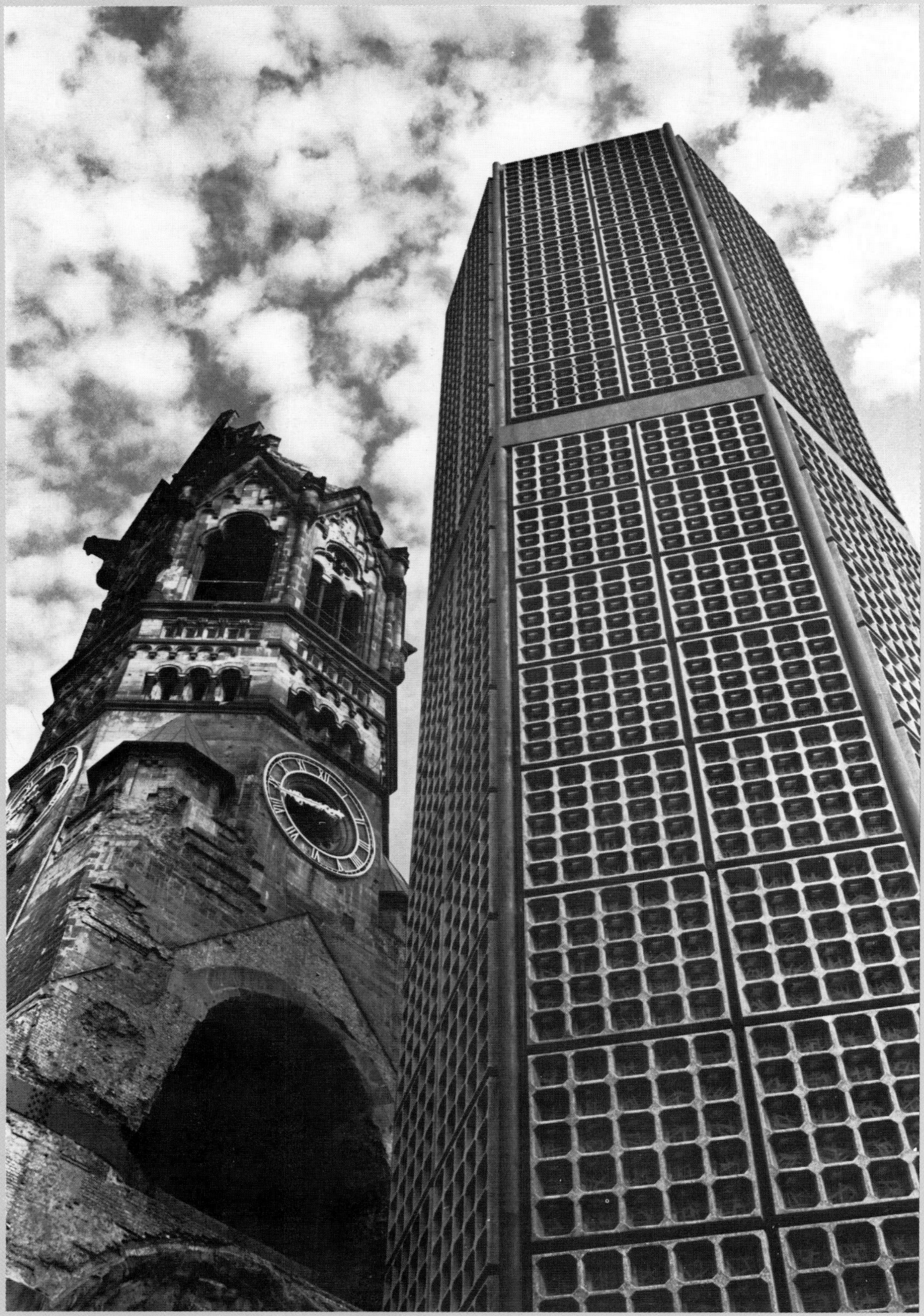

Kaiser Wilhelm Memorial Church Gene Nocon.

My start in photography was winning a photo contest in Germany. I submitted, in the pictorial section, a picture I had taken of the Kaiser Wilhelm Memorial Church in West Berlin. It won in that section as well as taking the overall grand prize. It was published in our local newspaper. A few days later I got a 'phone call from the Commanding General (I was in the army) and he asked if I would take some portraits of him and his family. I said, 'Yes, sir'.

On the scheduled day, I turned up at his house, introduced myself, and proceeded to set up. There really wasn't much to do. All I had at the time was a 35mm camera with a standard lens, a spindly little tripod, one roll of film, a bulb-type flash, and a packet of flash bulbs.

The General left me to set up while he rounded up his 'family'. Expecting him to return with his wife, Junior, Sis, and the dog, I was rather overwhelmed when two other Generals and five 'full bird' Colonels and their wives entered the room. The entire army division's top brass! I was then only a Private, and a very young one at that. What made it even worse was the fact that I had never ever taken anyone's portrait before.

But something rather extraordinary took place. For some reason I was no longer simply a Private – I was there because I was a PHOTOGRAPHER. I found myself telling the Generals and Colonels what to do – and they did it! Eventually I managed to position them all in the stairwell, and looking through the viewfinder I was satisfied that everything looked all right. But some moment of madness came over me. Just to see what they would do I told them all to move up one step. They did! I, a buck Private, had 'ordered' an entire army division to do as I said.

It makes a wonderful story when my children ask me what I did in the war. But I relate this true story because a photographer worthy of the title PHOTOGRAPHER should be master and ruler of his domain. It is not a cloak of omnipotence. It is an attitude of mind which assures those being photographed that he, the photographer, knows what he is doing. This instills confidence in those being photographed and assures them that their time is not being wasted.

The pictures of the Generals, incidentally, were a success – thank goodness!

CHAPTER ELEVEN

CHAPTER ELEVEN
Print Washing and Drying

The reason for washing the print is to remove the chemicals absorbed by the paper and the photographic emulsion. Washing must be done before drying. Otherwise, in time, the residual chemicals can stain or discolour the print. This effect can be seen to be immediate if the print is heat-dried.

Washing involves the immersion of the print in a bath or tray of running water. The paper base and emulsion softens and becomes swollen like a sponge. In this swollen state the circulating water washes away the chemicals. An effective wash requires frequent changes of water as well as movement of the print by manual agitation or by force of the running water.

Use of chemical washing aids such as Kodak Hypo Clearing Agent or Ilford Wash Aid reduces the washing time. These washing aids apparently change the composition of the fixer, making it easier to remove the residual chemical from the print.

The longer the print remains in the chemicals, the greater the absorption of chemicals. Therefore do not leave the prints in the chemicals any longer than the manufacturers' recommended time. Also avoid using hardeners in the fixer. Hardeners reduce the swelling of the emulsion and make it more difficult to wash the print effectively.

PRINT WASHING

There is little I can add to the technique of washing other than to describe my own methods. I use three washing trays. After fixing, the print is placed in the first wash tray of continuous running water to rid the print of most of the fixer. I leave it in there to wash, with intermittent agitation, for about 30 minutes. After draining, the print is placed in a second wash of running water for another 30 minutes, again with intermittent agitation. And finally it is put in a third wash of running water where it remains until I am ready to start drying. To my knowledge none of the prints I have washed in this way have discoloured.

Resin-coated papers, being plastic, do not absorb the chemicals and therefore require very little time to wash. Follow the manufacturers' recommended time for washing.

DRYING PRINTS

Depending on the needs of my clients I either air-dry or use a conventional, heated drum-dryer to dry prints. I air-dry prints when archival processing and drying is required. Air-drying prevents contamination of the print with any chemicals on the drum blanket. Drum-drying is faster and used for more immediate and commercial needs.

My air-drying method is simply to squeegee excess water off the washed print, place it with the print emulsion up on a large clean glassine envelope, and leave it to dry overnight. The print usually dries with curled-up edges. I then use a heated dry-mounting press to flatten the print. It has been suggested that a method of getting air-dried flat prints is to hang the prints back-to-back with the corners held together with wooden clothes-pegs.

Kodak Elite paper has to be air-dried. Unless the print made on Elite is toned in selenium toner, heat-drying reduces the density (the blackness) of the print. The cardboard thickness of Elite helps keep the print flat when air-dried.

Drum-drying is simple enough. I first squeegee the excess water off the emulsion side and then lay the print face down on the blanket. The excess water is squeegeed off the back side of the print as the print starts to revolve around the drum.

After drying, I place a large wooden board on top of the print and place weights on top to help flatten it.

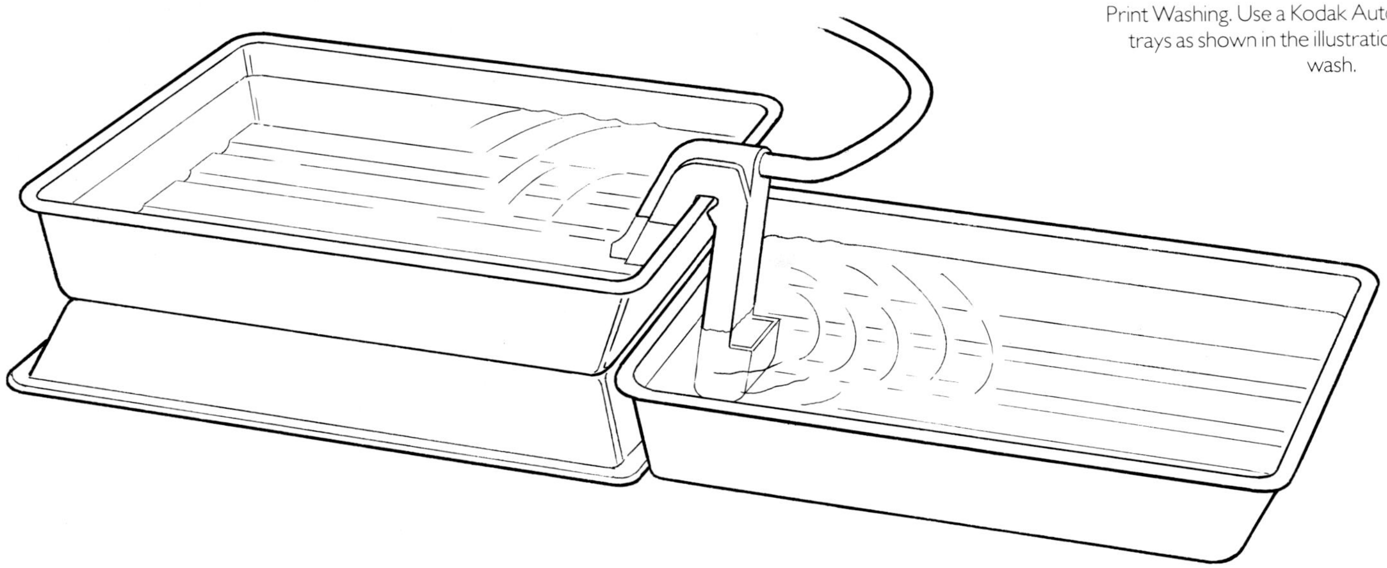

Print Washing. Use a Kodak Autosyphon with three trays as shown in the illustration for a two-bath wash.

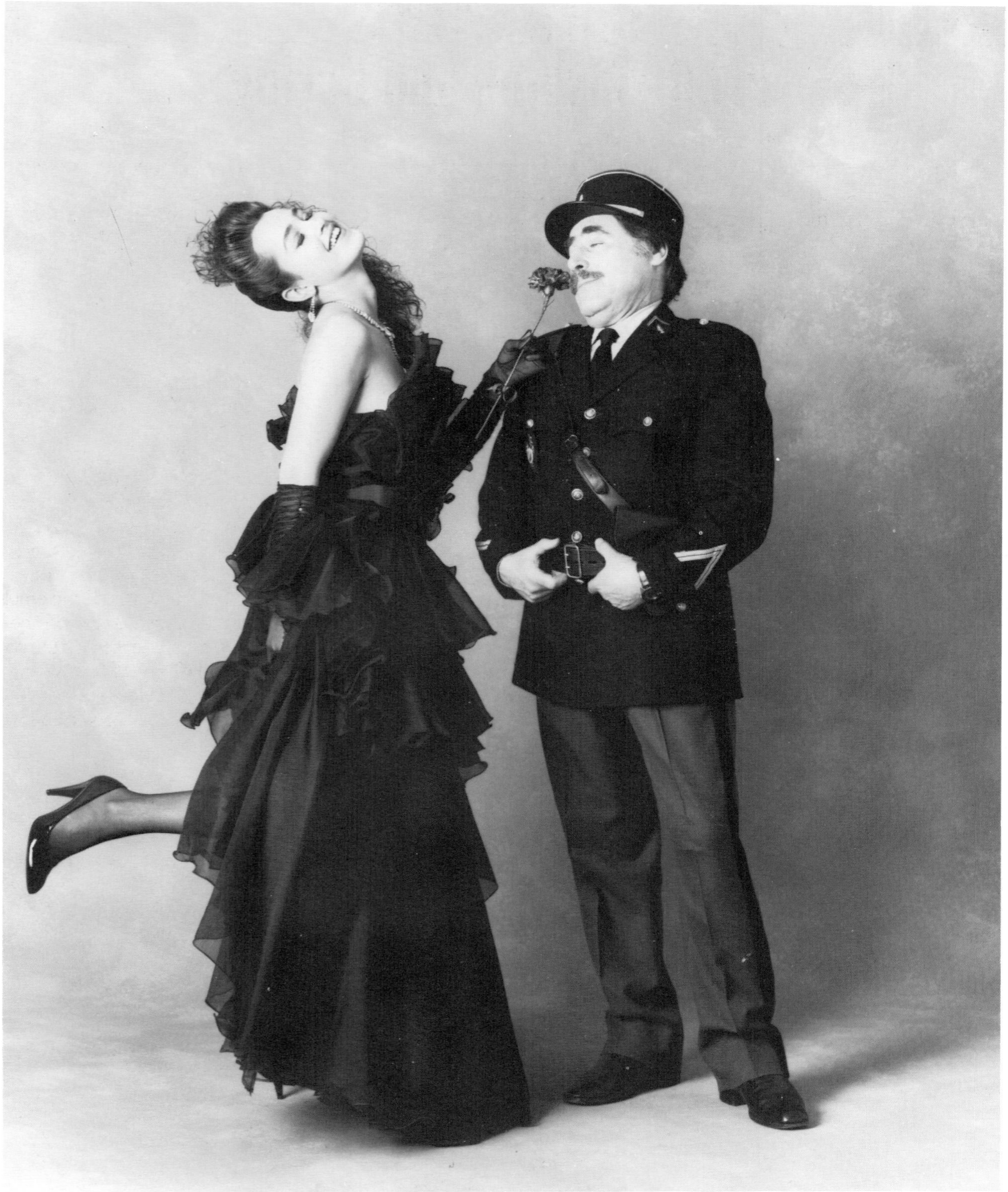

Heat-drying de-grades the black on Kodak Elite papers. It is recommended that the print be air-dried or selenium toned prior to heat-drying. The print above was heat-dried without selenium toning. Compare it with the print overleaf which was air-dried.

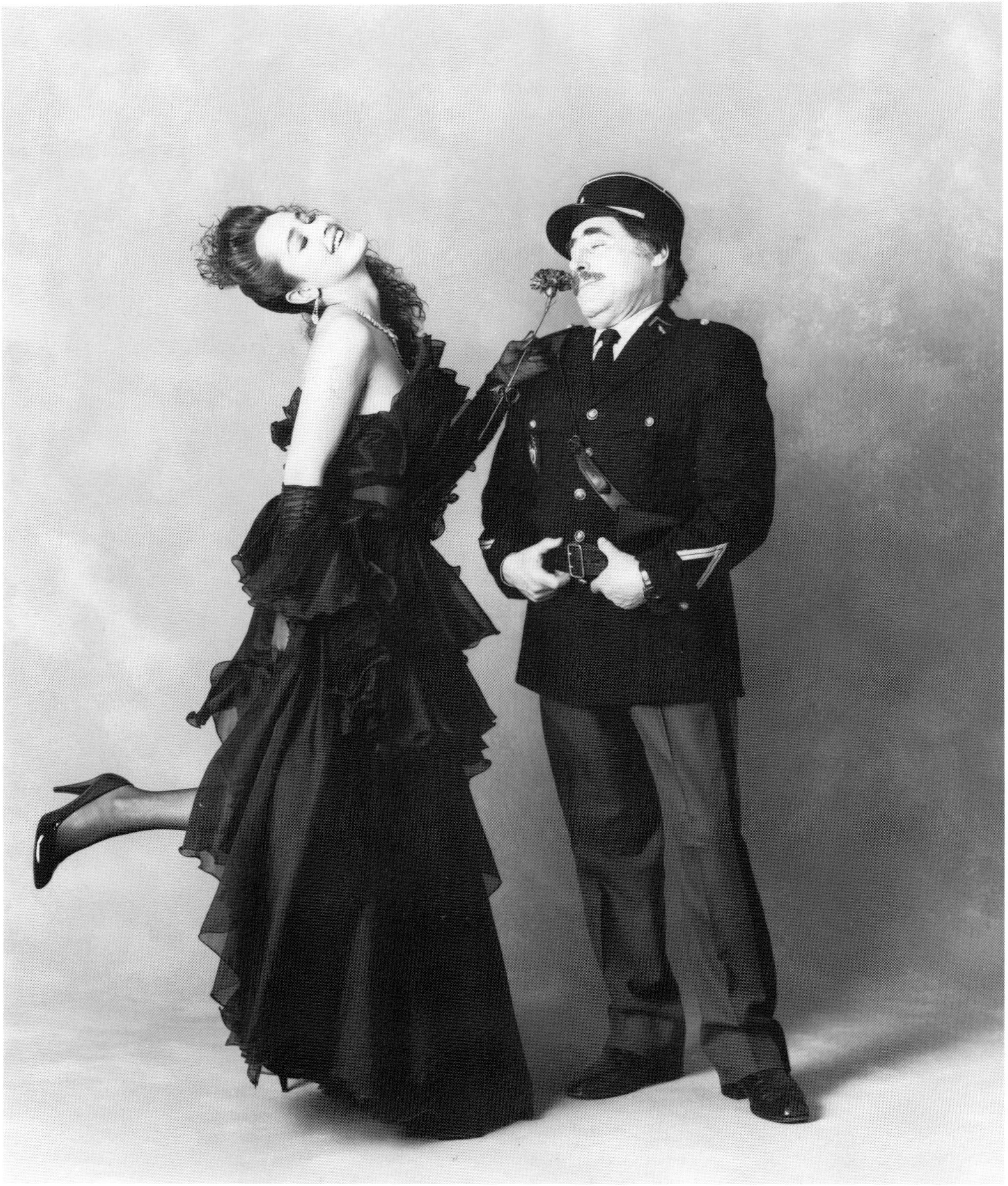

Parisienne Spring Benjamin Lee.

CHAPTER TWELVE

CHAPTER TWELVE

Why Things Go Bump in the Dark

The past eleven chapters have been a comprehensive discussion on the techniques of photographic printing. I have saved Chapter Twelve as a catchment area for all the other bits and pieces of information you may like to know.

THE EXPONENTIAL PROGRESSION OF EXPOSURE TIMES

If we begin with a basic unit of exposure of 1 second and double that to 2, this, by photographic convention, increases the exposure +1 f/stop. Doubling again to 4 seconds increases exposure another +1 f/stop. Double again to 8 and that increases the exposure a further +1 f/stop. If we continue doing this we will have an *exponential* progression of 1, 2, 4, 8, 16, 32, and 64. These values are the exponential progression of the base number 2. If we list these values alongside their equivalent exponential forms:

$$1 = 2^0$$
$$2 = 2^1$$
$$4 = 2^2$$
$$8 = 2^3$$
$$16 = 2^4$$
$$32 = 2^5$$
$$64 = 2^6$$

Notice that the exponents increase a unit value with each progression. Note, for example, that 2 seconds, equivalent to 2, is 1 f/stop more than 1. And that 4, equal to 2, is 2 f/stops more than 1. And 8, equal to 2, is 3 f/stops more than 1.

The intermediate values between these whole integers can be determined by finding the fractional exponential values. So an expanded list in ¼ exponential values is as follows:

$1 = 2^0$	$2 = 2^1$	$4 = 2^2$	$8 = 2^3$
$1.19 = 2^{1/4}$	$2.38 = 2^{1\,1/4}$	$4.76 = 2^{2\,1/4}$	$9.52 = 2^{3\,1/4}$
$1.41 = 2^{1/2}$	$2.83 = 2^{1\,1/2}$	$5.66 = 2^{2\,1/2}$	$11.32 = 2^{3\,1/2}$
$1.68 = 2^{3/4}$	$3.36 = 2^{1\,3/4}$	$6.73 = 2^{2\,3/4}$	$13.46 = 2^{3\,3/4}$

These values as they stand are too small to be manageable as exposure times. They only have to be multiplied by 10 to provide a useful range of exposure times:

10	20	40	80
11.9	23.8	47.6	95.2
14.1	28.3	56.6	113.2
16.8	33.6	67.3	134.6

I chose 10 as a multiple of the exponential values. You could choose any multiple. If, instead, I used 5 I would then get the exposure times of 5, 5.9, 7.1, and 8.4, followed by 10, 11.9, 14.1, etc. Hence the familiar:

F/STOP EXPOSURE TIME

5	10	20	40	80
5.9	11.9	23.8	47.6	95.2
7.1	14.1	28.3	56.6	113.2
8.4	16.8	33.6	67.3	134.6

I have already explained why arbitrary values of time prove to be confusing.

Some of you may be using percentages. Let me illustrate how that, too, creates problems.

If I had 10 seconds as an exposure time and I reduced the exposure by 50% the exposure time would be 5 seconds. But if I changed my mind and wanted to get back to my original exposure by increasing the exposure by the same 50%, my exposure time would only be 7.25 seconds! Madness.

ON APERTURE F/STOPS

The formula for determining the area of a circle is:

$$A = \pi r^2$$

Pi, π, is a constant. To simplify this discussion, for the time being just let:

$$A = r^2$$

So given a circle of unit area, $A = 1$, $r^2 = 1$, therefore $r = \sqrt{1} = 1$. If this area is halved (to represent a -1 f/stop), $A = r^2 = \frac{1}{2}$; r then equals

$\sqrt{1/2}$ which is equal to 1/1.4. Halve this area again so that A is now equal to ¼, then $r = \sqrt{1/4}$, which is equal to 1/2. Halve again the area so that A = ⅛ and $r = \sqrt{1/8}$ which is equal to 1/2.8. If this progression is continued you will see a familiar series of numbers begin to emerge:
1, 1/1.4, 1/2, 1/2.8, 1/4, 1/5.6, 1/8, 1/11, 1/16, 1/22, etc.

These are the f/stop markings on your camera lens! It helped me many years ago to consider that the 'f' in f/stop meant fraction. The smaller the fractional value – the smaller the aperture. Hence f/16 (1/16) is smaller than f/4 (¼).

FLASHING

The 'characteristic curve' of photographic film or paper is a graphic representation of the relationship of exposure and its effect on the density. These curves are determined experimentally using sensitometers and other photographic measuring devices and plotting the results of photographic density against the exposure:

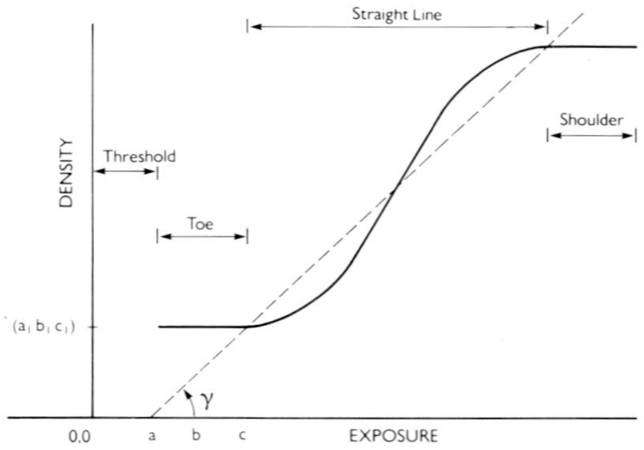

For exposures a, b, c, the corresponding density values are a_1, b_1, c_1. There is no change in density, therefore no highlight separation or detail.

The curve shows the relationship of density to exposure. The point where the density starts indicates that a certain amount of exposure is needed before the film or paper actually starts to produce a measurable tone. It is not a gradual build-up starting at 0 exposure, 0 density. The point where this tone immediately starts is the 'threshold' of the film or paper. Up until the threshold value the photographic paper will show no discernible tone.

Between the threshold value, the start of the curve, and the point where the curve starts to swing upwards is the part of the plot known as the TOE of the curve. The toe is that part of the curve which shows no changes in density with the change in exposure.

Beyond the toe, the curve now begins to show the most useful part of the film or paper: changes in exposure actually cause a change in density. This part of the curve is known as the STRAIGHT LINE.

The tangent of the angle this STRAIGHT LINE makes with the exposure axis is referred to as the 'gamma'. Gamma (γ) is a measure of the contrast of the paper or film. The greater the angle, the higher the contrast.

After the straight line the curve starts to flatten out, indicating that any further exposure no longer effectively increases the density. This part of the curve is the SHOULDER.

My reference to density, here, refers to blackening of the silver, i.e. the blackest part of the paper, or the densest area of the film.

If we restrict ourselves to discussing the characteristic curve of paper the TOE represents the lightest part of the picture, and the SHOULDER the black area. (For film the toe represents the shadows, the shoulder the highlights.)

The toe represents the highlight area of the print. This is the lightest part, just beyond the base white tone of the paper. But any variation of exposure in this toe part of the curve causes no change at all to the density. The density remains the same – this is referred to as 'compacted' highlights.

The shadow area is represented by the shoulder of the curve. Exposure variations in this part of the curve, like the toe, show no change in density. No density separation – no shadow detail.

Thus the most useful part of the paper is the straight line part as seen on the characteristic curve. The toe and shoulder are, for the most part, unusable. It is for this reason that we have to burn-in highlights and dodge-out shadows to fall within the straight line part of the curve.

Now that you know a bit about characteristic curves I can discuss the effect that flashing has on them.

Flashing changes the characteristic curve. Why it does this I don't know. I have discussed this with technicians of the major film and paper manufacturers, but there is no apparent explanation, only that it does change the curve.

Provided the flashing does not reach the threshold value the characteristic curve straightens out, losing the toe and shoulder! This means that exposure differences in what were once the toe and shoulder of the curve can now be seen to have separate density values, revealing the highlight and shadow details. After flashing the curve looks like this:

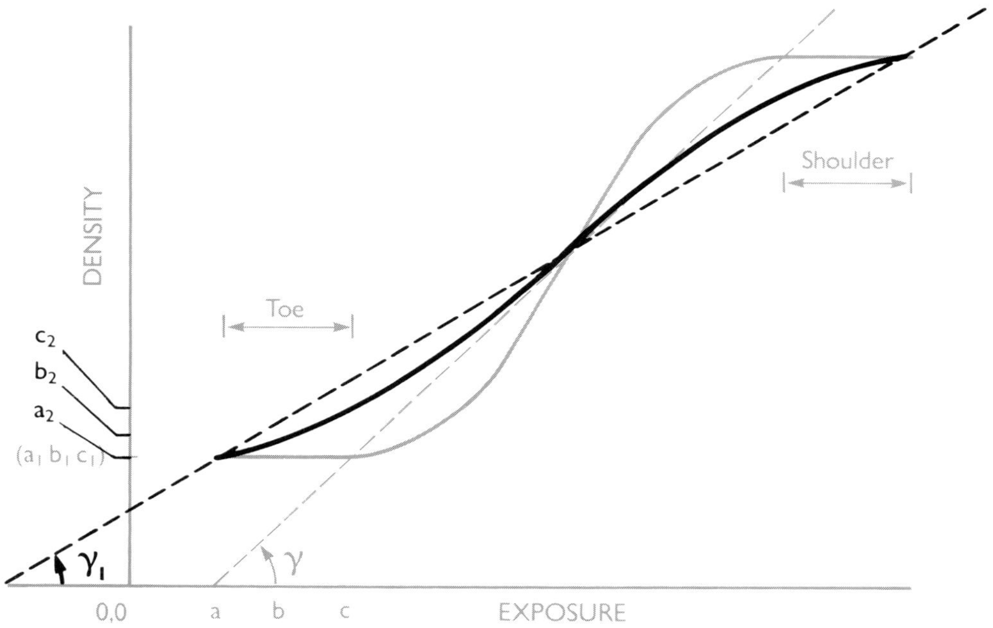

Flashed curve. For the same exposures a, b, c, the density values are a_2, b_2, c_2, which can be seen to be of different density. These changes represent the highlight detail.

Notice that for exposures a, b, c, on the un-flashed curve there is very little density change (a_1, b_1, c_1). But on the flashed curve these same exposure values can be seen with greater density values (a_2, b_2, c_2). These show up as tones on the paper and it is this greater separation in tones that provides highlight detail.

Flashing extends the useful part of the curve to include what was the toe and shoulder. Using the toe effectively increases the sensitivity of the paper. Because of this the basic exposure time can be reduced. By at least $-\frac{1}{4}$ f/stop. This means that the shadow area has a better chance of showing detail (because of overall reduced exposure). But the blacks remain black because a harder grade of paper, which is characteristically blacker, is used for flashing. Remember too that the highlight areas will also show more detail because of the change in the characteristic curve.

Flashing *reduces* the contrast. You can see this in the reduction of the slope (γ_1), of the flashed curve.

Flashing has been practised by photographers and printers since the technique was discovered. But it was all rather haphazard. Now that you know why and how it works, you will have much greater control over the technique.

CHAPTER THIRTEEN

CHAPTER THIRTEEN
Any Problems?

I have written almost everything I know about photographic printing, which should provide you with a greater understanding of the processes and a greater degree of control over the medium. In this chapter are just a few more bits of information which you may find useful.

STAINS ON PRINTS

Stains on the white borders of a print can be removed using a solution of about ½ a teaspoon of potassium ferricyanide and about 1 cup of water. I have never deliberately tried to stain a print so I cannot pinpoint what causes the stains . They are probably due to chemical contamination – I do not really know. Whatever the cause, this solution of ferricyanide can be used to remove the stain.

Use a piece of cotton wool dipped in the solution and apply it directly to the stain. Make sure the ferricyanide does not get on the image. I have a large sheet of plastic laminate on which to lay the entire print. This is propped up at an angle so the 'ferri' can be applied and the excess can drain down away from the image.

Leave the ferri on for about 30 seconds. Then use another piece of cotton wool with print fixer solution and apply that to the area of the stain. The fixer activates the bleaching action of the ferricyanide solution. Repeat this process if the stain persists. After removal of the stain put the print back in the fixer to clear what remains of the yellow ferri solution on the print.

With a print that is rather dark and flat, you can 'lift' the overall values by immersing the print in a tray of Farmer's Reducer (see Chapter Seven). This will clean up the highlights. Be careful that it does not bleach out all the highlight detail. Wash the print in running water just to get rid of the yellow colour, then put the print back in the fixer for about a minute. Wash the print as normal before drying.

WHITE GRAIN

'White grain' refers to the dust spots on the print. These should not be present if the negative was cleaned prior to printing. It takes more time to 'spot' white grain than it does to clean and print the negative properly.

Spotting involves using a soluble medium for

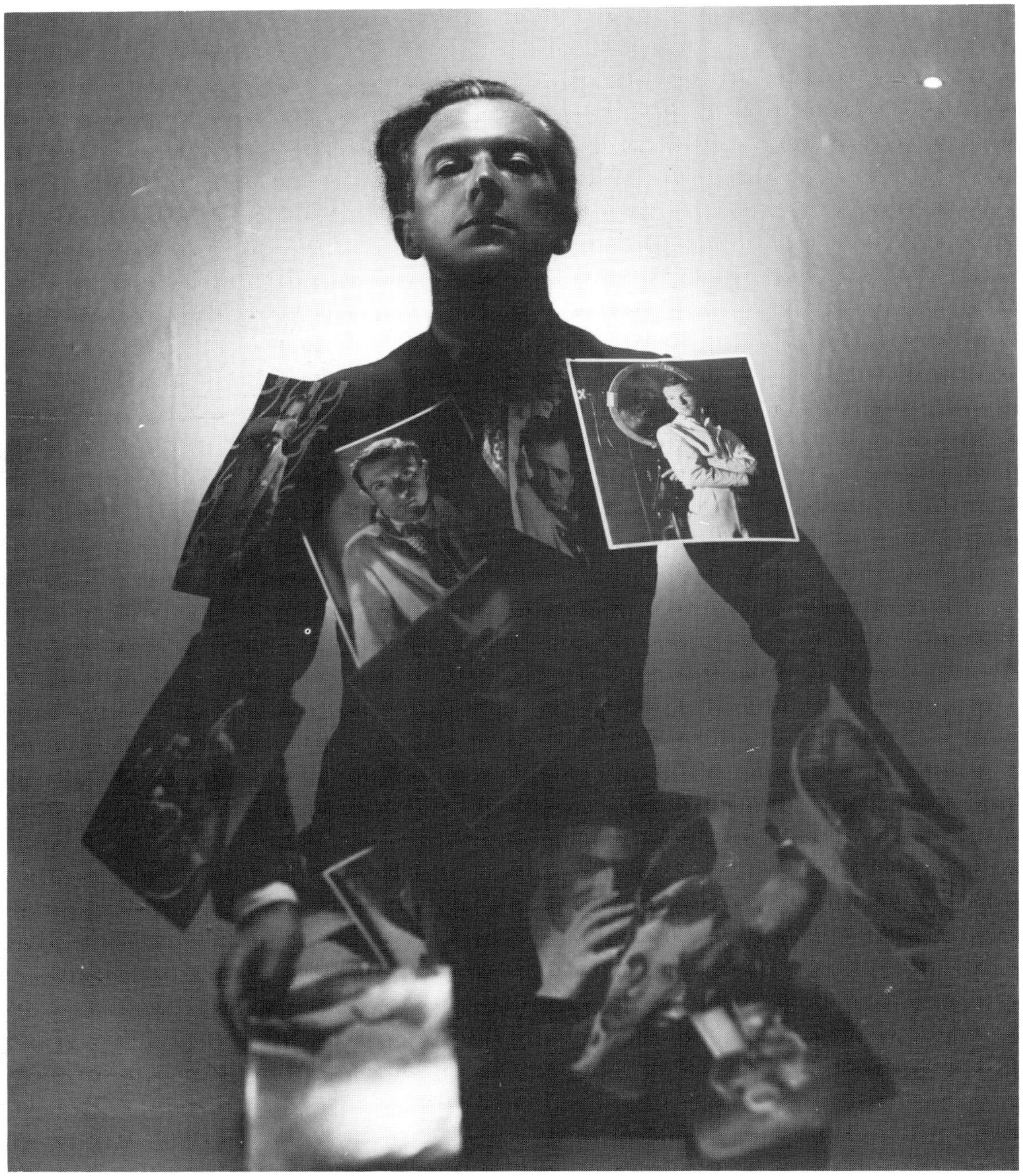

Unretouched print showing signs of damage on the negative. The illustration on the right shows the results of retouching and slight cropping to eliminate the blemishes.

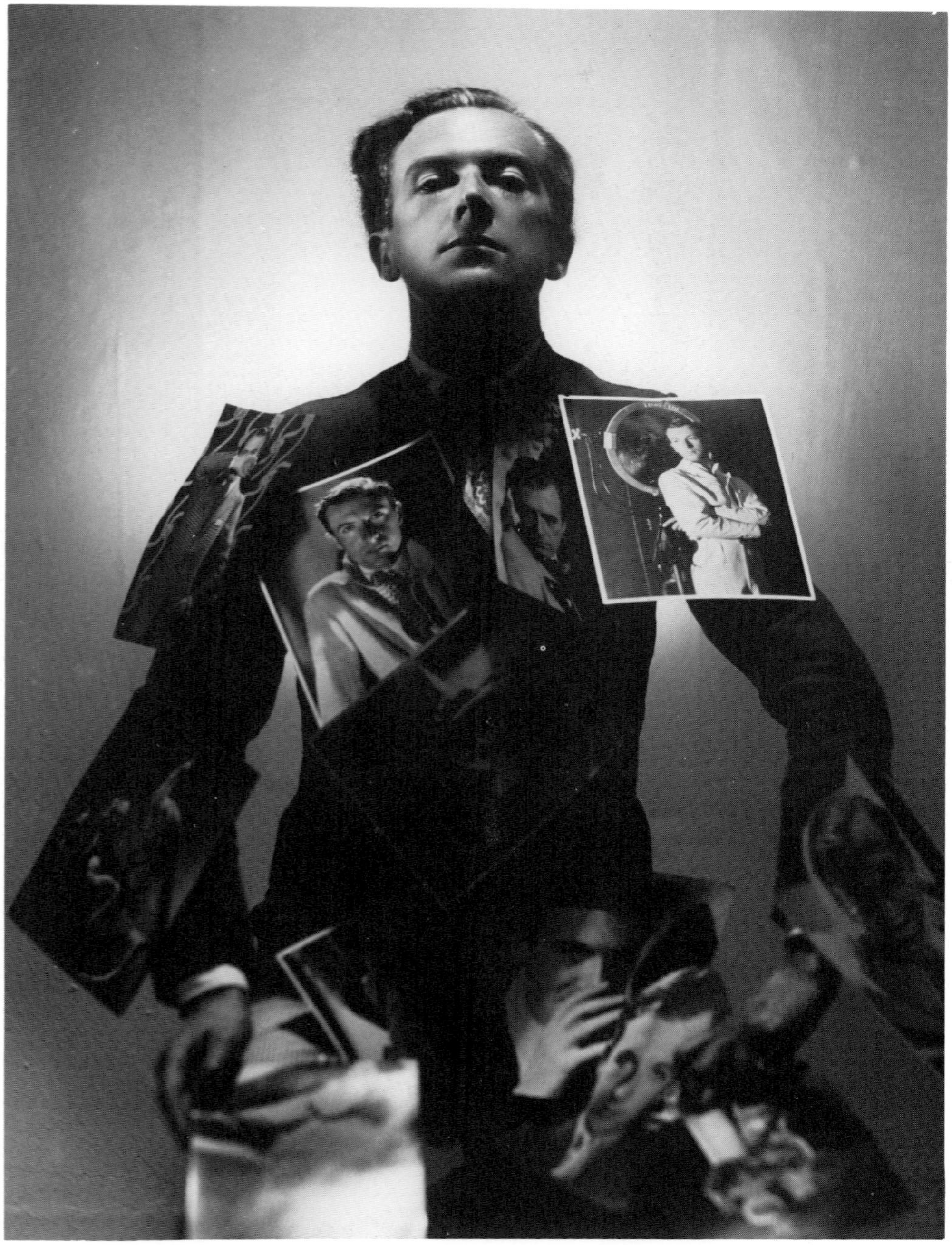

Cecil Beaton Paul Tanqueray.

literally putting spots on the dust marks to mimic the grain of the print. I use a spotting dye called Spot Tone which is absorbed into the emulsion. Ordinary water colour is not absorbed and appears to just dry on the surface of the paper. I use a very fine brush – No. 000 – to do the spotting. Match the tone of the dye to the print before applying it. The aim is to try and imitate and match the grain around the area to be spotted.

GRAIN

The 'grain' of the print is not the grain of the negative. The negative grain is the cluster of silver particles that prevent light from passing through. The grain you see on the print represents the holes actually present between the grain on the negative. When someone speaks of a grainy print, he or she is really referring to the 'holes'!

You cannot get rid of grain. It is the medium of the photographic image. Without it the image does not exist. It can be less obvious if you print a larger format such as a 4 × 5 inch (10.2 × 12.7cm) or 8 × 10 inch (20.3 × 25.4cm) negative, if you restrict the enlargement to small sizes, or if you use a slower, finer grain film.

BATCH NUMBERS

This refers to the emulsion 'batch' for a particular box or roll of film.

Photosensitive emulsion for film and paper is a chemical compound of silver bromide suspended and held together in a gelatine layer. Gelatine is made from animal fat which by its very nature is bound to vary from batch to batch of emulsion. This variation explains the inconsistent results between different batches of film or paper.

You will find, as I have, that the paper speed and the contrast will vary between different emulsion batches. These variations can be as much as ½ f/stop in the paper speed. The contrast, as well, can vary slightly between different batches. This is really nothing to worry about. But it is something of which you ought to be aware when doing 'print runs' (a large number of prints from the same negative). Make sure you have enough paper with the same batch number before starting a print run. If you have to use another pack or box of paper with a different batch number you may have inconsistent results. Test the new batch before continuing with the run of prints.

CHAPTER FOURTEEN

CHAPTER FOURTEEN
And Finally

Many years ago I had a bonsai – a tree in perfect miniature. It required care to maintain it in its miniature state. The seasonal changes affected the tree: during the summer it was in full bloom; in the autumn the tiny leaves would colour and eventually fall in a little pile at the base; during the winter the branches were barren; and as spring approached the little buds of new leaves would appear to begin another cycle.

The care and attention I gave to this miniature tree gave me a greater awareness and appreciation of trees in their natural state.

To me photographs are like bonsais. They are isolated images of reality enabling me to recognize and appreciate what perhaps I might have otherwise overlooked. A landscape photograph has a far greater impact than the reality of the land itself. A portrait tells more about a person than his actual presence. A photographic record of an event heightens the memory of it.

Alfred Stieglitz proposed the concept of 'Equivalence'. This suggests that there are levels or degrees at which the photograph itself has relevance to the viewer. At its basic level the photograph functions as merely a record of an object or an event. At the next level the photograph conveys to or creates in the viewer a certain feeling or emotion. It may remind him or her of personal incidents or it may capture the characteristics of a person with whom the viewer can identify. The final level is the mental image of the photograph when the actual photograph is no longer in view.

This concept of Equivalence guides my own decisions about what makes a good photograph. The first level is fundamentally a record. The second level is the personal association. And the third is the effect it has on my own perception.

I employ these thoughts when making a judgment about a good photograph. Beyond the record, beyond the personal association, it is the image which I remember when the picture is no longer in view. That, for me, is what makes an outstanding photograph.

It was Stieglitz, also, who was most adamant in dissociating photography from painting. When criticized by painters who said that his photographs were not Art, he replied: 'I don't know anything about Art, but for some reason I have never wanted to photograph the way you paint'.

I do not mind the association of painting with photography – I do not like the comparison. Photography should not have any pretensions to or make comparisons with the other arts to justify its existence. One is not better than the other. It is only the processes that make them different.

Photography appears to be an instantaneous process. Whereas other art forms, for example, painting and sculpture, require a conscious and time-consuming effort, the act of taking a photograph is completed in an instant. It is this idea of 'instant art' that perhaps causes the arguments over the validity of photography as Art. But the instantaneous moment of recording the image is merely the mechanical part of the process of photography.

The art of photography lies in the sensitivity to and awareness of composition, form, tone, and all those other qualities that can be attributed to art. It also requires an understanding of how to use the tools of photography: the camera, camera angle, camera lens, format, exposure, development, lighting. It is the time-consuming preparation and implementation of all these tools that constitutes the time factor in photography. All the elements that qualify a painting with regards to composition, tone, perspective, texture, and general aesthetic appeal, must be considered when the photograph is produced, before *and* after the picture is taken. The finished photograph is a culmination of all these elements.

Photographs endow the subject or object with a magic quality that does not exist in reality. They bestow upon the object a quality of light, a form, and a mood. All these attributes can be created in the printing – this, too, is a process which requires time and effort and which, again, we can associate with Art. It is for this reason that photographic printing should not be considered secondary to picture-taking.

Photography as an art form is open to much discussion. Perhaps this is more to achieve some degree of saleability or monetary value for photographers than to establish photography purely as an art.

It is understandable that 'vintage' prints are few

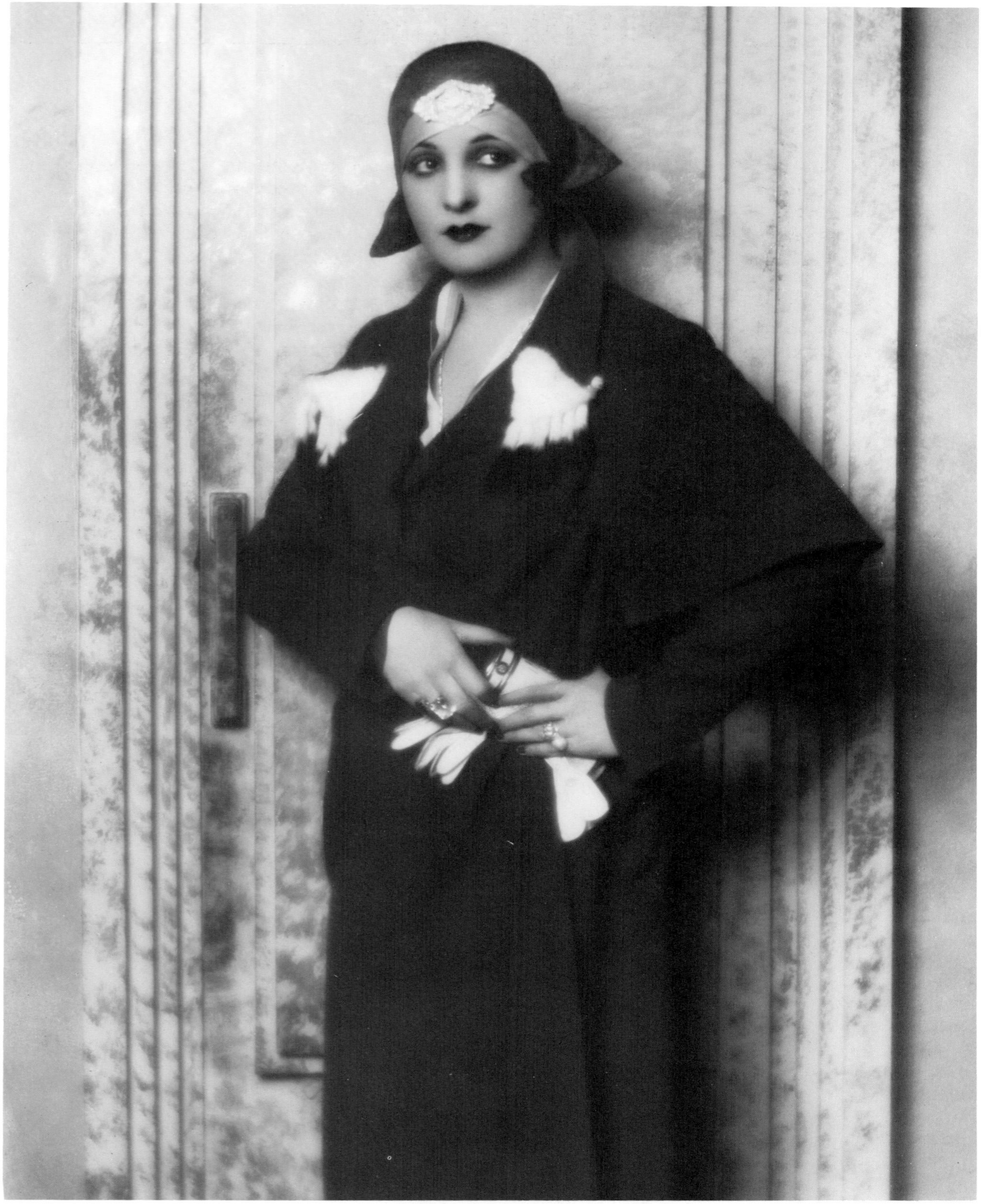

Gladys Frazin Paul Tanqueray.

in number, and for those who collect photographs the rarity plays a role in the monetary value of the print. But I do not believe this was a marketing exercise in those early days of photography. The nature of photography made it impossible then to produce prints in great numbers, and those that have survived the ravages of time are all that are left. But with today's equipment and available materials, it is possible to produce vast numbers of prints. As a photographic printer, the number of prints I can produce from the same negative is limited only by the number of sheets of photographic paper available. This, I suppose, is what concerns those who would like to buy a print as an investment. But photographs should not be looked upon strictly as an investment, any more than buying a radio or a car.

I do think that pictures have a value. My services have to be considered. The general cost of production. The time. The valued ability of the photographer. The value of the 'Name'. But I do not see that it is enhanced by such labels as 'limited edition'.

The history of Man is punctuated with visual 'records'. How much we value a photograph will come in time. Perhaps it is early days. I remember a cartoon drawing of two cavemen: one caveman had just finished a painting of a figure of some animal on the cave wall. Viewing his work he said to his companion: 'It may not seem like much now, but think how valuable it will be in 10,000 years.'

This book has described my personal approach to printing. I cannot endow you, the reader, with the subjective values of my own personal assessment of any specific print and cannot give you any golden rules. The variations are limitless. The examples shown can only illustrate what a change in tone, in cropping, in burning-in and dodging can do to a particular photograph. For your own pictures, only you can make those decisions.

This book can merely offer you some guidance. But what I have learned about photography is from experience. Besides taking pictures and working in the darkroom, it comes from talking with photographers and reading about other photographers and gaining some insight into the nature of their skills. It comes as well from visiting photographic exhibitions and looking through the many excellently produced photographic books. Your own experience coupled with your recollection of the photographs you have seen constitutes your own photographic vision.

In time, and with application, the mechanics of printing – the exposure, the dodging and burning-in, the cropping, the scale and positioning, the tone – will become skills which will enable you to enjoy to the full the art of photography.

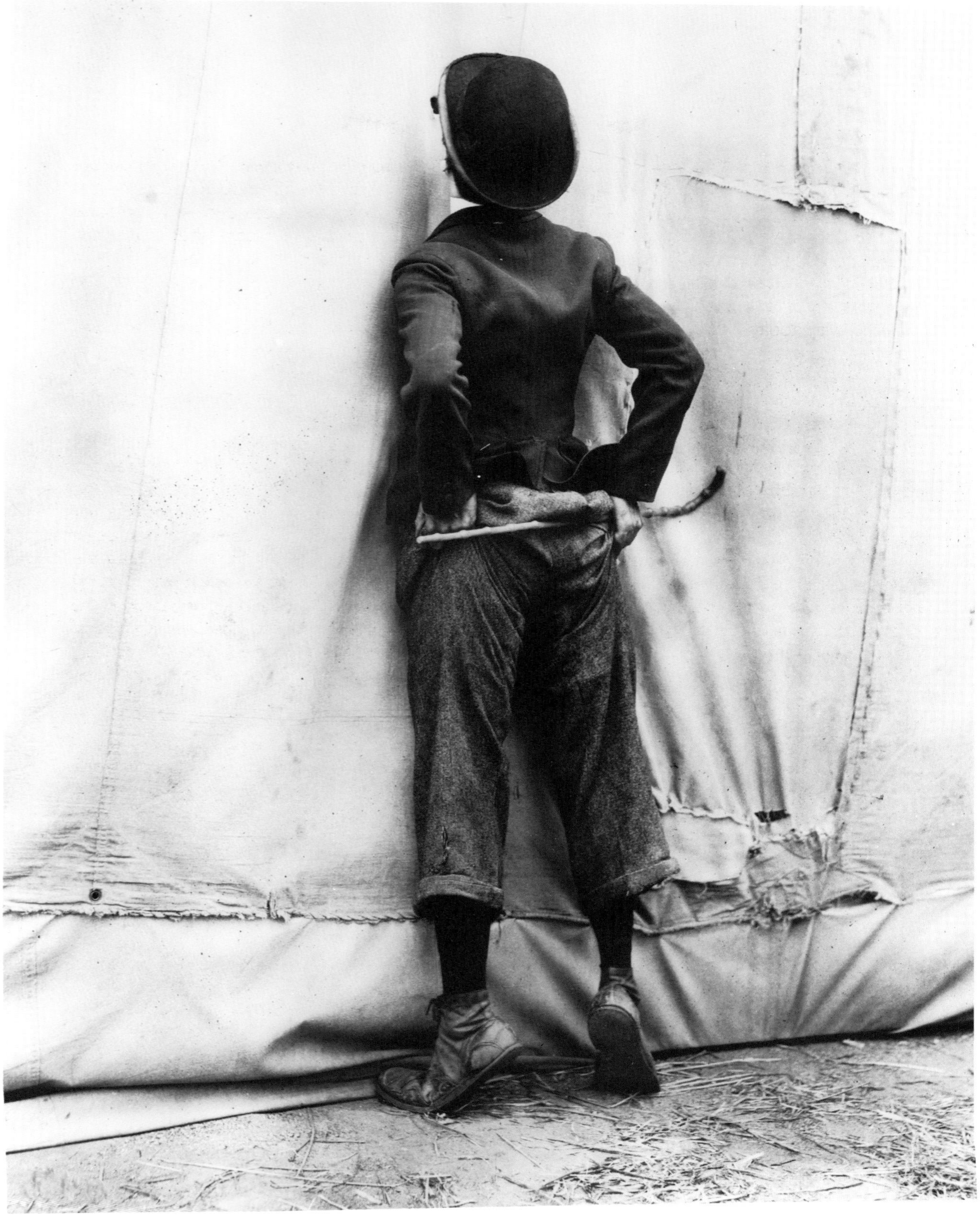

Charlie Chaplin, Courtesy of John Kobal.

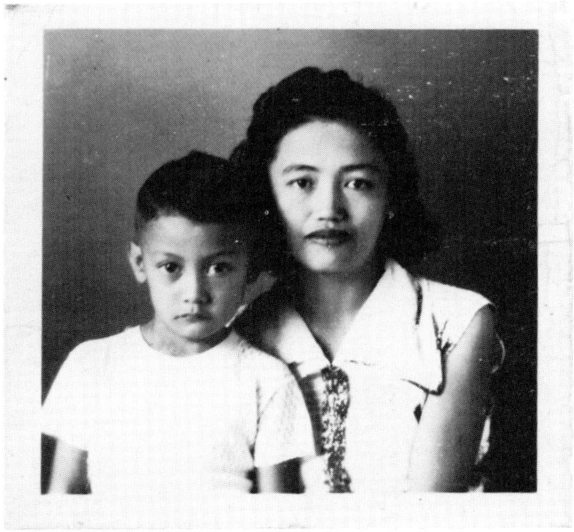

Mom and Me, photographer unknown. This is the only copy and is my most precious print.

ONE
RACER...and the rest

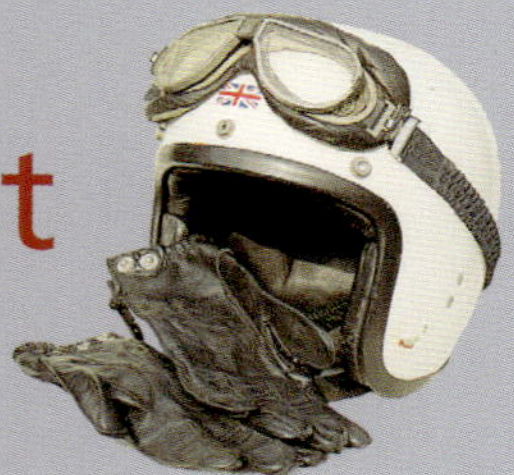

CONTENTS

REDLINE BOOKS

FOREWORD

In many ways Colin Seeley's life and experiences in Motorsport have mirrored my own. He started out with an engineering apprenticeship and he worked in the motorcycle trade as I had done at both the Vincent HRD company and with my father. He rode around on his father's Vincent sidecar outfit but in my case it was my mother's that I rode and he had a passion for competing both on and off the track. His life has revolved around two, three and four wheels just as mine has.

His personal successes racing sidecars on both the British and World championship scene show a high level of achievement between 1961 and 1967. More success followed when Colin retired to concentrate on his development of the Seeley motorcycles. He created the Seeley range powered by AJS and Matchless power units that he continued to produce and improve after the closure of the famous British AMC factory. The Seeley machines were 'the ones to have' if you were not riding for one of the factory teams and successes in British championships, the Isle of Man TT races and the World championship circuits followed.

The 70s brought a new challenge - the move to four wheels and his involvement with the highly successful Brabham racing car team. Thereafter that was mixed with the management of various successful motor race programmes such as working with Norton Rotary Superbike teams, Honda and Ducati.

Colin nowadays puts to good use the wealth of experience that he has gained over the years by acting as a consultant to numerous companies and circuits. What is important however, is that he still retains that competitive spirit and most importantly, that enthusiasm. This is particularly noticeable when he is around motorcycles. Recently I loaned him my MV Agusta World Championship bike to ride at a charity meeting and the sparkle in his eyes and the excitement in his voice said it all.

John Surtees MBE
Kent, 2006.

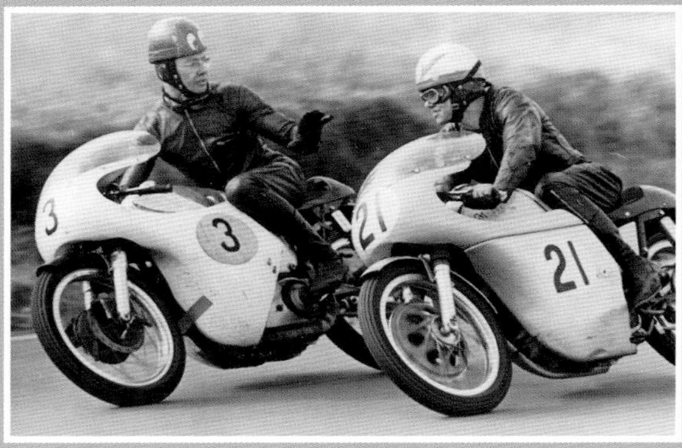

John Cooper and Dave Croxford.

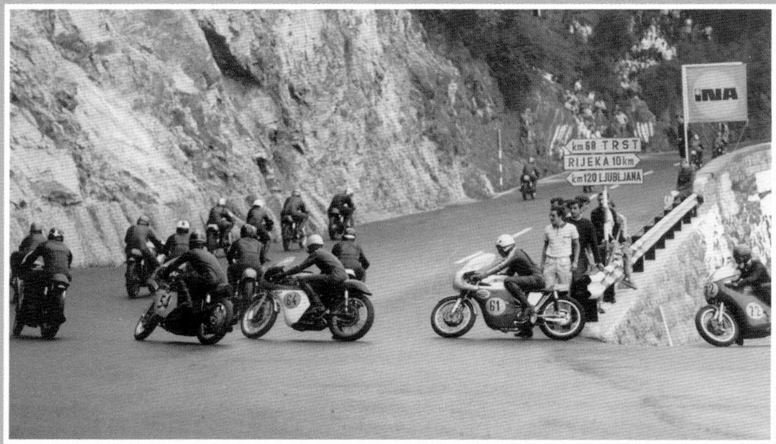

Yugoslavian GP 1969.

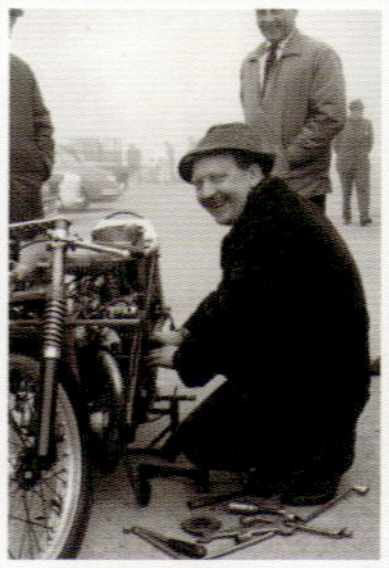

Charlie Rous.

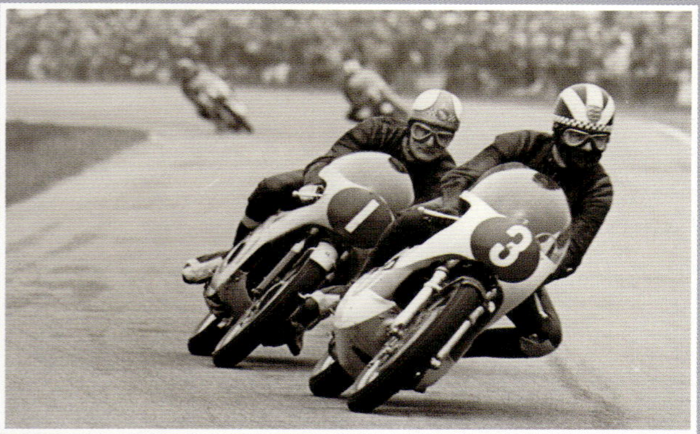

Phil Read and Mike Hailwood. Dutch TT, 1967.

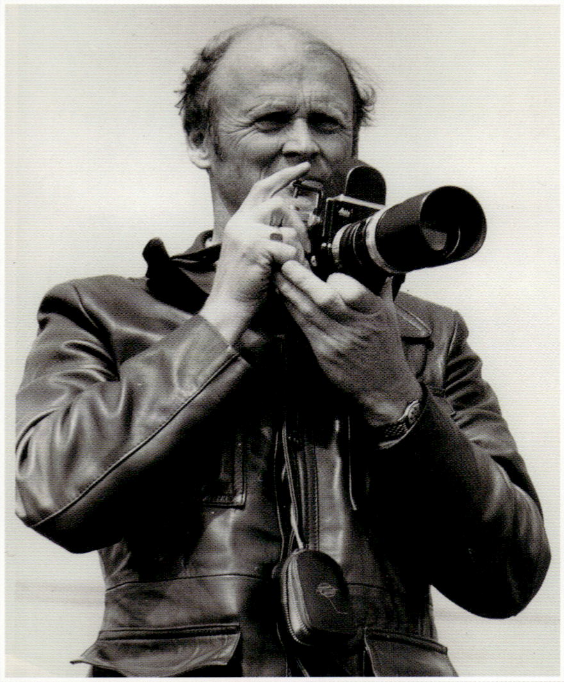

Nick Nicholls.

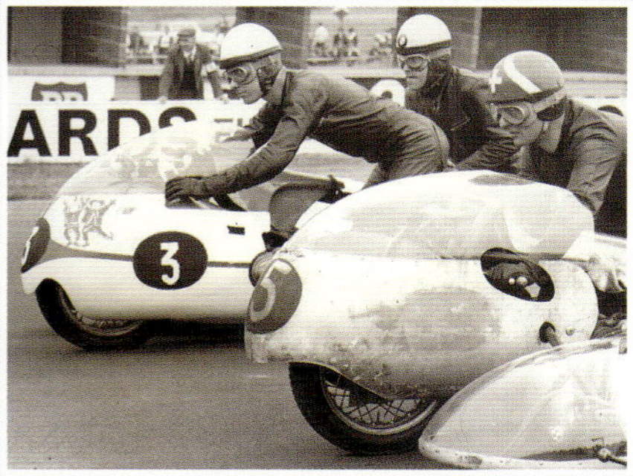

Deubel and Camathias, Brands, June 1963.

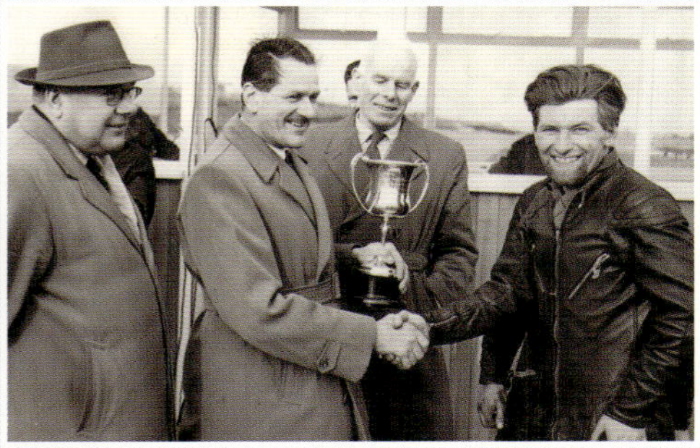

Angus Herbert, Eric Oliver, Les Schwieso, Norman Huntingford, Brands Hatch, 1962.

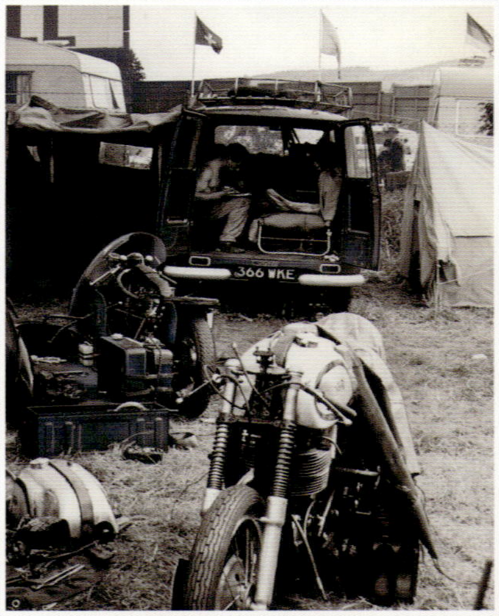

Belgian GP 1963.

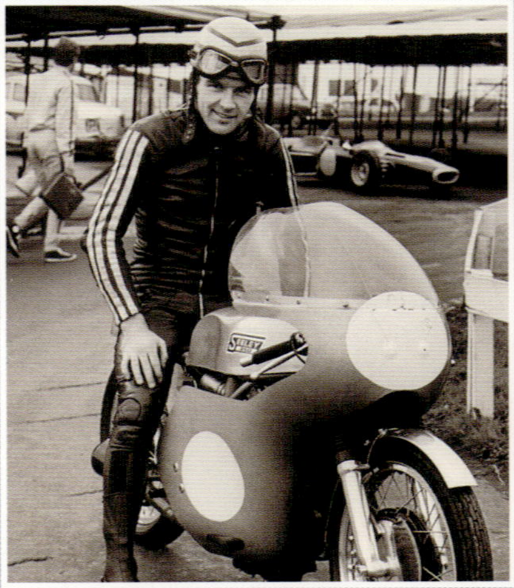

Ray Pickrell, Brands 1968.

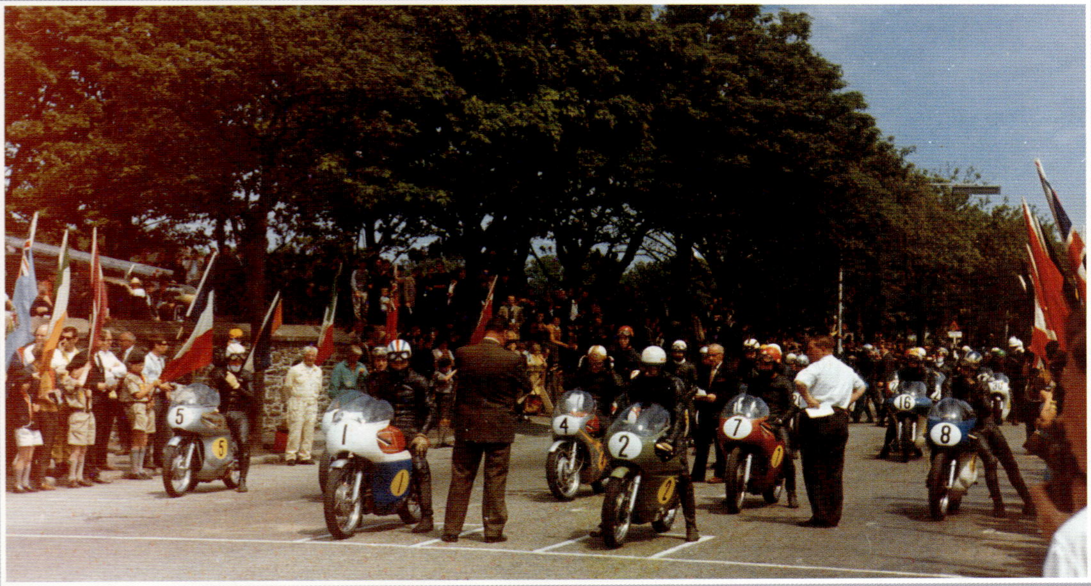

Isle of Man Senior TT 1967.

1 WHAT GOES AROUND COMES AROUND!

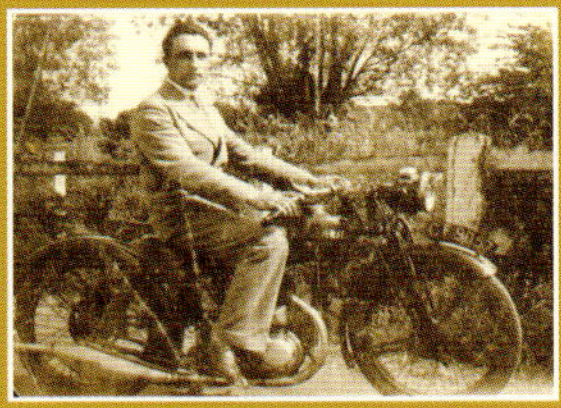

Percy on his Ariel.

The Goodwood Revival, 2001 was held to celebrate the achievements and victories of past motorsport heroes. I was fortunate enough to be invited as a guest rider for the motorcycle section, parading a rare ex-works AJS E95 Porcupine. Off the bike I was attired in period dress for the occasion, looking like an extra for an episode of 'Just William' in full schoolboy kit, evoking images and memories of my teenage years in post-war Britain.

It was in April 1951 that Goodwood hosted its one and only motorcycle race meeting and I was there, eager to see my favourite, George Brown on his 1000cc Vincent , riding to victory. I was disappointed; I left the circuit despondently, returning home to Kent to report to my father, an enthusiastic Vincent fan, the bad news. My hero had been beaten by the new Norton star, Geoff Duke, whose stylish riding along with the superior handling of his bike, had shattered my hopes for the day. I could hardly have dreamed that eventually I would come to meet and to know not only George Brown and Geoff Duke but many other motorcycle greats.

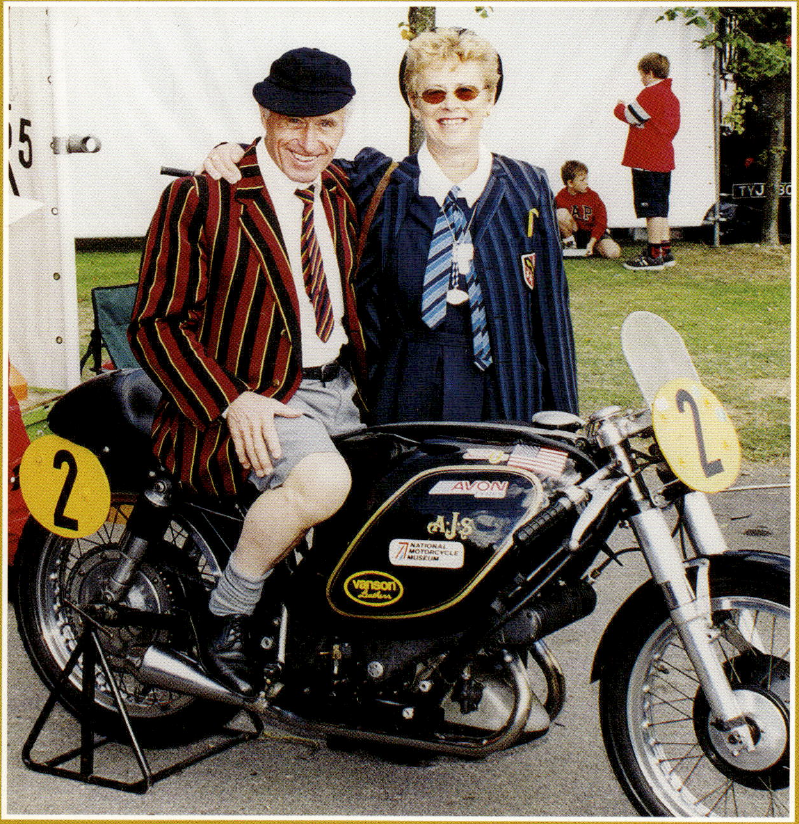

I suppose, now looking back, that all of the ingredients for my future involvement in the motorcycling world were present in the person of my father, whose interests and hobbies had a lasting effect on me. It was perhaps not so surprising that a quiet Kent lad should become so involved in such a demanding, competitive and often dangerous business.

My father, Percy Jordan Seeley, illegitimate son of Mr Jordan, a gentleman's jockey, was born 26th February 1905, not surprisingly in the Suffolk town of Newmarket. I had always thought that Jordan was a strange Christian name, mine being Colin Jordan Seeley and my Dad's sister's name Nora Jordan Seeley. It was not until the end of my father's life that the truth came out. Mr. Jordan had been drowned when his ship sank off the southern coast of Ireland whilst on his way to America to race horses. Percy was 4 years old and with Mr. Jordan coming from a wealthy family who lived in the Park Lane area of London, the name was retained in the vain hope that some money might come to my paternal grandmother. Anyway, Annie Seeley - Dad's Mother, married William Smith in 1913. He had fought in the Boer War and was to fight again, in the First World War. He was a kindly and loving man for whom I had great affection. Percy left school at 13 years of age, with no formal education but having a great interest in electrical items, in particular, wireless sets. He started building crystal sets, then medium wave sets with valves, and finally a straight six valve set with tuned anodes. Sounds like advanced motorcycle tuning! With this new set up and running, he was able to receive radio signals from America. By the time Percy was 16 he had quite a business going, building and selling wireless sets to the local gentry and business people. Unfortunately, at around this time, Marconi started marketing a range of wireless sets, and with his very limited resources Dad could not compete and needed to look for other ways of earning a living. These he found in helping with Grandad's horse-cab business, operating the projection equipment at the local cinema and of course spending time on his other love - motorcycles.

Colin and Eva at Goodwood, 2001.

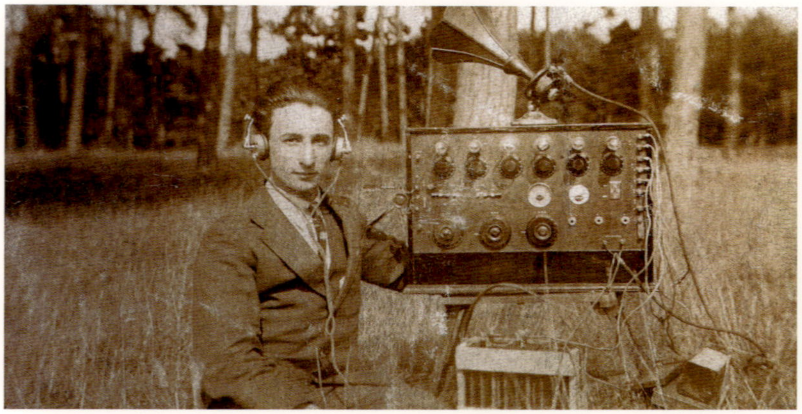

Percy on Newmarket Heath.

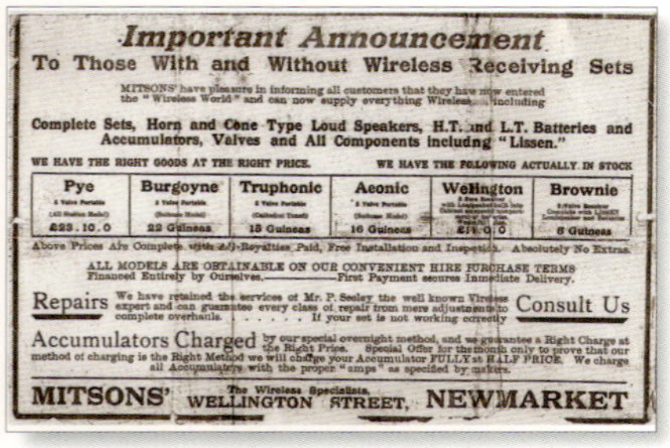

Important Announcement

To Those With and Without Wireless Receiving Sets

MITSONS' have pleasure in informing all customers that they have now entered the "Wireless World" and can now supply everything Wireless including

Complete Sets, Horn and Cone Type Loud Speakers, H.T. and L.T. Batteries and Accumulators, Valves and All Components includng "Lissen."

WE HAVE THE RIGHT GOODS AT THE RIGHT PRICE. WE HAVE THE FOLLOWING ACTUALLY IN STOCK

Pye	Burgoyne	Truphonic	Aeonic	Wellington	Brownie
£23.10.0	22 Guineas	18 Guineas	16 Guineas	£11.0.0	8 Guineas

Above Prices Are Complete with Royalties Paid, Free Installation and Inspection. Absolutely No Extras.

ALL MODELS ARE OBTAINABLE ON OUR CONVENIENT HIRE PURCHASE TERMS Financed Entirely by Ourselves.——First Payment secures Immediate Delivery.

Repairs We have retained the services of Mr. P. Seeley the well known Wireless expert and can guarantee every class of repair from mere adjustments to complete overhauls. . . . . . If your set is not working correctly Consult Us

Accumulators Charged by our special overnight method, and we guarantee a Right Charge at the Right Price. Special Offer for the month only to prove that our method of charging is the Right Method we will charge your Accumulator FULLY at HALF PRICE. We charge all Accumulators with the proper "amps" as specified by makers.

MITSONS' The Wireless Specialists, WELLINGTON STREET, **NEWMARKET**

At 14 Percy was riding a 1904 Minerva, when, on a Sunday trip to Norwich with a friend on the back and another alongside on a bicycle, the front forks broke pitching both Dad and his friend over the handlebars, fortunately without serious injury. Throwing the Minerva into the hedge, all three shared the bicycle for the 50 mile journey home, arriving next morning. Meantime, Dad's mother Annie was pulling her hair out. 'I'll kill him when he comes home. Where is that boy? Dammed motorbikes!' Eventually, Percy walked in through the door and all Annie could manage in her soft Suffolk accent was, 'Hello my dear boy, wherever have you been? Your dinner is ready.' All was forgiven. Nevertheless, father's motorcycling exploits continued, owning a four cylinder FN, followed by a Zenith, Rudge Multi, a Norton and others.

1928 saw a lack of employment in the Newmarket area, and wishing to explore other opportunities, Percy literally got on his bike to look for work in London. He managed to obtain a job soldering razors at the original Rolls Razor factory - many years before the infamous John Bloom took it over to build washing machines. Then, responding to an advert in a motor trade publication, Percy moved on, becoming employed as a motor mechanic with E. Davis and Son in Erith, Kent. His first couple of years were spent repairing and servicing the twin two-stroke Trojan vans and various motorcycles. Meanwhile, the Company decided to enter the radio and electrical business so with Percy's background it was a natural progression to manage the service department returning to his first love - the wireless set.

Whilst lodging in the Crayford area Percy met Hilda Victoria Elsie Ives, they fell in love and were married on the 9th February 1935. Percy was 30, nearly two years older than Hilda, a London girl born in West Ham. I was born at Iron Mill Lane, Crayford, Kent on 2nd January 1936, to be the only child of my parents. As a Capricorn I was destined to work hard for my living! I am told Grandfather Ernest Edwin Ives was a great engineer, working at the huge Vickers factory in Crayford. He was also a jolly good all round sort who loved a drink, but sadly I never knew him, as he died in middle age, from cancer. It is strange, but I often think of him and I would have just loved to have known him. 1937 found the family moving a few miles from Crayford to Bexleyheath for father to manage a new shop opened by the said E.Davis and Son with a wireless service department. Dad was still into motorcycles and now owned a 500 Raleigh Twin Port.

Soon the dark clouds of war were threatening over Europe and when hostilities were declared Percy was either too old or medically unfit to be called up for the armed services. Perhaps it was more important he was retained to fill and recharge the accumulators so that the old ladies could listen to the wireless sets that he had just repaired! So it was 'Dad's Army' or nothing and Percy was appointed as a local air raid warden - complete with tin hat, stirrup pump and bucket. Mother and father made a considerable contribution to keeping up morale in our area by arranging and running regular dances in the local church hall - St. Andrews, whilst the bombs fell. It was total black-out in those days, with shielded lights on the few motor vehicles around. Everything was on ration and everyone had air raid shelters - mostly Anderson corrugated steel shelters above ground, but ours was below ground at the end of the garden and made mostly of concrete.

I remember late one evening when I was about six, I was woken by the air raid sirens. Jumping out of bed I ran into my parents' bedroom calling out, 'Mum, Dad!' but there was no response. I remember being totally unperturbed and raced off down the stairs and into the garden making my way to the air raid shelter. The searchlights were

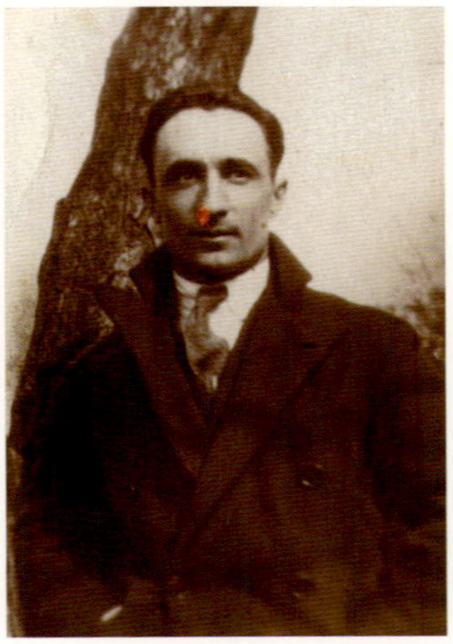

Percy Seeley.

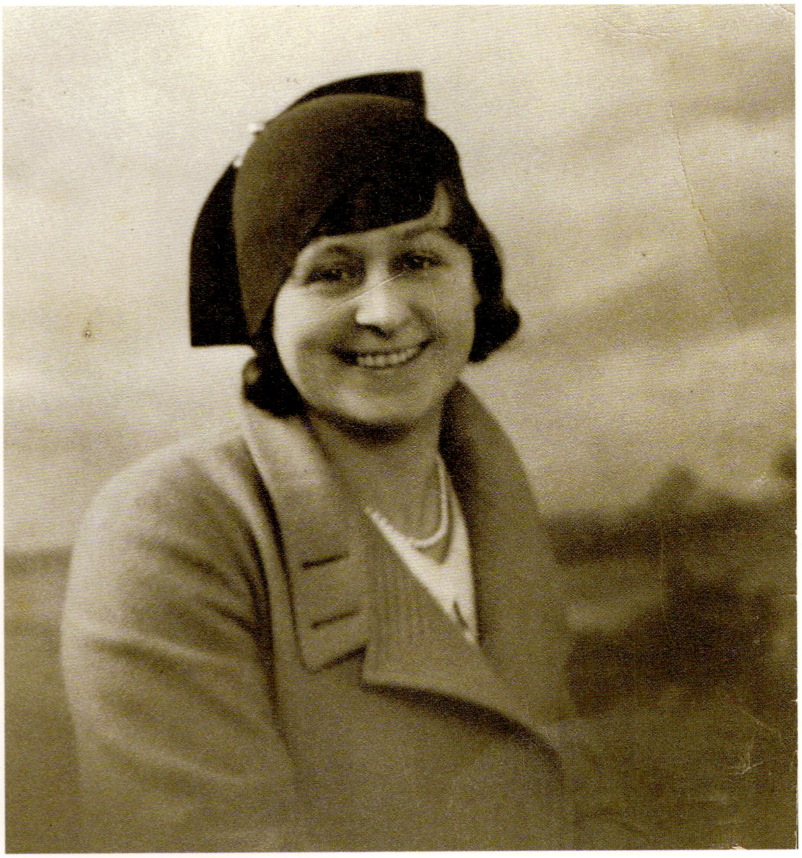

Hilda Ives.

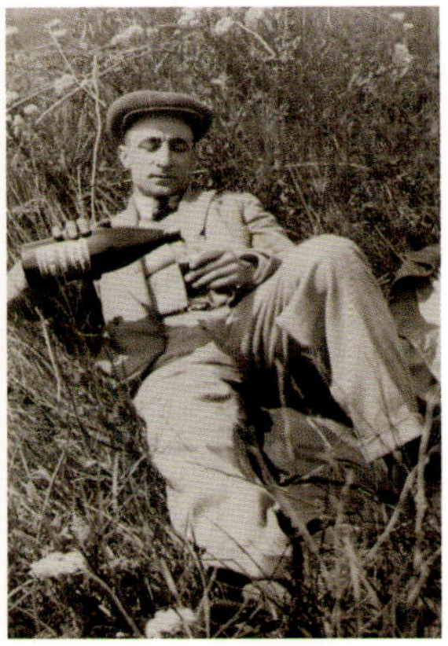

Percy relaxing with a drink after an air raid.

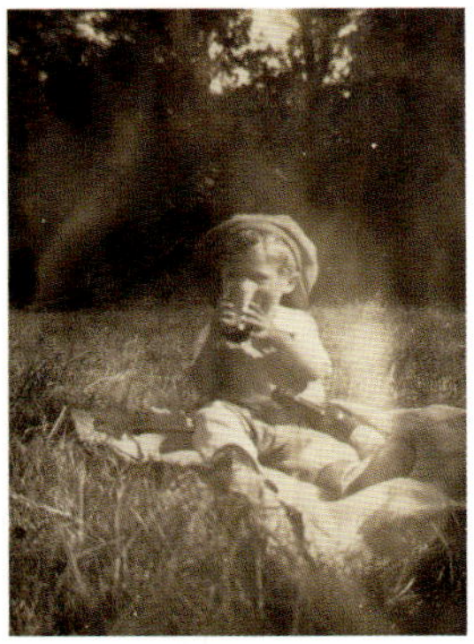

Like father like son.

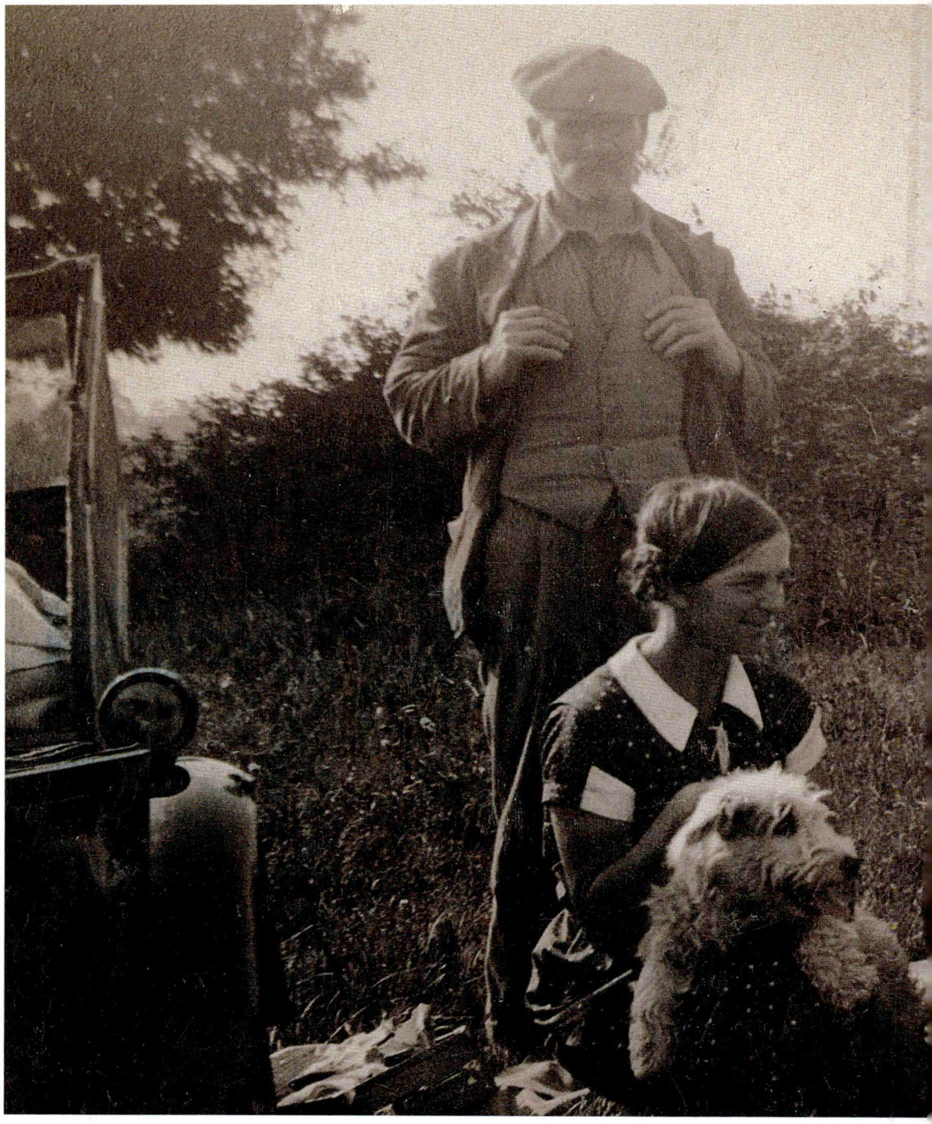

flashing across the sky and the local anti-aircraft artillery blasting away at the incoming German bombers. Safely down into the bowels of the earth I thought it was time for a small drink and raided my father's drinks cupboard. Meantime, an incendiary bomb had been dropped on the wool shop next door, setting the shop's stairs alight. So whilst Percy was dealing with this emergency having the stirrup pump working at maximum revs, I was busy down below helping myself to the gin. I didn't wake from my drunken stupor until the following mid-day. Must have been the start of my drinking habit! What a good excuse, pass the Scotch! Although Percy had built this really deep and strong air raid shelter, he had not allowed for the fact that when it rained heavily the LiLo airbeds, which he and mum slept on would be floating next morning. I was ok sleeping on my high bunk (with the drinks cabinet within easy reach!) Joking apart they were certainly desperate days. Much of our early schooling took place in the school air raid shelters with the lethal 'Doodlebugs' (flying bombs) passing just overhead. The steady drone of the jet engine cutting dead was followed by a few hushed moments - then a massive explosion. However, the spectacle of a Spitfire trying to shoot a flying bomb down was majestic. All of these sounds and sights remain vividly etched in my memory.

1943 found the family once more on the move, returning to Dad's homeland of Suffolk, and the small town of Brandon, less then twenty miles from his birthplace of Newmarket and a similar distance from Snetterton. At that time it was an operational airfield from where the American Flying Fortress bombers flew, subsequently to be the racing circuit at which my sidecar racing career would start, some seventeen years later.

The reason for this move to Brandon was that Percy had been offered a partnership with an old school friend (Harry Henman) to help run his retail business, selling cycles, radios, electrical goods and a forecourt selling National Benzole petrol - now there is a name to remember.

The local cinema was taken over once a week by the authorities for Italian prisoners-of-war and the same was done for the Indian soldiers, and they invited the local children to join them at the 'flicks'. The problem was that you had to sit right at the front and worse than that, we were not able to understand these pre-'Bollywood' films. Sadly, it was better to pay your sixpence and see the English speaking action. Harry Henman was

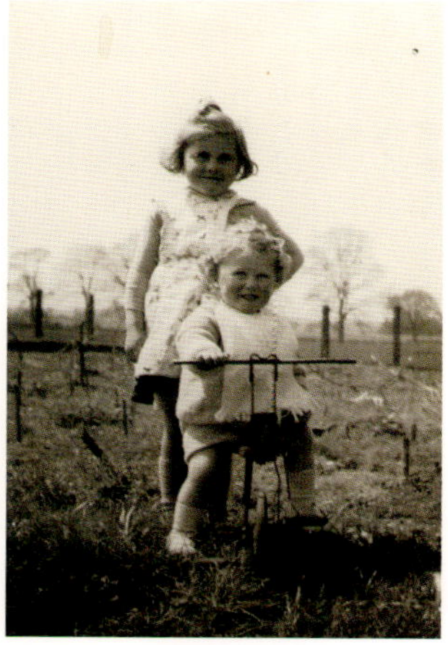

Already behind a set of handlebars, but no pillion for the girlfriend.

Grandad's brother's farm in Suffolk. Me between Mum and her younger sister Win.

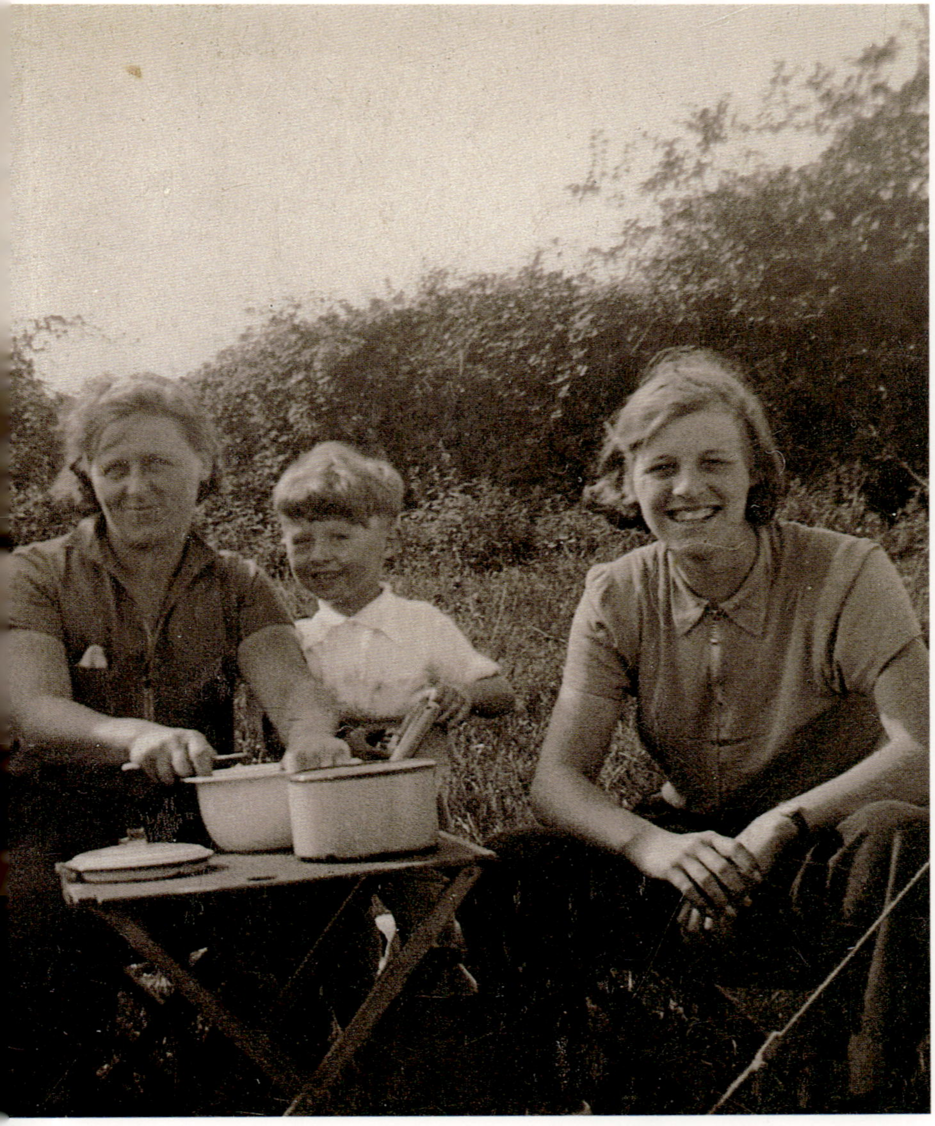

delighted by these visits to the cinema as the Indians used to park their bicycles in his garage area, and the small parking fee generated extra cash. It was an interesting period in my life with the River Ouse and the huge fir tree forest nearby creating great adventures for me, but despite my affectionate grandparents living close by I was missing my friends back at home - London was calling! In August 1945 the war finally ended amongst great rejoicing... Harry Henman had been keeping hidden a large trunk of fireworks for such an occasion and they were used to great effect at the wonderful street party which was to follow.

Unfortunately, the partnership between Percy and Harry was not working out as planned and Mother also wished to return to the North Kent area so again we uprooted, with a limited number of suitcases strapped on the back of Dad's Triumph Tiger 90. I often say 'what goes around comes around' and once more in 1946 Dad headed back to join E. Davis and Son to manage their shop in Nuxley Road, Upper Belvedere in Kent again selling bicycles, electrical goods, radios and now television sets. Our new home was a flat above the end of a terrace shop with a downstairs scullery and outside toilet, no bathroom, Valour paraffin stoves and coal fire for heating the tin bath for our weekly scrub. A mangle and washboard stood in the yard to provide us with an outdoor laundry. Even in these cramped circumstances I was allowed to keep pets. Both of my parents loved animals and so I learned to respect these so-called dumb creatures, having the opportunity to keep cats, dogs, pigeons, chickens and rabbits. Writing this brings back many memories, not all of them happy. I suffered with a weak bladder and regularly wet the bed at night, waking to ice on the inside of the window and a cold wet bed on many winter mornings, a miserable problem for any young lad. I suffered from bed-wetting until I was around fifteen years of age, along with being the worst possible traveller in cars, trains, buses and trams, managing to be sick after only a few miles. All most embarrassing - but fortunately for me my mother was very patient and understanding. Yet on motorcycles I was fine - how strange was that?

The bonus for living at Nuxley Road was another underground concrete air raid shelter and a wooden garage. Percy soon converted the shelter into a small machine shop with his Myford lathe, a wood turning machine and a polishing spindle, a machine on which

A day at the seaside.

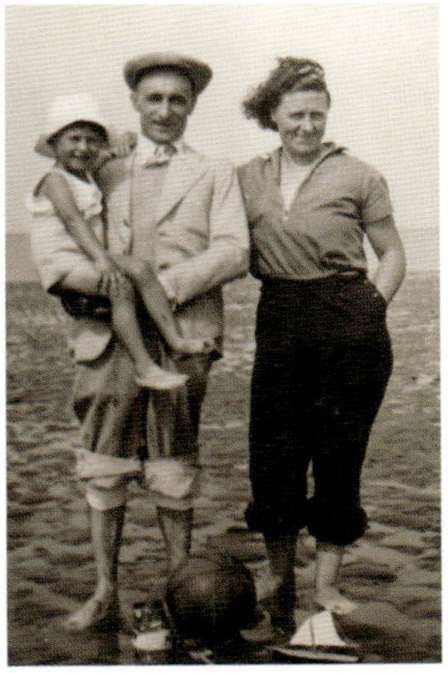

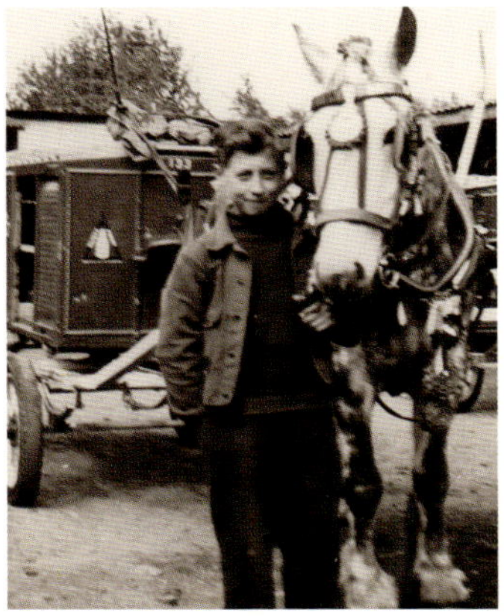

My Home Counties Dairies milk round.

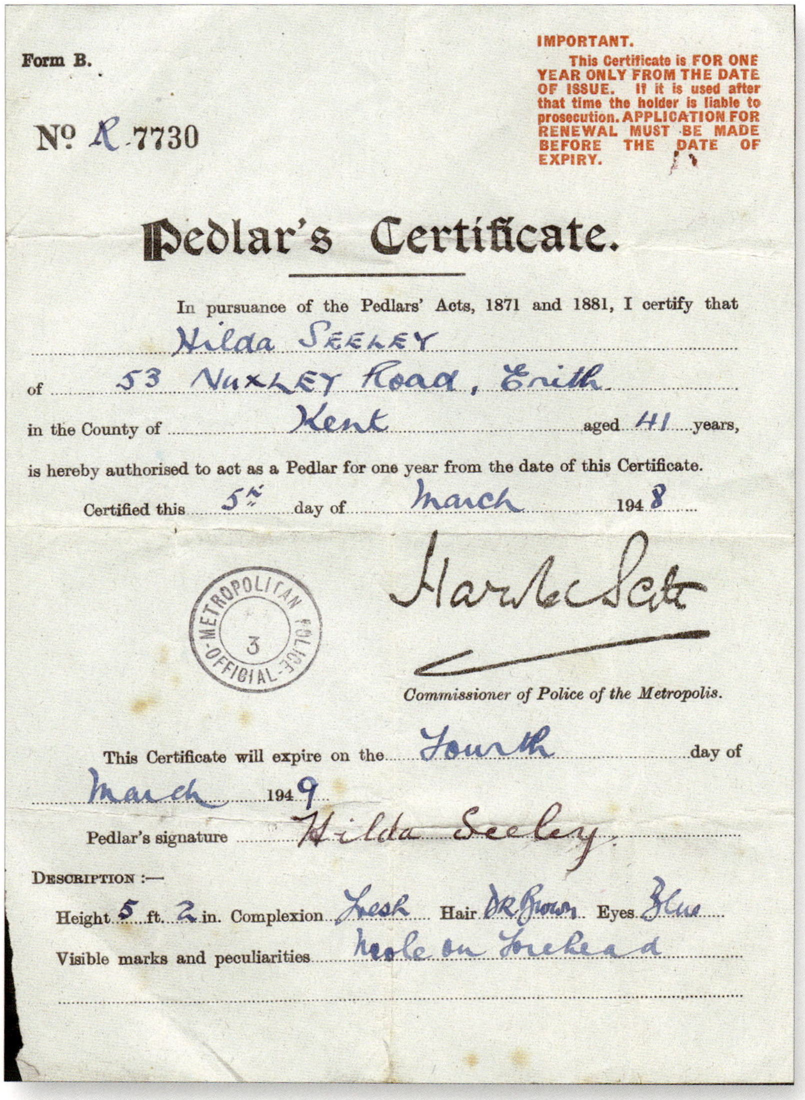

Form B.

IMPORTANT.
This Certificate is FOR ONE YEAR ONLY FROM THE DATE OF ISSUE. If it is used after that time the holder is liable to prosecution. APPLICATION FOR RENEWAL MUST BE MADE BEFORE THE DATE OF EXPIRY.

Nº R 7730

Pedlar's Certificate.

In pursuance of the Pedlars' Acts, 1871 and 1881, I certify that Hilda SEELEY of 53 NUXLEY Road, Erith in the County of Kent aged 41 years, is hereby authorised to act as a Pedlar for one year from the date of this Certificate.

Certified this 5th day of March 1948

METROPOLITAN 3 OFFICIAL

Commissioner of Police of the Metropolis.

This Certificate will expire on the Fourth day of March 1949

Pedlar's signature Hilda Seeley

DESCRIPTION :—

Height 5 ft. 2 in. Complexion Fresh Hair Dk Brown Eyes Blue

Visible marks and peculiarities Mole on forehead

Hilda's pedlar's licence.

I had an accident and still bear the scars! Times were tough for most in that period as everything was still rationed (including sweets) but I remember Grandmother Ives saying that if I did not ever take up smoking I could have her sweet ration. That was an offer I could not refuse and I have therefore never smoked, one of the better decisions that I have made in my life - thanks Granny.

Returning to Kent my schooling continued at the Northumberland Heath Secondary School in Erith. Although it was co-educational, in those days the girls were segregated. We boys were constantly gazing through the dividing fence.

I was of reasonable ability and enjoyed P.E., science, technical drawing and metal work and achieved good marks in class but I was useless at exams.

From the age of ten when I wasn't at school I was always working, doing an early morning paper round and a milk round on a Saturday, helping Dad in the shop serving customers and building and repairing bicycles. Saturday night was a treat, as Percy would let us borrow a television set out of the shop window display. We could watch for a few hours and return it later that evening. To fund Percy's wish to upgrade his motorcycle, my parents produced a range of hand painted butterfly calendars - the bodies turned on the wood lathe and the wings made of silk. Hilda would then go out on her bicycle complete with her official pedlar's certificate, issued by the police for selling goods door to door. This was typical of my mother, always hard working and totally supportive to Dad. She was a generous honest person, great fun but sometimes outspoken (a trait which some would say I have inherited). As well as doing her own job she always made sure there was a hot meal on the table for Dad when he had finished work.

Finally, the trusty Triumph Tiger 90 was part-exchanged for our first Vincent, a 1939 Vincent HRD 1000cc - 'plumbers nightmare' as it was known. Dad of course needed a sidecar, which he could not afford to buy so he decided to build his own. As you may have gathered Percy was a remarkable man in that he could turn his hand to any task from the building of early wireless sets, general electrical work, wood turning, metal turning, carpentry, mechanics, decorating, keeping tropical fish and building model aircraft. The list goes on. Many years later at the age of 80 Percy was still climbing a ladder to work on his cottage.

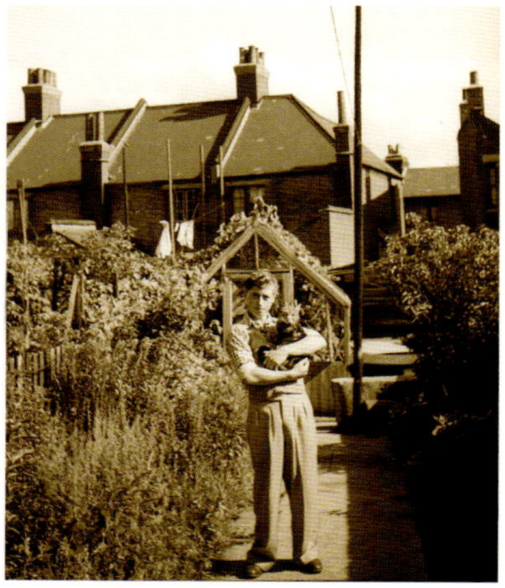

Outside the underground air raid shelter workshop at Belvedere.

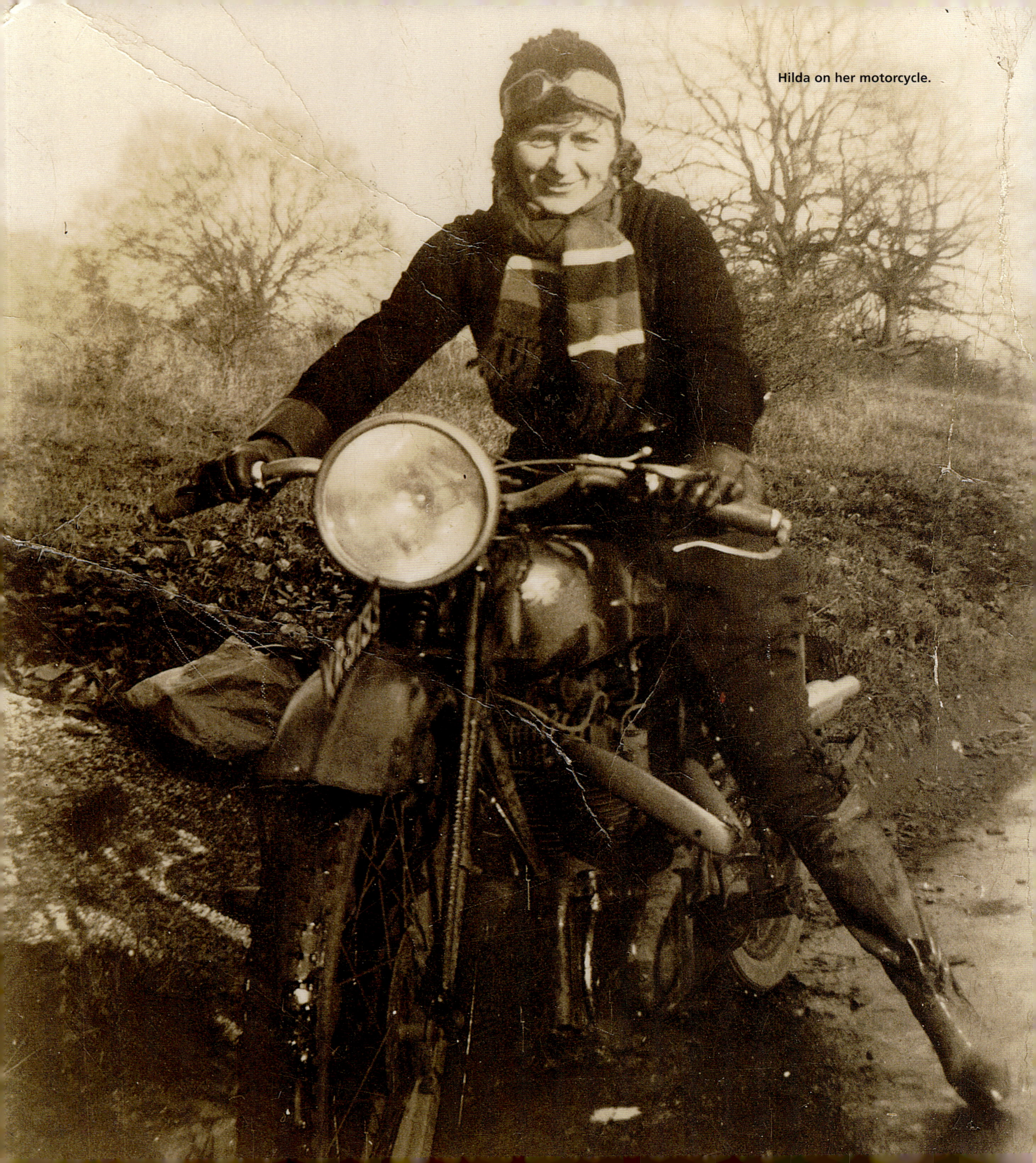

Hilda on her motorcycle.

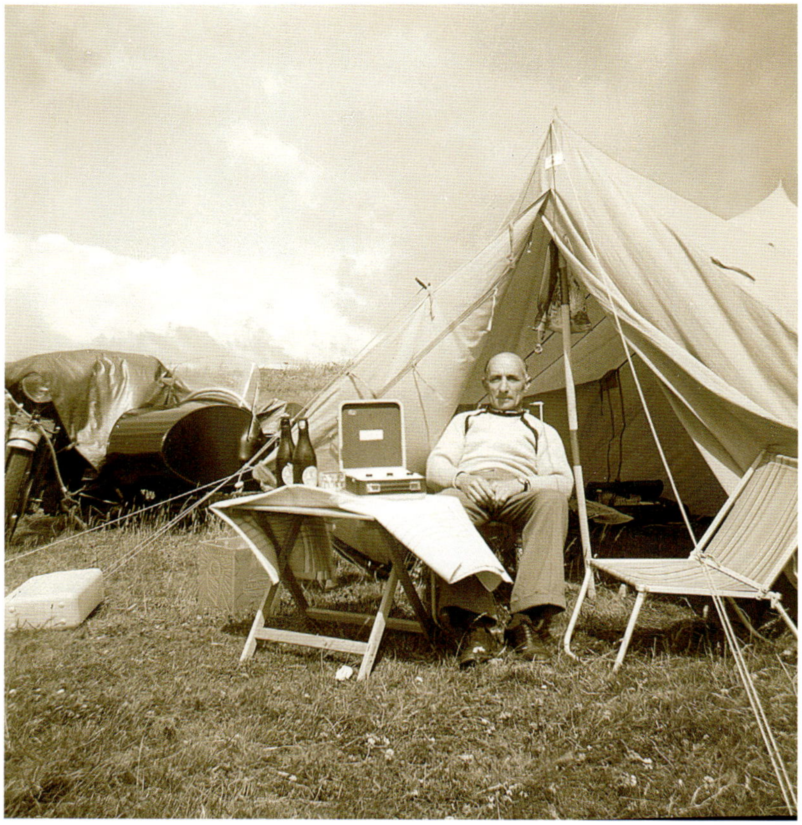

Percy and his HRD, camping at Lulworth Cove

With his plans drawn up for a sports single-seater sidecar with a sprung wheel chassis, a start was made working in the wooden garage now taken over by the impressive and gleaming HRD. In those days Percy did not have the benefit of acetylene and oxygen-welding bottles so used an old fashion large paraffin blow-lamp and a brazing hearth. These blow-lamps were not too safe and Percy did manage to have one blow up in his face resulting in scars on his neck that remained visible for the rest of his life. After many days and nights of work the finished product emerged into the sunlight. The timber-framed, metal covered sidecar looked fantastic and the sprung wheel chassis was a work of art.

Now at around 14 years of age with the sidecar outfit in action and our shared interest in model aircraft, we joined the Dartford Model Flying Club which met each Sunday on Dartford Heath.

Apart from the flying I really enjoyed these visits as I learned to ride the Vincent outfit - it was so exciting and great fun. Percy was such a good father - he had infinite patience and involved me in all of his hobbies. He was a generous, friendly man, willing to help anyone who was in trouble. He gave me so much encouragement and his teaching was invaluable. He even trusted me with his beloved Vincent-HRD. Although he was concerned for my safety, he would always be supportive.

In winter time Percy would completely strip the Vincent-HRD engine, 'decoking', replacing parts and rebuilding it with all external covers polished, so the unit looked immaculate when finished ready for the spring. With the shop closed on a Thursday afternoon, Percy would often ride to the Vincent-HRD factory at Stevenage to buy spares. On one trip he borrowed my uncle's Roadholder Norton' 500 and I was able to go with him on the pillion. We headed for the Blackwall Tunnel, when it started to rain and as we rode through the Plumstead area riding the tram tracks Percy called out 'hold on' because it was so slippery. His words had hardly left his lips when down we went in a heap, without injury, luckily, as flat caps do not give much protection. So much for the 'Road Holder' Norton. It was my first motorcycle crash but, fortunately there were not too many to follow. For me it was just one of the wonderful memories and experiences gained by having such an exciting and resourceful father.

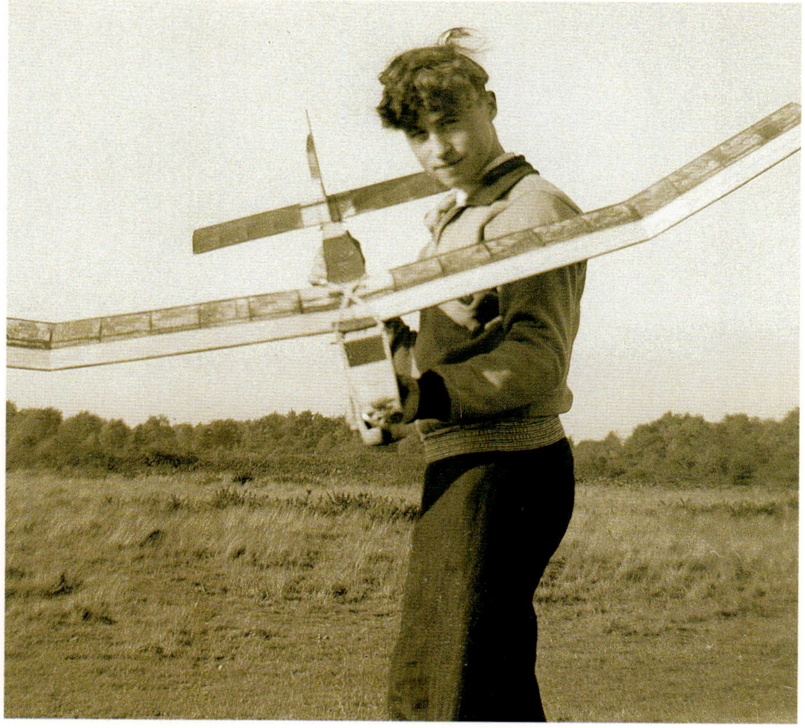

Model aeroplane flying on Dartford Heath.

Percy's sprung sidecar wheel.

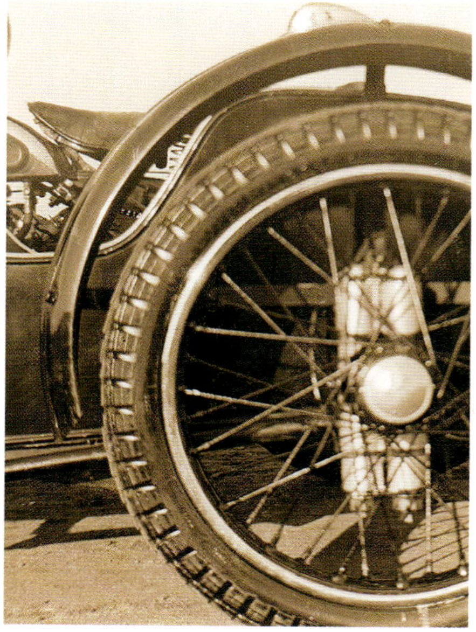

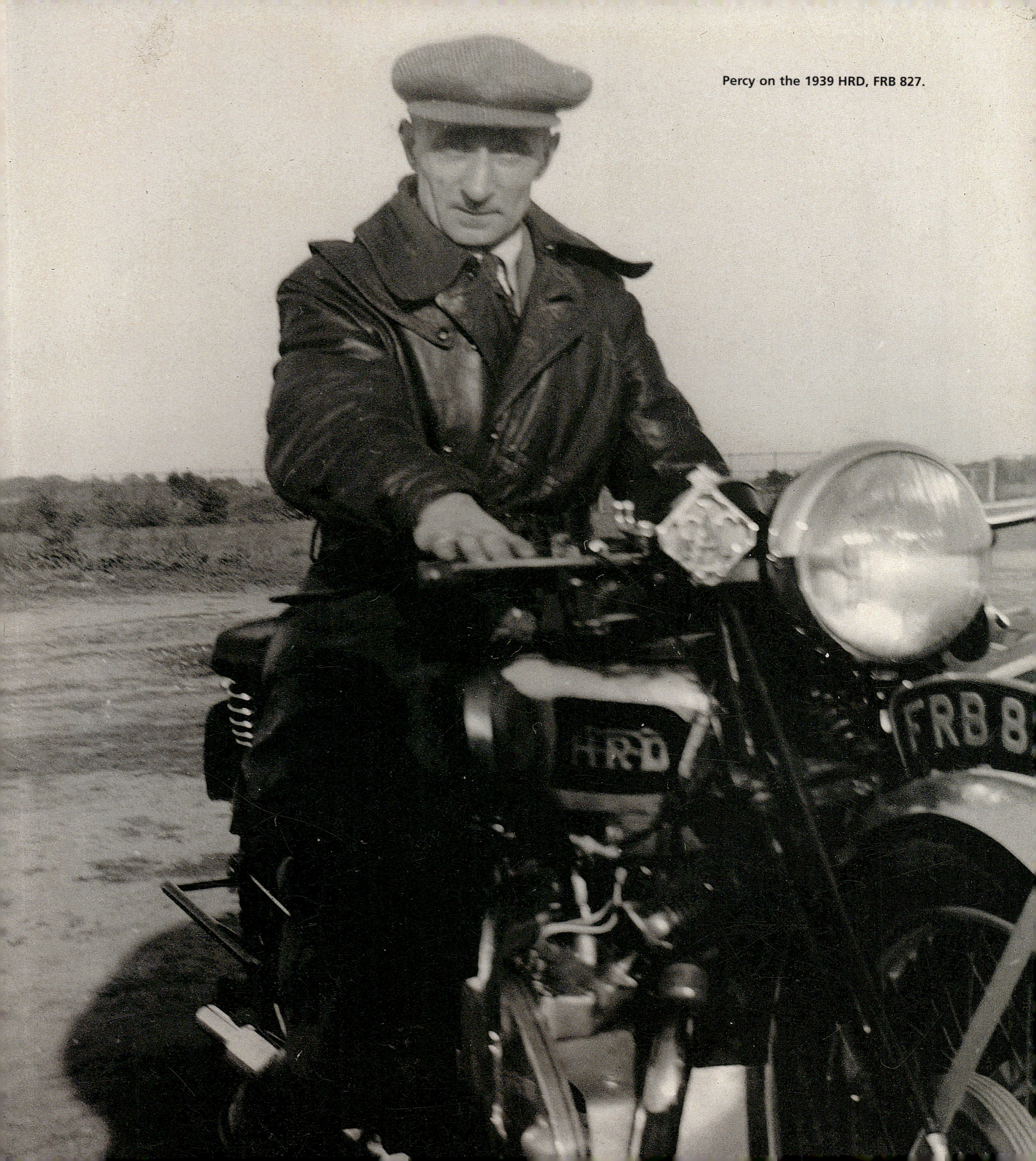

Percy on the 1939 HRD, FRB 827.

2 THANK YOU HALFORDS!

Meanwhile, working with Dad, I was becoming more and more involved with motorcycles. They soon started creeping into my schoolwork so that before I was fifteen I was writing technical accounts of the workings of our Vincent-HRD. This gave Mr Wedlock, my English teacher, a bit of a headache as he had no idea whether or not my writing was accurate. However, he must have seen something in it, as later on he brought his car, a Bond Mini three wheeler, to be serviced.

The North Heath School, as it was known, produced some very successful pupils, one being my classroom mate Doug Salmon, who is still a friend. He recently sold his very successful fine sheet metal company supplying the aircraft industry. Now he enjoys his two historic Bentley cars and travels the world.

I left school with no qualifications other than a fair assessment given by the headmaster, Mr. Pardy. I had planned to serve an apprenticeship in engineering (turner and fitter) joining the massive Frazier and Chalmers works in Erith. Needing to fill in time before I could start my apprenticeship at 16, I was placed in the marine office, which dealt with work carried out for the Ark Royal and other aircraft carriers, at £1. 25 per week. This Company employed hundreds of workers and had massive machinery and its own foundry. Meantime, I attended a weekly day class at the local technical college. In those days everyone rode bicycles to work. This company was just one example of many of the foremost firms throughout the British Isles who for the war effort were just fantastic in their patriotism. Design and production all happened without the use of any computers or sophisticated machinery we have today. I have always been fascinated by those war efforts and subsequent manufacturing achievements.

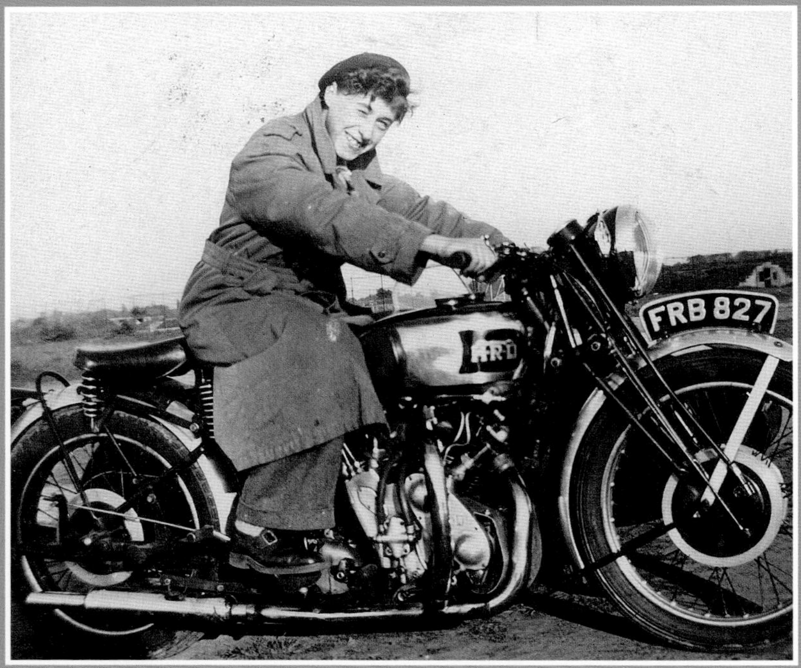

As my 16th birthday approached I was looking forward to receiving my provisional motorcycle licence, which would allow me to take the Vincent out on the road. I could hardly wait. My real passion in life was motorcycles and I therefore decided not to proceed with my apprenticeship - something I have partly regretted as it would have given me a better grounding for things to come.

Then with a family camping holiday planned at Lulworth Cove, Dorset and clutching my provisional licence, the Vincent was loaded up with camping gear and Mother in the sidecar. I donned my Corker crash helmet and took charge of the handlebars and the throttle. I kicked the beast into life and with Percy on the pillion we proudly left Belvedere on our holiday adventure. Some adventure it turned out to be as we only managed to get as far as Orpington - some ten miles - before the HRD started to collapse in on the sidecar. Instead of lean-out we had about a 3 inch lean-in! Totally dismayed we returned home, unloaded, then out came the fearsome blowtorch to straighten and strengthen the offending part of the chassis. Percy got it in the ear from Hilda, as no food or drink had been left in the house. Never mind, it was just one of those metal fatigue failures which was soon overcome, and with no further trouble, a good holiday was had by all.

With a picture clear in my mind as to my future, I jumped on my bike, as Norman Tebbit would say, and cycled round all the motorcycle dealers in the area in the hope of getting employment. It was very difficult. Nobody seemed to want this pathetic looking little boy with his rusty bicycle.

Me on the HRD, Dartford Heath.

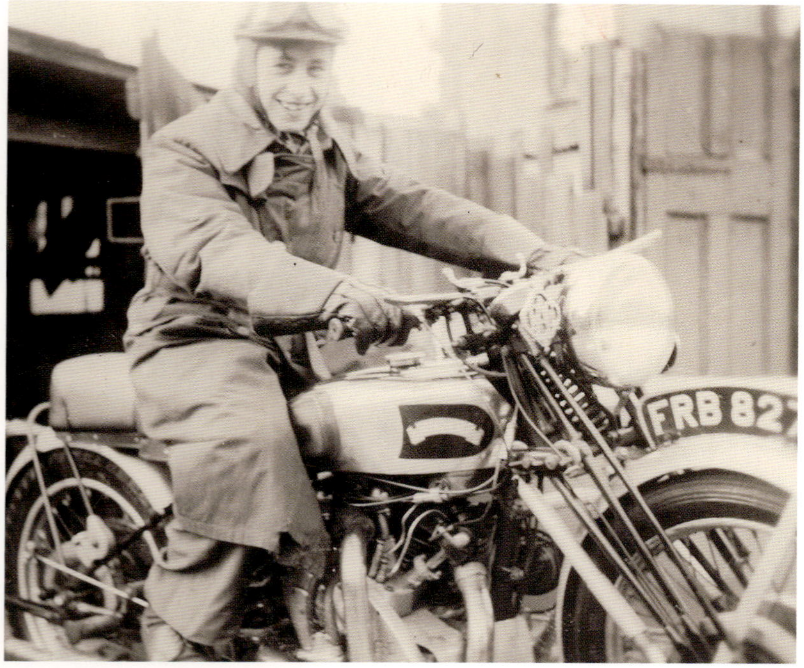

Setting out on my own for the first time without 'L' plates.

Finally, I struck lucky and was taken on at Harcourt Motorcycles situated in The Broadway, Bexleyheath - following in the footsteps of a certain Mr. B.C. Ecclestone, who by then had moved across the road to rent part of the Compton and Fuller car show room to sell motorcycles. Then later, with Fuller gone, Mr Ecclestone took over the whole operation trading as Compton and Ecclestone - the very start of the Bernie 'Titch' Ecclestone empire.

Armed with my provisional motorcycle driving licence I was, when allowed by Percy, eager and excited to ride the Vincent outfit, as I no longer needed supervision on the public roads. I soon joined the local Erith and District Motorcycle Club and proudly turned up on club nights with the gleaming Vincent. It was at this club that I was to meet Wally Rawlings, known as 'Gungy' Wal and his group of friends; Peter Morecock, Johnny Mack and Joe Chipperfield, all Belvedere boys apart from Wally who lived in Sidcup. The Club arranged a good number of 'club' runs, mostly on a Sunday to the South Coast. We returned on the old A20 to the Oakdene Cafe at the bottom of Wrotham Hill, this cafe being still around to this day. Club members would congregate at this venue on a Sunday night and most summer evenings, often just to sample the Oakdene's speciality, the piping hot 'All-on' consisting of ham, eggs, chips, beans and anything else that could be crammed on the plate. The food was just great and could even be smelt as you headed down Wrotham Hill. The Oakdene Cafe in those days was the vantage point for viewing the 'ton-up-boys' in the A20 action and there were a good number of those in our club. They included Gungy Wal and Johnny Mack with their 500 Ariel Red Hunters. Johnny's Ariel was highly tuned and immaculate fitted with a proper lighting system and dual seat with room for his long-suffering wife Joy. It must have been a nightmare riding with Johnny, flat out most of the time like a low flying stunt plane. Wally Rawlings' Ariel was different - not particularly clean, cycle lamps lighting, single seat (no-one would ride on the back) and the engine part Hartley, the Ariel specialist from Plumstead and self-tuned by Gungy.

Now you might be wondering how Wally got the nickname 'Gungy Wal' - well, he used to ride in an old flying suit, which was excellent for soaking up the oil that continuously sprayed out of the engine. Wally was not too worried about the state of his oily appearance, until one evening on a club run to Southend Kursel, as we approached our final destination his flying suit, fired by the heat of the exhaust, burst into flames. Fortunately, he put the fire out and was unharmed but seemed more concerned that his beloved flying suit had been destroyed, rather than the risk to life and limb. As you can well imagine we couldn't stop laughing, it was just so funny.

Meanwhile the time for my motorcycle test came round, booked to take place in Dartford. Confident it would be a breeze I was absolutely shattered when I failed. I had been so sure of myself. Although motorcycle racing was to be part of my future profession I had cut off some corners, and that is not allowed on public roads, and anyway how was the examiner to know I was to become some sort of racing star in years to come. Second time around and paying more attention, I passed my test. So pleased at the result I sped off to the Oakdene Cafe to pose in front of the waiting audience. The 'L' plates would no longer be flapping in the breeze, and at seventeen that was too much of an embarrassment. Of course there was another well-known bikers' cafe in the area, the infamous Johnsons at the top of Wrotham Hill on the A20. It was nearer to Brands Hatch and it was at Johnsons that the rockers and posers gathered decked out in their leather jackets and chains. We, the Oakdene crowd, thought we were a cut above the Johnson lot and had more riding skill on our faster bikes so would often show off as we raced home from the Oakdene to the Farningham roundabout, when flat on the tank a derogatory hand signal might be given to the sad lot outside at Johnsons. It was at this time that Gorse Hill, the A20 section down from the Brands Hatch entrance, was renamed Death Hill due to the amount of fatalities.

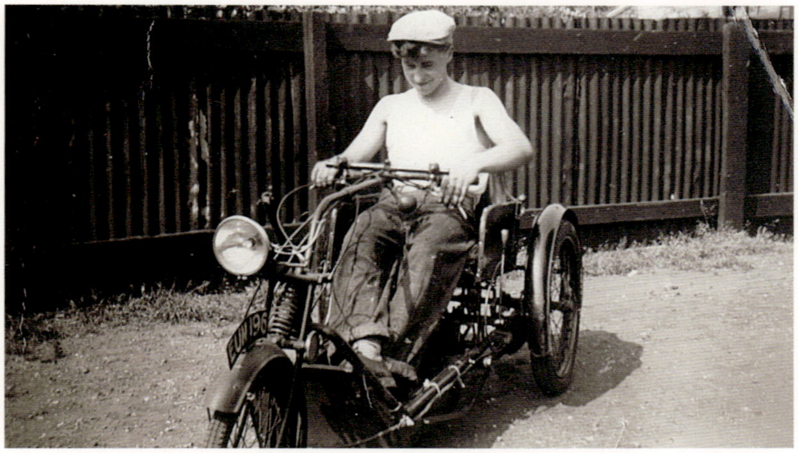

More practice on three wheels.

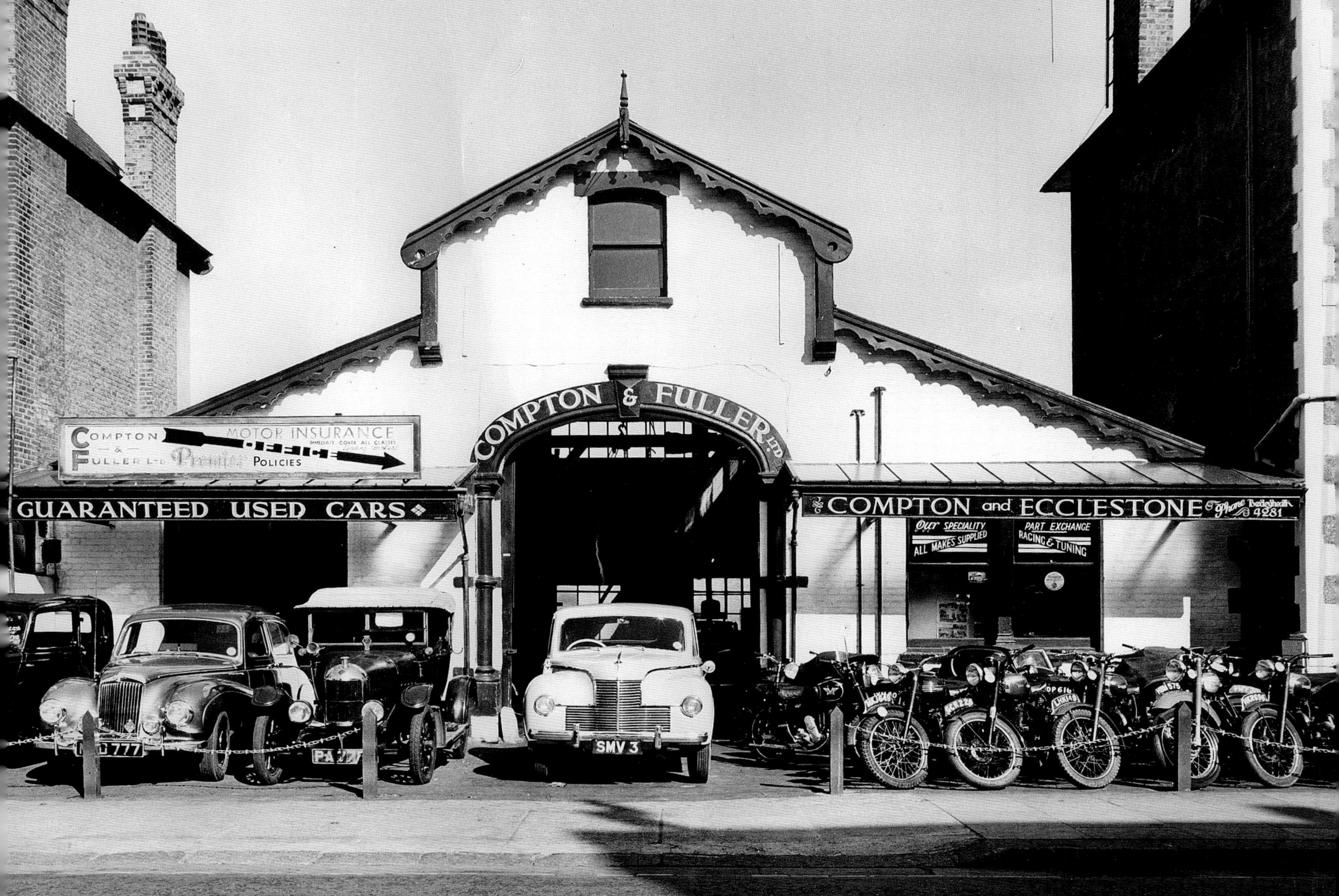

Bernie Ecclestone's first motorcycle showroom.

Bernie Eccelstone trying hard at Paddock Hill, Brands Hatch.

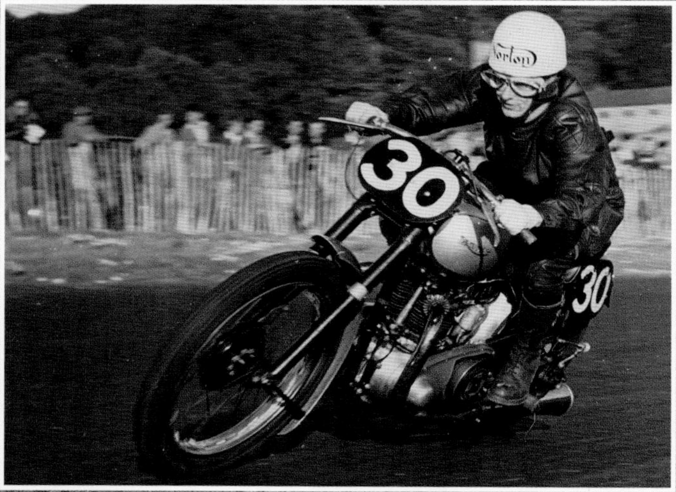

Perhaps I was very lucky not to be one of them, remembering in particular when riding pillion with our friend Peter Morecock on his 1948 Sprung Hub Grand Prix Triumph, we were pretty well out of control as it weaved at speed from side to side on the opposite side of the A20 trying to take the left hander that starts the descent to Farningham roundabout. In the gathering dusk I thought it was my lot as the Triumph wiggled under protest, the cycle lamp illumination hardly showed a glimmer despite the cycle dynamo connected to the front wheel, whizzing round at a high rate of knots. 'Phew' somehow I survived that frightening experience.

Riding Percy's Vincent HRD outfit was just as bad as I tried to keep up with the solo boys, often running out of road with nobody in the chair, numerous machine troubles, push rods jumping out, chains breaking and the cork clutch giving out - on two separate occasions I lost the sidecar wheel due to the axle breaking. 'Wrong material Percy'. I remember at one time, for whatever reason, riding with no sidecar fitted to the chassis and as many will know, you only had to look at a corner and the outfit would tip up, yet I was still racing my Oakdene mates. I often look back on those days and think my father must have been potty to let me loose on his Vincent. I was lucky to have survived that period, but it was to be good practice for the future. The Isle of Man TT at some later date posed little or no problem compared to the old A20 'Oakdene-Farningham' Grand Prix.

I didn't stay at Harcourt Motorcycles for long, as little was happening I managed to obtain a position at Halfords, again in Bexleyheath. Halfords in those days was of the old style with polished brass at the entrance and customers being addressed as Sir or Madam. The manager would stand at the front door with arms folded and if you arrived late he would give you the necessary dressing down. Detailed window displays were the order of the day. The amounts of cycle, motorcycle and car accessories held in stock were immense.

My period at Halfords left an indelible imprint in how to run a retail business, presenting a professional image combined with courteous and efficient service. This work experience probably had the most influence at that time on my future approach to business. Thank you Halfords!

Still keen to add to my knowledge of motorcycles and mechanics in general, I left Halfords to join the Penny School of Motoring, servicing their Morris Eight cars. Penny's at the time was located in Bexleyheath, now the site occupied by the headquarters of the Woolwich Building Society. Working at Penny's I learnt to drive and I passed my driving test first time, which was better than I had done riding the Vincent outfit on my motorcycle test. The boss of the Penny Company owned a Lanchester saloon, which was a fluid flywheel automatic model. One afternoon the foreman/mechanic was servicing this car when he asked me to sit in the driver's seat and rev it up. I jumped enthusiastically behind the wheel and put my foot down. There was a delay, then the fluid flywheel sprung into action resulting in this immaculate Lanchester leaping forward as from the starting blocks, smashing into the work bench with tools, oilcans and parts flying everywhere and with steam coming out of the bonnet. I thought it was time to move on - this job anyway had only been a stepping-stone.

Finally I managed to get the position I really wanted, joining the renowned company Schwieso owned by two brothers, Harold and Les, past stars of Brands Hatch grass track days. Their motorcycle business was based in Orchard Street, Dartford but as I joined them they were expanding and consequently moved to Lowfield Street, Dartford just off the A2.

Harold, the business man, was of portly stature, but always suited and smart. Les like their other brother Ernie was tall and strong looking. He was in charge of servicing and repairs and was a friendly and helpful man. Ernie tended to be a stern character, who kept himself to himself and just carried on with his work. I really enjoyed my time at Schwieso Brothers and my first job in the mornings at Lowfield Street was riding a good number of sale bikes round from the rear workshop to the front display area. This was

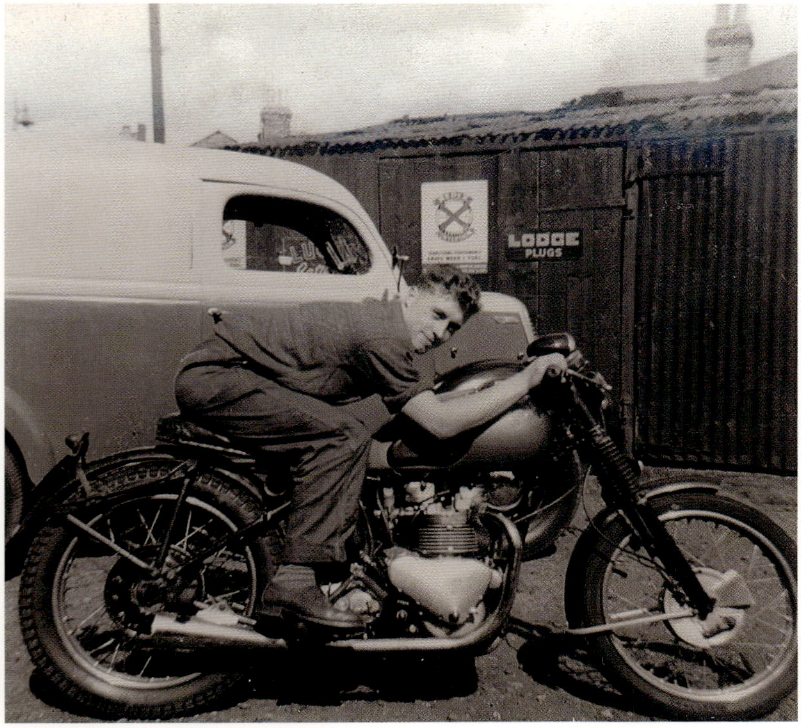

Posing on the Grand Prix Triumph.

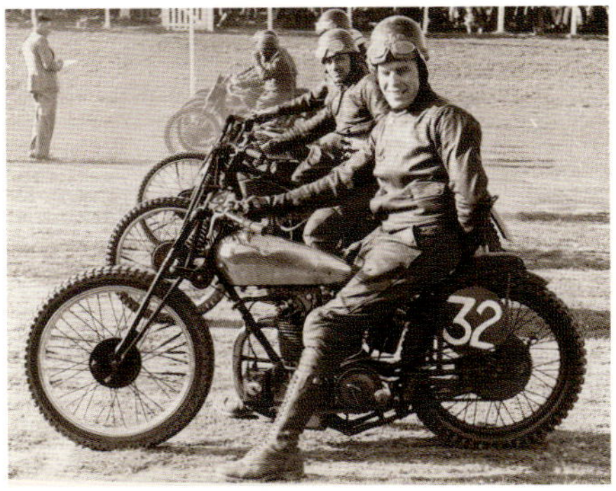

Les Schwieso on the Brands Hatch start line.

great, as I could ride a whole number of different machines and at the same time could chat up the local girls as they went to work in the morning and again as they returned home in the evening.

Working with Les in the workshop was good fun as his cheerful disposition made coming to work a joy. The large workshop was heated at the time by a single paraffin heater. One extremely cold lunch-time Les and I brought this heater into the office area for a 'warm up' - that bit was fine but what we did not know is that something had fallen against door of the office, so it would not open. Les and I were in fits of laughter imagining the vision of his brother Harold arriving with arms folded saying 'Les what is going on - why is this heater in the office?' Within minutes Harold did arrive saying word for word what we had imagined he would say. We thought it was hilarious but Harold just did not have a sense of humour and was certainly not amused. Schwieso Brothers quickly expanded and their business took on many different bike agencies, which gave me good working experience in the service department. Meanwhile now at $17\frac{1}{2}$ years of age with an ambition to eventually start my own business, I had for some time already been repairing motorcycles at home in the wooden shed in the back yard. Whilst working at Schwieso Brothers I had made contact with a friend, a certain Bill Patey, who at the time of writing is 83 and with whom I am still in touch. Bill ran the Joe Francis Motorcycle shop opposite Schwieso's in Lowfield Street and from whom I bought, at a 20% discount, all necessary spares for the repair work I was doing at home, my mother often helping out with a little back-up finance.

My small bedroom at home had become a store room, neatly stacked with tyres, oils, plugs, brake linings and all manner of items which at times did give me the problem as to how to get into my bed.

Looking back I am proud that firstly I never took any customer's repair work away from Schwieso Brothers whilst still working for them and also that I did not take any parts or spares that may have been conveniently lying around their workshop.

With National Service looming, at 18 it looked as if my business ambitions would have to be put on hold. As the medical appointment, one of the necessities before joining up, drew nearer I had resigned myself to the fact that I would soon be polishing brass

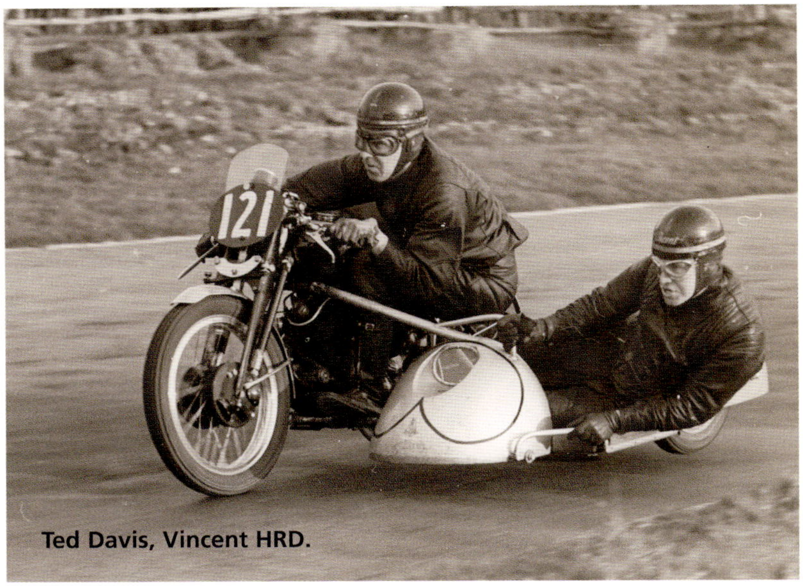

Ted Davis, Vincent HRD.

and painting the kerb-stones white with the rest of my peers. The Royal Air Force was my goal, thinking along the lines that I may as well learn to fly whilst in the forces. So with visions of Douglas Bader, lambswool flying jackets, leather helmets, goggles and shouts of 'chocks away' I went off to the Blackheath medical centre. 'Whoops,' down to earth and back to reality with a great bump. They had thrown me out on the grounds of having only qualified grade four at the medical - what a load of rubbish. I would not even have been accepted for 'Dad's Army' - what a blow to my ego. No going into action, when the orders 'scramble' were given and then flying off into the sunset.

Onwards and upwards my thoughts now turned to my intended motorcycle business, but with limited resources, suitable, cheap rentable premises were required. Luck was at hand because in Stapley Road adjacent to Nuxley Road was the old forge, then used for car repairs, but originally a blacksmiths. Shoeing of horses was still the order of the day - little did I realise then that a different sort of 'horsepower' would eventually take over the forge.

The premises at the time were being rented from the widow of the blacksmith, a Mrs. Ausden and the existing tenant agreed to rent me an end section fronting Stapley Road for 12s 6d per week - 62 pence or about one Euro in today's terms. So in August 1954 I was officially in business with the first milestone having been reached.

In those early days, even at 18 I did not have a motorcycle of my own, so I was still using Dad's Vincent, which had progressed from the 1939 plumber's nightmare to a 1949 Rapide and then a Black Shadow. It appeared not to matter too much as I could so easily have wrecked them whilst racing along the A20. Then Bill Patey offered me a 1936 250 MOV Velocette for £10. That was the good news, the bad news was that the bike was in bits and supplied in a box, so I took up the challenge, finally building myself an immaculate, if slow motorcycle complete with Brooklands Can (fishtail silencer for the uninitiated). The motorcycle repair business was proceeding nicely and meantime

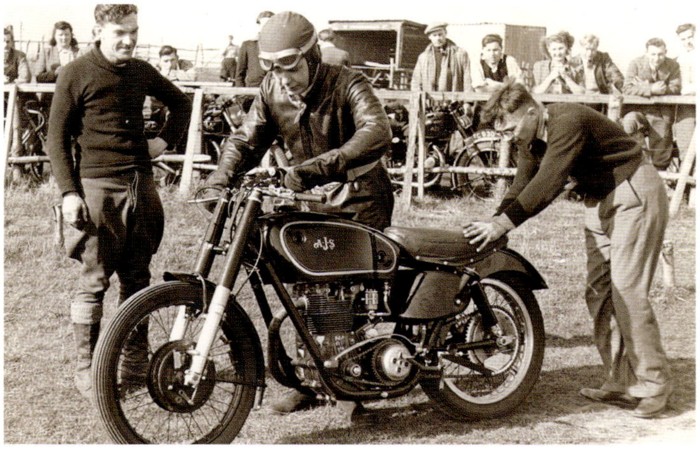

Jock West testing the early AJS 7R at Brands Hatch, March 1948.

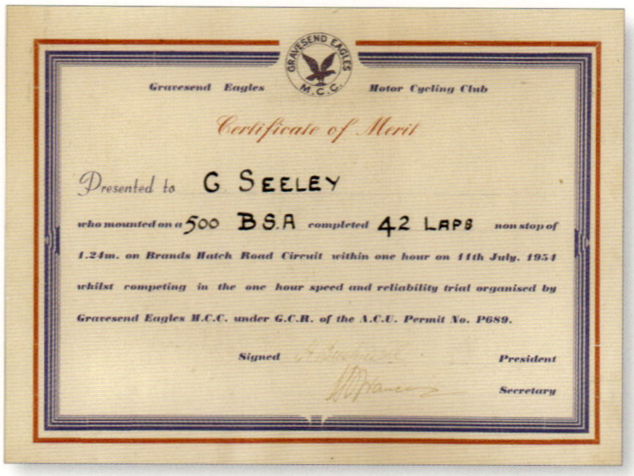
GRAVESEND EAGLES M.C.C.
Gravesend Eagles Motor Cycling Club

Certificate of Merit

Presented to G SEELEY

who mounted on a 500 B.S.A completed 42 LAPS non stop of 1.24m. on Brands Hatch Road Circuit within one hour on 11th July. 1954 whilst competing in the one hour speed and reliability trial organised by Gravesend Eagles M.C.C. under G.C.R. of the A.C.U. Permit No. P689.

Signed ______ President

______ Secretary

1954 BSA Star twin and my first taste of Brands Hatch.

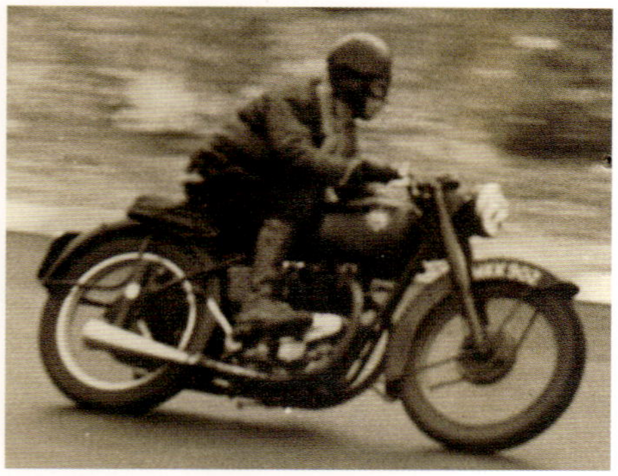

I had taken over the whole of the old forge when the head tenant stopped paying any rent at all to the owner. My transporter in those days was a v-twin side-valve Matchless outfit with a specially built sidecar in which to put a motorcycle. Nicknamed 'The Chariot' I had so much fun with it.

Come 1956 with trade increasing, I decided to open a motorcycle retail shop on the main road and suitable premises were found at 28 Nuxley Road, Belvedere, belonging to a local wealthy estate agent Harold Bennett and his wife Molly. I was too young at the time to sign a lease so my dad Percy decided to join me in this venture and signed up. So trading as C.J. Seeley (Sales) Ltd Motorcycle Specialist our first shop was opened with the Old Forge being retained as the workshop.

Agencies were difficult to obtain in those early days so sub agencies were taken for NSU, Zundapp and Rumi - pretty exciting eh? We also sold bicycles, clothing and accessories but as time passed by we were appointed main agents for Matchless, AJS, Francis Barnett, Ariel, BMW and Greeves.

I often think back to around 1949/50 when at fourteen I used to cycle to Brands Hatch shortly after it was transformed from a grass track into a road circuit going anticlockwise in those early days. Watching the Vincent HRD test rider and sidecar racer Ted Davis in action was inspirational. With the roar of the 1000cc v-twin engine the forks bending as Ted went through a corner in an opposite lock and his passenger hanging on for all his worth was, to a 14 year old, awesome. So inspirational! I watched this action thinking I would like to try that one day, if the chance came my way, not for a moment believing I would ever achieve the level required to race at Brands Hatch.

It was in 1954 I had my first taste of the Brands Hatch Circuit, riding a friend's BSA 500cc Star Twin in a one hour endurance event. Kitted out in a flying jacket, pudding basin hat, RAF goggles, horse riding breeches and DR boots, I was ready for action and achieved 42 non-stop laps in the hour and received a certificate of merit from the Gravesend Eagles Motorcycle Club. My first ever award. I was delighted to have finished and not thrown the bike down the road, you would think that I had just won a major race. Back home I was as pleased as punch to tell my parents how great it had been and how I would like to do that sort of thing again.

Due to the commitment of my new motorcycle repair business my road-racing career was put on hold. However, in 1957 I took in part exchange a 500cc Triumph Trophy

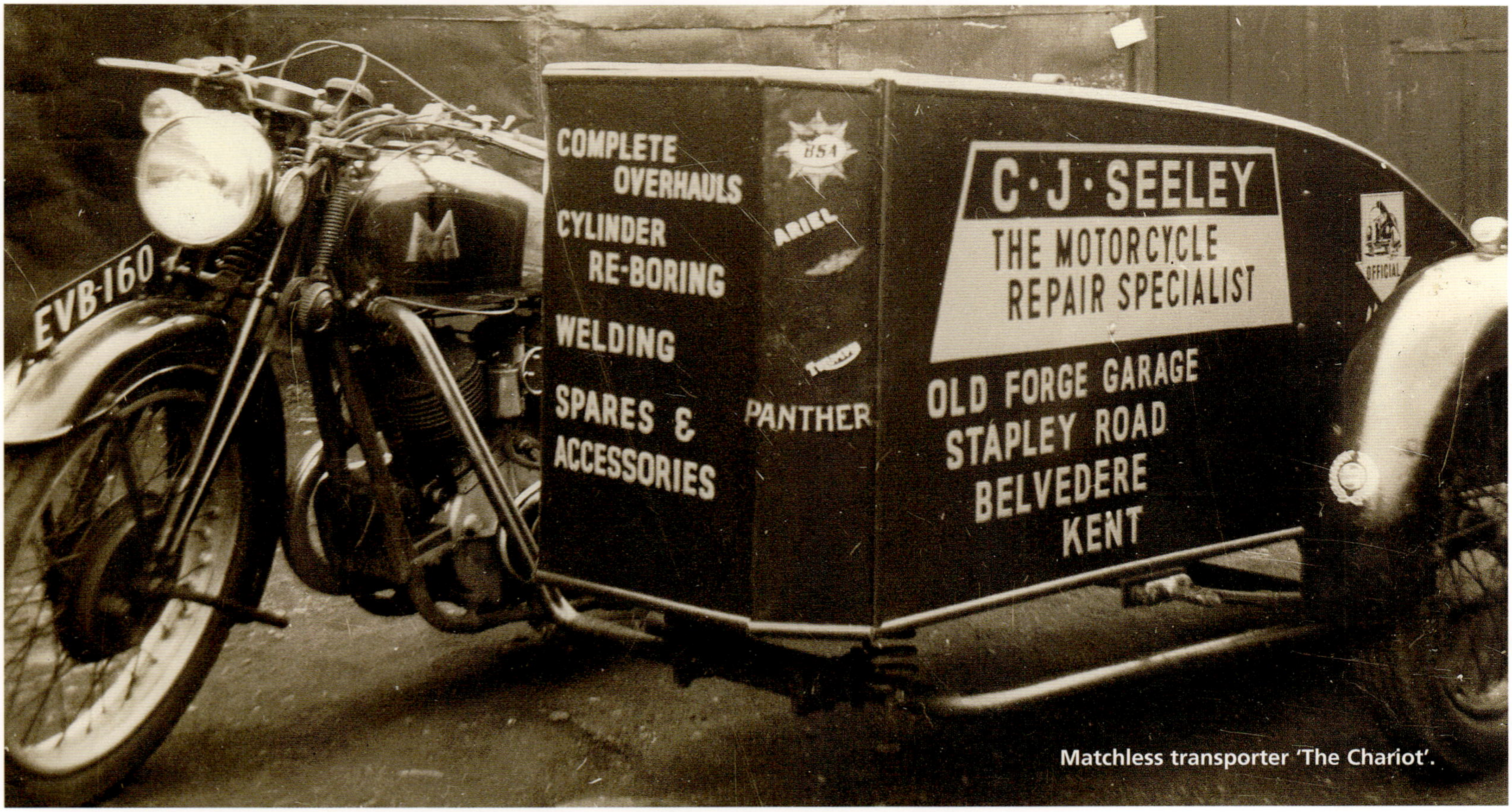

Matchless transporter 'The Chariot'.

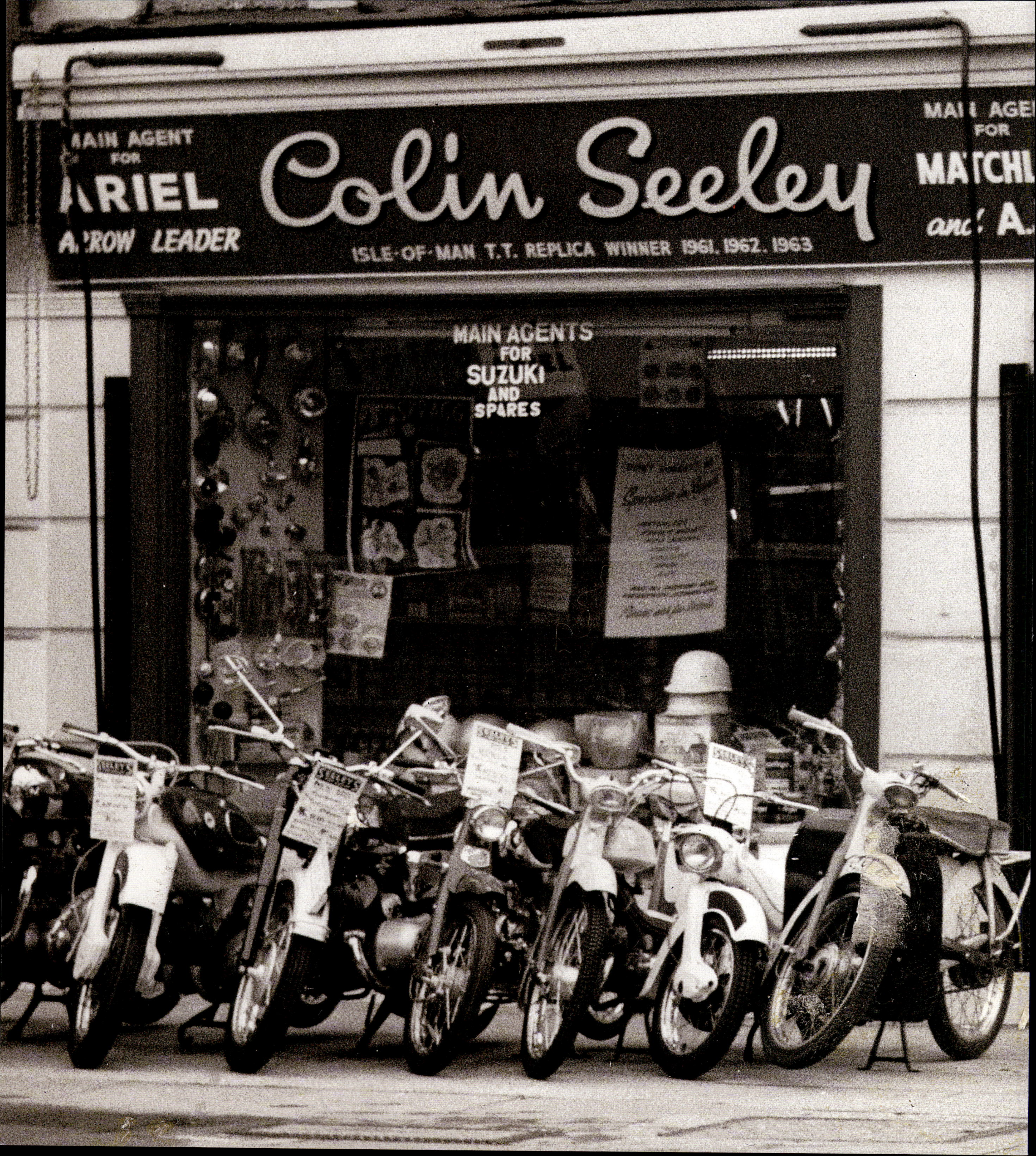
MAIN AGENT
FOR
ARIEL
ARROW LEADER
Colin Seeley
ISLE-OF-MAN T.T. REPLICA WINNER 1961. 1962. 1963
MAIN AGENT
FOR
MATCHL
and A.
MAIN AGENTS
FOR
SUZUKI
AND
SPARES

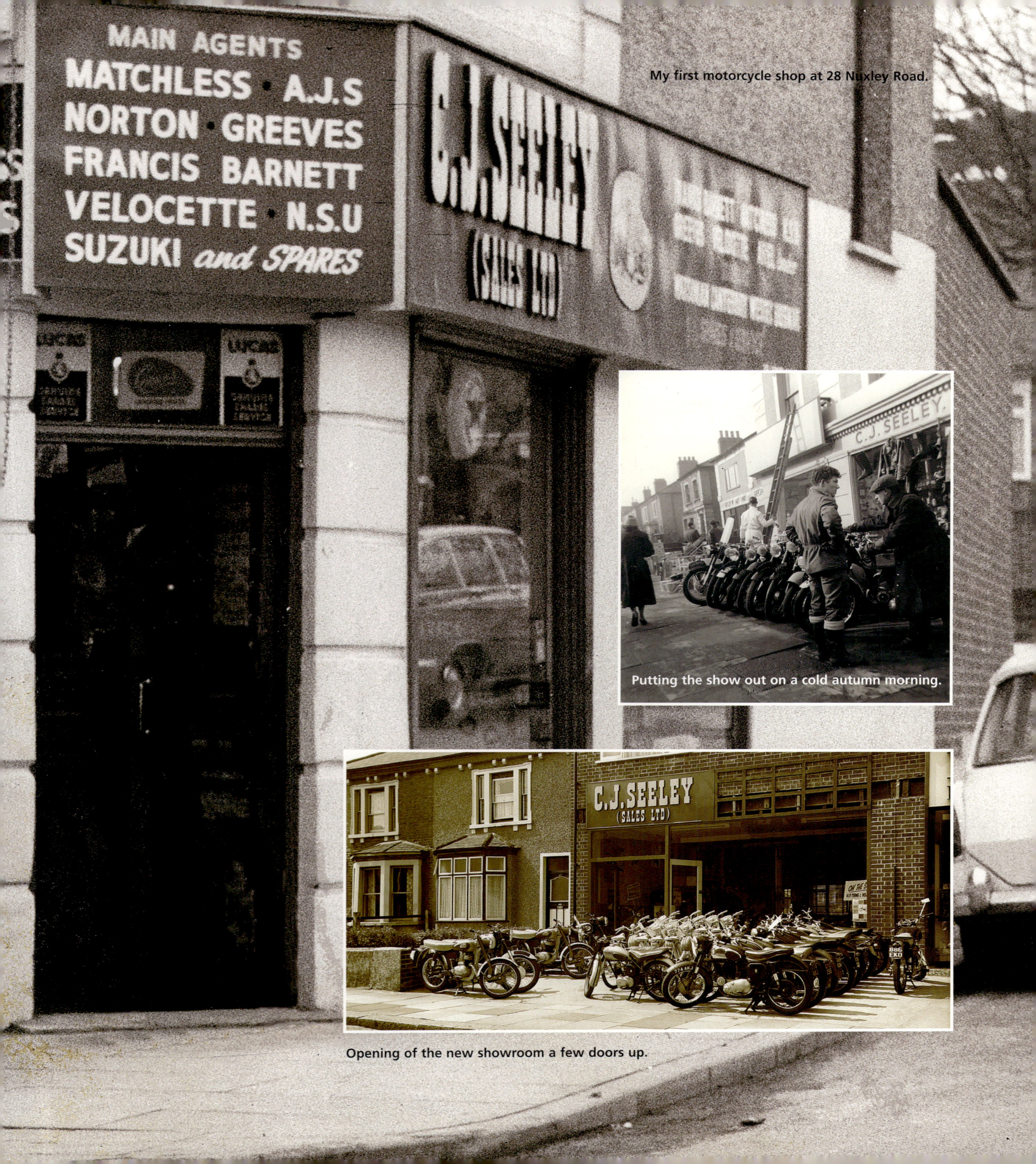

My first motorcycle shop at 28 Nuxley Road.

Putting the show out on a cold autumn morning.

Opening of the new showroom a few doors up.

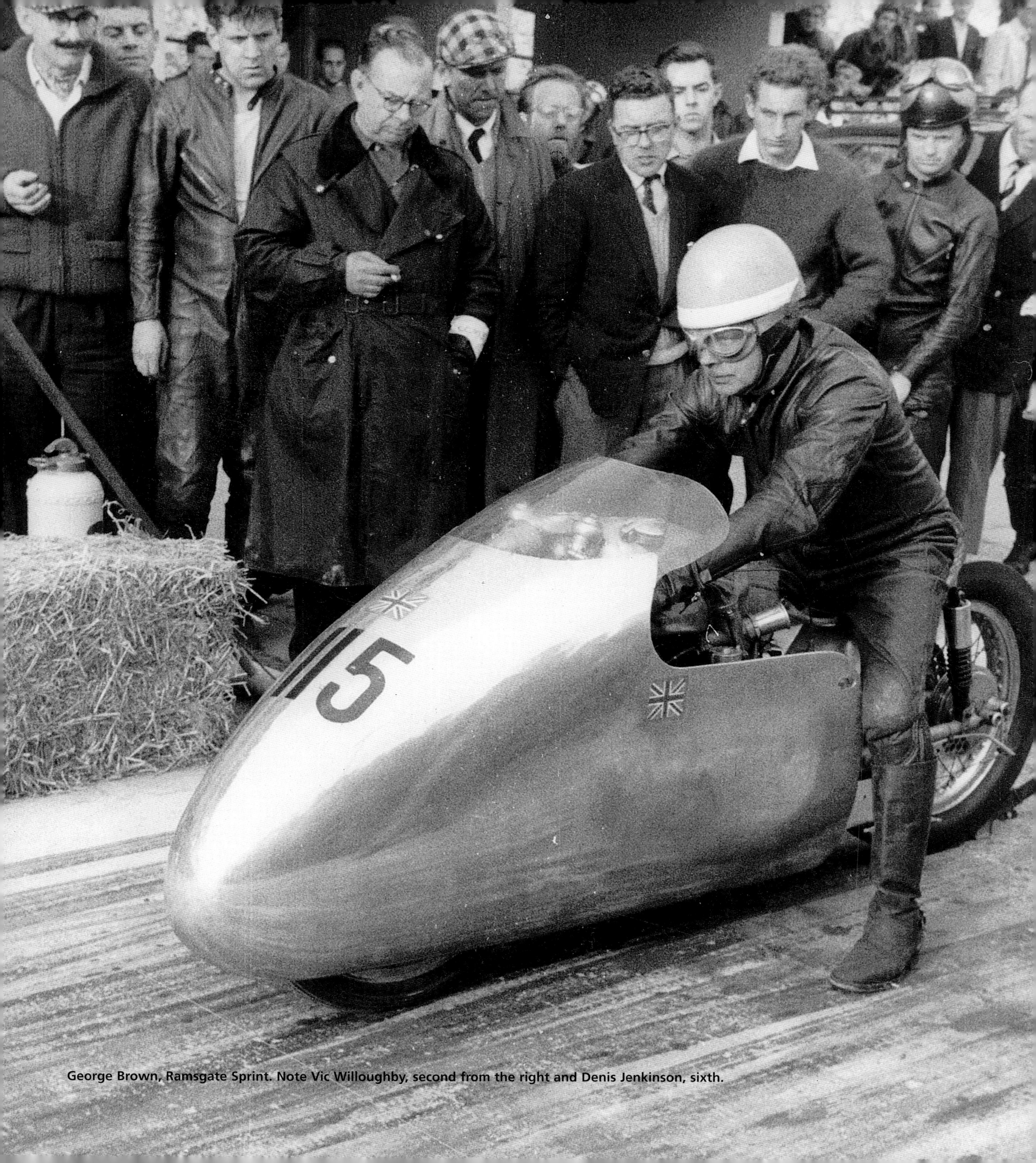

George Brown, Ramsgate Sprint. Note Vic Willoughby, second from the right and Denis Jenkinson, sixth.

Triumph Trophy 500 my first competitive machine.

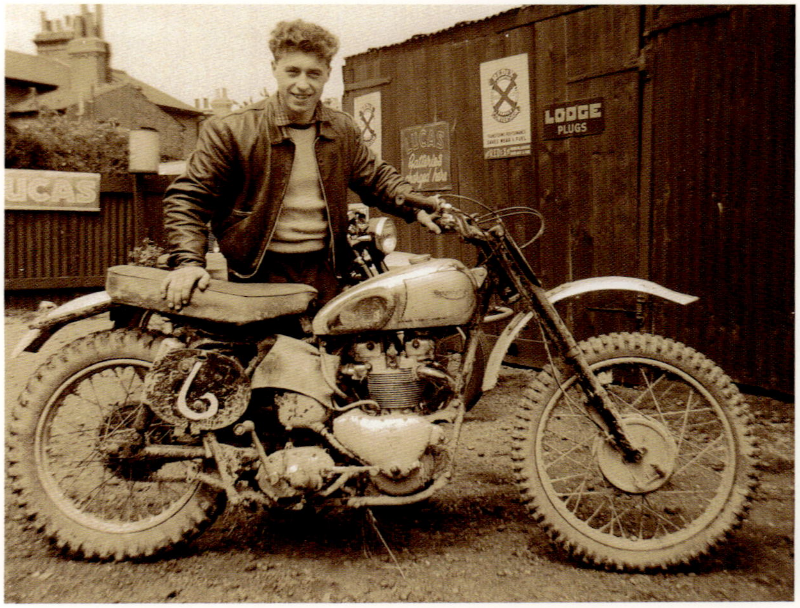

solo, which I decided to retain for scrambling. Entering my first event ever at Uckfield, East Sussex in May 1957, I achieved a fourth and fifth place in the heats. Then with the same machine racing grass track at Rhodes Minnis in Kent that June, I got two thirds and a second - again in the heats. As I have no details of the finals in either event I must have fallen on my head. Knatts Valley Hill Climb, situated close to Brands Hatch, followed, and then back to Rhodes Minnis in September with a third and second in heats and a fifth in the final - not bad competing against such grass track specialists as Jack Colver and Alfie Hagon. I finished that season with a road sprint at Ramsgate on the sea front with my hero George Brown competing. Finally, a scramble at Hurst Hill at Bramley in Surrey finished with a fifth in the heats - again, not too bad with great riders such as John Giles and Ken Heanes taking part. They were just fantastic. However, I fell off in the finals - obviously over enthusiastic. Certainly it was a most enjoyable first season's racing and very cost effective. What shame those days have long gone.

The 1957 AJS Scrambler.

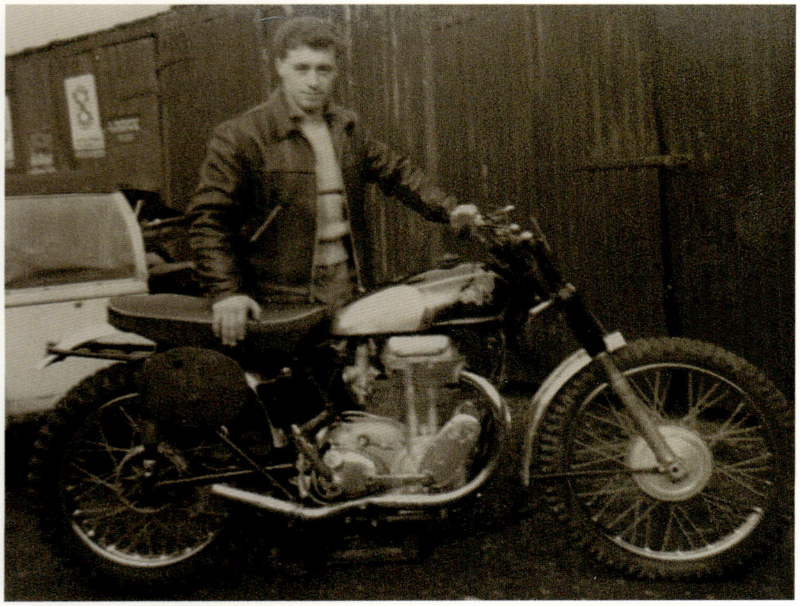

My association with the AJS and Matchless factory started in 1958 and being still unable to afford time or money to consider road racing, I bought an ex-works ex-Gordon Jackson 500 AJS scrambler direct from the factory. This machine for me was awe-inspiring and intimidating at the same time. Competing on this monster for the first time at a Brands Hatch scramble in February that year, my initiation ride on the slippery Kent chalk surface was totally hopeless. The next event in March, the Grand National Scramble held at Pirbright was no better. Following later in the same month was the March Hare scramble at Streatly, Berkshire at which I crashed heavily and injured my knee. Riding the AJS at the last event in April at Geddinge Farm, Wootton near Canterbury, my entry and results book states, 'one point for the team placing'. Rough! I had quickly come to the conclusion that the AJS was not for me. It is the only machine that I have not been able to control - it was an absolute beast. I take my hat off to the likes of Gordon Jackson and the speedy Vic Eastwood for their success on such a projectile.

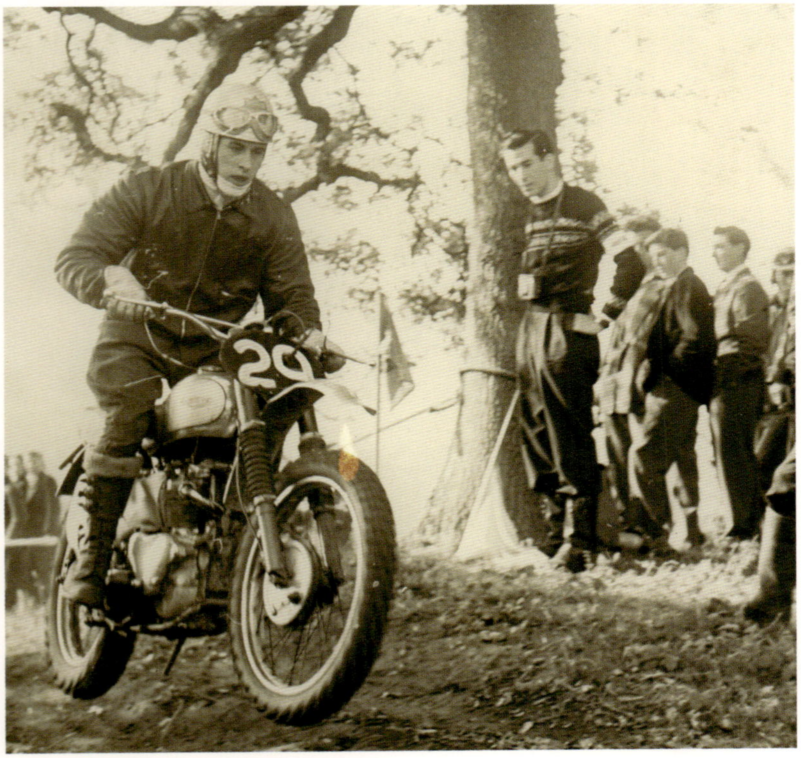

First scramble, Uckfield 1957.

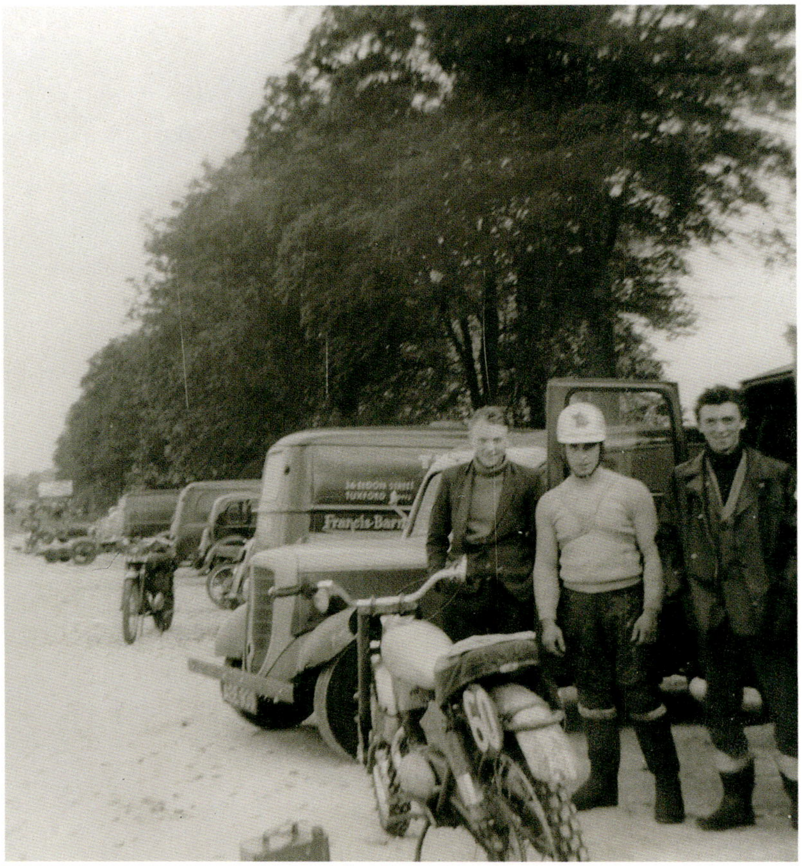

In the same year I had been appointed a Greeves agent so it was straight onto the Woolwich Ferry and down the A13 to the Greeves factory at Thundersley in Essex, requesting to see the Sales and Marketing Director, Derry Preston-Cobb, a cousin of Bert Greeves. Derry was severely disabled and hence the early fifties production of the Invacar invalid carriage designed around Derry by Bert Greeves, followed in the mid-fifties by the range of Greeves motorcycles. Derry was a great character having a tuned Invacar invalid carriage, which he often crashed off the road into a ditch. Derry, although suffering from a severe speech impediment, managed to be extremely outspoken and swore like a trouper. He was a very astute businessman and also extremely fair in his business dealings. The following example brings this to light:

Derry: 'What do you want, Colin Seeley?'

C.S: Answering in a mild and almost apologetic manner, 'Well, I have recently been appointed an agent for your Greeves motorcycles. To promote the fact that I am a rider agent I would really like to scramble one of your machines. I believe I can do a good job for Greeves, therefore, I am asking for some additional support and perhaps an extra discount?'

Derry: after a short pause and in a croaky voice, 'Fuck off.' Well, that was the start of

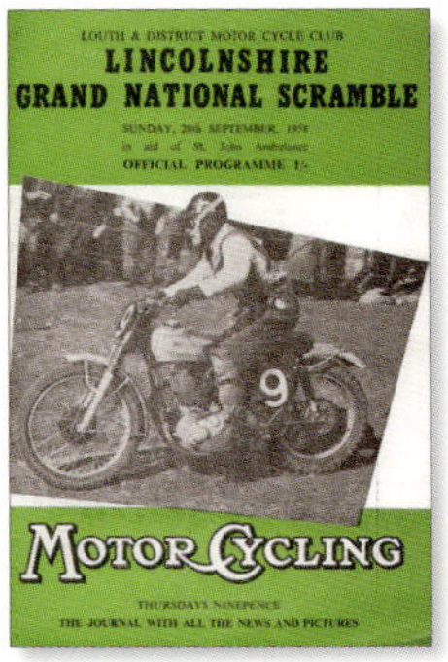

Cadwell Park, Lincolnshire Grand National.

an extremely happy relationship with Derry and Greeves Motorcycles. It was the time of the great Brian Stonebridge and Dave Bickers.

Entering my first event, at Canada Heights in June 1958, on a 197cc Hawkstone Greeves, by now a member of the Sidcup and District MCC, I achieved fourth in the heat and fifth place in the 200cc final. With a seventh in the 500cc heat, the final was stopped for whatever reason but I won the princely sum of ten shillings, 50p by today's earnings. I was back on course.

I continued riding Greeves, upping the performance by legally changing the fuel to Dope-alcohol and riding mostly at venues throughout the south with reasonable success. I ventured north to compete in the Lincolnshire Grand National held on the 28th September 1958, at the Cadwell Park Racing circuit. The scramblers' circuit was laid out partly alongside and partly crossing the tarmac track and hillsides, for which Cadwell is well known. I rode in eight races that day with second and third places in the 200cc event and a third and fifth in the 350cc event. I also took two tenth places in the 500cc event and finally eighth and thirteenth in the 500cc handicap events. An

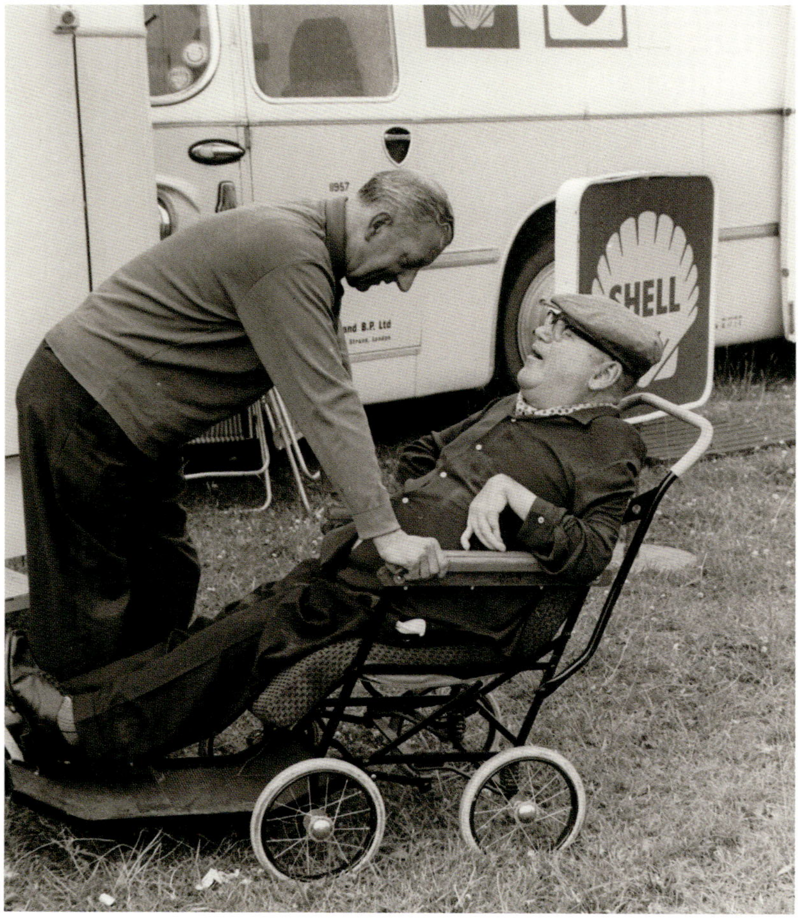

BP Competition Manager Harry Downing with Derry Preston-Cobb (in the wheelchair).

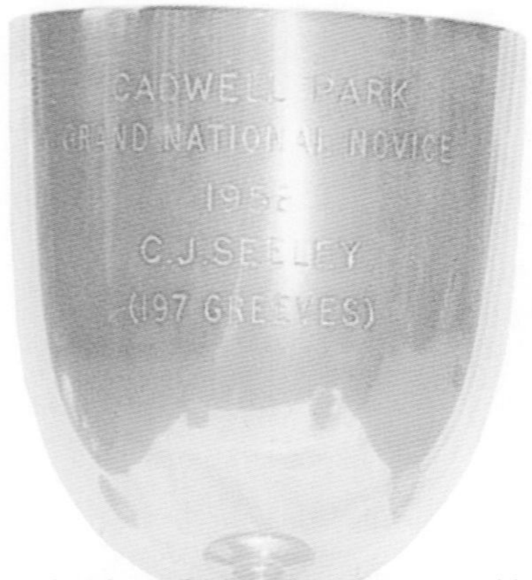

exhausting but thoroughly enjoyable day resulted in my being presented with my first award, The Lincolnshire Grand National Novice Trophy along with a monetary prize of £2 15s 'Fantastic!' as Murray Walker would say.

Further success followed that season with rides at the October Biggin Hill Double Five Kent event, which secured me a second, third and fourth place, along with thirty shillings prize money. Brands Hatch in November found me battling for the lead with Mike Jackson, Greeves, Ron Lindup and Alan Mayes with Mike finally the first under the chequered flag.

With the Earls Court Motorcycle Show on the following week Mike Jackson was delighted to have beaten me back to fourth place so he could claim his success to the Greeves bosses - what a sad person! Mike as a privateer supported by Greeves was to join the company in 1964 as a sales representative, continuing in this position until May 1969 when Greeves/Invacar lost its government contract to supply the invalid carriages. Combined with the lost supply of the Villiers engine units, which effected the production of the motorcycles and with the American market in decline, Greeves as a company folded in the mid seventies.

The same year - 1969 - Mike Jackson was invited to join Dennis Poore at his Norton-Villiers Company as European Sales Manager for the AJS - Stormer scrambler operation. Come June 1970 Mike was despatched to the USA to control the Norton-Villers operation at Long Beach California, distributing both the Norton Commandos and AJS Scramblers. Mike stayed with the Company as Sales Director until 1982 when he bought NVT through Dennis Poore. Then trading as Andover-Norton was built by Mike into a very successful distribution company for the motorcycle trade. This company was eventually sold in 1994 and my old adversary and friend Mike Jackson, then 56, turned his hand to journalism, special historic events organiser and auction consultant. In his own words 'an all round busy-body' - a good egg and a highly respected character within business and the sport.

My final scrambles event in 1958 was at the November Tunnel Hill Pirbright Grand National. I finished on a high with two thirds in the 200cc heat and final, a third in the 500cc heat and running fourth in the 500cc final when the engine seized.

So far so good. I was pleased with my progress and the Greeves suited my style but Derry Preston-Cobb was still swearing and jokingly shouting - 'You could do better!' By this time, towards the end of 1958, business was so busy that expansion was planned for 1959. By chance, near our existing shop a new building was being erected containing two separate and good sized shop units, with self contained flats above. I grabbed the opportunity to have a separate showroom for the motorcycles and now the sidecars that we were to stock - namely Watsonian, Canterbury, Wessex, Busmar, Swallow and Garrard, publicising Colin Seeley as the sidecar specialist. Needing additional staff and a secretary, I advertised in the local press, having my own ideas at 23 years of age for a secretary, perhaps around 18 with a slim line chassis and nice headlamps, and possibly with some ability, but this was secondary. Finally I came to my senses, having interviewed a number of young girls when I met up with Mrs. Marie Bull, a mature, friendly lady who agreed to join my then progressing company. Marie Bull was known to my landlord Harold Bennett and she proved to be one of the most efficient and loyal people one would ever wish to meet. She stayed with me through thick and thin for some 14 years. I have the fondest and kindest memories of her.

Also to join me was Wally Rawlings (Gungy Wal) as a mechanic, joining forces in the workshop with a local man, Les Grayston who was another Red Hunter enthusiast at the time - a total nut case - quick on the road and apparently quick in bed with his numerous girl friends. Les was tall and an extremely fit, strong individual who you would always want on your side. He also took up scrambling, riding Greeves but was often disappointed as I, being the little squirt out of the two, mostly beat him over the line, but we had great fun together.

My scrambling career continued into 1959 still with Greeves but now on a 250cc model riding in the first event at Canada Heights, in March of that year, gaining three fourths, a couple of seconds and a crash, not a bad start. Saltbox scramble the following week got me a third and fourth in two 500cc heats but two crashes in the finals. Must do better! Greenwich and District MCC organised a scramble at Brands Hatch in April '59. With six races in one day I gained a fifth and fifteenth in the heat and finals of the first 500cc race. I remember in that race that I stalled in a particular section and when I kicked the Greeves up again hooking it back into gear then dropping the clutch, the bike shot off backwards into the undergrowth with me hanging on in a somewhat

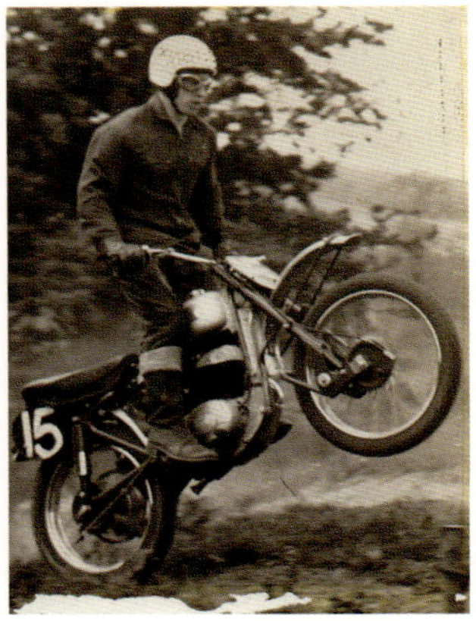

Me on the Greeves and Tim Gibbes on the AJS, Canada Heights.

Brands Hatch Scramble.

surprised manner. The two-stroke engine had fired up backwards hence the astonishment. No such mistakes in the second 500cc race resulting in a fifth place in the heat and a very satisfying fourth in the final and one pound prize money earned.

A number of other scramble events followed that season. I had rides at Bognor Regis MCC's Polegate Scramble - Heyshott, Sheerness and District MCC's Muswell Manor - Leysdown, Canada Heights and Dormans land (East Grinstead) etc. Overall for 1959 I was pleased with my results but did not set the world alight. However I was never too far from the front.

Whilst my business was doing well at that time, there was a lot of competition around with something like fourteen motorcycle shops within a radius of six miles. These included Joe Francis Motors, Schwieso Brothers, Cleares of Woolwich, Sharlands, Alan Trow (the Alan Trow who was to ride in the Slazenger Norton Team). Also nearby was Mr. Bernie Ecclestone, who in those days specialised in secondhand motorcycles - all highly polished and supposedly the best around! Mr. Ecclestone had the reputation for being spotlessly clean in his appearance and was always very smartly dressed in a suit.

I could not have managed that in those early days. The suits would have to come later. I was always rushing from shop to shop dealing with customers, then to the workshop to perhaps fit a sidecar, then down to AMC or over to Greeves at Thundersley to collect spares. Weekends were always busy, often starting at 6.00am on a Saturday morning by cleaning the shop and windows, 'getting the show on the road'. Gunking down and cleaning the second-hand bikes, to be ready for action, opening at 9.00am and closing at 6.00pm, Monday to Saturday, plus Sunday until lunch time, life was pretty hectic. I always believed that the quality of my secondhand bikes was second to none in the area, with superb service back up. Never mind Ecclestone.

Operating from our new showrooms, but still retaining the original premises for the spares and accessories department it was to be a good business year. Many AMC motorcycles were sold, in particular the G12 650cc twin Matchless frequently fitted with a sidecar, and for the solo ton-up-boys the sporty G12CSR and AJS 31CSR 650cc models.

It was the day of the NSU Quickly mopeds, for which we were sub-agents being supplied by the main distributors Deeprose Brothers of Catford. The NSU Quickly was an excellent moped with the basic model selling like hot cakes at £69.10s.

Another successful agency was for the advanced design 250cc Ariel Leader and Arrow models. Little did we know at the time of a certain Sammy Miller being employed at Ariel Motorcycles from 1957 until 1964 in the development shop. The Ariel Leader, launched in 1958, was for its day, so advanced with its excellent colour schemes, pressed steel frame, leading link forks, built-in legshields/screen, adjustable headlamp/indicators, stylish pannier boxes and engine covers. The bike handled extremely well on the road and was, from memory, a joy to ride. Combined with the superb spares back-up which offered an exchange service for many items including frames and forks, it was a great concept. Later a Golden Arrow was produced, a sports model without enclosed bodywork and screen etc. A version of the Arrow tuned by Hermann Meier and raced by Mike O'Rourke in the 1960 250cc Isle of Man TT finished in a very creditable seventh place averaging over 80mph. Sammy Miller partnered by Cecil Sandford finished second in the 200/250 class of the 1960 Thruxton 500 mile endurance race riding an Ariel Arrow.

Sammy, although previously owning a number of earlier motorcycles, and with his increasing interest in 'mud plugging' (trials) decided to build his own special, known as the SHS (Samuel Hamilton Special). In 1954 at 21 years of age for the first time he entered his SHS in the prestigious and challenging Scottish Six Days Trial.

Meantime Sammy's interest in road racing increased. Then the owner of a 1949 AJS 7R, in May 1954 he entered his first race, the Cookstown 100 and finished in a brilliant second position. This boy had talent! Sammy went on to race a variety of machinery including NSU, Ducati, CZ, Norton and Mondial, competing against the best at the Isle of Man TT, Ulster Grand Prix and world championship events. He finished third in the 1957 250cc World Championship - pretty impressive after only three seasons in racing. Intermingled with this road racing (1954 -1958), was his first love, trials, at which he was also showing great skills, especially riding his beloved Ariel 500 GOV 132. Later he became somewhat disillusioned with the road racing scene, and missing the relative peace and solitude of competing in trials, retired from tarmac racing.

We all have to make difficult decisions in life, and certainly in sport one has to concentrate on a particular area. Sammy went back to mud and I left mud to arrive on the hard surface.

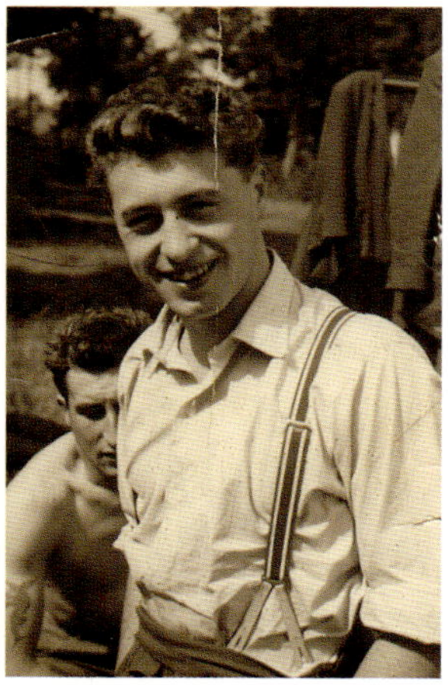

A fine pair of braces.

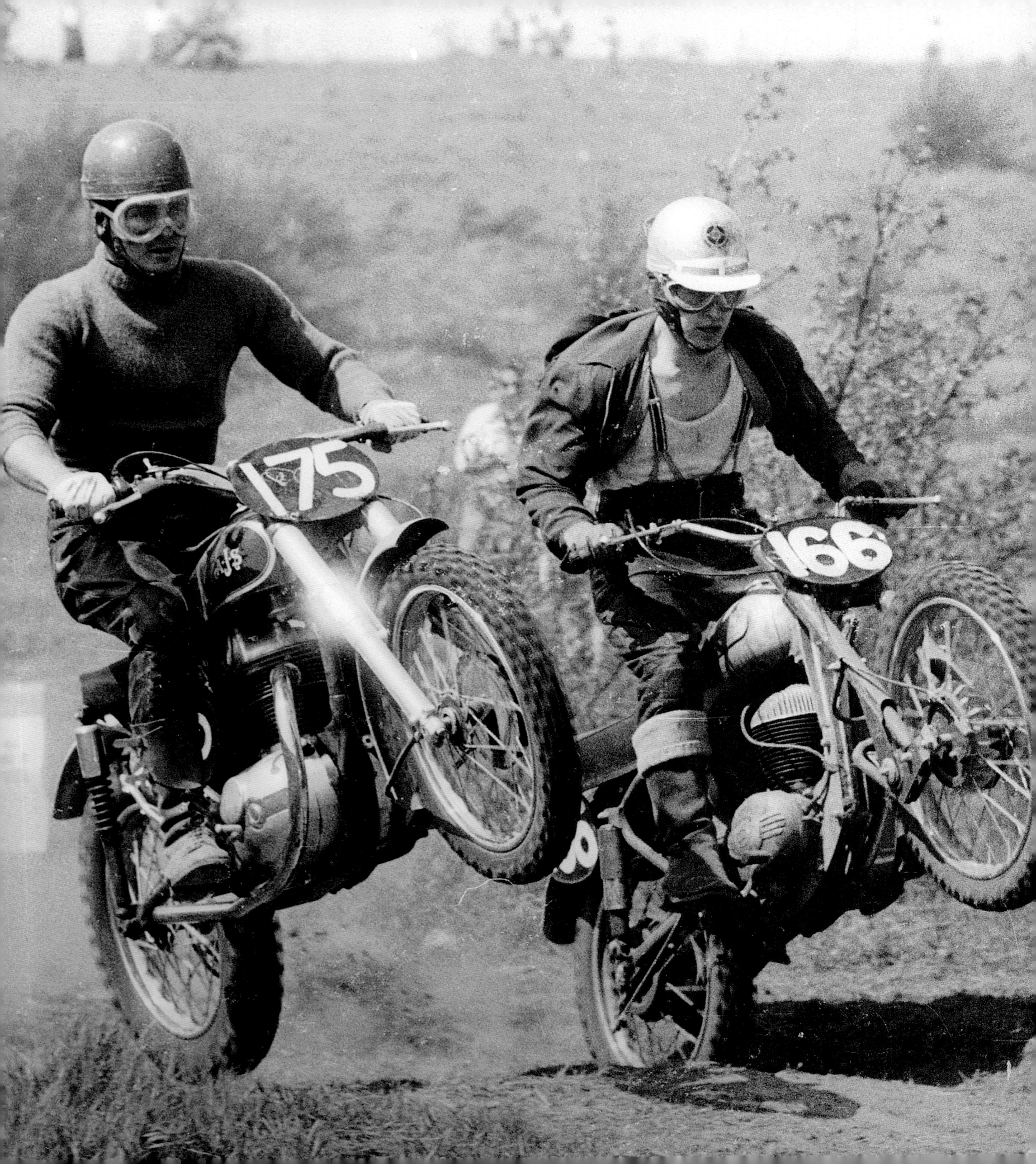
75
166

Sammy's sporting motorcycling successes would be hard to surpass particularly with his trials achievements. When visiting his impressive motorcycle museum at Bashley Manor in New Milton I gazed at the huge display cabinets sparkling with hundreds of trophies which brought it all to the fore. Sammy, apart from the sporting fame is a very astute and professional businessman, fair, but takes no prisoners. He is very outspoken on most subjects, or those items which are not, in his opinion, being dealt with correctly, but is highly respected amongst his fellow competitors and world wide friends. His contribution to the motorcycling world has been immense and I am proud to be considered a friend.

Another friend of mine and of the Wally Rawling's group was R.E. Rowe (Bob Rowe). Bob was a stylish and capable rider who at that time was sponsored by Bernie Ecclestone on two Steve Lancefield tuned 350 and 500cc Manx Nortons. In May 1959 I travelled with Bob and his wife Beryl to the Northwest 200 event in Ireland. Unfortunately, the weather was atrocious and in practice he was struggling on this high-speed road circuit coming in at the end of the session soaking wet and not very happy. When Beryl, one of the most supportive of wives but also fairly outspoken, said to him, 'You are not doing too well,' Bob turned round with a look on his face that you have to imagine and said, 'Beryl if you can do any f..... better then you had better ride the bike yourself!' It was at this event that I had the opportunity to meet Francis Beart and Bob McIntyre. With these Irish races traditionally held on a Saturday we rushed away after the event to travel back for Brands Hatch the next day, not such an easy journey with only the M1 motorway in those days. Ecclestone was in attendance at Brands to see his protégé Bob in action. Bob promptly fell off at the top of Paddock Hill breaking his collar-bone resulting in an ambulance ride to West Hill Hospital in Dartford. I remember going to see Bob in hospital as a passenger alongside Bernie who was struggling to see over the top of the steering wheel of his V12 Maserati. Bernie it appeared, was already in the money and enjoying a life style which he was never to lose. The memory of that weekend has never left me. It was ten years later that I revisited the Northwest 200 with Brian Steenson who then rode the QUB 500cc two-stroke single. Then 36 years later, again at the Northwest, I was with Ian Simpson who won the first race and set a new lap record riding our team's Castrol-Honda RC45.

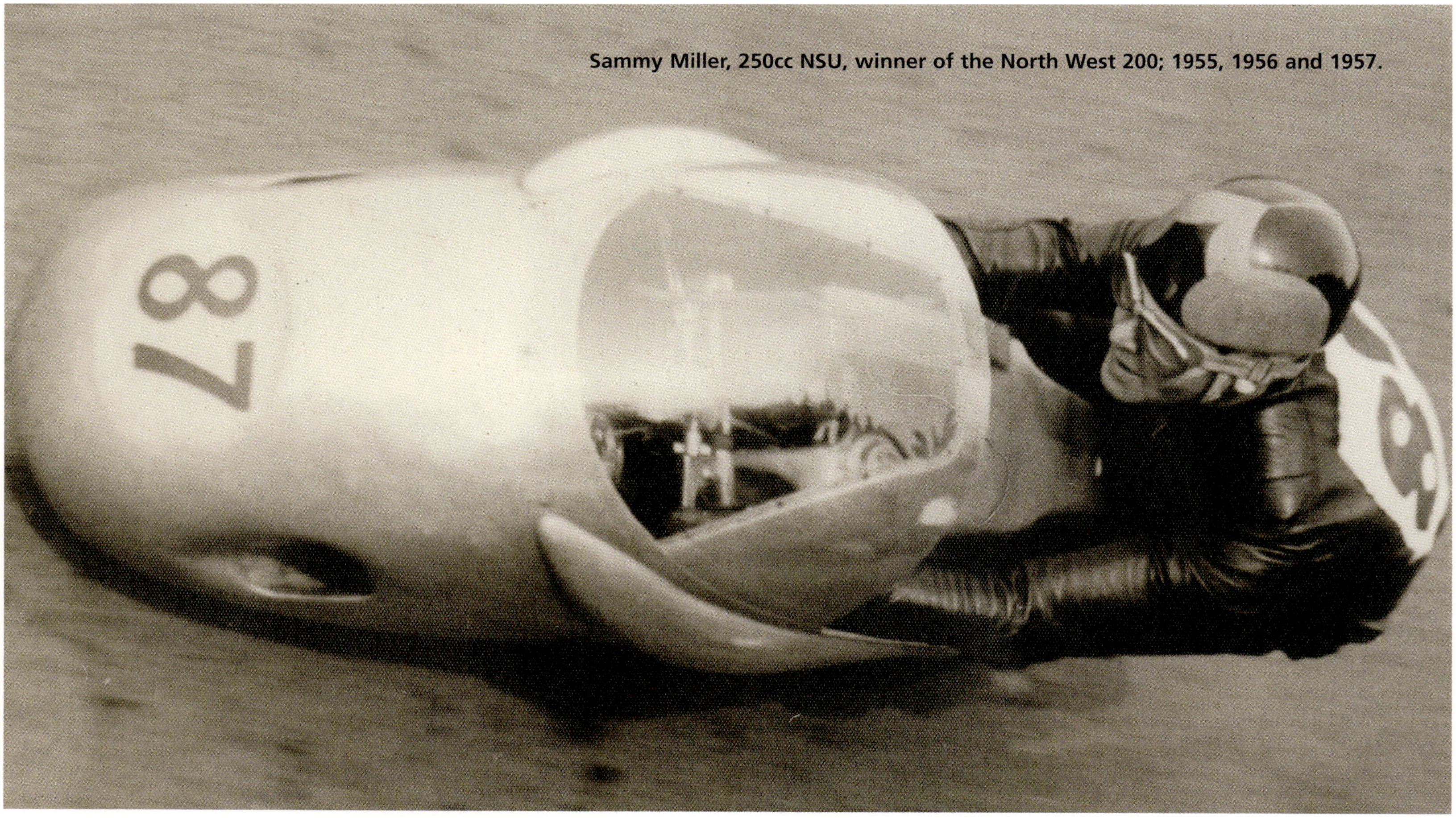

Sammy Miller, 250cc NSU, winner of the North West 200; 1955, 1956 and 1957.

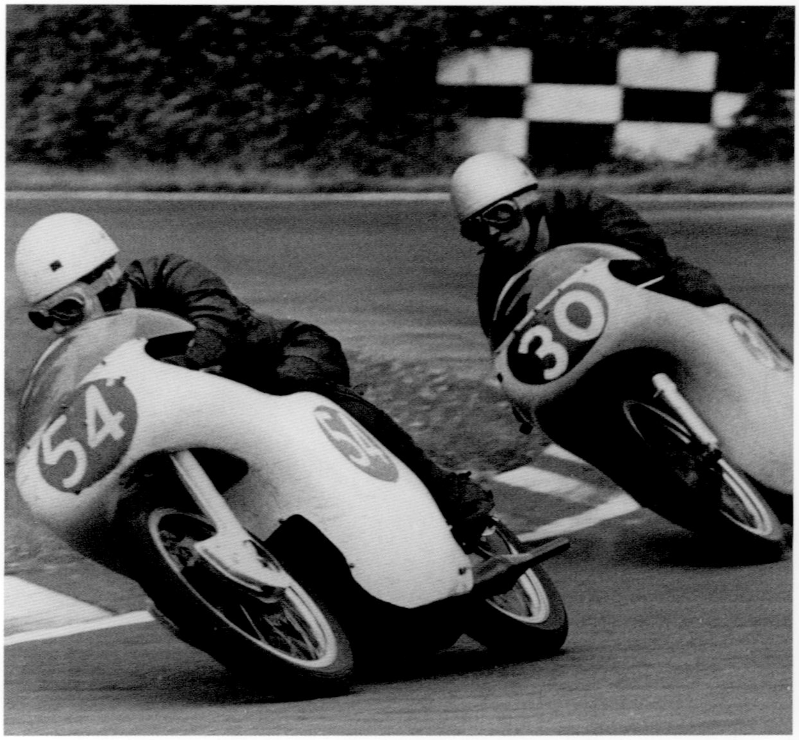

Mike O'Rouke (54) 249cc Ariel Arrow, Bob Rowe (30) 248cc Norton. Brands Hatch 9th July 1960.

Meanwhile my friend and employee, Wally Rawlings, had earlier in 1959 bought himself a 1948 AJS 7R on which, along with our friend Peter Morecock who also had bought a 7R, was to enter the Manx Grand Prix.

Rushing down Gorse Hill past Brands Hatch flat out was a little different, I might suggest, than rushing down Bray Hill at full speed, missing the kerb-stones by only a few inches. However, our Oakdene heroes would find out for themselves. For the 1959 Manx Grand Prix races there had been a huge increase in entries causing the committee to review their approach to the event. Therefore they requested that the Manx Government doubled their £2,000 grant to cope with the newcomers. The Autocycle Union agreed to an increase in the original start grid of 100 riders per race allowing every one of the 217 entrants a ride. A number of 350cc Junior entries would ride in the Senior 500cc event and this would include Gungy Wal, just one of the seventy-one newcomers to the Isle of Man mountain circuit. The 1959 event benefited from good weather conditions for the whole of practice and races. Notable leaders in practice for both the Junior and Senior races being Eddie Crooks, Tom Thorp, Peter Middleton, Roy Mayhew, Phil Read, Ron Langston and Michael Brookes.

The junior race was won by Peter Middleton after the talented Eddie Crooks, a friend to be in later years, broke down on the third lap when leading the race. This put Tom Thorp in front, who then broke down on the mountain section during the last lap. Finally, by courageously free-wheeling and pushing, Thorp, totally exhausted, staggered over the finish line, to sympathetic applause and forty-fifth place. Slotting into second place with a magnificent effort was that all-rounder, scrambler, trials rider and now road racer, Ron Langston.

Our friend Peter Morecock was also riding in his first Manx and finished fifty-seventh, midfield of the Junior Race at 78.27mph. For the Senior race, Eddie Crookes, several times runner-up in previous Junior and Senior races, got his revenge, despite stopping to fix a loose sparking plug lead. He won his first Manx Grand Prix Race at a record speed, 31 seconds ahead of second place man Tom Thorp, with Ned Minihan third.

Gungy Wal, riding his 350 AJS 7R in the Senior event, achieved a creditable fifty-fourth place, midfield at 75.30mph. How could he know that two years later he would be lapping the TT course quicker, lying on a sidecar platform?

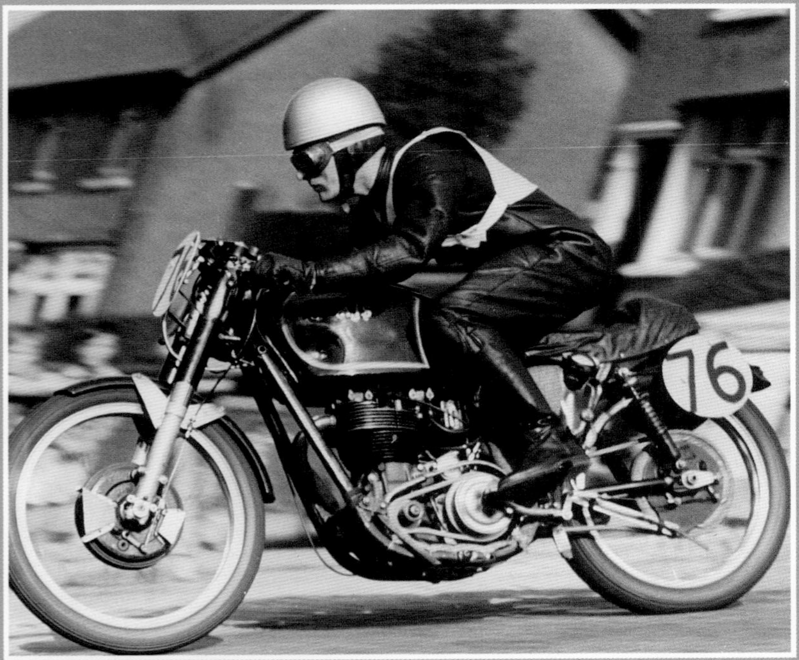

Peter Morecock, Bray Hill, 1959 Manx Grand Prix.

3 1960-61

YES, YES, WE LIKED IT!

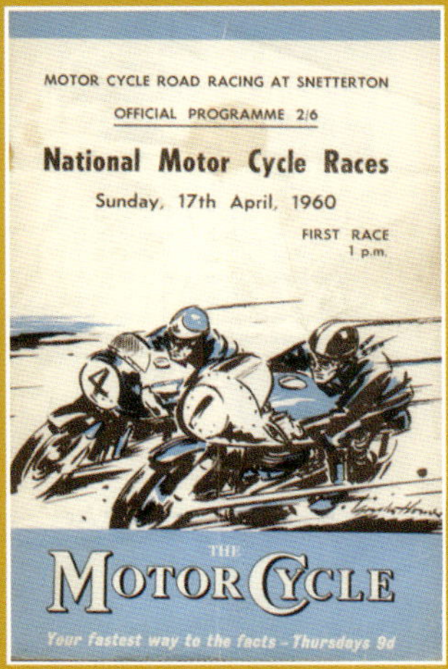

As the very busy season of 1959 - running the business, scrambling, visits to road race events - Gungy Wal's ride in the Manx Grand Prix - came to a close, I had time to reflect on my possible future career in sidecar road racing. Wally agreed to sell his 7R and put the proceeds into a joint venture with me, the purchase of a racing sidecar outfit to compete in the 1960 racing season.

Words like stupid, rash, dense, dim, foolish, daft were frequently suggested by his friends when Wally Rawlings agreed to be my racing passenger. Well perhaps Wally was rash, but certainly none of the other words applied. In agreeing to ride with me, Wally embarked upon a remarkable and very successful partnership. The great Eric Oliver later described 'Spiderman Wally' as the best passenger in the business. An accolade indeed.

Scouring the MCN and motorcycling adverts, we came across a so called ex-Eric Oliver Norton outfit, advertised by the man himself. To be honest it really was a heap, but the best we could afford at the time. Working on the outfit through the winter saw some improvement but the Manx engine did not seem to manage much above 6,500rpm.

In early 1960 you could regularly practise on a Wednesday afternoon at Brands Hatch for a couple of pounds, and the sidecars practised with the cars - interesting eh? So, suitably equipped with our new black Lewis racing leathers, ACU approved Cromwell helmets, Octopus goggles and for me knee high boots, off to Brands we trundled. We were somewhat apprehensive having no real idea what to expect - certainly for Wally being the acrobat on the side. After a number of hesitant laps, a pit stop and then back into action we both broke into a grin. Yes, yes, we liked it! In fact it was great. We couldn't wait to get a race entry as soon as possible.

We joined the Greenwich and District MCC, part of a club's combine, whose members organised the meetings at Brands Hatch, which proved to be invaluable. The club and members were most enthusiastic and helpful, with 'yours truly' being appointed to the race committee at a later date and even being the secretary of a scrambles event held at Brands, with Vic Eastwood as Star of the Day.

Our first road racing entry was accepted for the April 1960 event at Snetterton, Norfolk. We travelled from Kent on the day with the sidecar balanced on the roof rack of the Thames van, and the bike inside. My immaculate van still portrayed on the sides the scrambler rider image, but it was soon to be out of date. We were road racers now! Arriving at the flat, open and windy Snetterton circuit we unloaded and bolted the sidecar to the Manx Norton and prepared ourselves for action.

With practice at an end and all going well, we grabbed a coffee and a sandwich, then checked the outfit over. We were ready for our memorable moment. After being called to the assembly area, we anxiously wheeled the machine on to the crowded grid. There was a line-up of some 30 competitors including stars of the day such as Pip Harris, Jackie Beeton, Bill Boddice just to name a few - it was scary.

For a moment I wondered what we were doing there, I must have been demented. Riding a 250cc scrambler slipping and sliding in the mud was one thing, but the thought of rushing down the Norwich straight, at around 100mph amongst 30 crazy sidecar crews jostling for position, that was something else! It was too late now. We were being called to attention by the starter for the push start. Then all was silent as we waited for the flag to drop. A pause, a sudden roar of engines, the smell of Castrol R, and we were away.

It is a job to remember what happened in those next few laps. We were swept along in a sea of speeding metal, burning rubber and grim faced riders intent on ringing out the last ounce of power from their roaring engines. With the rush of all the noise and

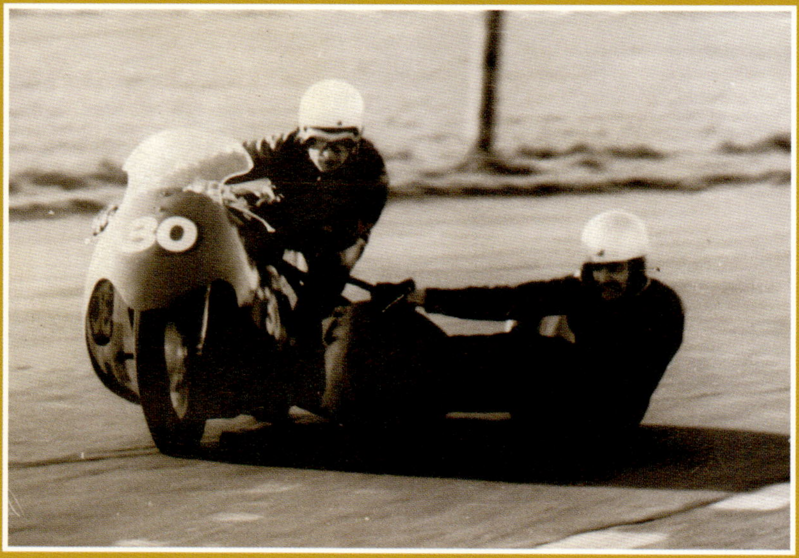

Snetterton, April 1960. First ever sidecar race meeting on the Norton.

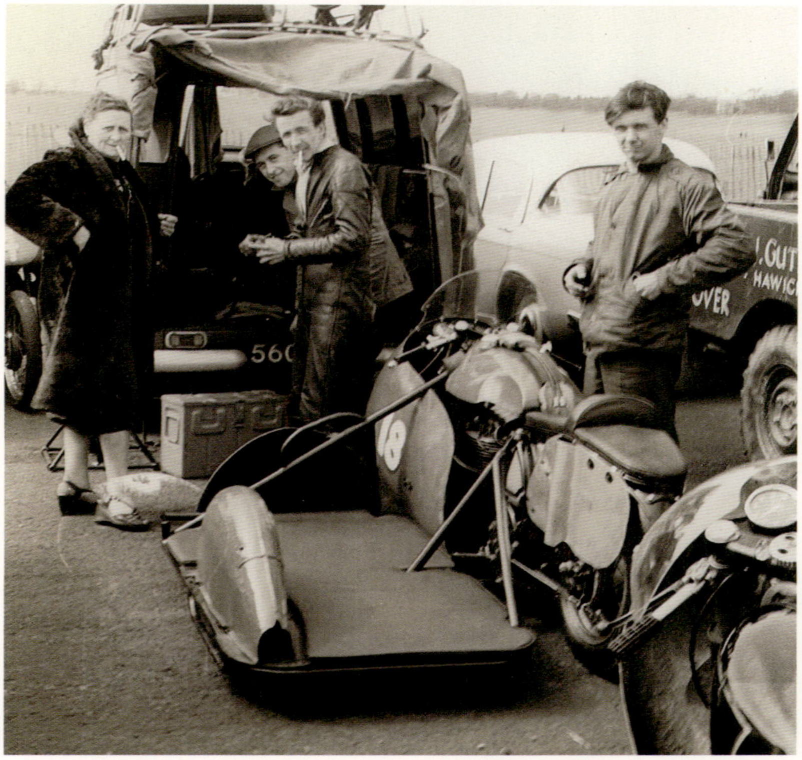

Hilda, Wally Dave and me at Charterhall.

the grit being thrown up from the track into our faces, Wally and I just concentrated on the job in hand. Suddenly the chequered flag was in sight. Thank goodness for that! We had finished in one piece and unbelievably in tenth place. Our first taste of this obsessive sport was sweet. The seeds had been sown. Our next event, still in April, was Charterhall, in the wilds of Scotland's border area, approximately 20 miles from Berwick-upon-Tweed. I believe it was another redundant airfield. Never heard of it? Don't worry, not many have! Once again with the sidecar strapped to the Thames van roof rack and the bike inside with provisions for this expedition, Wally did the driving and Peter Morecock was his companion. I travelled in my car with my long-suffering and ever-supportive mother and a certain young man Dave Downer. We finally arrived to attend our second Grand Prix - oops! sorry, unheard of national event with, would you believe, four 1000cc Vincents entered. Although Vincents were my first love I was not impressed to be racing against them. I do not remember much about the Charterhall event, other than the Norton refused to run over 6,000 revs, being more than a handicap against the Vincents, nevertheless remember that we managed a fourth place, beating three of them. We seemed to be getting the hang of this three wheeler racing.

Being new to the road-racing scene, we struggled in those early days to have our race entries accepted. That June, Mick Woollett, then editor of Motorcycle News and previously a sidecar passenger with Edgar Strub, had written a piece about the lack of fresh British star-quality sidecar crews coming through the ranks. So I immediately responded (see article below).

As Wally and I struggled to obtain any further race entries for 1960. and disillusioned with our Norton outfit, my thoughts turned to perhaps using a Matchless G50 for 1961 and as I was the rider agent it made sense. Also as Canterbury Sidecars produced a racing sidecar, and I was an agent, it seemed an ideal solution. With my mind buzzing I rushed off to speak with Jack Williams, the man in charge of the AMC racing department. Typical of me at the time, I expected an immediate and positive response to my bright idea, but Jack, who as a good engineer and a gentleman, was quite reserved about this proposal. Possibly, he hated the thought of a sidecar being attached to one of his beloved Matchless G50s that had been carefully hand built in the AMC race shop under his personal guidance.

'Just how badly do we need sidecar racers?'

MICK WOOLLETT has observed that British sidecar racing badly needs an influx of younger riders. Perhaps he and others who share this view would be interested to know what the young, would-be sidecar racers are up against.

I am 24 years of age and have been scrambling, etc, for about four years. This year I decided to take up sidecar racing and to this end I bought a Manx Norton chair outfit which had belonged to a well-known person. I completely dismantled the machine and rebuilt it at a cost of some £400.

Since then I have entered approximately ten meetings, submitting the entry forms as soon as I had received the regulations. But what happens? Cheque returned. "Very sorry—full up," the organisers say.

However, we did manage to get accepted for the Snetterton meeting on April 17, finishing tenth in a field of 31 starters—and this in our very first race! One other meeting for which our entry was accepted was at Charterhall (400 miles away), where we finished fourth in a field of 18 in the one race we could ride in.

If this is the only encouragement that can be given to us young sidecar racers there is only one thing left for us to do—go back to scrambling and other forms of cycle racing, then in about four years time there won't be any sidecar racing due to the lack of riders. As Mick Woollett has said, the class is already dominated by veterans.

I wonder what other young riders like myself think when they have their entries returned and then read articles such as Mick Woollett has written.

Upper Belvedere, Kent. **C. J. SEELEY**

★ ★ ★

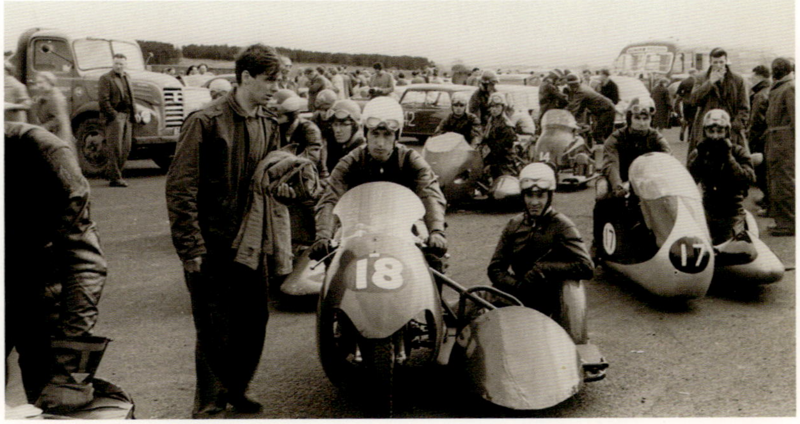

Charterhall assembly area.

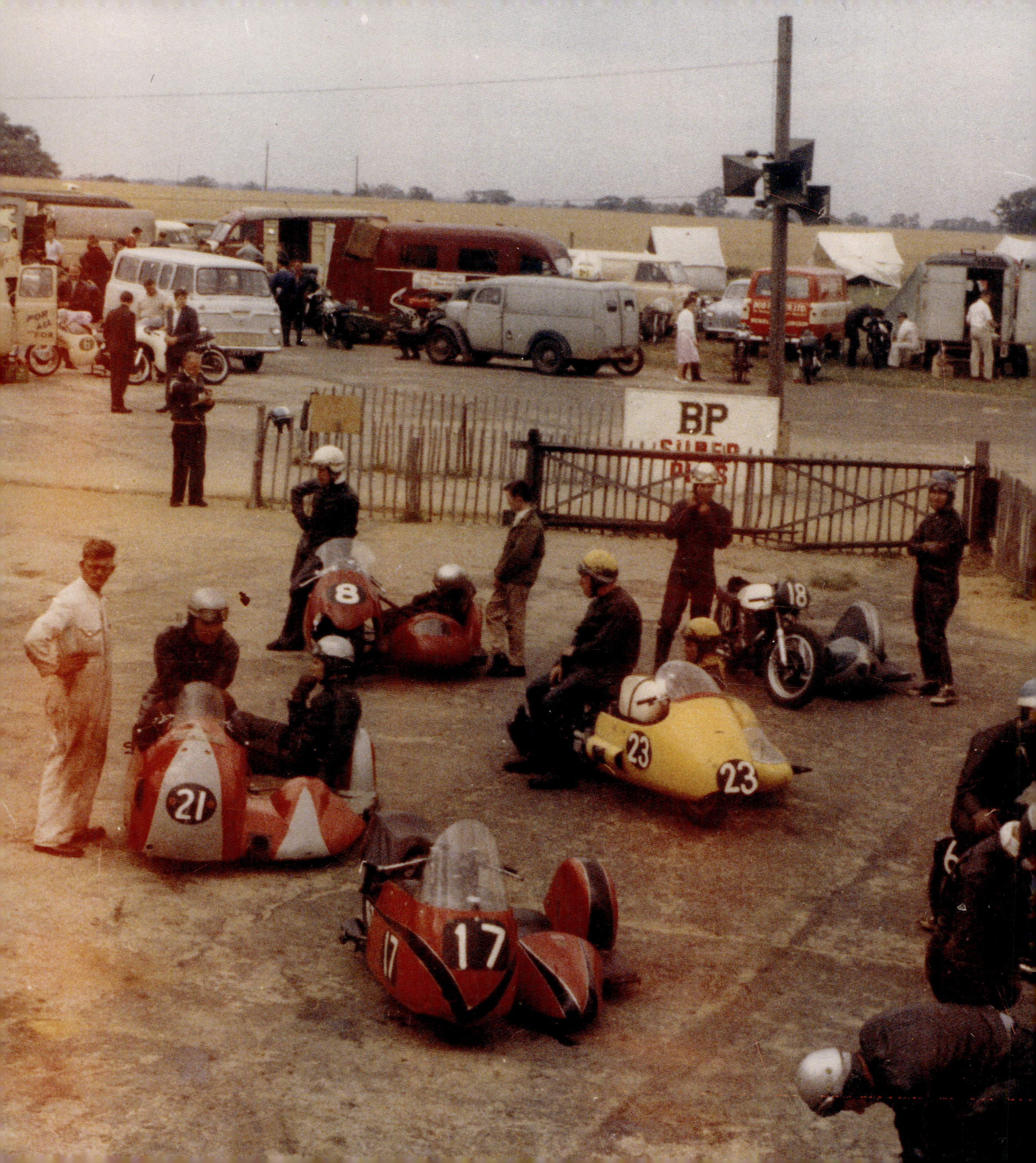
BP
8
18
23
21
17

Collecting my first Matchless G50, late 1960.

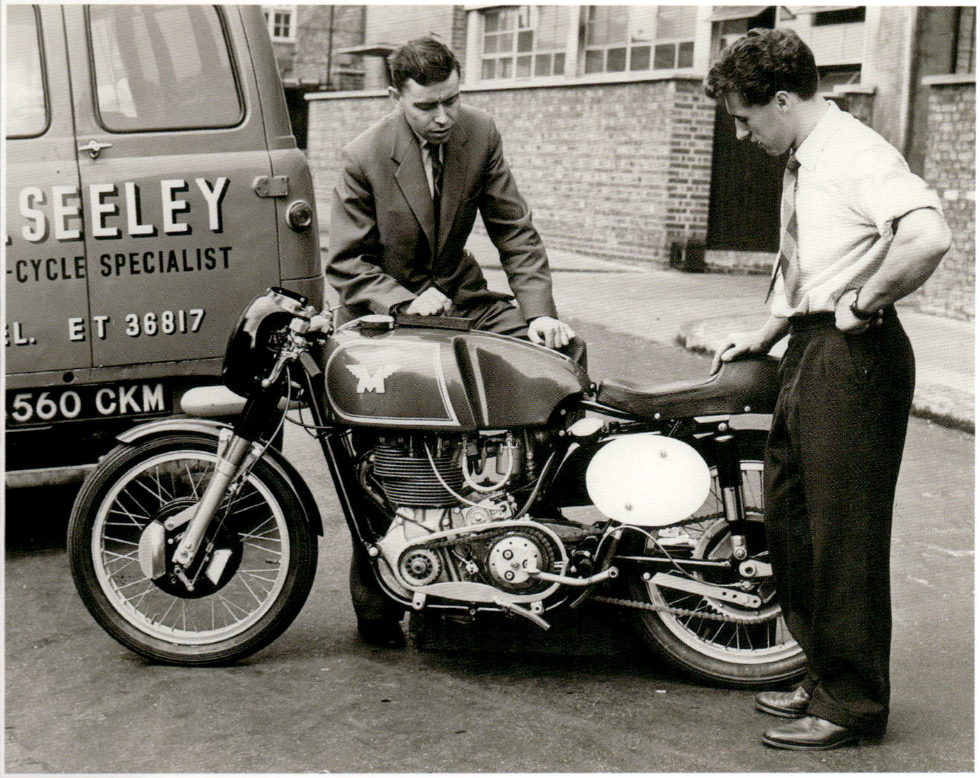

Nevertheless, I managed to convince him otherwise, and soon I was back to collect my first brand new gleaming Matchless G50 racer, which cost me, from memory, the princely sum of £360, a fortune in those days. Returning to the shop premises and unloading the magnificent Matchless, Wally Rawlings and I wheeled the G50 onto the side road, which was on a slope, and proceeded to take turns in coasting down the slope. We were just like kids with a new toy.

Soon the serious business of conversion began. Out came the hacksaw and the bike was completely dismantled. Thought was given to where the sidecar fitting lugs were to be welded. Being a self-taught welder this was to be my biggest challenge to date. There was no point in the Matchless going in one direction and the sidecar with Wally on board going in the other. Fitted on the rear was a sixteen inch wheel with an 18 inch to the front. As Avon Tyres, with whom we had become associated, did not make a suitable 16 inch front racing sidecar tyre, an 18 inch solo Avon was fitted.

The telescopic front forks were retained with Tom Mortimer employed at the AMC factory manufacturing a new top fork crown out of solid material to suit the altered malleable bottom fork crown. The fork springs were shortened and finally a strong steel fork brace was fitted in place of a mudguard. That was it - no fancy leading link forks for us.

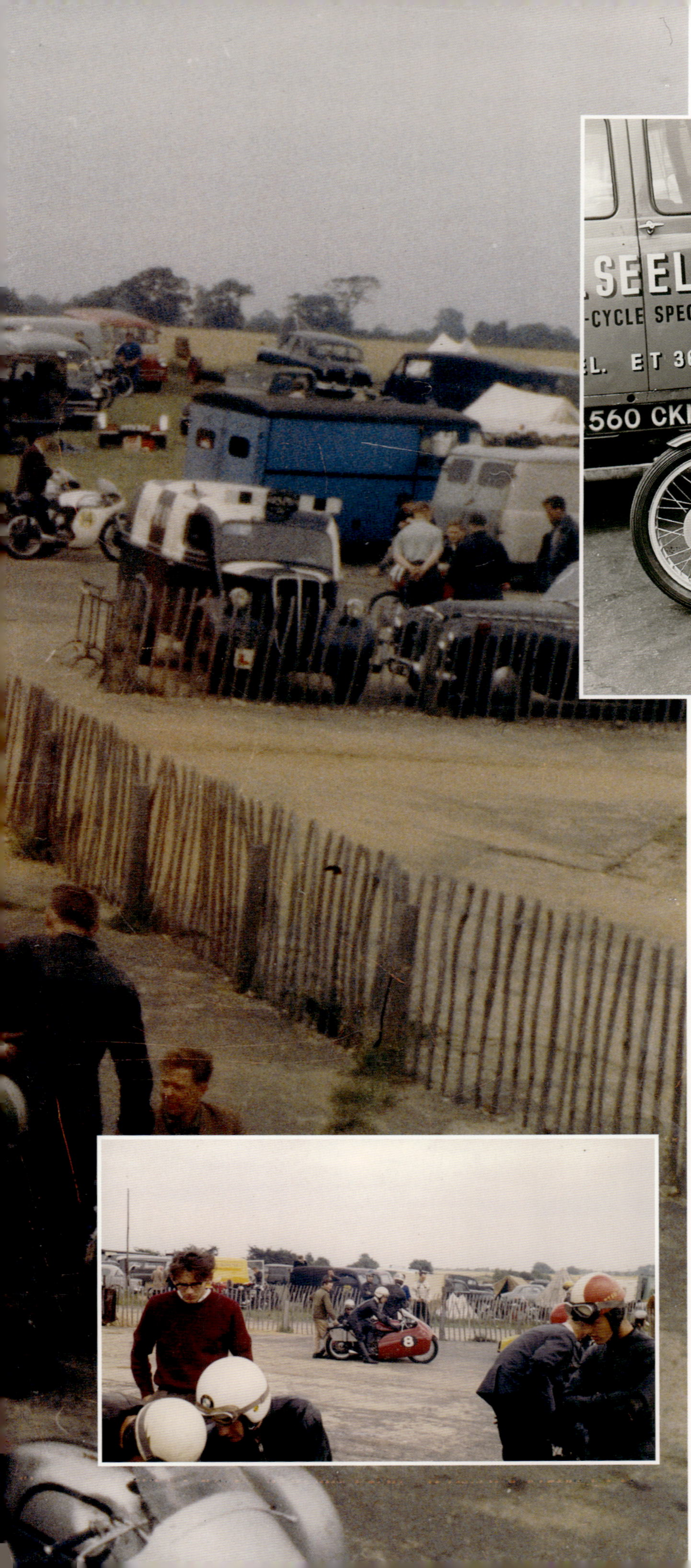

Snetterton 1960, number 8. Note, Pip Harris second in, bottom left hand corner of the inset picture.

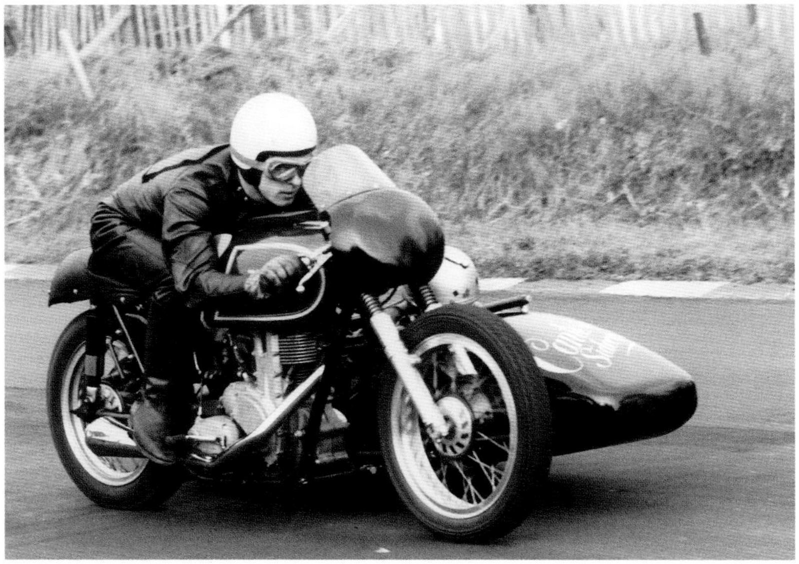

Testing the outfit at Brands, exactly as we drove it down the A2.

Hilda and Percy supporting our Brands effort.

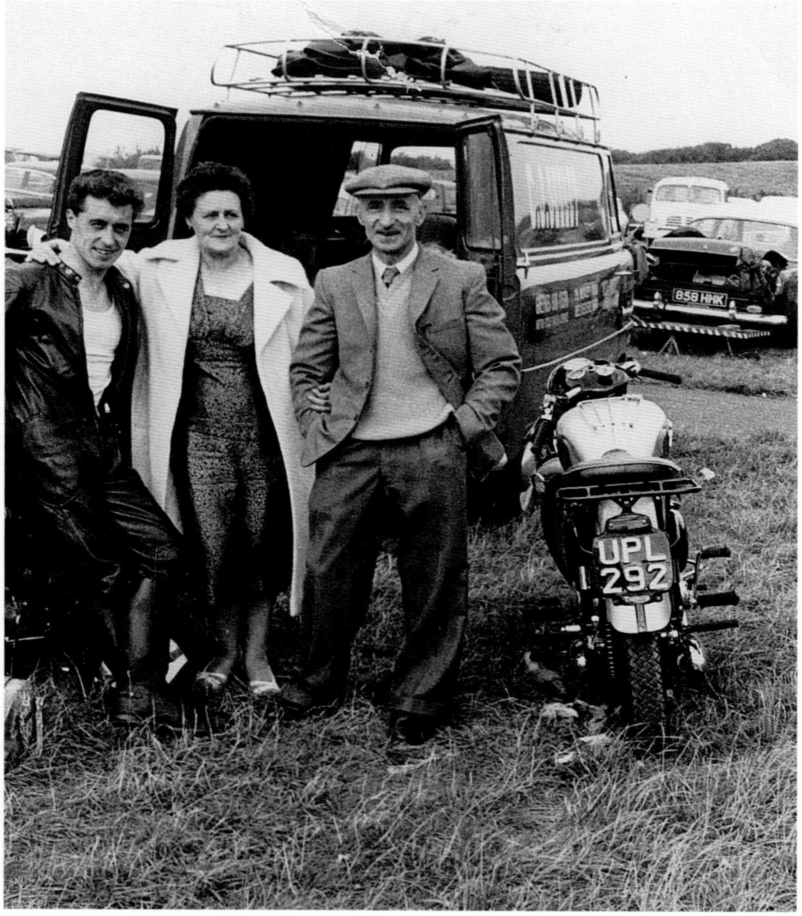

Thus rebuilt with no other alterations, and still with the original solo fuel tank, seat and brakes, the Canterbury racing sidecar was fitted. Eager to try out the results of our work, trade registration plates were bolted on and with a bung attached to the megaphone and Wally in the chair, we ventured out from Belvedere onto the main A2 London to Dover road. We rode to the tollgate at Gravesend and back - around 20 miles. It was simply great and a strange sight, but the police never caught up with us - can you imagine being able to do that sort of thing today?

After some Wednesday afternoon practising at Brands Hatch, our entry with a fee of £2 for the first Brands meeting of 1961 was accepted - hoorah let's go! The first appearance of our Matchless outfit with 'Canterbury Sidecars' painted in large lettering across the sidecar must have caused some amusement and interest among our rivals.

With the sidecar event up to 1200cc we managed a creditable ninth place and were lying third in the handicap race when the oil cap dislodged. We were pleased with our efforts and the Matchless was excellent with more to come. The teenager Colin Seeley, back in 1950 couldn't have imagined this scene, 11 years ago, as he looked over the fence at Clearways watching the sidecar outfits in action.

On then to Snetterton for the Easter Sunday event, 2nd April 1961 with 25 sidecar crews assembled on the grid for the 1200cc race. A mixture of Nortons, Vincents, Triumphs, BSAs and including the two top men, Pip Harris and Jackie Beeton on their BMWs. This was just our second outing with the Matchless and we gained a strong seventh place, three-up on our first visit to Snetterton a year before.

Then there was a rush home to attend next day the Easter Monday event at Crystal Palace. This was our very first visit to this dangerous circuit, which was enclosed mostly with railway sleepers, and with no run off areas. Solo entries, amongst the 100 in attendance were our friends Bob Rowe and Dave Downer, Ron Chandler (who some

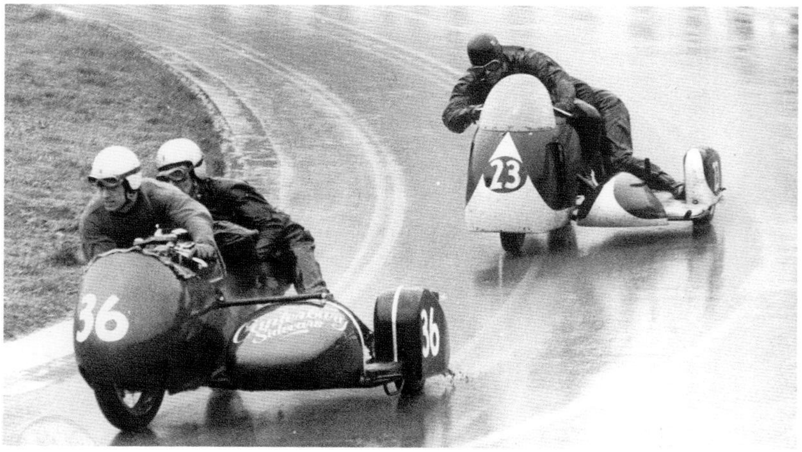

Wet action at Crystal Palace, third in heat, fourth in final, won £16. Number 23 is Derek Yorke.

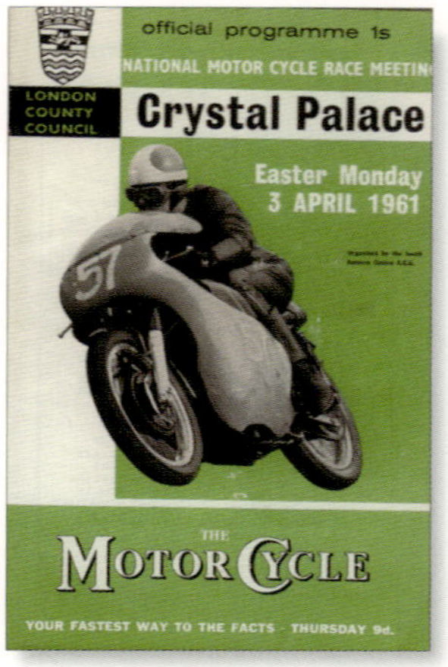

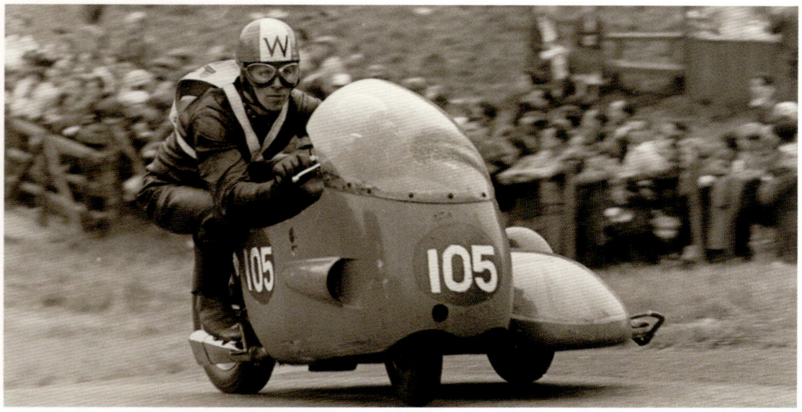

Les Wells, Cadwell Park.

years later was to race the Seeley product), Joe Dunphy, Griff Jenkins and Norman Surtees, brother of John - whatever happened to Norman? There was also Michael O'Rourke with the Ariel Arrow, who had achieved that fantastic seventh place in the 1960 250cc Isle of Man TT with that machine. For the sidecar events, three heats with full grids of nine outfits would be run. There were 27 competitors plus another 10 outfits as reserves and we were one of those crews. With such riders of the day in attendance Canterbury Sidecars' top man Pat Millard, E.A.G Vincent, Derek Yorke, P.J. Hardcastle were there. Also there was Les Wells, a real charger, who was at a later date to be killed tragically by crashing his van causing a gas bottle to explode. Les was a really good guy but super aggressive and quick on the track. Although I only knew him for a short time I perhaps unconsciously looked back and based myself on his racing approach. With the first three from each 5 lap heat going onto the 10 lap 13.9 mile final, for us it was going to be a tall order. Fortunately we were chosen from the reserves to compete in a heat. By then it was raining and so our first race was to be in wet conditions. With no front mudguard fitted, the spray was appalling, but what an experience! Hardly seeing in which direction we were headed, we skated to the finish in third place and a position in the final - phew that was lucky! With the rain still belting down, we removed the screen and fitted some canvas across the top of the fairing to act as some sort of mudguard, reducing the spray thrown into my face - proving to be only partly successful in the final event. Achieving a good start in the race, Les Wells, the star, soon came rushing by at awesome speed in the wet conditions and nearly scooped us up in the process. Dispensing with my steamed up goggles we were flying blind. Les Wells won and we struggled into a fourth place and £12 in prize money. A significant result, an indication of our racing future.

We entered for Mallory Park the next weekend, but had our entry rejected. In that case, I was going back on two wheels entering the April 100 mile Scrambles event being held at Tunnel Hill in Pirbright. Again my entry was rejected as they had a full house. I decided there and then that my days of riding on the rough were over. Around four years of fun and physical effort had honed my body into good shape, connecting with machine and throttle balance provided invaluable experience for my road racing career yet to come.

The month of May 1961 we were back to Brands Hatch as reserves in the programme for the Whit Monday event, held over the short circuit. We gained a fifth in the 500cc race, second place in the handicap and once more we were in the money, with £6 of winnings.

Our next racing venture was to be on a totally different level. Whatever gave me the idea I shall never know. Could it have been the fascinating BBC radio reports on the Isle of Man races that I listened to whilst repairing motorcycles was I just plain crazy or perhaps 'wet behind the ears'? From the start of the 1961 racing season, our results had given us sufficient points to obtain a restricted ACU International Licence. We had a whip-round for the entry fee of £9 and yes, entered our first Isle of Man TT sidecar race. Being new to the road-racing scene, having our entry for the TT accepted was for us, like being included in the team to climb Mount Everest.

Few alterations to our now faithful Matchless outfit were carried out other than we now had a custom-made apron for inside the fairing, stopping the spray, and an opening cut into the front nose of the sidecar for a screen to be fitted. Wally could then see the way forward.

So the great adventure began. With the Thames van duly loaded we were on our way to the famous Liverpool Docks and caught one of the Manx Steam Packet ferries. This at the time, was an experience all of its own. We were fortunate and after a smooth $3^1/2$ hour journey (it can be extremely rough), 'The Island' came slowly into view. With many stories told about the beauty of Mona's Isle, we were not disappointed, the view of Douglas Bay glistening in the midday sunshine was inspiring.

Docking with a bump, the whole harbour burst into life. The porters busy helping foot passengers, vans driven into position to receive the island's essential goods, whistles and shouting heard as the vehicles stowed away in the bowels of the ship were craned off along with the numerous motorcycles which had been stored on the deck in every conceivable nook and cranny.

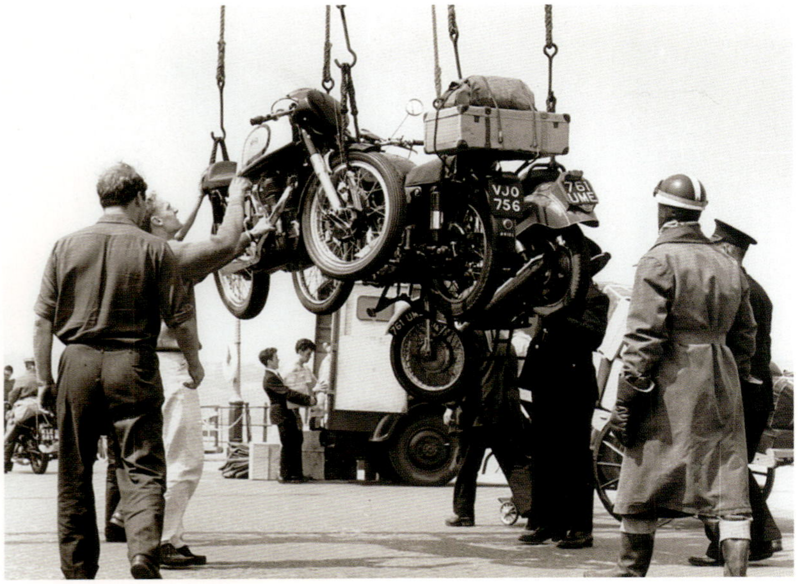

1960 Isle of Man TT, the horror of unloading the ferry by crane.

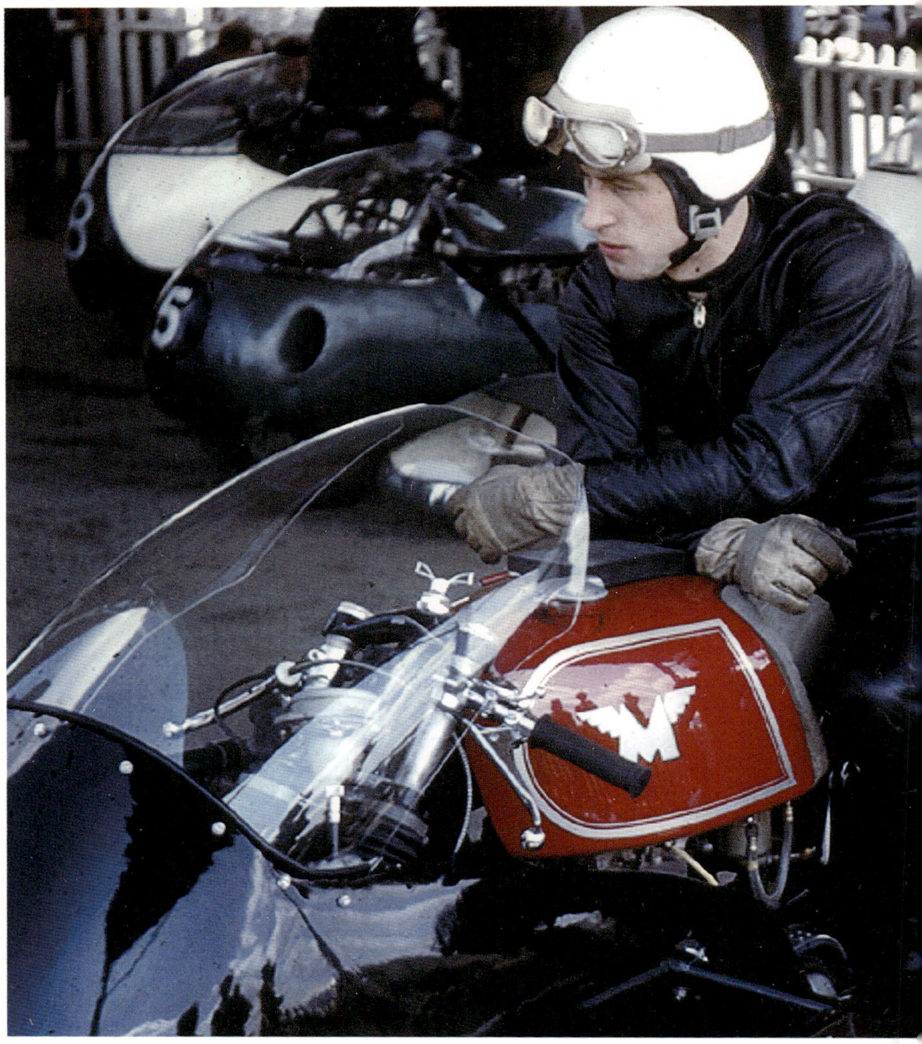

Safely unloaded from the ferry, our van was ready for departure from the hustle and bustle of the docks. We proceeded to our base camp, Beverley House, a private cottage at Mount Rule Road, Strang Braddan, a few hundred yards from the TT course at Union Mills. Mrs. Frances Clucas our host was to be 'mum' to us for a number of Isle of Man visits. Ma Clucas had a collie dog, which used to nibble at our heels and herd us to sit around the dining room table. Our host's home was open all hours. It didn't matter what time we came in at night or even in the early hours of the morning, she was always there to greet us with cries of 'Hello my boys!' By that time she would have downed several pints of Guinness - God rest her soul. If in one of her philosophical moods, we would have to sit and listen to her 'preachings', before retiring to the tune of 'my boys' ringing in our ears. Frances, although eccentric, was a great lady to whom we shall always be indebted.

Having the use of a large garden shed adjacent to Beverley House, we unloaded the Thames van, as we were eager to complete a lap of the TT course. From the start in Glencrutchery Road we proceeded in our van on a lap of the longest, most demanding and changeable course in the world. We had arrived to view our Everest and we were not to be disappointed. As we drove down Bray Hill it was hard to believe that most riders come down this hill in top gear with the throttle firmly held against the stop, hitting the bottom at speeds often well in excess of 140mph and missing the jutting kerb by inches. The rider is pushed down onto the fuel tank but in a split second the front wheel is pawing the air as the bike exits the dip on the way to Quarter Bridge.

Aghast, we continued down through Quarter Bridge, over Braddan Bridge and then 2 miles out from the start we arrived at Union Mills, our favourite spot-to-be with our local fans from nearby Strang always there to cheer. Then up the rise through the very fast section of Glen Vine, through Crosby and down past the Highlander Pub at great speed. No time for a drink. On to Greeba Castle and Bridge followed by another fast run into Ballacraine 7 miles out. From Ballacraine is the tricky and bumpy rock-lined Laurel Bank to Glen Helen section. The course then swings left, climbing past Sarah's Cottage onto the bumpy Cronk-y-Voddy straight 11th Milestone, down through Handleys arriving at the top of Barregarro. Rushing through the left kink at the bottom we were soon to be in Kirkmichael village, passing close by to the shops and houses, followed by Rhencullen, 15 miles out and a fast run to Ballaugh Bridge. Then following Quarry Bends, we sped onto the fast, but bumpy Sulby Straight. A tight right-hander over Sulby Bridge, through Ginger Hall, Kerrowmoar, Glentramman, Milntown and then we were down to School House and the approach to Ramsey, at sea level through Parliament Square up to the Ramsey Hairpin and then 24 miles out, the start of the mountain climb section.

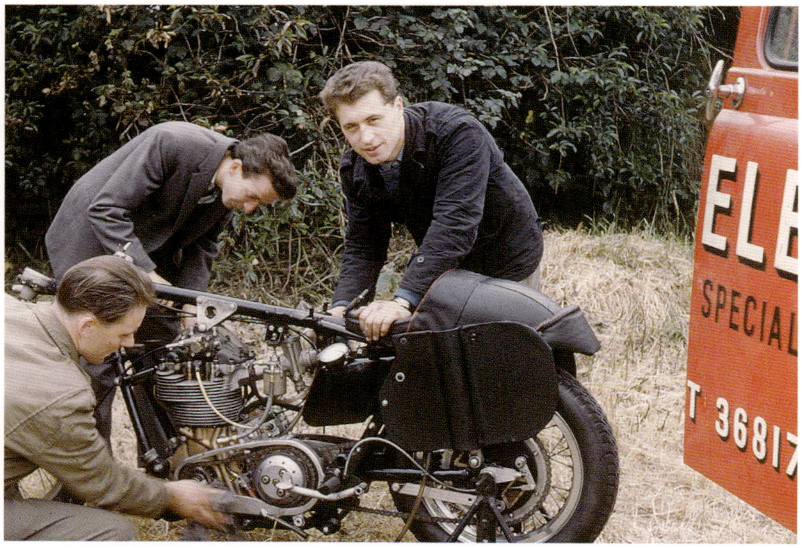

Working on the Matchless.

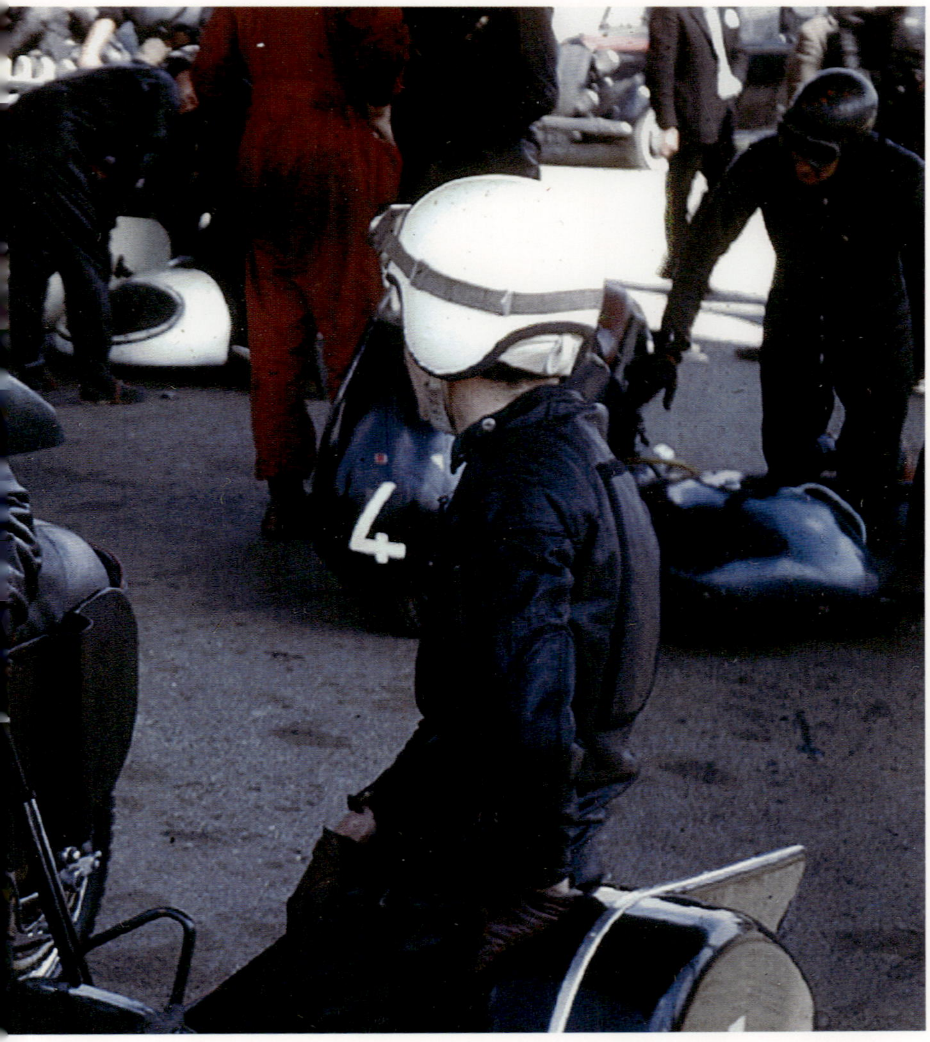

Waiting for action May, Brands Hatch.

The view at the Waterworks overlooking Ramsey Harbour is spectacular, but we had no time to stop and stare! Proceeding up to the Guthrie Memorial, now at 1,100 feet and still climbing, we carried on to the Black Hut and the Verandah section at 1,369 feet with a vast drop on the left hand side, before arriving at the Bungalow, 31 miles on, crossing the mountain railway lines and on to the highest point of the TT course.

Left at Brandywell there follows a gradual drop down to Windy Corner, 33rd Milestone, swinging left at Keppel Gate a fast run down past Kate's Cottage to the right hander at Creg-ny-baa still at 700 feet. We blasted down the very fast section, bordered by hedgerows, to the left-hander at Brandish, 35 miles out from the start - nearly home. Up the Hillberry and Cronk-ny-mona section we went, to the right-hander at Signpost, down to the tricky slow Governor's Bridge dip hairpin back out onto the Glencrutchery Road followed by the final run into the finish at 280 feet above sea level and 37.73 miles completed the TT course.

I realised after that first lap of the TT course that it had two distinct parts. The first part is the start down through to Ramsay passing residential homes, shops, pubs, colourful trees, green fields and hedgerows. Crucial knowledge is needed to achieve a quick lap with so many corners partly blind to your view and coming so quickly they allow very little room for error.

Once through the Ramsey hairpin and Waterworks you are out onto the mountain climb and the second part, the open section of bleak moors and mountainous landscape. Despite the climb the speeds are high and again intense concentration is needed, especially if misty conditions prevail. Hopefully, I have given some idea what faced us, and our fellow competitors with over 200 bends and corners to be remembered. The Mountain Course has, since its inception in 1911, been feared, loved, hated and admired throughout the world and we were there to experience it for ourselves. Having overcome the initial excitement of our visit and lap of The Island, it was time to sort out paperwork. So it was up to the start to confirm our entry and sign on with the ACU officials. Well it was similar to show business and 'Who's Who'. Unbelievably Geoff Duke drove the course car, and so close at hand were the racing heroes of the day - Mike Hailwood, Gary Hocking, Luigi Taveri, Carlo Ubbiali, Tom Phillis, Phil Read, Derek Minter, Alan Shepherd, John Hartle, Jim Redman, Bob McIntyre, Tommy Robb, Tarquinio Provini... they were all there! Sidecar aces Fritz Scheidegger, Max Deubel, Bill Boddice, Pip Harris and Chris Vincent and a certain Les Wells to name just a few, helped to make up the 200 plus entries. Many competitors and manufacturers were racing for those all-important World Championship points.

The sixties were certainly a very special period. I was totally unknown at that time but little did I realise that I was soon to know most of the top solo and sidecar competitors and my own named bikes would be racing around the TT course.

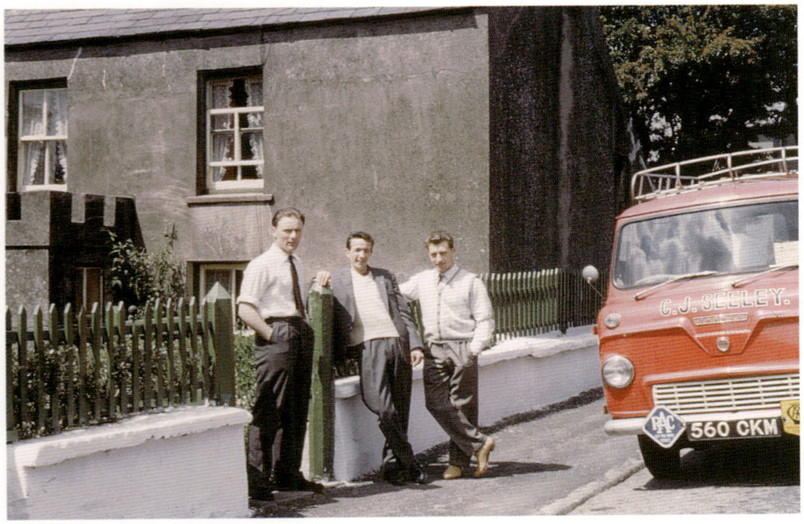

Frances Clucas cottage at Strang, Braddan.

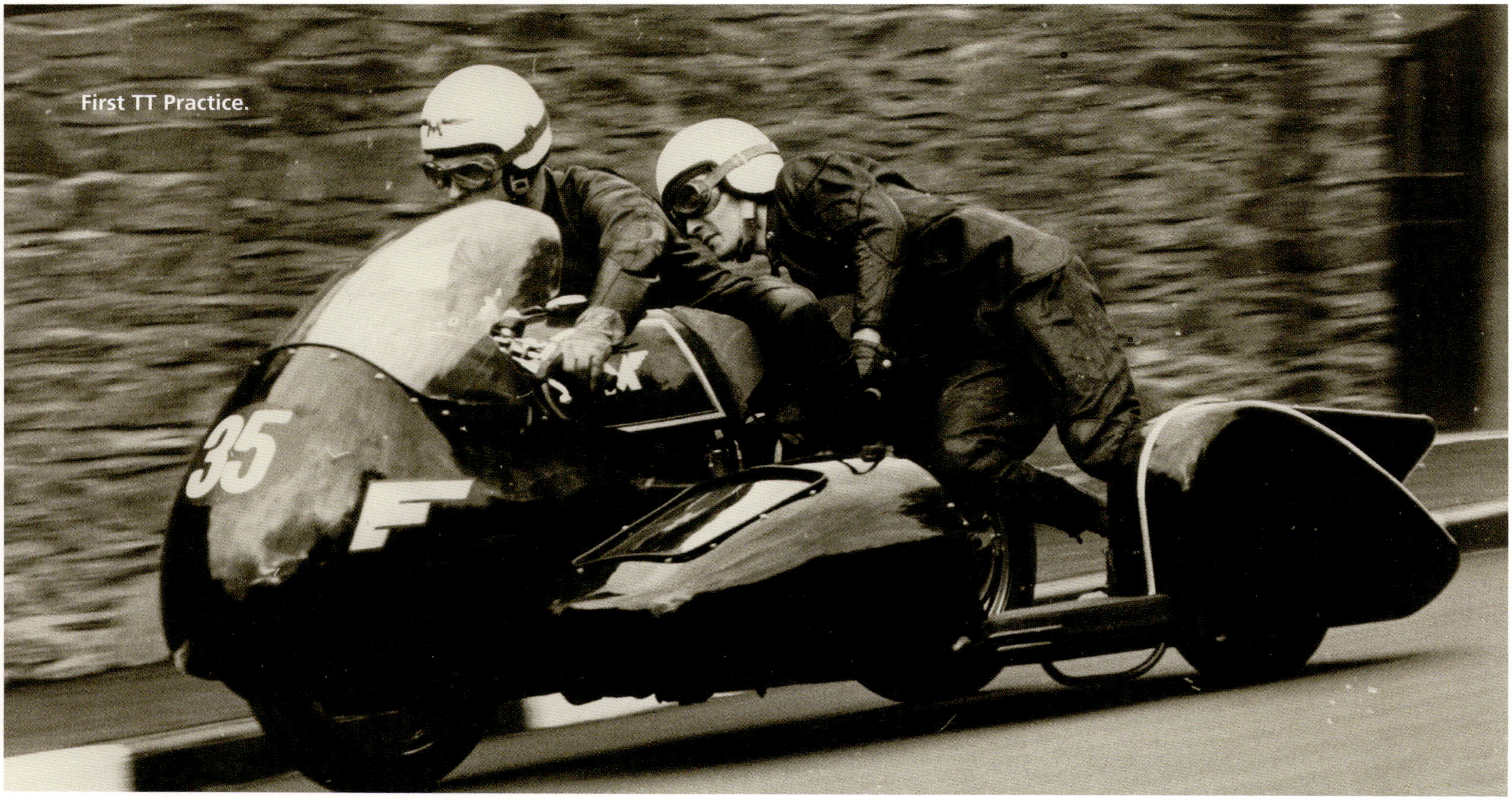

First TT Practice.

Back to the present, and having signed on we were allocated our race number, 35 from the 40 sidecar crews entered in the race. If in the first 10 finishers the previous year, you were allocated an early race start number, otherwise your start position was pulled out of a hat. With a number of non-starters the field was reduced to 32.

Starting at 10 second intervals, Wally and I, paired with another sidecar team, would be last away. Coming from the back often caused a problem as overtaking slower riders was particularly difficult with an outfit. In order to learn the course we would drive round at least twice a day in our Thames van, including one lap at night with headlamps dipped. That really made you concentrate, particularly as the van was being driven to the limit most of the time. Our first practice was scheduled for Saturday evening of June 3rd at the start of practice week. We had ridden up from our base at Strang to the start for the outfit to be scrutineered before the beginning of official practice. I enjoyed afternoon or evening practices as they reminded me of the A20 Oakdene days. Anyway, with conditions warm and sunny we must have adapted to the course pretty quickly as we finished the evening fifth fastest having completed 3 laps, (the full race distance). Not bad for our first attempt! Both Wally and I were chuffed to bits with our efforts and went back to Frances Clucas to give her the good news. She would be on the Guinness tonight!

The next practice session, planned for early Monday morning, was to be a rude awakening, rising at 3.00am to have a light breakfast, then sliding into a cold thin leather racing suit and pulling on boots making sure whilst half asleep we had picked up our helmets, goggles and gloves before walking out into the darkness like zombies.

By torchlight we opened the shed to wheel out the Matchless G50 outfit, trying to be as quiet as possible so as not to waken the Strang residents. It was a bit of a joke really, as we flicked the fuel tap on, flooded the float chamber, hooked into first gear, pulled back on compression, then within a few steps our G50 500cc single cylinder burst into life. Normally, with the open megaphone exhaust that beautiful noise is a joy to the ear, but at that time in the morning we were just trying to be quiet, but it is like trying to keep dry when you have fallen in a lake.

By then, we had woken the whole neighbourhood, including the bird population. Riding carefully on the public roads up to the start, the outfit was burbling and bouncing along on the bumpy roads. It did go through my mind how is it that we can keep the outfit on the track at that speed, but fortunately we could, as the stiff suspension begins to work. Now at the start and once more passed by the scrutineers, we were ready for action, despite the wet roads, dull conditions and mist on the mountain.

The starting flag dropped at 4.30am with Bill Boddice a front starter completing 2 laps on his Norton outfit. He summed up the TT course and conditions that morning, 'Well, it will certainly sort the men from the boys'. For us, I remember taking it easy on the first lap and thinking that it was bloody cold, wet and miserable. I wasn't a bit impressed by this insane practice period. Anyway we must have been gluttons for punishment. By the start of the second practice lap I had woken up somewhat, although by now the mist and fog had worsened on the mountain. Straight after completing that lap, for us it was a dash to the Cadbury tent for a hot chocolate before returning to base and bed. Later that day, Wally and I were in a Douglas coffee shop when our friend, Isle of Man resident and racer Sid Mizen joined us saying 'little Man' (that was his nickname for me), 'what do you think you were both up to in practice this morning - you crazy pair!' I was puzzled by this question until Sid showed us a copy of the TT Special newspaper in which it was reported that we had been fastest in that practice. Dream on! What a surprise and such a boost considering those poor conditions.

Throughout practice week the conditions varied with the Thursday morning sidecar period again awash with rain and mist, and visibility at Windy Corner down to some 10 yards. The Friday evening session however was held in near perfect weather with Fritz Scheideggar, BMW, Max Deubel, BMW, Chris Vincent, BSA, that man again Les Wells on the Norton, Pip Harris, BMW and Owen Greenwood, Triumph heading the leader board, which stood for the race. The final practice of the week was held Saturday evening, 10th June 1961. This was possibly the the worst session of a dismal week, heavy rain and mist on the mountain causing great concern and with the speeds well down it was Deubel from Scheidegger and Harris and, wait for it, Seeley/Rawlings in fourth spot - once more most pleasing. Wally and I had completed a total of 11 practice laps in the six practice periods, three of which we finished in the first six, the most laps of any crews and without any real incident.

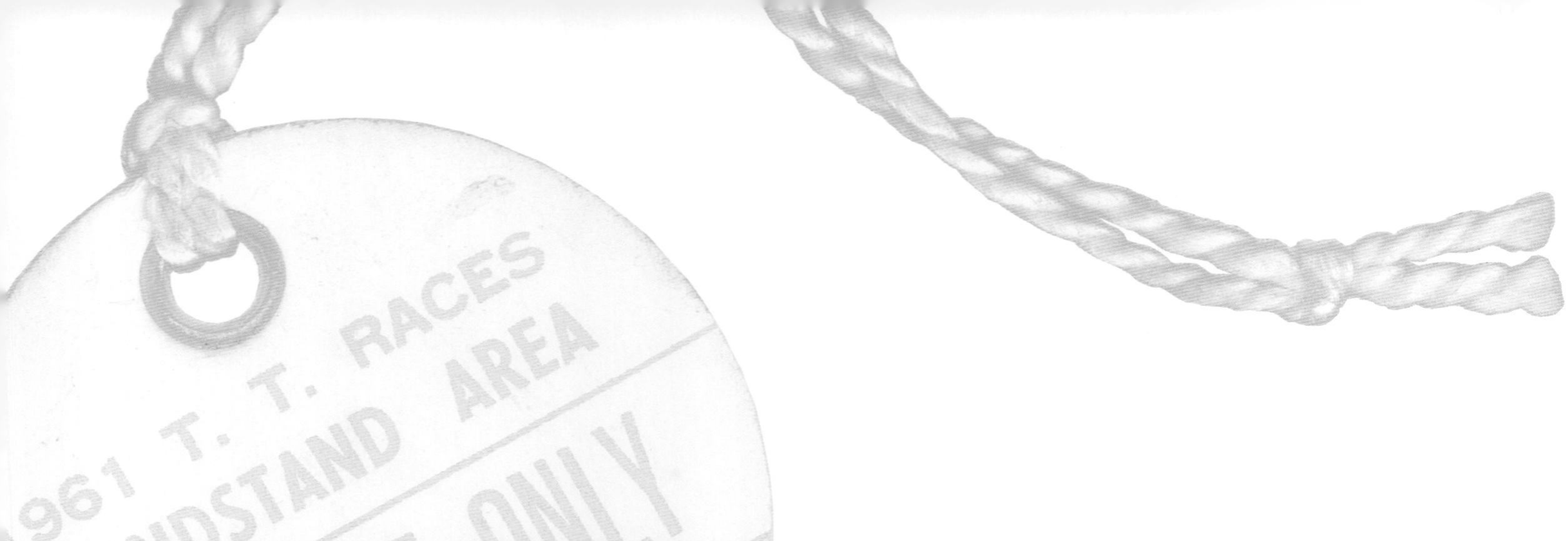

Wally as a passenger had adapted to the job in hand very well, despite the bruising incurred by the constant pounding. Stretched out on the sparsely covered platform, Wally weighing in at only 'nine stone nothing' at the very best, and built like a rake, had to pad out the inside of his race leathers to prevent him from being black and blue all over. Suffering a total of 14 laps punishment that year, it's a wonder that he did not have me up for 'GBH'. Unfortunately, that Saturday morning in the last solo practice session, 27 year old experienced Manx Grand Prix competitor Michael Brookes, riding in his first TT, crashed at Glentrammon, succumbing to his injuries the next day. This was the first fatality of the event that year and I cannot explain why, but this accident has always remained in my mind.

Sunday 11th June 1961 was final day for race preparation, the day before our race, Monday 12th June at 12.30pm. The Matchless G50 had been to date, totally reliable, but during practice week the staff at the AMC racing service, now interested in our progress, fitted a set of new piston rings and ground in the valves, free of charge. We on that Sunday changed the Castrol oil, checked the brakes and carefully looked at every item that could cause us a problem. We also scrutinised my welding on the sidecar fitting lugs which was still okay. Finally, we gave our chariot a good clean and polish.

Then, as was the custom, later that Sunday afternoon we rode the outfit up to the Grandstand start area for a final pre-race inspection by the scrutineers, surrounded by the enthusiastic fans waiting for autographs - but I don't remember being asked for ours at the time!

Once passed by the ACU scrutineers, the gleaming outfit was wheeled into a large marquee for storage overnight along with the rest of the competitors' machines. That was it, no more could be done. That practice week we had achieved more than we could have ever hoped for and tomorrow would be the real challenge, so back to Ma Clucas for dinner, tales and Guinness.

With the weather forecast good, race day dawned sunny with blue skies. The first race of the day was the 125cc event starting at 10.00am, in which Hailwood would spring a surprise by winning his first ever IOM TT by less than 8 seconds from Swiss ace Luigi Taveri. A historic first victory for the Honda Motor Company, in fact Honda took the first five places. Our race was not until 12.30pm, but because we were located inside the course at Beverley House, Strang and the roads closed half-an-hour before the first race, we had to be at the start area early.

For our first TT race I do not remember having any particular plans or serious ambitions other than trying to complete the 3 laps, 113.25 miles of this famous racing challenge, safely. Pat Millard's Norton/Canterbury had achieved an eighth place in 1960 and the management of Canterbury sidecars were quite rightly excited by this result. So, as a Canterbury agent I wanted to do better.

Many will be aware that when the Isle of Man TT started in 1907 it included sidecar racing. One famous competitor in the twenties was Graham Walker, father of the fantastic Murray. Although finishing second in the 1923 sidecar event, Graham was mostly a solo racer, achieving second place in the 1931 Senior TT and third in the Junior Race, riding Rudges. He achieved many high finishing places before he retired at the end of 1934. He then took to 'the mike' for the BBC and the man himself interviewed me in 1962 for the Schofield Isle of Man TT Sound Records. A photograph of this interview now hangs proudly on my office wall. Through a general lack of support for sidecar racing, the event was dropped in 1926 and not introduced again until 1954 when the 10.79 mile Clypse Circuit was opened using part of the mountain course.

With massed starts for the 125, 250 and sidecar classes, it provided a touch of mainland short circuit racing. However, in 1959 the Clypse Circuit was used for the last time with all racing returning, after a 34 year lapse including the war period, to the full 37.73 mile Mountain Course in 1960. Competing in that 1960 TT sidecar race at the age of 59 was Eric Oliver, four times World Sidecar Champion and a legend in his own lifetime. In a Wednesday afternoon practice session Eric, with passenger Stan Dibben set a new lap record of 79.71mph from a standing start. Then they crashed at Guthrie's Memorial, due to a fork steering head retaining bolt breaking. Although escaping serious injury, Eric had fractured a lumbar vertebrae and was advised not to ride again. So his TT was finished: and sadly, the end of a fantastic racing career. Nevertheless, Eric's lap of 79.71mph put

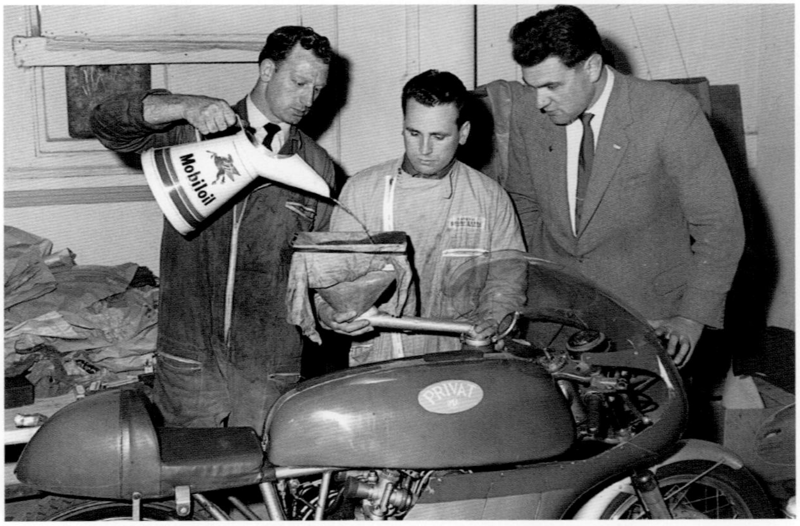

1961 TT, MV Agusta attention to detail Vittorio Carruana filters petrol, poured by Alf Gilbey with Mobil competitions manager Malcolm Edgar looking on.

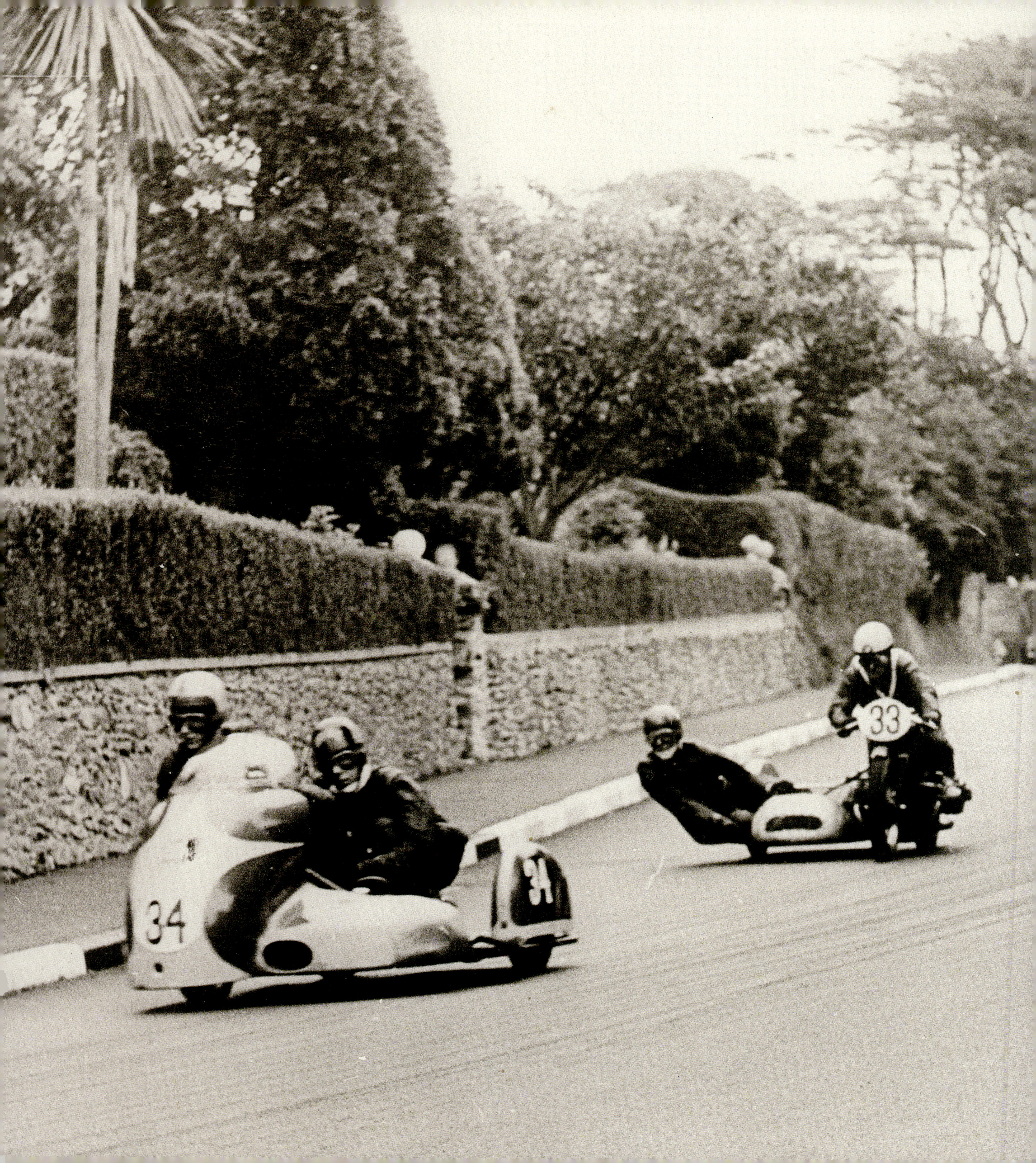
34
34
33

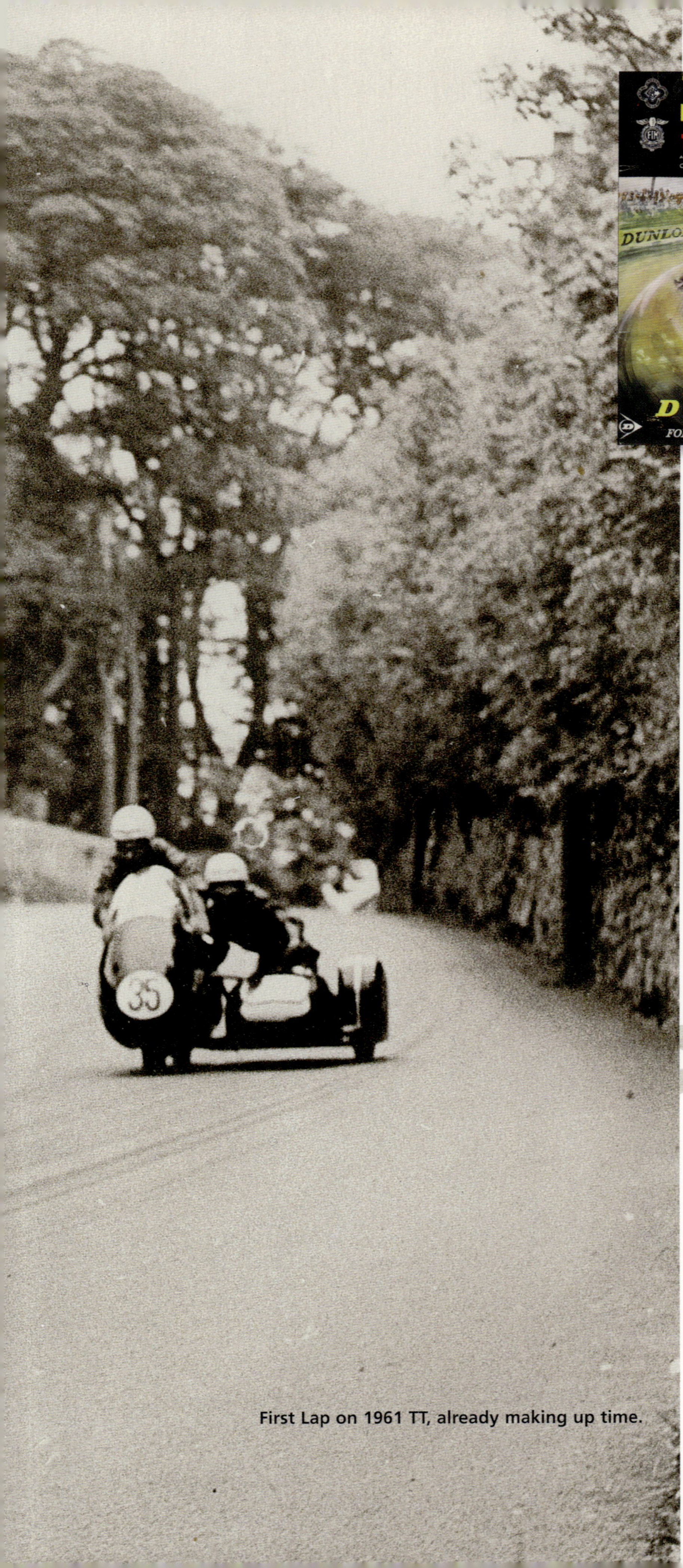

First Lap on 1961 TT, already making up time.

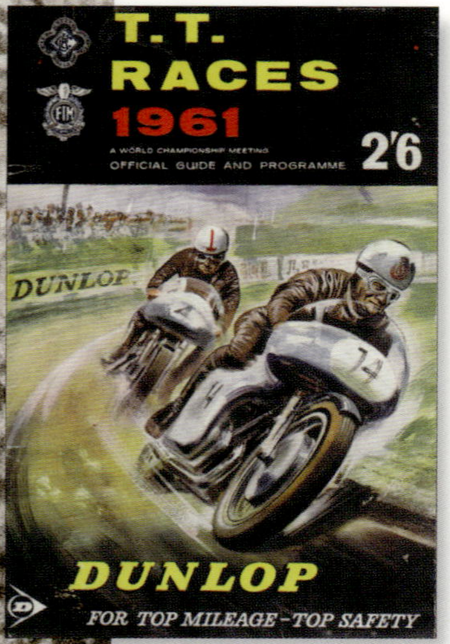

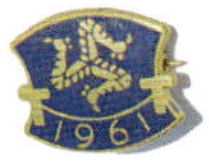

him in sixth place on the final practice leader board behind the BMWs and Chris Vincent's BSA. Eric at that point achieved the quickest single cylinder 500cc sidecar lap around The Island so it was my eventual ambition to try and beat this magic performance.

The 32 year old Helmut Fath from Ursenbach in Germany, racing sidecars since 1956, first raced the Isle of Man in 1959 finishing fourth on the Clypse circuit. In 1960 with passenger Wohlgemuth he was on good form, having just won the French Grand Prix, the first of that year's world championship events. Fath once more in competition with friend and rival Florian Camathias, who for the 1960 TT led the practice week from him. In the race itself Camathias led on the first lap with Fath only 7.6 seconds behind, same again on the second lap, but with Fath only six seconds back and a new lap record at 85.82mph. This was somewhat of an improvement on Freddie Dixon's 57.18mph 1925 sidecar lap record. Florian Camathias had first raced in the TT in 1957 riding a 250cc NSU in the lightweight solo event, then sidecars from 1958.

Back to the 1960 event, and Camathias was slowed down with engine trouble, finally finishing fifth. But for Fath, it was a great win with further successes to follow. Assisted by his passenger Wohlgemuth he became the 1960 World Sidecar Champion. Sadly Helmut was not to attend the 1961 TT due to a serious crash early that year racing at Nürburgring during which his passenger Wohlgemuth was tragically killed. A similar fate had befallen Florian Camathias that same year in a crash that resulted in his passenger Hilmar Cecco also being killed. Florian, although in attendance for the 1961 TT, was not competing, as he was nursing his left arm in a sling and limping badly. Wally and I were to become good friends with Florian over the next couple of years. The second place in that 1960 TT race went to Pip Harris on the BMW. Pip had raced on the Island since 1954. In third place was Charlie Freeman on the Norton with three TT events behind him and that man again, the builder from Walthamstowe, on the Norton, Les Wells in fourth position and A. Ritter on a BMW in sixth place. In splendid seventh place was Bill Beevers on his BMW. Veteran racer Bill had raced in the Isle of Man, apart from the war years, since 1935. He had competed in a total of 42 TT races both solo and sidecar events, including 36 races over the full Isle of Man mountain circuit, an absolutely extraordinary achievement. I was honoured to have known 'Gentleman Bill' who also acted as a travelling marshall in 1961.

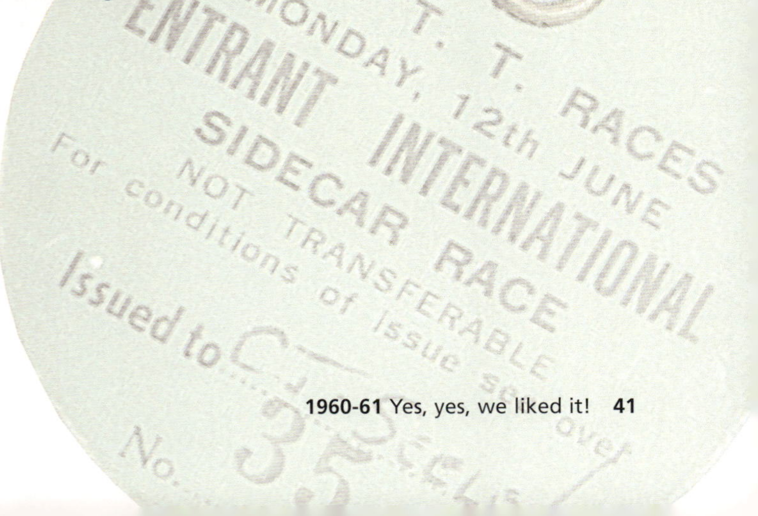

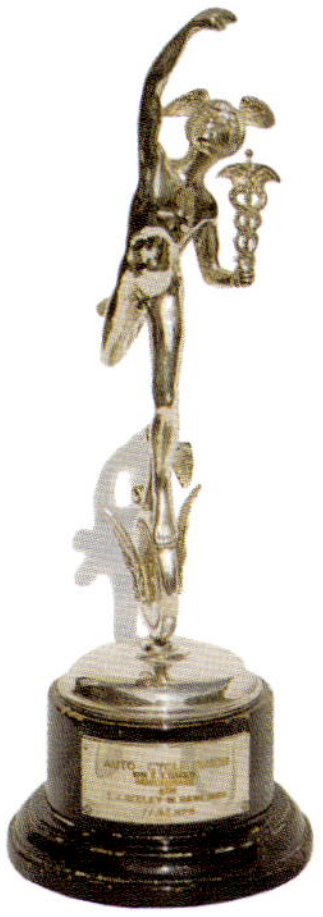

Suddenly, at twelve noon our race was nigh. The warm-up maroon was fired and within seconds the roar of 32 outfits burst into life, with crews warming engines, and taking a last nervous look over their machines. Did we put in enough fuel? Is the oil level okay? Tyre pressures? Checking the zips on our shiny Lewis race leathers and giving the goggles a final clean we made nervous last-minute adjustments to our helmet straps. The weather was still okay but there was some clouding over. We hoped that any rain would hold off. Then silence, as engines were shut down ready for the push start in pairs at 10 second intervals.

At 12.25pm the 5 minute to start maroon fired. No turning back now! Then it was all happening. The flag dropped and the first two away were Fritz Scheidegger's BMW and Charlie Freeman's Norton both pushing like mad, a roar and they were on their way. We being at the very back of the field awaited our fate with some trepidation. Then finally, it was our turn. Having selected first gear, I pulled back onto compression and then lifted in the clutch. We were ready, watching intently the official holding the stopwatch and in control of the flag. Then it dropped and within a few steps our Matchless fired into life and we were on our way. Rushing down the scary Bray Hill, my mouth was dry. It would stay that way for a few miles before the saliva would return and we had settled into some sort of rhythm. On corrected time Max Deubel had taken the lead from Fritz Scheidegger with Pip Harris third, all on BMWs. That's how it stayed to the finish. Meanwhile, Wally and I were making good progress gradually overtaking or catching up the opposition that had started in front of us to such an extent we accomplished seventh place on that first lap - only 75.5 miles to go.

Les Wells, who that same day became the proud father of a daughter, was during the first lap, in fourth place, on his Norton outfit, behind the BMWs (I told you he was good). Unfortunately he was forced to retire at the pits with a failed front brake.

The second lap for us was uneventful, no machine problems or hairy moments but we dropped to eighth place. We were holding steady for that all important last lap when I started imagining noises. Was it the big-end going, or had something fallen off, could we have run out of petrol? All sorts of things went through our minds with our concentration on a high as we approached the flat out and breathtaking Bray Hill. Within seconds 'swoosh' we were through the bottom dip, missing that protruding kerb stone by the necessary inches. No time to appreciate the many people gathered at that point. Then in a rush we arrived at Quarter Bridge, a slow sharp right-hand corner, where a great crowd was in attendance with encouraging waves from the TT enthusiasts. We quickly departed that section, over Braddan Bridge and soon swept through Union Mills. This was probably our favourite part of the TT course as our fan club of villagers and friends from the Strang area converged to give us a good cheer. This support was brilliant and great fun as we exited the Mills with Wally laying down on the platform and giving his feet a good waggle in acknowledgement of our well-wishers.

Soon we arrived at Ballaugh Bridge, 17 miles out, a full throttle approach, but down to first gear, ideally taking this hump-backed bridge under control. Taking off would result in the outfit crashing back to the tarmac, putting everything under undue stress, including us. Speeding on through the fast Quarry Bends onto the Sulby Straight then a few tricky parts before arriving at the slow approach into Parliament Square, Ramsey, a totally built up area with shops, houses and pubs, but a real favourite with the spectators. By now the informed crowds sensed that Charlie Freeman, Norton, and we were holding good positions, behind the four BMW mounted crews up front. They gave us waves and cheers of encouragement. As we accelerated out of the square we were on our way to The Mountain for the last time. Negotiation of the steep right hand Gooseneck is quickly followed by The Mountain Mile, a rising, flat out section. I had time to stare over the splendour of the distant valleys and hills of this magnificent region, through The Verandah with the valley to the left some scary 1,000 feet below. Then, once more over the railway lines at the Bungalow then onto the highest point of

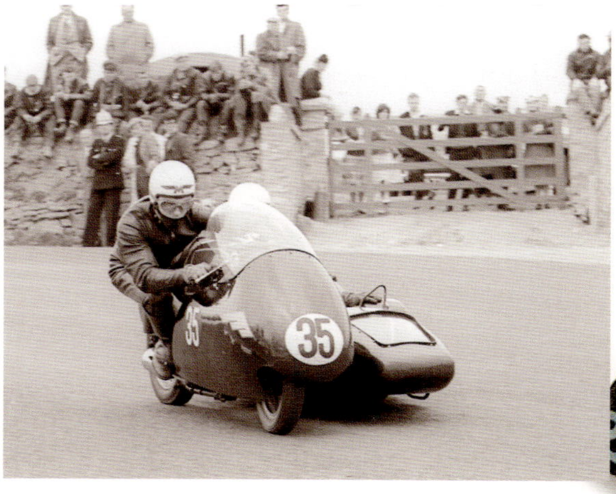

TT last lap at Signpost Corner

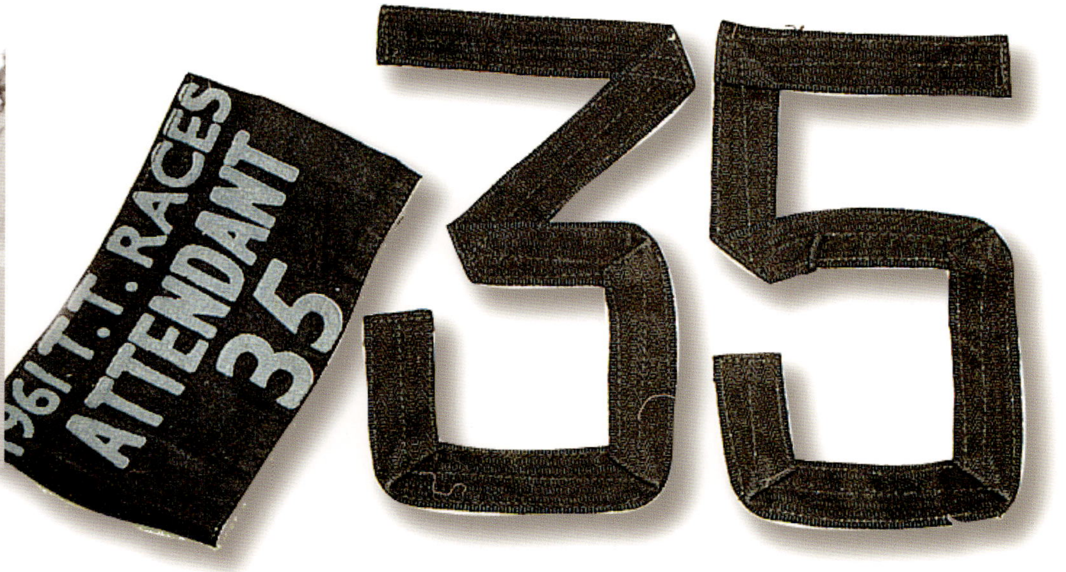

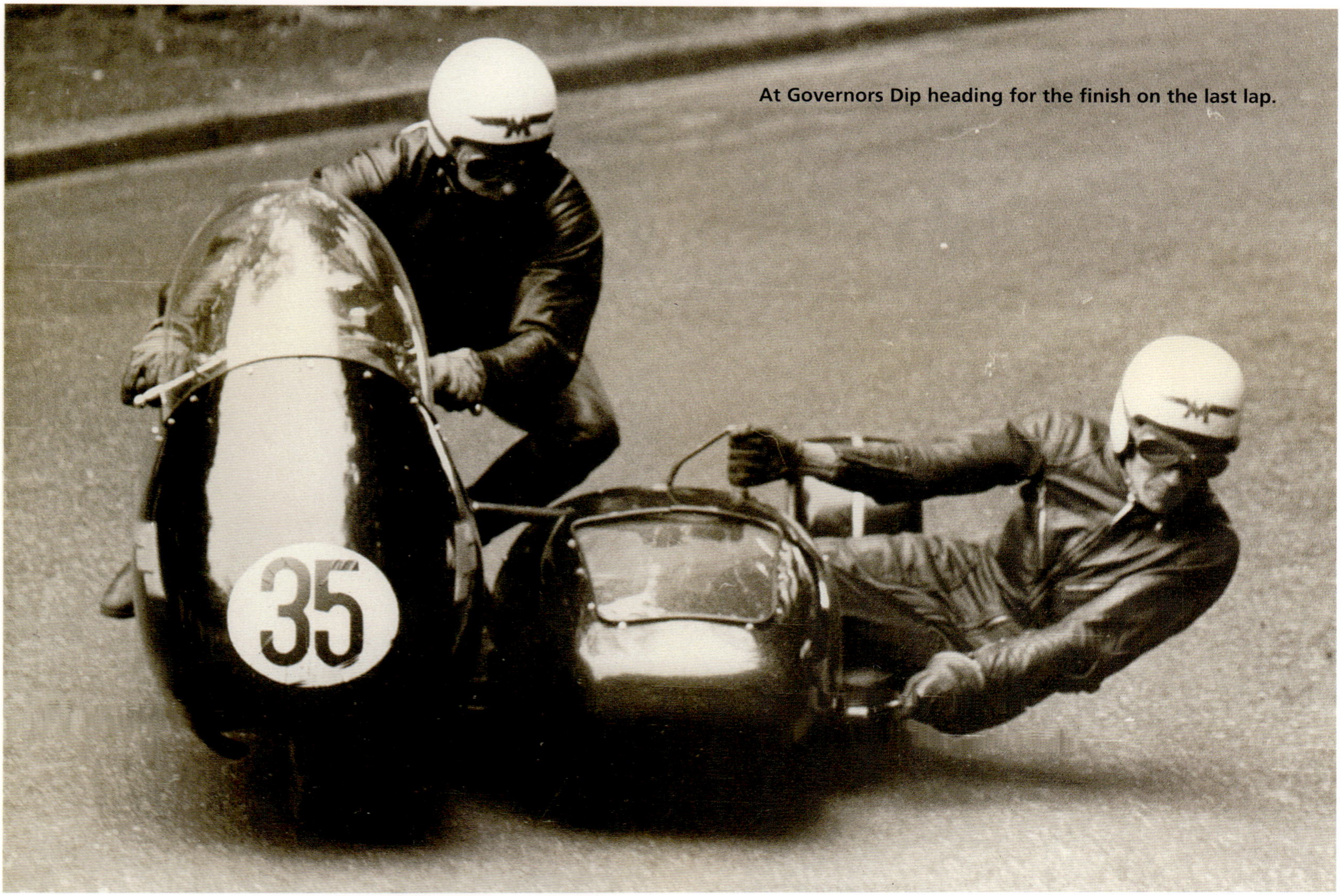

At Governors Dip heading for the finish on the last lap.

the course at around the 32nd Milestone, Brandywell, down to Windy Corner, Keppel Gate, and past Kate's Cottage on the way down to Creg-ny-Baa. Hundreds of people sat on the high surrounding grass banks waving their programmes. For us, so far so good, with only just over 3 miles to the finish, would we make it? What could possibly go wrong? Through Brandish then Hillberry, we fast approached Signpost Corner. Our light would now be on at the start and finish giant scoreboard so our pit crew would be getting excited. Then suddenly we were into Governors Bridge and the near-to-walking-pace hairpin. There was still time for things to go wrong. Many a rider has pushed in from here. However, we were okay. We accelerated out onto the Glencrutchery Road and just a few hundred yards to the waiting chequered flag. What a sight to behold at this famous start and finish, which had seen so many 'greats' past and present under the flag.

Charlie Freeman was in fifth spot. We were one minute behind in an unbelievable sixth place! Our first Isle of Man TT was fantastic. We had completed a total of 14 laps, 528.5 miles practice and race around this most awesome of circuits with our Matchless G50 outfit responding to our every demand. I now believed that Jack Williams - race chief at AMC would possibly change his mind about my racing a Matchless G50 and sidecar. I could not resist comparing my race lap times with those of 1960, with our times putting us in a hypothetical third place - pretty satisfying against such heroes.

Following the sidecar race was the five lap 250cc TT, at 3pm, with Mike Hailwood on the privately entered works Honda to do battle with Gary Hocking, riding a privately entered MV, with Bob McIntyre, Tom Phillis and Jim Redman all on works Hondas. From the start it was Bob McIntyre in front with a first lap of nearly 99mph average and a second lap of nearly the magic 100mph, Hocking was 25 seconds behind and leading Hailwood by 100 yards. These two had started together and after a terrific dice, lap 2 saw Hailwood in front of Hocking. Next time round Hailwood exceeded the 99mph lap but Hocking failed to complete the lap leaving Mike in undisputed second place on the fourth lap. McIntyre broke down before Sulby, leaving Hailwood to win his second TT that day on the Honda, having already won the 125cc race, the first ever TT win for Honda. Second was Tom Phillis then Jim Redman, Kunimitsu Takahashi, and Naomi Taniguchi in that order and all Honda mounted. A great, exciting and memorable race!

With the day's action over we returned to Beverley House, Strang to find Ma Clucas already on the Guinness and celebrating our success with, 'Halloo my boys, you was lovely through the Mills!' That evening we attended the official presentations held at the Villa Marina, rubbing shoulders with sidecar aces Max Deubel, Fritz Scheidegger and friend-to-be, Pip Harris.

With the presentations in reverse order, it was soon our turn to receive our Silver Replica. Silvers were awarded to riders finishing within 9/8 of the winner's time. Then came the Bronze Replica awards. The trophy awarded is a 10 inch high replica, a third size of the original winner's trophy first presented to the Auto Cycle Union in 1907. It embodies the figure of Mercury, the God of Speed.

For this year's sidecar race, only six Silvers were to be awarded and we were the sixth, plus £30 prize money. We felt so lucky and proudly we stepped onto the stage to receive our shining awards, shaking hands and waving to the knowledgeable audience. The end of a perfect day! Next day, basking in our 'new found glory', we packed up our tools, equipment and outfit ready for the journey home, but subsequently decided to stay to watch the Wednesday Junior and the Senior on Friday.

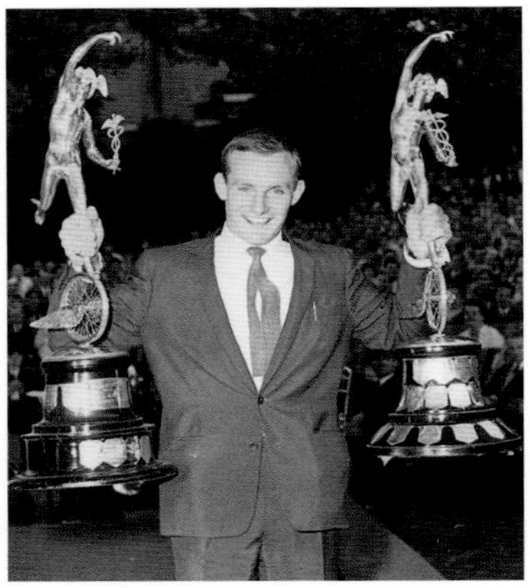

Mike Hailwood at the presentation.

Whilst in the Island on 10th June 1961 the Queen's official birthday, it was announced that John Surtees had been awarded the MBE for services to motorcycling. John was not in the Island having retired from motorcycle racing at the end of 1960 to concentrate on car racing but, not before winning in the period 1956-1960, six Isle of Man TT races and seven World Championships covering 350cc, 500cc events for the MV Agusta company. Driving for Ferrari he then won the 1964 World Formula 1 Motor Racing Championship. To date he is the only man ever to accomplish this, although this record could be broken by today's triple World Champion 22 year old Valentino Rossi who, with his special talent, has already shown serious ability in a car.

Junior race-day dawned perfect, with a scheduled start for the 6 lap race at 11.00am. The 80 competitors with their 350cc machines lined the Glencrutchery Road going through the regular procedure as described for sidecar races. Gary Hocking riding a privately entered MV was starting favourite, followed by Hailwood, Read, Minter and McIntyre. From the start it was that order for the first 3 laps after Bob McIntyre's Bianchi twin broke down at Sulby on the first lap. The fourth lap saw Hailwood's AJS in front from Hocking, Phil Read, Derek Minter, Ralph Rensen all on Nortons, with scrambler Ron Langston, AJS, in sixth place. Fifth lap and it was still Hailwood in the lead but now Read was second and Hocking third. It looked as if Mike might win three TT races in one week, this having never been achieved in the history of the TT at that point. It would also make him the first all-British winner of a Junior TT since 1954. However, it was not to be. On the last lap he retired at Ramsey with engine trouble, leaving Phil Read to take that honour and to win his very first TT race. Hocking, second followed by Rensen, Minter and Franta Stastny on the Jawa, with Roy Ingram in sixth place on his Norton. Bob Rowe was in twentieth place and another Silver Replica was added to his collection.

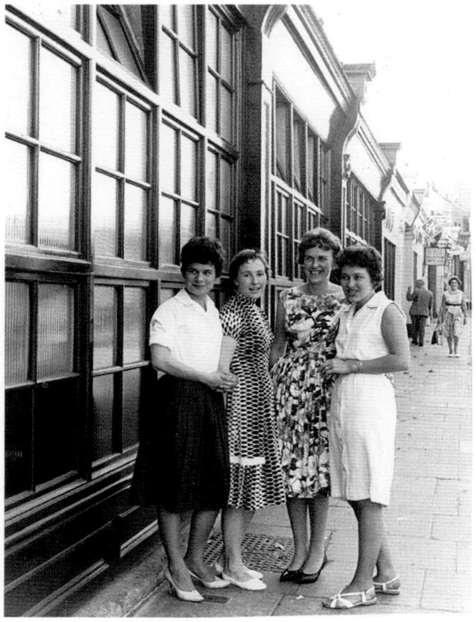

Joan and her colleagues outside the AMC offices in Plumstead Road.

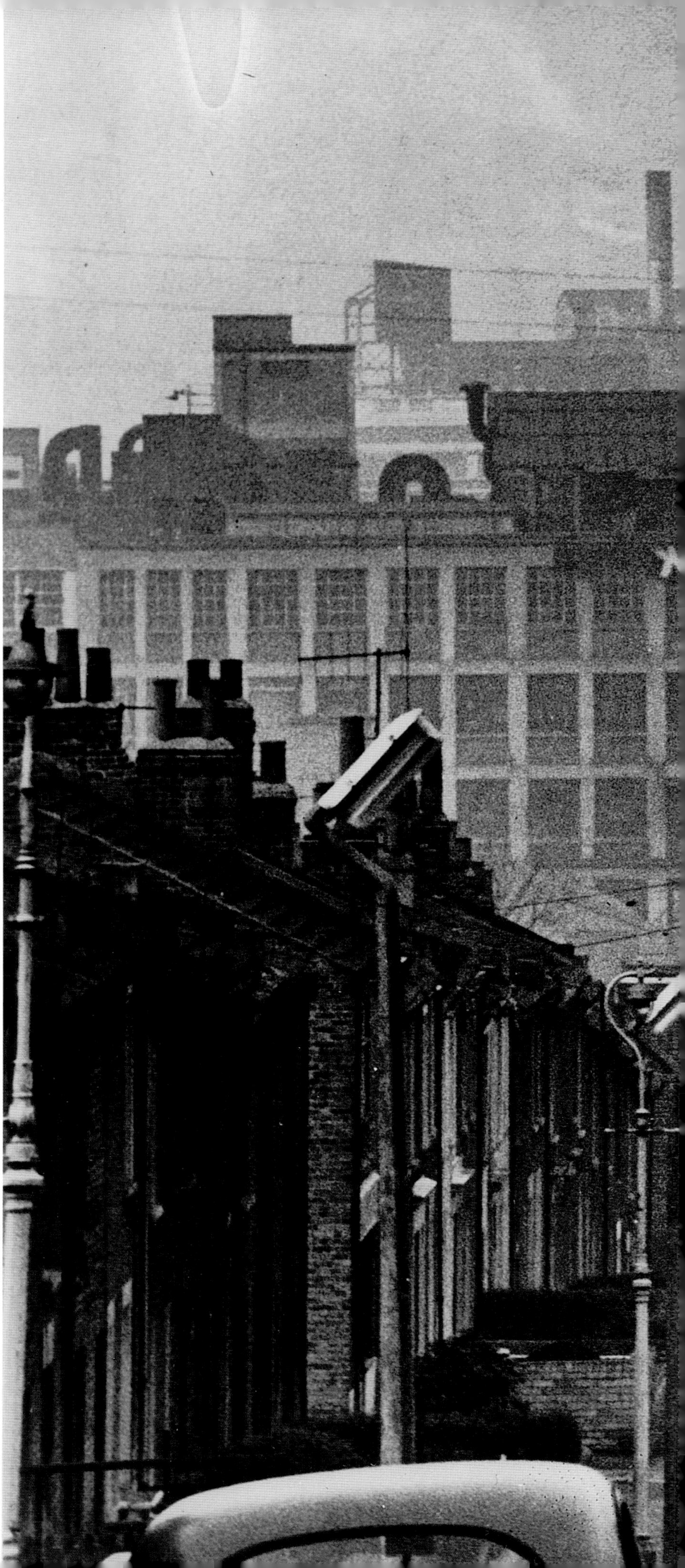

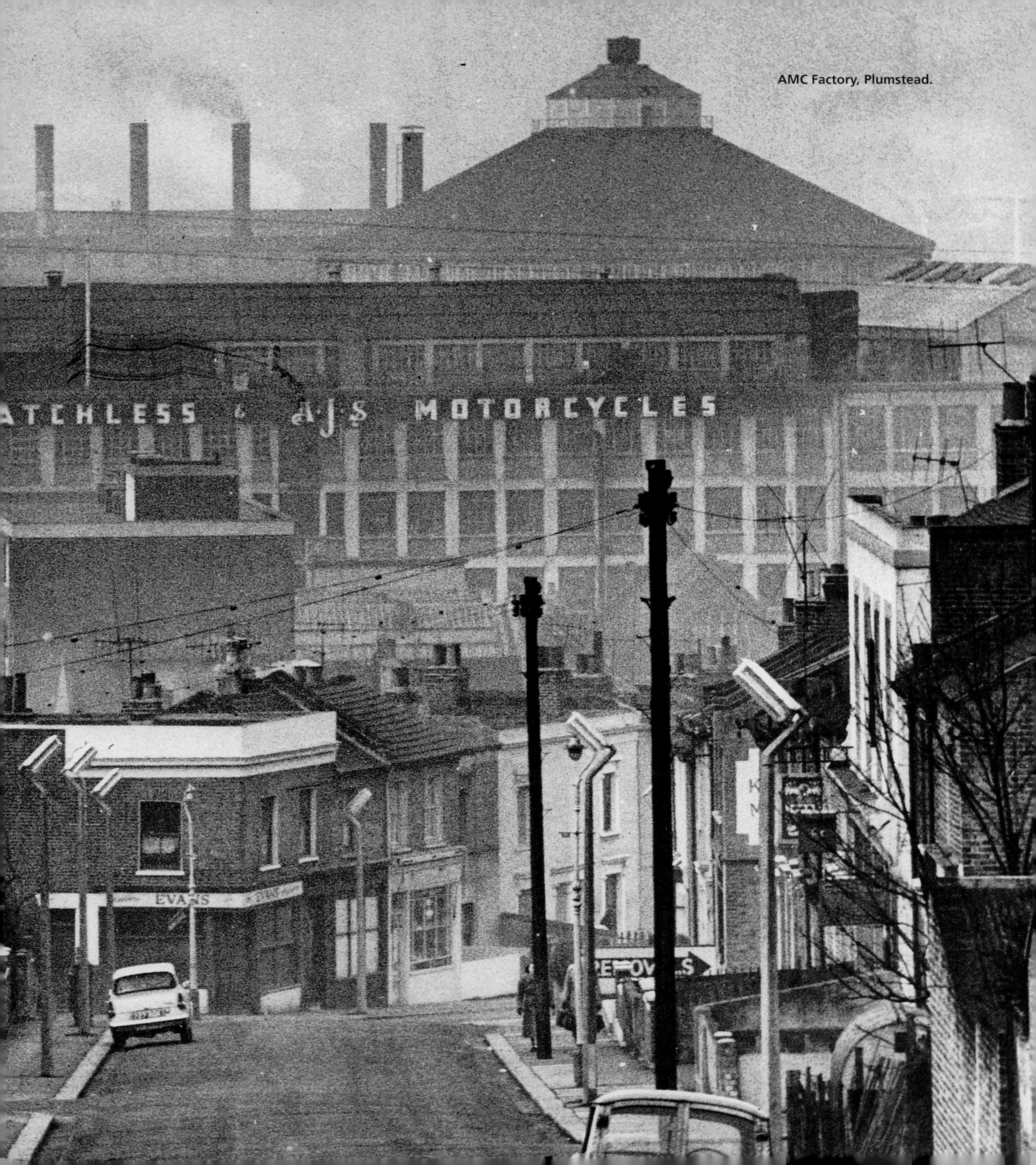

AMC Factory, Plumstead.

Tom Phillis on the experimental Norton Dominator twin.

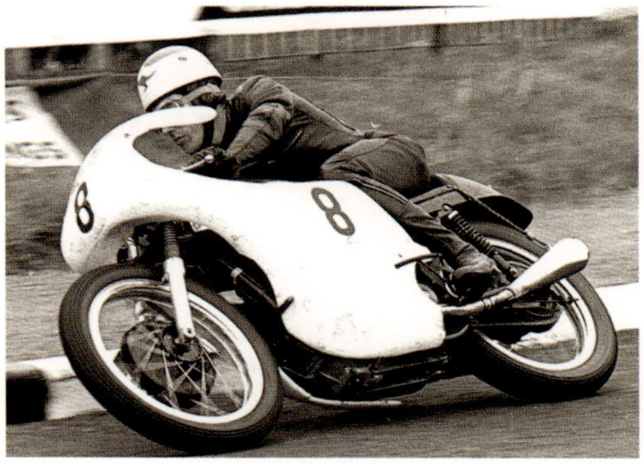

Senior TT all Norton rostrum; Phillis, Hailwood and McIntyre.

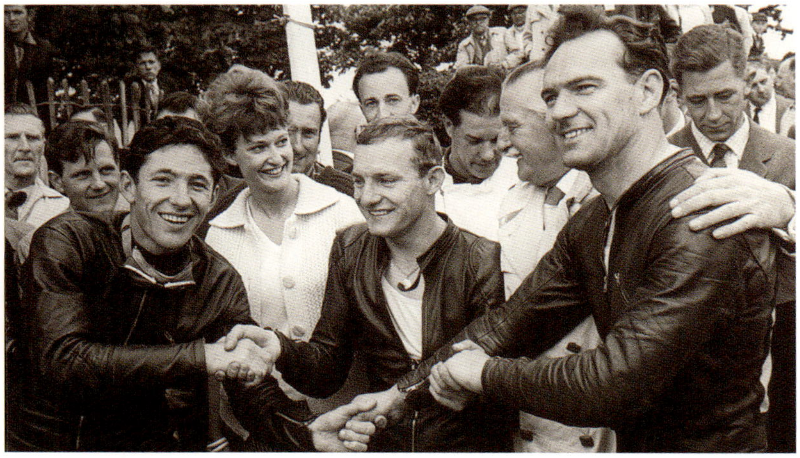

As our first TT fortnight was drawing to a close, it was finally, the prestigious Senior race held on the Friday for 500cc machines. The weather forecast for the day was not brilliant; bright periods in the morning, cloud and drizzle in the afternoon, visibility good with some damp patches under trees and a strong head wind on the mountain.

An additional five Manx ferry loads of enthusiasts had arrived from the mainland on Friday morning to join the thousands already lining the course. With once more a 11.00am start for this 6 lap 226.5 mile race the competitors were ready for action with all procedures followed. Favourites once again were Gary Hocking on his privately entered MV, with Hailwood, McIntyre, Read and Phillis all on Nortons. On the first lap it was that man Hocking again from Hailwood who lapped at 100.63mph with Read in third, McIntyre in fourth and Tom Phillis racing an experimental Norton Dominator twin in fifth place. Derek Minter, the first man to lap the Island course at 100mph on a single in the 1960 TT, was in trouble in ninth place and dropping back. By the third lap Hocking was still leading Hailwood but McIntyre was now in third. Fourth lap still saw Hocking holding a slender lead from Hailwood with Tom Phillis now third, Bob in fourth place, Phil in fifth and Ralph Renson sixth, with less than a second covering the first four, it was all so close.

At the end of the fifth lap Gary Hocking retired with sticking throttles, Phil Read on the last lap came off at the Gooseneck and retired. Minter pushed in from Governors Bridge to finally finish thirteenth. Hailwood won the Senior Race from McIntyre with Tom Phillis an incredible third on the Norton Dominator twin. Mike Hailwood achieved the three TT wins in one week and the honour of the first all-British Senior win since 1951.

At the end of a wonderful race with very few incidents came tragic news. Ralph Rensen from Liverpool, riding in the Isle of Man TT since 1955 and finishing that week in 1961 sixth in the 125 event and third in the Junior, crashed on the fifth lap at the 11th milestone. He died as a result of his injuries. A stark reminder amongst the joy of success that the Isle of Man TT course can hit back. It is to many, a mountain that has to be climbed, but sadly by its very nature, fatalities happen.

We said goodbye to Mona's Isle and it was back to business. What would be next on our calendar? Arriving home at Belvedere, we received a surprisingly rapturous welcome from friends, customers, family and the local press. 'Local boys make good' the headlines read. I often wonder what we would have received if we had actually won that TT event.

With only three weeks to go before our next race meeting at Brands Hatch on 9th July, it was back to reality. This brought some relief to Dad who had been taking care of the 'ranch' in my absence. The day after our return I was eager to visit the AMC factory and could not wait to show our Silver Replicas to Jack Williams and our friends in the race shop. With an original sidecar entry of 39 competitors for the 1961 TT made up of 15 Nortons, 13 BMWs, five BSAs, five Triumphs and our solitary Matchless - the factory had to be pleased. Certainly, they were delighted with our success, being the new boys on the block. Following the race shop visit I sped my way round to the administration offices at the front of the AMC factory, requiring a favour from Eric Ritson the sales manager - early delivery of a Matchless G12. Also it gave me the opportunity to chat up the office girls, in particular a certain Joan Anderson who I had been seeing for quite some time.

I dazzled the whole sales department with my enthusiasm and my sparkling TT replicas. I was never one to lose an opportunity and it gained me next day delivery on the G12 plus a further date with Joan. Also I was to be featured in the proposed 1962 Matchless motorcycle sales catalogue along with Joan as a model, what a result!

With the Brands Hatch meeting looming we pulled the Matchless Canterbury outfit from under the covers, changed the oil, checked the rocker clearance, altered the gearing, fitted some new Avon tyres and gave the machine a general check-over before the final clean and polish. Then once more we were ready for action.

This was our first race on the 2.65 mile long Brands circuit. Solo competitors included Mike Hailwood, Dan Shorey, Tommy Robb, Fred Neville, Phil Read, John Hartle and Derek Minter. We ourselves were up against Chris Vincent, Pip Harris, Bill Boddice and Fred Hanks on the front row, with us next to last on the fourth row behind Jackie Beeton and Owen Greenwood. We had managed the Isle of Man TT, but it can take a number of laps of short circuit racing to get back into the groove for the 'splash and dash' of the short races. This was still something we needed to learn. With the 8 lap

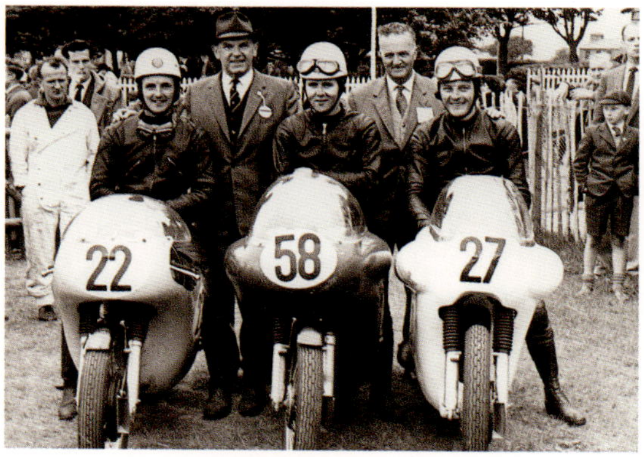

Senior TT, manufacturer's team prize for Matchless. Left to right, Derek Powell, Jock West, Billy McCosh, Jack Williams and Ron Langston.

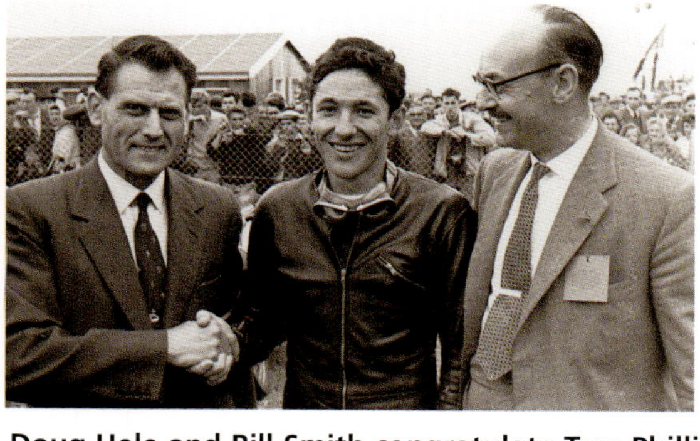

Doug Hele and Bill Smith congratulate Tom Phillis, who finished third on the Dominator twin.

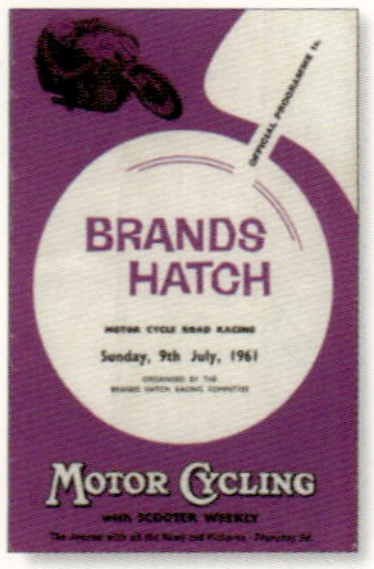

Close encounter at Brands Hatch.

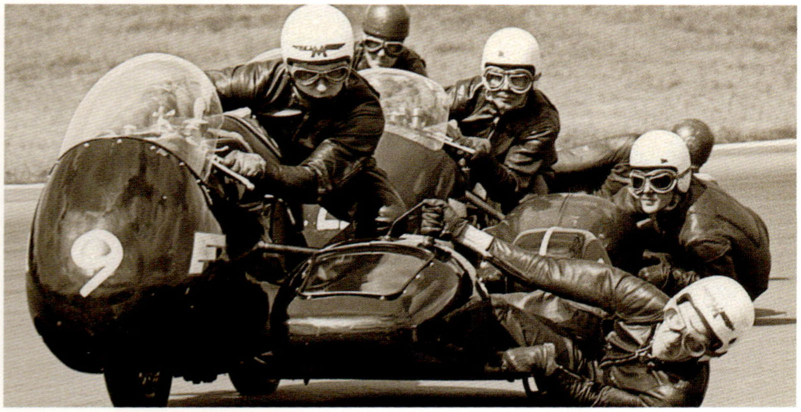

scratch race up to 1200cc, Chris Vincent on his 650cc BSA kneeler led from start to finish. Pip Harris on his BMW was in second place and we managed a reasonable fifth and then a fourth in the handicap race. This gave us a total of £6 prize money won from two races. Earlier that day at Brands Hatch it had been suggested that I might request from the then Manager/Director Mr. Hall some start/expense money. This at the time was all new to me, so slightly embarrassed, I knocked on Mr. Hall's office door. I remember he was a nice man, and I returned to Wally and my helper friends clutching a £5 note. This, added to our £6 prize money, made it a good day!

Later, on 30th July, it was off to Snetterton, for our third visit to this open ex-airfield 2.71 mile fast circuit. I really enjoyed racing at Snetterton as it had plenty of room, much needed as there were often 30 sidecar crews on the grid. Once through Riches and Sear corners we careered down the Norwich Straight, hoping we could slow down enough at the end to take the hairpin. Then on the return straight, through the tricky 'Esses' and onto Coram Curve, a really fast long right curve, brought you in those days onto the fast finish straight, which was just brilliant.

That day our faithful Matchless G50 was really singing. 27 starters on the grid for the 500cc race included the regular stars: Boddice, Vincent, Harris, Wakefield and Beeton. Gungy Wal and I achieved a very creditable and satisfying third place behind Pip Harris, BMW in first place, Chris Vincent, BSA in second, with Bill Boddice on his Norton fourth.

With 33 starters assembled on the grid for the 1200cc sidecar race, I remember Wally and I came from the back of the field to take an early lead. We were getting the hang of good starts. Pulling back onto compression then a good push and in a minimum of strides the G50 would burst into life. We finished this race in a most enjoyable fourth place, once again from Pip Harris, Chris Vincent and Jackie Beeton, BMW, the first single cylinder machine home once more. Les Wells would be proud of us. Also there was a magnificent £22 in prize money! So it was a stop-over in Newmarket on our way home to celebrate with steak and chips.

Fresh from our success at Snetterton, the Matchless outfit had its regular service before journeying north the following weekend for our first visit to Oulton Park, Cheshire. This event was an international and British Championship rolled into one. It attracted a strong solo field including Mike Hailwood, Alan Shepherd, Tommy Robb, Phil Read, Derek Minter, John Hartle, Bob McIntyre, Dan Shorey, Ron Langston and Fred Neville to name just a few, not forgetting our friend Dave Downer. The international sidecar event always attracted the continentals. Max Deubel, Florian Camathias, Fritz Scheidegger, Edgar Strub were there to compete against our best, Pip Harris, Chris Vincent, Jackie Beeton and Bill Boddice. So the racing would be tough.

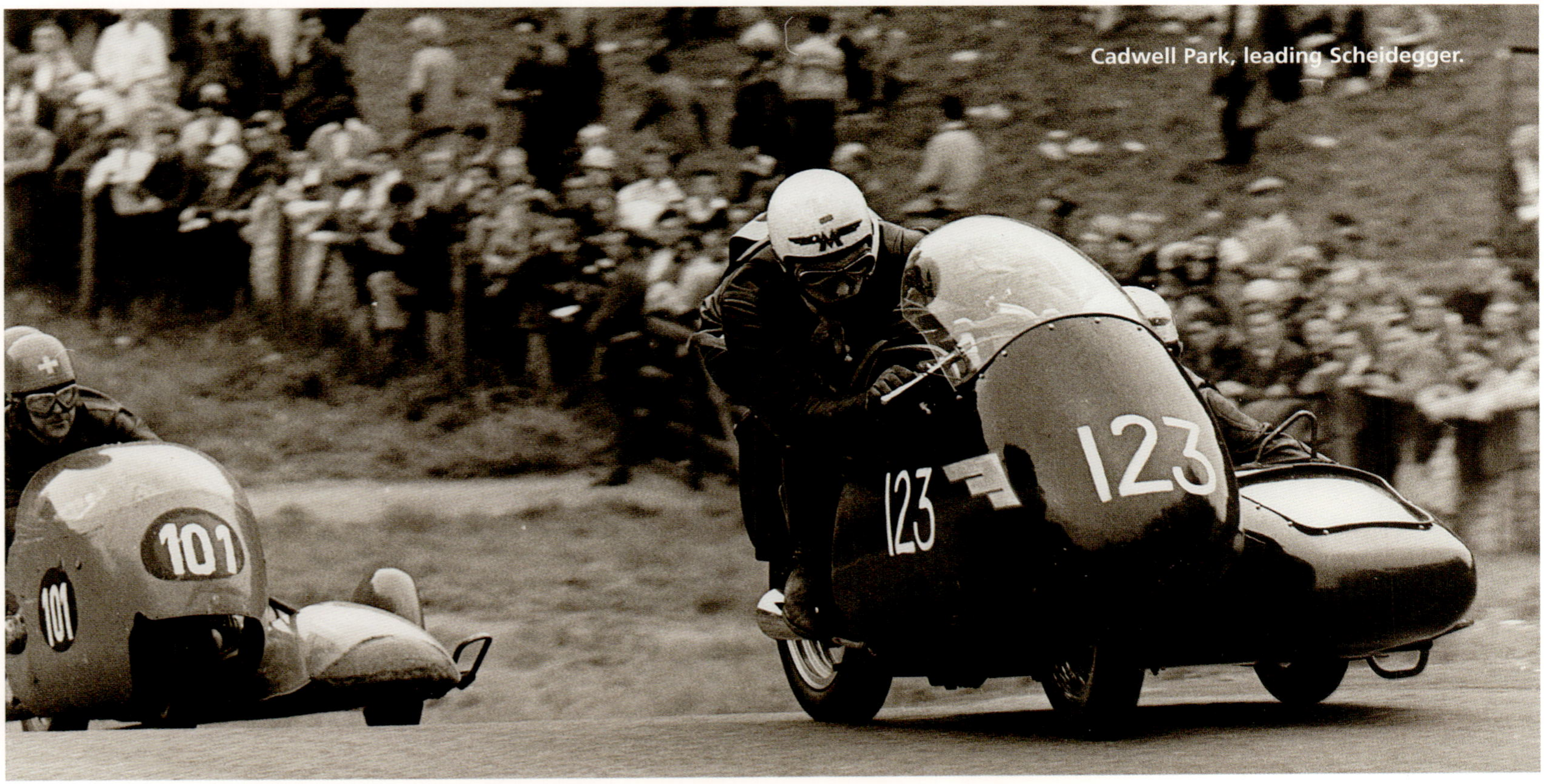

Cadwell Park, leading Scheidegger.

Mallory Park 1959, Mick Woollett and Dennis Jones

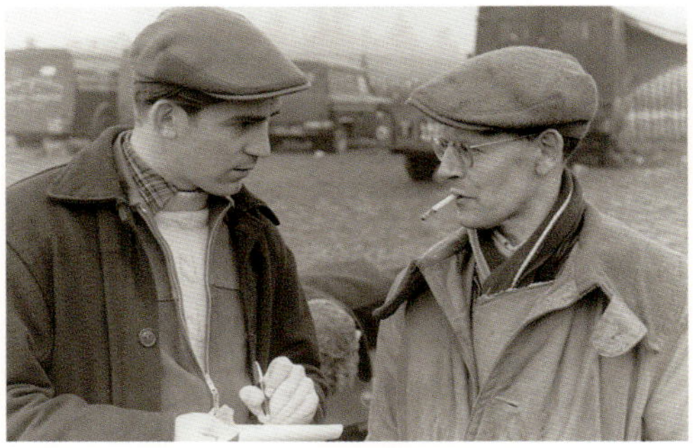

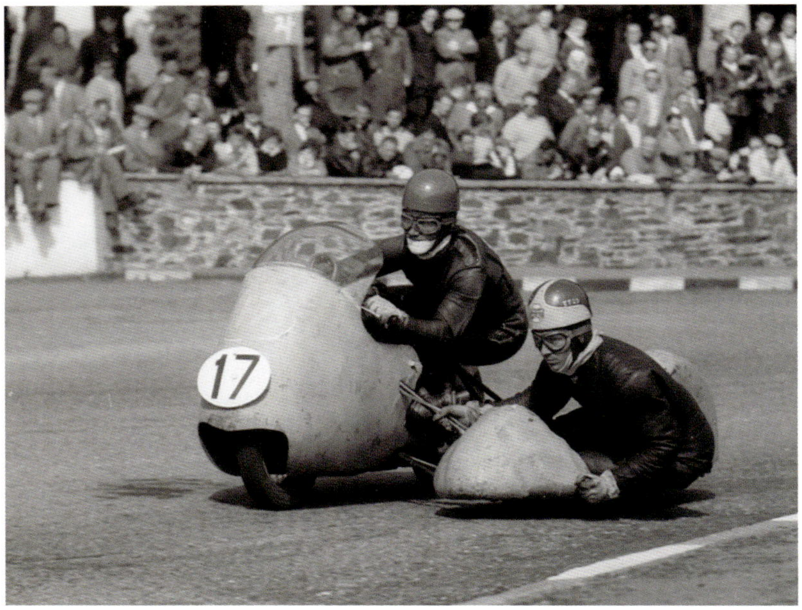

1959 TT, Edgar Strub, BMW, with Mick Woollett heading for 5th place.

Mick Woollett, then sports editor of Motorcycle News, who wrote the Oulton Park programme foreward, was reminded that he first visited Oulton Park back in April 1956 as a sidecar passenger to Cyril Smith and later to ride with Swiss rider Edgar Strub. Mick Woollett born September 1930, first became interested in motorcycles when his brother bought a model 18 Norton sidecar outfit in 1944. After completing his National Service in 1950 he bought his first machine, a 1938 350cc Norton model 50, from Whitbys of Acton for £55. A number of other machines followed and he was bitten. As a enthusiast he attended a number of continental Grand Prix events in those early days. With easy access to the 'stars' a friendship was struck up with Cyril Smith (1952 World Sidecar Champion).

Although Norton officially withdrew from Grand Prix racing at the end of 1954, Joe Craig continued to support Cyril Smith, who was employed by Norton, with the use of the ex-Ray Amm outside flywheel engines.

Mick became so impressed with the sport he finally gave up his job with the Alliance Assurance Company at the end of 1955, to passenger Cyril Smith in 1956.

Although a number of international successes were achieved, the 1956 TT saw the end of the Smith/Woollett partnership. Mick finished the season with Belgian rider Jack Wijns on a BMW, achieving seventh in the Belgian Grand Prix and sixth in the Ulster.

By then Mick was working as a freelance journalist for the infant Motorcycle News, joining them full time at the end of 1956. He combined racing with reporting for three seasons, mainly with the Swiss Edgar Strub. Quitting racing at the end of 1959 found Mick as Sports Editor for MCN, leaving in January 1962 to become Sports Editor of Motorcycling. When Motorcycling and The Motor Cycle Magazine amalgamated in 1967 Mick was promoted to Sports Editor, in 1976 Editor and in 1983 he was appointed as Editor-in-chief of Motorcycle and Classic Motor Cycle, retiring in 1985 when they both ceased publication. Mick 'The Scoop' Woollett as he was known, is one of the most respected in his profession, and continues his writing to this day with a good number of books and articles to his name.

The 2.761 mile Oulton Park circuit involves fast swooping corners, from the start into The Old Hall right hander descending down to the left hander at Cascades. Then it's near flat out through Island Bend slowing into the Esso Bend right-hand hairpin then accelerating onto the long undulating main straight. After dropping down to the fast Knicker Brook right-hander, the course climbs Clay Hill then sweeps left at this tree-lined section before the double right at Druids corner, - no room for error. Then it's a dash to the right-hander Lodge Corner. Finally, the Deers Leap section is like a big dipper, bringing one into the start and finish area.

I took an immediate liking to this circuit and it suited my style of riding. The Matchless G50 single cylinder could be kept on the boil, necessary to obtain good results against the more powerful BMW outfits. From sixth and seventh positions in the two races we finished sixth overall, not bad against the foreign and top British opposition on our first visit, collecting £15 prize money in the process.

As our racing career was taking off, my motorcycle business was also making good progress, with the AMC factory management pleased both with our sales of the AJS and Matchless motorcycles, and our continued racing success. Also my courtship of their sales secretary Joan Anderson had blossomed.

Suddenly, with no time for holidays it was back to Brands Hatch for the August 20th national event held on the 2.65 mile full circuit with no separate 500cc sidecar race, only up to 1200cc scratch and handicap races. We gained two rather unexciting seventh places.

Then it was a run of events through September and into October, firstly back to Snetterton on 3rd September for a national programme against the regular stars. It was a third again in the 500cc race and fifth in the 1200cc event with £18 prize money, less than on the last visit - so no steak and chips this time. The following week was to be our first road race visit to Cadwell Park, situated in the open countryside of Lincolnshire near Louth. It was three years previous that I had ridden at Cadwell Park, but at that time on my Greeves scrambler. Cadwell Park held the title of the oldest road race circuit

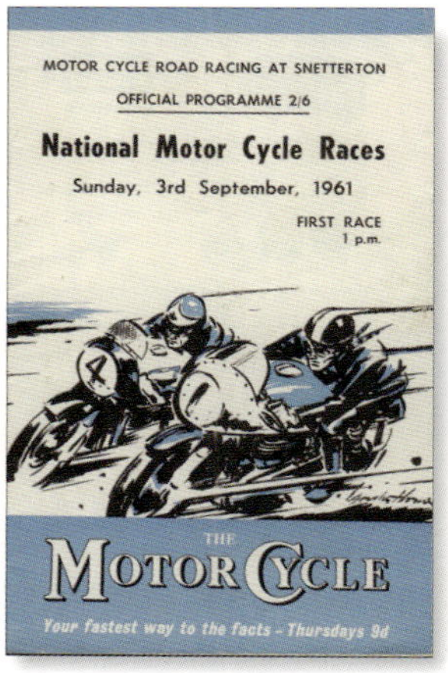

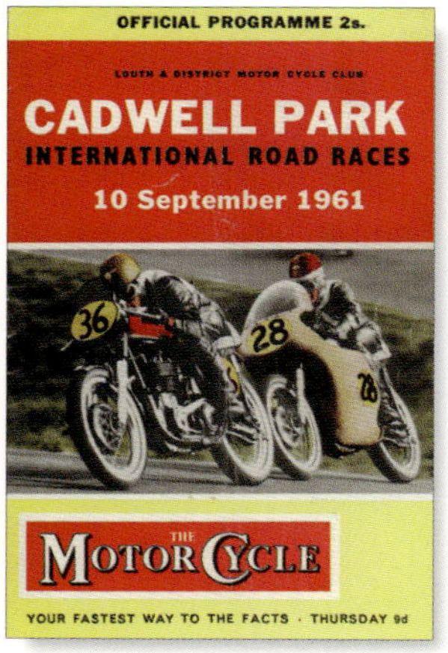

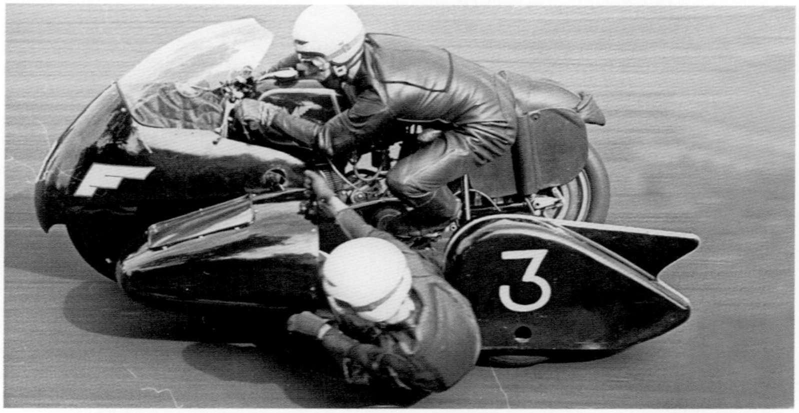

October, Brands Hatch 1961.

in the British Isles, excluding the Isle of Man TT courses. Established 1934, it was a short 3/4 mile track until 1953. It was then lengthened to one mile and finally in 1961 extended again to the 2 1/4 mile track as known today. The first event was run on the new circuit on August Bank Holiday Monday, 1961. Reading through the programme issued for the 10th September 1961 International Event I was amused by an advert promoting a company 'ECCLES SLAG', whose machines had laid the circuit!

This meeting had attracted many of the top solo and sidecar stars including Derek Minter, Alan Shepherd, Chris Conn, Percy Tait, Mike Hailwood, Dan Shorey, Jim Redman, Phil Read, John Cooper with Florian Camathias, Les Wells, Edgar Strub, Pip Harris, Chris Vincent, Bill Boddice, Fritz Scheidegger, Max Deubel and local specialist Charlie Freeman and Jackie Beeton. So we were once more to be racing in good company. I must be honest and say that Cadwell Park was not high on my list of favourite circuits, nevertheless we did not disgrace ourselves on this our first visit, finishing fourth in our heat behind Harris, Beeton and Wells. We finished seventh in the 10 lap final, behind Deubel, Harris, Wells, Freeman, Beeton and Scheidegger, then got a fourth place in the handicap event. A total of £5 prize money, it was just getting too much.

Then back to Brands Hatch on 17th September for our fifth visit that year. Once more the event was held on the long Grand Prix circuit, again with no separate 500cc sidecar race, but open up to 1200cc. We were not daunted, attaining a fourth in the main scratch race and fifth in the handicap. The four speed Matchless G50 again performed superbly.

Thankfully I had some good staff back at the business. Percy was aided by secretary Marie Bull and they kept the 'Empire' going whilst Wally and I were playing at racing. With Brands Hatch out of the way next it was up to Mallory Park for the international event on the 24th September 1961.

The Mallory Park circuit, located near Hinckley Leicestershire is a 1.35 mile course, needing special skills and a certain bravery to lap quickly but it has always provided exciting racing. The international events held in the UK at that time were fantastic, attracting riders from Australia, South Africa, Austria, Southern Rhodesia, New Zealand, Sweden, Germany, Switzerland as well as Norman Surtees from Sidcup. This event was no exception with Gary Hocking, Mike Hailwood, Bob McIntyre, Tom Phillis, Jim Redman, John Hartle, Phil Read, Alan Shepherd, Tommy Robb competing along with other top names including all the top regular foreign and British sidecar entrants. Mallory Park for us at this particular event, being our first visit, was a concentrated effort. Firstly, we needed to learn the intricacy of this circuit and then come to terms with the fact that one hardly had time to breathe in the rush. With a seventh in our heat and ninth in the final we were reasonably pleased.

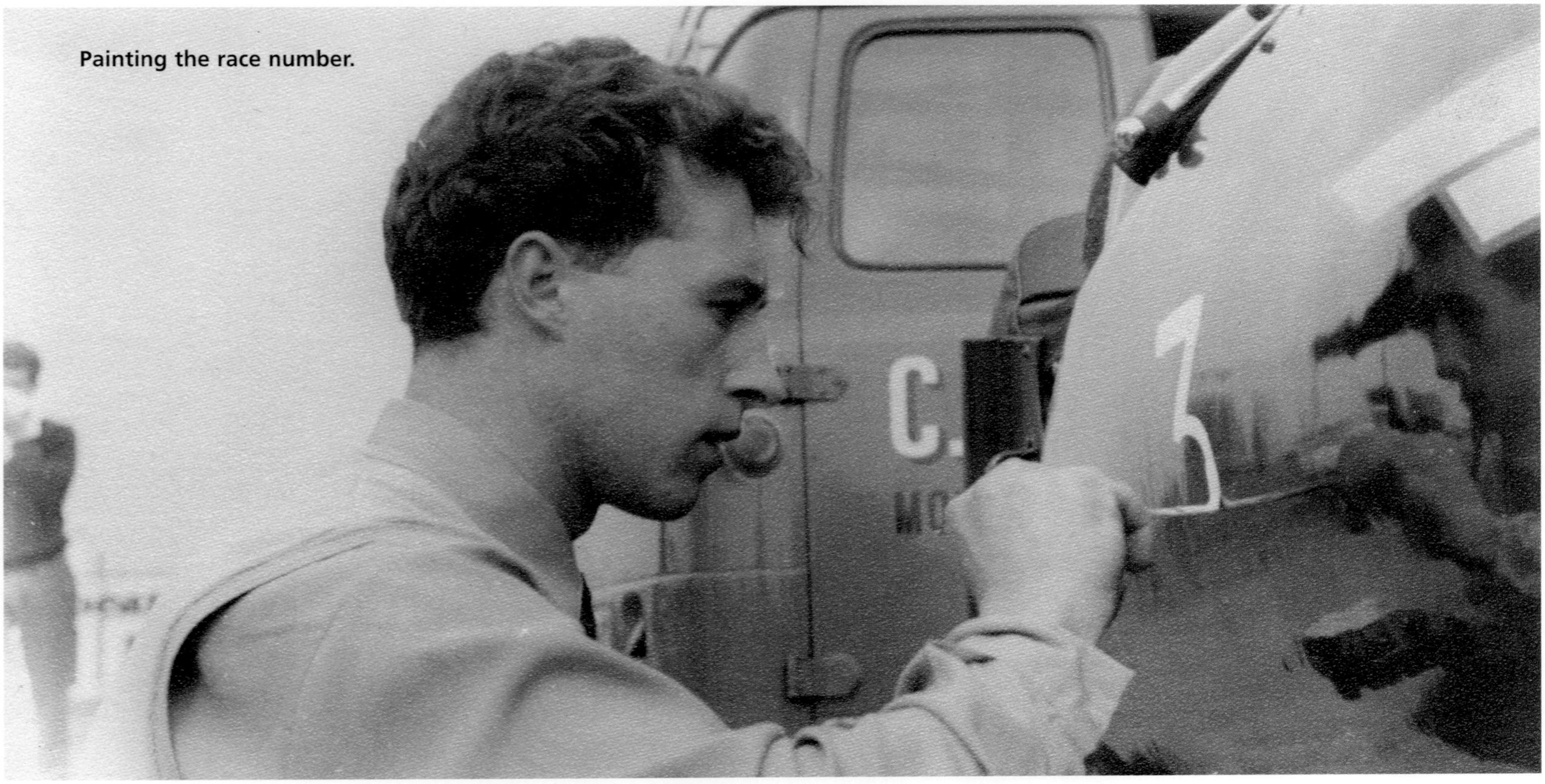

Painting the race number.

John Cooper, Cadwell Park 348cc Norton.

Serious discussion with AMC racing boss, Jack Williams.

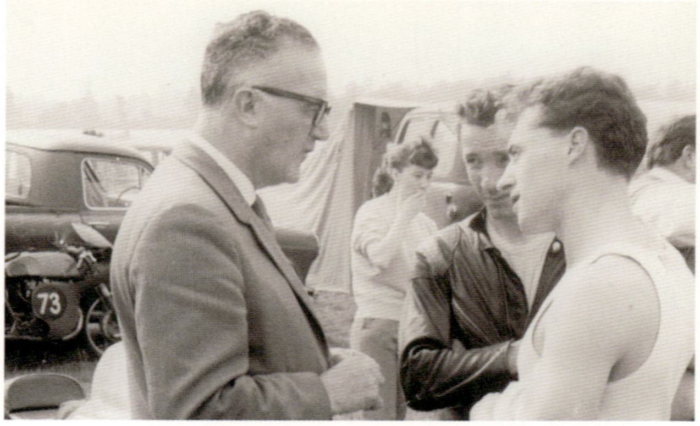

A fortnight later, on the 8th October, we were back to Brands Hatch for their last event of the year and our sixth visit this season. Again held on the Grand Prix circuit, many of the local solo riders were in attendance for this national event. Jimmy Cripps, Joe Dunphy, Ginger Payne, Dave Downer, John Taylor, Roy Mayhew, Dave King, Norman Surtees, brother of John and a certain W.D. Ivy. Little Bill was riding a 49cc Chis-Itom. These local boys were up against Phil Read, Mike Hailwood, Mike Duff, Derek Minter, Dan Shorey and John Hartle. Wally and I recorded a seventh in the unlimited scratch race and a third in the handicap, not so good, but our Matchless outfit was to hold good for our last event of a long season. The British Motorcycle Racing Club organised Guinness Trophy meeting was to be held at Snetterton on the 15th October. This was principally a clubman event, with a number of the sidecar crews being the competitors that we had raced against during the season. One such was Mike Rowell on a 499cc Norton, I believe a past winner of this sidecar race and favourite for that day's race. There were 27 other crews lining up on the grid.

Well Snetterton was our favourite circuit. With our good starting technique and our Matchless still on song, we romped away to win the 8 lap race from Mike Rowell with A.G. Vincent third. This was a satisfying conclusion to our first full racing season, finishing 27 races out of 29 starts. Our only two retirements had been down to a loss of an oil tank cap and then ignition trouble. Surely the Matchless G50 was here to stay and with £160 prize money won that year it was 'whoopee' and roll on 1962!

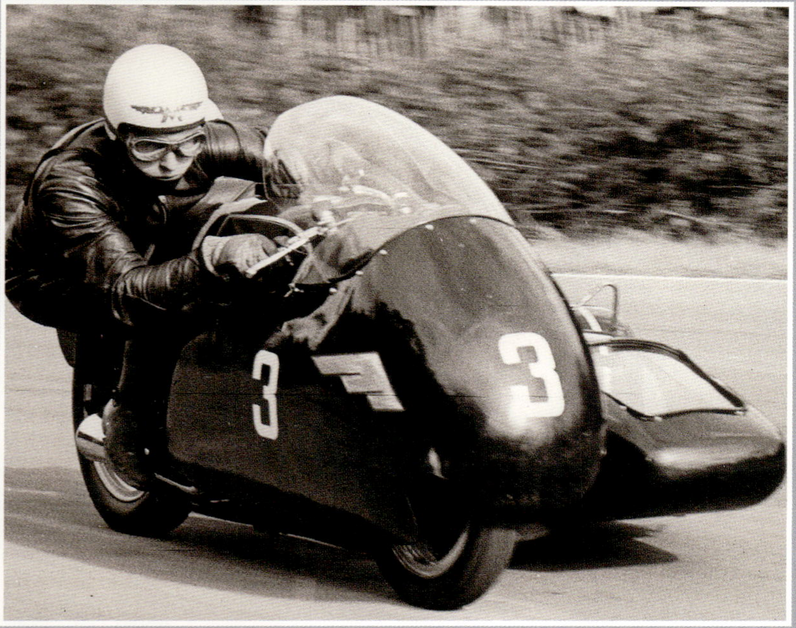

Druids Bend, Brands Hatch.

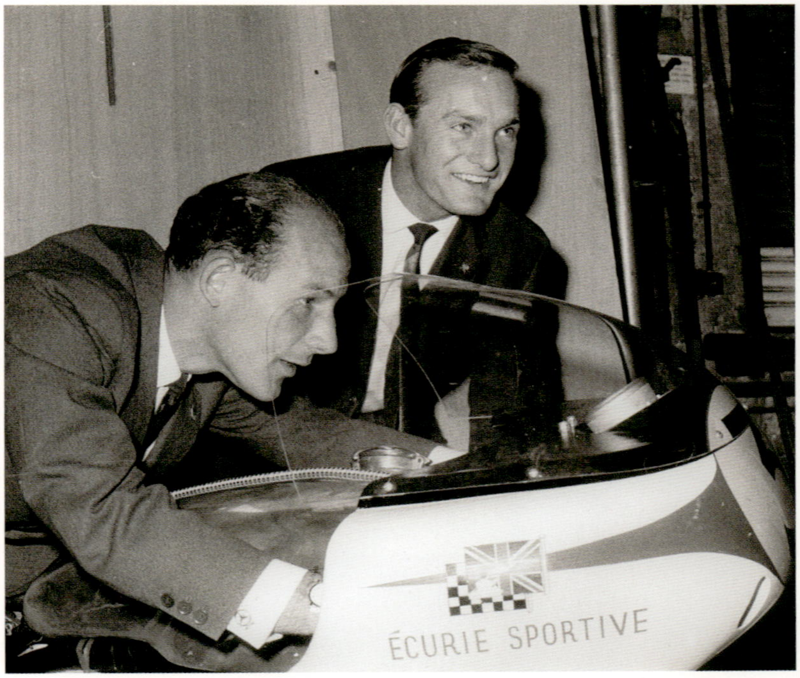

BBC TV Sportsman of the Year 1961, Stirling Moss, on Mike Hailwood's 1961 Senior TT winning Norton.

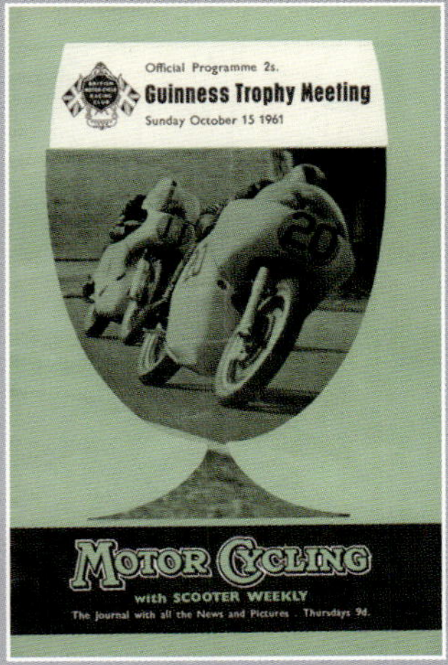

4 1962
OH! FOR THOSE DAYS AGAIN!

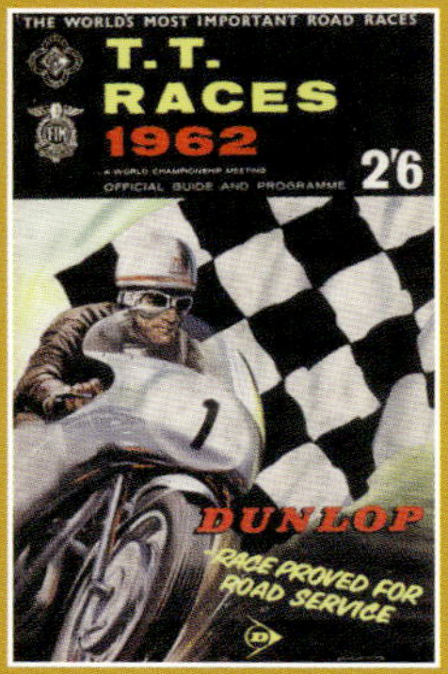

In February 1962 AMC announced improvements to their over-the-counter racing motorcycles, the 349cc AJS 7R and 496cc Matchless G50, more power, less weight, higher speed and increased reliability. The Matchless G50 had been introduced in 1959 to replace the G45 as a production racer. Prices in 1962 stood at; AJS 7R, £512 8s 0d including £92 8s 0d purchase tax, Matchless G50: £527 0s 9d including £95 0s 9d purchase tax. Oh! for those days again - great bikes - great value.

Encouraged by our reasonable success in 1961 and the increasing interest in our Matchless sidecar racing activities by the AMC management, we looked to making some improvements to the outfit for the 1962 season, with some 39 races sread over 21 events.

The Matchless/Canterbury outfit was heavy for its limited power of around 50bhp and had a high riding position. So, to the horror of Jack Williams, out came the hacksaw. I chopped a large lump out of the G50 frame seating position, lowering it at this point by some 6 inches, but causing a problem with the oil tank. A smaller one was constructed, but with restricted air space within the tank necessitating a larger breather pipe from the filler cap. The original beautiful fuel tank, the symbol of the Matchless G50 was reluctantly replaced with a fibreglass one, placed on the sidecar platform with an electric fuel pump to supply the carburettor. A much lighter and better shaped fibreglass sidecar nose and mudguard was fitted with the telescopic forks retained. With the continued support of Avon Tyres, the engine rebuilt, a lick of paint, and the Matchless motif proudly displayed on the front of the dustbin fairing, we were once again ready for action.

On Easter Sunday, 22nd April 1962, at Snetterton, the news came through that Les Wells, who had entered for that day's sidecar action had been involved in a road accident on his way to Pau in France for his international race debut. His van had skidded off the road at St. Vincent de Tyrosse and Les was killed instantly. His racing passenger, James Benge, had been seriously injured. 32 year old Les, who lived in Walthamstow, was a plasterer by trade and an amateur wrestler. In his eighth year of racing he was a formidable but fair competitor with many good results achieved, and was a sad loss to his family and to the sport.

With seven race events inclusive of 14 sidecar races under our belt already, our winter modifications to the G50 seemed to be paying off and the Isle of Man TT was once more in our mind. The entry fee of £9 was paid to the ACU and this time we carried a full international racing licence. It was off to the magic isle for our second TT, with our race to be held on Monday 4th June 1962. As they say in show business, 'What difference a year makes!' With a good number of consistent race results behind us, Wally and I were now being recognised as serious competitors.

Arriving in the Isle of Man was always special but the atmosphere for this world championship event was electric. The whole island was buzzing for the two weeks of motorcycle action. Once departed from the busy docks it was straight away to our regular base at Beverley House in Strang for Ma Frances Clucas to welcome her heroes. Once we had unloaded the racing outfit and equipment, like children, we could not wait to drive a lap of the TT course. Then we were straight back to the start area for the regulation signing-on, where we encountered once more the best motorcycle riders at that time in the world. Most had raced in the Isle of Man the year before, but a new team was the Suzuki Motorcycle Company. They were competing in the Isle of Man for the first time but with the experienced Ernst Degner and Hugh Anderson supported by Mitsuo Itoh and Frank Perris on board for the 125cc race.

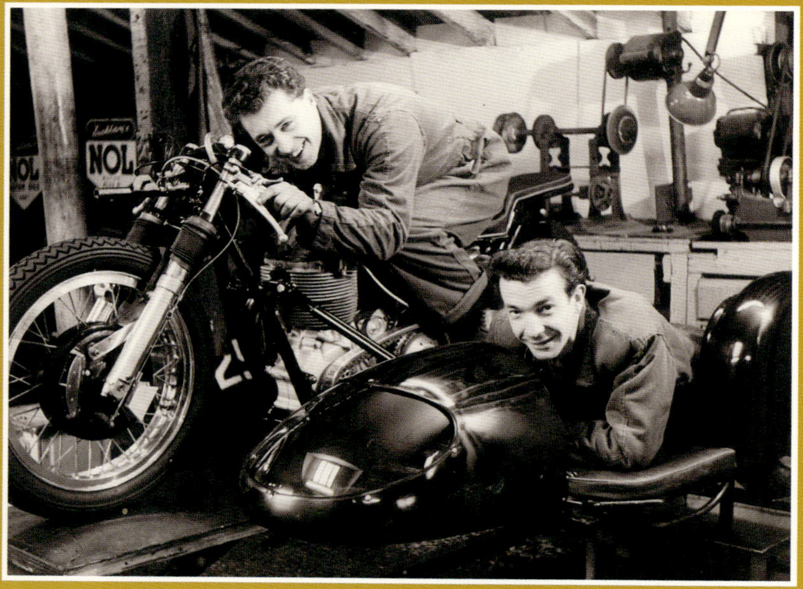

Matchless outfit alterations.

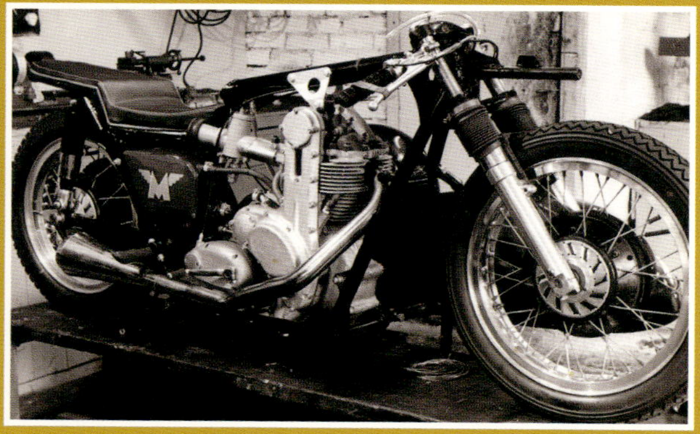

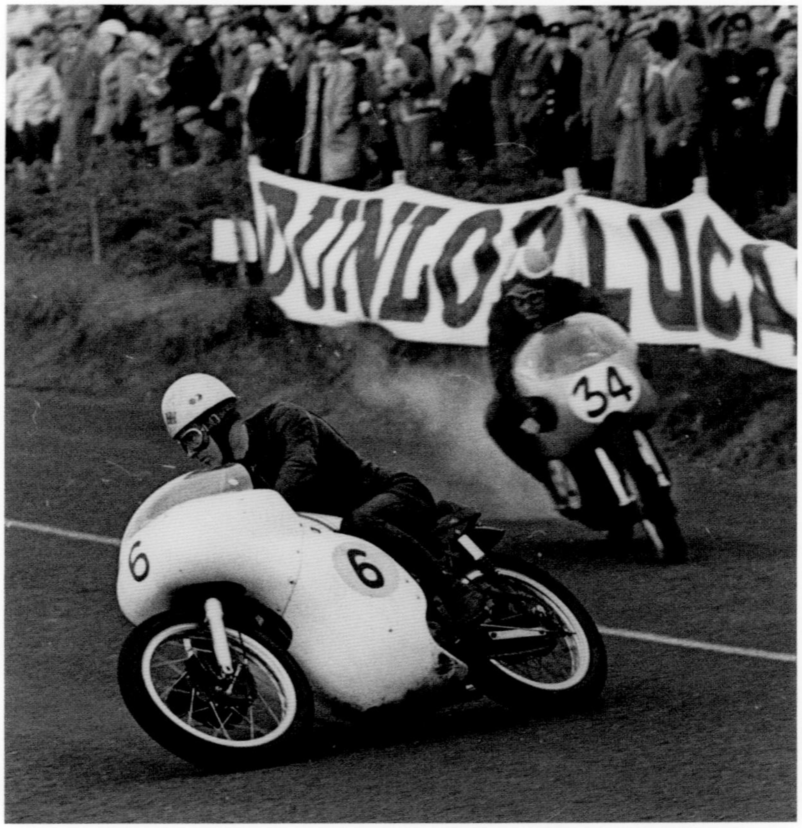

Ron Langston leading Franta Stastny, Ulster Grand Prix.

Entries for this year's sidecar race were down on the previous year, at 32 as against 39, non-starters reducing the field to 27. Amongst the notable non-starters was Fritz Scheidegger, second in the previous year's race, Charlie Freeman, fifth in 1961, and Pip Harris who had not entered.

Back in action and fully recovered from injuries incurred in 1961 and the sad loss of passenger Hilmar Cecco, was Swiss charger Florian Camathias. Florian, with his thick-lensed glasses always brought unexpected excitement and flavour to any event he competed in. Another sidecar race entry was from the multi-talented, International Six Days gold medal winner scrambler and solo road racer Ron Langston. Having ridden with success in the 1959/60 Manx GPs and the 1961 Junior and Senior TT races, he was competing again in 1962 in both Junior and Senior events. Ron, a good-looking man, hadn't been satisfied with his successes in most of the other motorcycle sport disciplines, so he thought he would try his luck at sidecar racing. Fortunately for us, he was not to get very far with the Ariel factory supported four cylinder sidecar outfit. With many problems during practice and the engine having just been rebuilt in time for the last qualifying session, Ron could only get as far at the Highlander on the first lap when the crankshaft broke, so that was that! The Ariel four was never seen or raced again!

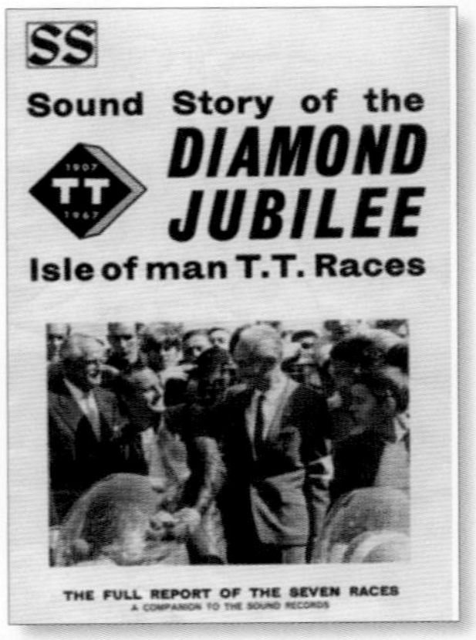

Graham Walker TT interview for Schofield Sound Stories.

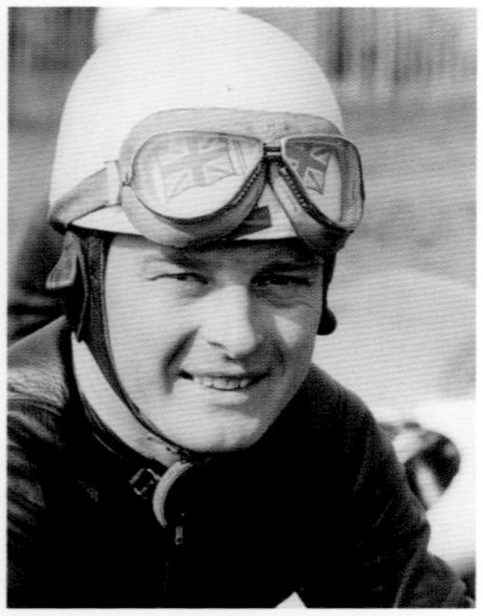

Ron Langston.

With a change to this year's programme, the opening race on Monday 4th June would be the 3 lap sidecar event at 11.00am, followed by the lightweight 250cc race with a start time of 1.30pm.

The lightweight 125cc race would now be 11.00am on Wednesday 6th with the 6 lap Junior 350cc at 1.30am. Finally, on Friday to complete the week, the first 50cc race to be run over the TT course, a two lapper, would start at 11.00am followed by the 6 lap Senior 500cc race at 1.30pm. If all competitors in the week finished, there would be 50,000 racing miles completed collectively.

Sunday, 3rd of June at 10.00am was the usual preliminary examination day of machines and riding gear and allocation of race numbers. We should have been prompt but we were late again. We just wanted to make sure everything was 'tickety boo' so we expected the fine imposed by the ACU. Luckily we had been allocated race No 7. We were delighted. With the weather clear and bright, a good crowd was in attendance, mostly hoping to get the attention of their favourite star for an autograph. For once ours was also requested by the enthusiastic crowd. Six of ours was a good swap for one of Mike Hailwood's.

Then it was an interview for the Stanley Schofield Productions Sound Stories by veteran TT racer and broadcaster, Graham Walker - father of Murray. These wonderful recordings as advertised were sold at 9s 6d.

With our faithful Matchless outfit fully serviced and ready for action it was parked in the pre-race assembly marquee then it was back to Frances Clucas to be herded up for dinner by her sheepdog.

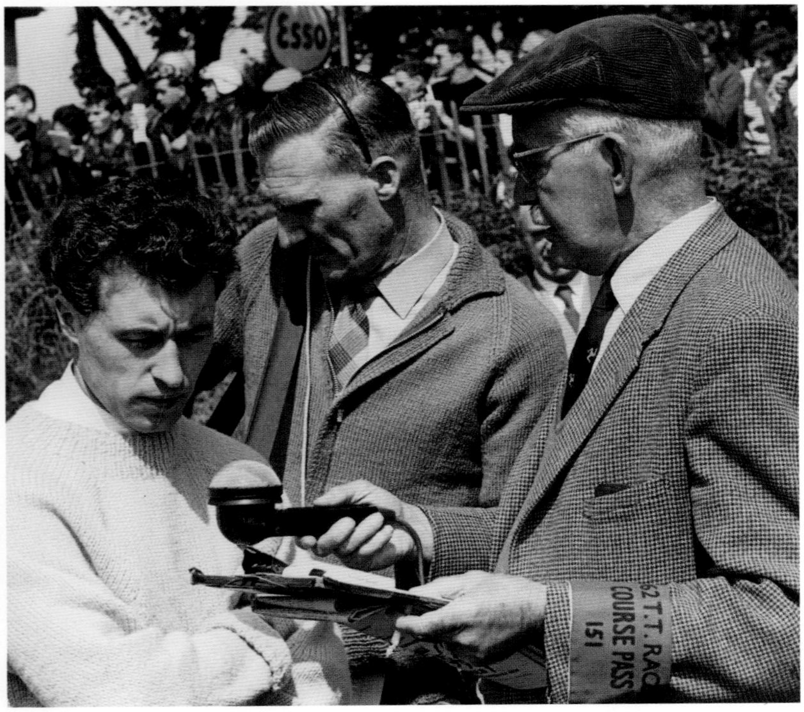

TT race action, Parliament Square, Ramsay.

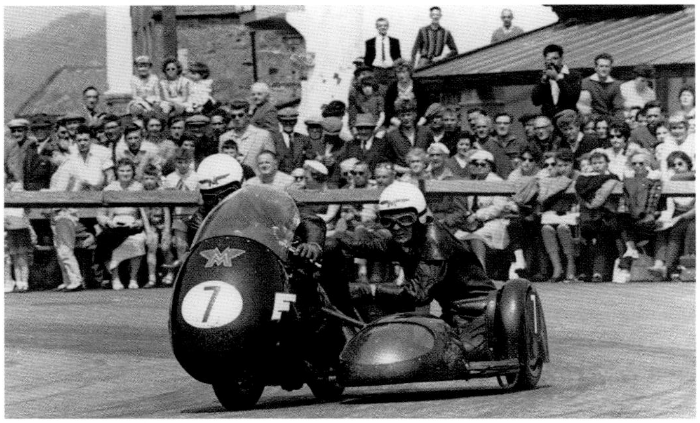

Next day dawned perfect and it was to stay that way with the whole Island bathed in sunshine. After breakfast we gathered our freshly-oiled leathers, polished helmets and boots and took best wishes from Frances, husband Tommy, daughter Diana and the assembled Strang gang supporters. Then we departed to the start in our Thames van, now displaying a sidecar action shot on the side.

At 10.30am the warm-up maroon fired into the blue sky and within seconds a roar of engines was heard and 15 minutes later the stop maroon fired, followed by the 5 minute to start warning. This time, being early starters, Wally and I were ready for the forthcoming challenge, but of course we still felt nervous and apprehensive of what was to come. Then came the one minute warning - then silence.

Fritz Scheidegger and Charlie Freeman, numbers 1 and 2, were non starters, 10 seconds, then it was the next pair up, Chris Vincent on his BSA and Max Deubel the works supported BMW rider. A further 10 seconds and Florian Camathias with Otto Kolle, both BMW, sped away. Then it was our turn alongside the BMW of Eric Pickup. The flag dropped and within a few steps we were away, rushing down Bray Hill flat out. That first lap for me is awesome. Once more my mouth was dry, but there would be no chance of a drink for at least 1 hour, 22 minutes.

On the first lap we had settled down to fourth spot behind the leader Max Deubel, then Florian Camathias and Chris Vincent with Otto Kolle just over a second behind and the Frenchman Claude Lambert sixth. On the second lap the irrepressible Swiss ace, Florian Camathias, although breaking the old lap record with a standing start speed of 89.72mph, crashed at Kerrowmoar just after Sulby Bridge, with his new passenger Horst Burkhardt coming off worse and suffering a broken right leg, a badly cut hand and shock. Deubel was still in the lead having established a new lap record from a standing start at 90.10mph. Vincent was second but with Kolle sneaking into the third spot ahead of us by only 3 seconds. Then sensation! Max Deubel was out at Ballig Bridge, just past Ballacraine, with engine trouble. So we all moved up one position with Chris Vincent BSA riding a faultless race to win his first TT at 83.57mph with Otto Kolle's BMW second 82.93mph only 8 seconds ahead of our Matchless outfit at 82.57mph, and gentleman Claude Lambert fourth, Hans Luthringshauser BMW came fifth, and in his first TT, Georg Auerbacher BMW took sixth. In seventh was Alan Birch,, Matchless, at 76.46mph, slower by 1.45mph than our average speed from the previous year, very satisfying!

With the accolade of a British win and us in a rostrum position they were happy British crews that stepped onto the raised platform at the start to receive the garlands and the applause from the Grandstand crowd. Wally and I were delighted to finish once again in the most demanding race in the world, and our Matchless had performed perfectly throughout. However, we were slightly disappointed to have been beaten into third spot by only 8 seconds, not much over the 113.25 mile race. An all British 1 - 2 would have been superb. Nevertheless, having increased our best practice lap time at 78.21mph by over 4mph with a fastest lap at 83.13mph and a race average of 82.80mph, it was very pleasing. I believe to this day that this is the fastest lap time for a single cylinder outfit around the TT course and at the time of writing it still has not been beaten. Our third place and the previous interview with Graham Walker would ensure that our achievement would be recorded on the Stanley Schofield celluloid and with £60 in prize money to come plus bonus payments, things were getting better and better.

It is difficult to remember exactly when and how I began my rapport with the solo riders. Generally, the sidecar crews kept to themselves, but I have always taken an interest in solo machines and riders. I believe that our association with friends like Bob Rowe, Dave Downer, Fred Neville and Sid Mizen - all solo men, certainly helped and provided an influence. I also would like to believe that our enthusiastic and professional approach to our racing had captured attention from a number of quarters.

The next race that Monday was the 250cc lightweight TT, run over 6 laps, not five as in the previous year, bringing this race back to equality with the Junior and Senior events. Entries for the TT races that year seemed to be down for some reason with the 250cc perhaps hardest hit, 37 entries against 72 in 1961 and non-starters reducing the field to 25. But there were 13 different makes of machines, although dominated by Honda.

Bob McIntyre, Honda was a favourite who had failed to win the previous year after leading the race and lapping just a shade under a 100mph before breaking down. He lead that year's practice from Minter, Redman, Phillis, Kitano all on Honda and Hailwood on a Benelli.

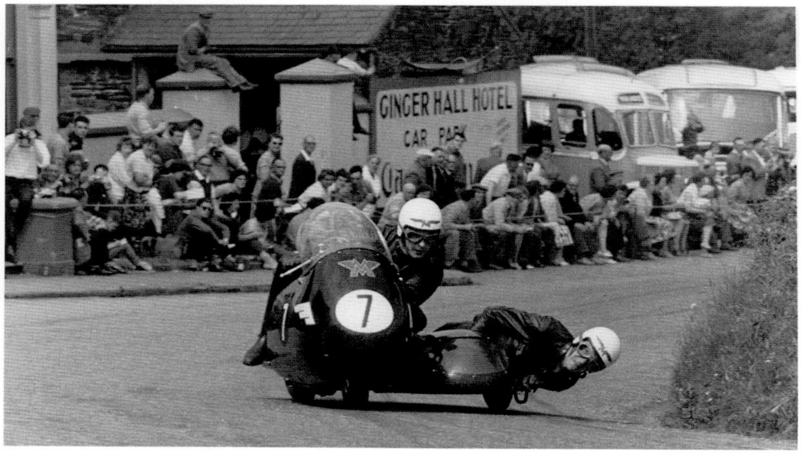

TT race action, Ginger Hall.

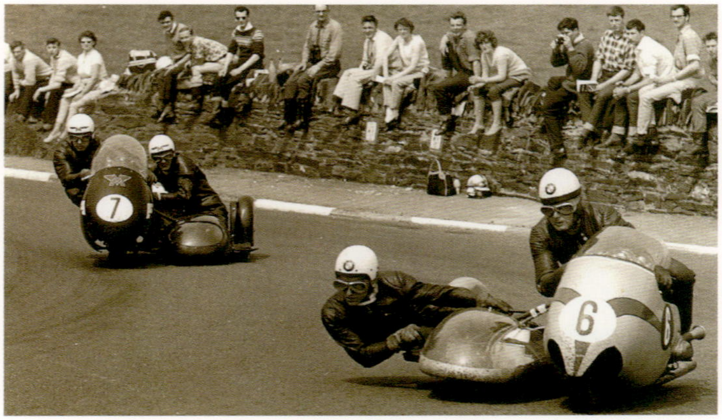

TT race action, Otto Kolle ahead of us at Sulby Bridge.

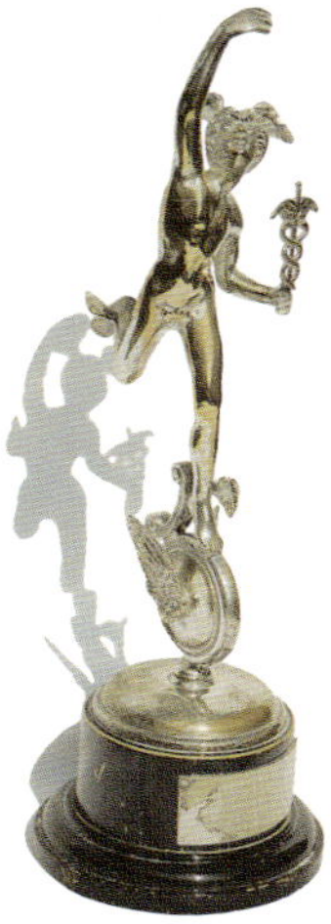

With riders lined up ready for the start sharp at 1.30pm and in ideal conditions the flag dropped with Hailwood and Minter first away. Minter led at Ballacraine but only 8 seconds ahead of a charging Bob Mac, who by Kirkmichael was in front. By the end of the first lap the race was lead by Bob McIntyre followed by Jim Redman, Derek Minter, Tom Phillis, Kitano and Mike Hailwood struggling with a slow machine. Bob McIntyre who was currently leading the 250cc World Championship, was out to seek revenge for his retirement in 1961 but was to suffer further bitter disappointment retiring on the second lap at Barregarro with a mechanical problem. Bob was destined never to achieve the results he so richly deserved.

In the second lap Jim Redman was leading from Derek Minter and Mike Hailwood, who never easily gave up, and despite the poor performance of the Benelli was in third place. Tom Phillis, who had lost a lot of time in the pits and at the end of the first lap to change plugs, had dropped back down the field.

By the end of the third lap Minter was in front of Redman but he overshot in the pits. Redman, by not stopping on this lap, went back into the lead with Hailwood still third and Phillis back up to fourth. At the end of the fourth lap Redman was still leading and pulled in for his pit stop with Minter in second and Phillis now up to third. Mike Hailwood rolled into the pits with a loose fairing. The mechanics pushed and tugged to remove the offending part, eventually wrenching it from the Benelli and Mike was on his way with a naked machine, loosing at least 2 minutes, only one minute in front of Arthur Wheeler, Guzzi. By Ballacraine on the fifth lap, it was level pegging between Redman and Minter but by the Mountain section, Minter was in the lead by 37 seconds on corrected time. As Minter flashed by the start line on his last lap, his lead increased to 50 seconds. Adding to Redman's problems, he came into the pits for a fuel top up as the filler cap was spilling fuel. Mike Hailwood, still running fourth, had to stop on Bray Hill to make adjustments, then finally retired with engine trouble at Braddan Bridge. What bad luck on that last lap after such an eventful race for him, but it just demonstrated what a real champion 'Mike the Bike' was, he never gave in easily.

Derek Minter, 'King of Brands' riding the TT course since 1957 and the first man to break the 100mph record on a single cylinder machine came in to win his first ever Isle of Man TT at 96.68mph. Jim Redman came second at 95.40mph and Tom Phillis third at 92.87mph. Arthur Wheeler, who had competed in an incredible 40 TT races since his first in 1949, came home in fourth at 88.72mph to equal his other best performances in 1953 and 1955. Despite the charge at the front by Minter and Redman neither had come near to Bob Mac's 1961 lap record. Nevertheless it was an exciting race despite only eight finishers at the end. All on Avon tyres, a 1 - 2 - 3 for Honda.

Racing over for that day, it was back to base at Strang and the ovation from our band of supporters. Frances Clucas was over the moon. She could not believe our success. Out came a crate of Guinness so she would be singing and dancing all that night.

Later, fed, washed and suitably dressed, it was once more off to the Villa Marina for the awards and presentations. Congratulations went to Derek Minter, like ourselves a Man of Kent. Less than four years later he would race the first Seeley Matchless. Wally and I collected our Silver Replicas, acknowledged the applause and left the stage still coming to terms with our success in 1961, and here we were again on the rostrum for 1962. It seemed like a fairy tale! Able once again to enjoy the 'Magic Isle' without pressure of racing and pose with our peers, we stayed on for the rest of race week.

Wednesday brought the 125 and Junior 350cc events with the first race of the day, the 125cc, attracting once again the top men. Bob McIntyre, Honda, Jim Redman, Honda, Ernst Degner, Suzuki, Mike Hailwood, EMC, Tom Phillis, Honda, Derek Minter, Honda, Luigi Taveri, Honda, Hugh Anderson, Suzuki, Tommy. Robb, Honda, Kunimitsu Takahashi, Honda, were just a few of the final 38 starters, but then McIntyre was announced to be a non-starter, a great disappointment for all! The 125 TT had been run on the Clypse course from 1954-59. When it returned to the full Mountain Circuit in 1960 it was won by Carlo Ubbiali on an MV Agusta at 85.02mph with the fastest lap at 86.13mph followed by Gary Hocking MV, second, Luigi Taveri, MV, third. In 1961, 'Mike the Bike', Honda won this event, raising the race speed to 88.23mph with Luigi

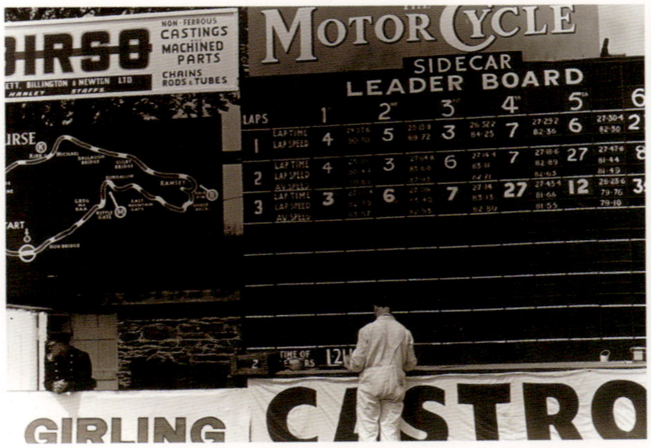

1962 TT; 1. Vincent, 2. Kolle, 3. Seeley.

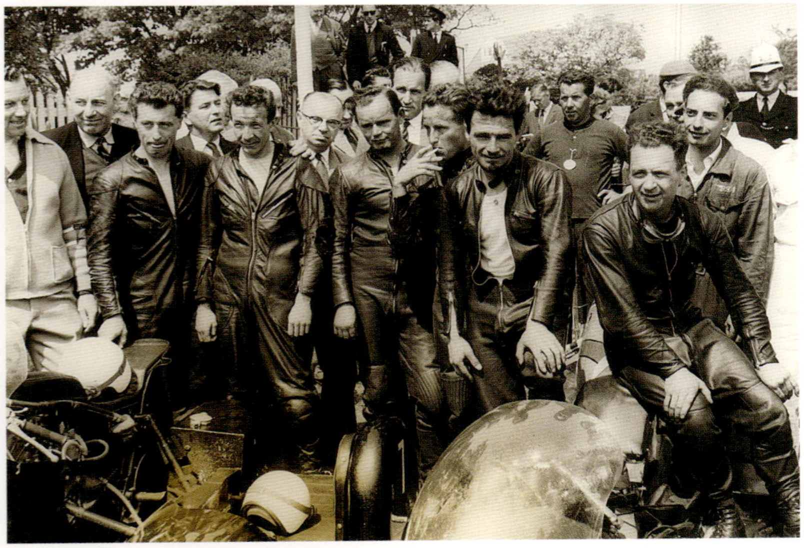

The finish; Me, Wally, Kolle, Marquardt, Vincent and Bliss.

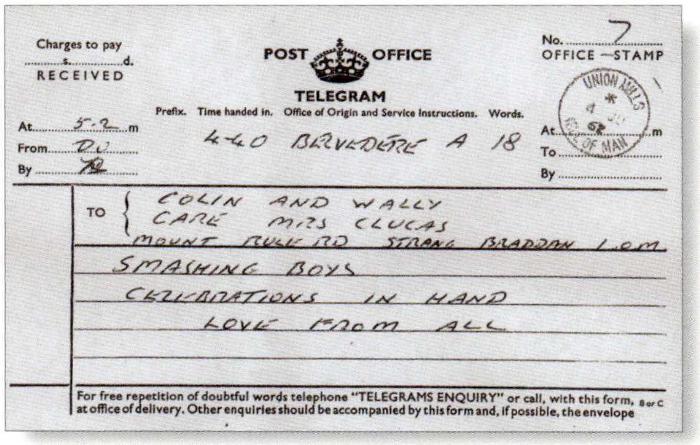
Charges to pay
s. d.
RECEIVED
POST OFFICE
TELEGRAM
No. 7
OFFICE —STAMP
UNION MILLS 4 JU 62 ISLE OF MAN
At 5.2 m
From DJ
Prefix. Time handed in. Office of Origin and Service Instructions. Words.
440 BELVEDERE A 18
TO { COLIN AND WALLY CARE MRS CLUCAS MOUNT RULE RD STRANG BRADDAN I.O.M.
SMASHING BOYS
CELEBRATIONS IN HAND
LOVE FROM ALL
For free repetition of doubtful words telephone "TELEGRAMS ENQUIRY" or call, with this form, at office of delivery. Other enquiries should be accompanied by this form and, if possible, the envelope

Taveri, Honda second with a record lap of 88.45mph, the talented Tom Phillis third and Jim Redman in fourth place.

With an 11.00am start and the weather holding, first away for the 3 lap race was Kunimitsu Takahashi, who unfortunately crashed his Honda at Union Mills on that very first lap, suffering head injuries and a fractured pelvis. The first lap leaders were Taveri, Honda 20 seconds ahead of Hailwood, EMC, Redman, Honda third and Tommy Robb, Honda just over 2 seconds behind, followed by Phillis, Honda with Minter, Honda in sixth place.

Luigi Taveri's first lap was a new record at 89.78mph and Mike on the British EMC at 88.58mph beat the previous year's record. At the end of the second lap the positions held for the first six, other than Tommy Robb who had got ahead of Redman by 10 seconds. On the last lap, with only 28 miles to the finish, Mike Hailwood retired at Glen Helen with engine trouble. Dr. Ehrlich, the EMC boss was disappointed but Rex Avery and Paddy Driver on the other EMCs were seventh and eighth, so all was not lost. Luigi Taveri, the diminutive Swiss crossed the finish line to win his first Isle of Man TT at 89.88mph, a record speed and a fastest lap of 90.13mph. Leading from start to finish, it probably was one of his finest hours. Tommy Robb was over one minute behind in second place followed by Tom Phillis, Derek Minter and Jim Redman in that order with Rex Avery EMC sixth with his team mate Paddy Driver retiring at Ramsay Hairpin. Ernst Degner, Suzuki finished eighth of the 20 finishers but this was a 'toe in the water' job for Suzuki, who would come back with a vengeance in 1963.

Luigi Taveri's successes continued that year with wins in the 125cc class at the Dutch TT, Belgian, West German, East German and Ulster GPs. The results combined for him to win his first World Championship, well ahead of Jim Redman in second.

For a 1.30pm start for the 6 lap junior race, the weather remained perfect for the 72 starters. Two manufacturers' teams were entered, Alan Shepherd, Hugh Anderson and Mike Duff for AJS and Derek Minter, Phil Read and Roy Ingram for Norton. Sharp on time the flag dropped and Tom Phillis was first away with Franta Stastny followed by the regular stars of the TT course. At the end of the first lap Gary Hocking, MV led Mike Hailwood, MV, by just under 12 seconds, breaking his own previous lap record of 100.09mph, the first junior 'ton' lap. Mike also beat the 'ton' with a lap of 100.05mph.

Sidecar TT presentation.

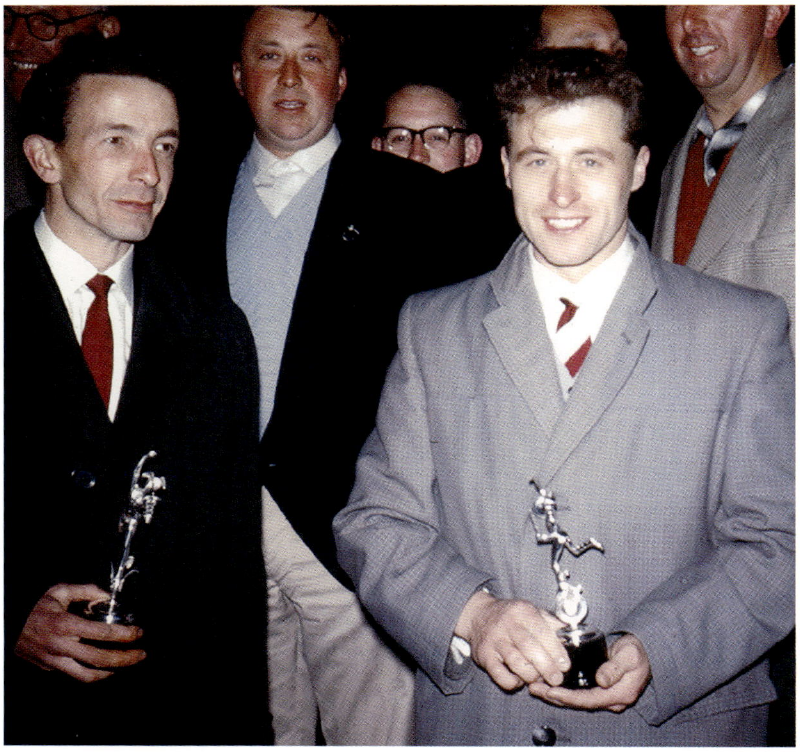

Tom Phillis, Honda was third, Bob McIntyre, Honda fourth with Alan Shepherd, AJS fifth and that man again Ron Langston sixth on the Norton. During the second lap, just under 9 miles out from the start, third place man, Tom Phillis had crashed at the rock-lined Laurel Bank section of the course succumbing to his injuries on the way to hospital. Tom Phillis had ridden the IOM TT course every year since 1958, fourth in the 1960 Senior event and third in 1961 but coming to a peak racing for the official Honda team in the 125cc and 250cc lightweight events in 1961/62. With three thirds and one second place he had been really knocking at the door for that number one spot. It was not to be for this likeable and talented Australian who would be sorely missed. The TT course once more reminded us that for the glory of the event an ultimate price can often be paid. This particular incident is another that has remained in my memory.

Then there was further tragic news. 28 year old New Zealander Colin Meehan riding his first Isle of Man TT had crashed on the second lap at Union Mills and was killed. Both of those unfortunate accidents had certainly marred an otherwise exciting race with a titanic battle between Gary Hocking and Mike Hailwood for first place. With Derek Minter out of the race early on, he was joined by Ron Langston, Alan Shepherd and Bob McIntyre, all suffering various problems forcing frustrating retirements. Skipping to the last lap at Ramsey, Mike Hailwood was still ahead on the road by 300 yards but still

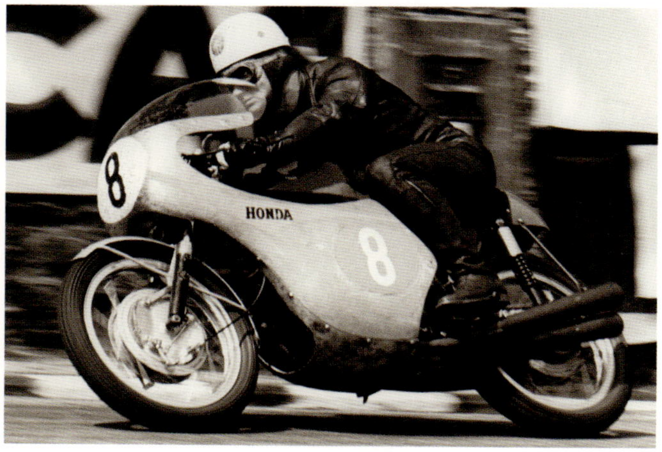

Bob McIntyre leaving Governors, 250cc TT.

Ernst Degner starts his victorious Suzuki in the 1962 50cc TT

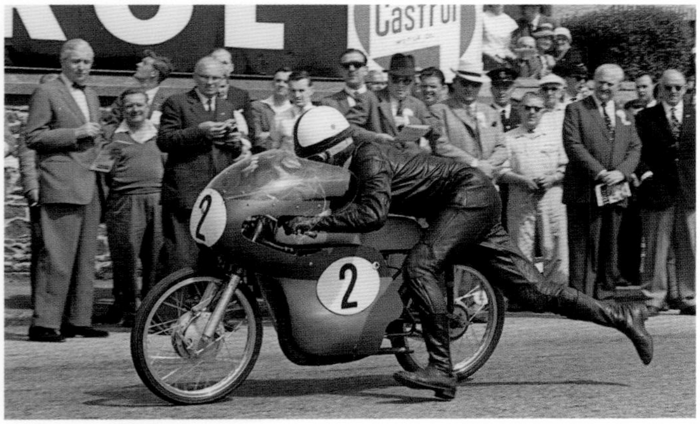

behind on corrected time at Keppel Gate. With about 4 miles to the finish Gary Hocking was ahead by 5 seconds in what was described as one of the finest post war TT races, but 'Mike the Bike' pulled out all the stops and arrived at signpost corner level-pegging. Then, after negotiating the slow Governors Dip it was a sprint to the chequered flag by the majestic Mike, recording in the process a new lap record of 101.58mph winning by only 5 seconds from the formidable 25 year old Rhodesian, Gary Hocking. The Saturday before, the Queen had awarded Hocking an MBE for his 1961 350 and 500cc World Championships. Third up in this Junior race was the popular Franta Stastny, Jawa. Roy Ingram, Mike Duff, Hugh Anderson completed the first six with the 1961 Junior Race winner Phil Read in a disappointing seventh place. It was obvious that he had some machine trouble, as his race time was well down from the previous year. I don't mind writing an excuse for our 'Prince of Speed'!

Friday Senior race day saw the introduction of a 50cc international racing class, a first on the Isle of Man TT course combined with the very first appearance of a lady rider, Beryl Swain. Previously, the only way that women took part in the racing was as passenger in the sidecar races. Suzuki were making a strong bid for this race with four riders, entering two-stroke specialist Ernst Degner, Michio Ichino, Mitsuo Itoh and Seichi Suzuki against Honda-mounted Luigi Taveri, Tommy Robb and Derek Minter. On the original entry list of 48 starters was little Bill Ivy riding a Chisholm-Itom. It was not until 1965 that Bill was to be a serious contender at the TT.

With Degner, Taveri, Itoh and Ichino leading in practice, it promised to be a good race. At 11.00am the 2 lap 50cc race was underway with Degner soon in a 15 second lead over Taveri, at the end of the first lap and averaging an astonishing almost 75mph. Georg Anscheidt, Kreidler, although down on top speed was playing his 12 speed gearbox like a fiddle to extract the best from his little machine lying fourth on the first lap behind Robb. Degner on his Suzuki increased his race average to over 75mph and came home to win from Taveri on his Honda. For Suzuki and Ernst Degner this was their first TT success. For Degner it would be the only TT win he would record. Then came Robb, Honda, Anscheidt, Kreidler, Ichino, Suzuki, Itoh, Suzuki, the first six followed by the Dutchman Jan Huberts, Kreidler, S. Suzuki, Suzuki and Derek Minter on the Honda. Beryl Swain, Itom finished a creditable twenty-second. Those works 50cc race machines were incredible for their design, workmanship and speed.

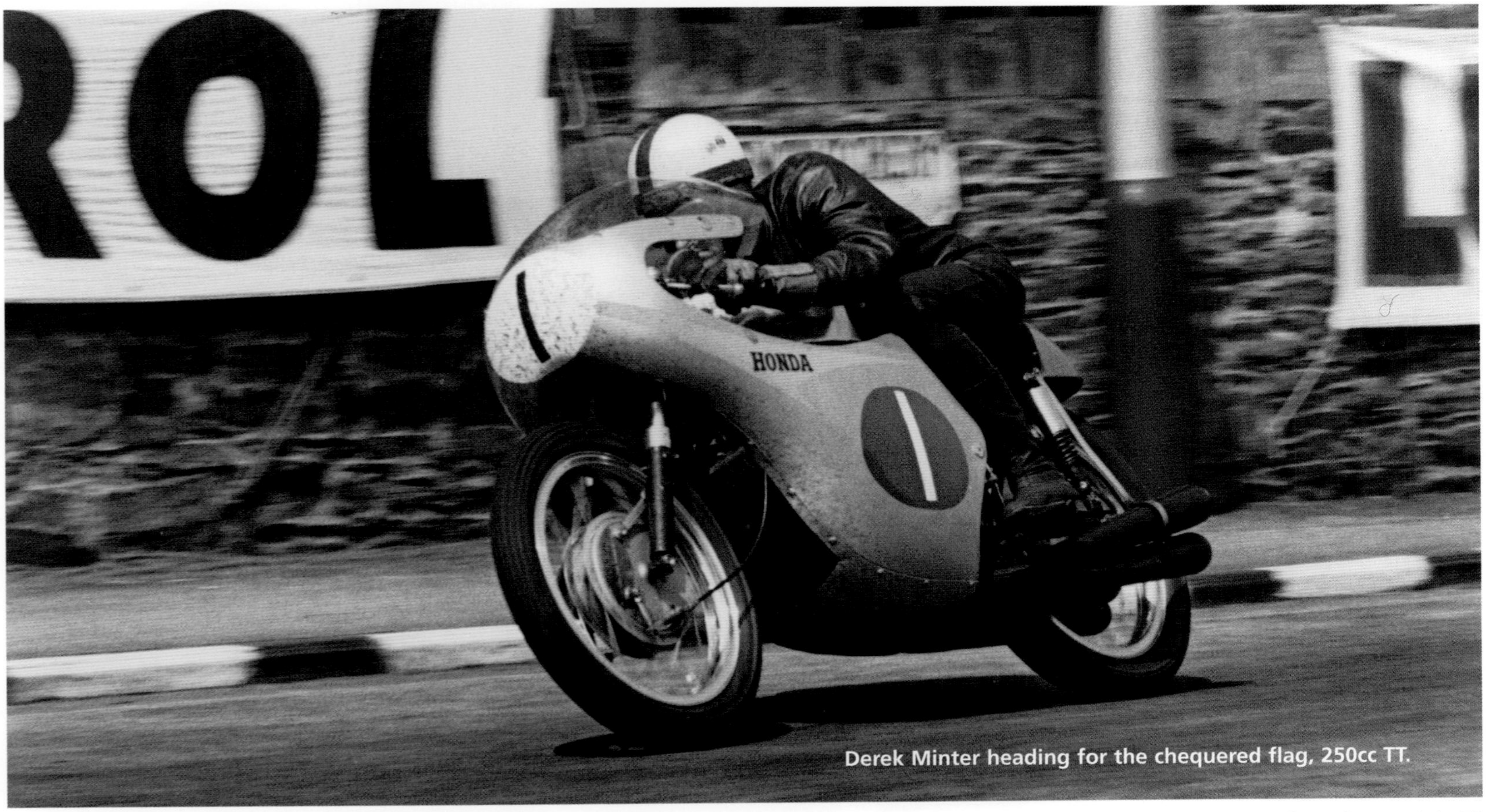

Derek Minter heading for the chequered flag, 250cc TT.

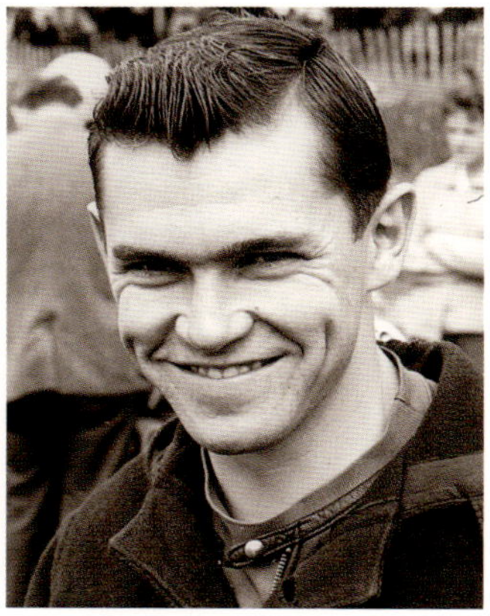

Gary Hocking MBE.

Next came the final race of a very busy fortnight. For the second time that week the main protagonists were Gary Hocking and Mike Hailwood, both on MVs. For this Senior race, Gary, first riding the Isle of Man TT in 1959 and since then achieving three second places in lightweight and junior events, had only won one TT, the 1960 lightweight 250cc race on an MV, so was keen to add to his single TT victory. Mike Hailwood on the other hand, first raced at the TT in 1958 and had won four TT races as well as achieving three other rostrum positions.

The 5 minutes to start maroon was fired for the last time that year. The final minutes ticked away and then sharp at 1.30pm the flag dropped for the start of the 6 lap event. Ron Langston alongside Alan Shepherd were first away. Then divided by the 10 second interval, off went Roy Ingram and Gary Hocking - Alastair King and Derek Minter - Bob McIntyre and Phil Read followed by Mike Hailwood and Paddy Driver. The first 10 were followed by the supporting cast, riders such as Jack Findlay, Jack Ahearn, Billy McCosh, Derek Woodman, Hugh Anderson, Mike Duff, Tony Godfrey, Billie Nelson, Chris Conn, Sid Mizen, Jimmy Cripps, Gyula Marsovszky, Dan Shorey, Tom Thorp, Ned Minihan etc etc. Such a wealth of rider talent made the TT races so exciting and brilliant in those days.

With the race well under way, Gary Hocking, despite some concerns for his MV, soon took the lead. Likewise 'Mike the Bike' was overtaking the slower front starters and made headway on Gary. He was only 1.6 seconds behind on the first lap but Gary fought back and increased his lead. Meantime, Alan Shepherd and Hugh Anderson retired on lap one, and Derek Minter on lap two. Mike Duff, Tony Godfrey, Ron Langston and Phil Read all fell by the wayside with mechanical problems. Mike held second place to the end of lap four but in stopping for clutch repairs he lost a valuable 13 minutes. This dropped him right back down the field. Gary led from start to finish and took the deserved accolade of his first Senior TT race win with the added prize of a new lap record of 105.75mph. Ellis Boyce was in second place and Fred Stevens in third followed by Bert Schneider, Roy Ingram and Brian Setchell.

Wally and I congratulated Gary Hocking MBE, when we saw him in town later that evening. Gary never returned to the Isle of Man and shortly after his Senior TT success he announced his retirement from bike racing. That was it for another year. It had been a wonderful fortnight, but a painful and sad one for some, with the ultimate price being paid.

Already packed for our journey it was the inevitable rush home, the circus was on the move, as like many competitors at the TT, we were due to compete at the Brands Hatch Whit Monday June 11th 2,000 Guineas international event. This was a great time for Brands Hatch with all the major events being held on the long Grand Prix circuit. Many solo stars of the day were there to compete, with the sidecar event also attracting many of the continental riders who had been at the TT.

Still on a high from our success, Wally and I were ready to take on the onslaught of BMWs. It is a known fact that after the Isle of Man some riders often took a while to get back the short circuit racing mode, Fortunately, I did not suffer with that problem, as proved by the twelve lap 31.80 mile sidecar race. It was a most enjoyable and fantastic race with crew man Wally and me in top form on our faithful Matchless, splitting the leaders Florian Camathias and Max Deubel. Finally, we finished in a very rewarding second place to the winner Camathias with the World Champion Deubel in third. As the only all-British crew and machine with six BMW outfits in the first seven places, we were pleased and proud of our efforts.

A 6 lap handicap race was to follow and once in the middle of a charge to the front we really enjoyed the scrap. When coming out of the left hander at Stirling's Bend, there

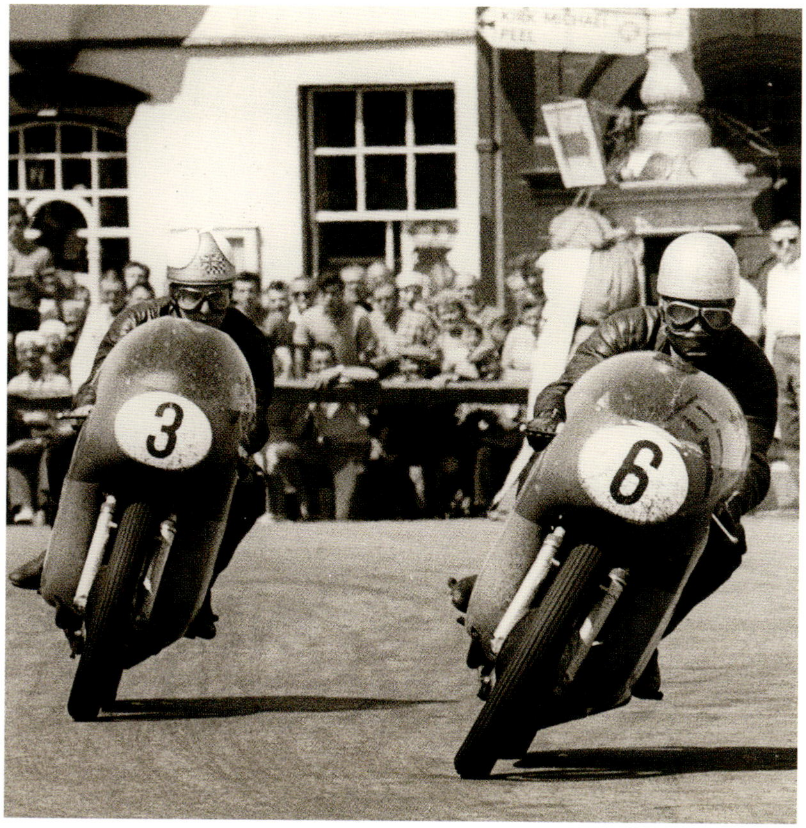

Junior TT, Hocking leads Hailwood at Parliament Square.

Joan in the AMC Catalogue.

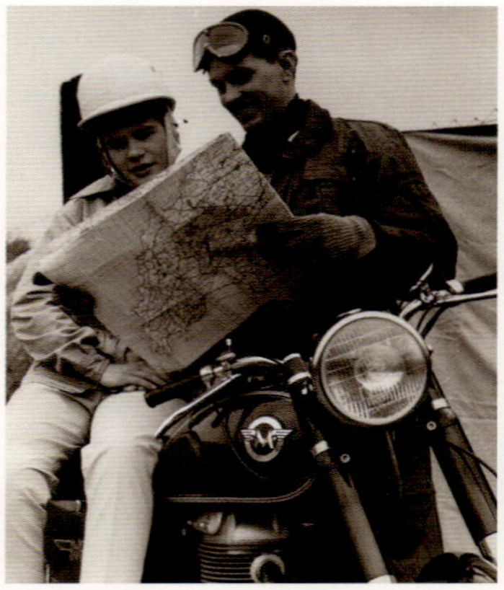

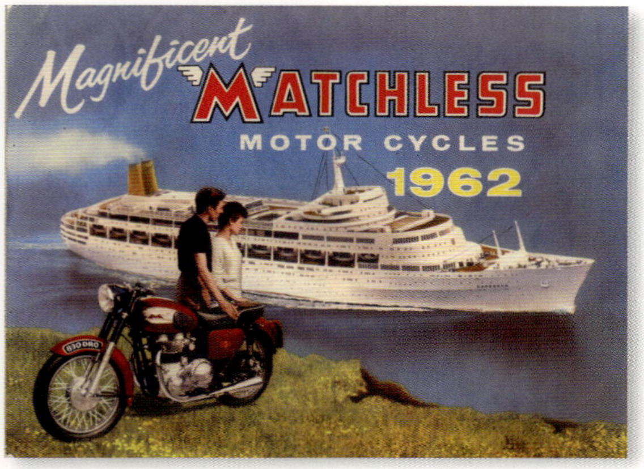

was an enormous 'bang' as the con-rod broke and came out through the crankcase and that was that! No complaints as our Matchless G50 had served us so faithfully having completed TT practice and the race without problems, With £100 prize money from our Brands effort we had funds for a deserved factory rebuild, or would it be a 'freebie'. We had given the AMC factory its best 1962 Isle of Man TT placing with a third, the next being Ellis Boyce's AJS ninth in the Junior Race and Derek Powell's Matchless ninth in the Senior event.

Next day after Brands Hatch, I could not wait to visit the AMC factory once more to show off our Isle of Man TT silverware. Jack Williams, race boss and his team were so pleased with our success and the AMC sales department responded by confirming that our achievements would be included in the 1963 sales catalogue. They requested that our Matchless outfit would be displayed at the Earls Court Motorcycle Show later that year. Last, but not least, AMC sales department secretary, Joan Anderson had accepted my proposal of marriage - hitching the sidecar in July that year of 1962.

Prior to the Isle of Man, I had sent an entry off to the Dutch TT organisers, hopeful of racing at Assen in Holland on the 30th of June, this to be our first continental race event if accepted. I had been disappointed when our application was rejected whilst in the Isle of Man, but that was before our race. Well, surprise, surprise, having finished third in the sidecar TT a telegram appeared to say that we were now accepted to compete at Assen... with an offer of £59 start money...whoopee!! My first reaction was to say stuff them, I am not going, but once I calmed down and took advice from friends we decided to attend.

We had to miss the 17th June Snetterton event so as to catch up with everything before departing for Holland. My motorcycle business was going from strength to strength still being managed by Percy, Marie Bull our able secretary and the rest of the loyal staff.

The AMC race department had rebuilt our broken engine from the Brands handicap race and a spare G50 engine was provided - they were certainly getting keen.

We booked on the British United Air Ferry flying out of Lydd Airport, Kent, and departed for Rotterdam, which was a great service in those days. Then we were driving to the famous Assen Circuit in the north of Holland for our next adventure into the world of motorcycle racing and our first short circuit Grand Prix - the Dutch TT. Our Thames van was now fitted with a custom-made side awning and a cover over the rear doors, made by the Tillett family. Inside, the floor and sides were boarded and a fold-back hammock was in place so one of us could sleep whilst travelling on an overnight journey - what luxury!

Once unloaded we took a look at this historic circuit, which reminded me of Brands Hatch, but on the flat. We took an immediate liking to this course with its fast sweeping corners yet sharp bends, a good mixture.

In the first practice I always remember Bill Boddice, Norton saying he would show us round the circuit, 'so follow me' was the order of the day. After a couple of laps I felt 'dear old Bill' was holding us up, so passing with a quick wave of thanks, Wally and I were on our way. Come the final practice we had once again along with Chris Vincent, split the BMW mounted contingent. Chris Vincent and passenger Eric Bliss recorded exactly the same time as Wally and me for joint sixth and seventh places, with Uncle Bill 6 seconds down. Those were the days of the British competitors, particularly abroad, helping each other and at the same time having fun!

The Dutch TT at Assen had an enormous following, as we were to find out. The night before the 'big day' we were woken in the middle of the night by general noise and hullabaloo. Peeking out of our steamed-up van windows into the darkness, featured against the moonlight sky was a huge stream of enthusiastic spectators marking their spots ready for Sunday's action. It was just unbelievable waking up the next morning to see 150,000 race fans already in place. The atmosphere was electric.

Ernst Degner, Suzuki won the 50cc race, Luigi Taveri on the Honda won the 125cc and Jim Redman the 250cc race with Bob McIntyre on the Honda in second place with

Quarter Bridge, start of the last lap.

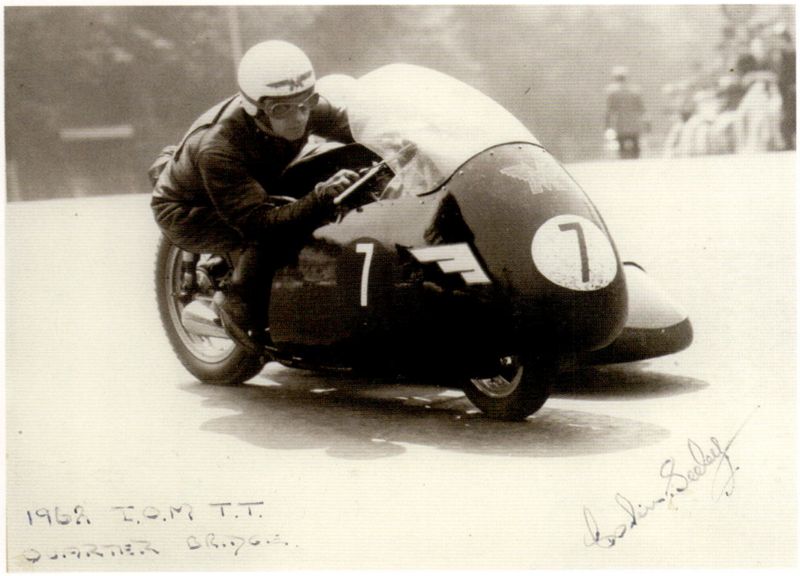

Joan and me.

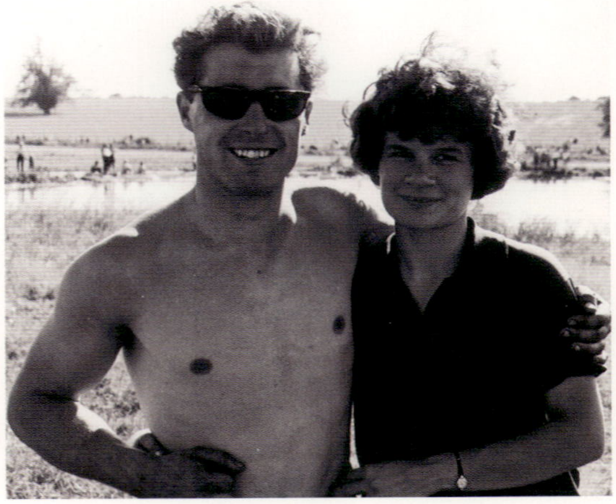

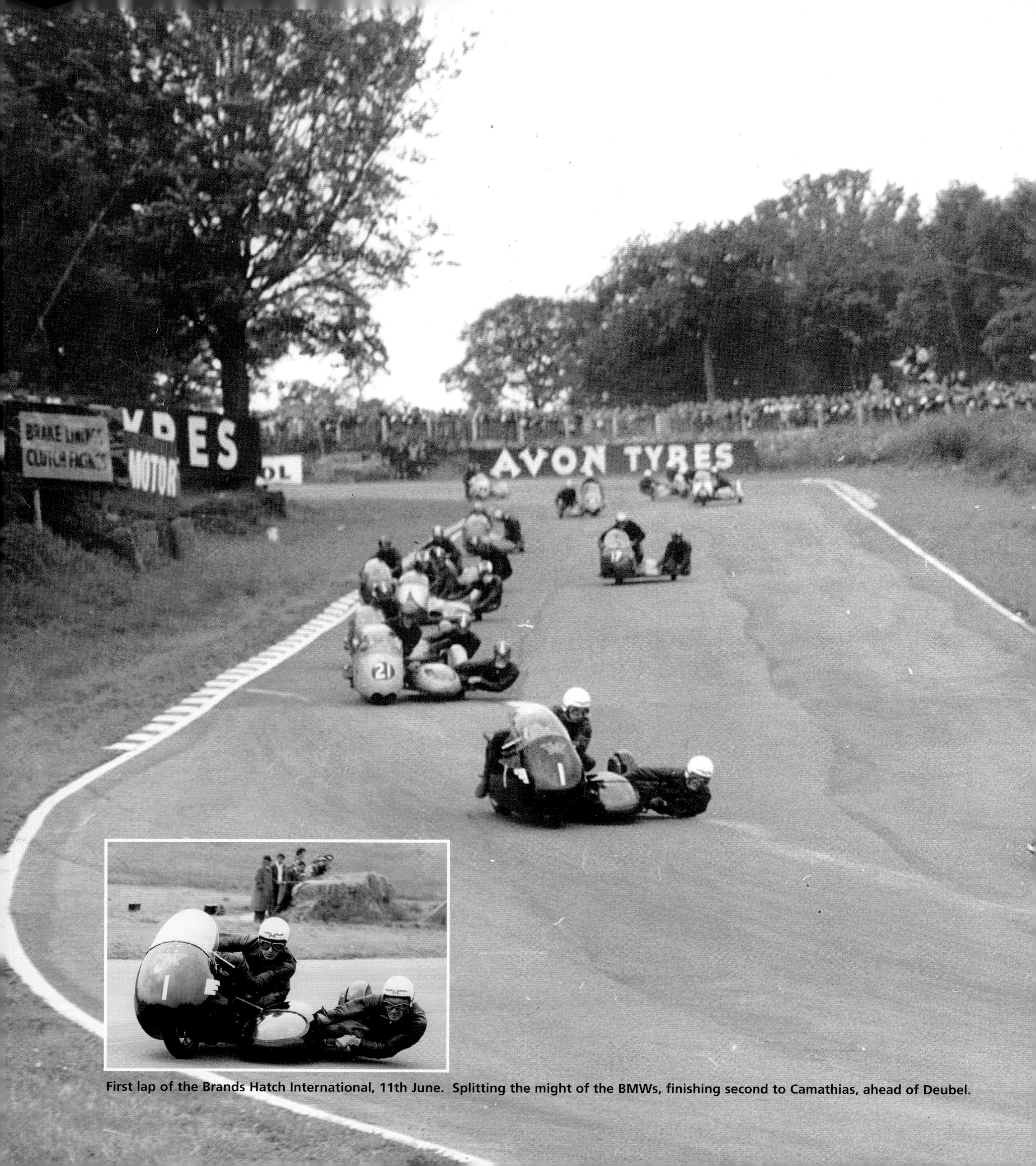

First lap of the Brands Hatch International, 11th June. Splitting the might of the BMWs, finishing second to Camathias, ahead of Deubel.

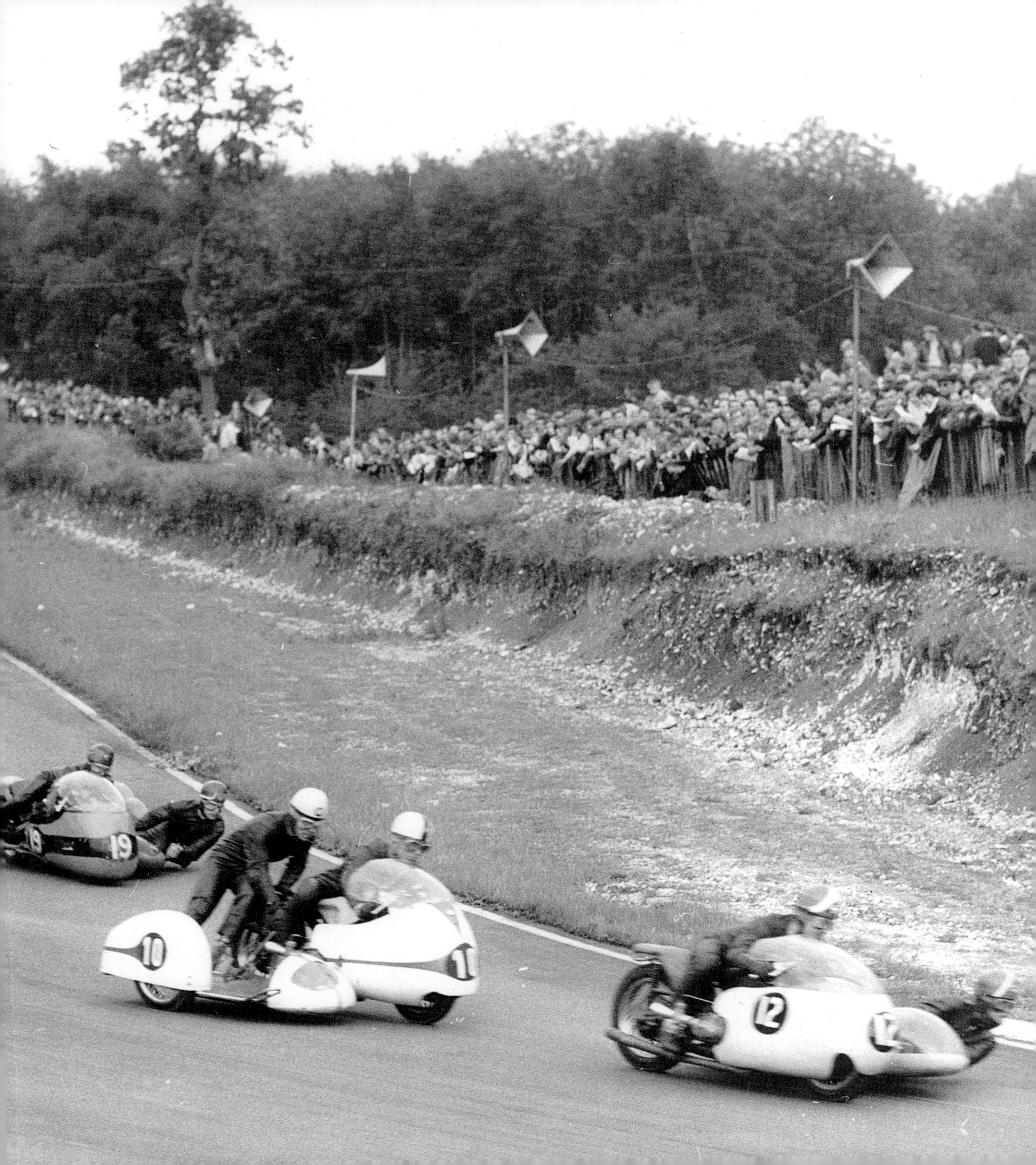
19
19
10
10
12
12

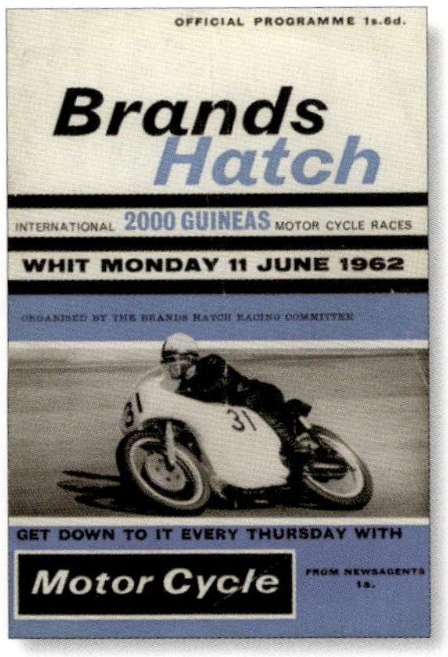

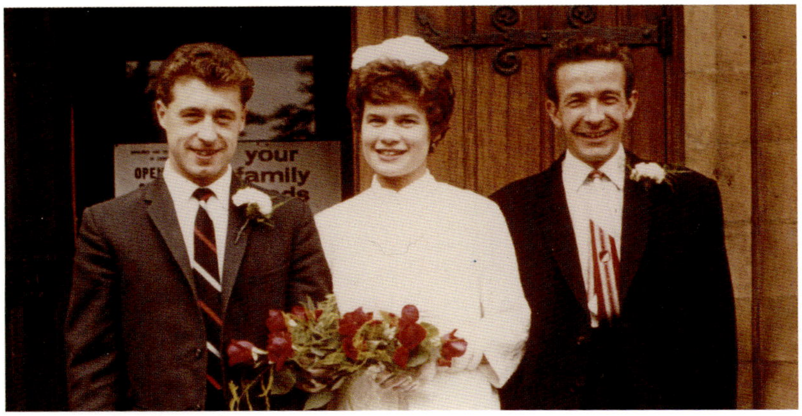

Our wedding day with Wally as best man.

Tarquinio Provini on the amazing Morini third. Jim Redman repeated his success in the 350cc race winning by some 20 seconds from Mike Hailwood on the MV with Silvio Grassetti, Bianchi, third. 'Mike the Bike' won the 500 event on the MV with Derek Minter on the Norton second and Phil Read again on a Norton third completing an all-British rostrum presentation.

Next was our race, the last event of the day, with the huge crowd of spectators still hungry for action. In those days interest in sidecar racing was enormous, and riders such as Max Deubel, Fritz Scheidegger, Pip Harris and Florian Camathias were held in high esteem by followers of the sport - in the same league as the solo riders.

Although race day weather had been cold and gloomy the many thousands of spectators had enjoyed some hot action-packed solo dicing and were not about to be disappointed by the sidecar race, which stole the limelight with an epic three cornered battle for the lead between Scheidegger, Camathias and Deubel. Chris Vincent was fourth, Wally and I sandwiched between five other BMW competitors, in eighth place. Scheidegger finally took a well-deserved win from Deubel, whilst we retired with only 2 laps to go, with a fractured oil pipe... disappointing!

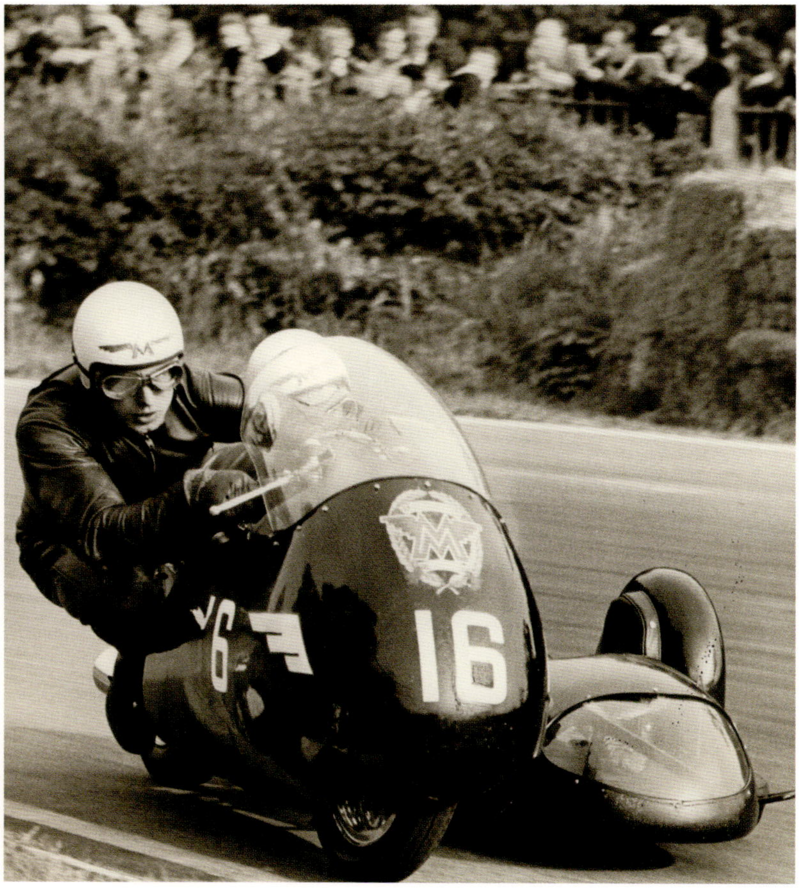

Traditionally competitors at the Dutch TT move on to the following weekend's Belgian Grand Prix held at the fast Spa Francorchamps circuit in the Ardennes. For us it was homeward bound, having entered Brands Hatch that next weekend. Also I had a wedding coming up. Wally and I had enjoyed our first race venture abroad and for sure we would be returning next year.

It was great to get home again after such a hectic month of June with time to collect our thoughts before Brands Hatch. By now for national events at Brands we were paid £20 start money and on finishing second that weekend to Bill Boddice racing his 750cc Norton twin, a further £10 was added to the coffers.

That same Sunday, 8th July, our close friend-to-be, Florian Camathias, had his revenge over Scheidegger and Deubel by winning the Belgian Grand Prix at Spa lapping the 8.75 mile circuit at the record speed of 105.29mph and setting a new lap record at 106.16mph. Florian was a specialist and so formidable on the very fast circuits.

Then perhaps the most important date, 19th July 1962, was my wedding day and consequently we had to cancel a race event at Castle Combe that same weekend. Marriage for a racer it is suggested often ruins a career, but in my case it enhanced my determination to succeed. My wife Joan proved to be my biggest fan and supporter for 17 years until her untimely death in 1979. After our wedding it was essential to give some time to business before Snetterton, the next race stop at the end of July, at which we recorded a second in the 500cc race and a third in the 1200cc event.

August 6th 1962 Oulton Park was the Auto-Cycle Union international and British Championship road race meeting. Another star-studded event but also a day of mixed fortunes, it started in glorious sunshine with a near-record crowd lining the 2.76 mile circuit. Hugh Anderson on his Suzuki won the 50cc race from Dave Simmonds, Simmonds-Tohatsu, Dan Shorey the 125cc event from Tommy Robb. However, it was to be mainly Derek Minter's day, winning firstly the 250cc race on the Honda four, then the 350cc race on the works development Norton after a battle royal with Phil Read, Mike Hailwood and Bob McIntyre on the 285cc Honda. McIntyre when in the lead, broke down leaving Minter and Hailwood in a close encounter to the chequered flag with Minter getting the verdict.

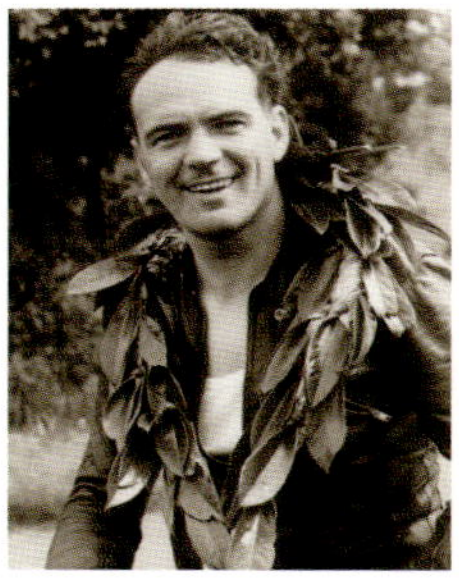

Everyones hero, Bob McIntyre.

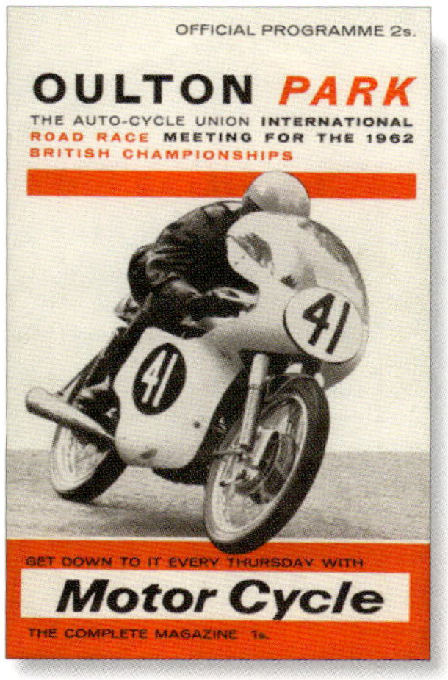

Brands Hatch 8th July.

Florian Camathias inspecting his tool box.

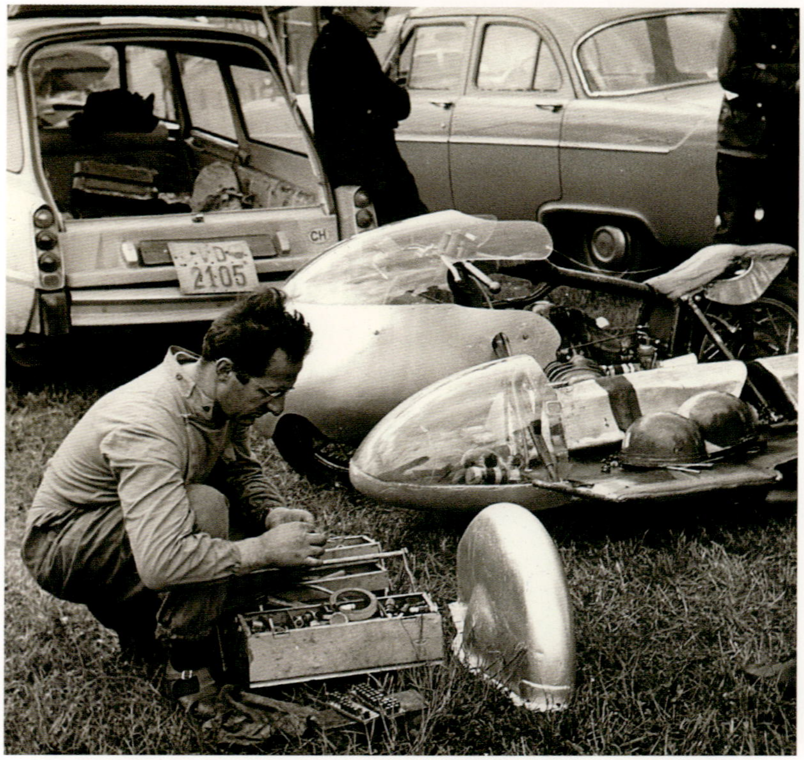

The rain started to fall during the first sidecar race which was won by Fritz Scheidegger with Max Deubel in second place. The second leg found the conditions slippery but Deubel was riding beautifully and soon overtook Scheidegger to win, but on aggregate time it would be Scheidegger from Deubel, with our all-British Matchless outfit and crew third and the British Championship title.

By the time we were acknowledging our success, the 30 lap 500cc solo race had started in teeming rain. From the start it was Phil Read from Hugh Anderson but soon Minter was ahead once more with Bob McIntyre at the halfway stage moving up to take second place with 10 laps to go. The rain was at its heaviest when the popular Scottish ace crashed heavily just after the left hand kink at the top of Clayhill. Derek Minter went on to to win from Read and Hailwood but no celebrations were to follow, for 33 year old Bob McIntyre would succumb to his injuries. This was a fateful day for the sport. McIntyre, amongst his many racing successes, had competed in 20 Isle of Man TT events winning both the Junior and Senior races in 1957 for the Italian Gilera team. Becoming the first man officially to lap the Island at over the 'ton', hoisting the record to 101.12mph. He was the idol of race fans for his 'tigerish' style, outstanding sportsmanship, quiet modesty and dour fighting spirit which never dimmed. His loss to the sport was a further reminder of the dangers.

Florian and Fritz Scheidegger, Oulton Park 1962.

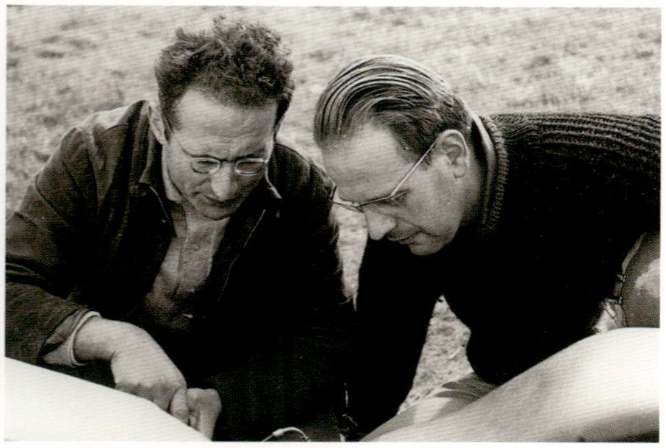

With our faithful Matchless G50 outfit, Wally and I continued to knock up successes at Brands, Snetterton and Cadwell Park in that order. Although at Brands in late September having a problem with the Matchless, Bill Boddice came to the rescue by lending us his spare Norton Dominator 750cc outfit on which we finished sixth.

On 9th September 1962 it was announced that Graham Walker, father of Murray, had died aged 66. Graham was a highly respected man. Born of Scottish parentage, he had been involved in motorcycling since his early teens, he was a dispatch rider in the First World War then became an accomplished international road racer competing in 23 IOM TT events. Graham had been Editor of 'Motorcycling' between 1938 and 1953 and combined this career with a vast number of other duties. Then, despite failing health, he continued his inimitable commentaries on radio, television, film and record. It was my privilege to have met this man, who had devoted his whole life to motorcycle sport.

On September 29th it was off to Liverpool for the races, no not horse racing, it was going to be a motorcycling Grand National. At the Aintree 'Century International' not all the top solo boys were in attendance, but the sidecar event attracted world champion Max Deubel and the 'Swiss Flyer' Florian Camathias, Jackie Beeton and Otto Kolle who had beaten us in the Isle of Man TT by some 8 seconds. It was our first visit to Aintree and in practice I remember at one section of the 3 mile course a queue of outfits at speed including Bill Boddice waiting to go through a particular right hand section which might have been the 'Anchor Crossing'. When arriving at this group I wondered what they were doing, 'hanging about', so I quickly shot down the inside and went to the front as we exited the corner. Dear 'old' Bill came to us after the practice to register a complaint, over what he did not know, he was just 'pissed off' that this upstart had beaten him to the draw and more would follow!

The 8 lap race provided us with another rostrum position and £37.50 prize money. Camathias was the winner with Max Deubel second.

Coming to the end of a busy season it was Mallory Park next day for the 1,000 Guinea Race of the Year international. After a night of gales and a morning of steady rain the 35,000 race fans were rewarded when blue skies appeared half-an-hour before the start of racing. Although Mike Hailwood was entered for the event, having planned to bring

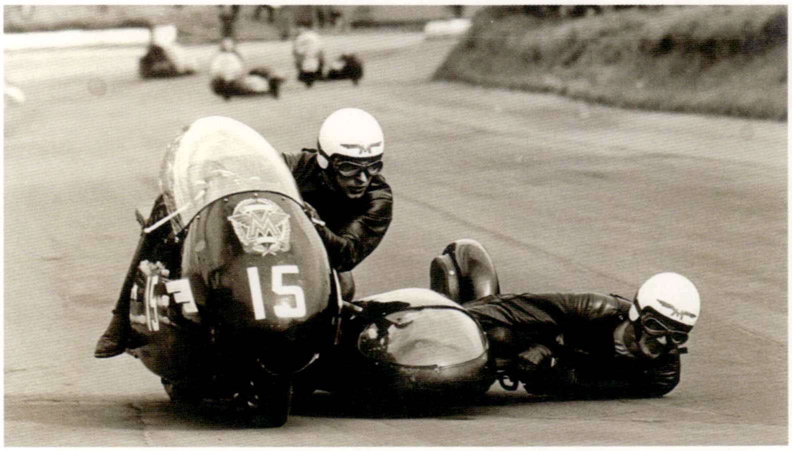

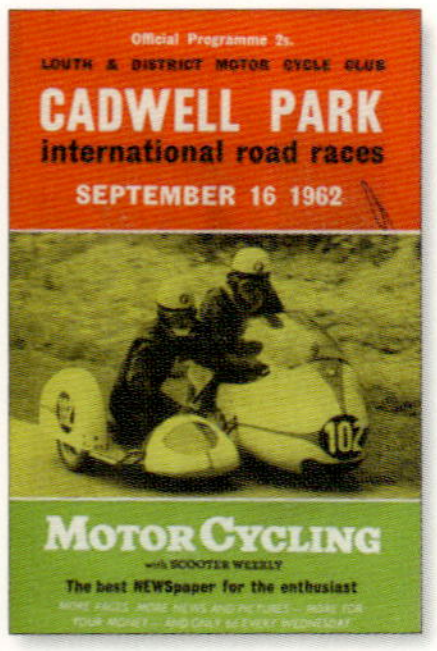

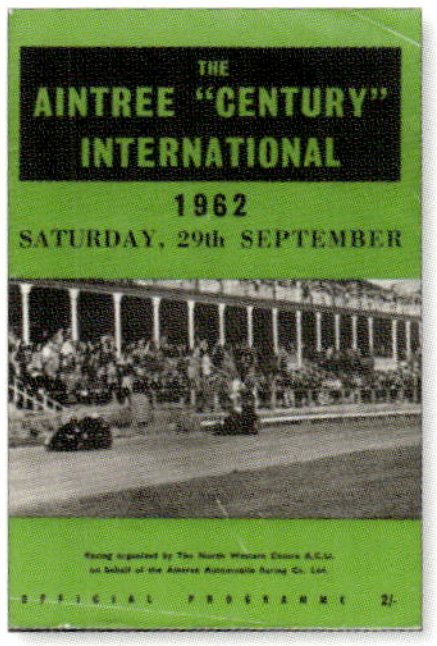

Race of the Year, Mallory Park, winning our heat.
We won £38, start and prize for the day.

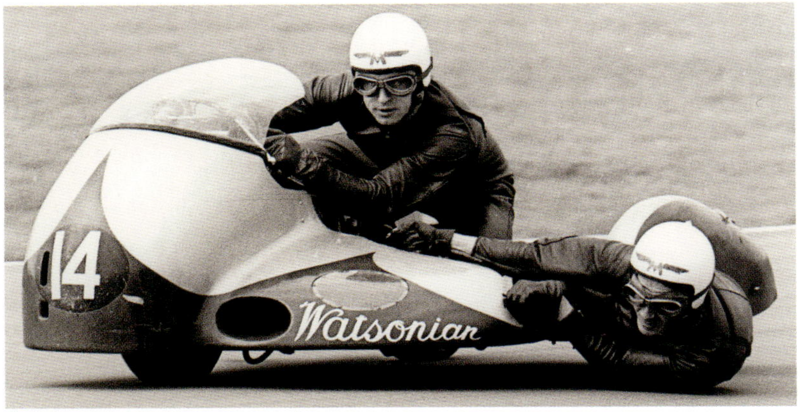

Action at Brands on the Bill Boddice outfit.

a 500 MV Agusta along, unfortunately he was recovering from injuries sustained at the Finnish Grand Prix, where in practice the water-cooled 125cc MZ had seized and thrown him down the road at close to 100mph. Miraculously he missed the trees which bordered the circuit and hit the straw bales, causing severe bruising to his chest and tearing muscles in his left leg so badly that he would be out of action for some time. Mike was disappointed not to be at Mallory Park as he had his eye on that thousand guinea prize.

So once more it was to be Derek Minter's day, winning the heat and the final of the 500 race from Phil Read, then first home in the 250cc race on the Honda. Finally he won the huge 'Crock of Gold' in the Race of the Year on his Norton from a stylish Alan Shepherd on his Matchless with John Cooper third on his Norton. Phil Read, having won the 350cc race, brought little consolation after crashing out of the Race of the Year whilst chasing Minter when in second place.

Victories in the sidecar events were shared between ourselves and champion Max Deubel, with Max winning one heat and ourselves the other. There was a fifth place for us in the 15 lap final, behind the winner, bespectacled Swiss Florian Camathias, Jackie Beeton, Fritz Scheidegger and a determined Charlie Freeman on his Norton fourth. After a race-long duel with us, Alan Thurgood on his Matchless came sixth. We received £15 start money, £3 for the heat win and £20 for our fifth place - £38 in all, whoopee!

Finally, it was Brands Hatch again for the last event of the season, held on October 14th. Unless the meeting was an international event at which the sidecar race would be restricted to 500cc capacity, all Brands Hatch sidecar races were up to 1200cc. So in racing our 500cc G50 Matchless, we had been at a disadvantage against the likes of Chris Vincent, Bill Boddice, Owen Greenwood and many others with 650cc or larger capacity machines. Also our 50hp G50 would be down by around 10hp or more against the BMW 'brigade'. So once again in the eight lap race over the 2.65 mile Grand Prix Circuit it was a fourth place behind winner Vincent, Boddice and Greenwood. We may not have won many races but we certainly kept those busy that did.

For this season two other riders had decided to follow my example and race a Matchless G50, Alan Birch and the other ex-Manx Grand Prix solo competitor Alan Thurgood. He was sponsored by the well-known Brands Hatch local, Don Overall. It had been obvious that we had been their target throughout the season and the ones to beat.

It was then time to 'hang up our leathers', the end of the season, time to reflect, time

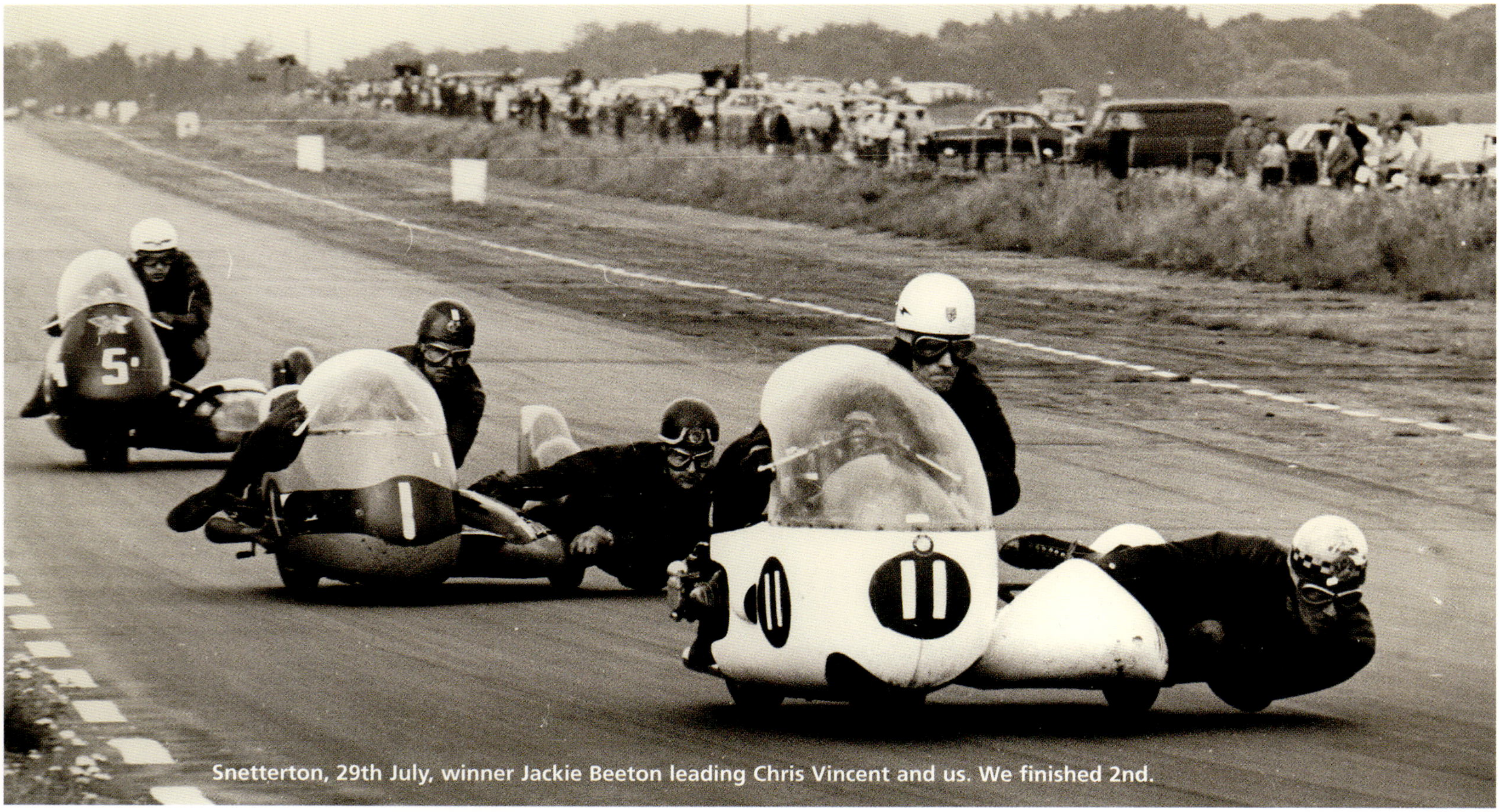

Snetterton, 29th July, winner Jackie Beeton leading Chris Vincent and us. We finished 2nd.

American visitors on the Matchless stand, Earls Court 1963

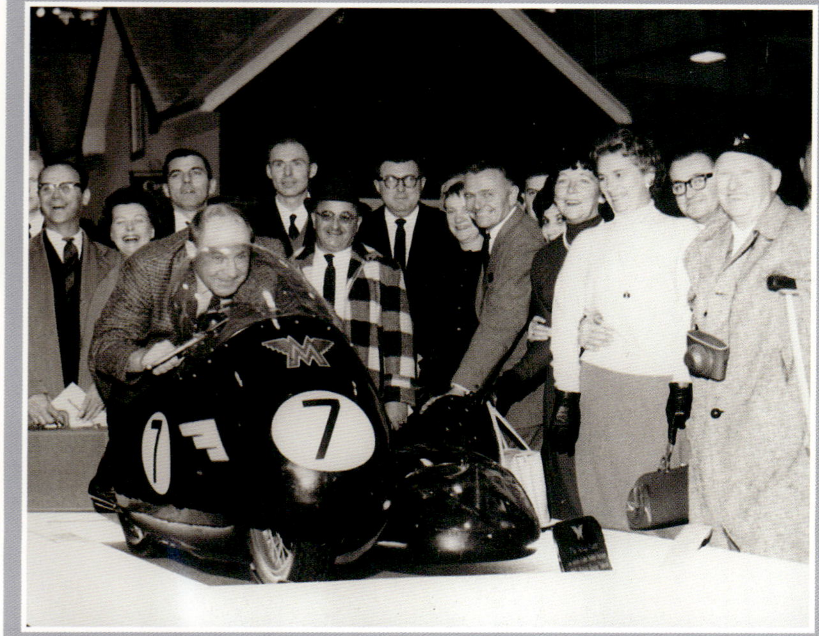

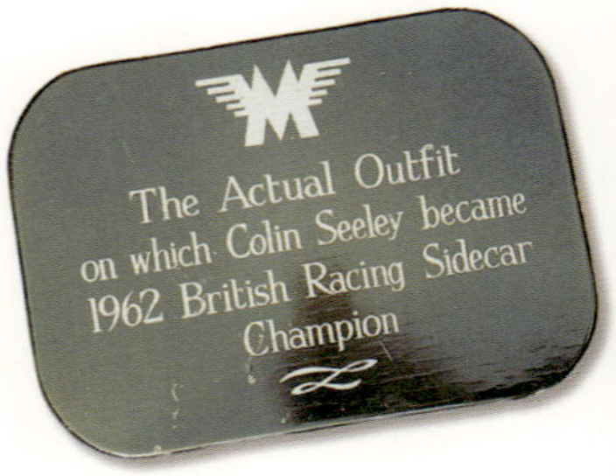

to rest, time to catch up with other important things in life. Our second race season had been unbelievable, we had started out with no great expectations apart from wanting to do well, safely, but to also enjoy our racing.

We had attended something like 20 race meetings from April to October, and had competed in 36 races, finishing in 32 with 18 top three placings, only one engine failure and a grand total of £758.50 in prize and bonus money.

Wally Rawlings had performed a fantastic job in the chair 'hanging on' at all times. We achieved third in the Isle of Man TT, Title of British Sidecar Champions, and ninth in the World Sidecar Championship.

Our Matchless/Canterbury outfit was displayed on the AMC stand at Earls Court, and what's more I even found the time to get married...

WHAT A YEAR! It was then back to shop work.

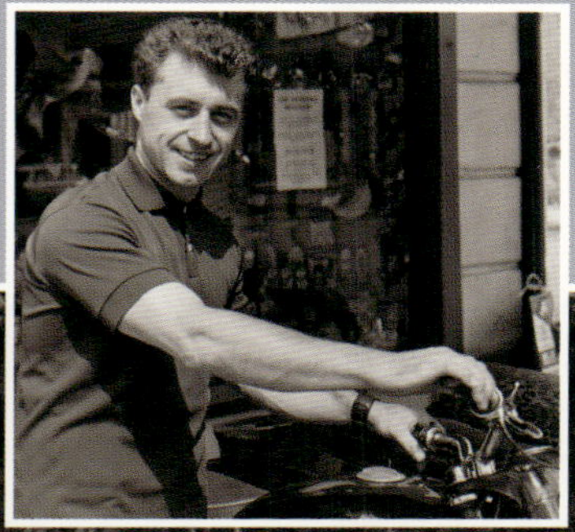

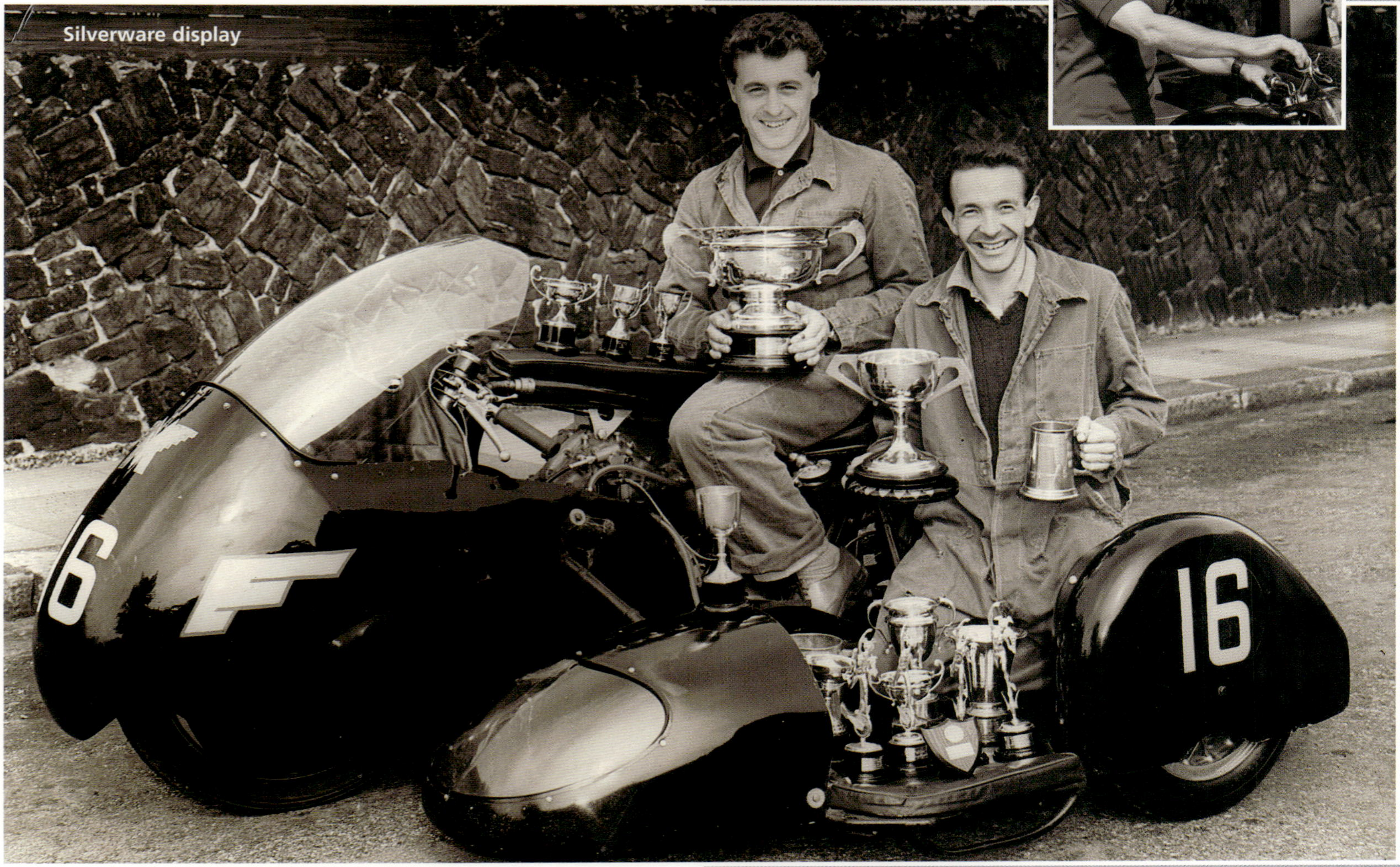

Silverware display

5 1963
GREAT FUN! GREAT DAYS!

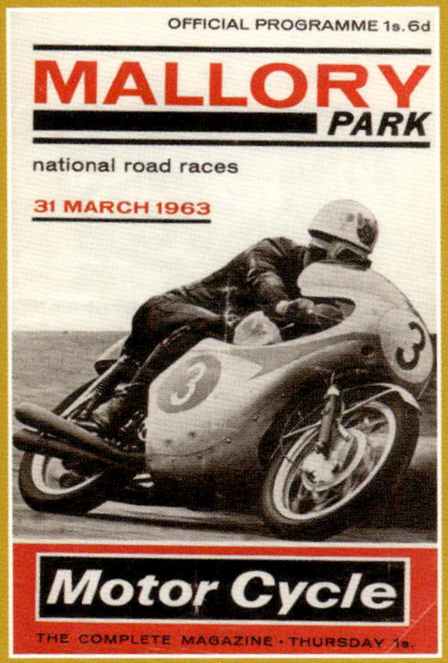

Following our racing success in 1962 with the Matchless G50, the bosses at the AMC Factory saw the benefit of the publicity generated by our track acheivements and granted additional works support. A spare G50 engine was supplied, and arrangements made to service all our engines at the factory free of charge throughout 1963. Furthermore, director Donald Heather agreed to have a special CSR 650cc twin engine be built to enable us to be more competitive in the unlimited races. Another G50 chassis was bought and prepared ready to accept the new motor which finally arrived in July. I hadn't thought about it before, but I suppose we had a title of 'official AMC works supported', quite nice!

We had also been approached by the famous Watsonian sidecar company, who were very keen to sponsor us with their racing sidecars. The Canterbury chassis had served us well but it was heavy and outdated compared to the lighter and neater Watsonian unit, so a deal was done with director Ron Bennett. Somewhat to the annoyance of Dickie Davies, Dunlop's competition boss we remained loyal to Avon Tyres, despite the fact that they could not supply an 18 inch flat tread sidecar racing tyre. 16 inch yes, as fitted to the back wheel but for two seasons we had used a rear 18 inch Avon solo tyre on the front wheel. This had worked fantastically, never giving us a moment's trouble ,wet or dry, and Avon Tyres would continue to support us. Dickie Davies really wanted us on Dunlop tyres because in 1962 we sometimes messed up their adverts for the British international events. They would get a 1 - 2 or a 1 - 3 depending on where we finished. All good fun!

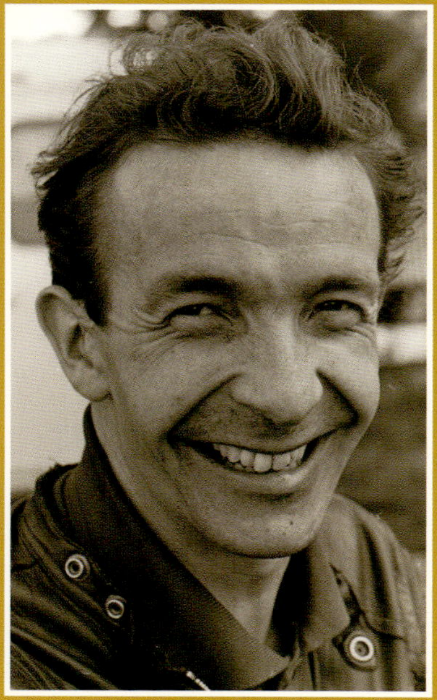

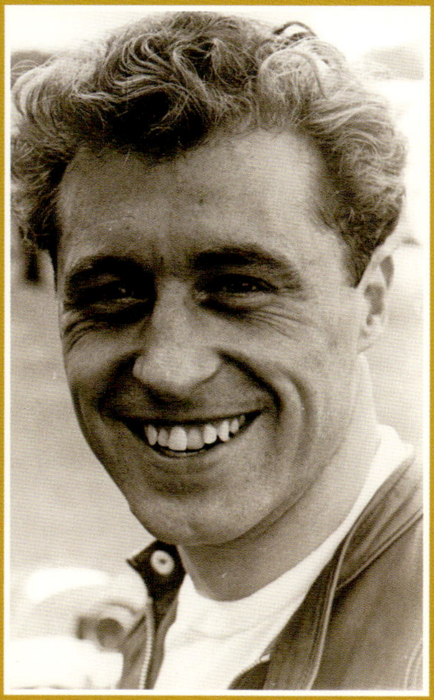

Wally and me .

Two Austrian Michael Schafleitner gear clusters were bought, a five speed and a six speed, as an option for certain circuits. Apart from other minor changes, the G50 outfit would remain basically the same as 1961-2 with telescopic forks - no leading link type for us, standard G50 solo brakes, and Castrol Oils provided the lubricants. Vic Doyle of Renolds supplied the chains, and Ferodo the brake linings. Once more we were ready to go.

Max Deubel was having a new racing chassis built by Ken Sprayson at Reynolds Tubes for his attempt on a consecutive third world sidecar championship. He was supported by BMW with works short stroke engines. Max then decided against using the Reynolds framed kneeler, and stayed with his sit up outfit, which had served him well.

1963 was the year of the 500cc four cylinder Gilera comeback, under a privateer label managed by Geoff Duke. The Gileras, last used in anger back in 1957, would now be ridden by Derek Minter and John Hartle, who had not raced since September 1961. He was chosen over Phil Read and Mike Duff, and was to prove his worth at the early March test, showing how to get round Monza at high speed in a stylish manner.

MV Agusta, provoked by Gilera's return to racing, sprang into action and officially decided to field Mike Hailwood, Alan Shepherd and Silvio Grassetti on 500cc fours, with grand plans to compete later that year in the 250 and 350cc classes with new machines.

Our plan for 1963 was to enter 25 meetings which would include six UK internationals and to spread our wings at six Grand Prix events.

A disappointing start to the season at Mallory Park on 31st March with a fifth and second place, was followed a week later by the 31st International Hutchinson 100 to be held at the fast 2.927 mile length Silverstone circuit. The Hutch was being sponsored for the first time by the Daily Express. This was our first visit to Silverstone but with over 200 entries, many were old hands. It is said that the British Motorcycle Racing Club spent £4,500 to organise and stage the event. The appearance of the Scuderia Duke

Minter on the 500cc Gilera, Good Friday at Brands.

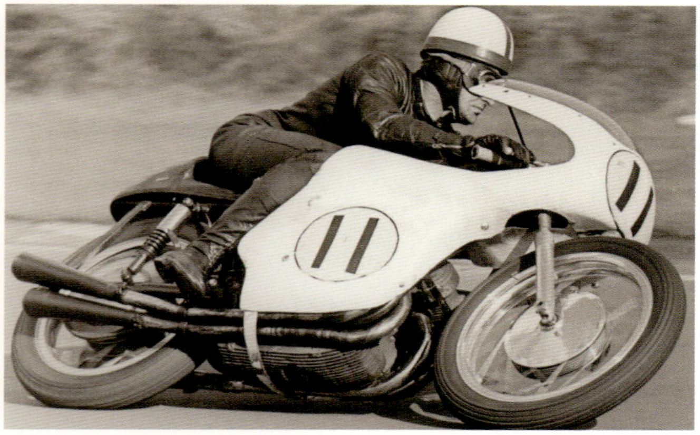

Gilera team had boosted the Saturday crowd to 25,000 and they would not go home disappointed. With the likes of Hailwood, Minter, Read, Woodman, Cooper, Redman, Duff, Bryans, Shorey, Robb, Avery, Dunphy, Butcher and Hartle along with Harris, Deubel, Camathias, Vincent, Scheidegger and Greenwood, it was sure to be a good show. The fantastic racing provided a fairly even spread of winners with Rex Avery, EMC winning the 125cc race from Tommy Robb with Ralph Bryans third. Jim Redman won the 250cc race on the works Honda and the Mellano Trophy, with Mike Hailwood, Ducati coming second and Ralph Bryans, Benelli, third. The 350cc Championship race was won by Mike Hailwood, AJS from Mike Duff, AJS, Phil Read, Norton third, Paddy Driver, AJS fourth Dave Downer, Norton in an impressive sixth position. Rex Butcher, Norton won the 500cc Spring Scratch Race. Then it was the big one, 49 competitors would line up for The Daily Express Trophy and BMCRC Championship Race. From the start Phil Read, Norton, who took the lead, but nothing was to stop on-form King of Brands, Derek Minter, Gilera, charging to the front to gain a comfortable lead, whilst his team-mate John Hartle was into a big fight with Read, who had tried every trick in the book to hold on to the flying Gilera, which he managed for 14 of the 18 laps. Read finished only 4.4 seconds behind John Hartle with an average speed of 96.68mph, a tremendous effort with next man home, Mike Hailwood on board a Reg Dearden Norton, gentleman Joe Dunphy fifth and Mike Duff sixth.

Now the sidecars, 25 outfits would come to the line for the 8 lap scratch race which found an on-form Florian Camathias, BMW, enjoying the open spaces of the Silverstone circuit. Although pushed hard by the long standing British ace Pip Harris and Ray Campbell, BMW/Watsonian, Florian posted the win from Harris with your very own all British crew and Matchless/Watsonian outfit joining our friends Pip and Ray on the rostrum with third place, Fritz Scheidegger, BMW fourth and Chris Vincent, BSA fifth, Claud Lambert, BMW sixth and Charlie Freeman, Norton seventh.

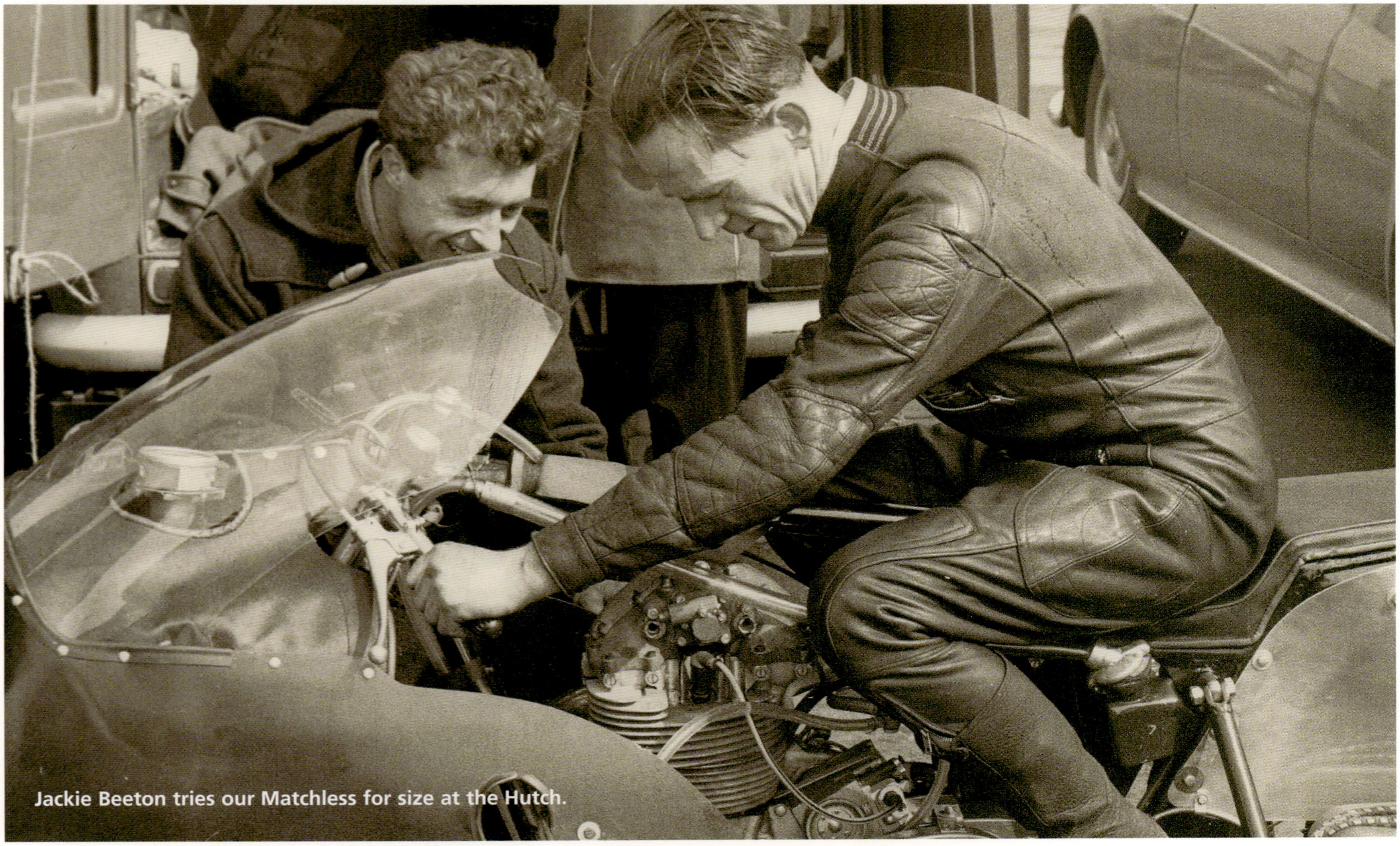

Jackie Beeton tries our Matchless for size at the Hutch.

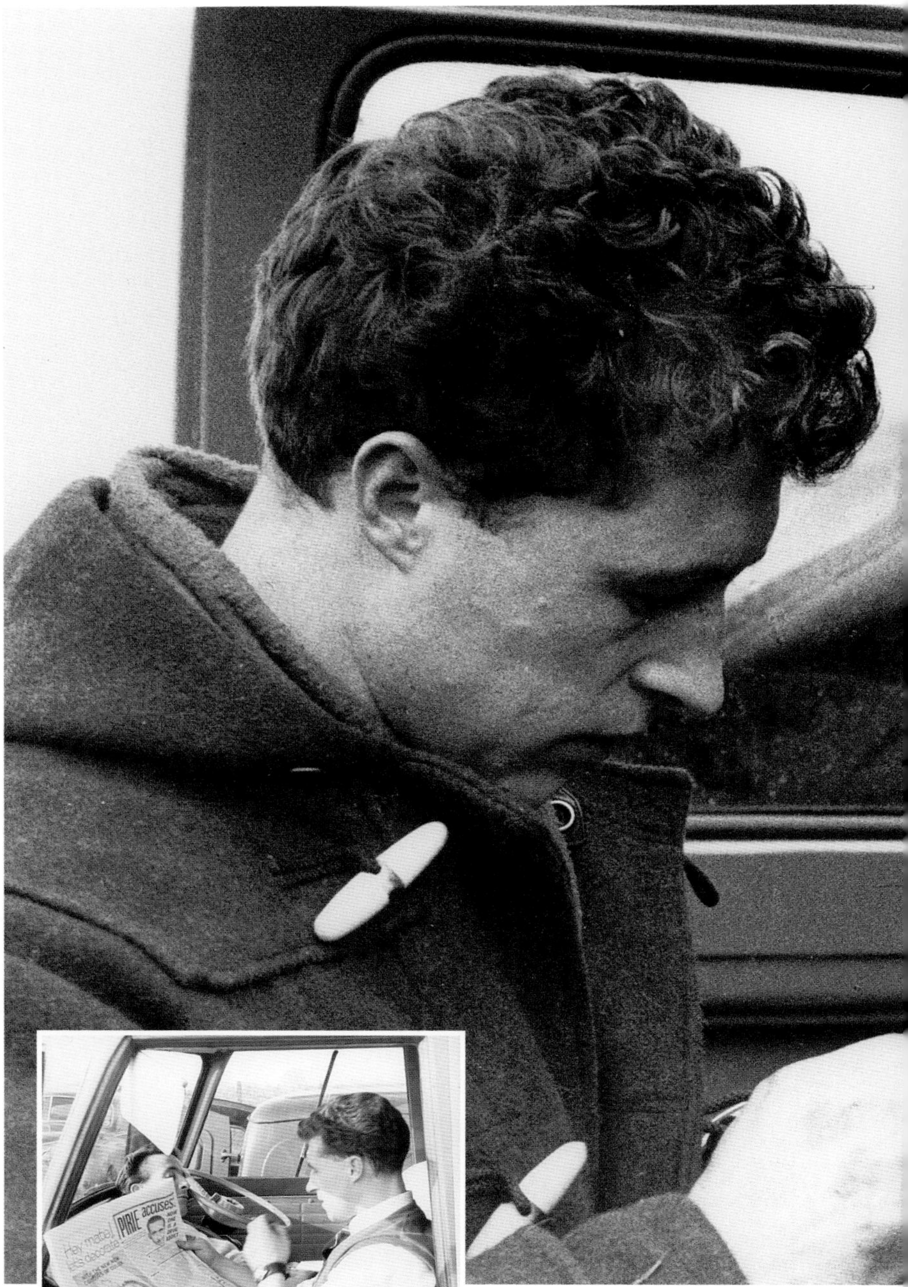

The afternoon 12 lap, 35 mile BMCRC Championship race turned out a 'hum dinger' with Camathias winning again after Pip Harris chasing him, was forced to retire with a collapsed sidecar wheel, letting Max Deubel through to second place. However, with ourselves and our Matchless G50 on form that day we hassled Deubel throughout to take our second rostrum position only 3.8 seconds behind the World Champion.

MCN's Charlie Rous reported, 'Even more fabulous perhaps were Colin Seeley and Wally Rawlings performances to finish third in both sidecar events on their single cylinder Matchless, gaining in the second race all the time on Champion Max Deubel.' It had been a brilliant meeting and I was proud of our performance and it's only in retrospect that I realise how fortunate we were to be racing in such company - it was just magic!

Following the Hutchinson 100 there was little time to prepare for what was to be one of the most strenuous racing weekends in the UK calendar. Easter started with Brands Hatch on Good Friday followed by Snetterton on Sunday and then Oulton Park, Easter Monday which entailed a real drag across country, without the benefit of today's motorways.

The Brands Hatch Good Friday meeting was covered by Mick Woollett. He reported that over 60,000 spectators had fought their way through the Easter traffic, in anticipation of a 500cc MV Agusta-Gilera 'clash of the giants' between Hailwood, Hartle and Minter. Unusual for Easter, it was a sunny dry day so the racing would be good.

The first race was the 10 lap 350 event held on the Grand Prix long circuit. The riders Minter, Shorey, Driver, Read, Hartle, Dunphy, Godfrey were all on the front row of the grid (only four allowed nowadays). It proved to be a great skirmish and the best race of the day. From the start Phil Read, Norton and Mike Hailwood, AJS tore ahead followed by Mike Duff, AJS. Derek Minter, Norton, always a bad starter, soon made it a foursome. Hailwood led into the last lap from Minter, Read and Duff then, exiting Clearways with the chequered flag in sight, Mike lost control of the AJS as it went into a hair-raising full lock slide and flipped over, catapulting him across the track nearly under the wheels of Minter's Norton. Minter went on to win from Read, Duff, Hartle, Driver and Dunphy.

Mike Hailwood, although miraculously escaping serious injury, had damaged his left wrist with a broken bone suspected. This prevented him from operating the clutch on the MV, putting him out of further racing that day - a great disappointment to all concerned, including the huge crowd.

The 50cc race was won by Dave Simmonds, Tohatsu, with up-and-coming Bill Ivy, Sheene-Ducson, second and Alan Dawson, Pope-ITOM third. The 125cc race winner was Tommy Robb, Honda, from Peter Inchley, EMC, and Fred Hardy riding the Frank Sheene tuned Sheene-Bultaco third.

The 500cc Redex Trophy Race had the 'King' Minter, Gilera, take the honours from Phil Read, Norton, after John Hartle, Gilera, was forced into the pit to change plugs. Paddy Driver was third by a tyre's width from young up-start Dave Downer riding the ex-works Norton Domiracer in a superb fourth in front of Joe Dunphy and Ron Chandler.

Then it was our turn. In those days grid positions for national events were allocated on merit and fortunately we were mostly on the front row. At that Easter Brands event it was no exception. We were alongside the crews of Pip Harris/Ray Campbell, BMW, Bill Boddice/John Tanner, 636 Norton and Chris Vincent/Keith Scott, 650 BSA with four other rows of sidecar outfits behind us. From the start Chris Vincent took the lead but

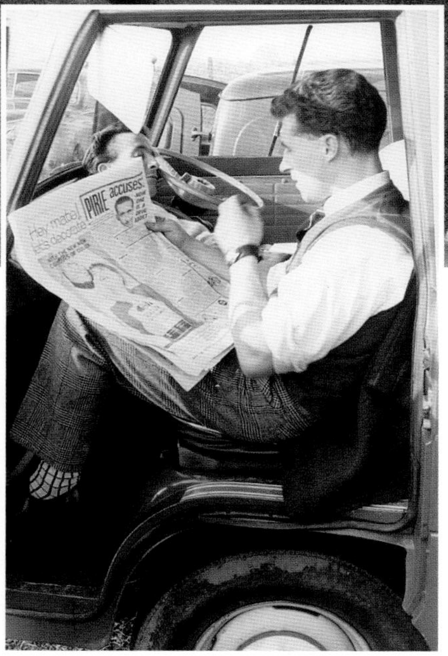

Calm before the storm at Snetterton.

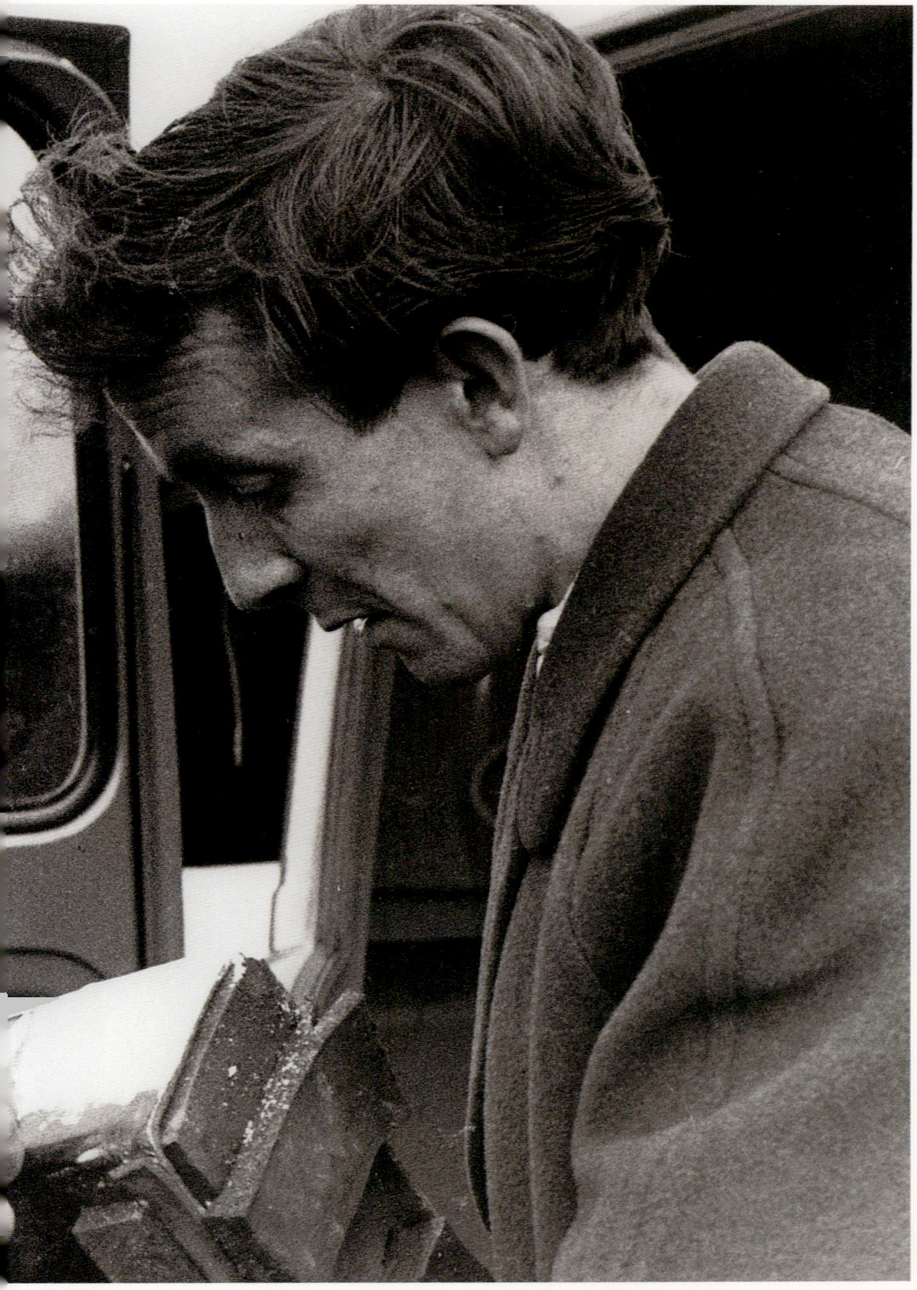

Team discussion, Wally you've got it wrong again.

was soon slowed by plug trouble, whilst Uncle Bill Boddice on his big 636cc Norton thundered through to win at a record speed leaving 'Gungy' Wal and me to have a race long duel with Pip Harris. Pip by name, Pip by nature, he 'pipped' us to the post for that second place, but we were pleased with our third spot. There was also a sixth in the handicap race, with £40 earnings in all!

Finally came the last big solo race of the day. Mike Hailwood watched from the sidelines and the Scuderia Duke Gilera team did not disappoint, with an impressive display of multi-cylinder sound and high speed lapping, the 'King' setting a new motorcycle lap record at 90.34mph and his team mate John Hartle second after some earlier encounters with Phil Read in third place. The Mint would have won £120 in prize money that day, plus start money.

We were looking forward to Snetterton on Easter Sunday, one of our favourite circuits. The international event had attracted Max Deubel and Florian Camathias. Arriving early Sunday morning at the overcast circuit it was to rain for the 500cc sidecar race. Normally, I had no problem racing in the rain as it often gave us an advantage, but on that day water somehow got into the works and we had to retire. The 1200cc race found the usual crews in front, Camathias adding to his 500cc race win by fronting Bill Boddice, Max Deubel, Chris Vincent and then 'yours truly' and Wally in that order.

Dave Downer was on good form, riding the Dunstall Domiracer. He finished third behind Dave Degens and 500cc winner the Swede Sven-Olav Gunnarsson. For many of us it was then a quick pack up for the long drive to Oulton Park, another favourite circuit.

The early morning drizzle did little to deter the enthusiasts flocking to the Cheshire venue for the Easter Trophy international sponsored by the Daily Express. Thousands packed every inch of the 2.76 mile Oulton Park circuit, eager to see the Gileras in action. They were not to be disappointed for Derek Minter, Gilera, shattered the lap record with at a speed of 91.86mph with John Hartle, Gilera, second, Phil Read again third and our friend Dave Downer, Domiracer, in a magnificent fourth.

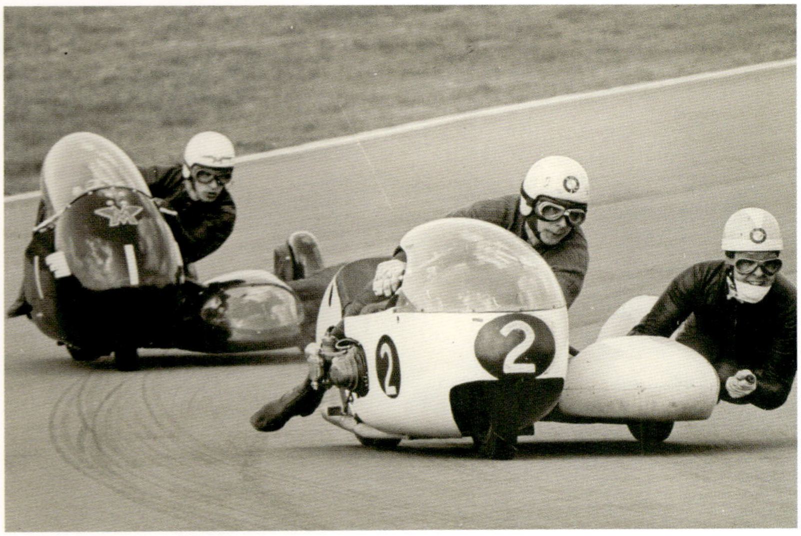

Pipped at the post by Pip Harris at Brands.

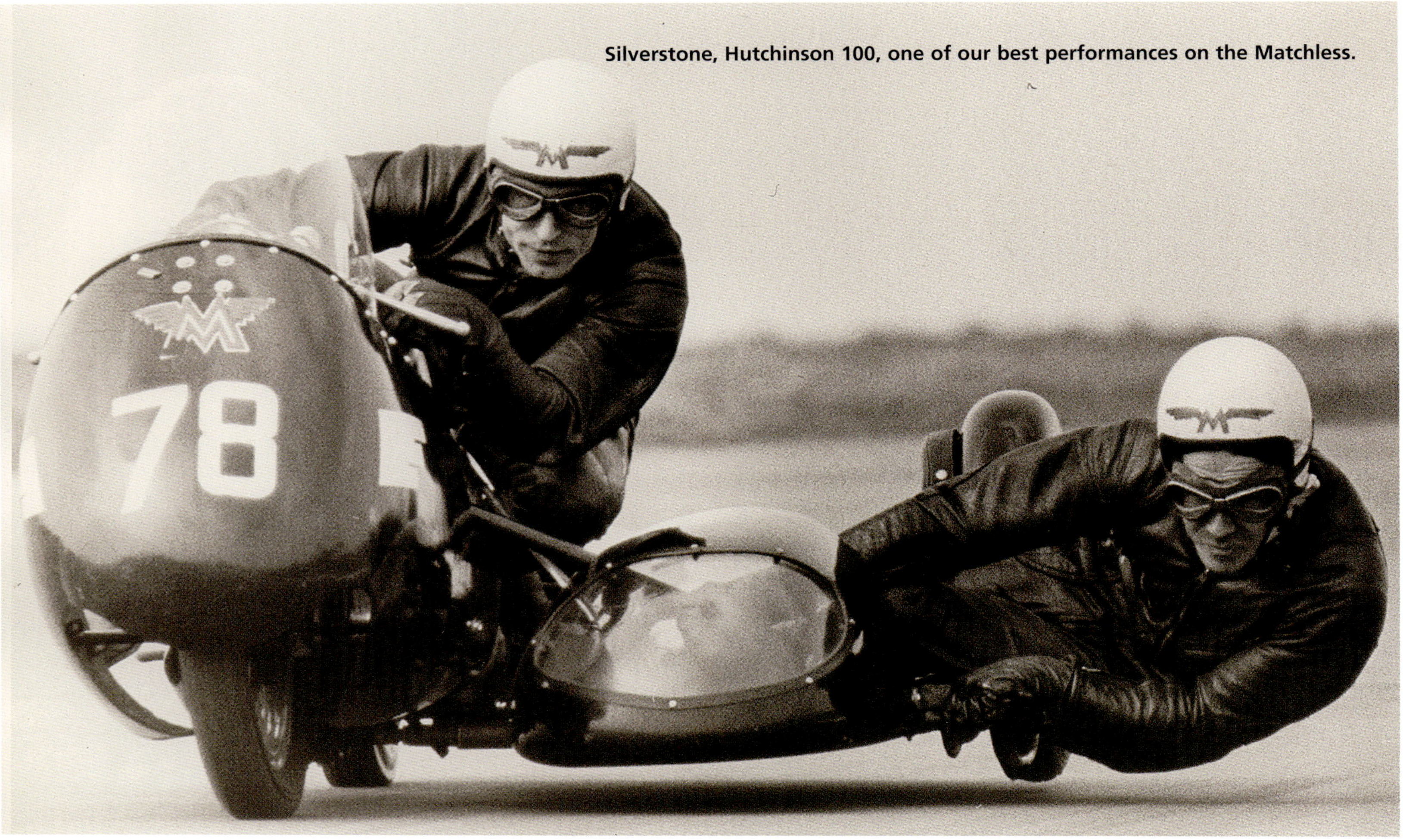

Silverstone, Hutchinson 100, one of our best performances on the Matchless.

It was another disappointing day for us, when holding a good fourth behind Deubel, Harris and Scheidegger, our G50 engine for once failed us with a main bearing problem. After an engine change we had some consolation with third place from Deubel in the handicap race. Earnings were £22 and we still needed to drive 230 miles home.

Derek Minter was on a winning streak having won both the 350 and 500 races, £175 in prize money, the Wirral 100 Trophy and start money. Well done to that Man of Kent.

Having a necessary break from that busy Easter weekend racing, it was time to catch up with my motorcycle business and arrange the necessary documentation for our trip in May to compete in Barcelona at the Spanish Grand Prix, held at the tortuous 2.35 mile Montjuich Park circuit. In those days a carnet was required, a customs permit for the temporary transit of goods, in our case racing motorcycles. The carnet needed to be stamped at each border, and not all customs officers were helpful, often asking us to unload the transporter. This was a complete pain when rushing from one event to another, also controls on foreign exchange were in place, often making life even more difficult.

On the day of departure to Spain with our Ford Thames van loaded with the Watsonian sidecar strapped on the roof rack the G50 and equipment inside and our friend from the Greenwich and District MCC John Juniper joining Wally and me to act as driver and mechanic, we embarked on the long journey to Barcelona which was something like a 1,700 mile round trip. Although there were no motorways in France we started off well by flying British United Air Ferries from Lydd to Le Touquet. It was a brilliant service in those days! On this first long trip abroad I remember that we were not that organised with food for the journey. Driving almost non-stop, our main sustenance was a banana or two with some French bread. (Never again though, as for subsequent journeys I produced a custom made food box which held a small Calor gas stove, coffee, tea, tinned food and all sorts of other provisions). Finally, arriving in the centre of Barcelona with no idea where to go, we drove around for a few laps, before asking a policeman where Montjuich Park might be. Once pointed in the right direction we arrived at the unbelievable tree-lined circuit, with pavements. Spectators were so close at certain points that they could nearly touch you! The paddock area was pretty grim, with local youngsters continually begging for food. I remember one young lad, standing on his head until he was blue in the face. We decided to blow our £45 start money on a hotel in the Ramblas area of Barcelona - a good decision.

The Spanish Grand Prix, the first of the year's classics, restricted the classes to 50, 125, 250cc and sidecar, the 350 and 500cc machines being too fast for such a potentially dangerous circuit. After two days of practice, at which for the first time ever, we suffered brake fade with our Matchless G50, large air scoops were made and the fairing cutaway for more air flow. That was the best we could do in the circumstances. Mick Woollett described the circuit as, 'one of the toughest in the championship calendar, it twists and turns round a rocky hill overlooking the seaport of Barcelona, a real test of riding skill which also demands the finest handling, braking and acceleration from a machine to be successful.'

Sunday race day dawned hot and bright with some 40,000 Spanish fans packing the rails around the circuit. The 50cc race started at 9.15am. The Spanish liked to get the racing over mostly before lunch. Hans-Georg Anscheidt, Kreidler after a race long duel, won from Hugh Anderson riding the works nine speed Suzuki. Ernst Degner who had been third, dropped out with ignition trouble. Another friend-to-be, the diminutive

Provini thrashes the works Hondas at the Spanish Grand Prix.

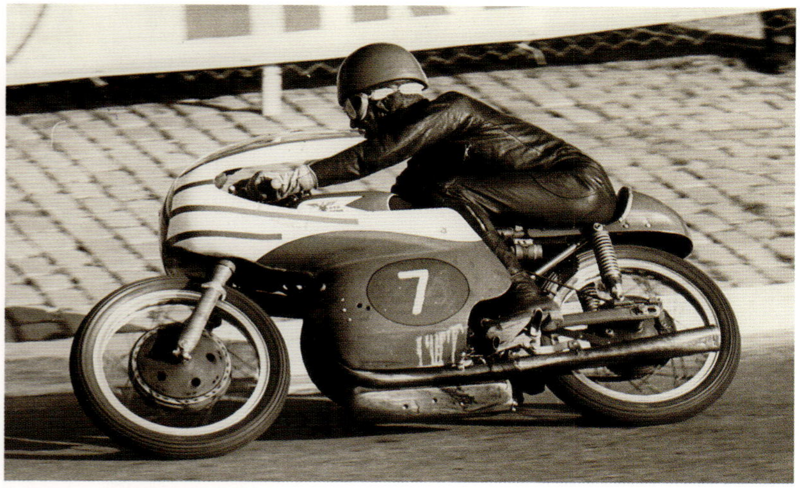

Luigi Taveri, won the 125 race from Jim Redman and Kunimitsu Takahashi all on Hondas with Peter Inchley, EMC fifth. The 250cc race found Tarquinio Provini on the fabulous single cylinder Morini in pole position. Jim Redman and Tommy Robb would be riding the works 250 fours with Taveri and Takahashi in support on production race Honda twins, all in an effort to stop Provini's run of success. On the start grid all the Honda boys were keeping an eye on Provini. Completely ignoring the man with the flag, Provini was already pushing, so the field shot off the grid not waiting for the formality of seeing the flag drop! The 33 lap race was a 'dust up' between Redman and Provini on the Morini matching the acceleration of the Honda four and the lap record was broken time and time again as they swapped places. Finally on lap 21 Provini went to the front once more to win by some 20 seconds, with Robb third. The headlines read 'Provini thrashes works Hondas'. Provini and the Morini had finally beaten the seemingly unbeatable Honda fours in a world championship event. The result was just fantastic and it was a privilege to have seen such action. Provini's riding style and determination were simply breathtaking.

Then it was our call. We had been standing in the shade trying to keep cool with the outfit covered over. Then pulling our race leathers up over our sweaty bodies and taking a last swig of water we rushed the Matchless to the line for the start of the 27 lap 63.57 mile race. The regular Grand Prix sidecar stars were all on the grid, mostly with BMW kneeler outfits and hydraulic brakes all round, including the sidecar wheel. We had neither luxury, but that would not stop us doing our best.

We all waited motionless in the glaring sun, the sweat already seeping into our wafer-thin leathers. Suddenly, the flag was down and with a roar we were away. We managed our usual good start, but soon ran into brake problems, really struggling to stop on the downhill hairpins. It was a complete nightmare and so frustrating, knowing we could mix it with the best even if we were down on power. Anyway, we did not give up and finally finished sixth in our second ever Grand Prix, but our first race finish. Max Deubel won from an on-form Otto Kolle, Florian Camathias came third. An impressive ride by Alan Birch, having given up his Matchless outfit to race an ex-Eric Pickup BMW, came fourth and Georg Auebacher fifth. Once again we were the first single cylinder outfit home. I suppose that was something!

In Spain our friendship with Florian Camathias was starting to blossom and would prove to be of great benefit. Soon it was out of the sweaty leathers and with the Matchless outfit packed away, it was the long haul home for Brands Hatch the next weekend.

Nobody could have known what tragedy would occur there that Sunday, 12th May 1963. The day had started well, the weather was fine and some good racing promised. Race one: the 350cc was once more a close encounter between Derek Minter and Phil Read who had led from the start, but the King had his nose ahead then slowed with oil on his boot. Read came alongside on the last lap to win by a whisker, with Dave Downer in fourth position.

Dave Simmonds won the 50 and 125cc races from a fast improving Bill Ivy who was second in both. The sidecar race was a further success for Chris Vincent, from Bill Boddice celebrating his 50th birthday and 30 years of racing and us third once more with Pete Russell and his very fast 998cc Vincent fourth. The 250cc race saw Derek Minter winning on the Cotton. Then it was the all important 10 lap 500 Redex Trophy race, producing a further win for the King from Phil Read, and with an impressive ride on the Dunstall Domiracer, Dave Downer who was just getting better and better, finishing third.

After the handicap sidecar race, it was the last event of the day, the 15lap 1000cc which turned into a gigantic contest between 'The King of Brands', Derek Minter and the rising star Dave Downer, on his super fast 650cc Dunstall Norton. Minter, riding his faithful 500 Manx Norton, was not about to give up his crown that easily, and it was 'nip and tuck' to the very last lap when the most horrific accident happened, Dave Downer was so close to Minter and could not avoid crashing when Minter went down at the Dingle Dell section. It was fatal for young Downer. The 'King' was down but injured. Everybody was just stunned by this tragic accident and for a while there was total silence. It was just too dreadful to comprehend. (See Dave Downer, page 88).

For the Scuderia Duke Gilera team and its challenge on the world 500cc championship, the Brands Hatch accident put their plans in doubt. Derek Minter was in hospital with a back injury and a broken shoulder as well as superficial cuts and extensive bruising. He was told that he could not hope to race again for at least four months.

Fritz Scheidegger.

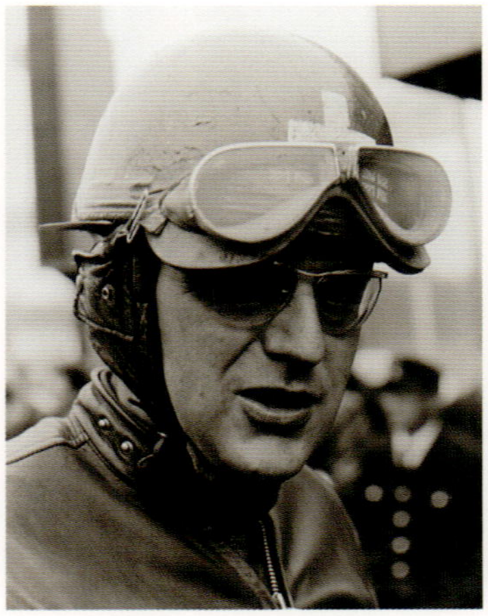

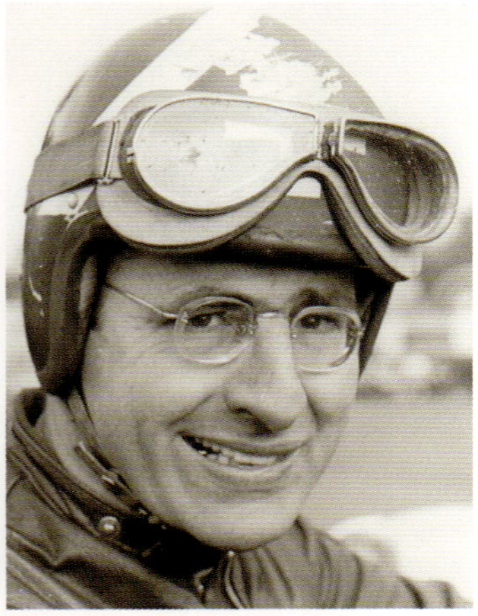

Florian Camathias.

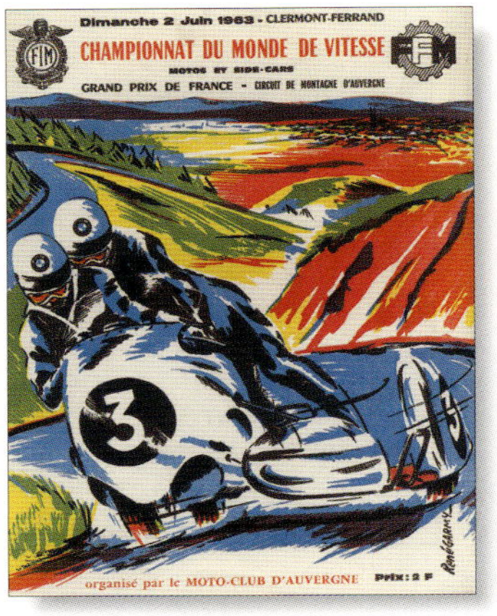

This accident would in fact wreck any chance ever of Derek winning a world championship. He made a comeback later that year to race the Gilera at the Ulster Dundrod Grand Prix, but had already missed three of the eight championship rounds that year. Although he scored a third place at the Ulster behind John Hartle's Gilera, and a second spot at the East German Sachsenring, it was 'Mike the Bike' Hailwood who would do most of the winning on the 500cc works MV Agusta. Phil Read, who had been signed to the 'Scuderia Duke' Gilera team, replacing Minter until his return, had taken up the challenge by finishing third in the Isle of Man Senior TT behind team mate John Hartle, who had also finished second in the Junior TT on a Gilera to winner Jim Redman on the works Honda.

Phil Read continued his charge by finishing second to Hartle, Gilera, in the 500cc Dutch TT, the Scuderia Duke team achieving its only 1 - 2 result that year. Then Phil scored a further second place behind winner Mike Hailwood, MV at the Belgian Grand Prix. It is always easy in retrospect, but perhaps Geoff Duke should have kept Phil Read in the Gilera team. Phil had such a good beginning, scoring in all his three championship rides. Perhaps the earlier commitment to Minter and loyalty by Geoff came into the matter!

Our next venture would be the West German Grand Prix, held on the original Hockenhiem Ring running anti-clockwise. The circuit was shaped like a bent sausage. From the start you raced up one side to a loop then down the other side in a fast left curve followed by a straight, a left kink then into a sharp loop before returning to the start. It was an extremely fast circuit, which of course suited the Rennsport-BMW outfits. Being the German Grand Prix, the BMW factory had a habit of issuing a few more works engines to the German boys, especially if there was a challenge from the Swiss or the British crews.

It was at the German Grand Prix that Florian Camathias gave us some advice on riding the fast circuit. He had certainly taken a liking to us and we appreciated his help. I distinctly remember Florian telling us to reduce the height and frontal area of the Matchless for the fast circuits, but it was difficult, as our outfit was still of the old style with a sit-up-and-beg riding position. Much to the annoyance of the Germans, Florian proved his point once more, winning the 100km race from World Champion Max Deubel with fast-improving Georg Auerbacher third. Florian at that stage was only two points behind Max in the championship.

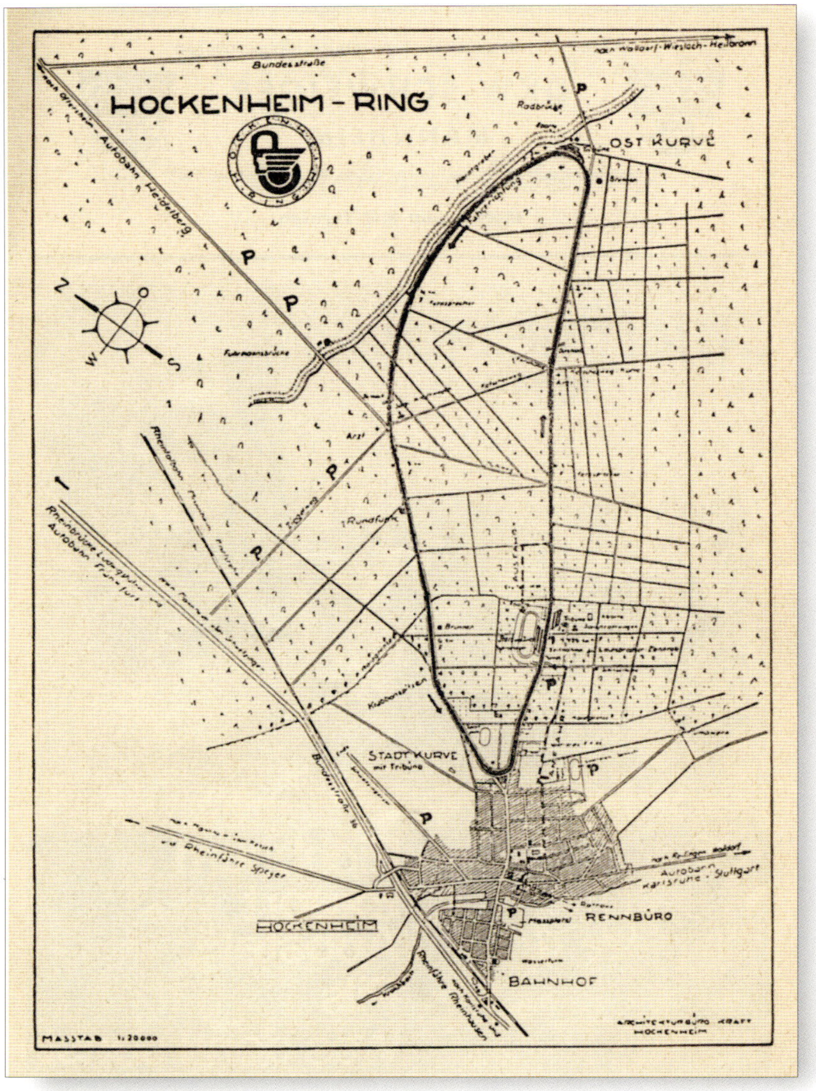

The original anti-clockwise Hockenheim Ring.

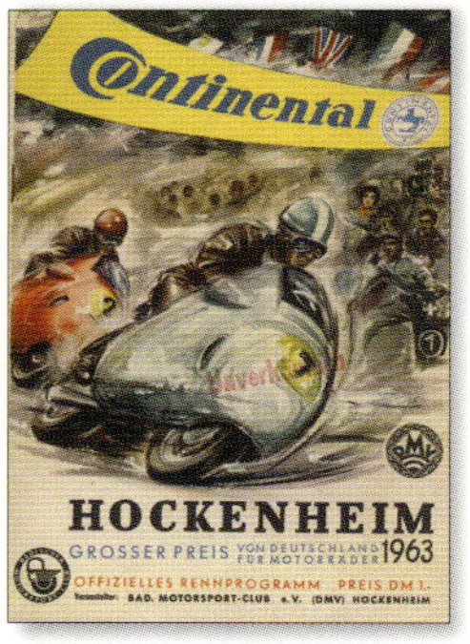

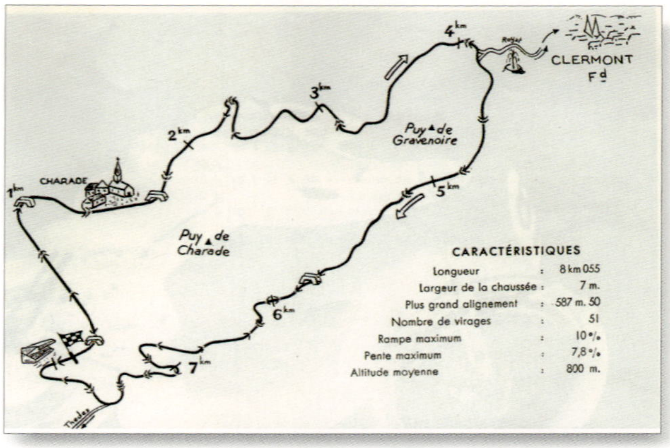

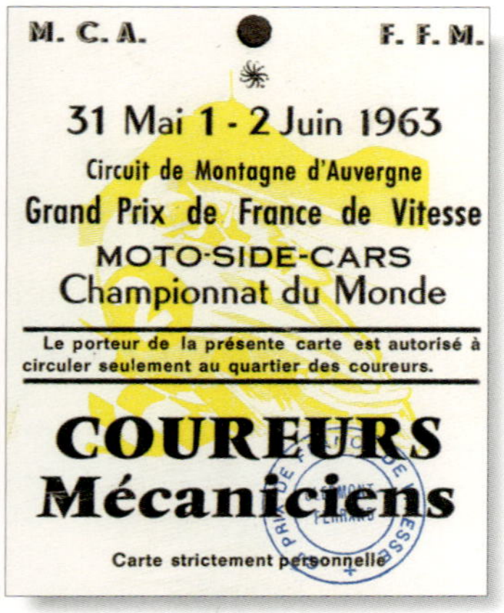

Clermont-Ferrand Circuit, and pass.

For our part, we were out of the points with an eighth place, still creditable from a field of 34 starters. The BMWs were just too fast for our single cylinder Matchless.

In the sixties, racing at Grand Prix events was always an excuse for a party, particularly after the official presentation of prizes. Once a few drinks were served it all seemed to get out of hand - dancing on the stage, the Australian contingent spreading itching power around all sorts of other pranks - all in good fun! I remember the gate being closed when I walked back to the paddock, climbing over the fence pissed out of my brain, I just fell into the back of the Thames van. Great fun! Great days!

We had not rushed to leave Hockenheim as we would travel direct to Clermont-Ferrand for the following week's French Grand Prix to be held on the tortuous 5 mile circuit, 2,400 ft. up in the Auvergne Mountains. This was another new venue for us and on inspection, what a circuit, with a rock-lined track, a down hill section of never-ending bends towards a half way point with sheer walls of volcanic rock on the right and on the left, nothing! It seemed there were only a few trees between the competitors and a thousand foot drop. Returning was not much better, just such a hairy circuit and a huge challenge. Were we mad or what?

The race day meeting opened in fine weather at 10.00am. In the 125cc race 18 riders had qualified for the grid, with Jim Redman in pole joined on the front row by Hugh Anderson, Frank Perris and Ernst Degner. The start was to be chaotic as a back marker jumped the flag, which triggered the front row and then practically the entire field jumped the start. Hugh Anderson, Suzuki, went on to a record-shattering performance in this 65 mile round the rocks race, Redman, Honda, second and Taveri third. Perris, Robb and Degner completed the first six. With that race over, a 3$^{1}/_{2}$ hour lunch interval took place (it could only happen in France) and then halfway through, the circuit was battered by a torrential thunderstorm which covered the track with hailstones and mud, washed down from the mountain sides making it treacherous. Finally, with lunch over and the rain abated, the 20 starters for the 50cc event came to the line for the 8 lap race. With only one championship point between pole setter Hugh Anderson, Suzuki, and Georg Anscheidt, Kreidler, it was an important race. From the start Anscheidt took the lead making the most of his 12 speed works Kreidler and he was never headed. Anderson and Itoh had fallen without injury, leaving Degner, Suzuki, second and Ichino, Suzuki, third. This placed Anscheidt five championship points ahead of Anderson.

I have said before, I was totally intrigued by the works 50cc racing machine, an engineering wonder, and to ride them to success certainly required great skill.

Following the first two races, the French Grand Prix was about to turn into a French farce. As the 250cc competitors lined up on the grid, the circuit was hit once more by torrential rain and the clouds cut visibility to a mere 20 to 30 yards. Firstly, the organisers, regardless of the conditions or thoughts of the rider's safety wanted to start the race, but the FIM steward Emil Vorster wisely insisted on sending the riders off on a lap of inspection behind the official car. Impossible to race was the view of Tarquinio Provini, and Jim Redman agreed, saying conditions were so bad that some top gear corners could only be taken in second. The organisers would be off their heads to start the race.

The organisation, never the best, almost ground to a standstill as a three hour postponement followed. By then, competitors including ourselves, were growing impatient, as we were racing at Brands Hatch next day and then directly onto the Isle of Man TT. The officials argued among themselves, tempers flared and the commentator took it upon himself to canvass riders' opinions over the PA system. For the solo boys racing was out of the question but world champion Max Deubel supported by Fritz Scheidegger thought the sidecar brigade should race. This brought cheers of approval from the fed-up wet crowd of spectators.

Finally, after a further inspection lap by the official car, the President of the jury announced over the PA system that they could not accept the responsibility of starting any racing in such bad conditions. His words were almost drowned by the angry jeers of the racing fans. Finally, to their credit, the organisers paid out the start money and a small amount of prize for us, amounting to a £38 10s pay-out all in. The whole event was a nightmare, but in all fairness nobody's fault, just a freak of nature.

Now loaded and leaving the French drama behind us, we embarked with a number of other competitors, on our overnight 500 mile journey through the French countryside. We had to make Le Touquet to catch the first British United Airways flight out next morning, to be at Brands Hatch in time to compete at the international event prior to the Isle of Man TT. I remember now having completed this trip three times, that it was really most tiring, racing a Grand Prix and then driving 500 miles overnight to catch a flight, hardly able to keep awake. Then there was a further 60 miles driving to compete at an international event. It was really stupid, but stupid we were, that's why we raced a sidecar outfit!

It was a great feeling to be back to our home circuit and the excellent organisation of the Brands Racing Committee, Greenwich M and MCC, Rochester and DMC and the Gravesend Eagles MCC Clerk of the Course Tony Lovett had arranged a late practice session for the bedraggled latecomers.

The 12 lap sidecar race was a humdinger, with our own Pip Harris stealing the show. Florian Camathias led for 2 laps before being displaced by the Harris/Campbell pairing who just drew away leaving Florian and Max Deubel in a bitter battle. Max suffered a partial engine seizure and dropped back behind Fritz Scheidegger, who then took second place when Florian suffered a flat on his sidecar wheel. Pip went on to win unchallenged, but Fritz equalled the 500 lap record in his efforts to reduce the gap. Max Deubel just managed to stay in front of our flying Matchless G50 to take third place. We were fourth in front of Otto Kolle, BMW, good enough!

Time to go home for some well deserved sleep, then we needed to get ready for the Isle of Man TT. Solo practice had already started on the previous Saturday. Arriving in the Isle of Man for our third TT event, the magic was still very much there. There was the same hustle and bustle of the docks as Manx boats were unloaded. Many competitors, like ourselves, had come from the previous events in France and Brands Hatch.

As we left the docks we turned onto the TT circuit at Quarter Bridge heading for Union Mills and viewed the banners displayed around the circuit 'Castrol', 'Dunlop', 'Lucas', 'Avon', 'Girling', 'BP', etc. This created a great feeling of excitement but also some apprehension. As we approached Beveley House in Strang, our host and 'cheer leader' Ma Clucas was already at the door. She must have been reading the smoke signals that we were on the way. She was so pleased to see us, especially when we gave her a crate of her favourite tipple! We had to spring into action, as we would be practising that very evening, Tuesday. Once unloaded, it was the obligatory signing on and the

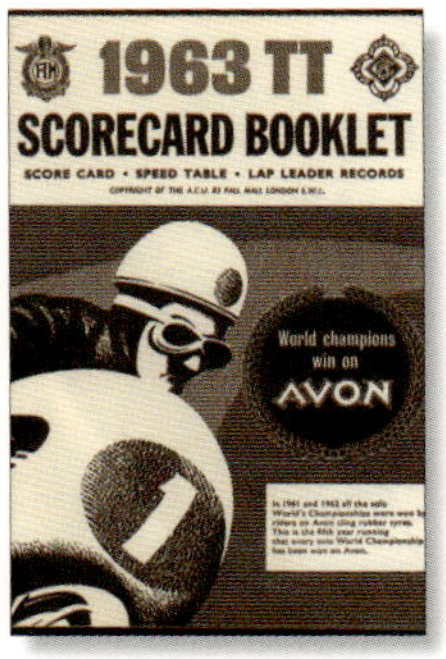

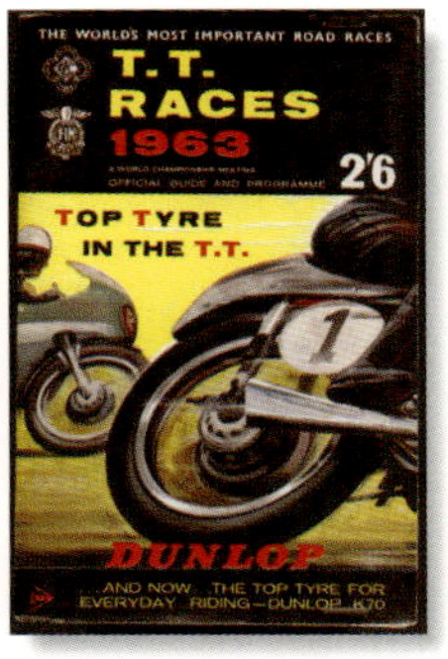

checking of riding gear. The supportive Greenwich and District MCC had kindly paid our race entry. Unlike in earlier visits, we were now considered serious contenders and this was certainly a good feeling. This respect was not only from the sidecar contingent, but also through our association with the solo competitors.

We discovered that our friend Florian Camathias, on his way to Liverpool had broken down at Hinckley. This fanatical man, never to be held back, unloaded his BMW-FCS racing outfit from his Citroen transporter and with Alfred Herzig in the chair, drove it with open exhaust to Liverpool, ignoring the looks of amazement from the police as he drove through the Mersey Tunnel to the docks - a fantastic story and absolutely true!

A couple of laps of the TT circuit in our van to refresh our memories, a check-over of the Matchless and the fitting of the Isle of Man gearing and some fresh Castrol Oil, and we were ready to go. As I have said, I loved the TT evening practices, as the weather always seemed fine. They were for me relaxed practice sessions. Perhaps they reminded me of the summer evening dashes along the A20 to the Oakdene Cafe in my youth. This particular practice would not disappoint as Deubel headed the leader board from the amazing Camathias and 'Master' Harris third, with me and Wally fourth. A good start, with 34 outfits out on that particular evening.

With our Matchless G50 fitted with a six speed Schafleitner gearbox specially for the TT I had certainly thought it was possible to lap the Island at around 85mph, having averaged 82.80mph for the whole race in 1962. We only needed to gain around 90 seconds a lap to achieve this speed. Our knowledge of the TT course was so much better, gaining so much experience in the last year made me confident that our goal was achievable. The six speed box would give us an advantage over the mountain section, keeping our single cylinder on the boil. I always thought the BMW competitors benefited over the mountain climb with their extra horsepower however from the start through the often blind corners and hedgerows to Ramsey, I thought we pretty well held our own.

Next day, Wednesday, was a further evening sidecar practice with Max Deubel once more at the front from Scheidegger, a fast-improving Alan Birch, BMW third at 81.62mph and ourselves fourth again at 81.27mph followed by Kolle and Auerbacher, the first six from the 38 outfits that had been out.

The third practice was scheduled for some unearthly hour next morning. (I personally never saw any real benefit to those early morning sessions, which were often extremely cold and miserable). As expected, next morning was no exception, dawning wet and horrible, so looking out at the conditions we took a vote to stay in our warm beds. We would hear the action as the outfits streamed through Union Mills. 'Shall we have another cup of tea? Pass the milk Wally'.

Out on the course, all had not gone well for practice leader Deubel, who in making one of his rare mistakes, on the second lap crashed at Sarah's Cottage, somersaulting the crew and the outfit. Max was not seriously injured - 'shaken not stirred!', however regular passenger Emil Horner was taken to hospital with superficial injuries. The final sidecar practice session held on the Friday evening was to be a laugh a minute, with our eccentric hero Florian Camathias taking off from the start without his passenger. All were 'gob smacked' as Alfred Hertzig stood in the road, watching Florian disappear in

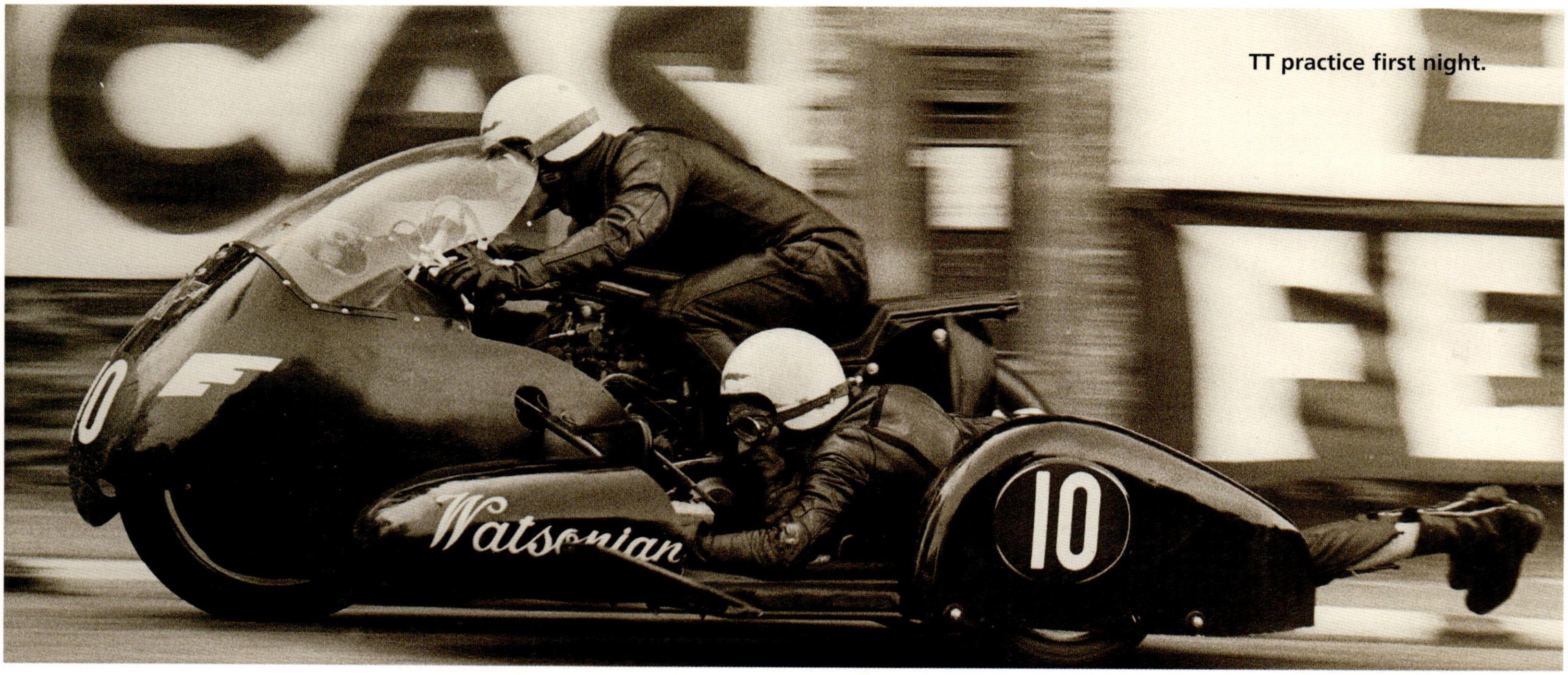

TT practice first night.

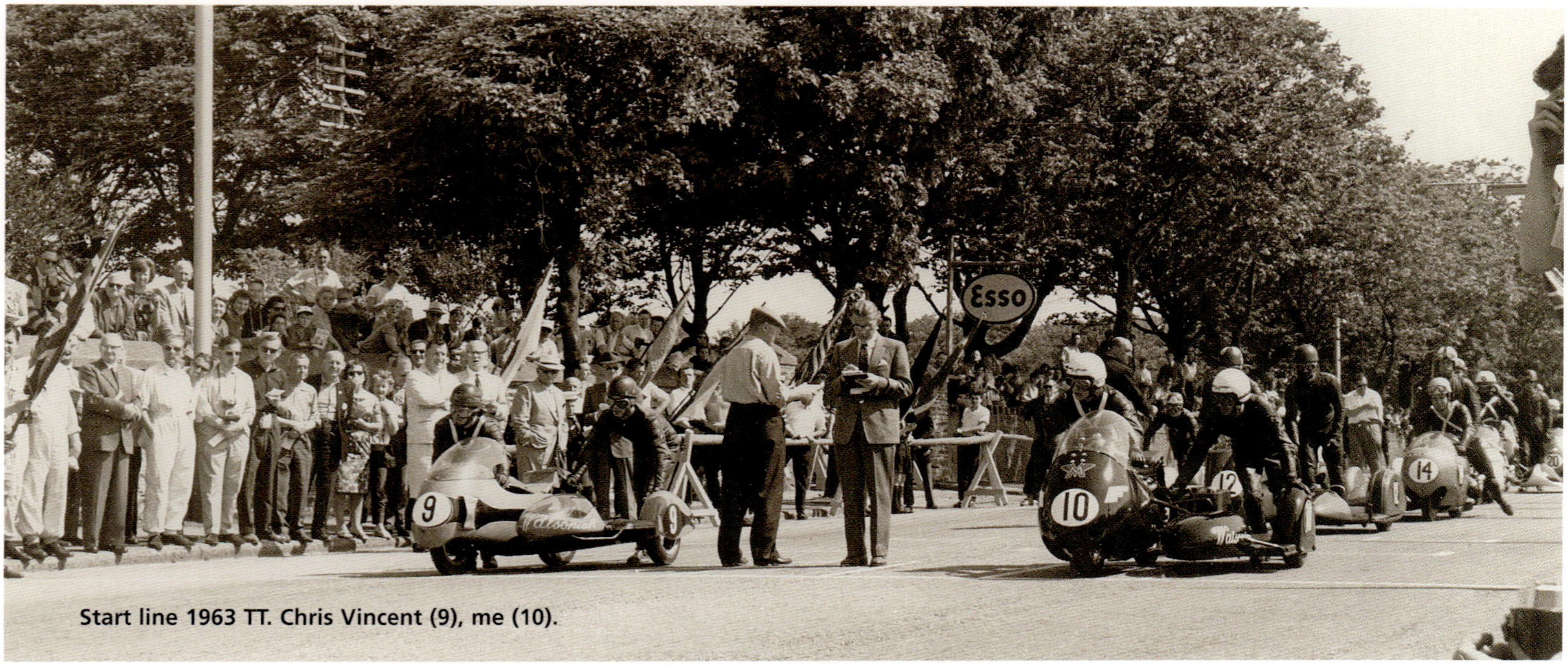

Start line 1963 TT. Chris Vincent (9), me (10).

a plume of smoke. Halfway down Bray Hill with the sidecar bumping up and down he wondered what was wrong, then, to his amazement realised that Hertzig was not there! Turning off the TT circuit at Quarter Bridge, Florian rode back through Douglas to collect his passenger at the start, acknowledging the applause for the grandstand entertainment. This incident did not faze Camathias whatsoever, going fastest that evening ahead of Scheidegger. With the sidecar practices over for that year, the first six on the practice table read Deubel, BMW, Camathias, FCS, Scheidegger, BMW, Birch, BMW, Seeley, Matchless, Auerbacher, BMW.

Following our usual procedure of double checking everything on the outfit prior to Monday's race, the engine had a once-over from the AMC service boys. We were ready, and once more we were late for the obligatory Sunday afternoon ACU weigh-in held at the race start area. The scrutineers soon gave our Matchless outfit the once-over, checked our riding gear, then we pushed our machine into the huge marquee for overnight storage. There followed a bit of posing for photographs, signing autographs then an interview for the TT Schofield record by Murray Walker. This tradition of interviews and commentary had been carried on from his father.

Monday 10th October 1963 at 11.00am, the, international sidecar race over 3 laps - 113.2 miles would start proceedings for that week's Isle of Man TT racing programme. The weather was so glorious that it had, the day before, melted parts of the tarmac on the course, so the 35 sidecar competitors coming to the line were warned of the danger.

World Champion Max Deubel following his practice crash, passed a medical check but his passenger Emil Horner was not able to ride. His place was taken by Englishman Barry Dungworth who had blown his own Norton up during practice. For Max it would be a tall order to perform as normal.

As in previous years, we went through the same start procedure, firstly wheeling out our outfit then waiting for the warm up signal. Then in silence all the competitors arranged themselves on the gird in pairs as allocated by race number.

British star and veteran racer Pip Harris with race number 1, was due to be first away, but had been struggling in practice with a mysterious misfire. To add to his troubles, having removed his BMW outfit from the marquee he discovered the sidecar glassfibre petrol tank had sprung a leak overnight. He was feverishly trying to repair it as the starting maroon burst over the sunlit scene. Bill Boddice beat Camathias off the line, but not for long, as the Swiss ace was soon ahead arriving at Ballacraine followed by Scheidegger. Number 10 at the start we were alongside the 1962 TT winner Chris Vincent - should be interesting. We awaited our turn, watching Kolle, BMW, Lambert, BMW, and Deubel, BMW, leave the start, 10 seconds later the flag dropped and we were away.

At Sulby Bridge, roughly half way round, Fritz was ahead of Florian by 9 seconds with Kolle third and us fourth, but at the end of the first lap it was Scheidegger, Camathias, Birch, Auerbacher, Kolle with us in sixth place. Our lap time was down on 1962 by over 1mph, which was disappointing. The second lap was no better, 1.25mph down. The G50 engine just wasn't pulling as it should, fortunately the six speed box was at least keeping us in contention. Florian Camathias, at 39 years of age, with fellow countryman

Florian Camathias and passenger Alfred Herzig and the FCS-BMW, a winning team in the Sidecar TT.

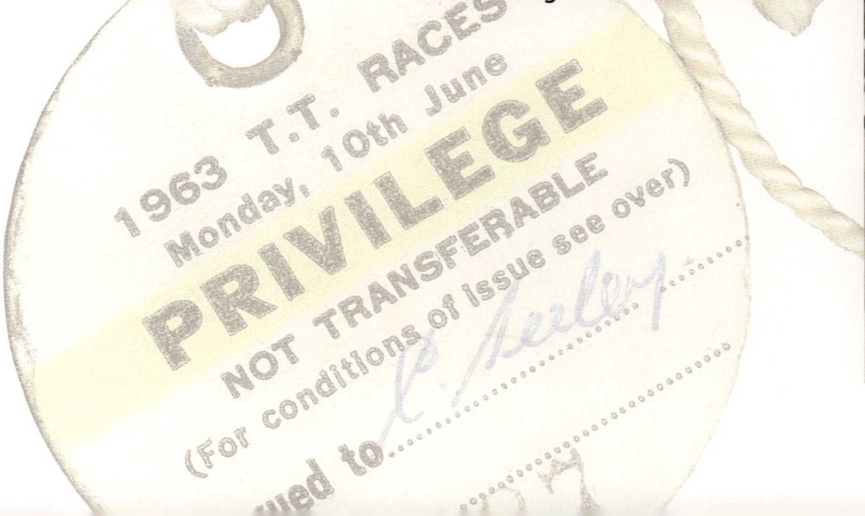

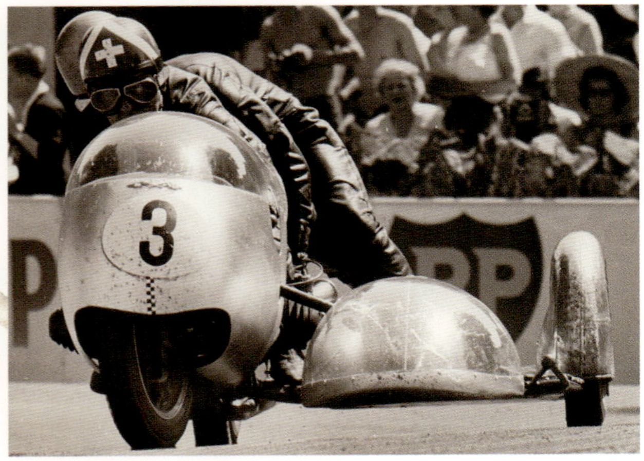

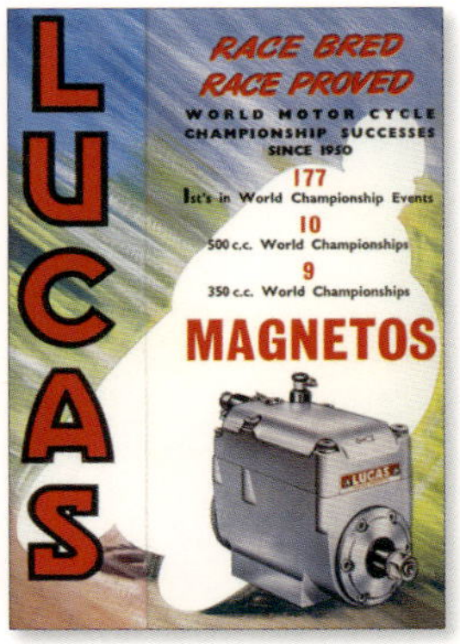

Low flying at Ballaugh Bridge.

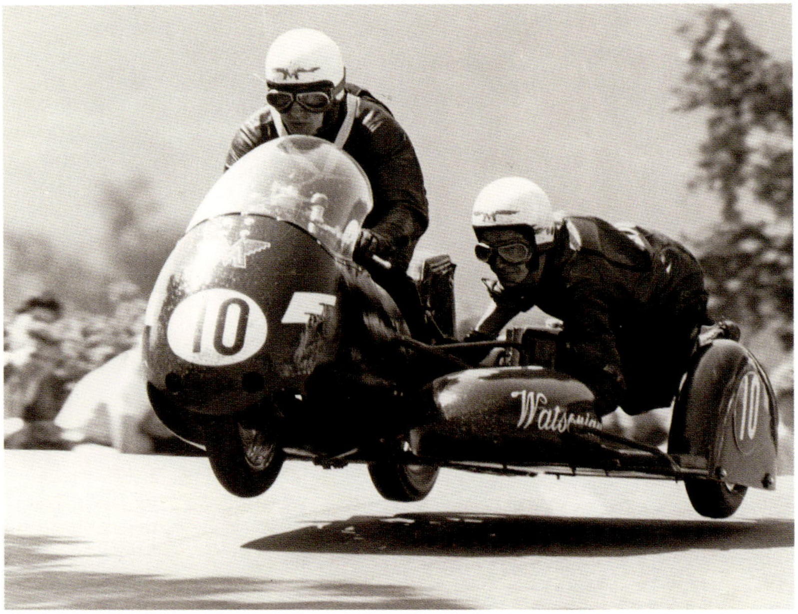

Alfred Herzig scored their first ever sidecar TT win at the average speed of 88.38mph, a new race record. Fritz Scheidegger and John Robinson finished second, 38 seconds behind, Alan Birch a fine third, Otto Kolle fourth at 82.75mph, which was slightly down on our 1962 race speed. Georg Auebacher was fifth at 82.56mph. With an ailing Matchless we came in sixth at 81.52mph. Owen Greenwood, Matchless G50 was seventh and with Deubel eighth, the only riders to receive Silver Replicas, 24 finishers out of 36 starters! Although very disappointed with our race speed, we took comfort from the fact we were the first all-British crew home and also members of the Matchless manufacturers' team prize (Seeley-Greenwood-Thurgood). Clasping our £25 start money, £30 prize and a Castrol Oils bonus of £50, that was it for another year regarding the Isle of Man TT. With sixth-third-sixth in three visits, at least we were consistent in racing on the most formidable circuit in the world.

The 250cc TT following our event would be interesting, as after a season's absence from the European circuits, Yamaha would be making another bid for top honours competing at the TT with completely new 40bhp plus twin cylinder 11,000rpm, rotary-valve, seven speed, two-stroke machines. Extensively tested in Japan by works' rider Fumio Ito, the Yamaha would certainly challenge the Honda 250 fours. Experienced TT rider, short circuit hero and joker, Tony Godfrey was chosen to partner Fumio Ito in that year's official Yamaha Team, supported by Hiroshi Hasegawa and Yoshikazu Sunako. After the first solo practice session a smiling Godfrey, back in the pits, described his first ride ever on the works Yamaha as 'terrific', confirmed by a start lap of just under 90mph.

After a week of practising, the positions stood with Redman and Robb, works Honda fours ahead of Ito, Godfrey, Sunako and Taveri. From the start of the 6 lap 226.4 mile race, Tony Godfrey, knowing this was his big chance to impress Yamaha, would give it all he had. On the first lap arriving at Keppel Gate, Tony was leading by 7 seconds, but at the end of that first lap, team mate Ito at 95.93mph was 4.6 seconds ahead of Godfrey, who had lapped in an impressive 95.63mph, nothing in it at that stage. Jim Redman was third, 13 seconds down on the leader but the Yamaha domination was not to last. Godfrey was forced to stop for adjustments on the second lap at Kirkmichael, loosing 2 minutes, dropping him down to seventh place. Finally, arriving back at the pits to fit new spark plugs Tony was shouting 'Out of the way I am off again, and back in the race!' By then he was well out of the running. Trying to make up for lost time, the buoyant Godfrey approaching Ramsey on lap 3, crashed heavily at Milntown, sustaining severe head, neck, and leg injuries, he was rushed to hospital in the Shell Oils sponsored rescue helicopter. The very first year of this rescue service probably saved Tony's life. Although surviving the crash, it would be the end of Tony's dream. This once more emphasised the very fine line in road racing between success, survival and misfortune.

Jim Redman went on to win his first TT from Fumio Ito after a very close encounter. The race was probably lost by Ito after a long refuelling pit stop, but he was rewarded by the best performance ever by a Japanese rider. Bill Smith, Honda, in an impressive ride, despite falling at Governors Bridge and remounting, made up the rostrum positions with works' Yamaha rider Hasegawa fourth and Tommy Robb fifth, after a long pit stop for plugs.

Unlike previous years we left the Island next morning having received our Silver Replicas the night before from the Mayor of Douglas at a well attended Villa Marina.

Leaving the Island early, we missed the Gilera race action, as John Hartle came home second to Jim Redman's Honda in the 350cc Junior. Then with 'Mike the Bike' in control on the MV, Hartle came home second in the Senior, with Gilera team mate Phil Read in third. These results brought encouragement to the Scuderia Duke Team.

A jubilant Camathias in charge of the Steam Packet ferry.

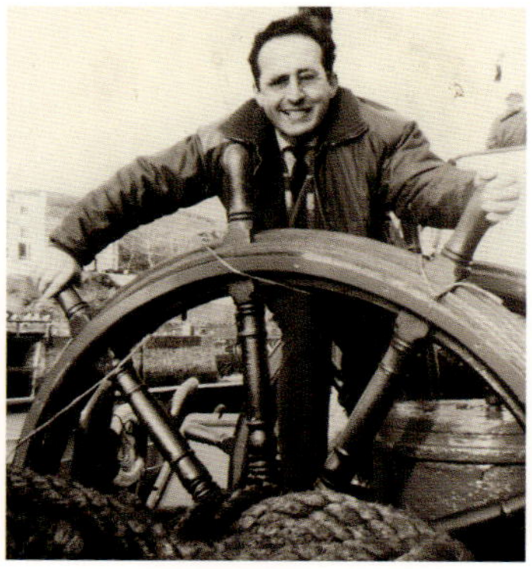

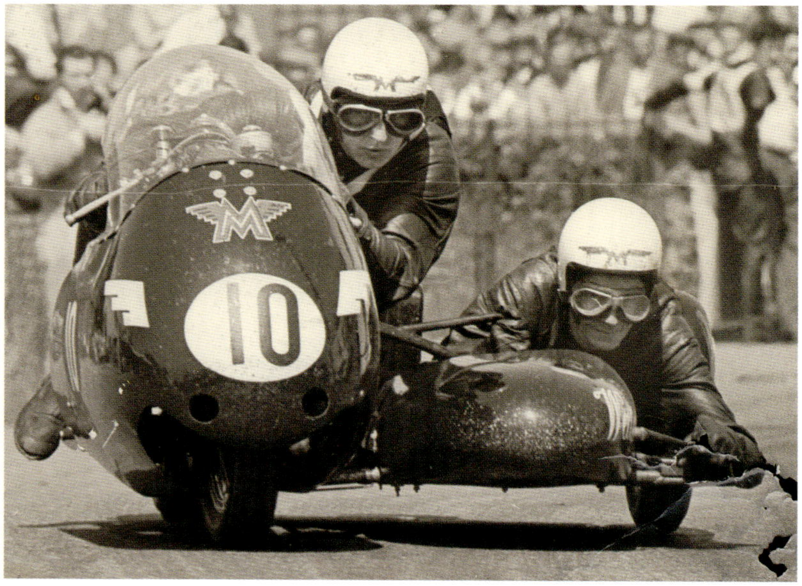

Parliament Square , Ramsay.

John Hartle (Gilera) on the way to second place in the Junior TT.

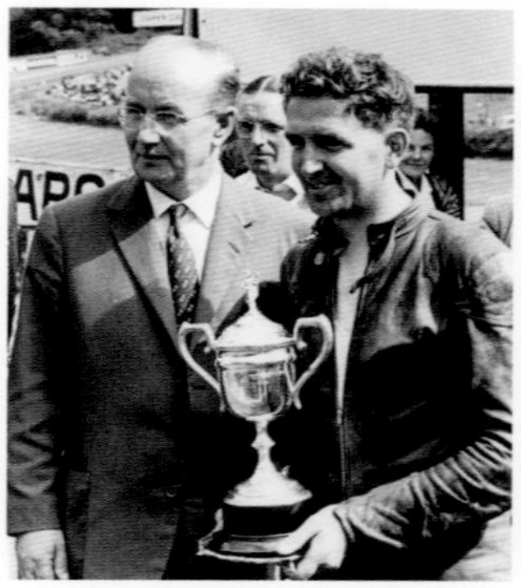

A retiring Mr Hall and Derek Minter.

Next stop, next weekend would be the traditional Mallory Park Post TT event, in the days when that venue attracted many of the international riders returning from the Isle of Man. Following a couple of seconds and a fifth at Mallory, our concentration was directed at the forthcoming Dutch TT and Belgian Grand Prix.

It was June 1963, that the first ever race training school was announced by Francis Beart and Charles Mortimer to be run at Brands Hatch, with rider instruction to be given by the regular successful Brands competitor Griff Jenkins. 16 days after opening, 500 enquiries had been received, with 140 riders registering. The school used 250cc Silverstone racers, with the initial cost being £17 10s, including registration and 12 laps of the circuit.

Also in June that year it was announced that Brands Hatch boss, John Hall was to retire at 66, handing over to John Webb and Dixon Cade. Gentleman John Hall had been there since 1948, overseeing the transformation from the original grass track into a tarmac circuit in 1950 then adding the additional Grand Prix circuit in 1960. John had built up a good reputation for fair play at Brands and it was sad to see him go.

After Mallory Park we had a good week at home before disappearing to the Dutch TT. Although I thought that I had neglected my motorcycle business, it was in fact running successfully. I was lucky to employ some loyal staff, overseen by my dad Percy and of course our racing success was bringing in extra trade and soon Suzuki would be added to our string of agencies. Then, even better, Joan was expecting our first child, due in December, if it was a boy perhaps he would be okay for the sidecar!

With the preparation of our Matchless outfit completed and the engine rebuilt at AMC, it was loading time again for departure to Holland for our fifth ever sidecar Grand Prix held at Assen, a great circuit in those days before the more recent alterations.

I mentioned earlier the complicated paperwork for customs and when Florian Camathias turned up at the Dutch border with the Gilera and MV Agusta works teams, they were held for seven hours. Even though the paperwork was in order, it seemed that a particular Dutch customs officer did not like racers or motorbikes and it took a telephone call from the Dutch organisers to the headquarters of the customs bureau to release the bikes. The Italian mechanics thought the delay was nearly worthwhile, just to see and hear Camathias throw a 'huge wobbler' and give the customs officer a piece of his mind.

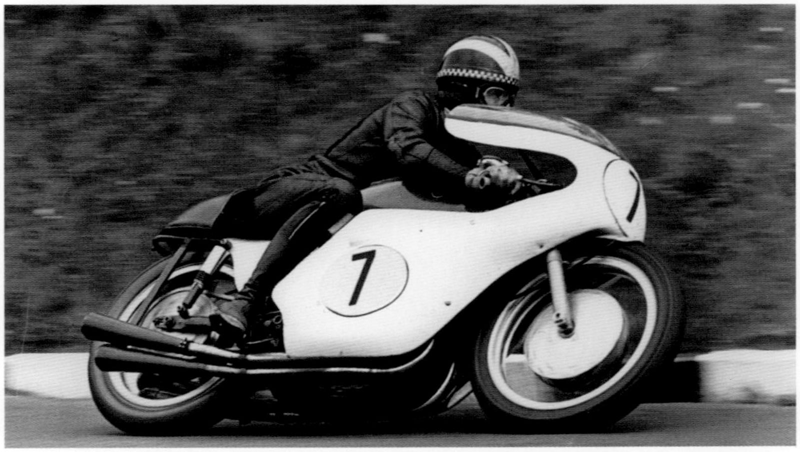

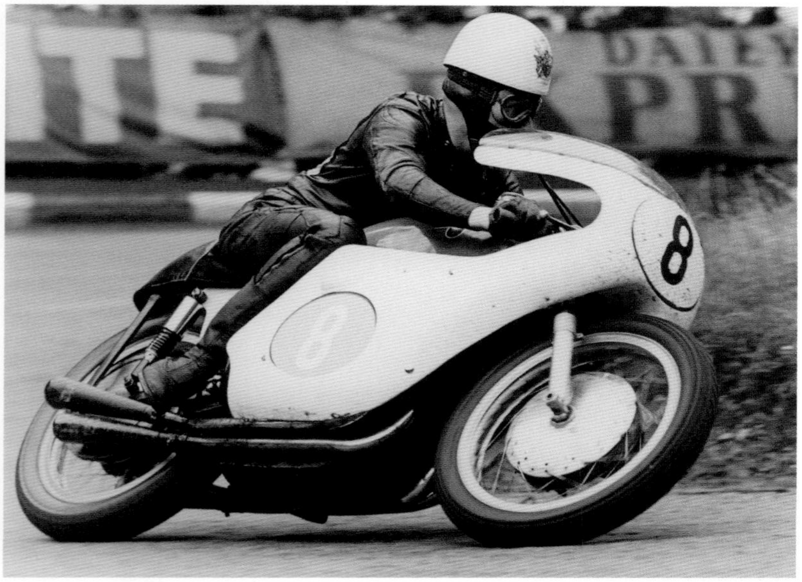

The Dutch TT was special as everybody, apart from the customs officer, was so enthusiastic. Along with most of the competitors we were camping in the paddock, although some had caravans. The camaraderie amongst the British solo and sidecar boys was excellent, the German crews keeping to themselves and the Swiss in the middle.

In qualifying we managed a very respectable fourth place, once more splitting the BMW flyers. The three days of all classes practice had attracted over 30,000 spectators. It was in Thursday's 500cc solo practice that Alan Shepherd, riding the Kirby Matchless, blew his G50 engine leaving him with a problem - no spare. The next morning, hearing of Alan's plight we decided to lend him our spare - the one that had taken us to third place in the 1962 TT. With little time for him to rebuild the Matchless, we provided the rest of the service and fitted the engine, just in time for that morning's last 500cc qualifying session.

For the Saturday race day with the weather fine, the regular estimated 150,000 race fans had packed into the nearly 5 mile, Drenthe Circuit. That year's Dutch TT 1963 would be the first continental Grand Prix to be broadcast by the BBC.

Racing started at 10.15am with the 350cc race, a promised close affair between Jim Redman, Honda, Mike Hailwood, MV, and Remo Venturi on the works Bianchi twin, but Venturi crashed early on, leaving Redman to win from Mike on a less than impressive MV. Next up was my favourite, the 50cc 'tiddler' event. Just watching those screaming 50cc machines with riders tucked in behind their fairings, wringing every bit of performance out of the machines, playing tunes on the multi-speed gearboxes, cranking over through the fast flat-out curves behind the pits area, was a sight to behold and sticks in my memory even today.

The actual 8 lap, 38.29 mile race would not disappoint, even though it would be a Suzuki walk-over, Ernst Degner taking the glory by 6.5 seconds from Hugh Anderson who had been locked in a race long tussle with Michio Ichino who took third place.

Phil Read, Gilera, on his way to third place in the Senior TT.

6 MOTOR CYCLE NEWS, Wednesday, July 3, 1963

ALAN'S QUICK CHANGE AT THE DUTCH TT

Paddock Gossip

BY CHARLIE ROUS

A MILD panic arose when Alan Shepherd blew up his works G50 Matchless engine during practice for the Dutch TT. And the engine on which he won third place in the 500 cc race was actually a spare motor lent to him by Colin Seeley, who retired in the sidecar race.

What happened was this. Soon after Alan's engine went "tinkle tinkle," he phoned the Woolwich factory. Unfortunately, a replacement works engine was not available, either in Jack Williams' racing shop or at entrant Tom Kirby's Hornchurch workshops.

So both Tom and Jack advised Alan to grab Colin's spare engine—a "pukka" works motor.

But the problem didn't end there. The spare engine incorporated a number of Seeley sidecar mods and Shepherd's engine plates had to be cut to suit. There was a spot of gearbox trouble too (Seeley uses four speeds while his six-speeder is being overhauled by the Austrian manufacturer) but, in the end, Shepherd used Kirby's five-speed box.

Nice to see such "esprit de corps" receive such a just reward as third place. But what's the betting Count Domenico Agusta is kicking himself for "sacking" Shepherd.

It should be remembered that, whatever may have happened since just before the TT, Alan is still under contract to race MVs. With Mike Hailwood out of the running, Alan would have been just the boy to chase the Gillies. Too bad for the Count!

Footnote: What happened to Shepherd's engine is still unknown. On Monday, it was still at London Airport and the customs wouldn't release it until today—Wednesday.

Morishita and Itoh in fourth and fifth, all five on the Suzuki works machines. Title leader Anscheidt, Kreidler only managed sixth place, dropping him to second spot in the championship title chase, behind Hugh Anderson.

The 250cc race was a walkover for an on-form Jim Redman, Honda four from the impressive Japanese Fumio Ito riding the works Yamaha into second place, with Tarquinio Provini, Morini not showing his usual form, coming third.

The 125cc race was a run-away victory for Hugh Anderson, Suzuki with team-mate Frank Perris third. Jim Redman, riding a production Honda, squeezed into sixth spot, then crashed, breaking his collar bone. Then came what promised to be a most interesting twenty lap 95.75 mile confrontation, between Mike Hailwood MV and the Gileras of John Hartle and Phil Read. Having recorded exactly the same speed through time trap at 149.1mph, it proved to be a disappointment. From the start with Mike leading the first two laps and recording the fastest lap, the MV broke down in the pits with a suspected broken piston.

From that moment it was a Gilera benefit parade, with Hartle taking the advantage by 4.6 seconds from team-mate Phil Read, Gilera's first classic victory since 1957, followed by Alan Shepherd in a well deserved third place riding the Kirby Matchless using our spare G50 engine which earned us £40 from Alan as a 'thank you'. When asked by a reporter what the Seeley G50 engine was like, Alan responded, 'Beautiful'. Our Manx friend Sid Mizen, Matchless finished eighth, despite having an anxious moment avoiding Austrian Rudi Thalhammer who dropped his Domiracer right in front of Sid.

Then it was us, the 'barrow boys' and the last race of the day. As we walked our outfits to the start line the engines already warmed, I was fully aware that we had absolutely no chance of winning with our Matchless outfit, but what we could do was give the BMW brigade some hassle. I was really enjoying the Grand Prix scene and though I respected the all-star opposition, I was not at all intimidated, and I was determined to do my best and wave the flag for Britain.

On the second row of the grid behind eventual winner Max Deubel, Scheidegger and Camathias. I made one of my finest starts, and led the whole field away down through the first swooping corners. Soon the main challengers were through, and we were back in fourth, but not for long. The G50 engine called enough under the stress, often 7,800rpm, (600rpm over the top limit for this engine) and it finally went 'bang' as the con-rod broke in half and went through the side of the crankcase. I said to Wally, 'I caught it quickly,' but Wally replied, 'Not quick enough,' as he looked through the hole in the engine with the daylight streaming through. 'Sods law' as they say, having loaned our spare engine to Alan Shepherd to finish third in his 500cc race, and now here we were sitting at the side of the track with the Castrol Oil pouring out of our wrecked engine.

Never mind, we soon drowned our sorrows having collected the £58 start money at that evening's official presentation at which Alan Shepherd asked if I would like to go with him to Italy next day travelling in his new MK2 3.8 Jaguar. Alan, who had a contract with MV Agusta, needed to clear the air with Count Agusta as to his future with that

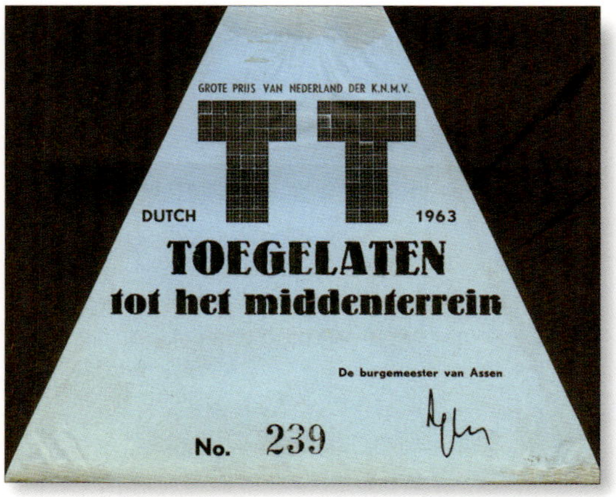

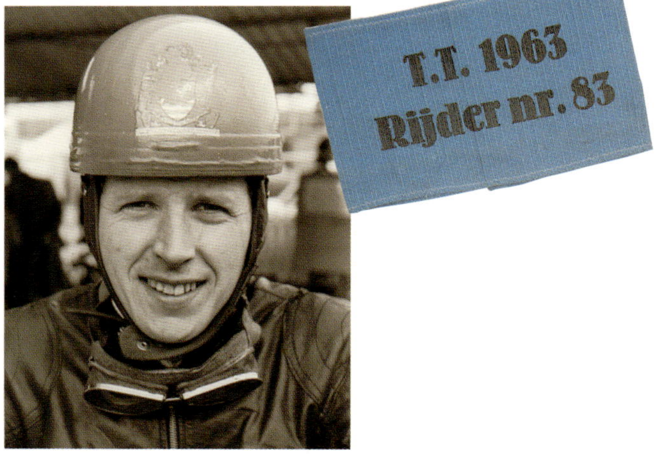

Alan Shepherd.

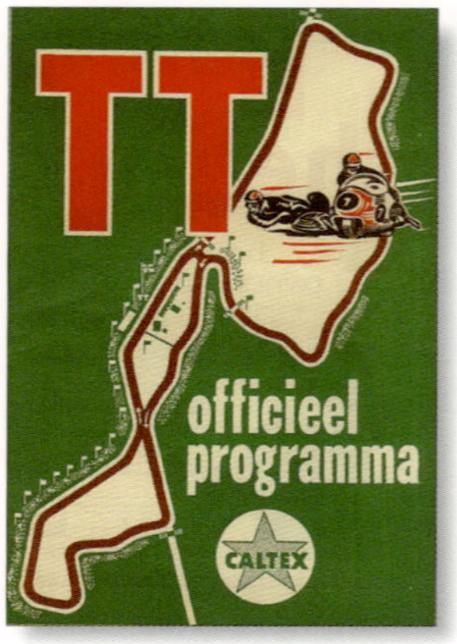

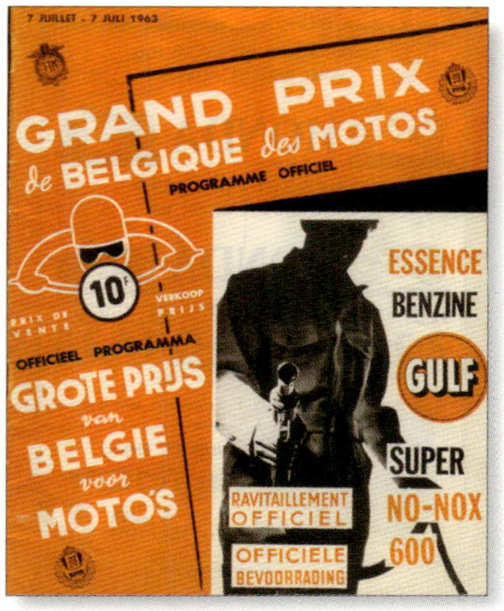

company. It would be my first trip to Italy and it was to be memorable. The Italian lakes in which we had a swim were glorious, then it was on to the MV factory at Gallarate.

I waited for Alan in the outer office, staring in awe at the magnificent display of trophies for something like 20 world championships, inclusive of 126 GP victories achieved in the period 1952 to 1962. Encompassing 125, 250, 350 and 500cc classes, and even more impressive were the specially made 22 copies of the full size Isle of Man TT trophies won by MV Agusta. Alan Shepherd's meeting with the Count did not go well. MV Agusta did not intend to supply him with machines for any more races that year, when he asked permission to race other makes was told that was not possible whilst he was under contract to MV, but if he wished he could end the contract. With little alternative, the contract was terminated by mutual consent. It was very disappointing for Alan, who was such a talented, stylish rider. We then left the Gallarate factory, driving direct to Spa in Belgium, for that weekend's July 7th Belgian Grand Prix.

Wally had driven to Spa direct from Assen along with the rest of the circus so we were already set up in the race paddock. This was our first visit to the ultra-fast 8.75mile circuit located in the thickly wooded Ardennes. Whilst I took an immediate liking to this circuit, it was not so good for our slower G50 Matchless, requiring a new riding technique to optimise lap times. Race day dawned dry and sunny and hopefully it would stay that way for the 80,000 spectators and the competitors, as the Spa-Francorchamps circuit had a reputation for unfavourable weather, it could be dry at the start and raining over at Stavelot at the opposite end.

The day's racing kicked off with the 'fabulous fifties', the five lap 50cc race being as exciting an event as any in this class. No distance separated the record-breaking leaders, all averaging faster speeds than the previous year's lap record. Newcomer to the class Isao Morishita, Suzuki would take the laurels by a 0.1 sec from Ernst Degner, Suzuki, with Hans Georg Anscheidt, Kreidler third with a record lap at 88.87mph, only 0.6 secs covering the first three. Hugh Anderson came fourth but still retained his championship lead, by one point from Anscheidt, a great race!

The 125cc race with no less excitement found Bert Schneider, Suzuki winning from Hugh Anderson, Suzuki, after Ernst Degner, Suzuki, having led in the early stages with a record breaking lap of 108.05mph, retired with a broken crankshaft.

The 250cc race had Fumio Ito taking full advantage of the fact that Jim Redman was still out of action after his crash at Assen, by scoring his first Grand Prix win and the first such success for Yamaha. It was a 1 - 2 for the works Yamaha team with Yoshikaza Sunako second. Fumio Ito also set a new 250cc lap record at 117.75mph.

With no 350cc event, next up was the premier 500cc race. Having well and truly cracked the motorcycle lap record at 124.91mph during practice Mike 'the bike' Hailwood and the MV four certainly started favourite. From the start of the 15 lap 131.41 mile race Mike was away from the pursuing Gileras of Hartle and Read and after 3 laps was half a mile ahead before slowing with a gearbox selection problem. Mike, never the man to give in, changed his riding tactics and increased his lead over John Hartle, who on lap twelve dropped out with engine trouble, leaving Phil Read in second, and that's how it stayed. Despite slowing down, Mike won by 1 minute 13 seconds, a huge margin. He averaged an impressive 123.99mph, a record, as was his fastest lap at 125.61mph. In third place, although having stopped to take on some fuel, was our friend Alan Shepherd on his Kirby-Matchless, then Fred Stevens, Australian big Jack Ahearn, Gyula Marsovszky and old mate Sid Mizen in that order.

Finally, it was the 8 lap 70.08 mile sidecar race. I was still looking forward to the event, even though we would be 'blown into the weeds'. The original fall out between BMW and Florian Camathias resulted in his outfit being called the 'FCS' Florian Camathias Special. BMW had, for the Belgian GP, supplied in addition to Deubel, both Fritz Scheidegger and Otto Kolle with works engines in their effort to defeat Camathias.

As I have said before, Florian was such a specialist on these very fast circuits and with his Helmut Fath tuned BMW engine he would certainly be the man to beat. There were only two points separating Max Deubel and Florian Camathias for the championship at

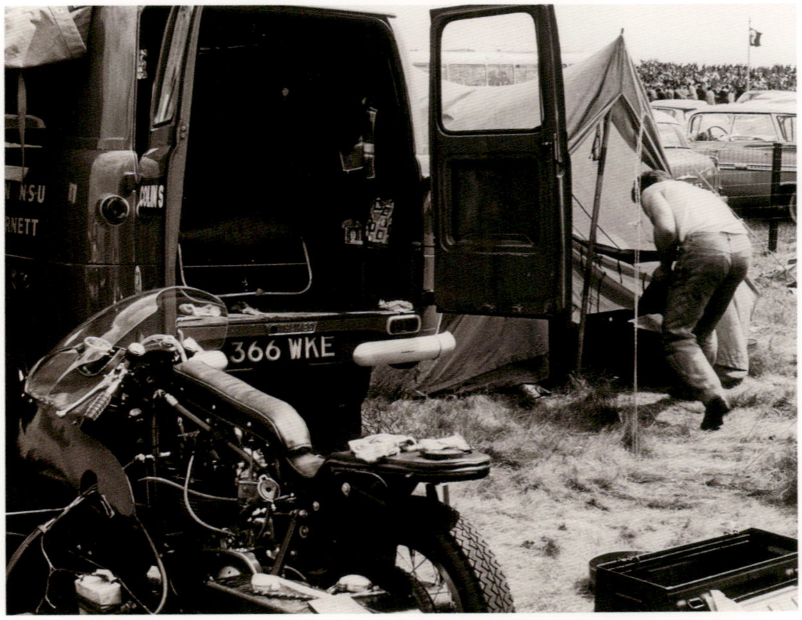

Home from home at the Dutch TT.

Leading at the start of the Dutch TT.

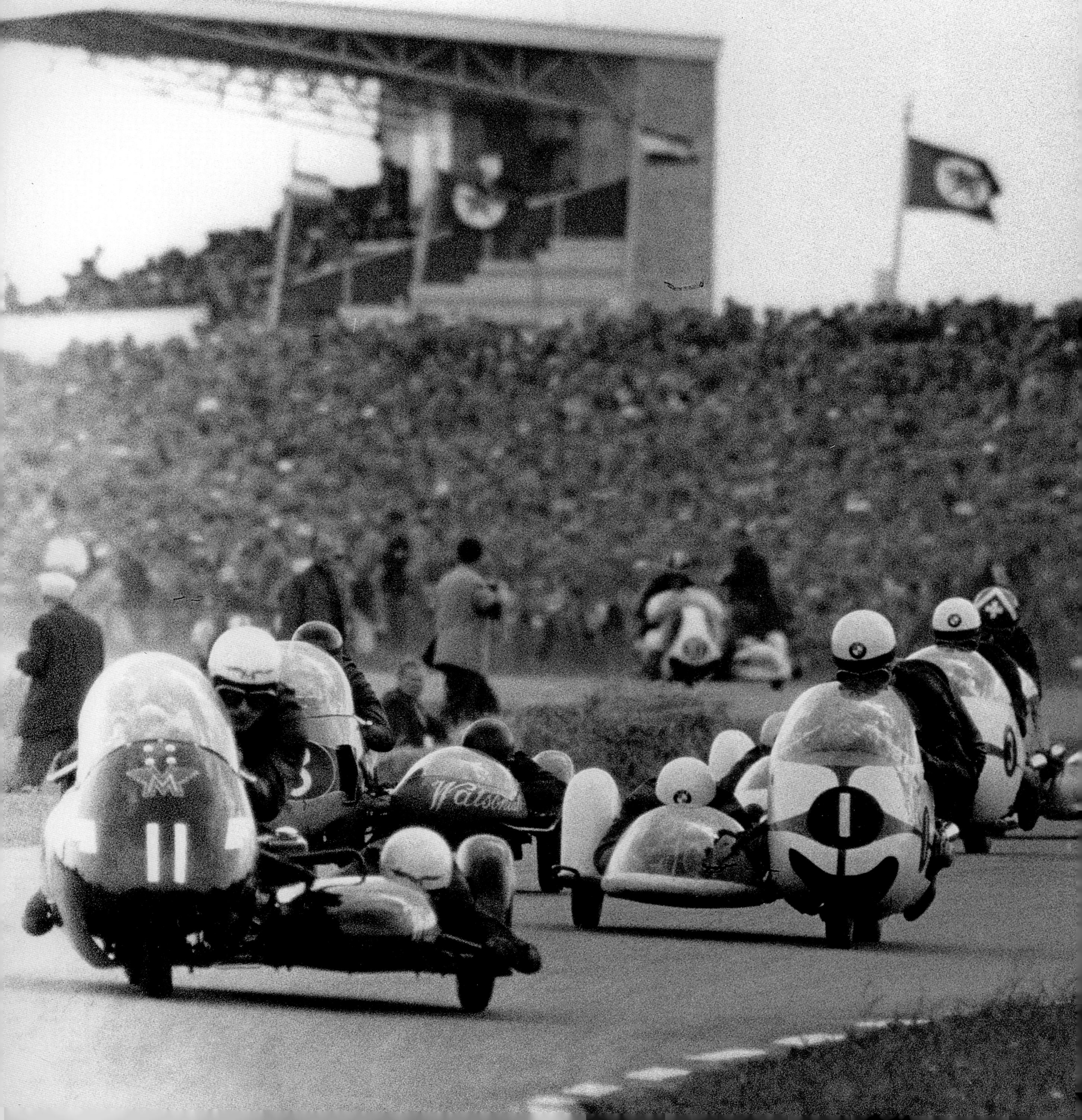

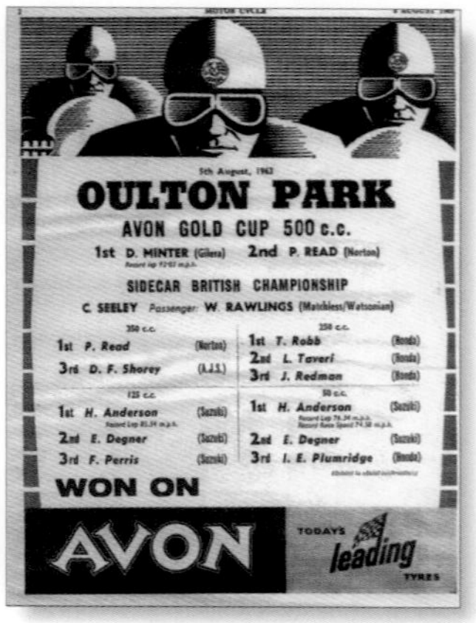

Leading Chris Vincent, October 14th, last event of the year, Brands Hatch on the 650cc CSR which then blew up.

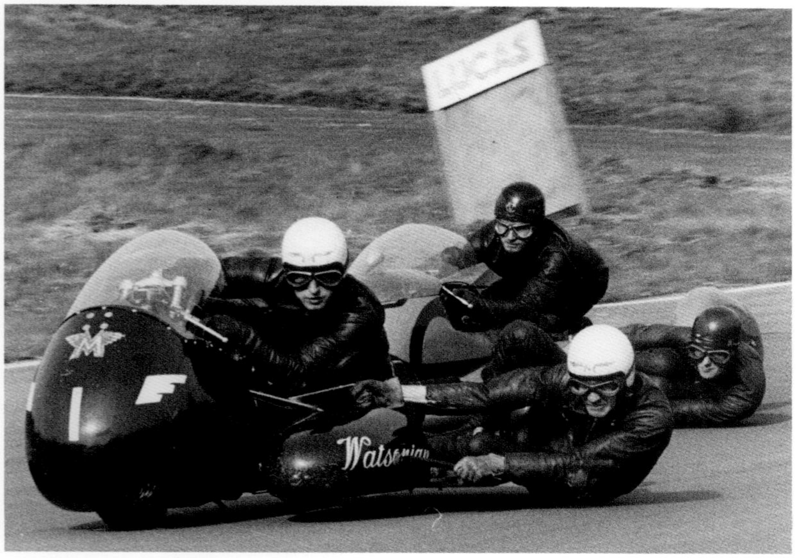

With Snetterton done there was still no spare time, as the next weekend was the all-important Oulton Park international for the 1963 British Championships. Once again the usual opposition would be in attendance with 32 sidecar race entries, although only 25 would be allowed to start. We were back on good form and confident with our G50 Matchless just flying in practice. Race one, 10 laps over the 2.76 mile Oulton Park circuit found Swiss 'ace' Camathias charging immediately to the front, making up for his disappointment at the Belgian Grand Prix. Max Deubel was second and that's how it stayed with us third ahead of Alan Birch's BMW. In the second 10 lap race, Camathias just disappeared, again leaving Deubel in second spot. Pip Harris, BMW had muscled in on the act and finished third with me and Wal a good fourth. From the two races on aggregate time we had finished third to Camathias and Deubel and for the second time in succession were awarded The British Sidecar Championship title. Again with our Matchless/Watsonian outfit we had more than split the ten BMW powered sidecar competitors in the event. My wife Joan along with our friends and helpers were overjoyed with our success.

Our fellow Kentish man, Derek Minter was back in action on the 500cc Gilera four, having recovered from the Brands crash in May, won both the Les Graham Memorial Trophy Race and the British Senior Championship, even breaking his own lap record at 92.03mph. Phil Read, Norton won the 350cc race and came second to Minter in the Avon Gold Cup event. Hugh Anderson, Suzuki, continued his winning ways in the 50cc and 125cc races with Ernst Degner, Suzuki, second in both. Finally, Tommy Robb, Honda, won the 250cc from Taveri and Redman, another great meeting and £65 and bonuses.

We were not finished racing yet, seven meetings were still to come; Brands, Snetterton, Cadwell, Brands, Mallory, Oulton and finally Brands Hatch again. A mixed bag of race results were achieved, notably a third place at Brands in August with the Matchless 650 CSR. Another 'bloody' second place was gained at a wet Snetterton early September to Chris Vincent and his BMW in the 500cc race, with Alan Thurgood on the Matchless third. Then when lying second to Chris in the 1200cc race with our 650cc CSR, we were forced to stop with plug trouble. However, Chris managed to get water in the works of his 650 BSA demoting him to second place behind the eventual winner, our friend and challenger Alan Thurgood - Matchless! Sods law again. A week later it was up to Lincolnshire for the Cadwell Park international. Cadwell not our favourite venue, nevertheless with our friend Florian taking the honours from Max Deubel and Cadwell specialist Charlie Freeman in third, our fourth place was, under the circumstances, very satisfactory.

At Oulton Park on October 5th for the McIntyre Memorial Meeting, riding our Matchless CSR 650 and having finished second in our heat to Bill Boddice, we would once more be running second to Chris Vincent's BSA in the final when our oil tank split, slowing us somewhat and letting Alan Birch, BMW, and John Crick 650 Triumph, through on the last lap and demoting us to a disappointing fourth place, and a total of £16 earnings.

Brands Hatch, 13th October was the last event of the UK calendar. We were competing with our Matchless 650 CSR and all set for a good performance in the 1200cc scratch race. Unfortunately in the earlier stages, as we crossed the start line, the 650 CSR decided to call it a day and just exploded, with bits flying everywhere, so that was that! A shame as the engine had potential, but the like would never see the light of day again, as the AMC factory was beginning to reduce its racing commitments. Nevermind, it had been a good season with 25 meetings attended and 46 races competed in with no crashes or injuries - luck had been on our side.

Although the world sidecar championships had finished for us at the Belgian Grand Prix, the solo championships had another six rounds to go. The Ulster Grand Prix on August 10th, on the tricky open roads of the Dundrod Circuit was to receive a tremendous boost. This famous event, which had been doomed to extinction faced with financial difficulties and lack of support from the Northern Ireland Tourist Board, attracted Mike Hailwood, MV Agusta, playing a lone hand against the contingent of the 'Scuderia Duke' Gilera team of Hartle, Read and with a Grand Prix comeback for Derek

Minter and Shepherd, Ulster Grand Prix.

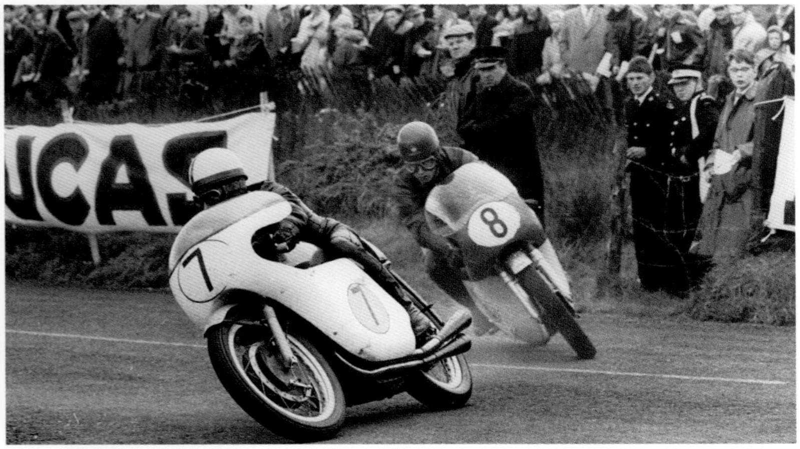

Minter it promised to be a huge attraction for the Irish fans. Magnificent, meteoric, miraculous Mike Hailwood, who as reported by Mick Woollett, led from the start to finish on the tough 7.5 mile Dundrod Circuit, winning at a record average of 99.27mph with a lap record of 101.28mph. The Gilera challenge fell apart as Phil Read crashed on the second lap. John Hartle was doing his best, still suffering from injuries sustained at Oulton Park, managing second place, 42.6 seconds down with a strangely subdued Derek Minter third, over 2 minutes behind 'Mike the Bike'. Derek had taken half the 128 mile race to shake off a very determined Alan Shepherd, Kirby-Matchless, who finished fourth.

A week after Ulster, the Grand Prix circus travelled to the East German Grand Prix, at the hilly 5.3 mile Sachsenring circuit, situated in Saxony, 150 miles south of Berlin, near the Czech border. This was a real road racing circuit, running through the town of Hohenstein-Ernsthal and the surrounding wooded hillsides. Gilera teamster Phil Read, still convalescing from his crash at the Ulster would not be competing at Sachsenring. The first race of that weekend was the 350cc held on Saturday afternoon after all the morning final qualifying sessions. The race run in brilliant sunshine, had Mike Hailwood MV blazing a trail that neither Luigi Taveri nor Jim Redman on their Hondas could touch, much to the surprise of many, who thought the 350 MV would be no match for the Hondas. Hailwood just stormed ahead to win the sixteen lap 86.80 mile race in a record time and with a record lap of 102.86mph with Taveri and Redman second and third.

For Mike this was to be a warm-up for the next day's action. Sunday was much cooler after overnight rain and a stiff breeze. First race of the day was the 125cc which was a walkover for that smooth-riding talented Hugh Anderson, Suzuki, who would, years later, race a Seeley G50 Replica in classic events. Hugh won his fifth 125cc Grand Prix, which combined with other successes, won him that year's 125cc world championship. This success would be the second manufacturers' title for Suzuki, the first being in 1962 with Ernst Degner winning the 50cc crown.

The 500cc race continued with an on-form Mike Hailwood, MV, having broken his own lap record in practice. Alongside him on the front row was John Hartle, Gilera, 3 seconds down on timing, with team mate Minter 7 seconds behind Hailwood. From the start Hailwood zoomed to the front, a good distance ahead at the first bend. Meanwhile Hartle was in trouble when at full bore into a right curve in pursuit of Hailwood, a newly fitted front mudguard became detached on one side and momentarily locked the front wheel, a most frightening experience. The wheel freed and he regained control, but the incident forced a long pit stop to remove the wrecked mudguard, which put him out of the running. Meanwhile, Hailwood not letting up, was taking 7 seconds a lap out of Minter who was easing away from Alan Shepherd. With Mike slackening the pace towards the end he finished nearly a minute ahead of Minter with Alan Shepherd third on the Kirby Matchless then Mike Duff, Jack Findlay and Vernon Cottle making up the first six.

Mike Hailwood, the 1961 250cc and 1962 500cc World Champion, on for the last race of the day, received the most colossal ovation, as reported by Mick Woollett, 'Hailwood had 200,000 East German fans at that Sachsenring Grand Prix rising to their feet cheering and waving as he scored his third victory of the weekend and the most popular win of that Grand Prix meeting, and possibly of his fantastic career, by winning the 250cc race riding the East German built MZ water-cooled two-stroke twin at a record speed of 98.30mph.' He was followed home by fellow Brit, Alan Shepherd, also on a works MZ, with Jim Redman on his works Honda four beaten back into third again. To complete the picture two other MZ riders finished fourth and eighth, a great result for MZ race boss, Walter Kaaden and a fitting end to a brilliant weekend's racing. The East Germans refused to grant Provini a visa to attend, could it be that the amazing 250cc Morini would have been too much of a challenge to the might of MZ!

In 1963 despite his motorcycle road racing successes Mike Hailwood was showing a keen interest to take up car racing for the 1964 season, but with his continued domination racing for MV Agusta and another world 500cc championship pretty well in the bag, he was persuaded by Count Agusta to stay with bikes. He was offered a lucrative contract, with the Count suggesting that MV might withdraw from racing altogether if he did not sign. Well, Mike signed on the dotted line, and the world of motorcycle racing benefitted, able to enjoy and follow the fortunes of this great star!

The decision by MV Agusta to compete in 1964, prompting the Gilera Arcore factory to continue with their racing comeback via the 'Scuderia Duke' Gilera team.

At the next Grand Prix, held at the end of August at the dangerous, tree-lined Finnish Tampere 2.24 mile circuit, a crowd of 30,000 waited in anticipation for the start of the 500cc race which climaxed the meeting. An all-action encounter was expected between Hailwood MV and Hartle on the lone 'Scuderia Duke' Gilera. From the start Mike was ahead of Hartle but only by a few yards. At the end of the first lap a gearbox problem hit the Gilera, then on lap ten of the 35 lap race, the gearbox finally called enough, and John coasted to a standstill. Hailwood carried on unchallenged to win his fifth 500 Grand Prix race of the year, Alan Shepherd was second, Mike Duff third and our jolly Manx friend, Sid Mizen fifth.

Mike Hailwood MV looked completely unstoppable in the 500cc class. The Gilera team of Minter, Hartle and Read just seemed out of luck most of the time and it would not change for the all-important Italian Grand Prix held at Monza on September 14th.

Friday 13th was the first day of official practice. John Hartle, cutting things a shade too fine, sped into the Grand Curve at 130mph clipping the kerb at the apex of the corner which flicked the rear wheel into a full lock broadside, causing the Gilera and John to skid for some 50 yards. Landing in some bushes saved him from serious injury, escaping with bruising and a broken bone in his right hand.

Come the start of the 35 lap 125.05 mile 500cc race on the ultra fast 3.57mile Monza circuit, Mike Hailwood was once more in a class of his own leading from start to finish. Some way back, Derek Minter and Phil Read's Gileras lay second and third until Remo Venturi, on the works 452cc Bianchi twin, from a poor start was on an unbelievable flyer, passing Read on lap four and Minter 7 laps later. The impressive Bianchi steamed away from the Gilera teamsters who both retired from the race with mechanical problems. Hailwood won at 118.07mph, a race record, with a new lap record at 119.99mph but only just beating John Surtees' MV record from 1960 at 119.21mph. So close! Unfortunately for the Bianchi camp, when in second spot Venturi retired in the pits on lap twenty-four with an undisclosed problem, leaving Jack Findlay, Matchless second and Fred Stevens, Norton third.

The 22 lap 250cc race was a real thriller, with a good mix of machinery on the grid. Minter and Grassetti rode Benelli fours. Redman, Taveri and Robb were on Hondas, Shepherd on an MZ, Provini and a new name coming through, Giacomo Agostini, both on the fantastic single cylinder Morinis. Alan Shepherd took the lead on the first lap, but was soon forced into a pit stop to change a plug whilst Agostini led from Redman, but Tarquinio Provini soon led and stayed there to win at 111.60mph from Jim Redman, 13 seconds down. Provini's Monza result made three Grand Prix wins so far that season, equalling Redman's three, there being only six points between them, with the advantage to Redman.

At the star-studded Mallory Park international Race of the Year on 29th September, Mike Hailwood and his fabulous 500 MV four brought in a near 50,000 crowd to see their British world champion in action. Although Derek Minter and Phil Read were back with their Gileras, once again they would be no match for Mike, in fact they would struggle with that tenacious Alan Shepherd on the Kirby-Matchless. The 25 lap 500cc race was a Hailwood benefit whilst Shepherd got the better of both Gileras to the cheers of the crowd. How the British love the underdog.

The 40 lap Race of the Year found Mike the Bike easily collecting the pot of gold. It was more like robbing the bank. After a race long battle with Alan Shepherd, Minter managed to take second place when Alan overcooked it at Gerard's Bend causing a 100mph broadside. Shepherd then settled for third, ahead of Phil Read, Redman and 'Mooneyes' John Cooper.

It had been one of our few bad days. Although winning our heat, from Deubel in the 500cc sidecar event, our Matchless G50 went sick in the final and the best we could do was a miserable ninth! Our Swiss friend, Florian Camathias steamed ahead to win from the rest of the BMW mounted challengers, Vincent, Harris and Deubel in that order.

The penultimate Grand Prix of that season would be at Buenos Aires for the Argentine Grand Prix on the 5th October. Only the main championship protagonists from Europe attended this meeting, which was just as well, as the event was to be controversial and a complete farce. Robbery, official evasiveness, and a complete lack of organisation were the order of the day, as reported by Mike Hailwood, Jim Redman and Alan Shepherd on their return. On the first day of official practice none of the officials turned up, consequently there were no flag marshals, first-aid men, ambulances or marshals to control spectators wandering randomly across the track. When Hans-Georg Anscheidt crashed, he was picked up by three British riders and treated by Kreidler personnel who fortunately had a first aid kit. The riders then refused to practice until a doctor was in attendance. The circuit was covered in dust and sand with the organisers making no effort to sweep it. Rider's clothing left in the official changing rooms was rifled during practice. A gold watch, ring and a considerable sum of cash were stolen. After protest from the riders, the officials said they would make good the losses - but they never did!

Despite all the set-backs, racing took place, Hailwood 'walking' the 500cc race. Tarquinio Provini won the 250cc in an incident-packed race with Redman, who had won the earlier 125cc event. Finally, Hugh Anderson posted another 50cc win to consolidate his championship lead over Anscheidt who had not raced due to his practice injuries, with Suzuki team-mate Ernst Degner second in that race. The meeting finished in darkness and was so late that the organisers put off the prize giving from that Sunday until next day. What a total 'cock-up'! A complete shambles, it was more like a gangster film from start to finish, according to Alan Shepherd. How they ever acquired world championship status, I will never know. Letters of protest were despatched to the FIM with the hope that they, the riders would not have to race there again. Their prayers would be answered as the world championship did not return to the Argentine until 1981, 18 years later.

It was all happening in October that year when Associated Motorcycles, manufacturers of AJS, Matchless and Norton motorcycles, announced that production of the over-the-counter race range of 7R, G50 and Manx machines would cease with immediate effect, although spares would be continued to be manufactured. The racing lineage of both Matchless and Norton can be traced back to the very first TT in 1907 when Charlie Collier won the single class on a Matchless and Rem Fowler the twin cylinder class on a Norton.

This strange decision was a serious blow to many British and European racers. Possibly the growing threat of MV Agusta, Gilera, Honda, Suzuki, Yamaha, MZ, Jawa, and Benelli was a reason, although most of those manufacturers at the time only produced limited amounts of works machines. Alan Shepherd proved this point by racing his privately entered Kirby-Matchless G50, finishing second to Hailwood's MV in the 1963 500cc world championship, one point in front of John Hartle on the Gilera four.

Hundreds of racing competitors would never be in a position to be offered a works ride yet they were the backbone of the racing scene. Then another bomb-shell was reported, Avon Tyres had decided to pull out of direct support of motorcycle racing because of steeply rising costs and a downward trend in the motorcycle market. Worse still, the Avon factory would no longer be making racing tyres for individual riders, although tyres could still be supplied for another season to one or more of the works teams who already used them. Since Avon commenced racing in 1949 its tyre products had played an important role in winning an impressive 37 world championships including every solo road race title since 1958, along with 151 world records.

It was a real shock for us as we were the only sidecar racers on Avons. It was time to throw our hat into the Dunlop ring, however their racing boss, Dickie Davies, might be pleased or tell us to get lost. Fortunately, he had respected our loyalty to Avon over the previous three seasons and our commitment to the sport. He therefore agreed to support us in 1964.

The high hopes for the 'Scuderia Duke' Gilera team never really materialised. They started off badly when Derek Minter had the unfortunate accident at Brands Hatch in May just before the first round of the eight round world championship commencing with the Isle of Man TT in June. Phil Read was brought in as a replacement to partner John Hartle. Although having some success, the combination of an under-funded budget, some crashes and mechanical breakdowns resulted only third, fourth and seventh positions in the championship involving the three riders Hartle, Read and Minter after his comeback. Their total championship points amounted to 51, while Hailwood grossed 56 points on his own. Nevertheless, it was a good effort and added spice and enjoyment to the racing scene.

It has been written that the Gilera factory were spurred on by the MV challenge, announcing an official come-back in 1964, in addition to any plans they had for 'Scuderia Duke' at that time. Gilera were keen to sign John Hartle, Alan Shepherd and Gilberto Milani. Meantime, one of the Gileras had been fitted with a set of Reynolds

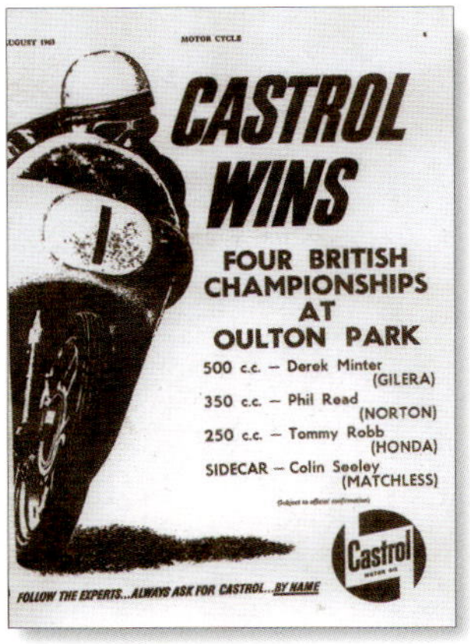

leading-link forks. Combined with advice from Ken Sprayson, would hopefully help to sort out the handling problems. A test was held at Monza, but the weather was so bad for the first two days, nothing was achieved. Towards the end of the week the weather was kinder, but Gilera's luck was not. Gilberto Milani, when rounding the long Monza Parabolic curve, came off when the rear drive chain broke. His leg injuries put him out of action for two weeks. John Hartle continued testing next morning but once again the conditions were bad and the test abandoned, a disappointment for the 75 year old Commendatore Giuseppie Gilera, boss of the famous Arcore factory who was in attendance.

Their racing plans then seemed to be put on hold, other than sending a four out to the Argentine for local star Benedicto Caldarella. The 'Scuderia Duke' team was disbanded and that was the end of Gilera's world championship comeback bid. Only memories were left of their success, having won six world championships in the 500cc class, 1950 and 52 with Umberto Masetti, 1953-55 with the master himself, Geoff Duke and 1957 with Libero Liberati.

Despite his lack of real success riding the 500cc Gilera four, Phil Read achieved two seconds and a third before Derek Minter returned to the team. Phil, very much on form, riding his 350 and 500cc Nortons, had recorded some very good results in between the Gilera excursions. As a consequence he was invited to ride the works Yamaha in the 125 and 250cc classes of the Japanese Grand Prix, the last classic of 1963, held at the Suzuka Circuit on November 9th. The Yamaha factory had been encouraged by its brief sortie into that year's European Grand Prix events, in particular with their 250cc model ridden by Fumio Ito. 1963 was Yamaha's rehearsal for a full scale world championship attack in 1964.

The final Grand Prix of the year, held at the 3.75 mile figure-of-eight Suzuka circuit, would be the first ever Japanese Grand Prix. The circuit, built by Honda and designed by Dutchman Jan Hugenholtz, would provide some interesting racing, although there was no 500cc event included. Over 150,000 enthusiastic Japanese jammed into every inch of spectator space around the circuit. Of course it would be an almost all Japanese racing machinery benefit, so that helped. The 50cc championship race was down to the wire. Anscheidt, Kreidler only needed to finish in front of Hugh Anderson, Suzuki, to clinch the title. However Honda, back for the first time that season, competed with a 50cc four-stroke twin, capable of 20,000rpm. The rider, Luigi Taveri just romped away from the field leaving Anscheidt in front of Anderson trying to keep up, when the Kreidler blew its big end. That was the end for the unfortunate Anscheidt and the European challenge. Hugh Anderson, finishing second, added this championship to his 125cc crown and the third championship for the Suzuki factory.

The 125cc race was to be a tough contest as Honda had overcome troubles with their brand new four cylinder model and in practice they proved a match for the incredibly fast Suzuki two strokes. From the drop of the flag, Redman, Honda and Anderson, Suzuki, shot into the lead. Taveri's race was short-lived as he retired his Honda with ignition trouble. Frank Perris, Suzuki was closing on the leading pair, Anderson dropped back with suspension problems and it was a dice with Redman to the finish, passing and re-passing each other, with Perris getting the verdict by 4 seconds from Jim Redman. This was Frank's first GP win of his career following second spot placings in the Isle of Man and the Dutch TT, it must have been contract time!

The 250cc race would not disappoint, with Redman, Honda, alongside Ito and Read, Yamahas. On the grid, adding a touch of glamour, Suzuki fielded three of their brand new fabulous square four two strokes ridden by Perris, Anderson and Degner. From the start, Ito and Read were well away with Redman in pursuit but behind on the first corner, Ernst Degner crashed heavily on his Suzuki four and it burst into flames. His burns and injuries would keep him in hospital for two weeks. Frank Perris on the other Suzuki four, having made a bad start, stopped at the scene to assist. Meanwhile at the front, the racing was fast and furious with the two Yamahas and Redman's Honda only inches apart on the last lap. Phil Read's Yamaha, which had been sliding around, went onto one cylinder, leaving Redman and Ito fighting to the flag with Redman winning by a wheel, and with it the 250cc world championship. Phil Read was home despite his problems, in a very respectable third place with that dedicated Italian Tarquinio Provini, Morini in fourth, beating the rest of the Honda and Yamaha 'gaggle' and gaining a well-deserved second place in that year's world 250cc title race.

The 350cc race although won by Redman on the Honda was a complete shambles. Unbelievably, only three riders came to the start line, so the result did not count towards

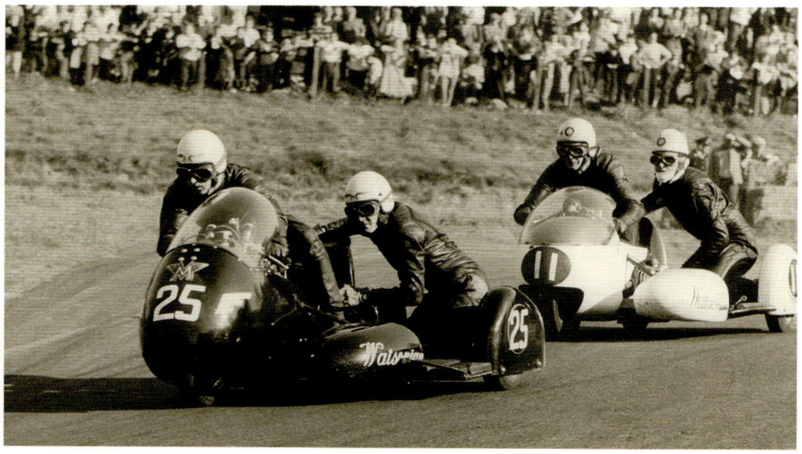

Cadwell International, September action.

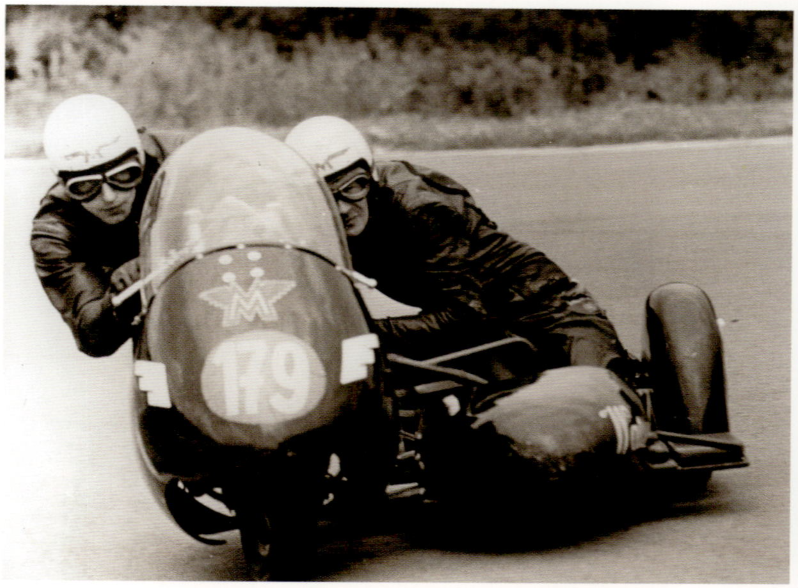

Matchless G50 action on the limit.

the world championship or anything else come to that, just extra pocket money for Jim!

Phil Read's efforts in the 250cc race at Suzuka were rewarded by a works' contract to ride for Yamaha in 1964. The contract allowed Phil to ride his Nortons when not required to race Yamaha - the best of both worlds for Phil - who duly signed.

With the end of 1963 nigh, Luigi Taveri the 1962 125cc World Champion and second place man this season, and winner of the Japanese Suzuka 50cc race had achieved all of this with Honda. The diminutive Swiss ace, to the surprise of many, signed with the German Kreidler factory in the 50cc class for 1964. He had given Honda fair warning that he wished to limit his racing to the 50cc and 125cc classes having finished third in the 350cc championship. He wanted to stay with Honda if terms could be agreed, but as time went on he became tired of waiting for them to make their minds up, and so signed for Kreidler. Honda can certainly manufacture racing motorcycles, but their way of running a team and making rider appointments are often strangely oriental.

John Hartle and Alan Shepherd, both highly talented riders were, according to reports, being considered by most of the manufacturers, along with all and sundry, so it would be lucky dip for these sportsmen in 1964.

Before writing this 1963 chapter, I hadn't realised just how much had happened. Reflecting on it 40 years later, what a fantastic, interesting but sometimes sad year it proved to be:

Our first full attempt at the World Sidecar Championship.
The begining of our long standing friendship with Swiss hillclimb champion and solo road racer Ernst Weiss.
The year of the 'Scuderia Duke' Gilera team.
The year our friendship blossomed with Swiss ace, Florian Camathias.
Barry Sheene was 12 years of age.
The return of Yamaha Racing to the world championship.
Our good friend David Downer lost his life.
'Mr. Cool' Max Deubel won his third World Sidecar Championship.
Florian Camathias lost his chance to win a world title.
We won our second British Sidecar Championship title.
Mike Hailwood's second consecutive 500cc World Championship with MV Agusta.
Jim Redman's second consecutive double world championship in the 250 and 350cc classes with Honda.
Hugh Anderson's first ever world championships with a double in the 50cc and 125cc classes for Suzuki.
Mike Hailwood announced he would continue racing motorcycles.
The year of the first Japanese Grand Prix.
Avon Tyres announced they were withdrawing from the sport.
Associated Motorcyles Ltd announced the end of racing motorcycle production.
The year BMW announced that they were withdrawing from racing.
'No more works' stated Deubel. Statement not believed!
Mario Sassi, first Gilera racing team member, 1911, killed in a road accident.
Mike Duff's son was born.
The Dartford-Purfleet Thames tunnel was finally operational.

1963 was the year that we were accepted by the solo and sidecar competitors alike for our serious and professional approach to racing. It had been fantastic mixing with the 'real stars' and a privilege to have ridden in the Grands Prix that year. I had come a long way since looking over the fence at Brands Hatch as a 14 year old!

Last but not least, in December our son, Colin arrived.

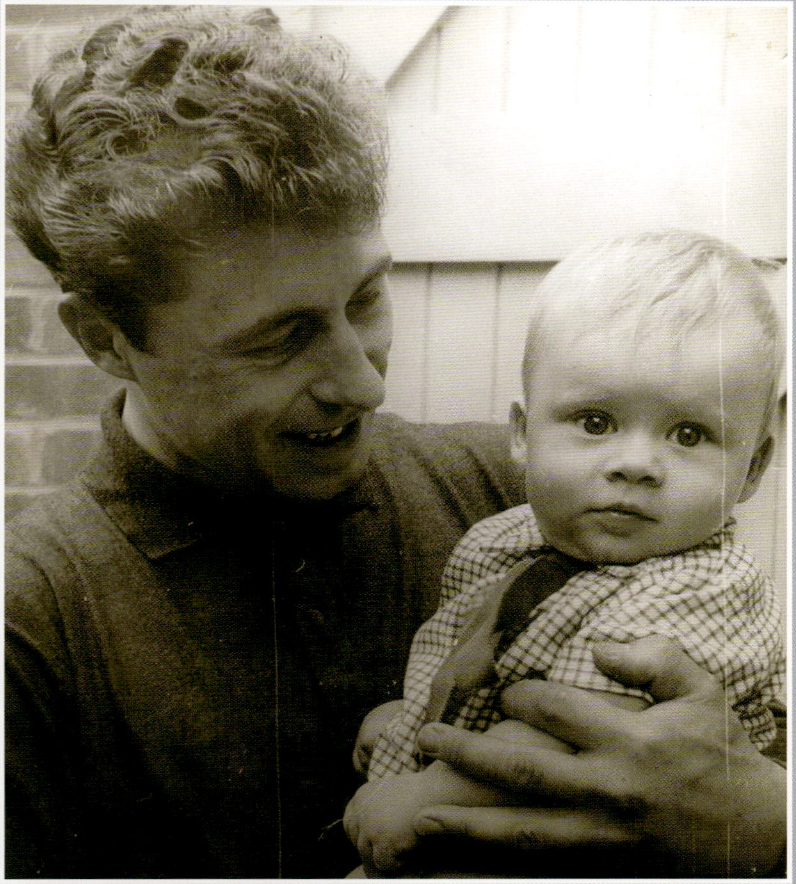

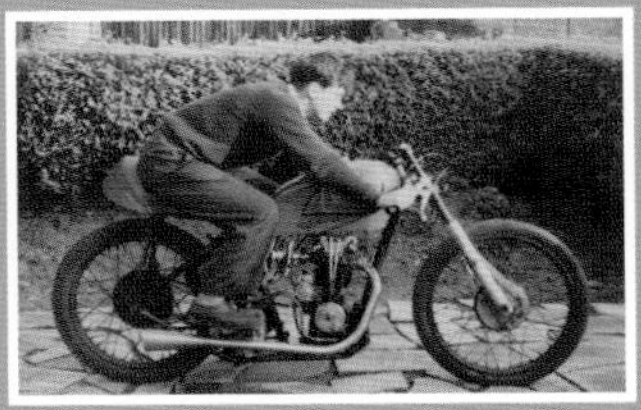

6 DAVID DOWNER, FORGOTTEN HERO

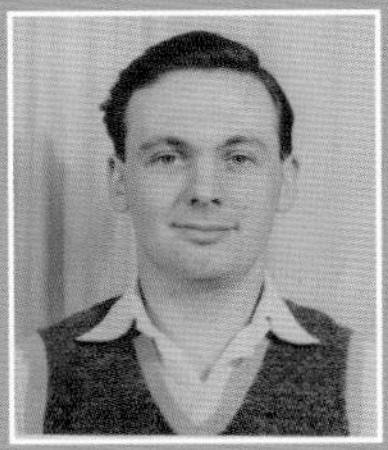

Dave aged eighteen.

Many readers may remember, that fateful day, May 12th, 1963, at Brands Hatch during the fifteenth and last lap of the unlimited race, the final race of the day, held on the long circuit, Dave Downer and Derek Minter were hotly contesting for the lead. Even today many still agree it was one of the most exciting races ever seen at Brands. At Dingle Dell corner, both riders crashed. Derek sustained serious back and shoulder injuries, but for 23 year old Dave, a star in the making, the accident was fatal. Everyone was completely stunned and the crowds stood silent and motionless. Dave's finest hour is sadly remembered as a tragic event.

David Leslie Downer born 21st November 1939 in Erith, Kent, was the son of an electrical engineer. David and his family lived at Lesney Park in Upper Belvedere, just 250 yards from a certain Jock West! 30 years Dave's senior, Jock was an all-round grass tracker and Isle of Man TT racer who became Sales Director for AMC.

Those early days of my motorcycle repair business had attracted the attention of this local Belvedere lad. At 14, Dave Downer was an inquisitive schoolboy who frequently called round to see what was going on. He would skid into the dusty Forge Works' yard on his own designed and constructed sprung frame push-bike. Dave asked if I needed any assistance with my work, as he was saving up for an old 250cc Rudge. I took a liking to this talented enthusiastic young man whose ambition was to be another Geoff Duke. I agreed he could help after school and at the weekends.

Dave left Erith Technical College at 16 and joined his best friend Mick Cossar at the huge Vickers factory in Crayford, Kent, as an apprentice in mechanical engineering. The Vickers factory had every conceivable facility for the manufacture of motorcycle parts, which was to prove invaluable to young David in the future when he needed to make spares for the race bikes. Having bought his first racing motorcycle, a 250cc Rudge, Dave and fellow racing friends attended the regular Wednesday afternoon practice sessions at Brands Hatch. They were so short of cash that they would only buy two practice passes between four of them. They also shared race leathers and helmets - it was a look-a-like job. What a scam!

David had no race fairing for the Rudge and tried making one out of papier-maché and chicken wire, which was fine until it rained, then it disintegrated. Sometimes he would invite his young sister Sandra along for the afternoon out at Brands, but would conveniently forget that he had no money so she was sent up to buy a gallon of petrol and the practice session ticket, after all, what were sisters for? As a member of the Erith and District MCC and eager for his first race action, David entered his initial event at Crystal Palace. He persuaded me to take him and his 250cc Rudge in my Ford van to the meeting.

This early 1958 event had attracted entries from Derek Minter, Brian Setchell, Rex Avery and Joe Dunphy with Mike Hailwood, Ginger Payne and Tom Thorp competing in the 250cc race.

David was totally unfazed by the opposition, not in any arrogant manner, but he had a confident style and believed in himself. That faith was rewarded with a notable sixth in the 250cc heat and a sixth in the final, which was won by Mike Hailwood with Ginger Payne in second place - an excellent start to Dave's racing career.

Fully enthused by the results Dave could not wait to race at Brands Hatch early in May. Another sixth place in the 250cc heat was followed by a crash in the final. Later that month came the Whit Monday meeting at Brands. The weather was rough with wet conditions prevailing, and in heat two of the 250cc event David and Ken Whorlow had a coming together whilst battling for the lead taking both riders off. Unhurt, they remounted and finished ninth and tenth respectively. Dave was now on his learning curve.

Often in those early days it was difficult to get race entries accepted, which was a problem I encountered at the start of my racing career. Dave suffered the same fate and

Dave at Brands, in the early days.

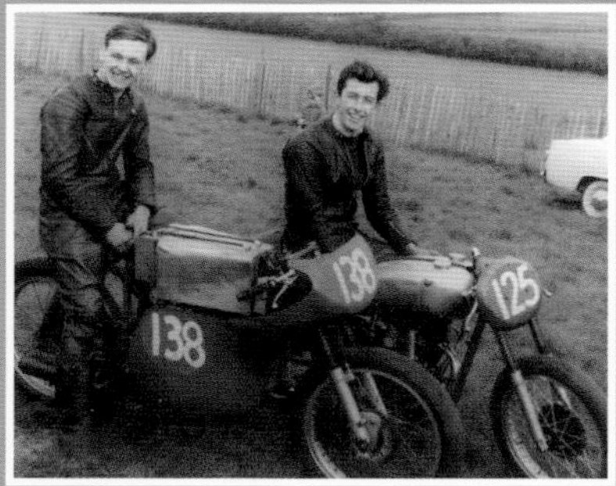

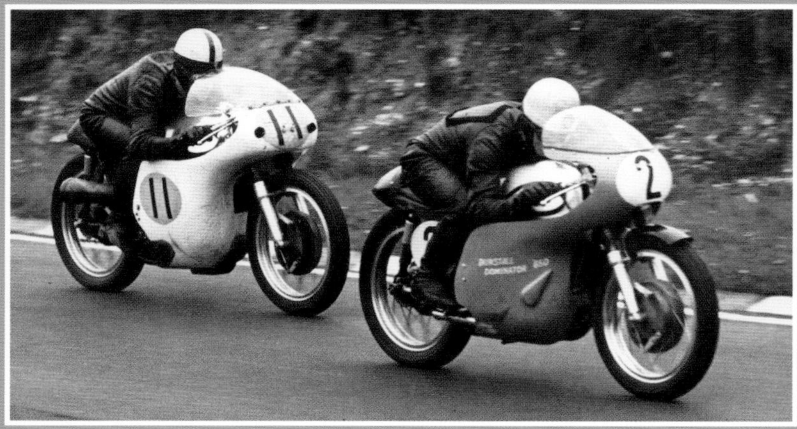

Dave leading Minter, Brands 1963

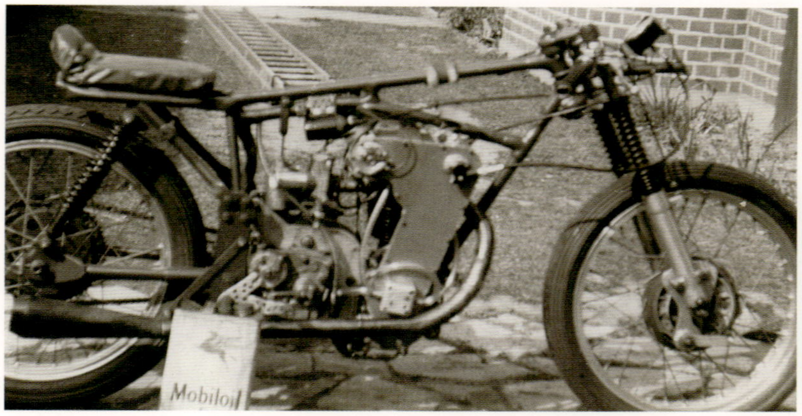

Dave's Desmo Rudge.

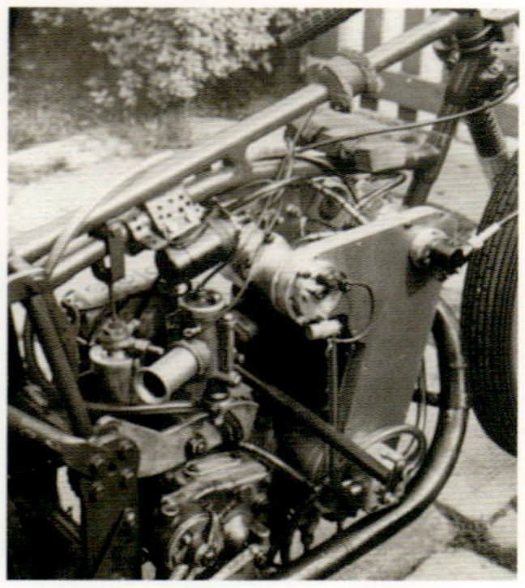

decided to travel the considerable distance to Charterhall in Scotland having been accepted for their July 1958 meeting. He had by now bought, with family assistance, another Rudge, but this time not for racing. It was a 500cc Ulster fitted with an open sidecar for transporting his race bike. Dave duly loaded the race bike, leathers, tools, provisions and anything else that could be fitted on board apart from the 'kitchen sink'. In addition a trailer was added for friend and racer Dave King to join the party with his special Norton. Certainly fully loaded, they embarked that Friday on their epic journey to the Charterhall circuit near Berwick-upon-Tweed. The journey north soon turned into a drama with the over-loaded Rudge continually breaking down. Broken wheel spokes was only one of the problems. Finally on the Saturday, approaching Charterhall, the Rudge expired. With no alternative they unloaded their race bikes and with friendly local police co-operation they rode these bikes the final miles to the circuit.

After a disappointing and non-eventful race meeting the two Davids managed a lift back with the race bikes to their broken Rudge, where after repairs, they slowly trickled southwards on the A1 arriving at Biggleswade, still a good distance from home, when the Rudge finally gave up. Totally dismayed, dirty, hungry and needing to get back for work they parked it in a local garage and caught a train, arriving home on the following Thursday - nearly a week later - some adventure!

As the 1958 racing season came to an end Dave Downer had grand ideas of improving his 250cc Rudge, but still on apprenticeship wages it was to be very much a self-help improvement project. Of course Dave would make good use of the Vicker's factory machining capacity and his fellow apprentice friends and supporters. Dave was nicknamed 'Mazda' because he was considered brighter than the light bulb of that name.

The alterations to his beloved 250 Rudge were to be major, converting this normal push rod model into a desmodromic version, all of his own design, a considerable feat in itself. The work started in November that same year. Later that month David, with work-mate and close friend Mick Cossar riding pillion on the repaired Rudge sidecar outfit, travelling to work in the thick fog-smog weather conditions, ran straight into the rear of a parked milk delivery lorry. The horrific crash resulted in Dave smashing his face on the lorry. Mick Cossar was thrust violently forward, knocking out the back of David's crash hat with his chin. His knees took a bashing as the Rudge's frame and forks folded from the impact of the crash. By chance and certainly with some luck, a friend was passing in a van and with a seriously injured David in need of immediate medical attention and no time to wait for a fog-bound ambulance, he was laid in the van and driven direct to West Hill Hospital. On arrival the doctors took one look at his facial injuries and immediately rushed him to the East Grinstead Hospital for specialist treatment. He had suffered a fractured skull, jaw and wrist, as well severe bruising.

Three weeks later he was discharged from hospital with his jaw wired, and was only able to feed through a straw. But persistent Dave was soon back working on the desmodromic conversion to his Rudge which was renamed a 'DDS' - David Downer Special. Disappointing race results in 1959 and 1960 were to follow, firstly due to recovering from the accident, and furthermore the need for time to develop the 'DDS' desmo machine. It was April 1960 that Wally Rawlings and I had entered the race meeting at Charterhall with friend Peter Morecock driving my Thames van. With our racing sidecar and dustbin fairing strapped on the roof rack we had room for Dave Downer's Rudge - sorry 'DDS' alongside our 500 Manx Norton. The latter part of 1960 saw Dave desperate to move on with his racing ambitions and with help from his brother Peter a 350cc Manx Norton was purchased from Monty and Ward for riding in that year's Manx Grand Prix. However, in this his first Manx race he stopped at Quarter Bridge on the first lap and finally was forced to retire. In 1961 due to a fall at Laurel Bank he was again forced to retire, fortunately without injury.

Meantime local Belvedere friend Paul Dunstall whose house backed onto the Bostall Woods and with part of their large garden extending into the woods, provided a convenient scrambles practice ground for me, in the period 1957-1960. Paul, having sold his 500cc Gold Star, a machine which at one time I used to service, bought himself

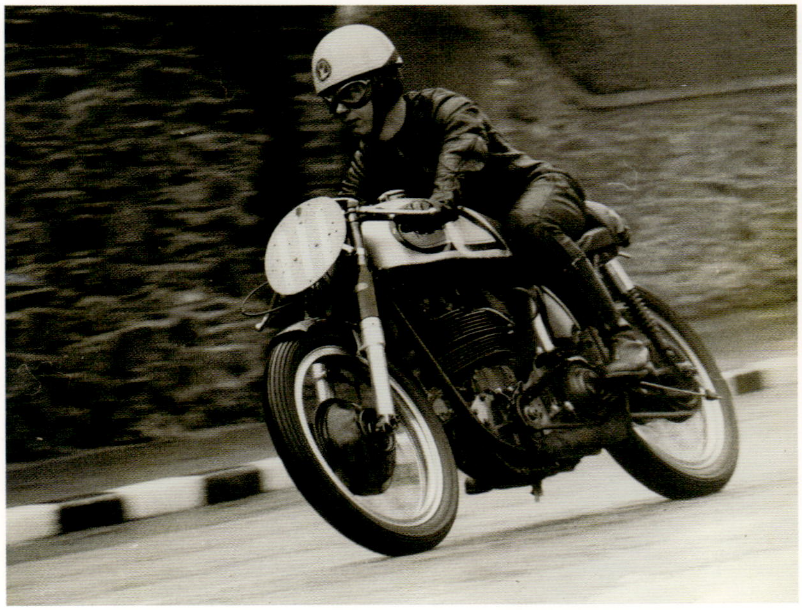

Dave at the 1960 Manx Grand Prix.

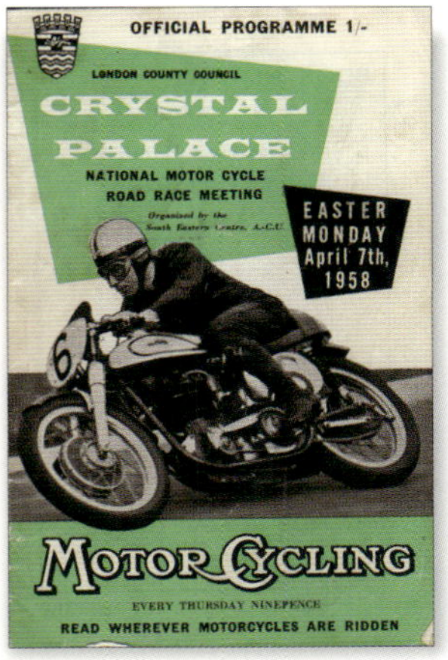

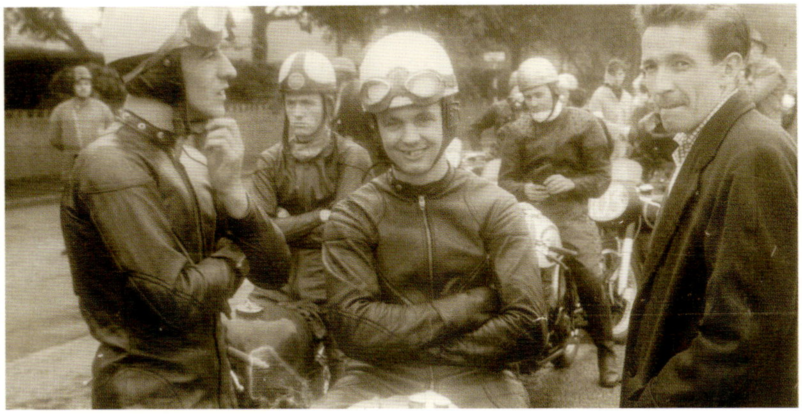

Dave at the start area,1962 Manx Grand Prix. Jimmy Cripps on the left and Wally Rawlings on the right.

a new 600cc Norton Dominator 99 in sports trim with a view to going racing. With the Norton 99 run in on the road it was completely stripped and rebuilt in racing trim for Paul's first race ever at Thruxton, Easter 1958, but with ignition problems it was a failed debut. For Paul's next adventure at Brands Hatch in July, a magneto had replaced the suspect coil ignition. Paul was a stylish rider and certainly had racing potential. He was the winner of the 1000cc novice event. Despite this success, with family pressures at the time, Paul quit racing to concentrate on the establishment of his motorcycle business, which was to become very successful. His Norton Commando racer was put on hold.

Then later a mutual friend, another local and talented rising star, Fred Neville convinced Paul to prepare the 600cc Norton twin for him to race in 1961. At the July 1961 Brands Hatch meeting held on the long circuit Fred Neville achieved a third place riding the Dunstall Norton Dominator, winner Derek Minter and Phil Read second. Then Neville achieved an outstanding victory at Brands Hatch, on the 20th August 1961 racing the Dunstall Norton. Sadly, the following month, September, Fred Neville was killed in the Manx Grand Prix riding the Tom Arter entered AJS 7R, whilst leading the Junior race by over two minutes in worsening rain lashed conditions. He crashed on the last lap at Greeba Bridge and succumbed to fatal head injuries. A tragic loss to his family, friends and certainly to the sport. Downer was also riding in the Junior race that year, 1961, but had a problem with his 350 Manx Norton from the start. In trying to make up time fell at Laurel Bank on the fifth lap, fortunately without injury.

Finally, in October 1961 at the last meeting of the year held at Brands Hatch, Derek Minter rode the Dunstall Norton 600cc twin finishing second to Phil Read in the rain-swept 1000cc race event. It was also 1961 that Tom Phillis had finished a fantastic third in the Senior TT on the works 500cc Domiracer.

Paul Dunstall, encouraged by the success of his 600cc Norton twin racer, immediately ordered one of the new 650cc Dominators announced by the factory for 1962. With Paul's knowledge, the 650cc version was soon modified to produce a very competitive machine, something I was to find out for myself three years later when I raced a Dunstall 650 in the 1964-65 unlimited sidecar class. Paul Dunstall, impressed by Dave Downer's total dedication and obvious riding skill, signed him for the 1962 race season to ride his 650cc Dunstall Norton, although David would continue to race his 250cc desmo DDS and 350cc Manx.

Meantime Derek Minter, similarly impressed by the Norton Dominator's performance, persuaded directors at Norton's Bracebridge Street to build him a 650cc version for the 1962 season which he was to race for the first time at Brands Hatch 20th April that year and won the 1000cc open event. For David Downer it was a non start at the first Brands meeting, an eighth spot finish on the 13th May, and a race retirement on the 8th July, all at Brands Hatch. It was then finally to be Dave's moment of glory at Brands in August winning from strong opposition with Tony Godfrey in second place he having taken over Minter's ride on the works 650cc Norton twin. This result rewarded the Dunstall team for its considerable efforts and faith in David's racing talent.

With renewed confidence Dave arrived next month in the Isle of Man for his third Manx Grand Prix event competing in the 350cc race on his Manx Norton. As had been our practice, learning the TT course in our van, David was to follow suit. However on one occasion driving his Commer van for a lap of the Island he approached the left hander at Kepple Gate where a bus had stopped. Going at some speed and committed to the corner he took prompt evasive action by taking to the opposite side of the road resulting in the van running up the steep banking and turning onto its side. Slipping and sliding with sparks flying the van was on its speedy way to Kate's Cottage. The van's windscreen popped out in one piece and the passenger door was ripped off. The passengers, shaken up like peas, were fortunately unhurt.

Having survived this accident Dave went on to become a race favourite in the 350cc event, having set the fastest lap in practice and unofficially breaking Ron Langston's 1960 350cc lap record by over 1mph at 92.76mph. As he stood behind the grandstand, naturally pleased with himself, his friends congratulated him on his achievement. The exalted and revered (by some) tuner Francis Beart, famous for his immaculate preparation and light-weight Nortons, with everything on the machines appearing to be drilled came by, pushing his 350 Norton. Dave, 'a cheeky little sod' with little respect for status said; 'Excuse me Mr. Beart do you know that I have just unofficially broken the 350cc lap record and your Norton is just not quick enough, you'll need to go home and drill some more holes.' Francis was not exactly renowned for his sense of humour and had no idea how to react to Dave's cocky comment. However, as he moved on his way, his sideways look said it all!

Interestingly much seemed to revolve round the letter, 'D' for riders Darvill, Dawson,

Fred Neville at Brands Hatch, July 1961.

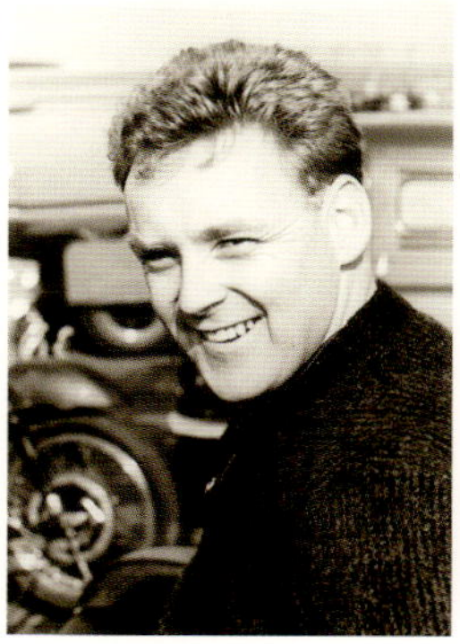

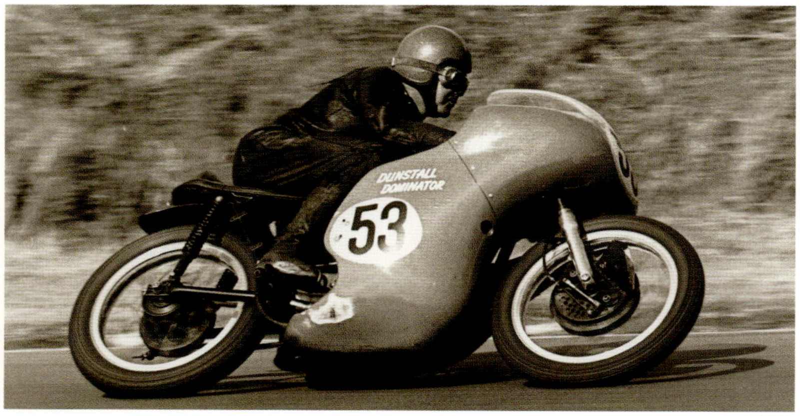

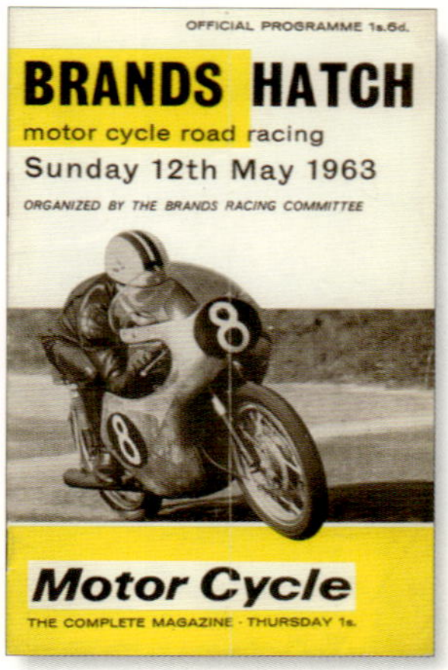

Minter leading Downer at Westfield Bend last corner before Dingle Dell and the fateful crash.

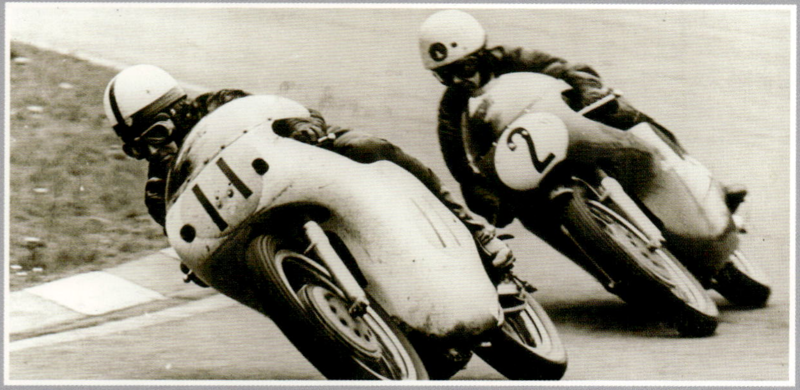

Downer, Duckett and Dunphy. The start of the Junior Race was delayed by one hour due to mist and rain on the mountain. It was to be Robin Dawson taking the honours from second place man Peter Darvill, both on AJS 7Rs. It was the first year that fairings were allowed in the history of the Manx Grand Prix. Despite this advantage, Ron Langston's 2 year old 350cc lap record was not broken and Dave retired on the fourth lap when in fifth position. The 'D' continued its success in the Senior Race with gentleman Joe Dunphy, Norton, winning from Peter Darvill, Norton. It was a most tragic Manx that year, with three riders killed in the Junior and one in the Senior.

Although another disappointing Manx Grand Prix for Dave, it certainly highlighted his all-round racing ability. Later that September it was back to Brands Hatch, once more racing the Dunstall Norton against Derek Minter on his official Norton 650cc Domiracer. The race was held, as was normal at that time, over the full 2.65 mile Grand Prix circuit. Minter got his revenge over Downer with Dave second and Phil Read third. Dave won £18 in prize money for his efforts and a huge £15 start appearance payment.

Further events followed at Aintree, Oulton Park and Snetterton before returning to Brands Hatch for the final time in 1962. Brands at the time was one of the very few venues, if not in fact the only one, to run an open 1000cc racing class. So David Downer was back riding the competitive Dunstall 650 Norton when leading the 15 lap race, thinking he had it in the bag, he was forced to retire. A very disappointing end to a very encouraging season, highlighting the performance of the Dunstall 650 Domiracer and his competence as a rider.

Much has been written and discussed about the unfortunate and tragic accident on the 12th May, 1963, at Brands Hatch, involving Dave Downer and Derek Minter. In 1963 Derek had been appointed team leader of the resurrected Scuderia Duke Gilera Team with John Hartle as team-mate. Derek at that time was considered the rider to possibly beat Mike Hailwood on the all conquering MVs.

The first non-championship clash was held on Good Friday at Brands Hatch on 12th April. Mike Hailwood having damaged his hand from a crash in an earlier race that day, did not make the grid with his MV 500 for the last race, the 1000cc open event. Derek Minter, Gilera, in winning from his team mate John Hartle recorded the first ever lap at over 90mph on the long Grand Prix Circuit.

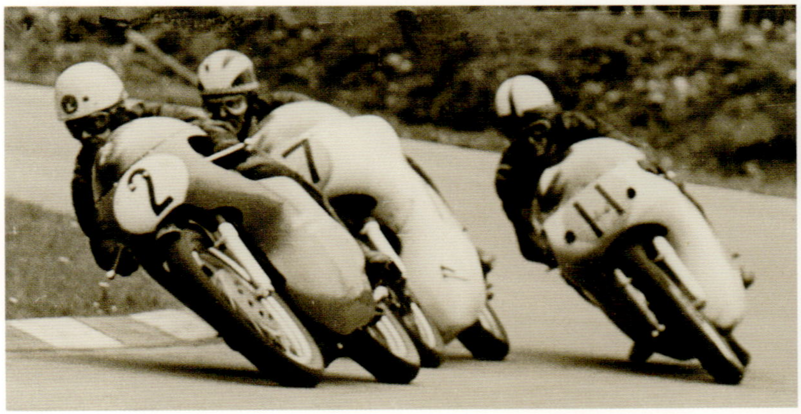

With only eight 500cc World Championship rounds that year, counting towards the World Championship, the first race was not held until the Isle of Man TT in June. Derek in his wisdom decided to compete at his regular track of Brands Hatch on the 12th May, due partly to only receiving a a small retainer from the Scuderia Duke Team who had received a disappointing lack of sponsorship. Also Derek felt a degree of loyalty towards his huge base of fans as 'King of Brands'. Having won the earlier 500cc Redex Trophy race from Read and Downer, riding his faithful 500 Manx Norton. Derek was aware that he could be under threat in the open 1000cc event from up and coming fearless Dave Downer on the powerful 650 Dunstall Norton.

In a discussion with a reporter/photographer, Derek said that he was there that day for the fans and to earn some money. Perhaps expecting to be beaten by Downer, foremost in Derek's mind would have been the forthcoming ride on the Gilera, being possibly his first or only chance to win a World Championship. In winning a championship often the throttle needs to work both ways and the brain to be fully engaged. Truly though, who is able to sit in judgement of a man such as Minter, 'The King'. He was the fastest man around the long Brands circuit. In the heat of the tremendous battle with the young pretender Dave Downer, Derek was never going to give up until the flag was passed, but in that race neither was to pass under the chequered flag because of the dreadful accident at Dingle Dell in the last lap.

Derek Minter, approaching 70 years of age, in an interview with Classic Racer Magazine, March/April 2002 issue, suggested that Dave Downer had accidentally run into the rear of his Manx Norton hitting the exhaust pipe which had caused Derek to go down followed by David. At the official inquest all the evidence pointed to Derek's machine having a substantial oil leak on that last lap. Smoke/oil/mist was seen coming from the bike and further along the track a Marshall positioned at the Dingle Dell corner, although not seeing smoke, saw Derek's rear wheel break away as the machine was banked over and with David so close he could not avoid the accident. Derek just missed the tree which Dave hit, resulting in multiple impact injuries.

Derek Minter provided written evidence but he did not attend the inquest. He said that on the last lap he had overtaken Dave on the Westfield Bend, one before the Dingle Dell corner, but he remembered no more until waking up in the ambulance and had no idea as to why he had crashed.

Finally, as Dave Downer left his family home for the last time, his father said to the driver of the hearse, 'Don't hang about. David never did when he was alive and he wouldn't want to now!'

Downer, Read and Minter at Westfield Bend, 500cc Redex Trophy race, May 1963.

7 1964

WHEN IT'S SWEET, IT'S VERY SWEET!

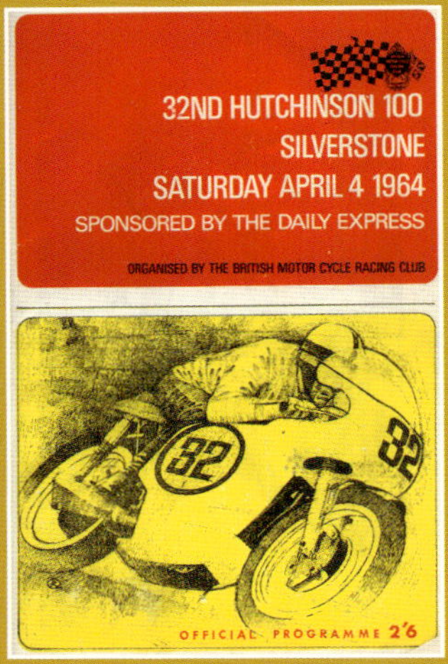

As rider-agent for the machines we sold, we had now raced the Matchless G50 for three seasons. However, it was becoming somewhat frustrating competing against the faster BMW outfits and it really was time to move on. The only problem was I could not really afford a Rennsport BMW even if it was possible to buy a good one, therefore, a decision was made to continue with the G50 but we commissioned Ken Sprayson of Reynolds Tubes to build a complete new outfit, lower, lighter and with leading link forks. That would be fine for the 500cc class but we would still struggle in the unlimited races against Vincent, Boddice, Greenwood and the others. In discussion with our local friend Paul Dunstall, he suggested that he would supply and support us with one of his fast 650cc Domiracers. He had agreed terms for 1964 with Manxman Sid Mizen to ride both 500 and 650cc Domiracers in the solo classes and as it happens Mizen was already to be sponsored by C.J.Seeley (Sales) Ltd on a 250cc Greeves Silverstone and a 350cc 7R AJS.

While Ken Sprayson was building us a new chassis for the G50, I took delivery of a Low Boy Domiracer rolling chassis and immediately started work on the conversion, including the construction of a sidecar chassis, which was chalked out on the workshop floor. The manufacturing of the chassis and the fitting to the Norton Low Boy frame was my first ever tubular welded creation. A set of Reynolds forks replaced the 'teles', the wheels were rebuilt with 16 inch rims and fairing and sidecar nose cone were fitted. This 'sit up and beg' outfit was something of a lash up, but proved pretty effective with the extra horsepower of the 650cc twin motor.

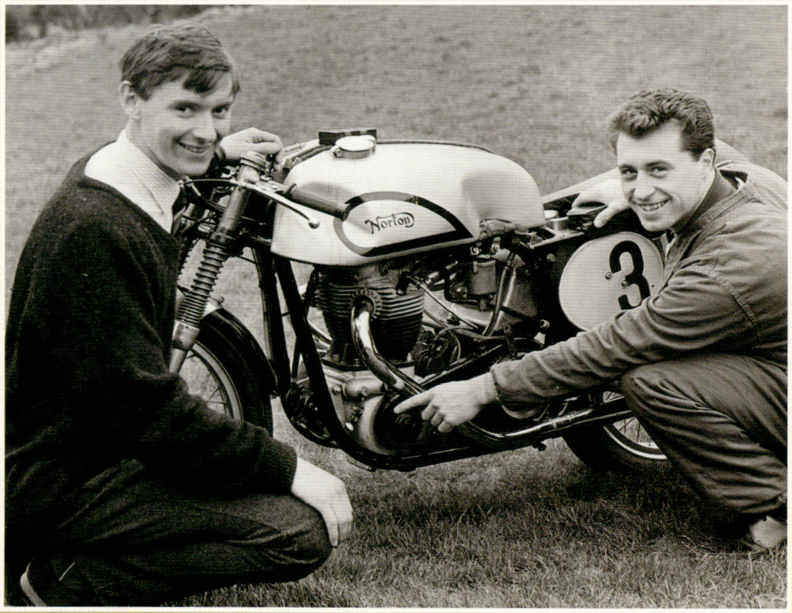

1964 was also the season that I supported and was the entrant for Greenwich Club member Norman Huntingford who would ride my 1963 Matchless/Watsonian outfit.

The race season started at Mallory Park on the 22nd March followed by the Easter meetings at Brands and Snetterton. Monday, 30th Oulton Park made four race meetings in nine days - which was a crazy schedule, and we suffered mechnical trouble at all of them.

To date, our new Reynolds/G50 outfit had been a disappointment. It handled well but for some reason just did not seem to go like our old Matchless. Next was the Silverstone Hutchinson 100 international on April 4th, at which all the regular foreign and home competitors would be in attendance. On the day foul weather darkened the British Racing Club's event although it failed to dampen the performances of the stars and supporting cast. The drama of the meeting was the late arrival of Florian Camathias, surprising all with the first appearance of his Gilera four cylinder powered outfit. Never a dull moment with Florian, but, troubled with a misfire in practice which was traced to a faulty battery connection, he failed to qualify. He therefore had to start from the back of the grid in both races. In the first race the tremendous speed of the Gilera outfit enabled him to storm past most of the 25 outfits, then as he passed Fritz Scheidegger at Coram Curve to take third place, he went into a spin like a top, catapulting passenger Alfred Herzig from the chair. Meanwhile, Wally and I were heading the field in the wet conditions having displaced Max Deubel from the lead, when only 300 yards from the finish flag we ran out of fuel and 'spluttered' to a stop, allowing Scheidegger to win from Deubel. We were devastated. It had been our big chance to finally win an international event, but a leaking float bowl resulted in failure.

In the second race, again from the back of the field, Camathias and his Gilera rocketed through to the front. Hertzig had cracked an ankle, so for this race his seat was occupied by Swiss solo rider, Roland Foell. However, they couldn't catch a flying Chris

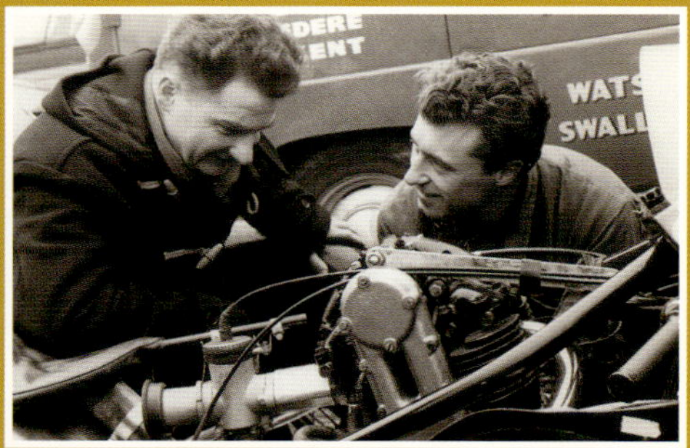

Ken Sprayson discussing the Reynolds outfit.

Paul Dunstall and myself discussing the Domiracer project.

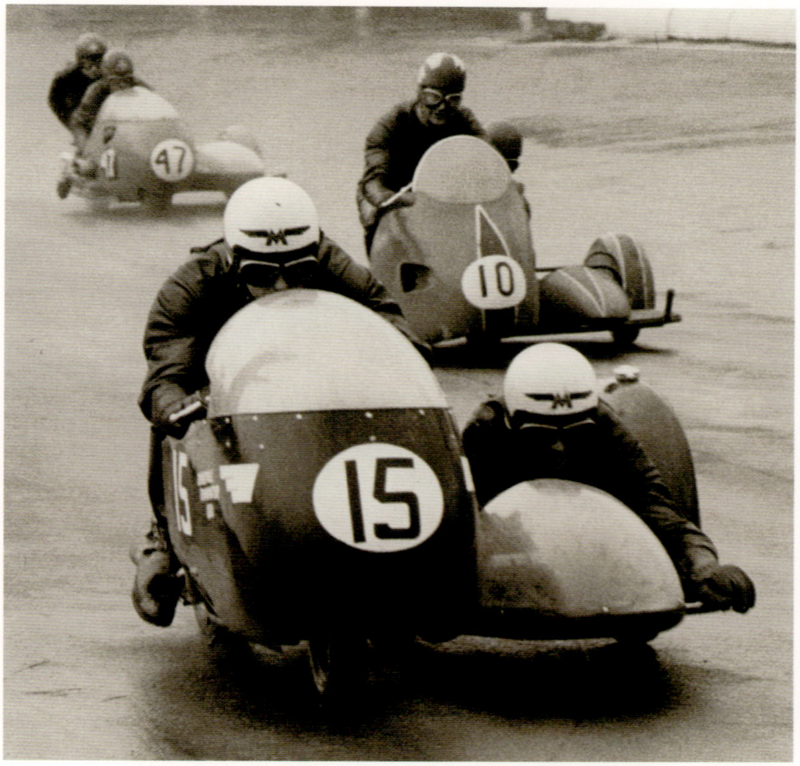

Mallory Park sidecar race of the year, leading Charlie Freeman and Fritz Scheidegger.

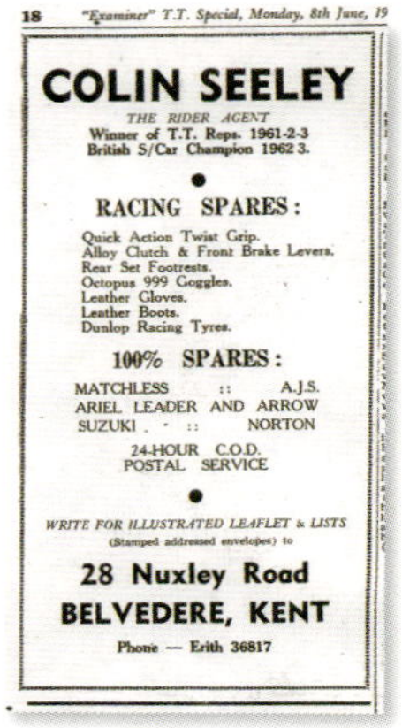

18 "Examiner" T.T. Special, Monday, 8th June, 19

COLIN SEELEY

THE RIDER AGENT
Winner of T.T. Reps. 1961-2-3
British S/Car Champion 1962 3.

RACING SPARES:

Quick Action Twist Grip.
Alloy Clutch & Front Brake Levers.
Rear Set Footrests.
Octopus 999 Goggles.
Leather Gloves.
Leather Boots.
Dunlop Racing Tyres.

100% SPARES:

MATCHLESS :: A.J.S.
ARIEL LEADER AND ARROW
SUZUKI :: NORTON

24-HOUR C.O.D.
POSTAL SERVICE

WRITE FOR ILLUSTRATED LEAFLET & LISTS
(Stamped addressed envelopes) to

28 Nuxley Road
BELVEDERE, KENT

Phone — Erith 36817

Vincent BMW who posted the win from Camathias, Deubel and Scheidegger. We, with our Reynolds/G50 outfit had held third place, but again we were struck with the 'gremlins', this time the float chamber fell off! Just not a good day - our luck was out.

Days later it was back to Mallory Park for the Sidecar Race of the Year, on April 12th, making six meetings in 22 days which included 15 sidecar races. We had no need to attend a gym for exercise as we were hardly off the bike. We were certainly race fit! This event was organised by the East Midlands ACU and sponsored by the Daily Mail, and was the first event of its kind with not a solo machine in sight. Such was the interest in sidecar racing in those days, despite the weather it attracted some 20,000 fans, and of course all the big names in sidecar racing.

We turned up in force with both the Matchless G50 and Dunstall Norton outfits aided by my friends from the Greenwich Club - John Juniper, Les Williams and Bill Savage. This time we were looking for some good results, but, once again it was to be mixed fortunes.

The 500cc race was won by Vincent/Scott followed by Scheidegger/Robinson - Harris/Campbell - Camathias/Foell - Deubel/Horner, all racing BMWs. We came sixth on the Matchless, once again the first single cylinder machine home. We then wheeled out the Dunstall Norton and won our heat in the 1200cc event, then in the final Chris Vincent BSA was once again first under the chequered flag followed by Pete Russell on the Vincent 1000cc. The third place would be hotly contested between Owen Greenwood, Terry Vinicombe and ourselves, fortunately, we came out best, with £15 in prize money, combined with the £3 heat win money, £5 of which went to Paul Dunstall as a contribution to the Norton's upkeep.

It was then the invitation only 25 lap Daily Mail Race of the Year, but the heavens opened so the race was reduced to 20 laps. From a superb start we found ourselves in the lead and the Norton was really 'singing in the rain', when, unbelievably, the sidecar nose cone came loose forcing us to stop and kick the dam thing off with 3 laps lost to the leaders. As a result, we finished eighth and out of money. It was 'pennies from heaven' for our mate Pip Harris and passenger Ray Campbell BMW who took the win and the £500 loot from Fritz Scheidegger, 10 seconds behind, who grabbed the £250 second prize.

We went home extremely disappointed, feeling we should have and could have done better. We were having more than our share of stupid problems and would need to sharpen our act if we wished to continue our racing success.

I discovered in writing this section that the Chief Scrutineer had been Alf Briggs, who in his younger days had been a very strong competitor in grass and road racing events. At the age of 50 in 1962 he had been appointed as the first Englishman to join the UK arm of Honda, or Hondis as it was called then. The company of Hondis was based in Nottingham and Alf Briggs was responsible for writing up the Honda instruction manuals for the UK. Later I would be dealing with Alf myself, when building the Honda TL 200 trial bikes in 1980. Alf stayed with Honda for 30 years, retiring at the age of 80. He was the oldest employee of Honda and highly respected in Japan and was on personal terms with Mr. Honda himself. Alf celebrated his 90th birthday in March 2003.

Our next event was the national at Brands Hatch, held on the 2.65 mile Grand Prix circuit, 19th April. The sidecar 1200cc scratch race had attracted Vincent, Boddice, Harris, Greenwood, Hanks, Birch, Thurgood and a fast improving Terry Vinicombe. Most competitors now had either 650 or 750cc motors so it was just as well that we had the 650 Dunstall Norton. Allocated race number 1, and on the front row of the grid we made a good start in the 8 lap dash. As described in 'Motorcycle' we made a full-blooded effort to hold Chris Vincent often sideways through Paddock Bend, but our outfit was not quite up to Vincent's superb 650 BSA, so once again we finished second

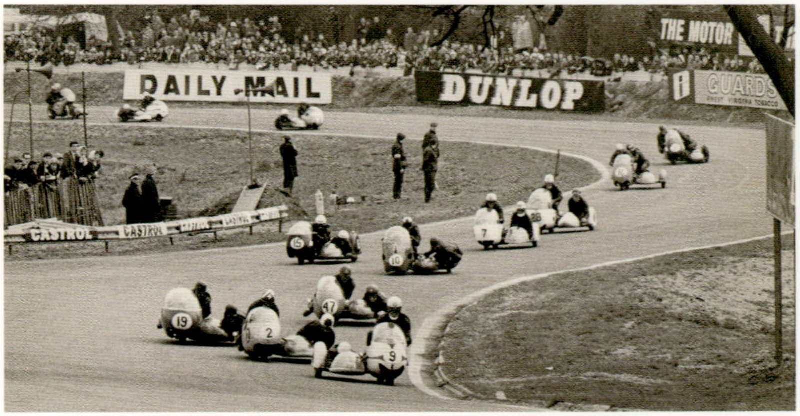

Mallory Park group action.

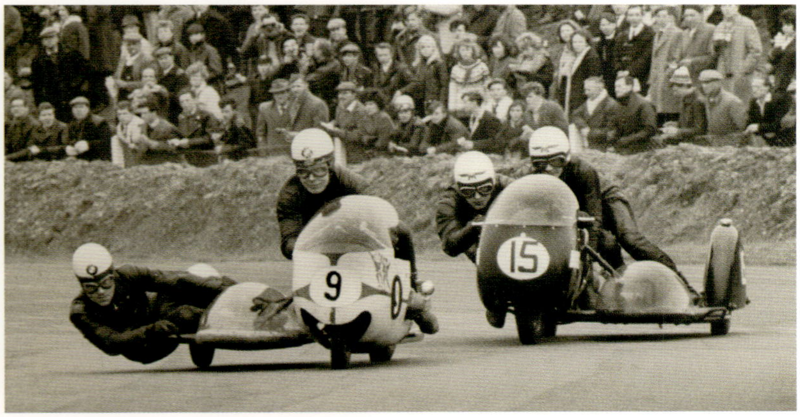

Max Deubel holding us off, 500cc race at Mallory Park.

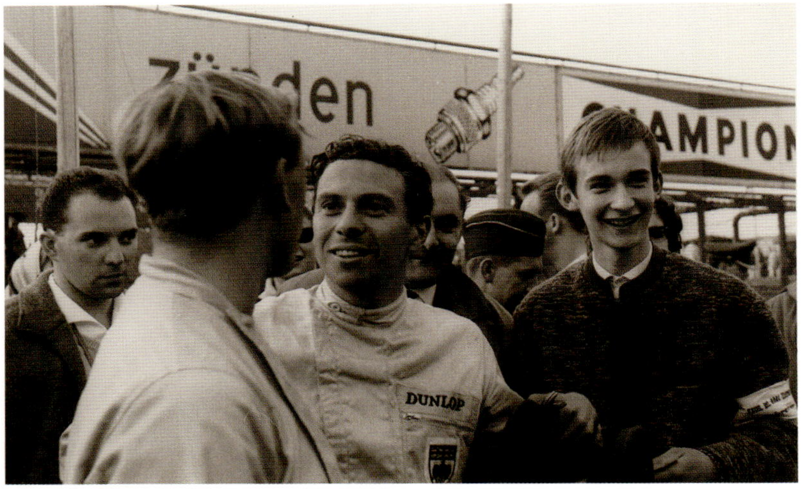

Jim Clark, winner, F2 car race Nürburgring.

to the 'Brummie' but beat Bill Boddice on his 750 Norton with Pip Harris fourth. So all in all, it was a satisfactory day, £215s entry fee, £30 start money, £18 prize money, from which Paul Dunstall was paid his commission of £9.

Of course whilst all this racing activity was taking place I still had a business to run, motorcycles to sell and repair, spares and accessories to be ordered, and decisions to be made! We simply did not have any spare time, as the following weekend would be our first European event of the season, a West German international held at the 7.75 km Nürburgring circuit on the 26th April 1964. This was a combined motorcycle and car meeting. 35 chairs were entered, including the usual stars plus a certain Klaus Enders!

The Formula 2 car race entry was impressive with the legendary Jim Clark in attendance, supported by his Lotus team mates Mike Spence and Peter Procter. Richard Attwood was driving for Lola, Alan Rees and Jochen Rindt driving for Brabham. Jochen, later in his career, would be managed by Bernie Ecclestone.

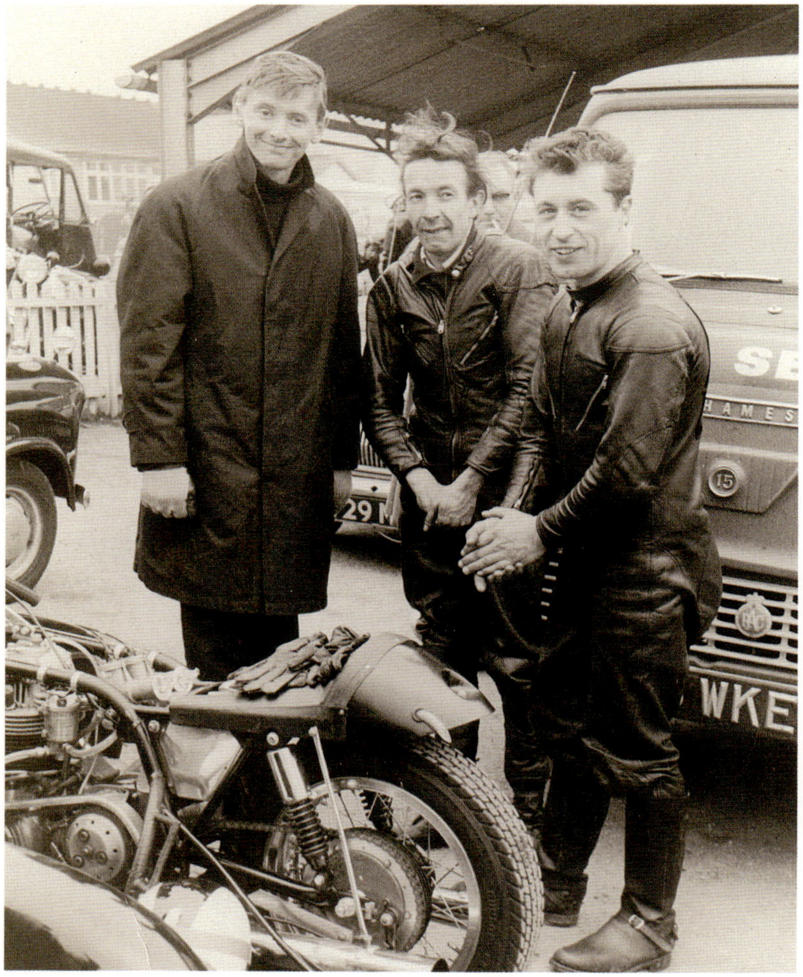

A happy Paul Dunstall after our second place at Brands.

The conditions at the circuit were freezing. I remember having a stinker of a cold and certainly it was not pleasant sleeping in the van, which was more like a fridge, so when our Swiss friend offered us accommodation in a local hotel, we accepted without hesitation. Ernst, who raced 350 and 500cc Nortons, also had a 250 Cotton which was carried on its side on the roof-rack of his van. As we drove out of the circuit courtyard and through a small low tunnel entrance, he completely forgot about the Cotton. The impact took the whole lot clean off. Amazingly, both roof rack and Cotton came off horizontally and landed straight down and undamaged. What a laugh! Ernst who I nicknamed 'Swiss twit', was such a comedian.

In the sidecar race itself, despite my stinking cold, I made one of our better starts on the Matchless G50, leading Deubel and Scheidegger on the first of the 10 lap race. My head cleared immediately and the cold was forgotten. Finally, we dropped back to sixth spot behind the BMW brigade, then the engine seized and that was that - another disappointment, luck seemed to have deserted us.

The following weekend was the Austrian Grand Prix at Salzburg, a 5.1km race on the autobahn, basically up one side and down the other. This event did not count towards the world championship but still attracted all the top chariot teams along with the solo boys. Schneider rode a works Suzuki, Rosner an MZ. Robb, Driver, Anscheidt, Hartle, Ahearn, Young, Shorey, Stasny and Findlay were all there. Sid Mizen was riding his 350, 500cc Nortons and our 250cc Greeves Silverstone. Bill Smith was another in the Continental Circus at that time. The 'joker of the pack' was Ernst Weiss. It was at this event that we got to know the local man, racer and farmer Rudi Thalhammer and visited the workshop of Michael Schafleitner, the gearbox 'supremo'.

In practice our problems continued when we lost the sidecar wheel, as the Reynolds chassis could not stand up to the pounding over the cobbles at the turn around section. As Wally was bouncing up and down in the chair, adding more bruising to his skeletal body, the sidecar wheel whizzed past, making it necessary to borrow welding equipment to carry out a repair. Back in business we achieved sixth position in the 51km

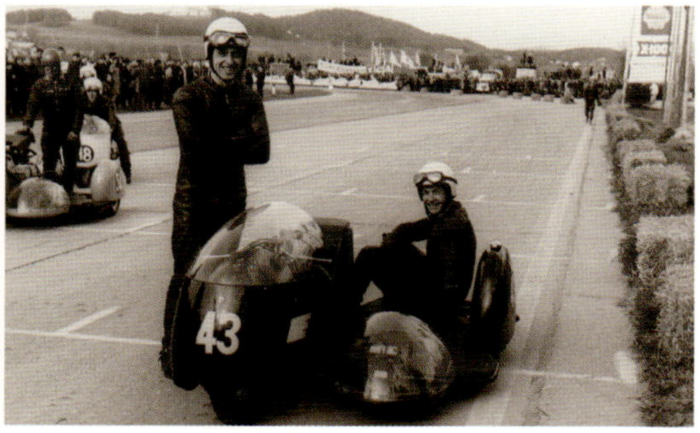

Austrian Grand Prix.

Florian's workshop two days before the French Grand Prix.

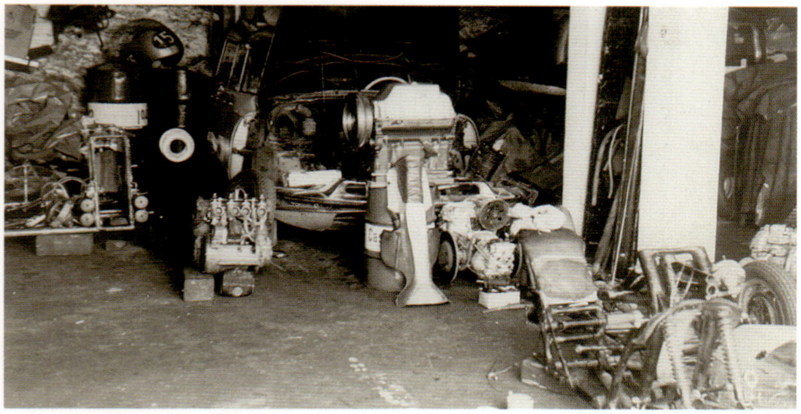

race but again were totally out-gunned by the BMW mounted aces. At that point I was very frustrated, for although the Matchless G50 had served us well for the last three seasons, with Wally and I both pushing the G50 to its absolute limit, often well over-revving. Clearly it was no longer competitive. Most times we were the best placed single cylinder sidecar crew at events and we knew that we had the ability to progress further. I believed that we had followed the likes of the great Eric Oliver, Cyril Smith and Pip Harris in racing a single cylinder machine, a situation I was proud of. We were never daunted by the opposition and our approach to the international and Grand Prix events was just as professional as the best. A little bit of trumpet blowing, but that's how we felt.

In the last race of the day, Ernst Weiss crashed his Norton in the 500cc event and apart from receiving a good shaking, broke his collarbone. Unfortunately, most of the circus was leaving that evening for the long overnight drive to St. Wendel in Germany for the followings day's practice. With Ernst bandaged up he was laid in the back of Trevor Barnes' caravanette for the journey. I took the controls of Ernst's van, loaded with race bikes and Wally drove our wagon, in convoy. Arriving bleary eyed next morning at St. Wendel, Ernst who was quite poorly, instructed us to take him to the home of a friend, who would be able to look after him. With Ernst settled, we went off to see what St. Wendel was about. The circuit turned out to be a 3.78 km dash around the town and past the shops, a tricky one, but it would suit our style.

This meeting was like a United Nations event with riders from England, Canada, Germany, Switzerland, Austria, Ireland, Isle of Man, South Africa, USA, Holland, Italy, Australia, New Zealand and Denmark. Having qualified well for the 20 lap race, hassling Florian Camathias BMW in the practice, it was imperative to get a good start. So with the narrow race grid congested with 23 starters and because it was a down hill start I suggested to Wally that I would stay on the bike and he could push. Well, best laid plans as they say, as the flag dropped flyweight Wally pushed for all he was worth but we hardly moved. I leapt off and joined in the pushing whilst most of the other competitors zoomed off around us. What a total cock-up, although we finally finished seventh behind the BMW-mounted troops, redeeming ourselves somewhat. Although just out of the prize money, £50 start money was some consolation.

Our friend Ernst Weiss was very unwell with a high temperature so we decided not to rush home, even though we were competing at Snetterton the next weekend. We then received a request from Florian Camathias to join him in a local restaurant for an evening meal, very nice we thought, yes we would be delighted. Well, as it turned out we were more than delighted, in fact ecstatic! Florian offered us the use of his Fath-tuned Rennsport FCS outfit. The plan was for us to ride shot-gun to support Florian in in his attempt to win that year's World Sidecar Championship, racing with the Gilera four. How could we refuse. This was an unbelievable offer coming at just the right time. Wally and I had both been feeling downcast regarding our racing future.

We certainly felt privileged that such a star as Camathias thought we were good enough to support his challenge. The sun was shining, we were so excited and could not wait to get home to spread the news. This was the chance that we had been looking for. The gloom lifted!

We would not make the Spanish Grand Prix that following weekend on the 10th May, as we were already committed to ride at Snetterton. We would join Florian in Switzerland immediately after that event giving us a few days before the French Grand Prix at Clermont-Ferrand, which would be our first event.

Finally, back home, although elated we were feeling knackered with all the travelling and racing. Work was now needed to prepare the G50 and Dunstall Domiracer for Snetterton that weekend, Wally and I always carried out the work ourselves. Snetterton was already the eleventh event that season and it was still only early May. It came and went with a third in the 500cc race and when heading for a win in the 1200cc class on the Dunstall Domi, the engine blew up. The gremlins were still with us.

Then it was the serious stuff, the forthcoming French Grand Prix. We were like a couple of excited schoolboys. With our luggage packed with race leathers and clean underwear we departed from Heathrow for Geneva and then caught the train to Montreux situated at the opposite end of the lake. We arrived at Florian's home town of Montreux on the Tuesday evening. Florian arriving back from Barcelona in high spirits, having won the Spanish Grand Prix with the Gilera four, he had made a great start. We had never ridden a BMW before, so Florian planned that we would test at a circuit in

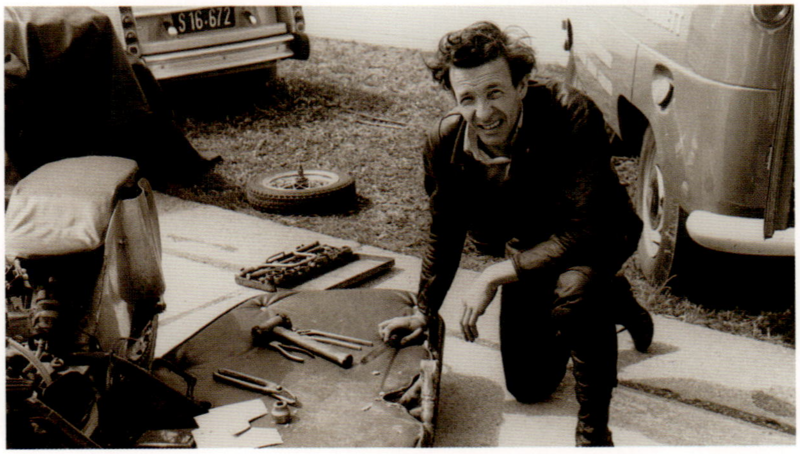

Wally helping with repairs to the sidecar wheel.

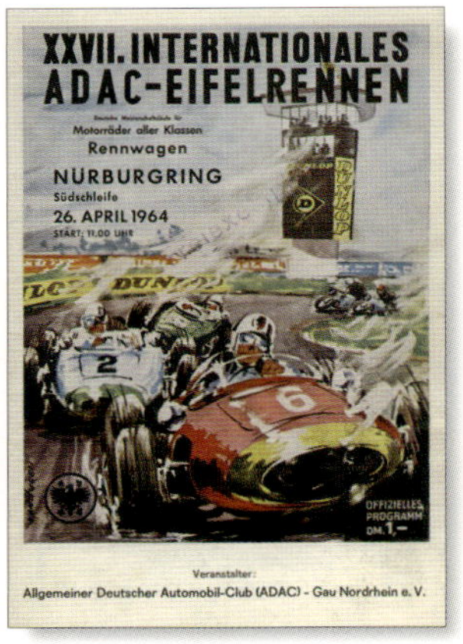

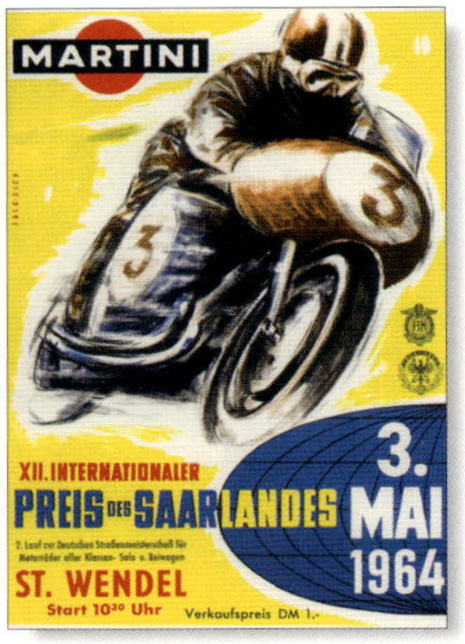

Germany before leaving for Clermont-Ferrand later that week. Well, that was never to happen as the Rennsport was in a dismantled state and required the gear linkage to be changed over. Florian also had the Gilera outfit stripped down and was carrying out some maintenance on his race transporter. On Wednesday nothing much seemed to be happening, people were calling into his workshop to say hello, then it was over to the local hotel by the lake for lunch - all very pleasant but we were not on holiday. Only Thursday was left to complete all the work. Friday was the first day of practice for the French Grand Prix. Thursday turned into a 'frenzy' in an effort to get all the work done and a late night, before all was loaded into the two special Camathias-converted estate car transporters. An early morning start was scheduled for the difficult cross country 200 mile drive to Clermont-Ferrand. When we arrived, the practice had already started so we had to take a back route to get anywhere near the pit area, and we had to wait until a session had finished to trickle down to the pits. As we waited, Florian holding his head said to Wally, 'I've got a headache', hardly surprising after the last two days hectic activity, what a man!

The 5 mile Clermont-Ferrand circuit, 2,500 feet above sea level has 51 bends, many acute and following each other in a succession of lefts and rights, uphill and down, often with a sheer drop on one side and a wall of rock on the other, was no place to master racing a Rennsport for the first time. Fellow countryman Chris Vincent, BMW had put up a good time in practice and was on the front row of the grid with Max Deubel. Not far behind were Scheidegger, Camathias, Auerbacher, Kolle and then ourselves followed by the rest of the field.

Race day dawned bright, hot and cloudless. With no 350 or 500cc events, the first of the day was the 125cc. One noteworthy non-starter was Alan Shepherd who had broken his collarbone in two places when his 125cc MZ seized in practice. From the start of the 13 lap race Anderson, Suzuki, was to hold a slim lead over Taveri, Honda, who was chased by Schneider, Suzuki, Redman, Honda, and Perris, Suzuk,i but Anderson was soon out when the Suzuki engine died. Schneider took the lead, but Taveri was soon back in front with a lap record, and that's how it stayed with Frank Perris third.

Then it was the incredible 50cc 'tiddlers' race, won by Hugh Anderson, Suzuki, from his close rival Hans-Georg Anscheidt, Kreidler.

The last solo race of the day, the 16 lap 250cc, would have Tarquinio Provini as a non-starter, having wrecked engines in both of his Benellis. The race would be a hotly contested event between the two main protagonists Phil Read, Yamaha, and champion Jim Redman, Honda. For the first 6 laps it was Read then Redman leading, pulling well away from Luigi Taveri, Honda, in third, with a tussle between Anderson, Frank Perris, Bert Schneider and the rest. Then halfway, Redman was forced into a pit-stop with the Honda four running on only two cylinders and that was his race run. Phil Read won his first race ever for Yamaha with the little Swiss ace Taveri in second place and Bert Schneider, Suzuki, making up the rostrum positions. Our Swiss 'twit' Ernst Weiss' Aermacchi, came in fifth. Then it was our turn and with our 'L' plates thrown away, we were ready for the 13 lap - 65 mile roller coaster race. As the flag dropped, Max Deubel made a head start over Chris Vincent who was determined to show who was boss on the day, by forcing himself into the lead but Scheidegger was right up with them, with a fast approaching Camathias on the Gilera four soon making four outfits in close formation. Not far behind we were having our own scuffle with Georg Auerbacher and Otto Kolle. On the fifth lap Chris Vincent went out and Scheidegger took the lead from Deubel. Whilst fanatical Florian soon gained second place from Deubel, we then got the better of Auerbacher and Kolle and started to reduce the gap between ourselves and Max Deubel. Scheidegger was troubled by petrol flooding from the carburettors onto the kneeler tray, saturating a still-raw wound on his knee. Camathias took the lead, heading for his second Grand Prix win with the Gilera powered outfit, when with only one lap to go he broke down and Scheidegger took back first place.

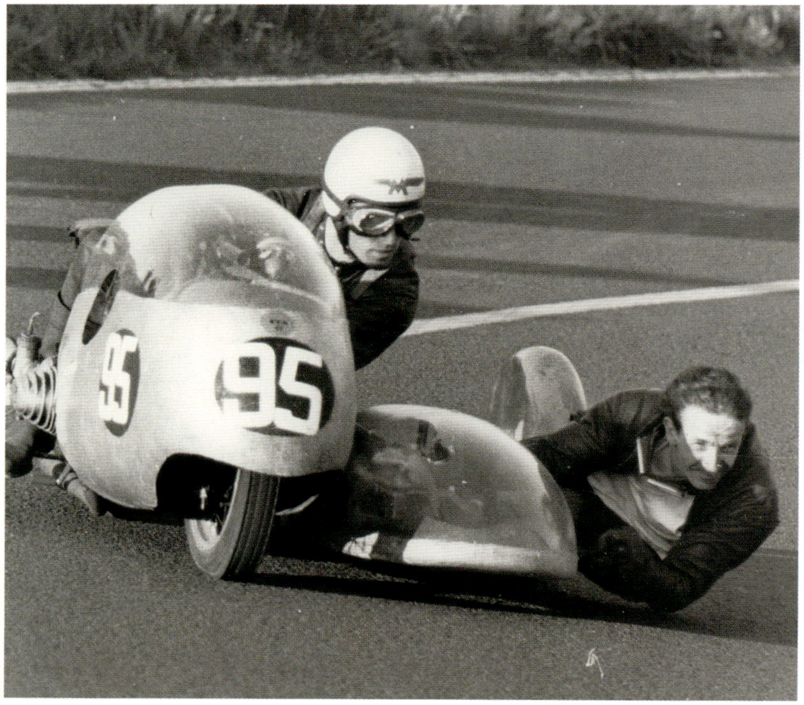

Where's his bloody hat gone?

Tommy Bowers from Dunlop with Franta Stastny, French Grand Prix.

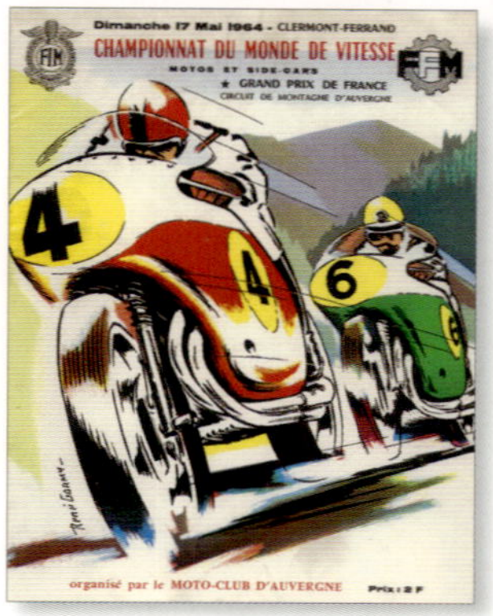

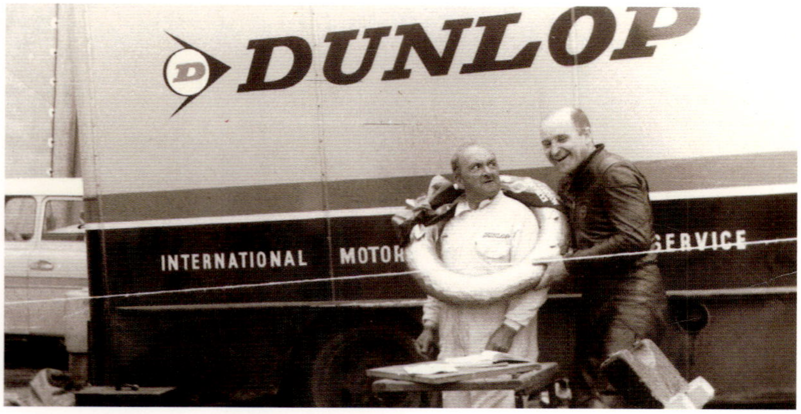

Meanwhile back in third, we were having our own drama. After one of the most hectic rides of our career, during one of the swift changeovers from left to right, Wally's helmet strap came loose and the helmet went flying down the mountainside. At the next left-hander I took a look at Wally hanging out and to my bewilderment he had no hat, I could almost hear Michael Cain in his cockney accent saying, 'Where's his bloody hat gone'. I remembered our early days on the A20, when Wally always rode without a helmet so I knew he would not worry, and with only a couple of laps to go, was it worth stopping? But out came the black flag, forcing us to pull into the pits for a replacement helmet. We had a quick angry discussion, then somebody plonked Sid Mizen's hat onto Wally's head and off we went, losing only one place to Georg Auerbacher and finishing in fourth. This was slightly disappointing when a third place in our first Grand Prix riding the BMW would have been so terrific. We collected our 900 francs of start and prize money, half of which we gave to Florian towards the upkeep of the BMW. It was a quick packing job as Brands Hatch beckoned next day for the International Whit Monday meeting.

There was the usual overnight drive to Le Touquet for the Airferry to arrive at Brands Hatch mid-morning. A fresh Pip Harris, BMW won the 12 lap sidecar scratch race with Chris Vincent second, Fritz Scheidegger third and ourselves fourth. That would do, as this had been our thirteenth race meeting since March 22nd. We had hardly been at home, where my son, my wife and my business beckoned.

We then heard the news that Florian had an accident on his way home to Montreux after the French Grand Prix. His love of animals caused an effort to miss a roaming deer on a mountain road. He crashed his Citroen Estate transporter. The vehicle containing the Gilera outfit rolled down the bank resulting in damage and injury to Florian, who suffered broken ribs. Nevertheless shaken but not stirred he would soon arrive at the Isle of Man TT for his next performance - you could not keep the bespectacled 40 year old Swiss racer down!

In the 10 days available after Brands, we decided to strip, check, repaint and rebuild the Camathias-owned FCS-BMW outfit in preparation for our fourth Isle of Man TT event. Certainly on paper this would be our best chance for success, so we did not need any problems. Arriving in the 'Magic Isle', the smoke signals were already out and our host Ma Clucas, Guinness in hand, would be ready to greet her boys.

Our friend and sponsor Florian Camathias finally arrived in the Island looking a bit second-hand from his road crash, with his ribs bandaged. As a requirement to ride in the TT races, competitors needed a doctor's certificate, so, unknown to the organisers, Florian signed his own.

The first practice, Tuesday evening, 2nd June, was a miserable session with persistent rain. Here we were with the machine on which Camathias had won the TT sidecar event in 1963, and it was raining. Despite a pit stop to change plugs, we were the only crew to complete the 3 lap race distance and third fastest behind Deubel and Auerbacher - a fair start. Florian and passenger Alfred Herzig completed only one exploratory lap on the Gilera, and did not figure on the leading board. Tragically, newcomers to the Island, Tony Baitup and passenger Brian Cockell crashed their Norton outfit on the first lap at Braddan Bridge. 23 year old Cockell from Bexleyheath, died as a result. For the Wednesday night practice the weather conditions were totally opposite. It had been a hot and sunny day and the evening conditions were just right. I remember proudly wheeling the FCS-BMW to the start line. The sun was still shining and so was our silver painted outfit. After our refurbishment work it looked just magnificent. Many comments were made as to our presentation and that surely we must now be in with a real chance of winning our first TT. Beating the likes of previous TT winners Max Deubel and Florian Camathias or Fritz Scheidegger who had finished second twice, would not be an easy task and I would not risk all to achieve it. Nine-tenths effort and commitment at the TT was always my strategy.

I just loved those evening practices, and despite 50 outfits competing, a clear untroubled 2 lap run resulted in a second place on the leader board, behind Deubel/Horner the German aces, with Auerbacher third and Camathias fourth, having lost his passenger Alfred Herzig who jumped back in unhurt at Governors dip, and the Gilera suffering a gearbox problem.

The next sidecar practice was scheduled for early next morning. Awoken by the alarm at some unearthly hour, I peered out into the darkness and the heavy rain. A decision was made to stay in bed, which was just as well. The session was cancelled.

Friday evening would be the last sidecar practice, at which Scheidegger would head

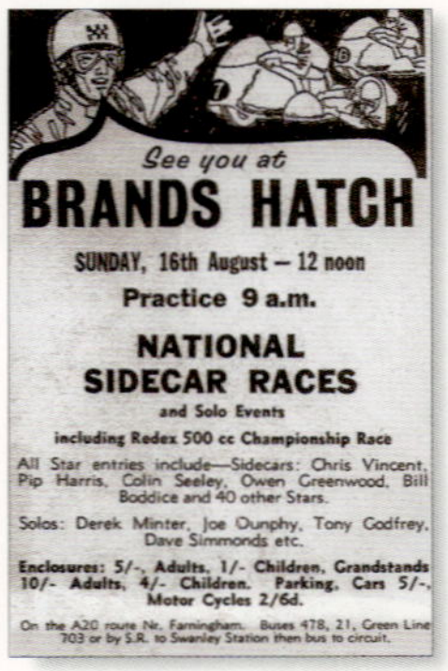

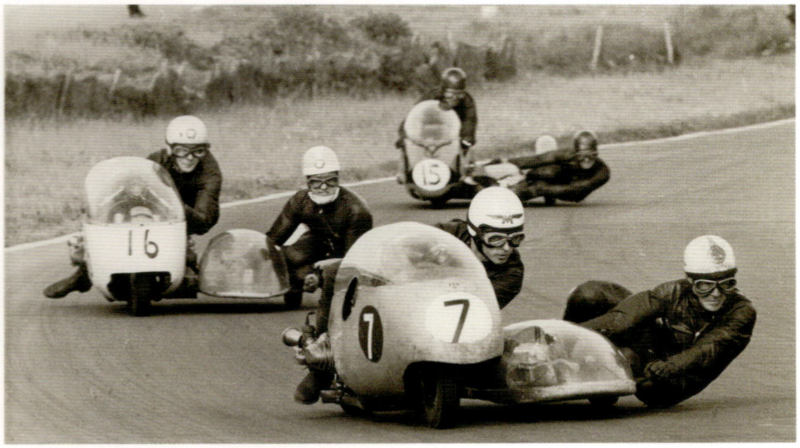

Fourth place at Brands, Wally wearing Sid Mizen's helmet.

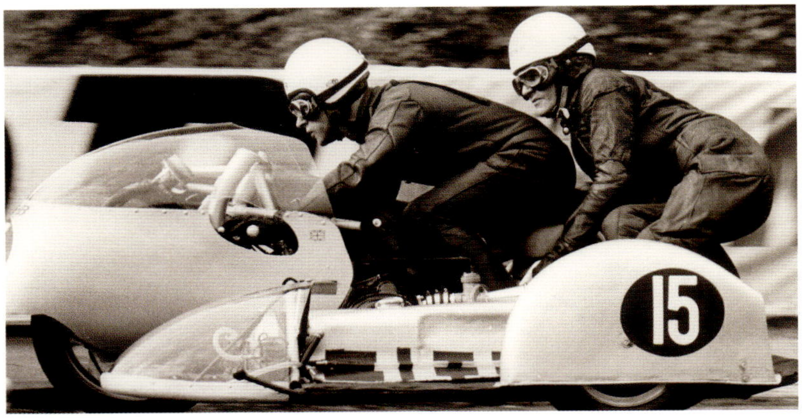

Last TT practice, Friday evening.

the list, although over 18 seconds down on our time from Wednesday night. Camathias was in trouble with a misfire. Chris Vincent was also having trouble and after only one lap we joined in with the lack of a second gear. Nevertheless, we had posted the second fastest time of the week and now felt confident with the FCS-BMW. Florian's troubles continued, and when working on the Gilera he had a fire incident from which he suffered burns to his forehead.

Apart from our own TT entry under the C.J. Seeley (Sales) Ltd banner we were supporting Sid Mizen racing our 250cc Greeves and Norman Huntingford with Pete Essery on the Matchless-Watsonian outfit.

After the obligatory machine check and Sunday weigh-in for the next day's race, we did a final lap of the TT circuit in our van, accompanied by Norman Huntingford and Peter Essery. I was trying to help them both with advice in riding this challenging course. I remember pointing out that there was no pressure on them, as there was on us with the expectations of success by our supporters. On arriving at Ballaugh Bridge, 17 miles out from the start I said to them both that although it was a fast approach to this first gear hump-backed bridge, it was better to come in a little slower and not leap the bridge, landing heavily. Then once over, accelerate hard, but in control. We then completed our tour, no more could be done.

The 3 lap 113.2 mile sidecar race with a 11.00am start would kick off the TT week, with a record entry of 56 charioteers, although non-starters had reduced the field to 46 which was still a record. As in the last three years, we had enjoyed the hospitality of Frances Clucas and the admiration of our fans from Strang who would all be cheering at their vantage point at Union Mills. This was the big one. How things had changed for us, we were now accepted as serious contenders. However part of our unwritten agreement with Florian was to support him on the track in his effort to win a World Sidecar Championship. I was therefore concerned as to what to do if we were ahead of him in the race. With 10 second start intervals and us starting one minute behind, it could get complicated. Anyway Florian said, 'Don't worry, just run your own race.'

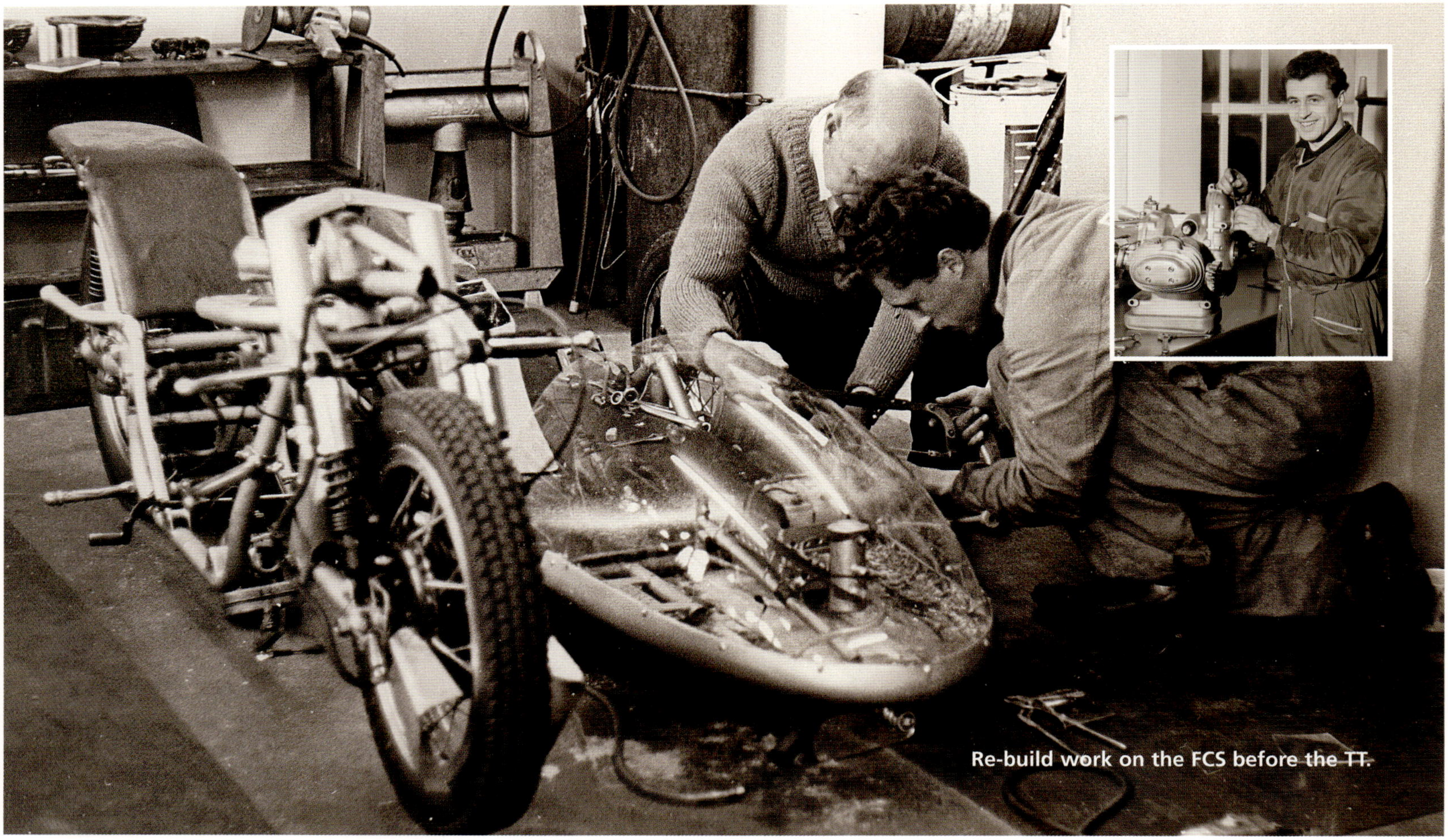

Re-build work on the FCS before the TT.

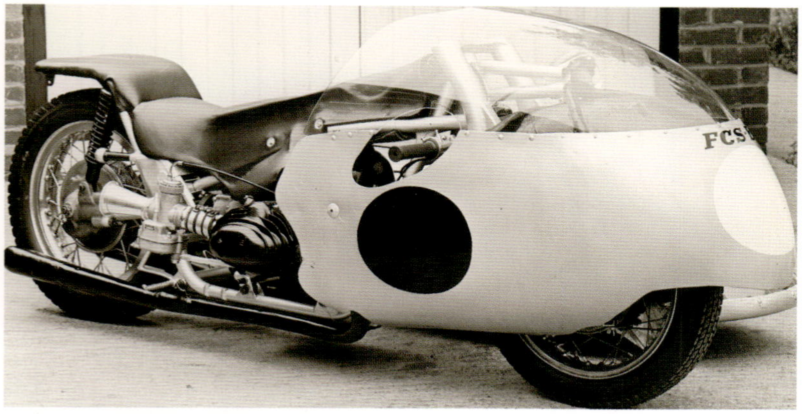

FCS rebuilt!

At the start we changed into our racing leathers and nervously exchanged pleasantries with other riders, mechanics and friends. The 10.30am warm up siren sounded. At 10.45am the siren blasted again for silence. The charioteers assembled on the grid in their allocated order. At 10.55am the 5 minutes maroon fired - no turning back. 11.00am the flag drops and Alan Birch, BMW, with Fred Hanks, Norton, open the 1964 TT races, followed 10 seconds later by Auerbacher, BMW, and Camathias with the Gilera four sounding fantastic as it left the line. Kolle, Scheidegger, Deubel also started in front of us. Only 90 seconds after the first starters, we are off alongside our old adversary Charlie Freeman, Norton. Swooping down Bray Hill 'in anger' for the first time on the FCS-BMW was breathtaking and my full concentration was needed. Camathias was at Ballacraine leading on the road by 4 seconds ahead of Georg Auerbacher. At Ramsey, Florian was half a minute ahead of Georg but only 5 seconds in front of Max Deubel, but by the end of the first lap Max was in front by around 4 seconds, Fritz third, Wally and I holding fourth place, despite a problem still with second gear.

Further back on that first lap our friends Norman Huntingford and Pete Essery, starting 4 minutes behind had caught a bunch of riders before Ballaugh Bridge. Norman was on a charge, having made up 1 minute 20 seconds on competitor Mick Potter when approaching Ballaugh Bridge, the very part of the 37.73 mile TT course which I had advised him on. With a number of outfits basically queuing to take the bridge, it appeared Norman went down the inside and collided with Mick Potter, causing a horrific accident from which his passenger, Peter Essery sustained serious head injuries and a broken arm. He never recovered, dying in hospital, paying a hugh price for such a mistake by Norman, who along with the other crews suffered superficial injuries.

On the start of the last lap Florian was still ahead on the road, but on corrected time Deubel had it by 12 seconds and with Fritz out, we were in third, well ahead of Kolle and Auerbacher. At the bungalow Florian and Max were together, then approaching Keppel Gate the Gilera outfit faltered, the engine dying caused by fuel starvation. So the race was in the bag for Max whilst Florian, never the man to give up, freewheeled down the descent to Creg-ny-Baa. Fiddling with fuel lines, trying to bring his Gilera back to life, at the right hand Creg-ny-Baa corner, Florian misjudged his coasting speed and ran straight into the steep bank smashing the race screen and tipping passenger Herzig out onto the road causing him a badly grazed elbow. Collecting themselves, they pushed off again, fortunately it was still slightly downhill at that point. As we flashed by at speed on our way to Brandish I wondered what Florian's thoughts would be as the Belvedere Boys, troubled only with a second gear problem but otherwise enjoying a incident-free race, took Florian's second place position riding the very outfit on which Florian himself had won the 1963 TT event.

The chequered flag was in sight and second place was ours, although averaging 86.76mph and 2 minutes behind Max Deubel, who recorded a winning time of 89.12mph, we were over 2 minutes in front of third man Georg Auerbacher, at 84.45mph, who was heard to say, 'That gentleman Seeley was very fast.' We were jubilant and Wally Rawlings as always, had performed with smooth precision. Our place promoted us to joint fifth in the World Championship, this second position followed our third place rostrum position in 1962 riding our faithful Matchless G50, which with an average speed of 82.8mph, would have given us still a good fifth position in today's racing.

A fast improving Terry Vinicombe, Triumph on the leader board with a fifth place, at 97.01mph, would join me some years later to work on the Seeley racers.

Then as we celebrated in the winners' enclosure, tremendous applause broke out and the grandstand crowd rose to their feet. A small figure pushing a red and white Gilera outfit appeared - Camathias, aided by an injured Alfred Herzig. The gallant pair had pushed in for some 3 miles, to finish fifteenth and be awarded the last of the bronze replicas. Although 15 minutes behind Max, Florian still averaged 74.48mph. Florian with his cracked ribs and exhausted from the race effort, not to mention his fire-damaged forehead, should have been awarded a bravery medal. His dedication to the sport was an inspiration to all.

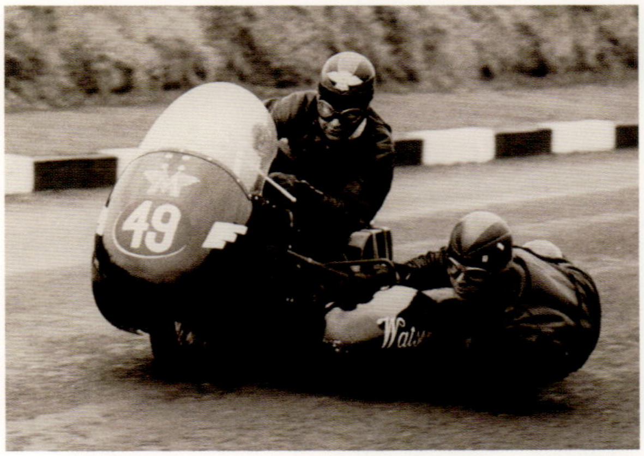

Norman Huntingford.

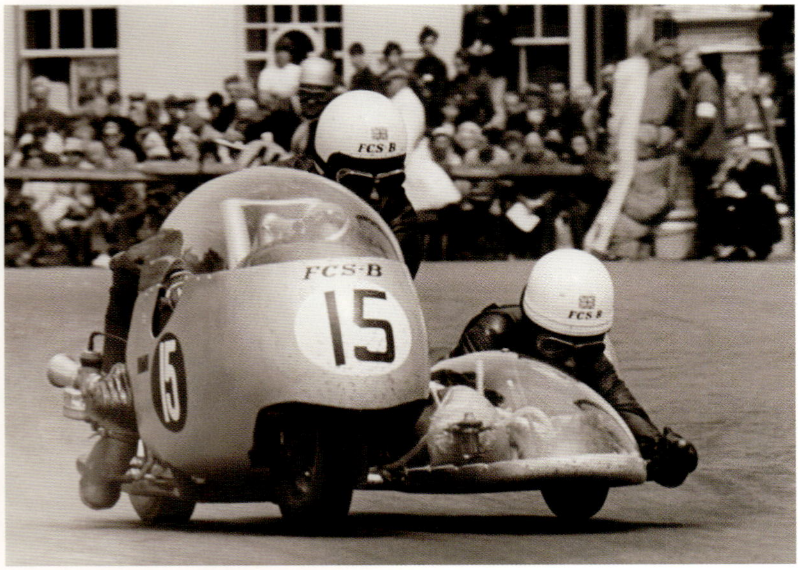

Coming out of Ramsey.

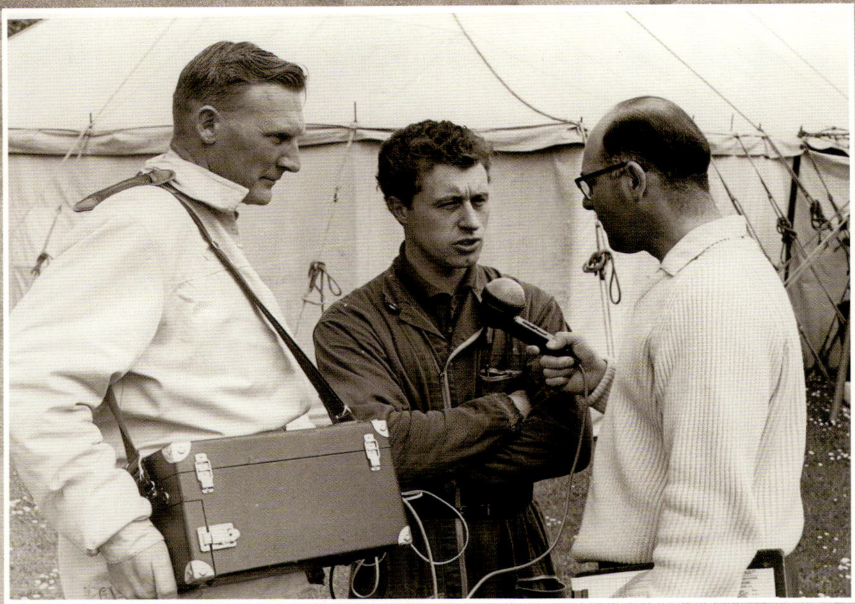

Murray Walker, TT interview.

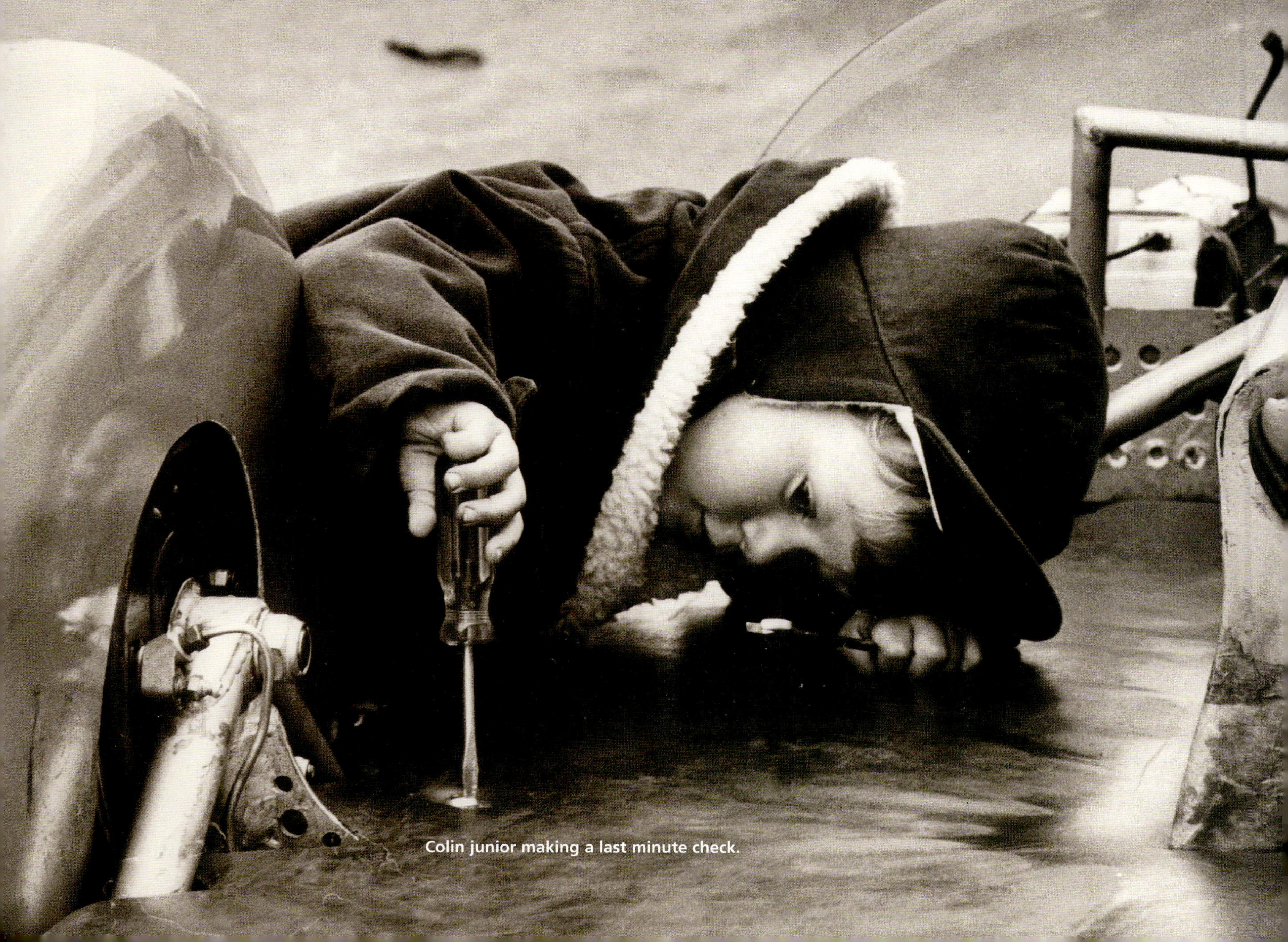

Colin junior making a last minute check.

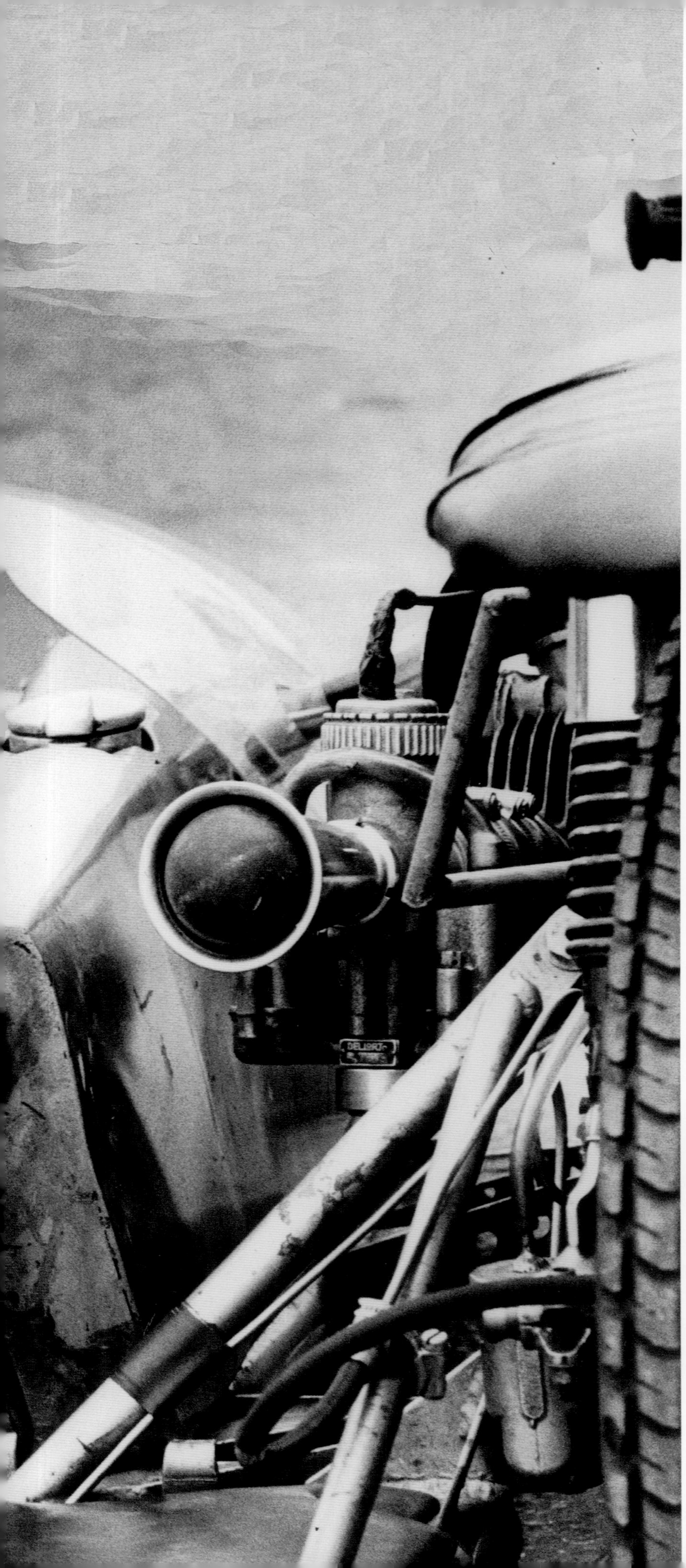

Camathias at Governors, on the lap before he broke down.

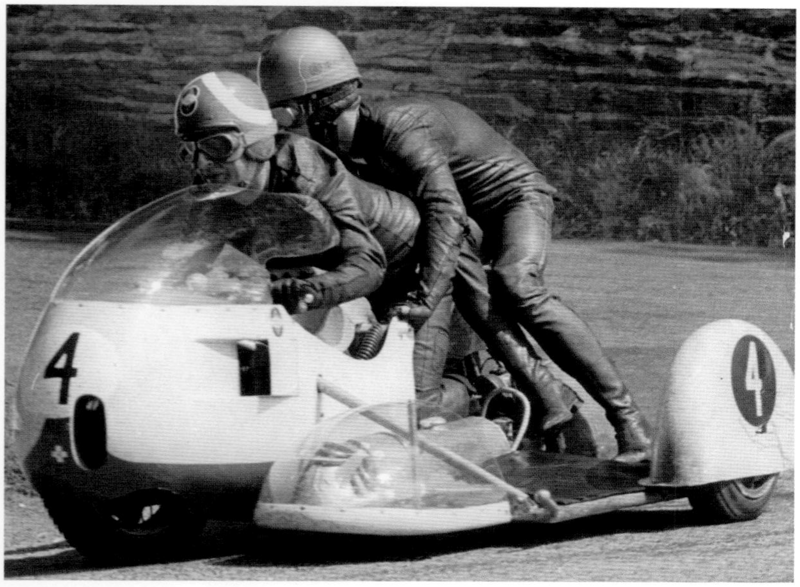

Financially this event had been our best to date; Start Money £25, Prize Money £84, Castrol Bonus £130, Girling Bonus £20, Hepolite Bonus £15, Ferodo Bonus £20, less payment made to Camathias £65, left us with £224.

As we enjoyed the immediate accolade we were unaware of Norman Huntingford's crash. A while later the information came through of the seriousness of the situation, putting an immediate damper on the proceedings. Motorcycle road racing can be likened to a portion of sweet and sour, when it's sweet it's very sweet but when sour often it's bitter with some very high prices to pay.

Following our sidecar race would be the 6 lap 250cc race with a 1.30pm start. From 95 entrants, non-starters had reduced the field to 65. The race would be a Jim Redman benefit, after Phil Read, Yamaha, his nearest challenger, though fastest in practice and riding like a demon, was forced to retire with spark plug problems, but not before setting the fastest lap at 99.42mph. All the other top runners, Provini, Ahearn, Schneider, Taveri, Duff, Robb and Perris fell by the wayside. Alan Shepherd, still recovering from a broken collar bone sustained in practice at the French Grand Prix, was examined by the ACU doctor who was of the opinion that he was unfit to ride. Alan immediately appealed and two days later, a board of doctors gave clearance for him to compete. Good news for Walter Kaaden the MZ team boss, who had travelled 1,000 miles with one mechanic, and four machines from eastern Germany. So what a reward when the tenacious Alan Shepherd brought the works MZ 250cc home in second place at 96.97mph, a brilliant ride with Alan never out of the top three throughout the 226.4 mile race. Alberto Pagani, Paton made up the rostrum positions.

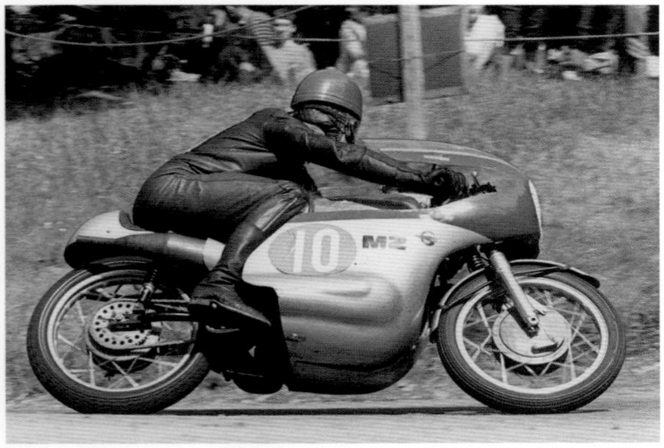

Alan Shepherd, 250cc MZ, second in the TT action.

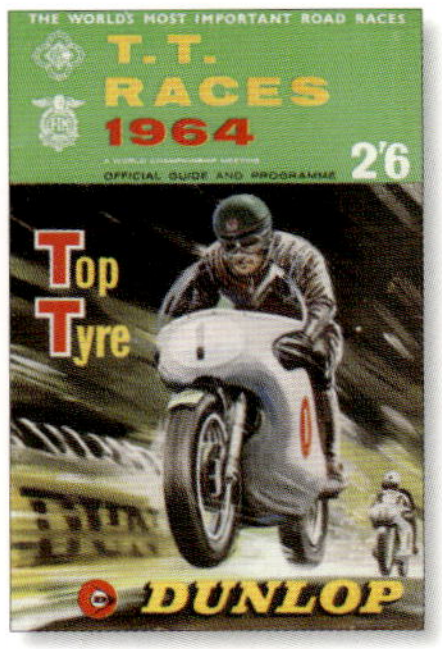

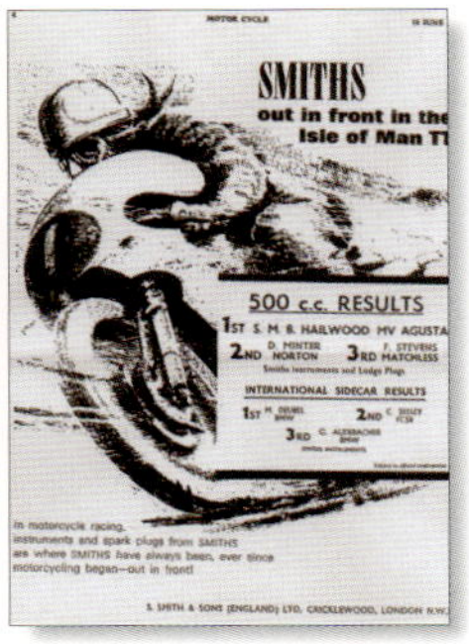

Arriving back at Beverly House, Strang, Ma Clucas was over the moon with our results. The Guinness was already flowing with hands in the air she was dancing around chanting 'My boys, my boys!' Frances Clucas was just great, she kept us fed, watered and entertained with her eccentric ways.

At that evening's presentation at the Villa Marina by the Mayor of Douglas, Jim Redman was heard to say that he was glad Alan Shepherd was riding with a partly mended collar bone, otherwise the race outcome might have been different. With a friendly dig at the unlucky Phil Read who had collected the fastest lap award, Jim attributed his own success to riding a 'reliable' Honda. Max Deubel, unwillingly at the microphone said that he spoke only a little English. Someone shouted, 'He takes some catching in any language!' 'The Belvedere Boys', so proud of our best ever achievement to date, received tremendous applause as we collected our Silver Replicas. Back to reality next day, helping to sort out Norman Huntingford's problems, and ourselves packing for the trip home.

The racing continued that week with the 125cc race held in ideal conditions on the Wednesday morning. Mick Woollett (Motorcycling) described it as one of the closest and most thrilling seen over the mountain course. A total of 60 competitors would start this 3 lap race. It would prove to be a 'battle royal' between the works Suzuki two-strokes of Hugh Anderson, Frank Perris and Bert Schneider and the new Honda eight speed four cylinder machines ridden by Jim Redman, Lugi Taveri and Ralph Bryans. Before the end of the second lap the Suzuki challenge had fallen away, the last of the Suzuki trio Frank Perris touring in to retire. Meantime, there was no letting up at the front with the Swiss ace Taveri getting the verdict by only 3 seconds from Redman, with Bryans third, a complete Honda benefit with a new lap record for Taveri at 94.18mph, his second IOM TT success.

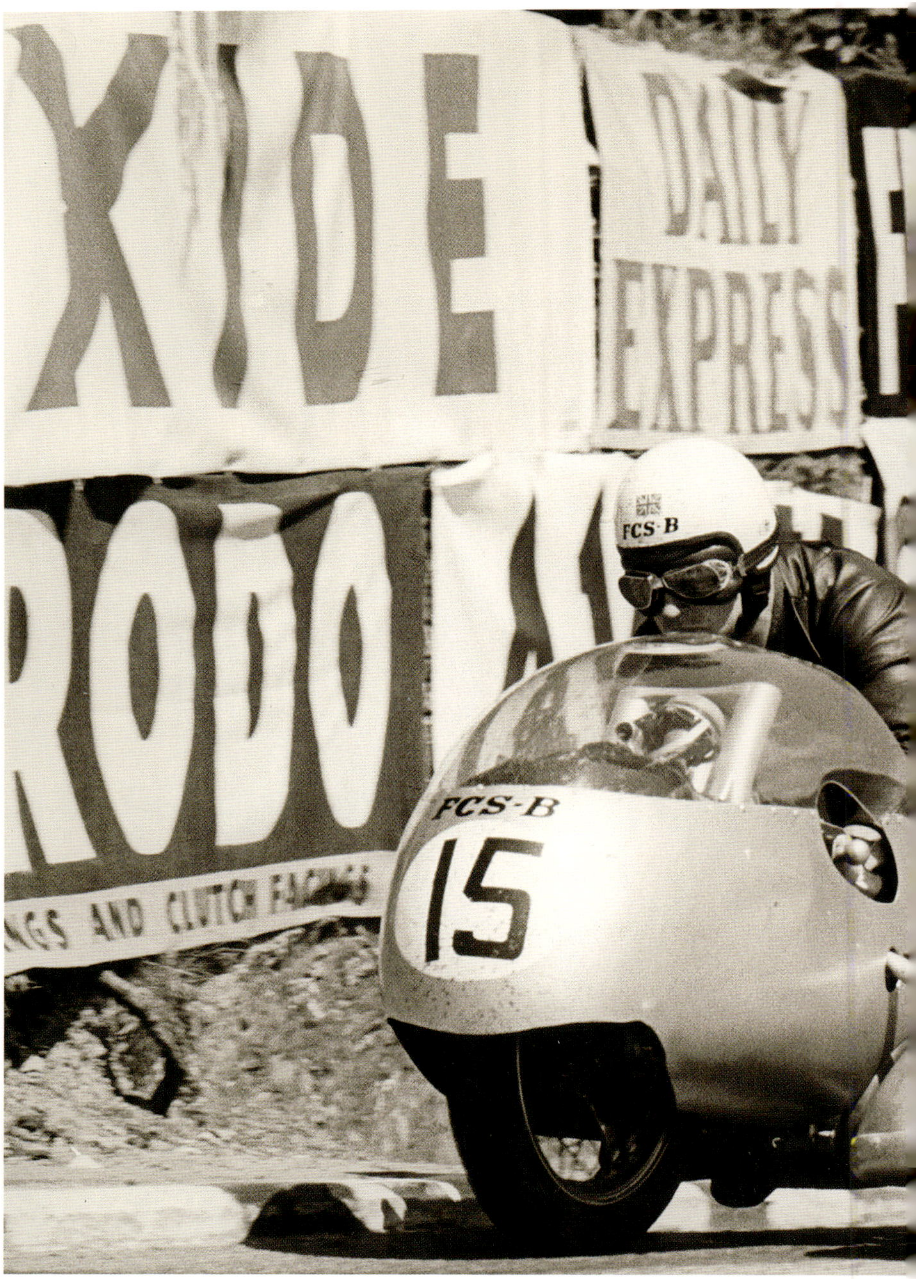

Out of Governors 1964 TT.

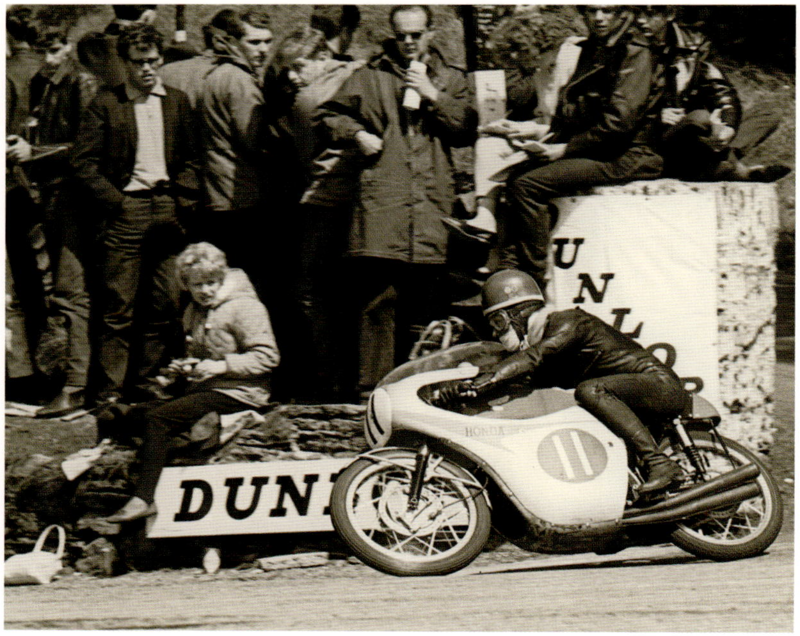

Taveri on his way to winning the 125cc TT.

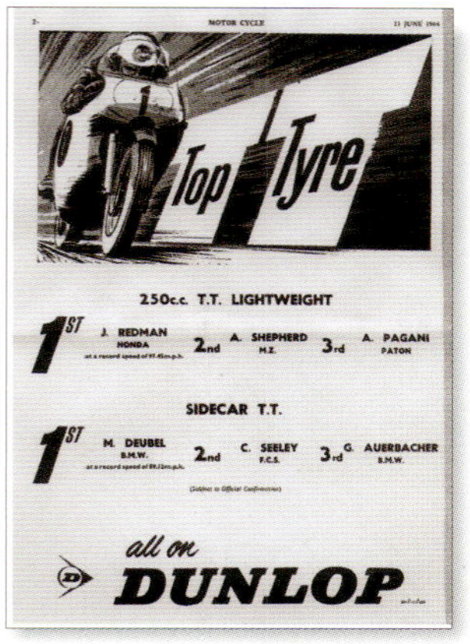

The afternoon 6 lap Junior 350cc race, although with 84 starters would be somewhat uninspired as Mike Hailwood, MV would be a non-starter, having not recovered from his attack of tonsillitis. The race was a runaway victory for Jim Redman, Honda. Derek Minter held third spot until the fourth lap when troubled by a broken inlet valve-spring, let Mike Duff and Phil Read by. It was a dust-up to the finish, with Read, Kirby AJS finally taking the second spot,11.8 seconds ahead of Duff in third. Derek Minter fourth and our man Sid Mizen, AJS, in an excellent eighth spot out of the 52 finishers.

Friday, the last day of TT fortnight, started with the 3 lap 50cc race. Once again the weather was kind, with little wind to knock the peak revs off the tiny engines. The race had only attracted 20 starters but a class field with nine works entries. If 20 machines were spread out around the TT course it would mean one machine every 1.88 miles - boring? not at all! World Champion Hugh Anderson, Suzuki a class act on the midget bikes was soon in the lead followed by team mate Mitsuo Itoh, Anscheidt, Kreidler third. On the second lap Anderson shattered the 80mph barrier lapping at an incredible 81.10mph. Anscheidt was now second and Ralph Bryans on the 20,000rpm Honda twin back in sixth place. With Hugh Anderson well on his way to victory, there was a fantastic

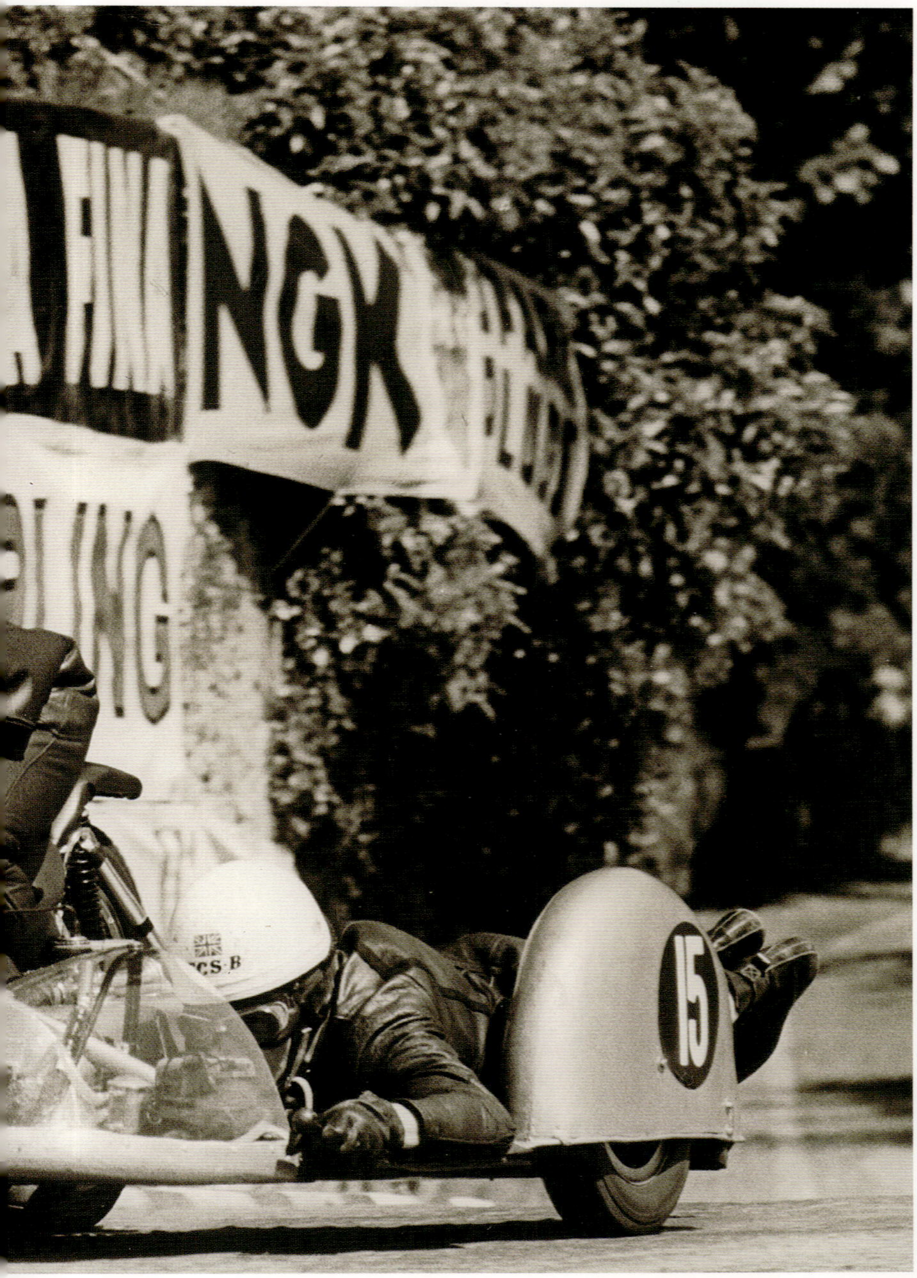

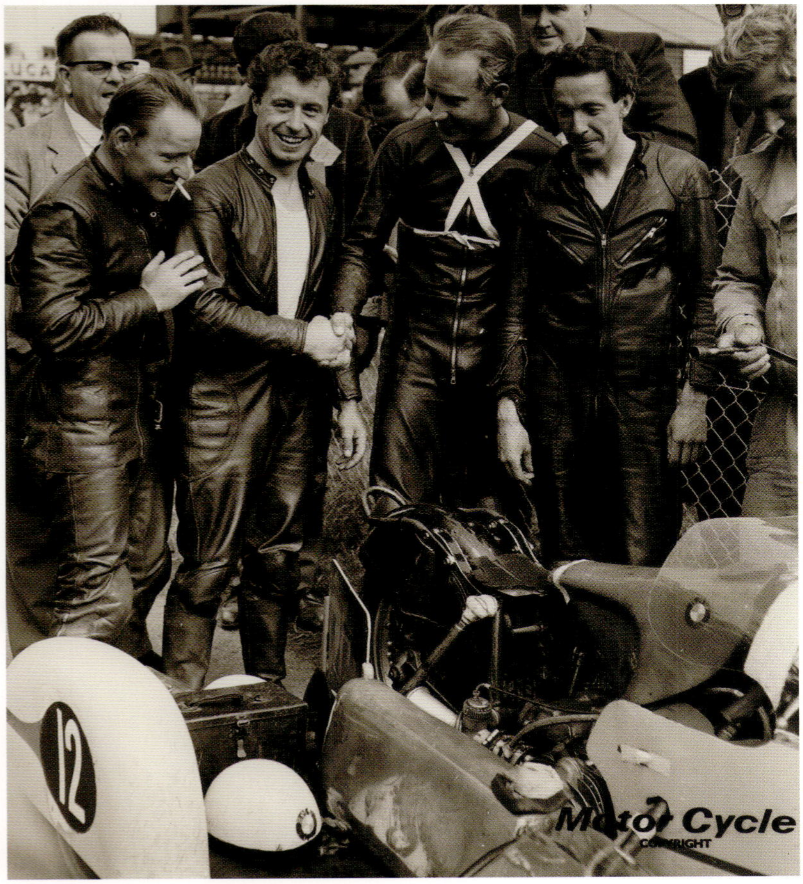

1964 Sidecar TT, congratulating Max Deubel, winner and current World Champion. Emil Horner, left and Wally on the right, we came second.

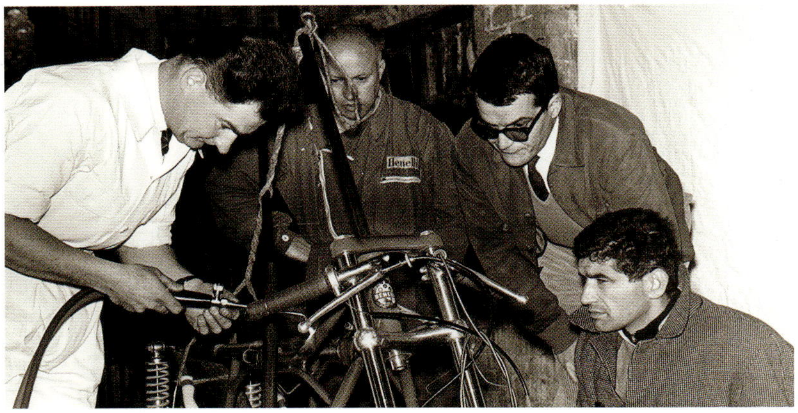

Ken Sprayson, works mechanic, Count Nardi Dei and Tarquinio Provini, with the 250 Benelli.

six man dice for the other positions. At Sulby Bridge Anscheidt still looked favourite but Bryans was making up ground fast on the 'screaming' Honda. Morishita, Suzuki, was trying with all his might to keep up and pushed Anscheidt down to fourth as Anderson won from that 'flying' Ralph Bryans second, Itoh, fifth, Naomi Taniguchi, Honda, sixth, and Luigi Taveri ninth and out of the points. Luigi never really got to grips with the Kreidler and would be back on a Honda 50cc the following year. Dave Simmonds, Tohatsu, was ninth, but well down on top speed, recorded at 88 miles per hour against Anderson's Suzuki at 103.2mph.

Finally, it was the 'big one', the 500cc Senior Race. Despite not being completely fit, Mike Hailwood, MV, would delight his fans by leading the 6 lap race from start to finish. Our friend Sid Mizen on the Dunstall Domiracer, fell at the first hurdle, slipping off unhurt at Quarter Bridge. The usual battle of the other 69 competitors mostly riding singles, was going on behind Mike's MV. With Phil Read out on the first lap, it was between Minter and Duff, then Duff was out and Minter, Norton held second place, unchallenged to the finish. Fred Stevens, Arter Matchless, third and Derek Woodman, Matchless, fourth enjoyed a race-long dice. Another man to watch would be the fast improving John (Mooneyes) Cooper who finished ninth. Mike Hailwood, although looking pale and admitting he felt wobbly, had just won his third Senior TT Race - what a man - another hero of the time!

Despite our own TT success we left the Magic Isle with some sadness. Our friend Norman Huntingford was still in Noble's Hospital recovering from his injuries, whilst Peter Essery would never return to his friends and family - a tragic end to the pair's TT ambitions.

On the return journey aboard the Manx ferry, up on the deck with the sea breeze in my face, I had time to reflect. Was the Isle of Man TT really worth the personal gamble, in fact was any of the road racing worth it? The rewards were mostly poor and the risks immense.

Even friends thought of us as completely bonkers, yet if we had been young fighter pilots in the Battle of Britain we would have been regarded as heroes and awarded medals for success and bravery. It was from the ranks of young racing motorcyclists that many heroes were taken and gave their lives for the country, so who can argue when racers risk their lives for the sport they love? The spirit of youth needs a challenge.

As for many competitors, motorcycle racing was like a drug to Wally and me. The ambition of preparing the best racing motorcycle in its class and the challenge of competing was compulsive, often beyond all sensible reasoning.

However as the Mersey Docks came into sight I turned the page, back to reality, home and our loved ones. Then there was Mallory Park that next weekend - yes, we were 'bonkers' and back on the 'merry-go-round'. Preparing the Dunstall-Norton for Mallory Park proved to be futile with a non-finish after an engine failure. Collecting our £25 start money we departed for home, where we should have stayed in the first place.

We really needed a rest, but there was no let up. We had set a hell of a race programme for ourselves and next was Brands Hatch on the 21st June. Paul Dunstall had rebuilt the Norton engine so our hopes were high, although it would not be an easy task against our regular adversaries, Boddice, Vincent, Harris, Greenwood and rest of the gladiators. Nevertheless, despite an intermittent misfire, we achieved second spot in an 8 lap scratch race behind Chris Vincent riding his invincible 654cc kneeler works BSA, and then a second in the handicap pursuit. A satisfactory day, with £58 start and winnings, less £14 commission to Paul Dunstall for his contribution.

Percy Seeley was still holding the fort at our motorcycle business, aided by our loyal staff, so a couple of days was spent going through business matters before departing

Dunstall Norton action, Brands 21st June.

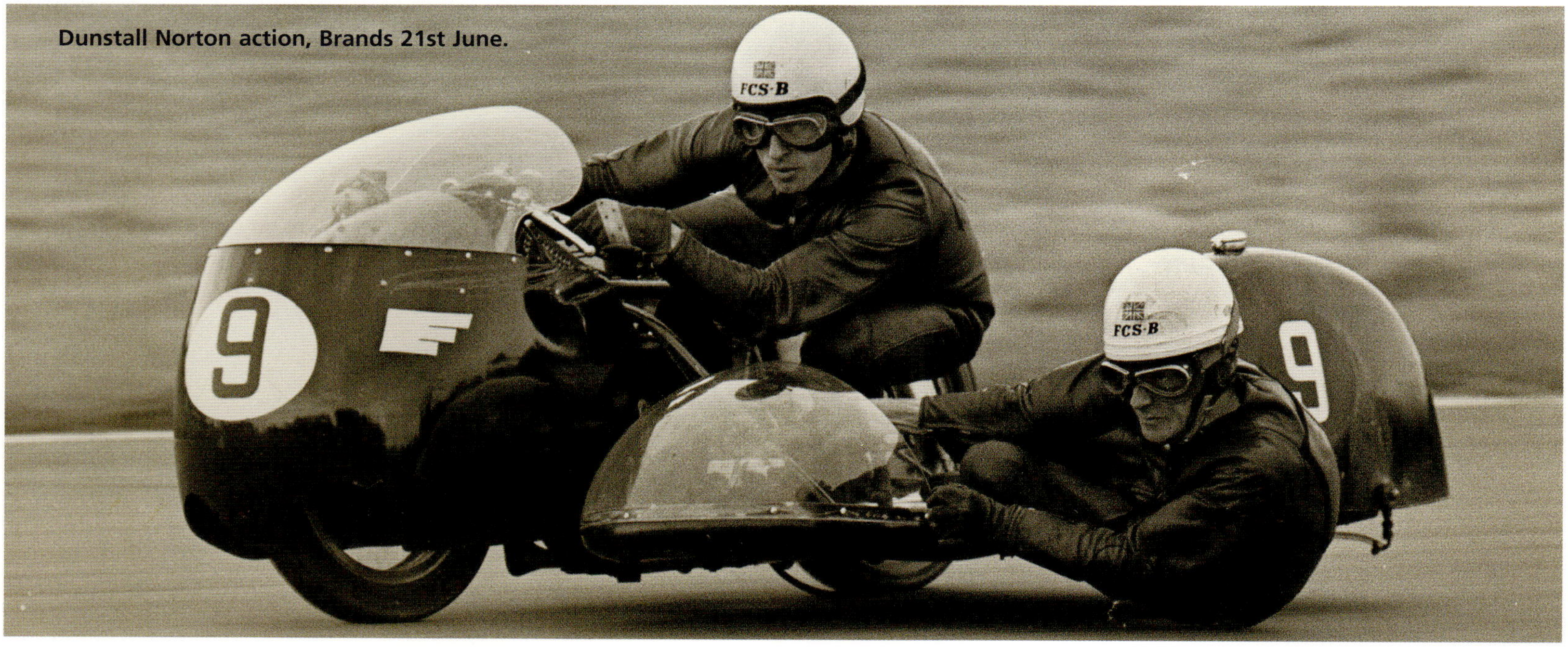

for the fourth Grand Prix of the season at the celebrated Stichting Circuit Van Drenthe Dutch TT at Assen in northern Holland. This nearly 5 mile long 'ear 'olers' circuit was a favourite for riders and fans alike. This would be our third visit to Assen for the Dutch TT. Perhaps we would finish the sidecar race this time.

In high spirits after our success at the Isle of Man TT and still having the use of the FCS-B, despite rumblings from the Gilera factory indicating that all was not well between themselves and Florian. Nevertheless, they continued to support him, leaving us in the hired gun position on Florian's BMW outfit.

For this meeting we were no longer slumming in the back of the van, Florian was the master in finding good cheap accommodation so it was Hotel de Kroon for us. With practice starting on the Thursday for the Saturday race day, not all would be well for a number of competitors. Ulsterman Tommy Robb, wife Noreen and young daughter in their Ford van on the A20 travelling to Folkestone were involved in a hair-raising accident with a lorry, causing the van to flip on to it's side, smashing all the windows and writing it off. Incredibly, apart from cuts and bruises, no-one was hurt. For the rescuers, panic set in when they found a crash hat under the lorry, believing a motorcyclist had been involved in the tangle. Tommy's helmet had been flung out of the window, in the crash. Panic over! Fortunately, with the Arter Brothers near Canterbury, sponsors of Mike Duff, it was arranged for Mike to transport the Robb family to Holland. Tough guys these racing motorcyclists. Tommy Robb went onto a third place rostrum position on his Yamaha in the 250cc race behind winner Jim Redman and Phil Read.

Unfortunately, there were a number of nasty crashes during practice, the first being Dennis Ainsworth, thrown from his 350cc Norton, suffering severe concussion and a broken collarbone. Then, leader of the 125cc World Championship, Luigi Taveri out on the works 250 Honda, crashed at high speed. He also suffered concussion and severe bruising which kept him in hospital until after the event.

Then, worse was to come. Our Swiss friend, 28 year old Roland Foell, in the very last 125cc practice session, entering the finishing straight lost control of his 125cc Honda. Following close behind New Zealander Ginger Molloy could not avoid Roland or the fallen Honda and crashed. Both riders were taken to hospital, Ginger suffering cuts and heavy bruising but Roland suffering head injuries to which, sadly he would succumb. Roland Foell was one of the most friendly and generous men you could ever wish to meet. Although born in Freiburg, Germany, he had spent most of his working life in Switzerland and raced as a Swiss. Roland came up the hard way, starting in 1959 as a sidecar passenger to Edgar Strub and Florian Camathias. Soon turning to solo racing, he was a regular competitor in international races with his favourite event the Isle of Man TT at which he first rode in 1961.

Only 16 days prior to the Dutch TT, Roland had ridden in both the 125cc and 350cc Isle of Man TT races achieving very creditable tenth and fifteenth places with bronze and Silver Replica awards. After the most challenging and dangerous race-course in the world, a relatively minor crash caused his death. Roland, an orphan, left no relatives but certainly a host of friends and admirers throughout Europe.

Practice for us had not gone as well as expected. There were no undue problems with the FCS-B, it was just us failing to get up to speed. In the last qualifying session we were back in eighth place, 10 seconds down on pole man, our sponsor Florian Camathias, 'Flo' as he was known. Chris Vincent, BMW who had put in a great lap, took second place, less than half a second down on Flo riding the faster Gilera outfit. Then it was Pip Harris, Fritz Scheidegger, Max Deubel, Otto Kolle and Georg Auerbacher, all the main competitors in the world championship sidecar series.

For the first time I was really disappointed with my effort, particularly as we had not gone any faster than the year before on the Matchless G50 outfit. It was not Wally's fault, it was all mine, I was behind the twist grip. On the Friday evening, back at Hotel de Kroon, we reflected on Roland's tragic accident, so out came the wine to toast him and drown our sorrows. Florian and Alfred were great company and a most enjoyable evening was had. Which was probably why we did not rush to the circuit the next day.

For that 1964 Dutch TT event, Mike Hailwood racing both the 350 and 500cc works MVs, had set himself a huge task as he was also due to race a BRM-Lotus car at Rouen, the day after. So Mike practised on the MVs Wednesday and Thursday, flying that night to Rouen to practice on Friday, then back the same day for the Dutch on Saturday, to win the 500cc race with a record lap and a second place in the 350cc event, to winner, works Honda rider, Jim Redman.

A week of heat-wave weather ensured another record was broken before racing even started, with nearly 200,000 spectators massed around the magnificent Assen Circuit. As reported it was three wins and six records for the 'Iron Man' Jim Redman on the works Hondas in the 125, 250 and 350 events with the 250cc race recorded as the best race of the day, a 17 lap 81.38 mile event. From the start after Alan Shepherd's MZ had gone out on the first lap, a race-long conflict took place between pole position setter, Phil Read and Jim Redman, and what a dice it was. They were practically locked together jostling for position dodging in and out of each other's slipstream. Then in the last lap, Read on the works Yamaha lead by a couple of lengths but Redman dived under him at the fast last left-hand kink and was a wheel ahead at the last corner. Read tried all he knew as they streaked for the line, but Redman took the flag by inches. Then it was the last race of the day, the 14 lap, 67 mile sidecar race. The huge crowd was still in place, sidecar racing being so popular in those days. The race was reported by Mick Woollett in 'Motor Cycling'. Colin Seeley, first Englishman to win a World championship sidecar race on the Continent since 1960 tells 'Motor Cycling's' readers the inside story of his success. 'I still cannot believe its true! After practising had finished, I was really downhearted. Despite all our efforts we were only eighth fastest, a full 10 seconds a lap slower than Florian Camathias and Chris Vincent.

'I had a lot on my mind. I didn't want to let Florian down. He'd lent us the FCS-B and expected us to do well. On the other hand I like to leave myself a safety margin, it's one thing to wreck your own bike-quite another to prang someone else's, especially when it's worth around the £1,500 mark! And the same applies to engines. I don't mind 'buzzing' my own, but I certainly didn't intend to over-rev Florian's engine.

'On the morning of the race I had intended to get to the circuit early to watch the solos. But Florian said that it would be far better for us to take things quietly away from the noise and heat of the paddock. All year I've had trouble with the twist-grip rubber slipping so I sorted that out by putting a couple of 6 inch nails up between the grip and the bar and taping the whole lot up.

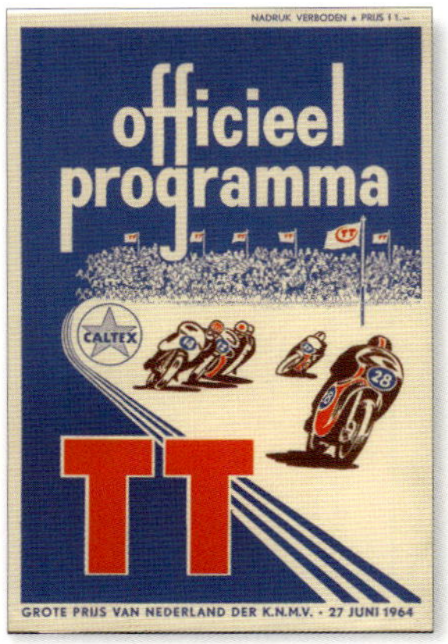

'We left for the track so late that we only got there as the 500s were being wheeled out onto the line at 3.25pm. We managed to get across the track to the paddock, but if we'd have been just a few minutes later, I don't know what would have happened because the sidecars were already being filled with petrol, a controlled system.

'Then we had one of those stupid hitches that tend to spoil racing - and to upset your nerves. When it was our time to drive out to the starting grid the official on the gate wouldn't let us onto the track. We'd forgotten to bring some form or other with us! Wally had to run back to the van for it - only to find that the Ford was locked!

'Just when tempers were on the verge of snapping they let us onto the track and we formed up on the third row of the grid nearest to the pit wall. It was to be a traffic light start so we needed to pay attention and I was determined to make a good start if nothing else. However, the FCS-B was not easy to push with the low-positioned handlebars enclosed in the fairing I needed to push with my right hand on the outside of the fairing cut out. Then as the engine fired up and I changed gear, immediately letting go of the throttle and quickly bringing my hand back inside the fairing I grabbed hold of the throttle once more. It sounds tricky and it was.

'The tension was rising as the lights went green, we pushed like mad and when the Rennsport burst into life we somehow managed to squeeze past Max Deubel and into the Esses we were leading, a repeat of 1963. In the scramble to start I had broken part of the screen with my right arm and when I tried to get back inside the fairing after the first 'right hander' my leathers had caught on the jagged edge. I freed myself after an anxious moment as we charged down towards the fast left kink and into a sharp right hander at the end of the straight. I didn't dare look back to see how close the pursuing pack would be. I just pressed on as hard as I could for nearly a lap before stealing a glance back. I couldn't see anyone! No one was more surprised than me - in fact I wondered where the others had all gone.

'Trevor Barnes was signalling for us in the pits and a very good job he did too - in fact apart from the Isle of Man TT this was the first short circuit race in which I had used signals. On the second lap Trevor put out the plus four second board and as we steadily increased our lead I began then to worry about Florian. Where was he? We were there

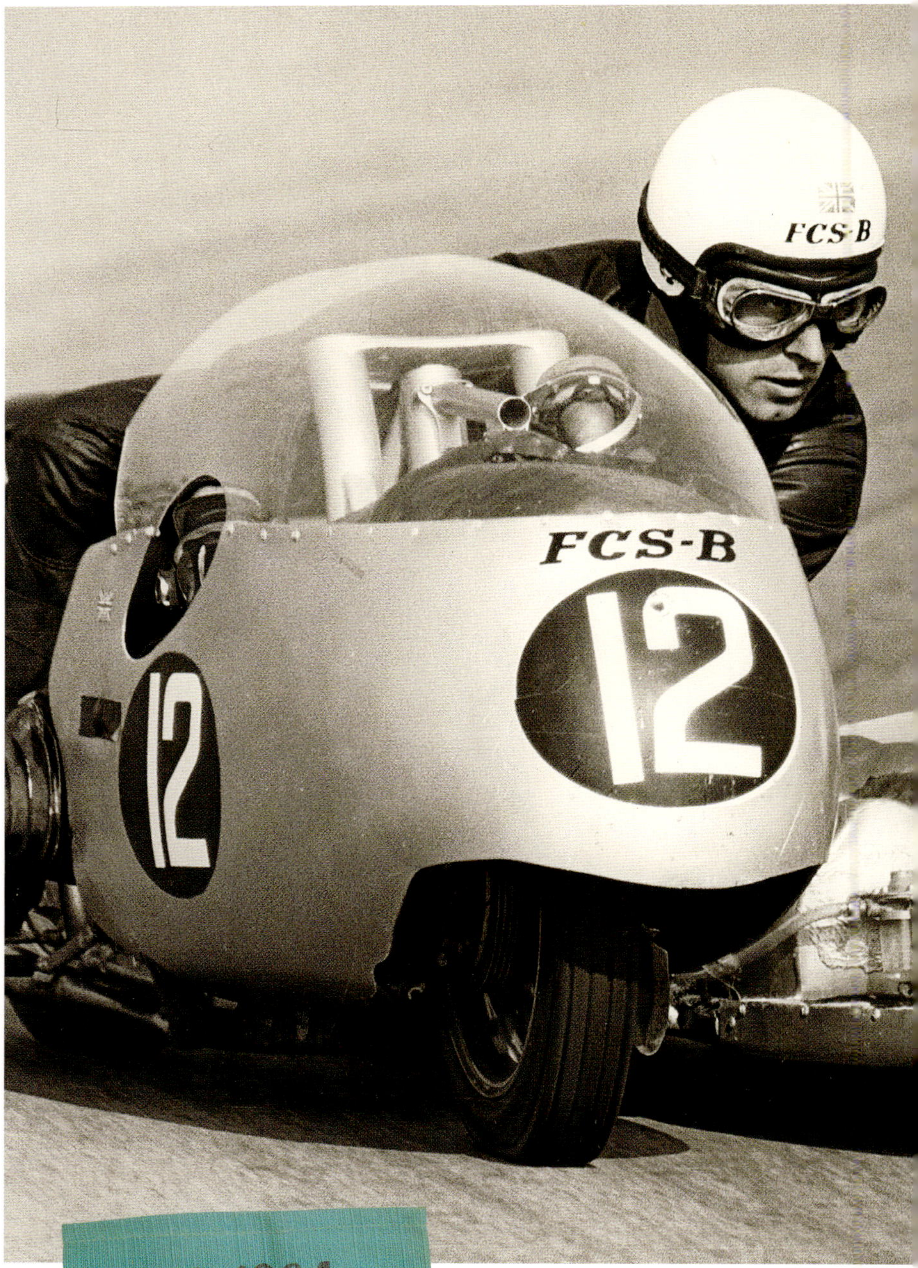

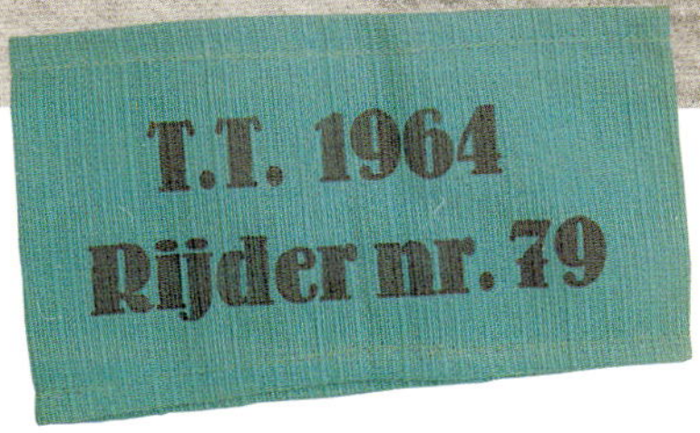

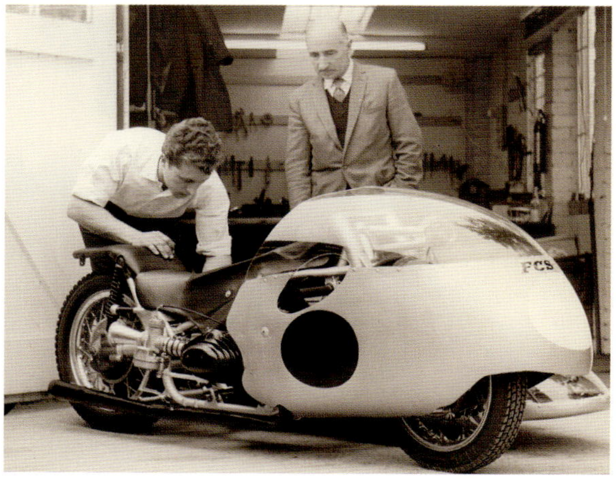

Percy looks on.

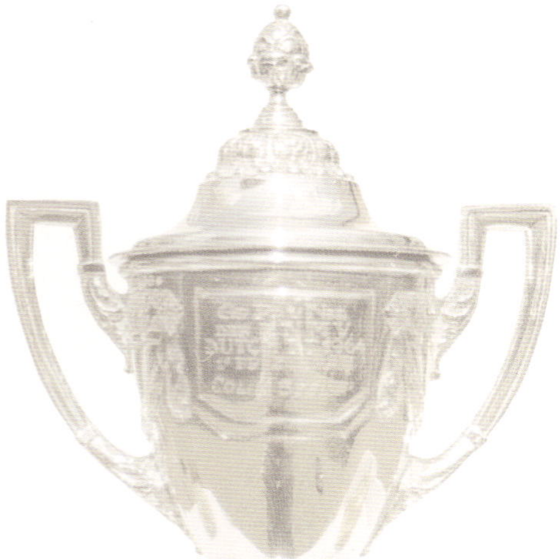

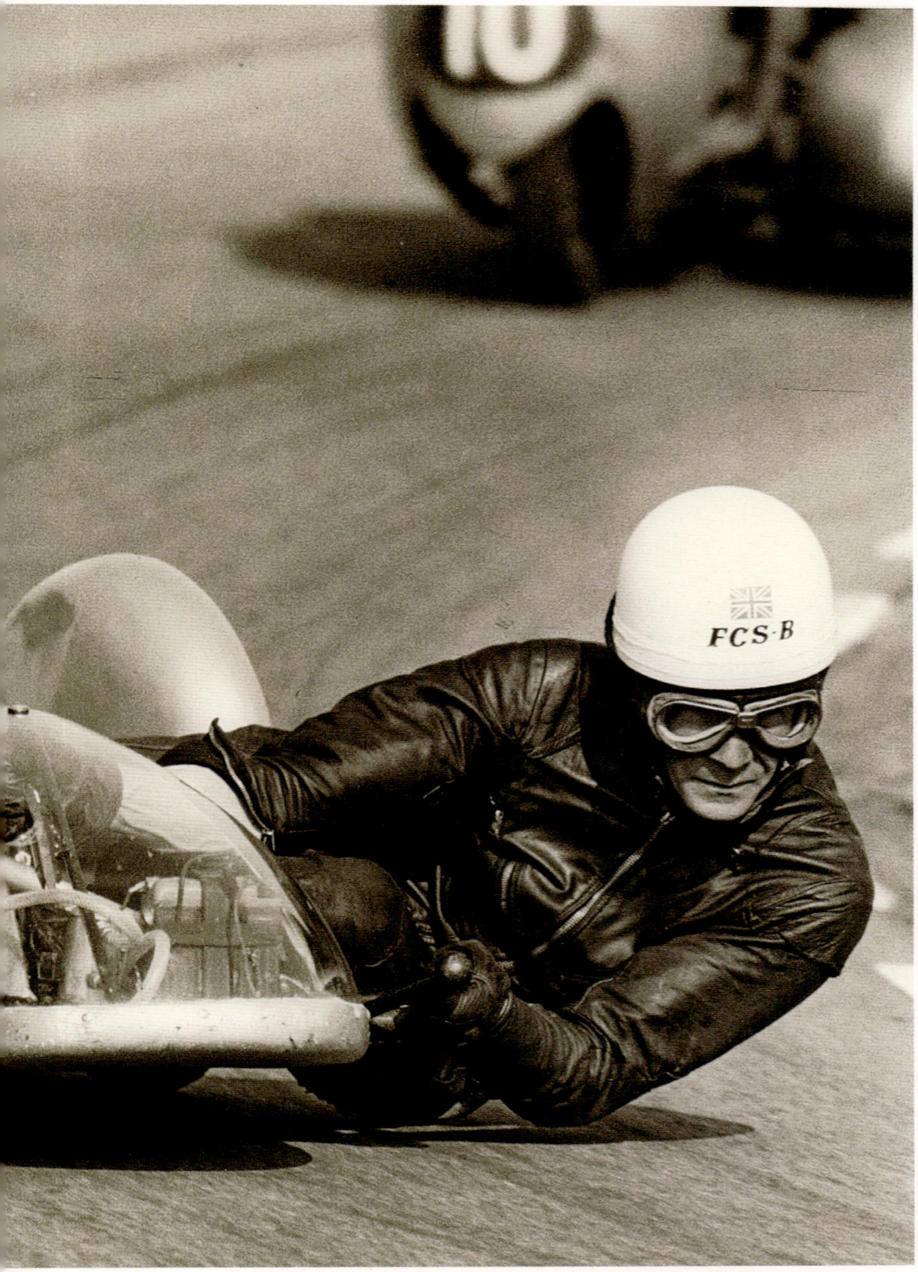

Dutch TT action.

to support him in his world championship endeavours, not the other way round. Well, Flo and passenger Alfred Herzig had held second place for 3 laps until displaced by a flying Chris Vincent then 4 laps later the Gilera outfit burst into flames when a petrol union came loose, spraying the hot engine with fuel. One moment they were racers, next moment they were fireman, fortunately putting out the flames without too much damage. By that time I had spotted them stopped out on the course with Flo waving us on, by then with Wally performing beautifully in the chair we were up to half a minute ahead of Chris Vincent. The Helmut Fath tuned BMW Rennsport long stroke engine, which I was told could be revved to 9,500 was running so sweetly and flying like a bird.

'It was the most fantastic race for us. We had the track to ourselves and we were having one of the smoothest and most untroubled races of our careers and unbelievably beating hands down the best sidecar racers in the world. It was a dream come true, but we still had one lap to complete and it was to be the most nerve-wracking! It would just be our luck for something to happen, just as it had done at Silverstone in April when we ran out of fuel on the last lap, when leading Scheidegger by 12 seconds. With the sun still shining and to the applause of that huge crowd it would be third time lucky as we came across the line to win our very first Grand Prix. Having eased the pace, 10 seconds ahead of Chris Vincent, a great ride by him but this time and for a change in our shadow, Fritz Scheidegger making up the rostrum positions with World Champion Max Deubel over half a minute behind well down in fourth place then Kolle and Auerbacher. Surprisingly, we had broken the lap record, knocking off nearly 13 seconds from our practice time and establishing a new race record in the process despite slowing up. Then the final icing on the cake, we had moved up to second place in the World Championship only three points behind the leader Max Deubel.'

Meanwhile, back in England my wife Joan and sister-in-law Shirley were out driving but had switched on the radio to hear the end of the BBC radio broadcast covering the sidecar race when Murray Walker, in his distinctive excitable style reported, 'Yes, it looks like we have a British winner of the sidecar Dutch TT, and yes we have! It's fantastic! A wonderful ride by Colin Seeley and Wally Rawlings!' Well Joan was so shocked she swerved the car and nearly drove off the road with excitement!

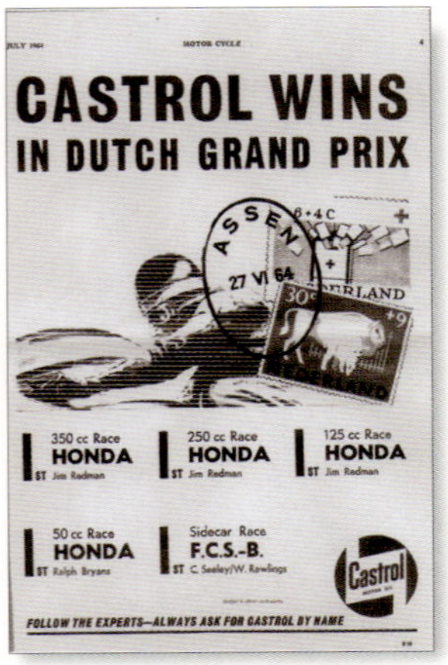

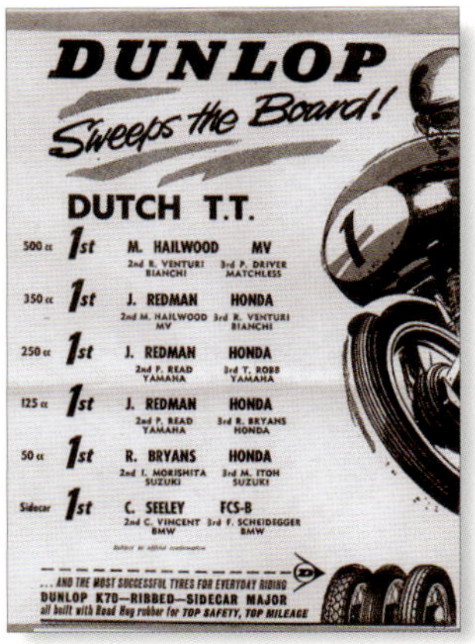

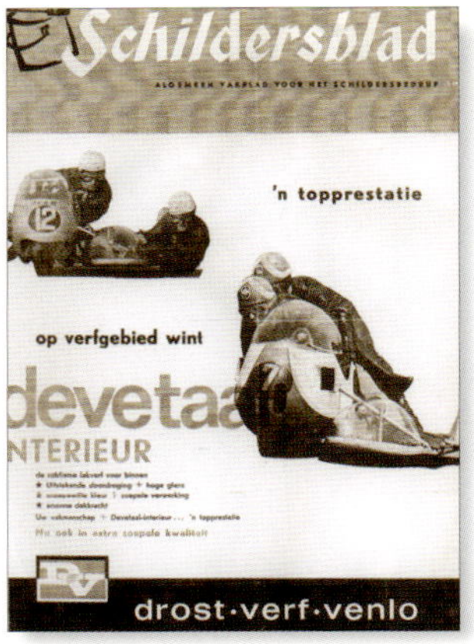

If Wally had not lost his bloody helmet at the French Grand Prix we would have got third, second and first in the last three Grands Prix on the BMW. But fourth, second and first was still pretty good. You would forgive us for being a bit boastful but it seemed a long way from racing at Charterhall in Scotland on that scrap Manx-Norton outfit in 1960. It would be 16 years before another British rider would win the Dutch TT and this would be the popular Jock Taylor who would take the World Title, in 1980 and I was there to cheer him on.

We were sad for Florian, he was not having much luck with the Gilera outfit. Much of the trouble arose from not paying enough attention to detail. But there was no stopping him, he took back the FCS-BMW directly after our Dutch TT win, to race it in France the very next day.

At the award ceremony that evening in Assen we were with Ralph Bryans, who had won his first ever Grand Prix, the 50cc event on a Honda. Jim Redman, Phil Read, Tommy Robb, Remo Venturi, Paddy Driver, Mitsuo Itoh, Isao Morishita, Chris Vincent, Fritz Scheidegger, were all there, but 'Mike the Bike' had dashed off to Rouen. It was a great evening in the company of so many great riders of that period.

Our earnings from this event would come in very useful; Start Money £60, Prize £125, Girling Bonus £10, Castrol Bonus £100, less payment to Florian £93, leaving us with £202.

We would meet Florian later on in the week for that following weekend's Belgian Grand Prix, but all was not well with Gilera. It looked more than likely that he would lose the support of Gilera so we would lose the use of the FCS-B and be relegated back to our Matchless G50. Anticipating this situation Florian, to give him credit, brought an older BMW outfit for us to use at the Belgian Grand Prix. It was on this machine that we practised with Florian on the FCS-B, still arguing with Gilera that he should continue to race their four cylinder engine outfit. Florian, if he could hold it together, would be the favourite to win on this fast 8.75 mile Spa-Francorchamp circuit.

Then we were invited with Florian to a dinner with the Gilera Team and their solo rider, the Argentinian Benedicto Caldarella. That evening, Gilera relented and agreed that Florian could continue with them at least for the Belgian Grand Prix. So it was all change, back on the FCS-B for us, but in missing the last practice it would be a tall order to race well on this fast circuit. A different riding technique was required. On these fast circuits Florian was the

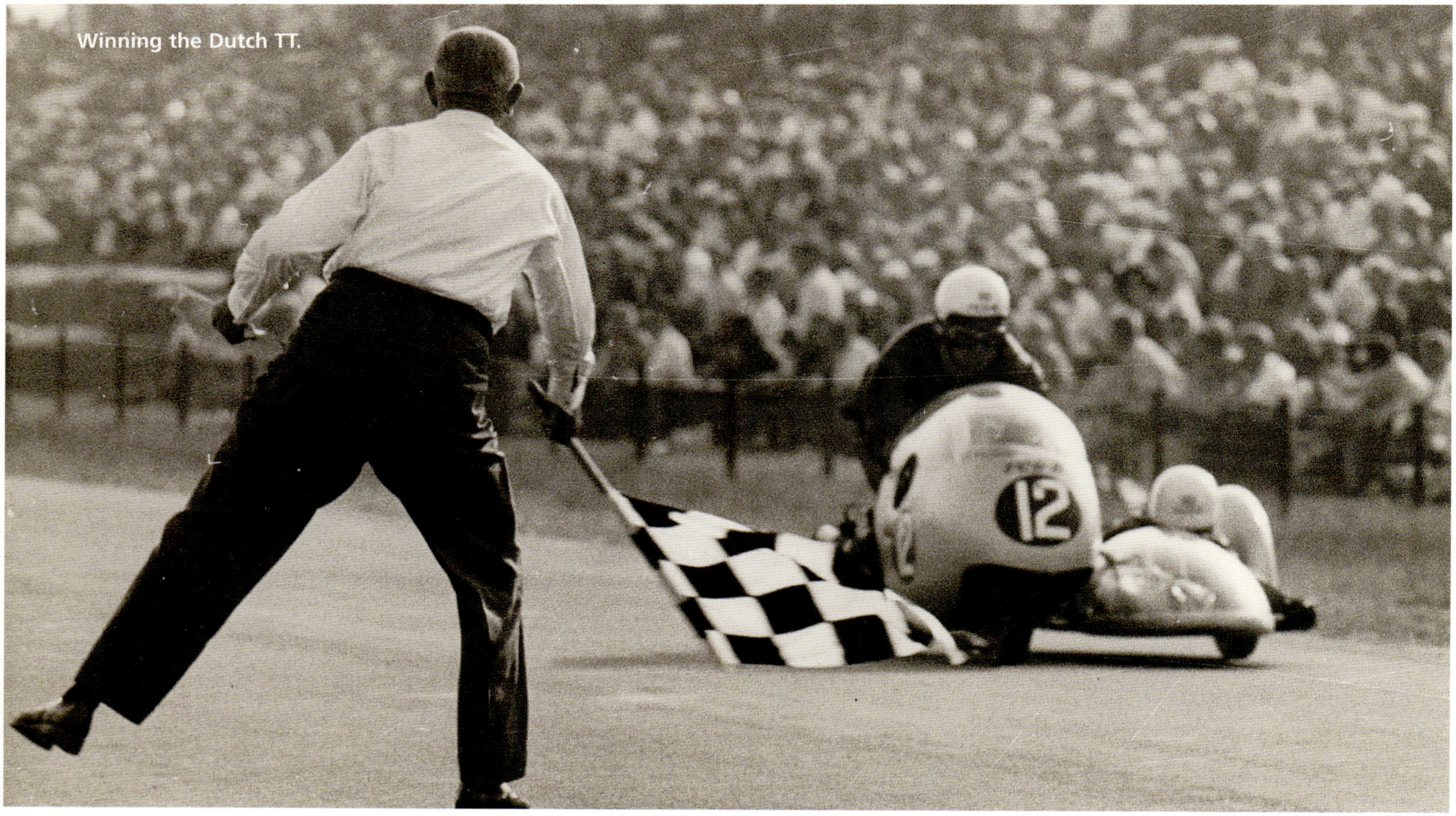
Winning the Dutch TT.

At Walter Joos' premises near Stuttgart, Left to right; Florian Camathias, Walter Joos, Wally and Trevor Barnes.

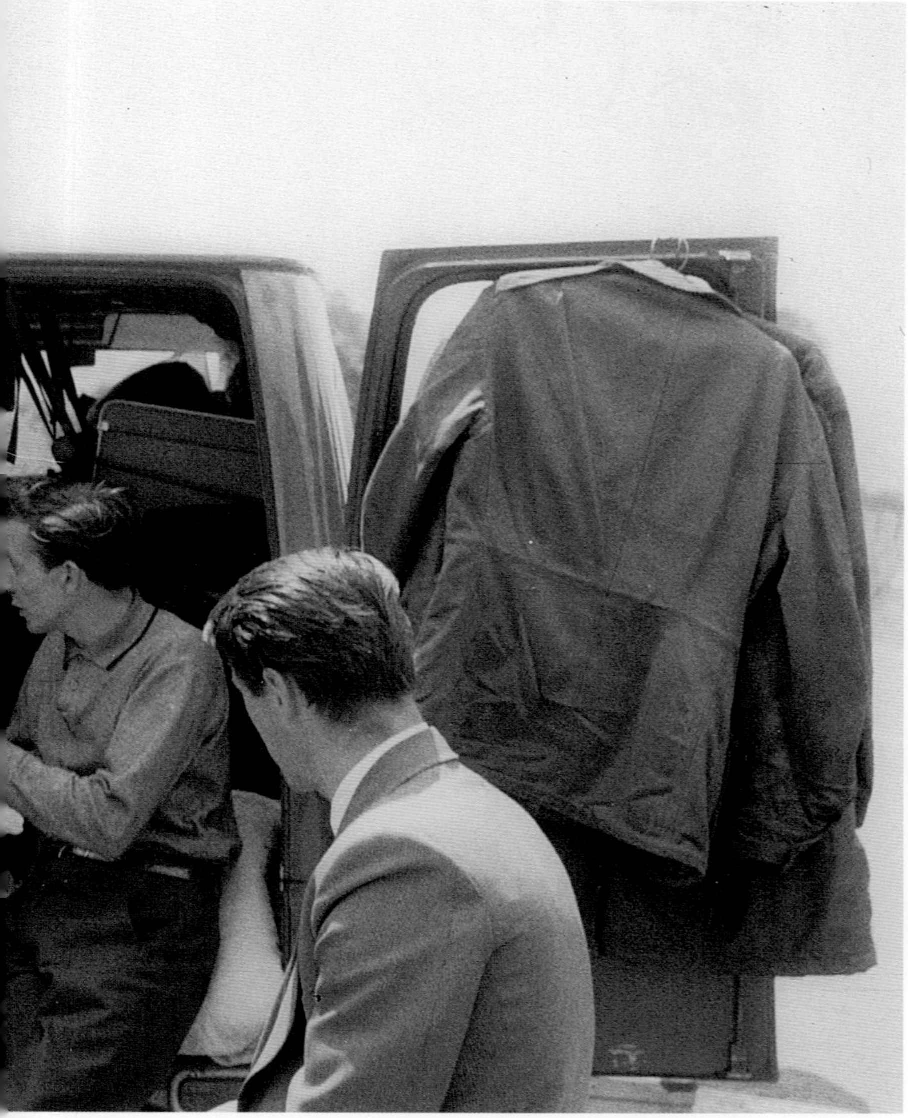

Our next important event was the August third British Championships at Oulton Park but we had to get to Stuttgart to collect the FCS outfit. With our friend Bill Savage, it was a non-stop return journey to collect the FCS but as we charged along the A20 near Charing in Kent a car came slowly out of a side turning, straight across the main road in front of us. With the brakes of the Thames van locked, we were heading for a big collision, but in the last seconds I threw the van sideways tipping it onto two wheels. As it hung in the balance I looked at Bill clinging on. The other driver seemed to be totally unconcerned and disappeared down the lane. We dropped back to earth with a thud, our sweets, drinks and sandwiches scattered around the van like gun-shot. And I thought racing was dangerous! No bones broken, we continued our journey.

At the home of Walter Joos in Stuttgart, with no time to spare, we loaded the outfit, had a coffee and were off. Next morning, back at Dover our other troubles started. Entering the custom area ready with the necessary sidecar outfit carnet document we believed the worst of our hectic trip was over. We still needed to return to Belvedere, collect all our equipment, and Wally, before driving the 230 miles to Oulton Park the next day. Our friendly customs officer asked if I was the owner of this sidecar outfit. I explained our circumstances but our friendly customs officer turned out not to be so obliging. He explained that I needed a letter of authority from Florian Camathias for the machine to be allowed into the country. I pointed out that this would be difficult, as Camathias himself was travelling to Oulton Park, and could be anywhere on the continent. Now came the official voice, 'Sorry Sir, step out of the van, we will have to impound the outfit.' I couldn't believe it! I explained the urgency of the situation. Surely he knew of Colin Seeley? Hadn't he heard the Murray Walker broadcast from the Dutch TT. I tried everything but our man stood his ground, not at all impressed. So I refused to move, which resulted in the van myself and the FCS outfit being impounded within the customs shed. What a drama! What next! Our only hope was that Florian would travel via Dover and not Sheerness. He could even be flying into Lydd Airport. What a cock-up! Bill and I were hungry, angry and tired. We paced up and down for a number of hours, when to our relief, Flo arrived at Dover to find us shouting the 1964 equivalent of 'I'm a celebrity, get me out of here!' Florian signed the necessary paperwork and we were free to go. Then it was the almighty rush to Oulton Park. This popular international bank holiday Monday British Championship event had attracted the likes of Minter, Read, Anderson, Woodman, Cooper, Duff, Shepherd, Redman, Provini, Perris, Marsovszky and the fast improving 'little' Bill Ivy who was riding an impressive list of machinery - 125 Honda, 248 Yamaha, 350 Norton and the Geoff Monty 500 Monard.

The sidecar races once again attracted World Champion Max Deubel with, Pip Harris, Camathias, Vincent, Boddice, Kolle and Auerbacher among the 29 entrants. For us it would be a disappointing meeting. After all the trouble, we only managed a fifth place in the first race, our friend Pip Harris, BMW getting the better of Deubel from Camathias, FCS and Chris Vincent, BMW fourth. In the second 10 lap race, Florian, on the, FCS, was back in charge, winning from Chris Vincent with Max Deubel third. We had to retire our FCS when the engine went on to one cylinder. After the Belgian and Solitude fiascos this was another set-back. From £30 start money and £2 prize money, we paid £16 to Flo and we headed home to Belvedere.

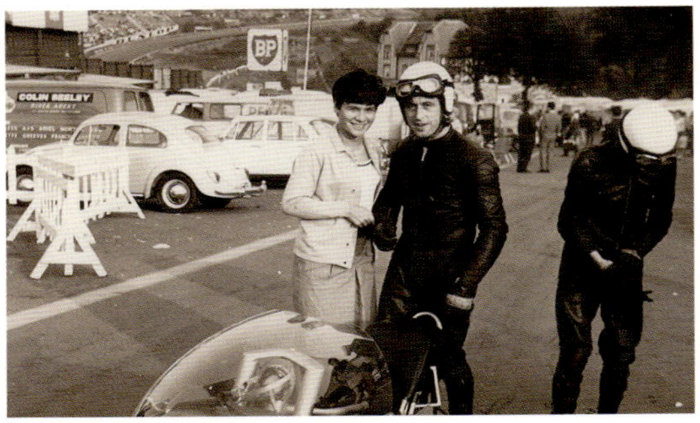

Before the sidecar race with Joan.

With hardly any let up in the racing programme it was a quick departure from Oulton Park, I felt I needed to spend a little more time with Joan, young Colin and my parents who were all so supportive of my racing career.

Brands Hatch was next on the calendar on August 16th, but we had work to do on both the second best BMW-FCS and the Dunstall Norton. Although a national meeting, Brands for a change ran an 8 lap 500cc scratch race as well as two heats and final of an 8 lap 1200cc scratch event. In addition as was popular in those days two heats and a final of a handicap race also 8 laps, five races in all, for which 48 outfits had entered. Chris Vincent was on form that day, but his BMW was not, leaving the challenge for the first place in the 500cc race, as described by 'Motorcycle', 'With Vincent out of the running, this only sharpened the appetites of Pip Harris, BMW and Colin Seeley, FCS who set about one another like mad dogs.

'Aided by the skills of passenger Ray Campbell the veteran Harris would match the youthful verve of Colin Seeley and Wally Rawlings by leading the 'Belvedere boys' by two seconds early on, gaining only an extra half second over the 21.2miles to take the win. Finishing third some half a minute behind us was Ray Pollard, BMW.'

With a third in the heat of the 1200cc event on the Dunstall Norton and £2 prize money, we were forced to revert to the BMW, as the Norton was playing up, resulting in a disappointing sixth in the unlimited final, and out of money. Never mind, combined with start money and our second place in the 500cc race we came away with £67 and had the privilege of racing head-to-head with with such a professional as Pip Harris. His credentials included fifth in the world championship as far back as 1953, third in 1956 and 1960. Pip, when all was right with his machine was an unbeatable, impressive gentleman racer.

Alan Thurgood riding the Don Overall Matchless, finished a good fifth in the 500cc event passengered by Bob Valance. Then in the handicap race, with us once more truly in his sights, swooping through the South Bank Bend onto the long circuit he lost control of the Matchless outfit resulting in an almighty crash into the bank under the overhead footbridge, suffering head and back injuries. This crash signalled the end of Alan's racing career. The luck which we had enjoyed racing a Matchless had not been with him in the same way. I admired Alan Thurgood, he was a tough competitor, a true sportsman and a friend.

Chris Vincent went on that day to win both heats and finals of the 1200cc events. Dave Simmonds, Tohatsu, won the 50cc 'tiddler' race, Bill Ivy, Chisholm-Honda, the 125cc. The 'King', Minter won both the 350 and 500cc races. There followed a break of three weeks before Snetterton on September 6th.

Meanwhile, Florian, overall winner at Oulton Park International meeting in early August, was racing later that month at the German International event at the Avus Circuit near Berlin. A huge crash resulted in the sidecar race being abandoned after only 3 laps. In the early stages of the race Camathias was chasing Chris Vincent on the North Curve, when he lost control and spun the FCS outfit. Max Deubel following close behind hit Florian, and Georg Auerbachar, unable to avoid the calamity, ran over Flo's passenger Alfred Herzig. It was a terrifying crash and both Florian and Alfred were rushed to hospital. Florian, with concussion and a suspected broken arm, would still be unconscious the following day. Alfred Herzig's days of passengering were over, as he

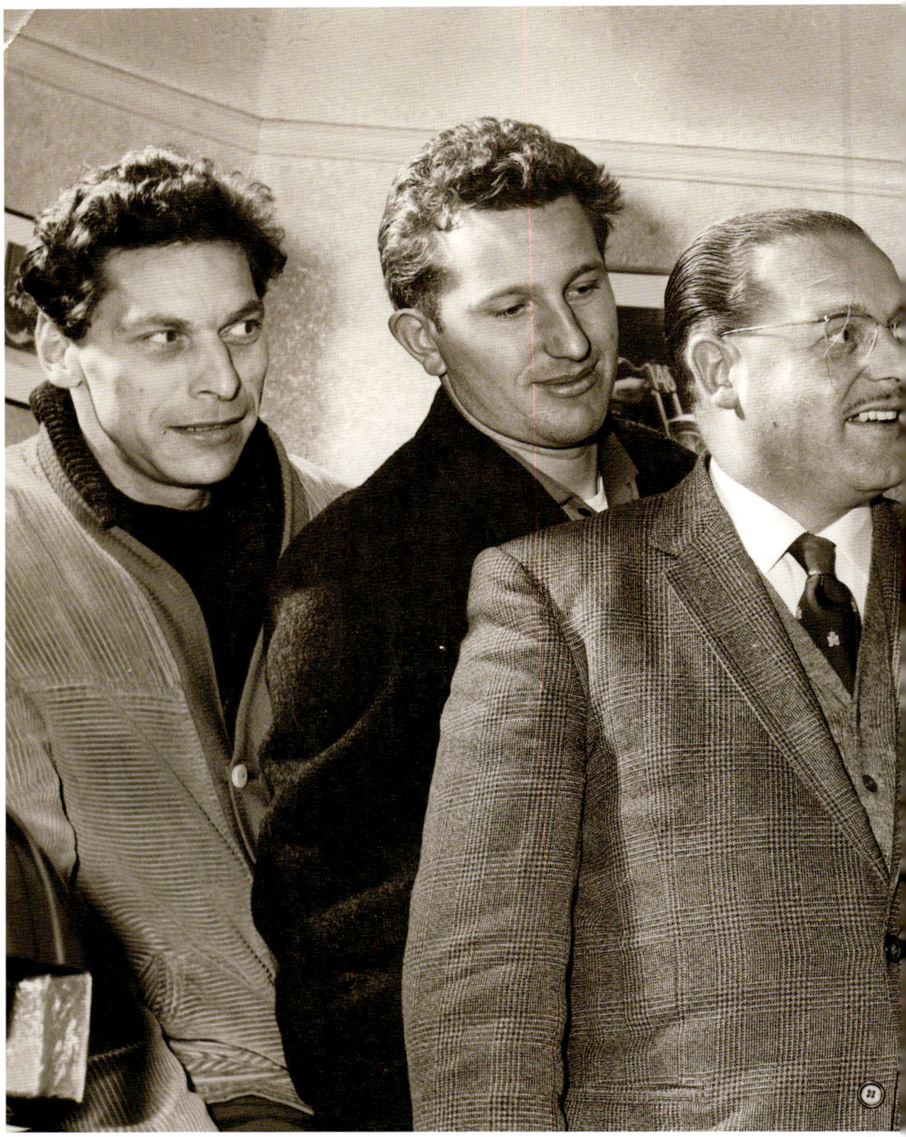

A gathering in London, left to right; Helmut Fath, Horst Kassner, Tom Kirby, Ernst Weiss, Florian Camathias, Roland Foell.

Dave Simmonds at Mallory Park with his Greeves.

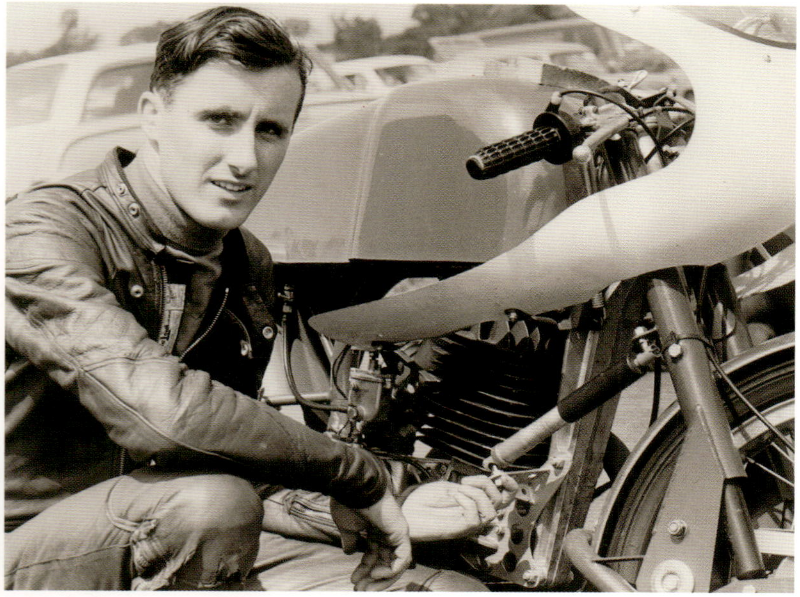

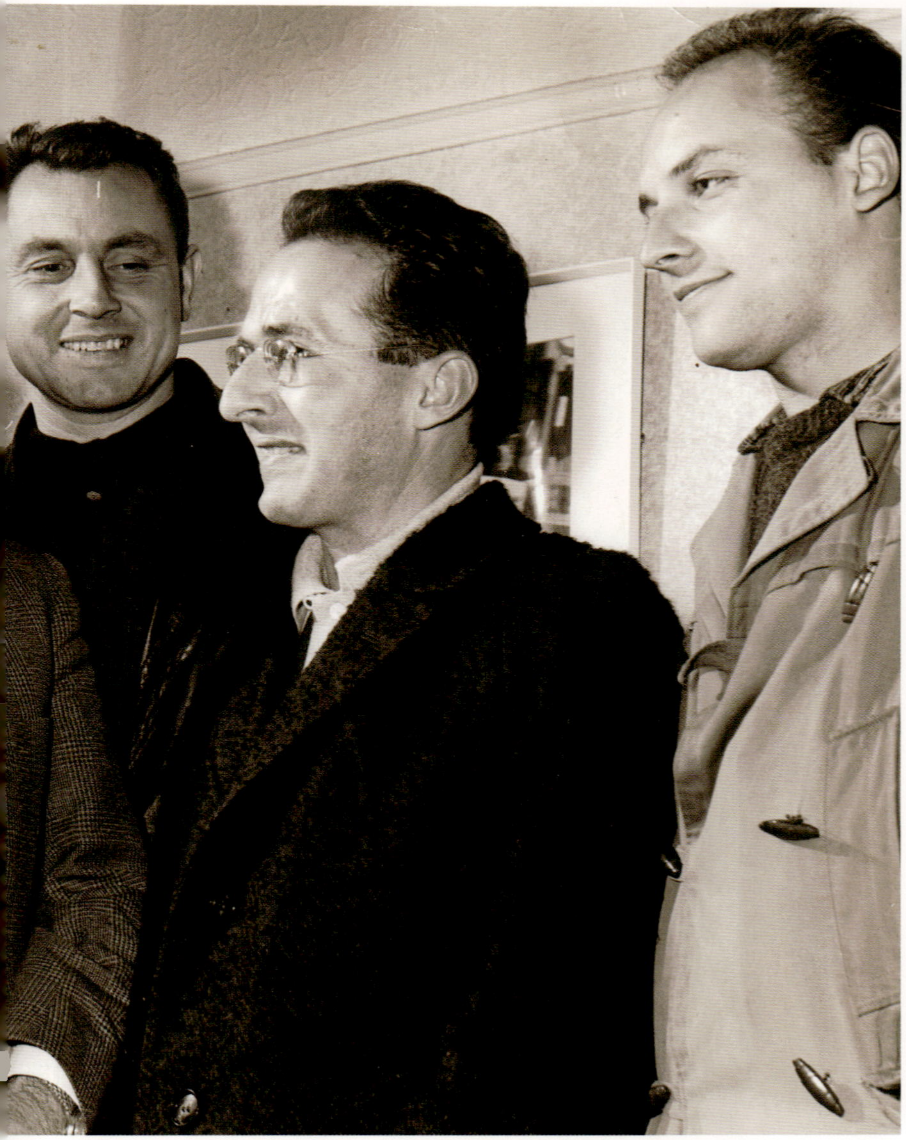

was to lose a leg. As well as all of this, the FCS-BMW (the oufit on which I had won the Dutch TT) had been virtually written off in the crash.

Florian was an unbelievable character. Within hours of regaining consciousness he had instructed his mechanic Walter Joos to arrange the return of the number two FCS. He had previously agreed to let us keep it to compete in the last British events, but his mind was on getting back to racing before the end of the season. Alfred Herzig, meanwhile, had two months in hospital recovering from that horrific crash. Florian was planning to race at Modena on the 4th October or at Madrid a few days later. Max Deubel, Otto Kolle and other competitors protested, insisting that Camathias should pass a proper medical at the circuit before being allowed to race. Florian often signed his own medical forms, and I am sure he had an official stamp made up in the name of some doctor from his home town of Montreux. On the 11th October, Florian was back, racing at Zaragoza in Spain, with a volunteer passenger ('poor sod') in the chair. However, in overtaking Australian Barry Thomson to gain third place, Florian again crashed, looping the rebuilt FCS, this time sustaining broken ribs and concussion - would he never learn?

For us, without the FCS, there was only the one outfit ready for racing, which was the 650cc Dunstall Norton. At the Snetterton 6th September meeting it was in the unlimited race that I made one of my rare 'cock-ups'. For the first 3 laps I was running head to head with Pip Harris, BMW who was in the lead with Bill Boddice third. On the fourth lap coming into the Esses the Norton appeared to go into neutral as I changed gear. I thought the drive chain had broken so I pulled in only then to realise what had happened. I had ridden four outfits in one season and had confused the gear positions. I had tried to change up instead of down, giving the feeling that something had broken as I coasted into the corner. I quickly recovered from my confusion, upped the pace and got a sixth place out of 31 competitors.

At Cadwell Park International a week later, with no 500cc outfit, a win in the 6 lap handicap sidecar consolation race on the Norton was the best we could achieve. The following weekend, September 18th/19th was the Scarborough International event. As we were not even offered a shilling to appear, we didn't, which suited us fine! The Scarborough Mountain circuit, although a favourite of many, was in my opinion too narrow, bumpy and dangerous. Scarborough had failed to attract the regular top International sidecar competitors, so it was Charlie Freeman, Norton, and Alwyn Maltby, Triumph, who would benefit. Alan Shepherd put in a good performance to win both 125 and 250 races on the works MZ machines. Phil Read, 251 Yamaha, won the 350cc race from 'Mooneyes' Cooper, Norton, who registered the fastest lap. Derek Woodman, Matchless, lead Chris Conn, Norton, over the line of the 500cc race and that was it.

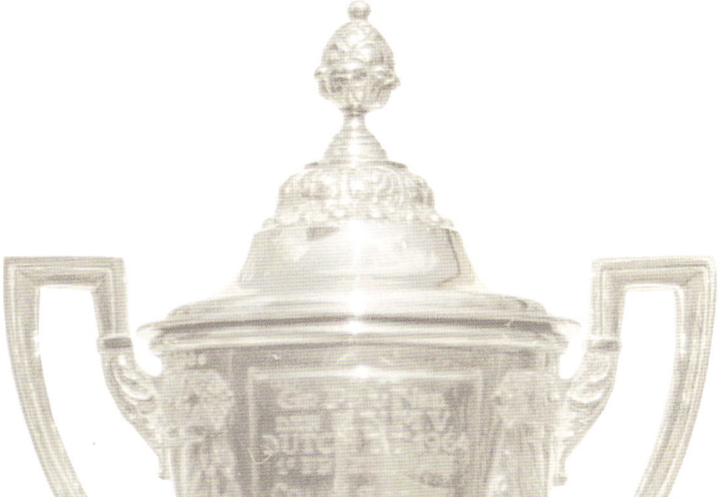

We much preferred to be at Brands Hatch for the Sunday 20th September meeting - our local 'Derby'. Back on course with our Dunstall Norton 650cc it was another good second to the BSA Flyer Chris Vincent.

Another weekend followed in quick succession, the Mallory Park International for which we had dragged out our Matchless G50 outfit, having fallen off the perch following our success on FCS-BMW earlier that season.

The sidecars would take second place to the solo boys, as supreme Mike Hailwood, four times World Champion riding the works MV attracted the biggest crowd ever to attend a post war road race meeting in Britain - all straining to watch a foregone conclusion! The 1,000 guinea first prize would be Mike's in the Race of the Year. He had won the first 500cc race with 'Mooneyes' second. Alan Shepherd won both the 125 and 250cc events on the MZ with the 350cc race going to Phil Read on a 251cc Yamaha, getting the better of Redman on a 305cc Honda.

The last race was the 15 lap final of the 500cc sidecar race with a 5.45pm start, for which we nearly needed lights. With Camathias absent, it proved a three way confrontation. At the front Max Deubel, BMW was in a British sandwich with Pip Harris, BMW leading and Chris Vincent on his BSA third. The British pair finally got the better of the World Champion so it was Pip, Chris and Max in that order across the line, with our trusty Matchless not far behind in fourth spot. With £40 start money and £15 in prize money it had been a reasonable day.

Whilst Camathias was considering his comeback in early October we were at our penultimate event, The Oulton Park National Cheshire Centre ACU Road Race Championships. From the 54 outfits entered only 24 were allowed for the 8 lap, 22 mile final. Fortunately, we came second in our heat to the BSA Flyer, Birmingham ace Chris Vincent, who also took the Laurels with us second in the final. £30 start money and £12 prize - whoopee!

Brands Hatch would be the conclusion to this exacting race season. The 8 lap scratch race for up to 1200cc outfits was held on the 2.65 mile Grand Prix circuit, as was still the regular case in those days. Our main challengers were Pip Harris with 'Mr. Smooth' Ray Campbell in the chair, Chris Vincent-Keith Scott, Terry Vinicombe-John Flaxman, Charlie Freeman with solo racer Billie Nelson as partner, Owen Greenwood-Terry Fairbrother, Alan Birch-Peter Birch.

Also competing were Bill Boddice-Eddie Bulgin and Fred Hanks-John Thornton. Bill, like Fred and Pip Harris seemed to have been around for ever. Boddice and Harris had first ridden the Isle of Man TT in 1954, and Hanks a year later. Like father like son, youngsters Norman Hanks and Mick Boddice would be out to show their fathers how to do it! Bearded John Tickle with wife Cathy in the sidecar were down as reserves, which would be a disappointment for this 'showboat' couple.

Racing our 'sit up and beg' Dunstall-Norton 650cc, although quick, we were no real match for the kneeler outfit of the BSA-Flyer and once more had to concede to the ace of the short circuits Chris Vincent. However we were pleased with our second place and our subsequent win in the handicap race - a good end to the 27 meetings attended and the 47 races started. With a payment of £73 start and prize money for this last meeting, less £2.15s. entry fee and a payment to Paul Dunstall, it still left us with some Christmas money.

During 1964 Florian Camathias had introduced us to the 1960 World Sidecar Champion Helmut Fath. This intense German from Ursenbach, near Heidelberg, made his international debut at the age of 25 in 1956 at Mettet in Belgium, finishing second to Cyril Smith, Norton, the 1952 World Champion. Later in 1956, he gained a fifth place in the Belgian Grand Prix, and an excellent third in the Solitude German Grand Prix. Helmut did not figure in 1957, but a third place in both the Dutch TT and Belgian Grand Prix gave him third place in the 1958 world championship behind winner Walter Schneider and Florian Camathias. 1959 found Helmut improving his Rennsport BMW by fitting his own-designed and produced con-rods and crankshaft. That year Fath finished fourth in both the French Grand Prix and Isle of Man TT and third again in the Dutch TT. In 1960 Helmut Fath with passenger Alfred Wohlgemuth sprung to world stardom on his home-tuned BMW, totally dominating the series by wins at the French Grand Prix, Isle of Man TT, Belgian and German Grand Prix with a second place at the Dutch TT, that year won by Pip Harris. Fast improving Fritz Scheidegger would finish second in that year's championship. The 1961 season started well for Helmut in winning the Spanish Grand Prix - the first that year, then at an international event at Nürburgring, he suffered an appalling crash resulting in the death of his passenger Wohlgemuth. Helmut himself received serious injuries to both ankles which certainly indicated an end to his racing career. However Fath and his doctors never gave up, and his ankles would be saved, although it would be five years before he would return to competitive racing.

Helmut kept busy during his convalescence, arranging the building of a new home which would include a ground floor workshop. It was here that the URS-Fath-four was born in 1963. This home-brewed project, aided by Dr. Peter Kuhn of Heidelberg University, would rule the world in 1968 and 1971. With an alleged fall-out with the BMW factory by both Fath and Camathias, the FCS was 'born' the Fath-Camathias-Special also instigating the manufacture of the Fath-four.

Helmut Fath was a good friend of Florian and he admired his total commitment to his racing. These two men were like 'peas in a pod', totally dedicated to their sport and obsessed to the extent that all normal reasoning, particularly in the case of Camathias, often went out of the window!

Castrol Oils supported the URS project in the earlier days and the help from the specialist factories, Karl Schmidt Pistons, INA Bearings, Bosch Fuel Injectors and titanium conrods from ICI England made a huge contribution to this home-grown venture. As the four cylinder engine was developed, Helmut never made any claims to its actual power output, only knowing that each time he wheeled the home-made portable dyno out into the local woods and ran the engine up to 14,000rpm, he managed to get more horsepower. Coca-cola, coffee, cigarettes and a working day of 14 to 16 hours would eventually take its toll on Fath's health. Engineer Horst Owesle worked full time on this ambitious project and local solo rider Paul Smetana would ride a planned prototype solo URS four in 1965.

At the other end of the spectrum, the Honda Motor Company had started in a wooden shack back in the early fifties, and first appeared on the international racing scene in Europe at the Isle of Man TT, in 1959. Hordes of Japanese team managers, designers and engineers scouted the TT circuit, shooting miles of film, taking note of anything that could be useful later. They were back in 1960, but still on a learning curve.

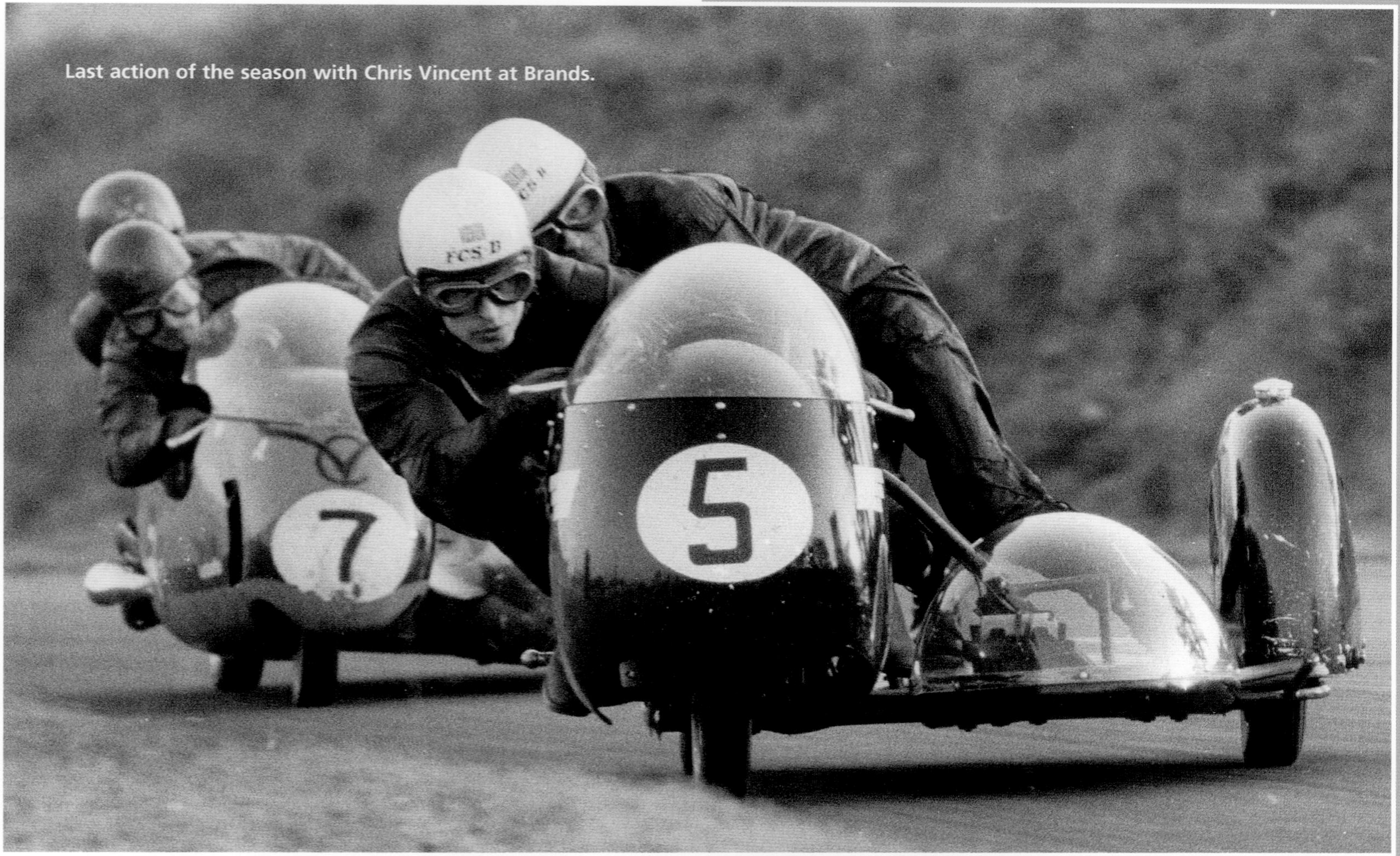

Last action of the season with Chris Vincent at Brands.

In 1961 Honda achieved its first serious success with 'Mike the Bike' winning the 125cc TT, and also a 1 - 2 - 3 in the 250cc TT event with Mike Hailwood, Tom Phillis and Jim Redman, with the same result in that year's 250cc World Championship. Tom Phillis would also win for Honda the 1961 125cc World Championship with Luigi Taveri, Honda, third. Honda was impressive, achieving by the end of 1964 nine World Championships including 77 Grand Prix first places and a massive 206 rostrum positions, which covered the 125, 250 and 350cc classes.

The Italian MV Agusta Factory won 13 Senior Isle of Man TT races between 1956-72 with Surtees, Hailwood, Hocking, and Agostini. Honda would win only two 500cc Isle of Man TT races with Hailwood in 1966 and 1967. Although it was very close between Hailwood, Honda, and Agostini, MV, in 1967 for the 500cc World Championship with five Grand Prix wins each, the second place positions gave Ago the championship result. Honda would have to wait until 1983 when Freddie Spencer gave them their first honours in the 500cc class, the Isle of Man TT no longer counting towards the championship.

The season over, it was great to fall into a routine with family and work. Wally swapped sitting for fitting chairs, as there was still a good demand for sidecars which were a specialist product. Many of the regular manufacturers announced their new models at the Earls Court Show in November. Bond, the three wheeler people launched their latest version a 246cc two or three seater drop-head model. Don't you just love those vehicles!

A Watsonian glass fibre Monza Sports sidecar fitted onto their Super Silk chassis would cost you £106 including purchase tax and if you required a new Triumph 650cc Thunderbird to go with it, add £308 7s 6d including tax to the cost. The man who opened the 1964 Earls Court Motorcycle Show started his racing career as a passenger in his father's racing outfit. John Surtees, seven times World Motorcycle Champion, only a couple of weeks before the show had, in a Ferrari, added the Formula 1 Car Grand Prix crown to his successes.

Phil Read on the 250cc Yamaha won his first ever world title, and in October his first son, Michael Philip was born.

It was also 1964 that Mr. Marples, Minister of Transport lost his job along with the Tory Government. He had shown a zeal and enthusiasm almost unequalled in the Ministry of Transport. Marples left behind 1,300 miles of new roads and a properly organised driving licence system.

Joan and I, now with young Colin, needed more space and a garden, so having bought the old forge workshops back in 1960 which had a plot of land at the rear, planning permission was obtained to build a bungalow. This would be another project for 1965.

Racing-wise we decided to try and buy our own BMW-Rennsport outfit for our Grand Prix aspirations so with a sad heart the G50 Matchless outfit that had served us so well would be sold on. Paul Dunstall was still prepared to supply and service his Norton 650cc Domiracer engines for our use in the UK unlimited classes.

With 27 race meetings in 29 weeks and 47 race starts in 1964, no wonder it had been such a physically demanding year. The constant mental pressure, the ups and downs, our first Grand Prix win, the loss of good friends, third place in the World Sidecar Championship, 1964 had been a 'hell of a year'.

8 1965
SEEMED LIKE A GOOD IDEA AT THE TIME!

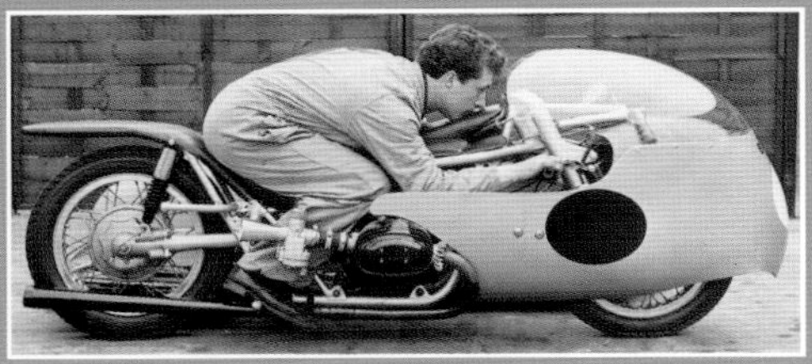

Astride the rebuilt BMW Rennsport

During the winter we had managed to purchase our own Rennsport-BMW sidecar outfit, but as a boxful of engine parts with a fire-damaged frame and chassis unit. This 'heap of parts' was subject to a complete restoration job, including re-styling the frame to match as near as possible the FCS-BMW we rode the year before. Unfortunately, along with a lack of experience of obtaining the best from the horizontal opposed overhead camshaft and shaft drive engine, we lacked any new engine and gearbox spares. As we found out in 1964, obtaining spares from the BMW factory was very difficult as one had to return any old parts before being able to buy replacements.

Before the opening of the 1965 season, Florian Camathias planned a trip to America in early March to the Daytona Speed Bowl to mount an attack on the World Sidecar Speed Records. I was invited as co-driver, in attempts on the long distance records, up to 12 hours in duration. Although the owners of the speed bowl made the circuit available free of charge, the project never really got off the ground.

So back to reality. Brands Hatch March 21st was the first outing for our revamped Dunstall-Norton 650cc Domiracer, now fitted with a set of Ken Sprayson built Reynolds leading link forks on this normal seating position sidecar outfit (no kneeler for us), originally just a quick lash up, although nicely built. Again, we would continue to hassle Chris Vincent throughout the season on his green meanie kneeler 650cc BSA.

At Brands a second place behind Chris in the scratch race, and a win in the handicap race with a fastest lap, with our friend Norman Huntingford on the Seeley entered Matchless second, was a good start. Our next event, 11th April, the Mallory Park International Sidecar Race of the Year, saw 56 sidecar competitors lined up to do battle in the nine events of heats and finals - such was the interest in sidecar racing in those days!

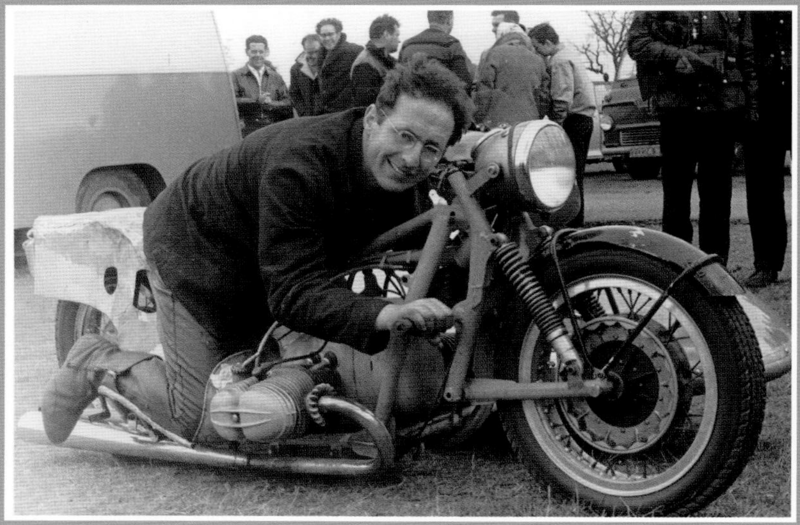

All the UK and international contenders were in attendance and not least our quirky Swiss friend Florian 'Flo' Camathias. Unknown to us, Flo had built an almost exact replica of his BMW racing outfit for use on the normal roads. Who in their right mind but this incredible man would even consider riding such a kneeler sidecar outfit. This freaky machine was powered by a BMW R69 engine, with handlebars nearly scraping the floor, and complete with number plates, lights and horn. Only Florian would attempt the 600 mile journey from Switzerland to my home and workshop in Belvedere. I will remember forever Flo's arrival. It was late evening, and we were loading our outfits for Mallory Park next day. In the silence of the night we heard the roar of Flo's contraption. A helmet displaying a Swiss cross popped up over the gate and a pair of thick-rimmed glasses glistened in the light. A voice in a heavy French-Swiss accent said, 'Good evening, do you have a bed for the night?' Did we have a laugh when we saw what he had ridden to England on! Franz Ducret, 'Flo's' new passenger had driven the converted Citroen transporter containing the race outfit.

Florian's plan after Mallory was to visit the Isle of Man with the road-going racer outfit to practise with his new passenger before returning to the island in June. Anyway, next morning, following 'Flo' riding his special outfit on the M1, he kept stopping and then re-starting rushing off into the distance, then repeating the action. We suddenly twigged, he was practising race starts on the M1 motorway - what a character!

For all his efforts, Florian failed to have a good day at Mallory, finishing in a lowly fourth in the 500cc race to winner and fellow countryman Fritz Scheidegger. Pip Harris, second at the time, retired with magneto trouble. Out for the first time on our BMW, we were stopped with a broken gearbox. However, we made amends in the 1300cc events, winning our heat on the Dunstall-Norton, then second once again in the final to the BSA Flyer, Chris Vincent. Then came the Daily Mail Race of the Year with £500 at stake for the winner. We led the first lap from Scheidegger and Vincent, Fritz then took the lead. Chris soon got the better of our Norton as it started to misfire, caused by collapsing valve springs and that was our race run. Chris arrived at the front winning the 'pot of gold' from Fritz, with Max in third place.

Within days came the Easter race meetings. That year would be busier than normal, Brands Hatch on Good Friday, 16th April, Snetteron Sunday, Oulton Park Monday and

Florian, at Mallory Park on his road going outfit.

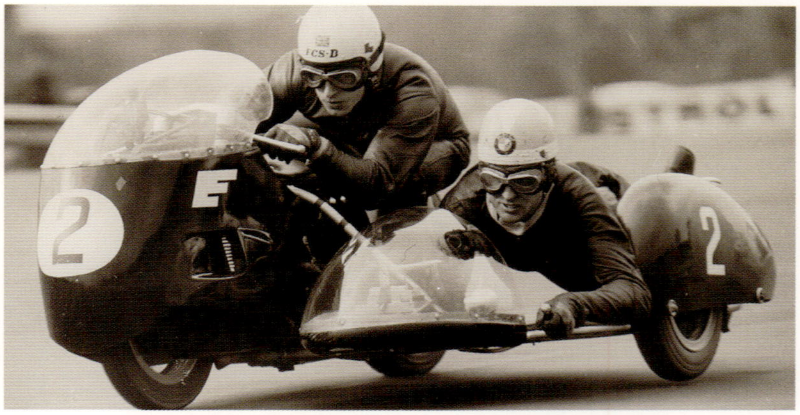

Mallory Park, Easter Tuesday with stand-in passenger Ray Campbell.

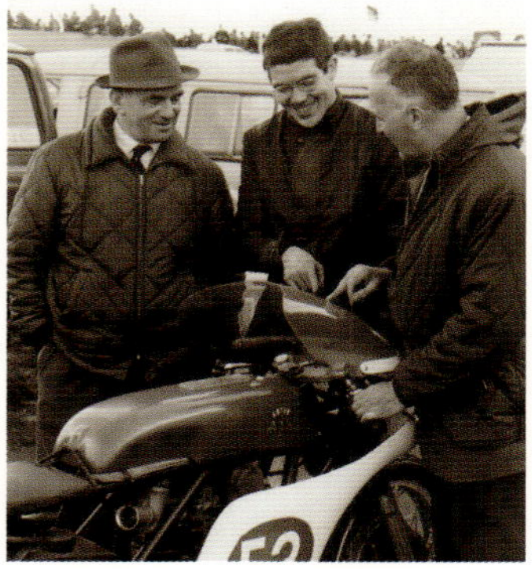

Mallory Park 1965, Tom Arter, Peter with his father, Jack Williams.

Mallory Park's Easter event on Tuesday. Four meetings in five days was crazy. At Brands on Good Friday, 50,000 fans witnessed Derek Minter at his best. On Ray Petty's Nortons, outclassing all, he won the 350, 500cc and 'King of Brands'. Bill Ivy won the 50cc race, second in the 125 with a lap record, second in the 250, then second to Minter in the 500cc race. If Minter was 'King', surely Bill Ivy was 'Crown Prince'. Chris Vincent took the honours from us again in the 1200cc race, with Pip Harris third. Sunday morning it was up to Snetterton, nearly a wasted effort when our BMW broke down. With a fifth in the 1300cc race on the Norton it was a bad day. Monday's Oulton Park International was no better, retiring our BMW in both races.

With Wally having gone straight home after Oulton Park to work on the BMW, I had a change of passenger for Mallory, the stylish Ray Campbell on loan from Pip Harris. Well, between us we had a good day, second in both heat and final. Out of my winnings of £53, £10 was for Ray Campbell's services and £10 for Mr. Dunstall. On Thursday we left for the German Grand Prix. five race events in nine days was totally ridiculous and perhaps ill conceived.

We were in trouble from the very start of that season, with our BMW failing to finish in the first three UK Internationals, and then at the German Grand Prix, at the Nürburgring, in late April, the year's first Grand Prix at which the 62.5 mile sidecar race would be held in atrocious conditions. It was more like a speedboat championship with the rain, sleet and snow decimating the field in the first few laps. Deubel, Camathias, Harris, Vincent, Kolle and ourselves were amongst many skidding to a halt, totally waterlogged. Fritz Scheidegger somehow managed to keep going, to win, riding without goggles, only his normal glasses giving protection from the spray. A new man on the block, Siegfried Schauzu, BMW, although half a minute astern, finished second and Arsenius Butscher going boatwise into third position. A calamity event for most of us and we were pleased to get back into the warm.

We travelled down to Austria for the following weekend's non-championship Austrian Grand Prix, another waste of time and effort following another breakdown. However, whilst there we made an agreement with Michael Schafleitner to be the UK Distributor for his excellent gear clusters.

Next came the Spanish Grand Prix held at Barcelona on the Montjuich Park Circuit. The best part about this meeting was the sunshine and the beautiful girls, both in abundance. Chris Vincent had driven the near 1,000 miles to Barcelona only to find that his race entry had not arrived, or was lost, or even put to one side. Pip Harris had his race application rejected, yet a number of 'no hopers' had been included. Who, I wonder, had upset Don Francisco Franco Bahamonde, (General Franco).

Wally and me with the BMW and Norton.

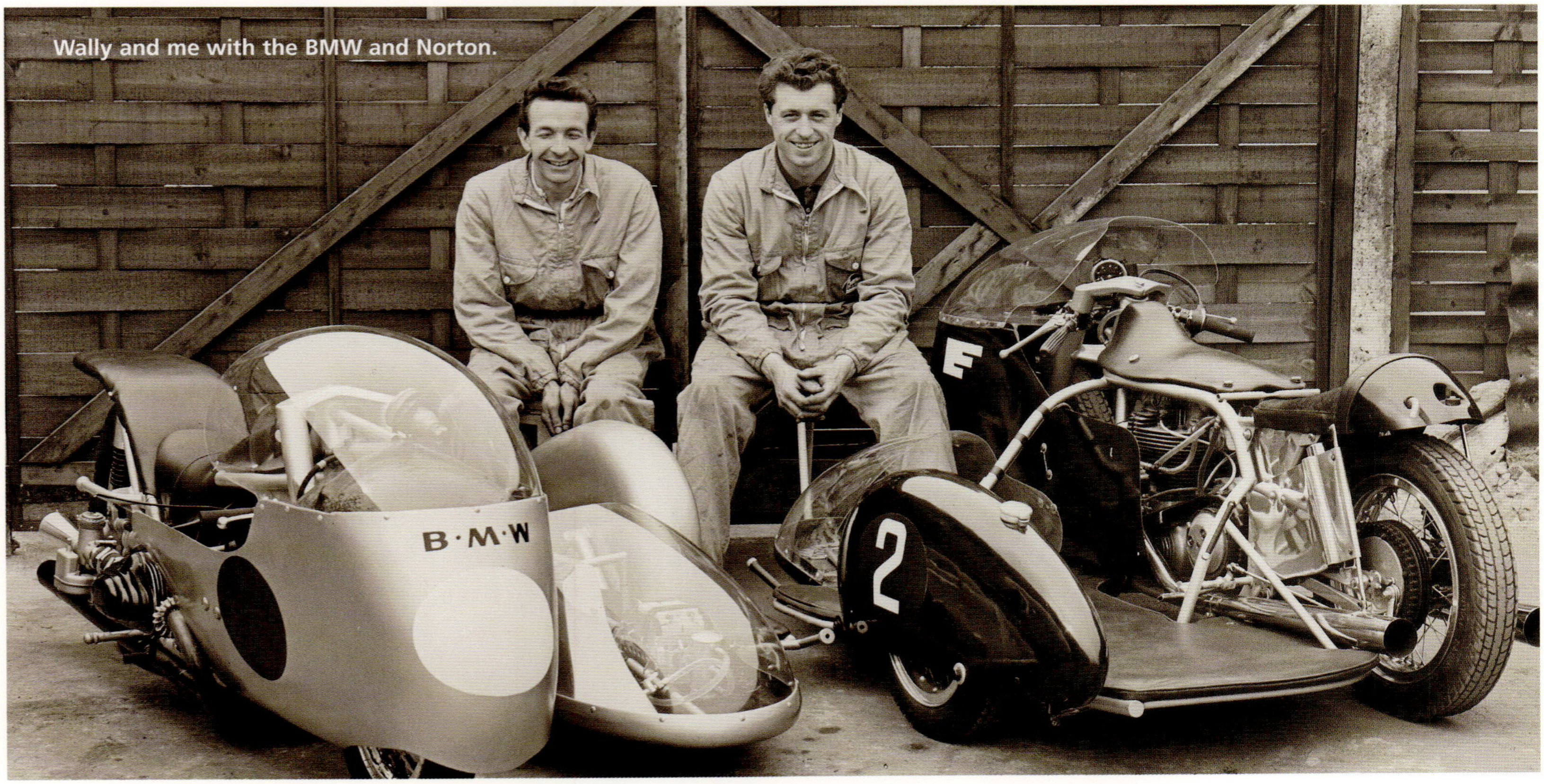

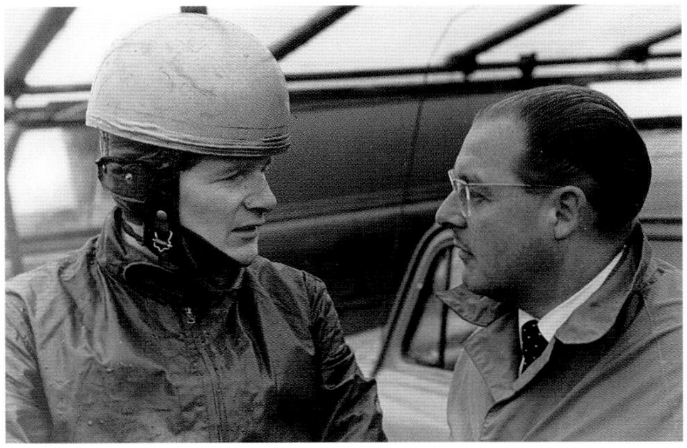

Terry Vinicombe and Tom Kirby, 'What do you think I should do Boss?'

In brilliant sunshine the day's racing started with the 50cc 'tiddlers' at 10.00am. It was suggested that the only thing ever rushed in Spain is the organisation of the Grand Prix, as later in the day everybody rushed off to the local bullfight. The 50cc race held over 14 laps had the Spanish crowd on their feet cheering their local hero Jose Busquets on a Derbi who took an early lead from Hugh Anderson, Suzuki, and Ralph Bryans, Honda. It would be a long encounter with Anderson getting the verdict from Bryans, and Busquets in a well deserved third, well away from Luigi Taveri and Kreidler ace Anscheidt fourth and fifth respectively.

Hardly had the 50cc riders dismounted when the 125cc competitors were wheeling to the line for the 10.40am race start. Hugh Anderson leapt from the 50cc to the 125cc Suzuki for 27 laps (63.6 miles) of hot tub action. This he achieved without a challenge, keen to get the race over so he could retire into the shade. Team mate Frank (gentleman) Perris put in a spirited performance from a slow start to come through in second place, with Derek Woodman MZ third.

The last solo race of the day was the 250cc Grand Prix with an 11.45am start. It was like a spaghetti western, a duel in the sun at high noon between the rising star, World Champion 'speedy-Read' and the man in the cloak and sombrero, World Champion from the late fifties, Tarquinio Provini winner over the last two years of the 250cc Grand Prix held at Montjuich. Provini was deep in thought as to how to keep this 'young pretender' at bay. The race, held over 35 laps (77.73 miles) would provide cheers, sweat and tears, as from the start Phil Read, Yamaha, and Tarquinio Provini, Benelli, set a fantastic pace in their wheel to wheel skirmish. Montjuich Park with its many twists and turns was said to be a favourite with Provini, but Read was able to match the challenge bringing to bear all his experience.

Read managed after a number of laps to pull away, but there was no shaking the tenacity of the fiery Italian. His machine no longer in the usual Italian red, but a dull battleship grey, seemed to take on the role of a destroyer and was soon back on Read's heels. Then Provini took the lead by a second but the 'canny' Read wasn't out of the picture. Their record breaking speed was such that in tearing away from the field they lapped fourth place man, Mike Duff, on the other works Yamaha.

With only 3 laps to go 'speedy-Read' moved ahead of Provini but it was all so close, a gigantic struggle. The master at Montjuich Park, Provini went all or bust. Screaming the four cylinder Benelli to its maximum, he hurtled into a bend and took the braking of the machine to a point of no return, locking the front wheel. He shot himself over the handlebars and out of the contest. This popular racer Provini had given his total commitment and no more could possibly be asked. The Spanish fans had enjoyed this encounter and were certainly pleased when their own hero, Ramon Torras brought his Bultaco home in second place, after a race long tussle with Mike Duff. Torras was the only rider not to be lapped by the 'flying' Phil Read. This race of the 'two aces' was a race to behold.

With the Spanish crowd still buzzing with excitement, it was time for the charioteers with a 1.00pm start for the 27 lap (63.6 mile) event. This would be a long race in the stifling heat, wrestling sidecar outfits around the tortuous Montjuich Park for an hour was no fun. The regular top German and Swiss crews were all in attendance, but Wally and I were the only top British sidecar crew, hence the complaints from our compatriots.

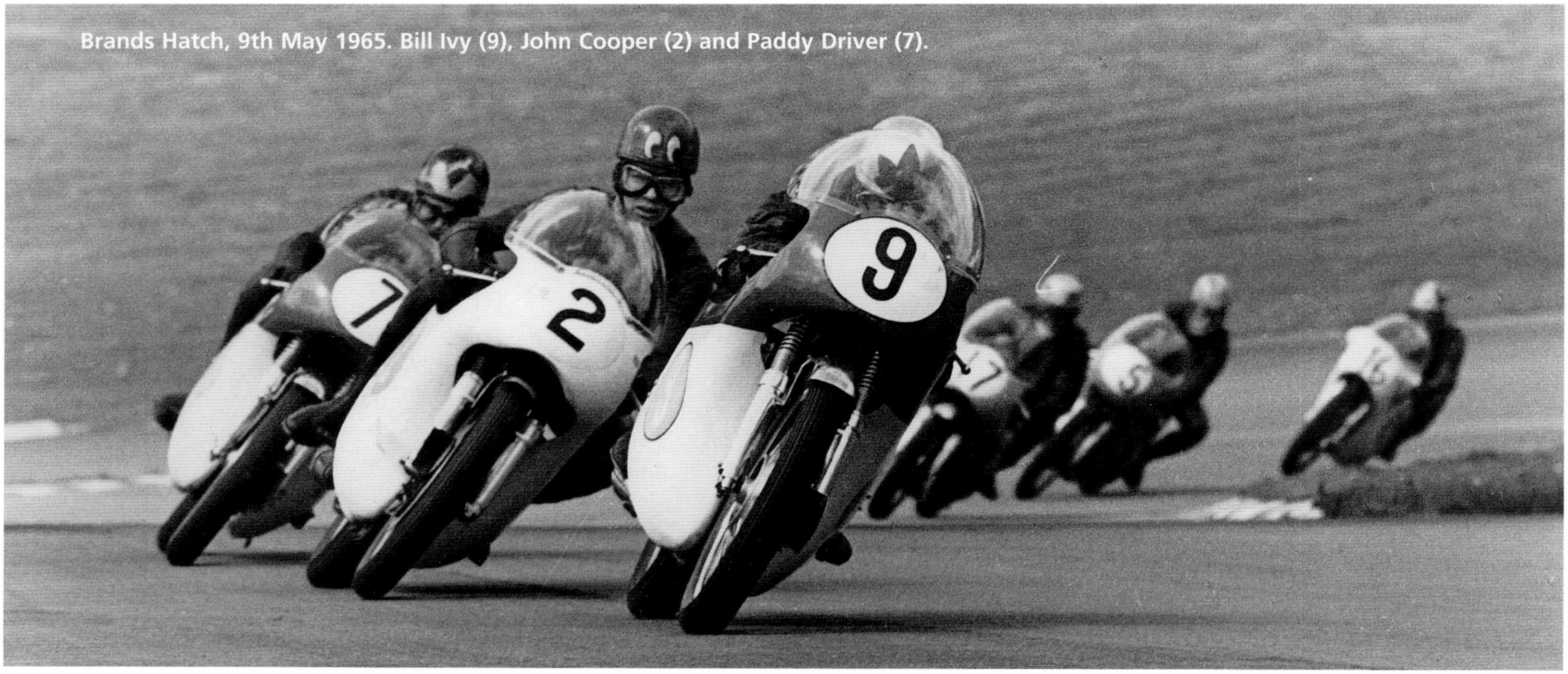

Brands Hatch, 9th May 1965. Bill Ivy (9), John Cooper (2) and Paddy Driver (7).

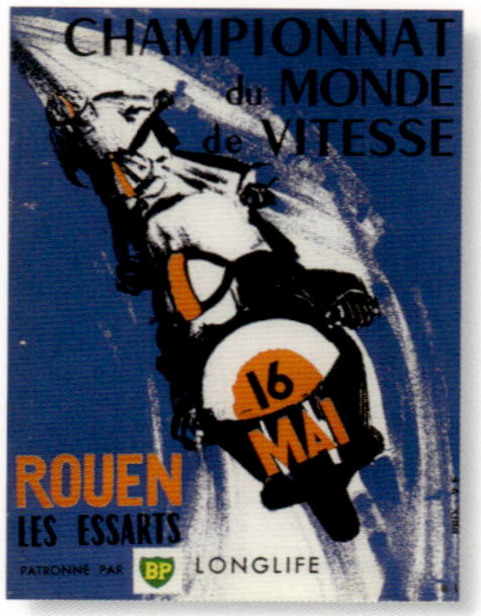

Camathias at Ballaugh Bridge, TT practice.

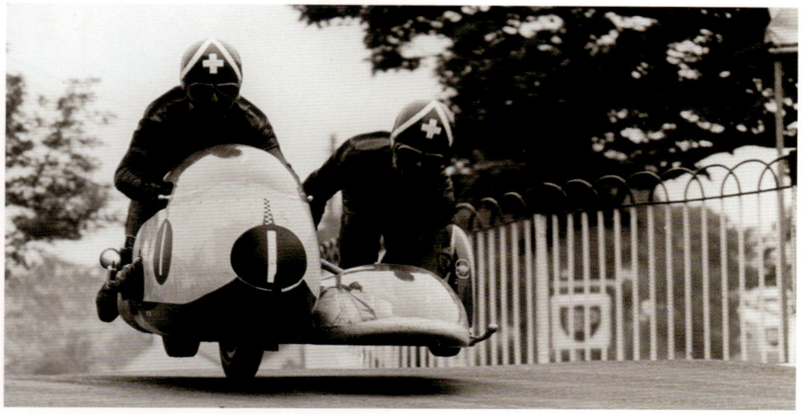

We were allocated race number 'one', not that it would do much good, as from the start our BMW suffered a misfire. Meanwhile our friend Florian Camathias, BMW, took the lead, but not for long. His ignition batteries broke loose and were finally lost overboard causing his retirement. Florian was once more all at sea because he did not pay enough attention to detail. World Champion Max Deubel went on to win from Scheidegger whilst we held on to a sixth place despite our problems, until we ran out of fuel on the very last lap. The enthusiastic Spanish fans dispersed, pleased with the morning's action and now ready for their siesta before the next highlight of the day, the bull fight!

We packed up for the long haul to Rouen for the following weekend's French Grand Prix. Camathias, back on form won from Scheidegger with the 'champ' Deubel in third place. Our own sixth spot was the first result with our own BMW, earning us £58 in start money and £30 in prize money. A total of seven international and Grand Prix events within six weeks combined with all the travelling, was already beginning to stretch us and drain our resources.

There was no let up. Directly after the French Grand Prix it was back to Mallory Park on May 23rd for another dash around on the Dunstall-Norton, second in the heat and third in the final earned us £50, less £7 10s to Paul Dunstall. We then had two weeks to catch up with motorcycle business matters and the family, and to prepare for the forthcoming Whit Monday 'Evening News' sponsored sidecar international event, to be held on 7th June at Brands Hatch. £350 prize money was up for the winner of the 500cc sidecar race which encouraged the continental stars to attend, as most were on the way to the Isle of Man for the TT the following week.

Sidecar racing was still attracting the crowds and the BBC mounted six camera crews around the circuit, the most ever to record the sidecar action line. We soon found that having a Rennsport BMW was one thing, but having the right one was another. Despite all our efforts, our bad luck would continue. Third in our heat at Brands would be it, with a further retirement in the main event. Our friend Pip Harris, who had rushed to our workshop in Belvedere between heats and finals to borrow and fit a new set of Dunlop tyres, returned to scoop the main prize of £350 - a good day for Pip, a bad day for Wally and me. Then it was a rush for most of the sidecar crews to the Isle of Man, where practice was already in progress.

We were plagued with trouble, in TT practice we failed along with Pip Harris and Bill Boddice to qualify for the race. So like three naughty boys we had to appeal to the ACU TT jury for permission to start. Camathias had suffered his own problems when there was very nearly a serious fire in his garage just before the second sidecar practice. As the finishing touches were being put to his BMW, a fire started inside the streamlining when a welding torch touched some oil and petrol, which had collected there. As Florian sprang forward to beat out the flames, he came almost into the line of the fire of the still flaming torch. His forhead was burnt and his hair set on fire. His eyes fortunately were saved by his glasses but the heat was so intense that they cracked! Florian beat out the flames, took himself off to be patched up and, although late for practice, still managed to put in 2 laps.

For the 3 lap race, a good start off the line was the highlight of our day. Our BMW was no match for the likes of Deubel, Scheidegger and Camathias. We were left in their wake on the first lap although managing to hold fifth place, then as we sped down Bray Hill on the second lap our Rennsport engine went kaput, with smoke billowing from the megaphones, forcing us to retire at Braddan Bridge to be spectators - a real choker. Perhaps we should have stayed with our Matchless. Our average speed in the 1962 event would have given us a respectable fifth place and the first all British crew home. Never mind it's always easy in retrospect!

The stylish west German World Champion, Max Deubel went on to win his third Isle of Man TT. Fritz came second and Georg Auerbacher third, after Camathias, an early leader, retired with a clutch problem. Norman Huntingford, back in action after his TT race accident the previous year, now partnered by Roy Lindsey racing the C.J Seeley (Sales) Ltd entered Matchless/Watsonian finished in a very respectable eighth place.

Following the sidecar event the lightweight 250cc race had attracted a record entry of 106 riders with an unbelievable 29 different makes of machines. With changes and non-starters the field was reduced to 76 with six manufacturers teams entered; Bultaco, Cotton, Honda, MZ, Royal Enfield and Yamaha. Jim Redman won his third consectutive TT on the works Honda. Phil Read almost stole the show with a standing start lap of 100.01mph (the first such speed for a lightweight machine) before retiring on the second lap. This left Redman to set a lap record of 100.09mph, ahead of Mike Duff, Yamaha, second and Frank Perris, Suzuki, third.

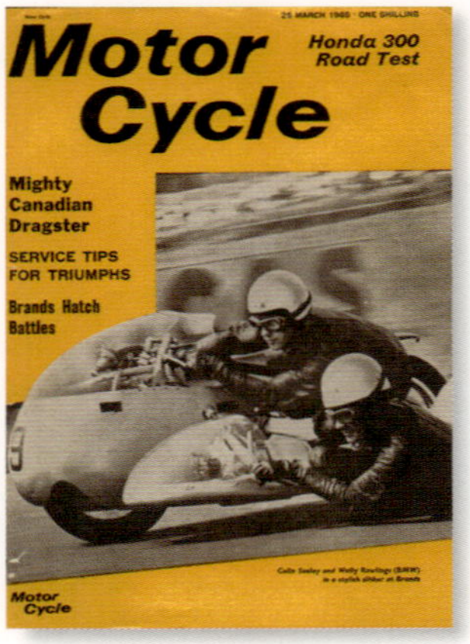

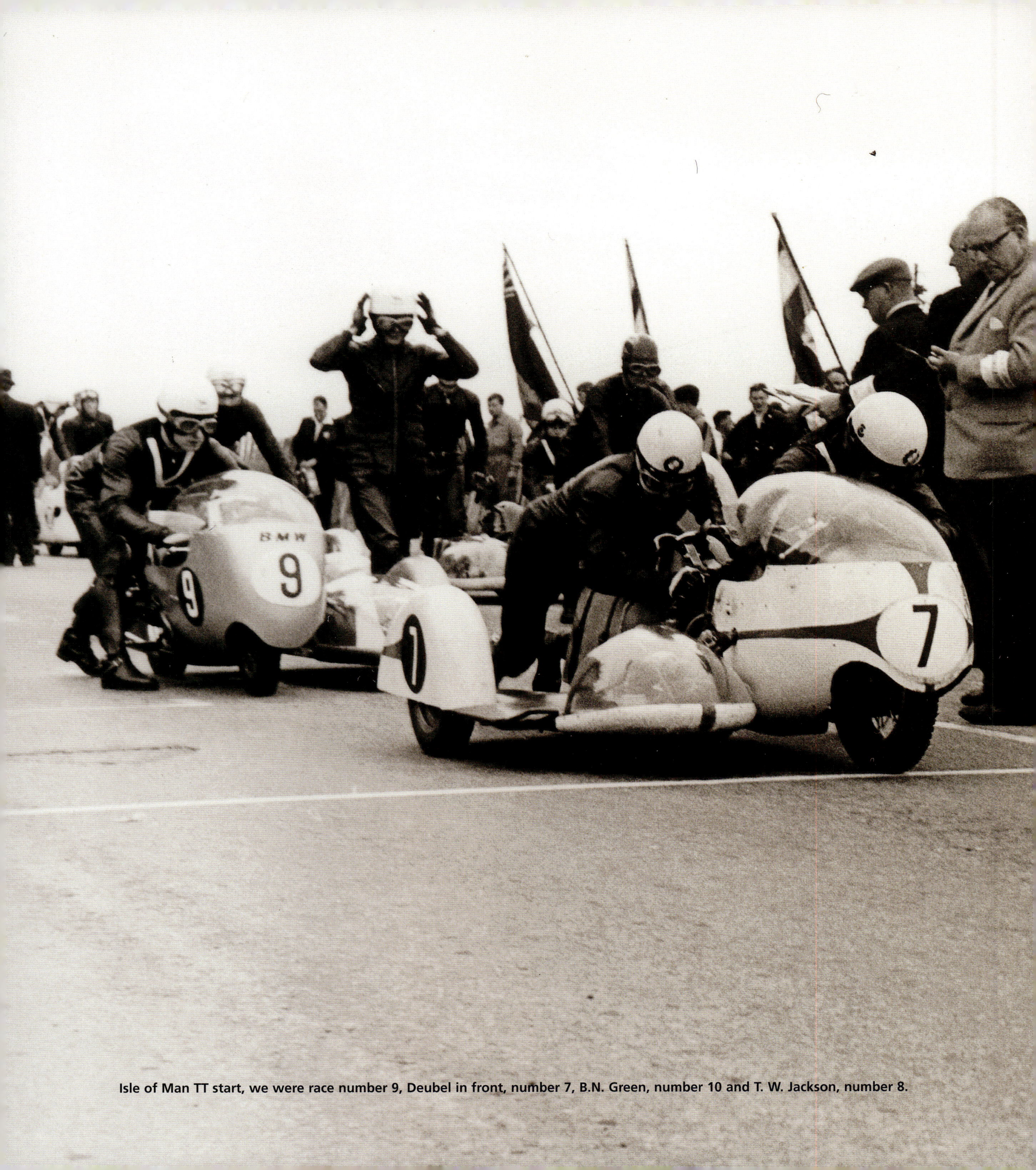

Isle of Man TT start, we were race number 9, Deubel in front, number 7, B.N. Green, number 10 and T. W. Jackson, number 8.

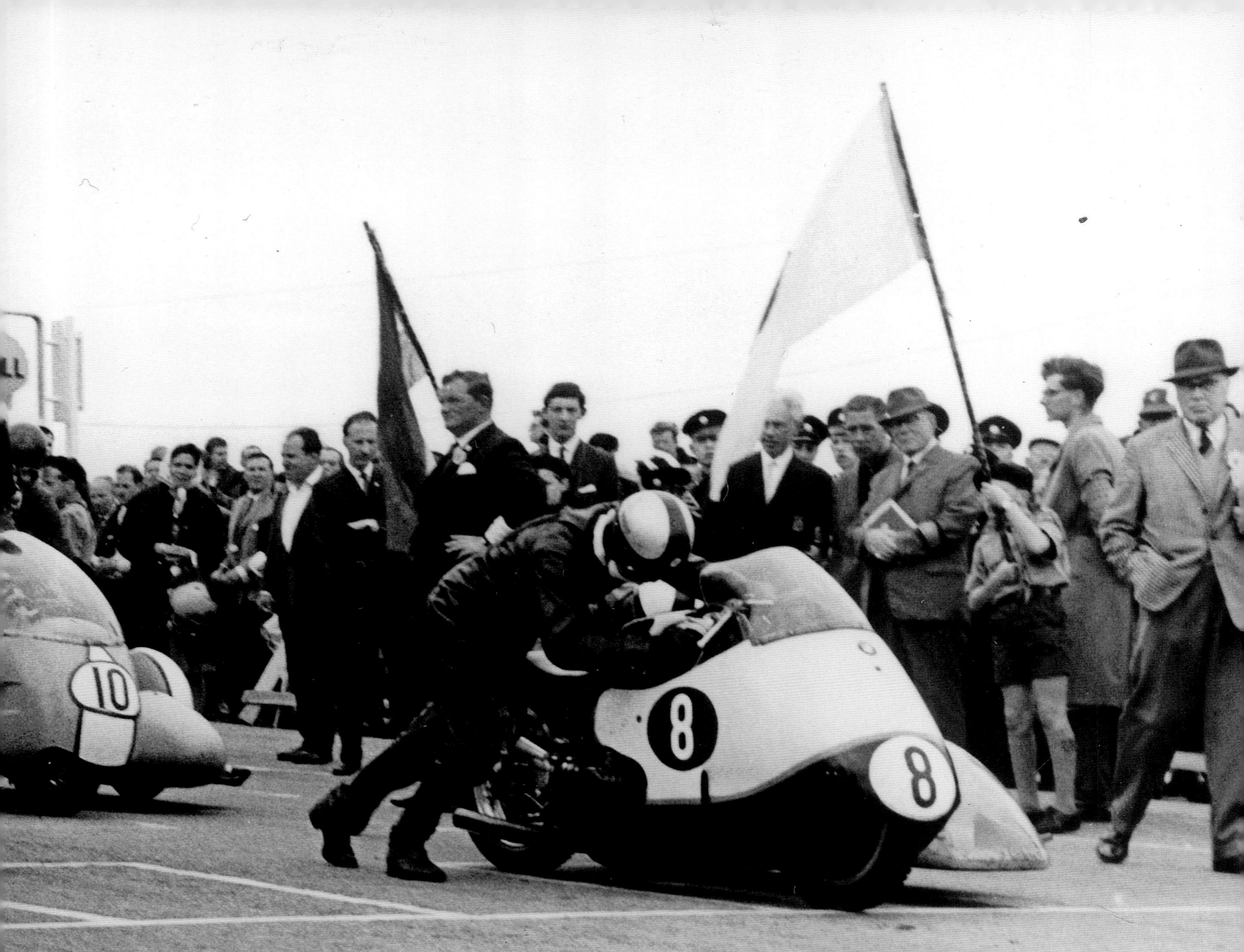

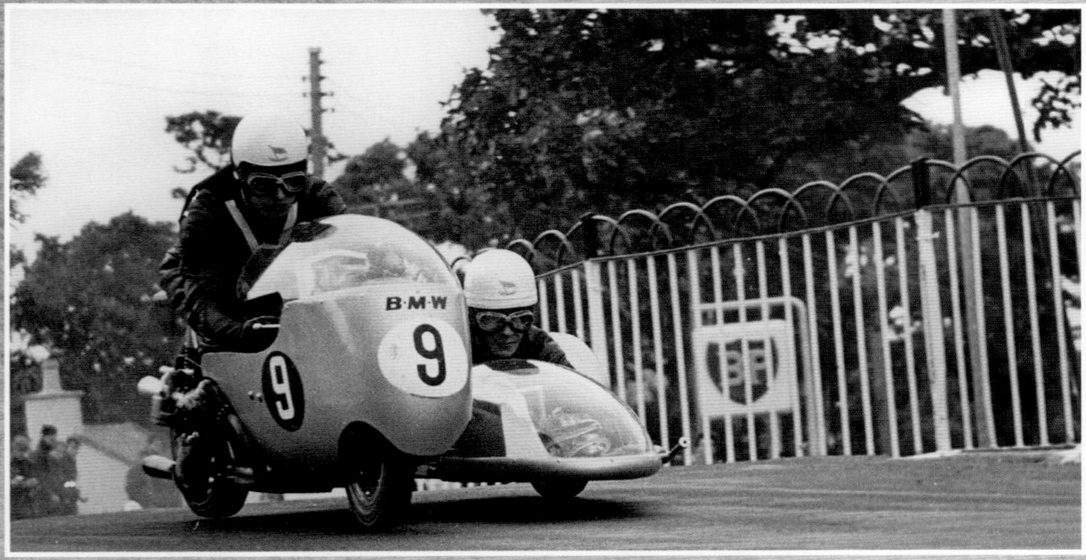

First lap Ballaugh Bridge.

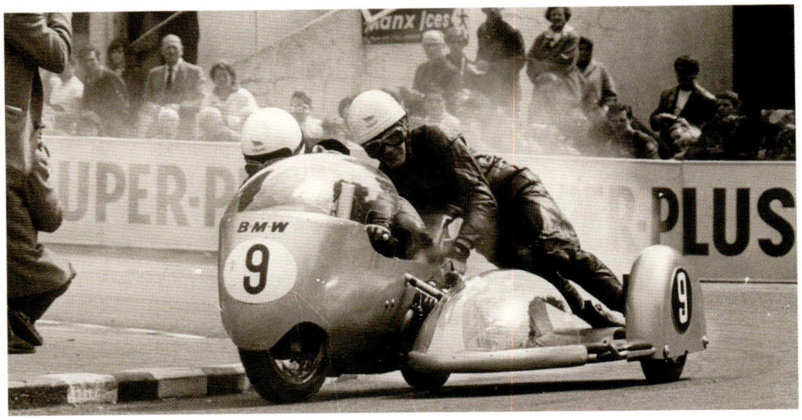

Second lap just before retirement at Quarter Bridge.

1965 saw the arrival in the Isle of Man for his first ever TT, the 23 year old Giacomo Agostini, fresh from winning his first ever major event, in the German Grand Prix, at the Nürburgring, riding the works 350cc MV and beating team mate Mike Hailwood. With so much expected of this handsome, talented newcomer and with so much to learn about the hazardous TT course, Italy's bright new star achieved at least 14 laps in practice and fourth fastest in the Senior 500cc, qualifying him to race with Hailwood, Minter and Griff Jenkins.

Alan Shepherd, forced to hang up his leathers after suffering serious injuries when testing for Honda at Suzuka in the previous October, had taken up a position with Castrol Oils competition department so would still be in action at his favourite event having ridden there first in 1959, finishing seventh in the Senior Race. The racing circus and the fans have surely missed Alan's remarkable talents on the race track, his incredible second place in the 1964 250cc TT on the MZ when riding injured, was sadly his last Isle of Man TT.

Amongst the huge trade support in those days for the Isle of Man TT, where points counted towards the World Championship, Reynolds Chains had to that point given excellent service via Vic Doyle and his merry men, providing a fitting service and free replacement chains. Unfortunately, the service was being abused by some competitors, who often arrived in the Island without any chains fitted on their machines. Therefore a nominal charge had to be introduced.

It was alleged that Phil Read, having been overwhelmed by requests for his autograph had produced a rubber stamp. Signing can be a problem - but a rubber stamp was surely no answer! There was often controversy surrounding this talented rider, seven times World Motorcycle Champion between 1964 and 1974 on 125cc, 250cc and 500cc machines, Phil's antics in business and in his private life have left much to be desired.

After a disappointing 250cc race, the 'Prince of Speed' Phil Read won his second Isle of Man TT, later that week. His first was back in 1961 on a 350cc Norton. In the 3 lap 125cc event of 1965, Phil on the works Yamaha rode to victory with an astounding record average speed of 94.28mph, beating the diminutive Luigi Taveri, Honda by 5.8 seconds with Mike Duff, Yamaha. third. Derek Woodman, MZ, was fourth, then little Bill Ivy on the other works Yamaha fifth.

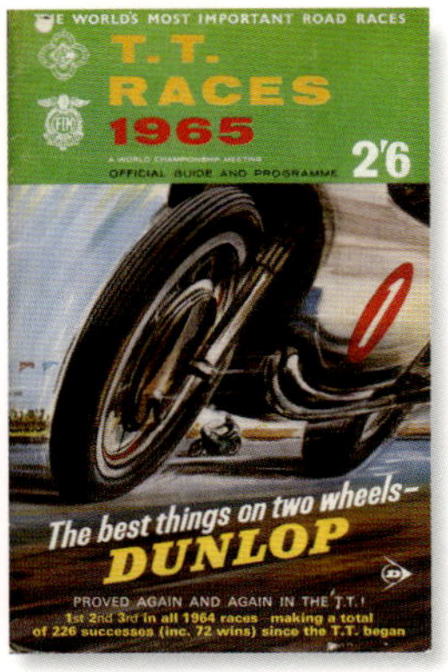

With little time to spare after the the 125cc race, it was action again for 'Speedy' Read, Duff, Ivy and Woodman all entered in the 6 lap 350cc Junior Race at 1.30pm. Hailwood, Redman, Minter, Provini, were also among the 90-odd starters. The first lap found Mike Hailwood, MV 20 seconds ahead of Jim Redman, Honda and breaking the lap record with a speed of 102.85mph, with Read third and Agostini fourth. The second lap was the same except Woodman, MZ had overtaken Ago but only by 0.4 seconds lapping at 99.38mph - pretty good for this under-funded East German team. At half distance Hailwood was still leading but a long pit stop at the start of the fourth lap cost him nearly 3 minutes, then a retirement at Sarah's Cottage with engine trouble. Derek Woodman held fourth until he retired on the last lap leaving Redman to win his third successive Junior TT. Phil Read riding an overbored 250 Yamaha, finished second at 99.35mph. This second spot plus his earlier win in the 125 race added up to 9 laps and 339.6 miles of racing, not a bad day's work! The smooth Italian 'Ago' having lapped his MV at 98.25mph, a dazzling first time performance, was in third.

Our man Sid Mizen on the Seeley-sponsored AJS 7R came in twelfth with friend and rider-to-be in the Seeley camp, Ron Chandler, AJS thirteenth, awarded the last of the Silver Replicas.

The final events of the TT week were Friday's 50cc and 500cc races when unfortunately, the Manx weather upset the day's proceedings. The 'tiddlers' race had attracted 37 entries, but non-starters including the Kreidler team, reduced the numbers to 23. The main contenders would be Ralph Bryans, the championship leader, and team mate Taveri, Honda against the Suzuki trio of World Champion Hugh Anderson, Degner and Itoh. In practice Anderson and team mate Degner had unofficially broken Hugh's lap record from 1964 lapping at just over 81mph but it was Ralph Bryan's practice lap at 82.46mph that set Honda's tail wagging and with a top speed of over 95mph it was just incredible how fantastic a 50cc engine could be.

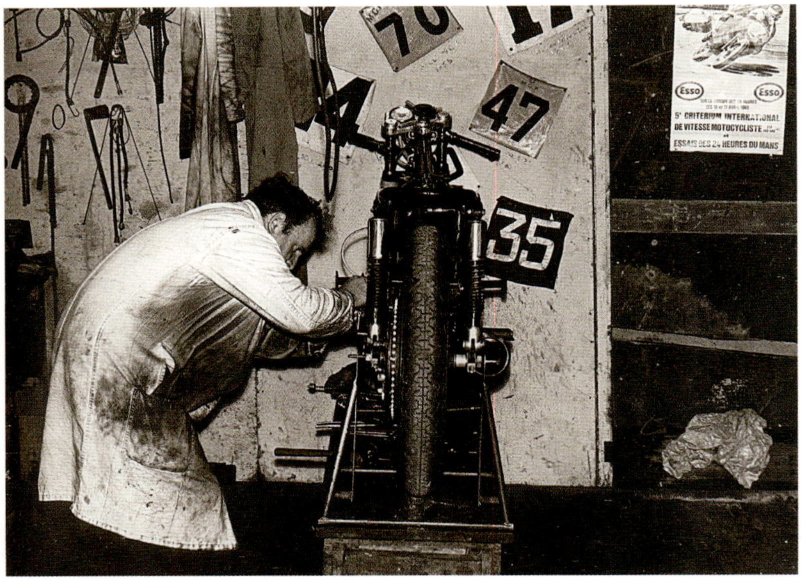

Sid Mizen before we got to grips with him!

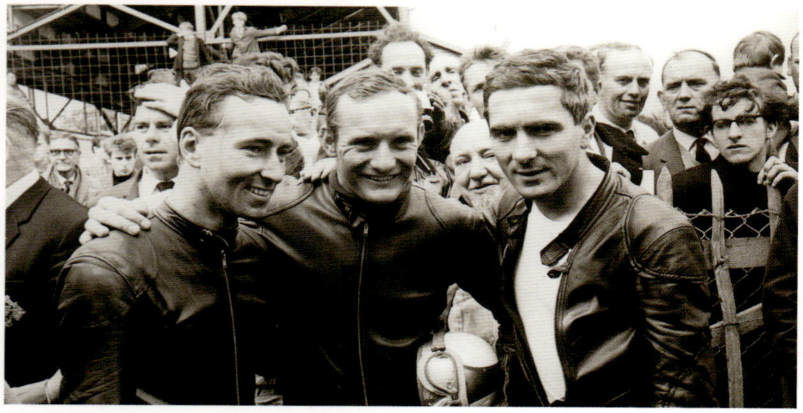

1965 Senior, Mike Duff 3rd, Mike Hailwood 1st, and Joe Dunphy 2nd.

At 10.30am the rain started, 20 minutes later visibility was down to 100 yards on parts of the mountain. A 30 minute delay was announced. At 11.15am the rain stopped. The 11.30am rescheduled 'wasp' start was on. With the number of non-starters, Luigi Taveri started the race alone, the next man 20 seconds behind, the TT course all to himself, wonderful, if it was not for the conditions. On the first lap Ralph Bryans was in trouble - well down in fifth place he retired at the Gooseneck. Meantime, Itoh, Suzuki, who held the lead on the first lap, was forced into the pits to change plugs. Taveri took the lead on the then drying roads, staying there to win his third Isle of Man TT event. Finishing well behind, Anderson took second place and Degner third. With only three Silver Replicas presented and no bronze it was a disappointing race. Then despite all the delays for the 'tiddler' race, the Senior started on time at 1.30pm The weather was cloudy at the start, some sections of the road were dry, some damp, some sunshine, strong winds, a nightmare unless you had three wheels.

'Mike the Bike' and 'Ago' on the works MVs were not expecting any real opposition. Of the 82 entries, 45 were riding Nortons and 26 Matchless machines. Londoner Joe Dunphy, sixth in practice, and Roger Hunter were the first pair to be flagged away followed 10 seconds later by Derek Woodman and big Jack Ahearn, then 'Mike the Bike' and Griff Jenkins, Derek Minter and 'Ago', then the rest of the field in pairs at 10 second intervals.

It was a slow first lap, as conditions, particularly at Ramsey, were terrible, with rain bucketing down. Hailwood and Ago led the first lap from Woodman, Matchless, Joe Dunphy, Norton, ahead of Griff Jenkins and 'Mooneyes' John Cooper, Norton, in sixth place.

On the second lap Minter retired at the pits with magneto trouble, Ivy and Cooper both retired with problems at Brandywell. It was reported that sleet was falling with the rain, yet at the pits the rain had stopped and a blue sky was approaching with some sunshine. Meantime, newcomer Agostini, not used to the changing weather conditions, came off at Sarah's Cottage, fortunately without injury. Fourth place man Griff Jenkins disappeared up the slip road at Governors.

On the third lap Hailwood, well in the lead from Woodman, also lost the plot and fell at Sarah's Cottage - what was the attraction of Sarah's? Mike's crash had bent the handlebars of the works MV and shattered the windscreen, undaunted Mike kicked the MV straight, remounted his battered racer and continued - still in the lead! A long pit stop sorted out some of the problems. Derek Woodman and Joe Dunphy were giving good chase in second and third on lap four. Then Woodman, after such a gallant attempt, retired with a mechanical problem and consequently had to push his machine in. 'Mike the Bike' Hailwood, our hero, won the Senior TT for the third year in succession and his seventh Isle of Man TT event. Joe Dunphy took a well deserved second place, his best TT result to date with Mike Duff, Arter Matchless making up the rostrum positions.

With another eventful TT over, the circus moved on, leaving this Island of contradictions. Love it or hate it, the 37.73 mile mountain course offers the ultimate challenge. Although calm returned to the Magic Isle, an undercurrent of controversy was growing between the organisers of the Manx Lottery Fund, established with the idea of providing the cash to finance the manufacture of a British 'world beater', and the motorcycle industries association which had other ideas!!

Somewhat in despair with our BMW after the Isle of Man TT, and with the Dutch TT looming up within days, which path should we take? Well, Florian came to the rescue, and lent us one of his Rennsport engines. Returning to Assen for the Dutch TT was always a pleasure, and it was a favourite circuit for most competitors. Having won the sidecar event in 1964 Wally and I had something to prove, but I was unsure our BMW was good enough. Although we now had a Camathias engine, it was surely not the best.

Race day saw 200,000 race fans thronging around the testing 4.8 miles of the Assen Circuit. Ralph Bryans, Honda would repeat his success of 1964, winning the opening 'tiddler' 50cc race from Hugh Anderson, Suzuki, with team mate Taveri, Honda making up the rostrum. In the 125cc race Phil Read, having won the Isle of Man TT lightweight, was on for a double, leading team mate Duff by 19 seconds. With little more than a lap to go, Phil was dramatically out of the race with a seized engine. Mike Duff produced the win for Yamaha only 2.6 seconds ahead of Suzuki's bright new star Yoshide Katayama. Championship leader Hugh Anderson recovered from a disastrous start to make third and 'little' Bill Ivy fourth.

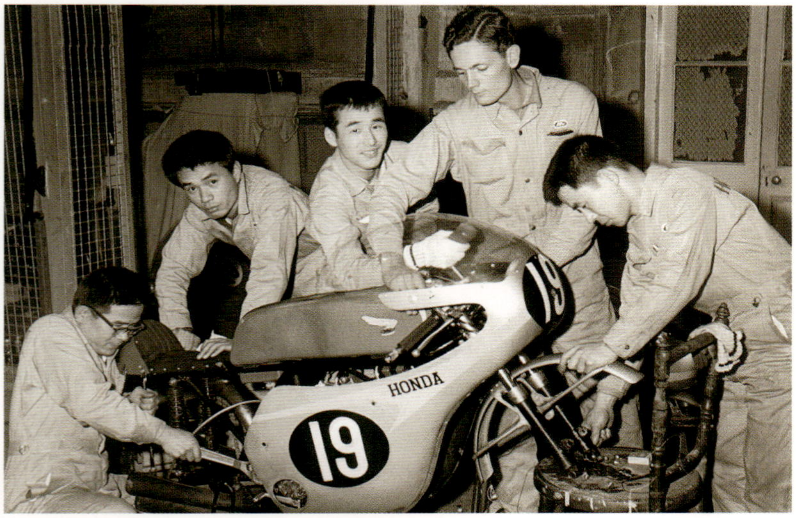

Isle of Man TT, work on Ralph Bryans' 125cc Honda headed by Nobby Clark, but not in the normal working conditions.

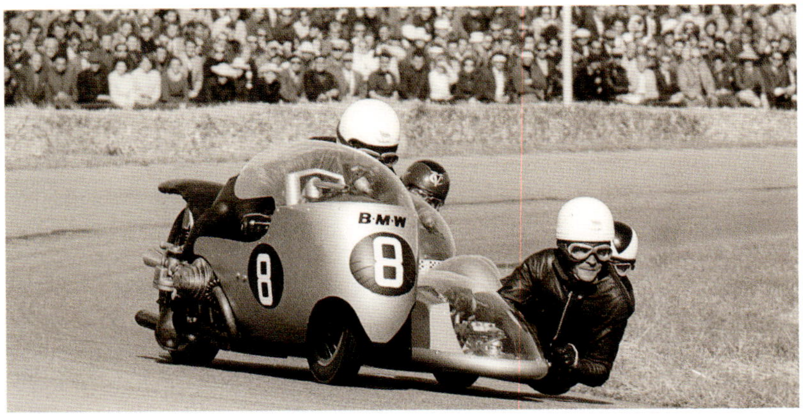

Dutch TT 1965, holding off Chris Vincent in the early stages.

'Speedy-Read', still racing the twin cylinder Yamaha 250cc, (the new four cylinder model was not quite ready for the track), continued his winning ways dominating the 250 race and showing his rival Jim Redman on the Honda six the way home. This was Phil's fifth Grand Prix victory that year, and Mike Duff, Yamaha completed the top three rostrum positions.

Jim Redman won the 350cc event from the MVs of Hailwood and Agostini. Mike Hailwood was back in charge for the 20 lap 500cc race, letting the new boy on the block, 'Ago', lead the early laps. At half distance Mike opened up, leaving the MV's latest recruit almost out of sight. Further back, the singles brigade had Derek Minter retire in the pits, Bill Ivy lost third spot when a plug lead came off and then, in fourth place with only 3 laps to go, 'little' Bill retired with a wrecked gearbox. So it was a 1 - 2 for MV, Paddy Driver, Matchless third, 'Mooneyes' Cooper, Norton fourth and our man, jolly Sid Mizen, Matchless tenth.

Then it was the turn of the 'wheel barrows' the 14 lap race providing the most exciting clash of the day. Who better to spark off such a race than action man 'Flo' Camathias? Partnered by Franz Ducret, 'Flo' made a superb start in a field of 15 BMW outfits and held the lead for 9 laps. Tailing him were Max Deubel and Fritz Scheidegger, closely followed by Harris, ourselves and Chris Vincent. Fritz overtook Max and started closing fast on Florian, and with 4 laps to go was out in front. Dramatically, Camathias had overshot a corner, taken to a slip road and crashed through a gate. Pip Harris retired with engine trouble, as did Max Deubel with only one lap to go. The Swiss gentleman Frtiz, partnered by John Robinson, took the chequered flag followed by Chris Vincent who got the better of us, put us into third position, our best result in 1965, on the BMW to date. Our mate Florian returned to the paddock cut and bruised, but full of enthusiasm, reliving every moment of a really great race.

We had an overnight trip to compete at Brands Hatch next day. Before leaving that evening, I collected our start money of £70 and the prize money of £85, which was given to 'Flo' for the loan of the Rennsport engine, which we would use at the following weekend's Belgian Grand Prix. A small number of solo riders also joined us in the dash back to Brands; namely Minter, Ivy, Driver and Chris Conn.

Our team of helpers had taken the Dunstall-Norton to Brands ready for the action. With Chris Vincent not returning for that event, perhaps we might have been in with a chance of winning, although Bill Boddice, the fast improving Terry Vinicombe and Pete Russell with the awesomely fast 998cc Vincent, would be no walk-over in the 8 lap race, held on the Grand Prix circuit. We managed our usual quick sprint off the line, and were leading comfortably. After several laps, much to my surprise, and annoyance, Owen Greenwood partnered by Terry Fairbrother in their 1070cc Mini Special came charging by. Despite all my efforts, I could do little to catch the flying duo and once more we had to settle for second. When Chris Vincent heard, he thought it was hilarious. What 'plonkers' we were to let this Mini Special beat us. I warned the 'Cocky Brummie' that his time would come, and Owen Greenwood would run round or over him if necessary.

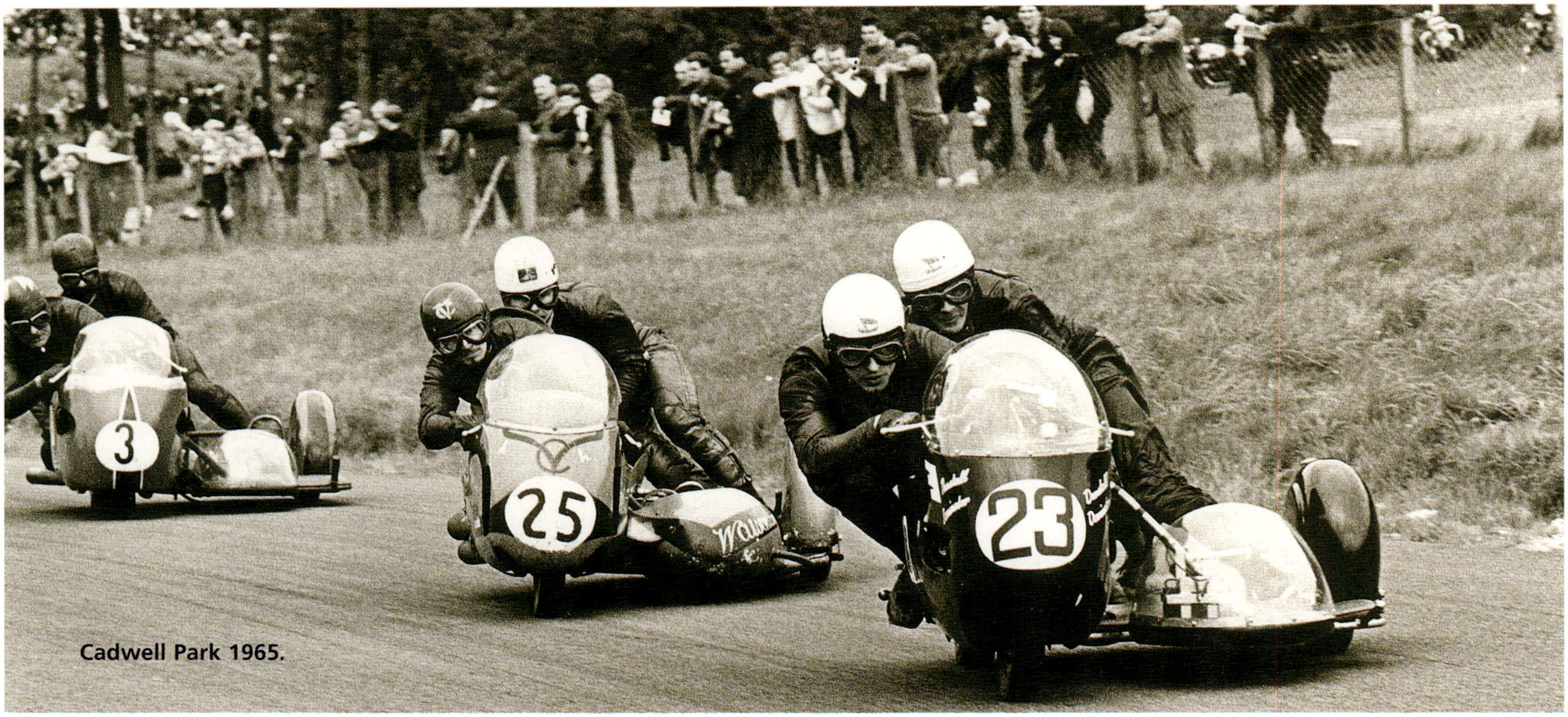

Cadwell Park 1965.

Letter from Jim Swift.

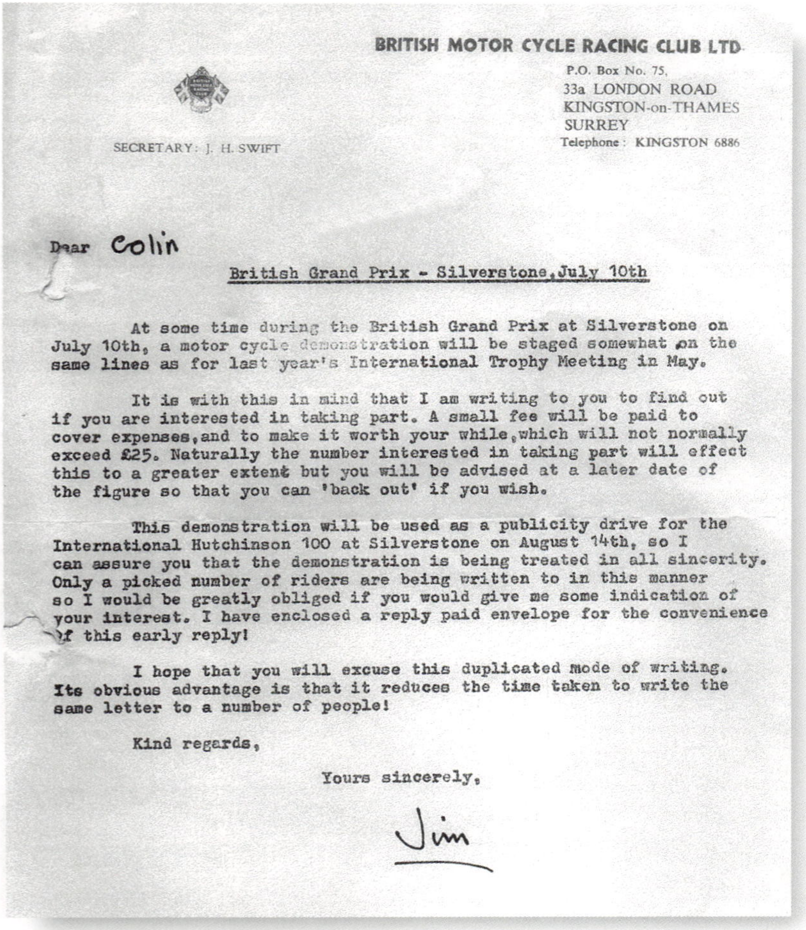

BRITISH MOTOR CYCLE RACING CLUB LTD

P.O. Box No. 75,
33a LONDON ROAD
KINGSTON-on-THAMES
SURREY
Telephone: KINGSTON 6886

SECRETARY: J. H. SWIFT

Dear Colin

British Grand Prix - Silverstone, July 10th

At some time during the British Grand Prix at Silverstone on July 10th, a motor cycle demonstration will be staged somewhat on the same lines as for last year's International Trophy Meeting in May.

It is with this in mind that I am writing to you to find out if you are interested in taking part. A small fee will be paid to cover expenses, and to make it worth your while, which will not normally exceed £25. Naturally the number interested in taking part will effect this to a greater extent but you will be advised at a later date of the figure so that you can 'back out' if you wish.

This demonstration will be used as a publicity drive for the International Hutchinson 100 at Silverstone on August 14th, so I can assure you that the demonstration is being treated in all sincerity. Only a picked number of riders are being written to in this manner so I would be greatly obliged if you would give me some indication of your interest. I have enclosed a reply paid envelope for the convenience of this early reply!

I hope that you will excuse this duplicated mode of writing. Its obvious advantage is that it reduces the time taken to write the same letter to a number of people!

Kind regards,

Yours sincerely,

Jim

It is well documented that I was opposed to the Mini Special. The rules at the time, and for many years before, allowed three-wheelers powered by motorcycle engines to compete in the unlimited sidecar events. My criticisms were not personally levelled at Owen Greenwood, for whom I had great respect as a hard-charging racer but also a clever and innovative engineer. Owen had manipulated the rules to his best advantage, but in my opinion had produced a very competitive three-wheeler racing car, which was not in the spirit of true sidecar racing. Owen's passenger, Terry Fairbrother, one of the nicest guys in the paddock, no longer needed to lean out into the air stream. This meant the Mini Special was as quick on left handers as rights and it could run up the inside of a passenger hanging out for the bend. This of course could be dangerous for the passengers. The controversy would rage on.

The Belgian Grand Prix, on the ultra fast Spa Francorchamps circuit, would provide us a sixth place at 101.35mph average, but winner Fritz Scheidegger took an early lead from his compatriot Camathias, although only yards separated the two Swiss drivers from Deubel for more than half the race. Florian then dropped back and Pip Harris came storming through to finish third, right on Max's tail. With three Grand Prix wins and three seconds now under his belt, Fritz was well onto winning his first well-deserved World Sidecar Championship. For the German 'cool' Max Deubel, winner of four world championships, his reign would soon be over.

The Belgian Grand Prix would be our last visit abroad that season. We returned the Rennsport engine to Florian, paid him the £40 hire and departed for home. It had been 17 meetings to date, but the following weekend, July 10th would be slightly different. We had been asked by Jim Swift, competitions manager of the (BMCRC) British Motorcycle Racing Club to participate in a sidecar demonstration race at the Silverstone F1 Car Grand Prix, with £25 expenses. We arrived with the Dunstall Norton to show those F1 drivers what racing was really about, and we won the demo. I think the F1 drivers thought we sidecar lot were a bit barmy - perhaps they were right!

My interest in solo racing had been spurred on by the Sid Mizen sponsorship. Although I was unaware of it at the time, my increasing involvement with the solo boys would be very beneficial later.

Although we had finished with the continental events for that year, we continued a busy race season at home; Snetterton, Hutchinson 100, Brands, Mallory, Oulton, Cadwell, Brands, Mallory, Oulton. Four of these were of international status. The Dunstall-Norton still continued to give us our best results in the unlimited classes whilst the BMW would still disappoint.

In the sixties, the 'Hutchinson 100' was followed enthusiastically. 'The Hutch' a popular abbreviation of the famous 'BEMSEE' event, the Hutchinson 100, takes its name from the club's oldest challenge trophy. Apart from the war years, it had been an annual event since 1925. In 1925 'The Hutch' was a hundred mile track event run at the famous Brooklands venue and was open to all who cared to enter.

Since the war, the event became a road race. The reward remained the same, the magnificent Mellano Trophy, a large silver cup originally valued at £200 and presented by Mr A. V. Mellano of the Hutchinson Tyre Company in 1925.

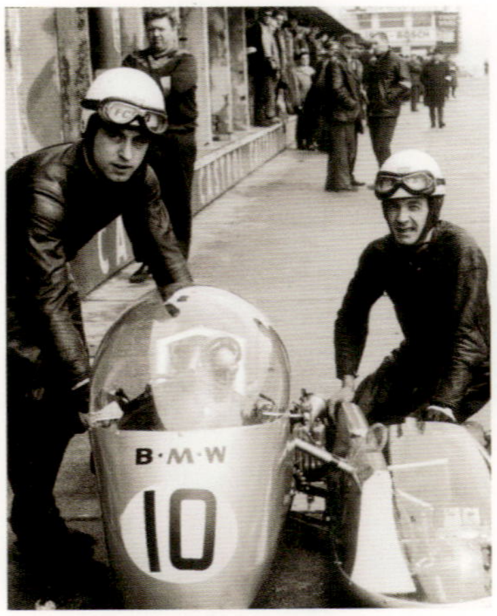

Awaiting practice, Belgian Grand Prix.

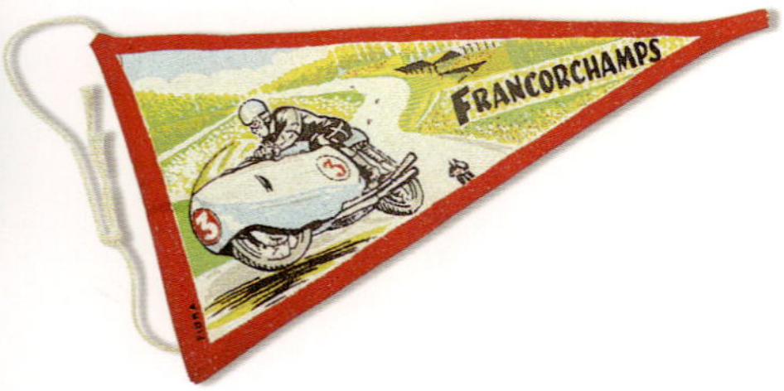

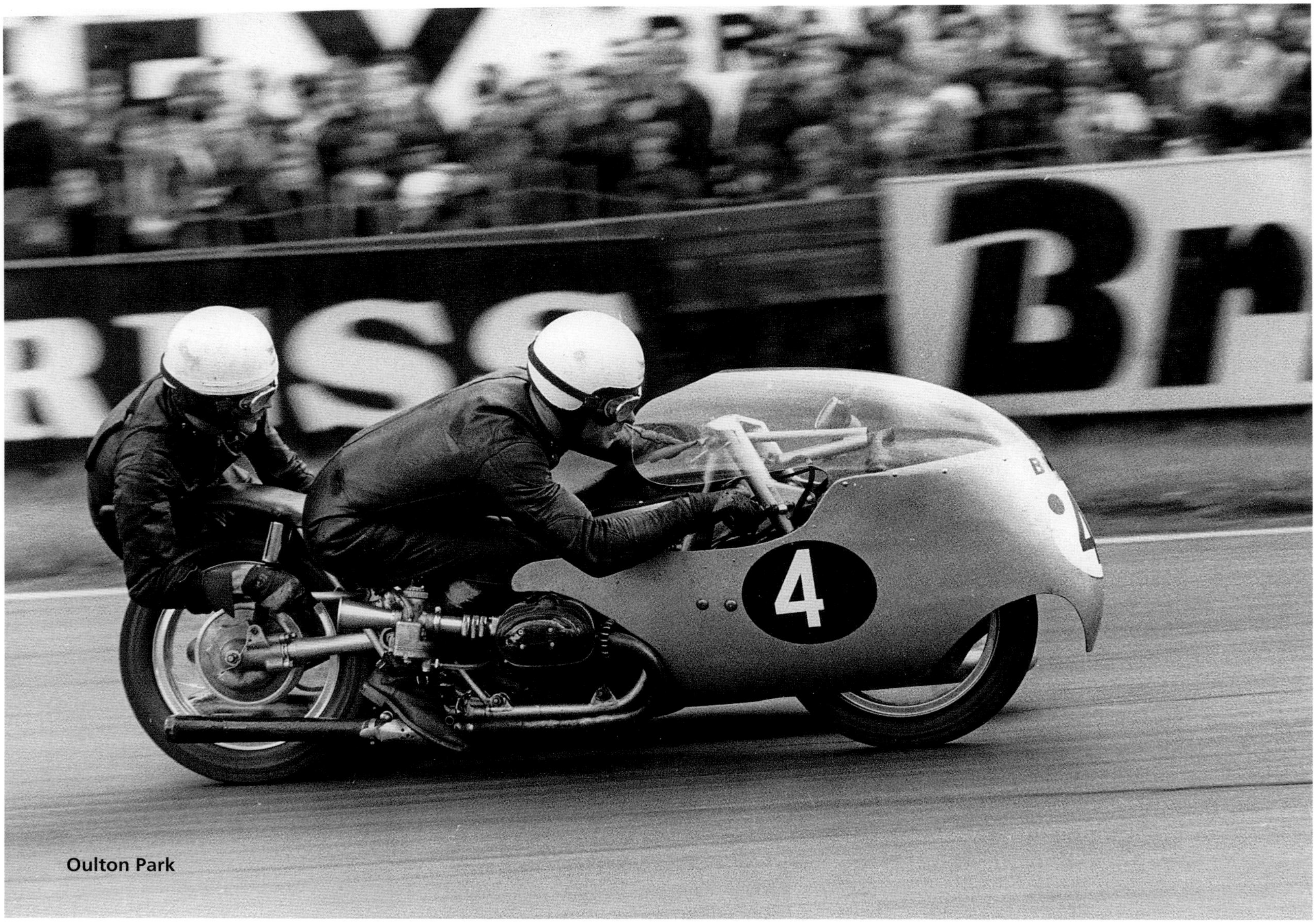

Oulton Park

Brooklands was one place in the British Isles where a motorcycle could be ridden on full throttle for hours on end if the rider and bike could stand the strain. An average speed of the order of 90mph for a distance of 100 miles was a severe test of man and machine. Consequently, the winning of BEMSEE's annual classic the Hutchinson 100 was an achievement of which the victor could be justifiably proud. The last of the Brooklands races was the 1938 event. After the war years the BEMSEE Club was homeless, for Brooklands was no longer available.

The Hutchinson 100 as a race was resurrected in 1949 at Silverstone, the first motorcycle race meeting to be held on this circuit. In 1963 the Daily Express took over the sponsorship of the meeting giving this historic event national prominence.

The 33rd International Hutchinson 100, organised by the British Motorcycle Racing Club and sponsored once again by The Daily Express attracted 30,000 spectators to Silverstone for this one day event, on Saturday 14th August 1965. These fans would not go home disappointed, despite the changing weather conditions. Many had come to see Mike Hailwood in action on the fabulous 500cc MV Agusta. 'Mike the Bike' proved once again he was master on the track, with breathtaking victories in three events. First riding a Tom Kirby 350cc AJS in a hard fought event he beat John Cooper and Derek Minter to the post. Then, perhaps even more impressive was Mike's ride in the 15 lap (43.9 mile) production machine race, riding a 654cc BSA Lighting. With 40 competitors on the grid in wet conditions it would be no walk-over. The race soon developed into a three-cornered dice between Hailwood, BSA, with Phil Read and 'farmer' Percy Tait both on Triumphs. First Read led, then Tait went ahead for 4 laps until he clipped a wall, after which Hailwood took over to win at an average speed of 83.19mph, proving once more that he could ride any machine, any time, anywhere and in any conditions.

The rain swept 125cc race was won easily by the world championship leader, the stylish Hugh Anderson on the works Suzuki, with team mate Toshio Fuji, the very first Japanese to race in a Hutchinson 100 event finishing second with our own 'little' Bill Ivy, Honda, third, beating the current 125 World Champion Luigi Taveri, Honda, into fourth place and Dave Simmonds, Tohatsu, fifth. Mike Duff, Yamaha, won the 250cc race from Read, Yamaha, and Derek Minter riding a Cotton, held third place until ignition trouble caused him to pull out with only 4 laps to go.

The 8 lap 50cc 'tiddlers' race had (I hate to say it), versatile Chris Vincent riding a works Suzuki on which he would perform with distinction, finishing second to Toshio Fuji, Suzuki, only one second behind. So close and beating Ansheidt, Kreidler, in the process. Fuji averaged 78.37mph, no less than 7.08mph faster than the old lap record and this margin won him the famous Mellano Trophy, awarded to the rider whose average speed exceeded the existing lap record by the greatest margin. Chris Vincent lost out only by the smallest of margins, being next in line for the Mellano Trophy after his two sidecar wins.

As was expected, in the 25 lap Daily Express Trophy BMCRC Senior 500cc Championship race, Mike Hailwood on the works MV, although playing around for a few laps with Minter, Read and Ivy, soon pulled ahead to his third victory of the day.

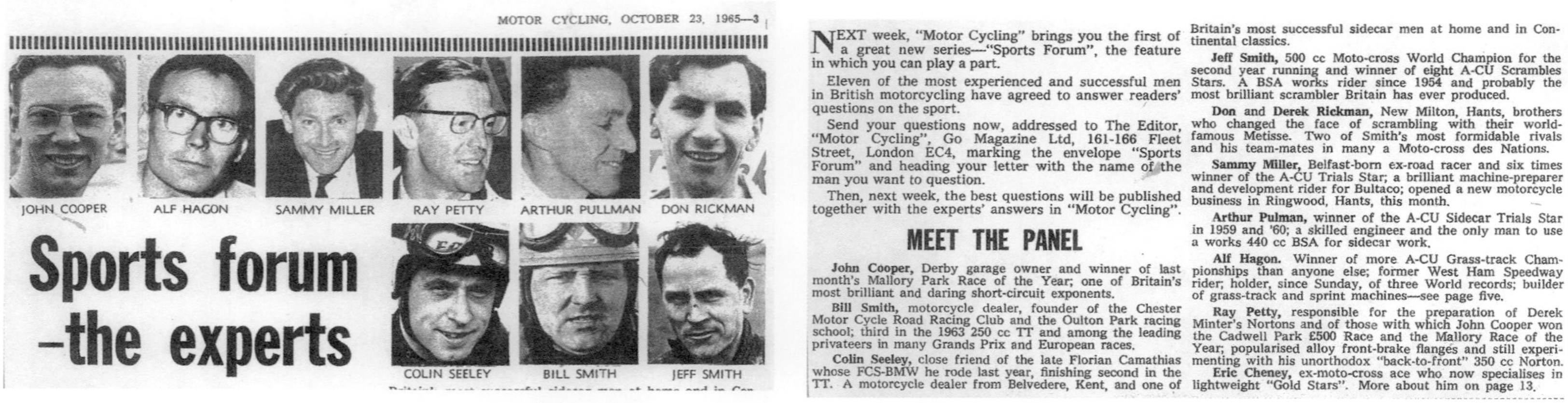

MOTOR CYCLING, OCTOBER 23, 1965—3

JOHN COOPER | ALF HAGON | SAMMY MILLER | RAY PETTY | ARTHUR PULLMAN | DON RICKMAN

Sports forum –the experts

COLIN SEELEY | BILL SMITH | JEFF SMITH

NEXT week, "Motor Cycling" brings you the first of a great new series—"Sports Forum", the feature in which you can play a part.

Eleven of the most experienced and successful men in British motorcycling have agreed to answer readers' questions on the sport.

Send your questions now, addressed to The Editor, "Motor Cycling", Go Magazine Ltd, 161-166 Fleet Street, London EC4, marking the envelope "Sports Forum" and heading your letter with the name of the man you want to question.

Then, next week, the best questions will be published together with the experts' answers in "Motor Cycling".

MEET THE PANEL

John Cooper, Derby garage owner and winner of last month's Mallory Park Race of the Year; one of Britain's most brilliant and daring short-circuit exponents.

Bill Smith, motorcycle dealer, founder of the Chester Motor Cycle Road Racing Club and the Oulton Park racing school; third in the 1963 250 cc TT and among the leading privateers in many Grands Prix and European races.

Colin Seeley, close friend of the late Florian Camathias whose FCS-BMW he rode last year, finishing second in the TT. A motorcycle dealer from Belvedere, Kent, and one of Britain's most successful sidecar men at home and in Continental classics.

Jeff Smith, 500 cc Moto-cross World Champion for the second year running and winner of eight A-CU Scrambles Stars. A BSA works rider since 1954 and probably the most brilliant scrambler Britain has ever produced.

Don and **Derek Rickman,** New Milton, Hants, brothers who changed the face of scrambling with their world-famous Metisse. Two of Smith's most formidable rivals and his team-mates in many a Moto-cross des Nations.

Sammy Miller, Belfast-born ex-road racer and six times winner of the A-CU Trials Star; a brilliant machine-preparer and development rider for Bultaco; opened a new motorcycle business in Ringwood, Hants, this month.

Arthur Pulman, winner of the A-CU Sidecar Trials Star in 1959 and '60; a skilled engineer and the only man to use a works 440 cc BSA for sidecar work.

Alf Hagon. Winner of more A-CU Grass-track Championships than anyone else; former West Ham Speedway rider; holder, since Sunday, of three World records; builder of grass-track and sprint machines—see page five.

Ray Petty, responsible for the preparation of Derek Minter's Nortons and of those with which John Cooper won the Cadwell Park £500 Race and the Mallory Race of the Year; popularised alloy front-brake flanges and still experimenting with his unorthodox "back-to-front" 350 cc Norton.

Eric Cheney, ex-moto-cross ace who now specialises in lightweight "Gold Stars". More about him on page 13.

Chris Vincent, with his regular 650 BSA kneeler, won both sidecar events, the first from Owen Greenwood, Mini Special, Camathias, BMW in third and us on the Dunstall-Norton fourth with Max Deubel fifth. It was a disappointing second sidecar race for us, as we were soon out of the running with magneto trouble, so it was Vincent from Scheidegger, Camathias, Deubel, Wakefield and Freeman in that order.

A 176 yard electronic speed trap was set up for this event:

Hailwood, 500cc MV	135.9mph
Read, 254cc Yamaha	133.3mph
Cooper, 500cc Norton	126.8mph
Camathias, 500cc BMW	123.7mph
Vincent, 650cc BSA	120.9mph
Seeley, 650cc Norton	120.9mph
Deubel and Harris, 500cc BMWs	119.6mph

The Works Suzuki Mopeds went through the speed trap at 97.3mph. Of special note from this great day's racing were the achievements of our talented Kent boy, the likeable Bill Ivy who made five race starts and finished five.

50cc race	4th on a Honda
125cc race	3rd on a Honda
250cc race	6th on a Cotton
350cc race	6th on an AJS
500cc race	2nd on a Matchless

A total of 78 laps or 228.30 miles of racing, it could have been 6 laps on the TT course - well done Bill, the rising star. Later that year BRDC (British Racing Drivers Club), issued a £25 bill for cleaning up the rubbish after a BEMSEE run club event. BEMSEE's secretary at the time, the feisty Jim Swift, was having none of it and told the BRDC where to stick their bill, resulting in BEMSEE being banned from Silverstone. The Hutch then moved to Brands Hatch in 1966. It would be 1996 before it returned to Silverstone.

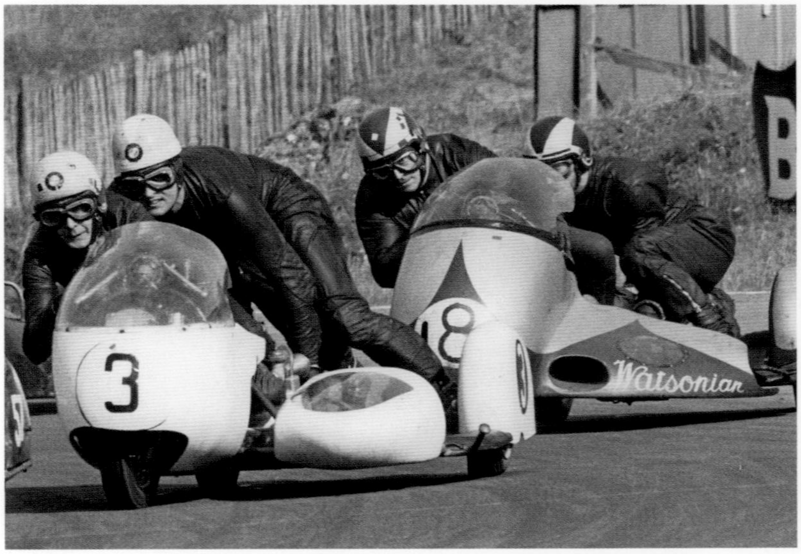

The day after The Hutch, at the Brands Hatch Sidecar Trophy meeting, there were 64 sidecar entries for this predominantly sidecar event. How times have changed, when today, there's not a sidecar outfit in sight on the national championship scene. Those where the days!

At this meeting, held on the 1.24 mile short circuit, there were eight heat and final sidecar races, so it would be a busy time for us all. Following the first solo race of the day it was the 500cc sidecar scratch race, over 10 laps and won by Bill Boddice after Pip Harris retired with a fuel problem. Tony Wakefield and Graham Milton, BMW were second and we were third.

Fresh from Silverstone the day before, I was out to get some revenge over the Hutch double winner Chris Vincent. Overnight Paul Dunstall had fitted a fresh magneto to our Domiracer to replace the faulty unit that caused our retirement in the second race at the Hutch 100. Our Dunstall-Norton was flying, beating 'Uncle' Bill Boddice with ease in our heat. The 10 lap 501-1,.300cc final would be a battle royal between Chris Vincent on his 'Green Meanie' 650cc BSA and 'Gungy' Wal and me on the all-black 650cc Norton.

From the start it was very close and we both pulled away from the rest of the field. For once I really thought we could get the better of the 'flying Brummie'. When rushing into the left hander at South Bank with a full right lock, drifting to the limit, the rear of the Norton swung round. Suddenly we were completely sideways and out of control at about 90mph. Wally was catapulted into the air for some distance, coming down running at what looked like around 60mph. Being built like a wafer, he just seemed to float down. Luckily Wal was 'shaken not stirred'.

Meanwhile, that split second of the crash seemed like a lifetime to me. I thought I must get off and away from the outfit as it was about to flip over. I remember pushing hard on the handlebars. As I flew though the air I felt 'I must roll, I must role' then I wondered if the outfit was going to land on top of me? Fortunately, it landed upside down in the middle of the circuit. But there was no time for me to move before the rest of the competitors came charging into view. I raised my arms in the air and remained motionless as outfits passed either side of me, including the dreaded Mini Special, but Owen Greenwood was not about to run me over. 'Phew' that had been a lucky escape 'lady luck' was on our side, just my pride hurt and a small hole in the back of my Lewis race leathers.

Pip Harris leading Boddice at Brands, 15th August.

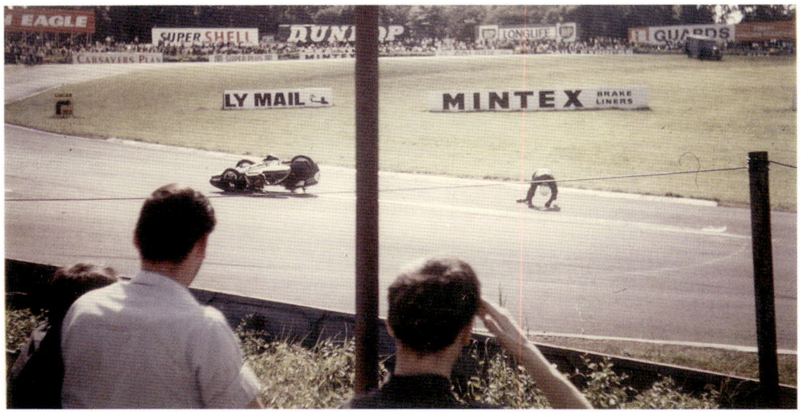

Looped it at South Bank, Brands Hatch, Wally bailed out earlier.

Chris Vincent went on to win that race with Owen Greenwood second and local boy Terry Vinicombe partnered by John Flaxman third. On examination of the Norton outfit it was found that the rear wheel hub bearing lock ring had come loose, allowing the wheel to move sideways on the spindle, a contributing factor in our accident. This was our first crash in five seasons of sidecar racing, so we had done pretty well up to now. Unfazed, we came out on the BMW for a heat of the handicap event - just for fun and to shake off the dust. The final was won by Boddice after early leader Harris retired once more. A good day for big-bore engines?

Following our upside down view of the world at Brands Hatch, we decided to stay upright for Mallory Park and the Sidecar Gold Cup meeting the next weekend. In sun-drenched conditions with our repaired Dunstall-Norton we won our heat and then turned the tables on Chris Vincent and won the 10 lap 1200cc final. Charlie Freeman came third and Owen Greenwood on his Mini Special fourth - very satisfying. Then in the 20 lap Gold Cup sidecar race, to a tremendous ovation Owen Greenwood and Terry Fairbrother with the controversial Mini Special finally broke the strangle-hold of Chris Vincent in the unlimited class. I enjoyed this result, Chris having 'taken the piss' out of me when we were beaten by the Mini at Brands Hatch earlier that year. It was a great race with all three of us breaking the 20 lap record set by Chris when he won the Race of the Year back in April. John Webb of Grovewood Securities presented the Gold Cup to Greenwood and, wait for it, a cheque for £30. For Wally and me it had been a good day, £38 in prize money plus £35 start, less £19 paid to Paul Dunstall for the Norton-Domi engine service. Other good results were achieved with the Norton at three other events before the last meeting of the season, The Evening News International Race of the South, held at Brands Hatch on 10th October 1965.

That Sunday was a fateful day for one of the sport's most colourful, unpredictable and legendary characters that Grand Prix and international sidecar racing had witnessed for many a year. Our fearless friend, Florian Camathias, affectionately known as Flo, lost control of his FCS-BMW during the 500cc sidecar race held on the Grand Prix circuit. Pip Harris had just taken the lead, when Flo's front forks collapsed causing an horrendous crash into the bank at Clearways resulting in 'Flo' suffering multiple injuries and a fractured spine which caused his death. His passenger Franz Ducret escaped with leg and head injuries, serious enough, but not life-threatening.

Pip Harris and Ray Campbell, unaware of the crash behind them, went on to win the 10 lap race with a new race and lap record for the 500cc sidecar class - such was the pace of the race. Chris Vincent who was close behind Florian as he crashed, managed to avoid the debris and finished in second place with Fritz Scheidegger third.

I distinctly remember watching the race action and crash from the riders grandstand at the top of Paddock Hill. We, with our own BMW would have been competing in that race. I cannot remember why, but we had withdrawn. Although our BMW had often been a disappointment and not as competitive as we would have liked, we always started

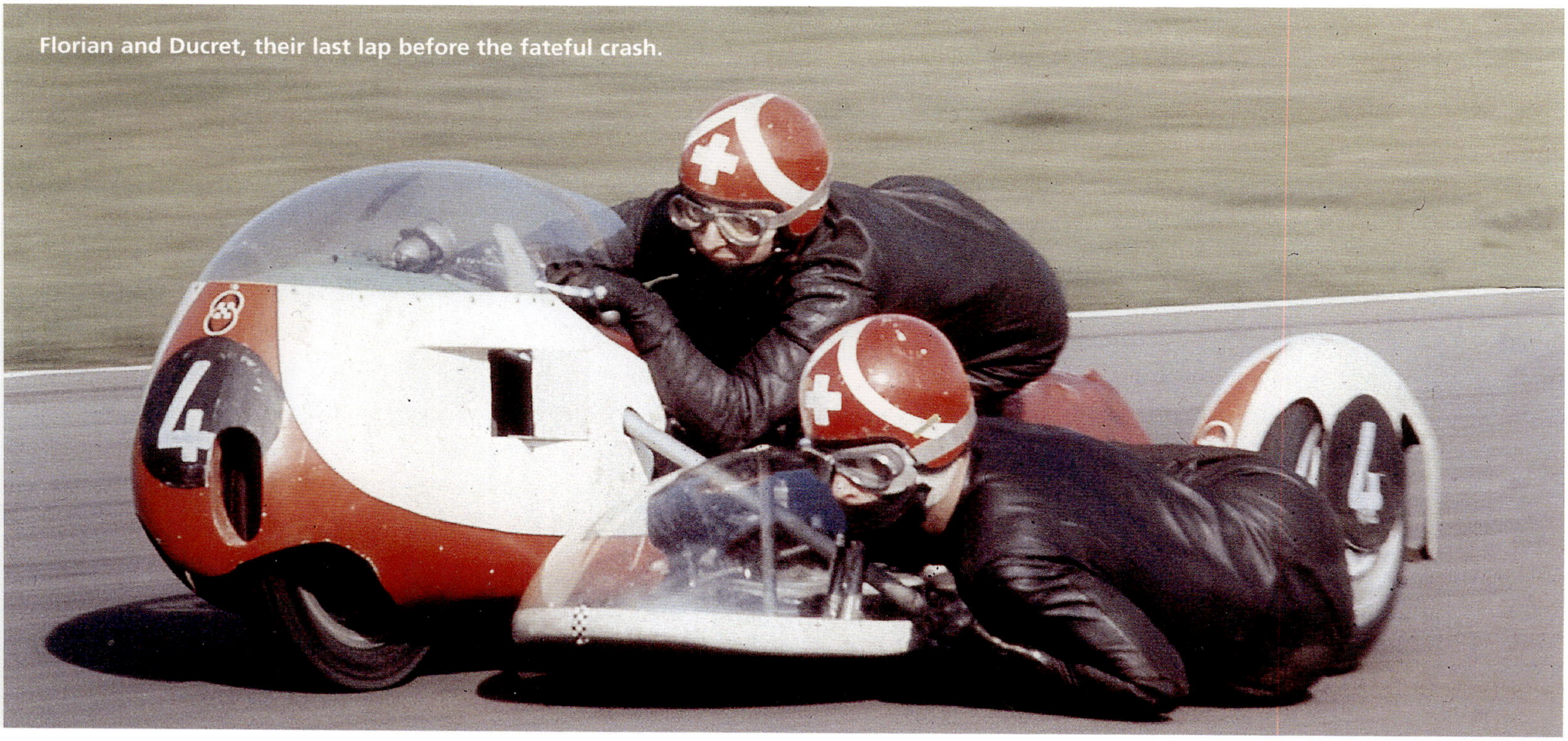
Florian and Ducret, their last lap before the fateful crash.

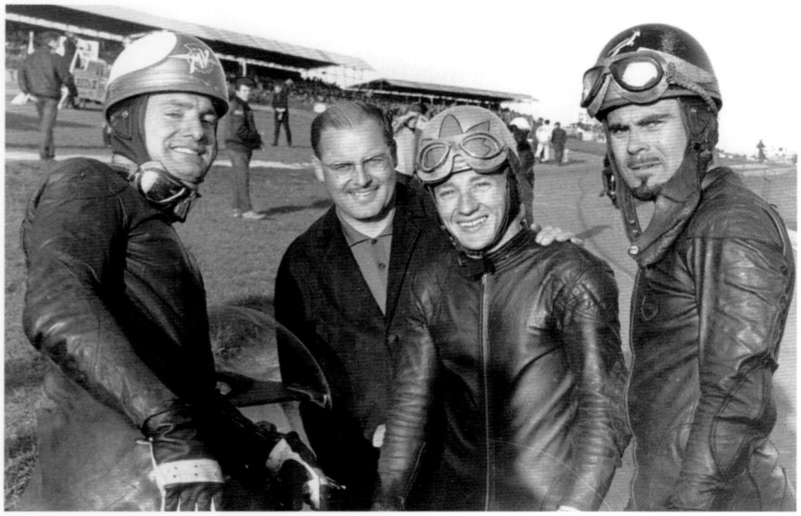

Smiles all round for the Tom Kirby team, after Mike, Bill and Paddy achieved a 1 - 2 - 3 in the Evening News Race of the South.

races we had entered. Had fate kept us out of the catastrophe? We shall never know!

In the following 1300cc 10 lap sidecar scratch race, Fritz Scheidegger and Pip Harris withdrew out of respect, but Wally and I, although subdued, decided to race the Dunstall-Norton and honour our friend. Chris Vincent won from Terry Vinicombe and we took the third position.

Florian Camathias was born in Laax in the province of Grisens on March 23rd 1924. He lived at Montreux, Switzerland by the lake where he and his wife Margarite ran a car and motorcycle repair business. He spent much of his boyhood mountain climbing but was soon bitten by the motorcycle bug, racing solo machines (125cc and a 250cc NSU) in 1947. In an early racing accident Flo fractured his skull but returned to the action combining sidecar racing with his solo career. In 1955 Florian broke 19 world records at the famous banked Montlhéry track near Paris. At his first Isle of Man TT in 1957 he finished ninth in the 250 lightweight TT on the NSU and third in the sidecar event on his BMW.

Speed was his total pre-occupation. Throughout Europe he raced at national, international, Grand Prix, Isle of Man TT, hill climbs and world record attempts. In 1963 he held 25 records. Nothing stopped this cheerful, optimistic giant among men when it came to perseverance.

Although I had tremendous admiration and respect for Florian I did not believe he was the most naturally talented rider of his time. Suffering bad vision hence the familiar thick lensed spectacles, combined with his often over exuberant style of racing contributed to more than his share of race accidents. However, there was no doubting his capivating charm, optimistic nature, daring beyond belief and great charisma, making the Swiss ace so appealing to his many fans and admirers. Ex-world sidecar champion Helmut Fath who tuned Florian's BMW engines, said, 'Flo is better than all of us.' On the fast circuits such as Hockenheim and Spa-Francorchamps, Florian was awesome and mostly untouchable.

Florian blamed the German BMW factory for a crash at Modena in 1961 when the front forks of his BMW broke and his passenger Cecco was killed, then the publication of a newspaper article caused a huge row between them. This prevented him racing in 1963 at the international race at Nürburgring. Camathias was bitter, recalling that he and Stirling Moss were the only recipients of special gold medals for three consecutive wins on the tricky Nürburgring Circuit. Neither Moss nor Camathias managed to become World Champions.

After the fall out with the racing department of BMW and with the row still simmering, Florian and his passenger Alfred Herzig proved themselves unbeatable at Hockenhiem's high speed West German Grand Prix in 1963. Racing the FCS-BMW they clipped 5 seconds off the previous lap record, going round at 111.34mph causing a few long faces at BMW. Then came Flo's proudest moment. When in his sixth attempt he won the 1963 Isle of Man TT. Officials of the Munich factory asked him to revert to naming his outfit a 'BMW' but Florian was adamant 'FCS-BMW' would stay. BMW was panicking as at that point, Florian was leading the World Sidecar Championship from their man, Max Deubel. After the Dutch TT, which Deubel won with Flo in third, Florian needed to win at the Belgian for his first World Championship title. Once more he demonstrated in his tenacious style just how good he was. He led the field by half a mile on the first lap and chopped 10 seconds off his own previous record, getting round Spa-Francorchamps at 109.86mph, but on the third lap with the race seemingly in the bag, the engine blew up. He coasted for 2 miles before Scheidegger came past to win. For the four times runner-up in the championship, it was a great disappointment and as events unfolded Flo's championship chances were gone for ever.

Flo never gave up trying, and was a huge favourite with the race fans who loved his showmanship, determination and true grit. It had been a real privilege for Wally and me to have known this special man, to have raced with him and to have been his friend. He was a man of great charm and kindness, and had shown such faith in our racing abilities.'Flo' we salute your memory.

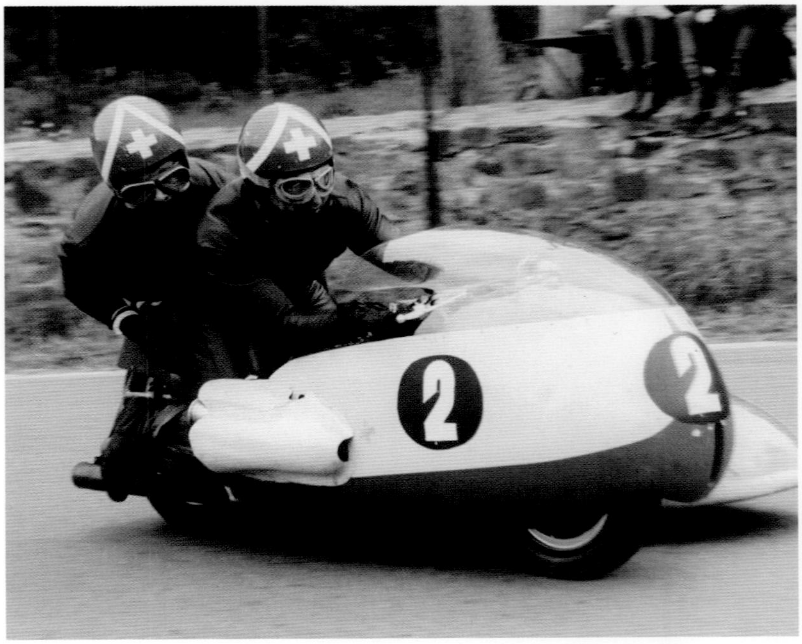

Camathias and Ducret at their last Belgian Grand Prix in 1965.

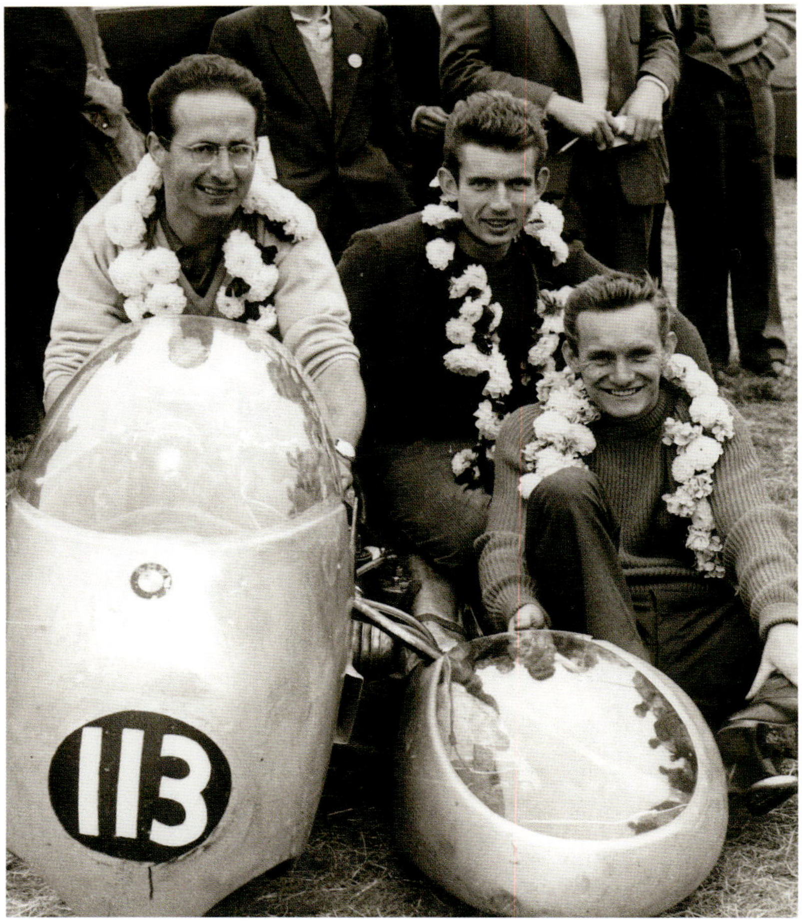

Camathias, Cecco and Hailwood, 1959 winners at Scarborough.

Madame Camathias, back in Switzerland requested that I deal with the arrangements for the return of Florian's body to his home in Montreux on the shores of Lake Geneva. Firstly, there was the unenviable task of the official identification. Then came the inquest where Chris Vincent, the race competitor nearest to Florian when he crashed, gave evidence. Other witnesses confirmed that Florian approached the Clearways Bend at speed when suddenly the BMW outfit veered off to the left and the sidecar came off the ground. Ex-Works Norton TT ace, Harold Daniell and I examined the machine. We confirmed that the bronze welding supporting the front fork leading link arms which retained the front wheel, suffered a catastrophic failure, leaving the machine totally out of control. A verdict of 'death by misadventure' was recorded for the Swiss ace.

Earlier that year, at the Spanish Grand Prix, looking closely at the front forks of Florian's BMW outfit, I found some small cracks, which I repaired for him. The outfit in question was not the one we had used the year before, but the one that had been built specially by Florian to suit the Gilera's four cylinder engine in 1964, then adapted for a Rennsport engine for 1965.

In those days I considered that generally the continentals were not as good at welding as the British, with Ken Sprayson of Reynolds Tubes leading the way in quality welding. I was not impressed by the construction of Flo's front forks, the leading link arms were too small in diameter leaving a reduced fillet welding area when attached to the cross moving member. Also, no strengthening gussets were welded in. Certainly a design failure!

I had pointed out my concerns to Florian but typically, he was always in a rush and it seemed that he overlooked my advice. Also, his crash at the Dutch TT in June, when he drove through a gate, could well have caused the start of a fork fracture. We shall never know!

It is ironic that the week before his death, Florian explained to Mick Woollett that he was racing without a fairing because of damage sustained in a recent crash in Avignon, which he hadn't repaired. Like Scheidegger, Florian often preferred to race without streamlining, so that if anything is broken or cracked it can be seen. The accident at Modena when the forks broke caused the death of passenger Hilmar Cecco and could possibly have been avoided if the fractures had been seen earlier.

It is strange and sad that just a week later after speaking with Mick Woollett an almost identical mishap to Modena took Florian's life. Florian's body was returned to Switzerland, in a sealed coffin. Grief stricken Maggie Camathias tried to lever off the lid but was restrained by friends. It was a harrowing situation as Flo's injuries were severe. The funeral was a huge event attended by hundreds of friends, fans, car and motorcycle race competitors including World Champion Max Deubel, Georg Auerbacher and fellow Swiss racing ace Fritz Scheidegger. I was there as a friend but also representing the British sidecar racing contingent.

After a long and moving service in a Catholic church in Montreux the draped coffin, adorned with Florian's helmet displaying the Swiss cross of which he was so proud, was carried some distance to the burial ground. Florian was placed close to Hilmar Cecco, his passenger in the 1961 crash at Modena. After the funeral, immediate family and friends gathered at the local lakeside hotel opposite Florian's workshop for a celebration of Florian's life and his contribution to motorcycle sport. It was hard to accept that all of that enthusiasm and commitment was lost to the sport.

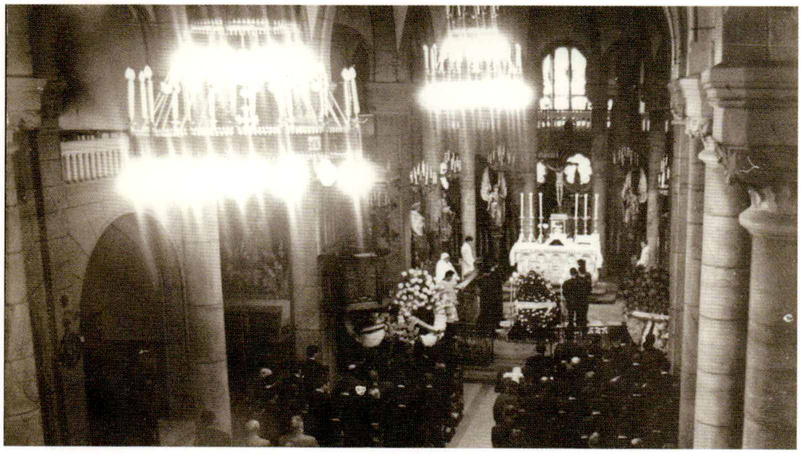

The funeral service for Florian Camathias.

The graveside tribute for Florian Camathias, at Montreux.

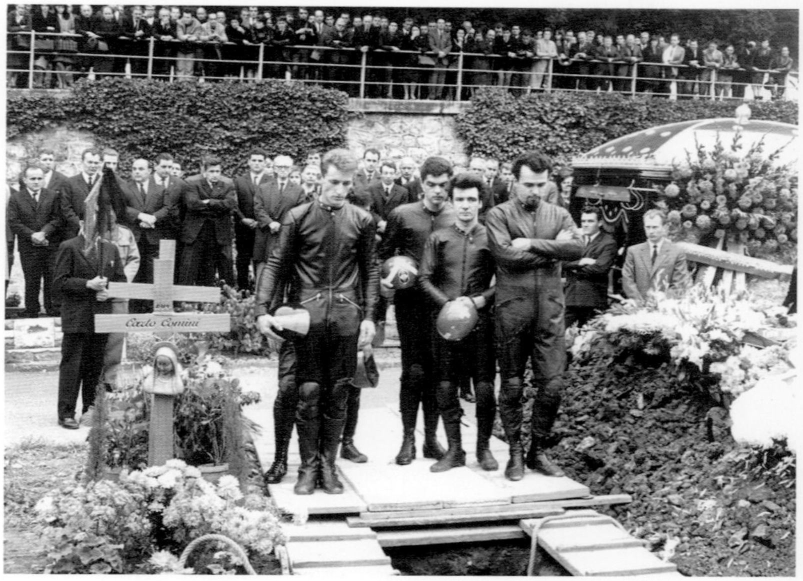

A strange thing happened a few weeks after Florian's death. My wife Joan visited, for the first time ever, a spiritualist meeting with the medium Joseph Benjamin, who she had never met. During the evening Benjamin asked if there was anyone in the audience who had a connection with the sport of motorcycling, Joan of course raised her hand and then Benjamin told her that a friend of her husband had recently been killed racing and this person was not of English nationality - she of course then confirmed the story of Florian being killed at Brands Hatch. Benjamin then assured her that her husband (me) would not die in a racing accident. It was a strange and scary experience. How could Joseph Benjamin have known of Florian's death?

For us it had been a hard and somewhat disappointing season. Busy, yes with 25 national, international and Grand Prix events combined with 52 race starts, but the year's racing had ended very sadly.

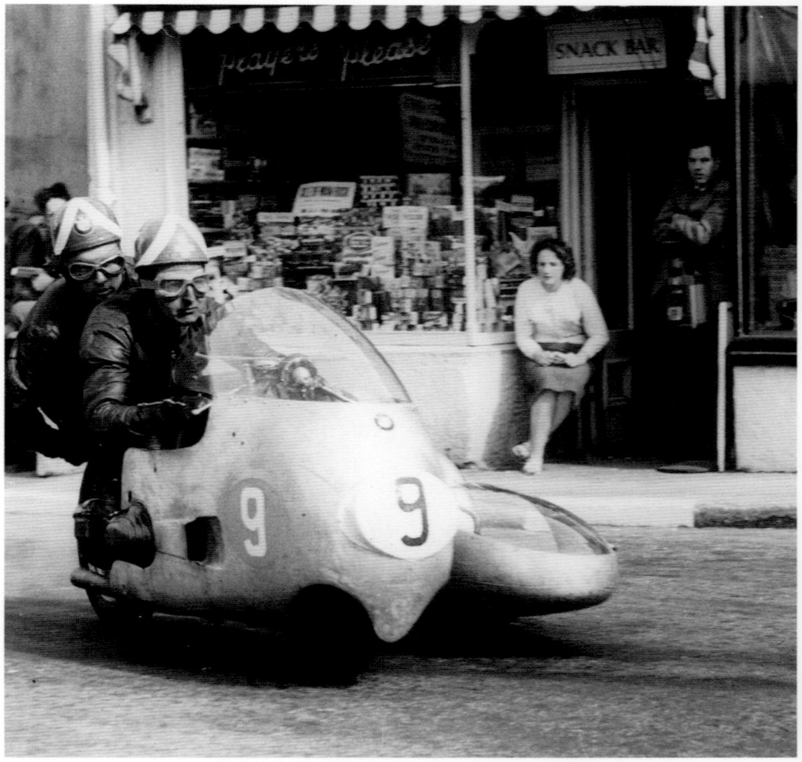

Camathias and Cecco going for second in the 1959 TT.

Camathias and Cecco, second place, Clypse Course, IOM TT 1959.

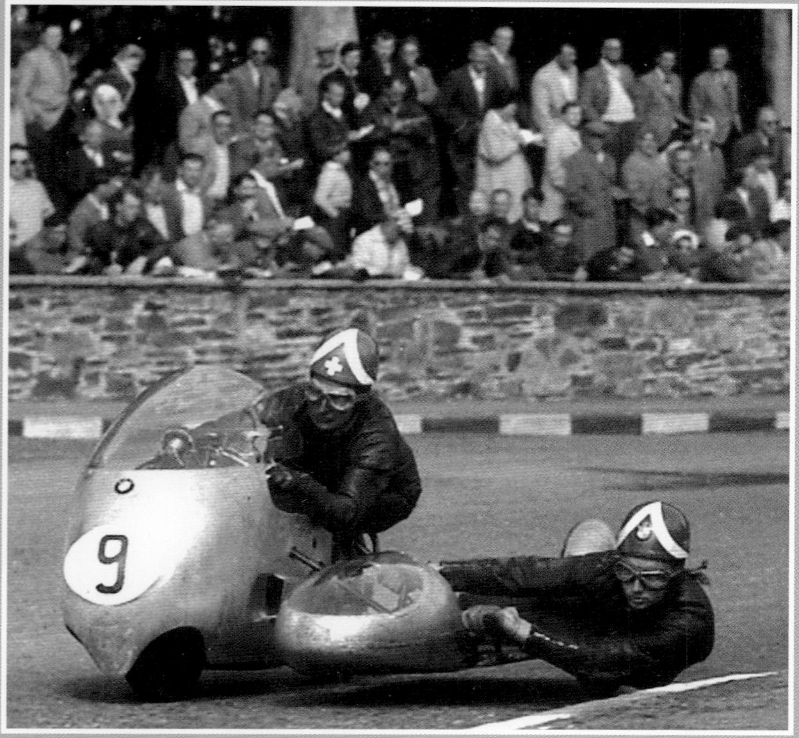

Meanwhile the bungalow I had been building during the busy race season, continued to take shape but it still needed a roof, amongst other things. The business was doing fine in between the hectic race meetings.

My thoughts now turned to the idea of building a small batch of solo racing motorcycles powered by AJS 7R and Matchless G50 engines. This adventurous decision would play a major part in my life for the next eight years and I certainly did not realise that the decision to build racing bikes would become such an important aspect of my work, it just seemed like a good idea at the time!

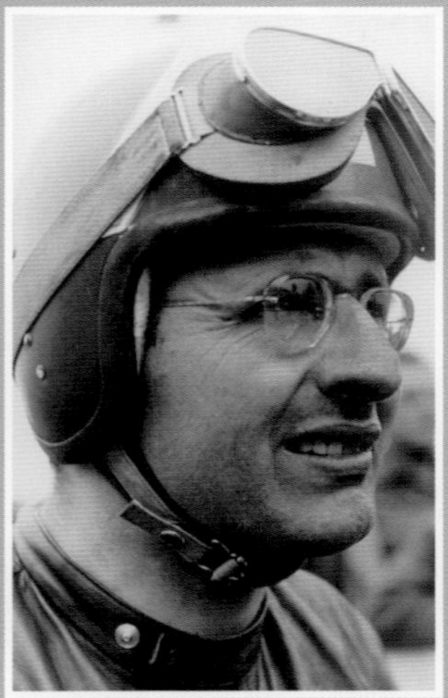

Florian 'Flo' Camathias.

9 1966
LIMITED RESOURCES, HIGH HOPES!

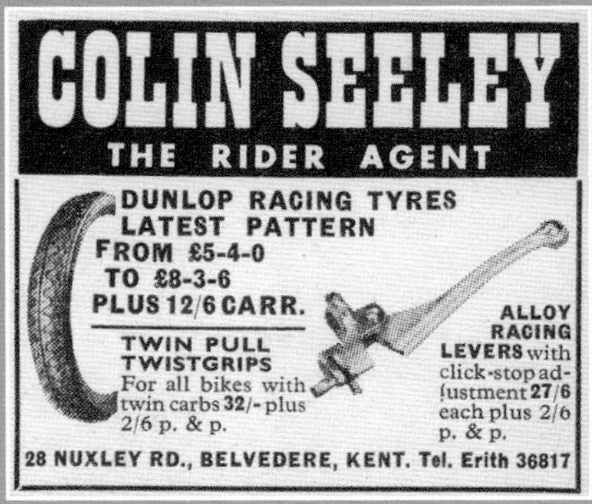

In early December 1965 I provisionally ordered eight 500cc and four 350cc engines from the AJS and Matchless factory (AMC) Associated Motor Cycles. The problem was the price at £275, plus £22 for a carburettor (replicas cost over £6,000 nowadays). The gearbox and rolling chassis would make the bikes too expensive, at around £700 complete.

Nevertheless, with agreement reached with MD Bill Smith at AMC, the project was to go ahead. I had no idea what type of race frame I would build. I just wanted something straight-forward lighter and simpler than the original frame unit. All I had was an acetylene welding set. I must have been fearless or even bonkers, but certainly optimistic!

A large flat surface table was hastily produced out of angle iron covered with a quarter inch steel plate top. A centre line was scribed. An adjustable fixture made by my friend Les Williams was then attached. The vertical threaded one inch diameter rod held the frame steering head in the desired position for the attachment of frame rails. That was that, no other jigs or fixtures. The early frames were all made entirely by hand, according to my sketches. My tube-bending equipment was not much better, a plumber's hand set with formers up to 1¼ inches in diameter. This was secured to a heavy steel bench cemented down in the works yard.

I remember bending the tubes for the first ever Seeley frame. I had filled the 1¼ inch by 16 gauge Renolds 531 tubing with silver sand to prevent crinkling. My muscles bulged as I pulled the tube around the cast iron former. Suddenly there was a loud bang as the former exploded into a shower of bits. It had crystallised in the cold winter conditions. Not a good start for the grand plan. So it was down tools and inside for the Christmas pudding.

Sid Mizen's Matchless G50 gave me the basic geometry. Wally Rawlings was the appointed engine builder and Eddie Robinson, who was renting part of my workshop with his Harrison lathe, was part of our small team. Eddie was developing his double-sided single leading shoe front brake.

Given time, I was confident that we could build a couple of competitive race bikes. I recognised the need to obtain the services of a capable rider. So I spoke with the 33 year old, five times 500cc British Champion and King of Brands, Derek Minter.

Derek was at a cross roads in his career. Most of his successes had been on a Manx Norton, the first rider to lap the Isle of Man at 100mph on a single cylinder machine, and the 1962 250TT winner on the works Honda. Along with newspaper criticisms that he was too old to change machinery, Derek's marriage was also troubled. The days of a slow start and coming through to win would soon be over. New boys like Bill Ivy, John 'Mooneyes' Cooper and 'crazy' Croxford had arrived on the scene.

Tom Kirby, also interested in Minter's services, was upset when Derek requested a test ride before making any decision. Minter wouldn't ask to try the Hondas if they offered him a contract, said Kirby, but Honda were on a different level. Well, I believe Tom Kirby was wrong in this respect. I was only too pleased for Derek to sample the goods first.

So in early January with Derek riding the Sid Mizen Seeley-Matchless, a comparison test took place at Brands Hatch between the Ray Petty tuned Nortons and the Matchless. Derek was favourably impressed with our efforts. He finally managed to test the Kirby AJS and Matchless racers but felt that being the team-mate of Bill Ivy in the Kirby Team could lead to an ego clash. So after consideration, Derek Minter agreed to join the Seeley Team. 'Colin Seeley is my own age, he is an active racer and knows the

Me and Minter inspecting the Seeley Matchless.

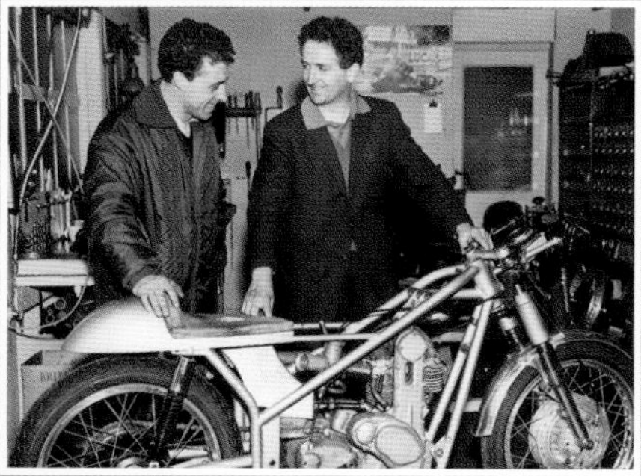

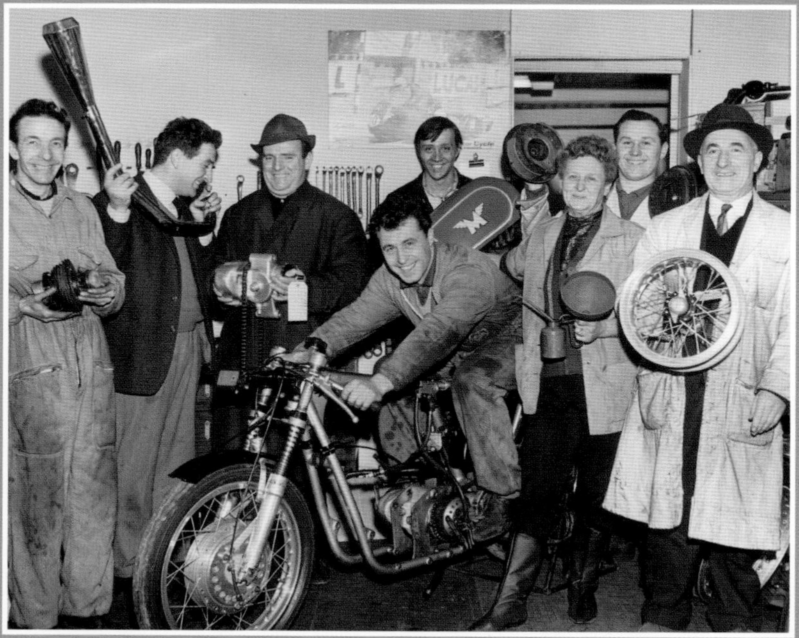

The Seeley musical team, left to right, Wally, Minter, Mizen, Carter, Hilda, Robinson, Percy and myself.

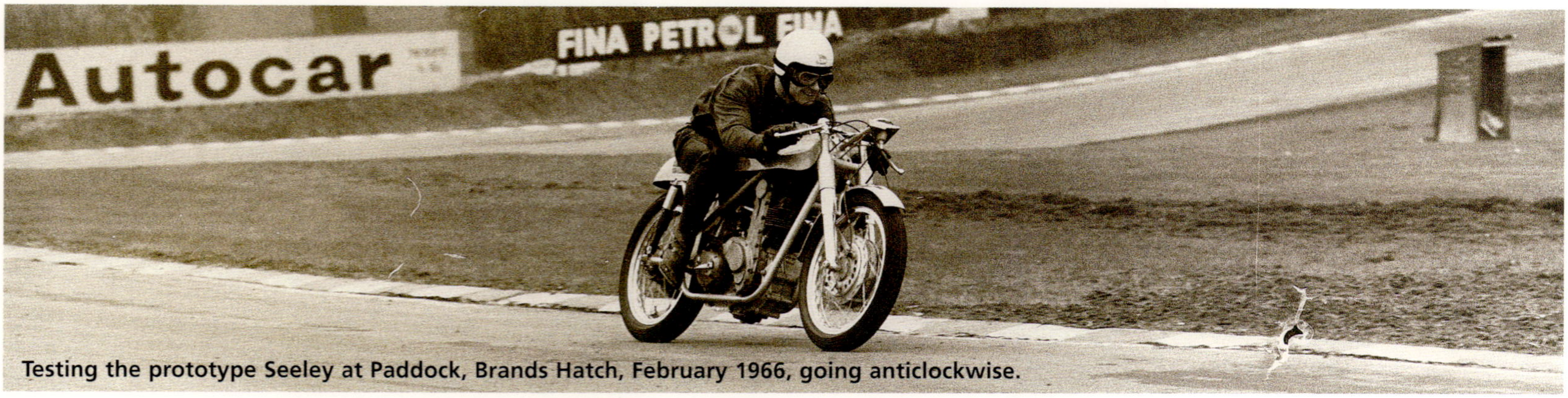

Testing the prototype Seeley at Paddock, Brands Hatch, February 1966, going anticlockwise.

present-day requirements. I think we will make a good team and I have been impressed by Colin's machines.' This hot news soon hit the headlines, with our man at the Daily Express, Leslie Nichol making much of the story. We were delighted to retain the services of the 5ft 6in road racing dynamo and fellow Kentish man!

We planned that Derek and I would race at all the major UK meetings and selective Grand Prix events. Derek would continue his association with the Cotton Motorcycle factory, sponsored by Veedol, by riding their 250cc machine.

The sponsorship and involvement of Sid Mizen and Norman Huntingford would continue under a new company name, Colin Seeley Racing Developments Ltd, established to deal with all racing matters and the production of the Seeley-AMC Racers.

Meanwhile with welding torch in one hand, contracts and telephone in the other, I had negotiated with Madame Camathias in Switzerland to purchase one of Florian's Fath-tuned BMW Rennsport engines, to be fitted into our outfit from the previous season. I still had high hopes of winning a World Sidecar Championship, but , at around £1,000, could only afford one of the number Florian had stored away. The Germans always had the advantage with BMW engines and spares, with the Swiss and we Brits second in line. Fair play? Not on your Nellie!

The next problem was oil contracts. Derek and I had long associations with the Castrol Oil Company but Castrol's competition chief, Malcolm Edgar had misgivings regarding Minter's change of machines and felt that perhaps the 'Mint' was past his prime. Castrol wished to continue supporting me and the BMW outfit, but Minter was not in their equation - disappointing! Then out of the blue we were approached by the American Veedol Oil Company to sponsor the whole team. It was a one year contract, arranged by their competitions manager Ian Smith, worth £1,000, plus oil supplies and free fuel from the Gem Petroleum Company for all home events including the Isle of Man TT. The official announcement was made at their headquarters, Sutton Place in Guildford, Surrey, home at the time to the Veedol Oil Company's major shareholder Paul Getty, said then to be the world's richest man.

This high profile event was attended by most of the motorcycling press including Leslie Nichol from the Daily Express. All this publicity attracted the attention of off-shore Radio Caroline who agreed to plug our team's progress throughout the race season, similar to the tie-up between Radio London and the Tom Kirby Team.

After all the hype, we donned our overalls to get the real work done. Sparks were flying in the welding shop, and the very first Seeley-Matchless was completed in time for Derek Minter to test at Brands Hatch in early February. Motorcycle News reported that this would not be any normal test, it was backwards at Brands! The Grand Prix Circuit in a reverse direction had been proposed as a neutral course for the International Hutchinson 100, to be held on August 14th after moving from Silverstone.

The Mint, as the current holder of the lap record the right way round at 1minute 45.6 seconds, 90.34 mph (on the 500 Gilera four in 1963), thought the 500cc lap times for the Hutch at Brands would be around 1minute 58 seconds at 80.84mph. (In August Hailwood, on the 350cc Honda would put up the fastest lap of the day at 1minute 49.2 seconds; 87.36mph.) The test went well for the Seeley-Matchless and MCN sports reporter Charlie Rous was very encouraging about our ambitious new project.

The Rickman Brothers, building their Metisse frames for the Kirby Team, were well ahead of us, having produced their successful motocross frames for a good period of time. We were just a garden shed operation in comparison, but our passion for road racing would eventually prove the difference between the track success of the two companies.

With the first event of the season looming, Mallory Park, Sunday March 6th, that week prior we burned the midnight oil to complete the brace of Seeleys. It had been 5am to bed on Tuesday, 3am Thursday, and not at all on Friday. Finally wheeling out the distinctive gold and silver Seeleys into the daylight was very satisfying.

Mallory proved reasonable for our team, but better for the Kirby camp ,with Bill Ivy winning the 500cc event on the Rickman Metisse-Matchless G50,giving this marque its winning debut. Dave Degens, Kirby-Matchless came second and Derek Minter third on the Seeley-Matchless, with race number 2, rather than his usual 11. Griff Jenkins rode the Dunstall-Domiracer in fourth ahead of the future master of Mallory, John Cooper on the Norton, with Chris Conn on the Matchless making up the first six.

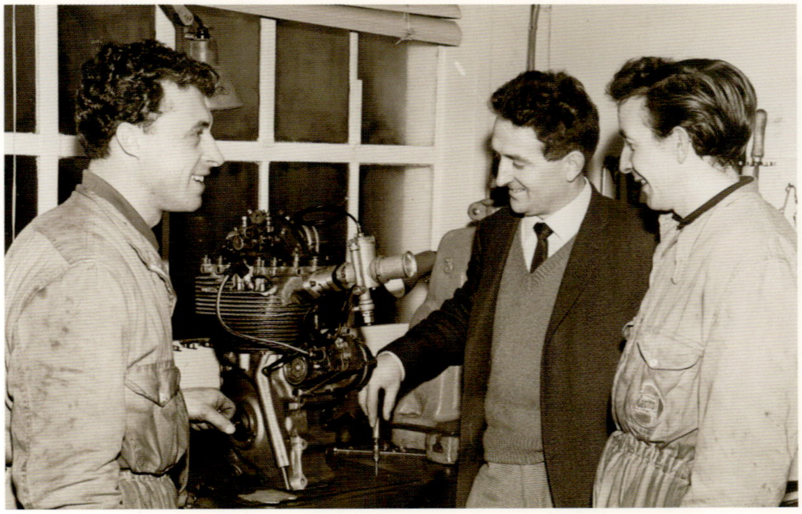

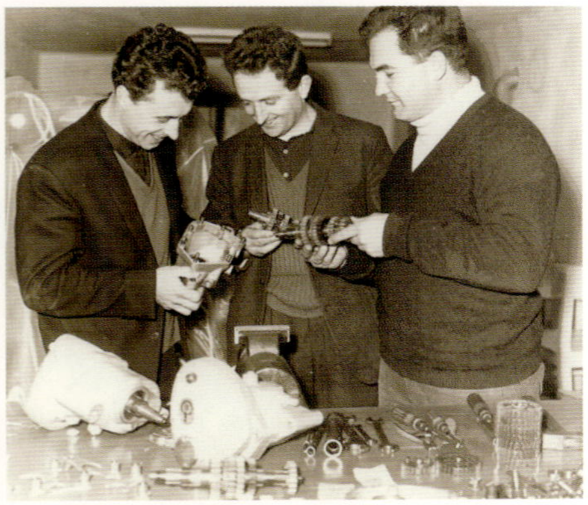

Michael Schafleitner with Derek Minter, Austria 1966.

Inspecting the G50 engine with Minter and Wally .

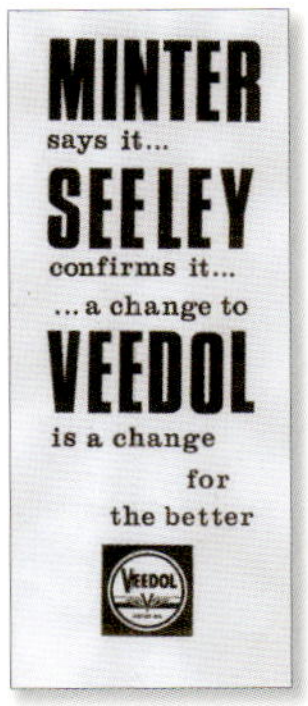

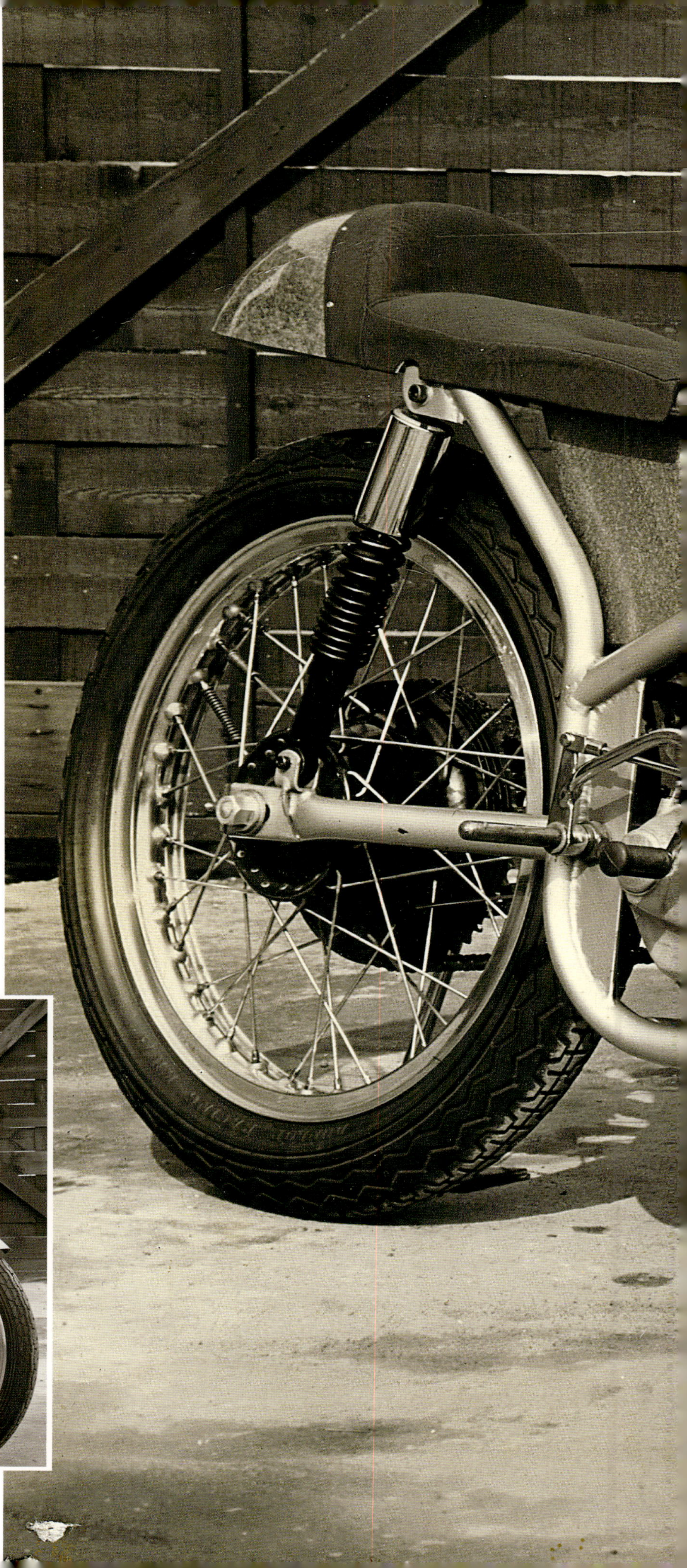

The first Seeley Matchless G50 with and without fairing.

The Mint had secured a third place on the Cotton in the 250cc event but the Seeley-AJS 350cc had a problem. With my BMW sidecar outfit now fitted with a Fath rebuilt Rennsport engine I used the two sidecar races for running-in. Our sights were on Brands Hatch the following weekend.

After our disappointment at Mallory Park we found that a piston ring had broken and the big end was faulty on the G50 engine. After rebuilding we needed to run in the engine before Brands. A quick trip to Snetterton and 17 laps sorted out the gearing and suspension ready for our return to Snetterton on the 20th March for the East Anglian Cup. My records show an oil change and a new primary chain fitted on the 500 before Brands Hatch, so important for Minter, Gungy Wal and myself. This was our favourite circuit, and a crucial event.

It was a wonderful sunny day with a huge crowd for this second national event of the year, run on the 2.65 mile long Grand Prix circuit and organised by the Brands Hatch Racing Committee. We were nervous and jumpy but much was at stake. It was not a good start. In the first event, the ten lap 350cc race, Minter shot away into the lead, but after two laps he was overpowered by Degens, Cooper and Chandler. Minter fought back to second place behind Degens. At the halfway stage, the Maidstone 'pocket rocket' Bill Ivy took the lead on the Kirby AJS-Metisse. Ivy won by two lengths from Dave Degens, Norton, with John Cooper, Norton, an equally close third. Minter finished eighth after trouble with the front tyre.

Then it was our turn. The wheelbarrows were on display. We were now concentrating on the BMW, having lost the support of Paul Dunstall's 650cc Domi-Norton engines. We had achieved reasonable success and good publicity with the Dunstall for us both, but Paul, an astute businessman, wanted to concentrate on the Domiracers and his

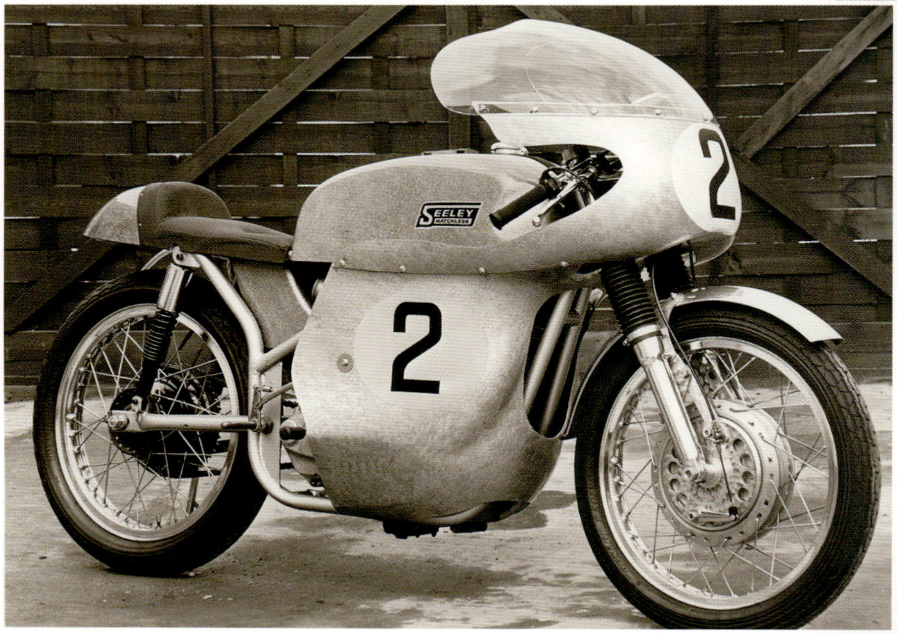

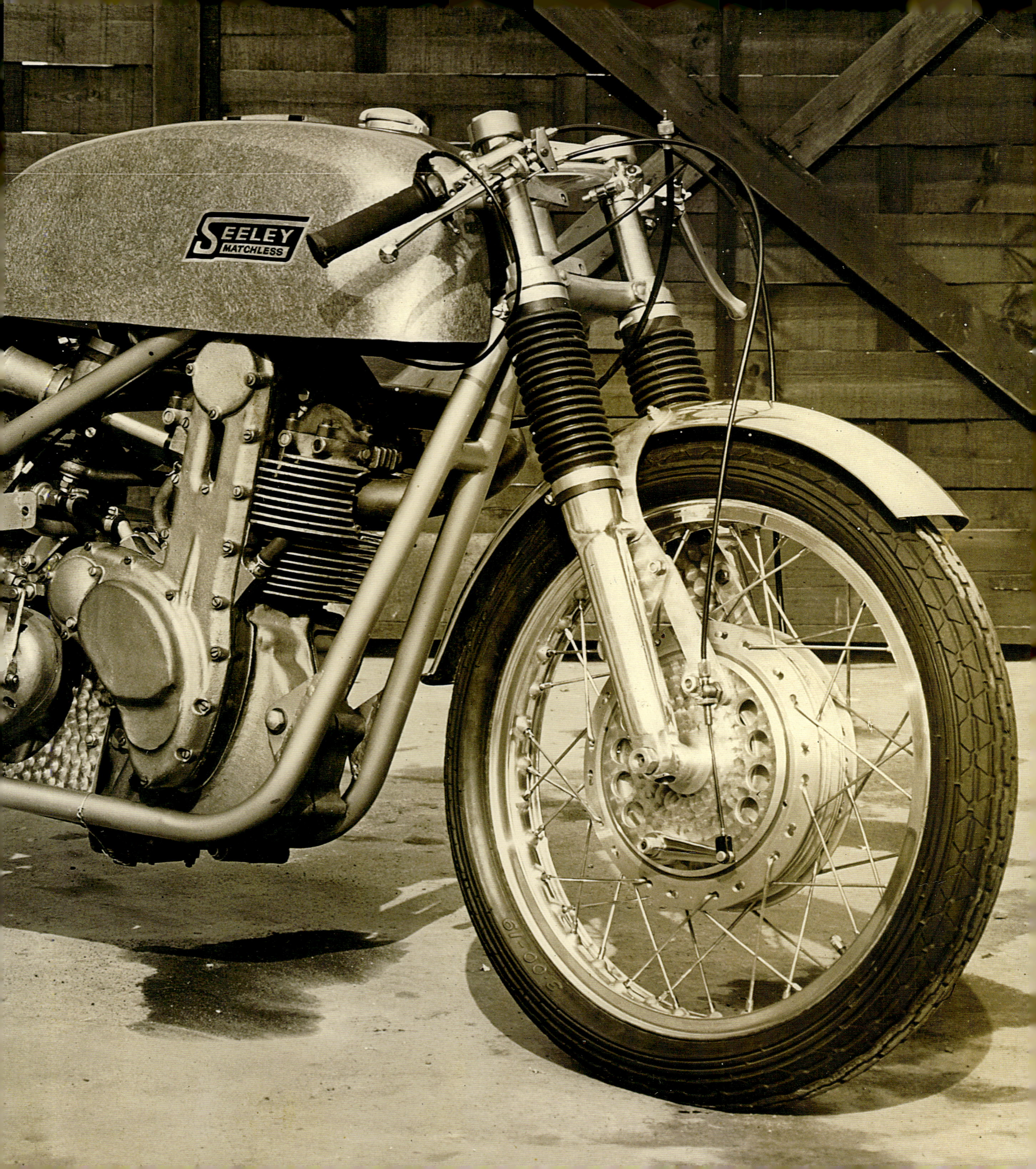
SEELEY
MATCHLESS

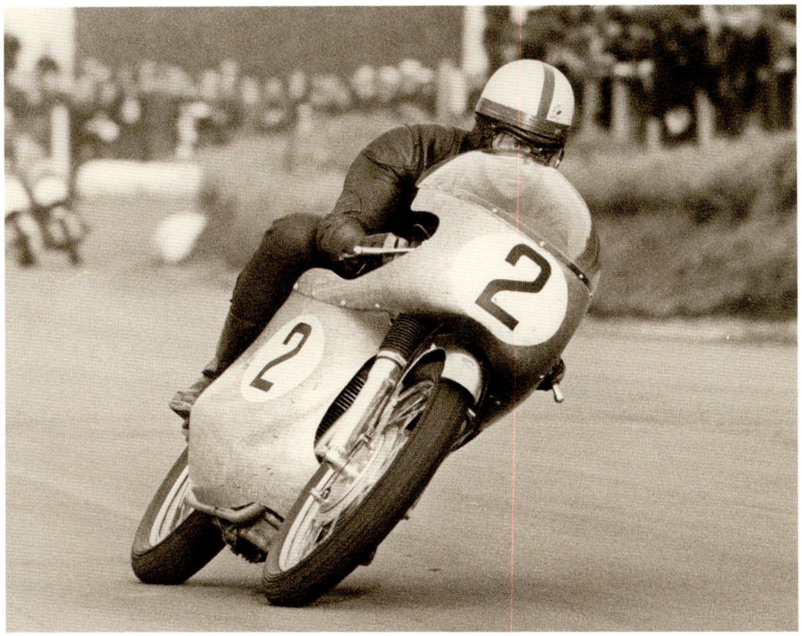

Minter at Mallory Park, Seeley - AJS.

goodies empire. Therefore, we were trying to conserve our one good BMW engine, we had a long season ahead of us. Once more at Brands the sidecar race was for up to 1200cc machines, which put the 500cc engines at a considerable disadvantage. Luck was on our side and we posted our first win of the season with the fastest lap, from Terry Vinicombe and passenger John Flaxman riding the Kirby 650cc BSA. The Kirby-Seeley needle was hotting up!

Minter didn't do so well in the 250cc race, coming in sixth on the Cotton. Rod Scivyer, Honda, won the 125cc, with Dave Simmonds, Tohatsu, second. Then came the first round of the prestigious Redex Trophy, a 12 lap race for machines over 350cc but not over 500 cc. So much depended on this race. Could the King pull it off? Watching and waiting was almost as bad actually racing.

36 riders assembled on the gird, no warm up lap, no tyre warmers and no clutch start. It was an all-action push start. As the flag dropped Minter hurtled away, alongside Little Bill Ivy on the Matchless-Metisse. Ivy snatched the lead into Paddock Bend and held it for some 4 laps then Minter slipped ahead, pursued by Degens, Matchless, challenging hard. After a 2 lap tussle, Degens got past but the determined Kentish flyer soon re-passed Degens and stayed there to win with the fastest lap, the King's first success for the newly formed Seeley stable. We were delighted. I ran through the paddock tunnel to give my wife a big hug. Joan was so supportive of our long hours and commitment.

The day finished as it started, with yet another tremendous dice in the 15 lap 1000cc event. A bullish Rex Butcher on the Dunstall 650cc Domiracer took the honours in a race long duel with Ivy second, Cooper, Minter then Griff Jenkins on a 500cc Dunstall-Domiracer. four first places out of seven events was a good day's work for the Kent boys. The sidecar race won us £30, Derek got £28 for the 500cc race and £16 for fourth place in the 1000cc event.

Brands filled us with confidence for Snetterton the next weekend. A new set of Dunlop Tyres was fitted to the 500 Seeley, nothing left to chance. (Nowadays, a set of tyres only lasts one race, not several as it was then!) The huge crowd at Snetterton basking in the sunshine would enjoy some superb racing. The first event was the 350cc, three heats involving a massive 120 competitors plus three reserves. The first 12 from each heat went through to the final. Derek Minter, Rodney Gould and Peter Williams won all their heats.

In the 10 lap final the 'Mint', who was getting the hang of good starts, stormed into the lead and Londoner, Dave Degens, on his incredibly fast Aermacchi tucked in behind. It stayed that way for 8 laps. Degens briefly took the lead but Minter wouldn't give up. The gold Seeley-AJS was running well and it was our turn for glory. The chequered flag was in sight and the race finished with Degens a few lengths astern, but rewarded with the fastest lap.

Taking a quick break from working on Minter's bikes, Wally and I comfortably won the 500cc sidecar race with the fastest lap from our friend and rival Pip Harris on his BMW. Then back to two wheels for the two heats of the 500cc event, The East Anglian Cup, 80 competitors entered with 14 reserves. Derek Minter, with his familiar race number 11, won his heat and John Cooper the other. Honours would be evenly shared in the 500 final as 'Mooneyes' stalked the Mint throughout the 10 lap race, and beat Minter, who suffered a split megaphone, to the finish line on the last lap. With two wins, a second place and a third for Derek in the 250cc race, it had been a good day for the Seeley Equipe and a happy drive home. Wally and I would use the break to get ready for our next important sidecar event, the Daily Mail International sidecar race of the year, held at Mallory Park, Sunday 3rd April.

With 58 sidecar competitors, all the usual protagonists were in action, the new popular World Champion, Fritz Scheidegger partnered by John Robinson, four times World Champion, the smooth Max Deubel and Emil Horner, Auerbacher, Vincent, Harris, Freeman, Boddice, Kolle, Vinicombe, Wakefield, Lambert and Owen Greenwood assisted by Terry Fairbrother with their controversial 1071cc Mini Special. However, the veterans, Greenwood and Fairbrother broke all the records to take the cash, winning the Daily Mail 20 lap race of the year and the £500 first prize. Fritz was second, Harris was third and

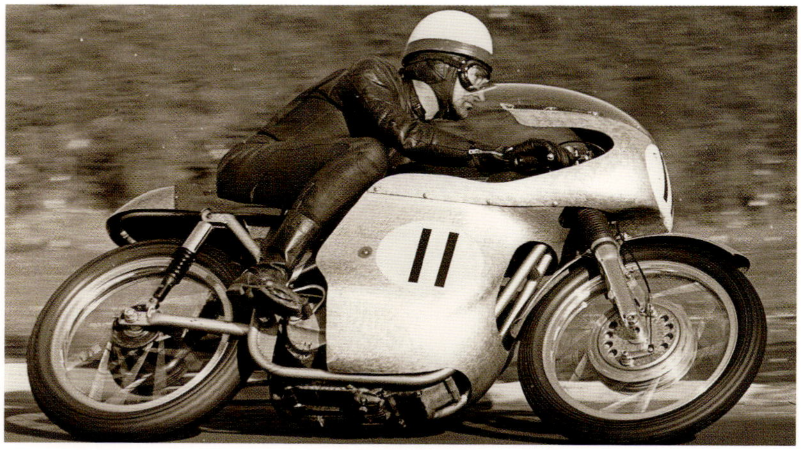

Minter at Brands, Seeley - Matchless.

8   MOTOR CYCLE NEWS, Wednesday, April 6, 1966

Don't overdo sidecar only meetings

says Colin Seeley

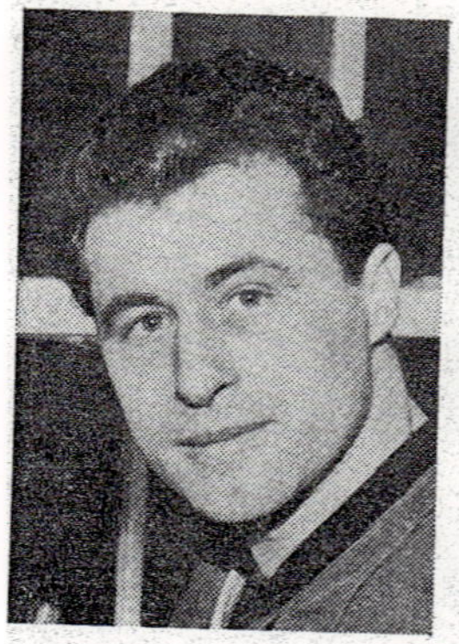

Colin Seeley

OWEN GREENWOOD'S £500 win at Mallory Park on Sunday has brought to a head the question of the whole future of sidecar racing in Britain. Should the Mini be banned? Are the sidecars only meetings killing the sport and is it fair that the new ACU championship should be in the up to 1300 cc class?

Colin Seeley, Britain's chief hope for this year's world sidecar championship, expressed the view of many sidecar men when he told me at Mallory: "This should be the last sidecars only meeting. It is played out. The crowd was down and entries were down and if carried on it will only harm the sport."

"The basic idea was good and we are very grateful to Grovewood for putting up the money, but there are not enough men or machines capable of providing close dicing. Sidecar racing should be something to be looked forward to at a meeting, now I think spectators are getting too much."

Colin went on: "My solution would be to divide the prize money up and perhaps have five races with £100 first prize or alternatively run it in conjunction with the solo "Race of the Year".

As far as the Mini is concerned, Seeley does not think it should be banned just because it is winning.

He says: "The ACU should have taken a more definite stand on it and either banned it from the start or created a separate class. Let's have car races for cars and sidecar races for sidecars. If we must have three-wheelers, then make them use motor cycle engines."

Finally, the British Championships and the fact that only 1,300 cc races count. Says Colin: "I think it is completely wrong. If we are going to continue with 500 cc races, let's have some points for them.

"Riders like Pip Harris and myself spend a lot of money on 500 cc engines. We rush back from the Continent to compete at British meetings. Let's have some recognition — why not two championships for both 500 and 1,300 cc?"

Gentlemen of the ACU and Grovewood, over to you.

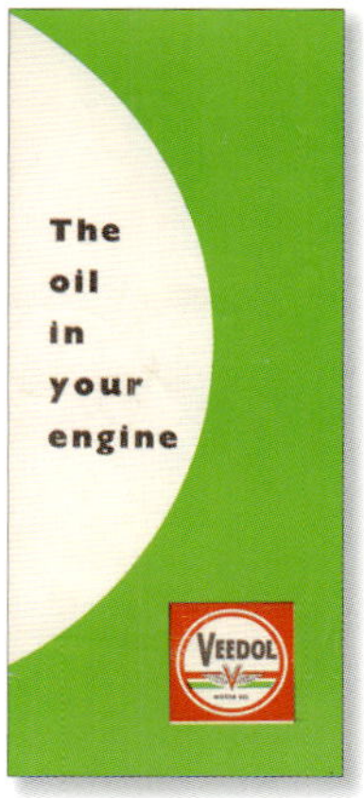

we were in a satisfying fourth place ahead of Chris Vincent and Terry Vinicombe on their 650 BSA outfits.

In an earlier heat, Max Deubel had just beaten us to the line in the 500cc 5 lap dash but we managed to get our own back in the 10 lap final, which was won by an on-form champion Scheidegger with Harris second, us third, then Max, Wakefield and Kolle, the first six. It had been good day for us, earning some very necessary prize money, a total of £147!

Bad news awaited us at home. On the first lap of the 500cc race at Le Mans our great friend, rider and supporter, 37 year old Sydney William Mizen had been killed. He had finished fourth in the 350cc event. Then in the 500cc, a close pack of riders swept on to the Muisanne straight when Alain Barbaroux's bike seized. Francois Berthand ran into him and Sid was unable to avoid the pile-up. He died in the helicopter before reaching hospital.

It was an emotional set back to our team. Although unmarried, Sid would be missed by his family. We had lost a good friend and would miss his wicked sense of humour. Sid, who had planned to retire from racing at the end of 1966, used to call me 'the little man', no respect!

With only four days to go before the hectic Easter weekend begining 8th April with the Good Friday 'King of Brands', work had to be completed on a 650cc twin Seeley-Matchless. The engine was prepared at AMC by Arthur Childs, a mix between CSR and G45 engine parts, fitted with Del 'Orto carburettors.

We wanted to give Minter a bit more punch for the 1000cc 'King of Brands' event, but our hastily prepared 650 proved to have insufficient ground clearance and Derek was forced to retire from the race. In trying to achieve the near impossible we had made a mistake.

The 'Maidstone Marvel' Bill Ivy won the King of Brands title for the Kirby camp, the crown held up only by his ears. The hard-riding Dave Degens, racing his home-built 650cc Dresda-Triton nearly stole the show, finishing a close second. Mike Hailwood on the 349cc Honda four had to settle for third spot.

The earlier 350cc race with 36 riders on the grid started the day's proceedings. Hailwood won with Ivy second. It had not been so good for Minter. At the push start Derek was about to swing a leg over the saddle when his foot slipped off the footrest, leaving him clinging to the Seeley. Somehow he climbed back on board the accelerating machine but lost vital time. He worked his way up the field to do battle with Cooper and Dunphy, finally finishing in a disappointing sixth place.

Once again it was the turn of the chariots, an 8 lap race over the Grand Prix circuit. A great cheer went up when it was announced that Owen Greenwood with the Mini Special would be a non-starter. With Owen out, there was nobody to challenge Chris Vincent on his 654cc green flying machine, which disappeared into the distance whilst Pip Harris' 500 BMW, ourselves, Vinicombe and Boddice, both BSA, disputed second place, which finally went to Pip, with us in another third position and £10 in prize money.

Derek Minter cheered us up by winning the 250cc on the little Cotton as well as a third position on the 500cc Seeley-Matchless in the Redex Trophy Race. In the last major race of the day , Derek came third again. This up to 1000cc event was a second win that day for the charging Degens. Combined with the two second places it was a good day for the London boy, £91 in all. Minter took home £43 plus undisclosed start money, probably £100. It had been a fair day for the Seeley Equipe, and a good day for Kirby. Dave Degens, Lancefield-Norton, stole the show, but not the crown jewels.

Sidecar Race of the Year, Mallory Park.

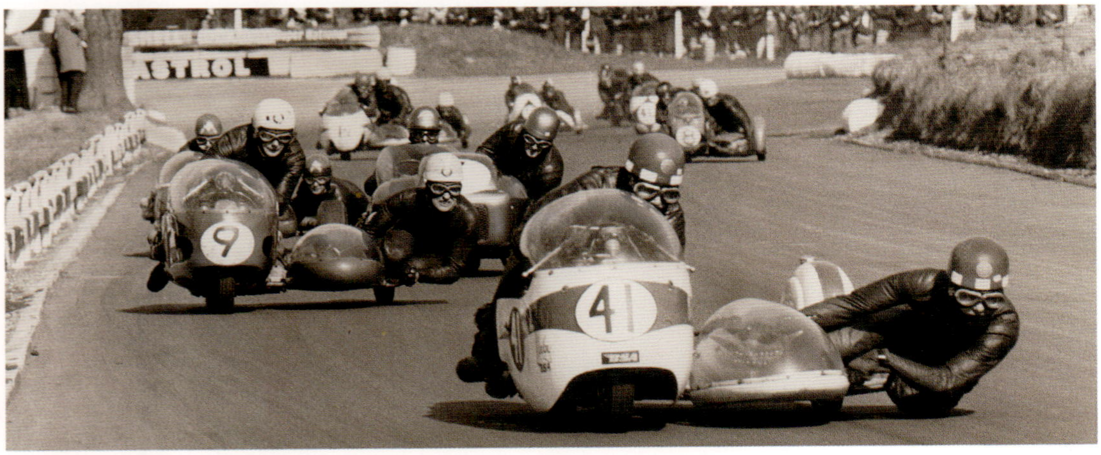

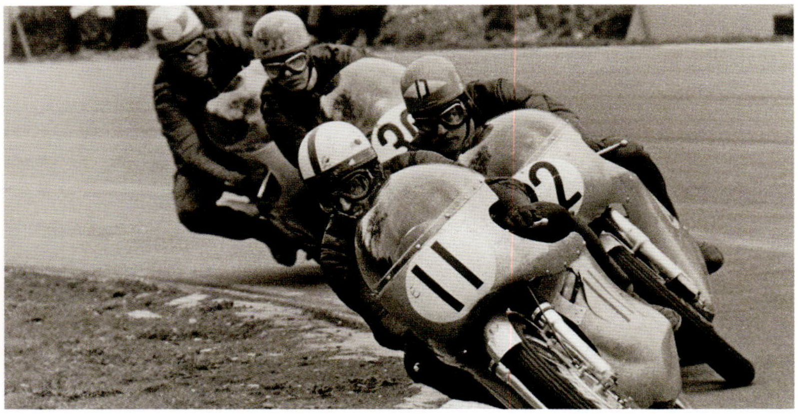

Minter, Degans, Jenkins and Croxford at Brands.

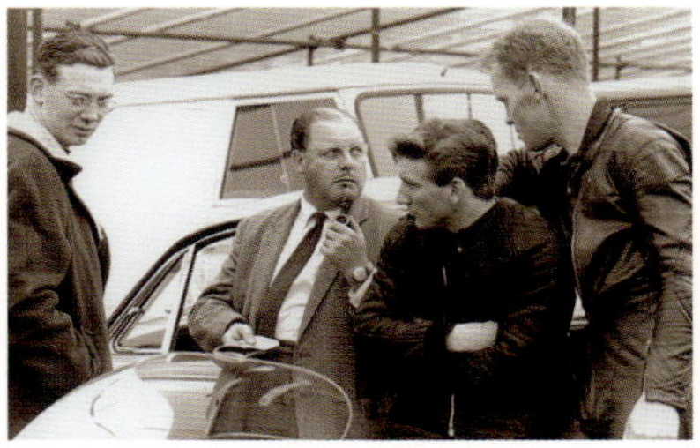

John Cooper, Tom Kirby, Bill Ivy and Chris Conn, Brands Hatch.

Mostly, the circus travelled straight to Snetterton for the Easter Sunday International 'Race of Aces'. But we were back to base in Belvedere with much to do. The shop was open for business, Percy and assistants still keeping the wolf from the door, although motorcycle sales were down.

Snetterton was best forgotten. In the 10 lap 350cc race as competitors lined up on the grid it started to rain. There was plenty of rubber on the track from the previous week's car race. The rain made it like an ice rink, particularly at Russell's corner where a chicane had been put in to slow competitors down from Coram Curve. In the opening laps Hailwood parted from his Honda at Russell's. A succession of riders fell like skittles, spinning on their backsides with more falling each time round. A frantic Tom Kirby was signalling Bill Ivy his last runner on wheels to slow down. Derek Minter took fright or perhaps just had the sense to pull in. Dave Degens on the Lawton Aermacchi returned to the pit area covered in mud, having gone scrambling at Riches Corner. It has been suggested that most of the ACU officials were out to lunch when finally Bob Havers got the red flag out after 4 laps and Peter Williams was declared the winner. It was like a scene from The Keystone Cops.

In practice for the 500cc sidecar race Deubel, Scheidegger and ourselves rushed our BMWs round the 2.71 mile circuit, all within the existing lap record, but it would prove nothing as it was still wet and slippery for our race. From the start Deubel took the lead, closely followed by ourselves and Pip Harris with Fritz well down midfield, but we were soon out with water in the works. Harris took the lead, tip-toeing around the track leading Max who spun the outfit accelerating out of Russell's. Emil Horner fell out, leaving Max travelling backwards down the circuit. Within seconds Emil leapt back into the chair and Max was off again, now back in tenth position earning the admiration of the crowd by working back to third place after Tony Wakefield's BMW also stopped with problems. So it was finally Harris, Scheidegger, Deubel, Vinicombe and our man, Norman Huntingford's Matchless in fifth place.

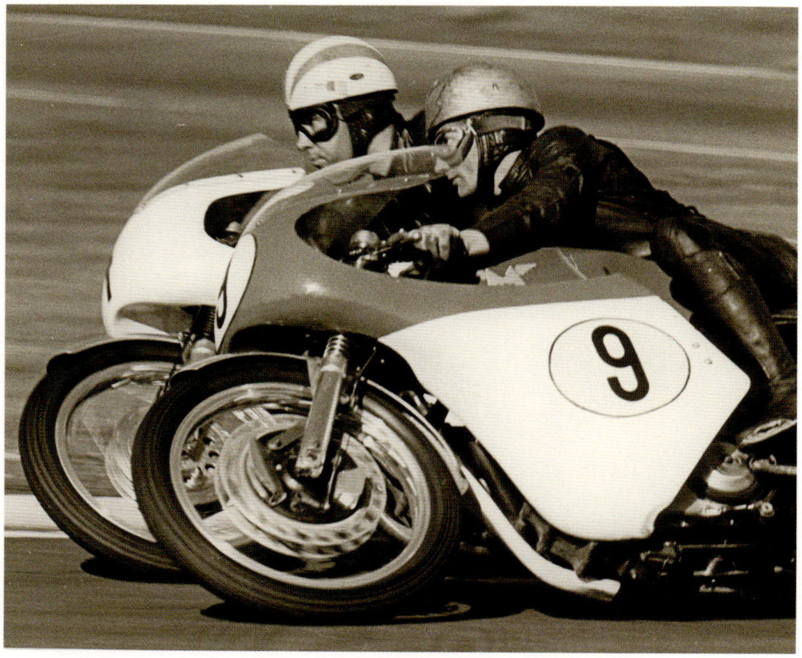

Ivy leaning on Chandler, heading for his 1966 King of Brands title.

The 77 competitors for the 500cc 'Race of the Aces' were split into two heats with the first 15 of each qualifying for the 10 lap race. Dave Croxford won the first heat. An unhappy Minter was left on the line when the Seeley failed to fire up. When he got going he was back in fourteenth, so far back he decided to retire. A shame, as the 'Mint' could have still qualified for the final, which was won by the Kirby team of Degens, Matchless, and Bill Ivy, Matchless-Metisse, second and credited with the fastest lap. I wasn't too pleased with Derek, I felt it had been an opportunity lost.

The 1300cc wheelbarrow race would be a further Chris Vincent benefit followed home by Harris, Fritz, Max, yours truly and Wakefield making the first six. The day was over and it hadn't been ours. Quickly, we packed up for the long weary journey to Oulton Park, Cheshire for the Easter Monday action.

Oulton Park's 2.761 miles circuit was another favourite for our team, in particular the 'Mint'. His race record at Oulton was almost as good as that of his home circuit, Brands Hatch. This Easter trophy international event, organised by the Wirrall 100 Motor Club and sponsored by the Daily Express, attracted 40,000 fans. The 125cc started the day's proceedings and was won by Tommy Robb, works Bultaco, after an initial tussle with Derek Woodman, MZ, who retired.

Then we were on, a 2.55pm start for the 22 lap 58 mile race. The champ Scheidegger won from Pip Harris and it was another third position for Gungy Wal and me, but with the satisfaction of beating Max Deubel and Chris Vincent. Then, with hardly time to get off the BMW outfit, we rushed over to help the Mint prepare for the start of the 19 lap 500cc race at 3.30pm.

Forty 500cc machines assembled on the grid, the riders pulled the bikes back on compression and adjusted their goggles, with their thoughts on the dash to Old Hall Corner. Wally and I, still in our race leathers, were watching intensely. The results of this race were crucial to our plans and we needed to even the score.

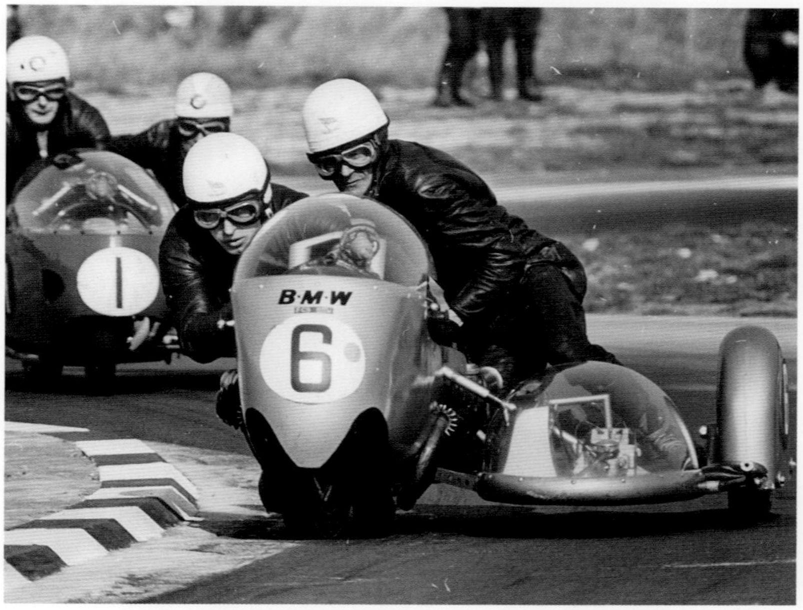

Winning ways, leading Pip Harris at Snetterton.

The flag dropped and Mooneyes Cooper took the lead at the first corner, closely followed by Griff Jenkins, Keith Heckles, Peter Williams, Joe Dunphy with Minter around the outside. After an initial tussle with Jenkins on the fast Dunstall Domiracer, a challenge from Mooneyes and Malcolm Uphill, Derek Minter sped ahead to score his first International win on the Goldfinger Seeley-Matchless, as reported on the day by Charlie Rous, followed home by Cooper, Jenkins, Uphill, Ivy and Stuart Graham. A superb result, The Wirral 100 Trophy and £100 prize.

With only minutes to spare after his victory, Derek dashed to the 250cc Cotton for another 19 laps around Oulton Park. The race itself turned into a two horse confrontation between the Mint and Derek Woodman on the works MZ. Using every trick in the book and with some incredible riding, Minter kept Woodman at bay until the last lap and the last corner, but there is no substitute for power and Woodman nipped by to take the win and the £50 first prize, with £30 for the Mint. Now Derek could have a well-deserved rest before the last race of the day, the 350cc event.

The final leg of the sidecar race was next, but we were in trouble. As we wheeled our BMW to the line we discovered a sump stud had broken, causing an oil leak so we were unable to start, a huge disappointment as I felt we could have finished in third position overall. Never mind, the 350cc event was more important. I did not believe that Derek was quite as confident with the 350cc Seeley-AJS 7R as with the Seeley 500, but time would tell.

Mike Hailwood was on parade with the private 349cc Honda four. Many fans had waited all day to see Mike the Bike in action and they would not be disappointed. Mike himself had waited all day for this race, although he was starting from the back of the grid due to being late for the morning 350cc practice. Mike and friends had been busy straightening the Honda after the Snetterton crash. From the start of the 19 lap 52.5 mile race Mike's progress was meteoric, despite a collision with a midfield starter. With a gesture of apology, Mike was soon at the front and winning. The crowd was delighted, but the regular stalwarts behind were in hot pursuit. The Kent Flyer from Blean would not be outdone, holding off the challenge of Londoner Degens on Steve Lancefield's Manx Norton swapping places continually until the intrepid Degens flung his immaculate Norton away at Cascades. The Mint went on to a fantastic second place finishing ahead of John Cooper, Peter Williams and Bill Ivy.

A 500cc class first place and a 350cc class second position to Hailwood in this international event was more than we could have hoped for. Our Seeley bikes had been built in little more than a garden shed. The disappointment of our sidecar race was put in the shade by the solo results. It would be an easy 230 mile drive home to Kent, a brilliant end to a frantic four days. But hold it! We still had the little matter of Mallory Park next day, Tuesday 12th April, the second such event.

This meeting tagged onto the end of such a busy Easter weekend, in my opinion was not good for anyone. Once again four meetings in five days was crazy! It was road racing overkill and it certainly doesn't happen nowadays.

Wally got a lift straight home to continue our work programme so I hired Norman Huntingford's passenger Roy Lindsey for the day, costing me £12. We came second in the up to 1200cc heat and third again in the final, to Chris Vincent and Peter Russell on the awesomely quick (when running properly) 998cc Vincent. We were awarded a magnificent £2 for second in our heat, and £7 for third in the 10 lap final. It was hardly worth the wear and tear on the BMW, and didn't justify another night in the Thames van. No caravan for us! Yes, our ace rider, the Mint had some luxury, a comfortable caravan!

Derek had a bad day too, problems with both of the Seeley machines and even the 250cc Cotton broke down. Tuesday's Mallory Park meeting was best forgotten.

We now had a break from racing but no time to ponder or despair. It was back to base to correct faults and improve our Seeley machines before Derek Minter went to Castle Combe at the end of the month. We would not be attending, saving our energy in readiness for Brands Hatch next day, lst May, our third visit so far that year, but for me very significant, promoted to commemorate our good friend Florian Camathias.

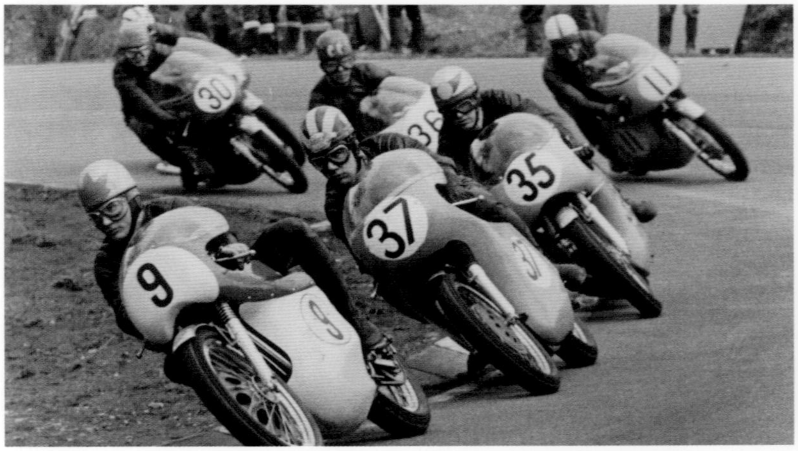

Bill Ivy 'King of Brands' (9), Rex Butcher (37), Dave Croxford (35), John Cooper (36), Derek Minter (11) and Griff Jenkins (30).

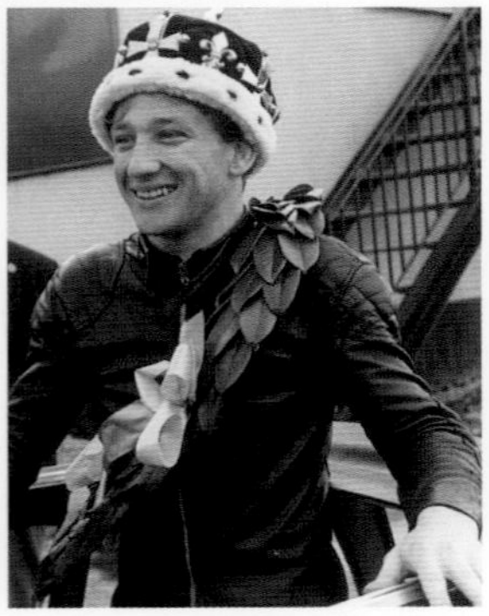

Bill Ivy 'King of Brands' 1966.

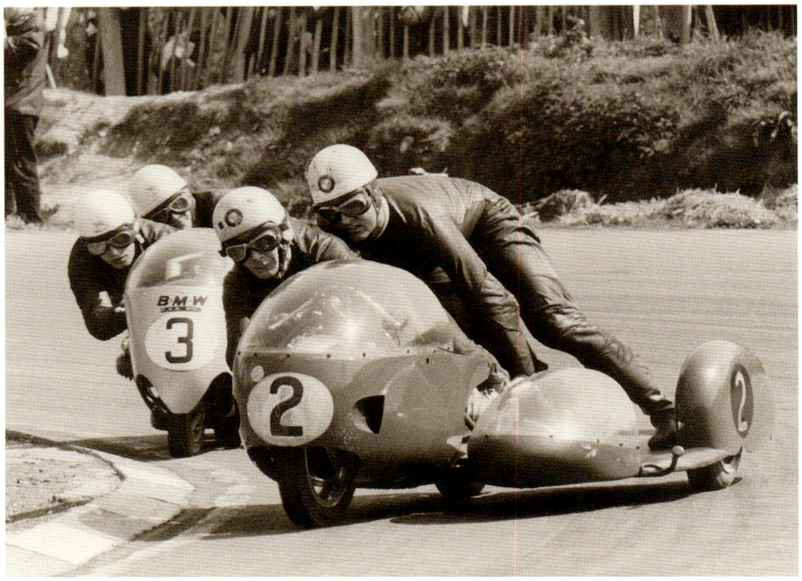

Brands Hatch 1st May 1966, Florian Camathias, 500cc race.

At Castle Combe, Minter, Seeley AJS, again failed to dominate, first place going to Selwyn Griffiths, AJS, in a close 350cc encounter, with the improving Croxford third. The scorching 500cc final saw the Ruislip racer Croxford, Matchless, wheel to wheel, with The Mint on the Seeley Matchless, but halfway through the 10 lap race Derek slowly dropped back to an eventual sixth placing leaving an on-form Selwyn Griffiths, Matchless, to take on the challenge. But at the chequered flag it was Croxford then Selwyn followed by Tom Phillips, Rod Gould and Ray Pickrell, on a trio of Nortons, all so close!

Next day at Brands Hatch before the Camathias Memorial meeting began, Madame Camathias, in the bright sunshine at Clearways, unveiled a plaque dedicated to Florian. 50 sidecar competitors, lead by Vincent, Harris and ourselves turned an impressive slow lap of the short circuit in final salute, a fitting tribute to this Swiss hero.

For this meeting there would be, for the sidecar competitors, a 500cc race, an up to 1300cc event, and a handicap race. I was riding the FCS-powered BMW and I really wanted to win the 500cc race. For me and for many Florian Camathias fans, this was a very emotional day. But with Pip Harris, Chris Vincent and the fast-improving Tony Wakefield with his passenger Graham Milton on their BMWs, it wasn't going to be easy.

This meeting was not only for sidecars, but supported by all the solo classes. With Derek Minter to look after it would be a busy day. My sights though were firmly fixed on winning the 500cc sidecar race and the Florian Camathias Trophy, but Pip Harris had other ideas. From the start he held a slender lead until a problem occurred. I was through in a flash to win from Harris, Vincent, Wakefield and Norman Huntingford fifth on his Matchless. Florian must have been looking down and pushing us forward. Wally and I were ecstatic, to us it was more than a 10 lap dash round Brands.

The 350cc solo event was a cut and thrust affair with Ron Chandler, AJS, leading, until the dashing Dave Croxford riding the Colin Lyster lightweight framed Norton came past, then promptly crashed. Minter on the Seeley was creeping up, but so were Mooneyes Cooper and Peter Williams. Degens on the Aermacchi took the lead and stayed there to win with Minter back in sixth place.

Then back to the sidecars for the heats of the 1300cc Camathias Memorial Scratch Race. From 54 sidecar competitors in three heats, 18 would go through to the finals. The 5 lap dash heats left no room for mistakes and with our 500cc BMW it not an easy task. Anyway, we won our heat from Wakefield, Greenwood and a young Mick Boddice.

The 10 lap final let in Greenwood's Mini menace, which had a tough job coming through to win. Wally and I got the better of Peter Brown and Norman Hanks on their 654cc BSA machines for second place, good as a win. None of the sidecar boys could live with 1071cc Mini monster. Two firsts and a second were just great, we did not need to wear out the Rennsport any further in a handicap race. Our prize earnings of £68 and start of £40 plus a treasured trophy were pretty good.

Not quite so good for the King, Minter had to settle for second place in the 15 lap 500cc race, beaten again by Degens on the fast Lancefield Norton. Then in the 20 lap 1000cc event Mooneyes got the better of him. Dave Degens had crashed heavily at Paddock Bend on the third lap sustaining a beating around his chest and ribs. Minter's only consolation was to beat Rex Butcher on the 650cc Dunstall-Norton and Croxford on the Oakley-Matchless. The race results for the Seeley Equipe were one sixth, one fifth, three seconds, two firsts. Not a bad day at the office.

Following Derek's reasonable success on the Seeley machines, we began to receive orders. Austrian Rudi Thalhammer, our Swiss friend Ernst Weiss and Helmut Fath for a German rider he was to sponsor, all wanted our race bikes. Engine supply from AMC was still a problem as they were suffering serious financial problems. Their long term situation did not look good.

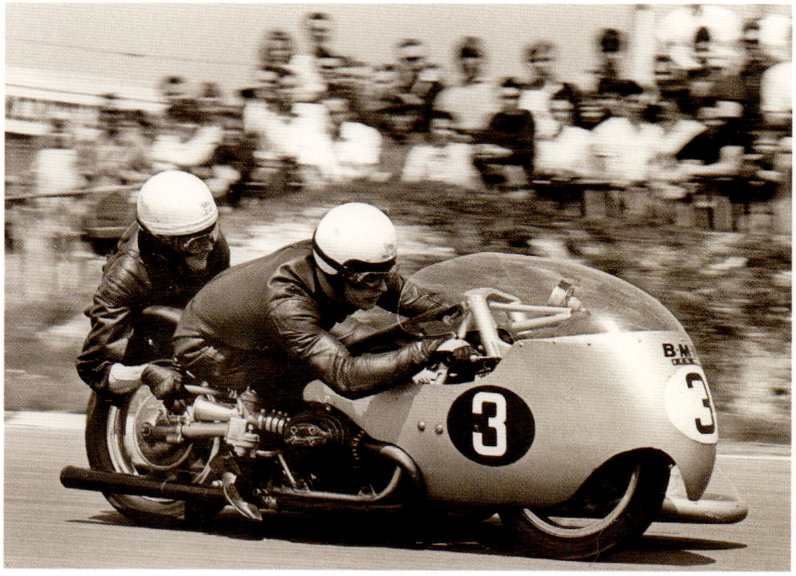

Paddock Hill Bend, Brands on the way to win the 500cc event.

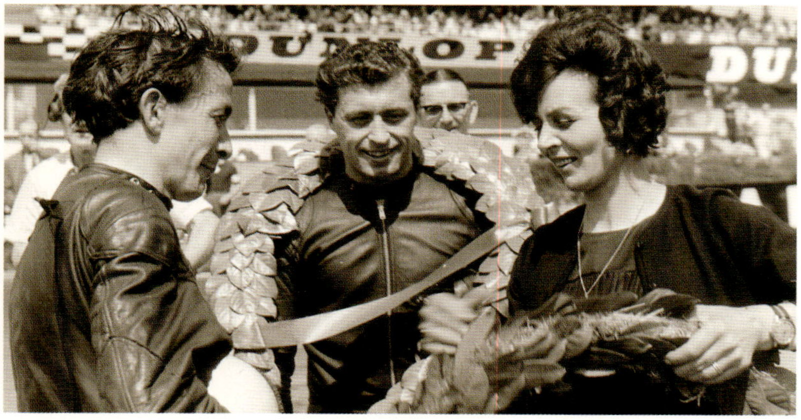

Presentation by Maggie Camathias after winning at Brands.

The Camathias Trophy presentation.

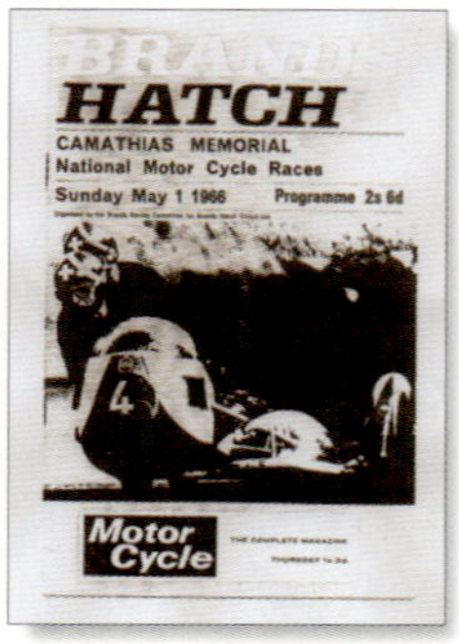

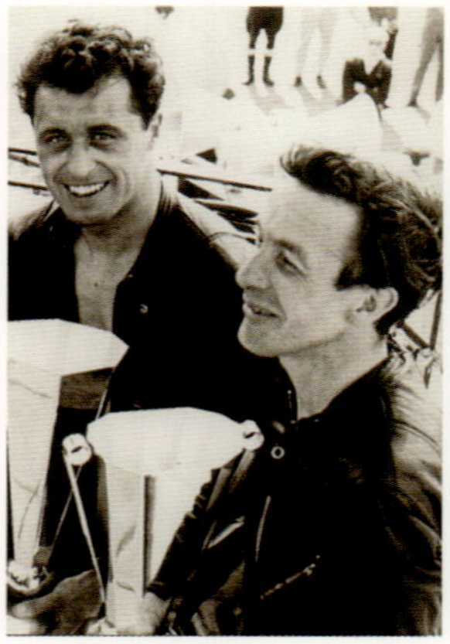

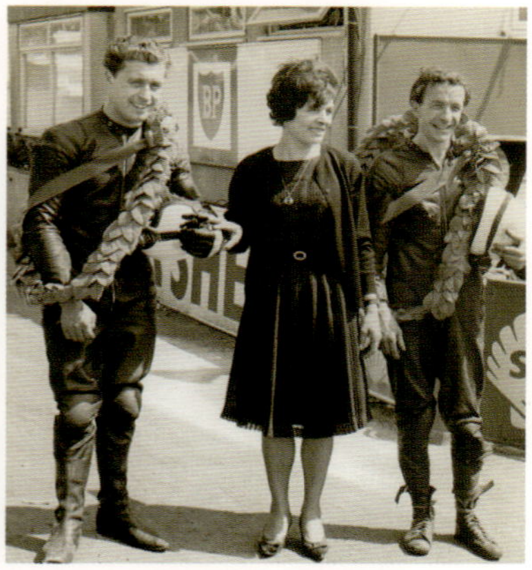

Me, Wally and Maggie Camathias.

Meantime, all our earnings from the sidecar racing was being put back into the race programme purchasing bits of machinery as we went, to speed up production. Those early days had their difficulties! But, nothing ventured nothing gained. We would be on this treadmill for some seven years.

Derek Minter! What can I say? His Grand Prix results weren't so impressive, his best placing fifth in the 1958 500cc World Championship (fourth Isle of Man, third Dutch TT, fourth Ulster Grand Prix).Then in 1962 he was placed twelfth, with a second at the 500cc Dutch TT.

After the fateful crash at Brands Hatch with Dave Downer, Derek finished third in the Ulster Grand Prix and second at Sachsenring giving him seventh in the 1963 championship and apart from a second place in the 500cc Isle of Man TT in 1964, that was Derek's World Championship aspiration over.

Derek on his day was in a class of his own, he was certainly on a par with Hailwood, Read, Hartle, McIntyre and many others. Unfortunately, there was more to getting a regular works ride than simply turning on the throttle. Derek was very outspoken, which is good coming from me, but picking the right moment is important and I don't think Derek ever learnt that. He would criticise product suppliers in public, including Dunlop Tyres who had given so much support, it was often very embarrassing.

I sensed that Derek was not happy with his performance on the Seeley machines. Certainly we had suffered teething problems, but every effort was being put into the solo machines. Our sidecar outfit mostly took second place.

With no classes for 350, 500cc or sidecars at the Spanish Grand Prix, our first Grand Prix that season would be the German, held on the rebuilt 4.2 mile Hockenheim Circuit on May 22nd. It was at this event Honda boasted that they would win every solo World Championship that season. The might of the 1966 works Honda Team was amazing. It made the Seeley racers look somewhat puny, but of course not every rider would have a works machine and race meetings always needed a full supporting cast of players, and a variety of machines.

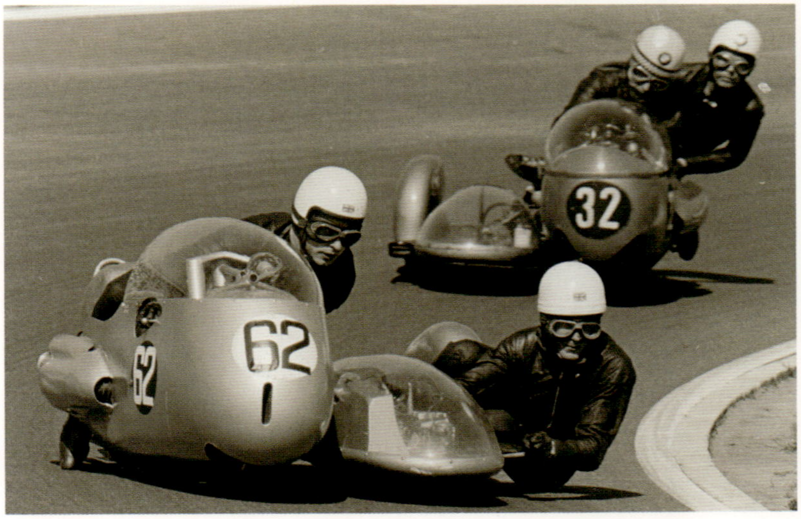

Race day at the new 6.768km clockwise Hockenheim circuit saw thousands packed into the newly built stands surrounding the twisty infield section around the pits complex. The enthusiastic German fans enjoyed a full sun-soaked race prgramme 50cc, 125cc, 250cc, 350cc, 500cc and sidecars. Honda didn't have it all their own way, as Hans-Georg Anscheidt won the 50cc race on the works Suzuki from Ralph Bryans, Honda, with Hugh Anderson, Suzuki, third and Luigi Taveri, Honda, fourth. Then it was Honda all the way, as Swiss ace Taveri won the 125cc race. Although Phil Read, Yamaha, led the opening laps of the 250cc race from Hailwood and Redman, he cast his Yamaha four away in the infield section under the noses of the Honda pairing, who with the only real opposition gone, gave a race long high-speed demonstration on the awesome Honda sixes, averaging just under 110mph with Mike pipping Redman to the post by a split second. The Maidstone Flyer, Bill Ivy brought home the other works Yamaha four in third place, just over 16 seconds down, a good effort, with Woodman's MZ fourth. Mike Hailwood then won the 350 event and Redman the 500cc race having taken the ride on the new Honda 500 four. The 28 lap race, totalling 116 miles was reduced to 23 laps due to the extreme heat. Redman led the 500cc race from start to finish, the Honda much quicker than Agostini's MV some 26 seconds behind, with Gula Marsovszky, Matchless, third.

For our team, Derek Minter finished a very creditable eighth in the 350cc race. The Seeley-AJS was the first single cylinder and non-works machine home, behind an array of works Honda, Benelli, Bianchi and Jawas. We were hoping for a similar result in the 500cc race. Unfortunately, we had filled the fuel tank of the Seeley-Matchless to the brim for the long race, but we had not considered that petrol expands in hot conditions and with the temperature still rising as Derek came to the start line, the fuel started to gush out of the filler cap. There was nothing we could do in time and were forced to withdraw.

The new World sidecar Champion Fritz Scheidegger, along with Max Deubel, were receiving support from the BMW factory and surprisingly in practice, both riders were forced to revert to their original BMW engines when the new works engines seized up. This situation did not stop Scheidegger achieving an easy win in the 15 lap race from ex-champ Deubel.

German Grand Prix, Auerbacher, Wally and me.

Rostrum, German Grand Prix.

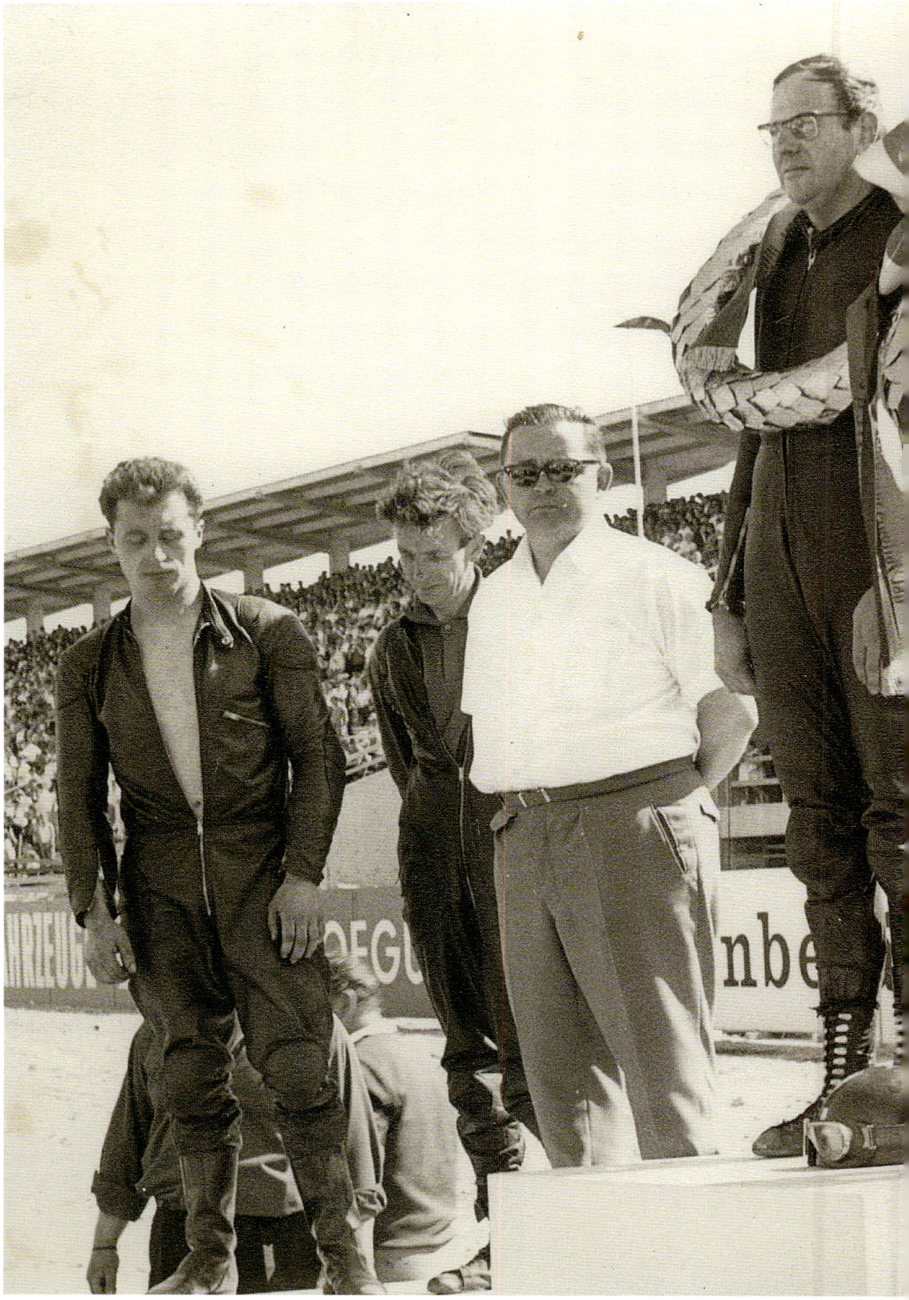

Earlier in the race, back in fourth, we were sandwiched between Georg Auerbacher and Chris Vincent. Chris soon dropped off the hot pace, and hot it was, as Georg and I were almost locked together. We did not quite have the speed to pass Auerbacher down the long straights and only made up time to pass Georg in the slower stadium section. Then he was back in front again. Lap after lap this was repeated. As the battle raged, I vividly remember how we streamlined Auerbacher, receiving a tow only a couple of feet from the rear of his BMW outfit, our front fairing almost touching his passenger's feet. As we charged down the shaded high speed sections I could see the reflection in our race screen of the Union Jack on the front of my white helmet. I was proud to be British and wanted to beat our German friend, particularly in the German Grand Prix

The sight of the Union flag reflecting in the screen gave me extra encouragement, so we kept on Auerbacher's tail, not letting up for a single moment, just waiting for Georg to make a mistake, and he did! In entering the twisty stadium section for the start of the last lap, Auerbacher over-shot and went dirt tracking just enough for us to pounce and slip past. By then I was worn out by the tough race and extreme heat. It was only the weight of my arm that kept the throttle open. How we completed that last lap in front of the determined German I shall never know. The gods were with us. We came over the finish line 2 seconds ahead, averaging 95.32mph and into third place.

As I stumbled off the outfit, I collapsed with heat exhaustion. My heart beat seemed quicker than our Rennsport engine in the race. I required the doctor's attention and had never suffered so much from racing before. Lack of sleep, the long hours of work on the Seeleys and Hockenheim's blistering sun had all taken their inevitable toll.

Hardly recovered, we packed up our kit, loaded the Rennsport and set off for another gruelling weekend, the French Grand Prix at Clermont Ferrand. The Grand Prix as before was followed the next day by the Bank Holiday Brands Hatch meeting, so another dash home. With no 500cc solo class at The French Grand Prix, Derek Minter would travel straight back to England.

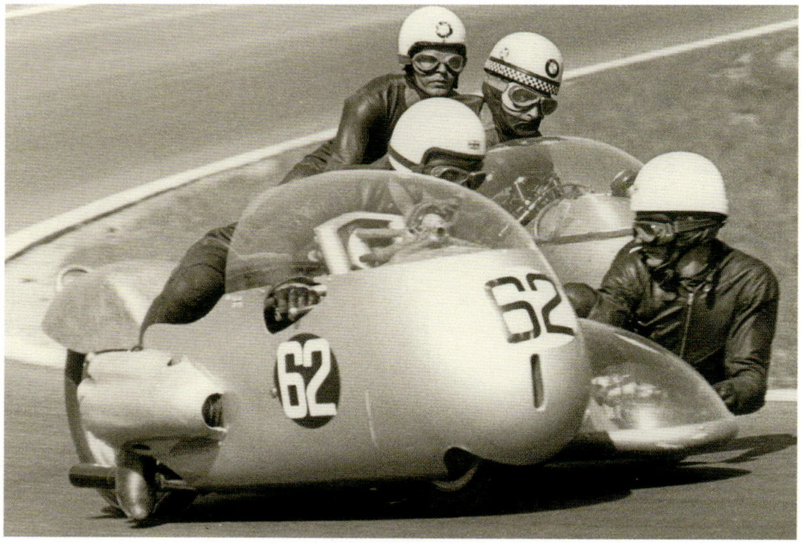

Action in the German Grand Prix.

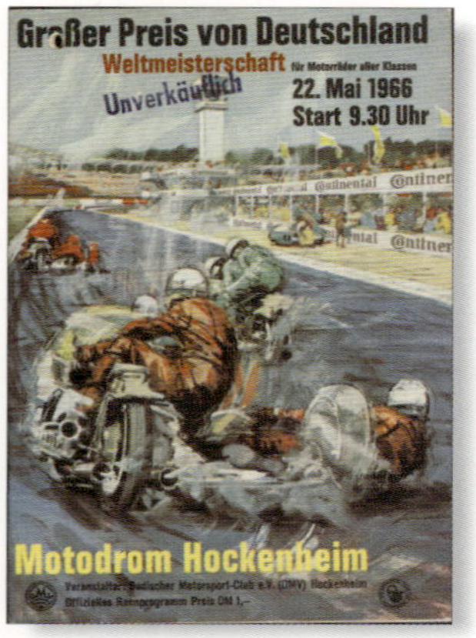

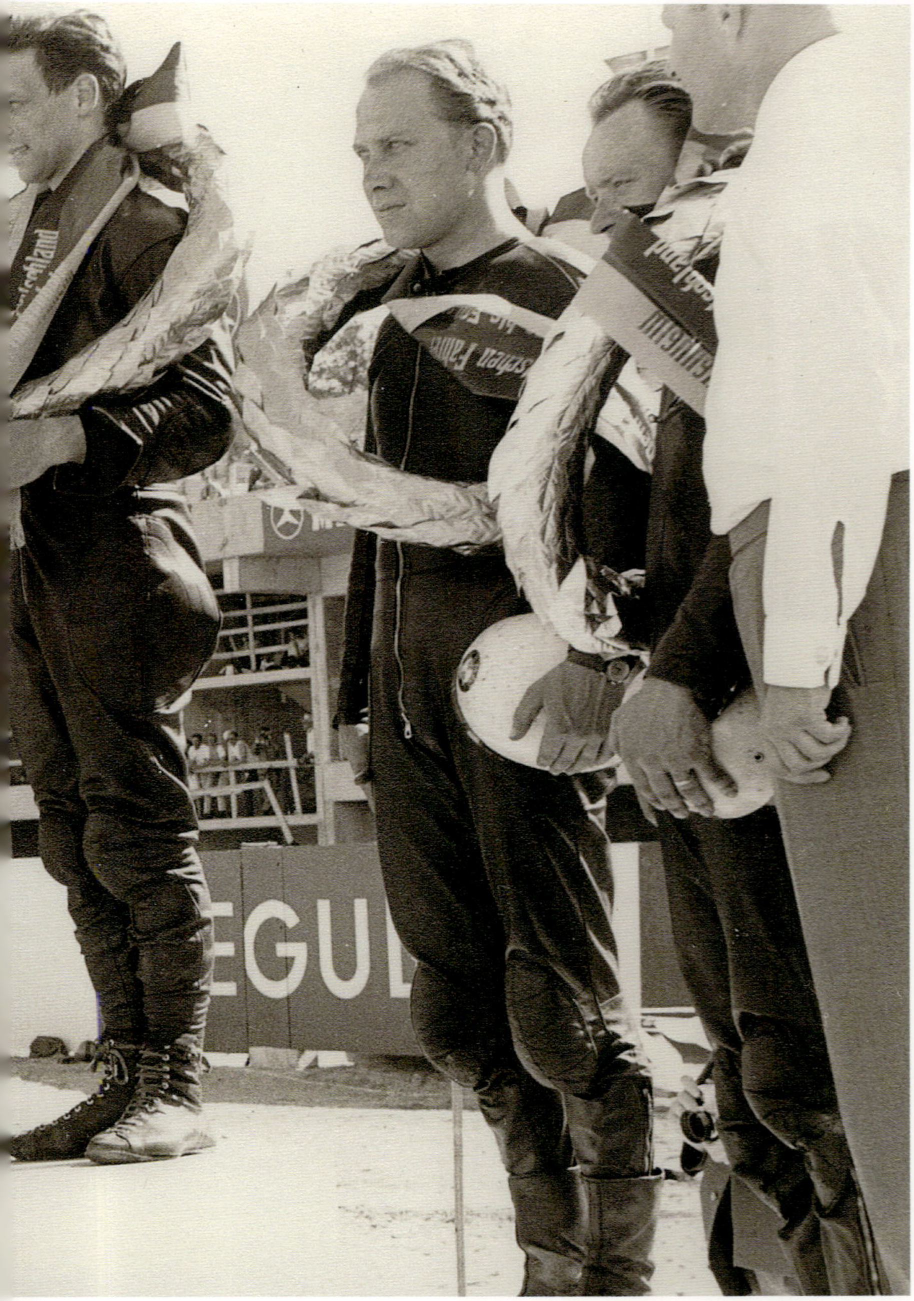

Norman Huntingford joined us on the trip to Clermont for our third visit to the mountainous, rock-lined 5 mile circuit, a challenge indeed. In those days you were expected to ride your machine down into the town centre for the official scrutineering and stamp of approval. This was really an excuse to promote the event, and the French were no different.

A big attraction would be Mike Hailwood, the Master returning to Clermont, his first visit since 1961 when he finished second in the 500cc race to winner Gary Hocking on the MV, the last year of the 500cc class until re-instatement in 1972. Mike also came second in the 250cc race in 1961 on a Honda behind Tom Phillis, also Honda. The 350cc class had already been dropped in 1961, not returning until 1966. Mike the Bike, already five times World Motorcycle Champion, would stamp his complete authority on both the 250cc and 350cc classes throughout 1966, leaving Phil Read, Agostini and Redman in his wake.

In brilliant weather the 30,000 spectators covering the gorse-covered hillsides were enthralled with Mike's dominant performance on the works Honda, but were disappointed with the lack of close racing in the solo classes. In fact the three-race-only programme, 250, 350 and sidecars had contributed to this situation, as it automatically forfeited the Suzuki, Yamaha and Honda works teams in the 125 class, nevermind the loss of the 50cc machines, ideally suited to Clermont. The French organisers assumed that Yamaha and MZ teams would compete in the 350cc race, and although listed in the programme, both teams denied they had entered.

Twenty-one competitors lined up for the 250cc race. With engines running a huge din (no silencers in those days) reverberated between the pits complex and the mountainside opposite. Many riders were not wearing their obligatory tie-on race number waistcoats. Gesticulating wildly and their faces going almost purple, the officials tried to explain that riders would be disqualified if they didn't don the jackets. The competitors felt that the jackets could come loose and be a danger. As tempers frayed the French federation officials were forced to have a quick re-think and within minutes announced that the waistcoats were optional. So quick as it started the French farce was over. This incident was a real pantomime and added a little spice to the day.

Finally, the 250cc race was under way with Mike the Bike sitting behind Redman, both on Honda sixes, for a couple of laps before taking the lead in the 18 lap 90.04 mile race. To witness the pair of works Honda six cylinder machines ridden by two of the best riders in the world, combined with the incredible sound of those multi-cylinder motorcycles, was just fantastic.

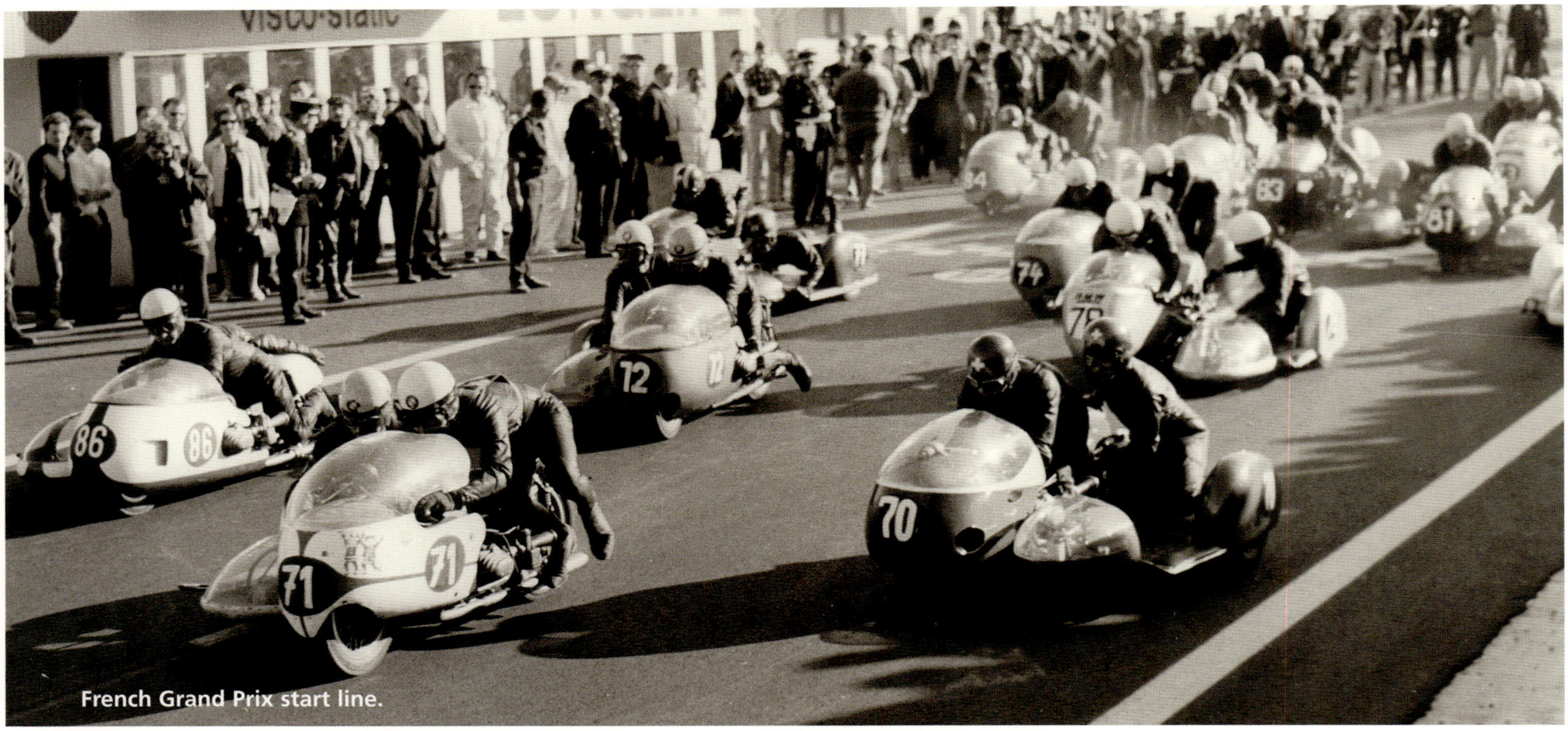

French Grand Prix start line.

Having taken the lead, Hailwood was relentless, winning from Redman nearly 46 seconds behind, with Phil Read third on the works Yamaha four, 1 minute 22 seconds behind Mike. Little Bill Ivy on the other works Yamaha on his first visit to Clermont, after a bad start dropped his Yamaha on the first lap, leaving Derek Woodman on his MZ to take fourth place.

Hailwood hardly left the winners rostrum when he was back out in action on the 350cc Honda four competing in the 20 lap 100.10 mile charge around the twisty French circuit. This time, with no French farce to delay the start, Mike romped away from his ex-team mate Giacomo Agostini on the MV three, winning by 19 seconds. Hard man Tarquinio Provini riding the Benelli four held third place in front of Redman, who was feeling unwell after the exhausting 250cc race and also had to contend with a sticking throttle on his 350cc Honda four. Then on lap 12 Provini's Benelli broke a crankshaft, leaving lucky Jim in third place but well behind. For Mike Hailwood it had been a dominating performance with lap and race records in both races.

Then with the sun still shining brightly, it was our turn to feel the heat as we wheeled our BMW to the line for the 14 lap 69.07 mile event. Racing the tough tortuous 5 mile Circuit De Montagne took a lot of concentration and physical effort. An experienced sidecar passenger was essential, there was no room for error and tucked down behind the screen the rider needed to trust his passenger implicitly. Fortunately, Wally and I had that relationship, and once more stood on the rostrum later that day for what I felt was one of our best performances ever. Florian Camathias who had given us our first chance on a BMW Rennsport outfit at this very event back in 1964 was in our thoughts, we didn't let him down.

As the flag dropped the sidecar crews started pushing for all they were worth. Then a burst of noise as the engines, mostly BMW, came to life, Swiss World Champion smooth Fritz Scheidegger took an immediate lead from Max Deubel and steadily pulled away. Deubel was on his own for 4 laps as Georg Auerbacher, Otto Kolle, ourselves and new boy, ex-solo rider Klaus Enders were head-to-head for third place. Then Enders blasted past, pushing us back to sixth place. Spurred on by this, I raised our game and got back in front of Klaus and Kolle, setting my sights on Auerbacher, shades of Hockenheim the week before. By now we were getting into the groove and our Rennsport was running perfectly. We were in control, it ran like clockwork. We sped by Auerbacher, with our next target ex-champion Max Deubel not far ahead. The crowd were brought to their feet as we finally caught Max on lap 9 and went ahead, a satisfying moment. Florian must have been looking down. Meantime, Fritz Scheidegger partnered by John Robinson, was in a class of his own, winning his second Grand Prix of the season. Our lap times became ever closer to Scheidegger's, causing great interest as we drifted the outfit at speed through the left hander after the start with a smoking rear Dunlop tyre. Klaus Enders cornered frantically to hold fourth place until in lap 10 he dropped behind Auerbacher and Chris Vincent after running out of road, then finally retiring.

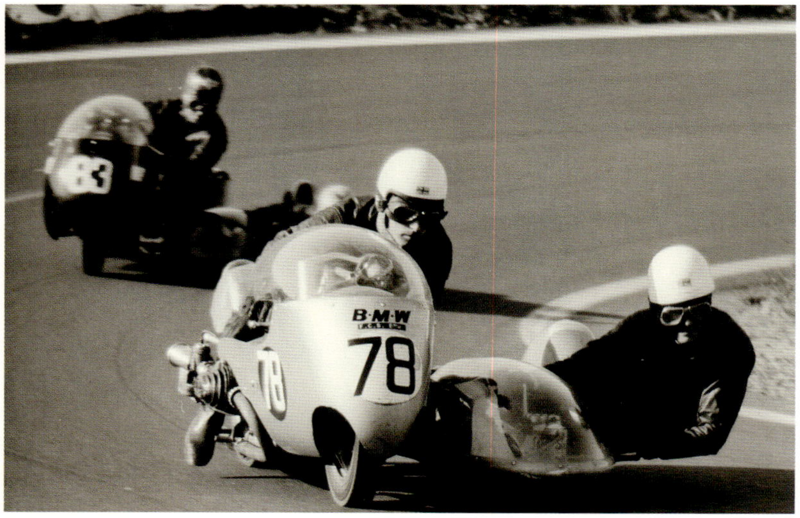

Lapping our team member Huntingford at the French Grand Prix.

Mike Hailwood, 350cc Honda Four, Brands Hatch.

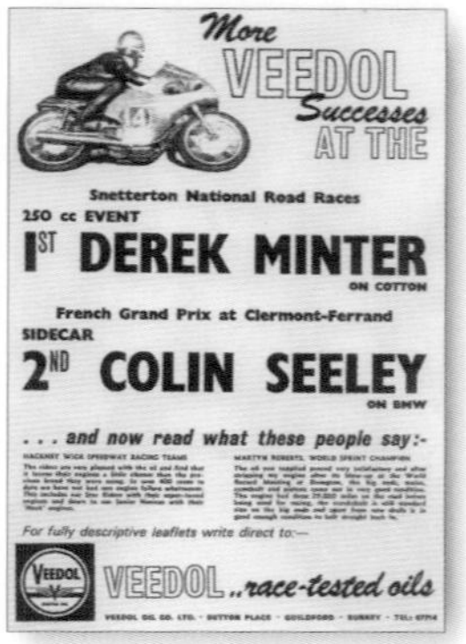

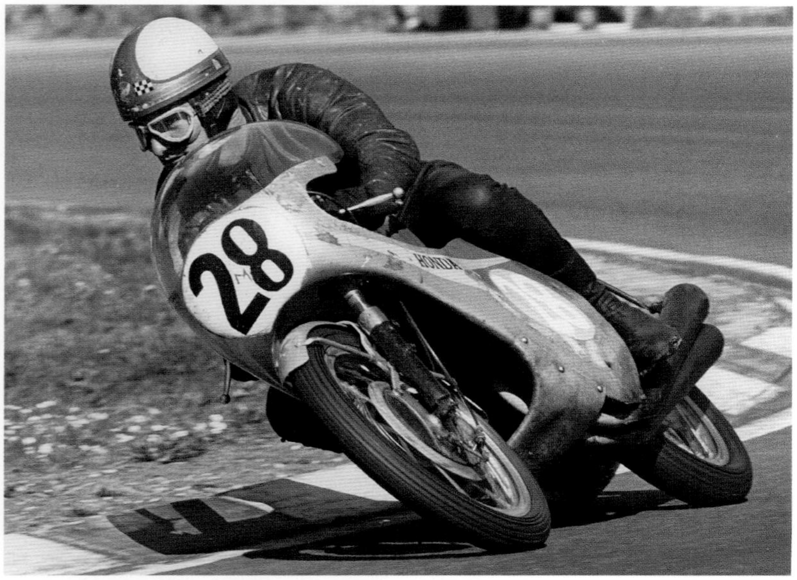

This time Wally kept his hat and we came home intact in a superb second place, once more the first all-British crew. Over 10 seconds behind came Max Deubel then Auerbacher, Vincent and Australian, Barry Thompson, all BMW mounted making up the first six places with our team mate Norman Huntingford, Matchless, in tenth place.

As we mounted the rostrum it was a proud moment when Madame Camathias presented us with our laurels, and we were joint second with Max in the World Championship. Then was the rush to load up for the arduous overnight journey to Le Touquet and the air freighter to Lydd in Kent for the Evening News International Meeting at Brands Hatch the next day.

It was another sun-soaked meeting at Brands Hatch held on the 2.65 mile Grand Prix Circuit and enjoyed by the 30,000 fans. The bedraggled racing circus competitors arriving from France after their overnight drive were kindly allocated 10 minutes practice for both the solo and sidecar events.

In the sixties, the international stars competed for the various world motorcycle championships, often on full works machinery, but would lower their sights to ride other motorcycles and entertain the home race followers. British riders Hailwood, Read, Ivy, Rob, Simmonds and Perris certainly were in that category. The British charioteers, although not receiving the same manufacturer's support, always made a huge contribution to the motorcycling race events.

Brands Hatch that Whit Monday would be no exception. Home favourite Mike the Bike Hailwood riding his private battered Honda 350 four, although having to start at the back of the field due to clutch trouble and needing a pusher, won The Evening News 20 lap main 1000cc event. A fast-improving stylish Peter Williams on the Arter Matchless came second followed by Croxford, Ivy, Minter and Chandler, all Matchless mounted.

Frank Perris, Suzuki, won the 125cc race from Dave Simmonds on his Tohatsu, Tommy Robb, Bultaco, third and another Maidstone boy Paul Smart, Honda, fourth. The other Maidstone boy 'Little Bill' took the 250cc honours on a 1965 twin Cylinder Yamaha from Phil Read on a similar mount, with Robb third again.

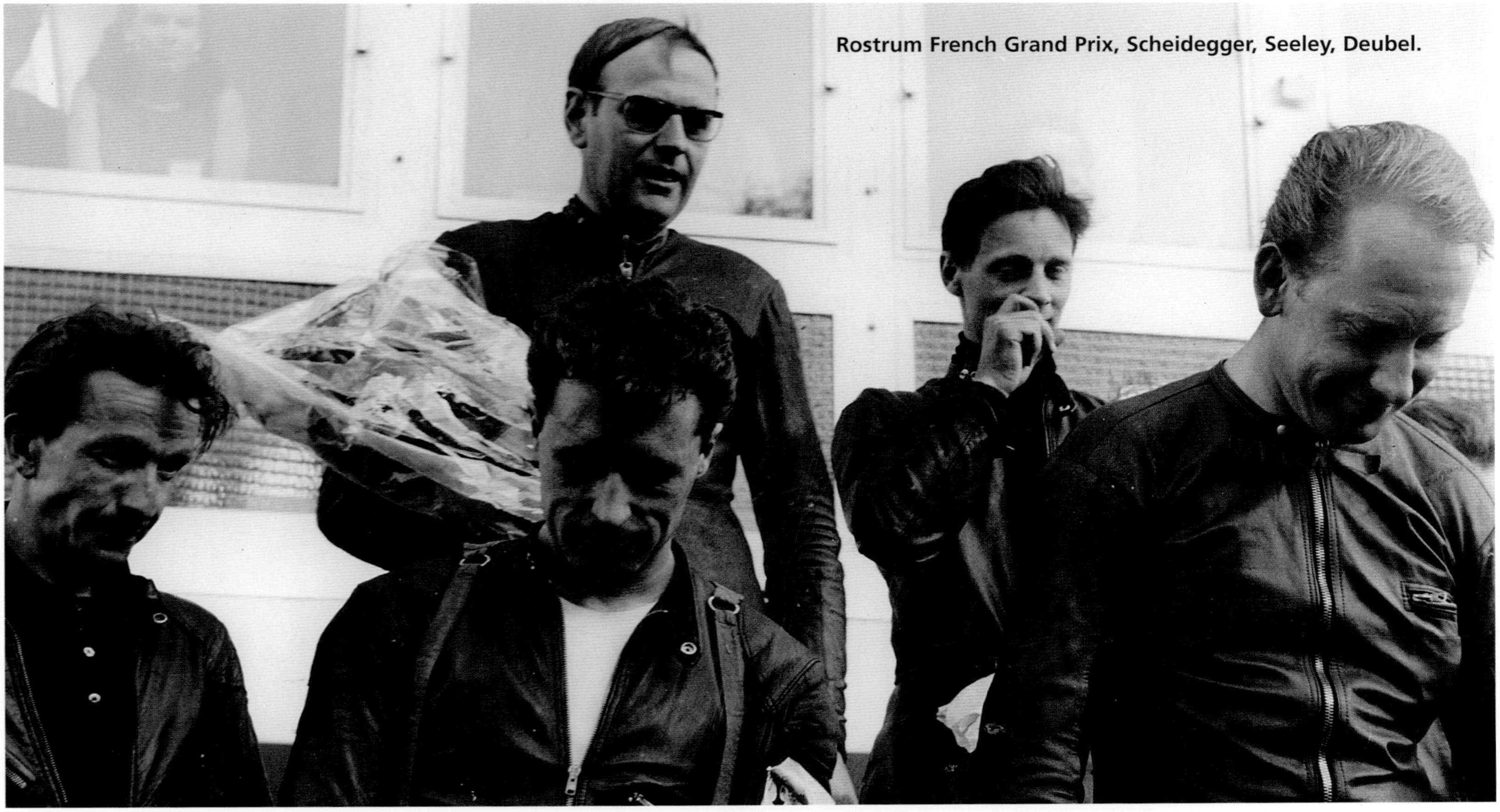
Rostrum French Grand Prix, Scheidegger, Seeley, Deubel.

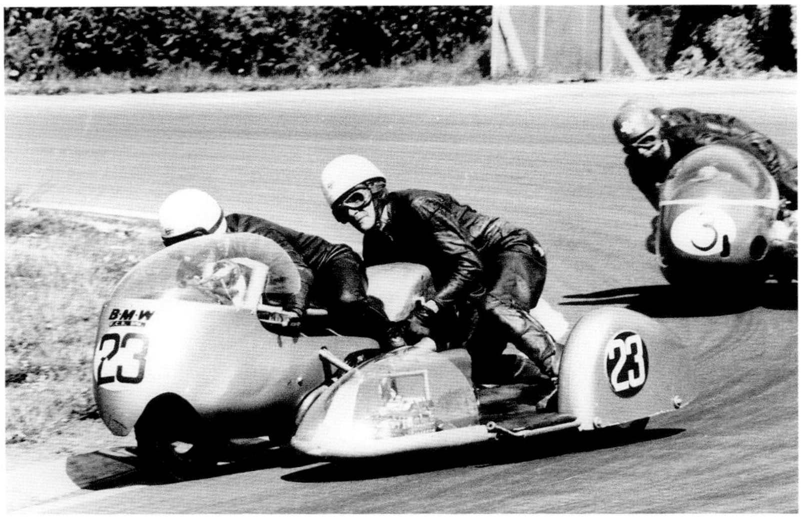

Leading at Brands, Whit Monday. Scheidegger won the event.

Then it was our chance for glory. Could we possibly beat or even equal yesterday's French performance? With Fritz Scheidegger and Max Deubel in attendance and Max perhaps looking for revenge, it certainly would not be easy. We got a flying start in the 10 lap 500cc race and held the Swiss gentleman at bay for a couple of laps, but there was no stopping Fritz that year and although we gave it our all, Scheidegger pulled ahead to win his third race in succession. We came home second, very gratified to beat ex-champion Max Deubel into third for the second time in two days.

It had been a really strenuous 10 days, but a third and second in two Grands Prix as well as an international second place was a great reward for our efforts. With our earnings from the German Grand Prix £153, French Grand Prix £128, Brands Hatch £85, this gave a grand total of £366 to invest in the Seeley project.

The day was not over, Minter was in trouble with the Seeley-Matchless and was a non-starter in the Redex Trophy event which was won by Peter Williams on the new lightweight Arter-Matchless. The 'Mint' bounced back in the last event of the day, the 350cc race, finishing fourth on the Seeley AJS to winner Phil Read on a 251cc Yamaha, Redman, Honda, second and Bill Ivy on a Kirby-Metisse third.

The day over, it was home to Joan and Colin. I was looking forward to my own bed, totally fed up with sleeping in the Thames van for nine nights and putting up with Wally's smelly feet. I enjoyed the Grand Prix scene but I always looked forward to going home. I loved being with the family, and had some catching up to do, just the little things in life, as well as business matters.

Next up on the racing programme was the Isle of Man TT in early June. Derek was often unhappy with the niggly problems on the Seeley machines and we were sometimes disappointed with his lack of commitment. We also knew he had agreed to ride the Gilera 500cc four in the Senior TT. This meant that relations were sometimes strained between Minter and ourselves. Then, the seamen's strike which affected the Isle of Man Steam Packet Ferry service caused the June TT races to be postponed until the end of August.

Next, was the Mallory Park International event on the 19th June, traditionally the Post TT on the Sunday at the end of the TT fortnight. This meeting normally attracted international riders who would attend on their way home from the TT, but not this time, so the meeting was renamed the Pre-TT International. Not many overseas competitors attended, mostly unknowns. Although Fritz Scheidegger, Auerbacher and Schauzu raised the profile in the sidecar event. Amazingly enough 20,000 fans turned up for this meeting, perhaps due to the TT delay.

Derek Minter was still holding on to his place in our Seeley Team and was entered in both 350 and 500cc races. Unfortunately, in the 500cc practice Derek crashed the Seeley-Matchless at the Esses. Then in heat one of the 250cc event Derek crashed the works Cotton at the same spot, bruising his chin and his dignity. Frustratingly, that was really the end of our partnership, no big argument, I just left it to Derek to make the decision. Steve Lancefield offered Derek his well-prepared bikes but a conflict about oil contracts put a block on that. So Derek reunited with Ray Petty and his beloved Nortons. We parted friends and are still friends to this day.

John Cooper won the 20 lap 500cc Senior Race of the Mallory International after a close run struggle throughout with crazy Dave Croxford often touching fairings round Gerards. Little did I realise how heavily I would be involved a year or two later with these rising stars!

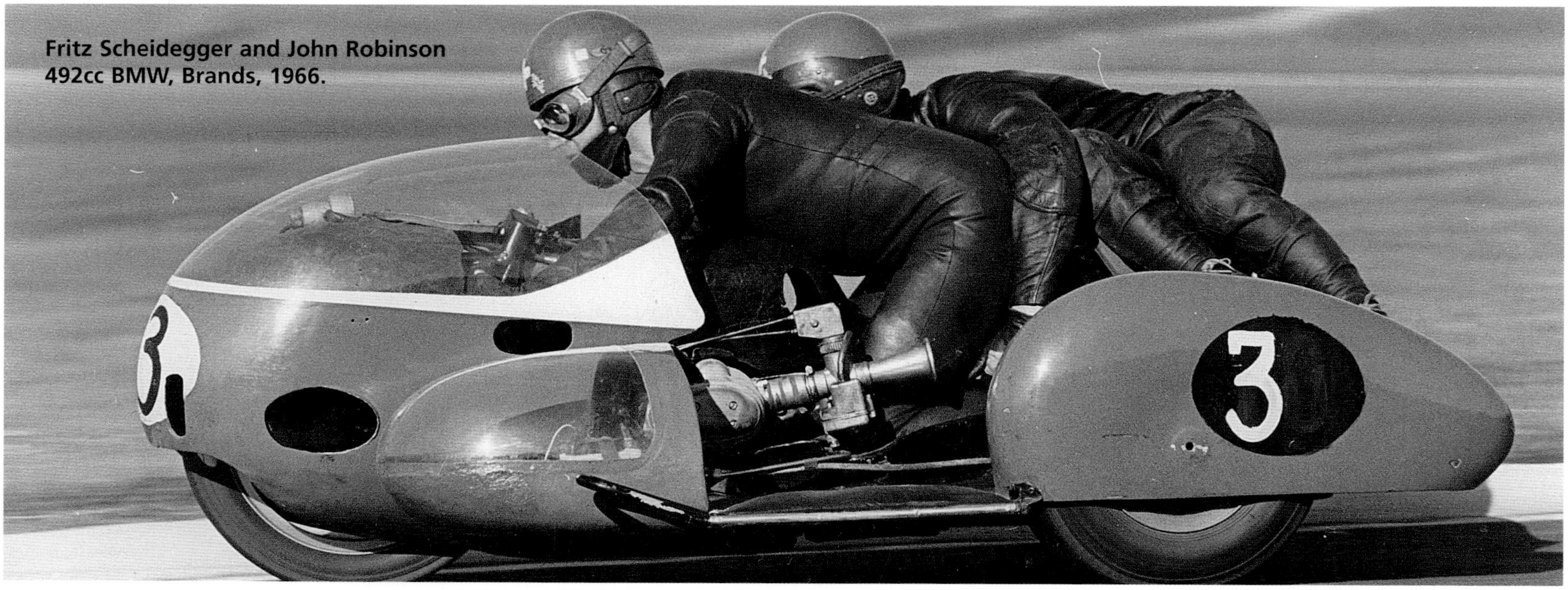

Fritz Scheidegger and John Robinson
492cc BMW, Brands, 1966.

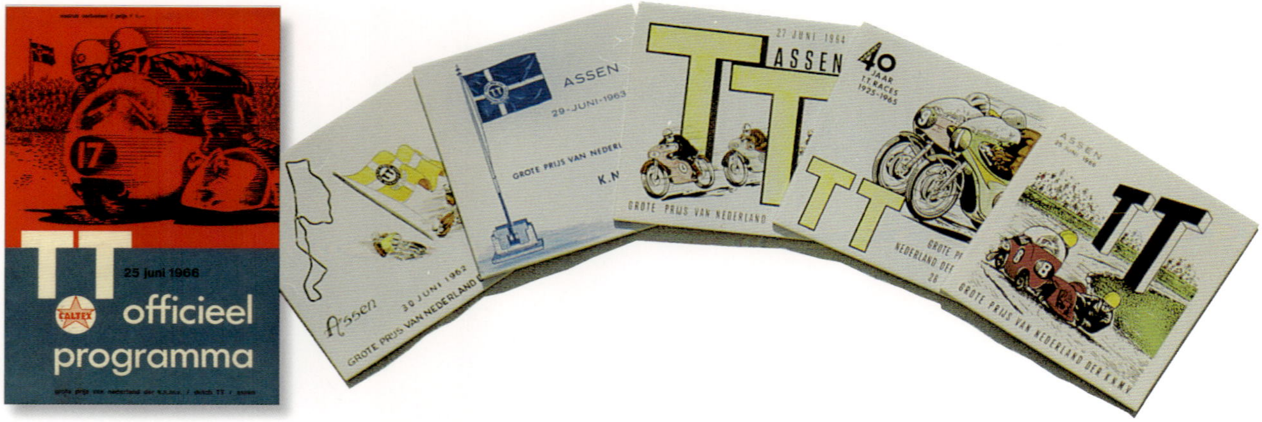

Before we could depart for home it was the 10 lap final of the sidecar race. The last event of the day would bring a little cheer to our team when another second place was added to our scorecard from the winner and champ Scheidegger. Fritz was just unstoppable, our team mate Norman Huntingford riding our old Matchless-Watsonian G50 outfit achieved a fine third place, his best to date, having beaten off the challenge of hard man Charlie Freeman, Norton. We cheered Norman on, never thinking this would be our last opportunity to do so.

In a day or two we would be off to the Dutch TT, followed by the Belgian Grand Prix a week later. It was strange as normally we would be coming straight from the Isle of Man TT for these two, but now it was the other way round, we would be going back, although at the time we didn't know if the Isle of Man TT was even going to take place. Derek Minter's departure took the pressure of us whilst we attended these Grand Prix sidecar events.

By Wednesday we left for Llydd Airport to catch the British United Air Ferry direct to Rotterdam, an excellent service. Norman Huntingford had joined us for this popular Dutch event. Norman, passengered by Roy Lindsey, was slowly gaining experience on the Grand Prix circuits and was handling the Matchless outfit to good effect.

After the Dutch TT practice, which put us towards the front of the grid, I spoke to Norman pointing out that from the start on the very first lap as he approached the fast left hand kink, with a ditch to the right, he should take a middle of the road position before approaching the 90degree right hander, as it was in those days. A tight line on that first lap would shut the door on the German competitors with sidecars on the right who would be trying to come up the inside. Then they wouldn't be able to push him off line or endanger Roy Lindsey, his passenger.

The Dutch TT held in Assen, northern Holland was always a popular event and despite the changing weather conditions, overcast and with some rain, the event had attracted around 150,000 very enthusiastic race fans.

The day started with the 50cc tiddler race proving a 1 - 2 for Honda, Luigi Taveri taking the honours from Ireland's Ralph Bryans, with Hugh Anderson, Suzuki, third. Our own pocket rocket Maidstone flyer Bill Ivy, Yamaha, took the 125cc race from the Swiss ace Taveri, Honda, who finished second just over 2 seconds behind, with Phil Read, Yamaha, making up the rostrum positions and the current champion Anderson, Suzuki, back in a lowly fourth place.

In the 250cc race, Hailwood was in a class of his own. Riding the Honda six he finished well ahead of Phil Read, Yamaha, with Redman, Honda, in third place. Derek Woodman kept MZ in the picture with a fourth place, with a stylish Bob Anderson, Yamaha, fifth and the Irishman you could not keep down, little Tommy Robb sixth.

The 350cc race was another walkover for Mike the Bike on the Honda four, beating off the challenge of Giacomo Agostini, MV, second with Renzo Pasolini on the Aermacchi third, John Cooper, Norton, eighth, Grand Prix stalwart Billie Nelson, Norton, ninth and Fred Stevens on the Hannah Paton thirteenth.

The FIM rules limited competitors to a certain race distance in any one day. Therefore Jim Redman was to ride the 500cc Honda four once more in that event but in a close encounter he just managed to hold off the Italian ace Agostini, MV, by 2 seconds. Franta Stasny, Jawa, was third and our own John (Mooneyes) Cooper, Norton, fourth, followed by Stuart Graham, Jack Findlay and Gyula Marsovszky in that order, all Matchless mounted. Fred Stevens, Hannah Paton, came eighth with Australian Jack Ahearn and Kel Carruthers, both on Nortons ninth and tenth.

Then it was our turn. Our fifth Dutch TT would not be easy. We were limited to one good competitive Fath-tuned long stroke Rennsport BMW engine. It had done us proud so far and I think the Veedol engine oil was so good it had helped the reliability. As the lights turned green we made a good start, but not good enough. Max Deubel took the lead on the first lap of 14, closely followed by Scheidegger, then me and Wal, Vincent, Auerbacher and Otto Kolle the first six. Then the Swiss champion was back in front and stayed there to register his third Grand Prix win of the season, Max second with us holding third place throughout 11 laps posting the second quickest time of the day behind Fritz. We speeded up with Deubel in our sights, well ahead of our old adversary Auerbacher, Siegfried Schauzu, Vincent and Kolle. With only 3 laps to go, we were forced to retire with a collapsed sidecar wheel, the first time ever for such a problem. We were bitterly disappointed, another rostrum position was in sight and a further four world championship points nearly in the bag.

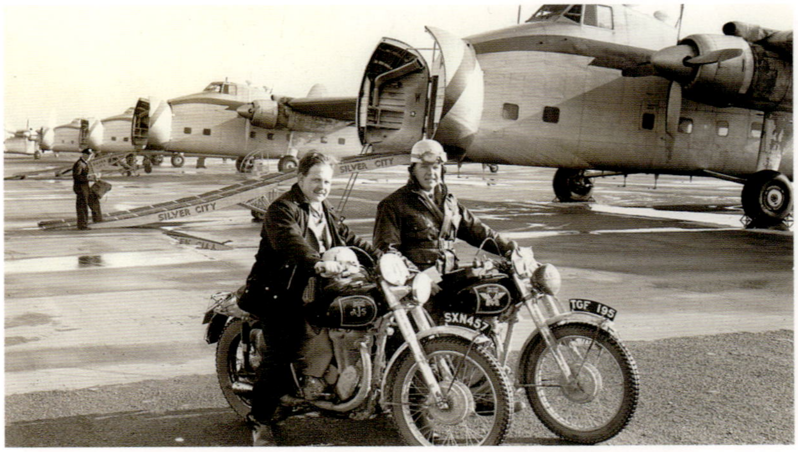

British United Air Ferries. Left, Norman Sharpe, right, Jock West.

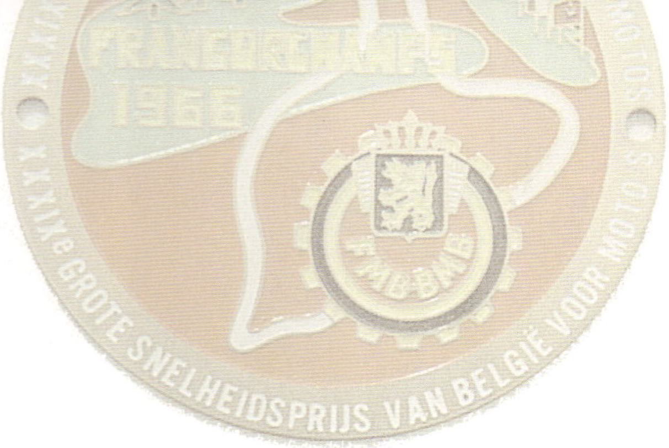

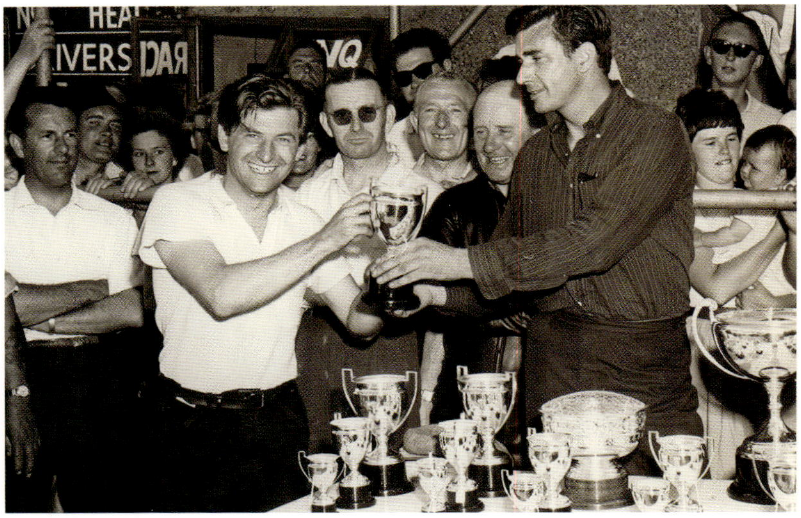

Norman Huntingford in happier days at Brands, being presented with a Winner's Trophy by actor Richard Wyler.

Then we were informed that Norman Huntingford and Roy Lindsey had been involved in a crash on the first lap. It seemed inconceivable that on the very point of the 4.78 mile circuit I had warned Norman about, particularly on the first lap, it appears a German competitor with an alleged reputation for ruthless overtaking went inside of Norman on that very corner, resulting in Roy having to pull himself back into the sidecar. The outfits touched and the Matchless was flipped over into the ditch. Norman was killed instantly. Roy escaped with injuries. 32 year old Norman was a most popular member of the Greenwich and District Motorcycle Club and a most enthusiastic racer.

Once again I had the unpleasant task of performing an identification. I remember him lying in his race leathers as if asleep with not a mark on him, his Colin Seeley racing gloves alongside. I stood speechless, so choked that Mr. Nice Guy Norman was no longer with us, greatly missed by his girl friend Ann Barrett, family and many friends.

The loss of Florian Camathias, Sid Mizen and now Norman, all within nine months, was difficult. I cannot explain how we dealt with such situations. We shared in a great sport, but it had its down side too. The racing circus would move on to the next event. Such happenings were pushed into the subconscious, it was the only way. However we would never forget!!

After spending a couple of days at Assen helping to deal with Norman's personal matters, making sure Roy Lindsey was okay and arranging for Ann Barrett to fly home, we moved on to Spa-Francorchamps for that following weekend's Belgian Grand Prix It would be a sparse event for spectators with only 250cc, 500cc and sidecar races being run. This famous 8.75 mile ultra-fast circuit located in the Ardennes was well known for its often adverse weather conditions and race day that year was no exception.

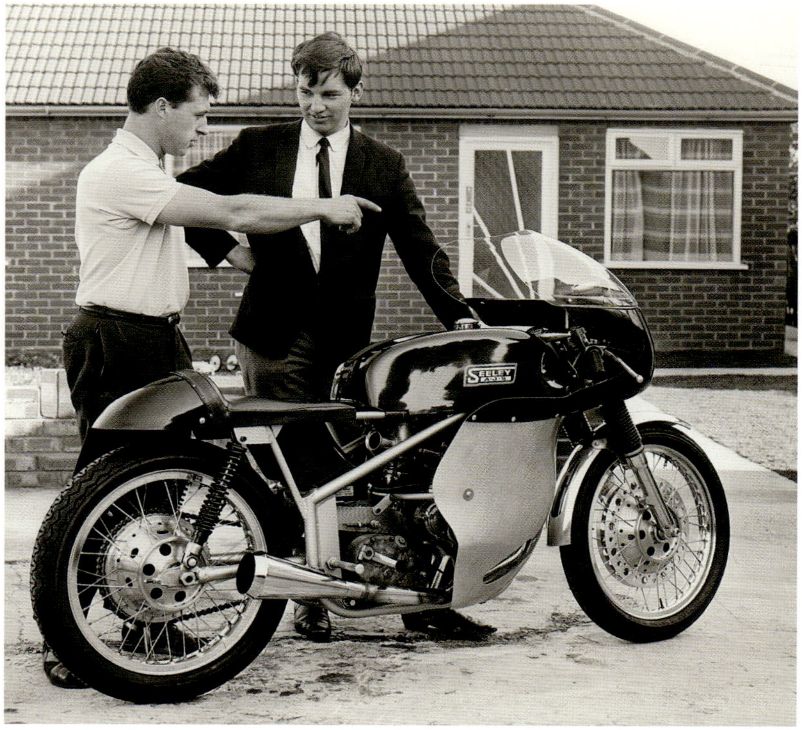

Hailwood continued his winning streak on the 250cc Honda six from Phil Read, Yamaha four, Redman, Honda, in third and Derek Woodman continuing his good work on the 250 MZ in fourth place.

As the 500cc riders came to the line for the 15 lap 131 mile race the clouds gathered. With the race well under way, the skies opened and there was a huge downpour with lightning flashes. The track was flooded in many sections and the conditions were simply awful. Today such a race would be red flagged and stopped, but not then! Hailwood on the big 500 Honda four retired from this absurd race with a combination of exposure and problems with the Honda gearbox. Jim Redman crashed breaking an arm. This injury contributed to his official retirement from racing that year. Derek Woodman joined a number of fallen heroes, just missing a telegraph pole, one of many lining the public road circuit. Treading carefully, Giacomo Agostini, MV Agusta, won the race, with Stuart Graham, Matchless, in second place from big Jack Ahearn, Norton, making up the wet rostrum positions.

In slightly better conditions, the charioteers came to the line for the 8 lap, 69 mile race. Once again it was the unstoppable Swiss champion Fritz Scheidegger who led the rest home, then Deubel, Auerbacher, Enders with us fifth in front of Tony Wakefield, the first six all on BMWs. It had been a sad few days. Wally and I just wanted to go home and collect our thoughts and readjust our plans for the future of Seeley Racing.

Back at base we had finished the building of a conversion to a Seeley framed 7R for customer Chris Stanger, boss of CDS Screws. Unfortunately, later that year he crashed the bike in practice for the Manx Grand Prix.

With reports in Motorcycle News that Derek Minter had returned to racing Nortons, we had received a number of requests from riders offering their services to the Seeley-Racing bikes. One rider in particular took our interest, the Bermondsey bill poster, John Blanchard, his name having been put forward by Sid Mizen earlier that year. John had

Chris Stanger collecting his Seeley AJS conversion.

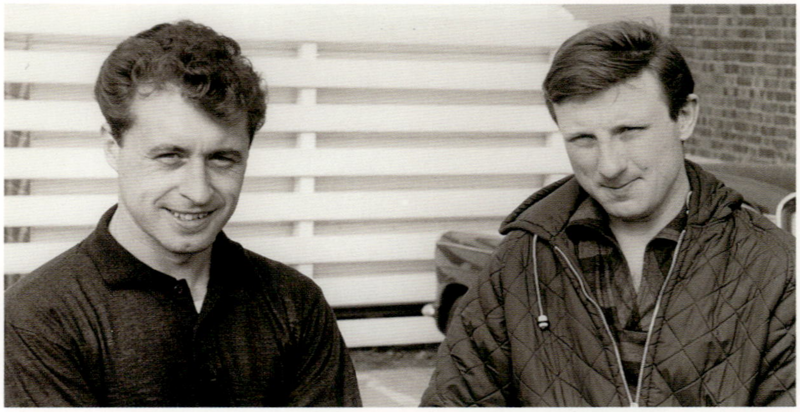

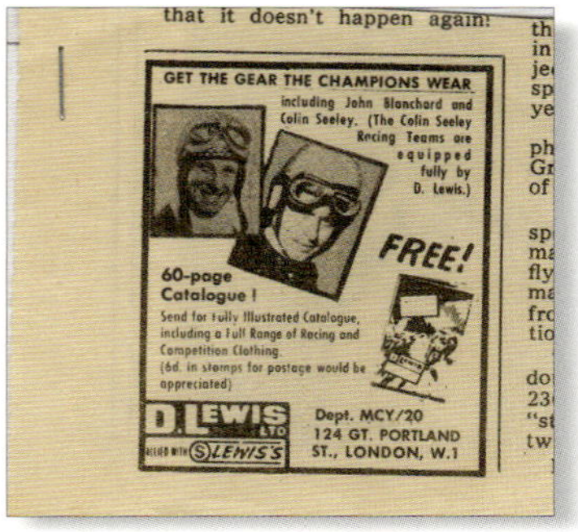

that it doesn't happen again!

GET THE GEAR THE CHAMPIONS WEAR

including John Blanchard and Colin Seeley. (The Colin Seeley Racing Teams are equipped fully by D. Lewis.)

FREE!

60-page Catalogue !

Send for fully Illustrated Catalogue, including a Full Range of Racing and Competition Clothing.
(6d. in stamps for postage would be appreciated)

D. LEWIS LTD
LEWIS'S

Dept. MCY/20
124 GT. PORTLAND ST., LONDON, W.1

John Blanchard and myself, meeting to agree terms.

been riding a number of machines including 250 and 350 Aermacchis early in 1965 then took over from Bill Ivy to ride for Monty and Ward on the 498cc Monard along with a 350 Norton and 250 Bultaco. This agreement had continued right up to the point when our Seeley machines became available. We had no part in John's leaving Geoff Monty. That was between those two parties. After testing with John, terms were agreed and Blanchard had his first competitive ride with the Seeley Equipe, (the Isle of Man TT still delayed) at the Brands Hatch 34th International Hutchinson 100 on the 14th August 1966. The event was held on the 2.65 mile Grand Prix circuit but in reverse, a strange experience I must say. Certainly it wasn't my personal preference although it would certainly suit Max Deubel and Helmet Fath with their sidecars on the right hand side.

Derek Minter meantime, on his Norton come-back, had won the 350cc race at Castle Combe in early July but had to give best to Peter Williams in the 500cc event.

Probably due to the confusion over Isle of Man TT there appeared to be a lack of continental competitors at the Hutch. This was particularly true in the sidecar events. The majority, including Scheidegger, opted to compete in a minor West German event. Nevertheless, Hailwood, Read, Bryans, Ivy, Anderson, Duff, Redman and Robb would be taking on the likes of Cooper, Minter, Pickrell, Gould, Jenkins, Tait, so many good names and talented riders, of course not forgetting our latest signing, John Blanchard.

With a nine event programme, the racing proceeded with a 10.30am start, can you believe, for the first of the up to 1300cc sidecar races. We were just about awake for the 10 lap dash. Max Deubel, despite having one of his rare crashes during Saturday's practice, completely looping his BMW outfit, 10 out of10 for style, soon took the lead when Chris Vincent's BSA developed ignition trouble. Max won from Terry Vinicombe's 654cc BSA, with Helmut Fath racing his fantastic home-brewed URS four cylinder outfit into third, and ourselves in sixth with only £4 prize money. For sixth spot it was hardly worth wearing out our one and only Rennsport engine, which we needed in good shape for the forthcoming Isle of Man TT. Mind you, Max Deubel only received £20 for winning the race!!

Much of our time and concentration was taken up by John Blanchard, who was making his debut on the Seeley-AJS in the next race, 20 laps for between 250 and 350cc machines. Mike Hailwood, on the 350cc Honda four predictably disappeared into the distance. Phil Read on a 254cc Yamaha had to pull in for a plug change then he slid off on the last lap at the top of paddock. All this excitement left ex-king, the Mint in second place. In a race long scrap with Degens, Shorey, Ivy, Williams and a certain Kel Carruthers, the paper hanger JB, Seeley-AJS, brought our machine home to an impressive third place. Hailwood-Minter-Blanchard, a great result. Were we pleased? Of course we were!

The stylish yet unpretentious current 125cc World Champion, Hugh Anderson won the 125cc event from team mate Frank Perris, both on works Suzukis, Anderson for his effort winning the Mellano Trophy.

Canadian Mike Duff, Yamaha, won the 250cc race from the champion Phil Read when Phil's Yamaha went sick. Minter, having dropped the works Cotton in practice was out of the race, and would be a non-starter in the 500cc, suffering a wrist injury when crashing the Cotton.

We then had a 15 lap race for production sports machines with a good number of top names taking part; Percy Tait, Ron Chandler, Dave Degens, Mick Andrew, Peter Butler, Dave Nixon, John Cooper, Joe Dunphy and many more. Syd Lawton had mentioned to John Cooper's sponsor Russ Warren, that if Cooperman rode the 654cc BSA Spitfire in the race, he would kill himself, it was out of control most of the time. However, our Derbyshire hero J C Mooneyes was being paid £100 by BSA to ride such a machine. The production race produced the most lurid racing of the afternoon. After a slow start Mooneyes battled his way through the field to catch early leaders Tait and Andrew on the Triumph T120 Bonnevilles and despite the rather alarming handling of the BSA, JC managed to get ahead 3 laps from home to a fine win in the circumstances, and wait for it, a £15 first prize, a pound a lap for risking his neck!

The second sidecar race took place with ex-champion Max Deubel taking the honours again from a strong challenge by Terry Vinicombe and passenger John Flaxman, with Peter Brown on the other 654cc BSAs third, Helmut Fath on the fantastic sounding URS fourth with Pip Harris and ourselves on the BMWs fifth and sixth.

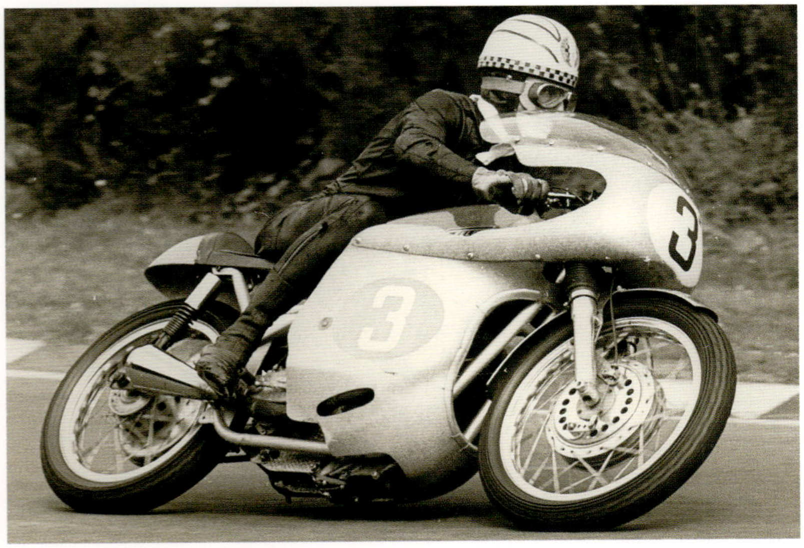

John Blanchard, Seeley AJS at the Hutchinson 100, Brands Hatch.

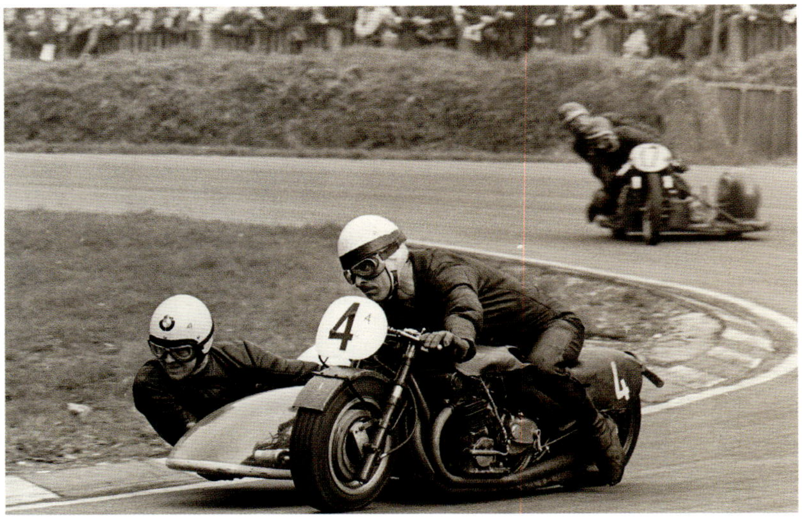

Helmut Fath, 500cc URS four, Brands, 1966.

I was reasonably happy with two sixth places, our job was out of the way. Now, it was the all important 500cc, 25 lap solo race, what could our 'Paperhanger' do in this race? Well, Blanchard was holding a good fourth spot when the Seeley Matchless G50 engine gave a loud grinding clonk, and that was that! What a disappointment, but he had performed well and done us proud. It was to be the Derbyshire flyer's day on his Norton winning the Evening News Challenge Trophy from Dan Shorey and Gulya Marsovszky after Hailwood, Honda, retired with gear box trouble and Peter Williams fell by the wayside, running out of fuel. Mooneyes won a grand £50. Apart from a couple of non-expert races, the day was over. The huge crowd had enjoyed some great racing on a very pleasant sunny day.

Much was happening in 1966, not only Route 66 and the World Cup, but winner of four World Sidecar Championships Max Deubel and passenger Emil Horner announced their retirement from racing at the end of that season. Max, a hotelier from Muhlenau, whose wife Iris was expecting their first baby, first hit the headlines in 1959 when he finished third in the German Grand Prix, then two years later supported by the Bavarian Motor Works (BMW) won the first of his successive world titles. With Deubel bowing out, the other German ex-champ Helmut Fath with his impressive 13,000 rev Fath-four was rejoining the fray after some five years absence following his bad crash in 1961.

In August the Grand Prix riders threatened to boycott the September Italian Grand Prix at Monza if the organisers insisted on including the notorious speed bowl section. The then recently formed World Championship Riders Association, WCRA was ready to fight its first battle over the proposed inclusion of the steeply banked bumpy oval section in the traditional motorcycle circuit, increasing the track length from 3.57 miles to 6.27 miles. Mike Hailwood, who was leading the revolt, was in a unique position being also a racing car driver and member of the Grand Prix Drivers Association who in 1964 after an hour's practice during which time several cars lost wheels, told the organisers they must cut out the banking or no one would start. Needless to say, they cut it out!

Since that occasion the Monza course was modified with chicanes inserted to slow down competitors approaching banked sections but both Giacomo Agostini and Remo Venturi, who had practised on the modified bowl, still condemned it as dangerous.

Rider power was having an effect, but whether the WCRA idea of having a closed shop grading list for 125, 250, 350 and 500cc solo Grand Prix competitors which race organisers would have to accept, was another controversial matter.

1966 was also the year of the prototype hush-hush 750cc three cylinder Triumph racers. There had been a tentative plan to race the Triumph at the Hutchinson 100 by Geoff Duke. The idea was dropped and the model demonstrated firstly at Silverstone to members of Triumph associates from America.

In a determined effort to clinch their first ever 125cc world championship that year, Yamaha flew over a four cylinder water-cooled racer for pocket rocket Ivy to ride at the Ulster Grand Prix. It was a slim chance to beat off the challenge of the Swiss ace Luigi Taveri, Honda, the 125cc specialist and 1962/64 World Champion. However, Bill Ivy and Yamaha would have to wait another year before winning their first World 125cc championship, as Bill crashed at the Hutchinson 100, sustaining concussion and a badly gashed back when an oil pipe on his AJS/Metisse split.

Husqvarna, the specialist Swedish manufacturers of moto-cross bikes, power saws and kitchen machines, who had won the 1966 250cc World Moto-Cross Championship, had planned to produce only 250 motorcycles of all sorts for 1967, but their American distributor, Edison Dye in California, ordered 1,000 scramble machines. This surprise order was followed by an order for a thousand bikes per annum from the Swedish army over the next 10 years. This caused some embarrassment to Husqvarna, whose motorcycle production to that point had made up only 1.2% of its total output.

In stark contrast, our own British manufacturing base was in decline. The writing was on the wall for Associated Motorcycles - AJS, Matchless and Norton with a receiver being appointed in August 1966. American distributor The Berliner Motor Corporation was called in to help save the situation. Dr. Joe Ehrlich, the EMC racer's boss, broke off negotiations to take over Cotton, the Gloucester motorcycle manufacturers.

The RAC had persuaded the officials of the new Tay Bridge, opened by the Queen Mother on August 18th, to slash the proposed toll charge for motorcycles from 2s 6d

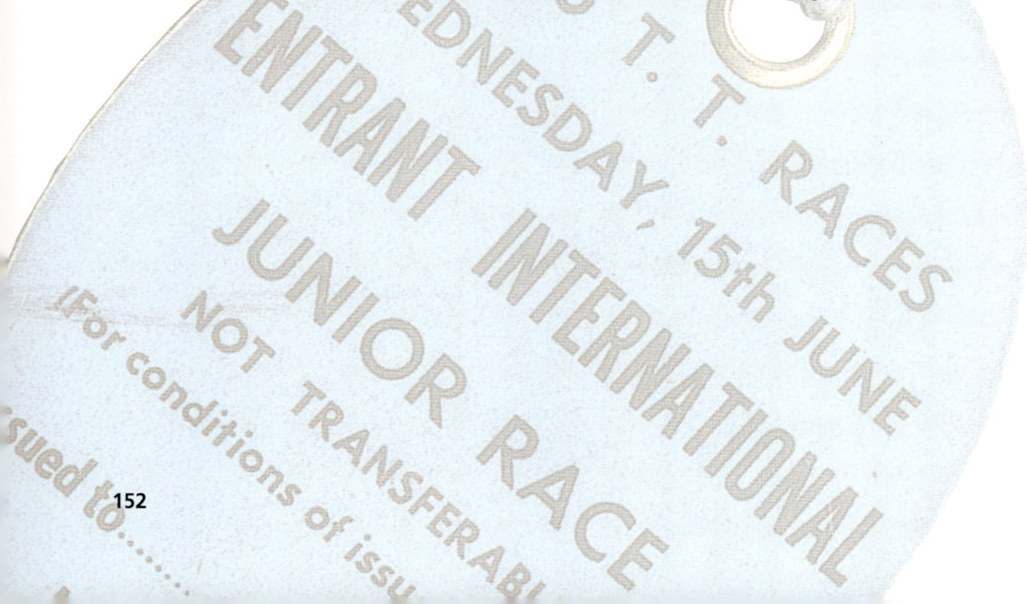

Left to right, Taveri, Redman, Bryans and reporter David Dixon 'ear-wigging' after the Isle of Man 50cc TT.

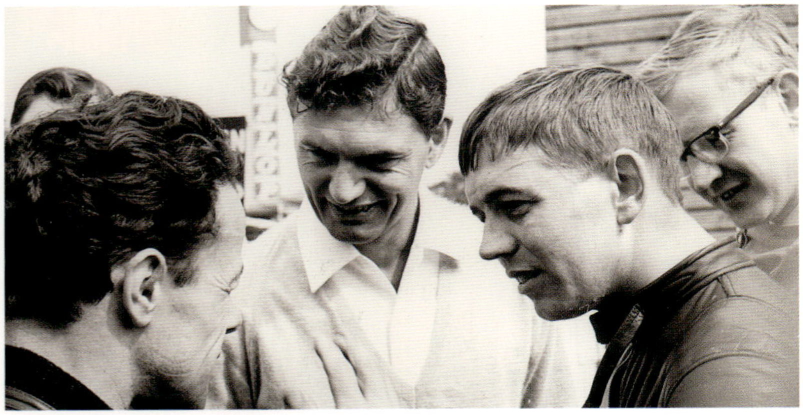

to a shilling. The reduced toll was a forerunner of what was achieved by the RAC at the Forth Bridge. What a year so far, but more drama was to come!

Directly after the Sunday's Hutchinson 100, many of the solo boys made their way to Northern Ireland for the forthcoming Saturday's Ulster Grand Prix held on the 7.41 mile Dundrod Circuit. With no sidecar class at Dundrod, it would be the ninth Grand Prix of the season for most of the solo competitors.

Although not always easy for certain works riders, the supporting cast of international privateers often found it doubly difficult. With so much racing, so much travelling and so much work needed on race machines by the riders themselves, it was endless pressure with the star factory riders mostly taking the top end of the prize money, leaving little for the runners up. The privateers existed on start money, hence the practice of 'start money special', pushing machines to the grid even if they knew they couldn't race, just to collect their money. Sponsorship was hardly known in those days.

At that time both the Ulster Grand Prix and Isle of Man TT played a major part in the world championship and even if a rider preferred short circuits, he had to race these circuits in order to be included in the world championship points system. So the extra challenge of racing on open roads with its increased risks was extra pressure for some. Rider safety would became a greater consideration and the last Ulster Grand Prix was held in 1971, with the last Isle of Man TT in 1976. Although both events continued, they were no longer considered for points in the world motorcycling championships.

Meanwhile, at the 1966 Ulster Grand Prix, 70,000 Irish fans braved the dismal weather to witness Mike Hailwood, Honda, trounce Agostini, MV, in both 350 and 500 cc events with lap and race records in both.

The paper hanger JB, Seeley-AJS, on brilliant form, was hotly disputing third place in the 350cc race from Franta Statsny and Gustav Havel, both on works Jawas, and Heinz Rosner, MZ, before a binding front brake forced John to retire.

In the 500cc race John on the Seeley Matchless again showed his determination, in what was reported as the hardest fought four cornered battle of the day, for fourth place, between Jack Findlay, Chris Conn and Peter Williams. Conn and Williams faded, then in the last lap of the 15 lap, 111 mile race, Blanchard led Findlay by a wheel, but the experienced Australian got ahead. In a last desperate effort John overdid things, and slid off without injury. Our Swiss friend Ernst Weiss brought his Seeley-Matchless home in sixteenth place.

Mike the Bike in winning the 350cc race, added that class to his World Championships, now seven in all including the 250cc title he had already won that year. Mike's seven World Championships equalled the great Carlo Ubbiali and John Surtees successes over that decade, 21 world championships between them all, some achievement!

After Ulster came the re-scheduled Isle of Man TT event, with much to do on the Sunday because practice would start on the Monday. Wally and I, supported by friends, had already arrived in the Island and had set up our usual base at Beverley House awaiting our star man John Blanchard who was entered in both 350cc and 500cc TT events. Ma Clucas was delighted to have her boys back and the Guinness was flowing.

Looking back now we had been extremely ambitious or perhaps just foolhardy in our first year of manufacturing Seeley-racers. With our limited resources we had high hopes to even consider entering the Isle of Man TT events, probably just the same naivety and optimism when entering our first sidecar TT in 1961. After our disappointment with Derek Minter, we were keen for the next challenge!

The 1966 Isle of Man TT would not be without incident, some funny, some not so funny and some tragic. Geoff Davison, the 1922 lightweight TT winner and founder of the very informative TT Special, died earlier that year.

Practice week began with the swearing-in of 700 volunteers as special police constables who would act as race marshals with the authority to remove people from the closed roads immediately before racing started.

The Monday morning first practice started with some excitement when Ralph Bryans' works 125 Honda caught fire near the 13th milestone and exploded, seconds after the Belfast rider had abandoned ship.

Next morning Hugh Anderson lapped his 50cc Suzuki at 32.2 seconds, better than his two year old record, averaging 83.03mph. Peter Inchley made history during the same session on the Villers Starmaker Special when he clocked an impressive 91.70mph, the first over 90mph lap for a British 250cc.

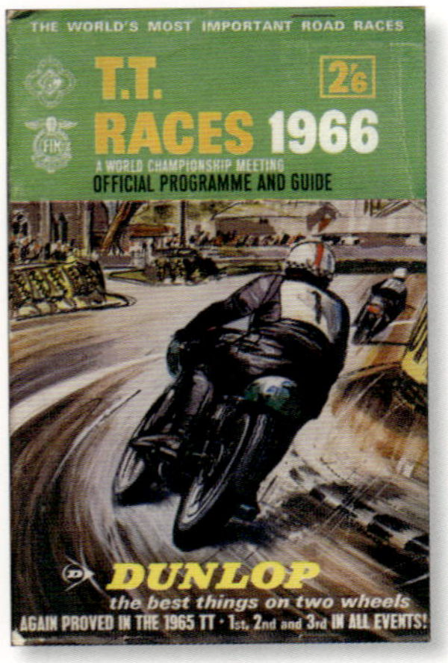

Rain slowed things on the Wednesday morning, Hailwood dropped the Honda 250 six at Braddan Bridge, when he braked sharply having missed a gear, without injury or serious damage. Franta Stastny was not so lucky when his 350cc Jawa seized on the full bore section before Quarry Bends. The circuit was dry at that particular point and the Jawa left a huge skid mark before smashing into a wall. Stastny miraculously escaped serious injury but was detained in the Ramsey Cottage Hospital.

John Blanchard rode without success in the 1965 Isle of Man TT on 250 and 350cc Aermacchis. This was his first competition in the Senior Class and he was proving his worth, up with the best of the rest in practice after Hailwood and Ago.

Despite our work load we were keeping the British flag flying in the dry Wednesday afternoon session sidecar practice, dominated by Max Deubel. One competitor Ron Wray, partnered by a Mr. Haddock, having stopped out on the course, phoned in to report that the engine of his Wray Special had fallen out! With Haddock in the chair they must have been all at sea! An engine fall-out is completely beyond my imagination.

On the Thursday early morning practice, Lucas provided amber flashing lights to warn of sun dazzle early morning and late evening, which often seriously affected the competitors at speed.

Tarquinio Provini double World Champion from the late fifties, known for his dazzling performances on the 250cc Morini, finished a very close second to Jim Redman, Honda, in the 1963 championship. Both riders won four GPs that year, but with the best six places counting, Redman got the decision with more second places.

The 34 year old Italian star, crashed his Benelli 350cc four that morning. It happened on the second lap of practice soon after leaving Kirkmichael, Provini was completely dazzled by the low rising sun and hit the bank at full speed in top, around 140mph. The Benelli was shattered, but Provini skidded down the TT circuit, his leathers completely worn away. With no marshals on the spot, fellow riders stopped to move the unconscious Italian while others informed marshals further down the track, a mile away. Tarquinio had to wait until the end of practice before the ambulance arrived to take him to Nobles Hospital in Douglas, where it was revealed that he had broken vertebrae amongst other injuries, and could not be moved for at least 10 days. The crash would prove to be the end of Provini's racing career. No more would we witness his spectacular riding style and skill.

As I write, I realise how much things have moved on regarding safety and medical care. The high quality race leathers, combined with body armour and back protectors, gloves with Kevlar, added ankle and toe protection in the boots have made a hugh difference. Most importantly, the technology invoved in modern full-face helmets make our sixties gear look positively prehistoric. The medical care now is beyond reproach. A doctor is in attendance within minutes and the rider is not moved until doctor and medical team are satisfied. Meanwhile, often the red flag is put out to stop practice or the race instantly, so as not to endanger the competitor further. This is all good news, although more needs to be done regarding circuit safety itself.

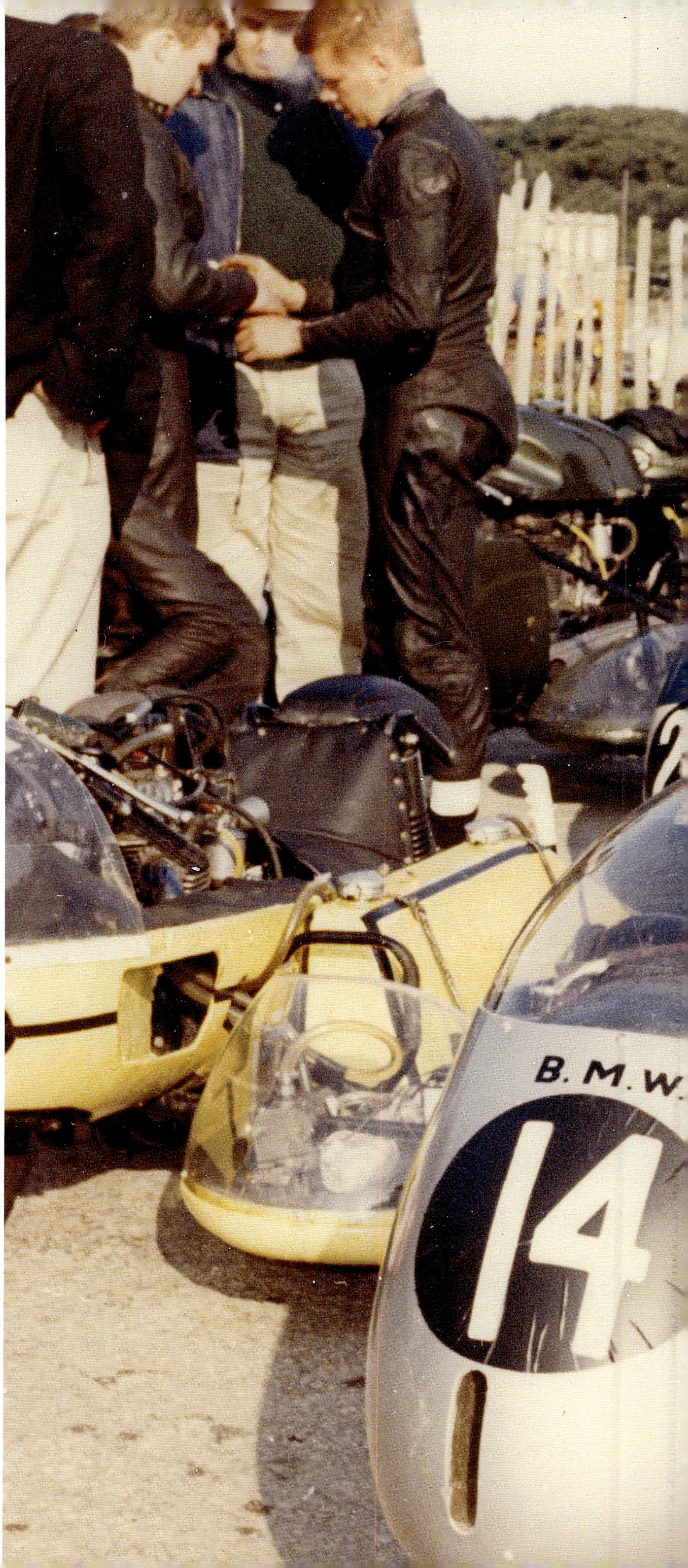

Patiently waiting for the start of evening TT practice.

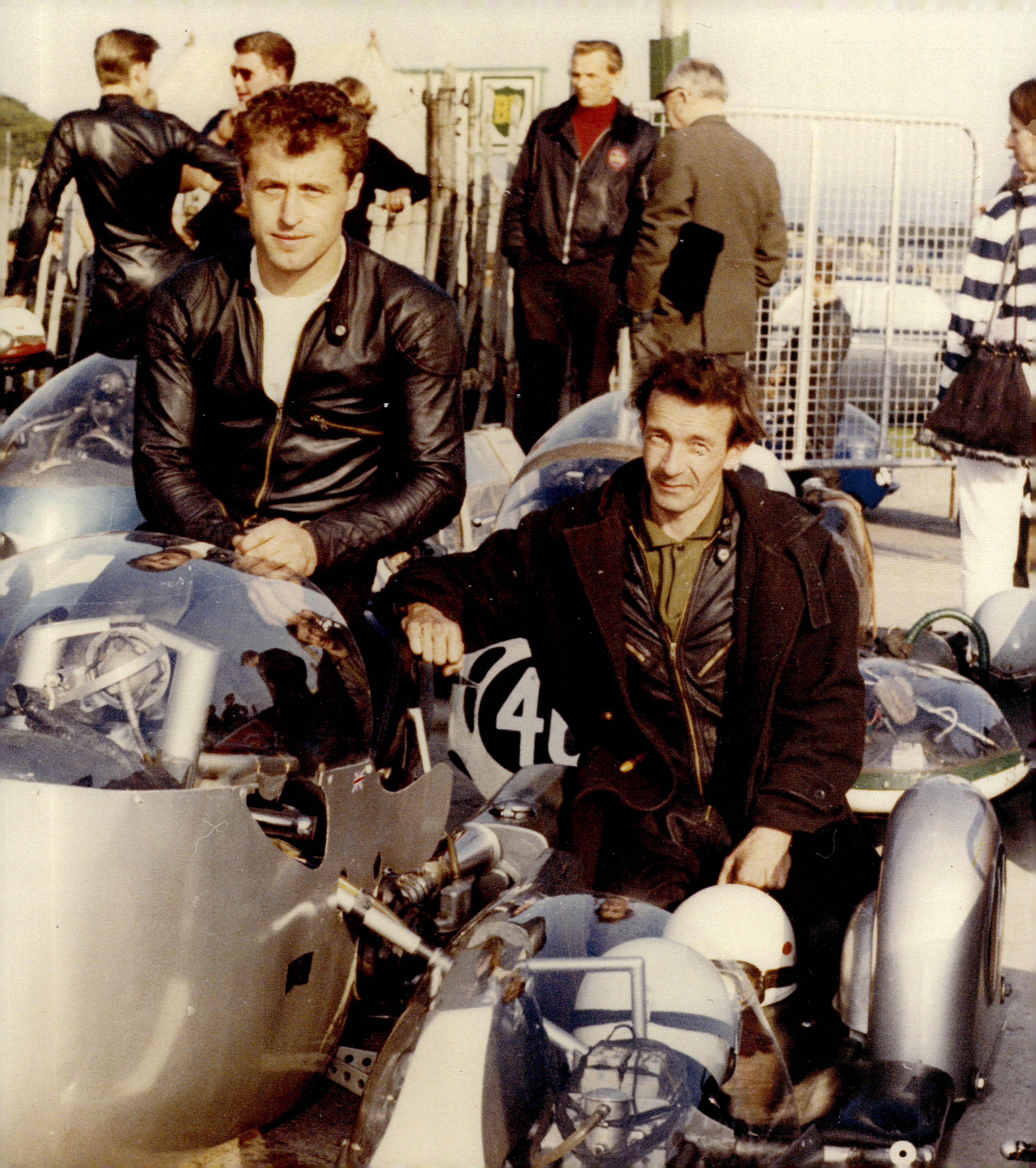

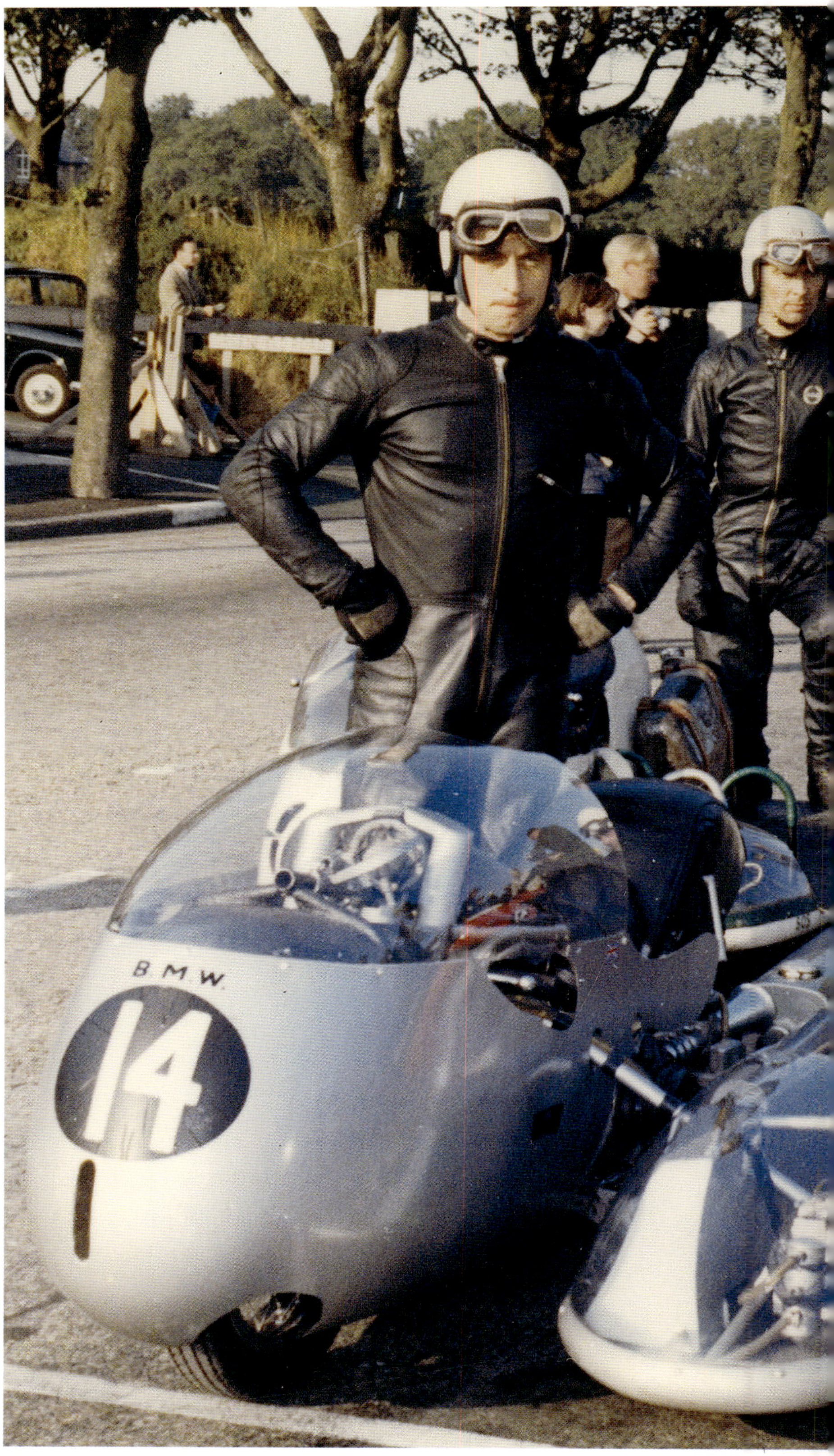

Derek Minter had arrived in the Island to ride the Gilera 500 four but was troubled throughout with handling of this seven speed multi. On hearing of these problems, some officials on the Thursday afternoon led a donkey to the door of the refreshment tent where Minter was having a cup of tea. The donkey refused to enter, so Derek came out and was assured by chief scrutineer Bob Havers that the donkey had passed inspection. Derek climbed on its back and to everyone's amusement the donkey refused to move, not with this jockey anyway, perhaps an indication of what was to come for Derek.

Following Provini's crash, the Benelli Team agreed that Minter could ride the spare bike, only to hear next day that the Benelli Factory had vetoed this arrangement. Then only a few hours later on that Saturday, end of practice week, Minter still struggling with the Gilera with his lap times not even in the first six, crashed at Brandish, breaking his wrist. Minter's luck had run out. I wonder how he felt when John Blanchard, Seeley-Matchless, finished on the Senior practice leader board, fifth fastest of the week.

On his first visit to the Island, racing a 125cc Kawasaki (Kawasaki's first time at the TT), 25 year old Toshio Fuji, coming out of Ramsey, crashed at Cruickshank Corner on the Friday evening practice. Fuji, the 1965 Hutchinson 100 Melano Trophy winner on a 50cc works Suzuki, was not thought to be seriously injured. Sadly he died two hours later from a ruptured spleen, another Isle of Man TT statistic.

Due to the re-scheduling of the Isle of Man TT after the seaman's strike, the sidecar and 250cc events would be run on the Sunday 28th August instead of the regular Monday start of TT race week.

In attendance as a spectator, Jim Redman, winner of six world championships and six IOM TTs, announced his retirement from racing. The 31 year old London-born Rhodesian joined the Honda Team in 1961, winning all his championships with Honda. Redman was known as a shrewd operator and often as the captain of the Honda race team, held considerable influence over riders to be included in the Honda Team. Other than 1961 in the 250cc class, Mike Hailwood, who rode mostly for MV, would not join Honda racing full-time until the 1966 season, the year Redman threw in the towel.

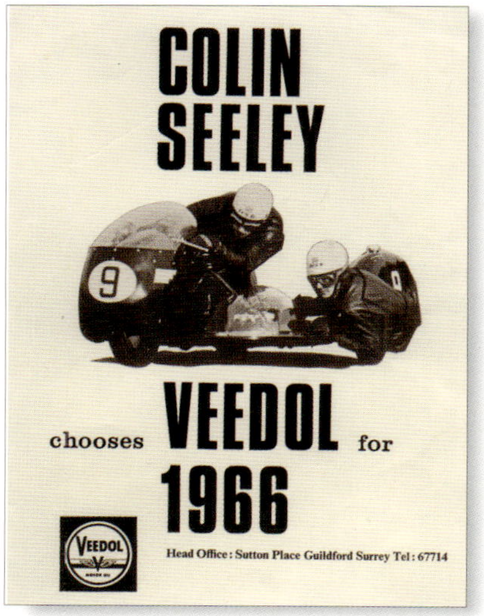

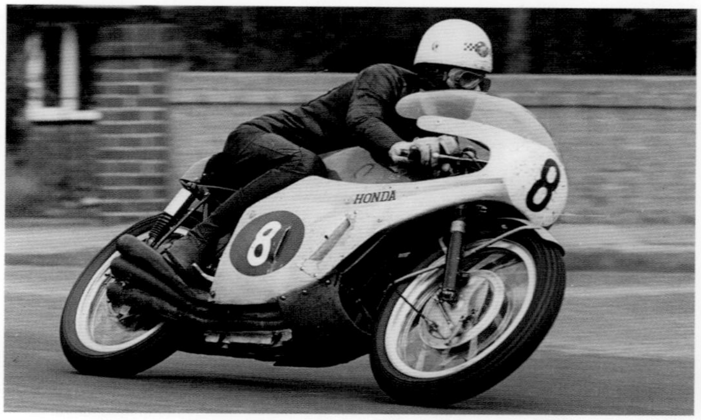

Stuart Graham on the Honda 250cc six.

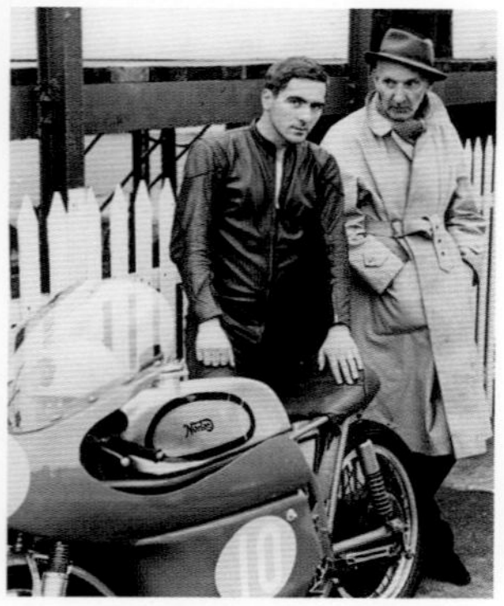

Joe Dunphy and Francis Beart awaiting the 350 TT start.

Honda refused to fire up. Graham tried again and again, then at the end of the pit lane, having flooded the carbs, against all odds the Honda six finally burst into life and he was away, having lost 2 minutes.

Meanwhile, Ivy was in the pits, but needed a plug change, which meant he could not benefit from Graham's lost time. At the end of the fourth lap Bill, still in third position, was forced to pit again, a broken carburettor was found, a failure by Yamaha, and that was that for little Bill.

Stuart Graham, Honda, came home second, over 5 minutes behind, with Peter Inchley on the Villiers Starmaker single cylinder racer making up the rostrum positions, averaging a very remarkable 91.43mph, the first time in 16 years that a British machine achieved such a success, and the quickest ever for a British 250 motorcycle. Peter collected the third and last silver Isle of Man TT replica, the rest presented with bronze replicas back to eleventh place. Dennis Poore, the new Chairman of the Villiers Engine Company was there to witness this achievement. Sadly, on the very last lap, veteran racer 47 year old batchelor Brian Duffy crashed when his Yamaha seized on the Mountain Box section. He was killed instantly, another sharp reminder.

With the sidecar race out of the way, we could now concentrate on John Blanchard as well as the Seeley-AJS and Seeley-Matchless on which John would ride in the Junior and Senior TT events. We had little idea of what to expect. Although the 'Paperhanger' had performed well in practice, just about anything could happen in such long races.

Wednesday began with the 3 lap 125cc race, scheduled for a 11.00am start. Unfortunately, the one thing predictable about Manx weather is its unpredictability. Dense fog blanketed the mountain section. A half-hour delay was announced, then another. Meanwhile, already at the grandstand start area awaiting the 350cc race, we were mingling with the stars, many of whom we were on first name terms; Read, Anderson, Duff, Perris, Bryans, Taveri, Hailwood and the Maidstone Marvel Bill Ivy. What a difference from our first TT in 1961 when we hardly knew anyone.

Finally, after almost three hours delay, the weather broke and the sun shone through. From an original entry of 77, 28 non-starters reduced the field to 49 lightweight machine competitors. Champion Hugh Anderson had lead the practice on a re-vamped short-stroke twin cylinder works Suzuki, lapping at 96.77mph, followed by Read, Taveri and Ivy, although we were told there were no team orders for Read and Ivy. It was a close call at that juncture, Phil having 26 championship points with one win, against Bill with 24 points and two wins. Both chose the twin cylinder Yamahas instead of the new vee-four. Hugh Anderson along with Fred Stevens started the race proceedings, Phil Read (No 10) starting 40 seconds behind and Bill Ivy (No 15) 30 seconds down on Read. On the first lap the main contenders were jockeying for position. Taveri, Honda, overshot at Ballacraine and lost 30 seconds, at Ballaugh Ivy caught Taveri, Read was alongside Perris, Suzuki, at Ramsey and leading the race on corrected time. By the end of lap one, Read was 18 seconds ahead, clipping 4 seconds off Anderson's old record, boosting it to 96.7mph. But it was the Maidstone Marvel, little Bill who was on fire. Despite hitting a wall at the Gooseneck and punching a hole in the screen, he was second at the end of that lap, tailing Read by 12 seconds and 4 seconds ahead of Anderson in third. Duff was fourth, Perris fifth. The works Honda four-stroke machines were unable to match the speed of their two-stroke rivals. Mike Hailwood was holding sixth place. On the second lap the leaders maintained position to Ramsey, but Read had slowed due to a momentary engine hiccup on the full bore Crosby section. Fortunately, the Yamaha picked up again but Pocket-Rocket Ivy had taken the lead by Creg-ny-Baa and was 8 seconds ahead into his last lap. Taveri was in the pits with all sorts of problems as the news came through that Ivy had shattered the lap record with an incredible lap of 98.55mph.

Ivy in the lead and now third on the road, was not letting up. He might just catch Phil Read who started 30 seconds ahead. At Ramsey, Read was still second on the road, behind Anderson. Approaching Guthrie Memorial, little Bill had team-mate Read in his sights and seemed determined to get to the finish first (was it rubbing salt in the wound, we all wondered). Through the Creg, it was Ivy leading Read as they fought their private duel down to Brandish, Read was well down to Ivy on corrected time. Realising there was nothing to gain, he dropped back, allowing Ivy to cross the finish line first. So it was Ivy, Read, Anderson, Duff, Perris and the works Hondas of Hailwood, Bryans and Taveri in that order. It had been a great race with 32 finishers. The manufacturer's team prize was awarded to Yamaha with first, second and fourth places, consolation for the team's poor performance in the 250cc race.

A crowd of well-wishers towered over the 5ft 3in Maidstone Marvel thrilled to have won his first Isle of Man TT and to have kept his World Championship hopes alive. But the 1964 125 World Champion, Luigi Taveri, having already won four Grands Prix and three second places that year, was still 18 points ahead of Bill Ivy, who now had three Grand Prix wins. It would be close.

Then at 4pm, before dark, it was the turn of the patient 350cc competitors. Never in the history of the TT had any race started so late in the afternoon. The original entry of 110 had shrunk to 70 starters. Non-starters included Redman, Read, Ivy, Minter, Provini and Duff. The Junior race promised the first clash of the week between the two main protagonists, the current 500cc World Motorcycle Champion Mike Hailwood and the rising Italian star Giacomo Agostini, yet to win a championship or an Isle of Man TT. In the Junior practice Hailwood, Honda, posted a time only a second faster than Agostini, MV, both lapping at over 101mph. As the machines warmed up conditions were near ideal. We were alongside our man John Blanchard somewhere at the back on the grid with race number 43. Cheshire's Bill Smith, AJS, was away first, followed by Griff Jenkins, Norton, then the first pairing, Australian big Jack Ahearn, Norton, and Londoner Joe Dunphy, Norton, followed 10 seconds later by Mike the Bike and Franta Stastny, Jawa. Agostini, MV, and Selwyn Griffiths, AJS, set off 20 seconds behind Hailwood who already had six 350cc Grand Prix wins that year, against Agostini's one win and four second places.

However, in the 500cc class, prior to the TT, both riders had two wins each, but Ago was ahead with four second places to Mike's one. So in the best tradition it was a tense battle. Drama on the first lap, Hailwood in trouble at Ballacraine, the Honda sounded rough and was forced to retire. Agostini, a class act despite no real opposition, opened up the throttles of the three cylinder MV putting on a great display for the thousands of fans, cracking Hailwood's lap record with a round of 103.09mph and beating Redman's race record by averaging 100.87mph for the 6 lap 226.4 mile event.

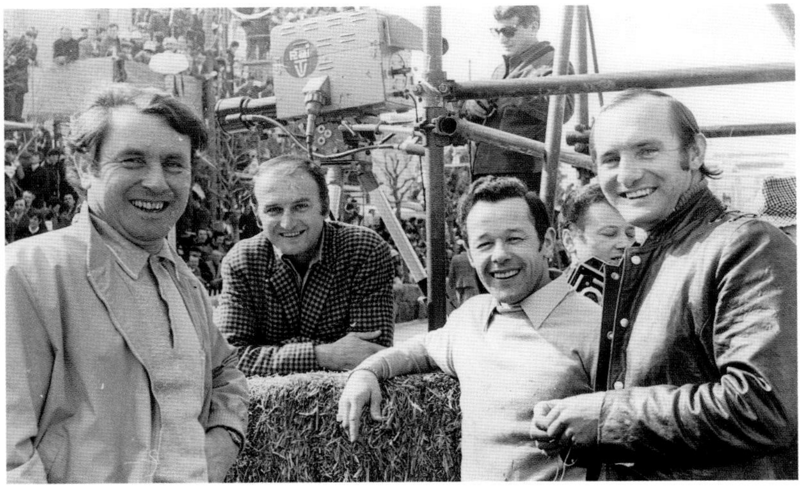

Left to right: Ernst Weiss, Frank Perris, Luigi Taveri and Mike Hailwood

Far behind Ago were the British bangers, with rising star Peter Williams on Tom Arter's Reynolds framed AJS a magnificent second, his first TT. There was a great dice for third place between Chris Conn, Jack Ahearn both on Nortons and Czech Frantisek Bocek on a single cylinder CZ. It was so close that the officials had Bocek on the rostrum, until the timekeepers decided otherwise. So Chris Conn was credited with third place, Ahearn 4.4 seconds behind in fourth and Bocek fifth. Then, much to our delight, the 'Paperhanger', with his head still down on the tank, came through to a brilliant sixth on the Seeley-AJS. The flag-man missed John, and he rocketed off down Bray Hill on his seventh lap, such commitment and with no lights. Griff Jenkins came seventh, Dave Simmonds, Honda, eighth and Franta Stastny, works Jawa, having spent three days of practice week in Ramsey Cottage Hospital following his crash at Quarry Bends, finished in an amazing ninth place. 37 finishers in all!

Two good results, but we were probably more pleased with John Blanchard's sixth place in the Junior than our fifth in the sidecar event. What could our Team achieve on Senior Day? JB had finished fifth in the 500cc practice week, so our hopes were high. We celebrated that evening after the presentations, JB proud of his first silver replica. Drink was flowing but JB, clutching his first Isle of Man TT Silver Replica, kept to his prison rations. It had been a standing joke that JB seemed to exist on such meagre rations. Certainly Ma Clucas could not make John out.

On that Thursday, over in America, Detroit dealer Bob Leppan became the fastest man on two wheels when he cracked the AMA recognised motorcycle speed record at 245.667mph on the Bonneville Salt Flats. His flying cigar shaped Streamliner powered by two 650cc Triumph engines ran on alcohol fuel.

Meanwhile, Friday's Senior Race was scheduled to start at 1.30pm. We needed to be at the Grandstand area early. As we were located inside the circuit we had to be across the TT circuit before the roads closed at 10.00am, with the 50cc International tiddler race kicking off at 11.00am. For the first time the 50cc race would start en masse, with 17 starters from the original entry of 31. Taveri, Honda, was leading the championship, at that stage two points ahead of Anscheidt, Suzuki, and three ahead of team mate Bryans, so this race was crucial. With the early morning clouds clearing it would be a dry race.

Right from the mass start Ralph Bryans streaked away with Taveri alongside. Seventeen screaming tiddlers rushed down Bray Hill on that first lap of three, making a wonderful sound. Out through Braddan Bridge 6 seconds covered the six factory riders, on the approach to Ballancraine. Hugh Anderson, Suzuki, outbraked the leading pair of Bryans and Taveri only to be repassed by Bryans at Sarah's cottage. Anderson's Suzuki nipped its pistons and lost the edge. At Parliament Square the Suzuki boys Katayama and Anscheidt were nose-to-tail, 20 seconds behind the Honda duo, with Anderson a further 10 seconds behind, caught by teamster Ernst Degner.

Over the start line on the first lap, the current World 50cc Champion Ralph Bryans was nearly 6 seconds ahead of Taveri and from a standing start had lapped in an astounding 85.15mph, chopping 1 minute 19 seconds off the record set two years before by Hugh Anderson. In fact all six front runners bettered Anderson's previous record. That all 17 competitors had completed that first lap was a record in itself. Bryans led from start to finish setting a new lap record of 86.49mph, an amazing achievement on a 50cc machine. The Swiss ace Luigi Taveri held second place to the end whilst for Katayama and Anscheidt it was all over, both retiring with engine trouble. Anderson finished third, with Degner, also with troubles, in fourth place. Tommy Robb, who had held fifth, had to change a plug up on the mountain section, which dropped him back to eleventh of the 13 finishers. Bryans was the first Irishman to win a TT since Reg Armstrong's Senior victory, on a Norton in 1952 and his historic result put him only one point behind championship leader, Taveri, with Anscheidt still in third place.

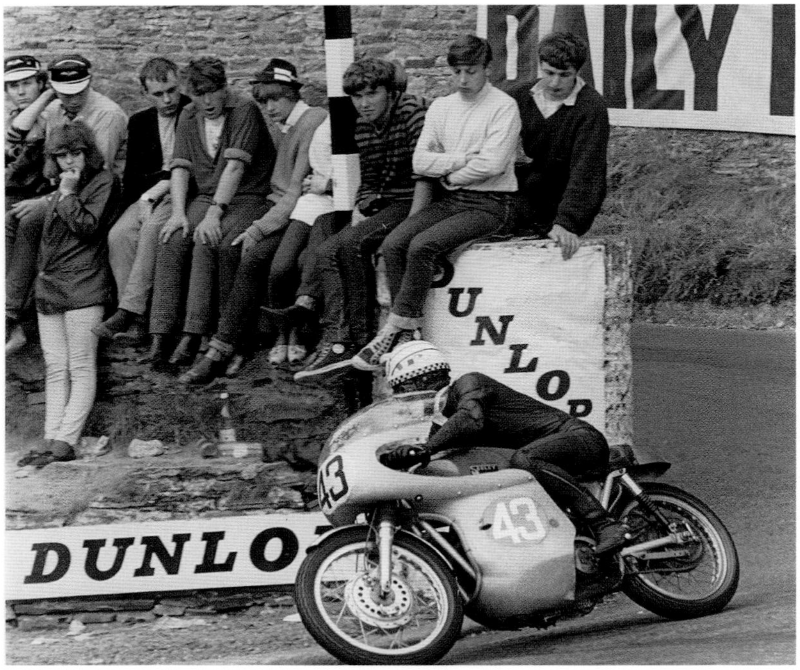

John Blanchard finishing the 350cc junior Isle of Man TT in sixth.

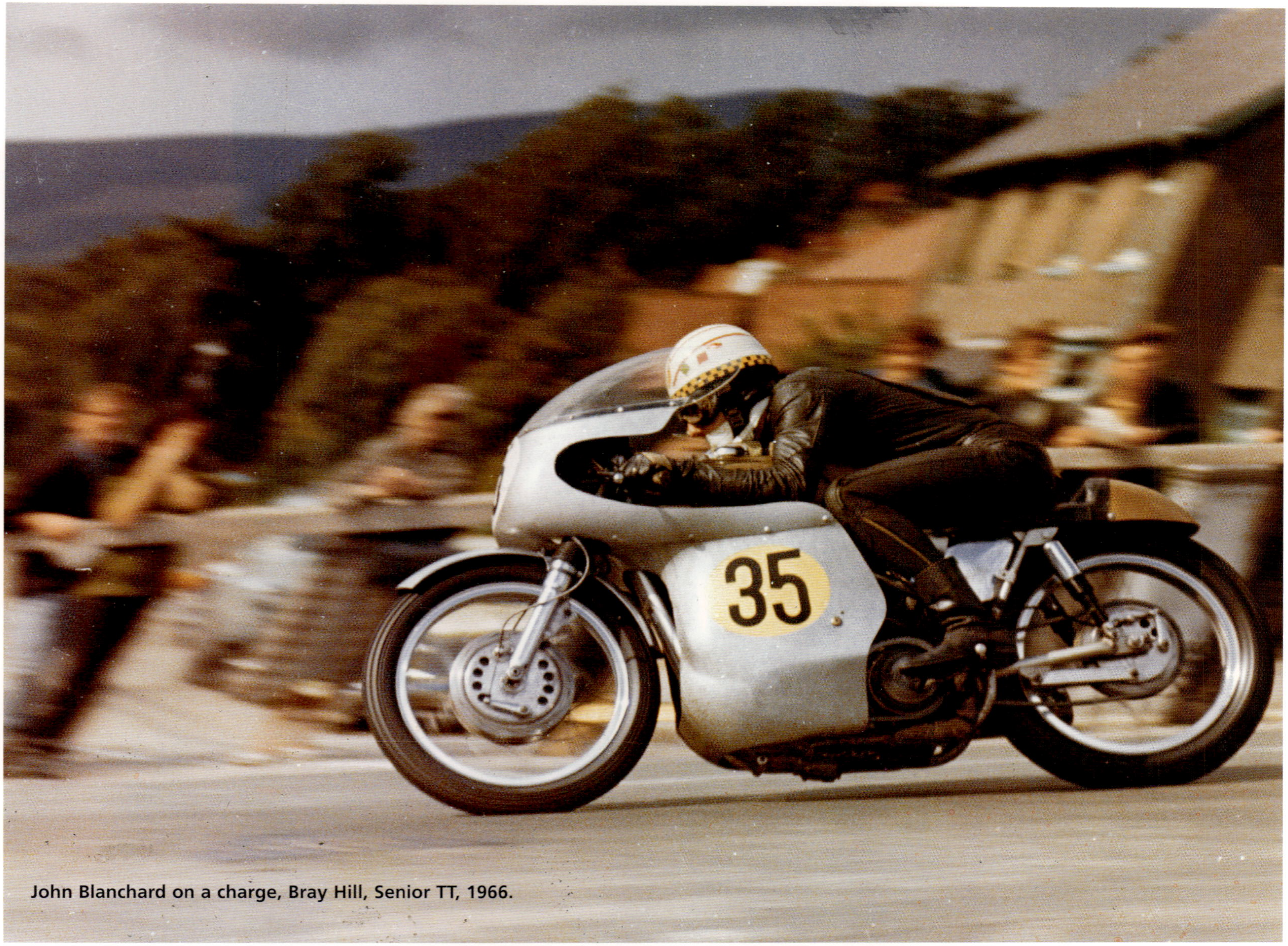

John Blanchard on a charge, Bray Hill, Senior TT, 1966.

With the National Anthem playing and the rostrum presentations over, it was the big one. 80 competitors were already warming up their machines. For the second time that week it would be a shoot-out between two of the most popular stars of that period, the people's champion, Mike the Bike Hailwood and the dashing Italian Agostini, the girls' favourite. As the competitors lined up on Glencrutchery Road, anxious eyes looked to the skies, low cloud and drizzle had swept across the Island at the end of the tiddler TT. But with 10 minutes to go, the sun broke through, the wind freshened drying the damp roads.

For the last time that week it was hush as the riders prepared for the start. We stayed with our man JB and the Seeley-Matchless, race number 35, until the last minute. Wally and I had done our bit. It was now all down to the 'Paperhanger'.

A moment's silence, down went the flag, and with a roar Hailwood's Honda four was 100 yards clear of starting partner Joe Dunphy as they disappeared down Bray Hill. Agostini, MV, smoothly left the start on a 20 second interval followed by the rest. At Ballaugh Bridge, Hailwood had gained one second on the Italian, and by Ramsey 5 seconds. But he was only one second ahead over the mountain section down to Creg-ny-Baa, showing how hard Ago was trying. The Signpost Corner lamps flashed on the Leader Board for Ago as Hailwood completed his first lap, then over 6 seconds ahead of Giacomo, followed by Peter Williams, Malcolm Uphill and John Blanchard.

On the second lap, Williams was in trouble. Uphill moved into third place and JB fourth. Hailwood broke his own lap record of 106.41mph from the year before on the works MV, now at 107.07mph. Ago, not to be outdone, also broke the old record by .27mph.

On the third lap, by Ballaugh Bridge Mike increased his lead to 15 seconds. Joe Dunphy, Malcom Uphill and Jack Ahearn retired with engine problems. At the end of the third lap, pit stop time, Hailwood was leading Ago by 22 seconds. Blanchard was in a nail-biting third place, 11 seconds ahead of Chris Conn. The 'Paperhanger' screamed in for his pit stop but it took ages to refill the tank. Wally had forgotten to remove the cap from the petrol refiller tank, causing an air lock. Our rostrum place was possibly lost because of this. Nevertheless, Blanchard was doing a great job, up with the leaders on every lap. Hailwood continued to dominate the race even when the rain came down to the north of the Island from Ballaugh, through to the start of the mountain climb. How Mike kept that hairy Honda upright is a mystery, and nearly 2 minutes ahead of Giacomo, who was having a front brake problem. The duel was over.

Mike the Bike came home to the cheers of the crowds and his ninth TT win, just one short of Stanley Woods record of ten. This gave Mike five Senior Race wins, beating the four scored by Woods and John Surtees. Perhaps more significantly, it was Honda's first Senior TT win and left them with a chance of the 500cc world championship, to be decided at the next weekend's Italian Grand Prix.

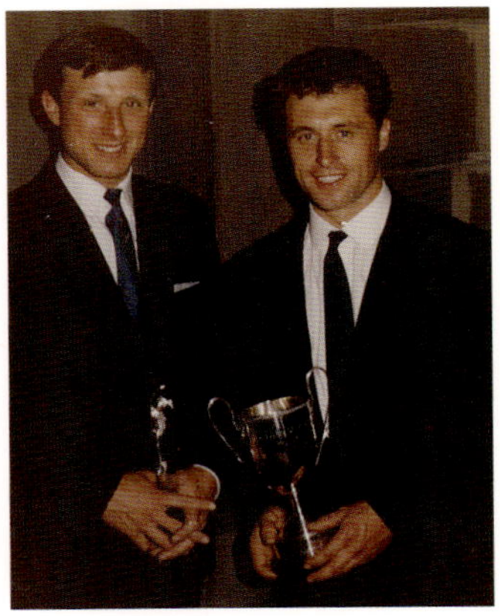

John Blanchard and me, TT awards.

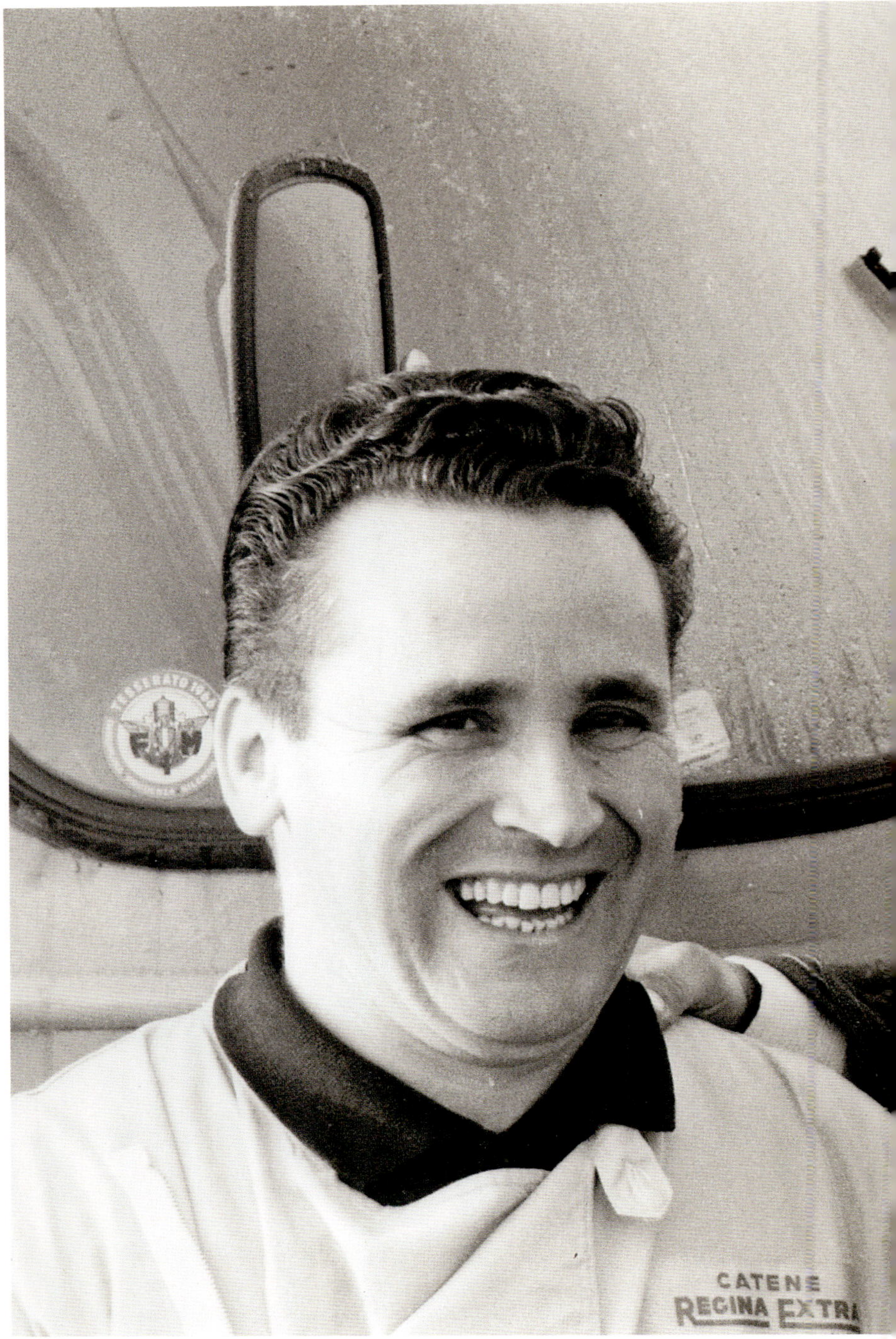

Giacomo Agostini came second to enthusiastic applause, and Chris Conn, who rode strongly throughout, made up the first three. John Blanchard brought home the Seeley-Matchless and into prominence with a magnificent fourth place. We could not believe it, a huge reward for all the effort and commitment put into those prototype machines. Our friend Ron Chandler, Matchless, finished in fifth then Stastny, Williams, Findlay, McCosh and Stanton made the first 10 of 30 finishers. Our Strang Gang supporters would be pleased and the Guinness would be flowing. Ma Clucas would be on a high, when she held a Silver Replica you would think she was holding the Crown Jewels.

The presentation at the Villa Marina that evening was special, with only 11 Silver Replicas handed out, the last going to another up and coming Australian, Kel Carruthers. Bronze Replicas were presented to riders who finished 12th to 21st. For the others nothing!

As we awaited the official presentations, I thought back to the mid-fifties when I ran my motorcycle repair business and listened to the BBC radio reports from the Isle of Man TT races. They were brilliant broadcasts, probably commentated by Graham Walker, Murray's Father. Those were the days of such stars Geoff Duke, Ray Amm, Ken Kavanagh, Dickie Dale, Fergus Anderson, Reg Armstrong, Rod Coleman, Bill Lomas, Jack Brett, John Surtees, Cecil Sandford, just a few of the greats that created TT history. It never occured to me that I would be on the Isle of Man myself, let alone building bikes which would finish in the first six of the Junior and Senior TT races. It was a boyhood dream come true.

With presentations in reverse order, it seemed ages before a grinning John Blanchard walked onto the stage to be awarded his Silver replica for fourth place, averaging 95.02mph. Colin Seeley Racing Developments was awarded the Motorcycling Cup, for the rider who had made the best performance in Senior, Junior and Lightweight 250 races. John's sixth in the Junior and fourth in the Senior events had earned £150 prize money. A good week for our team, three starts and three finishes, a total of 566 racing miles around the most demanding race course in the World, sixth, fifth and fourth places and three Silver Replicas, We hadn't done too badly!

We left the hustle and bustle of the magic isle on Saturday morning, on a fully loaded Manx Ferry with hundreds of motorcycling enthusiasts, machines, riders, helpers standing, sitting or lying all over the decks, no luxury on those boats. With the beer flowing, TT stories and experiences were exchanged. A sister ship passed, arriving for the Manx Grand Prix which that year followed the TT directly.

It was always rewarding to arrive home. The last three weeks had been completely exhausting. Our success in the Isle of Man had not been straight forward, Wally having to work hard on the AJS 7R and Matchless G50 engines, which had each required a couple of rebuilds. 12 racing laps around the TT course plus all the practising had taken its toll.

At the Italian Grand Prix the next weekend, the 11th September, no sidecar class would be included and we cancelled a trip to the Cadwell Park International a week later, giving us a hard earned break.

The Italian Grand Prix was the last round of the World 500cc championship. Mike Hailwood and his works Honda needed to win to keep the title he had retained every year since 1962. Results of the best five out of nine Grand Prix events counted towards the championship for 500cc machines. Agostini had 34 points in the bag against Hailwood's 30 from only four races, so Mike had to win for the eight points. Even if Ago

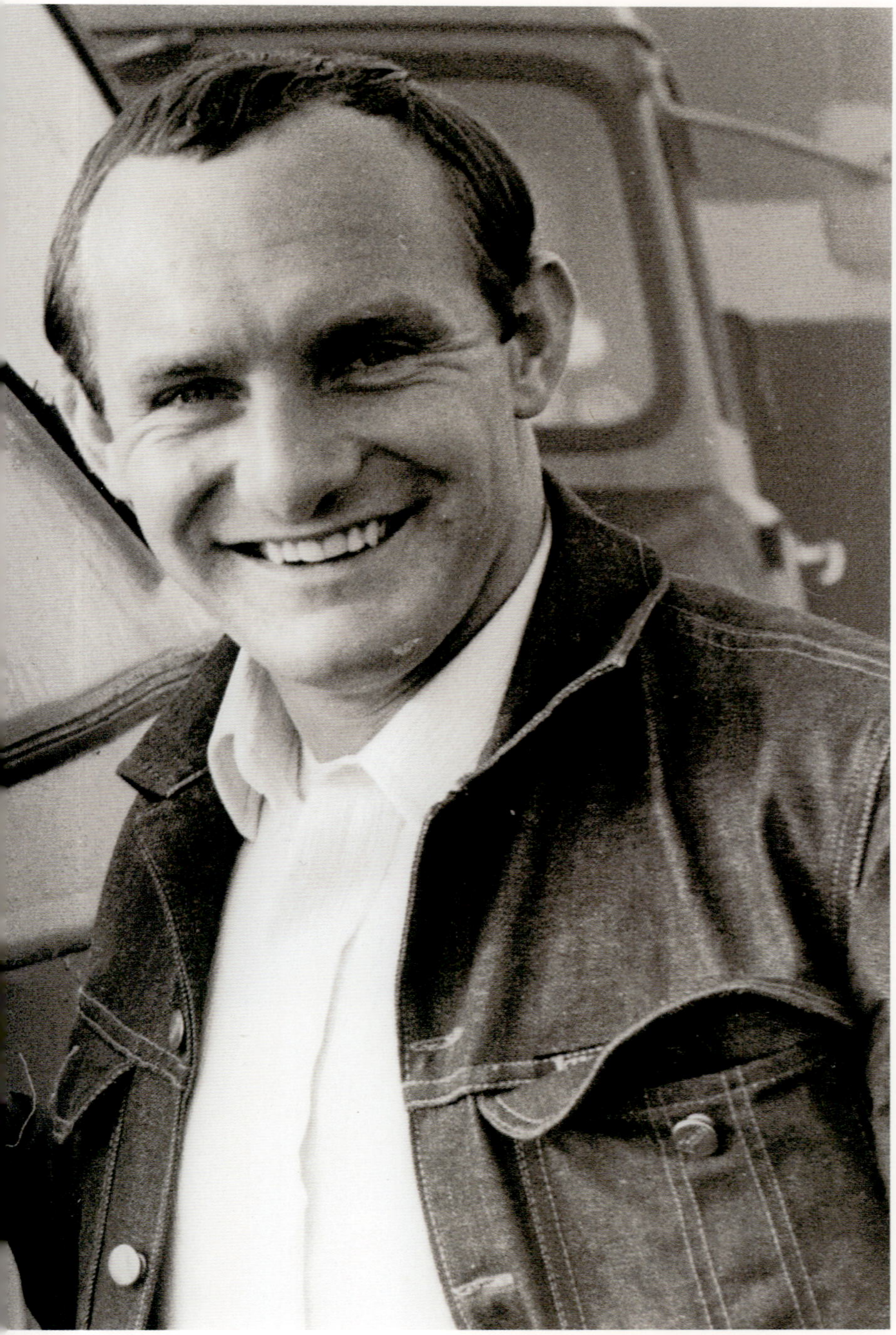

Hailwood with Agostini's MV mechanic Vittorio Carruna at Brands.

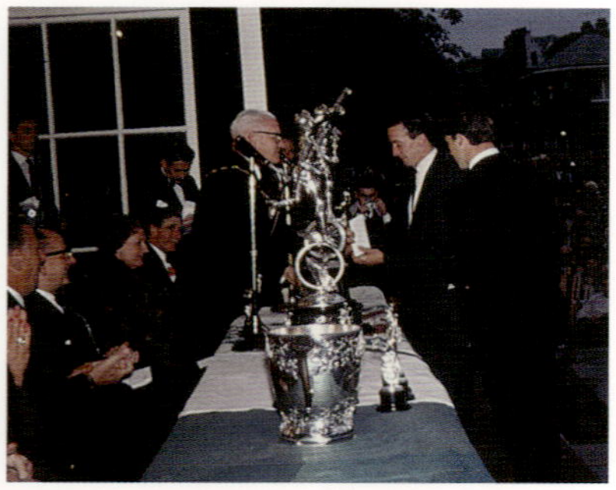

Wally receiving his last TT replica.

finished second, he could not better Mike's points score. If Ago won, and Hailwood was second, the best of five would give each rider three Grand Prix victories and two seconds, making them equal on 36 points. What would happened then, I am not sure. Anyway, it was not a problem. From the start of the 35 lap, 123 mile race, Hailwood rocketed away, Agostini, MV, was midfield but not for long, keen to show his best in front of his countrymen. By the end of the first lap Ago was on Mike's tail and soon took the lead but Hailwood, not the man to give in easily, just sat behind keeping the pressure up. On lap 6 the big Honda let Mike the Bike down, the engine went clunk with broken valves. Hailwood was beaten by the Honda not the MV!!

The championship was Agostini's, the first of many, the third Italian to hold the 500cc title joining Umberto Masetti, Gilera, 1950 and 52 and Libero Liberati, Gilera, in 1957. The cheering was deafening and the fans were ecstatic. Mike Hailwood, a true sportsman, was first to congratulate Ago commenting, 'Good luck to him, he has worked hard for the title and deserves it!' What was the efficient Honda Racing Team thinking of, arriving at Monza, with Mike's well-worn Senior TT machine, no spare engine and too few spares? Nobby Clarke, the Japanese-speaking Rhodesian and Mike's race mechanic, had already flown to Amsterdam to collect a spare lower crankcase half and gears after an oil leak had been discovered. In comparison, MV Agusta, determined to win that title, had complete spare machines in both 350cc and 500cc classes.

Honda had blown the chance of a magnificent clean sweep in all classes from 125, 250, 350 and 500cc. This situation was never to be repeated, and it would not be until 1983, 17 years later, that Freddie Spencer would win the 500cc World Championship for Honda.

Giacomo Agostini also won the 350cc race (Mike did not compete). The headlines in Milan that Sunday evening proclaimed, 'Agostini Mondiale!' Yes, the World was Agostini's oyster. It is incredible that 40 years later, Agostini is still held in high regard by the British fans and the motorcycle fraternity in general. How many present day riders will even be remembered, let alone held in such high esteem for so long after?

Back home that same Sunday, it was all action at Brands Hatch. Not road racing but the Moto-Cross Trophee des Nations. Spearheaded by the World 250cc moto-cross champion Torsten Hallman, Husqvarna, Sweden's team scored a convincing victory, their

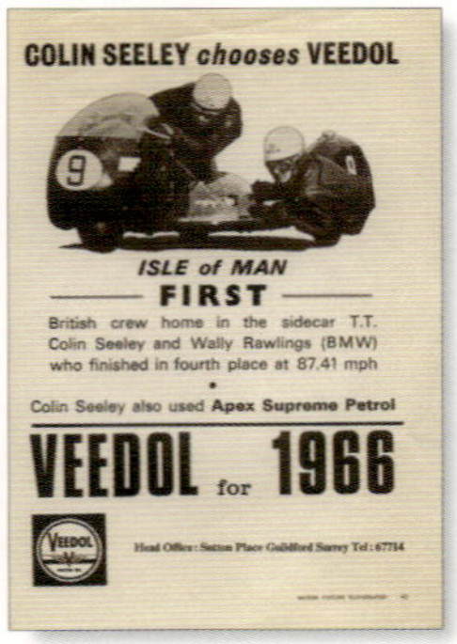

Motor Cycling

WEEK ENDING OCTOBER 22, 1966 No. 2945 WEDNESDAY 9d

COLIN BUYS

third in the series. Their nearest challengers were the British team who did well to notch second spot. They were led by Bryan Goss, Husqvarna, who was on top form, winning both legs by a huge margin, with two of his greatest rides against world class opposition.

It is often forgotten that Brands Hatch hosted such events on a 1 1/4 mile moto-cross track, this time attracting teams from Belgium, Sweden, Finland, France, Holland, Denmark, Czechoslovakia, Ireland and Switzerland. Such stars as Joel Robert, Derek Rickman, Dave Bickers, Chris Horsfeld and Ollie Petersson took part, a great event attracting a huge crowd.

A break from racing proved crucial to our future plans to manufacture the Seeley machines. Associated Motorcycles was in trouble and the receiver had to make cuts and sell off parts of the company. Hence the rumour spread that the 7R, G50 and Norton Manx racing department would be up for grabs. A number of meetings with the official receiver convinced him that Colin Seeley Racing Developments was the right company to continue the manufacture of such famous marques. Opposition from cash-rich parties was intense. Some predicted we would not last more than a few weeks in our efforts to continue manufacturing.

I held two ace cards. I had a long association with the AMC factory as a dealer and racer. Also, my earlier agreement with the factory to be able to produce joint-named racing bikes combined with our recent race results, led to a positive decision. We all understood this would not be a quick fix to pocket huge returns. I gave my word, and for the next seven years I fullfilled that promise.

I have never disclosed how much I paid for the take-over of all the 7R G50 and Manx racing spares, jigs, fixtures and drawings, but it was a fantastic deal. I would never get an opportunity like this again. It took two weeks and two vans to move everything from Woolwich to Belvedere, 6 miles away. The receiver could never have known, and nor did we, that in a small way we would change the face of UK motorcycle racing. Thank you for such trust!

Whilst the official agreement was being sorted out at AMC for the take-over, we still had some racing commitments. The Scarborough International on Saturday 24th September had been postponed from its original date, which clashed with the TT.

With a number of names missing in the solo classes, it would be a disappointment for the 10,000 strong crowd. The sidecar race had attracted Deubel, Scheidegger, Auerbacher, Schauzu, Vincent, Vinicombe. The anticlockwise narrow circuit certainly suited our German friends, and in the 8 lap 20 mile final it would be Auerbacher, Deubel, Schauzu and then ourselves. The World Champion Fritz retired with clutch trouble.

Desperate Dan Shorey won both 350 and 500cc finals with our 'Paperhanger' JB, Seeley AJS, fourth in the junior race and an excellent third in the 500cc event on the Seeley-Matchless, the challenge of Dave Degans, Kirby-Metisse, falling by the wayside on the first lap. With two fourths, one third and £68 of prize and start money, more funds for the manufacturing equipment, it was a reasonable day's work at a track I personally did not like, and would not return to.

Then was a dash across country for many competitors for the next day's Mallory Park International Daily Mail sponsored Race of the Year. These were the great days of racing at Mallory, the 1.35 mile circuit creating some fantastic close racing and attracting huge crowds. This event was no exception with a 5 mile queue of cars and motorcycles bringing some 50,000 fans. The chance to view the World Champions in action against the cream of the regular UK competitors was a great draw. Those days of regular appearances of international stars mixing with the local heroes have long gone, more's the pity!

Today's attraction was the newly crowned 500cc Italian World Champion, Giacomo Agostini, a rising star indeed, competing against our very own multi world champion Mike Hailwood, not forgetting Bill Ivy and Mike Duff on the works Yamahas. These champions were willing to risk their reputations against the likes of Peter Williams, John Cooper, Dave Croxford, Dave Degens, Joe Dunphy, Ron Chandler, Pat Mahoney, Chris Conn, Dan Shorey, John Blanchard, all hungry for success. For the world champions it was not always straightforward, but these men were not cotton wool champions, so accepted the risks. The thousands of British enthusiasts sensed that Giacomo Agostini would become as much a favourite in Britain as in his home country.

Practice took place in the morning for this one day event and with heats and finals for the 250, 350, 500cc and sidecar races, it was astonishing how it all fitted into a nine hour period. Was it a miracle or was it slick organisation? Nowadays it takes two or three days often for less racing - what has gone wrong? The day's activities kicked off with two heats for the 500cc races. As expected Agostini dominated the final with the stylish Williams second and fast improving Londoner, Dave Croxford, Matchless, third, beating home favourite John Cooper and the rest of the pack not far behind. Ago and Williams also won the heats of the 350cc event.

Hailwood's four cylinder Honda had to be rebuilt, so arrived too late for morning practice. So again Agostini had things all his own way, whipping the MV away from the start in fine style. Dan Shorey, Norton, double winner at Scarborough the previous day, out-paced Williams to take second place, while another Londoner, Joe Dunphy beat local hero Cooperman for third place.

Then it was the turn of British bulldog, Mike the Bike, riding the works 250 Honda six. Winner of his heat, Mike would be up against his mate the Maidstone Marvel, Bill Ivy, who had won the second heat on the works Yamaha. From the start Hailwood screamed away into the lead. Ivy made a poor getaway and took 4 laps to claw up to second position, but Mike Duff, on the other works Yamaha, was on a charge, closing fast on Little Bill and snatching second spot on the last lap. So it was 1 - 2 - 3 for the Grand Prix stars, with Isle of Man TT 250cc hero Peter Inchley on the Villers Starmaker fourth. Hailwood broke Phil Read's lap record by one second, averaging 89.67mph.

Then came the race that everybody had come for, the £1,050 first prize, 30 lap race of the year with invited riders drawing lots for their places on the grid. Agostini on the 500cc MV was in the midst of 28 starters, while Hailwood, on the 250cc Honda six was right at the back. After a delay and a fanfare by RAF trumpeters, the flag dropped and Hailwood streaked through from the back row to take the lead long before the pack reached Gerard's Bend.

Ago was not used to the hurly-burly of a British short-circuit start, and was stuck in the middle of the group. It took a number of laps for him to find his stride, but was still back in sixth place, as the British contingent would not move over. On the sixth lap Ago passed Chandler and Degens and set about catching the flying Peter Williams who was battling with Bill Ivy for second place. Ivy pulled away from Williams but Ago, on lap 12, took over, this was a World Champion in action. For a few laps it seemed as though the extra power of the big MV might get the better of Mike's lead. Meantime thousands were enjoying the spectacle.

The combination of the high-revving, high-pitched Honda with its six straight-through exhaust megaphones and the more subtle sound of the three cylinder MV was just fantastic.

By lap 24, Mike was holding off the challenge of the Italian ace when the valve of the rear tyre was torn completely out of the inner tube. Mike wobbled to a stand still. Unchallenged, Agostini went on to scoop the first prize and equalled Hailwood's old MV lap record at 91.69mph. Bill Ivy took second place and £500, with team mate Mike Duff taking third and £250, from Peter Williams on the last lap, John Cooper fifth, Chandler sixth, then Degens, with our 'Paperhanger' a close eighth.

With a total of £1,146 of prize money, plus reputedly the highest start money ever paid to a rider competing at a British motorcycle meeting, Giacomo Agostini would be even more attractive to the girls! Tommy Robb, Bultaco, won the 125cc event just getting the better of Dave Simmonds, Tohatsu, in a 10 lap thriller.

Finally, the 10 lap final of the 500cc sidecar race rounded the day off. We won our heat and Tony Wakefield his. Roy Lindsey, having recovered from the Norman Huntingford crash at the Dutch TT, joined me as a passenger staying to the end of the season. This allowed Wally Rawlings a rest, and more time for race engine preparations. From the start it was going to be another battle between World Champion Fritz Scheidegger, BMW, and ourselves. Fritz had taken the lead and there was little we could do other than keep the pressure up, resulting in Fritz almost breaking his own race record of 81.16mph winning at 81.11mph, so close. I was pleased with our second place and the £73, and Roy performed well. Scheidegger, now works supported, was always a hard man to beat. Third was Tony Wakefield, BMW, then Chris Vincent, BMW, and Max Deubel, BMW, in that order. Now we were ready for the final International Brands Hatch event that year, in two weeks time.

Despite all the focus on our racing activities I was still running our motorcycle dealership with Percy's help, although in 1966 trade was difficult with a drop in demand for motorcycles and a lot of opposition from around 15 motorcycle dealers within a radius of 7 miles.

Those were the days of the big London dealerships: Pride and Clarke, Claude Rye, Elite Motors, Geo Clarke, Whitbys, Rowland Smith, Slocombes, Glanfield Lawrence, TC Munday & Co (sidecar specialist), Raymond Way, Godfreys, Rivetts of Leytonstone (clothing specialist), of course not leaving out Comerfords at Thames Ditton, and certainly not forgetting the out of town big one, Stan Hailwood's Kings of Oxford, with 20 outlets throughout the UK. Then there was our racing sponsor, Lewis Leathers of Great Portland Street, London Lewis leathers were worn by all the champions in those days, so said Derek Minter!

Soon it was our final local Derby, the Evening News International Race of the South, on October 9th, held on the 2.65 mile Grand Prix Circuit. With nine races planned for the day, including two heats of 1300cc sidecar race, it would be slick organisation by the Brands Hatch racing committee and clerk of the course, Tony Lovett. Scrutineering started at 8.30am for the smaller classes and as they worked up the list, the practice started at 9.00am, with the two programmes overlapping and all finishing at 1.00pm. There was hardly time for a cup of tea and a sandwich as racing started promptly at 1.30pm.

25,000 spectators attended, particularly to see the new 500cc World Champion, Agostini competing against our own double World Champion that year in the 250 and 350cc classes, Mike the Bike Hailwood. Other top names included Remo Venturi on his

AMC RACE-RIGHTS

PRODUCTION of four world-famous AMC road racing models is to be re-started in the near future. For Colin Seeley has bought the manufacturing rights of the 7R AJS, G50 Matchless and the 350 and 500 cc "Manx" Nortons. And the Belvedere, Kent, sidecar racer plans to commence making them again as soon as possible.

Said Colin on Friday: "My company, Colin Seeley Racing Developments Ltd, is taking over the whole racing side of the now-defunct AMC company lock, stock and barrel. We have bought all the existing stock from the factory: drawings, jigs, castings and spares — the lot — and have acquired manufacturing rights for the racers."

Realising that AMC were failing, Colin first made an offer for the racing side of the business earlier this year. "They laughed at me then", Colin recalled, "but I'd got in first and I was ready to act when they finally folded."

More spares than expected

"Our first aim is to get the spares side sorted out," he continued, "and to restart the flow of spares that are in short supply. But I've been surprised by the amount of stock they had at the factory—far more than I thought.

"The second aim is to re-start the production of 7R and G50 engined racers — and eventually to bring back the "Manx" Nortons. The 7R and G50 will be of the Seeley-AJS and Seeley-Matchless pattern, built and sold by us this year with our own frames, hubs and brakes and Norton forks."

This week, Colin's shop and workshops in Belvedere are closed while his staff concentrate on moving the recently acquired stock the four miles from the AMC factory at Woolwich.

And, from now on, all inquiries regarding racing spares should be sent to Seeley.

"We'll be trying to help everyone, but I hope people will be patient until we get organised. When we have sorted things out, we are going to supply what the customer wants. If he wants an engine he'll be able to have it. He won't have to buy a complete machine or anything like that, and we'll continue to prepare engines for the lads".

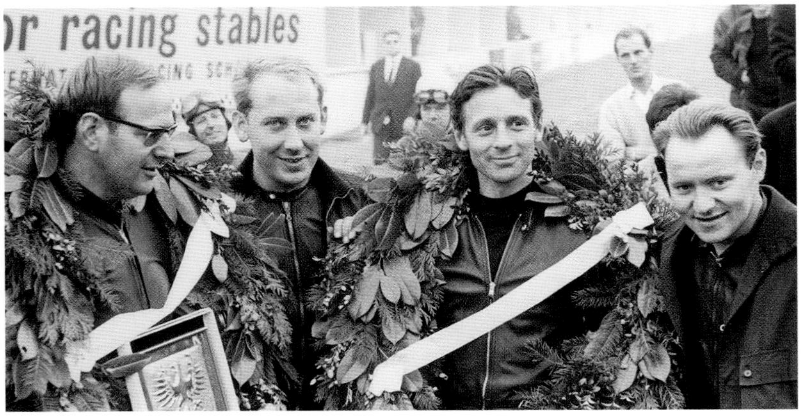

Left to right, 500cc sidecar winner Fritz Scheidegger, retiring champion Max Deubel, Fritz's passenger John Robinson and Emil Horner.

first visit to the Kent circuit, partnered by Frank Perris, both on Gileras, this event would signal the end of the Gilera Factories racing involvement. Gilera had made a major contribution to world championship racing winning six 500cc world titles, 1950 to 1957, inclusive of 31 Grand Prix victories. Apart from Ago, the foreign contenders found it difficult against the regular Brands Hatch scratchers. The action started with the 350cc race, Agostini leading from start to finish. Mike Duff, from a bad start was back on form and set the fastest lap, but wasn't quite able to catch the MV. Peter Williams, Arter AJS, came in third. John Blanchard, Seeley AJS, came sixth, beaten by Shorey and Croxford.

The first heat of the 1300cc sidecar event was won by Peter Brown 654cc BSA from Vincent, Deubel, Harris and a young Mick Boddice. The first nine went through to the final.

Race three, the ultra-lightweight 125cc race was won by Derek Chatterton, Honda, after leader Heinz Rosner dropped the little MZ at the tricky Druids Bend, Rod Scivyer second and Paul Smart, Honda, came third.

Next was the second heat of the unlimited sidecar event, but the dreaded Mini Special was competing and the partnership of Owen Greenwood and Terry Fairbrother, who surprise, surprise, won the heat. Scheidegger, Vinicombe, Wakefield, Bill Boddice and ourselves had little chance.

The final round of the Redex Trophy was race five, led at that stage by Dave Degens, one point ahead of Minter's 19 points, with Croxford third on 15. Britain's best would surely overwhelm the four participating continentals. It was Ago's first visit to the Kentish circuit, but with the 350cc race already in the bag, he led the Redex Trophy from the start, leaving the hungry pack well behind. 'Crazy' Croxford got the better of 'Desperate' Dan Shorey, Degens fourth, Chandler fifth, and from an appalling start Peter Williams edged ahead of Rex Butcher for sixth place. With Minter out of action for this event, Degens was handed the Redex Cup.

Then came the 20 lap Evening News Race of the South. Sir Robin Miller, now Chief Executive of EMAP, publishers of MCN and many other publications, was then the humble Motorcycle News reporter. This was the race everybody was waiting for, the encounter between the World Champions Ago and Mike. Miller called it 'the five second wonder', for that is how long the battle of the champions lasted.

Hailwood had rocketed his six cylinder 250 Honda away from the start but within 50 yards the clutch was in and Mike's right arm shot into the air signalling trouble. As the pack surged past the trouble was not hard to find, a broken connection rod dangled from the shattered crankcase. Agostini was completely unchallenged. The Gileras were never in the picture. Frank Perris in a dice for sixth place with Griff Jenkins, Dunstall Metisse, missed a gear, over revved the engine and the Gilera stopped with expensive noises. Team mate, Remo Venturi on the Gilera performed well to finish ninth. Agostini disappeared into the gathering gloom pursued by Peter Wiliams, Croxford and Chandler. The applecart was nearly upset when Degens on the Dresda Metisse blew past the local pack, but then retired with a broken chain. But it was to be cockney Croxford's day. He finished second, home just in front of Chandler, third and Peter Williams fourth, all Matchless G50 mounted. Dan Shorey, Norton, came fifth, with Griff Jenkins, Dunstall Metisse, sixth. Disappointment for Hailwood and the fans but a good race nevertheless!

Then it was the farewell to Deubel race, Max and passenger Emil Horner had decided to retire from racing. The four times World Motorcycle Sidecar Champion 1961-64 won a total of ten Grand Prix races for BMW and was a true professional, smooth in style and safe on the track. It had been a privilege to have raced against this German ace and occasionally to have beaten him.

The 10 lap race for outfits not exceeding 500cc would include Swiss champion Fritz Scheidegger who throughout 1966 had won every Grand Prix. With nine championship wins in all, Fritz and passenger John Robinson seemed unstoppable. I was never intimidated by the opposition or the venue, I just concentrated on the job in hand and that day, partnered by Roy Lindsey would not be any different.

From the race push start, Max Deubel set off as though he meant to win but Scheidegger was soon in front, closely followed by ourselves. The Rennsport was running beautifully and I was on fine form, determined to please my supporters. We pushed so hard that we set the fastest lap of the race, only 0.6 of a second outside the 500cc lap record, held by Pip Harris on his BMW from the year before. We just failed to get the best of the current champion, finishing second with the veteran British ace, Pip Harris, BMW, third, Tony Wakefield fourth, both on BMWs and the retiring champion Max Deubel fifth. A very pleasing result for us. With Hailwood's Honda broken, Mike Duff, Yamaha, left the opposition in the 250cc race behind. Rosner, MZ, on his first visit gave a good performance, hounded by Peter Inchley on that very fast Villiers-Starmaker. He finally went past for second place and Derek Chatterton, Yamaha, came third.

The last race of the day, the 10 lap final of the 1300cc three-wheeler race, had a 5.45 pm start. It was almost lighting up time. This race would not be easy against the Greenwood 1071cc Mini Special with its car tyres and twin wheel rear drive, so developed at that stage, it was almost unbeatable. Even Fritz Scheidegger could not hold back the Mini Special, which went to the front in a couple of laps. So, for the second time that day, it was Fritz and me battling for position. Fritz again pulled out all the stops to hold off our challenge. It was the controversial Mini first, the champion second and yours truly, partnered by Roy Lindsey who had performed extremely well, in a satisfying third place. Earnings that day were £60 start plus £75 prize money, a good result! The day was over, the lights out, well, not quite. Once we were packed up we piled in to the Atlantic Suite opposite the start line for a bit of a party, great days!

After Brands Hatch, the last British International, there was a two week break before the last round of the British Championships, held at Snetterton, one of my favourite circuits. The charge down the original Norwich Straight into the Hairpin got the adrenalin pumping and will remain in my memory for ever! I decided to give this event a miss and sent John Blanchard along with Wally to compete in the 350cc and 500cc solo races.

The pressure was on to conclude arrangements with Associated Motorcycles regarding the takeover of their racing department. Funds needed to be found and room made for all the jigs, fixtures and existing stock. It was an exciting time, and encouraged by the success of the first of the Seeley racing bikes, I could not wait to get going on the next stage.

In my absence JB performed well at Snetterton, third in the 350cc race, a fourth in the 500cc event, won by John 'Mooneyes' Cooper, Norton, who wrapped up both 350 and 500 British Championships that day.

Agostini with Dunlop Tyre boss, Derek Carpenter, Brands Hatch.

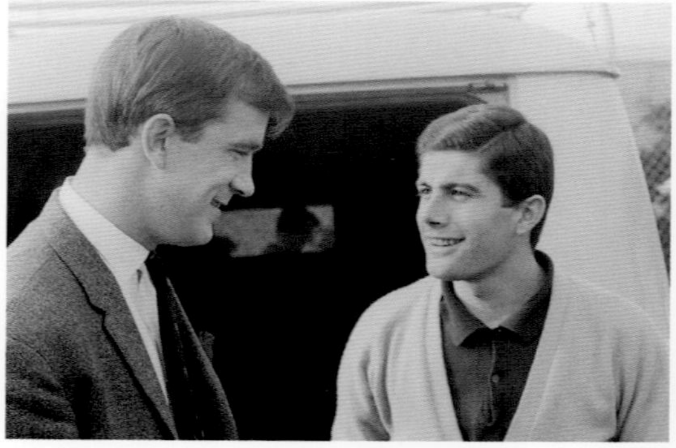

The very last event of the year (21 meetings that season), was the Mallory Park National. An Indian Summer, and no highly-paid works riders or factory machines to spoil the fun, no titles at stake, it was one of Mallory's best days racing in 1966.

As expected, local hero Mooneyes the new champion, was in the thick of things in the big classes, although finishing second in the 350cc race to desperate Dan Shorey. Cooperman hit back, winning the 500cc race after a tremendous duel with another fast improving competitor, Londoner crazy Croxford, who fell at the last hairpin hurdle, and in this hectic race no fewer than four riders shared the fastest lap; Cooper, Croxford, Chandler and Gould. So this 20 mile blast around Mallory Park finished with Cooper taking the gold from Chandler, Gould, Shorey, Degens and Blanchard sixth in that order.

With the first seven to the final from two heats in the up to 1200cc sidecar event, we would have our work cut out again racing the 500cc BMW. Only three of us out of the 36 sidecar competitors were racing 500cc machines. Nevertheless we won our heat by a second from Vinicombe, then in the 8 lap final, my BMW was slow to fire up. Perhaps Roy was not pushing enough. Owen Greenwood with his Mini Special eliminator forced through from the back of the grid and rammed the rear of our outfit. It was a light blow fortunately, but enough to put the Mini Special out of action with a jammed throttle. Despite our bad start we came through the field to finish in a creditable fourth place, just failing to catch Terry Vinicombe on the 654cc BSA outfit.

John Cooper, Dave Croxford and Ron Chandler were all destined to ride Seeley machines and bring further success to themselves and our product. The man who had just beaten me to a further rostrum position, Terry Vinicombe would join Colin Seeley Racing Developments as a constructor and welder in our frame department.

So, that was it, the curtain was down on the 1966 racing season, a frantic year. Aided by Wally and latterly Roy Lindsey, I was pleased with our racing achievements, five Grand Prix events including the Isle of Man TT, nine international and seven national meetings had resulted in 21 rostrum positions, six firsts, nine seconds, six thirds, three fourths, three fifths and a sixth place. We had done this with one outfit, no spare BMW engine or a supply of spares, and ended up third in the World Sidecar Championship, as well as best placed British sidecar driver. I felt proud to fly the Union Jack. On top of this, Seeley Racing Developments had had its first taste of success and was ready to move on.

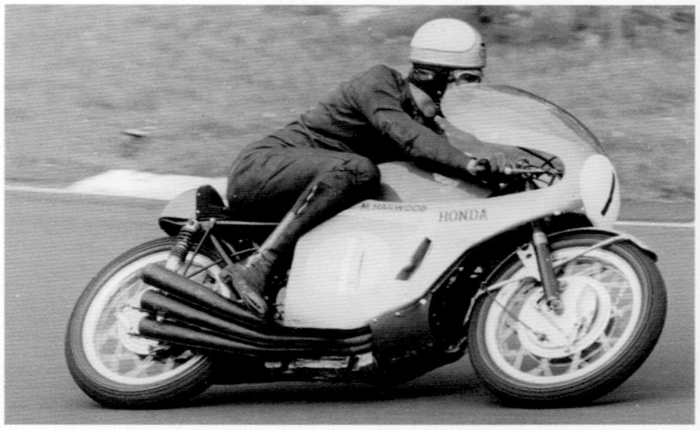

Hailwood on the Honda 250 six at Brands.

4—MOTOR CYCLING, NOVEMBER 5, 1966

SPORTS GOSSIP

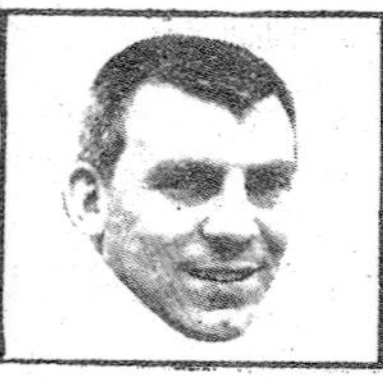

BY MICK WOOLLETT

SEELEY SAYS 'BAN MINI NOW'

COLIN SEELEY and many other top-line sidecar men want Owen Greenwood's Mini-Special to be banned from sidecar races. Said Colin at Mallory Park on Sunday: "I should like to see action taken now before the class becomes a complete shambles—now is the time for the A-CU to make a decision.

"Owen has had two good seasons with it, and this year he must have earned enough money to pay for it. Now the Mini with its four wheels and 1,071 cc four-cylinder engine is so superior to normal outfits that it simply clears off and leaves us.

"This means that competitors now coming into sidecar racing will be tempted to build themselves a similar machine — which would cost them a lot more than a normal outfit and would be dangerous to other competitors.

"This sport of ours is motorcycle racing. So let's keep it like that and insist that all outfits are powered by motorcycle engines. As it is, the Mini is a car — four wheels and all.

"Alternatively, if the A-CU and the organisers want the three-wheelers, let them start a separate three-wheeler class and let the sidecars get on with it on their own. But now is the time to decide, before more people start building them."

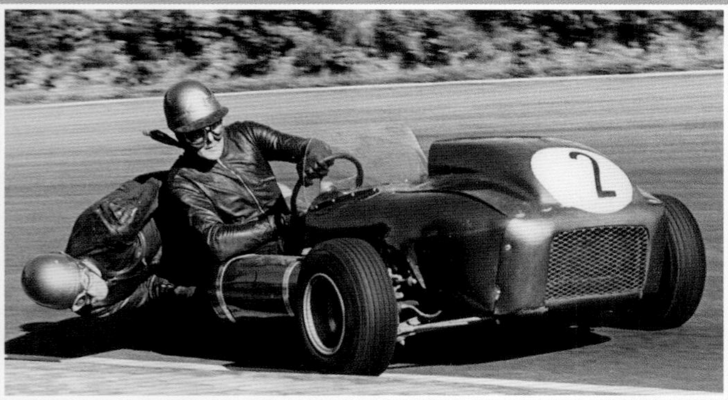

Brands Hatch 1966, Owen Greenwood and his Mini Special.

10 1967
WHAT A PERFORMANCE!

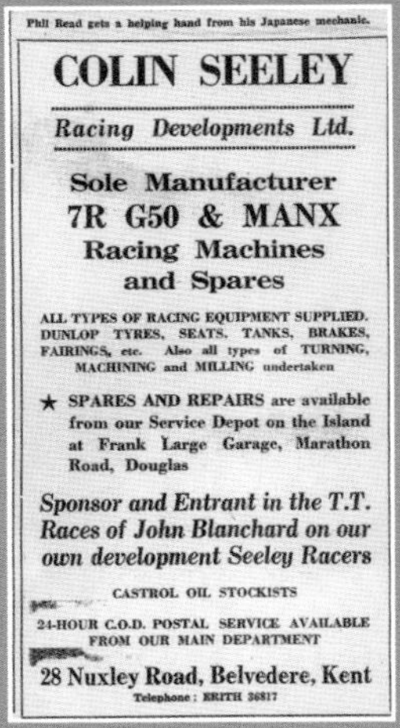

After all the discussions about the future production of Seeley Racing Motorcycles and the continuation of the illustrious line of race engine units, the 7R, G50 and Manx, it was time for the talking to stop and the serious work to start.

It was an immense task sorting out the mountain of parts, production jigs, the fixtures and hundreds of original blue print drawings. It was nearly Christmas and this was like the biggest present ever.

As AJS 7R and Matchless G50 racers had been out of production for three years and Manx Nortons for even longer, it proved a huge undertaking to persuade the many suppliers of components, raw castings, forgings, valves, pistons, magnetos, carburettors and so many other associated parts to re-start production or continue to supply, particularly since many of these companies were owed money by Associated Motorcycles Ltd.

I lost count of the number of trips I made to the Midlands where most of the suppliers were based. I would make my first call at 9.00am sharp carrying out as many other visits throughout the day as was possible. Although driving our Thames van, I made sure that I was always, 'booted and suited', smartly dressed in a suit and tie with shoes shining. I needed to entice these firms to trade with us as a new racing company. It was 'Mission Impossible', such a critical and intensive period, absolutely crucial to our plans and the future of UK motorcycle racing. Fortunately the Birmingham 'boys' came good and took a liking to the man from Kent and his enthusiasm.

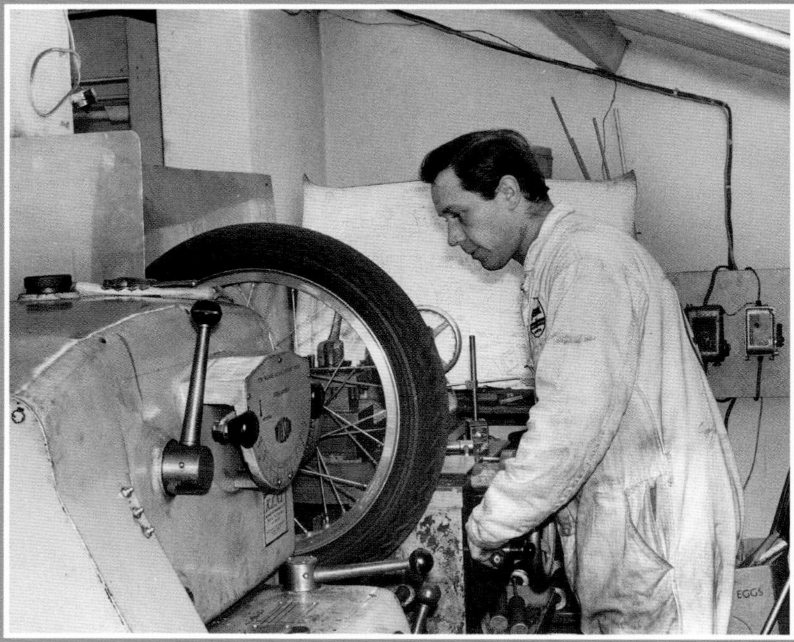

Eddie Robinson, wheel and brake specialist at work on a Wilson lathe.

Back in July I had taken on my first full time employee to work in our machine shop, alongside self employed Eddie Robinson. A local Vincent enthusiast Len Smith came to work on a big Harrison Centre Lathe (our first major piece of equipment) which would prove to be a shrewd move. As we expanded our production facility, Len who had joined our company as the highest paid at £24 10s per week (yours truly drawing just £18 per week) justified his position and as foreman became the corner-stone of our machine shop, with total loyalty and excellent engineering skills.

Prior to the establishment of CSRD Ltd we had promoted racing and sports equipment sales by mail order and a cash on delivery service. Alongside the G50 rebuilding service and spares a selection of the sundries and their prices makes interesting reading:

KLG spark plugs	£ 0 15s 0d (75p)
Lodge spark plugs	£ 0 10s 6d (55p)
Magnetic rev counters	£10 10s
AMAL racing alloy control levers	£ 1 6s 3d
Castrol R – Grade 40	£ 1 9s 0d per gallon.
Grade 20 or 30	£ 2 6s 6d per gallon.
Octopus Italian racing goggles	£ 4 9s 6d (my personal choice)
Dunlop 3.50 x 19 inch racing tyres	£ 7 17s 6d rear.
Inner tube.	£ 1 0s 6d

Colin Seeley racing gloves and a range of fibre glass products from Dick Jupps F1-Glass Company were some of the racing items offered.

As I was pleased with his performance, terms were agreed with 23 year old John Blanchard to continue as our works rider for 1967. With Roy Lindsey in the chair I planned another full season of national, international and Grand Prix, racing my Rennsport BMW outfit. As the best placed British rider in the 1966 World Championship, I still felt that I had a chance to win the title, not won by a British sidecar competitor since Eric Oliver in 1953. With the Veedol Oil contract coming to an end, we agreed with competitions boss Malcolm Edgar to renew our association with the Castrol Oil Company for 1967.

As Christmas approached it was my son's third birthday and it would be great to have a few days at home with 'young' Colin and Joan before embarking on the next part of our ambitious production and racing programme. As I write I now realise how crazy I was to believe we could achieve so much - something would have to give, and it did!!

New Year 1967 and Dr. Christian Barnard performed the first heart transplant. The Beatles released their Sergeant Pepper album, and only two days after my 31st birthday on January 4th, Britain's speed hero Donald Campbell attempted to be the first man to speed across water at 300mph.

His father Sir Malcolm Campbell, a First World War fighter pilot and celebrated 'speedster' was the first man to reach 300mph on land. One day enthralled in reading a fairy story to young Donald relating to 'Bluebird happenings' within days repainted his record breaking machine in blue then smart in the new livery renamed 'Bluebird' a legendary name that would go down in history. After all the dangers he had faced in his life, Sir Malcolm Campbell, at 63, died in his sleep in 1949. Donald who worshipped his father but lived in his shadow, vowed to keep the Campbell speed dynasty alive. Easier said than done at 23 years of age.

After various attempts Donald was awarded a CBE (Commander of the British Empire) for his first world record on water with Bluebird in 1955 and again in 1956. Then in 1960 he crashed at Utah, in America at 360mph pursuing a new land speed record. Four years later Donald Campbell CBE achieved his greatest success having recorded a remarkable 276mph on water. That same year, with his jet powered 'Bluebird' he raced across the Australian Lake Eyre Flats at a record 400mph. Campbell a most passionate man who believed that Britain was the greatest, was then at the height of his career, wining and dining everywhere, and determined to pursue his ambition of being the first man at 300mph on water.

The pre-war record breaking attempts of Sir Malcolm attracted considerable trade support in developing the tyre, oil and engine components. Donald continued to attract this support until 1964. After this time record-breaking was going out of fashion and sponsors were losing interest. Donald Campbell, committed to a record attempt felt there was no going back and with rising debts, had little choice but to go on.

Nine weeks had been spent at Lake Coniston - where chief mechanic 67 year old Leo Villa (who had also served Sir Malcolm) was often frozen to the bone as endless mechanical problems arose. A more powerful Orpheus jet engine was fitted, providing a further 1,000 lbs of thrust. With time running out fast Donald and his team, including friend and newspaper journalist Keith Harrison, just waited for the best weather conditions.

The evening before the chosen day, January 4th at Piers Cottage, Campbell played cards with Keith Harrison. Donald turned over the Ace then Queen of Spades saying, 'Somebody is for the chop, hope it's not me!' These cards were drawn by Mary Queen of Scots the night before she was beheaded.

Donald, a superstitious man, would not sleep easy that night. At the lake it was decided around 7.30am that it was a 'goer' and Bluebird was launched down the ramp,

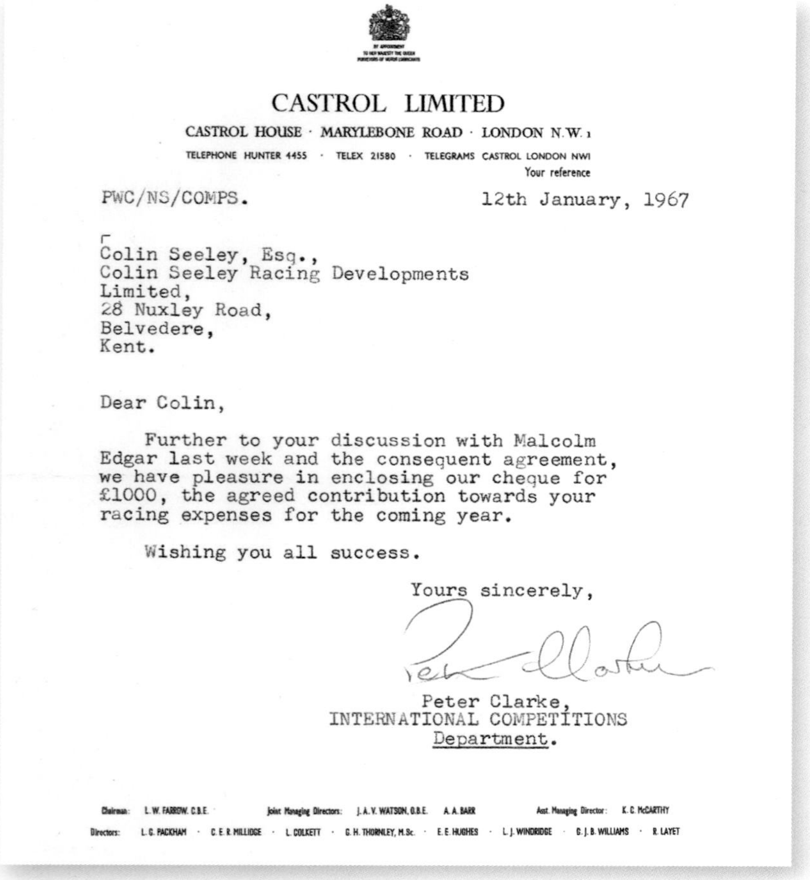
BY APPOINTMENT TO HER MAJESTY THE QUEEN PURVEYORS OF MOTOR LUBRICANTS

CASTROL LIMITED

CASTROL HOUSE · MARYLEBONE ROAD · LONDON N.W.1

TELEPHONE HUNTER 4455 · TELEX 21580 · TELEGRAMS CASTROL LONDON NW1

Your reference

PWC/NS/COMPS. 12th January, 1967

Colin Seeley, Esq.,
Colin Seeley Racing Developments
Limited,
28 Nuxley Road,
Belvedere,
Kent.

Dear Colin,

Further to your discussion with Malcolm Edgar last week and the consequent agreement, we have pleasure in enclosing our cheque for £1000, the agreed contribution towards your racing expenses for the coming year.

Wishing you all success.

Yours sincerely,

Peter Clarke

Peter Clarke,
INTERNATIONAL COMPETITIONS
Department.

Chairman: L. W. FARROW, C.B.E. Joint Managing Directors: J. A. V. WATSON, O.B.E. A. A. BARR Asst. Managing Director: K. C. McCARTHY
Directors: L. G. PACKHAM · C. E. R. MILLIDGE · L. COLKETT · G. H. THORNLEY, M.Sc. · E. E. HUGHES · L. J. WINDRIDGE · G. J. B. WILLIAMS · R. LAYET

looking like a jet plane without wings. Under the record attempt rules, two runs were required through a measured timed distance and the average speed taken. Finally, Campbell, who could not afford any further delays, fired up the jet engine, as friends, spectators and the press watched and waited. At 8.45am down the 5.25 mile long, half mile wide Coniston Lake the first run took place from the north end. Within 6 seconds Bluebird went from 30mph to 200mph and in another 5 seconds was out of sight, passing through the other side of the Swiss Longines timing markers set at a basic 250mph having reached a staggering 320mph. Even with its powerful water brake it took 2 miles to slow down. The official one way speed was 297mph, so only 6mph extra required on the return run and the record would be Campbell's.

Hardly time it seemed to wait for the lake's wash to subside and with no need to refuel, Donald Campbell headed for the return run, pushing Bluebird to the limit, through the first timing marker at 318mph. The record was his if he could keep it together, but despite carrying his lucky mascot (Teddy) 'Mr Whoppit' with only something like 150 yards, or a second in time to the end of the timed kilometre, he was to confirm his fatalistic obsession that he would die with his boots on, as Bluebird started to pitch from side to side and Campbell's voice came over the radio, 'I've got a bloody row in here… I can't see anything… I've got the bows up… I've gone!'

Bluebird's nose lifted and the wind pressure somersaulted the boat high into the air. It plunged to the bottom of the Lake, killing the 45 year old speed ace instantly. As the water settled, silence fell over Coniston. Donald Campbell CBE was posthumously awarded The Queens Commendation for brave conduct. The Campbell 'speed' dynasty had ended! Was it worth it? Was it necessary? Does it prove anything? These are always the questions asked after such a tragedy.

For the courageous Donald Campbell it was worthwile, a man who would push out the boundaries, knew great fear and conquered it. Other men climb mountains, sail alone around the world, ride in the IOM TT races and even orbit the globe. The human endeavour, courage and quest for speed is so often inconceivable.

Through our friendship with Florian Camathias we had met Helmut Fath, the 1960 world motorcycle sidecar champion. Following his crash in 1961 when his passenger

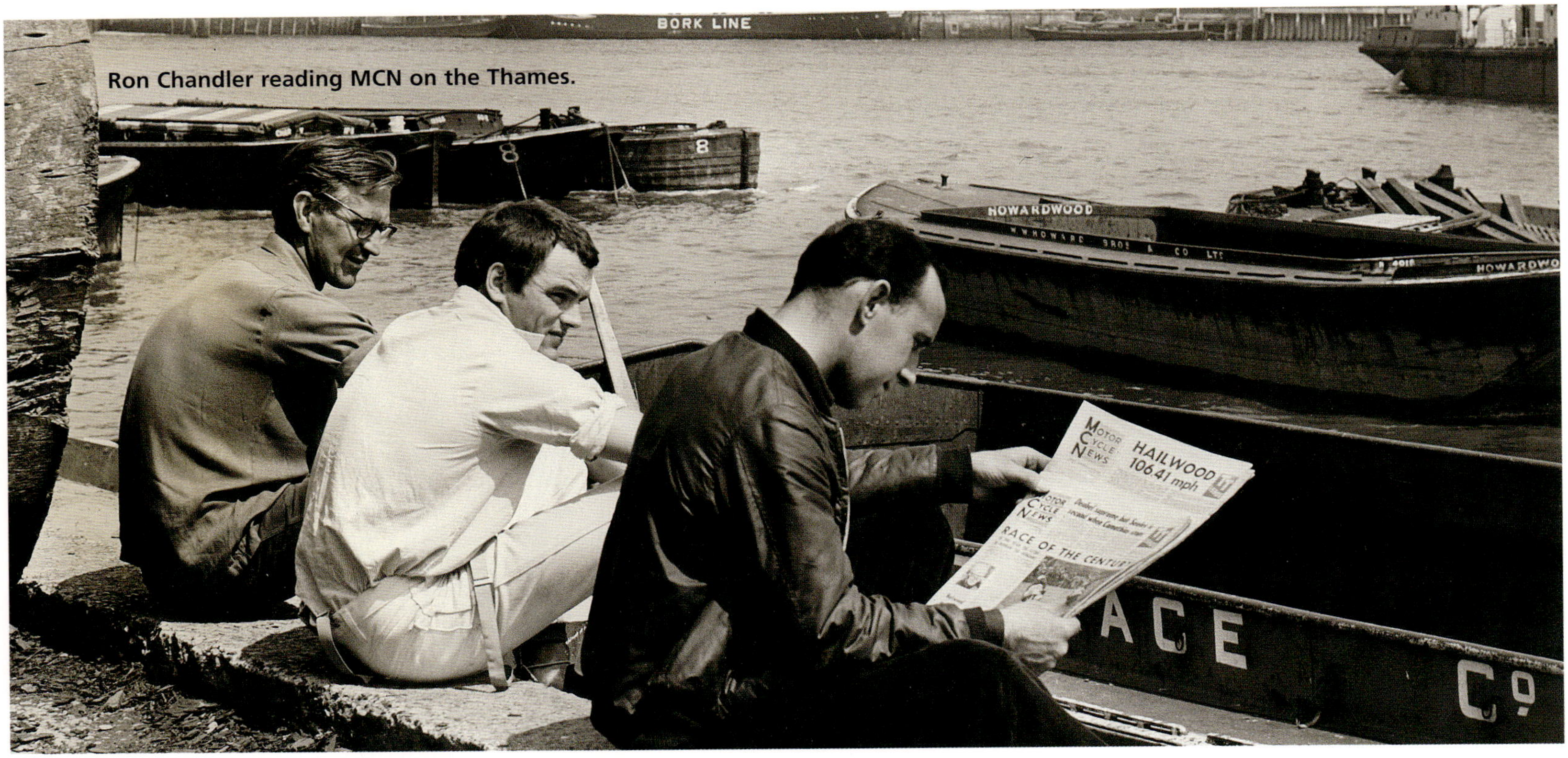

Ron Chandler reading MCN on the Thames.

Wohlgemuth was killed, Helmut was seriously injured and spent a year in hospital and was not fit to race for another five years. As a precision engineer, and with the assistance of university lecturer Dr. Peter Kuhn, Fath designed, developed and built the double overhead camshaft four cylinder engine, named the URS after Ursenbach, his village near Heidleberg. To raise funds for his project, Helmut continued to rebuild and tune BMW Rennsport engines, in particular for Camathias. Although Fath himself returned to racing in 1966. The URS engine was plagued by teething troubles and the solo machine, ridden by Paul Smetana, needed improvement, particularly in the chassis department. We were approached to consider making a new solo frame for this impressive multi-faceted engine. Blanchard, a fluent German speaker, was requested to test the existing machine in early January in secret at the Hockenheim circuit. The URS engine had been considerably improved with the addition of fuel injection. British electronics expert Jack Cooper, brother of sprinter and Triumph specialist Fred Cooper was in the process of manufacturing an energy transfer system for the 15,000rpm URS four, with a safety margin set at 20,000rpm. Fath was pleased by Blanchard's lap times but a broken valve brought the test to an end. JB was impressed, saying it was the most exciting machine he had ever ridden, but sensed some resentment from Smetana, the usual rider of the URS prototype. Smetana, from the same village as Fath, wasn't pleased when JB came along, lapped faster, then blew a precious engine!

Horst Owesle, engineer and Fath's right hand man, was also hoping to race a URS sidecar outfit in German non-championship events, which added to the tensions of that small team with such limited resources. The intense Helmut Fath had other ideas, figuring that a solo machine capable of matching the works MVs would attract the necessary financial support. Early in 1967 I was interested in helping Fath, as it was hinted that I might have a URS four cylinder engine unit at a later date for my continued challenge for a world sidecar championship title.

With Blanchard in Germany, I visited Michael Schafleitner in Austria with my Swiss friend Ernst Weiss to collect as the UK importer the first batch of those splendid five and six speed gear clusters which were expensive, but simply the best!

After breaking his association with sponsor Tom Kirby mid 1964, Ron Chandler continued on his own until 1966 when Tom's brother, Reg stepped in. With little love lost between the brothers it was a chance to prove a point for Reg!

Meantime, we became friends with Chandler, a regular top flight racing stalwart, and another man of Kent! Ron, as a close friend of the late Norman Huntingford, was aware of the support we had given, and decided he would give us the business of preparing his Matchless G50 and AJS 7R engines for 1967. Sponsorship from Reg Kirby Motorcycles based in Stanford-le-Hope, Essex would continue. With AMC factory engine builder Arthur Childs joining Wally Rawlings in our engine build section, the agreement with Chandler gave a great boost to our business.

27 year old Ron, a Thames lighterman (who's job was to steer huge barges up and down the river gateway to London), steered his Matchless G50 to victory in the 500cc event in the first meeting of the year at Mallory Park, on 5th March. Unusually for that time of year, gloriously sunny weather attracted 15,000 spectators who would witness the most dramatic race of the day, the 500cc final. 56 riders lined up for the two heats, plus six reserves including Barnett and Croxford, with the first twelve from each heat going forward to the final. Minter and Chandler won their heats. The final would be no push over with Degens, Gould, Hartle, Jenkins, Williams, Butcher, Shorey, Blanchard, Dunphy, Cooper and many more talented names in contention for the title. The 15 lap race proved a tremendous battle with Chandler, Cooper, Degens and Gould nose to tail at the start of the last lap. First Degens, Kirby Metisse, crashed at Gerards bringing down Gould, both escaping with a 90mph shaking. Down into the Esses, 'Mooneyes' Cooper, Norton, and Chandler, Matchless, were side by side but the lighterman held his nerve as Cooperman fell off. Ron went on to win the £30 first prize with an up and coming Alan Barnett, Matchless, second and Minter, Norton, third.

For the official Colin Seeley Racing Developments Team of ourselves and Blanchard it was not such a good day. We had problems with both solo machines, and in the 1000cc class final of the sidecar race we were shunted by Owen Greenwood in his Mini Special. I lodged a protest for the first time ever in the UK, alleging dangerous driving by Greenwood, making the point that the exposed front wheels of the Mini Special were dangerous and a serious accident could be caused. Once more, the ACU jury waffled and the protest was thrown out, but I had made my point!!

The following weekend was a first visit to Snetterton that season for the East Anglian Cup races – so many different titles in those days. Snetterton Circuit, a favourite, would be a disappointment that day. In pushing to start the BMW, a stone flicked up into the

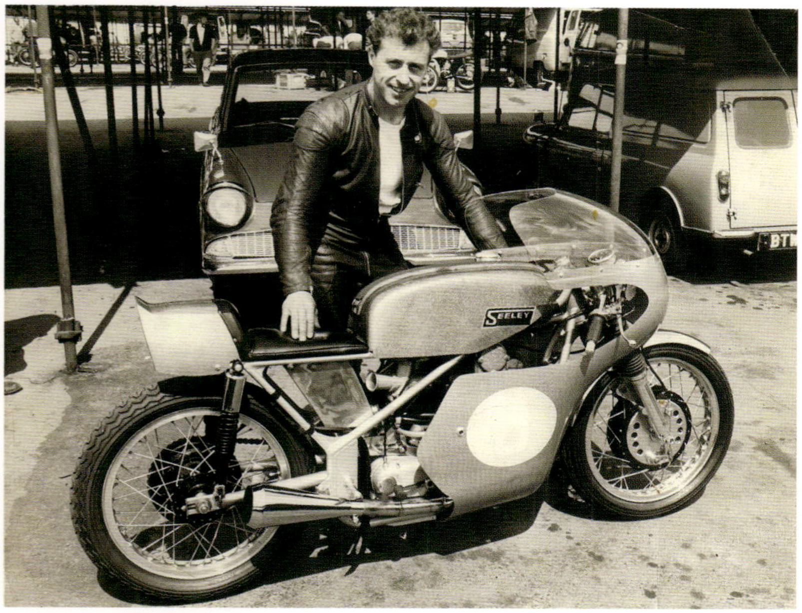

Testing the prototype Mark 2 Seeley AJS 7R, at Brands Hatch.

the 500cc race but as a start money special, having to pull in after a couple of laps. As we sat in his caravan that evening, after the day's racing Ron suddenly became ill, lost the sight in one eye and blacked out. John Blanchard, our German-speaking rider was found to assist. In hospital Ron was found to have concussion and a hairline crack in his skull. After treatment and rest he left hospital to recuperate at Helmut Fath's home for a couple of days before I arranged to fly him home, leaving Wally to drive his van and race bikes back to the UK. All part of our customer service!

A meeting best forgotten, other than Fath's superb efforts which plainly heralded the impending end of BMW's long domination in the sidecar racing class, which had amounted to fourteen consecutive world sidecar championships (1954-1967), twelve with German riders and two with Swiss ace, Fritz Scheidegger.

In the same inclusive period 1954-1967 the British boys hardly got a look in apart from Eric Oliver and Cyril Smith, Nortons, second and third in 1954, Pip Harris, Norton, third in 1956 and third again in 1960 on a BMW. Then amazingly, Wally and I got third in 1964 and 1966. BMW's domination would continue up to 1974 with Klaus Enders the most successful sidecar rider for BMW with a total of six world titles. Only interuped when the intense Helmet Fath took the crown from BMW in 1968 on the URS, beating Georg Auerbacher on the BMW. Then Fath's remarkable Ursenbach special ridden by Horst Owesle, partnered by Englishman Peter Rutherford put it across the works supported BMW of Seigfried Schauzu to win the 1971 world sidecar title, another slap in the face for BMW. Rolf Steinhausen's appearance in 1972 on the two-stroke Konig, would mark a decisive point in sidecar racing history. BMW's reign ended when Steinhausen took over the championship in 1975 and 1976.

In twenty-one seasons of sidecar racing BMW's commitment and support of such champions as Willhelm Noll, Willi Faust, Fritz Hillebrand, Walter Schneider, Helmut Fath, Max Deubel, Fritz Scheidegger and Klaus Enders won them nineteen World Sidecar Championships. My only criticism is that BMW weren't that helpful in the supply of replacement engine parts. As for buying an engine unit there was no chance for the likes of Pip Harris, ourselves and other British contenders who could have mounted a challenge to the German domination.

The start to our 1967 world sidecar championship challenge was very disappointing, caused by engine failures of our BMW. With the third round, the French Grand Prix nearly upon us and a serious lack of spares for our Rennsport engine, I said to Mick Woollett, 'If I can't get the bits and pieces needed to keep the BMW motor in top shape, I am flogging a dead horse, and it's no good pretending otherwise. A month ago I was dead keen to have another crack at winning the title, but I had to face two facts. First I would be a fool to neglect my business at a time of such demand for AMC spares. Second I haven't a hope in hell of taking the title with my present equipment!'

As part of our enterprising plans we announced that Colin Seeley Racing Developments (CSRD) would provide a continuation of the Isle of Man racing service for all 7R and G50 competitors following the tradition of the AJS and Matchless factory. This added to the frantic activity at Belvedere. John Blanchard would be competing in both Junior and Senior TT races and I would be attempting my seventh sidecar TT event.

Bill Wright was sorting out all the spares for the Isle of Man service and Wally was gathering the equipment required to provide a full engine rebuild facility for TT riders. Meanwhile, having pulled out of the French Grand Prix, I made a start on the Eddie Robinson pencilled URS frame.

A trend seemed to have started in the manufacturing of replacement frames. Following Ken Sprayson, Colin Lyster instigated his Italian-built lightweight Lyster frame to suit the mighty works 500cc Honda four, which with the original Honda frame was often unrideable. Honda racing was not impressed and the Lyster frame unit would not progress much further. Castrol Oils, celebrating their success with Honda at the German Grand Prix, were also delighted with 32 year old Sammy Miller, who with incredible skill on a 252cc Bultaco, won his fourth Scottish Six Days Trial. Was there no stopping this man!!

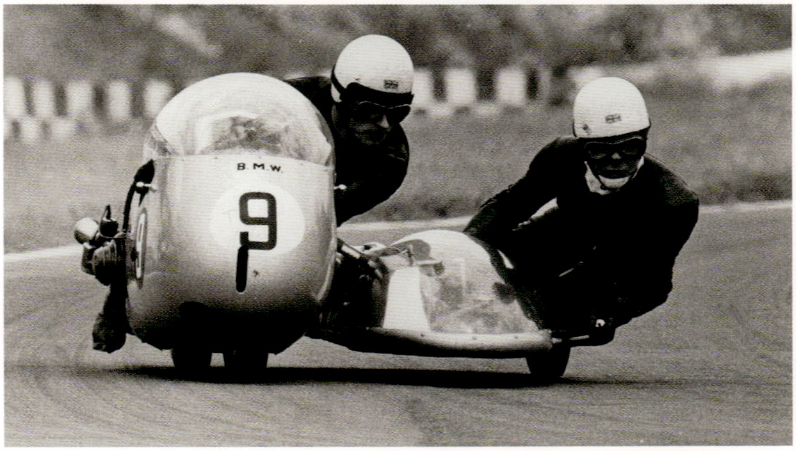

Brands Hatch May 29th, Roy Lindsey in the chair.

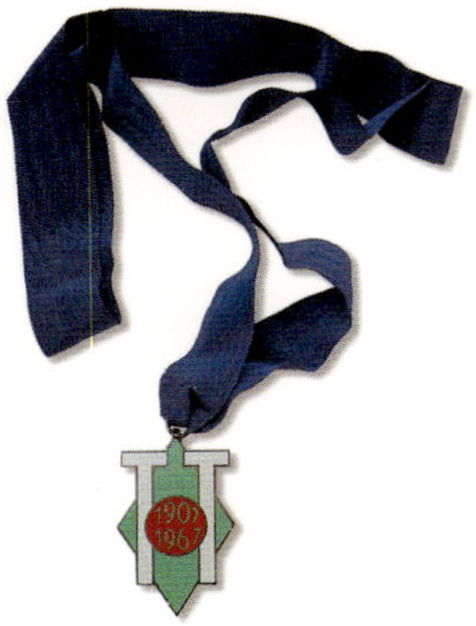

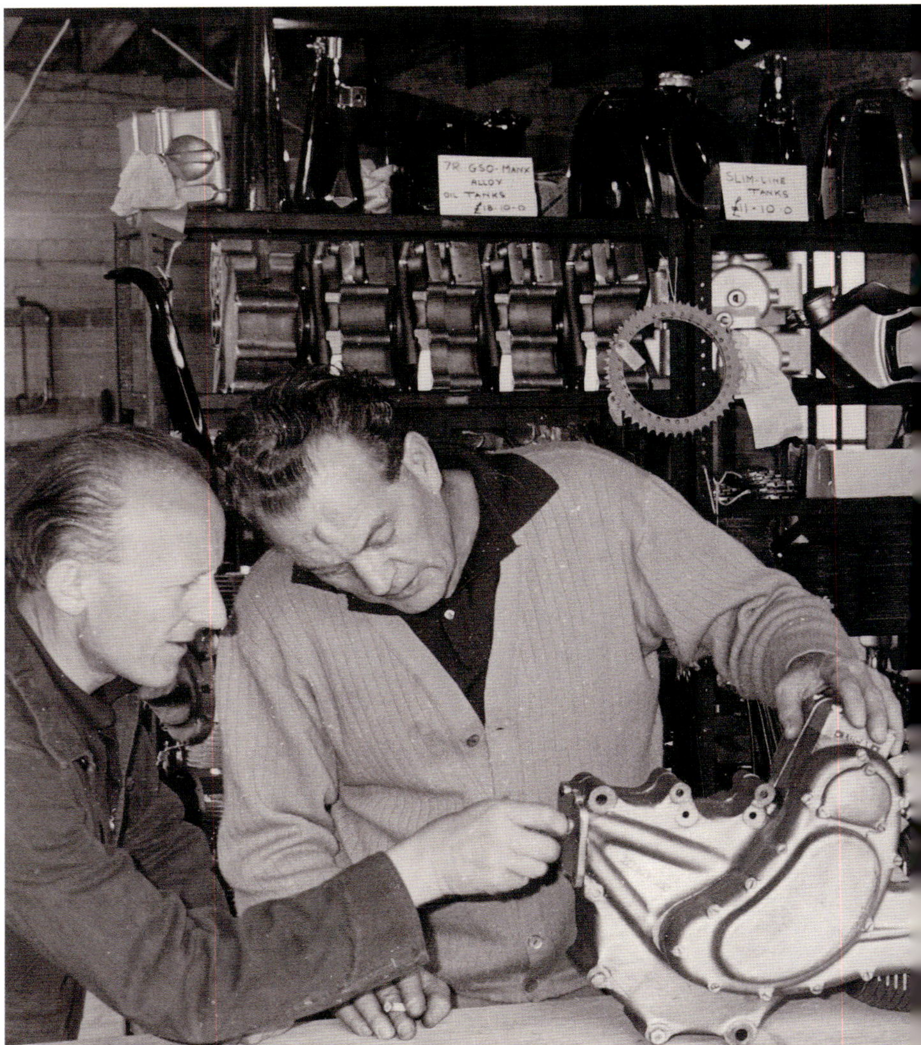

Isle of Man service department, left to right, Arthur Childs, Arthur Keeler, Bill Wright and myself.

The Isle of Man event was looming. It had attracted an excellent total entry of 573 competitors for the Diamond Jubilee TT, with a bewildering variety of machines from an incredible 39 manufacturers. Before the Magic Isle event and celebration, there was the little matter of the international North West 200 held in Northern Ireland on May 20th, over an 11 mile public road course starting at Port Stewart down to Coleraine, back to Portrush and then on to the finish back at Port Stewart. This was Ireland's second premier race meeting and was always well attended by enthusiastic fans from both sides of the border.

The event, organised by the Coleraine and DMC, found practice conditions atrocious and with no indications of race form. Race day gave little cause for cheer, with a high wind, inky clouds and chilly temperatures. However the hardy Irish fans turned up in their thousands, despite the FA cup final being that same day. Fred Stevens, riding the Hannah-Patons won both 350cc and 500cc races and in the Senior Race came within one second of smashing the late Bob McIntyre's absolute lap record of 106.86mph.

Despite a cloud burst as the competitors lined up for the 500cc event, the opening lap was a tremendous affair. Stevens was just ahead of a high speed wheel-to-wheel scrap between John Blanchard and Malcolm Uphill the popular Welshman and Rob Fitton, both on Nortons. Although all eyes were on Ian McGregor, riding the famous Joe Ryan Norton, his lap of 104.08mph bringing him from a slow start into fourth place before retiring on the sixth lap with a brake problem.

Our 'Paperhanger' JB revelled in this pure road race. Making up for his disappointment in the 350cc race when the primary chain broke on the Seeley AJS, he continued his tussle with Uphill, gaining a 24 second advantage then posting the second fastest lap of the race at 104.55mph to bring his Seeley-Matchless home into a brilliant second place in the 100 mile race, behind the ultra-quick Italian Paton twin of Fred Stevens. Malcolm Uphill came third followed by Peter Williams, Chris Conn and Ireland's Billy McCosh. Our team was in the money, as John had been paid £100 start shekels, then won £71 prize money plus a £10 bonus.

With the all important TT looming, the short circuit events still came in rapid succession, Mallory's International was Sunday 28th May, at which Ron Chandler, still feeling the after-effects of his German Grand Prix crash, rode his AJS brilliantly to win his 350cc heat and the 15 lap final from a challenging Pat Mahoney on a Kirby-Metisse, then it was Paul Smart and John Cooper, all very close.

The 500cc final provided a fitting climax to a wonderful day's racing, when the 'Paperhanger' JB on the Seeley-Matchless, fresh from his success in the North West '200' roared away from the start and held the lead for six tough laps until Peter Williams forced by on lap 10 of the 15 lap race. But Williams had eight frantic riders on his tail. 'Mooneyes' Cooper got his nose ahead for the start of the last, lap but Williams outpaced 'Cooperman' round the long sweeping Gerards bend to win. Percy Tait was third, just ahead of JB, followed by Rodney Gould and Joe Dunphy. Ron Chandler had to retire with front fork problems. Peter Williams on the Arter Matchless who won both the 500 and 750cc races at Mallory, took home the Winston Cup for setting the fastest lap of the day.

I had given Mallory Park a miss to prepare for the Brands Hatch International the next day, as well as preparing for our TT expedition. On the same day as Mallory Park, down at the 2 mile seaside Ospedaletti Circuit at San Remo Italy, my racing company might

TT service department with the prototype Mark 2 Seeley AJS 7R.

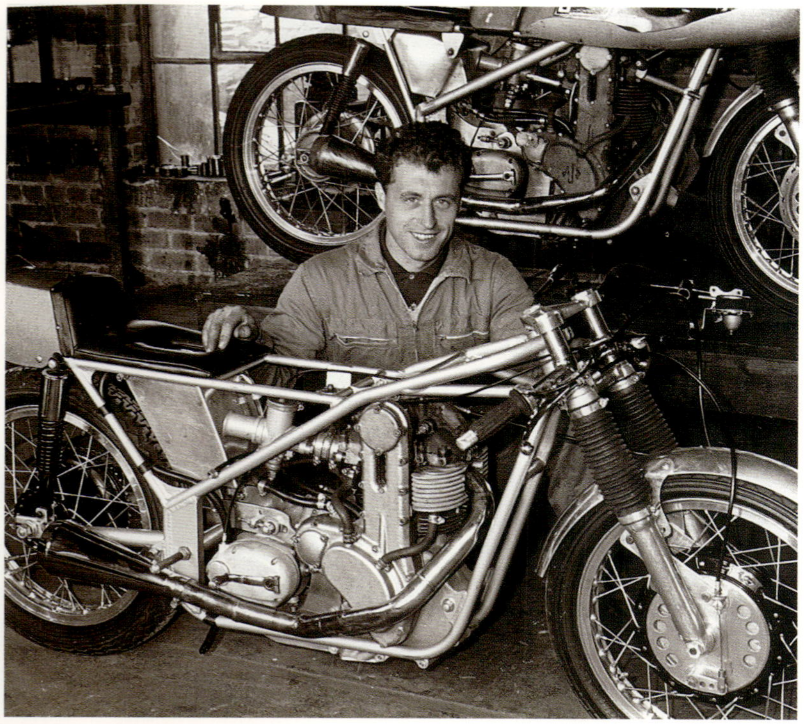

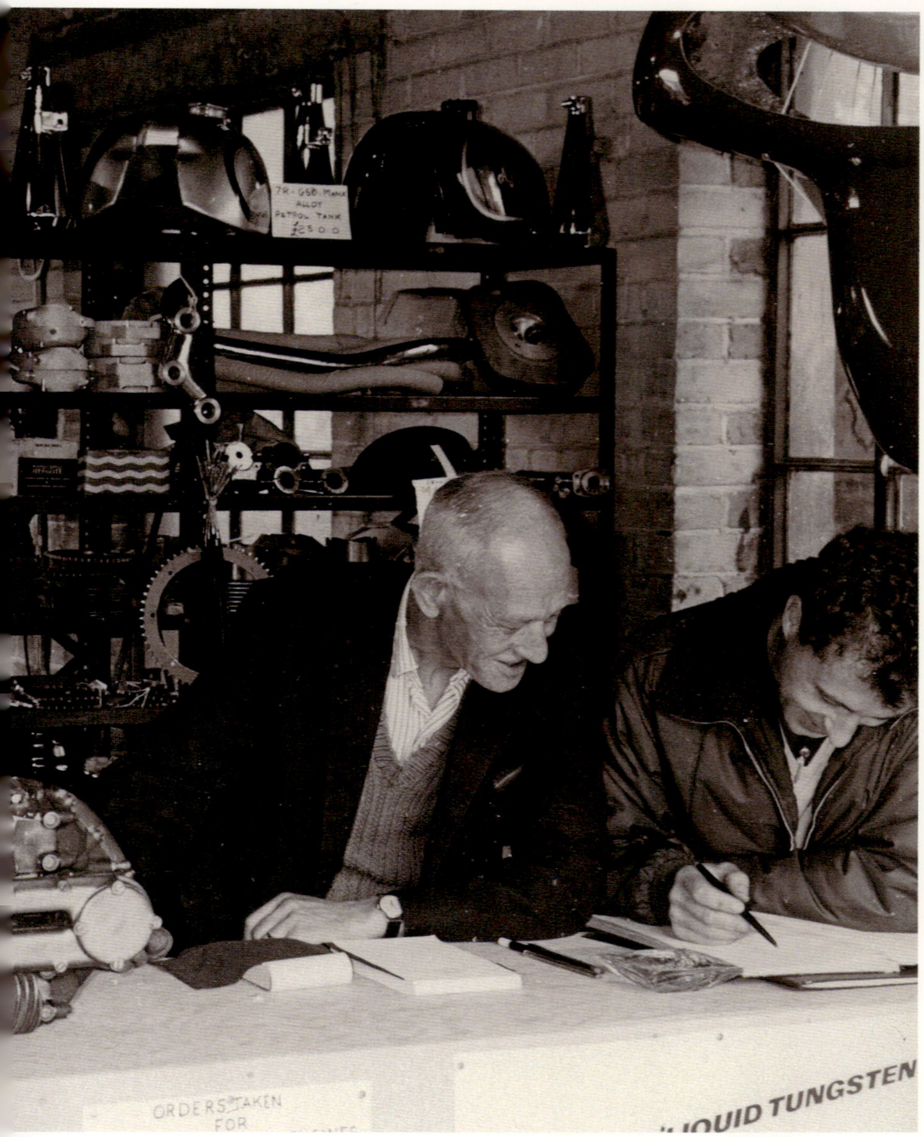

have enjoyed its first customer racing success but race leaders Paulo Campanelli, Seeley-Matchless, Jack Findlay, McIntyre Matchless, and Gyula Marsovszky, Matchless, all crashed in quick succession when a track marshall waved the wrong flag after a tank full of oil was spilt on a tricky section, causing havoc. Angelo Bergamonti, Paton, avoided the oil and won easily as the fallen trio remounted to finish with Campanelli finally fourth, such a shame!

The Brands event was run in fine sunny weather and attracted a crowd of around 25,000, probably to see their hero 'Mike the Bike' Hailwood in action before he, along with so many of the top British competitors, left immediately after for the Magic Isle and the TT.

Those were the days of the magnificent men on their flying machines. There were so many race meetings all over Europe and the UK and these riders dashed from one event to another, often overnight, doing thousands of miles of driving and still finding time to prepare their machines. Nowadays top level riders have at least two personal mechanics and 'loads of money', apart from many other advantages. The world champions of that period were not exactly cocooned! They were usually willing to take on any local aces and be counted! They were approachable and accessible and attracted thousands of followers (no Sky or Eurosport coverage in those days).

Back at Brands, the 10 lap 350cc race on the 2.65 mile Grand Prix circuit rewarded Tom Kirby's faith in Crayford's 21 year old Pat Mahoney. He won the event on the special short stroke, AJS, Kirby-Metisse from Paul Smart, Aermacchi, with Williams third on the, Arter-AJS, and Chandler sixth. Our man Blanchard, for the first time riding my prototype MK2 type Seeley chassis (to suit 350 or 500cc 7R/G50 engine units,) fell in the 350cc race. He did not like the machine, which was not a good start for the model I had thought about and built earlier that year. The idea was to reduce weight and produce a much neater machine. Fortunately the MK2 became one of the most popular chassis units in our range and was used by many. To this very day it is still copied and built to a high standard and with my approval by Roger Titchmarsh.

The 10 lap 500cc sidecar race, a poorly supported event, was a benefit for Helmut Fath and his four cylinder URS. Having bumped Pip Harris out of the lead, Fath went on to his first success with the URS and his first race victory since his serious accident in 1961. Pip Harris having been nudged by Fath tried to control his outfit and leaned heavily on the nearside carburettor, which eventually fell off, forcing his retirement. Roy Lindsey and I, being close to Pip, took second place but then again the dreaded gremlins bit, and for the third time we were stopped by a broken piston.

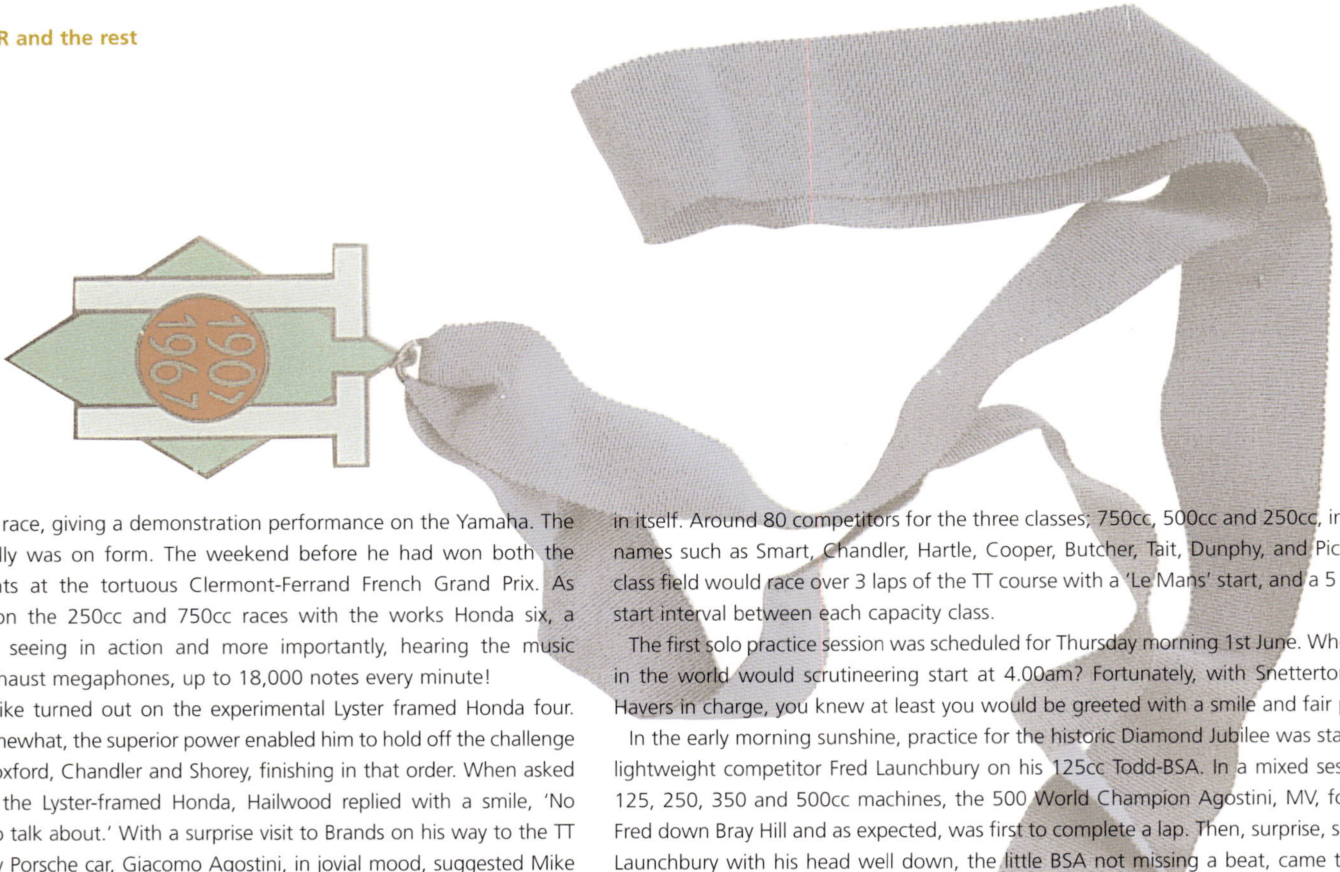

Bill Ivy won the 125cc race, giving a demonstration performance on the Yamaha. The 'Maidstone Marvel' really was on form. The weekend before he had won both the 125cc and 250cc events at the tortuous Clermont-Ferrand French Grand Prix. As expected, Hailwood won the 250cc and 750cc races with the works Honda six, a machine always worth seeing in action and more importantly, hearing the music chiming from the six exhaust megaphones, up to 18,000 notes every minute!

For the 500cc race Mike turned out on the experimental Lyster framed Honda four. Although it wobbled somewhat, the superior power enabled him to hold off the challenge of Williams, Cooper, Croxford, Chandler and Shorey, finishing in that order. When asked by Peter Arnold about the Lyster-framed Honda, Hailwood replied with a smile, 'No comment, it's too bad to talk about.' With a surprise visit to Brands on his way to the TT having collected his new Porsche car, Giacomo Agostini, in jovial mood, suggested Mike might like to sit out the Senior TT rather than ride the wobbly Lyster-Honda.

The enthusiastic crowd went home happy having enjoyed the smell of Castrol R and the roar of multi-cylinders. Helmut Fath and Wolfgang Kalauch came to stay with me in Belvedere that night before departing for the Isle of Man, where practice week had already started. Wally Rawlings and crew had left a couple of days before, loaded with equipment and spares along with our works Seeley-Matchless to be prepared for John Blanchard. The service department would be set up in the Frank Large Garage, Marathon Road adjacent to the Frank Large funeral premises, a bit macabre I must admit!

Our visit to the Isle of Man in 1967 would be most significant, both for my company (CSRD) and for myself, as I had made a decision that this would be my last sidecar TT. I would be retiring from sidecar racing soon afterwards. It had not been easy to convince myself. I loved my sidecar racing. Partnered by Wally Rawlings we had come from obscurity to one of Britain's best in the sport and I was very proud of our achievements. The turning point had been the obligatory Isle of Man TT medical check. I was told that my blood pressure was running at 100mph, well over the top! I would be in trouble if I did not slow down, so I made my resolution.

But first, there was some unfinished business. Could John Blanchard and myself, now partnered by Roy Lindsey, match our 1966 results? Would the Colin Seeley racing service be accepted and successful? We had much to prove, much to gain, but it being the Isle of Man TT, we also had much to lose – it was knife-edge stuff.

As usual, Wally and I were based at Beverley House, not wishing to upset our long standing host Ma Clucas, who provided light entertainment along with the 'gurgles' of Guinness. The rest of the crew, including Roy, stayed in Douglas. Helmut Fath, preferring somewhere quiet to work, shared the large garden shed in Strang, along with our BMW outfit, which I kept separately from the race service at the Frank Large garage.

The Isle of Man TT Diamond Jubilee 1907-1967 would be a special event, commemorating 60 years of illustrious action and so many great riders and characters… it's impossible to mention them all, over 2,000 gallant privateers and works riders have contributed to the excitement, drama, joy, frustrations and often heartbreak of the Tourist Trophy races.

The Diamond Jubilee saw the introduction of the first standard production machine race. Added to the itinerary at a rather late stage by the ACU, it would prove a winner in itself. Around 80 competitors for the three classes; 750cc, 500cc and 250cc, included names such as Smart, Chandler, Hartle, Cooper, Butcher, Tait, Dunphy, and Pickrell. A class field would race over 3 laps of the TT course with a 'Le Mans' start, and a 5 minute start interval between each capacity class.

The first solo practice session was scheduled for Thursday morning 1st June. Where else in the world would scrutineering start at 4.00am? Fortunately, with Snetterton's Bob Havers in charge, you knew at least you would be greeted with a smile and fair play.

In the early morning sunshine, practice for the historic Diamond Jubilee was started by lightweight competitor Fred Launchbury on his 125cc Todd-BSA. In a mixed session of 125, 250, 350 and 500cc machines, the 500 World Champion Agostini, MV, followed Fred down Bray Hill and as expected, was first to complete a lap. Then, surprise, surprise, Launchbury with his head well down, the little BSA not missing a beat, came through next and Fred completed a race distance of 3 laps. Only 29 riders went out for practice that morning. It seems many preferred to stay in bed. Shame, the early morning weather had been the loveliest locals could remember in 40 years of Manx Grand Prix and TT races. By the afternoon, riders out for practice had more than doubled, although many competitors still had not arrived. The session was headed once more by Agostini.

In the 500cc class our man JB was out for his first practice that year on the Seeley-Matchless, second quickest, at a respectable 96.48mph. Changing to his 350 MV Ago threw down a challenge to Hailwood after lapping at 101.33mph. The next morning, Friday, seven riders including Hailwood on the big Honda had set off before 5.00am but fog on The Mountain kept the speeds down and only 30 riders bothered to get out of bed. The evening practice was different, with 45 machines out for the 'tiddler' 50cc, 125 and 250 lightweight classes. Hailwood provided the fans with two fantastic laps on the Honda 250 six, both from standing starts, first at 104.27mph, then 105.12mph unofficially breaking the lap record. What a man!

For the riders and mechanics who made the effort to get up, Saturday's early start was a complete waste of time. High winds and heavy rain brought visibility down to 20 yards on the mountain section. Mike Hailwood walked into the scrutineering bay in 'civvies' looked up the rain-swept Glencrutchery Road and was not impressed. In fact nobody was. When ACU official Mary Driver announced practice cancelled, a cheer went up and the riders retired to the hospitality tent for a warm-up soup or coffee, courtesy of Nestlé.

With no action for two days, Monday June 5th was an early start to the serious business of preparing for the Diamond TT races. Itoh, Suzuki, headed the 50cc class, 'Little' Bill Ivy, Yamaha, the 125cc and Hailwood, Honda, the 250cc. The evening practice was the first viewing of the standard production machines with silencers, lights and horns. Norman Hanks, BSA A50, and former Manx Grand Prix winner Eddie Crooks, Suzuki T20, started this unique session. The big boys headed the list, former Junior TT winner John Hartle lapping in an impressive 94.76mph, Rex Butcher at 90.74mph and Ray Pickrell 88.26mph, all riding Triumph Bonnevilles. Paul Smart and Griff Jenkins, on Dunstall Dominators were fourth and sixth. Meriden sheep farmer, Triumph tester and all round good bloke, Percy Tait led the 500cc class on the Triumph T100 at 89.18mph. Percy at one stage was chasing Ron Chandler, Norton Atlas, to warn him of a broken oil pipe on the Norton from which serious trouble could arise - such chivalry in those days.

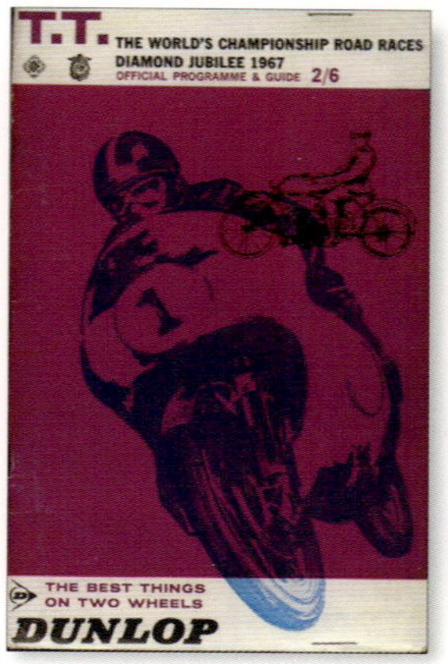

Tuesday morning was another early start for the scrutineers, Bob Havers overseeing 53 machines through inspection and onto the circuit by 5.00am. Although the session started dry, the unpredictable Isle of Man weather soon caused problems for the 140 Junior and Senior competitors on the course, the biggest turn out so far. Agostini, MV, led the Juniors and Hailwood, Honda, the Seniors. The weather proved little better for the Tuesday evening lightweight practice, with strong winds and driving rain. Conditions on the Douglas side of The Mountain were the worst Hailwood had ever known. Although there were several retirements there was only one casualty, the popular Jack Findlay crashing his 250cc Bultaco. His injuries put him out of action for about a month, depriving him of riding the immaculate Francis Beart Nortons. Despite conditions the 'Maidstone Marvel' Bill managed a lap of 98.52mph on the works 125cc Yamaha - just incredible - and for the fifth time in nine sessions 'Mike the Bike' headed a leader board, this time the 250cc class.

Wednesday's 7th June, sixth early morning practice was allocated to production machines. Although this event aroused interest, it was wondered if this class deserved another practice to itself. This was the tenth solo practice session and there hadn't been one yet for the record entry of sidecar competitors - a poor do in my opinion. Ex-Manx Grand Prix star Steve Spencer was on the leader board that morning putting his Triumph Bonneville ahead of John Hartle with Paul Smart up to third place with the Dunstall Dominator. Percy Tait was still top of the 500cc class and Frank Whiteway, Suzuki, leader of the 250cc machines.

The 745cc Atlas-Norton of Peter Inchley and Ron Chandler was not performing and would eventually be withdrawn. The stated reason was brake problems, but a misfire had plagued Inchley all week, eventually an electrical fault was diagnosed, but too late.

With four practice sessions already run for the Senior and Junior classes we were busy at our racing service, supplying spares, giving advice, repairing and servicing 7R and G50 engines, as well as keeping our own bikes in order. John Blanchard loved his road racing and saw the TT as the ultimate event. He had his eye on achieving the magic 100mph lap, which was certainly a possibility. All was not well however, as unfortunately, Blanchard was not too happy with the new prototype MK2 350cc Seeley and as practice week went on, our relationship deteriorated. John was spending too much time helping Helmut Fath and practising his German, which didn't help. I was under immense pressure and still had a TT sidecar race to contend with.

Finally, the eleventh practice period of the week was the turn of the charioteers and not before time, an evening practice, totally allocated to the 76 sidecar competitors. I loved the evening session, it was more enjoyable than the actual race. Roy Lindsey and I put ourselves to the test and blew away some of the frustrations of the week. Keen to get out on the magic circuit on our Rennsport BMW, we were first to charge down Bray Hill followed by Georg Auebacher and Terry Vinicombe. It was great to speed out to Union Mills. Where our fans, the 'Strang Gang' were to give us a wave. The long stroke BMW with new pistons was singing along at its maximum 9,000 revs as we dropped down past the Highlander pub. Happy with our progress we completed a 3 lap race distance, second fastest at 88.30mph, just 6 seconds down on an old adversary, Auerbacher, lapping at 88.66mph. As we approached the end of nine days of practice, the whole island was heaving. At the Grandstand start area it was 'open all hours'. Thursday afternoon, 8th June was to be the busiest so far, with the whole island seeming to shut down and the Islanders joining the visitors. Over 280 competitors turned out for the practice sessions covering all solo classes apart from the 50cc 'tiddlers' and production racers. The sidecar contingent added to extensive queues waiting for Bob Havers and his merry men of scrutineers to wade through the inspections.

'Mike the Bike' in the Senior practice, keen to show who was master, recorded the fastest time on the big 500 Honda four at 102.85mph. Ago was second at 100.24mph. An impressive effort by John Hartle on a Matchless-Metisse, lapping at 98.43mph, proved he was getting back on form. Hailwood on his favourite machine, the Honda six, an overbored version at 297cc, in the Junior practice unofficially broke the lap record at 103.24mph, 2 seconds faster than Agostini's record in 1966. Phil Read that afternoon headed the 250cc class and Katayama the 125cc practice. For the second time that week, the sidecar brigade went into action, Siegfried Schauzu the works supported BMW rider seventh in the 1966 Isle of Man TT, beat us to the post in this session, with Terry Vinicombe Kirby-BSA third. Chris Vincent retired at Ballaugh. Pip Harris was in some sort of trouble and Helmut Fath, winner in 1960, wasn't happy. The course was too bumpy for his outfit and bits were falling off. Over many years discussion had taken place about speeds over various sections of the course, but for this year The Examiner, TT Special newspaper thought they would try something different. Riders entering Parliament Square, Ramsay were timed to Governors Bridge, $13\frac{1}{2}$ miles away and covering The Mountain section. The 8 miles from Ramsey to the highest point on the course, the marshal's box at Brandywell, was also timed. This interesting exercise was carried out in the glorious conditions of that Thursday afternoon practice.

Georg Auerbacher headed the sidecars Ramsey-Brandywell with a time of 5 minutes 45 seconds. Enders was second at 5 minutes 48 seconds. We were third at 5 minutes 53 seconds and Schauzu fourth at 5 minutes 59 seconds, only four of us under 6 minutes. Then Auerbacher fell back with problems from Brandywell to Governors Bridge, leaving Schauzu quickest at 3 minutes 41seconds, Enders 3 minutes 49 seconds, and ourselves 3 minutes 56 seconds. Fastest total time from Ramsey to Governors was Klaus Enders at 9 minutes 37 seconds, Schauzu 9 minutes 40 seconds, then us at 9 minutes 49 seconds. Otto Kolle came fourth at 10 minutes 32 seconds.

Hailwood on the 500 Honda recorded 8 minutes 44 seconds for the $13\frac{1}{2}$ mile mountain section; Renzo Pasolini on the 350cc Benelli four 8 minutes 41seconds, Heinz Rosner 250 MZ 8 minutes 56 seconds and Yoshimi Katayama 125cc Suzuki 8 minutes 58 seconds. These were the fastest solo riders that afternoon, all very interesting!!

With another early mixed session next morning I gave the sidecars a miss to be there for John Blanchard, who put in a sterling performance at 98.29mph to put himself and the Seeley-Matchless into fourth fastest that morning, so back to the soup tent to celebrate. Meanwhile, the Italian star Agostini, not to be outdone by our hero Mike, recorded a shattering lap at 106.28mph on the works' 500cc MV. Hailwood, in an Italian sandwich, came second at 104.56mph, with Renzo Pasolini, Benelli, third, well down at 98.41mph.

Germany's talented ex-solo rising sidecar star Klaus Enders, problems all sorted, leapt to the top of qualifying at 89.54mph leaving his countrymen Auerbacher, Fath,

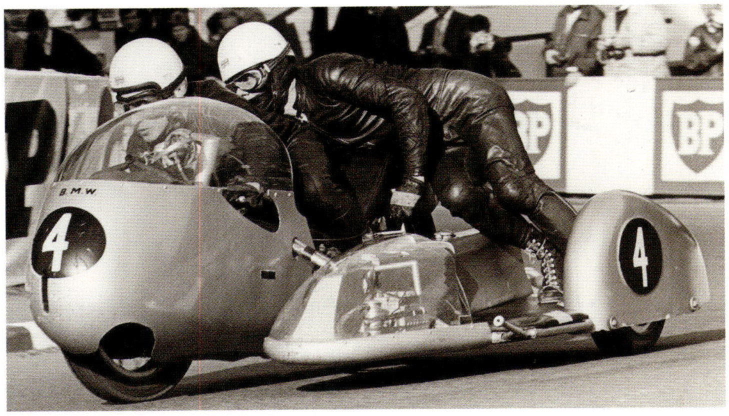

Isle of Man practice, Quarter Bridge.

Schauzu, Wolhfahrt and newcomer Attenberger in his wake. Friday evening was another solos only session for 125cc, 250, 350, 500 and production. The star that night, 'without the headlamps on' John Hartle, hurtled his Triumph-Bonneville around the TT course at a smart 96.30mph, nearly 2.5 seconds ahead of the other Smart, Paul who pushed the Dunstall-Dominator to a very creditable 96.15mph. Steve Spencer, Triumph Bonneville, came third at 94.50mph, all very impressive for production motorcycles.

The sixteenth and last practice qualifying session in a very busy 10 days was another dreaded early morning event. Getting up at 3.00am was not fun, but absolutely necessary to be at the start in time. I had completed two sidecar practice sessions so far, only 5 laps in total. I decided therefore to refresh our memories ready for the big day and my seventh Isle of Man sidecar TT event, Monday the 12th June. On this final practice session Georg Auerbacher clocked a very impressive 90.34mph outdoing Enders by 16.6 second., That may not sound much, but in 3 laps it amounts to almost a minute! Roy Lindsey had adjusted well to my style of riding, and I had settled for a slower 85.20mph lap, but still held third place that morning from Barry Dungworth, Pip Harris and Chris Vincent, all BMW mounted. Although we had not quite made the front slot, I lived up to my reputation as 'Mr. Consistent'. Two seconds and a third place in three practice sessions wasn't bad ending up third fastest overall with our private BMW. We were ahead of Schauzu, Fath and Vincent, which was very pleasing for my last racing venture around this famous course. John Blanchard retained his fifth place on the Senior leader board, a huge encouragement for our team!

During 10 days practice 78,238 miles were ridden around the TT course, a total of 2,081 laps with the scrutineers checking 1,511 machines. Until that Saturday morning the event had been trouble-free, with no serious injuries or accidents. Then a regular visitor and Isle of Man competitor, 51 year old Alfred Shaw crashed his 500 Norton near the Mountain Box. Sadly his injuries were fatal.

Although the day was marred by this accident, the official celebrations continued. Late that afternoon the Governor of the Isle of Man, Sir Peter H.G. Stallard, FIM representative Paulo Colombo, and the Auto Cycle Union's Norman Dixon officially opened the Diamond Jubilee TT races. The 43rd Royal Marine Commandos band led a parade of the Island's constabulary, the town band and the new Jubilee Standard Flag borne by a member of the British Legion. There was a procession of riders bearing flags of their nations, and groups representing the TT marshals and scouts, a grand affair and a nostalgic moment in the history of the Isle of Man TT. Although a lack of co-ordination between the procession controller and the grandstand controller regarding commentary left the packed grandstands without any understanding as to what was going on. The sight of the Douglas beach donkeys being led home across the course near the Grandstand and in front of the parade, added to the general confusion.

Saturday evening, the sun was still shining and the mountains sparkling clear. The production race, held over 3 laps of the TT course, set this unique event in motion. At 6.00pm the 52 competitors heard the words, 'Gentlemen please start your engines', and at 6.15pm the siren sounded for silence, requesting the machines to be wheeled onto the grid. It would be a 'Le Mans' start, the first group away the 750cc class, followed at 5 minute intervals by the 500s and finally the 250cc class. 6.30pm sharp the riders ran across the road, jumping on their bikes hoping to kick-start their lusty machines first time. Race favourite John Hartle, on the Triumph Bonneville was soon leading the pack, with Paul Smart way behind, having failed to fire up the Dunstall-Dominator immediately. In ideal conditions Hartle lapped at an impressive 97.16mph from a standing start, a good margin ahead of Steve Spencer, Griff Jenkins and Paul

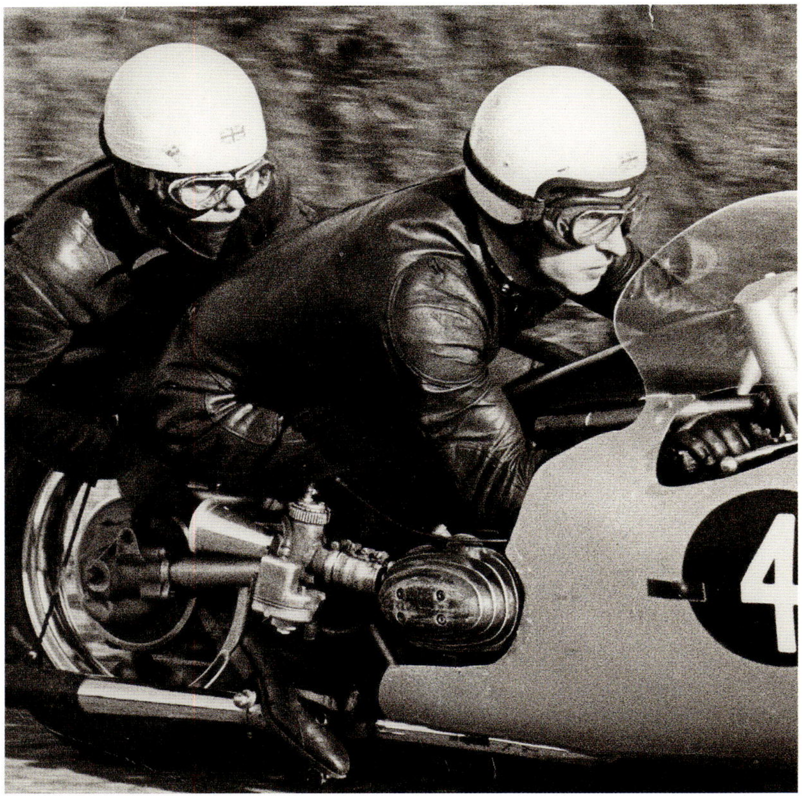

At the Gooseneck during evening practice.

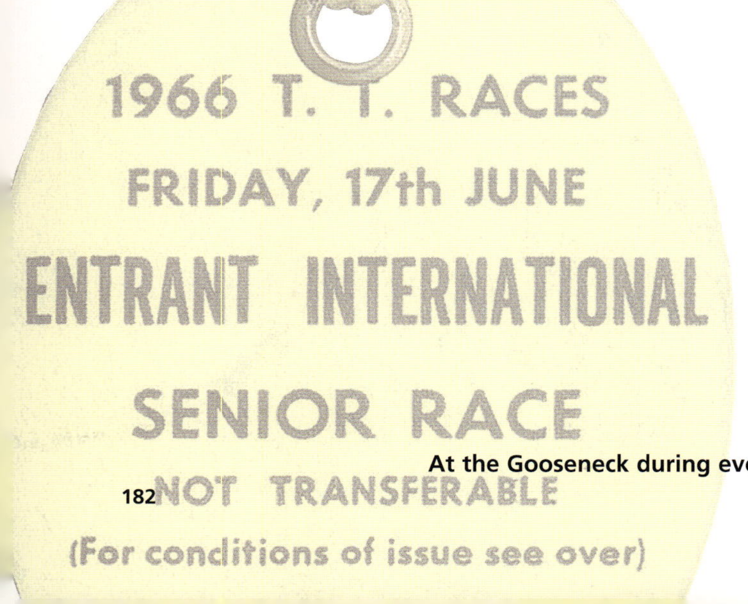

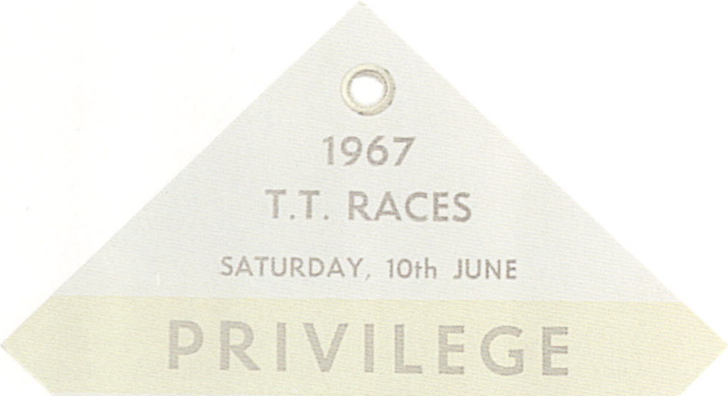

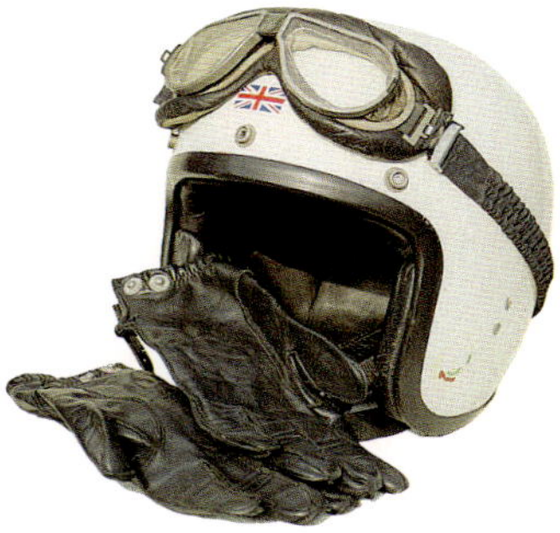

Smart who had pulled up to fourth. Rex Butcher and Peter Butler held fifth and sixth places on their Triumphs. Manxman Neil Kelly, Velocette, led the 500cc class after the favourite, 'sheep farmer' Tait, on the Triumph, suffered mechanical problems, then was out after falling in the mire at Appledene. Bill Smith was wheel to wheel with Tommy Robb leading the 250cc class, both on Spanish Bultaco machines. There was no stopping stylish John Hartle on the Geoff Duke entered Triumph-Bonneville. He led the race from start to finish, averaging an impressive 97.10mph and claiming the Double Diamond Trophy and £50 first prize. With Steve Spencer and Griff Jenkins both out, Paul Smart on the Dunstall-Dominator after his poor start brought himself up into a creditable second place at 94.60mph, 1 minute 51 seconds behind Hartle. Third overall and winner of the 500cc class in a fantastic effort on a Velocette and raising a big cheer from the locals was Manxman, Neil Kelly at 89.89mph with Keith Heckles on another Velocette second in the class, but sixth overall. In a very close finish, Chester's Bill Smith got the better of Ulsterman Tommy Robb in the 250cc class by 0.4 second, the pair finishing eighth and ninth overall. Tony Godfrey, Dunstall-Dominator, on his return to the Island after his serious crash in the 1963-250cc TT on the works Yamaha, finished tenth overall, a popular result. With 38 finishers, the production race was hailed as a great success, with all credit due to sidecar competitor and ACU man Fred Hanks for instigating the event.

Sunday, a day of rest, was more like 'Mad Sunday'. It seemed half of the Island, mostly visitors, were charging round the TT course, on motorcycles and in vans and cars – great fun but extremely dangerous. We were busy with the final preparation of our Rennsport BMW before the traditional 'weigh in' at the grandstand area in front of hundreds of fans waving their autograph books. I enjoyed this occasion, proud of the various immaculate outfits I had wheeled up for the weigh in over a number of years. 1967 was no exception. It was reported in the TT Special, 'Colin Seeley's BMW is a credit not only to himself and his helpers but to the sidecar fraternity as a whole.' Back at the Frank Large Garage our race service was very busy. After the huge commitment it was good to be so well received. Wally and I were still not happy with John Blanchard's approach to that year's TT, and I had even seriously considered withdrawing him from both the Junior and Senior races, but needed to have our sidecar event out of the way before making a final decision.

Race day, Monday 12th June was a perfect day, I couldn't remember otherwise in six sidecar races I had ridden previously. Were we lucky or what? That year's Diamond Jubilee sidecar event would be best yet with the record entry of 79 starters.

Back at Beverley House, Wally, our friend and helper John Juniper and myself enjoyed a hearty breakfast, cooked by that special lady Frances Clucas. We collected our gear together, and hoping that we would return safely later that day, we departed for the start area before the roads were closed.

In 1964, racing stalwart Fred Hanks made history by racing against his son Norman in the sidecar event. Bill Boddice repeated the process in 1966 competing against his son, Mick Boddice who would go on to future TT success. For the 1967 sidecar race Fred Hanks' whole family turned up, Fred, Norman and Roy all racing BSA outfits. Up at the start, the enclosure gates opened at 10.00am and the 158 riders and passengers supported by their mechanics, wheeled the outfits from the overnight marquee, and made final checks and adjustments before the 15 minute warm up at 10.30am. People were pushing and shoving in all directions in an effort to get started. Onlookers wandered into the way, amongst shouts of 'out the way', the roar of engines, the smoke, the commotion and officials trying to bring some sort of order into that small terraced paddock area. It all appeared a shambles. Suddenly the siren echoed through the area to stop engines and for competitors to assemble on the grid. Now there was no going back. In this, my last TT event, I really looked forward to a good result but I was apprehensive, so much could go wrong in a 3 lap 113.2 mile race, with mechanical failure, breakages and of course mistakes which can lead to serious injury, not only to oneself but the passenger who was scraping the ground much of the time, always needing complete faith in the rider's ability.

Knowing we had little chance against the top works supported BMW competitors. I decided to have a strong steady race, keeping my act together and going for a finish. As the seconds ticked away for 11.00am start, I remembered the only Swiss winners of the sidecar event, the late Florian Camathias in 1963 and Fritz Scheidegger 1966, whose passenger John Robinson survived the Mallory Park crash. Although still in plaster he was at the TT to see his old mates.

Seconds before the start, Roy Lindsey in his first TT riding with me, gave a nervous 'thumbs up'. I looked back at the queue of outfits behind us. We had been allocated the best start number yet, No 4. We were starting alongside our friend, the previous winner Helmut Fath on the ultra quick URS four, No 3.

The first pairing, Barry Dungworth, BMW, and Georg Auerbacher, BMW, were away and soon disappeared down Bray Hill. 10 seconds flashed by and the flag dropped for us. A few steps and our Rennsport burst into life and we were away, ahead of Helmut Fath. Chris Vincent, BMW, and Terry Vinicombe, Kirby-BSA, were next to leave, followed by Butscher and Enders with Schauzu further back at No 12.

Through Union Mills, the 'Strang Gang' cheered us. Helmut Fath, close by, passed us with some ease through the very fast Glen Vine section, but from Ballacraine onwards, having passed Dungworth, we were back on equal terms with him, glued to the tail of the high revving URS. The exhaust noise was ringing in my ears but we managed to hold him all the way to Ramsey. Once we started the mountain climb from Ramsey Hairpin, we could not match the superior speed of the Ursenbach Special and ex-World Champion, Helmut Fath sped into the distance to finish the first lap in fourth place at 90.21mph, leaving us in fifth spot with a lap of 88.58mph. Pip Harris, BMW, lay sixth, just over 6 seconds behind us. With 6 seconds covering the first three, Enders, Auerbacher and Schauzu, the race was hotting up. It was a battle between the three German BMW aces. Fath went out with engine trouble at The Bungalow on the second lap. Georg Auerbacher had taken the lead at 91,18mph, Schauzu passed Enders for second place and we were up to fourth. Suddenly I developed a raging toothache and once more a dragging clutch on the bike.

Then Auerbacher, on his last lap, dropped out at Ballacraine with a seized engine, a disappointment for this likeable German, as he would have won comfortably. Starting our last lap, for the last time we blasted down the breathtaking Bray Hill, the throttle absolutely back on its stop as I changed into top gear. Foolish or brave, I raced down Bray Hill 'flat out' in 1966 averaging 116mph from the start to Quarterbridge. I had

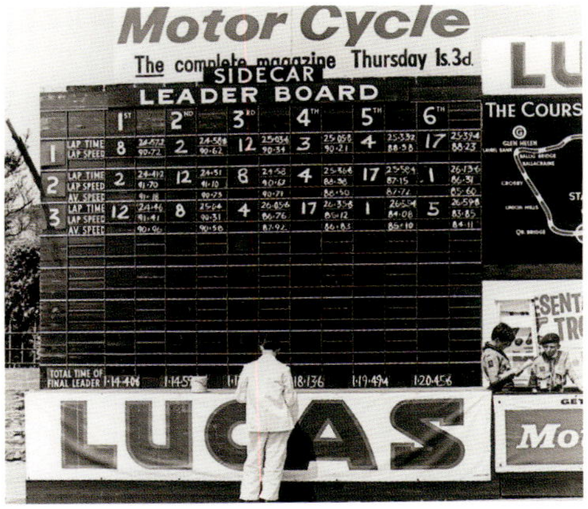

Final sidecar leaderboard.

always found this part of the long TT circuit daunting. Soon we were on to Braddan Bridge and the section through Union Mills, one of my favourites. The loyal Strang Gang gave us a final wave and Roy, lying in the chair, waggled his feet in response. Apart from the clutch drag and toothache, it was a trouble-free race, not a single hairy moment as we made our way to the finish.

On only his second visit to the Isle of Man, Siegfried Schauzu with passenger Horst Schneider won a record-breaking sidecar TT, averaging 90.96mph upholding the BMW dominance of this race. The formidable Klaus Enders with partner Rolf Engelhardt finished second at 90.58mph. Roy Lindsey my Liverpudlian passenger who had performed perfectly, helped me finally to finish third at 87.92mph, a bit disappointing but just about the quickest we could lap with our almost worn out Rennsport engine. The Germans always had the best parts! It was not sour grapes, it was a fact! Anyway, I like a moan. However, we had the consolation of being the first British crew home, and the third place rostrum position at the TT.

Our mate and long-time British sidecar hero, Pip Harris finished fourth 86.83mph on his worn out BMW, another British boy who suffered. Barry Dungworth, BMW, got a creditable fifth and the fast improving Kent boy, Terry Vinicombe, partnered by John Flaxman with the Kirby-BSA made it onto the leader board in sixth place at a brilliant 84.11mph. A total of 40 sidecar competitors finished the Diamond Jubilee Sidecar Race. Georg Auerbacher was awarded the fastest lap. The Club Team award was presented to the Greenwich Motor and Motorcycle Club with riders Vinicombe, Ellis and Seeley. As I stood on the rostrum with Schauzu and Enders I reflected on my decision to retire from racing.

As a lad learning to ride my father's Vincent/HRD all those years ago, I never imagined that I would race in the Isle of Man, let alone end up on the rostrum. With sixth place in 1961, third in 1962, sixth in 1963, second in 1964, retirement with engine failure in 1965 when lying fifth, fifth in 1966 and now third in 1967, I was pretty proud of my record. Riding the Matchless G50 outfit with Wally in the chair was very special. We were possibly the fastest single cylinder powered outfit around the Isle of Man TT

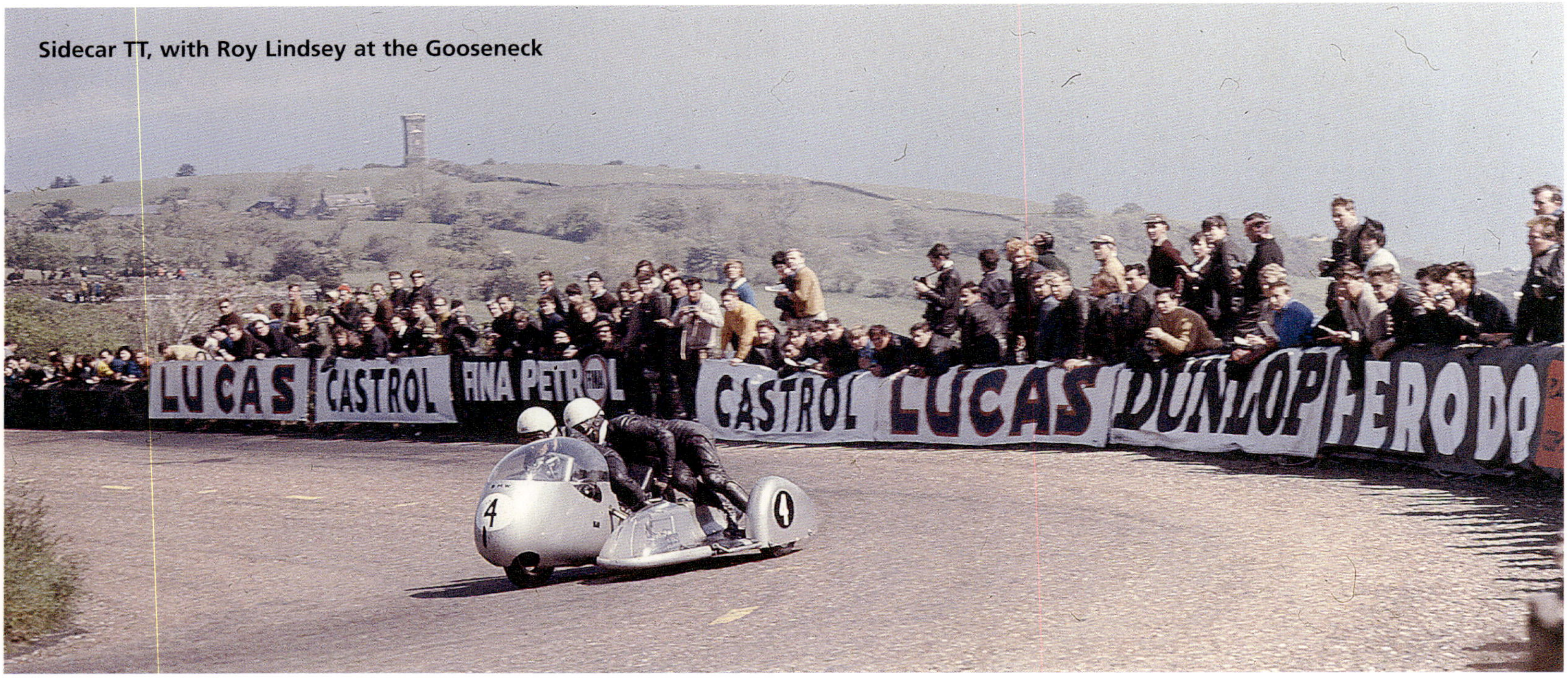

Sidecar TT, with Roy Lindsey at the Gooseneck

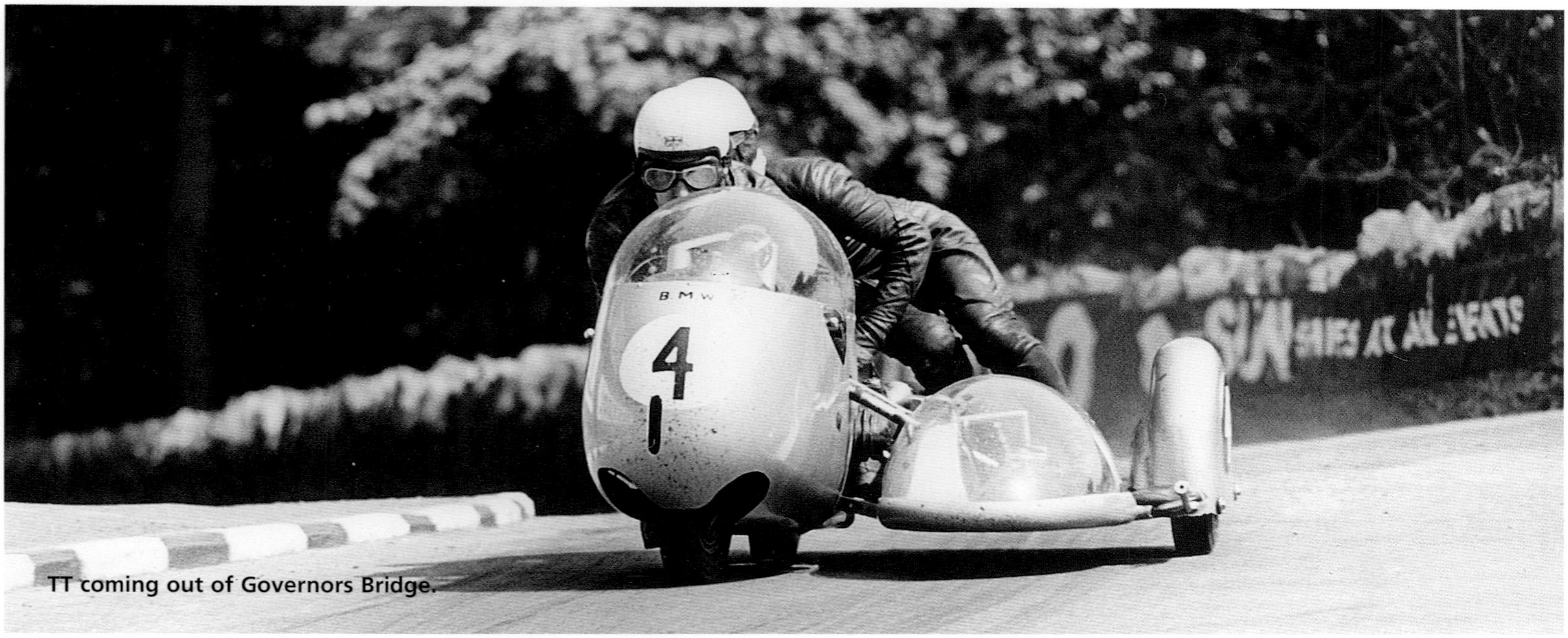

TT coming out of Governors Bridge.

course, at 83.13mph, back in 1962 we averaged 82.80mph for the race. I would miss the cut and thrust of the Grand Prix scene and being a real patriot, I was always proud to race for Queen and Country. Standing on a rostrum with the Union Flag raised was an emotional moment. I had made my contribution to the British sidecar scene in the sixties, not only in racing but just as importantly, known for an excellent standard of machine preparation and presentation.

The German domination of Grand Prix sidecar racing would go on for nearly a decade. British success followed when in 1972 Chris Vincent riding the Fath built URS-Munch finished fourth in the championship to winner Enders BMW. George O'Dell, Yamaha, although not winning a single Grand Prix, took the title in 1977, then the popular Jock Taylor, Windle-Yamaha, in 1980 took the title in a most convincing style winning four Grands Prix from Rolf Biland. Wally Rawlings and I had won the Dutch TT in 1964 and it would not to be won again by a British rider until 1980. When Jock Taylor partnered by Benge Johansson won this great Dutch event, I was pleased to witness his success and to offer my congratulations. Unbelievably it was seven years before the next British success, when Steve Webster won three World Sidecar Championships in succession 1987-88-89. A marvellous achievement!

We left the winners' rostrum and dealt with obligatory photographs and interviews. The first three sidecar outfits were wheeled into the scrutineers bay for the compulsory checking of engine capacity. This had been a tradition at the TT for many years, but a dammed nuisance for most of us, adding to our work-load. Cylinder heads had to be removed and then needed to be rebuilt. This does not happen at any other circuit unless a protest is put forward. I suppose it is all part of the TT tradition.

Sidecar TT rostrum, 1 Schauzu, 2 Enders, 3 Seeley.

Finally came the 6 lap 250cc TT starting at 1.30pm. The weather continued fine. Everybody's favourite, recording a practice lap of 105.12mph was Mike Hailwood on his most preferred Honda, the 250cc six cylinder. He was out to annihilate the opposition and record his tenth Isle of Man TT victory. Mike would start 10 seconds ahead of Bill Ivy and 30 seconds ahead of Phil Read. With team mate Ralph Bryans, also Honda six, Hailwood would have his main opposition, the Yamaha works pairing, behind him, leaving him a virtually clear road ahead. The Champion led the race from start to finish, although the first lap was very close, less than 3 seconds separating Hailwood, Read and Ivy in that order, all lapping over 103mph. At the end of the second lap Mike had pulled away from Read by over 12 seconds, and 21 seconds ahead of Ivy. Ralph Bryans held fourth from the East German MZ machines of Woodman and Rosner, with Dave Simmonds and John Cooper seventh and eighth on their Kawasakis. At the end of the third lap Mike pulled in and from his pit stop reported the Honda was handling badly, changed his goggles, refuelled and was well away before Read and Ivy arrived together.

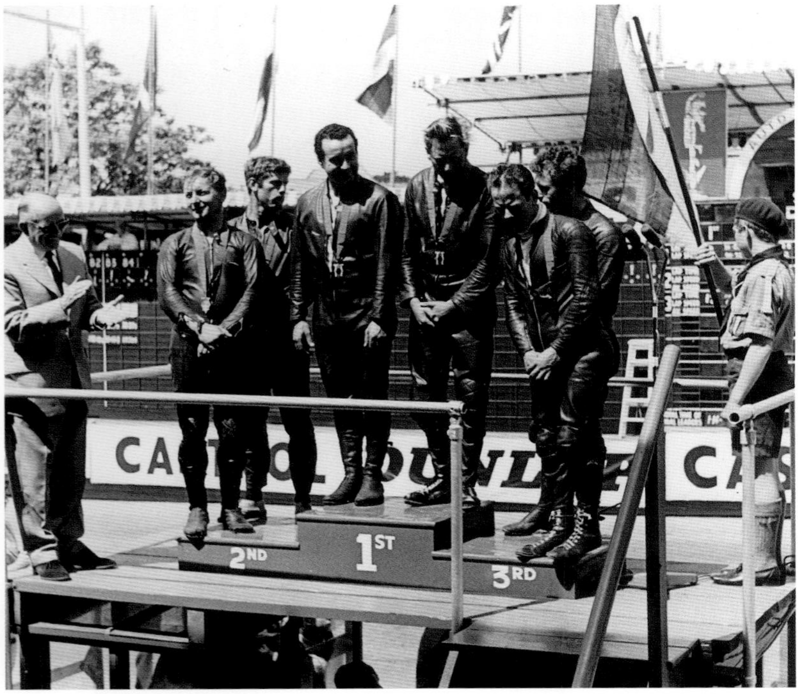

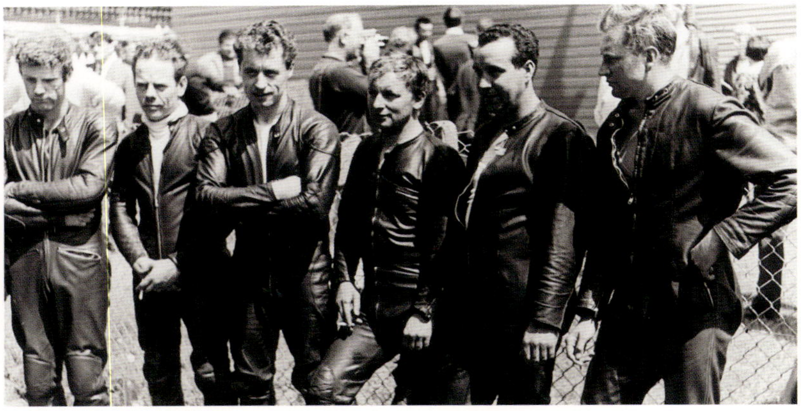

Left to right, Engelhardt, Lindsey, me, Enders, Schauzu and Horst.

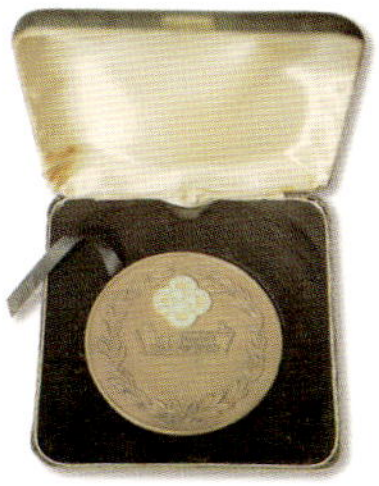

By noon, Hailwood, 30 seconds ahead of Phil Read, was on his way to equalling Stanley Wood's record. Despite poor handling of the Honda, Magnificent Mike won the 226.4 mile race at record speed averaging 103.07mph with the fastest lap at 104.14mph. Stanley Wood's 28 year old record of 10 Isle of Man TT wins had been equalled and gentleman Stan was in the grandstand to applaud our hero. Phil Read brought his Yamaha home into a well-deserved second place at 102.05mph, his first 250cc race finish on the Yamaha, having broken down in the last three Isle of Man TT events. Ralph Bryans, still mastering the Honda six, made up the rostrum positions. Dave Simmonds brought the Kawasaki home in fourth place whilst John Cooper, fifth on the last lap, had broken down and had to push his Kawasaki in from Brandywell to finish twenty-fourth, a great effort. Out of the original 250cc entry of 104, there were 30 non-starters with 29 finishers and not a single casualty. The Castrol sponsored rescue helicopter hadn't needed to spin its rotors - a very pleasant and exciting day's racing. Thousands of fans flooded back to their hotels, bed and breakfasts, homes or camping sites to enjoy a beer and exchange stories of the day. We returned to our favourite cottage, Beverley House, to the praise of the Clucas family. Frances would already be on the Guinness and be waving in the air chanting: 'My boys, my boys you were lovely through The Mills!' Frances Clucas was a wonderful woman, if a little eccentric. I would miss these visits in the future.

The presentation evening was to start at 9.00pm – a grand affair, but not at the familiar Villa Marina. It returned to the Palace Ballroom which had been used for the first public TT prize presentation in 1908. High ranking officers of the Isle of Man; the Mayor of Douglas, Clerk of the Rolls, S.J. Kneale CBE and the Lieutenant-Governor of the Isle of Man, Sir Peter Stallard KCMG, CVO, MBE would present the various awards. The evening was well-attended and the first presentation was for the production race. Ind Coope Ltd, brewers of Double Diamond, provided the 'Double Diamond' trophies, awarded to the first three finishers in each of the three classes plus £50 for the winners, £40 for second places and £30 for third: Double Diamond works wonders!! John Hartle received a great cheer. His overall win of the production race was a popular one.

Then it was our turn, the charioteers. Only the first ten finishers were awarded the Silver TT Replicas, the next eleven Bronze Replicas, and the rest?... nothing! Presentation was in reverse order, so we had a while to wait. Passenger Roy Lindsey received his first ever Silver TT Replica, I, my sixth and £50 prize money. It was a great moment for both of us and I was delighted to finish my racing career on such a high note! Then what a cheer for the 250cc race winner, the likeable, approachable 'Mike the Bike' Hailwood who nonchalantly walked up to collect the Tourist Trophy, a replica and the £100 prize money. With no racing next day, there was time for celebration and celebrate we did! In those days competitors raced hard then played hard, great days.

Now I would be able to concentrate on the rest of the week's business. Fortunately Wally Rawlings aided by Bill Wright, Arthur Childs and the loud-voiced Arthur Keeler had been busy with our race service.

The situation with John Blanchard had not changed, we were still daggers drawn. Finally, I blew a gasket and withdrew our Seeley race bikes from John. I had no plans at the time for anyone else to ride our machines, I was just mad, and stuck to my decision for Wednesday's Junior Race leaving Blanchard devastated. He did not believe I would do it and perhaps I had over-reacted, but I made my point. Meantime, John was lobbying Wally Rawlings, a more dispassionate person, to persuade me to change my mind. I took Wally's advice and relented, allowing John to compete in the 500cc Senior Race.

On Wednesday 14th June, the fantastic weather provided a glorious setting for a wonderful day's racing. Thousands of spectators, shirt sleeves rolled up, spread around the TT course in the sunshine, standing, sitting on walls, lounging on the grass banks, peering through hedgerows, leaning over fences, in the luxury of the grandstand, or sitting on the mountainside for the best view of all. The enthusiastic fans were at every vantage point for the start of the Diamond Jubilee lightweight 125cc event.

The 'Maidstone Marvel' Ivy, winner of the race in 1966 and fastest in practice at 98.52mph, was race favourite on the works Yamaha. It was rumoured that 'Little' Bill had been offered a bonus of £1,000 by Yamaha if he was the first man to lap at 100mph in the 125cc event. This would have been useful as during practice week, playing car racing with Hailwood sitting alongside, Bill crashed Mike's new Ferrari at Greeba Castle causing extensive damage. Mike discovered that his Italian comprehensive insurance policy was only covered for third party outside of Italy – Whoops! Bill would have to pay!

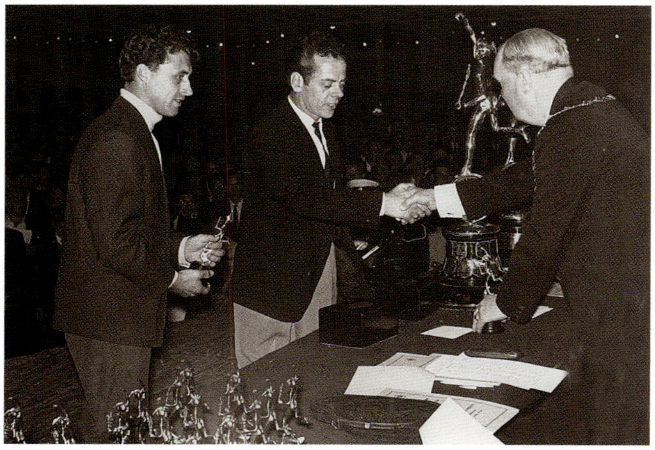

Sidecar TT presentation with Roy Lindsey.

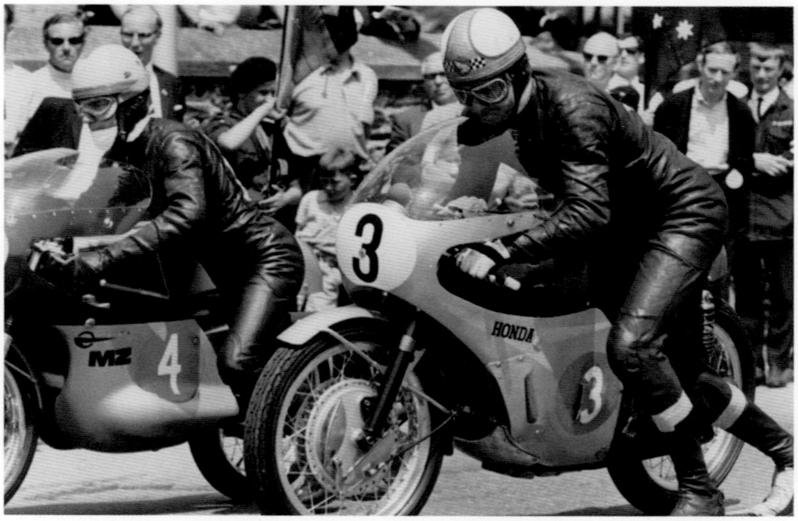

1967 Junior TT. Derek Woodman (4), Mike Hailwood (3).

Peter Inchley, on Terry Shepherd's Bultaco, and Stuart Graham, Suzuki, started the 125cc race as the flag came down at 11.00am sharp, the riders in pairs despatched at 10 second intervals. Next pair Tommy Robb and Australian Barry Smith both on Bultaco machines, were within seconds followed down Bray Hill by Bill Ivy, Yamaha. 'Prince of Speed' Read started on his own, 20 seconds behind Ivy, with Yamaha team mate, Japanese new star Akiyasu Motohashi starting alongside his fellow countryman Yoshimi Katayama, Suzuki, 10 seconds down on Phil Read. The main six started in the first twelve, out of an original entry of 63.

The blistering weather caused over-rich carburation on many of the temperamental two-strokes. The molten tar in many places also ensured that race and lap records remained intact. Nevertheless, the race turned out to be a David and Goliath situation, The favourite, Bill Ivy, slowed with engine trouble, retired when an electrode from the sparking plug fell into a cylinder of the mini four cylinder Yamaha. Suzuki also received a shock when their main man Katayama stopped at Sulby on the first lap with a sick engine, leaving their hopes resting on the underdog Stuart Graham, who after one lap was only 1.4 seconds down on the Prince with Motohashi third and Dave Simmonds on the Kawasaki holding fourth.

Stuart Graham, 25 year old son of the late great Les Graham, had much to prove. His father had won this 125cc event back in 1953 and Stuart perhaps wanted to cock a snook at Honda, who dropped him from their team in 1966. As the contest between Read and Graham raged into the second lap, on sheer riding ability Stuart had offset the speed difference between his twin cylinder Suzuki and Read's Yamaha four, gaining a second advantage half way round. Up The Mountain and down the other side there was absolutely nothing in it. Starting the last lap, Phil Read had a shock. His pit board showed he was down on Graham by 0.4 second - only a whisker between them. Down through the full bore Highlander section, Stuart Graham's Suzuki gave a cough and went onto one cylinder. Stuart thought his race was over, but suddenly his engine came back on two cylinders. It was momentary set back. Graham scratched like mad to draw level with Read, on time again by Ramsey. However, the double World 250cc Champion 'Prince' Read was not about to give up. He pulled everything out of the hat as he sped over The Mountain, the spectators waving furiously. By The Bungalow, Read had made up 2 seconds and the tension in the pits was electric as Stuart passed under the chequered flag. The seconds ticked by as Phil came into sight, his head buried into the fuel tank, his body tucked in, slipstreaming the warm air, to come over the finish line to win his third Isle of Man TT event, 3.4 seconds ahead of Stuart Graham, who had ridden brilliantly. He had pushed the 'Prince of Speed' to the limit, Phil's last lap was 98.36mph, just short of Bill Ivy's Yamaha lap record in 1966 at 98.55mph. Phil averaged 97.48mph for the 113.2 mile race on his Yamaha and his challenger Graham 97.40mph, impressive speeds for such little machines. Phil's team-mate, Japan's Motohashi, finished third in an impressive ride averaging 94.56mph. Overshadowed by the scrap at the front, 'Mr. Nice Guy' talented Dave Simmonds finished a fine fourth on the Kawasaki, at 92.08mph, and a certain Kel Carruthers, Honda, fifth, Jim Curry, Honda, sixth and Ulsterman Tommy Robb on a Bultaco seventh. Worthy of a mention was the plucky performance of little Gary Dickinson, probably the smallest rider competing in the TT that year. His Honda stopped at the 33rd milestone on the last lap. He free wheeled and finally pushed in to finish thirty-second, not last, still averaging 66.31mph. His heroic footslog earned the Solway Racing Club the team prize. The race heroes don't always have to be at the front.

By the time the lightweight 125cc winner's rostrum ceremony had taken place, the entrants for the 350cc Junior race were assembled for a 1.30pm start. The spectators hardly had time to calm down after the close finish of the lightweights, before Mike Hailwood, starting No 3, the Junior Race favourite, was zooming by on the sensational Honda 297cc six. The Isle of Man was the place to really appreciate the awesome sound of this high revving six cylinder projectile. It seemed as if the machine could be heard over the whole island – just magnificent. Added to this sound treat for the first 3 laps was the singing of Agostini's MV three cylinder, and Pasolini's Benelli four.

There was no stopping the Maestro that day. Mike was determined to win his eleventh TT, having recorded a standing start lap of 107.73mph leaving the 500cc World Champion Agostini in his wake. Ago could only manage a first lap of 103.73mph followed by an array of machinery Pasolini, Benelli, Rosner, MZ, Stevens, Hannah-Paton, Woodman, MZ, Pagani, Aermacchi, Conn, Norton, Williams, AJS, Milani, Aermacchi, Simmonds, Kawasaki, and Hartle, Aermacchi, the first 12 as the race progressed. Retirements came thick and fast; Renzo Pasolini out with a broken chain, Mike Duff, Steve Jolly, Malcolm Uphill, Joe Dunphy, Dave Croxford, Heinz Rosner, Ron Chandler also with a broken chain, Fred Stevens, our Austrian friend Rudi Thalhammer who crashed, Peter Williams on the fifth lap and up in sixth, Dave Simmonds on the last lap when ninth. George Fogarty (father of Carl) crashed at Milntown and was taken to hospital in the Castrol sponsored BEA Helicopter. In fact, out of the original 95 starters, only 36 finished.

On the last lap, Meteoric Michael who only started 10 seconds ahead of Agostini, was so far ahead of the languishing Italian, that Mike was well on his way to Ballacraine as Ago rounded Signpost Corner, miles back, for the start of his final lap. Although Hailwood eased the pace, he came across the finish line having well and truly trounced the opposition as well as the lap and race records. In the Diamond Jubilee TT he registered the fastest ever speeds around the historic Isle of Man TT course with an average of 104.68mph for the 226.4 mile event, and the fastest lap at 107.73mph, some achievement by the British hero. Finishing in second place, Italian sportsman Agostini accepted his defeat with grace and simply said, 'Mike was much too fast.' Derek Woodman brought his works MZ in third to the final rostrum position. Stanley Woods, whose record of 10 Isle of Man TT victories was now broken, was first to congratulate Hailwood and present the garlands, a fitting climax to a significant day's racing.

Following the not so smart move by the ACU to charge 7s 6d to attend the prize giving in the Palace Ballroom on the Monday evening, Production Race winner John Hartle forgot his ticket and had to pay for his entry. Mike Hailwood had to pay for his father, Stan to attend the ceremony. The cost for admission was reduced to five shillings for Wednesday's presentation and when ACU secretary Ken Shierson said that money spent by the visiting fans did not go into ACU pockets, there were cries of 'Rubbish!' The cost of competing in the TT was obviously a very sore point for the competitors.

Lap 5, the signal to Hailwood on Ago's position, 'minus 11 MV'.

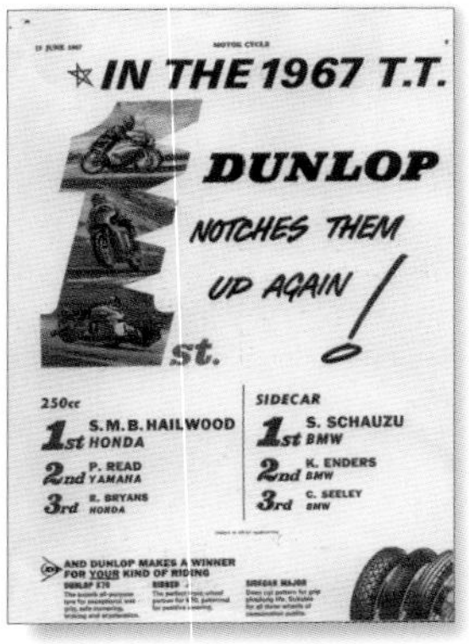

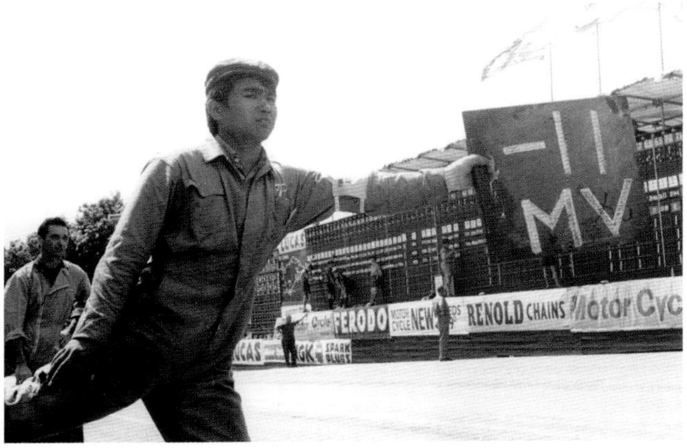

Thursday would be our last busy day at the Seeley Service, provided mainly for owners of AJS 7R and Matchless G50 machines, although we also supported Norton owners and in fact did not turn anybody away. Motorcycling's sports editor, Mick Woollett reported that, as usual with Seeley projects, the workshop area, set up in Frank Large's Garage was spick and span, a service counter concealing crates of spares, racks of larger items and an imposing array of special tools, along with a drill, honing machines and normal workshop equipment. Many agreed that it surpassed anything AMC had provided in the past – a compliment indeed.

Having agreed that John Blanchard could compete in the Senior Race, the finishing touches to the Seeley-Matchless took place before the check in later that day. Ron Chandler was in trouble with his own G50 engine, so we loaned him one of the spare works engines. Then, with most of the work completed, the drudgery of packing up our TT service began, ready to return to base in Belvedere, directly after the Senior Race. It had been 'open all hours'. All I wanted now was to be back with my family.

Without trade support the TT could never run. Reynolds Tubes' Ken Sprayson was non stop welding and repairing bikes. Dunlop's Tony Mills, apart from overseeing the supply and service of tyres, spent much time picking up nails and sharp objects in the paddock area to avoid trouble on the track. Vic Doyle and his team replaced and fitted Renolds Chains as required. Lew Ellis represented Shell, there was the Ferodo brake service, and Les Simms for NGK Plugs. Our sponsor, the Castrol Oil Company had competition manager Malcolm Edgar. He once left a box containing 500 booklets of demisting tissues in the warming up area Castrol hut. A few minutes later they had gone – mystery! The next morning a little boy approached six foot Malcolm, looked up and asked, 'Mister, do you have anymore of those little autograph books you were giving away yesterday?' Mystery solved!

The tiddler 50cc event held over 3 laps of The Mountain circuit kicked the day off at 11.00am, the only mass start of the week. The weather held good with blue skies as the 24 competitors screamed down Bray Hill. Fastest in practice the 1963 winner Mitsuo Itoh, Suzuki, was a non-starter having broken his wrist in a crash during practice. Suzuki was the only factory team entered with riders Stuart Graham, Yoshimi Katayama and Hans-Georg Anscheidt, Itoh of course out of action. Anscheidt was leading the world championship from the Japanese Katayama, Stuart Graham was the new boy. The Suzuki Race Team declared that Katayama should win, as they wished for an all Japanese victory. Well, best laid plans as they say. The 1966 German champion Anscheidt, on the first lap, led Graham at Ballacraine. Katayama had 'cocked up' his push start then had to to change a plug soon after at Quarter Bridge. Tommy Robb on a production Suzuki was third.

The two leaders, obeying team orders, were playing 'silly buggers' at the front waiting for Katayama to catch them up. By the second lap the 'race' degenerated into a farce, it was slow motion as Katayama painfully, slowly, caught the front pair at Ramsey on the second lap. As they raced over The Mountain section Katayama was neck and neck with Anscheidt. It was Keystone Cops. Yoshimi looked across at Hans-Georg's oil-sprayed rear wheel and rode straight into a ditch on the mountain mile. He was unhurt but rather embarrassed and the bike was bent. This left the door open for Anscheidt and Graham to get on with the serious business of racing. Then Anscheidt was in trouble, the little Suzuki cutting out on one cylinder and with oil leaking from a pump. He slowed, leaving Stuart Graham, fourth fastest in practice at 83.48mph, in an unchallenged lead. Third man Tommy Robb was 10 minutes and more behind as Graham came over the finish line, a popular win to bag his first Isle of Man TT, Stuart took the impressive 17,000rpm Suzuki twin round the TT course on that last lap at 85.19mph, near to the record.

In Diamond Jubilee year, this race had made a mockery of Grand Prix championship racing. In fact it proved to be the beginning of the end for 50cc 'wasp' racing, the last event held at the TT in 1968 and not attended by any of the main protagonists. Nevertheless this midget 50cc class of racing still held a sort of magnetism, certainly at the short circuits, to which it was better suited and would continue in the world championship series until 1983.

At the TT Honda Racing announced a full scale come back for 1968, including the re-introduction of their 50cc and 125cc machines to be ridden by Luigi Taveri and Ralph Bryans. They had hoped that Hailwood would stay to compete on the 250, 350 and 500cc Hondas. Well, none of those plans materialised. Honda had to wait until 1983 to head a championship table again with Freddie Spencer as 500cc champion. Not until 1990 and 1991 would they again dominate the 125cc class when Loris Capirossi took the titles for Honda.

After the debacle of the boring 'tiddler race' the patient fans were rewarded with an earth-shattering spectacle, the two greatest riders in the world, multi World Champion Mike Hailwood and colourful 500cc World Champion Giacomo Agostini, celebrating his 25th birthday. They battled for top honours in that 1967 Diamond Jubilee Senior TT race. The works Honda four was slightly faster but with poor handling, against the slower but smooth handling works MV three. It would be close.

In contrast to the 'Tiddlers', there was no lack of entries for the 6 lap 226.4 mile Senior Race, 116 in all. Non-starters brought the line up on the Glencrutchery Road down to 91 for the 1.30pm start. The grandstand flags fluttered briskly and the high thin clouds filtered the sun. The day was cooler with a north westerly breeze, 'Good news', as the course would not be affected by melting tar, ideal conditions for record breaking!

Wally and I were on the grid for the start of this historic event, overseeing our friend Ron Chandler, who would have the honour of starting first along with Malcolm Uphill who had taken over the injured Jack Findlay's ride on the Bear Norton. With Grassetti, Benelli, a non starter. 'Mike the Bike' was next up to the famous start line. The Grandstand crowd held its breath. The flag went down, Hailwood, race number 4, pushed the big Honda. Within a few strides it burst into life and Mike disappeared out of sight. Wally and I were still standing to one side as our man John Blanchard on the Seeley-Matchless wheeled to the line, with Australian rider Malcolm Stanton on a Manx Norton, starting 20 seconds down on Ron Chandler. Blanchard was intense. The flag was raised and in a couple of steps John was away, a perfect start, ahead of Stanton.

Peter Williams, Arter Matchless, and Switzerland's Gyula Marsovszky, Matchless, followed. Next was the Italian star Agostini, MV, No 9, starting 30 seconds behind Hailwood. Now the race was really on and the rest of the field followed at 10 seconds intervals. Agostini, resolute in his aim to reverse the Junior result, charged around the

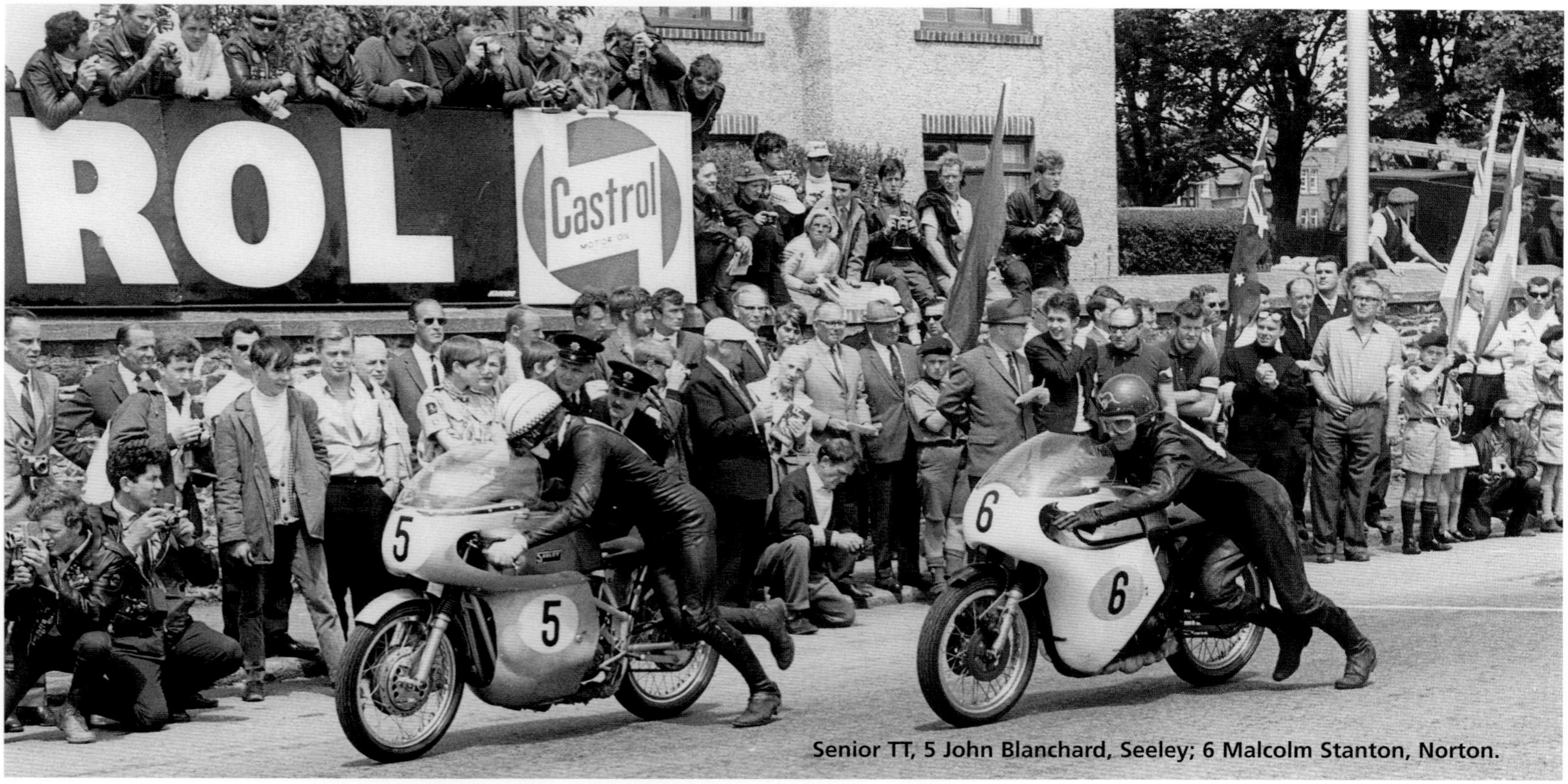

Senior TT, 5 John Blanchard, Seeley; 6 Malcolm Stanton, Norton.

TT course on that first standing start lap at 108.38mph, a new record, shattering Hailwood's 1966 record and the new absolute record set by Hailwood on the previous Wednesday. Agostini was the first rider ever to lap the mountain circuit at under 21 minutes. Mike, still coming to terms with the big Honda, not his favourite bike, posted a lap of 107.37mph, nearly 12 seconds down on time. Pasolini, Benelli, held third at 100.61mph but close by in fourth, Peter Williams had joined the 100mph club at 100.35mph, impressive from a standing start. Then it was our man, John Blanchard holding fifth place at 99.61mph from Malcolm Uphill, 7 seconds behind in sixth place. Ron Chandler, still feeling the effects of his German Grand Prix crash, had dropped back down the field.

Up front the heat was on. Hailwood came through to start his second lap with a thumbs down, but never the man to give up, kept the pressure on and was only 10 seconds down on Ago. By the end of the second lap Mike had broken the lap record once more, at 108.77mph. He was now under 9 seconds behind the Italian. John Blanchard riding the Seeley-Matchless to its limit also joined the elite 100mph club, lapping at 100.84mph and still holding fifth place.

The end of the third lap brought the crucial pit stop. Mike roaring up from Governor's Dip in first, chopped the throttle as he crossed the pit lane line. As the crew refuelled the Honda with six gallons, Mike called for a hammer to belt away at the throttle twist-grip which had worked itself loose.

Hailwood was still in the pits as Agostini arrived, his lead now down to 2 seconds. In spite of a long pit stop of some 47.85 seconds, which virtually wasted his efforts on the third lap. Mike was off, to the cheers of the crowd. Quicker, slicker Ago took on 4½ gallons of fuel, bumped the MV back into life after a 37 second pit stop. Blanchard, still in fifth place and having lapped again at 100mph, came in for his pit stop.

At the end of the fourth lap, Hailwood on the 'bucking bronco' Honda was still nearly 12 seconds down on Agostini who was relentless in his efforts to keep ahead. With Pasolini out of the race, Peter Williams moved up to third place and Malcolm Uphill got the better of Blanchard by 9 seconds.

Starting the fifth lap, the pit board read 'minus 11 MV'. Our champion rose to the challenge and by Ballaugh Bridge had cut Agostini's lead down to 2 seconds. By Ramsey, Mike somehow in this fantastic race had got ahead of Ago by a miniscule one second. The stylish Italian, his MV running impeccably, received his own signals at Ramsey, turned up the wick and at The Bungalow, had regained the lead by 2.5 seconds. Further back, race retirements were thick and fast; Kel Carruthers, Norton, Tony Rutter, Norton, Renzo Pasolini, Benelli, Dennis Gallagher, Matchless, Chris Conn, Norton, Mike Duff, Arter Matchless, Rob Gould, Norton, Dave Croxford, Matchless, Joe Dunphy, Norton, were among the eventual 54 retirements.

Hailwood, head down and wrestling the writhing Honda, flashed past the grandstand to start his last lap. Stop watches clicked away while the assembled group of mechanics, team managers, helpers and officials were awaiting Agostini. Seconds turned to minutes – what had happened? Everybody was anxious for news of the World Champion. Then good news, Ago was okay, his rear chain had worked loose, jumped the sprocket, and broken at Windy Corner near the 33rd Milestone – what cruel luck!

Agostini part freewheeled and pushed the stricken MV Agusta 5 miles to the start pit area, the gallant Italian receiving the cheers of the well informed and appreciative fans. The MV mechanics attempted to fit a new chain but were stopped by a pit official. It had been reported that Agostini took the slip road at Governor's Dip, which meant automatic exclusion. It was believed that the marshals were at fault as they had waved Ago into the slip road, unaware that he may wish to continue in the race. Meantime, 'Mike the Bike' was still struggling with a loose twist grip which kept slipping off the handlebar. A Hailwood fan stuck out an 'Ago out' blackboard, a signal Mike could hardly believe. His luck was in! Our team's luck was about to change. The 'Paperhanger' was riding brilliantly, with the Seeley-Matchless still in fifth place.However he retired at the Mountain Box on the same lap as Agostini, with a broken primary chain. John carried out a repair after some fans threw him a couple of chain links and pliers, but the chain broke again as John restarted. Asking the fans to keep well away, as no outside

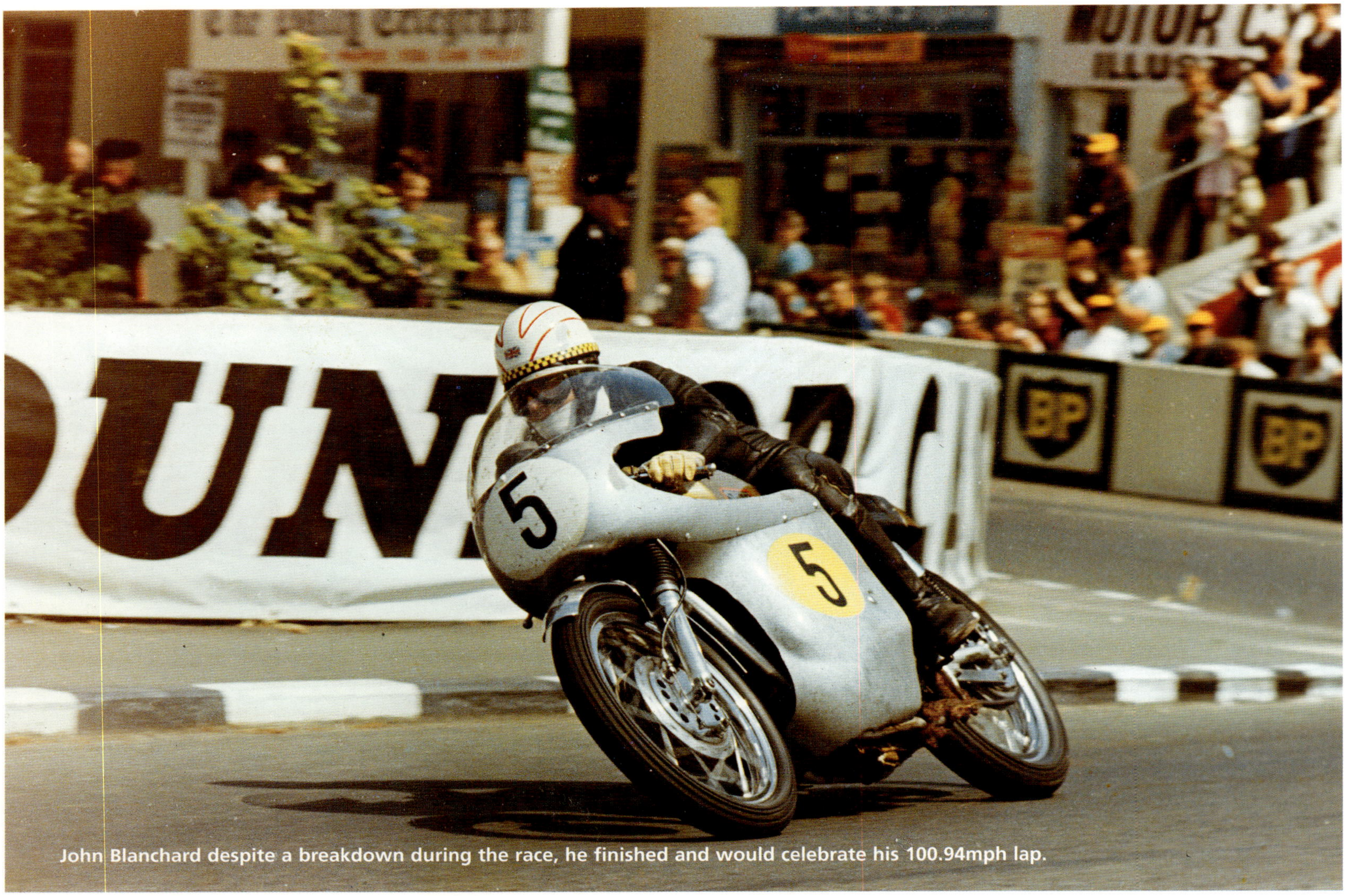

John Blanchard despite a breakdown during the race, he finished and would celebrate his 100.94mph lap.

assistance was allowed, John fixed the chain once again. So much time lost and still over a lap to complete with a primary chain that wasn't at its best. It was a miracle John got to the finish, although in a disappointing thirty-third position, not last, but of course well outside the awards, other than a collectable gold badge celebrating his 100.94mph lap. This in itself was a considerable achievement.

Meantime, Peter Williams in a faultless ride on the Arter-Matchless, was up to a well deserved second place as the 'Boys Own' superstar of his day Mike Hailwood acknowledged the thousands of waving spectators who were witnessing history in the making as the champion whistled across the finish line at an average of 105.62mph – a record, to score his second TT hat-trick and his twelfth Isle of Man TT victory. He was also the fastest man ever over the mountain circuit at 108.77mph, and this on a machine that nobody else could master, just awesome. Mike's last Isle of Man TT World Championship event was his finest hour.

The dazzling Giacomo Agostini, also loved and admired by British fans, had given Hailwood the race of his life, with nothing between these two great men, but the luck was Mike's that day. Williams claimed second place at 99.64mph and Steve Spencer, in his first Senior TT event, rode the Lancefield Norton at 98.59mph into a fine third place. Our new friend, John Cooper, Norton, came fourth at 98.20mph, Fred Stevens, Hannah-Paton, and John Hartle, Matchless-Mettise, made up the leader board. A steady ride by Ron Chandler got him into ninth place. The Senior Race had been a superb, momentous spectacle. It had been a privilege to have been involved and to have seen in action two of the most celebrated riders ever, Mike Hailwood and Giacomo Agostini. The action in Diamond Jubilee year, 1967 will long stay in my memory.

I was delighted with John Blanchard's riding ability. He had taken the Seeley-Matchless around the TT course at 100.94mph, however our personal relationship was on the rocks. It stuttered along until the end of August because of the agreement with Helmut Fath and our commitment to the URS project.

Meanwhile, our friendship and involvement with the 'Derby Flyer – Mooneyes' Cooper was developing. We loaned Cooperman our 350cc 7R Seeley for the Post TT Mallory Park event, as his Norton was out of action. John was in a good third spot, to winner Pat Mahoney when a split oil tank on the prototype MK2 Seeley caused him to drop back to sixth place. We couldn't have known that helping John Cooper would prove to be a passport to future success for the Seeley marque and a very long association with the bespectacled racing ace.

Our TT race service had proved a great success, but we were still financially stretched as we expanded our manufacturing operation. So, with some regret, the silver bullet BMW Rennsport outfit was put up for sale to raise much needed cash.

Back at Belvedere, out came the welding torch, to continue the construction of the Fath four chassis unit. The ambitious, fanatical engineer and sidecar ace Fath, had instructed that we should have the project ready for its debut at the Hutchinson 100 on August 13th. The Ulster Grand Prix was a week later, then Scarborough's Olivers Mount International a week after that on Saturday 26th August. Snetterton International Sunday was the next day, then Oulton Park International on the Bank Holiday Monday, making it three events in three days, with Helmut Fath himself racing at all meetings other than the Ulster Grand Prix, which had no sidecar class. In retrospect this was a totally unrealistic programme. It was too short a time period for such a complex project as the Seeley-Fath four, with the engine unit still under intense development. This was

Seeley-Fath four, the front down tubes could be removed to ease engine gearbox removal.

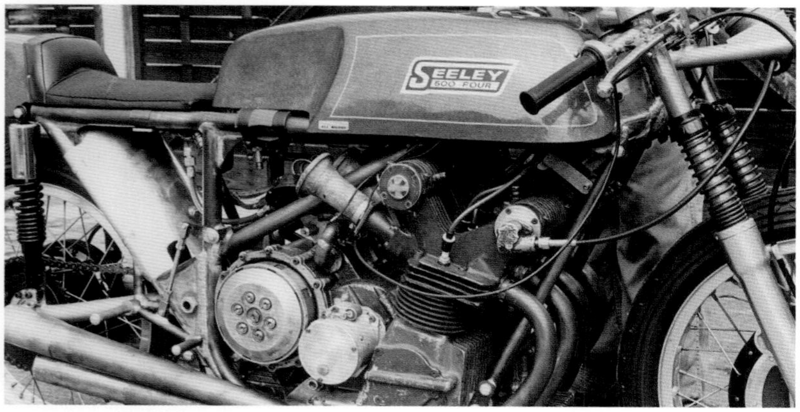

proved at the Dutch TT sidecar race on 24th June, when Fath retired with a broken piston. Arriving home afterwards he collapsed with pneumonia and was ordered to take a complete rest for a least two months. Well, it was like talking to a brick wall, although he missed the Belgian Grand Prix a week later, Helmut was soon back in his workshop, preparing the engine for the Seeley-Fath solo and getting ready for his trip to Finland, in August, a week before the 'Hutch', for the seventh round of the World Sidecar Championship. So far he had failed to finish in any of the five Grands Prix attended. What was driving this man? With the fragile relationship between John Blanchard and myself, I had withdrawn the MK2 350 Seeley prototype, just letting him ride the Seeley-Matchless 500cc, his favourite bike, whilst I concentrated on building the Seeley Fath four. We didn't realise at the time that Blanchard's successes on the works Seeley were over. His last competitive ride turned out to be the Belgian Grand Prix, in early July. Just before the flag dropped, an engine oil feed pipe broke and the Seeley was wheeled off the line. An ear infection prevented John from going on to the East German and Czechoslovakia Grand Prix meetings.

Helmut came to his senses for a short period, cutting back his visit to Finland to come to England to test the Seeley Fath four, in a private session at Brands Hatch. Despite problems with the ignition system and an over-geared machine, 50 laps were completed, mostly by John Blanchard, although I had the pleasure of a few laps on that impressive multi. Back at our works, the engine was removed for Fath to take back to Germany to be rebuilt ready for the forthcoming Hutchinson 100 and the rest of the whirlwind tour of the British circuits. The debut of the well publicised Seeley-Fath four was on the 13th August at the 35th International Hutchinson 100, run in a reverse direction on the 2.65 mile Grand Prix Brands circuit.

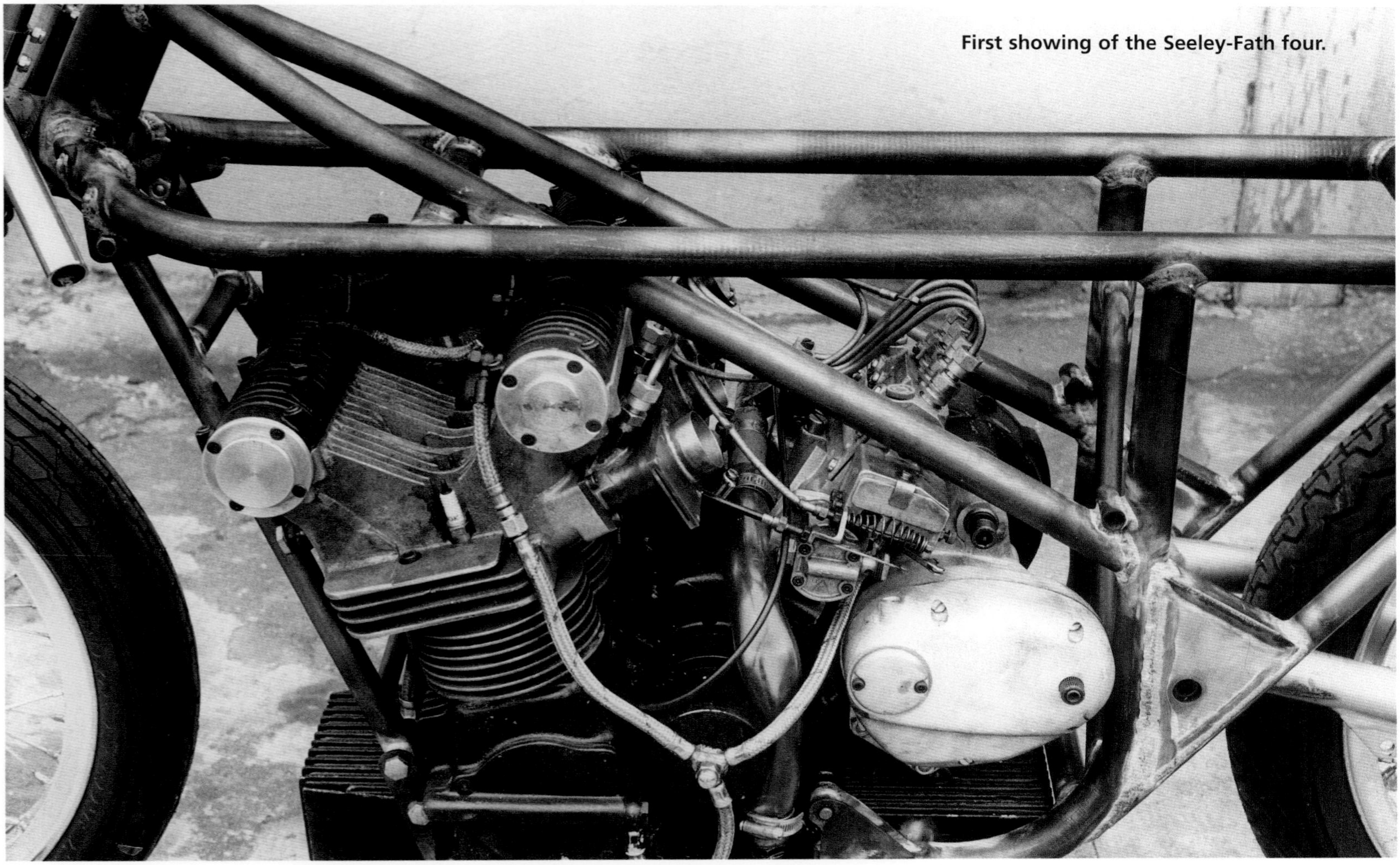

First showing of the Seeley-Fath four.

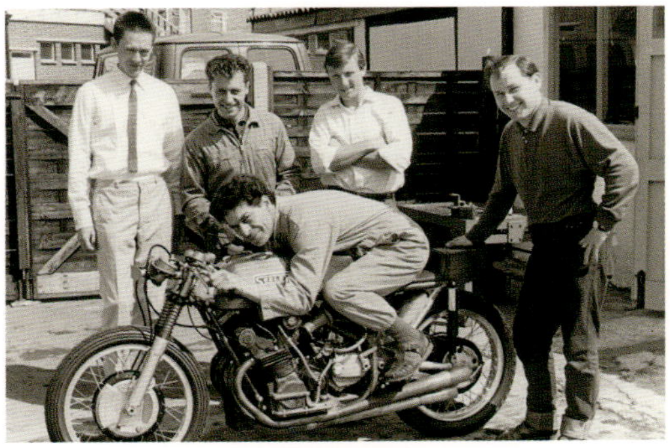

Left to right, Dr Peter Kuhn, me, John Blanchard, Eddie Robinson and Helmut Fath on the URS.

Helmut Fath turned up a couple of days early with the rebuilt URS multi, for the final fitting and adjustments to the Seeley chassis. I remember working through the night to complete it. Finally, the finished product emerged into the early morning sunshine. Helmut's passenger Wolfgang Kalauch stood alongside the Anglo-German effort. It looked magnificent, but would it go as well?

At Brands Hatch Saturday practice there was huge interest in the Fath entourage as the fantastic multi-cylinder powered solo and sidecar machines were unloaded. We may not have been ready to challenge Hailwood's Honda, but the Fath-URS could match it for noise.

A nervous Blanchard awaited his horse, for the Senior Championship solo practice for machines over 250cc and not over 750cc. We were in trouble, an air lock was causing a fuel starvation problem. After a lot of huffing, puffing, blowing and pushing the Fath four burst into life, and with a slightly hesitant rider it was out on the track.

I had not expected too much from the first public outing of the Seeley-Fath four. We needed more time to develop this machine, which I thought had great potential. Then as we all waited on the track side, it was calamity. After a few laps circulating with Ray Pickrell on the 745cc Dunstall Domiracer, Blanchard crashed the Fath four at Westfield. Ray reported that his Domiracer was doing about 135mph down the back straight on the previous lap when Blanchard came past, leaving him as if he was motionless. Unfortunately, in my opinion, Blanchard got carried away and had not taken into account it should have been 'steady as you go' on the first race event outing. He was going too quickly too soon. I was absolutely furious. The Seeley-Fath sustained considerable damage down one side and was brought back to us on the recovery truck. There was no alternative but to return to our works and try and sort out the mess and the flattened exhaust. John Blanchard blamed the low exhaust system for his crash, and certainly there was a problem to be solved there. When I made the original exhaust, Helmut who supplied the special tubing, was insistent that the pipes and megaphones be manufactured to an exact length. Unfortunately, for me, the tubing supplied was only enough to produce four pipes exactly, with not an inch to spare. With no real equipment to shape such exhaust tubing it proved to be a very difficult task.

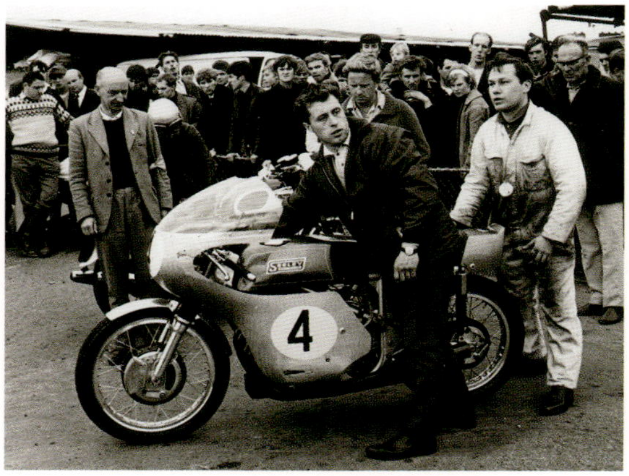

The URS at the Hutchinson 100.

Hutchinson 100, practice problems with the URS.

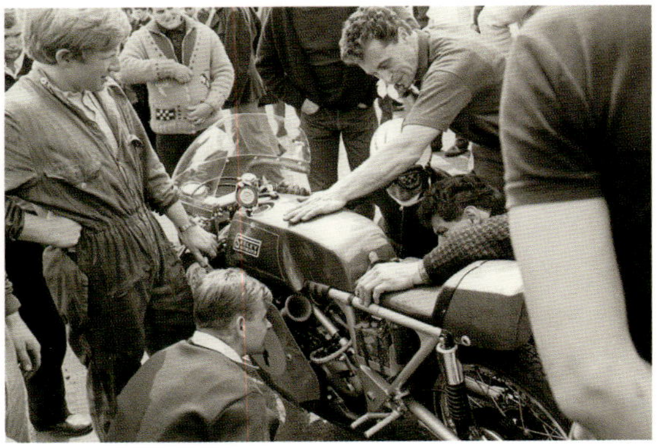

That Saturday Paul Dunstall supplied us with an array of exhaust pipes and megaphones but it was another overnight effort to recover the situation and be back at Brands Hatch next day. It was 4.00am when we all staggered out of the welding shop, with a job well done. With a ten event race programme starting at 12.00pm, practice was held in the morning. I was allowed to test the Seeley-Fath for a couple of laps on my own. Riding round Clearways and up Paddock Hill in the reverse direction was a strange experience. It was a powerful machine and if I fell off I would certainly be a laughing stock.

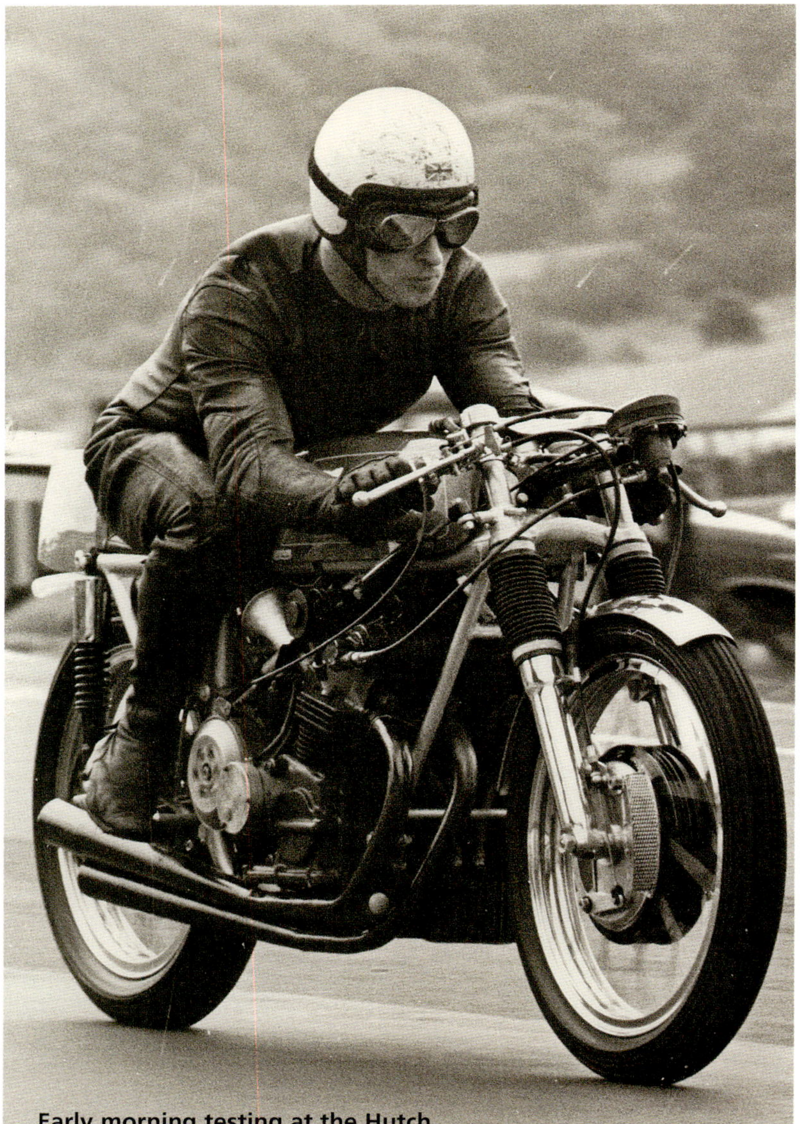

Early morning testing at the Hutch.

Hutchinson 100, John Blanchard and Ray Pickrell.

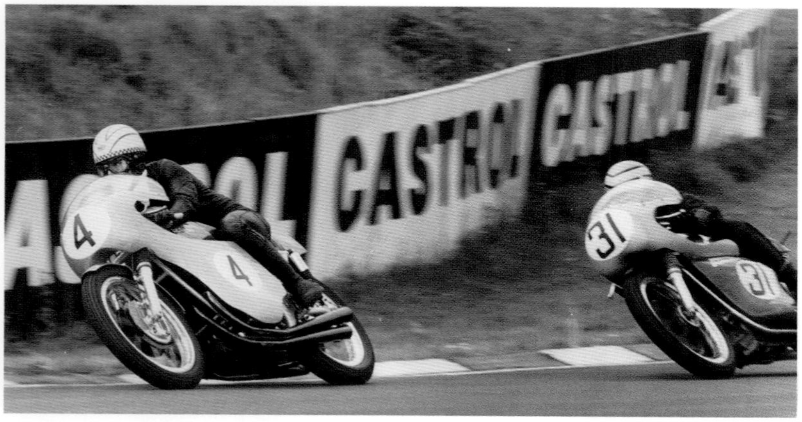

On Sunday, John Blanchard was warned he must go out to finish, with no heroics. In the first race he retired half way through the 15 laps with an oiled plug and in the second achieved a respectable ninth position after suffering a throttle problem. He had had to use the cut out button to stop the engine over revving. A reader's letter printed in MCN defended John Blanchard and criticised my actions over the Seeley-Fath situation. The letter described the bike at The Hutchinson 100 as handling like a 'drunken elephant on ice' and Blanchard falling off in practice was due more to poor handling than rider ability. Hurtful comments indeed! Perhaps the reader did not realise that Blanchard in the race was trying to control the Fath four on the cut-out button. A throttle stuck fully open was enough to make anybody wobble! With the URS engine performing better each time it went out, and the anti-clockwise circuit suiting the ex-World Champion, Helmut Fath cleaned up both 12 lap sidecar races. At least on that point Fath returned to my home that evening reasonably happy. Mike Hailwood's Honda six took the honours that day, winning both 250cc events and both legs of the Senior Races, in which John Cooper, riding our Seeley-Matchless, finished fourth overall.

Having worked so hard in the week running up to the Hutch 100 plus two nights extra working on the Fath project, I was tired, and also fed up with Blanchard, Brands Hatch practice was almost the last straw. John Blanchard was now wrapped up with the German contingent and the URS project. Colin Seeley Racing Development however needed to continue the promotion of our Seeley 7R and G50 machines. Therefore, I dispensed with the direct services of the 'Paperhanger' – (sacked if you like!). Although Blanchard would continue to ride the Seeley-Fath four as part of the agreement CSRD had with Helmut Fath.

The Mallory Park master, a star in his own right, the one and only 'Mooneyes', John Cooper joined us to ride the Seeley-Matchless and 350cc models for the remainder of that season and proved to be a prudent choice. His results on the Seeley-Matchless then the Yamsel would be almost legendary. We are still very close friends today.

After Helmut Fath had carried out service work on both the URS sidecar outfit (needed for Scarborough) and the solo machine, he and his crew left Belvedere for the long trip North and a boat for Northern Ireland for the Ulster Grand Prix at the 7.47 mile Dundrod Road Circuit. Not far behind, John Cooper with the Seeley-Matchless was also driving up the M1 on his way to the Ulster, Wally Rawlings having given the machine a quick once over after Brands Hatch.

The popular Dundrod Circuit first used for Grand Prix racing in 1953 attracted a record 80,000 spectators on the Saturday 19th August, race day with the first fine weather for years at this event. In practice, Blanchard, in his element at this pure road circuit, was troubled with a misfire on the Seeley-Fath four and failed to achieve one good lap in qualifying, ending up on the back row of the grid. Finally, after close inspection by Fath a copper fuel feed pipe to one cylinder was found to have a hairline fracture. Blanchard, having been sidelined in practice, watched Mike Hailwood riding the Honda 500cc four coming out of the start and finish corner. The tail end of the Honda waggled from side to side but Hailwood just whacked the throttle fully open and disappeared at a rate of knots into the distance as he changed into top gear.

Later that Friday morning Hailwood and Blanchard sat in the Castrol Service caravan. URS and Honda were both supported by Castrol. Mike Hailwood said, 'I see you are having some problems with your machine, I'll tell you what to do, for the next practice we will swap bikes.' Visions of riding the almost uncontrollable Honda four came into mind. Then there was laughter all round when Blanchard hardly paused before answering, 'No definitely not!'

The opening event on race day was the 350cc class, giving the Italian 500cc World Champion his first classic win of the year on the smaller works MV. Agostini's task was made easier by the absence of Hailwood, who had already tied up this championship. Ralph Bryans on the 297cc Honda six gave Ago a good run, the Ulsterman leading at one point, but 9.8 seconds down at the end, after the 112 mile race. Heinz Rosner on a 251cc works MZ held a lonely third place with his team-mate Derek Woodman fourth until the MZ developed magneto trouble and the Blackpool rider was forced to retire. Then back in fourth place Kel Carruthers riding an Aermacchi-Metisse was in a tremendous scrap with Ireland's rising star Brian Steenson, the 19 year old student riding a Ronnie Conn sponsored Aermacchi. It was looking like a photo finish between these two but a broken gear linkage on the Ulsterman's Aermacchi on the very last lap robbed Steenson the possibility of a place ahead of the future 1969 250cc world champion Carruthers.

The 'Maidstone Marvel,' Bill Ivy won the lightweight 125cc race on the works Yamaha, despite the tiny four cylinder two-stroke machine overheating. Ivy in the closest of races finished only 0.2 seconds ahead of 'Speedy' Read, both given the same average speed of 94.81mph for the 82 mile event. Stuart Graham on the works Suzuki was plagued with problems but finally made up the rostrum positions.

The 500cc race, which promised a confrontation between Hailwood and Agostini proved a disappointment. At the start, Ago, keen to get away and needing only one more win to clinch the 500cc championship title for the second year in succession, burnt his MV clutch on the line. When he realised he stopped and pushed the MV back into the pits. The clutch plates were replaced. As he left the pits, Ago was nearly 4 laps behind Hailwood who was romping away unchallenged at the front. The sportsmanship of the Italian star was not lost on the Irish fans who gave him tremendous encouragement despite the hopeless handicap. He finished twentieth.

Meanwhile, John Blanchard on the Seeley-Fath four was last away at the back of the grid but in an impressive $2\frac{1}{2}$ laps the 'Paperhanger' was up to third place, behind John Hartle on the Ray Cowles G50 Matchless. URS team 'Meister' Helmet Fath put out a signal to Blanchard to slow down, thinking John was well away from fourth place man Jack Findlay. Unfortunately JB was having problems with braking and stopping. He went through the speed trap at 144mph, only just over 8mph down on the works Honda four. The Findlay McIntyre-Matchless eventually got the better of Blanchard on lap 10 of 15, to finish on the rostrum with Hailwood and Hartle, but John Blanchard's fourth place was the first ever Grand Prix finish for the home brewed Helmut Fath – Peter Kuhn designed four cylinder motorcycle, causing Fath to shed more than a tear as John Blanchard flashed across the finish line. John Cooper brought the faithful Seeley-Matchless home in sixth place. Swiss friend Ernst Weiss was eighteenth on his Seeley-Matchless. John Cooper left the Dundrod Circuit immediately, for the overnight trip to his beloved Mallory Park event next day. 'Mooneyes' on the Seeley-Matchless won his heat

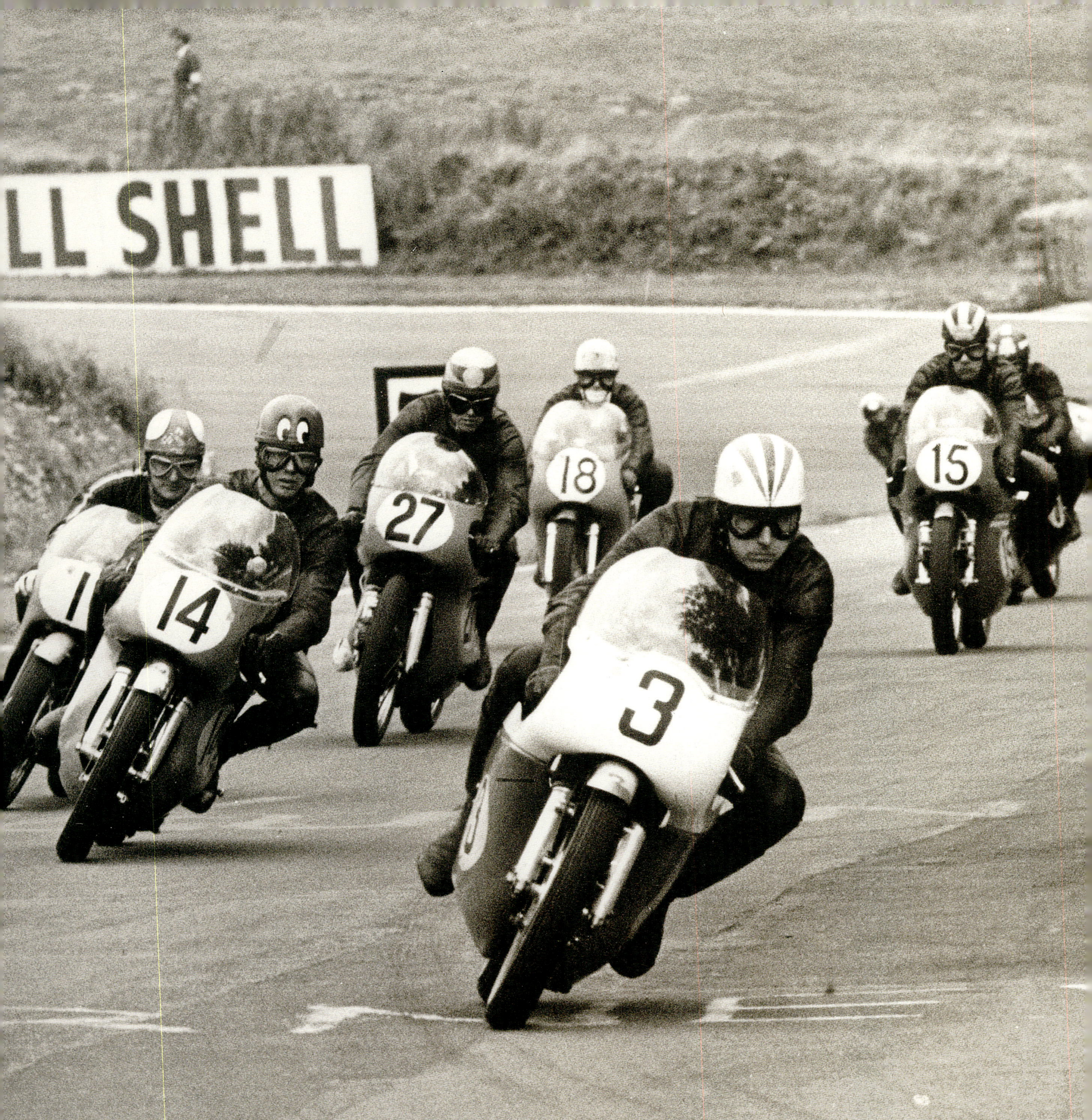

Hutchinson 100, approaching Druids in the reverse direction. Hailwood 1, Cooper 14, Croxford 27, Shorey 18, Chandler 3, Butcher 15, Pickrell 31.

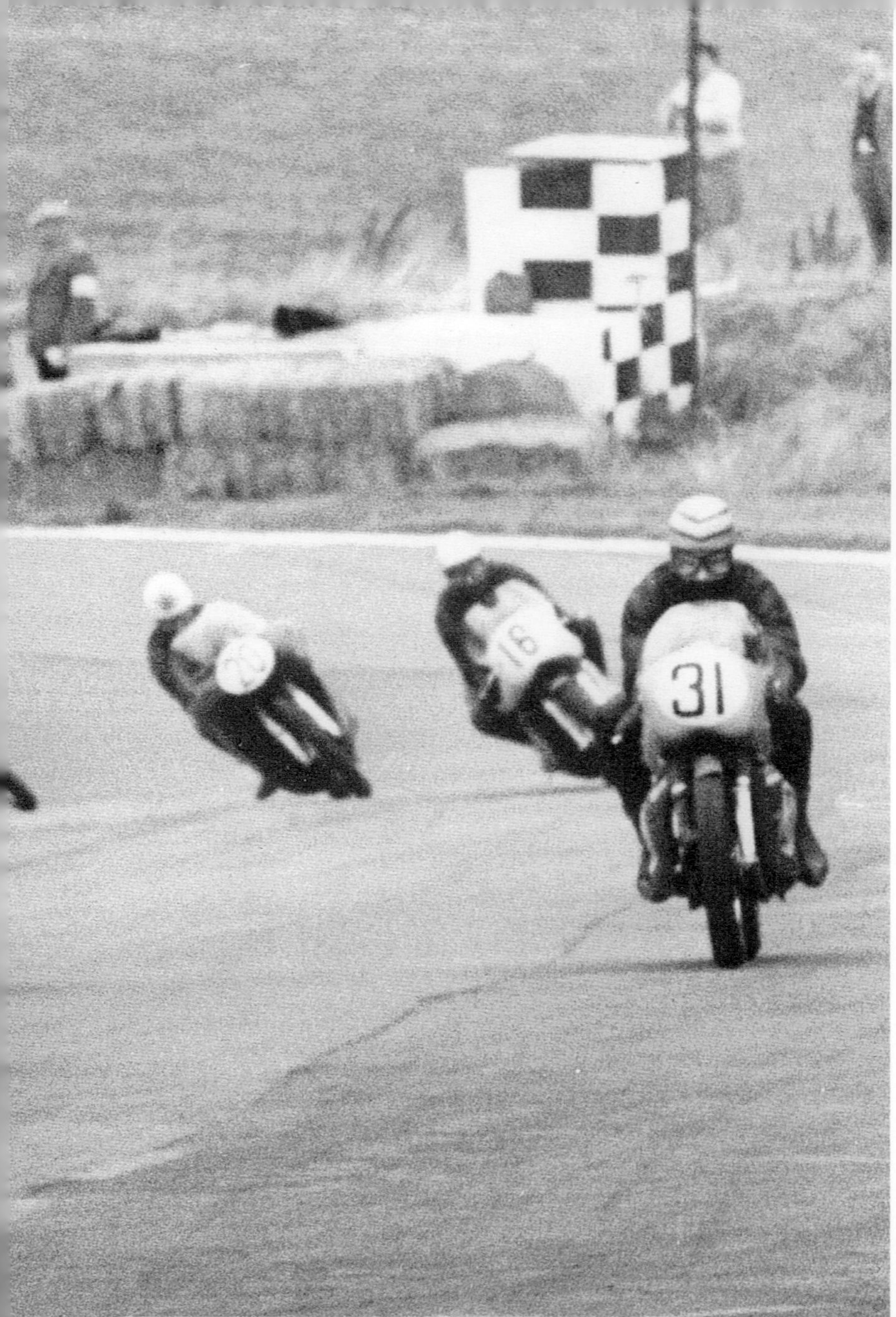

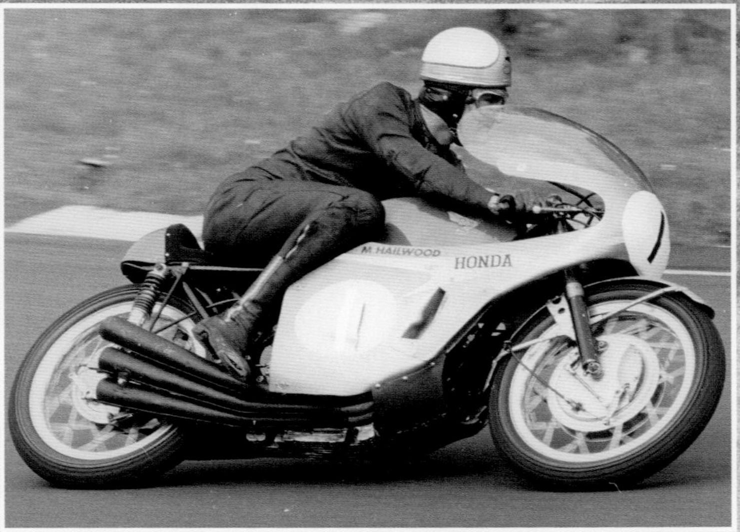

Mike Hailwood at the Hutchinson 100.

John Cooper carrying out some final tuning at Dundrod, Ulster GP.

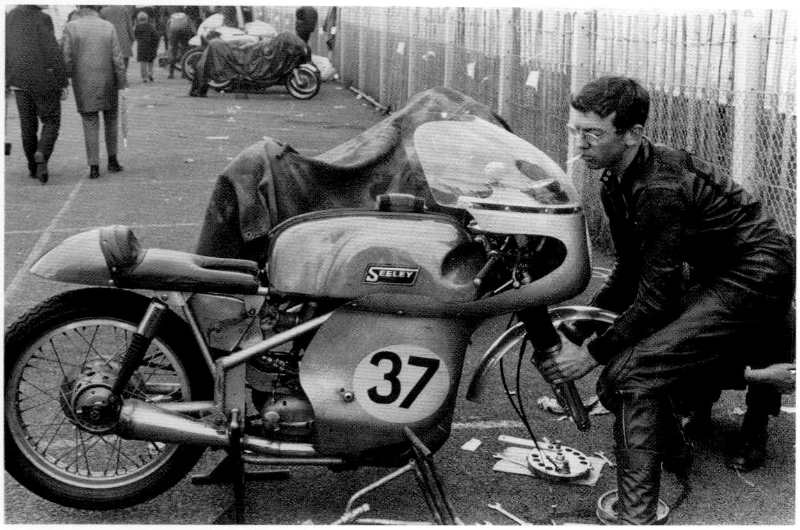

from Percy Tait on the fast works Triumph, then went on to win the 15 lap 500cc final, coming within a mere 0.8 seconds to Hailwood's absolute lap record held since 1962 on the works MV four. Barry Randle just snatched second place from our other man, Ron Chandler, who was having a little sleep on the last lap. 'It's never over until it's over'.

Once the furore of the first Grand Prix success for the Seeley-Fath had settled, Helmut Fath directed his concern to the braking ability of the machine. It was fitted with the Eddie Robinson dual front drum brake, manufactured by CSRD. It was at this point that trouble within the Anglo-German relationship began. Within the few days available before the next event, Scarborough, Helmut Fath arranged the loan of a Lockheed disc brake from Tom Arter via Peter Williams. In Scarborough Fath had been given the use of a small machine shop to engineer the change of brakes on the Seeley-Fath four. Mike Vaughan, the Lockheed technician in attendance must have thought it was Christmas, the Lockheed products already fitted on the Rickman-Metisse machines would now be on a Seeley framed racer. Not being present, I was completely unaware.

The Scarborough club's twenty-first international road race event held on the Olivers Mount 2.41 mile circuit on a glorious Saturday attracted 20,000 fans. 'Mooneyes' Cooper added to his successes, adapting well to the Seeley-Matchless (built originally for Derek Minter) and winning the 500cc final 8 seconds ahead of Dan Shorey, Norton, in second with John Hartle, Matchless Metisse, third. JC repeated his success from tenth place on the opening lap of the handicap race. Cooperman scorched round to win the 8 lap event with Dan Shorey second again. Having won his heat, in the main event John Blanchard, to his credit, rode the Seeley-Fath in a dazzling manner, fourteenth on the first lap, ninth on the second, he made his way through the field, setting the fastest lap of the race and in fact of the whole meeting. Then the Gremlins took over. The fork springs, hammered by miles around the bumpy Ulster Grand Prix course and now at Oliver's Mount were over-loaded. The fierce heavy front disc brake increased the problems of ground clearance for the already low exhaust system. This caused Blanchard to lose the front wheel and crash once more.

Helmut Fath added to his own list of successes with the URS outfit winning the main sidecar race from the World Championship leader Klaus Enders, BMW. On that Saturday, I was busy in the welding shop, producing the next Seeley G50 frame unit. The pressure of business prevented me from visiting Snetterton next day or Oulton Park on that Bank Holiday Monday.

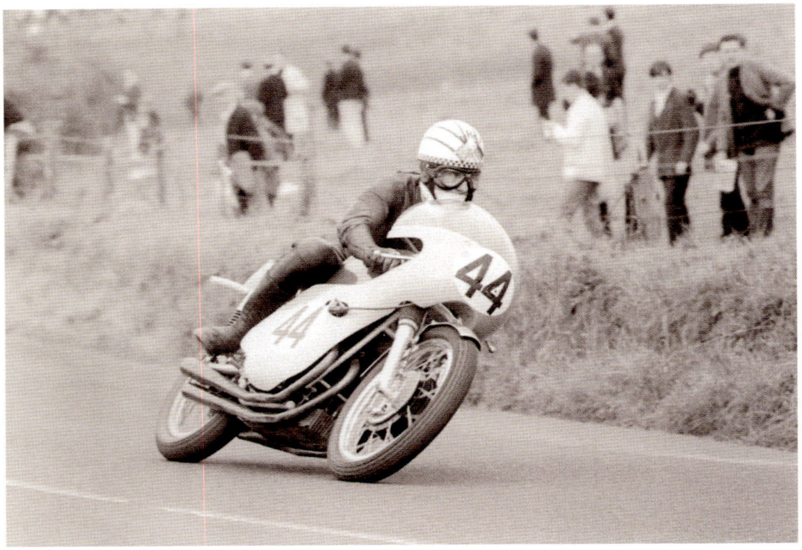

John Blanchard, Ulster Grand Prix, on the Seeley-Fath four.

A friend phoned and told me what had taken place, regarding the alterations to the Seeley-Fath and the fitment of a Rickman-Lockheed disc front brake. I was amazed. I'd had no communication whatsoever from Fath or Blanchard, let alone the opportunity to discuss a front brake problem, or the discarding of our Seeley-Robinson brake. Steaming, I left early next morning for Snetterton accompanied by Les Williams and John Juniper.

Although no longer riding our motorcycles, John Blanchard was still under contract to CSRD as part of the Helmut Fath agreement. CSRD held the entry for the Snetterton event with a promise of £50 start money from secretary and Clerk of the Course, Bob Havers. After discussion with Bob, I agreed to let the Seeley-Fath compete that day so as not to disappoint the fans.

Shortly after I had withdrawn the Seeley MK2 7R at the IOM TT from John Blanchard, he had purchased a secondhand early MK1 Seeley AJS for which I had loaned him a spare engine. At some point, possibly the Ulster Grand Prix, John had blown up this 7R engine. John denied this, but I wanted my engine back. So on that Sunday at Snetterton, and to avoid confrontation, I sent my friends to request the return of the engine but Blanchard refused. (John since has raised doubts that my recollections on this issue are correct). The refusal lit my short fuse and before the Seeley-Fath four had turned a wheel that day I reluctantly informed Bob Havers that I was withdrawing our race entry for the machine. I then instructed Fath and Blanchard to remove the engine unit from the Seeley chassis along with the offending Lockheed disc brake. The dung had hit the fan and we would go our separate ways.

The Colin Seeley Racing Developments Team had worked hard to design and build a rolling chassis to suit the complex URS multi cylinder engine unit. It was a huge commitment at a time when we could least afford the involvement. The manufacture of 7R, G50 engines, spares and frame units was our main priority.

As the whole unit had been supplied free of charge and on a loan basis, I did not believe it unreasonable that we be informed of any major cycle part changes. After all, it was a prototype machine and in my opinion a development project which could benefit us all in time.

Surprisingly, the project had shown early promise. The problem of low exhaust had been rectified back at base. A more powerful front brake may well have been needed for this fast and heavy machine however an examination of the Robinson dual brake revealed incorrect adjustment. It had been working as a single sided brake, not dual as intended, no wonder Blanchard could hardly stop at the Ulster Grand Prix! John Blanchard thought it unfair that he had had to cope with this experimental motorcycle mostly on his own. Fair comment but Wally Rawlings was now looking after John Cooper and the Seeley-Matchless. With no spare personnel or budget it was just not possible to provide a mechanic for him. The big mistake had been attending so many events in so short a space of time, but that was Fath's doing, not mine!

I had always blamed Blanchard for the introduction of the Rickman-Lockheed brake. Rickman Brothers were our direct competitors in the manufacturing of racing bikes, so fitting a Lockheed brake, with which Rickmans were associated, was like shooting ourselves in the foot in our efforts to sell the Eddie Robinson designed drum brake.

In a recent interview Blanchard said that the whole matter at the time went out of control and had gone over his head. In retrospect, the fanatical Helmut Fath was probably the main force behind the front brake changes. In his eagerness he hadn't considered the commercial implications of his actions. Fath was highly inventive and talented, but at all costs he was determined to prove to the critical German press that he hadn't been wasting his time on the home-brewed URS. Failure was not a word in Helmut's vocabulary. Thinking back, I believe Fath's hint that I might eventually receive the use of a URS engine for my return to world championship sidecar racing was never really in the equation.

In retrospect, I probably overreacted to the Seeley-Fath four situation. I was perhaps just as intense and blinkered as Fath. I was also criticised by the British press for my plan to continue the production of AJS and Matchless racing components. Much was at stake for both of us.

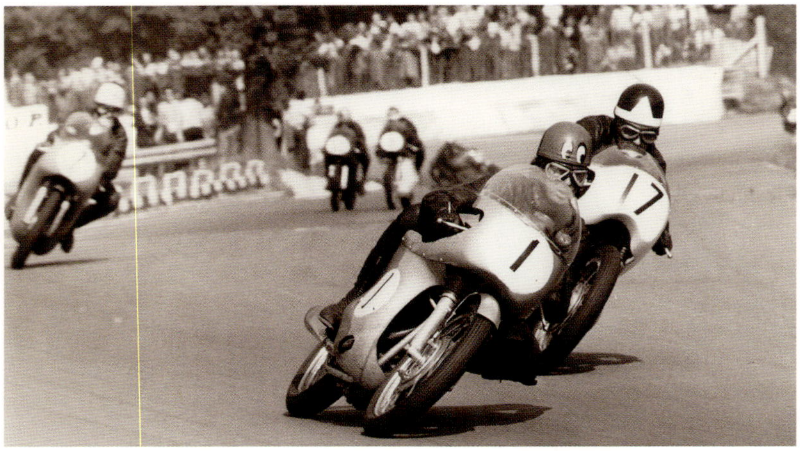

John 'Mooneyes' Cooper 1967.

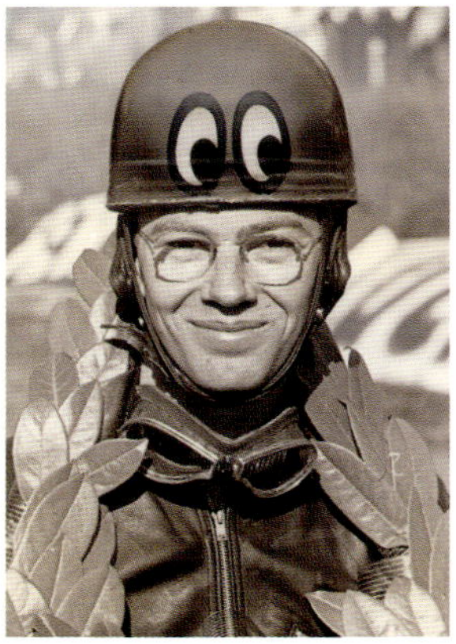

John Cooper, Leaning on Percy Tait to win at Mallory Park.

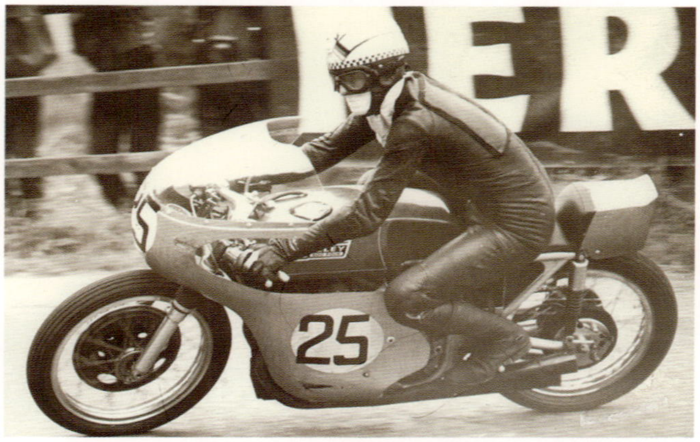

Lockheed front disc brake on the Seeley-URS, at Scarborough, which caused all the trouble between myself, Fath and Blanchard.

Helmut, on the URS sidecar outfit improved each time he ventured onto the track, breaking the long domination of BMW in the 500cc sidecar class. I believe he thought similar results could be quickly achieved with the solo URS. German speaking Blanchard was willing to chance his luck in this mission, having stated, 'My ambition is to prove the URS for Helmut.' Fath did not like my criticism of the head strong Blanchard and considered him as the only URS solo rider. After the Snetterton fiasco I decided to go to Oulton Park next day in an effort to redeem the unfortunate situation.

The bright spot for our sponsors, Castrol Oil at Snetterton was when Mike Hailwood on the 250 Honda six won the Castrol Challenge Trophy from Phil Read, Yamaha, with new race and lap records, in fact breaking the absolute course record by over 3mph.

Fath, having won the 500cc race at Snetterton from Pip Harris, BMW, was lying second to Chris Vincent in the unlimited race when he retired with a blown engine. When I arrived at Oulton Park, Helmut was busy changing engines, in fact fitting in the solo URS unit taken out of the Seeley Fath the day before. After all the work Fath failed to finish either race legs, so he was not too happy. He had little to say other than that was that for the solo URS machine that year, and he would do it himself in the future. Convenient for him, perhaps realising there was still much to do to make the URS reliable. Not so convenient for my company, left with a chassis unit only suitable for the URS.

Why we allowed a situation to get completely out of hand and wreck the indisputable potential of the Seeley-Fath four. I shall never know, the spout had come off the teapot and was not able to be glued back on.

The only bright spot for us on that hot and humid holiday Monday, attended by 30,000 fans, was our new signing, John (Mooneyes) Cooper, who won the 8 lap Les Graham Memorial Trophy Race from Minter and Hartle. Then in a stylish manner on the Seeley Matchless, he led from start to finish to win the Avon Gold Cup 19 lap event, to be awarded a gold watch and the £100 first prize.

Ron Chandler was in action at Crystal Palace that same day, winning the 500cc event on the Rawlings tuned Matchless from Joe Dunphy with Charlie Sanby third. It had been a traumatic weekend for me. The outcome was disappointing but it was time to move on, so much to do and so little time to do it.

Castrol competitions manager Malcolm Edgar congratulates Mike Hailwood on winning the 250cc Castrol Challenge Race at Snetterton with a record race speed of 92.68mph and record lap of 94.35mph.

In the tradition of Associated Motorcycles we (CSRD) were to provide a service in the Isle of Man for the Manx Grand Prix competitors. I was up to my ears in work. We were also preparing for the forthcoming Earls Court Motorcycle Show, mid September, having booked a stand in the Motorcycle News 'market place'. This would be our first show after the AMC takeover and an important opportunity to display the new Seeley products along with the replacement 7R, G50 and Manx Norton parts.

August 1967 was a month of announcements, BP the British Petroleum Company confirmed after many years of involvement that they were withdrawing from sponsorship of the sport. Motor Circuit Developments, controllers of the main racing circuits throughout the UK, decided to stop paying start money to the top semi and full

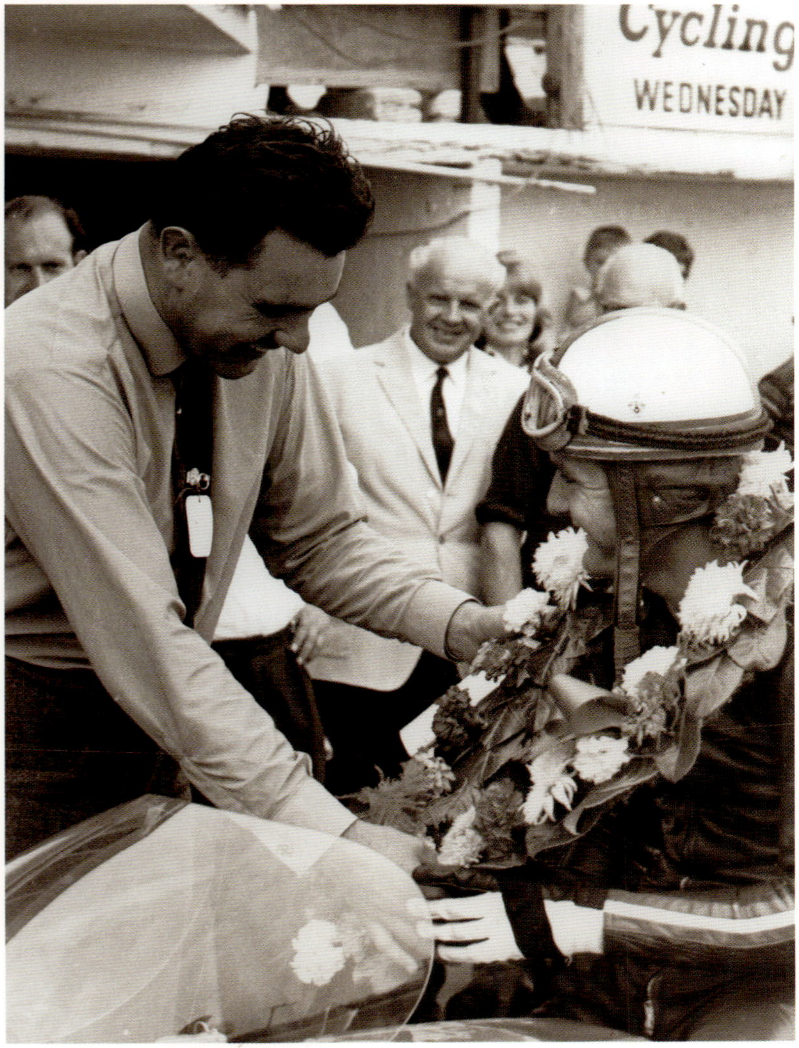

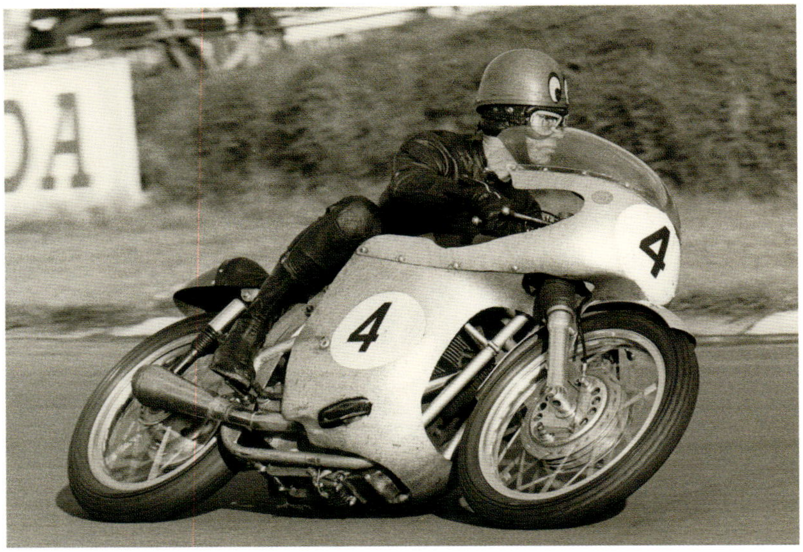

John Cooper on winning form at Brands Hatch.

time professional riders at national meetings. This decision caused concern for many British competitors who thought they could not afford to continue in the sport. Derek Minter decided the axing of start money was the last straw and he would retire at the end of that season. In fact he would 'pack it in' there and then if he could find somebody to buy his Nortons at £500 apiece. Reads Ltd of Leytonstone (Honda dealers) declared plans to produce a 72bhp 500cc twin cylinder-racing engine, in association with the Weslake Car Engine Company. I was asked to comment on this ambitious project by Ray Creek, Director of Reads Ltd. Unfortunately, Ray had little idea what such a project involved, and ill-advisedly began advertising the engine unit as the most powerful 500cc engine in existence apart from works machines – sounded great on paper! Reads were also inviting enquiries in Britain and from overseas, for what turned out to be another enterprise that eventually ended 'on the rocks'.

Enthusiastic London motorcycle dealer Vic Camp was appointed British importer for the range of Ducati machines, models from 50cc, 160cc, 250cc through to the 350cc Sebring Roadstar, costing a whopping £288. Minister of Transport, Barbara Castle denied that she intended to bring in compulsory training for learner riders. The good news that August was that the Duckhams Oil Company, with competition manager Ron Carnell in charge, would extend their involvement in road racing for 1968, supporting 'up and coming' riders.

Road racing continued unabated. Only days after the Scarborough, Snetterton and Oulton Park weekend there was a choice between Italian Grand Prix or Brands Hatch National, both on September 3rd. Brands Hatch it was, where Derek Minter, on what we thought would be his 'swan song', showed his old style and skill as the one-time 'King of Brands' by winning the fourth round of the 500cc Redex Trophy on his Norton after a tremendous 10 lap, race-long scrap with Dave Croxford, Matchless, and Cooperman on the Seeley-Matchless third, Dave Degens, Dresda Triton, fourth place and Alan Barnett on the Kirby Matchless Metisse in fifth.

'Mooneyes' Cooper was a triple winner and the star of the event. First he won the rain swept 10 lap unlimited 1000cc race on the Seeley-Matchless in a close encounter with Dave Croxford. Then, on his 350cc Norton, he won the Junior event from Croxford, Chandler and Minter in that order. Dave Croxford a man to keep an eye on! He then clinched the 15 lap unlimited event on the Seeley from Croxford with Chandler third, great results prior to the Motorcycle Show!

The Earls Court Motorcyclorama Show, sponsored by the Daily Express, opened on Saturday 16th September 1967 for eight days, two months earlier than usual for some reason. The opening day clashed with the World Speedway Championships final held at Wembley which attracted some 75,000 fans, with only 14,000 visitors to Earls Court! Swedish ace Ove Fundin became the only man to win the World Speedway title five times.

The next day, Sunday 17th September, in an all action week, thousands of fans swarmed to Mallory Park for the Daily Mail sponsored International 'Race of the Year'. 40,000 enthusiastic racing supporters turned out, eager to witness the contest between the champions Hailwood, Agostini, Read and the 1967 125cc champion elect, Bill Ivy.

The huge crowd was not disappointed. Agostini on the works MV kicked off the proceedings in heat one of the 350cc to 1000cc Senior Race. Ago left the fans gasping when he struggled to fire up the MV, managing to finish fifth in the 5 lap dash, but it was enough. John Cooper won his heat and Hailwood, without a suitable capacity machine, left 'Mooneyes' on the Seeley-Matchless as the main opposition to Ago in that race. John Cooper, not a man to lose an opportunity, took an early lead, whilst Agostini jostled his way through from his third row grid position, nipped under the flying Derbyshire man at Devils Elbow, and with the superior speed of the MV pulled away from Cooper, who on the Seeley held his second place from Ray Pickrell on the 750cc Dunstall Domiracer in third. Fast improving Dave Croxford fourth, was holding the sheep farmer Percy Tait, Triumph, in the pen for fifth and Barry Randle, Norton, made up the first six. Earlier in the race the ill-fated John Hartle crashed the Ray Cowes Matchless at Gerards Bend, broke his left arm, damaged his ankles, and sustained concussion.

Hailwood was in action for the first heat of the 250cc – 350cc Junior Race, providing that day the first distinctive sound of the 297cc Honda six. Mike made no mistake in his heat; nor Ago, so the 15 lap final was the first clash of the champions. Hailwood rocketed into the lead staying ahead of Ago and Phil Read and that's how it stayed. Paul Smart, Aermacchi, beat off the challenge of a charging Griff Jenkins for fourth place with Ron Chandler in fifth.

Mike Hailwood, Honda, was the victor again in the 250 race, Phil Read on the Yamaha twin no match for Hailwood, way behind with Derek Woodman, MZ, third. This race counted towards the Castrol Championship series and this win ensured victory for Mike who was handed the £500 winner's cheque, despite a final round to be held later at Brands

Then it was the big one, the 30 lap 40.5 mile Daily Mail 1,000 guinea Race of the Year for invited riders and machines, 175cc to 1000cc. Well, there was no holding back our British hero 'Mike the Bike', performing at his fantastic best. There was huge excitement as the three main contenders lined up at the front of the grid, Hailwood on his 297cc Honda, Agostini on his 500cc MV, with Read on his Yamaha 250 four. Behind the front trio were all the regulars; Cooper, Ivy, Croxford, Randle, Tait, Uphill, Shorey, Minter, Pickrell and Smart to name just a few. The race bikes were pulled back on compression waiting for the drop of the flag.

It was hush, suddenly the flag was down. Everybody was pushing, then the first sound, the fantastic Honda six burst into life and Hailwood shot into an immediate lead, putting yards between himself, Read and Ago. 'Speedy' Read kept ahead of the big MV for a few laps but soon gave way to the quicker machine as Ago pursued Hailwood. Delight for us when John Cooper on the Seeley-Matchless came round in fourth place and held that position to the very end. Best of the non–works men, 'Cooperman' along with Ago and Read were the only riders not to be lapped by the master. Mike Hailwood crossed the finish line to the cheers of the huge crowd 15.2 seconds ahead of Ago. It was Mike's fourth 'race of the year' victory, scooping the thousand guinea first prize, Agostini received £500, Phil Read in third £250 and John 'Mooneyes' Cooper £150. Bill Ivy and Dave Croxford made up the fifth and sixth position.

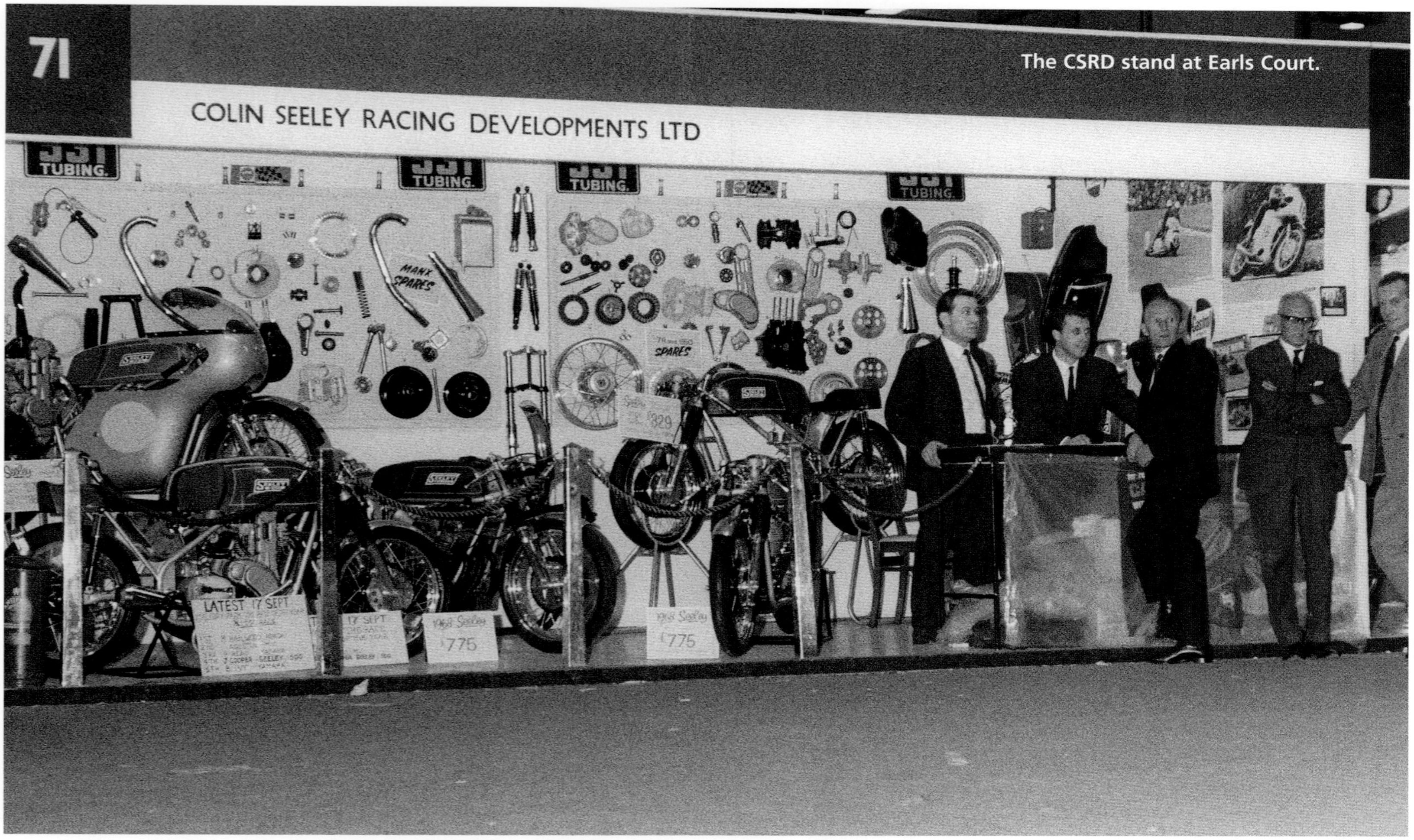

71 The CSRD stand at Earls Court.

The last solo race of the day promised to be a rousing encounter between Bill Ivy and Stuart Graham in the 125cc ultra lightweight class. Unfortunately, Ivy after giving pre-race entertainment by riding in the reverse direction up Devils Elbow in an effort to clear the plugs on the works Yamaha, then back on the start line wiping his goggles on the starters flag, retired with oiled plugs after only one lap. Stuart Graham posted his first short circuit win on the works Suzuki, but in style, leading from start to finish and establishing a new race record. Derek Woodman, MZ, was in second place and Kel Carruthers, Honda), third. With a total of eleven solo races and three sidecar events for the attending fans it had been a great day. They now flooded across the circuit to mob the champions and winners in the greatest of good spirits.

Back at Earls Court, our Colin Seeley Racing Developments stand had proved a great attraction with a number of orders placed for our MK2 Seeley racers and frame kits. The MK2 Seeley was 'amongst the neatest bikes in the show' according to 'Motorcycle'. Perhaps this caused the Rickman Brothers to reduce their rolling chassis unit by a huge £100, down to £295, under-cutting our product by £34. Our complete Seeley-500cc G50 Racer, fitted with a four speed box was listed at £775, or with a Schafleitner five speed box, £890. Fairings were extra, but each machine was personally run in by the boss, my regular job on a Wednesday afternoon at Brands Hatch, great fun!! I was proud that our Seeley racers were ready to race straight out of the box - all part of the service. We offered a total of six self-construction kits to suit the conversion of a standard Matchless G50 or AJS 7R at prices starting at £85 for a frame, swinging arm, Girling damper units, footrest and brake pedal. With a seat, oil and petrol tanks, retaining straps and engine plates the price was £120. Add front forks, clip-ons, head races, chain case and alloy mudguard, the price went up to a whopping £175. With the full Monty which included the wheels, exhaust system, fairing, control levers, cables and all sorts of other 'bits and pieces' it was listed at, wait for it, £329.

John Cooper, impressed by his successes on the Seeley-Matchless, decided for 1968 to switch completely from the Nortons on which he had made his name, to the Seeley product. John would buy his own bikes but we would take a special interest in supporting him. Wally Rawlings would maintain the engines. John Cooper, 'Mooneyes', was our first customer for complete Seeley racers and it was a big break-through at that time for our small company.

Joe Parkhurst, editor-in-chief and owner of the American 'Cycle World' Magazine, placed his order for a Seeley-G50, followed by regular customer Ron Chandler, still supported by Reg Kirby, who would race Seeley machines in 1968. I was still keen to have our own works supported rider, it was the best and quickest way to improve the product and I had my eye on the Ruislip racer Dave Croxford.

The work was endless, our machine shop bustling with activity. Len Smith controlled the day-to-day production: cylinder heads, crankcases, con-rods, cam boxes, cylinders, flywheels, rockers, brake drums, fork sliders, gearbox shells, the list was endless. We hardly seemed to get over the Motorcycle Show when the last major international event of the year was upon us. The Evening News Race of the South was held at Brands Hatch on October 1st. Once more it was a well publicised clash of the titans, Hailwood and Agostini, the newly crowned 500cc World Champion achieved at Mosport in Canada the previous weekend. It could not be have been closer. With five Grand Prix wins each, Giacomo Agostini got the verdict by one second place more than Mike the Bike - disappointing for Hailwood who almost had a clean sweep that year, having already cleaned up in both the 250cc and 350cc classes, the results were a near repeat of 1966.

At Brands Mike, riding his favourite 297cc six cylinder Honda would trounce the Italian on the three cylinder MV in the 350cc race, with 'Desperate Dan' Shorey, Norton, riding out of his skin, beating the ex-King Derek Minter and snatching third place, with Dave Croxford and Rex Butcher fifth and sixth. The 'Maidstone Marvel' Bill Ivy, already winner

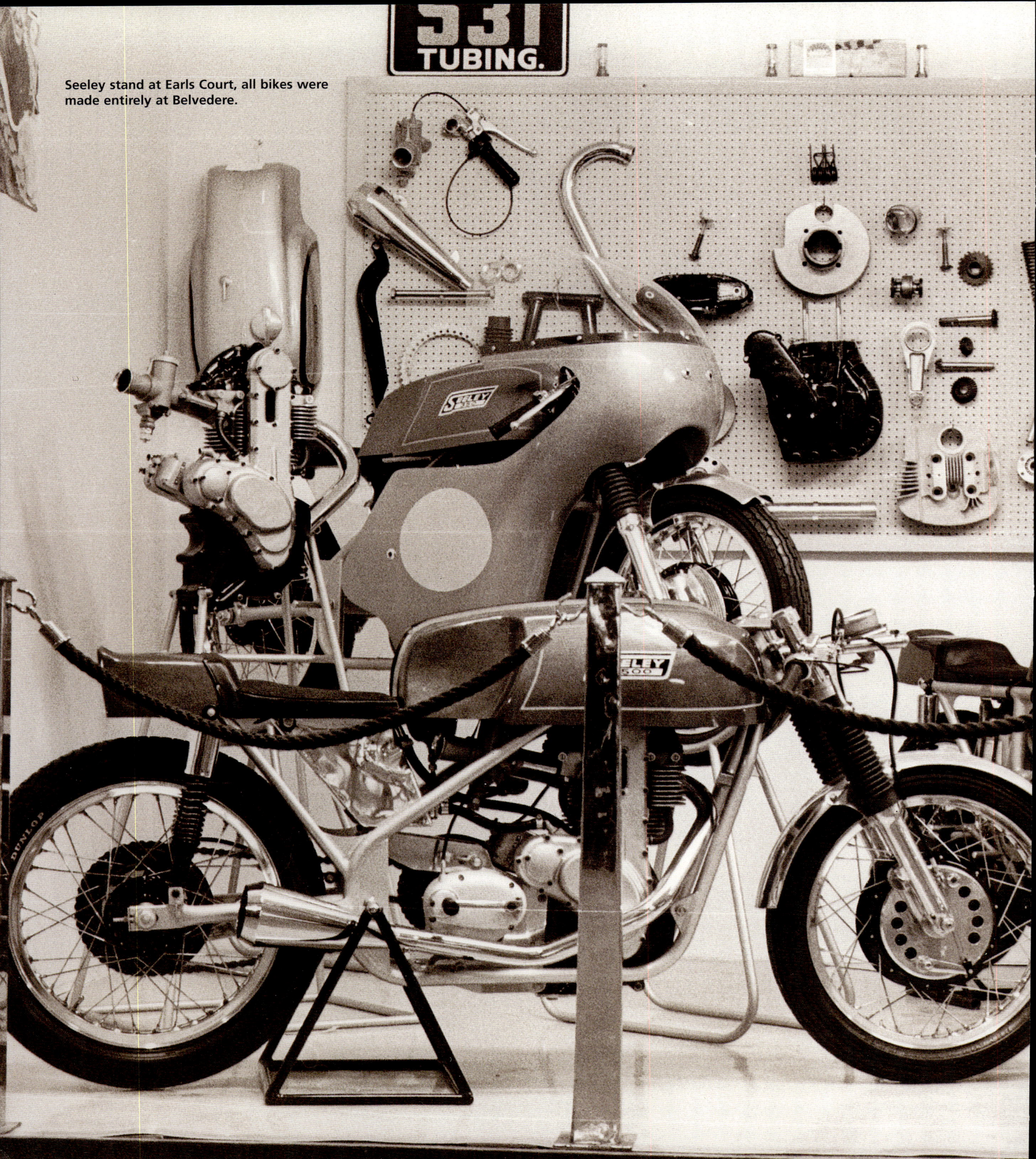

Seeley stand at Earls Court, all bikes were made entirely at Belvedere.

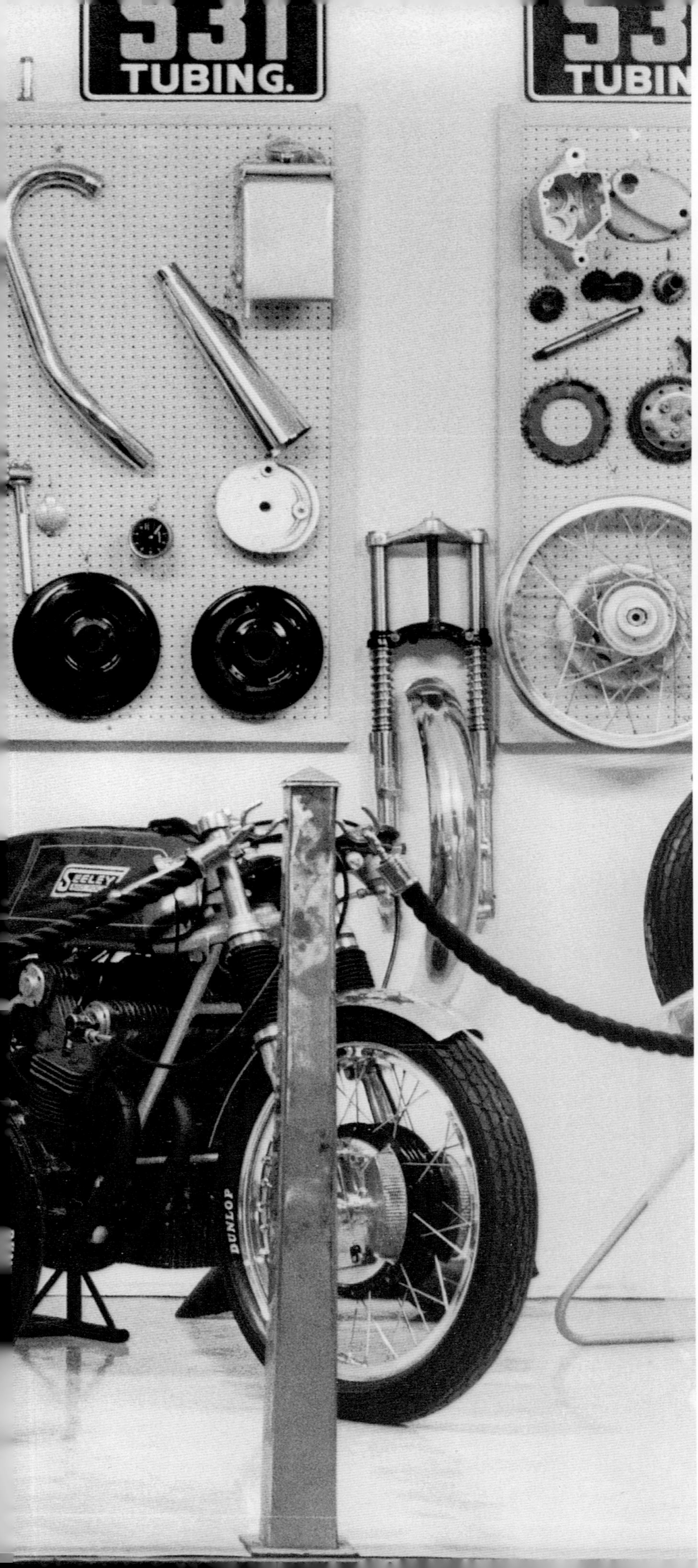

Joe Parkhurst and me at Earls Court.

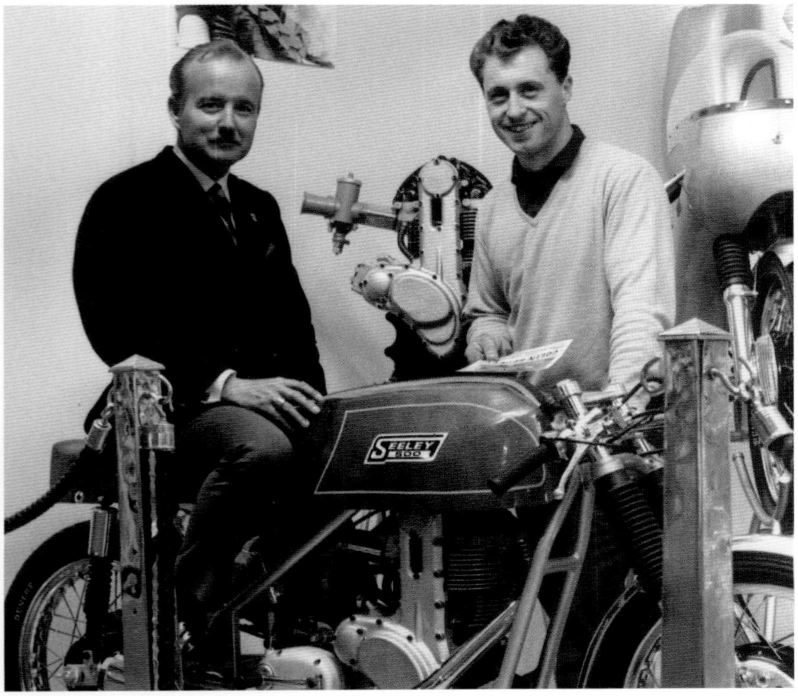

of seven 125cc Grands Prix that year and soon to be handed the 'Crown' with only Japan to go. On the works Yamaha he romped to an easy win in the 125cc.

With Hailwood out of the 500cc Redex Trophy Race, it should have been a benefit event for the Italian World champion. Relentless pressure from the British boys wringing the last bit out of their single cylinder machines, resulted in a rare occasion on the third lap when Ago crashed out down the notorious Paddock Hill, causing skinned hands and a badly bent MV. Most embarrassing, and a disappointment for the huge crowd. Meantime, in perhaps the best race of the day, the last round of the Redex Trophy was a photo finish between Shorey and Minter with 'Desperate Dan' getting the verdict. In third place the 'Ruislip Rebel' Dave Croxford gained the vital points to secure the Redex Trophy and £100. Ron Chandler on our Seeley-Matchless came in fourth, with Steve Spencer and Alan Barnett making up the first six places.

Helmut Fath on the four cylinder URS was a run-away victor in the 500cc Deubel Trophy Sidecar Race. The BMWs of Pip Harris and Tony Wakefield were no match for the four cylinder. Although Derek Woodman, MZ, led the field on the first lap of the 250cc Castrol Trophy Race, 'Speedy' Read, Yamaha, soon had the event 'stitched up' leaving Derek Chatterton, Yamaha, in a good second place, with Dave Degens, Aermacchi, third.

Then came the 'clash of the giants', the twenty lap Evening News Race of the South. Unfortunately, with Agostini out of action the race was somewhat an anti-climax. Hailwood on the formidable Honda six rocketed into an unassailable lead from Phil Read on a 250cc Yamaha. A determined Minter, riding like he would never retire, challenged Read for a number of laps but finally settled for third place, but this time ahead of Dan Shorey. Our man Ron Chandler brought home our Seeley Matchless in an excellent fifth spot and Alan Barnett on the Kirby Matchless-Metisse sixth. That was it, another race day over, always a great atmosphere at Brands. Many of us retired to the Grovewood Suite for food, drinks, the music of jazzman Chris Barber and time to relate the tales of the day.

Hardly believable, but the early October Race of the South was not the last event on the British calendar for 1967. Three more nationals followed at Snetterton, Brands Hatch (again), then finally Mallory Park on October 29th. There had been at least 20 national and international UK events, not including the Northwest 200, Ulster Grand Prix, and Isle of Man TT, or any of the Grand Prix meetings favoured by the British contingent, such as the German Grand Prix, Dutch TT and Belgium Grand Prix. With so many competitors racing in a minimum of two events, a good number would compete in 40 to 50 races in one season. When you consider all the travelling, wear and tear on machines and riders alike, they were a brave and hardy breed who played such an important part in our sport at that time.

Our racing service at the Isle of Man TT and Manx Grand Prix and our plans to produce new racing motorcycles led to the Isle of Man authorities inviting us to move our operation there. The Manx government was keen to attract light industry and ours would help to keep the TT and Manx Grand Prix races going. At that point we were not ready for such a move, but we wouldn't rule it out for the future. At the Brands Hatch International we returned the dummy engine unit to Helmut Fath following the Earls Court Show. We remained on speaking terms, but there was no reconciliation either over John Blanchard or the Seeley-Fath four. The project, as far as I was concerned, was dead. We stripped the frame unit of all useable parts and it was left to gather dust.

'Magnificent Mint' was the headline in 'Motorcycle' as described by David Dixon of Derek Minter at Snetterton on October 15th. No-one would have known Minter was planning race retirement as in his heat of the 500cc race, Derek pulling Isle of Man gearing and making full use of a strong tail wind down the long Norwich Straight left Croxford and Barnett locked in combat well behind, and broke the lap record in the process. In the 1000cc event Ray Pickrell, on the Dunstall Domiracer 745cc, in the lead from the second lap. also broke the class lap record to win from Dan Shorey with Ron Chandler on the Seeley-Matchless ahead of Dave Croxford, and Rex Butcher on the other Dunstall Norton in fifth. Dan Shorey, Norton, after a great scrap with the regulars, won the 350cc race, half a second separating Shorey, Croxford and Degens on the last lap with Minter fourth. Derek Chatterton, having his first outing on a new Kawasaki twin, notched fifth place.

For the last race, the 7 lap, 18.97 mile, 500cc event a bitter wind was blowing. At the end of the second lap just over 2 seconds covered the first nine riders and the race looked set for a long struggle, but a rain squall split the pack. Croxford took advantage and broke clear, but bravery overcame discretion when the 'Ruislip Rebel' rambled at great speed across the field on the outside of Riches Corner. The Matchless G50 was not meant for scrambling! That let Alan Barnett (returning having broken his leg at Castle Combe back in April) in with a chance, but Ron Chandler, in close formation, kept the Seeley steady and soon took the lead. The crafty Minter in scintillating style on his Petty Norton, having eased the pace in the earlier damp conditions, steadily gained on the two front men. On the last lap he coolly steamed past Alan Barnett, then Chandler the current holder of the King of Brands title. Minter received a well deserved ovation from the hardy spectators who had also braved the conditions. Rodney Gould, Joe Dunphy, and 'Desperate Dan' Shorey, recovered from his near crash earlier in the race, came over the finish line almost abreast and in that order.

Finally, came the fifth and last race meeting at Brands Hatch for that year. The man from Kent, after a career of 14 years, wasn't giving up his crown too easily. After a close encounter with Dan Shorey and Dave Croxford, Minter won the 350cc race. In the 500cc event, held over 8 laps of the 2.65 mile Grand Prix circuit, the 'Mint' led an inseparable group of Shorey, Croxford, Chandler and John Cooper chopping and changing, trying every trick in the book. Then Shorey, riding so well at that time, edged past the 'King' 2 laps from home, but Minter snatched the lead back. On the last lap, to the dismay of Kent fans, 'Desperate Dan' dived through to take the chequered flag from Minter just a machine's length ahead. John Cooper and Ron Chandler, both Seeley-Matchless mounted, came in third and fourth, Alan Barnett fifth and Australian Kel Carruthers Matchless-Metisse sixth.

Headlights were a distinct possibility for the 1000cc solo final as the autumn evening

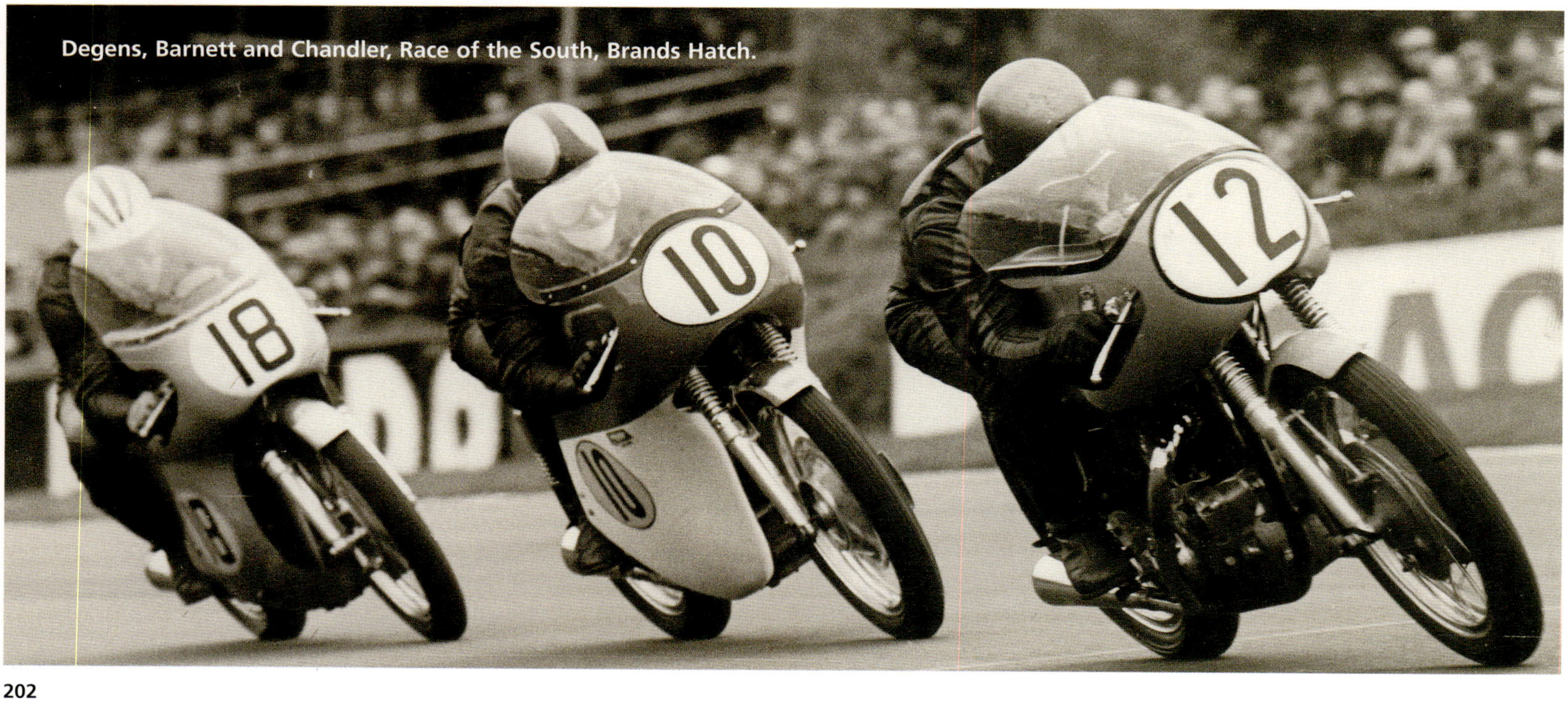

Degens, Barnett and Chandler, Race of the South, Brands Hatch.

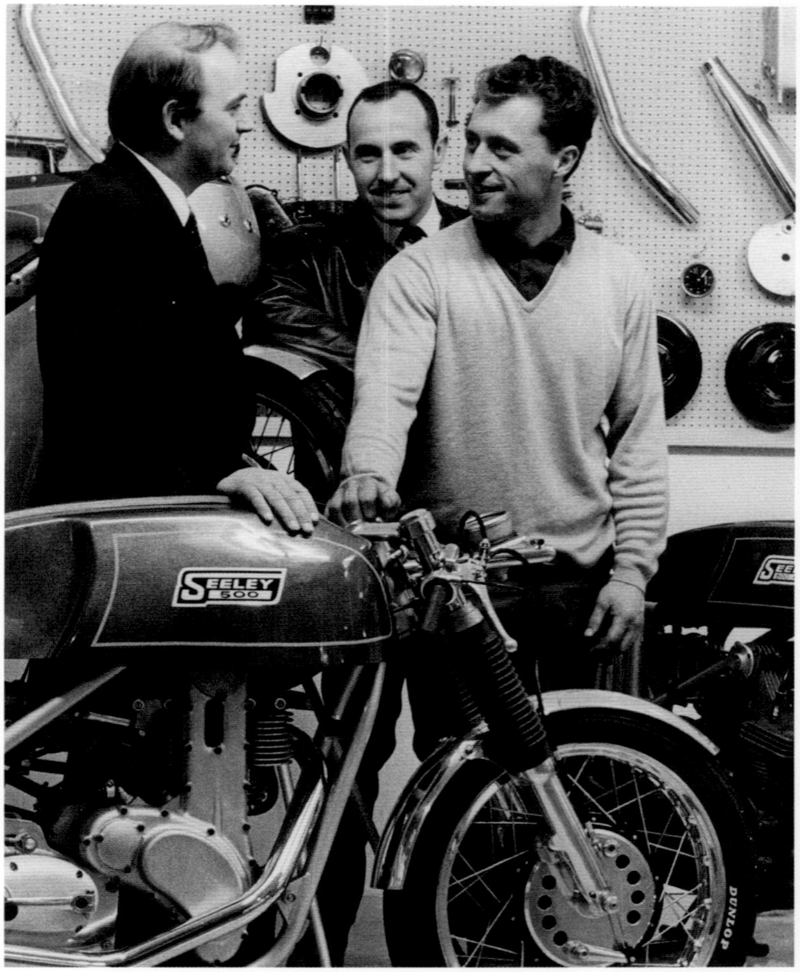

MCN reporter John Brown and Ron Chandler at Earls Court.

closed in. The big guns were out for this race, Minter on a 647cc Norton Domiracer, Ray Pickrell on the 745cc 'rocket ship' Dunstall-Domiracer and Dave Degens 649cc Dresda-Metisse. Derbyshire's 'Mooneyes' Cooper on the 500cc Seeley-Matchless had his own ideas, gaining a 4 second lead after 2 laps of the 8 lap event, but then as darkness fell, Minter proved that he knew his way round the Brands Grand Prix course with his eyes closed. He picked off the opposition until 'Cooperman' was in sight. He swooped by to take a standing ovation and his final chequered flag. John Cooper was followed by Pickrell, Degens, Croxford (who would join the Seeley camp in 1968) and Chandler's Seeley-Matchless made up the first 6. For Derek Minter it was a well-deserved final win.

Derek had been sometimes ill-advised, sometimes misguided, sometimes too outspoken. However, never in dispute was his ability. He had raced a wide range of motorcycles on a variety of circuits throughout the world, including the Isle of Man TT, where he had achieved the first 100mph lap for a British single cylinder machine and was winner of the 1962 250cc TT on a Honda. Derek, in his time, was one of Britain's best. Always approachable, he would be known forever as the 'King'.

By November 1967 I was literally down in the dumps. I spent a morning burrowing through the council rubbish tip. During a clean up of our engine and gearbox assembly bay, two brand new sets of Schafleitner five speed gear clusters had somehow been thrown into the bin and taken off to the local tip. I was mortified. Money was tight and delivery time was long from Michael Schafleitner. There was no alternative but to find these clusters. I tracked down the disposal truck but the load had already been compressed and dumped on the tip. The rubbish site operators could not believe their eyes. Amongst the diving seagulls a lone figure scratched around in the horrors of household waste. It was like trying to find a needle in a very smelly haystack. To everyone's amazement, not least mine, I found the gear clusters and saved the day. On returning home Joan would not let me near the house until I was hosed down.

Around that time, I agreed to build a G50 powered sidecar outfit for regular sidecar competitor Dick Hawes. This would be a winter project fitting in between producing the Seeley solo machines. Having so enjoyed racing my own G50 Matchless outfits, this order from Dick Hawes set me going. Perhaps I could build two outfits and return to racing in 1968. In fact I had already written to Honda in Japan, suggesting that they supply me with a works 500cc Honda four type, as used by Hailwood that season. I would win Honda a world sidecar championship. This was my greatest ambition at the time, but Honda didn't reply, perhaps just as well. I had enough on my plate and was already over-extended. It's difficult to step out of the ring, and even more difficult to stay out!!

Despite Hailwood's success for Honda, with five world solo championships, and very nearly six, Honda withdrew works support, so no longer required his services and didn't return to the Grand Prix scene until 1983. 1967 had seen the last of the battles between two of the greatest motorcycle champions ever, Mike Hailwood and Giacomo Agostini.

The Ruislip Rebel, Dave Croxford.

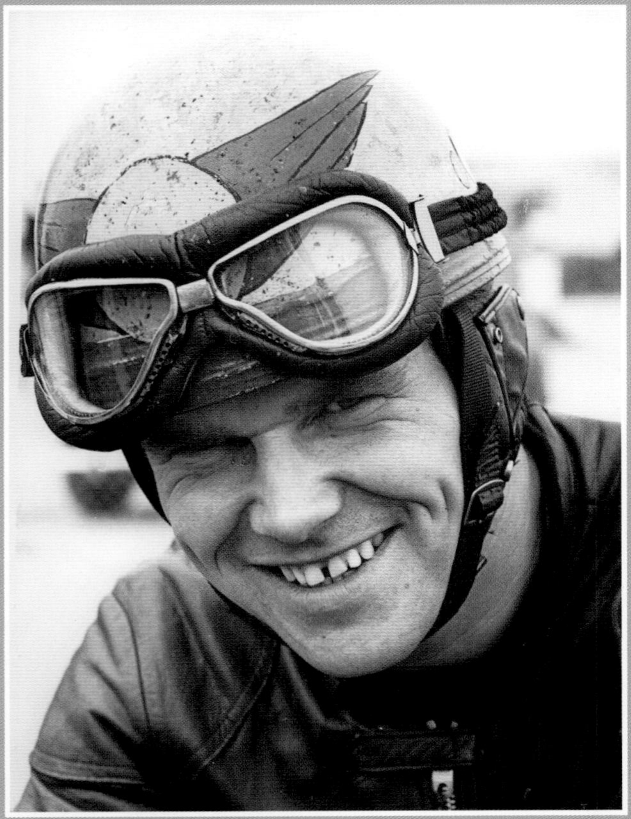

11 1968
WITHIN A WHISKER!

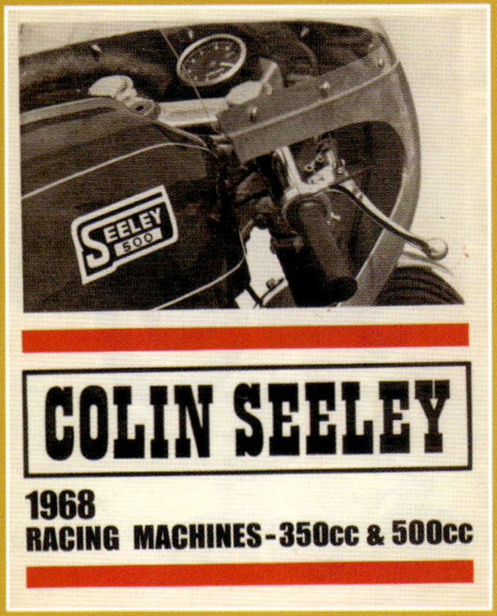

The year began with Mike Hailwood being awarded an MBE (Member of the British Empire), joining John Surtees, Jim Redman and Gary Hocking. Freddie Frith and Geoff Duke were holders of the higher honour of OBE (Order of the British Empire). I often wonder why Hailwood, the 1967 250 and 350cc World Champion, and winner of more world titles at that time (nine in all) than any other British rider, and one of the greatest ambassadors of our sport, did not receive the higher award too. I suppose some official in the honours department that year didn't consider motorcycle sport as too important. Perhaps there were some civil servants and fashion designers who needed an OBE that year… for me there have been many omissions. Why not Sir John Surtees, seven times World Motorcycle Champion and the only man to achieve a unique double by winning the 1964 Formula 1 World championship with Ferrari? Why not Sir Geoff Duke, six times World Motorcycle Champion – a hero of the fifties and a true gentleman of our sport? Why not Sir Sammy Miller, road racer and the greatest trials rider, who over many years has made a huge contribution to the business and sport of motorcycling?

Ron Carnell, Duckhams Oils Competition Manager signed Sammy Miller, the works Bultaco star for 1968, the first ever trials rider to be supported by them. For enthusiastic Ron Carnell, who would over the years become one of the most respected trade support men in the paddock, signing Sammy Miller to Duckhams was an early achievement.

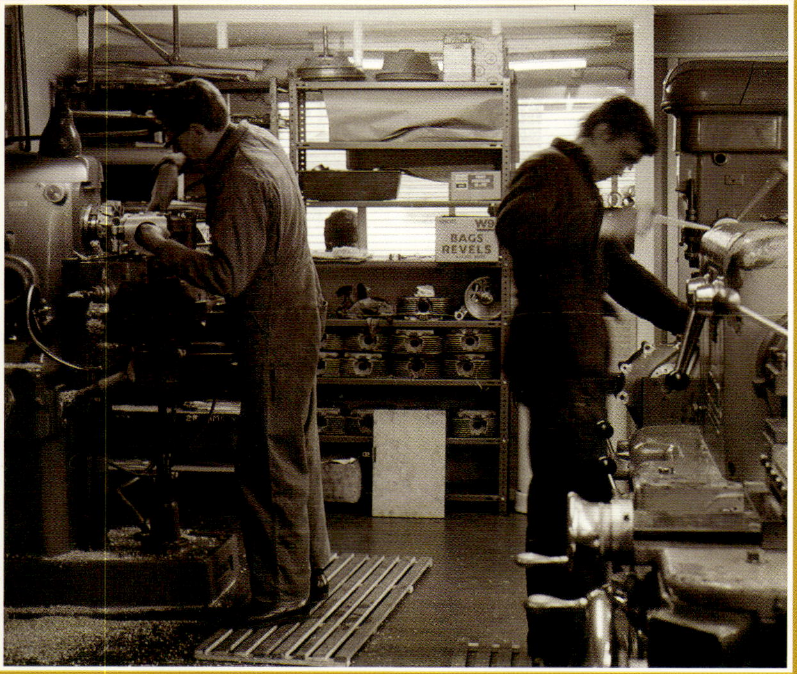

Local boy Ron Carnell, born 1936, went to the local Blackfen School along with Brian Whitehouse, chairman of the vast Kent based Whitehouse Garage Group. Opposite the original Whitehouse Garage at Blendon, Bexley was a café run by the father of scrambler Vic Eastwood. While still at school Ron joined the Blackfen Hammers Cycle Speedway Club, racing alongside another youngster, Ginger Payne, a future Brands star.

With motorcycles his first love, Ron left school to join AMC at Woolwich as an apprentice, helping make small parts for the race AJS Porcupines. Although he loved the work, Ron was desperate to purchase his own motorcycle and could not exist on 7s. 6d. per week, so he left to join the print business for the extra cash, but soon National Service was calling and Ron was posted to Cyprus and into the Ordnance Corp, where he was in charge of stores and helping prepare the Army's motorcycles for the forthcoming International Six Days Trial, a job from heaven.

After National Service Ron returned to print with the local Kentish Times newspaper, and with money in his pocket, he bought his first trials bike. He joined the Sidcup and district MCC and won a number of local trials, and reported on them for the newspaper. By 1966 the Duckhams Oil Company had moved their headquarters to West Whickam and advertised for a technical writer. Ron Carnell applied for the job and was immediately offered the position.

BP and Shell Oil Companies pulled out of sponsorship for the 1968 season and this provided an opening for the smaller Duckhams Company with its limited resources. In late 1967 Ron had been promoted to the motor sport division and with the Duckhams caravan would be a familiar sight at most events for many years to come. Ron Chandler, Rex Butcher, Peter Williams, The Boyer Racing Team and Helmut Fath were all added to the Duckhams Party for 1968, along with Colin Seeley Racing Developments and Dave Croxford who we had decided to support.

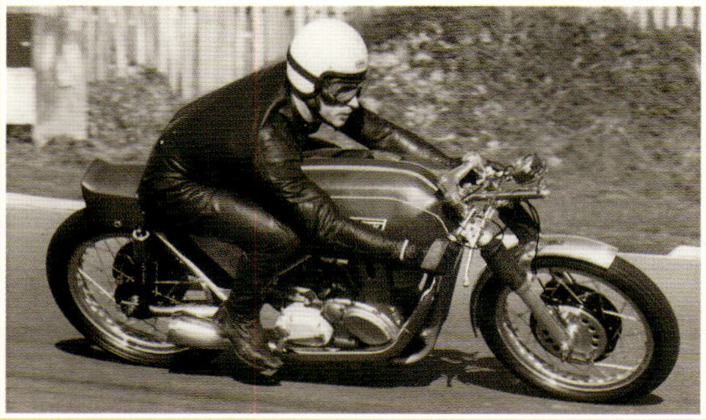

The manufacturer proving his product, the 500 Seeley at Brands.

Seeley machine shop in action, Len Smith, left and Mick Carter, right.

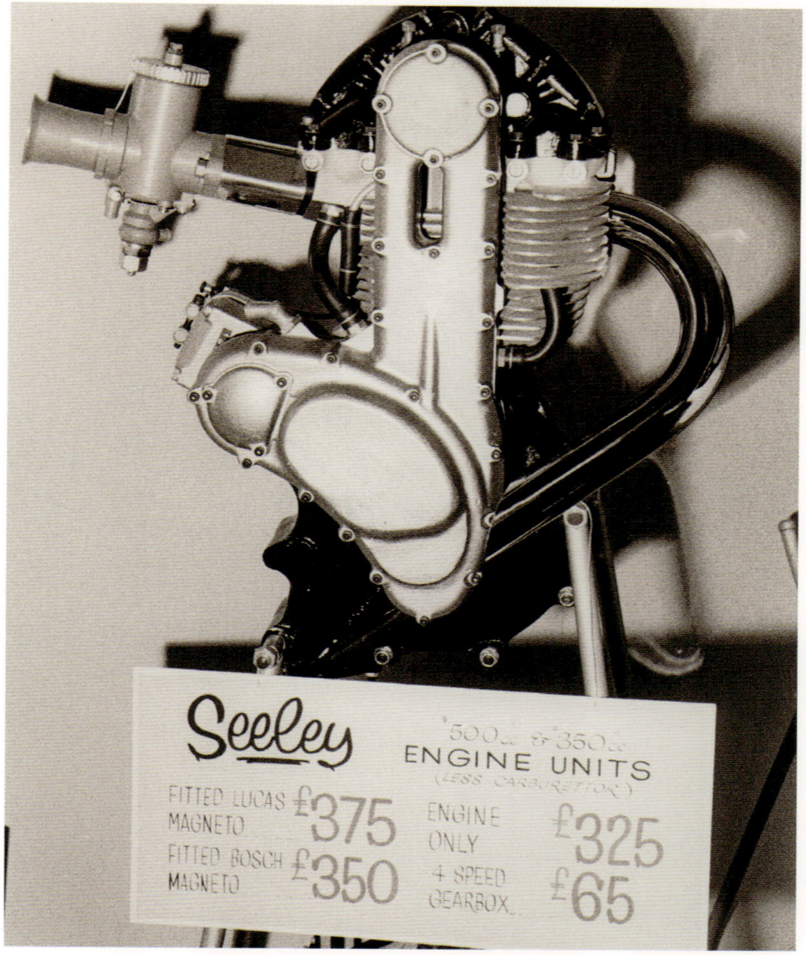

Seeley engine unit on display at Earls Court.

Tragedy struck the Jawa Factory when works rider Gustav Havel, travelling to work late in December 1967 on a hack version of the new 350cc 4 cylinder two-stroke racing machine, was involved in an accident. As the street lights went out, a woman walked into the road directly into his path. He sustained fatal head injuries and died on New Year's Eve. The woman escaped with two broken legs. By an unfortunate coincidence, Czech road racer Stanislav Malina had been killed in a similar accident two years before. The full weight of Jawa's racing programme would now be on the shoulders of the likeable Franta Stastny.

Despite Helmut Fath stating in late August '67, that there would be no more URS Solo that year and he would anyway do it himself, a Rickman version was shown to the press by the end of December '67. It was tested at Hockenheim within days by John Blanchard who reported that he was delighted with the Metisse frame, that nothing touched down, it did not wriggle and the brakes were particularly good. Snow put an end to the test that day, but would the Fath-Metisse end up on the slippery slope?

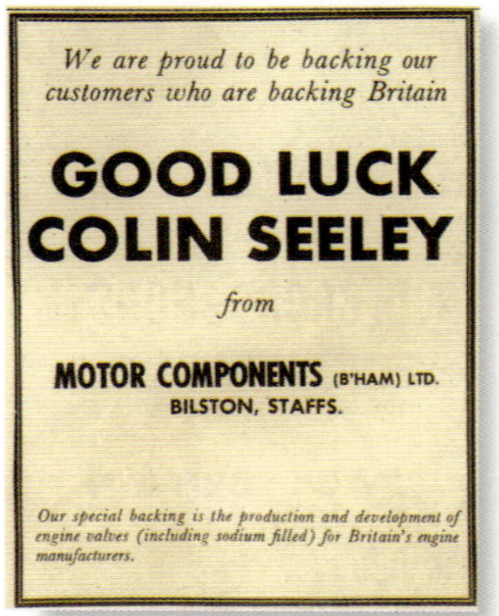

A foot and mouth epidemic in Britain had brought trials and scrambles events almost to a standstill for over two months and would possibly threaten road racing.

Then it was engine news, Rhodesian Colin Lyster, announced a cut-price twin cylinder engine designed to outpace the ageing Manx Nortons and Seeley-Matchless G50 machines. 60bhp, 65lb in weight and at a proposed price of £300 it would cost considerably less than a new G50 unit. Routine servicing would cost peanuts in comparison to the crippling expense of maintaining a Manx or G50, claimed Lyster! The Lyster engine looked exactly what it was, half an ugly Rallye Imp car engine - £300 for an untested conversion, never mind the claims made. A Seeley G50 500cc race engine complete with Lucas Magneto and Amal GP Carburettor tried and tested cost £375 – no contest.

Weslake's Mike Daniels informed the press that the Read-Weslake 500 would not be ready to run until March and it was doubtful whether a batch of engines would be ready in time for the Isle of Man TT.

At Belfast's Queens University the 32 year old Dr. Gordon Blair ran his first ever designed two-stroke engine, a 122cc unit, set to spin at between 12,500 – 13,000rpm, very ambitious but that was Gordon Blair for you!

The Honda Motor Company, after weeks of indecision, finally pulled out of official support for Grand Prix racing but with some 138 Classic Grand Prix victories and 16 World Motorcycle Championships between 1960 and 1967 it was certainly some achievement. 1966 was the most successful year for Honda, 29 Grand Prix victories with 'Mike the Bike' completely dominating the 250cc class winning ten of the twelve races and six out of ten in the 350cc class, combined with three wins in the 500cc class, keeping Agostini on his toes, a total of 19 Grand Prix successes that year for the champion - an awesome performance by the British hero Hailwood. Jim Redman was the most successful rider for Honda in that period with six world championships pipping Hailwood at the post by one. Lugi Taveri followed winning three championships, with Tom Phillis and Ralph Bryans one each. A sad passing of such a great era, no more the scream of the exhaust from the high revving multi cylinder four stroke engines.

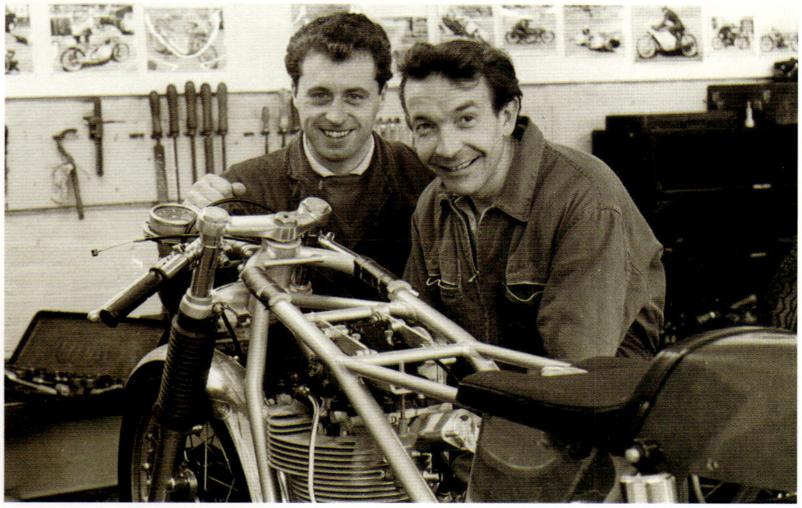

Come on Wal, let's get this job finished!

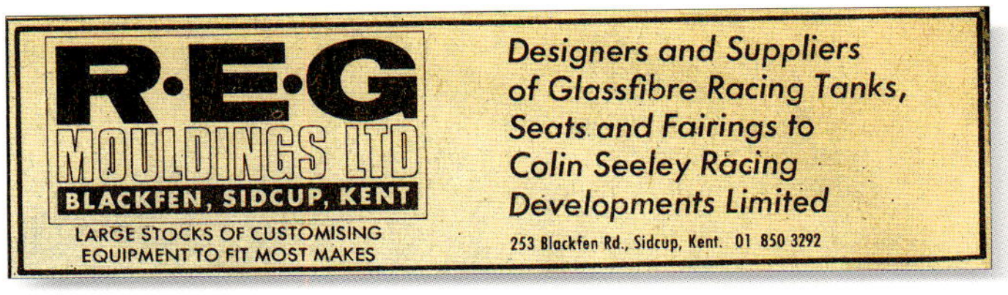

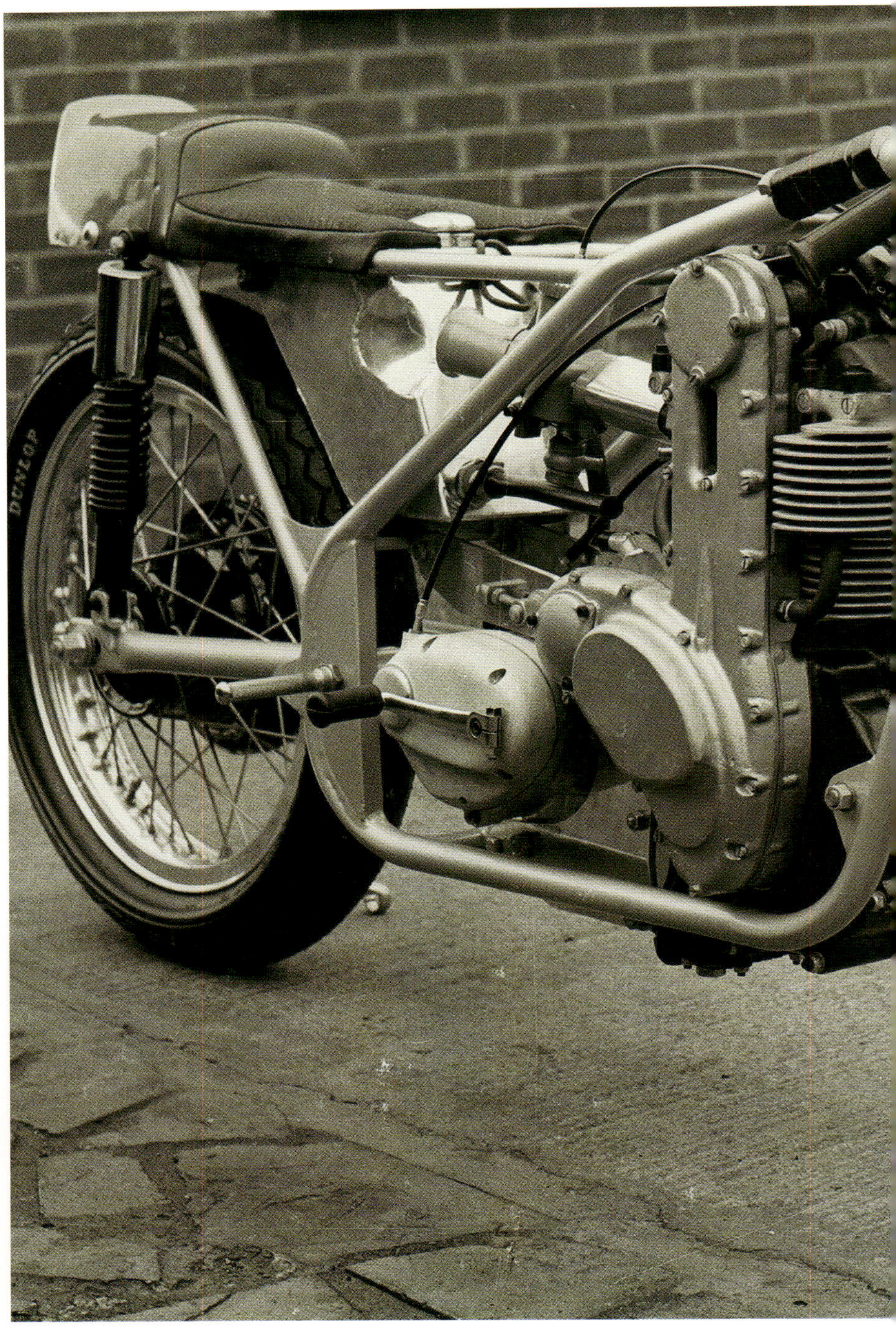

First of the Seeley Mk2 models.

For the 1968 Isle of Man Sidecar TT the ACU introduced a 750cc class to be run in conjunction with the world title points scoring 500cc race. A unique evnt held on Saturday evening, 8th June. Prize money would be the same for each class, £150 for the winners, £105 for the second and £75 for third place.

If there was not a busy enough racing programme in those days the ACU, (after continued pressure from Chris Lowe, a Director of Brands Hatch), gave the Brands Hatch Racing Committee permission to hold a road race meeting on Sunday December 29th 1968. Ken Shierson, ACU secretary said permission had been granted on a one-off basis and the future position would be examined.

Then, there was more startling news from the ACU, who seemed to have woken up to changes in the sport. British riders would be allowed to carry advertisements - but when, how and precisely what was still uncertain at that point. Some ACU officials warned of problems riders might encounter from the race circuits regarding advertising.

The display of our products at Earls Court back in September '67 had combined with some excellent race results that season. Ron Chandler won the ACU 500cc British Championship from John Cooper by one point. We had a good number of orders for our Seeley MK2 models, which was great news for the employees who would be kept busy producing engine parts and all the necessary bits and pieces. The machine shop was humming, as was my welding torch, trying to keep up with demand.

I was under enormous pressure, trying to oversee the whole operation, planning our racing programme, now with the 'Ruislip Rebel' Dave Croxford on board, and continuing single handed to manufacture the frames. I was working with little

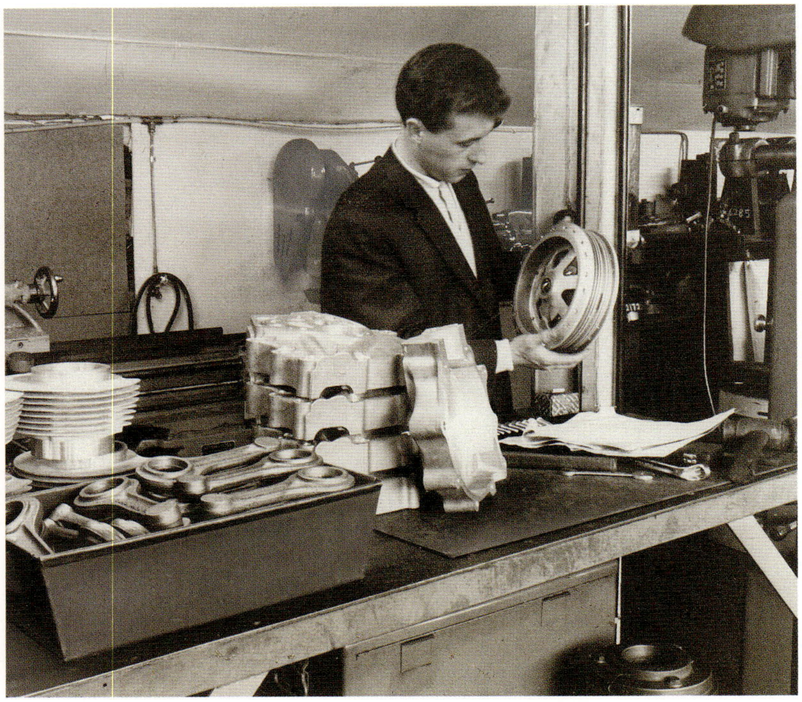

Close inspection of components by the 'Boss'.

Ron Chandler tries the bike for size.

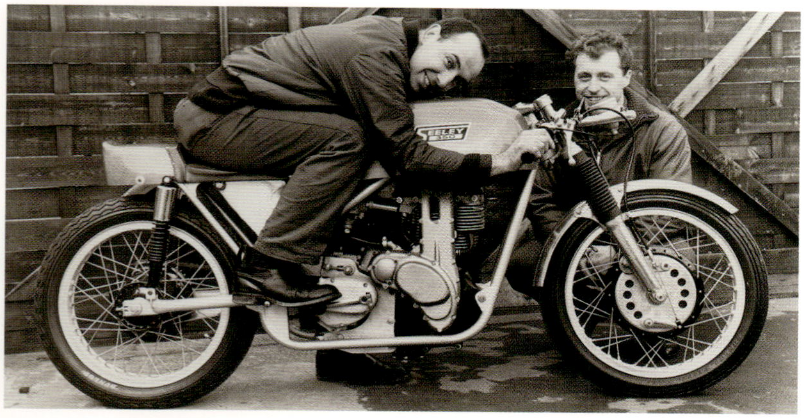

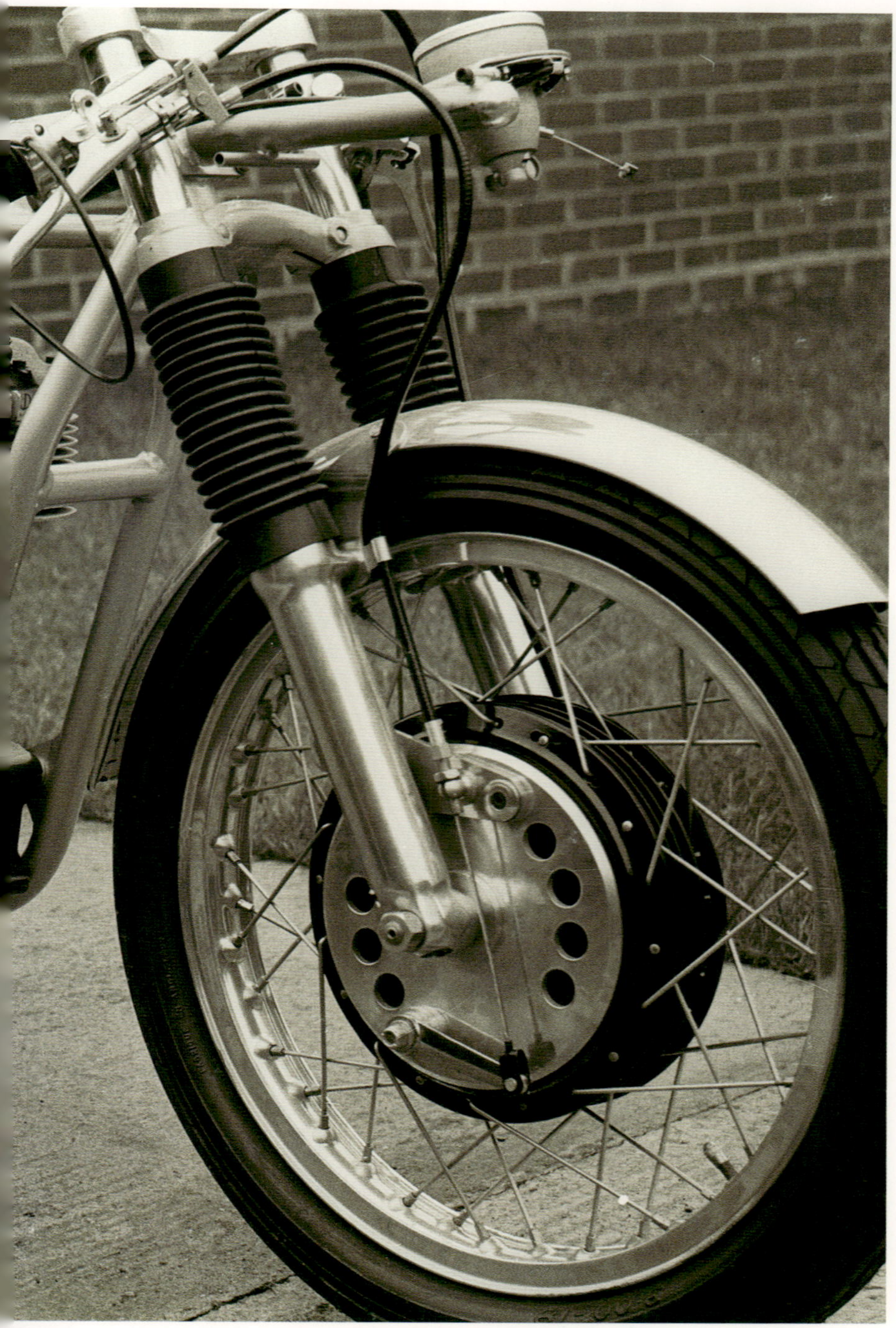

equipment, no jigs or fixtures, only a surface table with an adjustable steering head gadget attached. The Reynolds '531' tubing was still being bent by a plumber's hand bender - a difficult process. All the early Seeley frames were truly hand built, the frame tubes measured, cut, bent then individually filed and fitted for a perfect mitre joint. Every single bracket and gusset plate was hand produced, then held in place by magnets before welding together with No 1 sift bronze welding rods. The swinging arm pick up point was welded last, to make sure that the swinging arm would be correctly at right angles to the steering head. It was hours of work for just one frame and I often worked long into the night to fulfil an order.

I needed support in the production of frames, but resources were limited as all of our cash was invested in machines and equipment for the manufacture of engine and associated components. As an official stockist for Reynolds '531' tubing, I had contacts there and approached Ken Sprayson for help. The highly respected Sprayson, through the Reynolds Tube Company, agreed to build a batch of the Seeley MK2 frames. Firstly, Ken needed to produce a detailed drawing as I had only been working from my original sketches. I would continue to make frames but the arrangement proved invaluable and gave me the necessary breather. Thank you Ken!

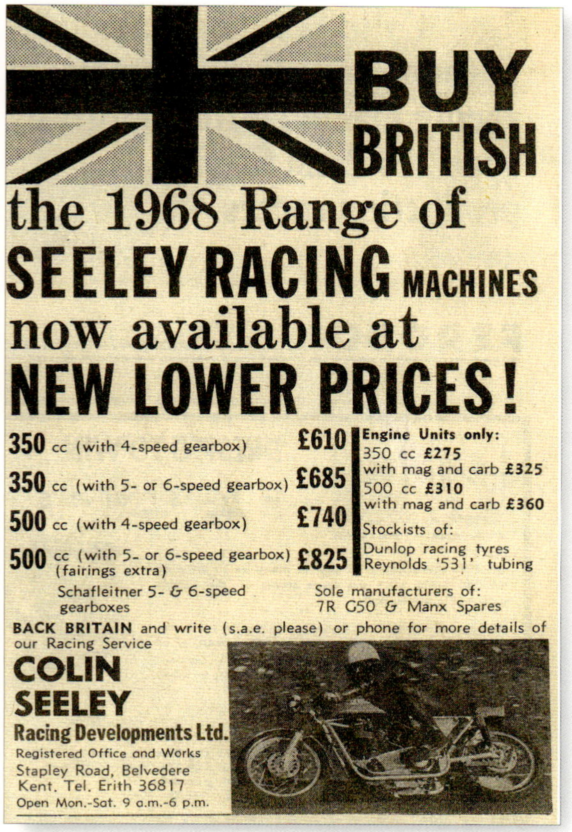

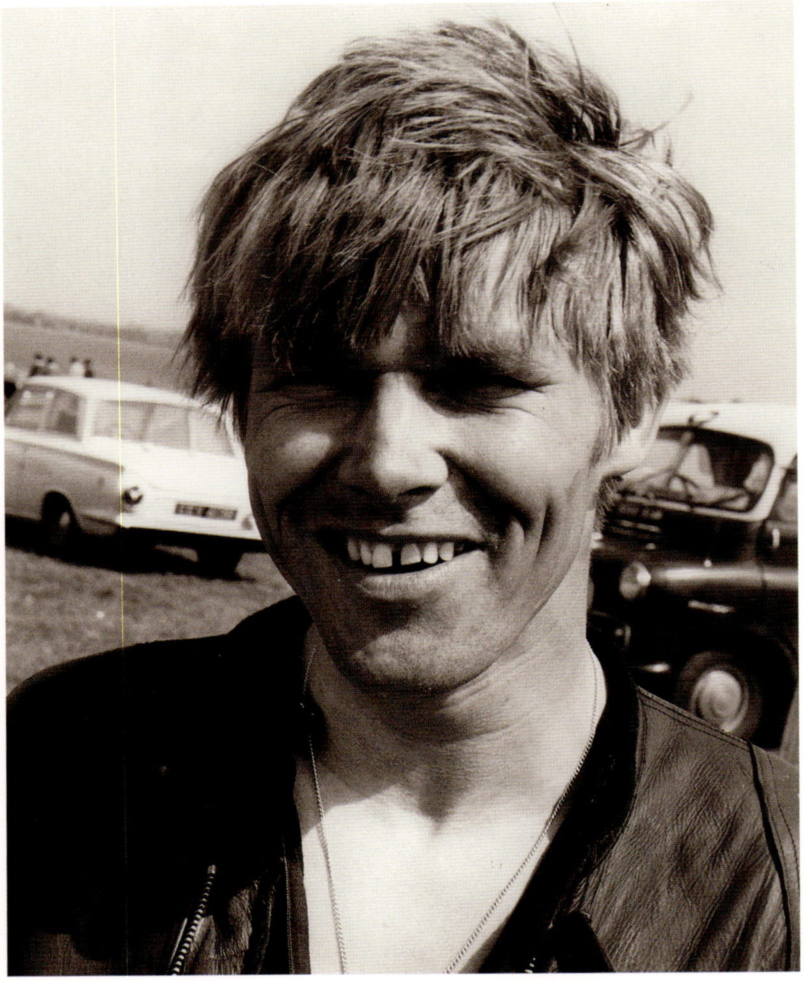

'Cheeky Chappy' Croxford.

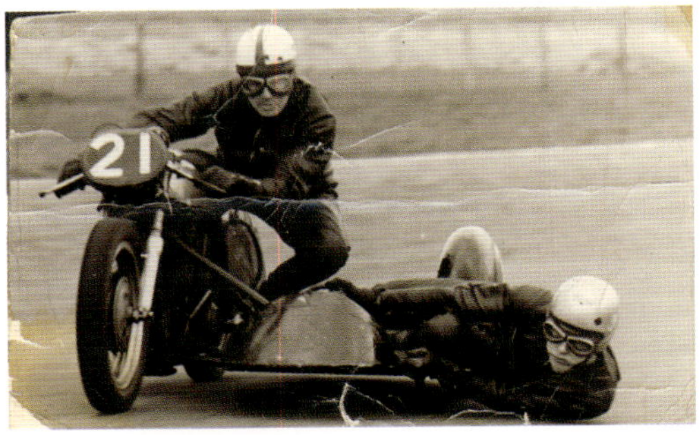

Ken Longman with Dave Croxford in the chair.

In February 1968 I announced a price reduction of our Seeley products, the exact reason for which I can't recall. I suppose I was concerned about rising opposition, particularly the threat of the Aermacchis in the 350cc class. I reduced the price of our Seeley-7R without fairing, from £760 to £610. The Seeley G50 was reduced by £20 to £760. At that price it would be two Seeley G50s for the price of one £1,630 500cc Paton Racer with change left over.

The Norton Villiers Company announced plans to build a batch of 250cc Villiers engined racers under the AJS name. These were to be replicas of Peter Inchley's special on which he finished third in the 1966 lightweight TT. After much publicity this came to nothing, demonsrating what a tough business building racing bikes was!

Londoner 'Cheeky Chappie' Dave Croxford, although still sponsored by Charlie Oakley, in 1968 began a long association with the Seeley Company. Dave was born July 1941 in Hammersmith, left school at 15 with no particular qualifications other than 'good with his hands' (handy for holding handlebars later on). Serving a five year apprenticeship as a tool maker, Dave had developed a keen interest in motorcycling, like so many lads of his day. He would wander to the Ace Café where all the motorcyclists used to congregate, and there got to know sidecar racer Ken Longman. He suggested that Dave might like to act as passenger on his Manx Norton outfit, – 'Yes mate why not?' was the answer, so from mid 1960 starting at Brands Hatch in June, Croxford was hanging about holding a wheel down. In that same year Dave had been banned from driving for a year for speeding at 90mph on his Gold Star. With time to spare that season, Dave built himself a 500cc Triumph-Norton solo special, going to Monty and Ward to buy a five speed gearbox, as he thought. He was unaware that Geoff Monty regarded neutral as one of the gears – so in fact it was a four speed.

Once back on the public roads, now on the Triumph-Norton with featherbed frame, Dave's aspirations to show the rockers how to ride came to an abrupt end when he crashed. Captivated by the racing scene, Croxford thought it might be wiser and safer to go racing, with the Triumph-Norton now rebuilt in competitive trim. In 1961 Dave entered his first solo event at Charterhall in Scotland. He drove 500 miles to Charterhall in his Nova-Racing (sign written) Comma van. After practice, through a ballot system, he ended up on the front row of the grid for his first ever solo event alongside Mike Hailwood, Bob McIntyre and Alastair King. Croxford thought he'd hit the big time but in reality he was only dipping a toe in the water. As with ourselves, race entries for beginners had always been difficult. Despondency sometimes set in, when the organisers did not realise what talent they were missing!

Croxford managed two more events that season on the Triumph-Norton, both at Brands Hatch, before going back to Geoff Monty to part exchange the Triumph for a 500 Manx Norton. He rode this for the first time at Snetterton on 3rd September 1961, bringing his tally to four meetings in that year. Wally and I had competed at fifteen meetings that same year, but were a year ahead of him career-wise.

Croxford, with his new love, the Manx Norton, got an entry for the Brands Hatch restricted event in April 1962, but only as a reserve rider. The same day, 1st April saw the first national meeting held at Mallory Park attracting 50,000 fans to witness the shoot out between Hailwood, Read, Minter, Shepherd, McIntyre, Driver and King.

Next stop for Dave was Snetterton on the 22nd April when for the first time ever in Britain, Mike Hailwood rode the works' MV, bringing thousands of spectators to the airfield circuit. Hailwood, equipped with both Italian 350 and 500cc 'fire engines' was supreme. His nearest competitor in both races was rising star Roy Mayhew with his AJS and Matchless machines. It was only a week on from the Snetterton meeting I remember Roy Mayhew crashing heavily on Devils Elbow at Mallory Park resulting in concussion. Two weeks later, May 13th, the 30 year old Londoner, a dock foreman married with two children, was on brilliant racing form back in action at Brands Hatch, but failed to negotiate Paddock Hill bend. The crash caused serious head injuries. He was taken to Dartford's West Hill Hospital, but did not survive. I witnessed that crash. Roy, at full throttle along the top straight, never sat up for the corner nor did he ease off to take the bend. Did he have a mechanical failure on the Matchless, or was it a result of ongoing concussion after the blow to his head at Mallory Park two weeks beforehand? We shall never know. 1962 was a poor year for Croxford – lack of entries – lack of money! But 1963 would prove to be a slight improvement for his racing ambitions, again on the Manx-Norton, although still only two meetings, at Brands Hatch in April and May. Then while working at Cyril Bennett's motorcycle shop in Ealing, the late Roy Mayhew's Matchless G50, gleaming in a silver finish came up for sale at £365. Dave thought, 'That's mine,' and persuaded his mother, Edna to sign as guarantor for the hire purchase. He raced the Matchless at Mallory Park that same month and said, 'It's as good as anybody's out there.' six more meetings were attended that season but with no mention in the press that the 'Ruislip Rebel' had been on the track.

1964 saw Croxford in positive mood, having married Pauline in March and had race entries accepted on a regular basis. He was also pleased with the performance of the Matchless G50. At Brands Hatch grid positions were mostly determined by previous performance, so in April Dave found himself on the third row of the grid for the 500cc

Seeley, Chandler and Cooper, testing at Brands.

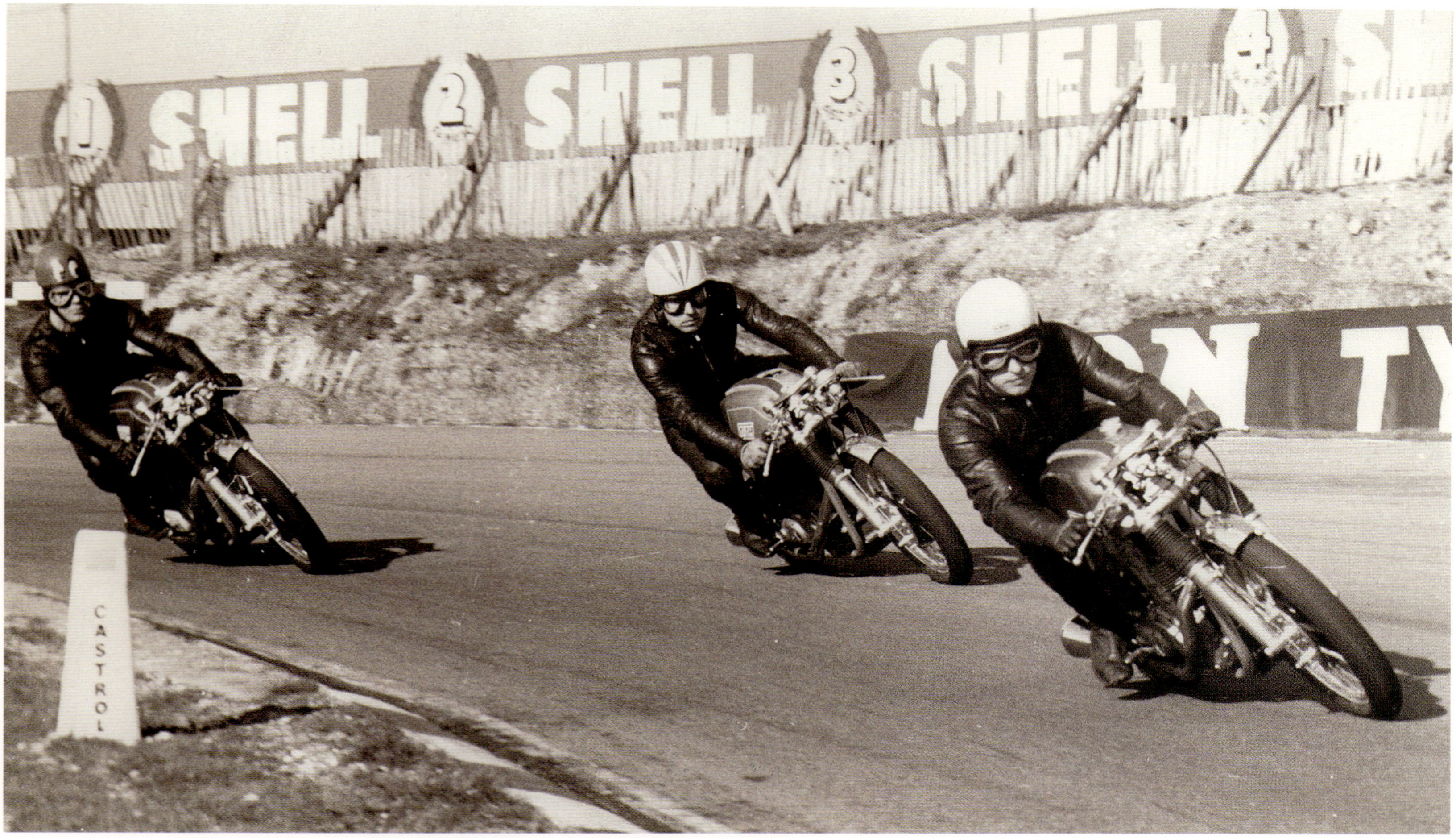

Redex Trophy Championship. At Brands Hatch in June he was listed as a reserve, then at the August event he was put onto row four. After six meetings Dave was still not featured in the top results or even mentioned in the race reports, but at Brands Hatch on 20th September, placed on the second row for that day, he achieved a fourth place in the Redex Trophy and a creditable fifth in the unlimited event, behind winner Derek Minter, Degens, Cooper; finally a mention in dispatches!

Prior to the next meeting at Oulton Park in early October, the Elektron crankcases of the Matchless needed to be replaced because of cracks, a regular problem in those days. AMC were making stronger aluminium types, but more costly. Croxford was again out of money so asked Motorcycle News (MCN) sports reporter Charlie Rous if he could give a mention in MCN that 'a poor, likely London lad with great race potential' was looking for support. Within days a cheque for £100 arrived and Dave dashed straight down to the AMC factory to purchase the new cases.

The generous benefactor was Charlie Oakley, a butcher from Westborough, Newark in Notts. He was to support Dave for four years and recognised that Dave ideally needed two machines, and instructed him to purchase a 350 AJS 7R. For Dave it was 'pennies from heaven'. The ex- Griff Jenkins' 7R was bought from Francis Beart. Dave thought it looked good, but it was not quick enough and in fact performance was extremely disappointing. Nevertheless, it gave him an extra ride and was first used at Brands in mid-October at the last meeting of the year.

The early sixties brought a profusion of new solo racing blood. Competition on the track was fierce and certainly Croxford had found that out, but for this tough likeable Londoner things were about to change. At Brands Hatch in March 1965, Dave had been moved up to the second row of the grid in the 500cc Redex Trophy event. He finished fourth to winner Minter, Dave Degens and Joe Dunphy. A sixth place in the 350cc event and another sixth after an excellent ride in the 1000cc event behind winner Degens, Minter, Ivy, Lewis Young and Dunphy. Croxford was now getting the regular front men in his sights, proving the point once more at Brands in April for the King of Brands meeting where he scored fourth in the 350 event, and fifth in both 500cc and 1000cc races.

By now Dave now had his International Racing Licence and the international 'Race of the Aces' at Snetterton was next, followed by three more meetings before the 1965 Isle of Man TT. In which he entered three events, the 250cc on a Pearce and Nichols NSU, and the 350 and 500 on his regular bikes. As a newcomer to the Island, the course was a shock to his system. When asked if he knew his way around he replied, 'Well, I follow somebody, and when they change gear I change gear, when they brake I brake'. 'So what do you do if they fall off?' Only Croxford could have answered as he did, 'I fall off too!'

Anyway the 'Ruislip Rebel' didn't fall off but brought his 250cc NSU into eighteenth place. Asked if he had any trouble with flies, he answered 'No, I never caught any up.' In the 350cc event he retired with machine failure. The 6 lap Senior event was run in appalling conditions. Hailwood on the MV, crashed at Sarah's Cottage and remounted to win with Joe Dunphy second and Mike Duff third. Croxford brought his Matchless into a very respectable eleventh place, with 31 finishes in all. After the Isle of Man TT an abundance of short circuit events would follow, making a total of around 14 meetings that season. The 'Ruislip Rebel' was now on the ladder to success, runner-up to John Cooper in the 1966 500cc ACU British Championships and winner of the 1967 350cc ACU British Championship.

I had no plans to run an official works rider in 1968. We already had John Cooper and Ron Chandler supporting our race efforts with their private Seeley machines. Croxford,

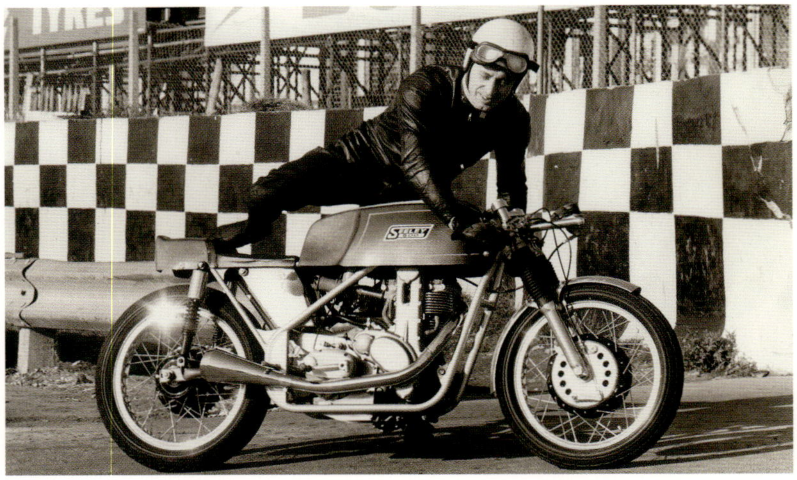

after a ride on John Cooper's Seeley towards the end of the '67 season, was so impressed that he decided to buy a Seeley MK2 frame kit and covert his AJS 7R hopefully into a more competitive machine. We supplied a Seeley rolling chassis in early March 68. It was soon built and tested at Brands on a Wednesday afternoon – Dave's regular jaunt. He took to the Seeley instantly and decided to fit the 500cc G50 engine. This decision would be a turning point for Croxford that year.

Wally Rawlings and I had taken a great liking to this exuberant character. He was totally committed to AMC type machinery, and he liked a Guinness! Encouraged by Dave's attitude, Wally built a 636cc G50 version which fitted into his original Matchless G50 chassis, for him to use in the unlimited capacity classes.

Mallory Park – 3rd March the first event that year, wasn't a good start due to a verbal 'punch up' with Rex Butcher after a tangle at Gerards Bend in the 250cc race. Nevertheless, in the 1000cc event Dave brought his Seeley into third place behind Ron Chandler, Seeley, second and winner Ray Pickrell on the Dunstall Norton. John Hartle, back after a six month lay off, on a Metisse Aermacchi won the 350cc event from Rex Butcher on a Kawasaki and Ron Chandler Seeley-7R third. two thirds and one second for the Seeley camp wasn't too bad a day's work!

At Snetterton a fortnight later Croxford came fourth in the 500cc race, then took third place at the end of March, riding the 636cc Seeley-Matchless at Oulton Park. Travelling overnight, he competed next day at the Lydden Circuit deep in Kent, but was it worth it? In the 350cc race he threw the AJS down the road, resulting in severe bruising. He needed a pusher for the main race, the 636cc Seeley-Matchless not being the easiest of machines to start at the best of times, but the courageous Croxford came through from the back to take the victory from Charlie Sanby and Steve Jolly.

Although Honda had officially pulled out of racing, their riders still had some use of the machines with Hailwood persevering with the big Honda four. Unhappy with the Lyster frame built the previous season for this powerful machine, Mike had turned to Ken Sprayson in the hope that he could come up with a way to control this projectile. Sprayson took up the challenge and a new frame was designed and built in time for Rimini in Italy on the 24th March.

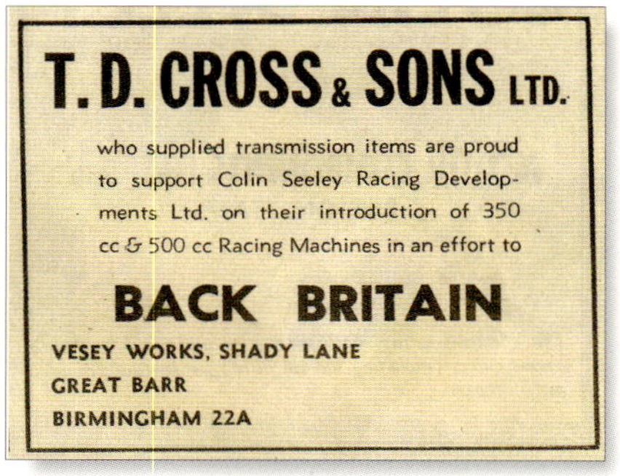

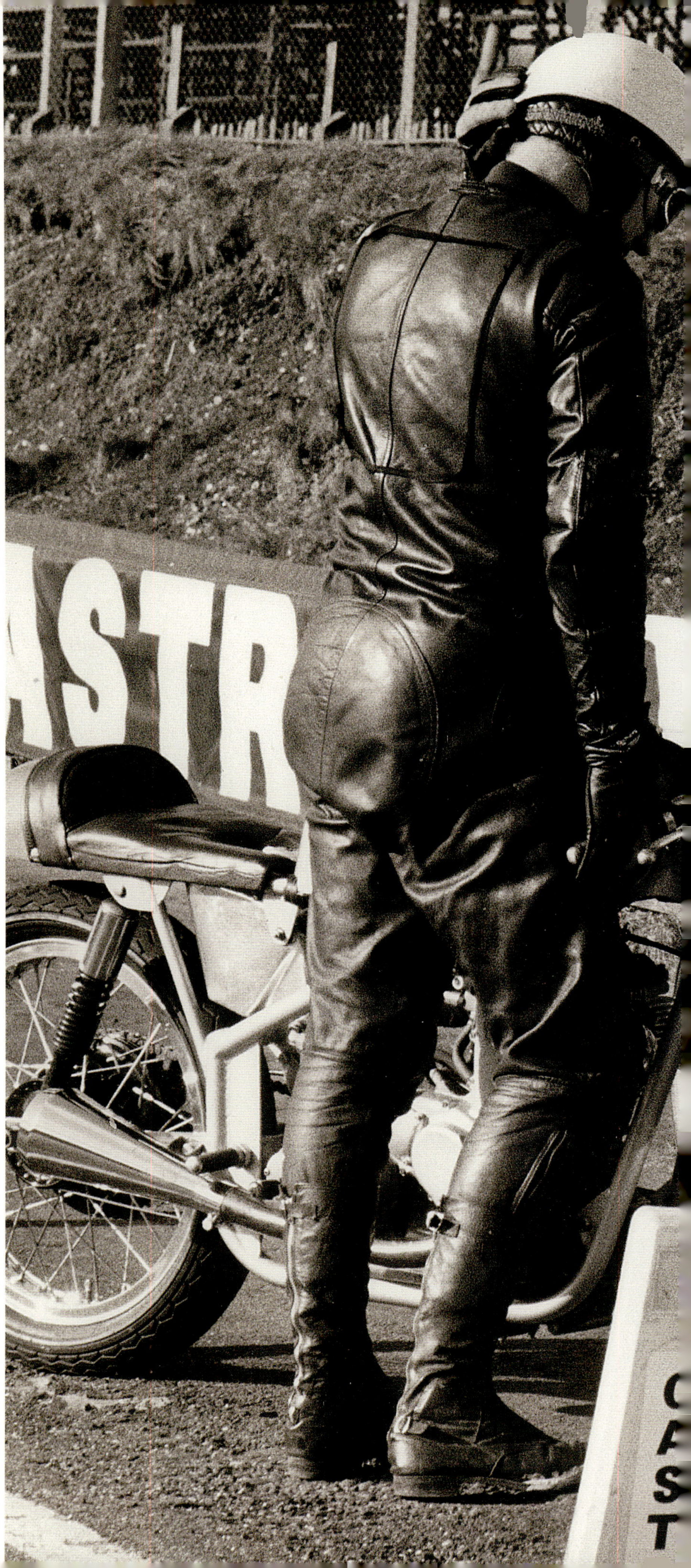

Test day at Brands, David Dixon, Ron Chandler, me and John Cooper.

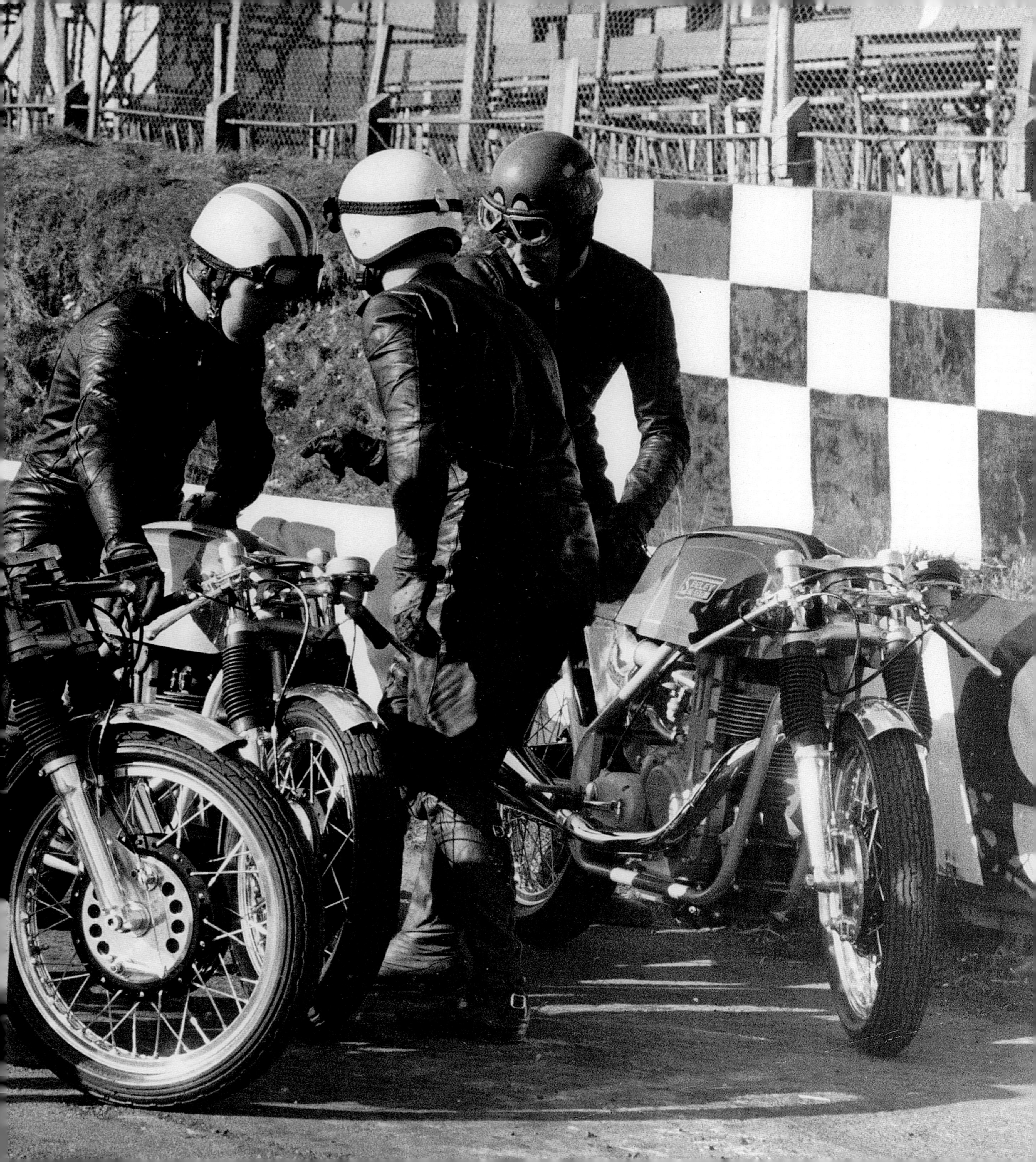

Seeley machine line-up.

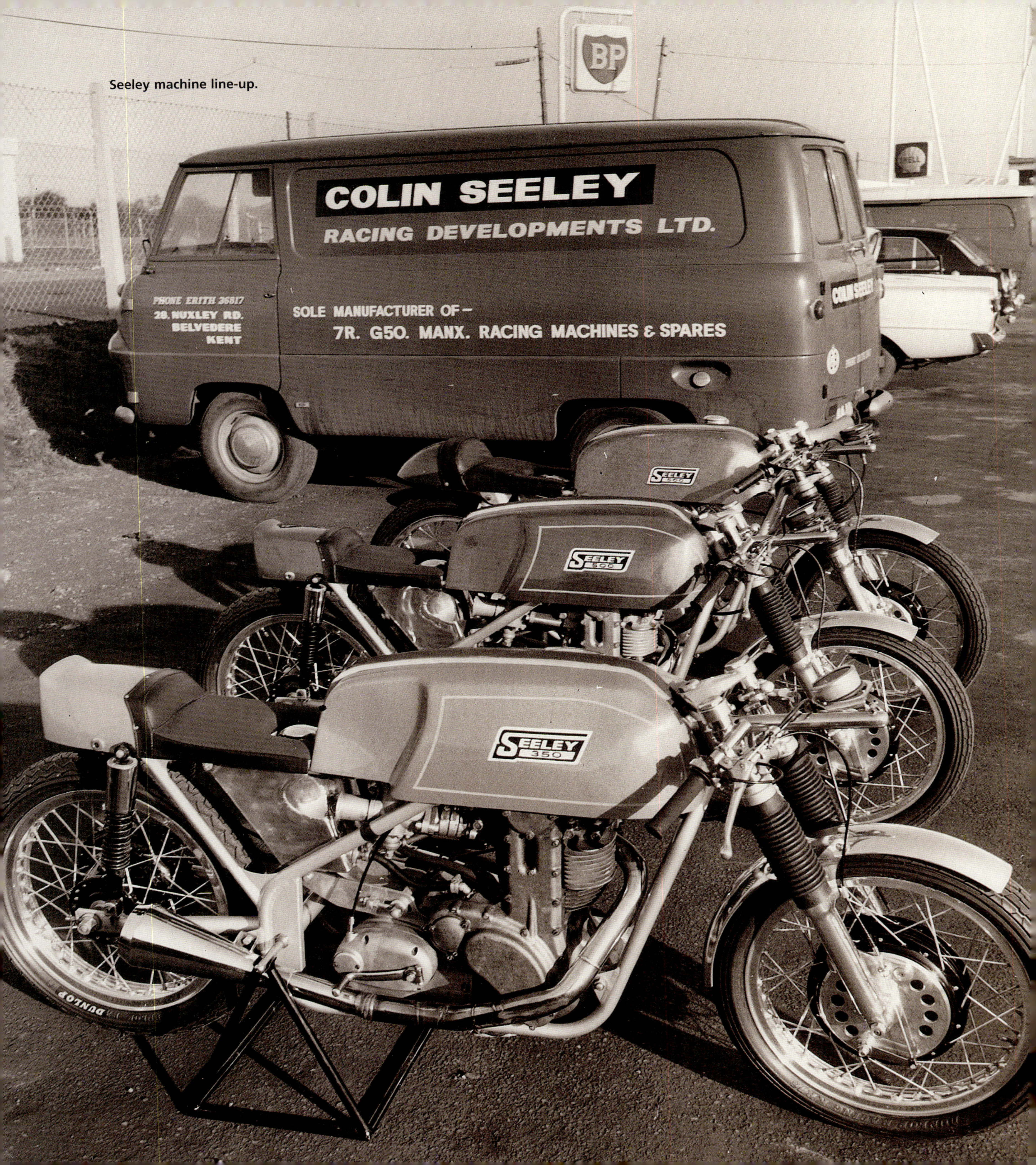

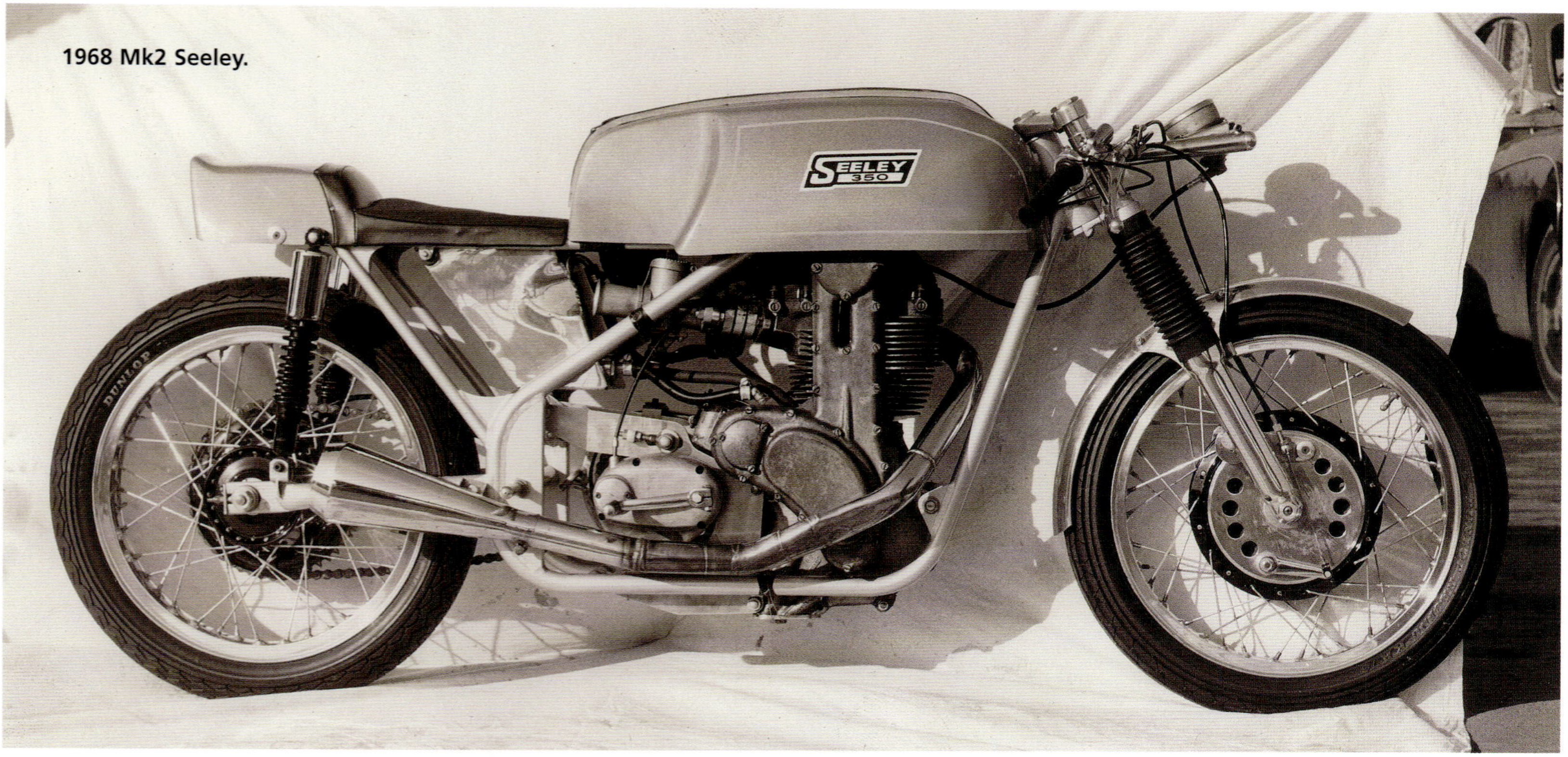

1968 Mk2 Seeley.

In the 28 lap 500cc race Hailwood was heading for victory on the Honda-engined special (HRS), almost 30 seconds ahead of Agostini, MV. Ago, desperate to stay with Mike, twice ran out of road, caused by brake fade. With Agostini back on track, Hailwood crashed his newly framed Honda (HRS). Half a lap down, he remounted and in a vain attempt to catch Agostini, broke the lap record finishing in second place, ahead of John Hartle's Matchless-Metisse, who showed his old style in a faultless ride. The streets were lined with enthusiastic fans who enjoyed the scrap for fourth place between Paolo Campanelli, Seeley G50, and Australian Kel Carruthers, Norton. Campanelli finally gained fourth spot when Carruthers also ran into brake trouble, with Spaggiari, Ducati, coming in sixth.

On Good Friday at Brands Hatch, 12th April 1968, Croxford collected the King of Brands title and scored his first ever race win at the Kentish circuit. In 1967 Ron Chandler took the crown in a one race decider, but this time the title would be determined over the 350cc, 500 and 1300cc events through a points system. It was no easy victory for the Guinness drinking 'Ruislip Rebel' with all events held over the long Grand Prix Circuit. The first race, a 15 lap 350cc event, was a tough opener. Kawasakis were in abundance, ridden by Martin Carney, Derek Chatterton and Dave Simmonds, who had already won the 125cc race that day. Alan Barnett, Kel Carruthers and Griff Jenkins provided a titanic struggle for the lead. For 12 laps Carruthers kept the mob behind, but an ignition fault on the Drixton Aemacchi put him out of the running, leaving only half a second covering Carney, Barnett, Simmonds and Croxford, and that's how they finished. Griff Jenkins came fifth with Chatterton making up the first 6. A good start, but there was no respite for Dave. The 15 lap 500cc race would be a hairy affair between himself, Barnett, Uphill and Gould, but Dave was really getting to grips with the Seeley G50 and after 6 laps had worn the opposition down and headed off to win, 4 seconds ahead of Malcolm Uphill, Rod Gould and Griff Jenkins, all on Nortons. Pat Mahoney and Martin Ashwood, both Matchless, came fifth and sixth. Alan Barnett had crashed at South Bank, so missed out after a spirited effort.

When the competitors lined up for the final solo race, the 15 lap 39.7 mile 1300cc event, the King of Brands title lay between Croxford and Jenkins, with Dave having a 4 point lead. Croxford was out on the 636cc Seeley-Matchless but it was off song from the very start, leaving him back in fifth place on the opening lap. Ray Pickrell, on the 750cc Dunstall Norton, and Alan Barnett 654cc BSA-Metisse were also having problems. Pickrell, trying to hold his position, went into a colossal slide entering the Bottom Bend and lost two places, finally retiring with an engine misfire. Croxford, keeping his head down, brought himself up into second position behind winner

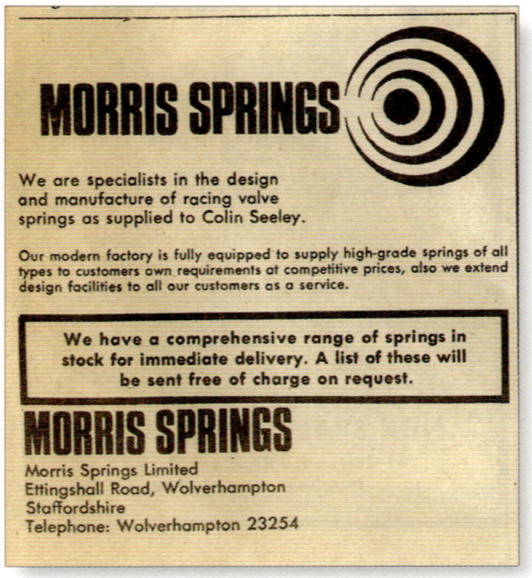

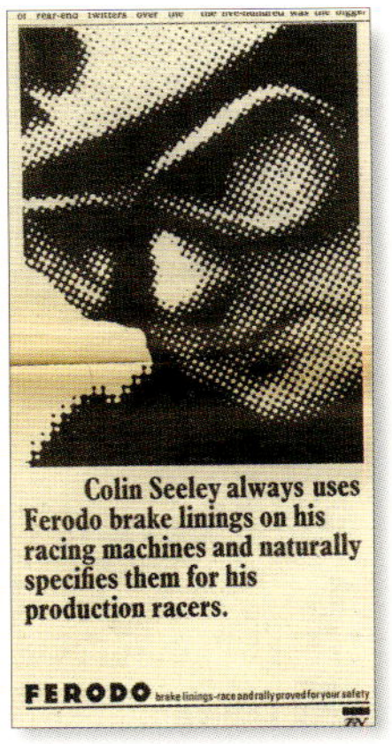

Uphill, but ahead of Gould, Barnett, Ashwood and Geoff Barry in sixth. A first, second and fourth place gave Dave Croxford the title and a kiss from Angela Scoular, star of 'Here We Go Round the Mulberry Bush' and more important, £250 in prize money, followed by a rush to the bar!

The 'Ruislip Rebel' continued his success that Easter weekend. On his Seeley G50 he added the Master of Mallory to his titles, and by then the cash register had rung up £685 in prize money – keeping the Londoner smiling.

In April 1968 America's stunt man Evel Kneivel named the day for his jump across the mile-wide Grand Canyon - September 2nd, America's Labour Day, but first he needed to recover from multiple fractures caused by a 150ft crash landing at Las Vegas. Only Kneivel could come up with a plan to use a rocket assisted Triumph equipped with a parachute for the attempt. Meanwhile the Czechoslovak Jawa factory announced its plans to race their 385cc 4 cylinder two-stroke development machine in the 1968 Grand Prix events with veteran Franta Stastny. American film star Clint Eastwood arrived at Brands Hatch to test ride a 750cc Norton, bought direct from the Norton-Villers factory.

The Thruxton national race meeting, on 21st April 1968, saw racing return to this circuit after a three year lapse. Easter Monday 1950 the Southampton and District MCC held the first motorcycle meeting on this disused wartime Hampshire airfield. Early in the sixties the Thruxton track surface deteriorated but for political reasons no major restoration work was undertaken and racing was discontinued after 1965. Then in 1967 through into 1968 British Racing Circuits Ltd created a superb new track. It was 2.356 miles long and a uniform 48 feet in width completely resurfaced, with earth banking for spectator protection and a pit complex with control tower. In glorious sunshine, 10,000 spectators found the new facilities to their liking and enjoyed the excellent racing.

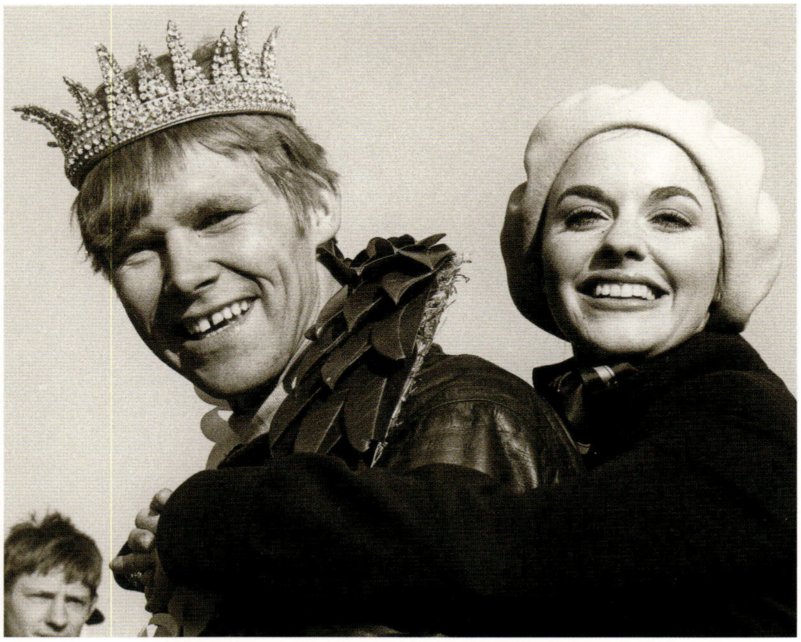

And excellent it was for Croxford. After a 250cc warm-up race in which he finished third on a borrowed Aermacchi. He then dominated the main events on his Charlie Oakley sponsored Seeley G50, winning both heat and final of the 10 lap 500 race. It was not easy, a race long tussle with the flying Welshman Malcolm Uphill, Norton, Alan Barnett on the Kirby Matchless-Metisse and Percy Tait, Triumph, were not far behind. Lap after lap the leaders chopped and changed. Uphill broke free from Croxford, then Barnett, but the on-form 'Ruislip Rebel' was having none of it and slipped by again in the final bend to take the chequered flag for the first 500cc final win, on the revamped Thruxton Circuit – 'hurrah!' The popular Malcolm Uphill took second spot from 'The Enforcer' Alan Barnett with the sheep farmer Tait fourth.

The 10 lap 1000cc race was a repeat of the shindig between Uphill and Croxford with Brian Ball, Seeley G50, not far behind, but approaching fast from a poor start, Percy Tait would be the cat among the pigeons. From the half way point another carve up ensued, places swapped on every bend until on the last lap Croxford pulled his rabbit out of the hat, and scratched ahead to win by a whisker from Tait and Uphill third, Brian Ball bringing his Seeley in fourth, ahead of Ray Pickrell, 750 Dunstall, and Paul Smart, Curtis-Domi, in sixth.

With four wins altogether and fastest laps in both finals, Dave Croxford added 'Master of Thruxton' to his 'King of Brands' and 'Master of Mallory' titles. he was on a high and so were we. It was 'just what the doctor ordered' to promote our racing efforts. The day was not finished however. Gravesend's talented Terry Vinicombe riding the Kirby sponsored 654cc BSA, won the sidecar event. The quietly spoken Vinicombe would soon be joining us to work as a frame builder.

A week later at Castle Combe, Percy Tait, who Croxford had tipped for the title that season, gave the him a riding lesson. Firstly, the 125 and 250 events took place in dry conditions on the 1.84 mile Wiltshire circuit. Former Manx Grand Prix winner Gordon Keith, Yamaha, won the 250cc race and pulverised Peter Inchley's old lap record, in fact Keith's fastest lap of 90mph also broke Derek Minter's 350 lap record on a Norton at 89.27mph.

Dave, having won both his heats for the 350 and 500 events, started as one of the favourites but the heavens opened. It wasn't singing in the rain for the competitors,

1968 King of Brands, Dave Croxford with Angela Scoular.

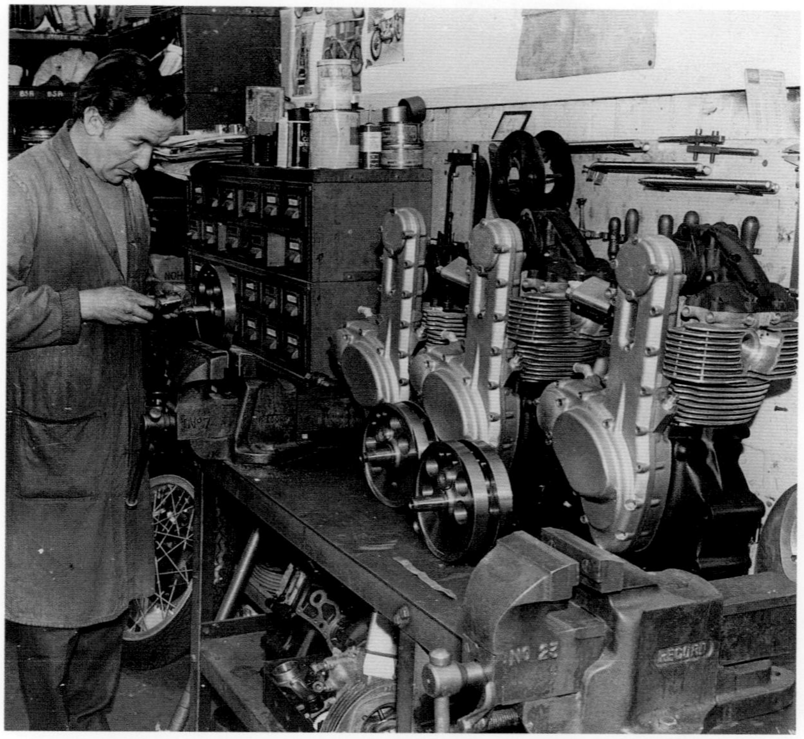

Wally Rawlings overseeing the engine department.

including Croxford who was riding Syd Lawton's Aermacchi in the 350cc event and leading the race. Despite warnings from a track marshall furiously waving his flag, Crox crashed at Camp Corner, the last bend before the finish, then slithered down the road on his backside, waving to the fans.

The 10 lap final of the 500cc race turned into an epic dual between the 'Ruislip Rebel' and the sheep farmer after Welshman Uphill joined the spectators in the Hillside. Croxford sped ahead of Tait, but Percy, a wet weather specialist (something to do with farming I expect), hit back with a remarkable display of skill as they both rushed side by side to the treacherous Camp Corner on the last lap, where so many had fallen that day. In clouds of spray, Tait on the works Triumph chanced the outside line, a hairy manoeuvre, but he managed to get away with it to beat Croxford, on the Seeley G50, to the line, and score his first well-deserved national victory that year. Tom Phillips and Tom Dickie on their Nortons, took third and fourth. A monsoon event almost best forgotten!

These were still the days of dashing from one event to another. Croxford rushed from Castle Combe to Lydden in Kent for the next day, Sunday's non-championship meeting. Riding the 500 Seeley, he won the 12 lap dash from Brian Kemp, 305 Yamaha, with Martin Ashwood, 649cc Metisse, third.

A week later, 5th May, Dave Croxford got his revenge over Percy Tait at Mallory Park. Croxford confirmed his Master of Mallory title by winning the main 30 lap 500cc event. The 40 mile race, which saw John Cooper, Seeley, retire with magneto trouble, was a nip and tuck affair between Barry Randle, Norton, and the 'Ruislip Rebel'. Randle got ahead but try as he might, could not shake off the Londoner. With a touch of class and 2 laps to go, Croxford slipped by to take the win on his Seeley G50 and the £100 first prize. Percy Tait came third, then Barnett, Spencer, and then Mahoney sixth collecting £14.

With the Isle of Man TT approaching in June, talented New Zealander Ginger Molloy a Bultaco works rider, was in print complaining about the ACU, controllers of the TT event, over the matter of expenses. Ginger Molloy, a respected professional rider racing in Europe since 1963 and attending just about every classic meeting in Europe including the Ulster Grand Prix, was keen to compete in the Isle of Man. He alleged that the ACU was not willing to pay any more than the £15 expenses being paid to British competitors, even though they called it the greatest race in the world! Ginger Molloy was no 'holiday maker'. Already that year, prior to the TT he had finished fourth in the 250cc German Grand Prix and second in 125cc and third 250cc Spanish Grand Prix. Pretty impressive, but not enough it seemed, to tempt the ACU to offer more. How much was the official New Zealand ACU Team paid?

The famous North West 200 was held on Saturday 18th May. Firstly, Ralph Bryans on a 250cc Honda six delighted the Irish fans with the fantastic sounding straight through exhaust machine. The fastest motorcycle in attendance, it screamed past the MCN speed trap at 138.5mph and recorded fastest lap of 109.23mph, shattering the absolute track record on the Portstewart-Coleraine-Portrush Circuit. Unfortunately for the likeable Ulsterman, Bryan's Honda was in trouble not only with loose carburettors, but oil on one side of the rear tyre. Dropping back to tenth place after a pit stop Ralph fought back to a final fourth place, leaving Rod Gould, Yamaha, to win with the fast improving Brian Steenson, Aermacchi, second, and Jack Findlay, Bultaco, third. Cheshire's Bill Smith won the 350cc race on his 305cc Honda but only by a whisker from Steenson, Aermacchi, who was performing brilliantly and set the fastest lap. John Hartle, also on an Aermacchi, rode the North West for the first time and made up the first three. It was obvious to us that at these very fast circuits the Seeley-7R 350cc was no longer fast enough, being as much as 7mph down on top speed against the Aermacchi machines. At that point we just didn't know what could be done.

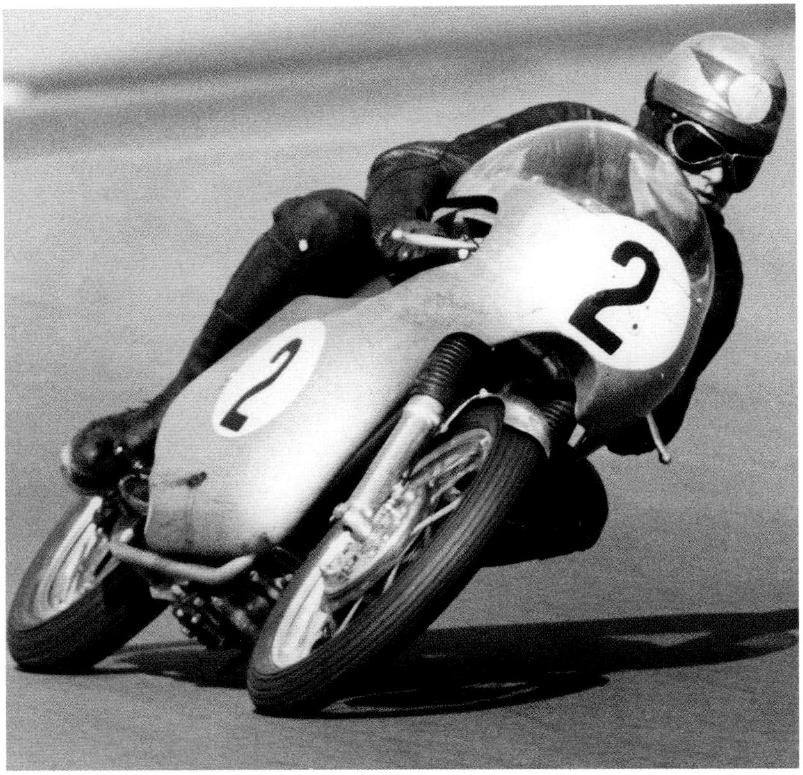

Dave Croxford, 500 Seeley, Mallory Park 5th May 1968.

Then it was Cooperman's turn in the 500cc event. four machines would go through the speed trap at exactly 133.3mph, John Cooper, Seeley G50, Ron Chandler, Seeley G50, Rob Fitton, Norton, and Peter. Williams, Arter Matchless, with Billie Nelson on the Hannah Paton just heading the list at 1mph faster. So it would be a close encounter in the 9 lap, 100 mile race. Rob Fitton, fastest in practice, led the group from the start but Australia's Kel Carruthers was just ahead by the end of the first lap. Although there was no separating the first ten riders, Peter Williams went into the lead after Fitton went out with gearbox problems. In a race described as the best ever 500cc event seen at the Northwest 200, on lap 3 it was Williams heading 'Mooneyes', then Findlay from Nelson, Chandler, Carruthers, Hartle and Gould, up to eighth spot after a bad start - a fantastic high speed race with some of the best competitors in the business.

Gradually, the stylish Williams, 'Cooperman' and Chandler drew slightly ahead but then on lap 7, calamity struck for Ron Chandler. In lapping a slower rider he was brought off his Seeley G50, sustaining a broken collarbone, then Billie Nelson on the Paton lost time when he over-shot and disappeared up a slip road. At the start of the last lap Williams gave a 'thumbs down', passed the pits then 4 miles later pulled in, suffering double vision. With John Cooper finally in the lead, the rest of the opposition fell away leaving 'Mooneyes' at his brilliant best, the most original Seeley G50 (built for Derek Minter two years previously) first under the linen with the fastest lap at 107.45mph. Nelson, back on track, finished second with Rod Gould third. The end of a fine days racing and the thousands of Irish fans went home very happy.

For John Cooper, Billie Nelson, Rod Gould and others there was no time for celebrations, Cadwell Park International races were the next day. A nightmare journey from Belfast, the Irish Sea crossing isn't always pleasant, then the early morning long drive from Liverpool across country to Louth in Lincolnshire. Arriving at Cadwell around 11.00am there was no time to spare. It was a rush to prepare the bikes, change the gearing and be ready for the delayed practice. Fortunately, for Cooper it was worth it. Although Phil Read on the 251 works Yamaha took the honours and £100 first prize in the 175cc-1000cc event held over 15 laps of the long circuit, Mooneyes on the faithful Seeley G50 took second place and £60, and our Ruislip man Croxford, Seeley, made up the rostrum positions and £40 in cash.

Mike Hailwood on the 500cc works engined (HRS) 'special' Honda, was still struggling with handling the beast. He won £30 for fourth place, can you believe it? For sure some separate payments were made to the stars by Cadwell's boss Chas Wilkinson, who despite a huge crowd of 49,000 spectators would be cringing, and rubbing his hands like Fagin as he passed the envelopes over.

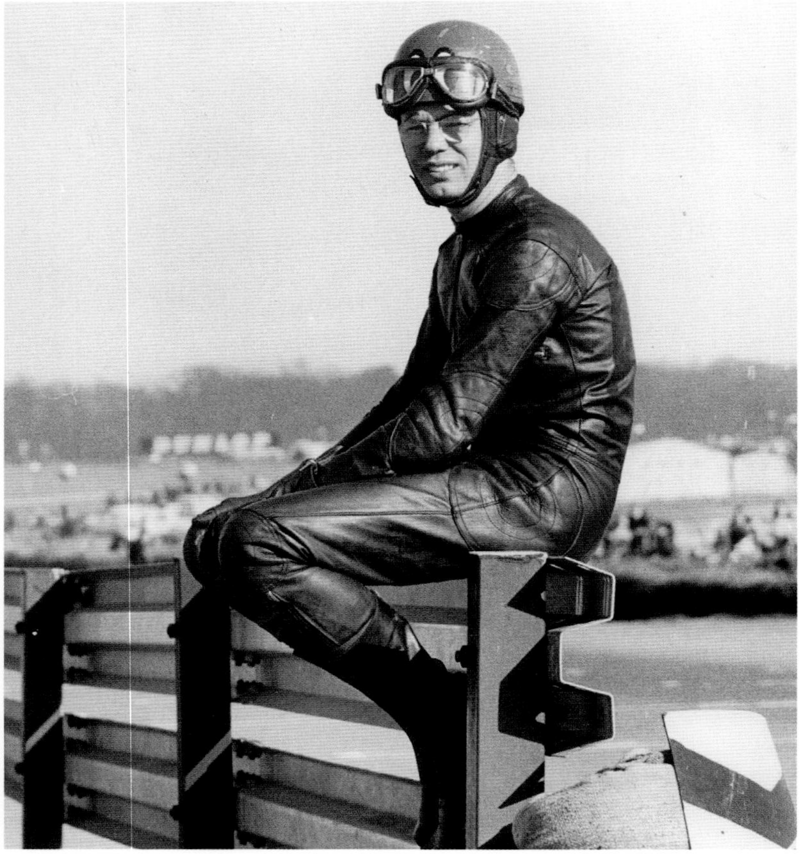

John Cooper, awaiting the action.

Ex MZ teamster Derek Woodman with his new Seeley.

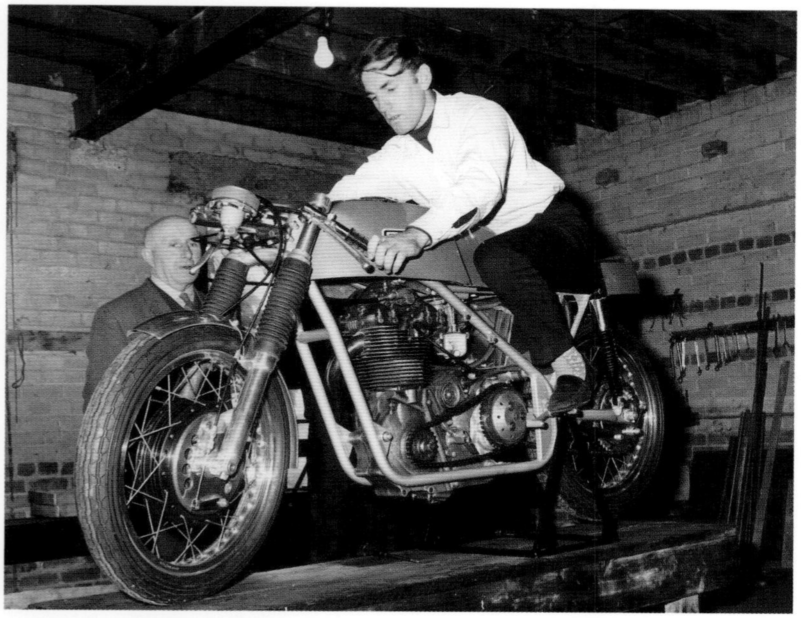

Meantime, Croxford continued his winning ways. Back to Lydden at the end of May he retained his Lord of Lydden title, taking victory in both 350 and up to 1000cc events, but could he keep up this momentum, that was the question.

Sidecar racer Dick Hawes, also sponsored by Reg Kirby, had received delivery of the newly built Seeley G50 500cc kneeler outfit to compete in that year's Isle of Man TT with passenger Jim Mann. Seeley machines had been entered in 350, 500cc and sidecar events, perhaps unique for such a small manufacturer. Once more we would support the TT races with our race service, perhaps believing it would be easier than the year before when I was competing. Wrong! As a growing company we were busy and it was a huge logistical problem to assemble all the necessary race spares in time. The packing and selecting of necessary tools, deciding which staff we could spare and sorting out transport, boat and hotel bookings, it was a most disruptive time to our normal order. Fortunately secretary Marie Bull and machine shop foreman Len Smith held the fort and kept the machines turning.

Friend and regular runner Ron Chandler had decided to miss the TT. He had raced since his crash at the North West 200, but felt that hundreds of miles around a bumpy TT course would not be good for his recently broken collar bone. Then good news which would strengthen our Isle of Man TT challenge was that ex-works MZ teamster, Blackpool's Derek Woodman would join the list of Seeley owners. His regular sponsor Jim Ball had bought him a 500. This enabled us to enter a manufacturers team in the Senior TT comprising John Cooper, Derek Woodman and Brian Ball. Ken Sprayson would be operating his regular Reynolds Tube TT Welding Service. NGK would have four men in attendance, Vick Doyle would be representing Renolds Chains as usual, and Lew Ellis representing Shell would be there to hand out the mix of oils and fuels to the required specification.

Supporters of the TT since 1907, Dunlop would have a team of fitters and technicians in the Island as well as a stock of some 1,420 race tyres which in those days were supplied completely free of charge! What a difference today, at a British superbike weekend the Dunlop Company turn up with three pantechnicons holding 2,200 tyres with around 10 fitters and technicians, a service for which the majority of competitors are charged.

Our Colin Seeley Service Team arrived in the Island and set up in Frank Large's garage, opening for business on Friday 31st May. Back at home that Whitsun weekend it was unbelievable that three major meetings were taking place, particularly as so many riders would be competing in the Isle of Man. The first mainland event was at Mallory Park on the Sunday, and if there had been any doubts about the ability of Croxford to hold it together, they were dispelled that weekend when the 'Ruislip Rebel' dominated the 500 race on his Seeley, winning a superb race from Peter Williams, Arter-Matchless, who finished ahead of Dan Shorey, Rod Gould, Barry Randle and Ron Chandler, Seeley, sixth, still in pain from the North West crash. For the same day the organisers had dreamed up a new idea, a two rider shared production race and team event on sprint lines, a challenge between a Mallory Park team and 'the rest'. Croxford and Pickrell winning the race on the Dunstall 750, provided some thrilling action, but with a compulsory pit stop the race degenerated into a time keepers' nightmare, all good fun!

Next day, Whit Monday, was a two-prong attack by the Seeley camp. 'Mooneyes' was in action at Cadwell Park and action it was. He scooped a hat trick of wins, the 250cc race on the Padgett Yamaha from Steve Jolly and Tom Phillips, then both the 500cc and John Player Championship events on the 500 Seeley, with fastest laps in both.

John Cooper had brought the latest version of our Seeley 350 to Cadwell, but with the TT days away and a lack of time to deal with all aspects of our TT involvement, I asked him not to use our new bike but save it for the TT Junior race, a prudent decision as it turned out. Meantime, on the same day back at Brands Hatch was a celebration of 40 years of motorcycle racing, supported by the 'Evening News' and organised by the The Brands Racing committee comprising the Greenwich M&MCC, Gravesend Eagles MC&MCC and Rochester, Chatham & DMC clubs. It was nearly 17 years before that John Surtees, graduating from the role of sidecar ballast-boy to his father Jack, scored his first win there in September 1951, racing a Vincent 500cc Grey Flash.

The first two races were held in the dry, giving the improving Kel Carruthers a win in the 125cc event. Then it was the Evening News International Race for machines over 101cc but not over 1000cc, originally to be run over 30 laps of the Grand Prix circuit, a 79.5 mile race incorporating a pit stop. Unfortunately, the petrol tanker bringing the fuel for the intended pit stop broke down, a blessing in disguise for the competitors, the event was cut to 20 laps. Ray Pickrell on the Dunstall Domiracer had his day of glory with a faultless ride, grabbing £300 and being awarded the Evening News Trophy by American folk singer Bobby Gentry. Griff Jenkins, on the 750 Curley-Norton, finished second, but only a machine's length ahead of that man again the 'Ruislip Rebel' bringing the 500 Seeley into third place and collecting £100, followed by Pat Mahoney on the other Curley 750cc Norton, Peter Williams, Arter Matchless, and our man Ron Chandler. 500 Seeley, making up the first six. For Banbury's Dan Shorey it was a meeting to forget, as he crashed and broke his collarbone.

Torrential rains came down for the start of the sidecar race which was won by Pip Harris after Chris Vincent retired with water in the works, truly a complete wash out. The track dried a little for the 350cc Junior Race, with another win for the Australian Carruthers on an Aermacchi-Metisse, and Croxford on his Seeley-7R third. After a disappointing ride in the 1000cc event Rex Butcher riding the lively as a kangaroo, 750cc Francis-Norton, Rex won the 250cc race on an Eddie Crooks' Suzuki.

The last challenge of the day was a 10 lap round of the 500cc Redex Trophy. On a wet track Croxford once more displayed his skills and determination, leading the pack from the start. 24 competitors behind were keen to knock the King of Brands off his throne. In the best race of the day, the 'Ruislip Rebel' held off the challenge of Williams, Ashwood, Mahoney, Uphill and Chandler until the last lap, when Uphill, with thoughts of the £100 first prize, in a desperate attempt came charging up to Croxford then side by side into Druids. Uphill then sneaked ahead as they approached Bottom Bend but the Welshman would not be singing in the hills that day, but joined them in the hillside, as he lost control of this Manx Norton and gracefully pirouetted into the mud. Croxford was very close, but fortunately avoided him, although having to grass cut with the Seeley G50, managing to get back on track and go on to a further 500 race win (14 so far that season). Peter Williams once more took second place followed by Martin Ashwood, Pat Mahoney, Ron Chandler, Seeley, fifth and Graham Sharp in sixth.

With a total of £240 prize money that day neatly folded into his pocket, Dave dashed to the bar for a well-deserved Guinness, whilst others dashed off to the Isle of Man for the TT practice week, which had already started. It was a brilliant weekend for the Seeley Racing Company, with wins at each of the three circuits in the 500cc class, a great encouragement to all involved.

I had missed all the Whitsun short circuit excitement and action as I was already in the Island with Wally Rawlings and our service staff. The finishing touches had been put to Derek Woodman's Seeley and we were all surprised when the combined practice times from the Saturday and Monday that Whitsun weekend listed Derek as fifth fastest in the Senior practice headed by Agostini and Hartle on MVs, Barnett Matchless-Metisse, Steve Spencer Matchless then Woodman and Brian Ball both on Seeleys. A good start to the fortnight!

As usual, practice week was feverish, with so many competitors for the eight TT events, so much practice, so much drama, so much work, hordes of mechanics, helpers, friends, family and hangers-on, thousands of enthusiastic fans arriving at the 'Magic Isle'. The endless sound of motorcycles turned the Island into an arena of electric intensity. On a warm day hundreds would be paddling in Douglas Bay, whilst not far away competitors were hurling themselves down Bray Hill at horrendous speed – what a contrast. It could all be a scene from a huge film epic.

John Cooper arrived at the TT from his successful day at Cadwell Park. Our service team, lead by Wally, immediately jumped into action to give the Seeley G50, here for its third TT event, a once over before John's first practice. With the increasing competitiveness of the Italian Aermacchi machines, we were trying to stem the tide and produce a lightweight 7R Seeley on which 'Mooneyes' could ride for us in that year's Junior Event.

John Hartle first figured in the Grand Prix scene as far back as 1955 with a second place on his 500 Manx Norton to winner Bill Lomas on the works Moto Guzzi at that year's Ulster Grand Prix winning the same event in 1956. In 1958 Hartle partnered Surtees on the works MV machines finishing second to him that year in both 350 and 500 World Championships. The following year Hartle on the works MV finished second again to his team mate John Surtees in the 350cc World Championship. Then for the 1960 Isle of Man TT Senior Race again partnered Surtees on the works MVs, but the double World Champion came across the finish line to win his sixth TT event leaving Hartle once more in second place.

John Hartle, a talented rider and a true professional, 10 years on from those first rides on the works MV multis, was, in 1968 offered the chance to race once more at the TT on those special machines, although again as a possible support rider, this time to World Champion Giacomo Agostini. Nothing much seemed to have changed for Hartle! John would be racing the 350cc 3 cylinder model in the Junior Event and have the 500cc 4 cylinder for the Senior Race.

At the end of practice week, Saturday 8th June heralded the start of the TT race week, a 6.00pm kick off. Was this football under floodlights? No it was the sidecar TT, but with a difference. That year the event would be run concurrently as a two part race, firstly the 500cc class for competitors competing in the World Championship. After a 10 minute interval the newly introduced 750cc class runners would follow. Although a record entry of 90 crews for the race was received, non-starters reduced the field to 43 in the 500 class and 36 in the 750, 79 outfits in all with 158 crew members lined up along the Glencrutchery Road. Nowhere in the world could you witness such a line-up for one sidecar race, it was pretty impressive.

Our interest was in Terry Vinicombe on the 654cc Kirby-BSA (he having joined our company), and Dick Hawes on the Seeley 500. Despite the early morning rain the day turned into a scorcher so the conditions were ideal for evening racing. As we awaited the start of the 3 lap race, the first time in eight years that I was not on the grid with a dry mouth facing that frightening rush down Bray Hill, I had very mixed emotions - pleased that I was no longer under that pressure, but a little sad to be no longer in the fray, mixing it with the best charioteers in the World.

In the drama-packed 500cc International Sidecar TT, World Champion, Klaus Enders, BMW, starting number 1, left no doubt that he was out to win his first Isle of Man event, lapping on the first circuit at 93.73mph (a new record), and even quicker on the second at 94.04mph, leaving Siegfried Schauzu, BMW, on corrected time, 1 minute 22 seconds behind. The fast improving Johann Attenberger, BMW, in his second TT event, was up to third place at 89.57mph. After Georg Aerbaucher, our old adversary in so many Grands Prix, retired with a broken fairing, Helmut Fath, URS, took fourth place with Luthringschauser, BMW, just over 4 seconds behind in fifth. The chequered flag was held ready for the expected flying Enders, however it was Schauzu's light that came on first on the giant scoreboard, indicating he was at Signpost Corner ahead of Enders who was pushing and coasting after the Rennsport engine went kaput! Schauzu, with passenger Horst Schneider, took the finish, his second successive victory at the TT, collecting the trophy and £100 with a race record average speed of 91.09mph. Attenburgher, second at 89.47mph was awarded £70, and £50 for third placed Luthringshauser at 87.60mph. A subdued Fath, lapping slower than he had done in 1967 when racing against me, came fourth at 87.28mph. John Brandon who had bought my BMW was fifth, at 82.43mph slower than my 82.80mph average on the G50 in 1962. Dick Hawes, despite stopping to make adjustments at Laurel Bank and removing sticky tape from his leathers which had restricted blood flow to his arm on the last lap, brought the Seeley outfit home in tenth place at 77.44mph. Silver Replicas for Dick and passenger Jim Mann with £20 prize money, the last but one crew being handed Silver Replicas.

In the true tradition of the TT Klaus Enders and passenger Rolf Engelhardt having broken down on the very last lap coming over the last section of The Mountain, pushed into the finish, receiving huge sympathetic applause for their tremendous efforts and a final eighth place. 25 competitors from the 43 starters of the 500 race finished the course.

I cannot resist comparing lap or race times at the Isle of Man TT. My average speed on the FCS BMW in 1964 was 86.76mph and would still have placed me fifth in the 1968

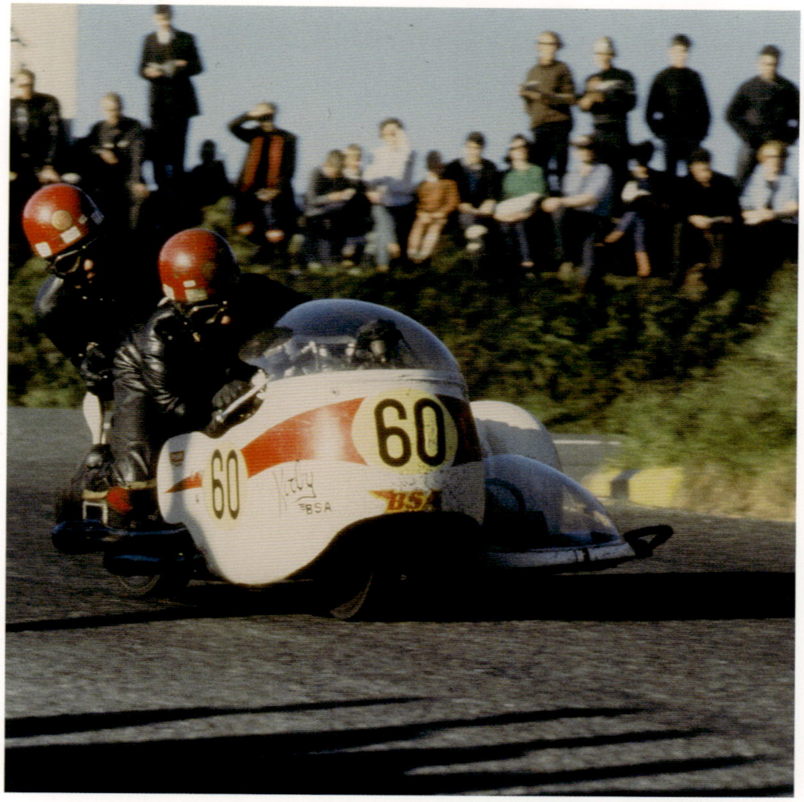

Winning ways, Terry Vinicombe and John Flaxman on their 654cc Kirby BSA at Signpost Corner.

race, my speed of 87.92mph in the 1967 TT would have placed me third. Perhaps I should not have stopped – who's being silly now?

Despite all the excitement of the 500cc race, the 750cc event had not gone unnoticed. Chris Vincent with Keith Scott in the chair, raced his 654cc BSA kneeler outfit starting as favourite, but 31 year old Gravesend boy, Vinicombe with John Flaxman holding the wheel down presented a remarkable challenge. On the first lap the flying 'Brummie' put in a brilliant lap of 89.07mph leading Vinicombe by 18 seconds, but Terry was not hanging about either, speeding his Kirby-BSA round at an impressive 88.03mph – well ahead of third place man Norman Hanks, BSA. Then Chris Vincent was out, stopping at Kirkmichael on the second lap with an oil leak. Terry Vinicombe, then unchallenged, rode a faultless race, reduced his speed and comfortably brought the Kirby-BSA home to win at 85.85mph, his first major TT success, and winner of the first ever 750cc sidecar race held in the Island, with Norman Hanks, BSA, second and Peter Brown, BSA, third, a BSA 'clean sweep' of this class. There were 22 finishers from the original 36 starters in the 750cc race.

On Monday 10th June, the start of TT week as it used to be, was the last appearance of the fascinating 50cc machines at the Isle of Man TT. With no more support from the Honda, Suzuki or Kreidler factories, although Spanish Derbi were trying to fill a gap, there weren't enough top quality entries to warrant a 3 lap 113.2 mile race. Nevertheless, on a bright sunny day at 11.00am, 33 starters rushed down Bray Hill from a mass start, perhaps providing the most exciting moment of the whole event. The race favourites that year were Angelo Nieto and Australian Barry Smith, both on Derbi machines. Smith soon took the lead and stayed there after Nieto crashed at Baaregarroo. At 72.90mph, Barry Smith, Derbi, won the Avon Challenge Trophy and £50, his speed well down on Stuart Graham's 1967 lap time on the works Suzuki at 82.89mph. Clive Walpole, Honda, was second at 67.26mph and Ernest Griffiths, Honda, third 66.20mph.

Now the serious stuff could get underway. The 6 lap 250cc TT had an original entry of 102, of which 81 came to the line at 1.30pm. With no works Hondas or Hailwood, Yamaha was the favourite with Phil Read and 'Little' Bill Ivy. Although team mates, there was a certain rivalry between these two stars. They arrived at the Isle of Man TT equal on points in the 250cc World Championship, having won a Grand Prix each so far that season – it would be a game of chess. Mike Hailwood was watching from the sidelines wondering if his mate 'Little' Bill could pull off the big one and give Yamaha its first 250cc TT victory.

Well, it seemed so. On the first lap of six the Maidstone 'Marvel' took the works 4 cylinder Yamaha around the scary 37.73 mile TT course at a fantastic 105.51mph, breaking Hailwood's lap record and leaving 'Speedy' Read 14 seconds behind, having lapped at 104.35mph. Renzo Pasolini on the Benelli was next through, ahead of Rosner on the MZ. Race retirements were coming thick and fast; Paul Smart, Mike Chatterton, Irish star Brian Steenson crashed at Union Mills receiving superficial cuts, Martin Carney was in the pits with a broken gear lever. With both works Yamahas coming in after lap 2 for refuelling, Phil Read pulled back some time on Ivy, then at the end of lap 3 Bill Ivy slowed having caught his foot under the foot rest causing a painful ankle injury, and Read was ahead.

Drama on the fourth lap, Phil Read stopped at the Mountain Bungalow with a flat rear tyre. He managed to struggle back to the pits but his race was over, joining the other retirements Kel Carruthers, Gordon Keith, John Williams, Tony Godfrey, 50 in all failed to make the finish, including 23 year old New Zealander Ian Veitch, who crashed at Glen Vine and sadly died as a result of his injuries.

Meantime, the 125cc World Champion, Maidstone's 'pocket' rocket Bill Ivy was in control. To the delight of thousands of fans he brought the Yamaha across the finish line to give the company its first ever victory in the 250 class of the Isle of Man TT. Pasolini finished second, over 2 minutes behind with Heinz Rosner on the works MZ third. Malcolm Uphill, Suzuki, Rod Gould, Yamaha, and Bill Smith, Yamaha, made up the first six in that order with our friend 'Mooneyes' Cooper in eighth on the Padgett-Yamaha, giving him valuable practice for Wednesday's Junior TT ride on the Seeley 7R. Bill Ivy pocketed £200 in prize money, and of course the lightweight Tourist Trophy.

Alongside the racing programme much was happening. We were very busy with our TT racing service, to which race commentator Peter Arnold paid a visit for an inspection and interview for a cover story he was asked to write for the Island's Examiner TT Special. Then, out of the blue, we received a request from an Australian film company. Could we lend them a race bike to which they could connect a movie camera? The crew had been given special permission to film some racing action at Windy Corner on Thursday, the day before the Senior event. Riders would include Jack Findlay, Kel Carruthers, Barry Smith and John Cooper, would they be actors or stuntmen – on the day I was not sure!

Back to the serious business, Wednesday's production race was followed by the 350cc Junior Race in which 'Mooneyes' would be competing on our latest Seeley 7R. Favourite for the 750cc Production Race and overall winner in 1967, John Hartle once again rode a 649cc Triumph Bonneville. Hartle, fastest in practice at 96.61mph, thought his main challenge would come from Ray Pickrell on the 746cc Dunstall Dominator who had lapped at 94.92mph. With non-starters the 750cc class was reduced to 14 runners, twelve for the 500 class and the majority of 20 covering the 250 class – 46 machines in all.

The 3 lap race was to have a Le Mans type start and a 5 minute interval between each class. At 11.00am sharp, BSA works rider Tony Smith kicked his machine into life and was away. By the Bungalow Hartle was leading Pickrell by 15 seconds, but less than 2 miles on, John Hartle crashed at, would you believe, Windy Corner and was being attended by a doctor. Meantime, Ray Pickrell completed the first lap, well in the lead at 96.55mph from Billie Nelson performing well on the Bert Saunders' Norton Atlas with a speed of 94.04mph, but 38 seconds down on Pickrell. Tony Smith was third and Paul

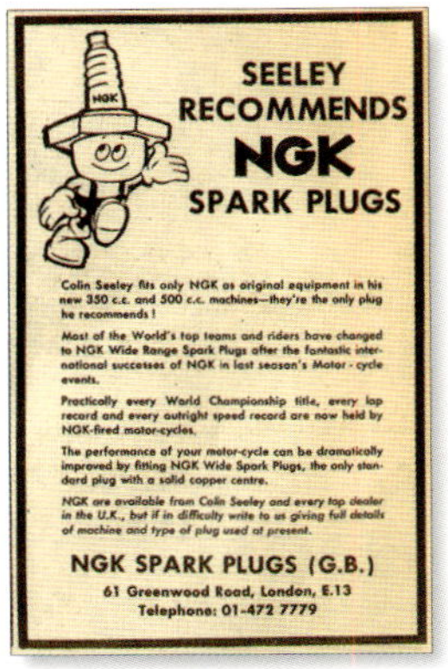

Smart on the works BSA Spitfire held off his friend Rex Butcher, Triumph, in fifth place, but was soon out of the running, along with six others in the 750 class. So it was Pickrell in for a well deserved victory, averaging a storming 98.13mph and collecting the Double Diamond Trophy and a huge £50 first prize, Tony Smith, second, then policeman Graham Bailey, the Welshman Uphill and finally Tony Godfrey collecting £10 for fifth place.

Journalist Ray Knight, Triumph, broke the 500 production lap record with a 91.03mph and won his class averaging 90.09mph. John Blanchard, who we had not seen much of since our fall out in 1967, finished second on a 500cc Velocette, ahead of Dave Nixon, Triumph, third. Trevor Burgess brought the 230cc Spanish Ossa home winning the 250cc class at an impressive 87.21mph. Only 28 finished out of the original 46 starters.

John Hartle, slightly concussed and suffering a cut hand, was unable to start in the following Junior Race. It was a huge blow for the popular Hartle who in practice had been most impressive riding both the 500 and 350 works MVs. John thought the 350cc 3 cylinder MV the most fabulous machine he had ever ridden and had lapped at 104.26mph. His fairy tale comeback had taken a turn for the worse. Would he be fit in time for Friday's Senior Race? With Hartle out, the Italian 500cc World Champion Giacomo Agostini had it all his own way in the Junior Race although Renzo Pasolini on the works Benelli four put up a spirited performance. There had been 111 entries for the Junior Event, but non-starters reduced that to 86 - still a good field with many star names.

The weather was dry with a little mist on the mountain. At 1.30pm Jack Findlay on the Francis Beart Aermacchi, with Selwyn Griffitths on the Ray Cowles AJS started proceedings. After a 20 second interval, Hartle and Agostini were due to start but with Hartle out, Ago was on his own, soon leading on the road as well as the race. He completed the first lap at 106.03mph, not beating Hailwood's record lap of 107.73mph set the year before. Agostini didn't need to break any records. Pasolini, Benelli, in second place on that first lap at 103.15mph was 30 seconds behind, with Heinz Rosner a minute down on him. John 'Mooneyes' Cooper on our Seeley started alongside Derek Woodman, Aermacchi, and was well adrift. The second lap was the same; Agostini, Pasolini, Rosner, Carruthers, Smith, Findlay with Woodman up to seventh, but 'Mooneyes' nowhere in sight. On the third lap Rosner retired with engine trouble bringing the Australian Carruthers up into third, but not for long. Kel's Aermacchi gave a cough and stopped at the 21st Milestone. Most riders were in for their pit stop at the end of lap 3. Even allowing for slowing down into the pits, Agostini wasn't letting up, averaging 106.26mph for the first 3 laps. Pasolini in second was well behind, then Bill Smith, Honda, Jack Findlay and Woodman now up to fifth and chasing hard. TT newcomer Alan Barnett was in sixth place and Irishman Brian Steenson, also a TT newcomer having recovered from his crash on Monday in the 250cc event, was in determined mood and up to seventh ahead of Uphill, Grotefeld and Jim Curry. Finally 'Mooneys' after a successful pit stop, came into the picture.

Motorcycle News had set a speed trap between Creg-ny-Baa and Brandish Corner. Agostini, MV recorded 146.3mph, Pasolini, Benelli 142.9mph, Rozner's MZ 137.4mph with most of the Aermacchi's clocking 123.3mph. Our Seeley was well down at 116.9mph. Was 'Mooneyes' asleep? By the end of the fourth lap 'Cooperman' must have been wringing the best out of the Seeley 7R, moving up to seventh place. Back at the pits we were all excited, we so needed a good result in the 350cc class. Then it was the final lap. Ago was still ahead of Pasolini, Smith, Findlay and Woodman but the pace had upped and 'Mooneyes' slotted into a leader board position in front of Jim Curry, Alan Barnett and Steenson. The last lap was crucial. We had no doubts about our Derbyshire man, John would not take undue chances but would the Seeley keep going surrounded by those Italian Aermacchis? Amazingly 'Mooneyes' had come through the field to pressurise the riders battling for the positions fourth back to tenth. We waited nervously as the Italian star Agostini crossed the line to win his second Isle of Man TT event, averaging 104.78mph for the 226 mile race, only just beating Hailwood's 1967 race record of 104.68mph. Ago collected the Junior Tourist Trophy and £200 first prize. Renzo Pasolini, in a faultless ride, brought the works Benelli home in second place. Clocked at 152mph at The Highlander, Renzo averaged 102.65mph for the race. Bill Smith, Honda, made up the rostrum positions. Then our friend Derek Woodman on a damned Aermacchi came fourth at 93.46mph just holding off John Cooper's challenge on the Seeley by 11 seconds in a brilliant fifth and £75 averaging a respectable 93.35mph. Jack Findlay dropped back to sixth as his Aermacchi engine started spluttering

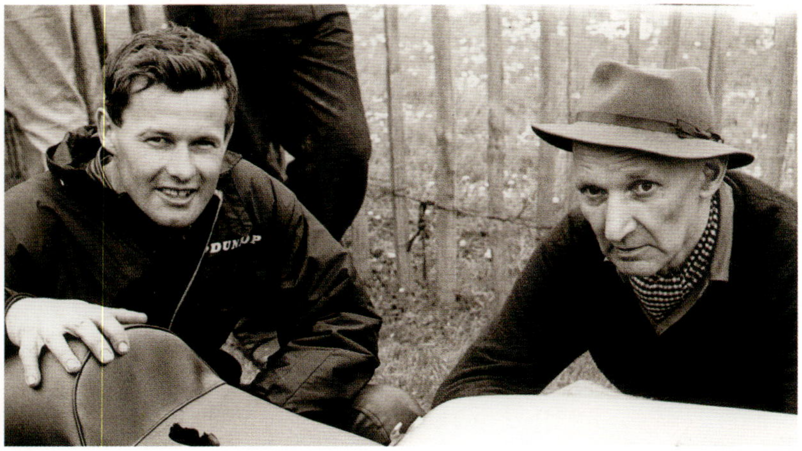

1968 Junior TT, Jack Findlay and the ever smiling Francis Beart.

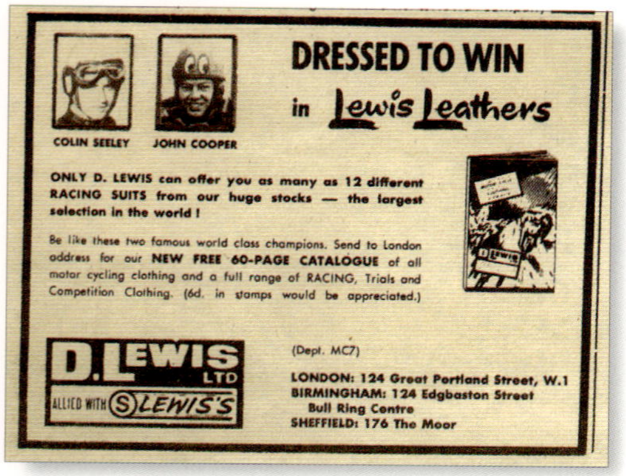

John Cooper, Seeley, 1968 Junior TT, Parliament Square.

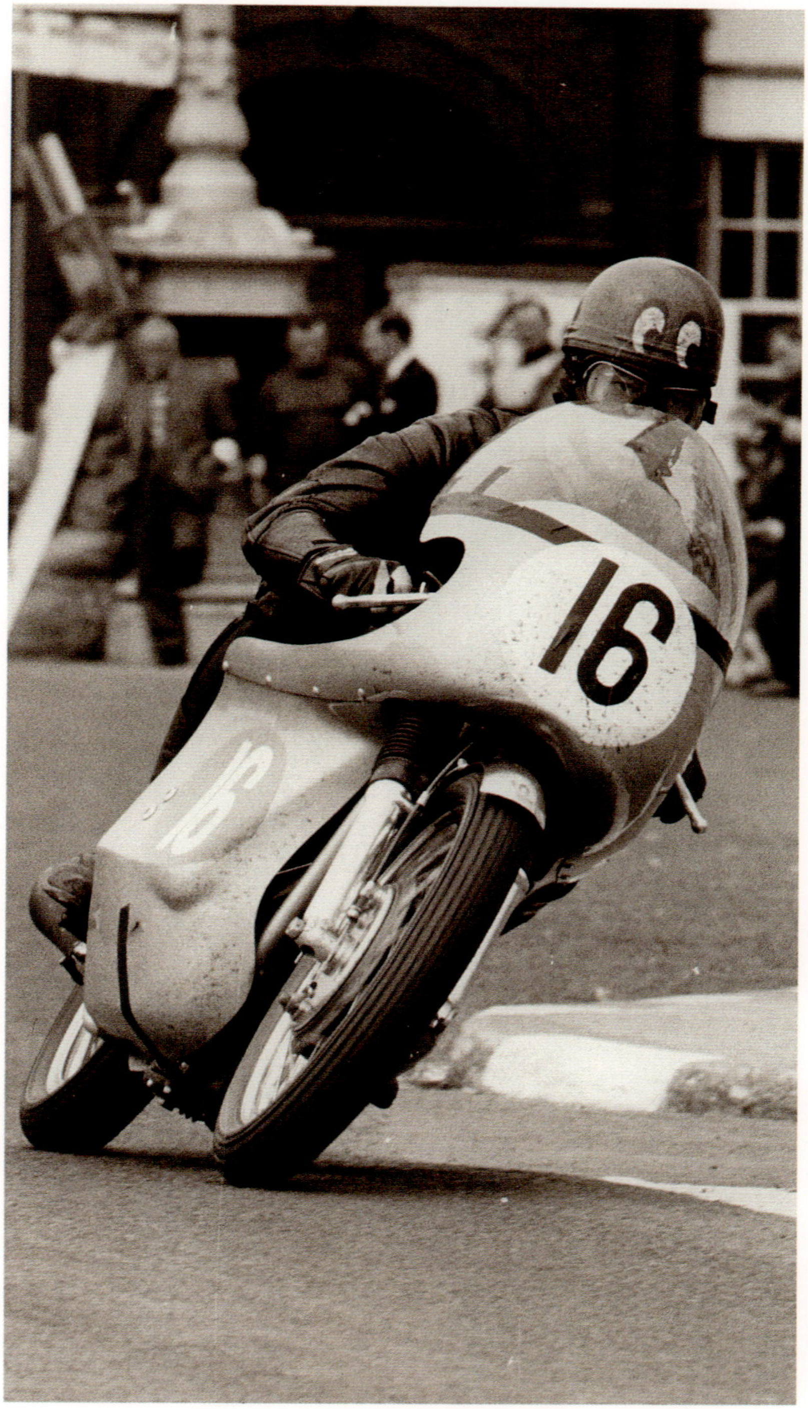

approaching the finish line. The rear tyre had worn a hole through the seat. Jim Curry Aermacchi seventh, Alan Barnett on the Kirby Metisse an impressive eighth, Brian Steenson Aermacchi ninth and Malcolm Uphill, Crooks Suzuki made up the first 10 places.

Forty competitors finished from the original 86 starters, with some 19 350cc Italian Aermacchi machines entered in the Junior Race although perhaps not all started. Our Seeley 350 7R finished fifth, with only one Aermacchi ahead and so very close. The whole Colin Seeley team was delighted. Thank you 'Mooneyes', not just the Mallory Park specialist as many had thought.

Thursday was the day for the final fettling of our Senior Team machines. After a rush of last minute customers we started to pack up the equipment and store the spares away for the return to Kent on Friday evening. Two weeks in the Island with all of its stresses and strains was long enough. However, first there was some film action at Windy Corner. That part of the mountain TT course was closed by the police, then after the usual delays associated with filming, a camera was finally attached to our 350 Seeley. The director gave his instructions and then sent the riders back down the course, ready to return when commanded, as if in competition. The Director shouted, 'Action!' The cameras rolled. In the blazing sun, high in the hills you wouldn't have been surprised if Clint Eastwood appeared on horseback from round the corner. Instead, different horses came rushing into view, the riders side by side as they swooped into Windy Corner. 'Cut!' shouted the director, sending the riders back for repeat action. Again the clapper board came down, 'Action!' and our TT heroes rushed towards us. Swoosh through the corner, looks good and the director is pleased. Then deciding an action shot the opposite way round would be just great. The riders assembled ready for a racing return. Riding the wrong way round on any race circuit, even with practice, can be strange and difficult.

The group of riders came through Windy Corner headed by Monday's 50cc TT winner, Australian Barry Smith riding a Thompson's Suzuki 250. As the bunch exited the corner, Barry was right on the road edge and skimming the fence. I remember thinking as I recorded the proceedings on my 8mm cine camera, Barry is going to crash. The Suzuki struck the fence and flew into the air, leaving Barry spinning in the middle of the road. The Aussie film director jumped up and down, 'Cut! cut!' That's a 'Wrap' believing that fellow Aussie had perhaps put on a special performance for the camera. Fortunately, Barry Smith was unhurt apart from cuts, bruises and his pride, but we all had a good laugh at his expense.

Friday 14th June, fortunately not the 13th, dawned warm and sunny. In fact the conditions were perfect and remained so for the 3 lap 125cc lightweight event, then the 6 lap Senior race. The 125cc race with a start time of 11.00am was dominated by the factory works Yamaha pairing of Luton's Phil Read and Maidstone's Bill Ivy. 'Speedy' Read had won this event on a Yamaha in 1965, then Ivy in 1966, pushing Phil back into second place. In 1967 Phil got his own back, taking the victory with Bill retiring so what could 'Little' Bill do now to even the score?

The usual start procedure, at 10.30am the siren sounded for the warm-up whilst the Royal Marine's display team performed in front of a packed grandstand. Extra thousands of spectators had arrived for Friday's events perhaps encourage by the marvellous weather with no rain all week. At 10.45am 47 competitors from the original 58entries came to the line. Dave Simmonds, Kawasaki, alongside Phil Read, Yamaha, were the first pair away, followed in 10 seconds by Martin Carney, Bultaco, the British 125 champion, and Derek Chatterton, Mondial, the 250 British Champion. Bill Ivy started on his own, 40 seconds behind Read. On corrected time at Ramsey, 'Little' Bill was five seconds ahead of Read, reduced to 4 seconds by end of lap one – nothing in it!

On the second lap the Maidstone Marvel sped flat out down Bray Hill at 131.4mph on the miniature engine 4 cylinder Yamaha. What was in the mind of this little man from Kent? Like many of us small men, perhaps he needed to prove something, and in this race our hero certainly did, taking the 125cc Yamaha (hardly a BSA Bantam) around the TT course at an unbelievable 100.32mph, breaking his 1966 record of 98.55mph, and achieving the first 100mph lap on a 125cc machine. Bill Ivy joined Harold Daniells (first to achieve a 91mph lap) and Derek Minter (on a 500cc Norton first to lap at 100mph), as another record breaker.

'Speedy' Read also broke the old record lapping at 99.76mph, pretty awesome for this pair of champions, but they were in a race of their own. Third placed man Kel Carruthers, Honda, was well behind. Then on the last lap at Ballaugh Bridge, Read was only one second behind Ivy, and by Ramsey was ahead by 5 seconds. 'Little' Bill had slowed considerably. Was he in trouble or was it simply team orders? Phil Read, through signpost corner came tearing across the line to win his third 125cc TT event with a new race record of 99.12mph. He collected his award of the lightweight 125 Tourist Trophy and £75 prize money. The Maidstone 'rocket' Ivy, with the Yamaha going off song, took a disappointing second place with blistered hands but had still averaged a phenomenal 97.78mph, and £40 for all that effort.

The versatile Kel Carruthers brought the Gates Honda home third to be awarded £35, but what a difference in speed, at 86.69mph - still pretty good for a 125cc twin production Honda. Tommy Robb, Bultaco was fourth, followed by Gordon Keith then Steve Murray. Only 21 finished out of the 47 starters. It had been history in the making for the two Yamaha stars. 1968 was the last year these fabulous 125cc works multi-cylinder Yamahas would be seen at the TT and with tragedy striking Bill Ivy in 1969, he would never return to the Island.

With the excitement of the lightweight event over 85 competitors for the Senior Race were already assembled in the paddock area. John Hartle had passed a medical examination the night before, following his crash in Wednesday's production race and was allowed to start in the 6 lap Senior on the works MV. Two manufacturers teams are entered, one for Norton with riders Tom Dickie, Barry Randle and Don May, the other Colin Seeley Racing Developments with John Cooper, Derek Woodman and Brian Ball.

J.C. 'Mooneyes' was competing on the most original Seeley G50, built early in 1966 and now owned by him. It had been ridden at the TT that same year by John Blanchard achieving fourth place. In 1967 it joined the 100mph club when in fifth place, before a broken primary chain put Blanchard back down the field but still with a finish. The Seeleys of Woodman and Ball, which made up our team, were customer bikes.

The race was due to start at 1.30pm, the wail of the siren at 1.00pm indicated the warm up procedure and at 1.15pm. the roar of 85 engines stopped, leaving plumes of exhaust gases and the smell of Castrol R drifting through the paddock and grandstand. We helped wheel out the trio of Seeleys onto that famous grid. Cooperman, number 11 was starting 50 seconds back from the first man Gyula Marsovszky. Fred Stevens, Hannah Paton was a non-starter. Derek Woodman, our next man, was number 17, 13 seconds back on J.C. then Brian Ball, number 30, a minute down on Woodman, so our riders were well spread out. Waiting for the start, the nerves kicked in. I looked down the Glencrutchery Road towards the top of the scary Bray Hill, almost inviting the riders to blast down with the throttle absolutely held back on the stop. As ex-TT competitors, Wally and I understood the feeling of apprehension, then pats on the back for good luck and the grid was cleared of friends, family and mechanics.

To the delight of the crowded grandstand, World Champion Giacomo Agostini made a perfect start on the big MV. The 4 cylinder burst into life and the 4 exhausts chimed a perfect note as the Italian fire engine disappeared out of sight down Bray Hill. Rising star Alan Barnett, Kirby Matchless Metisse, a TT newcomer and third fastest in practice with an impressive lap of 100.08mph would surely be on the leader board. John Hartle, on the MV, 70 seconds behind team mate Ago, left the line alongside Griff Jenkins, Matchless. At Glen Helen, nearly 10 miles out on that first lap, Agostini as expected, was first through followed by Carruthers, Findlay, Tait, Uphill and John Cooper who had caught Marsovszky. At Ballaugh, Griff Jenkins on the Ray Cowles Matchless, was reckoned to be in second place just ahead of Hartle who was having problems with an MV down on power, but worse, the six speed gearbox was playing neutrals much of the time. Then Griff Jenkins came through to start his second lap in third place, with Agostini ahead of the brilliant Alan Barnett. John Hartle, planning a pit stop at the end of that lap, approached the high speed Cronk-ny-Mona left-hander leading to Signpost Corner. In his wisdom he kept the MV in a higher gear than normal to avoid a box of neutrals and got into an uncontrollable tank-slapper at around 100mph, glanced a kerb and then crashed the works MV, completely flattening one side of the machine. Fortunately John was able to walk away from this pile-up with abrasions and his pride seriously hurt. He was totally devastated. Hartle's chance to hit the big time once more had probably gone for ever. We all felt so sorry for this dedicated racing professional – it was a sad turn of events.

On the first lap Derek Woodman's Seeley was holding fourth place and John Cooper seventh but as in the Junior Race, Mooneyes was just warming up. The 23 year old Alan Barnett having lapped at 98.63mph on that first lap, had his glory cut short at the top of Barregarro on his second circuit when the exhaust system on Kirby-Metisse broke up. Worse for third place man Griff Jenkins, going like the wind on the Ray Cowles machine, he crashed heavily at Glen Helen, which brought the helicopter into action to whisk him off to Noble's Hospital.

Meanwhile 'Mooneyes' had woken up, catching and passing Woodman to take second place. TT newcomer Brian Ball came from nowhere into sixth place, 36 seconds down from Percy Tait's Triumph in fifth. By the end of the third lap 'Cooperman' had lapped at 99.55mph on the Seeley, the fastest single cylinder lap of the race with Woodman on 98.01mph Our riders were holding second, third and fourth places. Could the manufacturers team prize be ours?

When Agostini came in for his pit stop, he jumped off the MV and was looking at the rear of the machine. Drama indeed, is Ago in trouble? The mechanics adjusted the rear chain, refuelled, and he was back in the race, having lost only two minutes. Race

Brian Ball, second on his Seeley, Senior TT.

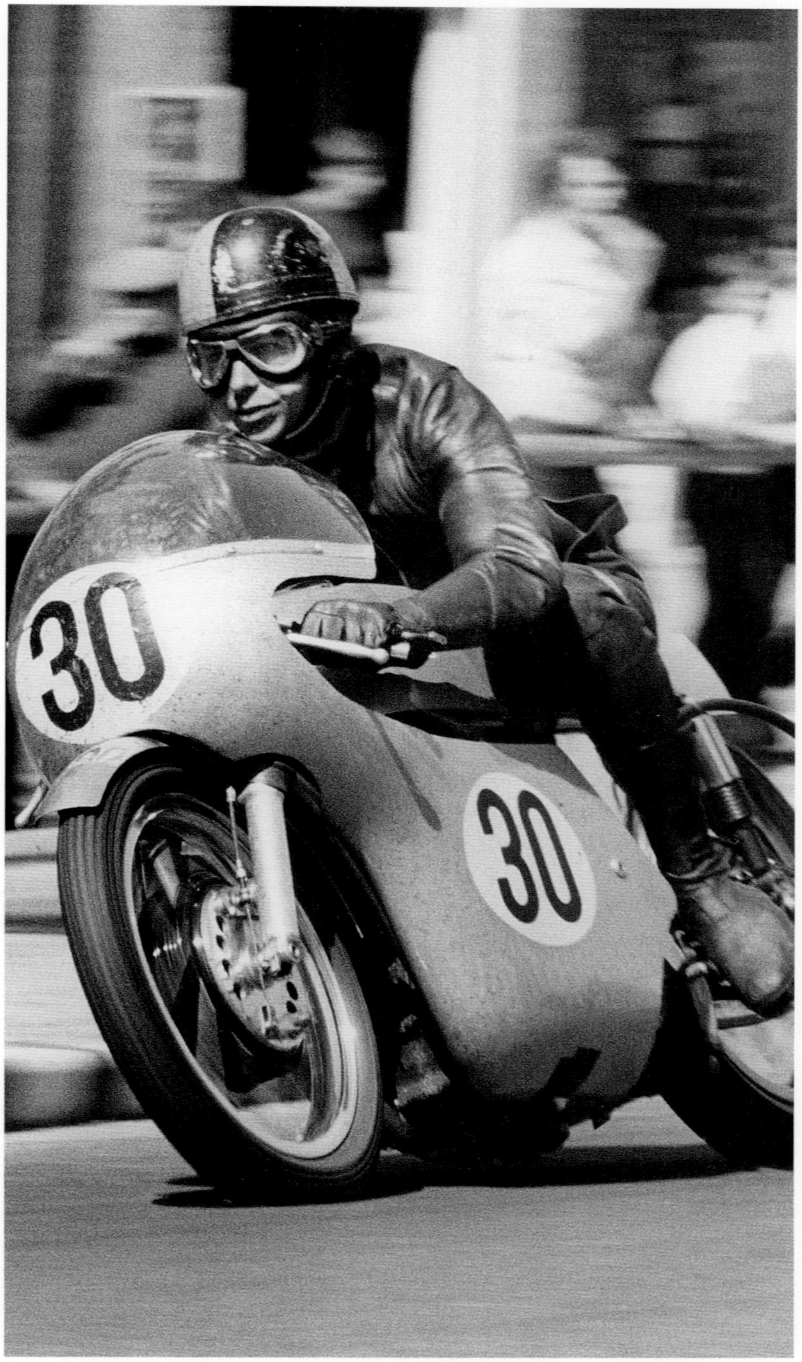

retirements were coming in thick and fast; Percy Tait, engine trouble, Marsovszky, broken clutch cable, Rod Gould on the other works Triumph, covered in oil, Vin Duckett ran out of road at Governors, then Crayford's Pat Mahoney crashed his Oakley Matchless in the same place, Malcolm Uphill crashed at Ramsey, tried to keep going with a broken handlebar and the Norton covered in oil but was black flagged. Peter Williams retired the Arter Matchless, Tom Dickie had a broken chain on the Petty Norton – and so the list went on! Then on the fourth lap Derek Woodman slowed on the Cronk-y-Voddy straight with something banging on his leg. It was the rear damper unit, the top retaining bolt had come loose letting the damper move on the frame spigot. He stopped and adjustments were carried out, dropping Derek down the order, but we were still in with a chance of the manufacturer's award. Brian Ball in second place was having his own problems, the megaphone had fallen off the Seeley, reducing the power. The gear lever had shed its protective rubber so he was struggling to change gear, skinning his toes through the effort. John Cooper put in another good lap at 99.45mph, lapping the same speed as Agostini on lap 5. Into the last lap Ago sped up but he wasn't going to make any mistakes, as this could be his first Senior TT success.

Then with our prize in sight, sensation! John Cooper stopped at Sulby Bridge. Having a 3 minute lead over Brian Ball in third place, news came through that John was okay, but the Seeley G50 had a broken crankpin and that was that for the Derbyshire ace, having his best Isle of Man TT so far – so disappointing. Fortunately, Brian Ball, riding a very determined race on his Seeley, moved up to hold second place from Barry Randle by the narrowest of margins - 0.04 of a second as they came under the finish flag. The 500cc World Motorcycle Champion Giacomo Agostini crossed that famous finish line on the MV to win his first Senior TT and another £200, his first double TT success and a very popular result. The likeable Italian star won every 500cc Grand Prix event in 1968.

Cheshire's Bill Smith was fourth, followed by Bernard Lund, Kel Carruthers, Billie Nelson, and Rex Butcher eighth, on a Seeley made up of a borrowed Ron Chandler Seeley chassis and a brand new G50 engine brought direct from us. Blackpool's Derek Woodman brought his Seeley home into ninth spot and £55 prize money, a great effort by Derek after his problems. 37 finishers meant that more than half of the competitors were littered around the TT course.

For the 125cc lightweight and Senior events MCN had set up their speed trap on Bray Hill. Quickest and bravest in the Senior Race was the British pairing of Griff Jenkins and Alan Barnett, Matchless, both clocking 134.3mph. Suprisingly enough Agostini, MV, was slower at 133.33mph followed by John Cooper, Seeley, 132.4mph and Woodman, Seeley, sharing a speed with Charlie Sanby, Norton, at 130.4mph. Out of 55 Senior riders that were checked, the slowest was Bergamonti, Hannah Paton, at 115.4mph. Only the first four Senior riders bettered the speed of the Maidstone 'Marvel' who took the 125cc lightweight Yamaha weaving and shaking down the big dipper at an incredible 131.4mph, 3mph faster than 'Speedy' Read. No wonder the fearless Ivy lapped the TT course at just over 100mph. Early that week in the 250cc event, 'Little' Bill went through the Motorcycle speed trap at the Highlander on the works Yamaha at 147.5mph, only 10mph down on the 500cc MV clocking 157.9mph, the highest recorded at that time, but 17mph quicker than Derek Woodman on his Seeley.

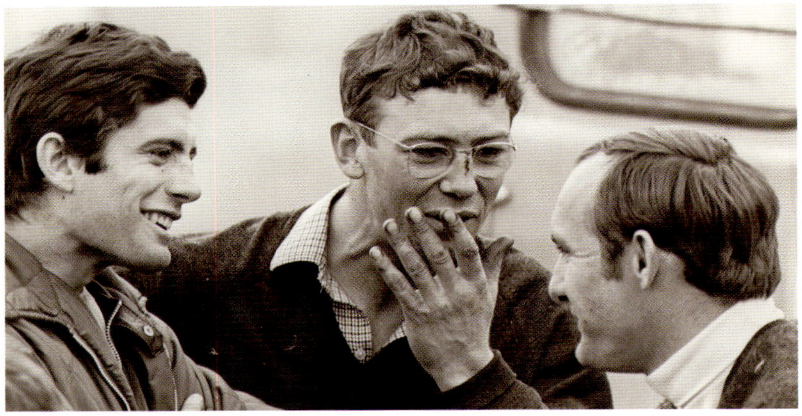

Ago, Cooper and Hailwood talking tactics at the Mallory Post TT event.

Back to the end of the 1968 Senior TT event - we were disappointed not to have achieved the manufacturers award but it was no fault of our riders who had all ridden magnificently. I was upset for 'Mooneyes' who had ridden so well only to lose his second place with engine trouble. Derek Woodman, the experienced Grand Prix competitor, had kept his cool and despite the dramas had brought his Seeley to the finish, an outstanding effort. The surprise of course had been Brian Ball, winner of the lightweight Manx Grand Prix in 1967 but a newcomer to the higher profile TT races. Brian one of our first customers for a brand new Seeley MK2 G50, rode with such determination in spite of problems, and was rewarded with a brilliant second place to World Champion Agostini, receiving £100 and the Ray B Westover Trophy for the best-newcomer. You cannot do better than that. Brian's success was the best ever for the Seeley product at the TT and his finish position matched my second place in the 1964 sidecar TT, although on a BMW! Altogether five starts with Seeley machines at the TT had resulted in four finishing places, one second, a fifth, eighth and a ninth. 'Not three bad', as my Swiss friend Ernst Weiss would have said.

As mentioned, Mike Hailwood was at the Isle of Man TT reluctantly as just a spectator, however enjoying the atmosphere, without the commitment of racing. The withdrawal of the official Honda Team left Hailwood with little option for that year's Grand Prix events. At the time there was much talk of Mike retiring from bike in preference to a car racing career, but he was insistent that was not the case. He had raced cars at various times, competing in Formula 1 some years back for the Tim Parnell team. Currently he was co-driving a GT40 Ford with Eddie Nelson in long distance sports car events. However, he definitely did not fancy Formula 1 car racing, 'It's far too hairy, far too easy to get yourself hurt.' It is clear that much of the fun had disappeared from his racing. Everyone from the factory bosses down to the youngest spectators always expected Mike to win. This was highlighted at the 1967 TT, when Honda demanded that Hailwood rode three classes 250, 350 and 500. He was out practising in nearly every session, tumbling out of bed at 4.30am and hardly ever getting a decent night's sleep. Although it was reported that Count Agusta might offer Mike an MV for 1969, in reality Hailwood's motorcycle Grand Prix career was over.

Meantime, in 1968 he would continue to have fun on his private Hondas, proving the point at the Mallory Park International Post TT event. In front of a huge shirt-sleeved crowd of 30,000 or more, Mike the Bike on his favourite 297cc Honda six, was at his brilliant best, winning both the 350cc event and the 250-1000cc race. TT double winner Giacomo Agostini MV only figured in the 500cc race after Hailwood had elected not to ride the Reynolds framed 500cc Honda four, but Agostini did not have an easy time. Alan Barnett, Kirby-Metisse, fresh from his efforts at the TT and riding like a man possessed, hounded Ago throughout the 20 lap race. Barnett himself was being targeted by 'Mooneyes' Cooper on the Seeley, with a fresh engine fitted after the TT failure. But it would be Barnett's day, setting the fastest lap ever for a single cylinder around the Leicestershire track, and in the last lap he held off 'Cooperman' by the narrowest of margins, 0.2 seconds by a heart-leaping dive around Devils Elbow taking

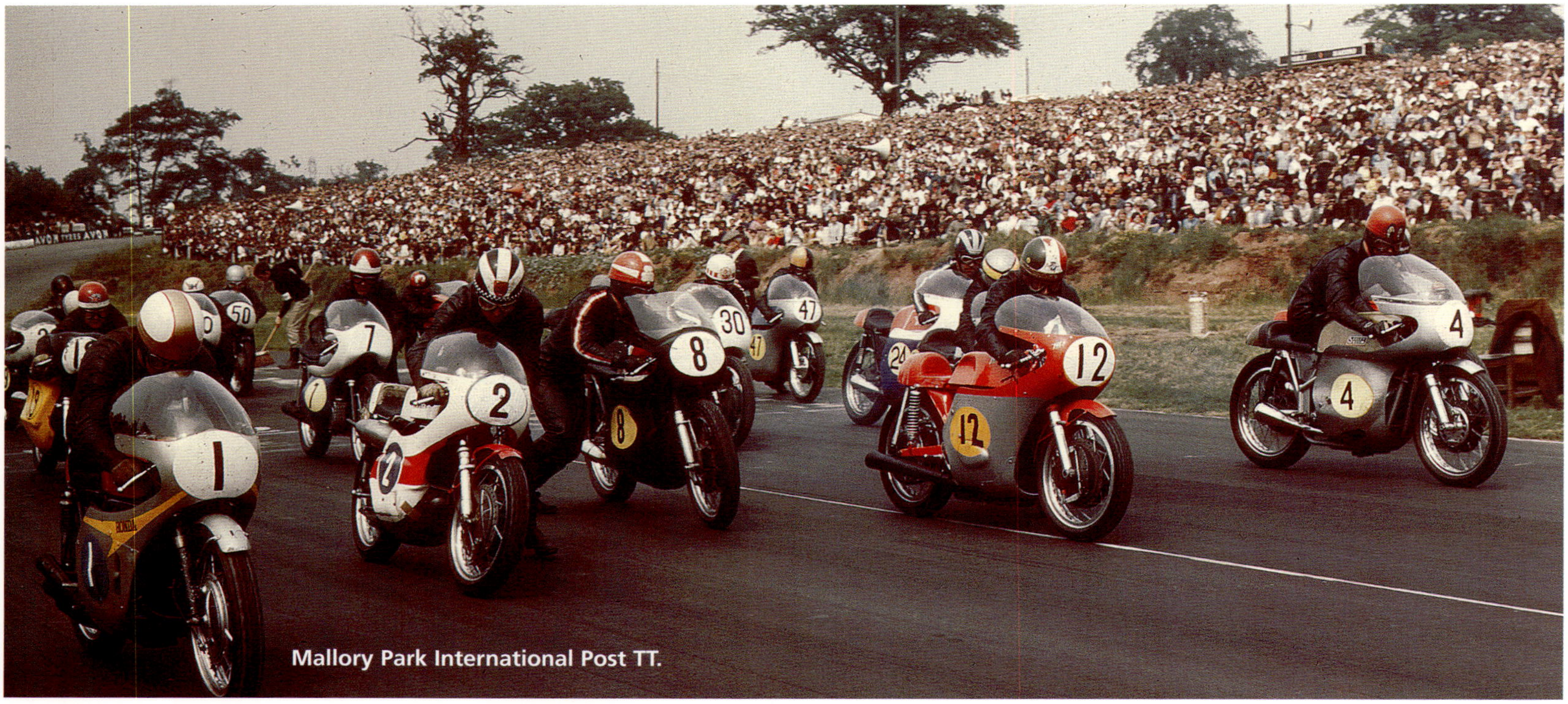

Mallory Park International Post TT.

Barnett outside of Cooper and across the line by a whisker, less than 3 seconds behind the World Champion, a brilliant effort by both Barnett and Cooper. Ago passed under the chequered flag and apart from receiving the winner's laurels and a cheque, he was presented with a 26th birthday cake and a bottle of Champagne, which as a true sportsman, he shared with the two British aces, who had provided such a sensational dice for that second spot. Pat Mahoney, Matchless, recovered from his TT crashes, came fourth, Rod Gould, Norton, fifth with Ron Chandler, Seeley, sixth.

The enthusiastic fans were treated that day to a feast of sound. There were so many different cylinder configurations, and Ralph Bryans added to the tune with the 5 cylinder 125 Honda, winning the lightweight event from Stuart Graham, Suzuki, and that man who kept popping up in the results, Kel Carruthers, Honda, third.

The 250cc race found the Yamaha works duo of Read and Ivy again in a head to head, but the two did not have it all their own way. Rod Gould on a Bultaco framed Yamaha twin, split the two champions for a lap or two. Bill Ivy held the lead until Read on the last lap squeezed by, but the Maidstone 'Marvel' fought back and claimed the flag by a hair's breadth with Rod Gould third. Such was the pace all three jointly shared the fastest lap.

Veteran sidecar ace our friend Pip Harris partnered by John Thornton, BMW, dominated the 500cc sidecar event. It had been a star-studded day, but also a day of problems for the organisers, Motor Circuit Developments, who owned most of the major circuits. A riders' strike, the first I could remember, was in the offing, over start money. 13 of the 24 qualifying riders refused to come to the starting line for the main 1000cc race. They objected to the amount of money being paid to Hailwood, Agostini, Read, Ivy, Bryans and Graham to appear while they, the regular British circuit competitors, received nothing under a new system brought in that season; no start fund as prize money was to be increased. The trouble was, the stars on works machinery were taking both the start and prize cash.

For general manager, Chris Lowe it was an embarrassing moment. The slow handclap from the huge crowd forced him to capitulate and discuss the riders grievances. They agreed that for the remaining international events start money would be paid to the regular stars, but for national events there would be no start 'gold', only an increase of the prize fund.

It was certainly a different sort of excitement and set tongues wagging. In addition, the threat of an immediate cut in national fixtures by Motor Circuit Developments due, they said, to poor crowds, was after an investigation lifted at least for 1968. Circuit entrance fees in those days for the major events at Brands was 10 shillings (50 pence in new money) and for the RAC British F1 Grand Prix, 20 shillings (£1) and 20 shillings for a covered stand seat. I believe that they were right as we had far too many meetings. For those competing in major national and international British events, the North West 200, the Isle of Man TT and selected European Grand Prix meetings it was very costly in time and money, and a logistical nightmare. How different things are now. Competitors in those days were, in my opinion, real pioneers.

Within days, many riders were attending the 23rd June Snetterton International event, with classes covering 125, 250, 350 and sidecar. The main race was for machines up to 1000cc, not your few laps, but a 50 lap special, 135.5 miles in all with a compulsory pit stop to take on a gallon of fuel. A good number of big twins entered; Ray Pickrell 745cc Dunstall Domiracer, Rex Butcher 650 Domiracer, Rod Gould 745cc Dunstall-Metisse and Percy Tait on the works Triumph to name a few. John Cooper and Brian Ball with their 500cc Seeleys might find it difficult on such a fast circuit. Unfortunately Brian failed to get his Seeley started. 'Mooneyes' however, was away from the start and into the lead but Pickrell soon caught and passed him, the Seeley no match for the speed of the big Norton twin. Cooperman held his pace, keen to make up for the TT. He kept the revs down and romped home to win this experimental race and £200 first prize - double what he would have won for the second place at the TT and only about half the distance. Pickrell's Domiracer fell by the wayside with magneto trouble, and sheep farmer Percy Tait brought the works Triumph into second place and collected £150. Where does he keep coming come from? It was that bloody Australian again Kel Carruthers, 500 Norton, claiming third place and £100 - good earnings for the first three!

Back at base things were moving at a pace. The service team had returned from the Magic Isle and the analysis of our efforts took place. Had we covered our expenses? What stock had been sold? What needed to be replaced?

Terry Vinicombe, returning victorious from the 750cc sidecar TT, would be picking up the welding torch to support me in the frame shop. My motorcycle retail shops had long gone, it was all manufacturing, and fresh machinery seemed to move into the Old Forge works each week. Every piece of space was taken up with centre lathes, radial drills, milling machines, a capstan lathe and a grinding machine. Of course extra staff was needed to work all this equipment. The cutting coolent dispersed a fine mist as the lathes churned out parts, the spirals of magnesium collecting up suddenly burst into flames. The continued whirl of machinery and the waft of paraffin stoves all added to the special machine shop atmosphere. Our successes on track were thanks to John Cooper, Ron Chandler and Dave Croxford, not forgetting new recruits Brian Ball and Derek Woodman. Things were just humming and I could hardly believe our good fortune.

After Snetterton, many competitors dashed off to the following weekend's Dutch TT, the fourth round of the World Championship. This popular event attracted a Seeley contingent of John Cooper, Ron Chandler, Rex Butcher and Derek Woodman, but the results were mixed for the quartet. 120,000 sun drenched fans enjoyed a great start to the day when local Dutch lad, Paul Lodewijkx surprisingly grabbed victory in the 50cc race from double World Champion in that class, the all-conquering Hans Georg Anscheidt.

The Maidstone 'Marvel' Ivy continued his winning ways in a high speed demonstration on his works 250cc Yamaha. 'Little' Bill lapped all but five riders in the 17 lap 81.3 mile race, beating 'Speedy' Read across the line by half a wheel and recording the fastest lap. Unfortunately, the situation was reversed in the lightweight 125cc event, at the start Kent Andersson's MZ reared up on the back wheel and landed on 'Little' Bill's foot, trapping it on the footrest. Although our brave soldier carried on for a couple of laps and caught 'Speedy' Read, Ivy was forced to retire. He collapsed in the pit lane and was taken to hospital with a suspected dislocated ankle. With only six points from four Grands Prix, Bill Ivy's 125cc world championship aspirations were going out the window.

As expected, Giacomo Agostini, MV, cleaned up in both the 350 and 500cc events, but good sportsman and showman that Agostini was, in the 20 lap 500 race he joined in with some Mallory Park style racing in the opening laps with Cooper, Findlay, Williams

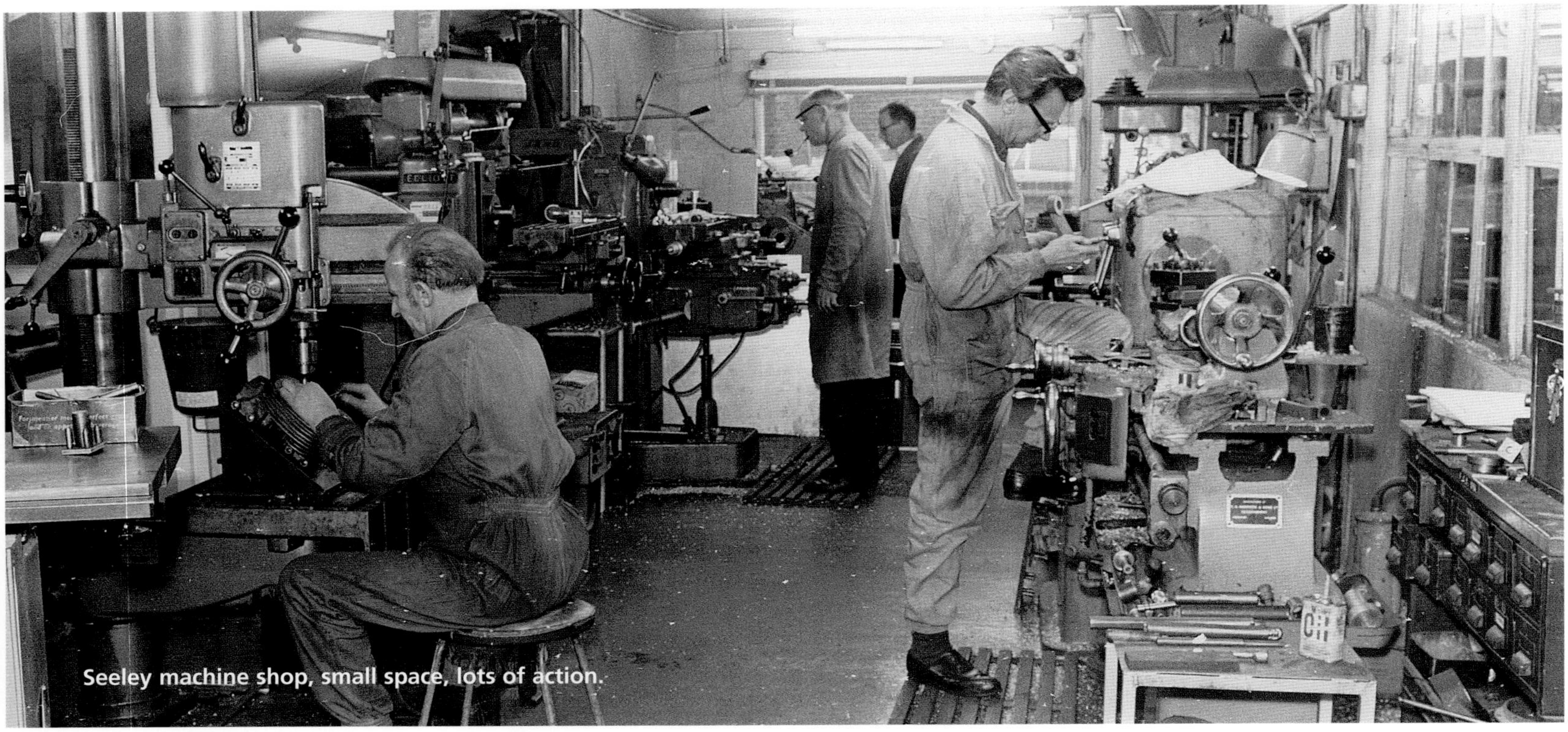

Seeley machine shop, small space, lots of action.

and Billie Nelson in varying order snapping at his heels. To a gasp from the crowd, Jack Findlay, McIntyre-Matchless, took the lead for a lap then the Italian champion decided the game was over and settled down to a runaway victory, but good fun while it lasted. The battle for second place raged on with Billie Nelson on the twin cylinder Paton faster down the straights than the singles. Unknown to Nelson, the Paton was steadily shedding its oil through a breather, the engine finally seizing, but not before smothering the following group in oil. Derek Woodman and Rex Butcher, although up with the leaders, went out with engine problems on their Seeley G50 machines. Fortunately 'Mooneyes' was still up at the front on his Seeley with Ron Chandler not far behind. Finally, Jack Findlay took a well deserved second place in a very close finish, with 'Cooperman' only one second behind. It was all very close. Peter Williams, Arter Matchless, was a second down on Cooper. Aussie Carruthers came in fifth, followed by Chandler, Uphill, Gould with John Hartle, back on a Matchless-Metisse after a poor start and regaining his confidence following his disastrous Isle of Man TT, a lap down in ninth place.

The Dutch TT was the third round of the World Sidecar Championship but with two rounds already gone, the current champion Klaus Enders was not having a good time, nil points so far. Winner of the Dutch TT the previous year, Enders must have wanted to win this one to have any chance of repeating his world championship success in 1967. Siegfried Schauzu was leading, at that stage one point ahead of Helmut Fath and his URS, with Attenberger on his BMW in third. Well, from the start of the 14 lap event Klaus Enders, BMW, was soon in front, perhaps believing his luck had changed. Not so, the relative newcomer Johann Attenberger, BMW, fought back to take the lead from the World Champion, breaking the lap record by an impressive 5 seconds, and taking the chequered flag by a split second from Enders. Schauzu could not match the pace, nearly one minute behind, but making up the rostrum positions.

After the presentations and celebrations in Assen that Saturday evening, the Grand Prix circus started moving on for the traditional following weekend's Belgian Grand Prix. A stream of vans, cars and caravans trickled towards the Spa Francorchamps circuit, an awesome fast course of 8.76mile in length, but a favourite for many. four events only would be held; 50cc, 250cc, 500cc and sidecars. We would be represented by 'Cooperman', Woodman, Chandler and Bo Granath in the 500cc race. At the end of June, Jack Findlay suggested racing the 500cc 3 cylinder 'Cardani' at the Belguim Grand Prix. It was designed by Daniele Fontana the brake specialist and built jointly with Jack Findlay. It had been tried at the Spanish Grand Prix back in May but had suffered a vibration problem. Preak power was estimated at 13,000rpm with an output of 71bhp, great on paper! 100,000 fans in ideal conditions would witness some Spa high speed action. Firstly champion Hans-Georg Anscheidt on his ex-works Suzuki, made no mistakes that weekend, winning the 'tiddler' 50cc race at an incredible average speed of 93.49mph turning the tables on the Dutchman Lodewijkx, Jamathi, the previous week's winner.

Bill Ivy, the favourite for the 250cc race, led the championship from Phil Read by 24 points to 14. From the start of the 9 lap 78.8 mile race both 250cc four cylinder works Yamahas failed to function properly. Phil Read needed a plug change on the first lap, leaving 'Little' Bill to pile on the pressure, coming within a whisker of the lap record and setting a fastest lap of 125.35mph before retiring with ignition trouble a couple of laps later. Read dropped back to 17th, and although the Yamaha was still off song, it was still quicker than most, catching the MZ of Heinz Rosner at the beginning of the last lap and going ahead to win by 7 seconds, a brilliant effort by 'Speedy' Read – motto – 'never give up'.

For the 500 solo event, in practice Giacomo Agostini took the 3 cylinder works MV round at a fraction under 130mph average, unofficially breaking his own lap record. Surely this would be another Italian benefit day, as there was just nothing that weekend to match the speed of Ago and the MV. In the 15 lap 131.4 mile race, Agostini lapped everyone except second place man Jack Findlay, on the McIntyre-Matchless (rather than the Italian Cardani as planned), nearly 4 minutes behind lapping at 118mph. There was a lot of concern about running out of fuel in such a long race, often at full bore. An application for reducing the distance was turned down, but a pit stop for some was allowed, which was unusual for such a race. Derek Woodman going so well on the Seeley, when in third place called into the pits for a splash and dash. On restarting he managed to hold the third spot as the following group appeared; Rob Fitton, Cooper, Gould, Williams, Dodd and Carruthers. Finally, the Blackpool ace came over the finish line to give the Seeley Racing Company its second Grand Prix rostrum of the week. Cooperman, Seeley, was sixth, Chandler ninth and Sweden's Bo Granath, Seeley, fourteenth. For us it was a great result. Agostini averaged 124.85mph for the race and broke his own lap record with a lap of 128.58mph - pretty quick for those days.

The last event of the day was the fateful sidecar race. From the start of the 8 lap 70.1 mile sidecar race, Helmut Fath on the 4 cylinder URS, took a commanding lead and was within a whisker of the lap record when the URS started to misfire and he was forced

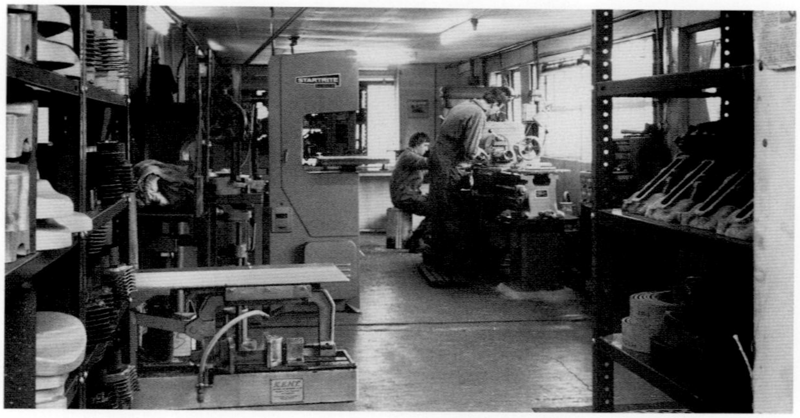

Seeley machine shop from the other end.

to retire. Klaus Enders and Siegfried Schauzu were both out, having blown their BMW engines, leaving championship leader Johann Attenburger jousting with Georg Auerbacher throughout the race. On the very last lap, coming out of the very fast right hand curve downhill section into the flat out Masta Straight, it is suggested Attenberger's BMW clipped the kerb and he lost control. Johann Attenburger and passenger Joseph Schillinger shot off the road, flying through the air over spectators before crashing into a garden bordering the circuit. Both men were killed instantly. This was a horrific accident, a great shock and perhaps one of the worst incidents for the close knit sidecar competitors. Georg Auerbacher, who I knew well, won the event. It must have been a hollow victory for him, and a very sad day for our sport.

Back home 7th July 1968, the same day as the tragedy in Belgium, it was the other end of the spectrum - 'joy and ecstasy' for Kent boy Vic Eastwood who won the 500cc British Moto-Cross Grand Prix at Farleigh Castle in Wiltshire. For Eastwood it was a 10 year old dream come true, a lifetime ambition. Riding in atrocious conditions, pouring rain and ankle deep mud, watched by 17,000 rain soaked fans, Vic won the first leg. In the second, riding with a rear flat tyre for much of the race he came through in true British style to win his first ever world championship event on the works Husqvarna. That same weekend in Ireland, Irish rising star Brain Steenson continued his progress, winning the 500cc race on his 350cc Aermacchi at the Skerries '100'. We would get to know Steenson in 1969. The following weekend I travelled to Switzerland in our Thames van with my wife Joan and son Colin, then 5 years old. It was a visit to our friend Ernst Weiss, in Zug near Zurich. Ernst would be coming with us to Italy to help us to purchase a Bersani Colombo hydraulic pipe bending machine. We desperately needed it. At £470 plus £365 for tooling, it was a lot of money, but one of the best investments we would make. Ernst, a regular hill climb competitor, would first be attending a meeting at Genorrosa in Switzerland, an event that Mike Hailwood thought would be fun, competing on the 297cc Honda six.

With road circuit racing banned in Switzerland, hill climbing on tarmac roads was the next best thing, but no easy path as Mike the Bike found out. The day itself was brilliantly hot and my son Colin, in his imagination was revving his little scooter until red in the face as he watched the competitors ascend the hill. In practice, Hailwood knocked 13 seconds off the record for the 6.25 mile climb with its 80 bends. Through a couple of small villages, it was the hairiest, most difficult and dangerous event that he had attended. Ernst Weiss, a regular hill climber and good friend of Mike, won the 500cc class on his Seeley, clinching the Swiss hill climb title. Mike Hailwood, on his first official run, arrived at a spot halfway up the course to find that a ramp which previously was laid over some railway lines had been removed, and nobody had thought to inform the starter or riders. As the screaming Honda six hit the railway lines, Hailwood was thrown over the top of the screen. He hit the road, splitting his crash hat in two, and broke his collarbone in the process. As he lay dazed, three other riders crashed at the same spot. About 40 competitors crashed in all. Next day the tenacious Hailwood said, 'It was fantastic, there were bikes everywhere, hanging out of trees, through hedges, I have never seen anything like it, it was enjoyable – but never again!' Fortunately, apart from the shake up and 'busted' collar bone Mike was okay. Joan, myself and Colin had a great time, in the company of friends including Ernst and Mike, who were great fun together.

Next day we were off to Italy with our interpreter Ernst Weiss to sort out our order for the tube bender. The trip was a success, the machine ideal as was the manufacturer, and the UK importers Funditor Ltd acted very professionally throughout the transaction, and the eight week delivery time was certainly worth the wait.

Sachsenring, East Germany. 14th July, was the next Grand Prix, the sixth event of the season. I had never visited this very popular meeting as no sidecar event for the championship was held there. With so many restrictions in East Germany at the time, the Grand Prix was a must for much of the population. 200,000 spectators flocked to view the action. People were everywhere, sitting up specially constructed poles with seats, hanging on the fences – 18,000 people in one grandstand alone, and every conceivable space taken around the 5.25 mile closed road circuit by the enthusiastic fans. Just four events would be held; 125, 250, 350 and 500cc. We would be represented in the 500cc event by John Cooper, Ron Chandler and Derek Woodman on their Seeleys.

With temperatures in the nineties, the 125cc race brought immediate drama. Bill Ivy on the works Yamaha pulled into the pits after the first lap. The Yamaha mechanics couldn't decide which spark plug to change. Finally 'Little Bill' was away last in the field, whilst 'Speedy Read' was well ahead of everybody. The Maidstone Marvel, never a man to give up, sped through the opposition breaking his own lap record and was the first rider to lap Sachsenring at over 100mph on a 125cc machine. Phil Read, the championship leader in that class took the win, with Bill Ivy a well deserved second.

The 250cc race was another close run affair between the two Yamaha teamsters, but team orders dictated Ivy should win, and after 80 miles of high speed racing, lapping at 103mph, the pair came over the line together, 'Little Bill' getting the verdict by half a wheel. Heinz Rosner gave the locals some cheer bringing his MZ home in third.

Giacomo Agostini on the 350cc 3 cylinder MV totally dominated his race, Heinz Rosner, MZ, second to more cheers, Kel Carruthers, Aermacchi, third, Ginger Molloy, Bultaco, and Derek Woodman, Aermacchi, fourth and fifth. Ron Chandler had an oil pipe break on the Seeley 7R and was pitched off the bike. Bruised and shaken, his day was over.

Finally, the big one, 107 miles of racing. The extreme heat did not stop the 1967 500cc World Champion, Agostini on the works MV disappearing into the distance setting a new lap record of 109.79mph. The usual gaggle of competitors followed, scrapping for the lower positions. Unfortunately, our Blackpool ace Woodman could not get his Seeley G50 started. He pushed it the length of the pits before it fired up, leaving him at the back of the field and well down. After 6 laps Derek gave up, a great pity. Alberto Pagani, Linto, held second place from Jack Findlay, Arter-Matchless. John 'Mooneyes' Cooper on the Seeley held off the challenge from Billie Nelson, Hannah-Paton, and took a fine fourth place. Londoner and British privateer Godfrey Nash, on a Dudley-Ward Norton, rode brilliantly to pick up his first ever championship point for sixth place, ahead of Peter Williams, Keith Turner, John Hartle and Dan Shorey. The rest of the field trickled home with Bo Granath, Seeley, 2 laps down in fourteenth place, although not last. Giacomo Agostini, who had averaged 105.73mph for the race, was already celebrating his third 500cc World Championship. With only four more events to come he was unbeatable.

It had been a sizzling Sachsenring. The huge crowd dispersed and the circus was packing up to move on to Czechoslovakia for the following week's Grand Prix. The Brno Classic was no picnic, with mixed weather on a skidpan circuit in dire need of resurfacing. Agostini was very critical, describing the circuit as very dangerous, even worse than when he rode in a cloud burst at the Imatra Finnish Grand Prix.

The 125cc race started the proceedings and once more all eyes were on Yamaha aces, Read and Ivy, who it is alleged were still riding to team orders. In the 69 mile race, Bill Ivy, tailing Phil Read, came a cropper on a second gear left-hander when skidding on a wet patch. 'Little' Bill and the Yamaha crashed through a gate and disappeared into a clump of trees. Ivy received treatment and injections for pain in hospital. Then this intrepid man, with a chance of clinching his first World 250cc championship, arrived back at the circuit, black and blue but determined to compete in the 250cc race. Phil Read won the 125cc Czech Grand Prix that day, making sure of his first ever 125cc World Championship title, three titles in all at that point.

It seemed that the 'Prince of Speed' would not play the game in the 250cc race. From the start Read rocketed into the lead. 'Pocket rocket' Ivy took a lap to pass Rosner, MZ. Still in pain from the earlier crash and with an almost useless front brake, Bill pressed on, but even though Read eased his pace, that's how it finished, a double win for Read and a championship to celebrate. As one can imagine, Bill Ivy was less than impressed and lost his temper with the 'Prince of Speed'. During the heated argument, Read was heard to say, 'I am tired of hanging back for Ivy to win!' The flabbergasted Ivy, hardly able to walk, was carried to the rostrum then back to the paddock. Yamaha had won both the 125 and 250 manufacturers championship titles, so there would be no team orders. Now it was be open warfare. They each needed two more wins to secure the 250cc riders world championship.

The rest of the day's racing seemed bland in comparison. Agostini wrapped up the 350cc World Title, completely dominating the 350cc race and becoming the first Italian to win both titles in the same year.

The 500cc race, held over the 112.5 miles of this dodgy circuit found our man 'Mooneyes' making a fantastic start on the Seeley. He came round on the first lap in second place to Ago then dropped a position to Pagani on the Linto. Faster but not so reliable, it soon pulled out with a dropped valve. 'Cooperman' was back in business. Perhaps he could bring the Seeley G50 into a further rostrum position. Unfortunately, as the rain came down, he lost control and crashed into a lamp post, miraculously suffering only minor cuts and bruising. The sump plate was knocked off the bottom of the engine and the bodywork scratched, certainly a lucky escape all round. Jack Findlay finished second, and Gyula Marsovszky on his Matchless third – another eventful meeting over.

Back home on Saturday that same weekend, the 'Ruislip Rebel' Croxford kept to his winning ways at Castle Combe. His Seeley G50 was across the finish line only inches ahead of a persistent Barry Randle, Norton, in the 500cc final with Tom Dickie, Norton, third. With the fastest lap, Croxford equalled the lap record.

On Sunday in a Clubmans' event at Snetterton, two young men would go mostly unnoticed. A certain George O'Dell, having won the first sidecar race that day on the 650cc Triumph outfit, finished race two in second place having suffered a misfire. George O'Dell many years later, in 1977, brought the world sidecar championship title back to Britain, the first time since Eric Oliver in 1953. Surprisingly, O'Dell did not win a single Grand Prix in his whole career but his consistency paid off. The other unknown was a young Cockney, Barry Sheene on his very first visit to the Snetterton track, and racing his father's special Bultaco. A reasonable impression was made that day in the 125, 250 and 350cc events. Five starts achieved a second, third, two fourths and a fifth position, making his dad, Frank very proud, a good day.

Back in Brno, Agostini was enjoying the title of double World Champion. What a contrast between the two riders at that point few realising that six years later Sheene on a 500cc Suzuki, would be competing against Agostini in the Grands Prix, grabbing the 500cc world title in 1976 and 1977... Almost a rag to riches story.

It was all happening that weekend. In France a determined and unflustered 24 year old BSA works rider John Banks finished second in the first leg of the French Moto-Cross Grand Prix to winner Roger Decoster, CZ. Then, in the next 50 minute race, a magnificent Banks reversed the result, leaving Decoster back in third with Bengt Aberg on the works Husqvarna in second. This brought John Banks his first ever Grand Prix win and moved him up into third position in the world championship.

Earlier that year the ACU had decided to allow sponsorship and advertising. The John Player Cigarette Company jumped in with £4,000, lots of fags and some gorgeous girls, all helping to brighten the British road racing and moto-cross scene.

Back home from Italy, I was invited to judge along with Vic Camp and Tom Kirby at Brands Hatch for the 'Stars of Tomorrow' meeting on the 29th July 1968. Our association with Mike Collins began here. Riding his own machines, a 350cc AJS and 500cc Matchless, he achieved second and third places in a great day's racing. Collins, 24 year old boilermaker, was a local boy from Crayford now in his third season of racing. He was chosen by the panel as the 'Star of Tomorrow' and was awarded the Ecurie Sportive Trophy. I instantly took to this bespectacled young man, slight of build with a good disposition, another version of John Cooper. I decided I would like to support his racing career, and would never be disappointed by this decision.

John Cooper, after his 'big off' at the Czech, gave the Finnish Grand Prix a miss. He came home for us to give the Seeley G50 a check over, as hitting lamp posts was not what our bikes had been designed for. Within days 'Mooneyes', unfazed by his dramas, was back at Snetterton showing he was still a man to beat, winning the 250cc race on a Padgett Yamaha. Then on our works lightweight 350 Seeley, he put in a tremendous performance, winning the 350cc event by 100 yards from Ian Richards, Yamaha, Tony Rutter, Norton, Barry Randle, Norton, Ray Pickrell, Aermacchi-Metisse, and Dan Shorey, Norton, finishing in that order, an important result for Colin Seeley Racing Developments.

Then in the 10 lap 1000cc race he scored another brilliant win on the 500 Seeley. It was not easy, Alan Barnett riding the 654cc Kirby BSA-Metisse was right up with John. With only one lap to go, Barnett crashed at The Esses leaving Cooper unchallenged. Paul Smart on a 647cc Curtis-Norton came in second, followed by Derek Chatterton, Tom Dickie then Brian Ball on his Seeley G50 fifth. As John crossed the finish line the Seeley G50 spluttered to a halt with a failed Lucas magneto. Unable to effect a repair in time, Cooper was robbed of the chance to win all four major solo events. The 500cc race was won by Percy Tait, Triumph. Dick Hawes on the Seeley G50 outfit came third in the 500cc sidecar race, making it a very successful day for our marque.

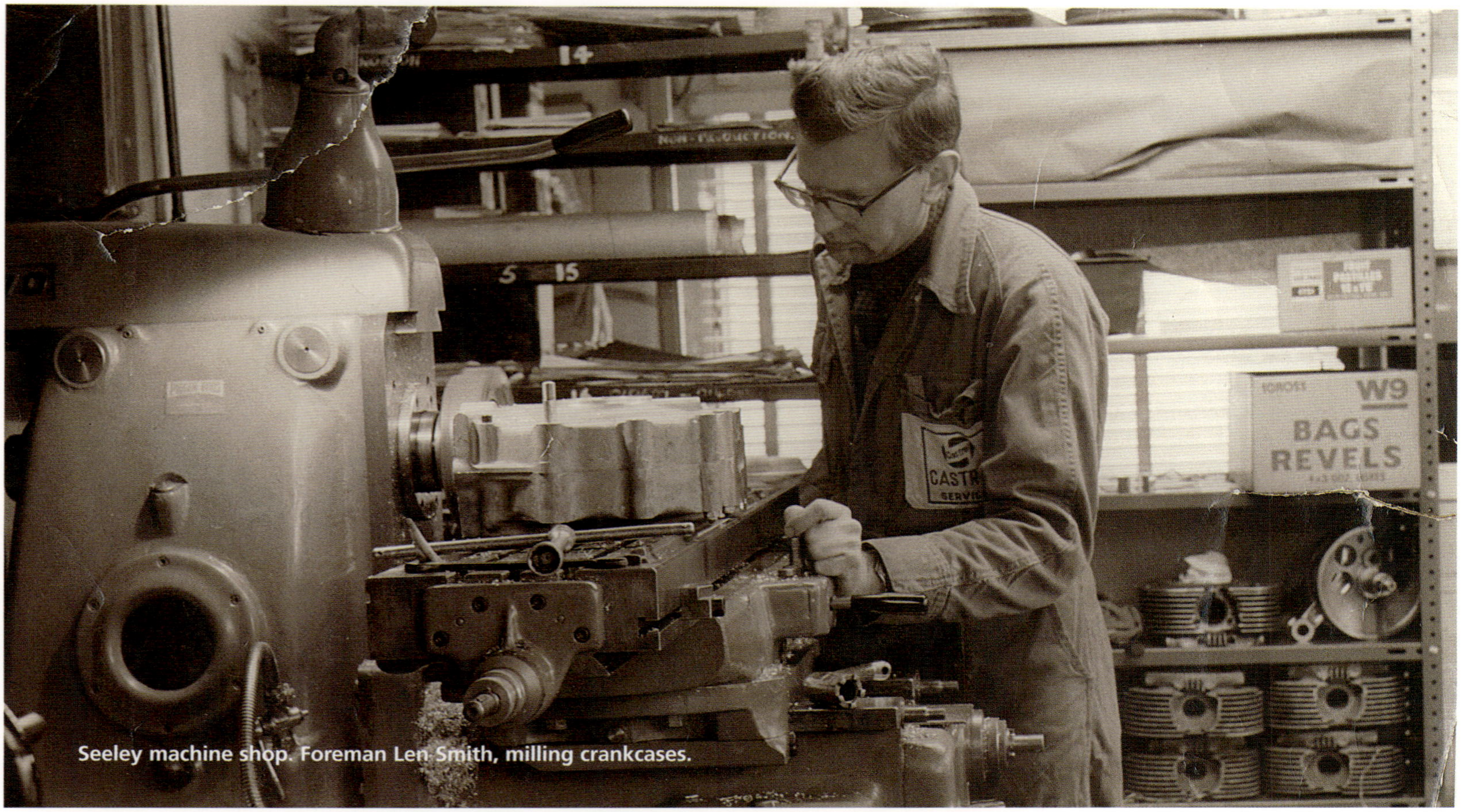
Seeley machine shop. Foreman Len Smith, milling crankcases.

Over at the Finnish Grand Prix at the tree-lined 3.74 mile Imatra circuit alongside the Russian border the power struggle between Read and Ivy continued. David Dixon described the 125cc race as a tense struggle between the Yamaha pairing. With team orders thrown out of the window, not an inch would be given or expected. After Read gained a flying start for the 20 lap race, it took Ivy 7 laps to get onto his tail but at the expense of his front brake. Adjustments were needed and the pit stop left 'Speedy' Read unchallenged, winning his sixth 125cc Grand Prix that season.

The 250cc race was important for the Maidstone 'Marvel'. With four wins, one second place and 38 points against Read's three wins, two seconds and 36 points, and with only three races to come, it was very close. Unfortunately fate worked against 'Little' Bill. On a wet track Phil Read shadowed Ivy in the early part of the 23 lap 250cc race then nipped ahead. Trying to keep up the pace, Ivy squirted the works Yamaha too hard and spun off, resulting in further injury to his leg hurt in the Brno crash. This was a frustrating set back to Ivy's 250cc championship aspirations. Read won the Finnish race well ahead of Heinz Rosner, MZ, in second. There was no 350cc race at the Finnish meeting, so the 23 lap 500cc race came next. Some 21 bikes lined up, including the first appearance in a classic of two six speed 492cc 4 cylinder Russian Vostok machines, ridden by Nikolia Sevestianov and team mate Endel Kiisa. They proved to be a sensation in the race.

World Champion Giacomo Agostini, MV, really without any serious challenger once again put on a sporting show in the earlier laps, encouraging the Russian Endel Kiisa on the Vostok to stay in his shadow. Then 'cheeky boy' the unknown Russian passed Agostini, but not for long as the well stretched Vostok blew up, leaving team mate Sevastianov battling for fifth place with John Dodds and Derek Woodman on his Seeley G50. Up front, Grand Prix regular Jack Findlay riding in his usual unyielding manner, was keeping Ago in sight, even making a pass before Agostini pushed the button and disappeared into the distance. Findlay swapped second place with Billie Nelson on the Hannah-Paton, then Nelson dropped back with a loose fairing. Derek Woodman pushed by neatly catching Findlay on the McIntyre-Matchless. Woodman slipped past Findlay into second place, but Jack promptly struck back. They were side by side on the last lap, only a mile from the flag, when Agostini, lapping both riders, cocked up Woodman's plan of swooping round the outside of Findlay on the last corner. So Agostini added to his tally of 500cc Grand Prix successes that season, eight in all, with race and lap records for the Finnish Grand Prix. Jack Findlay got second place, just a split second ahead of Derek Woodman, who had ridden brilliantly bringing his Seeley G50 into a further rostrum position for our company. Fantastic! Russian Nikolai Sevestianov, in a fine effort, brought the Vostok four home in fourth place ahead of Dodds, then Marsovszky, Nelson and Carruthers.

Finally, to round up an eventful day, Helmut Fath with his home built URS 4 cylinder sidecar outfit was back on track, winning the sidecar race having led from start to finish setting, race and lap records and putting himself into the lead of the world championship.

Mike Hailwood, having recovered pretty well from his collarbone injury suffered at the Swiss hill climb, confirmed he would race at the Hutchinson 100 on the 11th August. He hoped to have his 297cc six cylinder Honda, after a rebuild at the factory, to use for the 350cc race and unlimited events, but thought there would be a separate 500cc race. Hailwood was still very concerned about the handling of his Reynolds-framed 500 Honda four and arranged with mechanic Nobby Clark to bring the unofficial works Honda special to our works in Belvedere for our opinion, hoping we might be able to help with some improvements. On inspection, I felt that Ken Sprayson hadn't had time to build a frame capable of dealing with the 90 horsepower Honda race engine. The quality of the Reynolds frame was not of course in question. However, I felt that the swinging arm and frame pick up point were not stiff enough, so if exaggerated, when the power was applied, the rear chain connected to the unit construction engine unit just pulled the rear wheel out of line, causing this awesome bike to be almost unrideable. I am sure given adequate time, ideally not in the race season, a suitable frame unit could have been built, either by ourselves or Ken Sprayson. We had already managed to build the Fath-four with no undue handling problems. But we were never given the opportunity, although through no fault of Mike Hailwood.

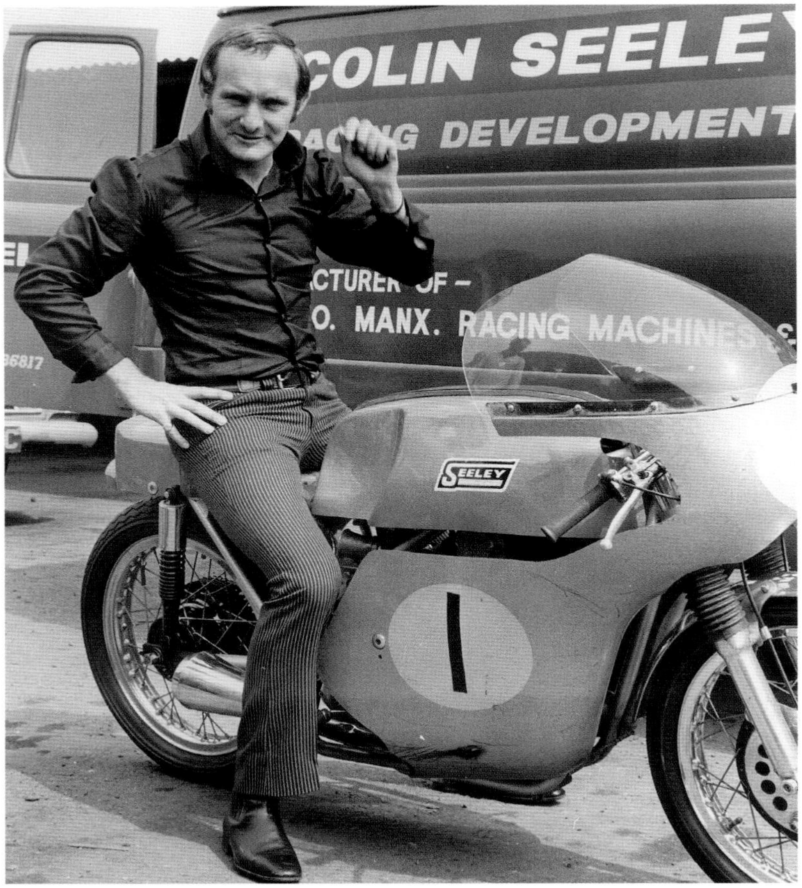

Mike at Brands Hatch, trying the Seeley before the Hutchinson 100.

Despairing of the situation and not wanting to ride the big Honda at Brands, Mike asked if we could help with a Seeley-500. We were delighted with the prospect of the multi-talented World Champion riding a Seeley. That was the good news. However, we had no spare Seeley to race. Everything was committed as we tried to keep up with customer demand. However, the day was saved when Dave Croxford offered Mike the use of his Seeley, a generous gesture by the 'Ruislip Rebel'. Having given the bike a once over back at works, we arrived for Saturday's Hutchinson 100 official practice. Hailwood had not ridden a single cylinder machine for some years, but it would make no difference. In the first practice session for big bikes, Mike was soon hammering round, leaving the rest struggling in his wake. Wally Rawlings and I were impressed with his performance, but then it dawned on Hailwood, there was no separate 500cc class that weekend. Both big races were open to bikes from 175cc-1000cc. Naturally, he chose his favourite machine, the 297cc Honda six, which he could ride in the 350cc race as well as the two main races. Speaking to 'Motorcycle' sports editor Mick Woollett, Mike was most apologetic saying he felt a right twit for putting us to so much trouble, never dreaming that there would not be a 500cc race. He said he was genuinely delighted with the way the Seeley went. 'It was grand to be back on a bike that really steers'. He was so fed up with the 500 Honda that he wanted to ride a Seeley at The Daily Express International Meeting at Oulton Park in September. Perhaps this was Mike's way of thanking us for the trouble we had gone to that weekend.

Hailwood was vocal about the 500cc class, which he said should be reinstated at the Hutch, to allow many top-class competitors with only 500cc machines to have a share in the prize money and to join in with the usual excellent racing in that class.

The 36th International Hutchinson 100 on the 11th August was sponsored by The Evening News and circuit commentaries were by Peter Arnold and Eddie Dow. Mike Hailwood did not disappoint his fans, playing a great tune on the Honda six, winning the 350cc race and both legs of unlimited events, leaving the likes of Read, Ivy, Pasolini, Gould, Cooper, Pickrell and Tait fighting for position.

We hardly seemed to have had a minute to spare. Our return to the Isle of Man with our racing service was imminent, this time for the Manx Grand Prix, due to be open for business on Saturday 24th August, once again at Frank Large's garage. Looking back, with limited

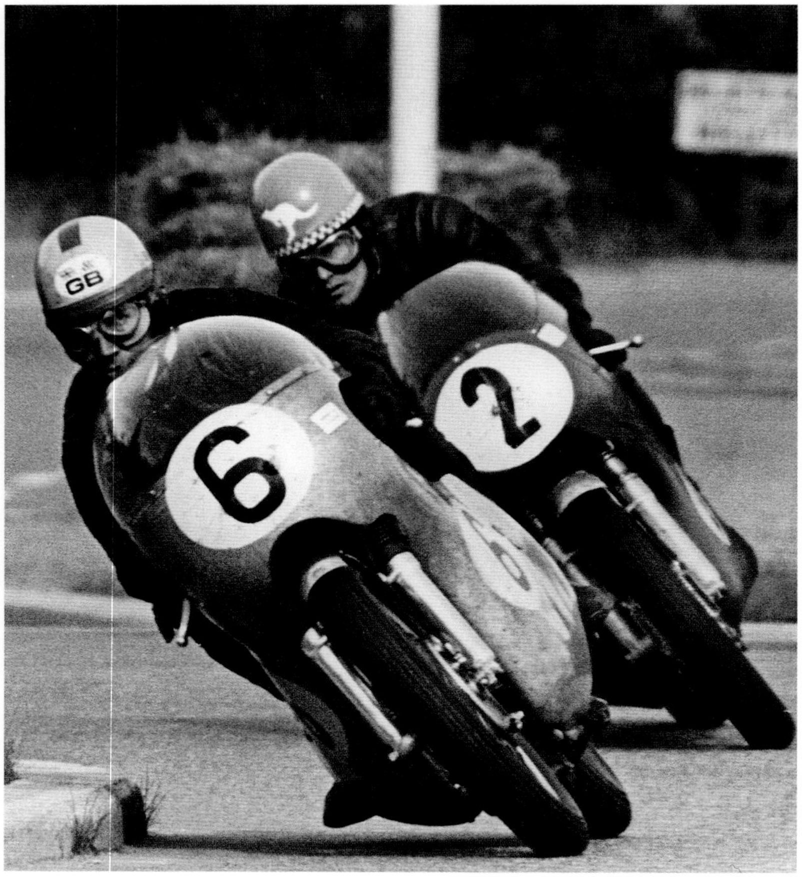

Derek Woodman, Seeley, leads Jack Findlay, McIntyre Matchless, in a fight for second place at the Finnish GP.

John Hartle receives the Fred G. Craner Trophy from Mike Hailwood. The trophy was awarded each year to the best Briton on a British bike in the world championships. Hartle won it in 1967 on a Ray Cowles Matchless finishing 3rd, as he had done in 1960 on a Norton.

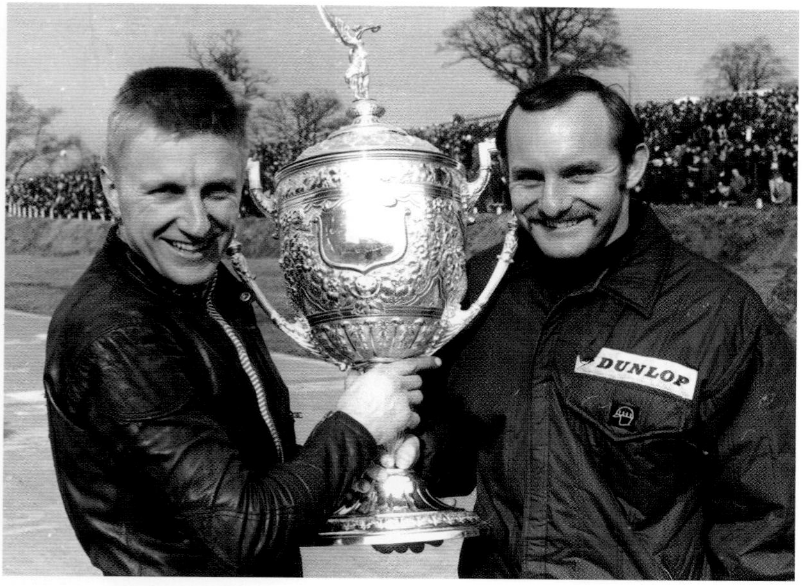

resources, financial and otherwise, I don't know how we managed such a schedule. It was so intense, all a complete blur, a massive challenge. I was absolutely flat out trying to satisfy orders. Thanks to the success of our loyal unofficial riders John Cooper, Ron Chandler and Dave Croxford, improvements and developments were ongoing, with never a dull moment!

We were concerned about TT sidecar winner Terry Vinicombe who had joined the company as a welder and frame builder. He was suffering extreme pains in his legs, making walking difficult and very painful. Terry was forced to miss some events. I knew from experience that standing all day welding was pretty awful for the legs, and did not help Terry's condition.

In the never ending round of race meetings it was another dash for competitors from Brands Hatch to Ireland's Ulster Grand Prix, 17th August at the Dundrod Circuit. It was the here that the 'Maidstone Marvel', Bill Ivy turned the tables on 'Speedy' Read by scoring a double win in the 125 and 250cc events on the works Yamaha. five wins and one second place in the 250cc championship put Ivy two points ahead of Read, with only the Italian Grand Prix to come.

In the 250cc race John Cooper on the Padgett-Yamaha was in a scrap for fifth place between Malcolm Uphill and Kent Andersson. With only one lap to go 'Mooneyes' lost control at Quarry Bends. The huge crash resulted in a visit to the Royal Victoria Hospital where John was admitted overnight needing 15 stitches in his right hand and 30 in his left arm. Giacomo Agostini continued his winning ways in the 350cc event, ahead of Aussie Carruthers with Irishman Steenson third. Agostini repeated his success in the 500cc race. With 'Mooneyes' and the Seeley out of action. Rob Fitton (BSc) the 40 year old Leeds Civil Engineer followed Ago home riding his Manx Norton. Fitton in a quiet boast said his was the fastest Norton in action, not having been passed in a straight line in five years. Rob Fitton, who started his racing at Cadwell Park in 1947, described himself as a holiday racer rather than potential star. Two years earlier he had competed on the continent, mostly at smaller road race events, with a fair amount of success. The second place in the Ulster Grand Prix was probably the best finish position in a major race for this quiet likeable Yorkshire man, 'I have always raced as a sideline to my work, motorcycling has spoiled my career and my career has interfered with my racing!' John Hartle took third place ahead of Percy Tait on the Triumph.

After the Ulster, another rush back to Mallory for the 'Mallory Park v Brands Challenge'. In those ludicrous times there were only a few days for competitors to carry out necessary race preparations. Bank Holiday weekend's International event, on the 31st August at Scarborough, then, the Snetterton International on the 1st September was followed by Oulton Park International, Cadwell Park, Thruxton and Crystal Palace nationals on the 2nd September. three internationals and three major national events over three days was somewhat crazy!

For Saturday's International Gold Trophy meeting at Scarborough, 10,000 spectators were joined by a BBC TV audience, but a cloud descended over Olivers' Mount. In the second heat of the 500cc Gold Trophy, a 6 lap dash. John Hartle, having the previous lap set the fastest time and making up for a poor start on his Matchless-Metisse, accelerated hard up Quarry Hill from the Mere Hairpin and caught John Blanchard who at that very point unexpectedly slowed. Caused by a missed gear selection, Hartle then so close to Blanchard with other riders roaring up behind had little option and only a split second to decide which side to take. With no room available, he took the left and caught his handlebar in Blanchard's fairing, causing them to crash. Blanchard was unhurt, but unfortunately the 34 year old John Hartle careered across the grass verge and went head first into the footbridge scaffolding, resulting in immediate death. This fatality was a great shock to the motorcycle racing fraternity. John, from Moulton, Northampton, first made his mark in 1955 with a second place at the Ulster Grand Prix. He achieved many successes, his best in 1958 finishing second in both 350 and 500cc world Championships on the works MV. John Blanchard, hardly the most popular rider in the paddock, was considered at fault for his part in the Hartle crash. Blanchard and I were not on the best of terms at that time. Although an intense competitor, Blanchard was not in my opinion, a rider who would cause undue danger to others, or himself come to that. I believe the critics of Blanchard regarding the unfortunate Hartle accident were unjustified. It was, in my opinion, an ill-fated accident, and would not be the last. Riders do tangle in competition, thankfully most of the time with less serious outcomes. Perhaps the organisers and the Autocycle Union who issued the track licence should have accepted some responsibility for not requesting adequate protection at certain points around the very narrow Olivers Mount Circuit.

Competitors in those days, including myself, did not have track safety high on their list; we just rushed from one meeting to another, oblivious of safety issues. Although never perfect, things have certainly improved over the years. The riding gear complete with body armour, the full face high quality helmets, protective gloves and boots are very different from the black skin tight wafer-thin leathers and gloves and the pudding basin crash hats as we used to call them. No longer does the St. Johns ambulance with a 'dinging bell' crawl to the rescue. Nowadays a 4 wheel drive Audi A4, with doctor and medical crew standing by are supported by the circuits' own medical centres. Emphasis is on safety, but the nature of our sport means accidents happen, and some sadly are fatal.

For some strange reason, John Blanchard was asked to identify the body of John Hartle. Already in shock, he left the Scarborough Circuit in a complete trance, and needed to be rescued later that day from a train station. Charlie Sanby had taken care of Blanchard's race bikes.

One gladiator lost, another combatant would be brought on. It was no different that Saturday at Olivers Mount. The 500cc Gold Trophy Race was won by Billie Nelson, Norton, in a close encounter with Croxford, Seeley, and Dan Shorey, Norton, in third. John Hartle was on everybody's mind that day, a true professional – sadly missed.

Sunday 1st September was the International Race of Aces on the 2.71 mile Snetterton circuit. Mike Hailwood, having flown back from South Africa for the weekend's racing, was in record-breaking form, winning the 350cc and 1000cc events on the 297cc Honda six, with lap records in both. He then switched to the Reynolds frame Honda 500 four, more suited to this fast open circuit. Hailwood benefited from the big Honda's

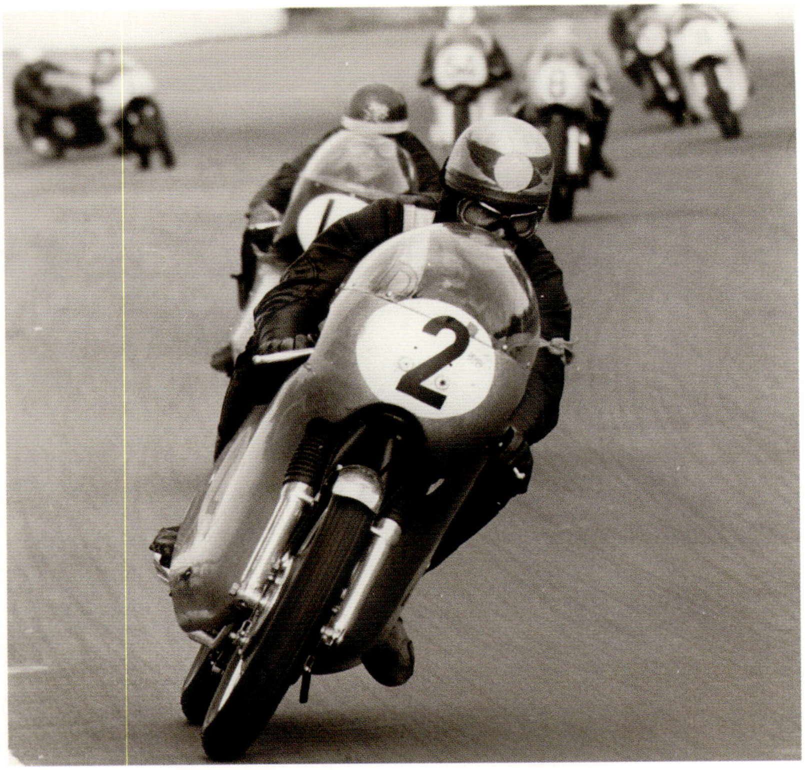

Dave Croxford leads Pat Mahoney, Mallory Park, 25th August 1968.

acceleration and top speed and was able to 'wobble' around the corners, relatively speaking of course. There were 50 competitors for two heats of the 500cc event, with the first 12 from each heat into the 10 lap final. John Cooper back on his Seeley G50 after his nasty crash at the Ulster, took heat one and Hailwood took the second.

With rain threatening, Mike Hailwood was determined to get this race over quickly, as on a skid pan the Honda would be unrideable. As the flag dropped Mike screamed into the distance, leaving a trailing group of Alan Barnett, Croxford, Cooper, Tait, Mahoney and Peter Williams having a skirmish for the other placings. A hair-raising six sided dice for second spot was eventually won by Alan Barnett, Kirby-Metisse, outwitting Croxford, Seeley, in the final sprint to the line. 'Mooneyes' Cooper, Seeley, was fourth, followed by Percy Tait and Pat Mahoney sixth. 'Mike the Bike' set another lap record – three wins in one day – what a man!

'Speedy' Read won both 125 and 250 races, whilst Bill Ivy had mechanical problems with his Yamahas. Helmut Fath on the URS was an easy winner of the 500 sidecar race from Pip Harris, BMW, then on a welcome return to the track of our employee Terry Vinicombe with John Flaxman in the chair posted a third place in the unlimited race.

Another day over, the circus quickly dispersed, many heading for Thruxton in Hampshire, and some to London's Crystal Palace, the rest travelling north to Cheshire's Oulton Park, an awkward journey from Snetterton in those days.

At the Hutchinson 100 Mike Hailwood had indicated he would like to race a Seeley at Oulton Park. Anticipating Mike would keep to his word, and not one Seeley that could be begged, borrowed or stolen, and with only two weeks of available time working with a reduced team, (staff had been committed for the Manx Grand Prix Racing Service), we built a brand new MK2 Seeley, although we had to use one of our spare G50 engines. It was a tremendous effort by everybody and was put together in time for me to test at Brands Hatch on the Wednesday prior to the holiday weekend. So what joy when 'Mike the Bike' confirmed his intention to race a Seeley at the Oulton Park International event. This was a huge boost for us at Seeley Racing and an unimaginable privilege to have the World Champion astride our bike. Phil Read, hearing that Hailwood was to ride a Seeley, thought he would do the same and approached us for support. He told the press that talk of him racing a Norton at Oulton Park was rubbish, even a good Norton was outclassed by a 'Seeley' so far as short circuit racing is concerned.

It was very gratifying to hear such praise from Phil Read, but being so hard-pressed, we were unable to help. The 'Prince of Speed' even offered John Cooper £50 for the loan of his Seeley! He was willing to borrow a Norton from Ray Petty for 'Mooneyes' to ride instead. But it was 'no dice' from the Derbyshire 'Ace'. When Ray Petty learnt what Phil Read was playing at and that the Norton was not for him, Petty cancelled any arrangements between Read and himself, saying, 'I am not going to be messed about like that!' Perhaps Read's outspoken controversial manner was coming home to roost, as nobody seemed keen to help. Finally, he managed to borrow an ex Kirby-Matchless from Austrian Christian Godetz who lived in Wales. So, a 'head-to-head' with Hailwood was now on the cards.

The 2nd September Daily Express sponsored Oulton Park International event would prove to be quite a day for Seeley Racing, but not before a drama. In Hailwood's morning practice the engine crank pin broke. Wally Rawlings and I were devastated. We could not believe it after all the hard work. With no spare engine all we could do was ask around in the paddock. Chester motorcycle dealer and accomplished rider in his

Helmut Fath and Wolfgang Kalauch in action on the URS.

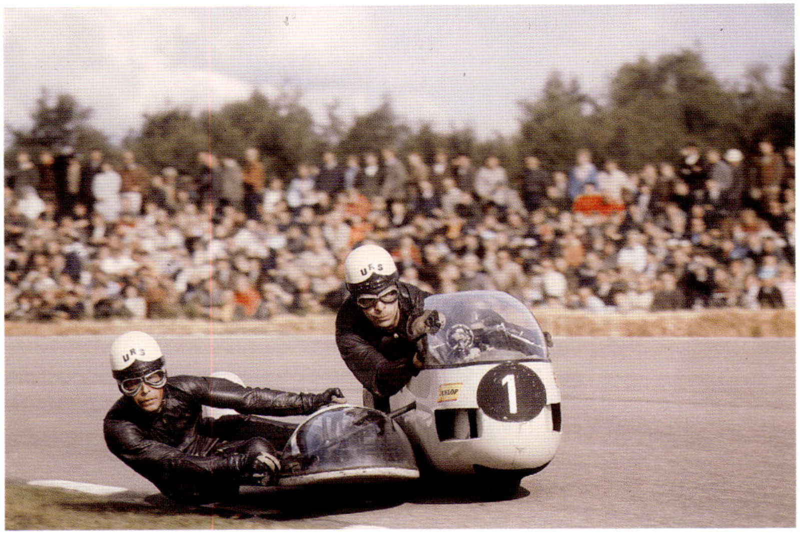

own right, Bill Smith came to the rescue. 'I've an old Matchless G50 engine back in the shop, it has not been touched since AMC overhauled it back in 1963 but you are welcome to borrow it.' With a quick 'Thanks Bill!' I rushed off to Chester leaving Wally to strip the Seeley. Good job there were no speed cameras in those days. The Thames van was flat out for most of the 20 mile round trip. The return journey was a nightmare, battling with thousands of race fans queuing to get into Oulton Park. Finally, I got back with an oily dirty Matchless G50 engine, literally covered in cobwebs. Ron Carnell had a two gallon can of petrol, which was tipped into an old cut open oil drum to give the 'mucky' engine a good wash. Mike Hailwood had other commitments, and sitting in the Duckhams' caravan was unaware of the drama over a replacement engine. So when I reported to Mike, I said 'Not to worry, we have a spare engine with us, but it is in the development stage!'

Around 35,000 fans packed into Oulton Park, such was the attraction of the Grand Prix boys supported by the top stalwarts of British short circuit racing. The lightweight 125cc race started the afternoon's proceedings and gave the locals some cheer when Stuart Graham, Suzuki, beat off the challenge of Ralph Bryans, Honda five, and Dave Simmonds, Kawasaki, in third. Phil Read was a non-starter and 'Little' Bill Ivy out on the first lap with a seized engine on his Yamaha. The 8 lap 22 mile Les Graham Memorial Trophy race was a warm up for many riders who would be competing in the Senior 500 event, including John Cooper, still recovering from his accident and getting back to his best. Sheep farmer Percy Tait on the works Triumph led the flock from start to finish, although he had a close encounter with Peter Williams, who took second place from 'Mooneyes' on the Seeley, followed by Rob Fitton, Mahoney then Shorey sixth. The anticipated clash between Phil Read and Bill Ivy in the 250cc race and the continuing feud between the Yamaha teamsters fizzled out when Read, having made a spectacular wheelie start, pulled away from 'Little' Bill, then slid off at Lodge Corner, at the end of the second lap, without injury. The Maidstone 'Marvel' took the £60 prize, ahead of Ralph Bryans on the 250cc Honda six, never being able to live with Bill Ivy.

The first of the 500cc sidecar races had Helmut Fath URS four take a record-breaking win from Wakefield, BMW, with veteran Pip Harris, BMW, third.

Then what thousands had been waiting for – Hailwood on the 297cc six in the 19 lap 350cc Castrol Trophy event, had some fun sitting on the tails of Kel Carruthers, Aermacchi, and Ginger Molloy, Bultaco, then shot of into the distance breaking Derek Minter's old 350 and 500cc lap records. £80 prize money and another trophy for Mike.

Tony Wakefield won the rain-swept second sidecar race from Fath, who was struggling to control wheel spin on the multi-cylinder URS. Over-all victory went to Wakefield, just 4 seconds ahead of Fath in second with Georg Auerbacher third.

Why should Mike Hailwood and Phil Read, multi World Champions want to revisit their roots and race single cylinder machines? Was it just rivalry, proving who might be the best? It was a huge risk, racing works bikes with their awesome performance at this type of event. As 'Hurricane' Hailwood demonstrated on the Honda six in the 350cc race, just playing around with the opposition was one thing; but at street level with tough competitors such as Cooper, Williams, Tait, Randle and Carruthers all there to snap at the champions' heels ready to pick up any pieces; was another. As Hailwood said, he was in a no win situation; if he won it was expected, if he didn't he would be rubbished.

The last race of the day was the 19 lap 52.46 mile Senior 500cc event. We had concerns for Mike on the Seeley, he'd hardly had any practice due to the engine failure and the fitting of a replacement unit, details of which were really sketchy. Nevertheless, Mike Hailwood on a Seeley so unfamiliar to him, lined up on the grid alongside John Cooper, Phil Read and 38 other competitors spread out behind. It was still the days of the push starts, therefore anything could happen. It was tense. The track was still wet and we were nervous as hell. This was an important race. Hailwood would not want to be beaten by 'Speedy' Read, with much to be proved at that point. The flag went down, and the 'Prince of Speed' made the best start, but Cooperman, also out to prove something, was soon beside Phil Read. Then Hailwood, settling in, passed the pair, took the lead and pulled away. Back in the pits we could hardly look, my heart was pounding. 'Mooneyes' continued his duel with Read, so it was a possibility that we could achieve a 1 - 2 result, or nothing at all if things went wrong. Then 3 laps before the end, Phil Read on the Kirby-Matchless ran out of fuel, leaving Mike the Bike to huge applause, a true winner on the Seeley, 9 seconds ahead of John Cooper who had brought his Seeley into a brilliant second place ahead of Percy Tait, Peter Williams, Rob Fitton and Bill Smith, who had loaned us the G50 engine, in sixth. A delighted Mike describing the race as great fun, had enjoyed every minute. Even allowing for some slides in the damp conditions, marvellous Mike Hailwood once more demonstrated his versatility and his champion quality, on and off the track, the people's favourite. Ron Carnell from Duckhams Oils who had supported us that day, Wally Rawlings, myself and friends were absolutely on cloud nine, such a wonderful result. Mike had certainly fulfilled his promise, and our own John Cooper, in his richly deserved second place – was fantastic. Hailwood received £100 first prize and 'Mooneyes' £60. Mike was also presented with the Avon Gold Cup along with an Omega gold watch, which he immediately presented to me, a treasured possession to this day. A truly generous gesture from a great sportsman. His parting shot was, 'I don't know what you are doing with that development engine but it's not working – oops – the original engine is much better!'

The long drive home was pleasant, reflecting on one of our most memorable race meetings ever. Elsewhere that Bank Holiday Monday the Ruislip 'Rebel' Croxford on his Seeley at Thruxton put Alan Barnett, Kirby-Metisse, in his place by winning both 500cc events plus a second spot in the 350cc event. The talented Terry Vinicombe in record-breaking mood, won two sidecar races. At Crystal Palace Ron Chandler on his 350cc Seeley won the 350cc event from Rex Butcher, Kawasaki. Ray Pickrell, 750cc Dunstall Domiracer on his debut at the 'Palace' watched by 7,500 sun-baked Londoners, having won the production race, won a round of the Players No.6 Championship for machines 351-1000cc. Ron Chandler brought his 500cc Seeley into second place with Welshman Uphill third.

I must admit to being a 'wee' bit boastful, but Seeley Racing with our team of riders, over three days of competition, out of 13 starts had achieved 13 finishes inclusive of 11 rostrum positions; four wins, four seconds, three thirds, a fourth and a sixth – remarkable results over a remarkable weekend. Number 13 might be unlucky for some, but not for CSRD!

Following his fun rides at the Oulton International on the Seeley and Honda six, Hailwood received an offer to partner Giacomo Agostini on a 500cc works MV at the Italian Grand Prix on 15th September. The Italians misunderstood Mike's reply.

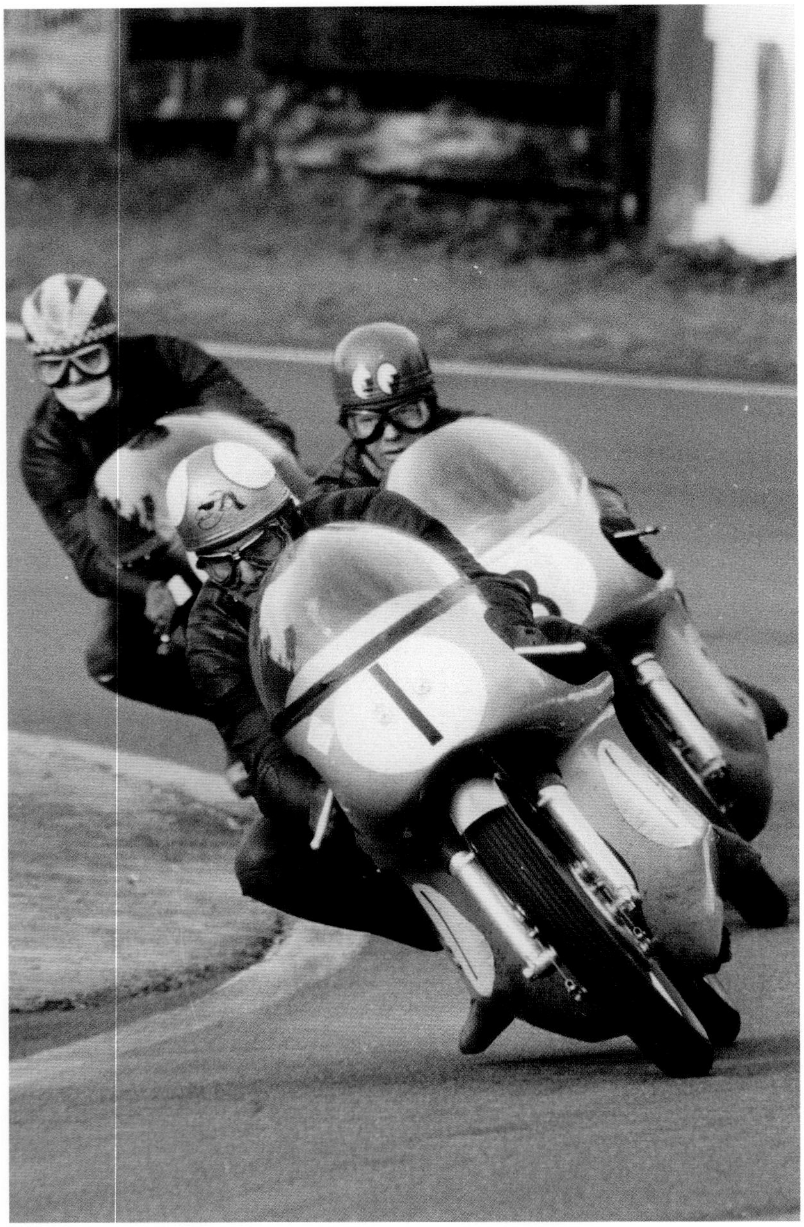

Hailwood, Seeley, winning the Avon Gold Cup from John Cooper, Seeley and Phil Read, Matchless, at the Daily Express sponsored, Oulton Park International, 2nd September 1968.

Believing he did not wish to ride the MV, consequently the consistent Aussie, Kel Carruthers was approached. It was not until Hailwood arrived in Italy that the MV Agusta race management realised their mistake and that Mike was available. Carruthers, who had performed so well on an Aermacchi that season, was then offered a works ride by that factory for the 350cc Italian Grand Prix race.

Over in Gothenberg Sweden at the Ullevis Stadium, 45,000 fans witnessed 28 year old New Zealander Ivan Mauger beat the rest of the world to be crowned the World Speedway Champion, an 11 year ambition fulfilled. Fellow countryman Barry Briggs, despite a temperature and riding against doctor's orders, finished runner-up. Ivan was presented with a child's bicycle, a transistor radio and a cheque for £250, such were the rewards in those days.

At Brands Hatch on the 8th September it was not much better for Derek Minter at the national event, supposedly a benefit meeting for the retired 'King of Brands' the very first of its sort for a rider. With proceeds of the main grandstand being awarded to Minter, unfortunately only 3,500 spectators turned up, the smallest gate of the year. A miserly 135 seats were taken in the grandstand. At ten shillings each it would hardly keep the 'Mint' in luxury, and was very disappointing for Minter who thought he was worth a little more. Nevertheless, it was packed track action on the 1.24 mile short circuit. Ron Chandler and Dave Croxford brought their Seeleys home 1 - 2 in the 350cc race, Ray Pickrell third on an Aermacchi. In the 1000cc event Croxford on his Seeley 500 took an early lead and held the advantage until Pickrell on the 750 Dunstall-Norton went ahead. But Croxford tucked into Ray's slipstream ready for the last lap challenge when the G50 engine called enough, and the rebel was out of it. Alan Barnett took second place from Roy Francis, 650cc Monard, third, Pat Mahoney Matchless led Martin Ashwood on the Arter Matchless with Chandler, Seeley, making up the first six. With Croxford out of action for the 500cc race, Alan Barnett won with Ron Chandler again in sixth. The lack of fans perhaps proved that there were just too many meetings and all so close together!

Over at the Manx Grand Prix our service team had been busy, trying to help all and sundry. With no Seeley machines competing, there was consolation in the 500cc event, when 19 year old Nigel Rollason brought his Seeley-Metisse home into third place and was awarded the newcomer's prize, Scotsman John Findlay, having won the Junior Race two days earlier, made it a double.

On Sunday 15th September the bespectacled grass track and sprinter ace Alf Hagon, who I had raced against in my early days, set a new fastest ever terminal speed at Santa Pod, taking his 1260cc JAP over the finish line at 157.73mph, the best ever recorded by a motorcycle at the end of a standing quarter-mile. Tragically the day before, down at the Brighton Speed Trials, 29 year old Ian Ashwell, a star 1000cc class sprinter, tipped to break George Brown's course record, somersaulted his supercharged Vincent Special at 160mph. The fairing had probably broken loose and jammed the front wheel. Only yards from the end of the kilometre course Ian hit a concrete bollard and was killed instantly, the first post war fatality at this event. The meeting was abandoned as a mark of respect.

That same weekend, at the rain swept Italian Grand Prix there was more drama. On Wednesday before the meeting, Mike Hailwood realised that his 350 and 500 three cylinder MVs were noticeably slower than Agostini's bikes. Then on the Friday, Count Agusta ordered Hailwood to let Agostini win both his races. Mike, the multi World Champion, refused to play second fiddle to that year's double World Champion. Later Hailwood reconsidered and offered to play the game in the 350cc race, providing he and Ago could ride their own race in the big class but the answer from Count Agusta was a resounding no. On the Saturday morning, Hailwood was fed up and on the verge of abandoning the meeting when the Benelli Factory offered him a 500cc Benelli four. The official factory rider, Renzo Pasolini, was prepared to stand down to let Hailwood ride his bike, but the Pesaro Factory mechanics had been working all night to assemble a second machine in time for the Saturday practice. Mike accepted the offer and lapped within 1.4 seconds of Ago's time. Delighted with the handling he prayed for rain to even the odds against the superior performance of the MV. Overnight and into the Sunday morning, rain lashed the 3.5 mile ultra-high-speed Monza Circuit, leaving it treacherously slippery, and conditions did not improve during the day.

The Maidstone 'Marvel' Little Bill Ivy won the 125cc race, Phil Read having fallen off and remounted to finish second. Astounding was the average race speed of Ivy on the works 125cc Yamaha, 106.4mph .07mph quicker than Agostini's 350cc race win average. Bill Ivy's fastest lap at 108.82mph was just over 1mph down on Ago's fastest lap. Awesome in such conditions! This was to be Bill's very last Grand Prix win. In the 250cc event which Ivy needed to win from Phil Read to achieve his second world championship, the alleged feud between the two ended when Read won the 250cc race from Ivy, some say in defiance of Yamaha orders. Phil added the title to the 125cc crown already clinched and his first ever double World Championship success. Equal on points at the end of that championship chase, with five wins and two seconds each, and three non-finish positions for both riders, the six best results out of the 10 championship rounds that year counted. With 46 points each, there was nothing between the two Yamaha teamsters yet the title was handed to Phil Read – a real puzzle!

The answer was provided when, for the first time in the history of the Geneva based FIM the sport's governing body, it was decided by secretary Jacques Hartman to add together all the finish race times for each rider. No football penalty shoot out! No toss of the coin here! 'Speedy' Read arrived at Monza with 14.3 seconds in hand over Ivy. There was little in it at that stage, but in the race on drying roads, Bill Ivy was eager to keep Read in his sights for a last lap challenge. Perhaps unaware how this championship would be decided if they both finished, he overdid things at the Parabolica Curve and lost valuable time, leaving 'Speedy' Read to break away to the finish line in the 22 lap race, averaging 110.73mph with a fastest lap of 113.22mph, and more important for Read, 1 minute 51 seconds ahead of Ivy. That time, added to the 14.3 seconds in hand, gave Phil an overall time advantage over six races of 2.53 minutes, amazing! Handing the title to Phil Read.

Finally that day the 35 lap, 124.95 mile 500cc event was held in appalling rain, which was what Hailwood had ordered, but it would be his undoing. From the start Mike on the Benelli four tucked in behind Agostini only inches astern in the spray. Renzo Pasolini, Benelli, was third, two seconds behind on the first lap. On the third lap Hailwood, braking for the Parabolica Curve crashed the Benelli - so embarrassing. He tried to restart but the bike was full of sand and Mike's day was over. An event to forget for him, the first time since 1958 that Hailwood ended the season without a single world championship point.

To the delight, but not surprise of the Italian fans, Agostini, MV Agusta, won the 500cc race at 110.73mph average, with Pasolini, Benelli, second at 109.92mph and Bergamonti, Paton, making up the first three. Ron Chandler and Campanelli on their Seeleys finished tenth and twelfth, helping to put Seeley fourth in that year's 500cc manufacturer's championship.

That same weekend Dave Croxford, newly crowned 1968 British 500cc champion recorded another double on his Seeley. At the mile long East-Kent Lydden Circuit he won both the 350 and 500 events.

Back at the Forge Works we were not just sitting on our hands. I had grave concerns for the Seeley 7R 350cc model. Although the 7R engine had great qualities and even fitted into the Seeley MK2 chassis, it was often being out-performed by the Italian Aermacchis. Eddie Robinson came up with the idea of the MK3 type frame with no front down tubes. I built a prototype light weight version for John Cooper to ride at the Daily Mail Mallory Park International Race of the Year on Sunday 22nd September. The rolling chassis was intended solely as a 350cc and not as a multi purpose frame. It featured a single front brake, smaller rim and tyre sizes, narrow rear chain and sprockets and as much

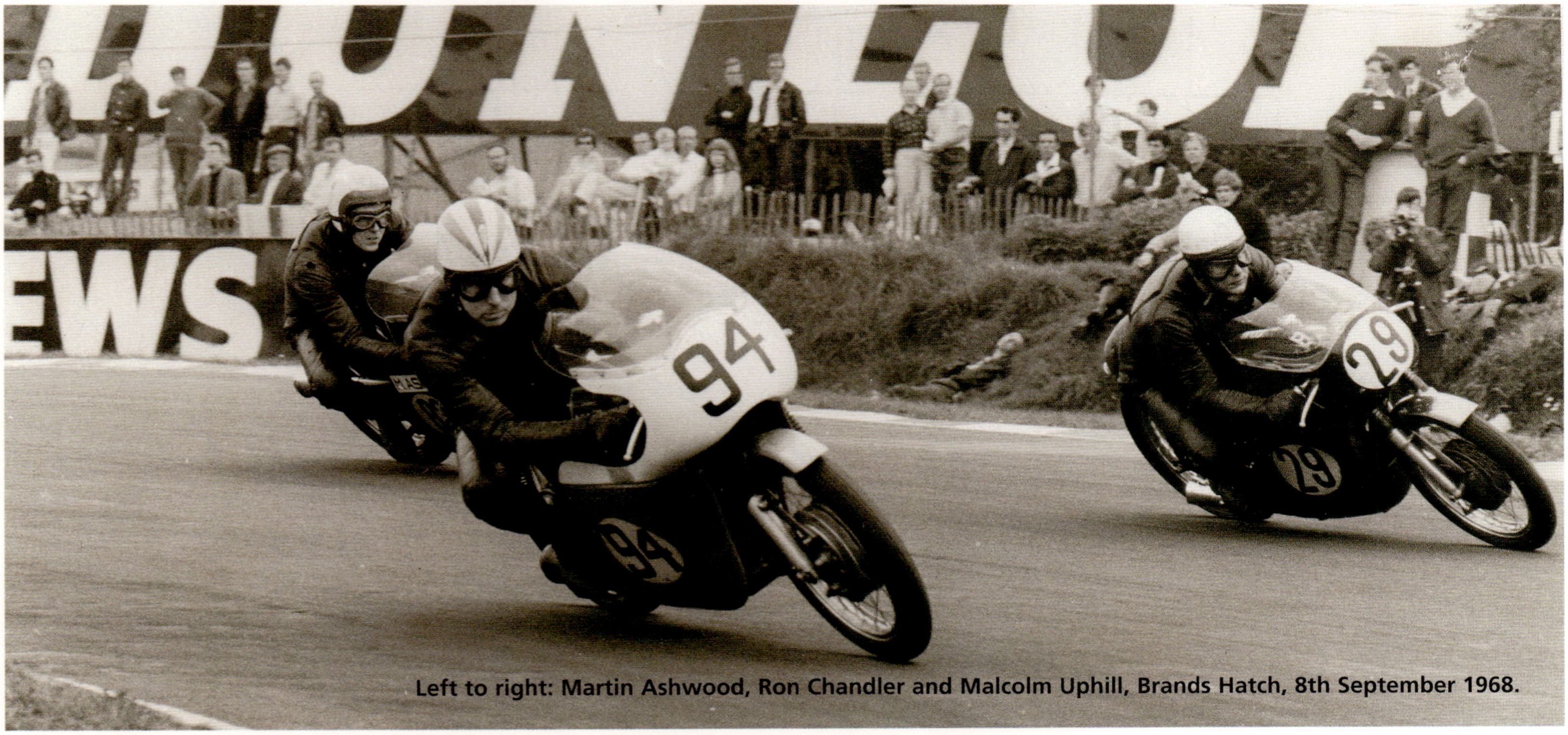

Left to right: Martin Ashwood, Ron Chandler and Malcolm Uphill, Brands Hatch, 8th September 1968.

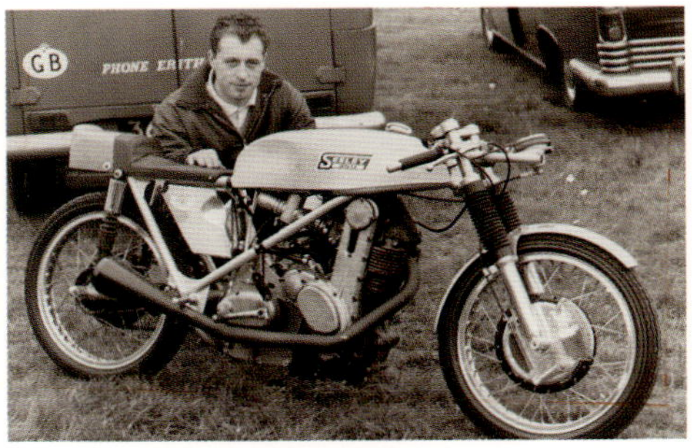

Mallory, Sept 1968 with the lightweight 350cc built for John Cooper.

Bill Ivy finished 4th on John Cooper's Seeley-G50, Redex Trophy, Brands Hatch 29th September 1968.

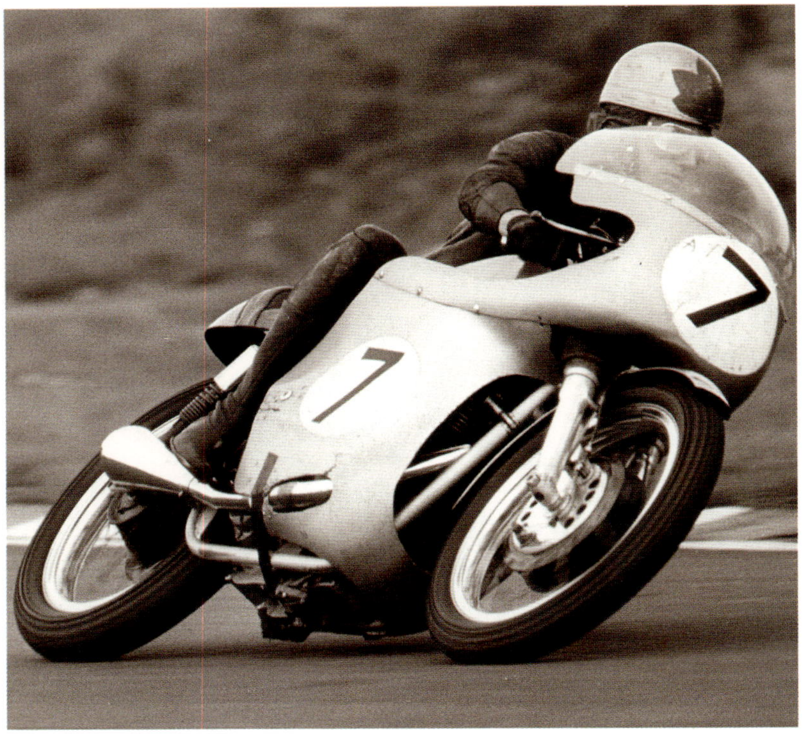

magnesium in the engine as possible. Lightened (less oil and fuel) by 21lbs (9.53 kilos). Total weight was 259lbs (117.48kilos) including the fairing. Wally Rawlings had performed his magic on the engine in an effort to improve top end performance, so we were hopeful. I thought a further 10lbs (4.54kilo) could still be trimmed, eventually making our Seeley 7R competitive for the 1969 season on a power to weight basis.

In heat one of a wet Junior Race, won by Agostini, MV, 'Mooneyes' Cooper, battling with Kel Carruthers Aermacchi and others for third place, slid off at the Esses. Although only bruised, 'Cooperman' pulled out of the day's racing as he was still recovering from his Ulster injuries. Disappointing yes, but John was pleased with the lightweight Seeley. 'It's a joy to ride,' he declared. The 30 lap Race of the Year for machines 100cc – 1000cc was dominated by marvellous Mike on the Honda 297cc six, scooping the £1,050 first prize. Agostini, MV, was in second place for £500, Barry Randle, Norton, in a well deserved third and £250 followed home by Alan Barnett, Percy Tait on a 750cc Triumph, then the Ruislip 'Rebel' Croxford, in trouble with his own bike, rode John Cooper's Seeley into sixth spot, for £75.

After the embarrassing celebrated riders strike over expenses at the earlier Post-TT Mallory Park meeting, Chris Lowe announced a sliding scale of start money for the Brands October 6th International. This astute move would avoid an awkward situation at the prestigious Evening News sponsored Race of the South, at which World Champions Agostini, Read, Ivy and Hailwood would be performing. Of course someone would have to pay, so admission charges were raised from 10 shillings to 12 shillings and 6 pence.

It had been a very busy season but it was not over yet. 20,000 spectators turned up at the Brands, Evening News International, held on the 2.65 mile Grand Prix circuit, the last chance that year to see the world champions in action, and all in the same race. Agostini, Read, Ivy, Hailwood were joined by Croxford, Barnett, Carruthers, Gould, Smart, Shorey, Tait, Chandler, Pickrell, Mahoney, Simmonds, Avery, Butcher and Robb – so many great names, not forgetting the sidecar boys Vincent, Boddice, Harris, Vinicombe, Hanks, Schauzu, Wakefield and Brown. Certainly, exciting racing was promised.

The 350cc race starting the action saw Maestro Mike, despite a broken finger on his throttle hand, take his revenge over Agostini. On the 297cc Honda six, Hailwood led the 10 lap race from start to finish taking the £50 prize money as well as breaking his own lap record. The Italian World Champion Ago in second place collected £35, but behind, a fearsome struggle took place between Kel Carruthers, Aermacchi Metisse, Alan Barnett, Kirby-Metisse, and Dave Croxford on our prototype lightweight Seeley. It was wheel to wheel until the last lap when Carruthers gained the advantage to snatch third place from Barnett with Croxford fifth and £15 for all that effort, ahead of Tony Rutter, Norton, sixth.

The 125cc event renewed the struggle between Luton-based Phil Read and Maidstone's Bill Ivy, both on works Yamahas. Neither gave an inch and both broke the lap record by nearly 5mph, whilst fighting off the challenge of Stuart Graham on the Suzuki. Graham led Phil Read for the first 3 laps leaving 'Little' Bill recovering from a poor start and an engine cut out at the hairpin. On the fourth lap 'Speedy' Read went into the lead, but the Maidstone 'Marvel' dug deep, caught and passed Stuart Graham and took the lead from Read on lap 8 to record his last ever victory on the Yamaha, an exciting race with Phil Read second, Stuart Graham third and Dave Simmonds, Kawasaki, fourth. Prize money; first £30, second £25, third £20, fourth £15.

The final of the 10 lap Redex Trophy for machines over 350cc but not exceeding 500cc had 40 competitors on the line. Agostini was there on the MV, but Hailwood didn't have have a suitable machine. Seeley racing was represented by our regulars Ron Chandler, Dave Croxford and a new face, and competing in his first race on a single cylinder machine for two years riding John Cooper's Seeley G50, was the Maidstone 'Marvel' Bill Ivy.

The Brands Hatch 'scratchers' led by Croxford, Chandler and Barnett held Agostini at bay for a couple of laps before he picked them off one by one for his first win at Brands that year. The World Champ was just too good. The trio behind scrapped furiously, with nothing in it until the last lap, when the Kemsing star Chandler, perhaps trying too hard, crashed his Seeley at Clearways leaving Croxford chasing Barnett to the flag and third place. Bill Ivy, riding a steady race brought the 'Mooneyes' Seeley home in an admirable fourth place. Our 1968 British 500 champion, the Ruislip 'Rebel' Croxford added more points to the Redex Trophy Championship he was leading. The 20 lap Evening News Race of the South for machines up to 1000cc allowed 'Mike the Bike' to play a tune on his favourite motorcycle, the 297cc Honda six. The exhaust note was as incredible as his performance. The 38 competitors on the start line had a wide variety of racing motorcycles; Norton, Yamaha, Suzuki, BSA, Aermacchi, Seeley, Triumph, Harley Davidson, Egli-Vincent, Monard, MV Agusta and Honda. At the start the machines are all pulled back on compression. The front row of Agostini, Ivy, Read and Hailwood looked intense as they waited for the flag to drop. Zoom! they are away in seconds. In the early laps a blanket would cover the champions, their antics having the huge crowd yelling with pleasure, the four best racers in the world at that time. Then the master Hailwood took the lead equalling Derek Minter's long standing 1963 lap record of 90.34mph on the Gilera 500cc four. A lap later he broke the record by 0.6 of a second or half a mile per hour, earning him a £100 bonus. Agostini had no answer to Hailwood's charge but pushed Read back into third place. Ivy had retired the 250 Yamha with plug trouble when in fourth, allowing Ray Pickrell, 745 Dunstall, in after his battle with Tony Smith. Having his best ride to date at Brands on his 650cc BSA, despite a misfire in the closing stages, Tony took fifth spot. Alan Barnett on the Kirby 500 Metisse secured sixth place after Croxford, riding the Reg-Curley 650 Domiracer, dropped back with a loose fairing, Percy Tait on the 750 Triumph earlier holding seventh, dropped back with a flat battery into sixteenth place.

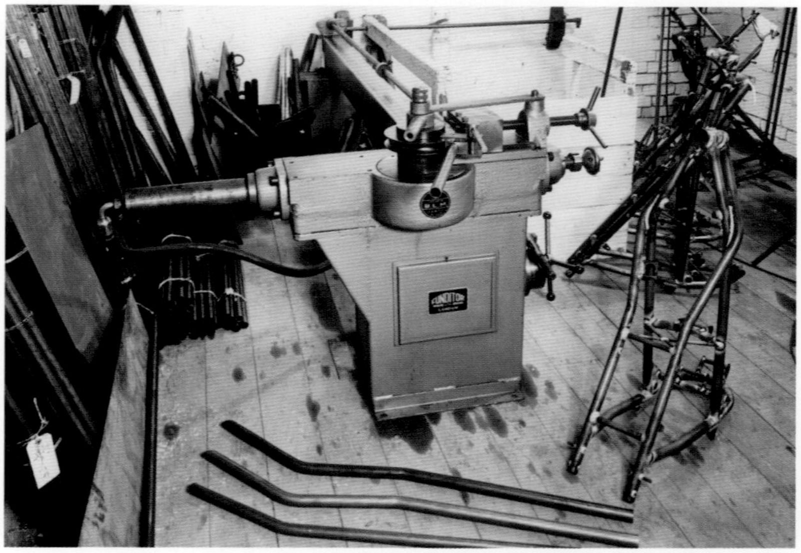

Bersani Colombo hydraulic pipe-bending machine.

Our friend, veteran sidecar racer and still top of his profession Pip Harris, BMW, won the 500cc sidecar event from Tony Wakefield, BMW, with TT winner German ace Siegfied Schauzu, BMW, third, and Dick Hawes on his Seeley G50 outfit coming home in fifth, a good result.

In the last solo race of the day, the Ivy-Read duel was on again with swords drawn. The 250cc race was fought wheel to wheel on works Yamahas for 8 of the 10 laps. Then, with a record lap, 'Speedy' Read squirted ahead to win by a few yards. A disappointed Ivy who I am sure wanted to win the 125 and 250cc events in front of his home crowd, announced his retirement from motorcycle racing. He said he was just too sensitive to put up with all the bickering and back-biting existing in the atmosphere of world championship racing. The talented, diminutive 26 year old 1967 125cc world champion Bill Ivy had been in racing nine years in all, the last three years with Yamaha. He left Brands Hatch that day for the very last time, saying he was no longer interested in the sport and never wanting to race again. 'The only thing I am thankful for is that I am alive. There have been times when I thought racing would leave me before I left racing.'

At 5.45pm the final of the up to 1000cc Evening News Sidecar Race of the South concluded the day's action. 18 outfits lined up for the push start. In the 10 lap race Chris Vincent started as favourite but the 'Brummie' suffered an early misfire with his BSA powered outfit. Meanwhile up front a tremendous battle raged to the flag between the 654cc BSA machines of Peter Brown and Terry Vinicombe, Brown just getting the verdict by a few yards from our employee Terry Vinicombe aided by John Flaxman. The veteran ace Pip Harris, BMW, made up the rostrum positions. Gerry Boret, 998 Vincent, and Norman Hanks, 654 BSA, were fourth and fifth, with Chris Vincent storming through from the back to the cheers of the enthusiastic fans, into a well earned sixth place. The day was over. The crowd dispersed, happy with a good 12s 6d worth of champion's action.

Back at the Forge Works we waited with excitement for the delivery that second week in October of the Italian Bersani Colombo tube bender. The purchase of a tube mitre machine had already considerably reduced the amount of hand filing work associated with frame manufacturing, The bender would enable us to improve production yet maintain the quality.

Around that time, Leslie Nichol of the Daily Express wrote a scathing story about The Isle of Man lottery, formed to raise capital for a British world beater. £7,000 was contributed towards the wonder bike but then the lottery folded – was there anything to show for that £7,000, or did anybody care?

It might be the middle of October but the race action continued. Ruislip 'Rebel' Croxford was established as the Lord of Lydden on his Seeley 500 in the unlimited race after a 12 lap tussle with Brian Kemp, 745cc Kirby Norton, and Roy Francis, 649 Monard. Already winner of the 250 and 350cc events, Brian Kemp was not about to give up his Lord of Lydden, but whilst overtaking Croxford at the Devil's Elbow he ran wide, believing Croxford would not be able to re-pass. Kemp hit the bumps and when the front wheel lost grip, he crashed. Brian Kemp, nursing his injured wrist afterwards said, 'I should have remembered Croxford knows how to pass where no one else would dare to tread.' Croxford just failed to set the first 70mph race speed for the tricky twisting track by only three fifths of a second, but averaging 69.95mph was a new track record. In the 350cc race on the Seeley, Croxford split the Padgett-Yamahas of Kemp and Terry Grotefeld to take second place.

John 'Mooneyes' Cooper changed his mind about no more racing that season. In 'just one for the road', 'Mooneyes' was in devastating form at Mallory Park on 20th October. On the Padgett-Yamaha not only did he win the title of 250cc British Champion but in the 350cc race he rode our lightweight Seeley 7R to perfection and first place. Croxford, Seeley, got the better of a hard riding Paul Smart, Vic Camp Ducati, to take second place. In the 500cc event, the early laps saw a Seeley 1 - 2 from Percy Tait, Triumph, then Croxford retired with engine trouble leaving 'Mooneyes' unassailable, bringing his Seeley G50 home under the linen first, ahead of Tait, Barnett, Randle, Hunter and Ron Chandler, Seeley, in sixth. It was a great day for the Derbyshire 'Demon' the bespectacled, 'Cooperman'!

On the never ending 'merry-go-round' a week later it was back to Brands Hatch for the Kentish 100 Races. Dick Hawes offered me his Seeley G50 outfit for this event. Perhaps stupidity took over, I accepted the challenge of a provisional comeback after a 16 month lay-off. More importantly, could the 'Ruislip Rebel' take the honours in the Redex Trophy Championship for 500cc machines on his Seeley G50? On the 1.24 mile club circuit this was an event of many heats then the finals. Although prize money was offered, it was a meeting of trophy race names from the past; Hartley, Neville, Slazenger, Mayhew and of course more currently Redex.

There were four separate 5 lap heats of the Slazenger Trophy sidecar event for machines up to 1300cc. Only the first three finishers got to the final, a tall order for passenger Roy Lindsey and me to qualify. Kindly the Brands Racing Committee allocated us race number 2. Chris Vincent, our old adversary was quite rightly issued race number 1. After such a lay off, I was extremely apprehensive about this ride and felt like a complete novice! Although I had built the Seeley, it was a kneeler outfit of a type I had not raced before. Even fitted with one of our Seeley G50 636cc engines, I was not convinced we would be competitive. Well I was never to find out. The 636cc unit wasn't running to its best (good excuse) and we failed to make the first three in our heat, perhaps a blessing in disguise. I must have been crazy to consider a racing comeback. Too much of a gamble, too much at stake, with so much going on at Colin Seeley Racing Developments. That meeting 27th October 1968 would be the last time my name would appear in a programme as a serious competitor.

Derek Chatterton, Yamaha, leading from start to finish made it look easy winning the 250cc final. Rhodesian Mike Taylor delighted sponsor Ted Broad by bringing the Broad Yamaha into second place after Paul Smart, Yamaha, slowed with a puncture on the last lap. In the 350cc Neville Trophy final Dave Simmonds on a 349cc Kawasaki surprised everyone by winning, but Alan Barnett on the Kirby-Metisse, in finishing second took the 350cc British Championship title from nearest contender Jim Curry, Aermacchi-Mettise, who was back in sixth place, having to win to have any chance. Two heats of the 500cc Redex Trophy had 27 competitors in each, with the first 14 to the final. Alan Barnett, Croxford's nearest competitor all season, won heat one and Croxford heat two, so it was all or nothing in the 10 lap final.

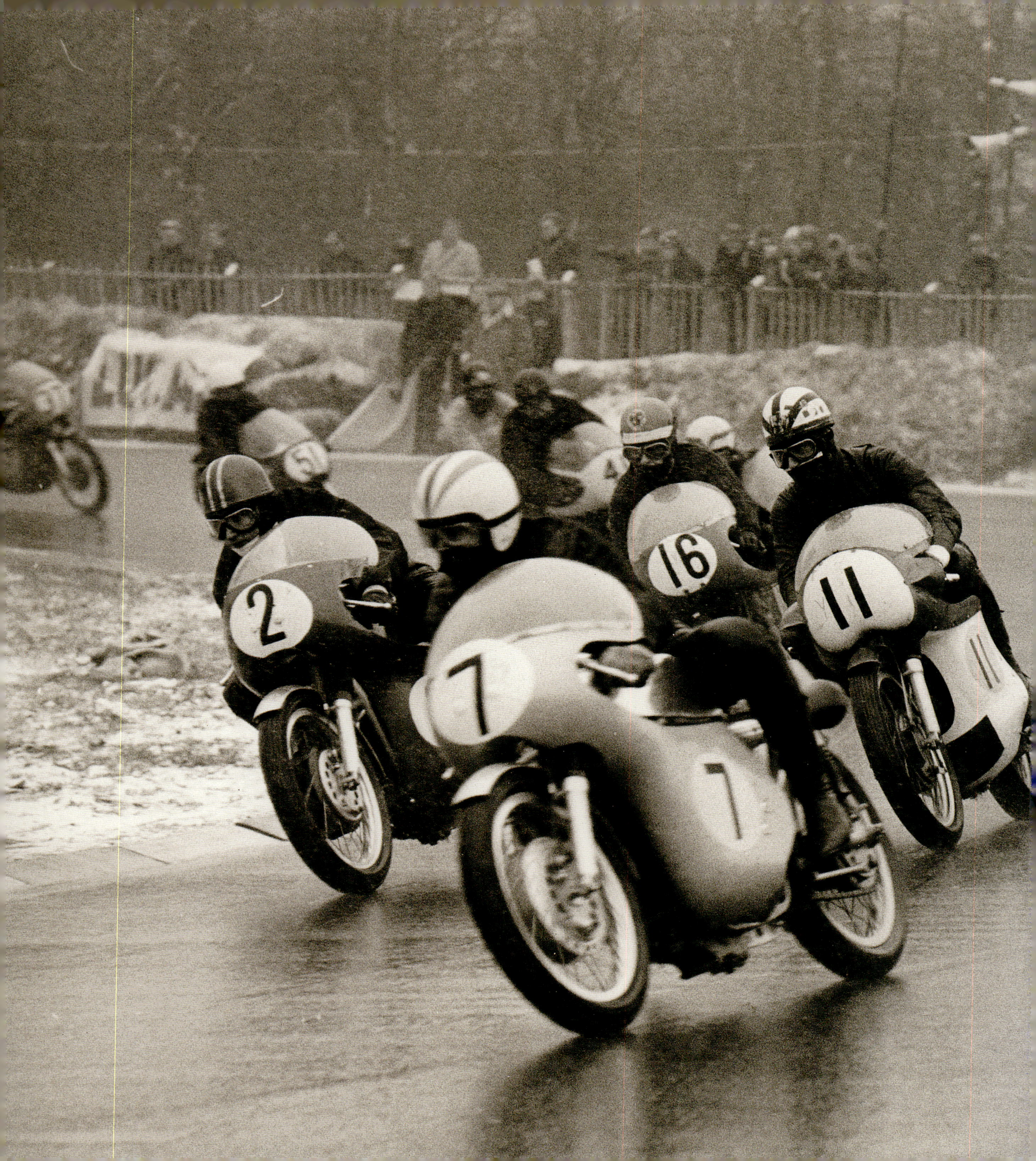
2
7
16
11

Ron Chandler at Brands with the prototype Mk3 Seeley.

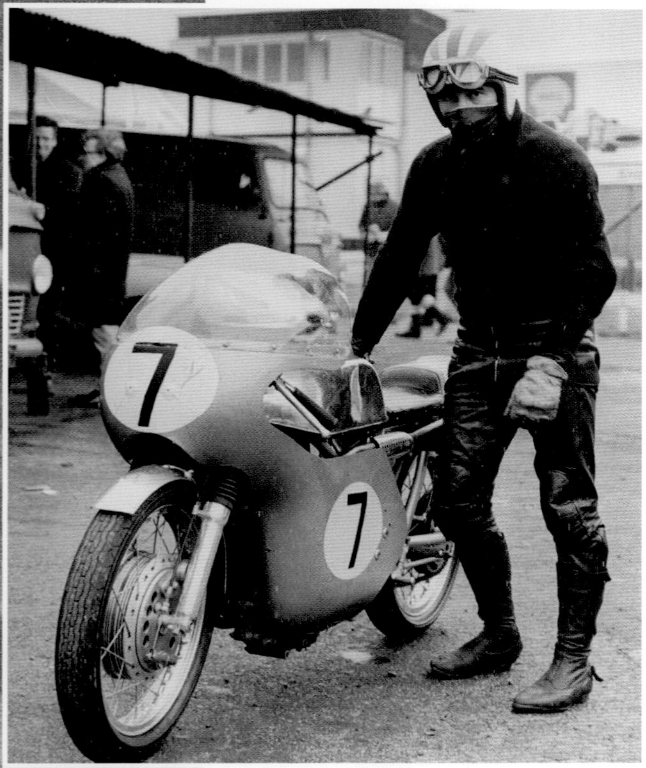

The Guinness-drinking, cigarette-smoking, likable Londoner Croxford made no mistake in that last round of the Redex Trophy. He stormed ahead from the start, the £100 prize reflecting in the race screen, bringing his Seeley G50 over the finish line ahead of Ray Pickrell, who on the Dunstall Domiracer collected £30 for his efforts, Alan Barnett £20 for third, Ron Chandler and Mick Andrew, Seeley, fifth and sixth, awarded £10 and £8 respectively. Barnett's consolation was the Grovewood award for the most improved rider of the year, well done Alan! A delighted Dave Croxford collected the Redex Trophy £100, plus £40 prize money, and also £30 for second place in the 1300cc final on the 745 Curley-Norton. Ray Pickrell, on the big Dunstall Domiracer had turned the tables on Croxford. The talented Mick Andrew on the 745 Kuhn Commando took an impressive third place.

The finish of another great day's racing found the Birmingham 'speedster' Chris Vincent, BSA, winning the sidecar race from a determined Gerry Boret on his 998cc Vincent. Terry Vinicombe and John Flaxman brought their BSA into third place. Terry's ongoing health problems eventually landed him in hospital. I believe that this meeting was the last the talented 1968 750cc Isle of Man TT winner Vinicombe would be seen in action!

1968 had been a year of endless race meetings. From March to December there had been at least 30 national and internationals in the UK alone. Many competitors were racing in two classes or more. The number of actual races started was just astonishing. The versatility of riders in those days, jumping from one machine to another, just had to be admired.

For me the year had been like a scenic railway, something different every day. The on-track success of the Seeley product seemed like a dream, but the reality was thanks to the efforts of my work force, all committed to producing the best, often in the shortest possible time. Many top riders had committed themselves to racing our machines.

I like to believe that we received this support on the track because we were totally devoted to our business. Nothing was too much trouble to support our riders. We always had an ear for suggestions and ideas to improve our bikes, and always the greatest enthusiasm. That was our big secret.

Ron Chandler leads the pack in the snow at Brands Hatch.

With racing for 1968 pretty well over, the rumours and news would continue: Tom Kirby announced he would only support and run with Alan Barnett for the 1969 season. Within weeks he would test ride the 500 Weslake-Metisse. The Weslake engine unit claimed 65 bhp at 11,000rpm. Although still not in production, it was being costed at £850, the price of a complete brand new Seeley five speed G50, with £25 change!

The last of Britain's 250cc road racing machines, The Greeves Silverstone, was finally dropped by the Thundersley Essex factory, four years after its introduction, joining the Cotton Telstar and DMW Hornet which had already gone. These machines had all played an important part in providing affordable racing in Britain at that time.

The famous Gilera concern had difficulties. Having run into financial problems a receiver had been appointed, 280 of the 550 workers were now on short time. Back home, probably following the unfortunate accident to Ian Ashwell at the Brighton Sprint, the Sunbeam Club, fearful of accidents, axed their annual Ramsgate Sprint on the promenade. The new venue for 1969 was to be Lydd Aerodrome.

With Castrol Oils cutting their support for 1969, and the reduction of works Grand Prix teams, larger than life Castrol competition manager, Malcolm Edgar left to set up a self-drive van hire business.

Eire's Mondello Park race circuit, opened in 1968, was to be upgraded for 1969 from a three-quarter mile to one mile track at a cost of £20,000.

The cigarette manufacturers certainly were taking an interest in our sport with Carreras, part of Guards and Rothmans Group confirming sponsorship of five events at MCD circuits for 1969.

December brought us more good news. Mick Mooney, the sponsor of Irish rising star, the dynamic Brian Steenson, ordered a new Seeley G50. Steenson in the final year of his engineering degree, would continue to race the 350 Aermacchi on which he had been so successful in '68, into 1969, but he would also be racing the Seeley under the Irish Racing Motorcycles Ltd banner. Queens University technician Ray McCullough and Steenson would be joined by newly signed Tom Herron – a name for the future.

No, the unbelievable year for Seeley Racing was still not over on the track. With hardly time to get over the turkey and Christmas pud our star men Chandler and Croxford were about to be snow ploughs at the 29th December Brands Hatch 'Yuletide' meeting. With a start time of 2pm it was a 'huge!' programme of three 5 lap heats of the 125-1000cc event. The first nine from each heat ran in the 10 lap final, followed by two 5 lap heats of the unlimited capacity sidecar race – the first six from the heats to the 10 lap final and then home! With prize money of £200 for the solo winner, £120 for the second and £80 for the third there was certainly an incentive, but the snow fell continuously throughout the $1^1/_2$ hour programme.

Some 66 solo riders had entered for this one race final, but only 27 would go through, the rest perhaps well pleased that they were no longer racing in winter wonderland. The 'Ruislip Rebel', not intimidated by the conditions, could see through the snow flakes that £200 first prize, just right to cover his Christmas 'fags and booze'. Croxford, riding his regular Seeley G50, made a lightning start in the final and was still there as the pack tiptoed round Druids. Heading into driving snow on the bottom straight, Ray Pickrell on the 745 Dunstall handled the powerful twin as if it were on skis. He took the lead and

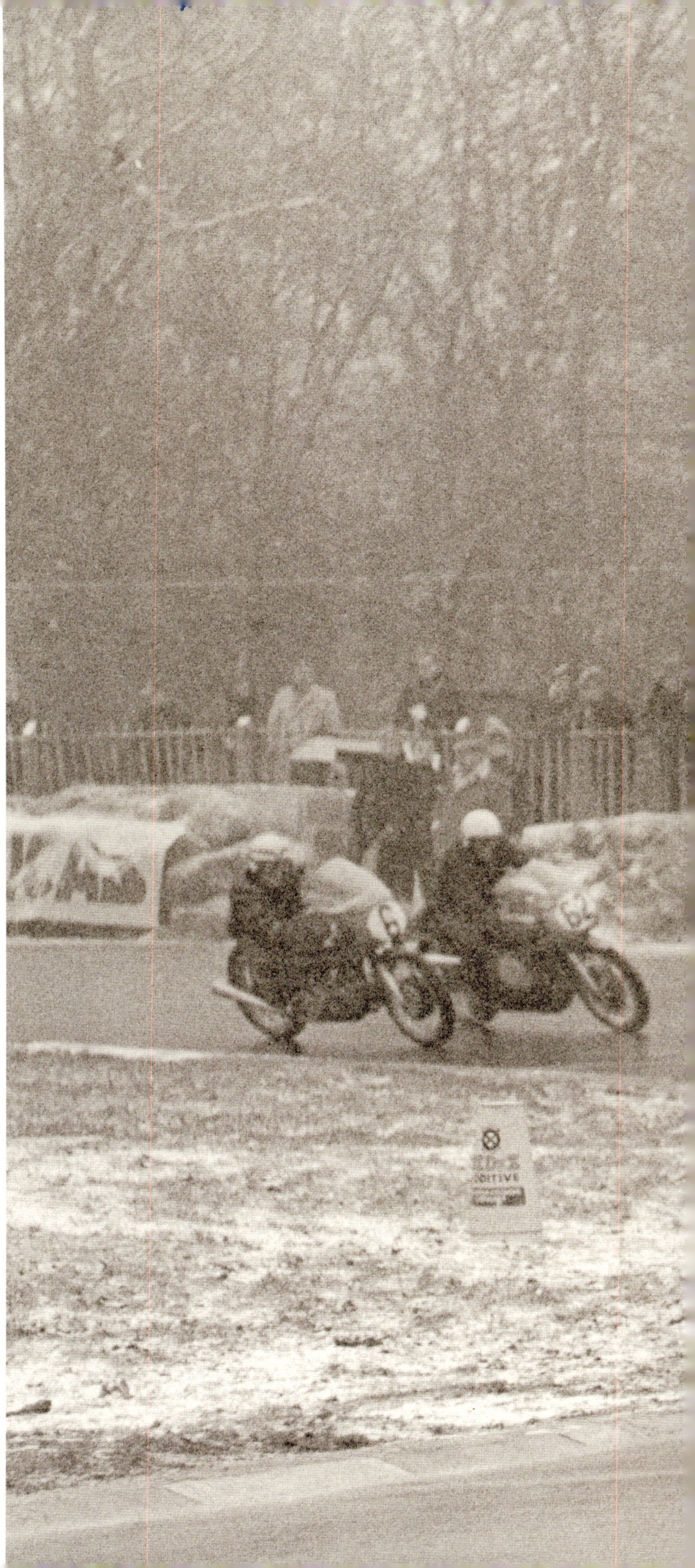

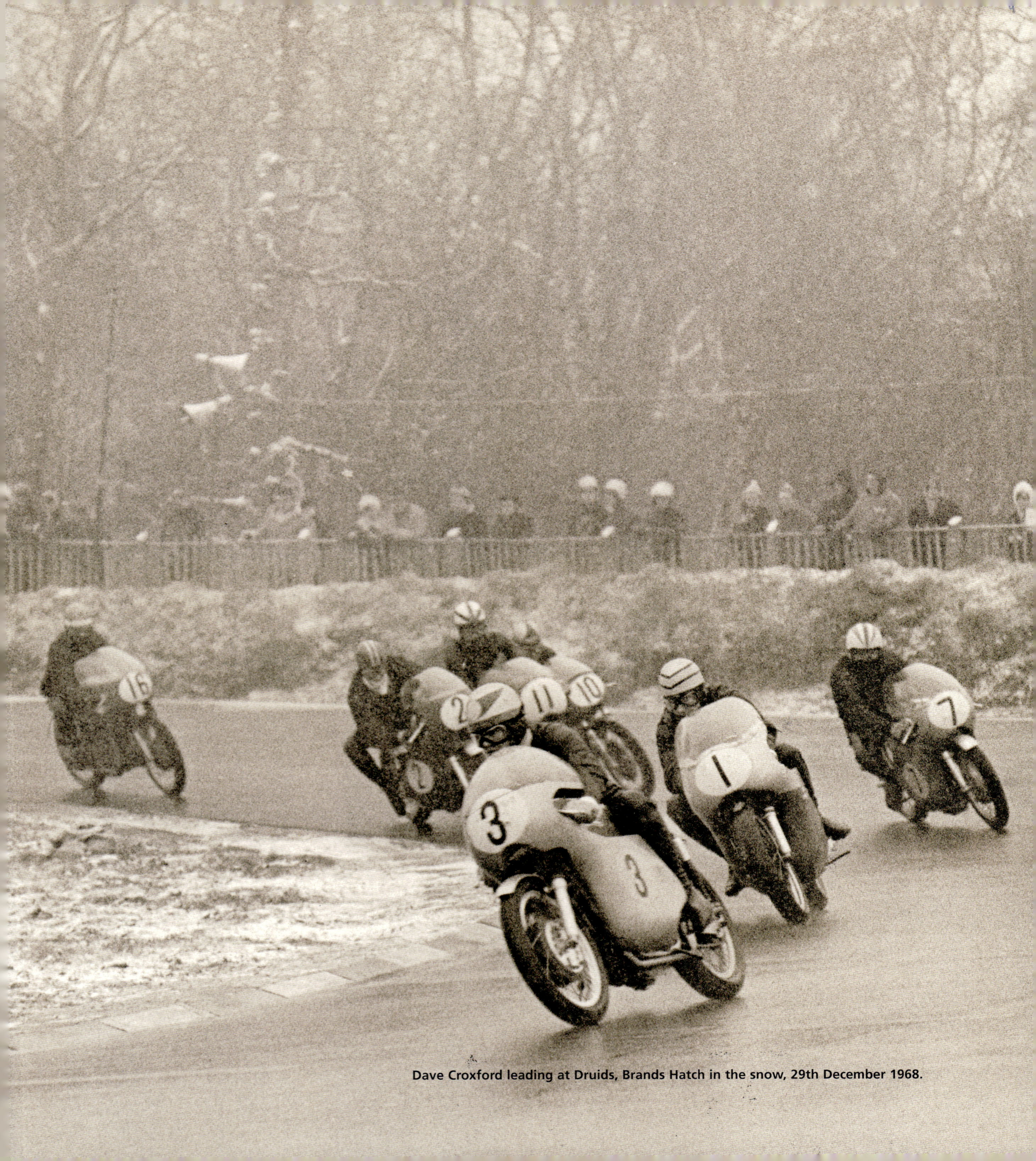

Dave Croxford leading at Druids, Brands Hatch in the snow, 29th December 1968.

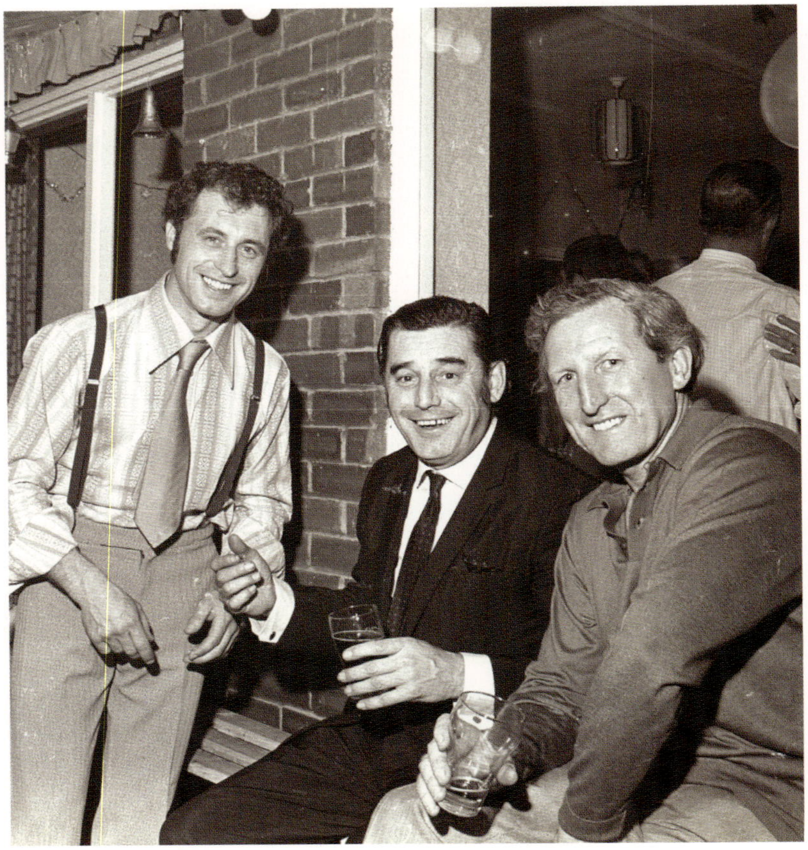

Me, Leslie Nichol and Vincent Davey (Gus Kuhn).

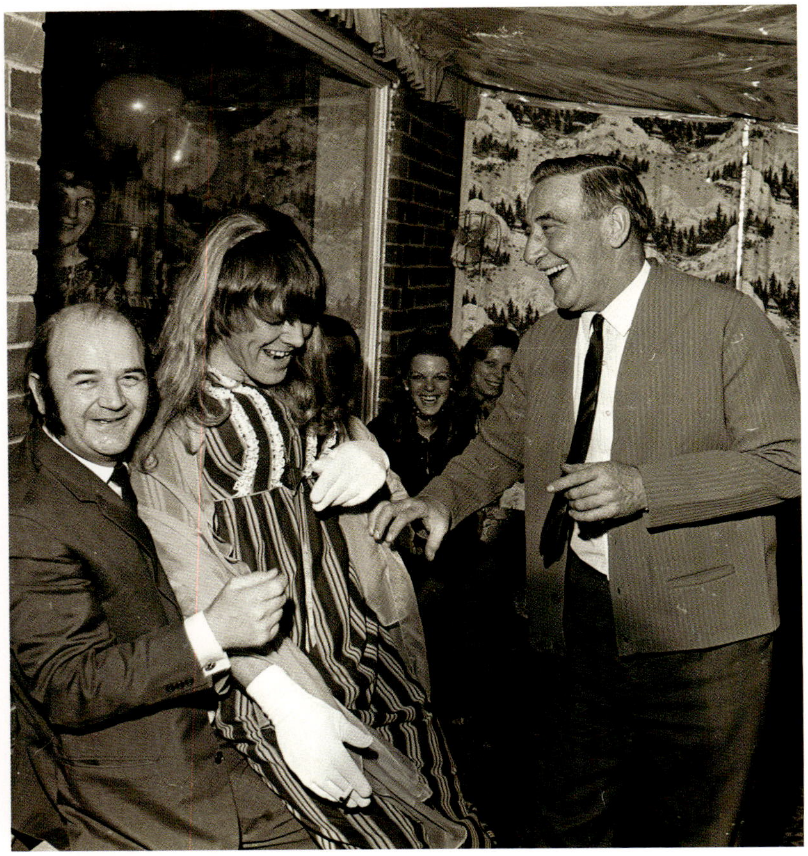

Left to right: John Brown, Dave Croxford and Jack Peddleton.

Croxford and Chandler tucked in behind. Alan Barnett, Brian Hunter, Coleshill Matchless, and Mick Andrew on the Gus Kuhn Seeley completed the leader board. Pickrell and Croxford pulled away then the Dunstall went onto one cylinder and Ray shuddered to a halt. 'Davy Crockett', now back in front had more time to wipe the snow from his goggles, and with Ron Chandler enjoying the handling of our lightweight Seeley 500, they crossed the finish line in first and second – a nice little earner for the two Londoners, with Brian Hunter third from Alan Barnett who slid off at Paddock Bend, with only 2 laps to go. Geoff Barry and Mick Andrew on their Seeleys came in fourth and fifth, and a certain Barry Sheene showing his worth with his skates on in the extreme conditions, finished sixth on a 282cc Bultaco, picking up £30.

More to come on that ridiculous day, the three wheelers had yet to perform their pirouettes in the slush. Chris Vincent as usual took the lead, but didn't allow for Andy Chapman who had taken over driving the controversial Greenwood Mini. Chapman in relentless mood, swirled the Mini three-wheeler through the drifting snow to catch Vincent, who couldn't see further than his back wheel as there was so much spray. So it was a complete surprise to Chris when the Mini swept by and took the £150 first prize plus £50 for the fastest lap. Chris Vincent's pride and pocket were both hurt. Remember how he took 'the piss' out of me when I was first beaten by the Mini, then driven by Owen Greenwood? Dick Hawes, riding the Seeley outfit fitted with our 650 twin CSR engine, finished a fine third, ahead of Norman Hanks and Mick Boddice.

This absurd day of racing in the extreme elements was actually a great end to a fantastic season of racing for the Seeley Company. Now it was time for me to celebrate at home with Joan, young Colin, and our many guests including riders, sponsors and friends alike!

1968 MAJOR ACHIEVEMENTS FOR SEELEY RIDERS:

DAVE CROXFORD:	36 Rostrum positions including 25 firsts
	King of Brands
	Master of Mallory
	Master of Thruxton
	Lord of Lydden
	500cc British Champion
	500cc Redex Trophy Champion
JOHN COOPER	North West 200 winner
	5th Isle of Man Junior TT
	3rd 500cc Dutch TT
	6th 500cc Belgian TT
	4th 500cc East German Grand Prix
BRIAN BALL	2nd Isle of Man TT
DEREK WOODMAN	3rd 500cc Belgian Grand Prix
	3rd 500cc Finnish Grand Prix
MIKE HAILWOOD MBE	1st Oulton Park International

DEREK WOODMAN and **JOHN COOPER**

seventh and eighth final positions in the 500cc World Championship.

Seeley fourth in World 500cc Manufacturers Championship

Dave Croxford, Ron Chandler, John Cooper, Brian Ball, Bill Ivy, Mick Andrew, Geoff Barry, Derek Woodman, Dick Hawes, Mike Hailwood MBE. all contributed to the fifty-nine rostrum positions inclusive of 38 first places. Overall there had been eighty-one positions in the first six.

THE RACING BIKE (£7,000 worth) THAT NEVER WAS

MOTOR CYCLING | LESLIE NICHOL

COLIN SEELEY is an industrious and inventive young engineer, currently striving to boost his own motorcycle factory.

He echoes the thoughts of Britain's racing fans when he asks angrily: "What has happened to the so-called British world-beating hope that certain sections of this country's industry planned to build?

"The scheme was launched about two years ago, backed by an Isle of Man lottery.

"I'm told the lottery folded, and only £7,000 was contributed towards the wonder bike.

"Well, what have we got to show for that £7,000, or doesn't anyone care? I do—especially when we have riders like Mike Hailwood sitting on the sidelines.

"It has been a costly night and day enterprise for me, building the only 500 c.c. racer that can be bought complete in Britain.

"Racing is my business. I don't say I could have built a world-beater—but I would have given the British public something for £7,000.

"My team re-built and re-styled our new 350 c.c. Seeley inside three weeks. We're short of cash for experiment.

"So we are, like a lot of other racing fans, annoyed that there never has been any official explanation. Isn't it time we had one?"

Enthusiasm

Seeley is no desk-bound executive. He is a former British sidecar champion who is stepping out of retirement to race again.

The men who planned the seemingly lost British record challenger should note his enthusiasm.

These include Sir Alfred Owen, millionaire industrialist who saved the B.R.M. racing car, his technical director Peter Spear, the British Cycle and Motor-cycle Industries Association, and officials of the Velocette organisation.

At the inauguration of the new enterprise, Spear stated: "There will be no big public unveiling. No fanfare of triumph until the bike is definitely known to be competitive."

Since then there has been no official statement saying whether or not the hoped-for racer has been scrapped.

Maybe it is considered that the racing fans of this country need no official explanation.

Starved as they are of any hope of parading a British grand prix winner—I think they do.

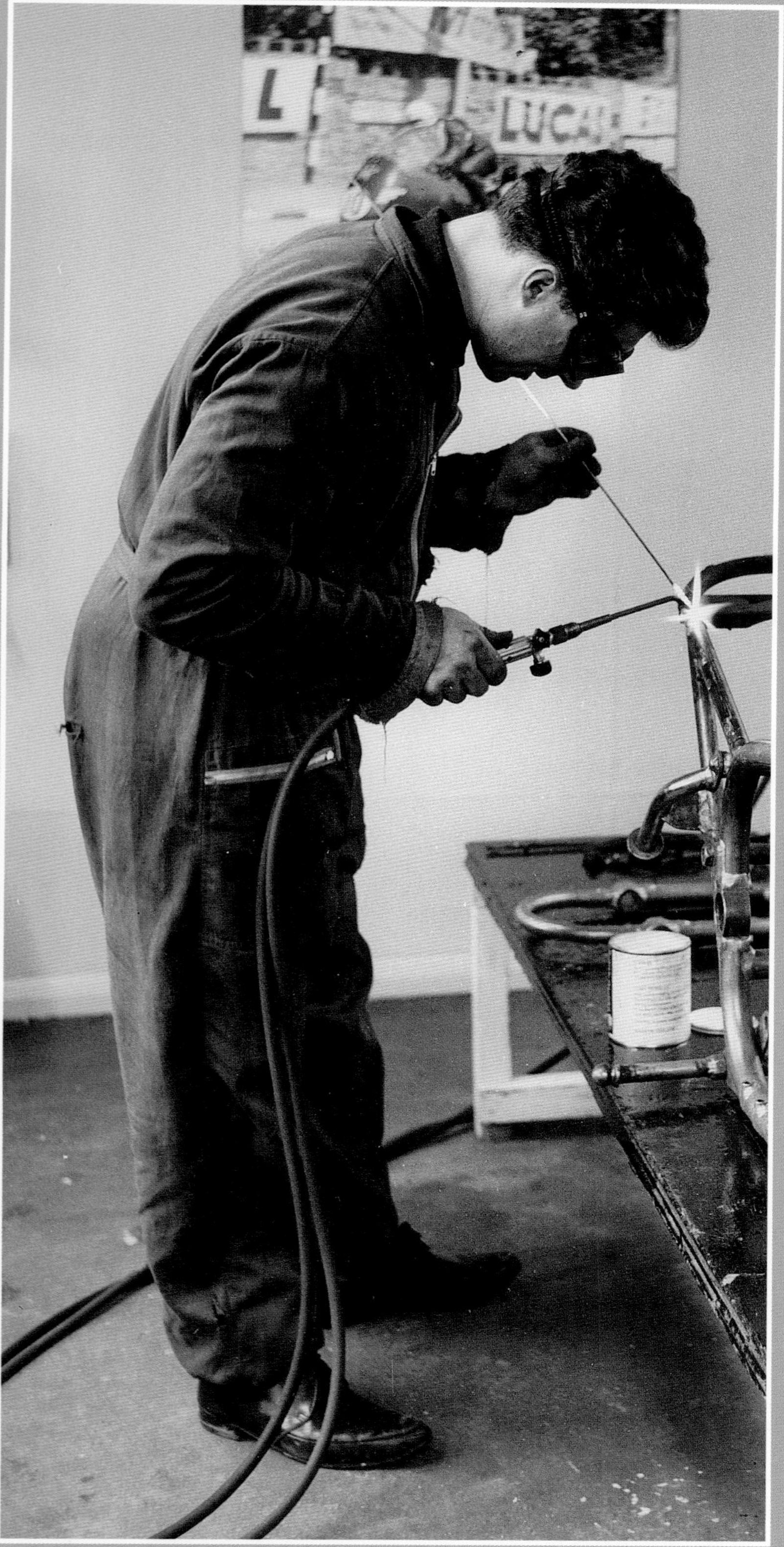

The boss's work is never done.

12 1969
DUCKING AND DIVING!

1969 had a sad start. My friend and employee, the sidecar racing ace, Terry Vinicombe died in January at 31, following a blood disorder. He was a great loss to Maureen his wife of two years, and his sidecar passenger of five years, John Flaxman. Colin Seeley Racing Developments would also miss Terry's considerable skills as a fabricator and our sport had lost a fine competitor. Terry, a member of the Gravesend Eagles Club, was best remembered, apart from other successes, for winning the first ever Isle of Man 750cc Sidecar TT in 1968 with John Flaxman.

Chairman of the Autocycle Union competition's committee for the last 18 years, and secretary of the South Midlands Centre, John C. Lowe also died in January, aged 64. Bob Lowe as he was known was described by Union Chairman Norman Dixon as 'hard working, extremely conscientious and scrupulously fair, one of British motorcycling's most respected figures.'

That same month editor of the Bantam Racing Club's magazine Alan Godfrey was killed while testing a 250cc Cotton at Brands Hatch. He was 22.

However, January was also a re-awakening for the racing fraternity. Bikes were wheeled out for the first time since being thrown into the shed at the end of the last season. Cobwebs removed, there were engines to rebuild, new tyres to be fitted – endless jobs to be attacked!! Could a new bike be afforded? What solo classes should be entered; 125, 250, 350, 500 or 750cc, club, national, international racing. Grand Prix, Irish Road Race Meetings, Isle of Man TT and Manx Grand Prix, choices, decisions, activity throughout the land, phones ringing, hibernation over!

Hundreds of racing motorcycles were stripped down, thousands of parts awaiting re-assembly, all frantically coming together in time for that first event. Like an ant hill, there wasn't much to see until the sun came out. Sadly, for Terry Vinicombe, Bob Lowe and Alan Godfrey the excitement of a new race season was over, a stark reminder to us all.

Our staff had increased along with plant and equipment. Each week the orders kept flowing in, making it difficult to manage business matters as well as building frames. I was lucky to attract AMC manager, 39 year old Ken Burnside to our organisation.

Ken was born at Westcliff-on-Sea in Essex, and when he was three moved to Bexleyheath. Later, but before me, he attended Erith's Northumberland Heath Secondary Modern School. Just before his fifteenth birthday he started work at the Woolwich Arsenal but after a few months as the second World War came to an end in June 1945, he decided to join the Navy, signing up for a 12 year stint. As a young seaman, Ken was allocated a home base at Chatham but was soon sent north to the Orkney Islands and Scapa-Flow for several months of high seas, winds and severe weather, a great introduction to seamanship. He was dispatched on a tour of the far east on HMS Constance, to Hong-Kong, Japan and Australia ,serving there for four years. After an urgent telegram reporting his 43 year old mother was very ill, he flew home, unfortunately not in time. His mother's death was a great shock for this 19 year old. As his father was also ill, Ken was granted six months compassionate leave. Finally he cut short his agreed Navy contract after five years service.

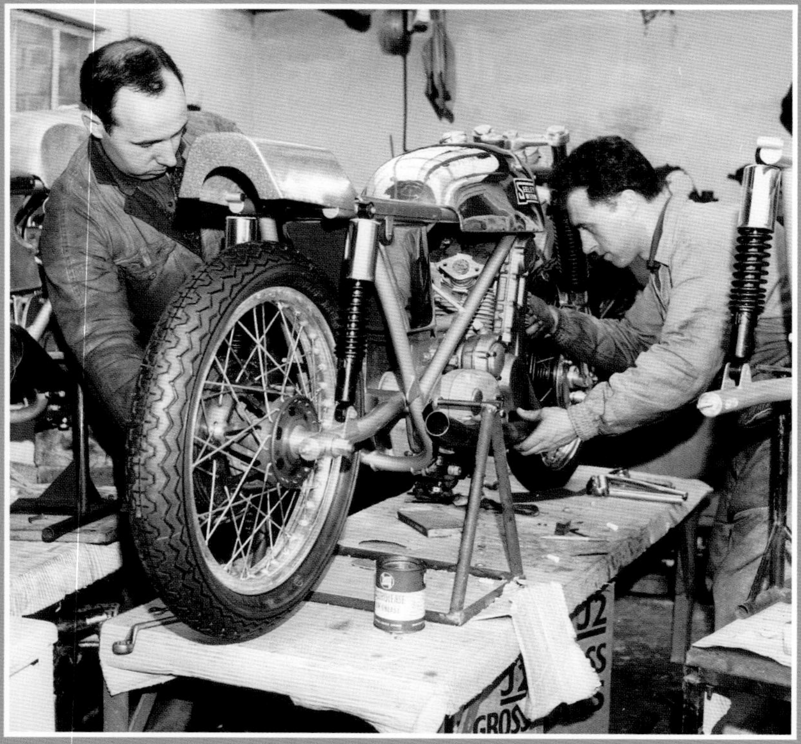

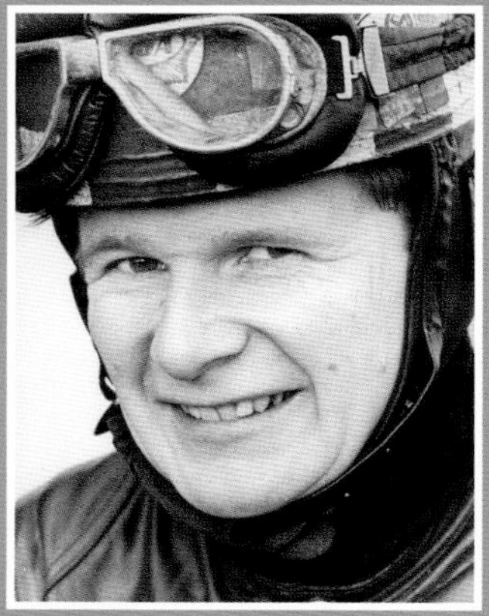

Terry Vinicombe.

Ron Chandler helping out.

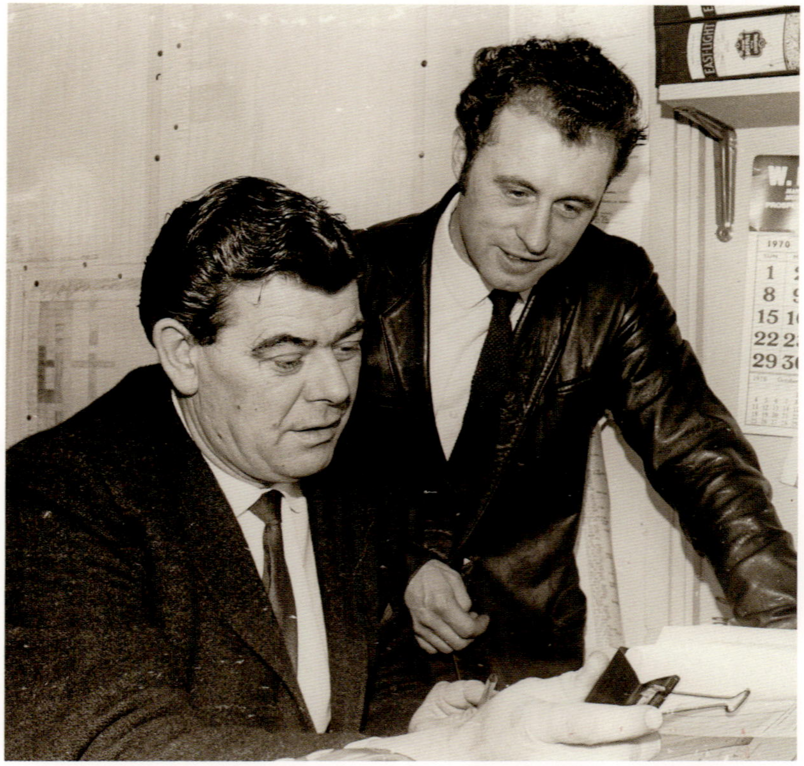

Me with Ken Burnside.

Needing a job, Ken intended to apply for work back in the Woolwich Arsenal, but on his way there he passed Plumstead's AJS and Matchless motorcycle factory. Attracted by the idea of joining the motorcycle industry he popped in and was offered a storeman's job at 2s 8d per hour, with a 3d. an hour bonus – not much but it was a start. Burnside took a real liking to his new position and rose through the ranks firstly joining the buying office, with over a 1,000 tons of various steel held in stock at any one time, promoted to control of export packing and dispatch and then finally production manager.

Jack Colver, a grass track star, a man I had raced against but never beaten, was in charge of the AMC motorcycle repair section. His father Bertie Colver, then approaching his eighties, was still working in the prototype department. Skills in those days were respected and valued, – nowadays for the more elderly it's work at B&Q or nothing.

Fred Neill at 73 in 1969, celebrated 50 years of service at the Matchless factory. In 1919 Fred was the chief tester, rode in the 1923 Junior TT and competed both as a trophy and vase team member in the International Six Day events. With 32 years as AMC service manager, and several books to his name, Fred had no intention of retiring.

Joint founder of the Matchless factory was MD Charles Richard Collier, 'Mr. Charlie' as he was known to most of his employees. Ken Burnside said he was the nicest person one could ever wish to meet. Charlier Collier won the very first Isle of Man TT on a Matchless single in 1907. He died 23rd August 1954 aged 69, the very month I started my motorcycle repair business.

Charlie was the last of the Collier brothers. His 34 year old half brother Bertie was killed in October 1941 after a motorcycle accident when testing his newly designed AMC teledraulic forks, as fitted to the Matchless G3L during the war. Harry Collier dying from an illness in 1944 aged 60. Sadly none of the brothers witnessed one of the best post war production periods 1954-1959 when 60 machines or more each day left the Woolwich factory and with 75% allocated to export, the home market waiting list was up to nine months. Unfortunately the handsome profits and record sales would not last. The accountants had taken over, led by Donald Heather. After the death of Charlie Collier, Heather cancelled the works racing programme and development, preferring to pay shareholders, rather than invest in new designs. With motorcycle sales declining in the early sixties, the situation started to look bleak for the industry. Sir Norman J. Hulbert MP joined the board as Chairman in November 1962 and proclaimed AMC was on the way to recovery. Perhaps he and his directors believed that buying the Norton concern for a suggested million pounds was the answer to their problems. That decision would prove an important factor in the final demise of the AMC Group.

The hybrid motorcycles subsequently produced totally confused the market, the dealers and the loyal customers of both AJS/Matchless and Norton Motorcycles. It was a costly mistake, setting AMC onto a downhill path. In 1966 the Sunday Times reported the AMC company to be £2.2 million in debt, then in August that year Barclays Bank called in the firm of Kenneth Cork, official receivers, to sort out the catastrophe! It took two more years for the shutters finally to close on the Plumstead factory. Industrialist Dennis Poore became involved in a most complicated takeover of the manufacturing and distribution rights of James, Francis Barnett, AJS, Matchless and Norton – a better story-line one could not have written. Years of skill and dedication by the founders of AJS and Matchless – AJ Stevens and the Collier Brothers, along with the loyal work force at Plumstead were allowed by directors of the AMC Group to fall into the abyss. In my own experience of many years of association with AMC, many of the directors were just shadowy figures in the boardroom with no passion, no commitment, no direction and often no real understanding of the business.

Ken Burnside, with 18 years at Associated Motorcycles had seen the rise and fall of this great company. The situation was crumbling fast with no rescue plan in sight. He reluctantly gave in to my persistence and joined Colin Seeley Racing Developments as General Manager, in control of the day to day running of the works and responsible for the purchase of raw materials. As well as Ken's vast experience, he brought other key workers from AMC to Seeley Racing.

Despite our success in 1968 with the MK2 Seeley framed 7R and G50, we decided to adopt the Eddie Robinson designed MK3 type frame as it was easier to manufacture was lighter and the engine could be removed and replaced in a very short time. The MK3 frame unit proved more versatile and with the fitting of Norton Commando engines for the Gus Kuhn Race Team, it became successful and reliable, although the MK2 Seeley is still seen as a favourite by enthusiasts.

Down at New Milton, Hants, the Rickman Brothers were 'all singing and all dancing' with the announcement of a four valve per cylinder 700cc conversion kit to suit 650cc Triumph engines. Designed by the Weslake Company and based on the Read Weslake racer, it was claimed the conversion would boost power of a 650cc Bonneville from 47bhp to 70bhp. With an American order for 1,000 Triumph kits, and the debut of the first Read-Weslake Metisse 500cc racer, business was booming for this progressive firm. With exports worth £100,000 Rickmans moved into a new 30,000 square foot factory. It made our efforts seem puny in comparison, working out of our ramshackle 'Old Forge' building with less than 2,000sq ft of floor space. Nevertheless, we were already producing a complete racer, (an ambition of Rickmans). Double world champion Phil Read having tested and raced the 500cc Weslake Metisse, decided to buy a financial interest in the project from Ray Creek of Reads of Leytonstone (no relation), forming Read Weslake Developments Ltd. Phil would soon find out that racing in a factory team with all the support was a different matter from making your own bike! Even Peter Williams was trying to get in on the act, having Ken Sprayson build a leading link Reynolds frame unit to suit the 500cc Weslake twin. Before it had even turned a wheel there were murmurs of a British world beater - so much misguided optimism!

First Seeley Mk3.

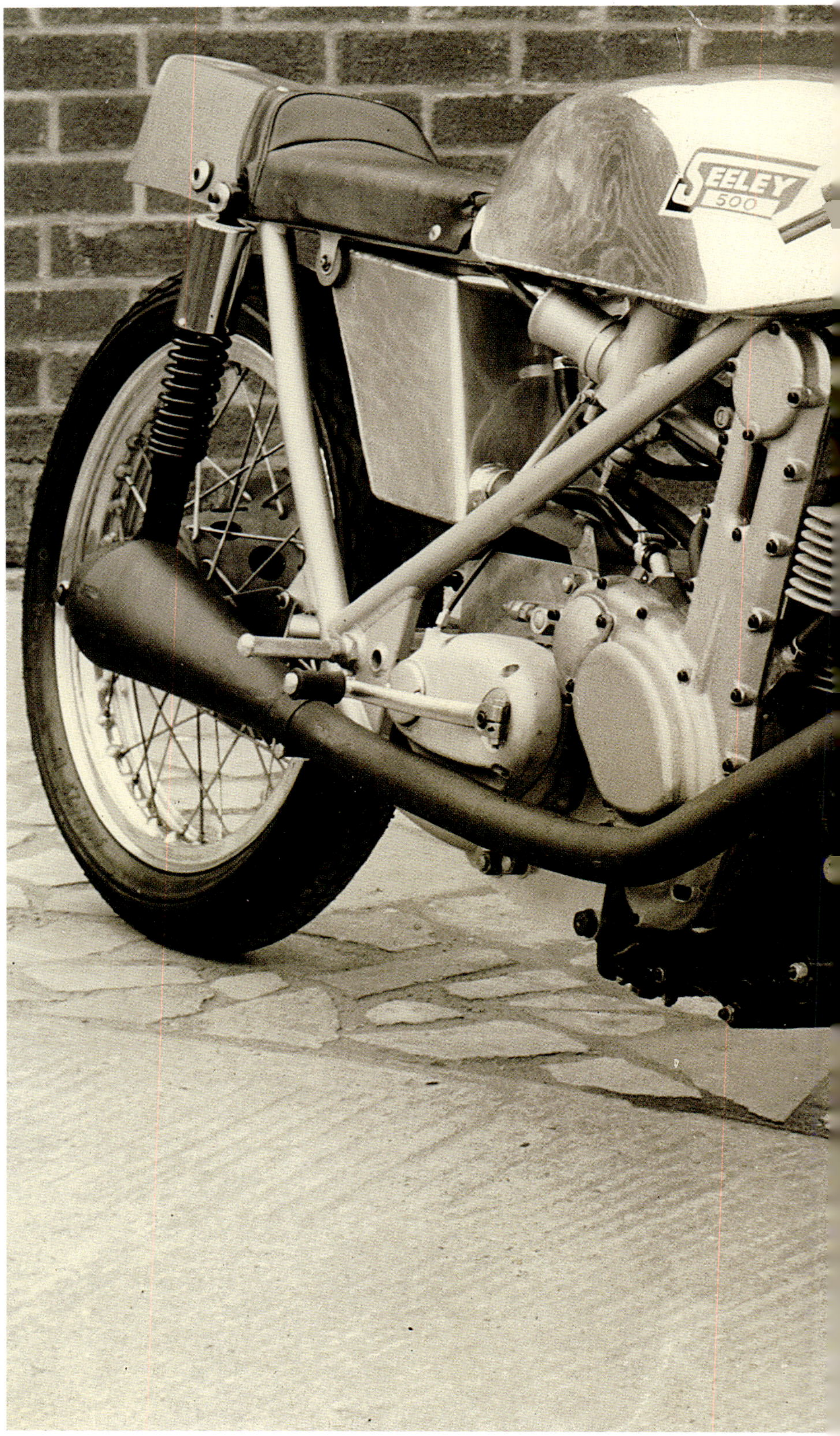

Local boy Micky Collins, winner of the 'Stars of Tomorrow' award at Brands Hatch in 1968, joined Ron Chandler as another test and development rider with us. Micky, a talented rider with huge potential was likeable and enthusiastic.

The 'feather in our cap' for the 1969 season was the order from Vincent Davey (boss of Clapham's Gus Kuhn Motors), for a brace of Seeley 350 and 500 machines for his newly established race team. Dave Croxford would join the talented Mick Andrew in the Gus Kuhn Team. Meanwhile, work would be carried out for the Gus Kuhn team on a prototype Seeley MK3 Norton Commando 750 racer.

John Blanchard having left us after the Fath-four debacle in 1967, spent 1968 somewhat in the wilderness of his racing career, until Essex motorcycle dealer Bill Chuck offered to sponsor him on a pair of MK2 Seeleys. Blanchard joined Brian Steenson, John Cooper, Ron Chandler, Derek Woodman, Steve Jolly, Rex Butcher, Mick Andrew and Dave Croxford as representatives of Seeley Racing on the track, we were out in force!

Yamaha had withdrawn their official works team at the end of 1968, Phil Read having won both 125 and 250cc World Championships, with Bill Ivy very close in both series. Despite that, Ivy, the 1967 125cc World champion for Yamaha was told not to expect any works machines as a gift - a smack in the face for this courageous ace. In 1968 at the Brands Hatch October Evening News International he had announced he had finished with the sport. For the 1969 season both Ivy and Read were offered the use of 250 and 350cc Yamaha production twin-cylinder racers but neither accepted. Read said he could not afford to compete in world championships at his own expense, as the 1968 season had cost him over £2,000. He would however consider racing Yamahas in selected meetings, if there was any start money! Yamaha were spending their money elsewhere, opening their own figure-of-eight 3 mile test track in the hills near Hamamatsu at a cost of around £1.25 million pounds.

No matter how good you are, it's very easy to get onto a downward slope when your future is uncertain. Possibly Bill Ivy was in that situation, hence his decision to retire. But once a racer, always a racer, and having had a couple of months out, the 'Maidstone

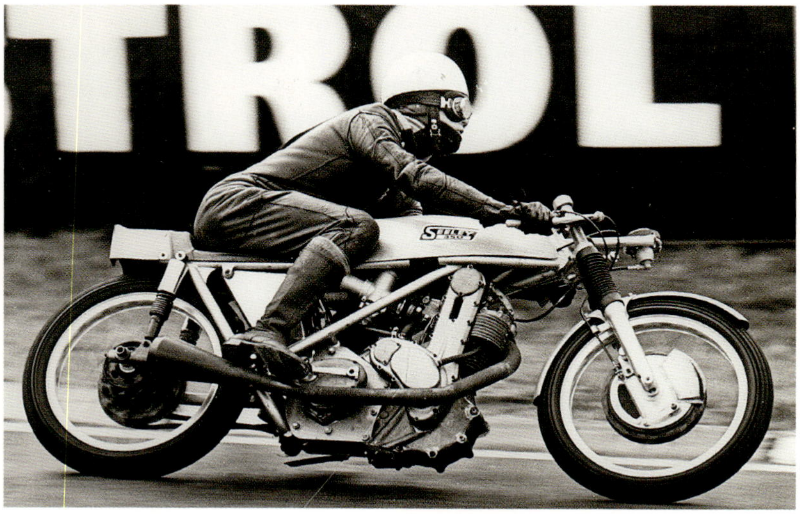

Micky Collins, 350cc Seeley, Brands Hatch practice, 18th January 1969.

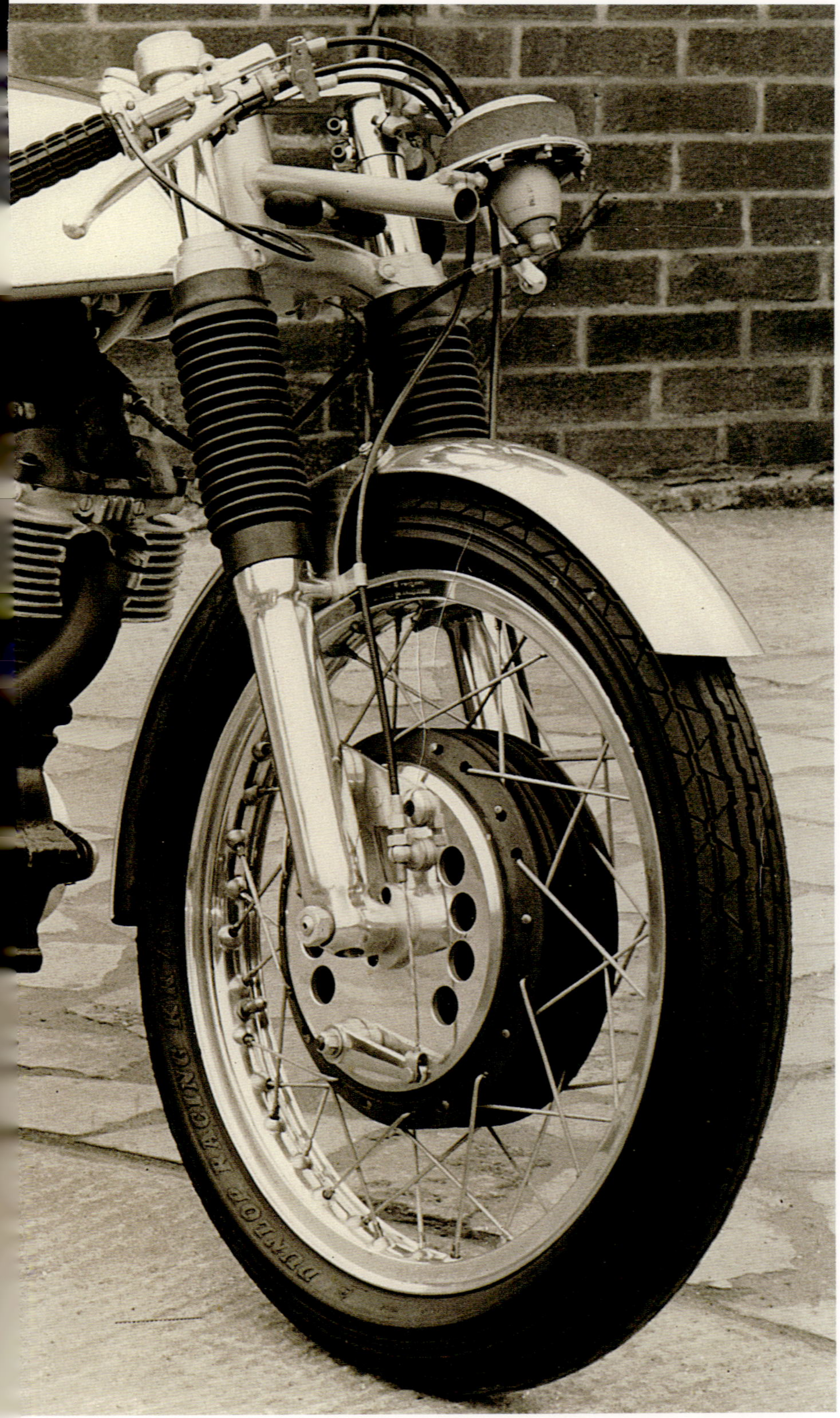

Marvel' bought himself a Formula 2 Brabham-Cosworth Ford racing car. The light was switched on again for this talented, committed man from Kent. Then the Czechoslovakian Jawa Factory offered him a works 350cc vee-four two-stroke to use at selected events.

Ivy planned to race the Brabham in the European Trophy series, open to non-graded drivers, along with other car events making 14 races in all. It would be a tall order to combine both, but perhaps encouraged by his good friend Mike Hailwood, he accepted Jawa's offer, becoming the second British rider to race an official Jawa factory bike, the first being George Patchett back in the 1930s. Mike Hailwood, nine times World Motorcycle Champion (1961-1967), in January of 1969, himself disillusioned for different reasons and accusing the FIM of having antiquated racing rules, announced his retirement from motorcycle racing to concentrate on his car racing career. The people's favourite, Mike-the-Bike would surely be missed, there must have been something in the water as the 31 year old scrambles-moto cross ace Dave Bickers also announced his retirement from the sport after 10 years of Grand Prix racing. He won the European Championship in 1960 and 1961 and six British titles in his career.

In 1969 ex-AMC employee, Jack Emmott, running his own racing supply business, introduced something new to his range - a super high-octane petrol used in aircraft piston engines, and known as Avgas. It had an octane rating ranging from 115 to 145, and was ideal for high performance two-strokes and priced at 10 shillings (50p) per gallon. Incredibly, it was available from Emmott's terraced house in Dupree Road, Charlton. Nowadays British Superbikes use a controlled octane fuel at over £13 per gallon.

Castrol Oils took over the support of Sammy Miller from Duckhams and also invested £1,750 in sponsoring the 1969 ACU British Road Racing Championships, with £200 apiece for the winners of each class at the end of the season, £100 for runners up and £50 for the third place men.

Another 1969 snippet; celebrating his 65th birthday was German Ernst Henne, who had achieved 76 world speed records between 1929 and 1937 for BMW. In 1931 Henne blasted his 750cc supercharged BMW through the timed kilometre at 149.33mph to take the world record. In 1936 Henne, who had pioneered full streamlined enclosure, riding a 500cc supercharged BMW, notched up an incredible 169.02mph at Frankfurt. The Nazi regime's desire for prestige in sport gave enthusiastic backing to such ventures.

Kawasaki, as part of their publicity drive to promote their completely new 500cc three cylinder supersports two-stroke in America, announced support for Dave Simmonds racing the model at the Daytona 200. More importantly 1969 would prove to be Dave's most successful Grand Prix season. Racing the works 125cc Kawasaki, he eliminated the opposition, winning 8 of the 11 Grand Prix events with two second places and only one retirement – a well deserved result for this popular Englishman.

Whilst Associated Motorcycles were going down the pan, up in the Midlands the BSA-Triumph Group thought moving into a stately home might be an answer to their problems. Umberslade Hall in Warwickshire provided a cosy retreat for an amazing 240 people working on design and development of new motorcycles for the group, headed at the time by Mike Nedham BSc. Mike had joined BSA in 1968 from Rolls Royce and was enthusiastic about this establishment, explaining the company needed a divisional engineering headquarters located within easy reach of the three main factories at Small Heath, Redditch and Meriden. David Garside had worked on rotary engines at Rolls Royce and he joined BSA to continue this work. BSA were keen to develop a new type of engine. Garside then moved from the BSA research centre at Kitts Green to Umberslade Hall. Later in 1969 Brian Steenson BSc, having graduated from Belfast University, joined BSA at Umberslade, recommended by Dr. Gordon Blair who via the University had been developing a 250cc twin-racing engine with support from BSA, a project CSRD would become involved in. Steenson worked in the research department under Mick Martin, brother of Brian Martin, BSA Competitions Manager and the moto-cross ace.

I visited this impressive stately home, with peacocks strutting the grounds, to discuss the supply of alloy tanks for their works moto cross bikes. The chief buyer Stan Hackett suggested that my company, CSRD, could be a sub-contractor to the research department, machining prototype engine parts and producing frames. Meanwhile, I secured an order for six tanks, at £35 each, considerably cheaper than the £90 they had been quoted elsewhere.

Harry Sturgeon had taken over the automotive division of the Birmingham Small Arms Company (BSA) from Eric Turner in 1964. As chairman he was considered to be taking the company in the right direction. Unfortunately, in 1966 Sturgeon then in his late fifties, was stricken by a brain tumour from which he never recovered. This was sad news for the family of Harry Sturgeon, and sad for BSA when Lionel Jofeh was appointed as Divisional Managing Director to succeed Sturgeon.

Lionel Jofeh, brought in from the aircraft industry, it was alleged by many, set the group onto a disastrous path. Adding to the problems in 1969 was the American launch of the Honda 750cc four. America, the Groups important and lucrative export market, would suffer after Soichiro Honda celebrating 10 years of marketing in the USA with one million sales confirmed the five speed, electric start Honda 750cc Four would sell for an average of £100-£150 less than the BSA Rocket 3 or Triumph Trident. By the end of June 1969 Honda had exported 5,000 CB750 models to Canada and the USA with production running at 2,000 units per month. Meanwhile, Lionel Jofeh, who may have instigated the move to Umberslade Hall, supported the Ariel 3 wheeler project. Using a 50cc Anker Dutch engine of which 20,000 were ordered, with two wheels at the back, one at the front and hinged in the middle, this project had women in mind. The idea, which had some merit, turned into a £2 million pound calamity. Eventual sales were mostly to dealers, who could not sell them on.

Later, in 1970 came the prestigious launch of the ill-fated 350cc double overhead cam twin cylinder five speed model, known as the BSA Bandit or Triumph Fury. At the London Dorchester hotel, over 500 worldwide dealers and importers were in attendance. Despite the 'pomp and ceremony' and Irish comedian Dave Allen telling the jokes, this did not prevent the tide of doom and the inevitable. Funds were evaporating fast so production of the Bandit/Fury was put on hold for two years and finally only a small number were produced. The Japanese must have been having a good laugh!!

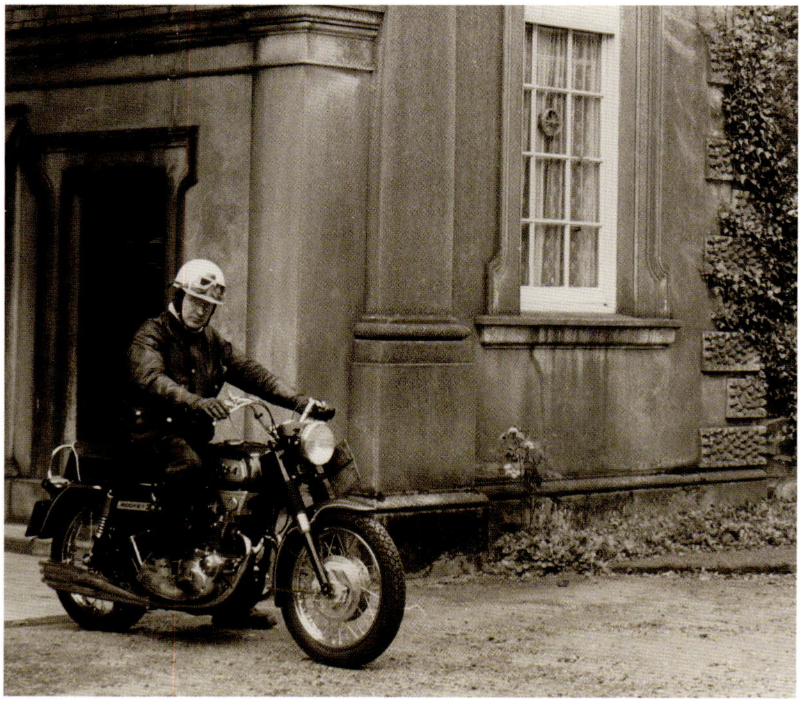

David Dixon at Umberslade Hall, testing the prototype BSA triple.

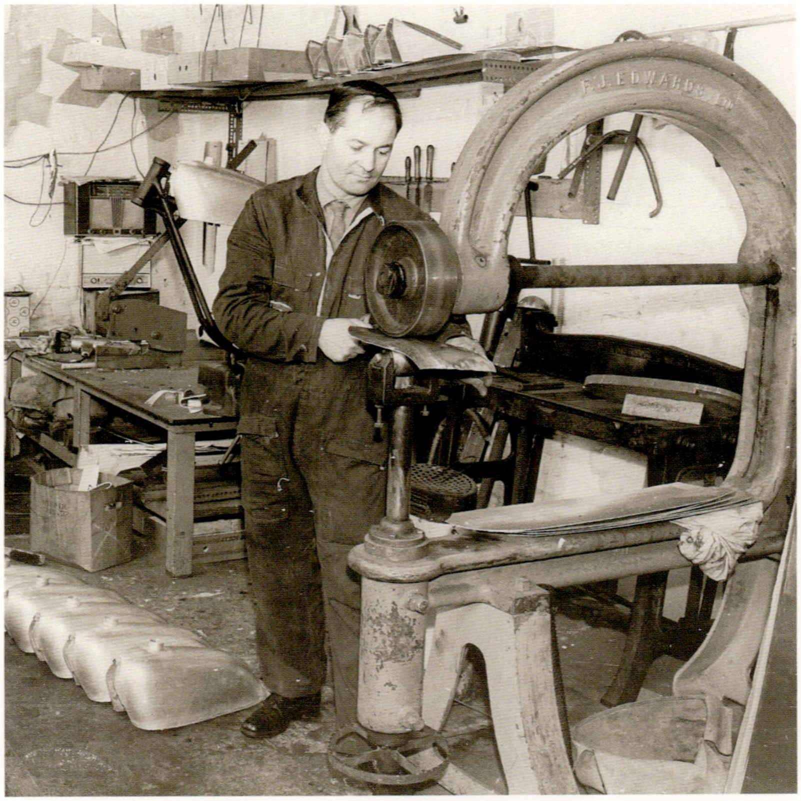

John Pearson making magic with aluminium.

In 1971 the racing arm of the group provided a little hope when Dick Mann on a three cylinder 750cc BSA won the Daytona 200, followed home by Gene Romero Triumph with Don Emdes BSA third, a clean sweep. Later that year John Cooper put his three cylinder 750cc BSA in front of the then-current World Champion, Giacomo Agostini, MV, at the long remembered Mallory Park 'Race of the Year'. Then Cooper outsmarted the Americans, winning the world's richest motorcycle road race at the Ontario Speedway on the BSA Triple - 250 miles of racing to take a prize purse of £6,040 in the Champion Spark Plug Classic.

The Company had tried to do too much too soon - sweeping changes in their models caused huge delays in design and development. This left assembly lines at Meriden and Small Heath often standing idle during the crucial winter period of 1970/71. Some $40,000 per month was spent on advertising in the USA to boost demand only to be met with a drastic shortfall on supply of machines. An £8.5 million loss in 1971 caused Lionel Jofeh to resign, and, for a job badly done he was reputedly given a £35,000 handshake - nice one!!

In November '71, my previous sidecar racing fellow competitors and employees of BSA at Small Heath, Mick Boddice, Peter Brown and Norman Hanks were among the 2,200 redundancies. A couple of weeks later Chairman Eric Turner announced that the Redditch works, in production since 1920, was to close. The 450 workers were offered jobs at Small Heath, which had just shed 2,200 workers! 'Slumberslade' Hall, (as known to the inmates), was also affected. Umberslade Hall and all those dreams of wonderful things, put into the darkness again, shrouded in emptiness and mystery for what might have been. The nickname was very apt according to Lawrie Watts, top technical artist at the time, who described his visit to Umberslade. Peering into the gloom and grandeur of this stately home, he recognised a colleague he hadn't seen for quite a while and greeted him by saying 'I thought you'd died some time ago!' Perhaps unfairly it summed up the BSA - Triumph group at that point. By the end of 1972 there were only nine out of the original 240 workers left at the stately home. The casualties included Jack Williams who had left the sinking AMC Company to join BSA! The one project and person surviving was David Garside and the rotary engine. Within months the whole company fell into the twilight zone, and the only signs of life at Umberslade Hall were the long feathered peacocks once more free to roam the grounds unheeded. Then in July 1973, with government assistance, industrialist Dennis Poore took over.

However, getting back to 1969, at which time we had 16 employees including John Pearson. John, a man with highly skilled hands could sculpt aluminium into exquisite shapes, hence all Seeley models would now be fitted with alloy fuel and oil tanks. Young Micky Collins along with Ron Chandler put the prototype MK3 though its paces at Brands Hatch, clocking up some 500 miles. With the loss of Terry Vinicombe I was struggling once again to keep up with frame production and was working very long hours! Concrete floors, fabricating and welding, did little for my legs and would cause me problems later.

The first road race of 1969, in near zero temperatures, was at Brands Hatch on 2nd March. Dave Croxford, now part of the Gus Kuhn racing team, carried on where he had left off in December. On the Kuhn Seeley, he won his heat and the final for the 500cc Redex Trophy event from Ray Pickrell Dunstall-Domiracer in second. Team mate Mick Andrew and Brian Hunter, both on Seeleys were fourth and fifth. Ray Pickrell got his own back on the big Dunstall-Norton in the 1300cc event. Local boy, Crayford's Pat Mahoney riding Joe Henderson's Aermacchi, put up a spirited performance to hold off Alan Barnett and win the 350cc event. Riding brilliantly, young Londoner Barry Sheene on a 125cc Bultaco, despite the plug lead coming adrift a couple of times, finished a close second to John Ringwood, MZ, with Jerry Lancaster, Honda, third.

Three days later Bill Ivy tested the latest 350cc four-cylinder Jawa racer at Brands and lapping just outside the lap record, was duly impressed with the bike's performance.

Less than a week later the British championship contenders arrived at Oulton Park where controversy hit this Castrol-sponsored event. Clerk of the Course, Vernon Cooper, reduced the all-important 350 and 500 events from 10 to 8 laps as poor weather conditions were expected. This ridiculous decision was made early morning and the day turned out perfect. Although the final instructions made clear the reduction in laps, most competitors referred to the printed race programme.

In the 500cc race Dave Croxford, Kuhn-Seeley, won his heat with Alan Barnett, Kirby-Metisse, close behind all of the way. As they swept into view to complete 8 laps, Barnett was just ahead. To Croxford's surprise the chequered flag was out, leaving him in second place with team mate Andrew, Kuhn-Seeley, third. Fresh from his win at Brands, Pat Mahoney was equally surprised to see the flag in the 350cc race. He had slip-streamed Tommy Robb, Aermacchi, throughout and was preparing to pounce on the last of the 10 laps. Croxford on a new Kuhn-Seeley 7R finished fourth holding off the challenge of hard-charging Brian Steenson, Aermacchi. The organisers were quick to point out that the changes in race distance had been notified in the final instructions, very convenient but robbing the fans of race action.

The circus then packed its bags for Snetterton the next day, a Pickrell-Dunstall benefit in both 500 and 1000cc events. Dave Croxford and Mick Andrew on Kuhn-Seeleys were third and fourth in the 500cc race, then second and fourth in the unlimited event. Dick Hawes on the Seeley G50 outfit got second place to winner Tony Wakefield, BMW, in the 500cc sidecar race. Over at Cadwell Park that same Sunday, the Derbyshire Flyer 'Mooneyes' Cooper recorded a fine double on his Seeley 7R and Seeley G50. three wins, three seconds, two thirds and three fourth places, not bad for the Seeley marque that weekend.

Within days on 16th March, Alan Barnett, Croxford, Pickrell, Tait and Mahoney were battling once more at Mallory Park's first national meeting. The 350cc race was a

Dave Croxford.

humdinger between Pat Mahoney, Aermacchi, Barnett, Kirby-Metisse and Croxford, Kuhn-Seeley, in the 15 lap scrap. Barnett got the verdict with Mahoney second and Croxford third, but all so close the timekeeper could not separate them.

The 1000cc race was a cliff-hanger. This time Percy Tait, Ray Pickrell and Tony Smith, 654 BSA, joined the pack along with the front runners of the 350 event. Alan Barnett made the early running on the 500 Kirby-Metisse then with 5 laps to go the mob in pursuit led by Tony Smith and Croxford caught the Kirby runner. On the last lap as they swept into the long right-hander at Gerard's, the 'Ruislip Rebel' held a narrow lead over Tony Smith's big BSA. As they rushed down the back straight the Kuhn-Seeley engine cut out dead with a magneto failure. Croxford coasted to a halt, having recorded the fastest lap along with Percy Tait. Tony Smith was victorious, just ahead of the 'sheep farmer' Percy Tait, Alan Barnett, then Ray Pickrell 745cc Dunstall-Norton. My old adversary Chris Vincent continued his winning ways in the sidecar event, BSA's first and second with Peter Brown ahead of Tony Wakefield, BMW, third.

Also on 16th March at Rimini Circuit the Italian race season kicked off with Renzo Pasolini scoring a double in the 250cc and 350cc events on Benelli machines. Pasolini, racing in his home town received huge support. The crowd roared as he beat Giacomo Agostini, MV, in a close fought 350cc encounter over 22 laps of the 2 mile long seaside circuit. The world champion Agostini making no mistakes in the 500cc race, winning from Angelo Bergamonti, Hannah Paton, Alberto Pagani, Linto third with Paulo Campanelli, Seeley G50, in fourth place.

For the 'King of Brands' meeting, competitors requested that straw bales be put in front of the steel barriers at the top of Paddock Hill to improve safety. This request was refused on the grounds that the car drivers complained that their cars suffered less damage hitting the steel barriers than straw bales. ACU's Ken Shierson said there was no need for straw bales as the bank had been moved back. It was stale-mate. A great help from our sports representative. Human life - car damage!

The Rickman Brothers continued with their latest project - an association with Friedi Munch - and fitted the 500cc twin double overhead camshaft Horex designed engine into their Rickman rolling chassis. Castrol confirmed support of the 497cc Weslake racing engine with a substantial cash payment to Harry Weslake, the 70 year old head of the Weslake Engineering Company. This would boost Phil Read's partnership in this project and the plan to market a Read-Weslake Metisse racer.

Easter heralded the opening of the Brighton Motorcycle Show at the Metropole Exhibition Centre. Star of the show was the brand new Honda CB750 four. A small show in comparison with Earls Court, it attracted 18,000 visitors in the first three days over that Easter weekend and nearly 33,000 in all. Although my company was not represented we were listed in the reports and 'Motorcycle' buyers guide as the only British manufacturer of complete road-racing machines:

347cc Seeley 7R Racer	£685. 0s. 0d.
496cc Seeley G50 Racer	£825. 0s. 0d.
Complete racer less engine and gear box	£329. 0s. 0d.
Basic frame assembly	£ 85. 0s. 0d.

The Easter weekend also brought success for the Seeley marque. Derek Woodman won the Oulton Park International 500cc event, Micky Collins the 350cc race at Snetterton, Ken Redfern the 350cc and Steve Jolly the 500cc event at Cadwell Park. Mick Andrew won the 350cc race at Crystal Palace, and in Ireland, Brian Steenson was taking well to his new Seeley 500, winning the 500cc race with the fastest lap and a new record at the popular Kirkistown short circuit.

On the 13th April in north eastern Italy, the fifth in a series of international races was held at Cesenatico, a street circuit. In the 350cc event Giacomo Agostini, MV, after suffering four defeats in a row beaten by 'arch-rival' Renzo Pasolini, Benelli, was out to get revenge. In the 55.92 mile race, Pasolini led for the first 3 laps then a determined Ago got ahead but Renzo was soon back in front, cheered on by his fans. As the pace quickened, Pasolini's riding became more lurid, and coming upon back markers, Ago took his chance and shot ahead to take a well-deserved win. Bill Ivy had his first competitive ride on the works 350cc Jawa four, coming home in seventh place. The Jawa was plagued by a misfire then finally seized, not a good start, and perhaps a taste of what was to come. Agostini continued his winning ways that day with an easy win in the 500cc event with John Cooper bringing the first ever Seeley G50 home in sixth spot with Paulo Campanelli's Seeley seventh. 'Little' Bill Ivy's problems were not over. His riding kit was stolen from his car after the Cesenatico event so it was a call to Mike Hailwood for help.

In mid-April one of the most celebrated and controversial motorcycle designers, 82 year old Granville Eastwood Bradshaw died, and in the same week originator of the Cotton Motorcycle Company, Bill Cotton passed away aged 78, at his Gloucestershire home.

Sixteen national and international events had already been held within eight weeks, plus of course numerous club meetings, and next up would be the third round of the Castrol sponsored series at Wiltshire's 1.84 mile Castle Combe Circuit on the 26th April. The enthusiastic boss of Gus Kuhn Motors, Vincent Davy and his team took another step towards his aim of winning both 350 and 500cc British Championships when Dave Croxford took the honours in the 500 event putting his Kuhn-Seeley ahead of Percy Tait and Alan Barnett, with Mick Andrew in fifth despite being rammed at the start. In the 350cc race the fast improving stylish Mick Andrew on a brand new Seeley 7R, delivered only days earlier, took the race by storm, ahead of tough guy Pat Mahoney, Aermacchi, Alan Barnett, Kirby-Metisse, with Croxford in fourth place suffering a collapsing rear wheel. Young Micky Collins, Seeley, was ninth in front of Dennis Trollope, Aermacchi, tenth.

Immediately after Castle Combe the Kuhn team dashed off to the Lydden Circuit where on the following day Andrew gave his Seeley 7R another win in the 350cc race. Crox came second. Then both on 750 Norton Commandos, Croxford won ahead of Andrew second, and Barry Ditchburn, 650 Triton, third.

That same weekend, in Holland at the International Tilburg event, 25,000 fans were delighted when local ace Jan Kostwinder, riding a brand new TR2 Yamaha, held off the challenge of John Cooper, Seeley 7R, who although recording the fastest lap and leading in earlier laps, could not match the speed of the Yamaha - a sign of what was to come. In the 500cc race on his Seeley 'Mooneyes' was master, although Godfrey Nash, Norton, put up a spirited performance, with Steve Jolly on his new Seeley G50 third.

'Mooneyes' was one of our most loyal customers and fast becoming a good friend. He was reluctant to give up riding the delightful Seeley 7R, and it was delightful. The original designed AJS 7R engine was a great, reliable, smooth engine and fitted to the lighter

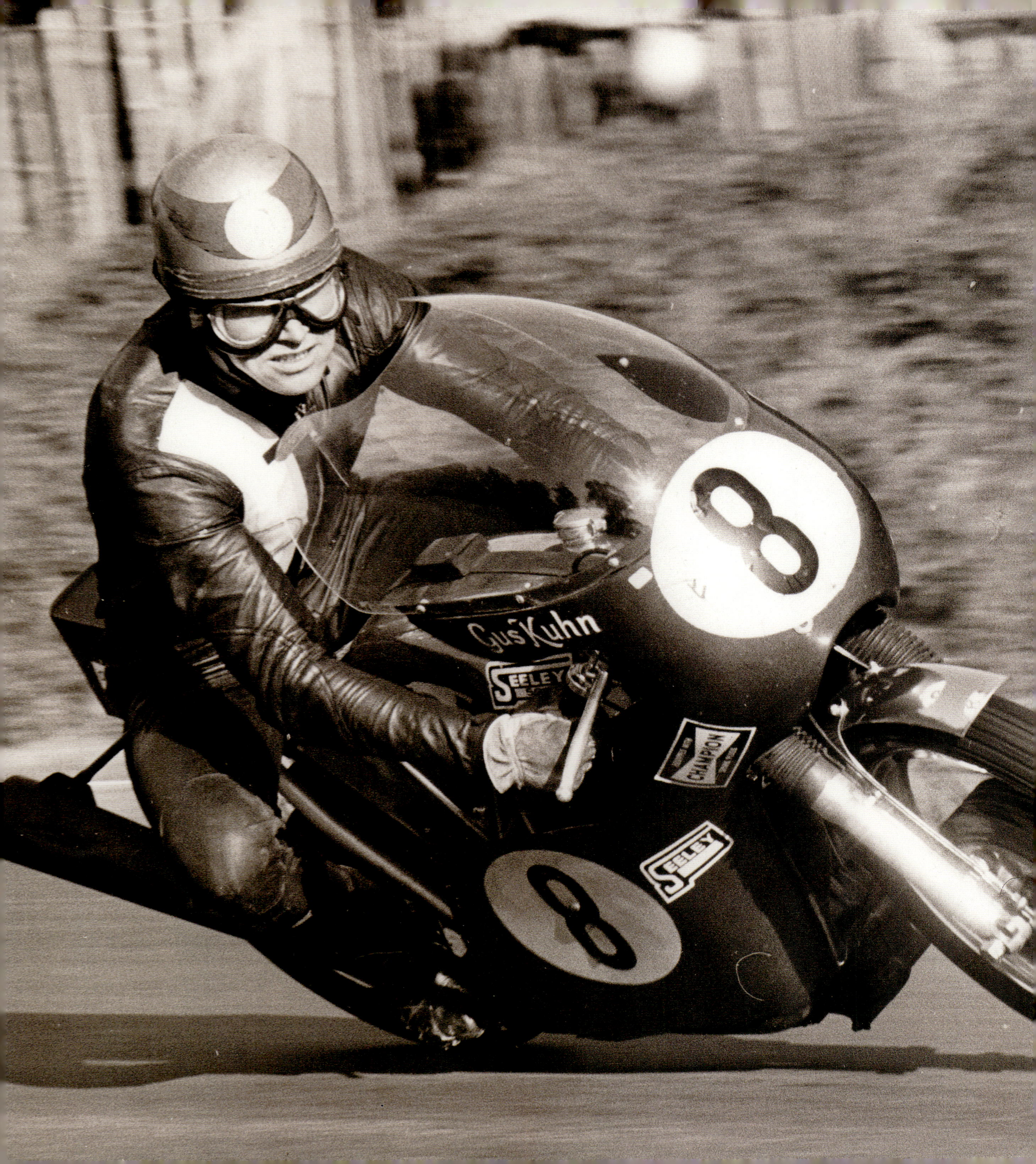
8
Gus Kuhn
SEELEY
CHAMPION
SEELEY
8

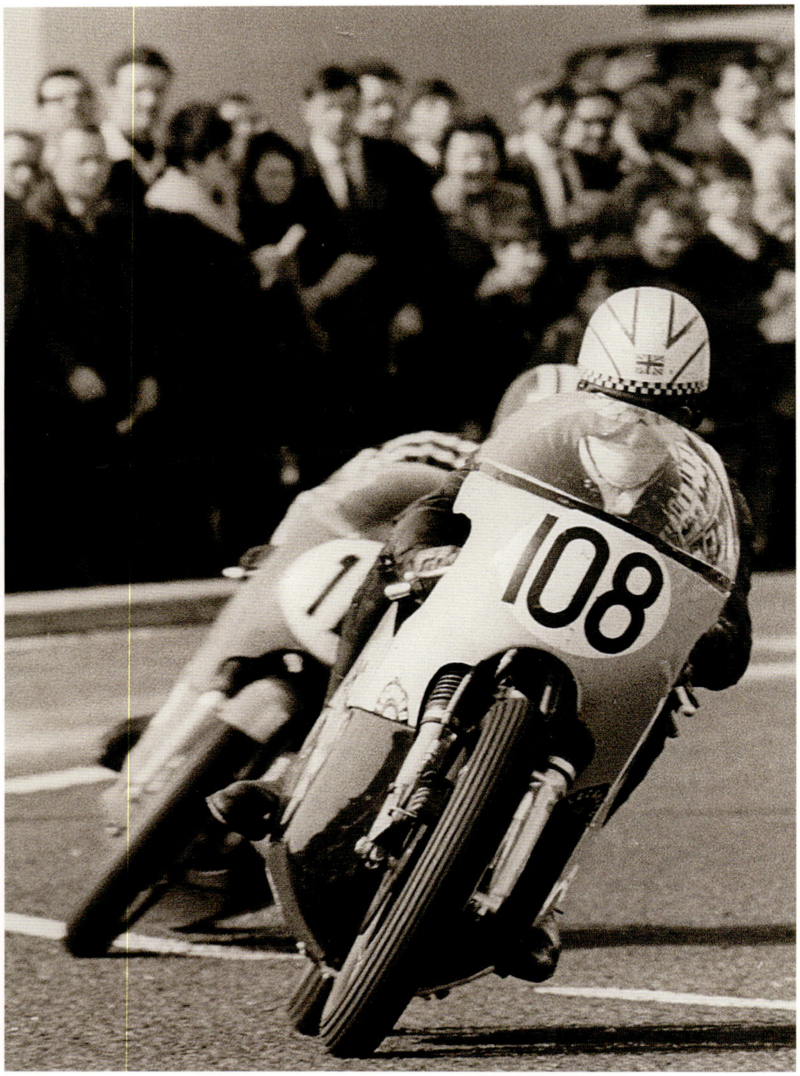

John Blanchard, Chuck - Seeley G50, winning the North West 200, at an average speed of 102.6mph, just ahead of Brian Steenson, on the Mick Mooney - Seeley G50.

smaller Seeley chassis unit, provided a machine which was a joy to ride, but falling down on performance against the incoming 250 and 350cc Yamaha twins. So we understood when John Cooper ordered a pair of new Yamahas. However, we were not finished yet, and later that season I would work on an improved lightweight Seeley 7R version.

In May 1969, the ever-progressive Dennis Poore, boss of the Norton-Villers Group announced that Alex Issigonis, the designer responsible for the record-selling BMC Mini, although continuing to work for British Leyland, would join Norton Villiers as a consultant on the design of new machines. Alex Issigonis filled the post left by Director of Engineering, atom scientist Dr. Stefan Bauer, who had moved to the BSA-Triumph Group – Umberslade Hall! The appointment of Alex Issigonis was perhaps largely to do with publicity, Dennis Poore had been at Cambridge with Issigonis.

The true design work at Norton-Villiers was being carried out by the talented Bob Trigg and his team. In fact, a while after the demise of Dennis Poore's empire Bob Trigg would join Yamaha and was responsible for the styling of the well received LC250 and 350 machines and played an important part at Yamaha in many designs up to more recent times.

Derek Carpenter, after 10 years with the Dunlop Motorcycle Division moved to the commercial department with 24 year old Paul Butler taking his place. Butler is now race director of Moto-GP, working alongside partner-in-crime, the very astute and ambitious Mike Trimby.

The 1969 version of the Hannah-Paton 500cc six speed twin racer claiming 60bhp at 10,000rpm arrived, with replica models available later in the season priced at £1,750, twice the price of a Seeley G50 but the Paton bike looked good – how good was another matter.

At the German Grand Prix, held in blistering sunshine at the ultra-fast Hockenheim circuit, on 11th May, 100,000 spectators saw Bill Ivy back in action on the Jawa 350cc four. Determined to answer criticism from the factory regarding his commitment to Jawa, the 'Maidstone Marvel' was on sparkling form, giving Giacomo Agostini a run for his money in the 23 lap 96.72 mile 350cc event. On the works MV, Ago piled on the pressure. 'Little Bill' could only finish second if the seizure-prone Jawa kept going. With only one lap to go, the Jawa faltered, but Ivy feathered the throttle with one hand and with the other waited to grab the clutch lever. Just over the finish line, the engine stopped, not a seizure but an empty fuel tank. Lucky for our hero, and with team mate Franta Stastny bringing his Jawa into third place, it was a good result for the Czech factory.

The association with Brian Steenson had brought us into contact with Dr. Gordon Blair who with Mervyn Johnson had designed a 250cc two-stroke racing engine. I was asked to build a rolling chassis for this unit, expected to product 55bhp at 12,000rpm. Production of the Seeley 7R and G50 range kept us pretty busy, but I was keen to be involved in new projects. At Belfast University we discussed the project and collected a dummy engine. I met up with Brian Steenson and Raymond McCullough, a very capable rider and knowledgeable technician who worked with Dr. Blair. It was interesting but some of the discussions were beyond me. I had left school at 15 with no qualifications and felt nervous as I walked the corridors of learning. All those academics were above my head. My visit would coincide with the North West 200 meeting that Saturday, the 24th May, so I chose to stay for one of Ireland's best road race events. What a joy it was. John Blanchard on his new Chuck-sponsored Seeley G50 delighted the 45,000 spectators lining the 10.7 mile Port Stewart-Coleraine-Portrush Road circuit, coming home ahead of the dogged Irishman Brian Steenson on his Mick Mooney sponsored Seeley G50. He had pushed Blanchard throughout the 96.3 mile race. Blanchard was on top form and led from start to finish, averaging 106.26mph with a new race and 500cc lap record at 107.69mph. Percy Tait on the works Triumph held third place until caught by Tommy Robb on a Joe Ryan Norton, then Dennis Gallagher, Matchless, and John Cooper, Seeley. 5th, Ron Chandler 7th, Bill Smith on the Hannah-Paton after a poor start made ground, but ended in disaster when oil on the rear tyre caused him to crash. Then the Triumph suddenly died, and Tait retired leaving the popular Irish star Tommy Robb in a rostrum position. Gaining first, second and fifth positions for my machines was a great result. I went home very pleased, as did Rodney Gould, having won both 250 and 350cc events with record laps in both. That bank holiday weekend the fourth round of the British Championship was held on the Sunday at Mallory Park, and the Evening News Brands Hatch event and Cadwell Park on the Monday.

Mallory Park gave mixed results. In the 350cc race Rex Butcher, Quaife-Seeley, Croxford, Kuhn-Seeley, and Pat Mahoney, Aermacchi, each took turns as pacemaker until Cliff Carr, Yamaha, came through to break the pack and claim the lead, leaving Croxford and Mahoney scrapping for second. Then on lap nine the chain fell off the Seeley and although Crox stopped to refit it he was out of the equation - shame! So it was Carr from Mahoney with Dave Simmonds, Kawasaki, third. The 'Ruislip Rebel' was soon back in action and won the 1000cc race on his 500cc Kuhn-Seeley, Paul Smart, 750 Norton, and Barnett, Kirby-Metisse, second and third. No stopping Croxford that day. On the 750 Kuhn Norton, Dave won the 30 lap production race from Ray Pickrell, 750 Dunstall. Over at Snetterton Combine's national event, Ivan Hackman won the 500cc race on his Seeley G50.

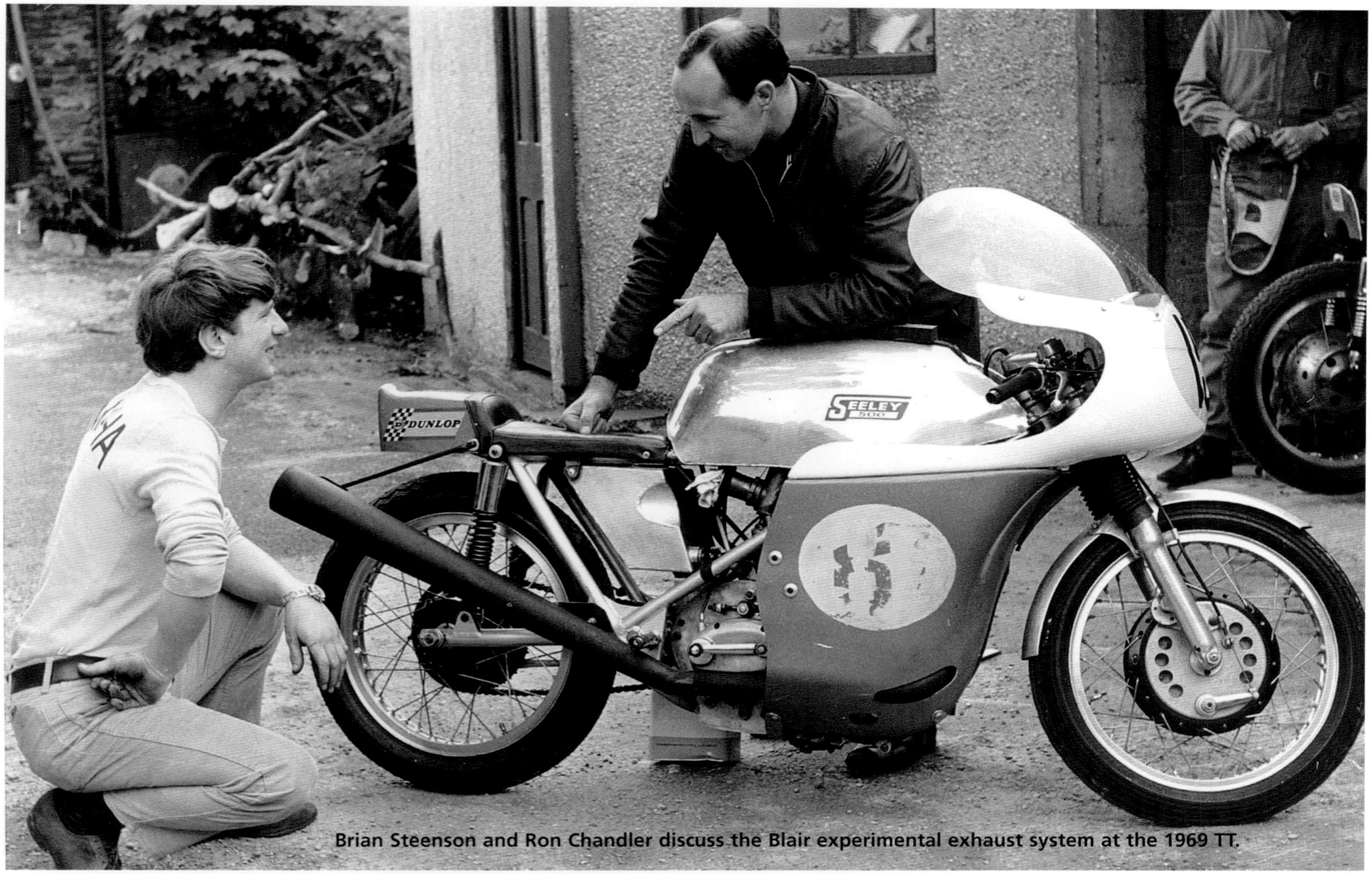

Brian Steenson and Ron Chandler discuss the Blair experimental exhaust system at the 1969 TT.

On Monday 26th May at Cadwell Park misfortune hit John Cooper. On the last lap of the 350cc race on his brand new Daytona Yamaha, while trying to regain the lead from Terry Grotefeld's Daytona Yamaha, he crashed at the Gooseneck, sustaining concussion and a suspected broken collarbone. This put 'Mooneyes' out of the Isle of Man TT for that season. In the same race Steve Jolly who had bought Cooper's Seeley 7R and had fallen the day before at Mallory Park, finished in fourth place.

On the same day, over at the Evening News sponsored Brands Hatch meeting held on the short circuit, honours would be truly shared, Stuart Graham, Suzuki, winning the 125cc race with a record lap from World Championship leader in that 'tiddler' class Dave Simmonds, Kawasaki, Barry Smith, Derbi, third with Barry Sheene, Bultaco, ahead of Chas Mortimer in fifth spot.

Rod Gould took the 250cc race on his Yamaha but could not repeat that success in the 15 lap 350 event. Phil Read, the current World Champion on his first visit to Brands that season, riding a stock TR2 Yamaha, made an appalling start. He then tore through the field to catch Gould and Ivy just as Ivy's Yamaha went sick with ignition trouble. Read, on a charge, soon slipped ahead of Rod Gould. A great dice for third place was taking place between local boy Pat Mahoney, Aermacchi, and the Gus Kuhn pairing of Croxford and Andrew. Then Mahoney, approaching Paddock Hill at speed crashed, miraculously with no bones broken. Croxford, Andrew, Chandler and Butcher took third, fourth, fifth and sixth places on Seeley 7Rs, an encouraging result.

The 20 lap 500cc Redex Trophy race was another battle between the Metisse rider Barnett and Seeley regular Croxford, with Dave getting the verdict by half a wheel, Ron Chandler, Seeley, third with Andrew and Brian Hunter, Coleshill-Seeley, fifth and sixth. The 1000cc class Evening News race was split into two 20 lap legs. Ray Pickrell, 750 Dunstall, won and Croxford on his Kuhn-Seeley came second in both. Final result was Pickrell, Croxford, Chandler, Butcher, Hunter and Ashwood; second, third and fifth for Seeley, not bad! Over the holiday weekend Seeley bikes had achieved nine rostrum positions including four wins; 18 races with riders in the top six and no engine failures. I was very proud of this achievement. My excellent work force was producing a quality product. After all the sweat and tears, good results were rewarding and a great encouragement to all at Colin Seeley Racing Developments.

Amongst all the excitement of racing, family affairs were also moving on. Joan was expecting our second child, due towards the end of the year. For the Isle of Man TT we would again be providing a full racing service from Frank Large's premises in Marathon Road, Douglas. This service put great strain on our limited resources but I considered it part of our original responsibility.

The epic of the Read-Weslake Racer continued. Phil Read decided to scrap the Metisse frame assembly and build the prototype engine into a Ken Sprayson Reynolds frame. Phil Read quoting, 'The Weslake-Metisse is too heavy at 315 lb, this is far too much. The Weslake engine with gearbox, weighs only the same as a Seeley G50 unit, yet our bike is 45 lb heavier. Our bike is meant to be a Grand Prix racer and we could not afford to carry the extra weight.' This just showed Phil Read's lack of experience regarding development. The Rickman Metisse frames were not the problem. 'Motorcycle' Sports Editor Mick Woollett had written on this subject. 'I agree that commitment to getting the anticipated running and performance of the Weslake engine should have been a first priority. Talk about giving this ambitious prototype its first outing at such events like the Northwest 200 and Isle of Man TT was unrealistic. It showed lack of experience by Phil Read, racing motorcycles is very different to developing and producing them.'

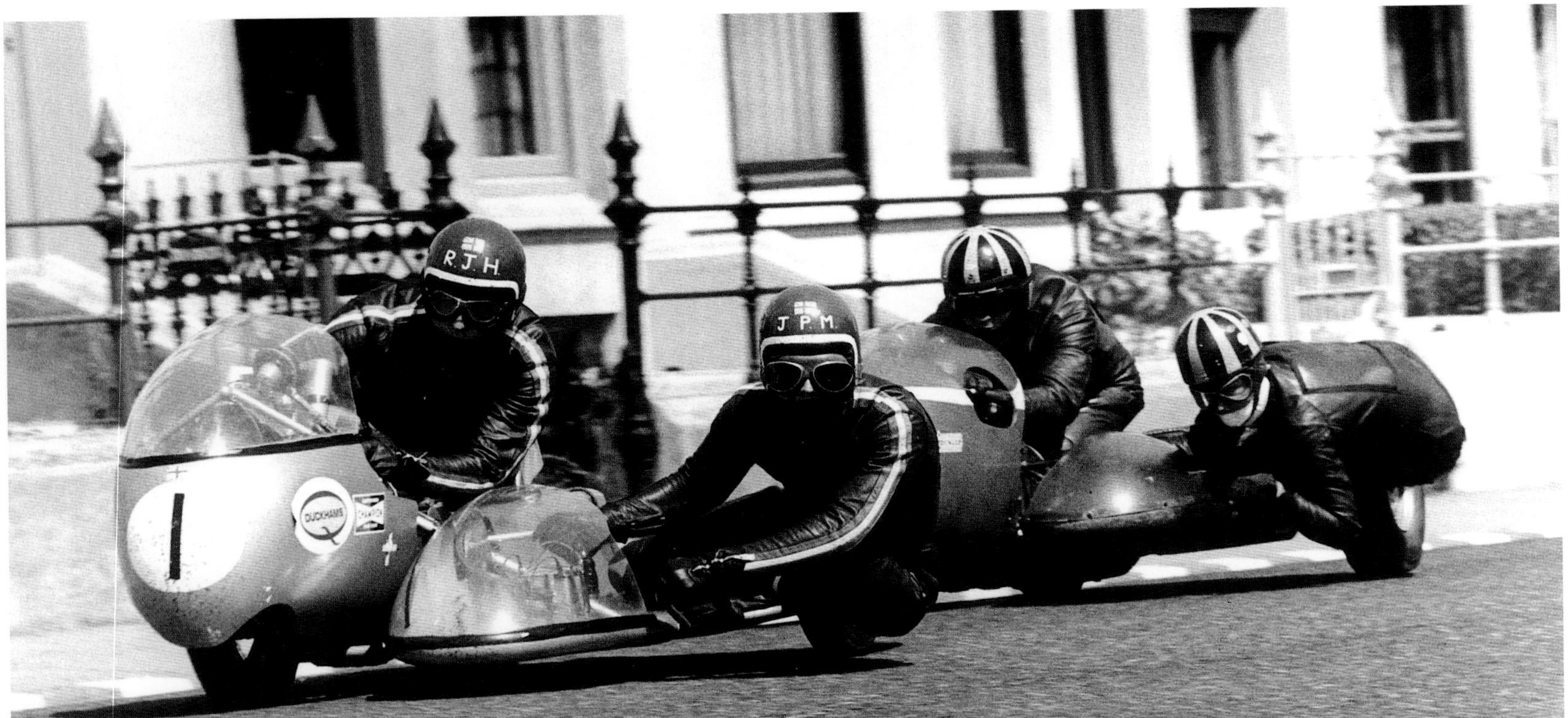

500cc Sidecar TT. Dick Hawes, Jim Mann 496cc Seeley, leads Norman Hanks and Rose Arnold, 500 BSA at White Gates.

Dr. Gordon Blair took an interest in the exhaust system fitted to our Seeley G50 machines. We had been fitting the regular system, which had suited the G50 for years and there seemed no reason to change. In discussions with Brian Steenson, Blair hit upon another design, which was longer. With the extra length front pipe and a 2 inch longer megaphone, the exhaust pipe needed to come straight down from the cylinder head, not swept back as normal. This allowed the long megaphone not to protrude beyond the rear wheel, keeping within the regulations. Ron Chandler tested the computer-designed prototype system, which proved very satisfactory, reducing the main jet size from 410 to 360. This allowed an increase in miles to the gallon without affecting top end performance. If anything, it gave an improvement to the bottom end, and mid range running was smooth, with good pickup and very little megaphonitis. We decided to fit these Blair systems to the Seeley machines of Woodman, Chandler and Steenson for the 1969 Isle of Man TT Senior event. Derek Woodman would justify this decision by speeding through the 'Motor Cycle' race speed trap placed at The Highlander at a 132.4mph, the quickest single cylinder machine recorded that week and less than 2mph down on Angelo Bergamonti with the Paton twin and 3mph down on Pagani riding the Linto. Agostini, of course was quickest at 150.6mph with no need to go faster. Ron Gould on the production 750cc Triumph was second quickest at an impressive 140.1mph, with Derek Woodman third quickest, putting the 250cc MZ through the speed trap at 138.5mph.

CSRD had been working on a new full race fairing suitable for high-speed circuits. Our alloy man, John Pearson created an aluminium prototype. Sections were cut from flat sheets, rolled and shaped, welded together, rolled again, cut to shape, more added, welded, rolled again, some parts beaten into shape, then finally fettled - a long painstaking process. Finally I was pleased, John had produced a prototype from which fibreglass moulds could be made. Fairings were produced in time for the Isle of Man TT and fitted to Woodman's, Dickie's and Steenson's Seeleys.

In 1969, for the first time in its 62 year history, the Isle of Man TT attracted over 600 entries - in fact 623 for the seven races, with many competitors turned away. Seeley Racing had an interest in the 350cc Junior, 500cc Senior and 500cc sidecar events. Before racing had started controversy arose, particularly in the Junior class. Among the 120 entrants, 18 machines had been named as specials when in fact they were manufactured machines. This name-juggling was to give publicity to sponsors, but meant that the actual machine manufacturer lost out. Rex Butcher entered his 350cc Seeley as an Oakley-Quaife. Bill Chuck Motorcycles had bought two brand new Seeleys for John Blanchard and having paid out £1,700, he felt he had the right to call the machines whatever he liked, and said, 'Having paid Colin Seeley, I don't see why he should get the publicity.' I didn't agree. They would not dare to try this tactic on the larger manufacturers. I took the matter up with the ACU, the sport's controlling body. I suggested that anyone who changed the name of my machines would actually be entering them under false pretences. Also, these owners couldn't expect after sales service or spares from me. Fortunately, for once the ACU backed my complaint. Rex Butcher said, 'If to get vital spares and service from Colin Seeley I need to change the entry to the name on the tank… fair enough!' Bill Chuck, probably with advice from John Blanchard, followed suit – drama over!

For the second year running, the TT races started with the 750cc sidecar event on the Saturday evening – 7th June, 6 pm. 81 competitors entered for this 3 lap race with 69 starters. Sadly, Terry Vinicombe 1968 winner would not be among them. Confounding the cynics 'Sideways Sid', West Germany's Siegfried Schauzu racing a 560cc BMW romped away to win, leading from the start and averaging 89.83mph with a fastest lap of 92.06mph. Schauzu's nearest challenger was Chris Vincent, 650, who retired on the last lap with transmission trouble, BSA honours being saved with Peter Brown taking second place at 85.65mph, and Bill Currie 650 Triumph third at 81.72mph. I should have been there, my average race time in 1962 would have given me third spot. Sorry, I can't help comparing!

Monday June 9th I always considered the traditional start of TT week. Dick Hawes partnered by Jim Mann was racing the Seeley G50 outfit. Out of 75 entries for this 3 lap, 113.2 mile sidecar race a record field of 69 started. In bright sunshine, Dick Hawes racing number one alongside Hans Luthringshuaser, BMW, were first away. At 11.00am sharp, Hawes on his pristine Seeley outfit rocketed from the start leading the German as they headed for Bray Hill. Wally Rawlings and I, now as spectators, watched our past adversaries disappear into the distance in billows of smoke. The struggle at the front was between the giants of Grand Prix racing; Klaus Enders, Helmut Fath, Georg Auerbacher, Siegfried Schauzu, and at the end of the first lap that was the order with Enders lapping at 92.54mph. BMW took five of the first six places but Norman Hanks BSA was next with Dick Hawes in eighth. Then Auerbacher was out with a fuel blockage at the end of the second

1969 TT, Steve Jolly and Wally Rawlings.

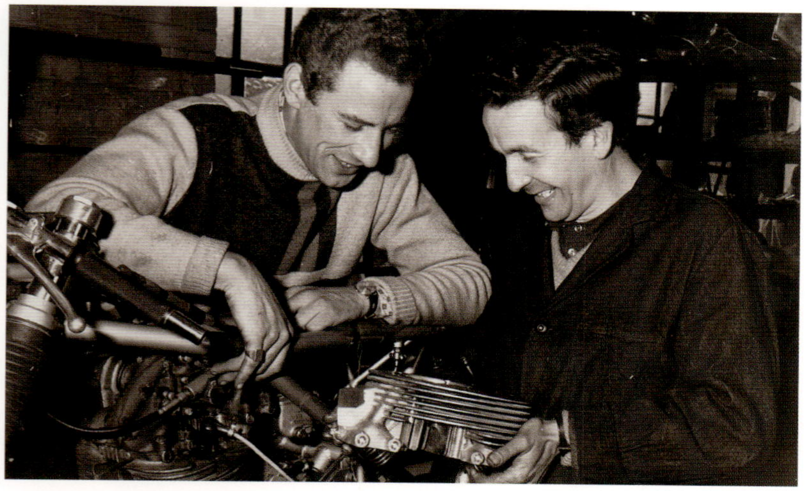

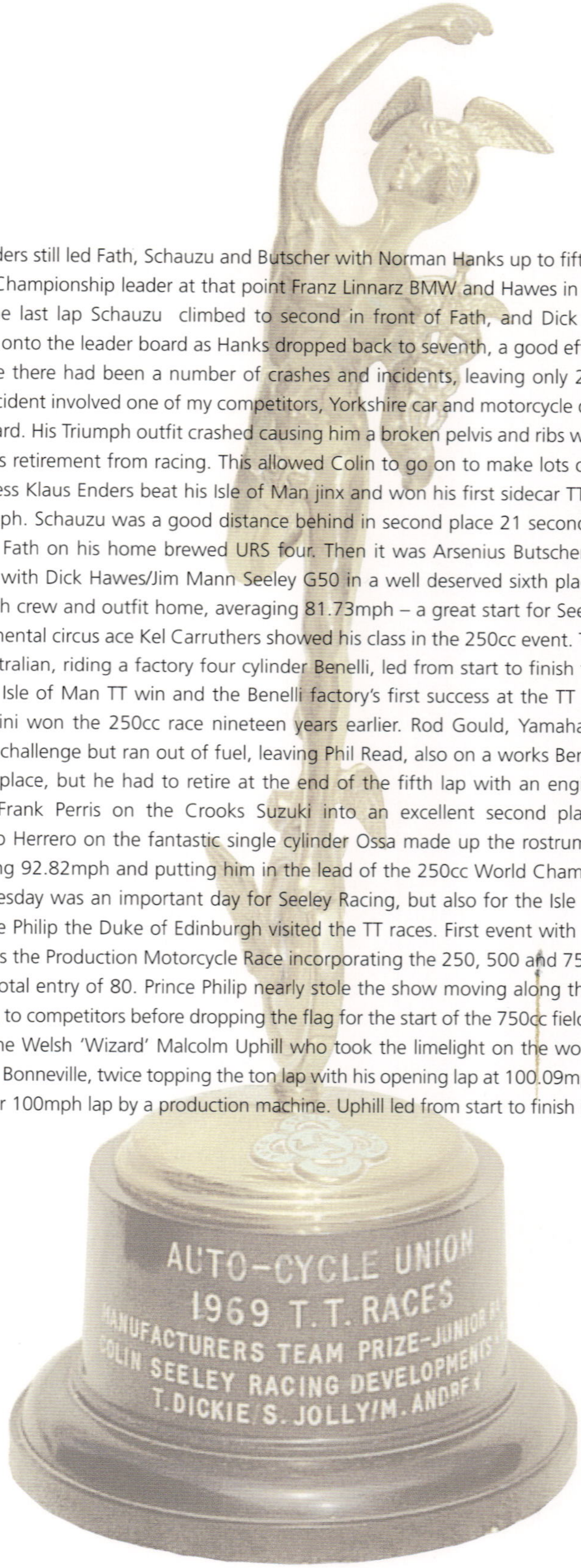

lap. Enders still led Fath, Schauzu and Butscher with Norman Hanks up to fifth, ahead of World Championship leader at that point Franz Linnarz BMW and Hawes in seventh.

On the last lap Schauzu climbed to second in front of Fath, and Dick Hawes got himself onto the leader board as Hanks dropped back to seventh, a good effort. During the race there had been a number of crashes and incidents, leaving only 26 finishers. One accident involved one of my competitors, Yorkshire car and motorcycle dealer Colin Appleyard. His Triumph outfit crashed causing him a broken pelvis and ribs which would force his retirement from racing. This allowed Colin to go on to make lots of money!

Faultless Klaus Enders beat his Isle of Man jinx and won his first sidecar TT, averaging 92.48mph. Schauzu was a good distance behind in second place 21 seconds ahead of Helmut Fath on his home brewed URS four. Then it was Arsenius Butscher and Franz Linnarz with Dick Hawes/Jim Mann Seeley G50 in a well deserved sixth place, the first all-British crew and outfit home, averaging 81.73mph – a great start for Seeley Racing.

Continental circus ace Kel Carruthers showed his class in the 250cc event. The 31 year old Australian, riding a factory four cylinder Benelli, led from start to finish to give him his first Isle of Man TT win and the Benelli factory's first success at the TT since Dario Ambrosini won the 250cc race nineteen years earlier. Rod Gould, Yamaha, put up a spirited challenge but ran out of fuel, leaving Phil Read, also on a works Benelli four, in second place, but he had to retire at the end of the fifth lap with an engine seizure, letting Frank Perris on the Crooks Suzuki into an excellent second place. Spain's Santiago Herrero on the fantastic single cylinder Ossa made up the rostrum positions, averaging 92.82mph and putting him in the lead of the 250cc World Championship.

Wednesday was an important day for Seeley Racing, but also for the Isle of Man TT, as Prince Philip the Duke of Edinburgh visited the TT races. First event with a 11.00am start was the Production Motorcycle Race incorporating the 250, 500 and 750cc classes with a total entry of 80. Prince Philip nearly stole the show moving along the start line chatting to competitors before dropping the flag for the start of the 750cc field. However, it was the Welsh 'Wizard' Malcolm Uphill who took the limelight on the works-entered Triumph Bonneville, twice topping the ton lap with his opening lap at 100.09mph, the first ever over 100mph lap by a production machine. Uphill led from start to finish in the 3 lap race setting another record by averaging 99.99mph for the event, with a fastest lap at 100.37mph. Paul Smart, Norton Commando, despite finding unwanted neutrals on the first lap, managed a brilliant second place at 99.37mph average, Bill Penny, 444 Honda, won the 500cc class, and Tony Rogers, Ducati, the 250cc event.

With the sun still shining, causing molten tar on some mountain sections, competitors assembled in Glencrutchery Road for the 2.00pm start of the 6 lap 226.4 mile Junior 350cc race. This was an important one for us. Our Seeley 7R machines were under threat, in particular from Italian Aermacchis. The 120 entries were reduced to 100 starters. Seeley would be represented by Mick Andrew, Steve Jolly and Tom Dickie, entered as our manufacturer's team, supported by Rex Butcher and Ron Chandler. It was disappointing that John Blanchard, second fastest on his Chuck Seeley in the Senior practice to Ago, would be a non-starter in both races. John rode a Norton-Commando in practice for the Production Race and lapped at 95.71mph then crashed at Kerrowmoar sustaining injuries to his hand which put him out of the running for all the events entered. Blanchard loved his Seeley 7R, a bike he felt could be ridden to the limit. He had finished sixth and fourth in the 1966 Junior and Senior events, then recording a Senior Race lap at 100.84mph in 1967, all on Seeley machines. John certainly knew his way round the TT course and wouldn't have been far behind the leaders, but it was not to be.

It was a nervous wait at the start. The Duke of Edinburgh had been introduced to the riders on the front ranks and was to flag the first pairing away, Rex Butcher, Seeley, and Barry Randle, Norton. Giacomo Agostini, MV, third off, cantered to an easy win when his only real opposition, Rod Gould and Phil Read both on TR2 Yamahas, fell by the wayside with engine troubles. Kel Carruthers on one of five works Aermacchis entered, held second place until the last lap, when the engine died. Dramas, retirements, it was a job to keep up with the action. Finally, it was all over, Agostini recording his third Junior Race victory with the hard charging Irishman Brian Steenson, Aermacchi, second, ahead of Jack Findlay, Beart Aermacchi, who was slowed down by a loose suspension bolt. Only 53 of the 100 starters finished the course.

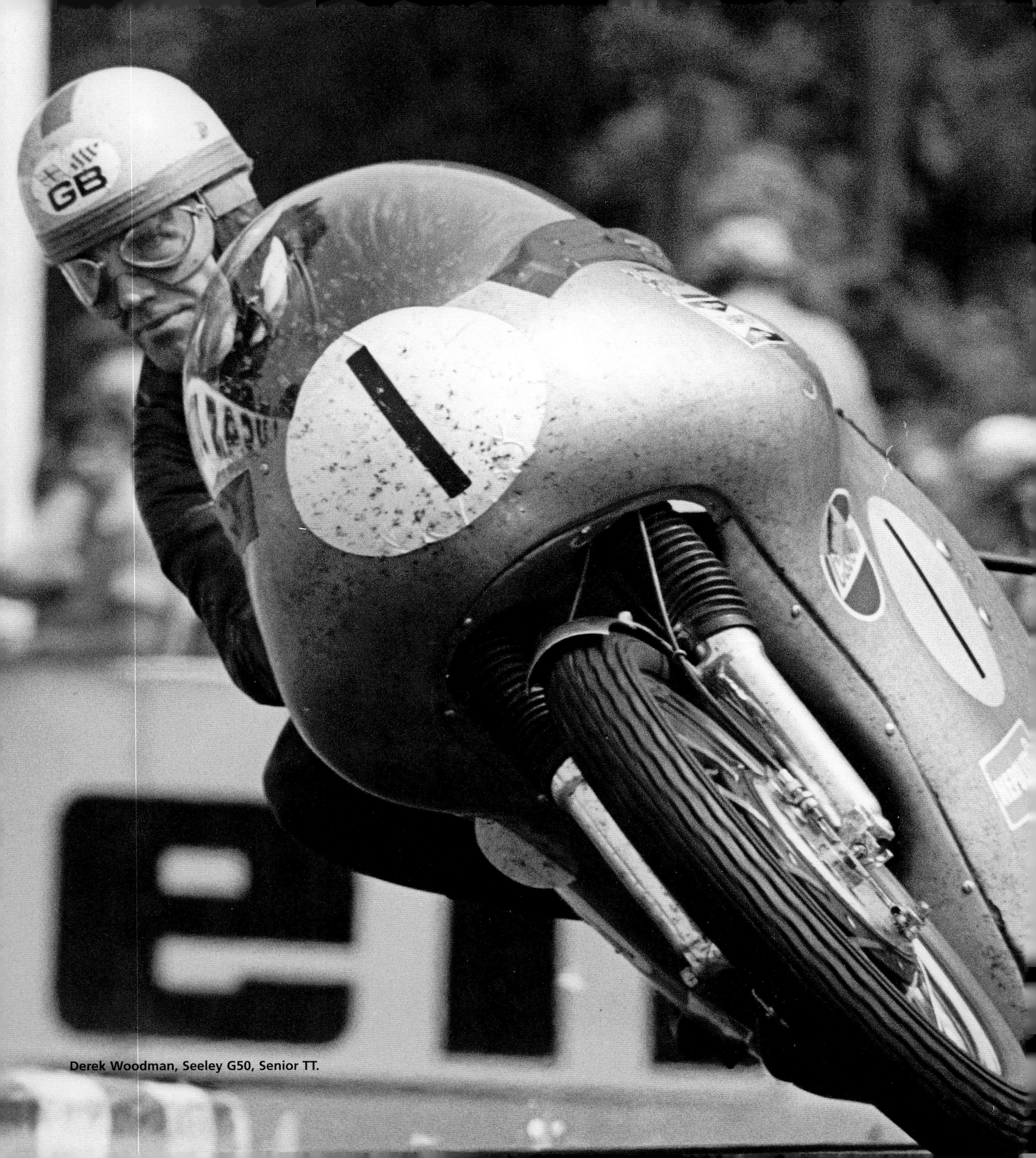
Derek Woodman, Seeley G50, Senior TT.

Brian Steenson, Seeley, Senior TT.

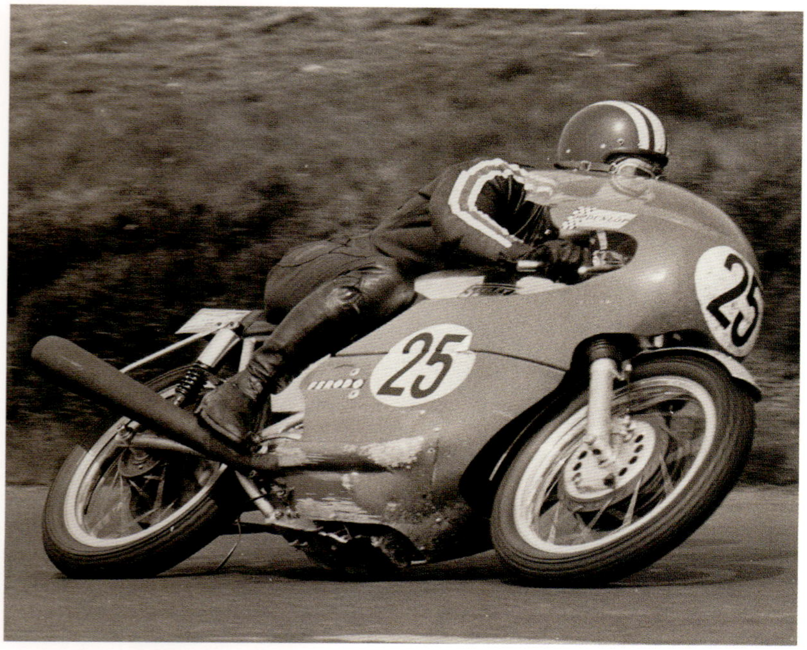

Out of the five Seeley 7R machines in the Junior Race, only Rex Butcher was forced to retire. Mick Andrew, Kuhn-Seeley, on his first visit to the Island finished ninteenth, Steve Jolly thirteenth, Ron Chandler twelfth with Andrew's team mate Tom Dickie bringing his Kuhn Seeley home in a great fourth place, which resulted in Colin Seeley Racing Development winning the manufacturer's team prize, an award I treasure to this day. It was a fantastic boost for my small company – drinks all round that night!

Thursday was back to reality, finishing last minute jobs for customers riding the Senior, then packing and preparing for home on Friday evening. Again it had been a long fortnight, but worth it.

Friday's Senior race day was another hot and sunny one. In fact it was the hottest TT week on record. By the Friday there were problems around the TT course with molten tar. Fortunately a westerly breeze cooled things down in time. Things started at 11.00am with the lightweight 125cc event. Dave Simmonds, World Championship leader, having dominated practice delighted his fans leading the 3 lap race from start to finish, bringing the eight speed water cooled 125cc disc-valve twin with a power band between 12,000-14,000rpm, home to give himself and Kawasaki their first Isle of Man TT success.

Out of 115 Senior TT entries, 97 came to the line. Unfortunately, injuries prevented two of our main hopes, John Cooper and John Blanchard, winner of the Northwest 200, from starting. However, there was still an impressive line-up of nine Seeley machines, ridden by Derek Woodman, Tom Dickie, Brian Steenson, Charlie Sanby, Brian Hunter, Steve Jolly, Ron Chandler, Mick Andrew and Vin Duckett. As expected, Giacomo Agostini, on the works 500cc 3 cylinder MV cruised to victory in the 226 mile race, admitting with a smile that he did not need to go any faster. Alan Barnett on the Kirby Metisse put in a sizzling lap of 100.03mph to consolidate second place. Derek Woodman, Seeley, had a race long encounter with Tom Dickie, Kuhn-Seeley, for third place. Trouble with the front brake adjuster and oil from an over-filled oil tank meant Woodman finished 20 seconds down on Dickie, who took third place. Ron Chandler took an excellent sixth after a tussle with Brian Steenson who crashed his Seeley at Creg-ny-Baa. He was taken by helicopter to hospital with facial cuts and a broken collarbone. Steve Jolly took seventh place and Vin Duckett twelfth. The Italian challenge of overbored factory Aermacchis, Paton and Linto machines fell away, whilst Mick Andrew, Kuhn-Seeley, retired with a broken primary chain. Tony Godfrey, who had taken over Brian Hunter's Coleshill Seeley, retired with a broken oil pipe in the pits and Charlie Sanby riding John Cooper's Seeley was out at Ramsey with engine trouble. So that was that, the Isle of Man TT was over for another year.

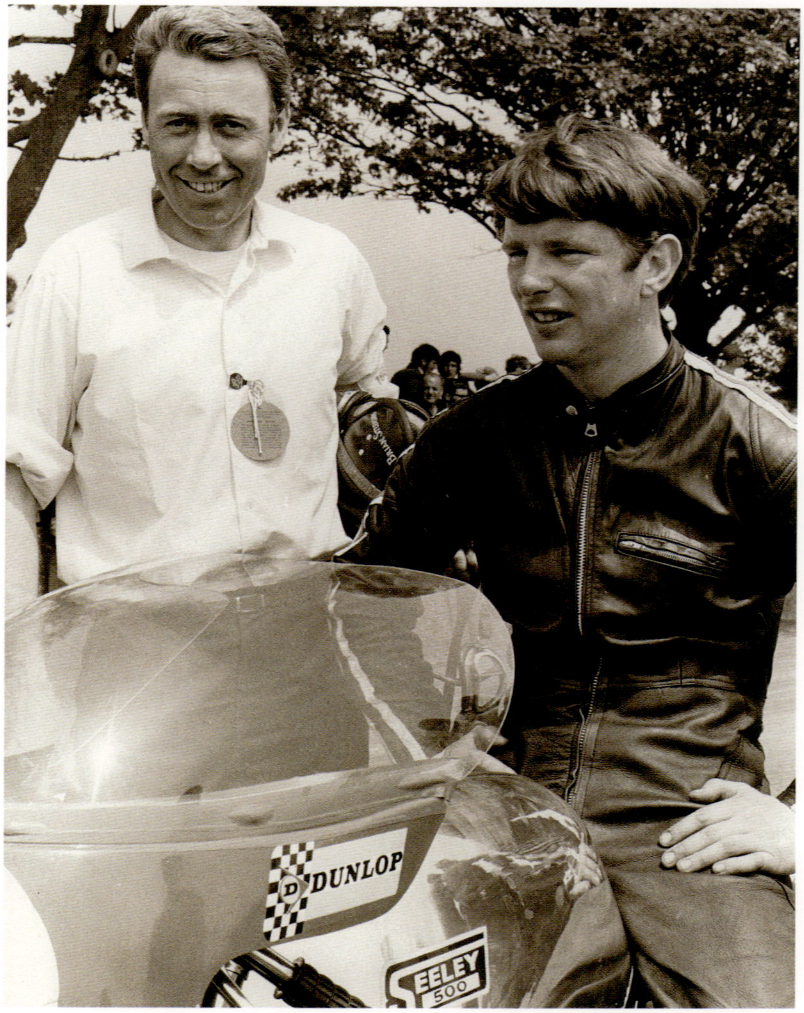

Brian Steenson at the start of the Senior TT.

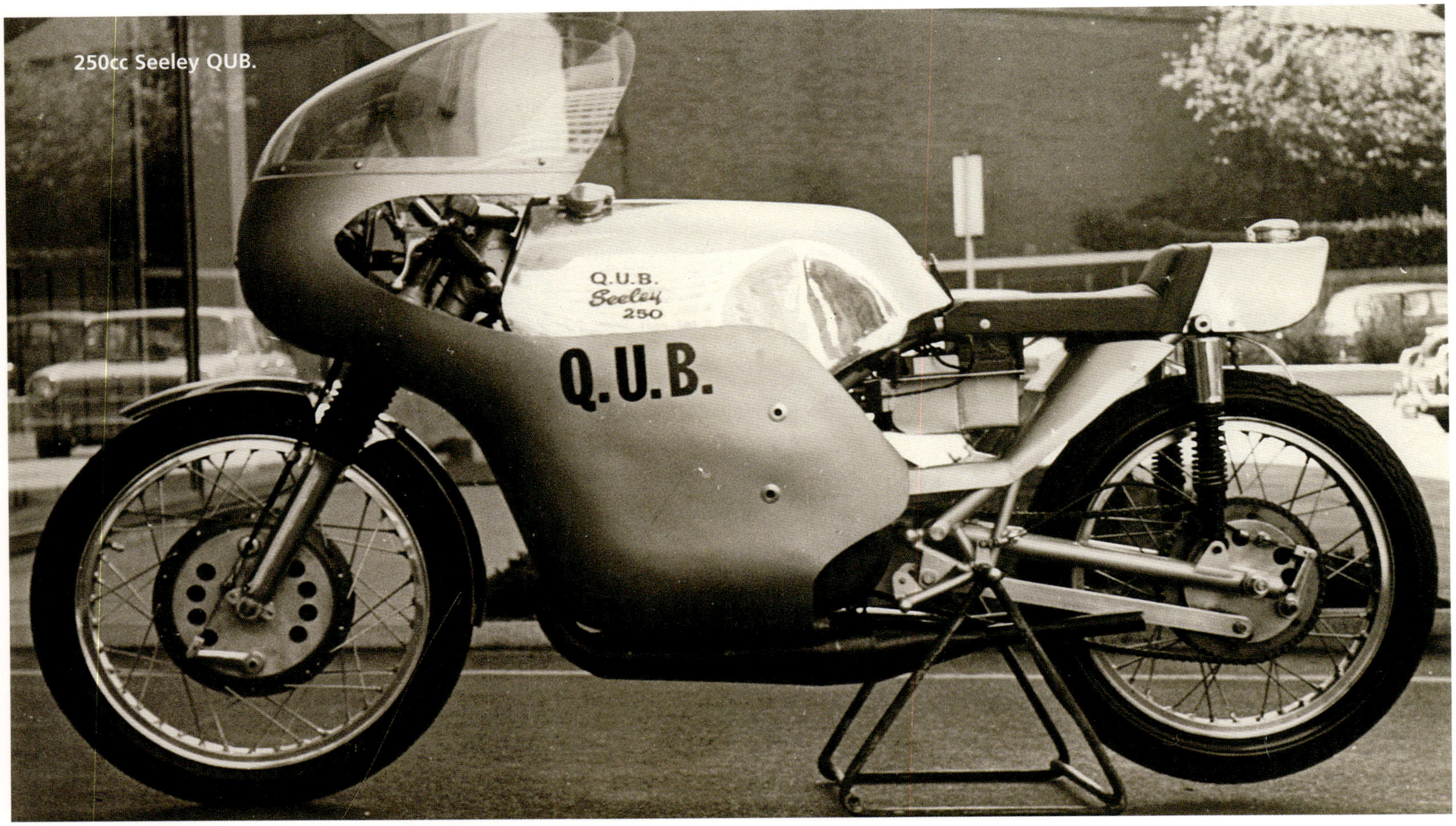

250cc Seeley QUB.

Seeley Racing had done pretty well: sixth in the 500 sidecar event; fourth, twelfth, thirteenth and ninteenth in the Junior 350; third, fourth, sixth, seventh and twelfth in the Senior 500 event. There had been 10 finishes out of 15 races for the Seeley machines, with only one engine failure. The Joe Craig Trophy was awarded to Tom Dickie for the best aggregate performance on a British machine with fourth in the Junior and third in the Senior on the Kuhn-Seeleys.

During the Isle of Man TT fortnight, a memorial seat dedicated to the memory of our friend and rider, Sid Mizen was unveiled by racing sponsor Syd Mullarney and blessed by the Rev R.H. Bertie Reid. The seat was located at Union Mills, near Sid Mizen's birthplace. A gentleman of our sport, Frank Perris, having finished second in the 250 Isle of Man TT event on the Crook's Suzuki, decided to retire from racing and return home to Durban, South Africa. Back in 1965 he finished second in the 125cc World Championship on the works Suzuki, winning two Grands Prix at Sachsensenring and Brno, and securing four second places and two thirds. Winner that year had been the unstoppable Hugh Anderson, Suzuki, with seven Grand Prix wins.

John 'Mooneyes' Cooper, in a mood and still recovering from injuries received at Cadwell Park, decided to sell his new Yamaha machines and also a new 500 Seeley. Did this mean he intended to retire? 'I haven't decided yet,' was his reply. 'I might race again when I am fit.' But the Derby ace still hung on to his original Seeley 500cc. Time would tell. We had not seen the best of 'Mooneyes' yet.

Eddie Robinson had pencilled a design to suit the 250cc QUB engine unit whilst I had been away. I soon got cracking to construct the frame unit, John Pearson created a great looking alloy tank and our bike assembler Mick Carter arranged the rest. In a few days our team had produced a very pleasing Seeley QUB 250CC, ready for shipment to Belfast for testing and its race debut in early August.

After at least two weeks in the Isle of Man, you would expect most competitors would be going home for a rest. No chance! The Mallory Park Post-TT International meeting on the Sunday 15th June, directly after the last TT event attracted many contenders. Double TT winner, world champion Giacomo Agostini was one of them. With all respect, Valentino Rossi or any current Grand Prix competitors would be unlikely to chance their reputations at Mallory. To the delight of a huge crowd, Rod Gould, making up for his TT disappointment, won both 250 and 350cc races then in the main 20 lap 1000cc event, Agostini made a poor start, allowing Gould, on top form to head the MV rider across the line to take his third win of the day with the 'Ruislip Rebel' Croxford bringing his Kuhn-Seeley into third.

A week later it was the fifth round of the British Championship at Thruxton, with Alan Barnett still on a high from his second place in the Senior TT. David Dixon of 'Motorcycle', reported the 500cc race as one of the best ever seen at Thruxton. Barnett won the 500cc event on the Kirby-Metisse, just ahead of Croxford, Kuhn-Seeley, after earlier leader Mick Andrew, Kuhn-Seeley, went grass tracking. Percy Tait on his first ride since breaking his collarbone at the TT, held onto third place with the Triumph. Barnett now held 55 championship points, Croxford 49, and Andrew 24. For a heat of the 1000cc race Alan Barnett made a winning debut for the Rickman Triumph Metisse, fitted with the 683cc Weslake eight valve conversion. In the final lap a misfire caused by sparking plugs not having been tightened slowed him down. Brian Kemp on a 750 Curley-Norton won from Croxford on the 500 Kuhn-Seeley with Paul Smart, 750 Francis-Norton, in third place. Barry Sheene's name kept popping up. He won the 125cc race on a Bultaco from Martin Carney on Terry Shepherd's special.

Earlier in the season the press made much of the Italian Linto machine, a twin cylinder 500cc built with the use of many Aermacchi components and said to produce 64bhp at 10,000rpm. Lino Tonti who had worked at most of the major Italian factories and in 1969 was technical director of Moto-Guzzi, designed the Linto. The whole project was financed by Umberto Premoli, a racing enthusiast and car dealer in Varese. Alberto Pagani who had put the prototype through its paces in 1968, and finished second to Agostini, MV, at the East German Grand Prix, was joined by 'Aussie' Jack Findlay as an official rider in 1969.

A batch of 15 bikes, with a price tag of £1,300 each, was planned. These machines it was suggested would sound the death knell for the British singles. Certainly the Linto had

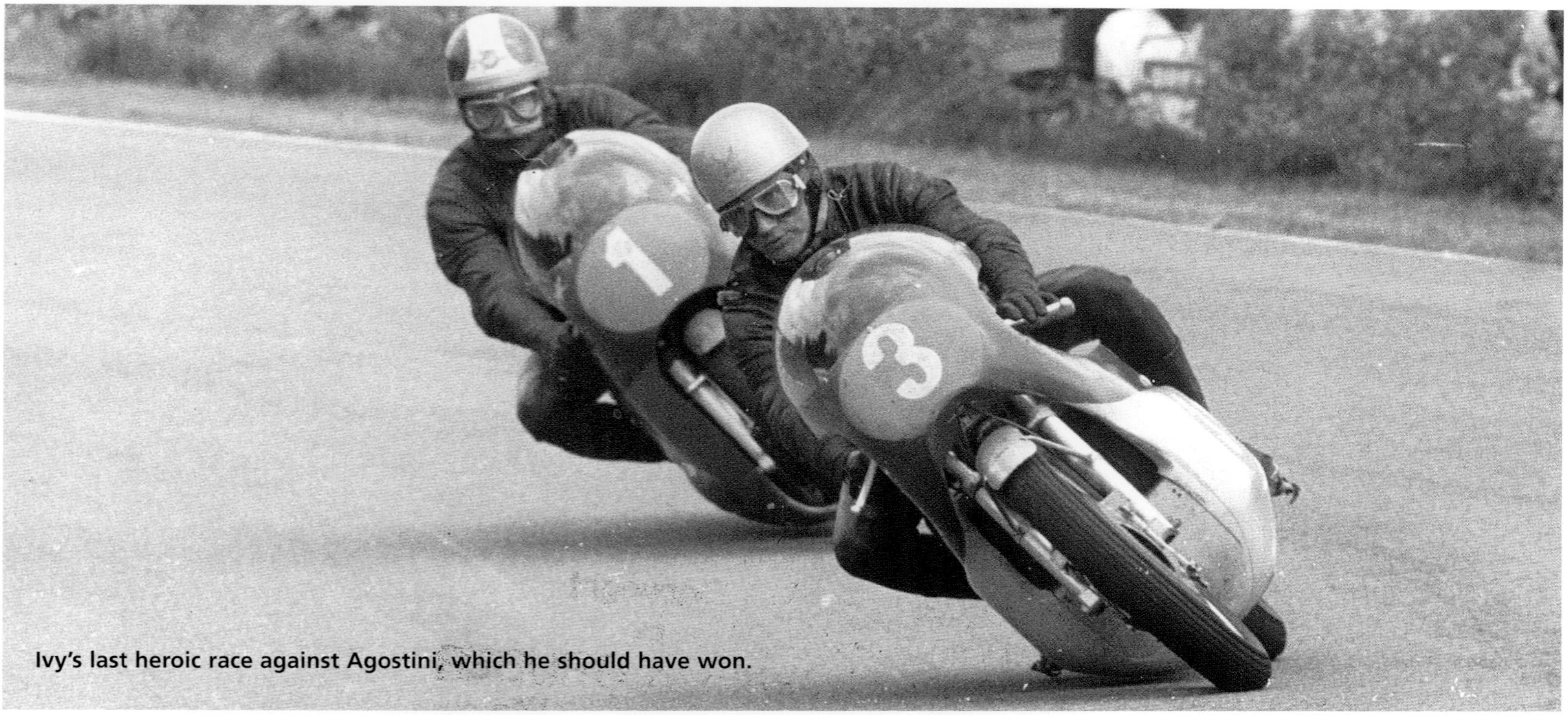
Ivy's last heroic race against Agostini, which he should have won.

a good turn of speed, but reliability was another matter. Jack Findlay while testing at Monza at the end of 1968, had a high speed crash when the Linto seized. More problems followed with a failure of parts. Then at the North West 200, Jack Findlay was halfway round on the first practice lap and approaching 160mph when the Linto went bang. The primary gears stripped, fortunately for Jack not resulting in a locked rear wheel. With no spare engine, that was Findlay's Northwest over! Although scoring a fine third place in the German Grand Prix prior to the Northwest 200 and Isle of Man TT events, Findlay didn't receive the support required from Umberto Premoli, who was more concerned about the bad publicity over Linto breakdowns. With no Linto machine available for the Isle of Man TT, Syd Lawton came to the rescue, providing Jack with a 382cc Aermacchi for the Senior race. Findlay was in fourth spot on the second lap when he struck trouble. Ironically, the dogs on the fourth gear stripped, forcing a retirement. Alberto Pagani, riding the only Linto in the race, in sixth place on the first lap, only got as far as Barregarro second time around before the Achilles' heel of the Linto bit. Failure of the primary-gears forced retirement.

Jack Findlay, a professional racer, was not impressed and when Linto didn't get a machine to him in time for the Dutch TT, he returned to the Lawton-Aermacchi. Perhaps the truth was that Umberto Premoli was struggling to look after the private riders who had paid good money for Linto machines which were proving unreliable. Replacement of faulty components free of charge was stretching financial resources, causing any plans to support Jack Findlay to fall by the wayside.

The Dutch TT, 28th June, was popular for fans and competitors alike. The star of the meeting for the record crowd of 150,000 was, our man, Bill Ivy. Riding the fragile four cylinder works' Jawa, the talented speed star in the 20 lap (95.75mph) 350cc event provided the best entertainment and excitement of the day when he took the lead from the Italian double World Champion Giacomo Agostini on the works MV and clung to it for 2 laps. When the Jawa started to misfire Ago went ahead, but the Jawa chimed back on all four cylinders and the dice was on again. By lap 12 'Little Bill' was back in front, the huge crowd going wild! The Italian star was in trouble with cramp in his throttle wrist. He looked beaten as Ivy drew away, but not for long. Again the Jawa ignition system played tricks, back on three cylinders, and Ivy back to second place. Ago put on the pressure to win, recording a new lap record at 91.38mph, faster than he would go in the 500cc event, such was the pace. Rod Gould held a secure third until the last lap, when a big end failed on the Yamaha twin. Silvio Grassetti (Yamaha) would take third place nearly 2 mins behind 'Little Bill' on the Jawa. Helmut Fath, the current world sidecar champion powered his four cylinder URS outfit all the way to his second win that season, and the lead of the championship. Again I can't resist comparing my winning race times from 1964. Being ahead, I slowed down, but still averaged 78.74mph, which would have given me third place in the 1969 event. My quickest lap 5 years earlier was less than 2mph average down on Helmut Fath with the fast URS.

Agostini seemed to stroll the 500cc event. Peter Williams, Arter Matchless, returning to racing after a six week lay off following his Thruxton crash, achieved a smooth second place with Alan Barnett competing for the first time on the continent in an excellent third on the Kirby-Metisse. Our best results were Ron Chandler eighth, Dan Shorey thirteenth and Paul Smart eighteenth on the Seeley machines. Johnny Dodds had blown his Linto up, leaving the other Linto riders Gyula Marsovszky and Keith Turner in sixth and eleventh. Jack Findlay brought the Syd Lawton 382cc Aermacchi into a superb fifth place. Dave Simmonds continued his winning ways on the Kawasaki in the 125cc event from Kent Andersson, Yamaha, increasing his lead even further in the championship.

Pasolini and Carruthers on the works Benellis dominated the 250cc race after Rod Gould, Yamaha, who had led for the first 6 laps, stopped to change a plug, finally finishing fourth behind the Spanish ace Santiago Herrero, Ossa, in third.

Back home in 'sunny' Darlington, the Gus Kuhn Team arrived at Croft for a round of the British 500cc championship. Mick Andrew was accompanied by June Hewston from his home town, Ware in Herts. They had been married just the day before. Andrew won his first 500 race on the Kuhn-Seeley from a hard charging Ken Redfern, Norton, who split the duo of Andrew and Croxford at the last corner. With his third place the 'Ruislip Rebel' Croxford went ahead in the 500 British Championship, four points in front of Alan Barnett with Andrew now up to third.

In early July the boss of Morini in Bologna, Commendatore Alfonso Morini died, aged 72. One time sponsor of Agostini and Provini, Morini was the first manufacturer to spot the potential of Agostini and signed the brilliant youngster to ride his famous single-cylinder 250cc machine for 1964 after losing Provini to Benelli.

The Grand Prix circus moved on to Belgium for the following Sunday's high speed event held at the 8.8 mile Spa Francorchamps Circuit. With no 350cc class, the 'Maidstone Marvel' would not be in action on the Jawa, nevertheless, some brilliant high speed racing would be enjoyed by the record crowd of 120,000.

Aussie Barry Smith, Derbi, continued his success. Having won the 50cc class of the Dutch TT, would win his second of the season from Santiago Herrero, Derbi, by just 6 seconds, averaging an amazing 89.91mph round the Francorchamps circuit. Dave Simmonds showed his class in the 125cc event, 7 laps of 'ducking and diving' with Kent Andersson, Yamaha, Cees Van Dongen and Dieter Braun on their ex-works ten speed Suzukis. The Kawasaki could not match their speed on the straights, but Dave could ride round the opposition on the fast flat out bends. He finally got the verdict by only 1.7 seconds from Braun, at an average of 106.89mph, with Van Dongen third a good way behind.

The 8 lap 250cc was an exciting race between Rod Gould, Yamaha, the Benellis of Carruthers and Pasolini, and until this season unknown outside Spain, 25 year old Santiago Herrero riding the single cylinder disc valved air cooled works Ossa. Herrero started racing in 1963 with a 50cc Derbi, won numerous races in Spain and finished runner-up in the 1965 championships. Having joined the Ossa Company in 1966, he notched the 1966/67 and '69 national championships. 1968 was his first year attending the classics where he concentrated on learning the circuits and developing this fantastic single cylinder two-stroke. Herrero's riding style reminded me of the great Tarquinio Provini's, tucked in, head down, controlled aggression, but very stylish.

Rod Gould lead the first lap of the 8 lap 250cc race by 3.5 seconds but by the third lap all four riders were together Carruthers leading Gould, Herrero and Pasolini, Heinz Rosner, MZ, fifth well ahead of Kent Andersson, Yamaha. Suddenly Pasolini and Rosner were out and with 2 laps to go Carruther's Benelli lost its edge. Gould and Herrero whipped past into the final lap, Herrero then 'dusted up' Gould at Eau Rouge, Gould returned the compliment, riding round Herrero on the Coco Bends, but the dashing Spaniard would have none of it and pushing the Ossa to its limit crossed the finish line just half a second ahead of Rod Gould averaging 117.96mph for the 70.09 mile race with Carruthers just over 10 seconds down to bring the factory Benelli four into third place.

The 13 lap 113.89 mile 500cc race would as expected be a walk-over for Giacomo Agostini on the works MV, pulverising both the race and lap records with a fastest lap of 130.66mph. The world's fastest motorcycle lap time previously held by Bob McIntyre at Hockenheim on the works Gilera 12 years before in 1957 at 129.48mph. Impressive at Spa was the performance of Percy Tait on the works Triumph, coming home in second place, averaging 116.58mph, being the only rider not to be lapped by the flying Italian. Alan Barnett came in third on the Kirby-Mettise. Gyula Marsovszky had borrowed a Linto engine from Alberto Pagani. Despite problems with the Linto, Gyula fought through to a heroic fourth place, ahead of Ron Chandler Seeley in fifth spot. It was ironic that Jack Findlay without his Linto works bike, borrowed the Arter-Matchless from Peter Williams and was up with the main group on the fourth lap when something locked up on the normally reliable Matchless at 130mph and he once more found himself spinning down the circuit, escaping with cuts and bruises. Later on, inspection revealed a broken fork leg had caused the accident. It certainly had not been a good season so far for this likeable Aussie.

The intense German ace World Champion Helmut Fath on his home built URS four screamed around the Francorchamps circuit at an 111.97mph average, 33 seconds ahead of Klaus Enders, BMW, and with a new lap record of 112.73mph, the best of British, Graham Milton, BMW, came sixth.

Next stop on the Grand Prix circuit was the East German event, held on the 5.4 mile Sachsenring Circuit running through the town of Hohenstein-Ernstthal. All solo classes were run 50,125, 250, 350 and 500cc. 200,000 sport-starved East German fans flocked to the circuit. On the wet Saturday morning practice, 12th July 1969, a black cloud descended over Sachsenring. In the 350cc practice, the talented 'Maidstone Marvel' Bill Ivy was killed. The engine of the four cylinder works Jawa seized as Ivy shut off for a 90mph left-hand curve entering the town of Hohenstein-Ernstthal. Bike and rider slid a good distance on the wet road before striking a concrete fence not protected by straw bales. Ivy's helmet seemed to come off before the impact. He was rushed to hospital. Sadly the doctors were unable to save him. The loss of the 5ft 3in racing dynamo was a shock to the racing fraternity and the fans. Bill Ivy was the second famous rider to be killed at Sachsenring, Jimmy Guthrie being the first, killed in 1937 when leading the 500cc race. During a 10 year racing career the 27 year old had served his apprenticeship racing a 50cc Itom for local dealers Chisholms of Maidstone then Frank Sheene became involved, followed by Geoff Monty and Tom Kirby. With such interest, the 'Pocket Rocket' could hardly fail and Ivy certainly did not disappoint. Although physically small, Bill Ivy stood head and shoulders above many of his contemporaries: runner-up to Luigi Taveri, Honda, in the 1966, World 125cc championship on the works Yamaha, winner of the Spanish Grand Prix, Dutch TT, Isle of Man TT and Japanese Grand Prix then, still with Yamaha, holder of the 1967 125cc World Championship crown, with eight GP wins and not forgetting his third place in the 250cc Championship that year. In 1968 he was runner-up to Phil Read in both 125 and 250cc championships, achieving seven GP wins that season, in all, 21 GP successes to his credit, totalling 37 rostrum positions. His racing skills, his dedication, his courageous commitment to the sport and off track antics with Mike Hailwood would be sorely missed. Bill Ivy, the approachable champion, we salute your memory.

As always, the show would go on, but not before riders pressed the organisers to put more straw bales at the danger points around the circuit. Jack Findlay, Rod Gould and Santiago Herrero advised where bales should be located. At a later meeting of the FIM jury, officials agreed it would be beneficial to take advice from top competitors before practising started at all meetings in future.

What a pity it took the loss of such a champion to kick-start this action. Even now organisers often have their heads in the sand over circuit safety. Motorsport by its very nature is dangerous, but loss of life in areas and situations where safety could be improved was not acceptable then, and is not acceptable now in my opinion.

The morning of race day was damp but did not deter the huge crowd of enthusiastic East German fans. Santiago Herroro gave Angel Nieto, both works Derbis, a run for his money, finally finishing a close second to Nieto, the challenger for the 50cc crown. Then, 'As the 350cc starters came to the line, a wreath was laid on the grid from where Bill Ivy would have started, being second quickest in practice. A few words were spoken. The crowd stood in silence and Sachsenring seemed at that moment a very grim place indeed.' The scene was reported in 'Motor Cycle' by Mick Woollett. Team mate Frantiesk Stastny and the Jawa Team had withdrawn as a mark of respect.

Without the challenge of Bill Ivy, the 350cc race was somewhat uneventful. Agostini, in his own time, won easily on the MV leaving Rod Gould and Heinz Rosner in his

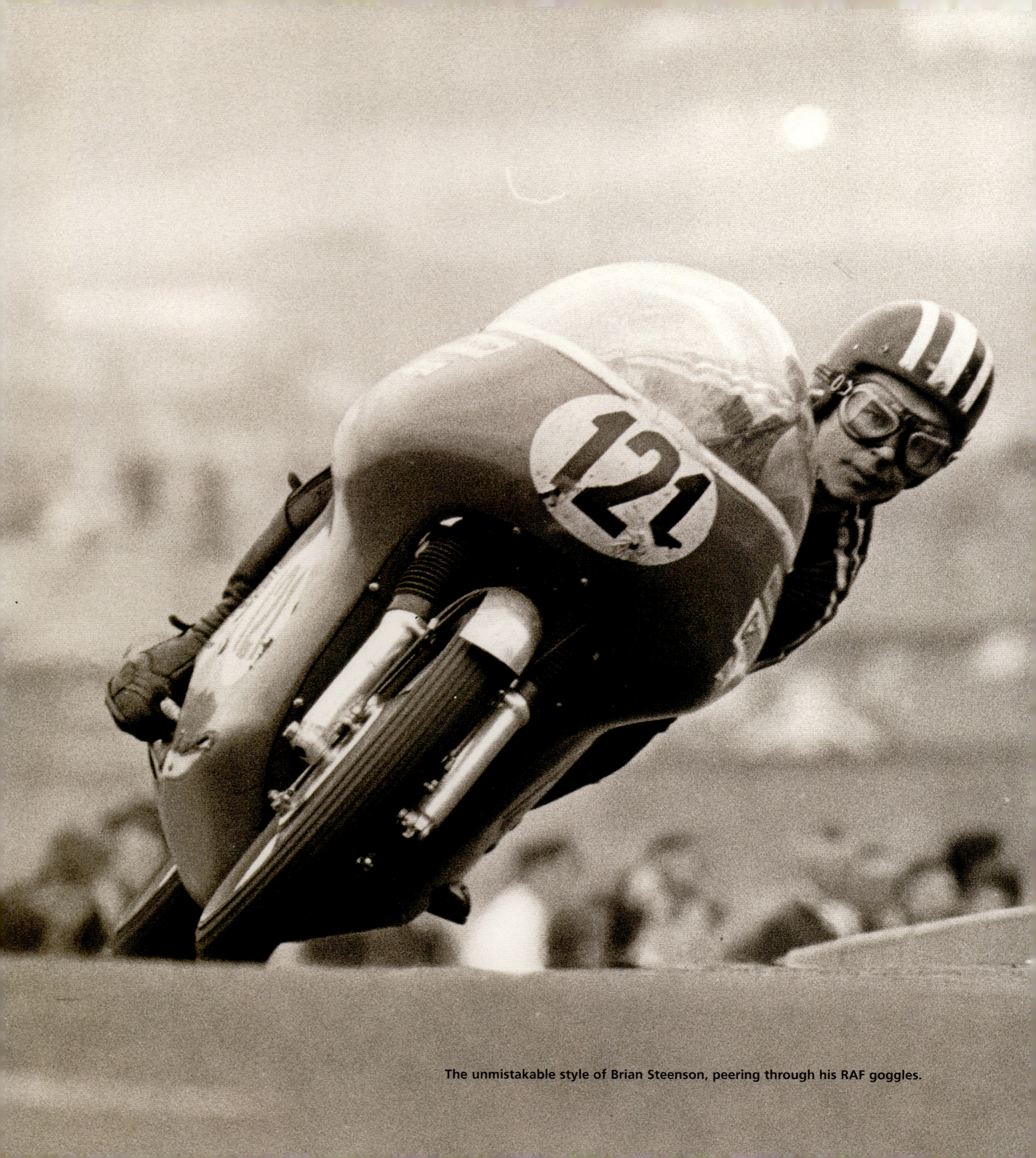
The unmistakable style of Brian Steenson, peering through his RAF goggles.

wake. The drizzle had stopped by the time the 125cc competitors came to the line. Dave Simmonds, the bright spot for the British contingent, won the lightweight event on the Kawasaki. His fifth Grand Prix win that season and not to be beaten, the 29 year old racing ace from Stanwell would join the ranks of World Champions, his first title and a first for Kawasaki. Dave was a very popular rider in the paddock, talented on and off the bike, his mechanical skills beyond any doubt. It was a double celebration, as Dave was to marry Julie Boddice, daughter of Bill Boddice – the sidecar-racing veteran.

As the competitors lined up for the 500cc 20 lap 107 mile race, the rain returned. Two Russian four cylinder Vostoks were in the field. Mick Woollett described them as rather old fashioned in appearance, 'with rather scruffy looking engines in frames that surely would make Colin Seeley weep, big and badly made.' Jack Findlay was back on a Linto after much pressure and effort from a French journalist Christian La-Combe, aided by members of a French film crew who had been filming Findlay's exploits as a racer for a full-length documentary. So it was Findlay, Pagani, Marsovszky and Ellis on the twin cylinder Linto machines. But would they all last the course? Unfortunately not! The two works riders followed by Marsovszky were soon out with mechanical problems leaving Steve Ellis on the lone Linto to finish third, but only after keeping the revs down to 8,500rpm instead of 10,500rpm.

Giacomo Agostini, MV three, won his seventh consecutive 500 Grand Prix which gave him his fourth successive world 500 title, equalling Mike Hailwood's record set on the MV Agusta fours in the early sixties. Billie Nelson brought the Hannah-Paton home in second place, ahead of Steve Ellis.

After more drizzle and a half hour delay, the competitors gathered for the last race of the day. From the start of the 15 lap 250cc race, Heinz Roszner, MZ, gave the home crowd something to cheer about, taking a 50 yard lead. Second time around Herrero and Pasolini caught the leader, next time Spain's new boy took the lead on the Ossa from Pasolini, Benelli, leaving Rosner back in third place. Rod Gould, Yamaha, up to fourth was ahead of Kent Andersson and Kel Carruthers. Then Gould slid off, Rosner called into the pits for a plug change and fell back to sixth. But to the delight of the East German crowd their man and machine fought back up to third place. At the front Santiago Herrero held on until a mile from the finish, when Renzo Pasolini on the works Benelli four pulled out of the Ossa's slipstream and sneaked by to take the win by a machine's length. Pasolini was ecstatic, punching the air for joy as he crossed the line, but the Spanish star, Herrero had increased his lead in the World Championship Table.

Back home the gregarious Irishman, Brian Steenson missed his graduation ceremony at Belfast University to compete at the Isle of Man Southern 100 meeting. Although retiring in the 350cc event with plug trouble on his Aermacchi, the newly appointed Bachelor of Science won the 500cc race, a round of the British Championship, and then the Southern 100 event on the Mick Mooney Seeley G50, with fastest laps in both.

Ivan Hackman scooped the prizes with his 500 Seeley at Cadwell Park, second in the first event, then with a third place in the second race, was a certain Mick Grant racing a Jim Lee 500 Velocette.

Politics, noise and 'do-gooders' all joined the effort to ban all motor sport on Sundays. Sir Cyril Black MP proposed a ban as an amendment to the Sunday Entertainment Bill. A statement issued by the Baptist Union of Great Britain and Ireland called for a ban on noisy entertainments: 'Examples include motor-cycle scrambles which can be heard over many square miles.' Fortunately, the proposal was defeated 9 votes to 2 – drama over!

So many important events clashed with each other or came in rapid succession; Isle of Man TT, Dutch TT, Belgian Grand Prix, East German Grand Prix and a week later the Czech Grand Prix, and there was the all important British Championship series. Many of the British private professionals wanted to show their talents at the Grands Prix, but it was very difficult. Money was tight, travel expensive, and there were often problems with customs officials in those days. There was never enough time to prepare race machines, and anyway you can only be in one place at a time – manic, yes!!

Within a day or two of the tragic East German Grand Prix came the surprising decision by Jack Findlay to take over 'dead man's shoes' and race the fragile, unpredictable 350cc four cylinder Jawa. No doubt his frustration with the Linto factory had something to do with it. Particularly after finishing second in the 1968 500cc World Championship on the McIntyre Matchless, Jack Findlay may have made a hasty decision. In practice for the Czech Grand Prix after just 2 miles the Jawa's cooling system leaked onto the rear tyre causing Jack to crash, resulting in a broken collarbone and putting him out of racing for three weeks.

Sunday 20th July was race day for the Czech Grand Prix. The 95.32 mile 350cc race had the 90,000 race fans on their feet when Englander Rod Gould on his privately entered Yamaha two-stroke twin, which had been plagued with trouble in practice, gave World Champion, Giacomo Agostini on the works three cylinder MV, one of the hardest races of his season. From the start Gould rocketed ahead then the Italian ace got in front, Gould being troubled with a weaving Yamaha not suited to the fast bumpy bends. Nevertheless he re-passed the champion. On lap 6 the tenacious Gould, although recording the fastest lap of the race at 98.5mph, could not hold the hot pace on the poor handling Yamaha. The MV's superior performance was just too much. Agostini in winning his sixth consecutive 350cc Grand Prix race that season, clinched a further World Championship disappointment for Gould, but a stupendous effort by this privateer. Agostini continued his winning ways in the 500cc race, way ahead of the popular Hungarian-Swiss rider Gyula Marsovszky bringing his Linto into second place with Bohumil Stasa, CZ, third and Banbury's Dan Shorey, Seeley, in fifth, his best championship position so far that season.

There was disappointment for the Spanish star Santiago Herrero in the 250cc race. After leading the first lap, he retired the Ossa with engine trouble, leaving his close rival Renzo Pasolini, Benelli, to take the honours ahead of Rod Gould, Yamaha, and Aussie Kel Carruthers, Benelli.

Our other British hero, Dave Simmonds faced defeat in the 125cc race, his Kawasaki not able to hold the speed of Dieter Braun's ex-works Suzuki twin until Dieter ran into trouble with gear-selection problems, letting Simmonds through for his sixth Grand Prix win that season.

Following Bill Ivy's death, attention was turned to helmets. If Bill had been wearing an American styled helmet which most agreed gave more protection than the old fashioned 'pudding basin' type, it might been saved his life. Even Ken Shierson,

Big Jack Wren a methodical, dedicated professional.

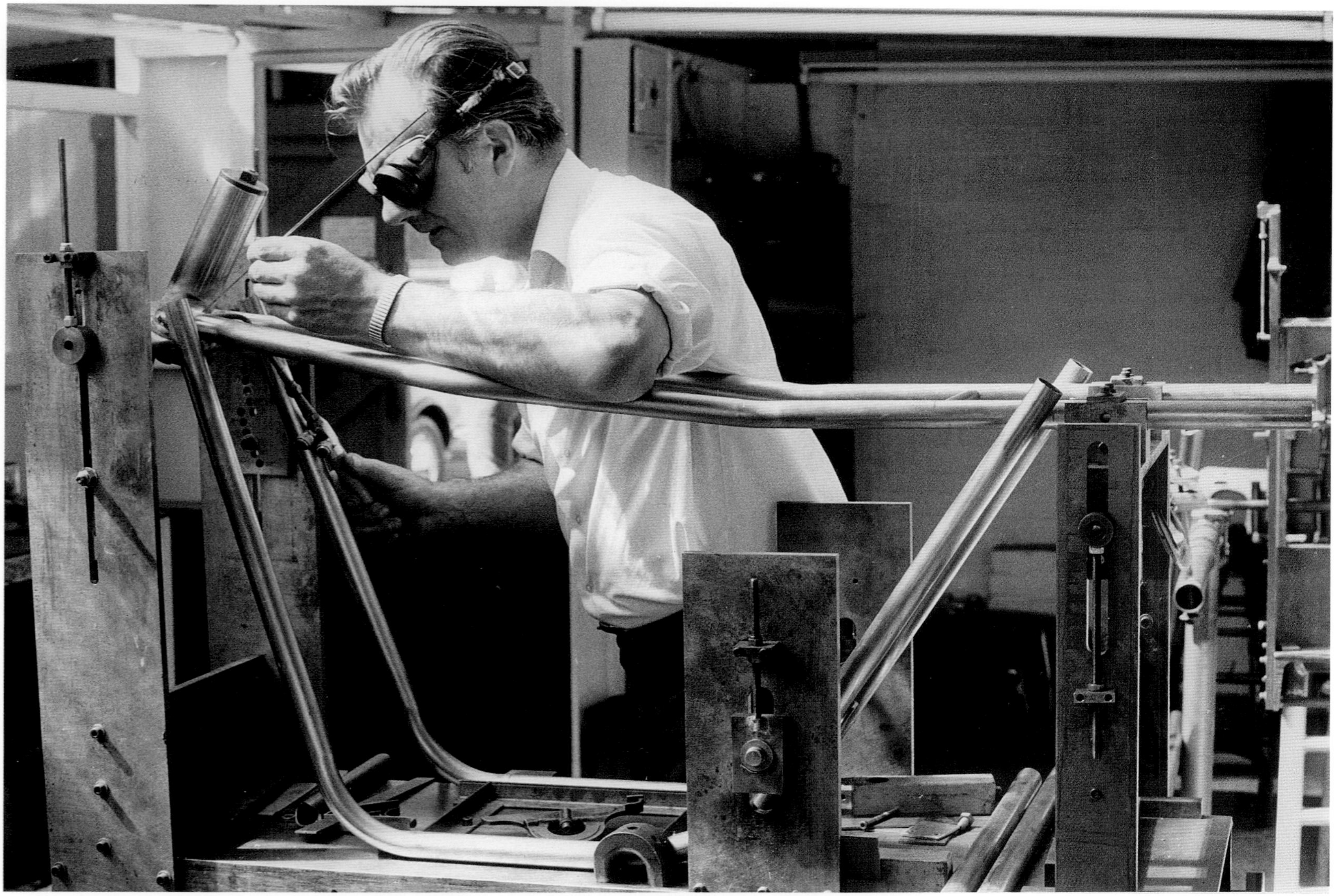

Secretary of the ACU, was convinced that the American styled space helmets were safer. This view was supported by John Cooper and Rod Gould. From 1958 in my own scrambling and road-racing career, I wore an American open face space helmet. However many competitors were reluctant or slow to change. How different are things today – riding gear has improved almost beyond recognition. Looking back, it is almost unbelievable that we raced in wafer-thin skin-tight leathers and gloves, the boots not much better. The leathers prevented loss of skin, but not much else – scary!!

Many racing stars attended the funeral of Bill Ivy at the Ditton Parish Church near Maidstone on the 23rd July; Mike Hailwood, Luigi Taveri, Phil Read, Stuart Graham, Alan Barnett, Ralph Bryans, Rex Butcher, Paul Smart, Peter Williams, Tom Kirby, Frank Sheene and myself, as well as members of the Chris Barber jazz band, among many who came to pay their respects to a brilliant sportsman. Forever in my memory is the occassion in 1965, arriving at Brands Hatch with my Dunstall-Norton outfit for a Wednesday afternoon practice. For some reason I was without a passenger. I asked Bill if he fancied a few laps in the chair, 'Sure!' was the answer. After the session and back in the paddock, Bill jumped out of the chair shouting, 'Never again!' Well now it was never again for this racing ace.

Meanwhile, in Southern Germany the likeable Swiss Gyula Marsovszky, then second in the 500cc World Championship, crashed his Linto during practice for the Frieburg Hill Climb. He suffered concussion, a punctured lung, broken ribs and collarbone. As a full time professional privateer Marsovszky was typical, needing to compete in as many events as possible to earn a reasonable living.

The 500cc Read Weslake twin project begun in 1967, with further modifications was tested by Phil Read at Snetterton in July '69, but was still not ready for competitive action, and still headed in the direction of failure.

At Woolwich the very last Norton left the Plumstead AMC factory - a sad end for such a historic company, world famous for its manufacture of AJS and Matchless motorcycles before the takeover of Norton. The five storey building would soon be demolished, but the memories would live on. Over many years there had been such an excellent range of motorcycles produced at Plumstead, with countless racing and competition successes. With Dennis Poore's takeover of Norton, production was moved to a new facility at Andover at which racing ace Peter Williams would be employed to head a new road racing development. With the closure of AMC, Seeley Racing Company was able to employ additional expertise, Jack Perkins taking control of our grinding department, Nobby Clark polishing, Charlie Bonner milling. Bob Cakebread design draughtsman, with Jack Wren and Denny Barnes lifting the weight of producing frames from my own shoulders.

Although everyone involved was essential for the progress of the company, one man worthy of a special mention was our new signing John Wren. After National Service John left the army in 1957. With no particular skills but living in the Plumstead area he

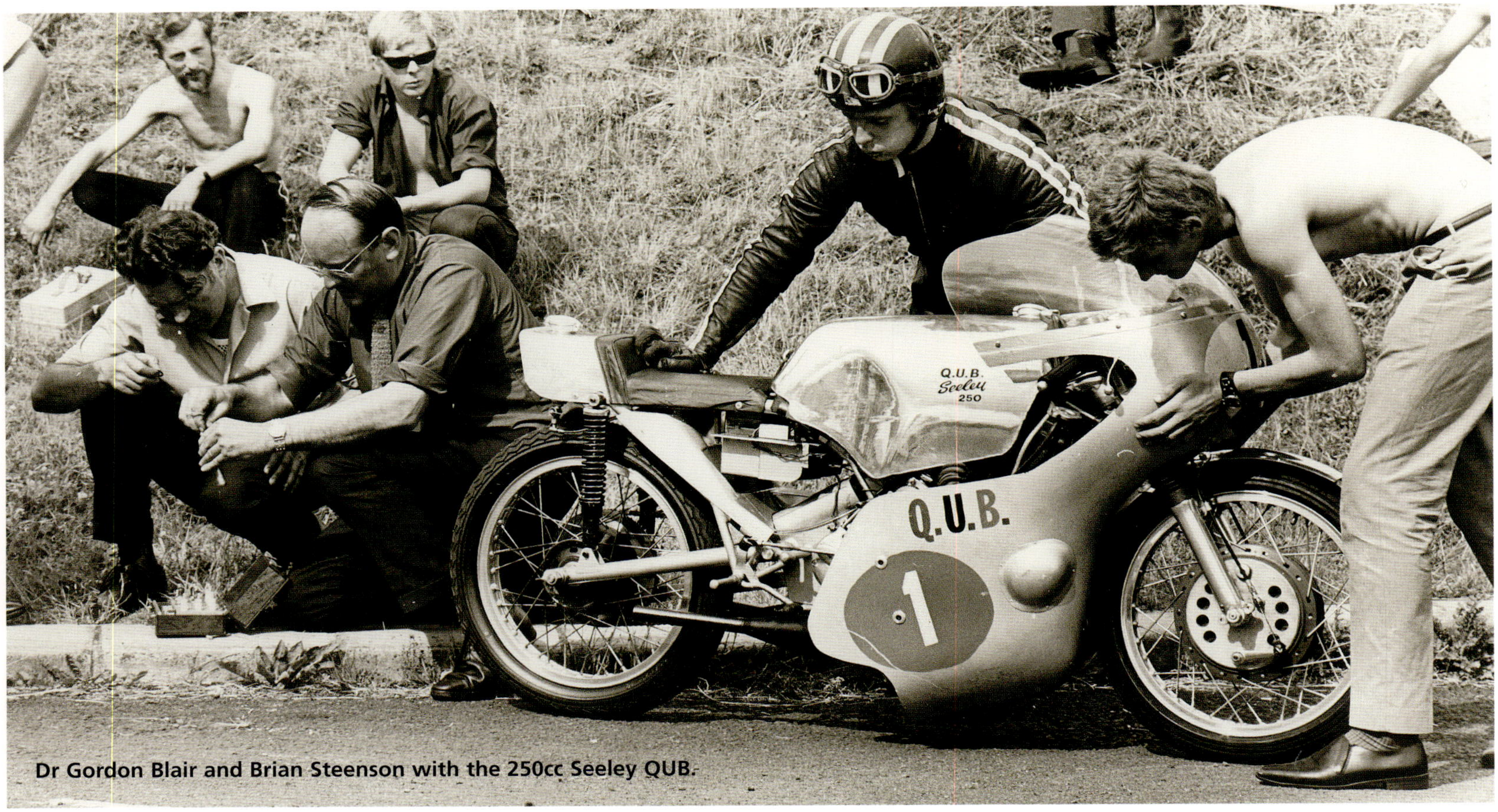

Dr Gordon Blair and Brian Steenson with the 250cc Seeley QUB.

applied to the AMC Factory. The only job available was store-man, which he gladly took. Months later, volunteers were requested to join the busy welding shop. John jumped at this opportunity and the training that went with it. His first serious production job was welding 92 pairs of headlamp brackets per day. 22 welders worked in that smoke-laden department and with several Johns in the department, John Wren became Jack and at 6ft 2in 'Big Jack', a name that would stick throughout his working life. Jack made great progress with his welding skills and was promoted to steel welding the prestigious 7R/G50 racing frames, possibly the Matchless G50 machines I had raced in my sidecar days had been welded by Big Jack. By 1965, with the AMC factory in decline, production of the 7R and G50 racing machines ceased. Jack moved on to AMC scrambles frames intended for the American market. These frames were bronze welded, and gave him further skills and expertise that he would bring eventually to Seeley Racing.

CSRD was expanding fast. We were bursting at the seams, every available space occupied by machinery, work benches, assembly area, raw materials and finished parts store, office space, customer reception, all somehow squeezed into the tiny Forge Works premises. Fortunately, I had managed to rent a small two storey building behind a flower shop. It was in this building on the first floor that my prize piece of equipment was located, the Italian Mandrell tube bender, along with a tube mitre machine which saved much of the intensive hand filing. Downstairs, John 'the tank' Pearson had his alloy tank department, a small, self-contained production unit.

Jack Wren reminded me of our original discussion when he applied for the job as a frame maker. We both gazed at an existing Seeley frame, and I explained that that was what I wanted, quality welding and a quality product, OK! Straight to the point, as I looked up at the 6ft 2in gentle giant, Just show me what you can do and with Danny Barnes, another ex-AMC welder in support, you will be given virtually a free hand in the frame shop. For Big Jack this was an another opportunity. With no formal training in either welding or management, Jack took it with both hands, pleased as punch to get the job involved with racing. He liked our handmade product and the fact that we could see the results of our handiwork on the track. With Bob Cakebread designing versatile production frame jigs, the whole operation of frame making moved onto another level. No longer would I be struggling with a plumbers hand bender or shaping and filing by hand whilst pressurised by the rest of the racing business. Manager Ken Burnside monitored day-to-day needs, but one particular day a staff meeting had been arranged at the Forge Works at morning tea break. All the staff gathered and we waited for the appearance of Big Jack and Denny. The frame shop was some distance away and both men decided to have their tea break before wandering down for the meeting. I was pretty impatient in those days, so I jumped into my car and drove off to the frame department. With a squeal of tyres and brakes, I burst through the door shouting, 'What the f... are you doing, we are waiting for you!' Big Jack remembers jumping into my Ford Capri without a word. I drove back at about 80mph, arriving to the 'jeers' of the rest of the team. Soon it was laughs all round and all was forgiven. How could anybody be angry with the unflappable Jack Wren who worked in such a methodical, dedicated and professional manner!

A fortnight later following the Czech Grand Prix the continental circus moved to Finland for its 3rd August Grand Prix around the 3.7 mile tricky bumpy tree-lined Imatra Circuit. Controversy hit this meeting when most of the top competitors threatened to strike if the sidecar race was run between the solo events. FIM recommended that three wheeler races be staged last for safety reasons. Double World Champion Agostini also requested the change pointing out that rubber and oil shed by the sidecars was another hazard on an already risky circuit. Typically, the organisers refused to budge. Amazingly, the FIM jury also rejected Agostini's plea. That Saturday evening, the top men signed a petition for the programme to be changed otherwise they reserved the right to pull out. The jury finally bowed to the riders' demands, but why should it take such a situation to bring officials to their senses! The Finnish event itself produced no surprises. In the 350 and 500cc races Agostini was in total control. The newly crowned 125cc champion, Dave Simmonds, on honeymoon with Julie Boddice, was in impressive form, bringing his Kawasaki home to its seventh Grand Prix win that season, 8 seconds ahead of Gunter Bartusch on a works engined MZ.

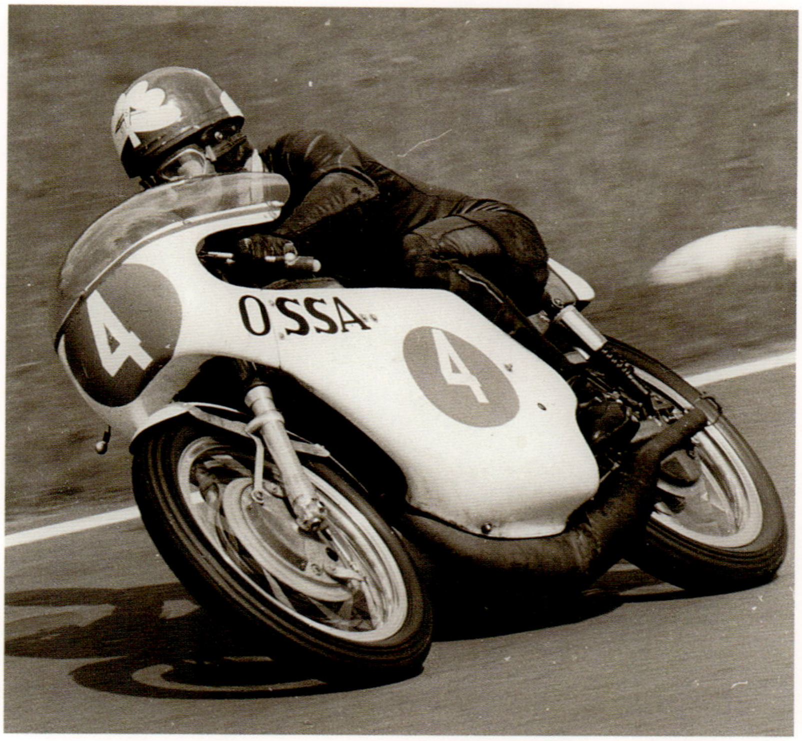

Santiago Herrero, 250cc Ossa, won the 250cc race in brilliant style.

Highlight of the meeting was the 250cc six way dice. Heinz Rosner, MZ, took the lead, but only for one lap as the MZ came to a halt with a broken crankshaft. The Spanish bombshell Herrero, Ossa, took over from Gould, Yamaha, Pasolini, Benelli, and Andersson, Yamaha, until lap 12 when Kent Andersson got just ahead. On lap 14 of the 21 lap race, championship leader Santiago Herrero, striving to clinch his championship bid, slid off on a slow corner, remounted and rode to the pits for repairs, but back in the race was a lap down. Pasolini also crashed. The on-form Rod Gould in second place on the last lap, was forced to retire with a broken crankshaft. For Sweden's Kent Andersson, splendidly attired in brand new white leathers, it was no lucky win, breaking Mike Hailwood's 250 lap record for the 3.7 mile circuit - an outstanding effort racing an over-the-counter TDZ Yamaha. Gunter Bartusch, MZ, managed second place ahead of Kel Carruthers who kept his championship hopes alive on the works Benelli.

Five Linto machines were entered in the 86 mile 500cc race. Agostini, MV, kindly let Keith Turner lead for a number of laps, but was soon out, breakage of the primary gear once more the cause. This let Paul Smart, Seeley, riding without goggles because the strap had broken, into second place. Behind Maurice Hawthorne, Linto, John Dodds, Linto, and Billie Nelson, Paton, battled for position. Then drama as Hawthorne's Linto sprang an oil leak – so he was out, soon followed by Dodds and Jack Findlay – the Lintos continuing to be unreliable. Steve Ellis carefully brought the sole surviving Linto home into eighth place. No joy for Paul Smart. The crank pin broke on the Seeley, leaving the talented 'Mr. Nice Guy' Billie Nelson, Paton, to finish in second place ahead of Godfrey Nash, Norton, in a fine third spot.

Finally, came the last race of the day, the controversial sidecar event for Fath. With three wins and one third to Enders, two wins and a second place to Helmut, he was in line for his third World Championship title and a win would do it. Fath was partnered this time by the versatile Billie Nelson, and led from the start. Mick Woollett described the race as awe-inspiring with the outfits drifting and sliding over the bumps as the crews struggled for control in the 17 lap 63.69 mile race. Fath was in a class of his own, pulling out a tremendous lead over Georg Auerbacher, BMW, who cooked his brakes, leaving the stylish Klaus Enders in second place. Having broken his own lap record, Fath himself was in trouble as an ominous trail of smoke appeared, a broken oil pipe the cause. A dejected Helmut was forced to retire. Klaus Enders took the win and a two point lead in the championship. With only the Ulster Grand Prix to come for the sidecar title – it was all to play for!

1968 World Champion Helmut Fath, along with many other competitors at the Finnish Grand Prix, decided to compete at the 2.24 mile Keimola Circuit 9 miles from Helsinki just two days later. This was just one of those 'top up the coffers' events, but it ended in calamity for Fath and passenger Billie Nelson. While leading Auerbacher and Enders and with only 2 laps to go, again an oil pipe fractured spewing oil everywhere. Helmut eased the pace in the hope of nursing the stricken URS four to the chequered flag. This was a huge mistake. On a fast right-hander the oil-starved engine seized solid causing the outfit to spin out of control throwing both men onto the track. Fath sustained fractured ribs and right leg and Billy Nelson a broken leg and right ankle. Fath's championship hopes were gone, handed on plate to BMW's Klaus Enders, Billie Nelson's chances of bringing the Hannah-Paton into a third place or even a second in the 1969 World 500cc Championship were also gone, he would be out of racing for three months at least. A huge price had been paid once again, just trying to achieve results, cover costs and earn a living.

In Ireland a week before the Ulster Grand Prix the Seeley-QUB 250cc ridden by Brian Steenson was given its debut at the mid-Antrim 150 meeting but it was disappointing for Dr. Gordon Blair and his crew from Queen's University. The QUB failed to complete even one lap after slipped ignition timing caused the little twin to run on one cylinder. The ebullient Steenson, fast becoming Ireland's top road racer, in a 350cc race dominated by Aermacchi machines, won the event on his Aermacchi after a tough race against Cecil Crawford and Ian McGregor, followed by winning the 500cc event on his Seeley G50.

Back at Brands Hatch the same weekend, preparations were taking place for Sunday's British Motorcycle Racing Club's International Hutchinson 100, run as usual, anti-clockwise on the 2.65 mile Grand Prix circuit. The meeting attracted the regular top solo British riders but controversy reared its head, this time over the entry of the home sidecar stars, with the BMCRC secretary Jim Swift refusing to pay any start or expense money. When asked if German riders Georg Auerbacher and Klaus Enders, on route to the Ulster Grand Prix, could produce a race on their own, with no real competition, or would it be just a demonstration! Jim Swift responded with, 'I'm not worried about sidecars, I am relying on the solo machines to provide the action!' Such a statement from an official was disgraceful, and a stab in the heart of British sidecar racing! Mr. Swift was obviously not aware of the part three wheelers had played in the historic Hutchinson 100 event over many years. Then a u-turn, Mr. Swift made an offer to Chris Vincent via his sponsor Peter Chapman. To Chris Vincent's credit he declined on principle and in sympathy with other British sidecar competitors. As a result there were no British drivers capable of challenging the Germans. Ironically, Georg Auerbacher won the massive Mellano Trophy with his winning speed average in the 1300cc race nearest to the existing lap record. Although at the time the trophy itself was worth around a thousand guineas, it was not retained by the competitor. A small replica but no money was offered - not much use to my old opponent gentleman Georg, who was seriously considering retiring at the end of that season, because prize and start money was decreasing at every turn.

The Hutchinson 100 had failed to attract foreign solo competitors other that the rising Spanish ace Santiago Herrero with his incredible single cylinder works 250cc Ossa. However, 25,000 sun baked fans enjoyed the day and witnessed our only World Road

Racing Champion that year, Dave Simmonds bring his Kawasaki home first in the 125cc from Barry Smith, Derbi, and London boy Barry Sheene, Yamaha-Bultaco, third.

In the 350cc race Rod Gould maintained his brilliant form, with Phil Read second, well in front of Mick Andrew's Kuhn-Seeley in third place. Then suddenly Read was out with machine trouble, leaving the flying Gould to break Hailwood's lap record. Then with only 2 laps to go, Gould crashed at Druids Bend on some oil and was out. In a hectic dash to the finish the Gus Kuhn Team rider Andrew brought his Seeley 7R first under the chequered flag, beating Alan Barnett and Peter Williams with team-mate Croxford, Kuhn-Seeley, in fifth place ahead of Paul Smart, Yamaha, sixth. Santiago Herrero showed his true colours when riding his 250cc Ossa in the first leg of the unlimited Evening News Race. Chasing the big bikes, the Ossa's crankshaft broke. With no spare machine it seemed his day was over, but undaunted, Santiago and his mechanic set to and stripped the engine and fitted a new shaft in less than two hours, just in time for the 250cc race, his main event. The dazzling Spaniard made a brilliant start leading the 12 lap event from start to finish leaving the current double World Champion Phil Read, Yamaha, in second with Maidstone's Paul Smart, Yamaha, in third spot. This was an astounding victory for the Spanish star on his first visit to Brands Hatch.

Then in the 15 lap second leg of the Evening News Trophy, Herrero on the 250 Ossa would mix it with the local aces on their big bikes, finally finishing fifth, an unbelievable result in an event totally dominated by Rod Gould, 350 Yamaha, who won convincingly both legs. Rising star Mick Andrew on the 750 Kuhn Commando registered two brilliant second places, and Paul Smart on the 750 Francis Norton was third overall. Rex Butcher, giving the 700cc Weslake-Rickman Metisse an airing came fourth with our man Croxford on the 500 Kuhn Seeley fifth, ahead of Percy Tait.

Mick Andrew added to his successes on the day winning the 20 lap production race on a 750cc Norton-Commando from Tony Smith, 650cc BSA Spitfire, Rod Gould, 650cc Triumph Bonneville, Ray Pickrell, 750cc Dunstall Dominator, Peter Williams, 750cc Norton Commando, and Percy Tait, 750cc Triumph Trident, in sixth place. This was no walk-over, the best were there, so great cheer for Andrew's sponsor, the Clapham dealership boss Vincent Davey of Gus Kuhn Motors. Despite the fiasco over the sidecar event, the day had provided some great racing and the crowd went home happy.

The following week was busy. I went to Northern Ireland for The Ulster Grand Prix, a meeting in total contrast to my local Derby at Brands. I was to stay with Dr. Gordon Blair to discuss the 250cc Seeley-QUB project and other schemes in the pipeline. I would also be supporting Brian Steenson, competing in the 500cc Classic on his Seeley G50.

Looking back, I suppose that many of the international competitors were oblivious to the political situation in Northern Ireland, in fact many mainland UK riders, including myself, had not taken on board the unrest that was simmering in Belfast prior to the forty-first Ulster Grand Prix. Racing was our business and we just wanted to get on with the tenth round of the World Championship that year. At the eleventh hour, Bertie Mann the Clerk of the Course received an urgent phone call from the Government Minister of Home Affairs, stating that with immediate effect all assemblies of people had been banned. This meant the cancellation of the Grand Prix and the possible end to this historic road race event, leaving Bertie Mann and his committee with a potential debt of up to £10,000. Faced with this dramatic situation, Mann strongly argued the case that the ruling should not apply to sporting events, finally managing to reverse the Government decision and allowing the Grand Prix to go ahead. What a nightmare for him, his band of supporters and competitors alike. On race day itself, an hour before the start, an anonymous note threatened trouble during the races, if certain flags were flown. Fortunately the organisers had anticipated this risk and the trouble was avoided.

Santiago Herrero must have thought racing was a simple affair after being caught up in the Belfast riots. A faction had threatened to burn down the hotel in which the Ossa Team were staying, so Herrero thought he should move out. Unable to drive through the barricaded streets that Friday evening, Santiago unloaded his Ossa. Once the locals realised that Herrero was a Grand Prix competitor they hoisted the Ossa over the obstructions. Then in a terrifying journey the Spaniard dodged the shots and rode the bike through the burning streets to the race paddock 5 miles away, arriving in such a rush that he braked too hard and fell off. Undeterred, our hero borrowed a van and returned to Belfast to rescue his team mates. He left his Ossa in the hands of his chief rival for the 250cc World Championship, Kent Andersson, great trust between competitors.

The previous day I had been in town with Leslie Nichol from the Daily Express. On hearing gunfire, we peeped around a corner to view the confrontation. It reminded me of London during the Second World War, but in Belfast the gunshots were pretty close. It was very sad and unbelievably dangerous.

Saturday's Ulster Grand Prix race day could not match the drama on the streets with smoke still billowing from the fires lit during the riots. Nevertheless, the show went on. Perhaps the Grand Prix provided a release valve for the troubles if only for a day or two. Motorcycle road racing had a long tradition in Ireland, where public roads could be closed to provide racing between kerb stones, hedges, trees and houses, immense excitement for fans with a common interest regardless of religious background. That Saturday morning, 40,000 enthusiasts lined most of the 7.4 mile undulating rather narrow Dundrod Circuit, the crowd down by 40% on 1968. Waiting for the 10.15am start of the 50cc 'tiddlers' race , the fans bought 20,000 of the official souvenir programmes.

With some trepidation 27 riders came to the line for the first ever appearance of 50cc machines at the Ulster Grand Prix. Apart from this new class, this was racing with a difference, as there could be trouble spilling over from Belfast. No worries though, the Irish fans respected the performers, and only a caterer's van was attacked by some rioters. MCN reporter John Brown and photographer Jim Greening, on their way to the event were challenged by army personnel wielding Sten guns, which gave them a bit of a shock, I can imagine them both shaking in their boots, 'Sorry officer, I think we're in the wrong road'.

The 6 lap 44.4 mile race for the magnificent miniature 50cc machines would more than justify their inclusion in the Ulster Grand Prix. For nearly 4 laps Angel Nieto on the works Derbi duelled for the lead with Dutchman Paul Lodewijkx, Jamathi. Initially the Spaniard just had the edge but in the fastest lap of the race at an astonishing 83.39mph average Lodewijkx closed in and took the lead. They passed and re-passed then Nieto, trying to pass inside through a sweep of bends lost control. The Derbi shot sideways and literally knocked the Dutchman's wheels from under him, causing the Jamathi and jockey to rocket over a hedge leaving Nieto and his Derbi bowling down the track. Fortunately, neither rider was

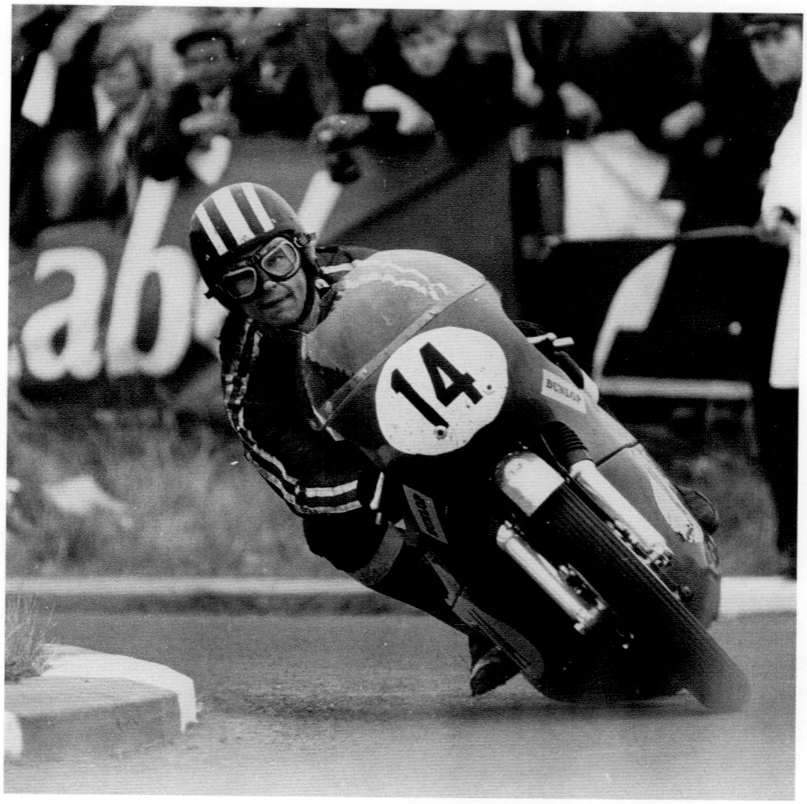

Brian Steenson, Seeley G50, 2nd place behind Agostini at the Ulster Grand Prix. A brilliant ride averaging 98.60mph.

badly hurt. Nieto was able to remount and finish the race still in the lead averaging 80.20mph Paul Lodewijkx could only look through the hedge as fellow Dutchman Jan de Vries brought his Kreidler home in second place, way ahead of Frank Whiteway, Crooks Suzuki.

Brian Steenson entered the prototype 250cc QUB-Seeley in the lightweight event and had completed some practice laps. But it was decided to withdraw it as Gordon Blair's design needed further development. The Irish star could concentrate on his Aermacchi in the 350cc race and the 500 Seeley in the Senior Event. 250cc World Championship leader Santiago Herrero had a bad weekend. After his adventures in Belfast he was on the verge of clinching his first world title in the 15 lap 250cc race. Holding third place to a flying Kel Carruthers on the Benelli and Rod Gould, Yamaha, Santiago overcooked it at Wheelers Corner and disappeared through a hedge, fracturing two small bones in his hand, a blow to the Spaniard's title hopes and certainly a meeting to forget. Despite some scattered drizzle, Carruthers rode a faultless race to win at 93.61mph with a fastest lap of 98.87mph from Kent Andersson. Rod Gould broke down again. In a brilliant ride Queen's technician and local man Ray McCullough brought his Yamaha home third only 7.4 seconds down on Kent Andersson.

The 350cc race as expected was a runaway victory for the Italian 'champ' Giacomo Agostini, MV. Rod Gould looked like being Ago's strongest rival but Heinz Rosner on the MZ had other ideas, keeping ahead of Gould who retired once more with engine trouble, the Yamaha proving fast but unreliable. Brian Steenson was dicing for third spot with Cecil Crawford when his Aermacchi seized, a major disappointment for his home crowd. Tony Rutter, Yamaha, took fourth ahead of Stastny, Jawa, and the popular Irishman Tommy Robb, Aermacchi, came in sixth place with Steve Jolly, Seeley 7R, in twelfth position.

For the 101 mile 500cc race Agostini again reigned supreme. The field of 36 starters including Ron Chandler, Malcolm Uphill, Jack Findlay, Percy Tait, Brian Steenson and Alan Barnett kept in sight of the champion for a short time before he shot off into the distance. Soon the Italian ace was blasting his MV to a record-breaking ride, leaving the Irish fans in awe of his racing skill, not only winning at an average speed of 103.74mph but breaking Mike Hailwood's 1967 lap record held at 105.71mph on the Honda. Ago recorded 107.66mph, not much in real time, but enough to take the record. Just behind was our own Brian Steenson who had held an impressive second place throughout. He brought his Seeley G50 home at 98.60mph average, the only rider not to have been lapped by Ago. Uphill took third place, after John Blanchard on his Chuck-Seeley retired with engine trouble on lap 6. Ron Chandler was sixth with Steve Jolly eleventh on their Seeley machines. Agostini for his spectacular performance received the Ulster Grand Prix Trophy, a souvenir and £100, matching the prize money for the 350cc race. Steenson was awarded a souvenir and £75, 15 shillings or 75p per lap. Prize money was paid down to fifteenth place, Ron Chandler received £15, Steve Jolly £5 and of course souvenirs, such were the rewards.

Finally came the sidecars, in a race re-introduced after a lapse of 13 years. The expected clash between Helmut Fath and Klaus Enders was not to be with Fath injured from his Finnish accident. Georg Auerbacher was also out of action after a practice crash. Klaus Enders, the new champion won the Ulster Grand Prix easily from Siegfried Schauzu in an uninspired race. BMWs took the first five places with Dick Hawes bringing his Seeley G50 outfit home seventh – not bad! Klaus Enders took the Grand Prix Trophy, souvenir and £100 but prize money went to the first six places. Dick Hawes got £15 and the other finishers – nothing!

Delighted with Steenson's performance the university arranged a party that evening. Dr. Blair, Ray McCullough, sponsor Mick Mooney and other well-wishers attended. The Irish certainly know how to enjoy themselves, it was a great evening free from the tensions of the last few days. I left the party with Gordon Blair. Driving home we were reminded again of the troubles, brought to a stop by armed soldiers at a check point. It was strange and spine-chilling, certainly not pleasant. Fortunately for me I would be flying home next day leaving the troubles behind, such a sad state of affairs for my Irish friends.

Away from the track, rumours were flying. Agostini was considering, or perhaps had been instructed, not to ride in the last two Grand Prix events of the season, the Italian and Yugoslavian. Instead he competed in the end of season British International meetings Oulton Park, Cadwell, Mallory and Brands. Count Agusta was irritated that the Italian Grand Prix had moved from its traditional home of Monza to Imola, so was making a point. An Italian Grand Prix without works MVs seemed inconceivable. The race organisers were anxious that without their 'star' Agostini, the crowd could drop by as much as 20,000! Despite pleas from the Italian Motorcycle Racing Federation and the newspapers, Count Agusta stuck to his decision, if it was no to Monza, there would be no MVs and no Ago!

On his way home from Ulster Ago accepted an invitation to visit the Norton-Villers Factory at Thruxton to discuss the possibility of racing a factory 750cc Norton Commando in major production events for the 1970 season. He turned down an offer that day to test ride the Hutchinson 100 winning Gus Kuhn Commando, declining on the basis of his contract with MV. Could you imagine this super star racing a Norton-Commando? I couldn't see him somehow, in the role of a production bike rider.

Racing circuits Castle Combe and Thruxton were under threat once more. Ministry inspectors, local councils and any other non-motor sport individuals that wanted to jump on the bandwagon, made noises to close them down.

Our hectic pace continued, manufacturing Seeley models and the many associated parts for older AJS 7R and Matchless G50 machines. For the third year running we were preparing for September's Manx Grand Prix event, to provide a full racing service. As before, this operation put tremendous strains on our resources, particularly with three

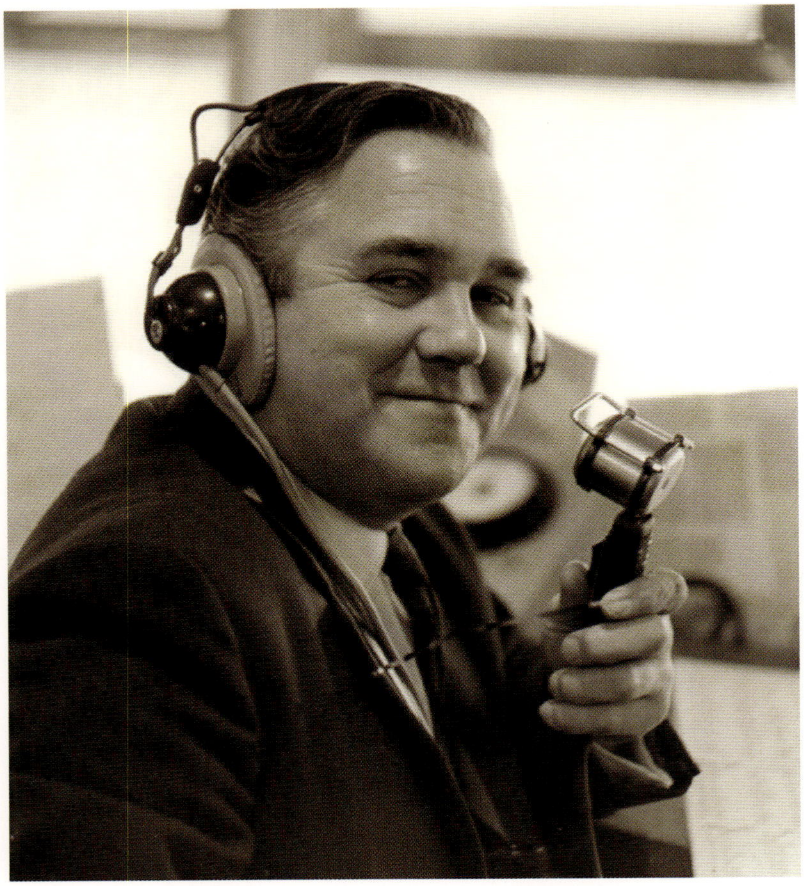

Peter Arnold, a real enthusiast for our sport of motorcycling.

major international events in September and the end of August Snetterton meeting, with Crystal Palace next day, Bank Holiday Monday 1st September. It was rumoured that Mike Hailwood would compete at the Mallory Park 21st September Carreras 1,000 guineas International Race of the Year. Mike had been offered a number of machines but he called me to say he would like to race a Seeley G50 for this event. What a compliment! A multi World champion waiting to ride our machine meant more pressure, but we would relish it.

Sadly, in the Isle of Man first day of practice week for the Manx Grand Prix, 30 year old Gordon Taylor was killed on the second lap of the 350cc practice. He crashed his 325cc Kawasaki at Alpine Cottage near Ballaugh. Then further bad news, 'Mr. Nice Guy', freelance journalist, commentator, broadcaster, 49 year old Peter Arnold died in Northampton General Hospital. His car left the road near Towcester in the early hours of Tuesday morning travelling from his regular commentating engagement at Reading Speedway. The inquest revealed Peter had suffered a massive heart attack, crashed his car, then died following a coronary thrombosis in hospital. Peter Arnold, born Alan Baxter, adopted his more familiar name while working in the theatre for 10 years as an impersonator. He served with a night fighter squadron during the war and was decorated for bravery. He also produced several RAF stage shows. A keen sportsman, Peter tried his hand at speedway and grass track racing. he had interviewed myself and passenger Roy Lindsey for the Stanley Scofield TT record in 1967 – my very last Isle of Man TT in which we had finished third, me with raging toothache. Peter's first wife died in 1966 leaving a 5 year old son Paul. The day after the accident he was to have married Maureen Vinicombe, widow of sidecar racer Terry Vinicombe. Peter had limitless energy and humour and was so well respected, a man for all seasons.

Seeley products were now in great demand. The last Manx Nortons had been produced at Bracebridge Street back in 1961. Of course the Norton had been enormously successful over the years and was still a favourite for many competitors. Despite the importance for us of AJS 7R and Matchless G50, I had visited Birmingham many times and arranged the continued supply of many Manx Norton components. This was not easy, as so many were still owed money from the defunct Associated Motorcyles Company. Finally, with our continued financial constraints, we felt that we were not able to give the necessary justice and full commitment to the Manx Norton project. We decided to sell complete all existing stock, blue prints, jigs and fixtures, plus manufacturing rights. Although this was well reported in the motorcycle press, there was no flood of offers. Disappointed, I even offered the well known Norton tuner Ray Petty a deal on a sale or return basis lending the drawings, jigs and fixtures to Ray with the promise to support the effort throughout. This would have given Seeley-Racing a lesser commitment, but still some control. The cash would have been very useful, but at least we would be working with someone who knew Nortons through and through. Unfortunately, much to my amazement and even now I'm still amazed, Ray Petty turned down my offer. As a well respected specialist Norton tuner, perhaps he was overawed by such an undertaking, a shame, as I was convinced it would have worked well for both of us as well as the Manx Norton owners.

Many competitors in the Isle of Man rested after a busy practice week awaiting the 250, 350 and 500 Manx Grand Prix events of 2nd and 4th September. Over on the mainland the excitement continued, with race meetings that Bank Holiday weekend, Snetterton Sunday 31st August, Oulton Park, Crystal Place and Cadwell Park, 1st September.

The Race of the Aces was held on the 2.71 mile Snetterton Circuit, previously a World War II USAAF bomber base, now with competitors bombing down the Norwich straight. At this meeting John Cooper made a comeback after recovering from his Cadwell Park crash back in May, but 'Mooneyes' choice was not an easy route, having been offered the chance by Mike Hailwood to race the mighty 500cc Honda four.

Snetterton always provided fast exciting racing and some surprises. Chas Mortimer, Villa, beat off the challenge of the improving Barry Sheene to win the 125cc race. Phil Read just got the better of Rod Gould in the 250cc event. Cliff Carr, Yamaha, inherited the 350cc race after Phil Read was a non-starter, and Rod Gould who in his 350cc heat had broken Mike Hailwood's year old absolute lap record by 0.2 seconds, only completed a lap on his Yamaha, retiring with a dead ignition. This left Cliff Carr battling with Mike Hatherill, Aermacchi, and the dashing Londoner, Sheene who got the better of Hatherill to take second place.

The 500cc race would be interesting. Percy Tait and John Cooper both won their heats. Our main hope lay in the hands of Croxford, Smart and Brian Steenson on his first ever visit to Snetterton. I stood beside Cooperman's wife Helen, vividly remembering the 500cc race start, 'Mooneyes' accelerated the big Honda off the line and it went into an uncontrollable tank 'slapper', the handlebars seemingly wrenched out of his hands. It looked inevitable that the Derbyshire ace would crash, but somehow he regained control of the wobbling Honda, which was some sort of miracle. Despite this fright John Cooper brought the Honda home fourth behind winner Percy Tait, Dave Degens second and Paul Smart, Seeley, third. Steenson had held second place but went out with a broken primary chain.

In the 500cc Sidecar race our old friend and adversary Pip Harris, BMW, in a close encounter with Tony Wakefield also BMW, was at his best on the Snetterton track and took the win from Wakefield, breaking Helmut Fath's lap record by 1.6 seconds in the process with a lap of 85.73mph.

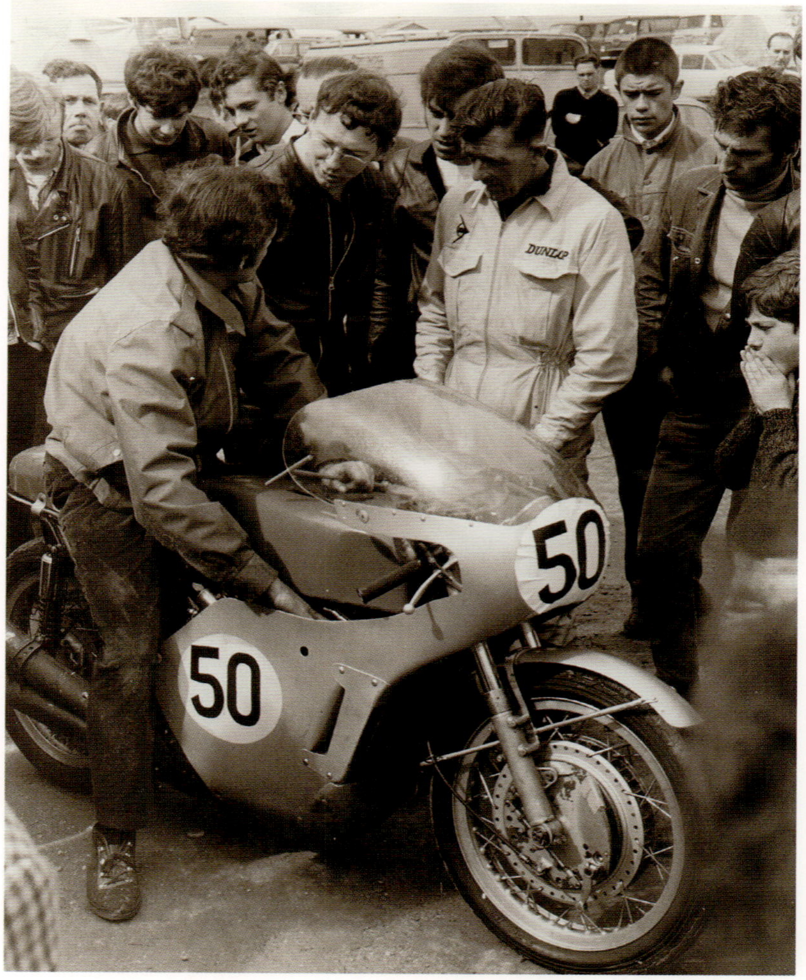

31st August 1969. Honda works mechanic, Nobby Clark on the Honda 500 four, chats to John Cooper who rode the machine.

In the 10 lap 1000cc Race of the Aces, Rod Gould charged ahead on his 350cc Yamaha to equal his earlier lap record. Behind him a fantastic eight strong battle for second place raged between Paul Smart and Brian Kemp on the 750cc Nortons, Percy Tait on a 650 Triumph Bonneville then Peter Williams, Steenson, Croxford and Cooper on 500s with Tony Rutter on his 350cc Yamaha. Only 1.4 seconds separated this group until the last lap when Rutter and Croxford broke away. Rutter just got second place from the 'Ruislip Rebel' who brought his Seeley home third, John Cooper, Honda, fourth, next Percy Tait, then Steenson, Seeley. Then the competitors dispersed for Monday's events!

I dashed home to spend a few hours with my wife and son before disappearing to Crystal Palace next day for the final rounds of the 350 and 500 British Championships. The 1.39 mile Crystal Palace circuit, lined with railway sleepers, was certainly not for the faint hearted. The British Motorcycle Racing Club organised the event on behalf of the GLC, with Clerk of the Course and Secretary of the meeting the controversial Jim Swift. ACU time keeper in charge was Harry Shuttleworth and one of the stewards was Sir Geoffrey Tuttle KBE,CB,DFC,FRACS, Chief Scrutineer Ernie Woods, and announcer, Allan Robinson MBE.

The Kent boys were out in force; Chandler, Smart, Butcher, Ashwood, Ditchburn and Mahoney all juggling for those final championship positions. The London fans and the BBC TV viewers were not disappointed. With a programme of 13 races including three for sidecars, it was non-stop action. Mick Andrew in the first production race of the day, ahead of Charlie Sanby and Pete Butler the eventual winner, crashed his Gus Kuhn 745 Norton Commando causing him a painful back injury which sidelined him for the rest of the meeting. Crayford's Pat Mahoney who lay second to 350cc title leader Derek Chatterton who had 'ducked' Crystal Palace to race at Cadwell, was without a 350cc machine, having fallen out with his sponsor. Pat, never a man to miss an opportunity, approached Vincent Davey, the Kuhn team boss for use of Andrew's 350cc Seeley, resulting in a four Seeley line-up for that championship race.

The all-important 500cc final was to be a close run contest between Croxford and Alan Barnett but unfortunately for the Tom Kirby team, Barnett was out of action with a broken arm from Thursday at Snetterton. When testing a prototype Triumph-Rickman Metisse, prepared by Rickmans, a gearbox cam plate indexing plunger bolt had dropped out allowing oil to spray onto the back wheel. This was a huge mistake, and the start of a suggested rift between the parties. Of course 'Crox' the 1968 British Champion benefited from this situation but he still needed to finish the 15 lap race around the tricky Palace track to grab his second title. Ron Chandler, a Palace specialist, brought his Seeley home first in a 'ding-dong' race, just ahead of Paul Smart on Joe Francis' Seeley with the Ruislip Rebel home third, securing the Castrol sponsored British Championship title. A 1 - 2 - 3 for Seeley Racing and our second British 500cc championship. Alan Barnett secured a championship second place, a disappointment for this likeable competitor, with Mick Andrew bringing his Kuhn Seeley into third position.

In the final round of the 350cc championship, from the drop of the flag, Graham Sharp, Aermacchi, led a terrific battle for 2 laps but 'Crazy' Croxford, Kuhn Seeley, with nothing to lose, overtook John Blanchard, Chuck Seeley, and Ron Chandler, Seeley, hung on in close formation. Croxford then overcooked his braking at the sharp right South Tower Corner, which led onto the start and finish straight. The British 500 champion hit some oil, possibly spilt by those damned sidecars, and crashed out! Blanchard, very close, grabbed his brake and clutch at the same time, and in the panic of avoidance his Seeley 7R engine over revved and the valves kissed, leaving him to join the bruised Croxford at the trackside. Ron Chandler came home to his second win of the day, recording the fastest lap ahead of Charlie Sanby and Graham Sharp, with Pat Mahoney finishing fourth on the Kuhn Seeley which clinched him the 350cc British Championship, 4 points ahead of Derek Chatterton with Alan Barnett in third. Martin Carney, Kawasaki, was fourth with our men Andrew and Chandler making up the first six. The day was not over for the Thames lighterman when Chandler brought his Seeley home first in the 15 lap 1000cc event. With both Kuhn riders out of action, Pat Mahoney took over the 745 Kuhn Commando and rode well for second place, beating off the challenge of Paul Smart on the 745 Francis-Norton. With a hat trick for Chandler and £130 prize money and a further British Championship for the irrepressible 'Ruislip Rebel' it was certainly time to celebrate, 'fags and Guinness' for Croxford, champagne for the rest.

Up at the Oulton Park international the anticipated duel between Rod Gould and World Champion Giacomo Agostini on his first visit to the Cheshire Circuit was dashed on the first lap of the 19 lap 350cc race. Gould from a superb start took the lead from Ago on the works MV, then crashed at the fast Knickerbrook section. Rod escaped with concussion, sprained wrists and a cracked right elbow. For the fans the excitement was over, and the Italian Ace cruised to an easy victory ahead of the 1968 double World Champion Phil Read, who didn't seem to be sparkling in 1969. However, a few days later at the Italian Grand Prix at Imola 'Speedy' Read won both 250 and 350 events on his Yamaha. Luck was on his side in the 350cc. Silvio Grassetti on the surviving works Jawa took the lead after Read was forced into a pit stop to secure a loose exhaust pipe. He rejoined in third place. Grassetti confident of winning his first ever Grand Prix, with several laps to go started waving to the crowd. The lack of concentration was his

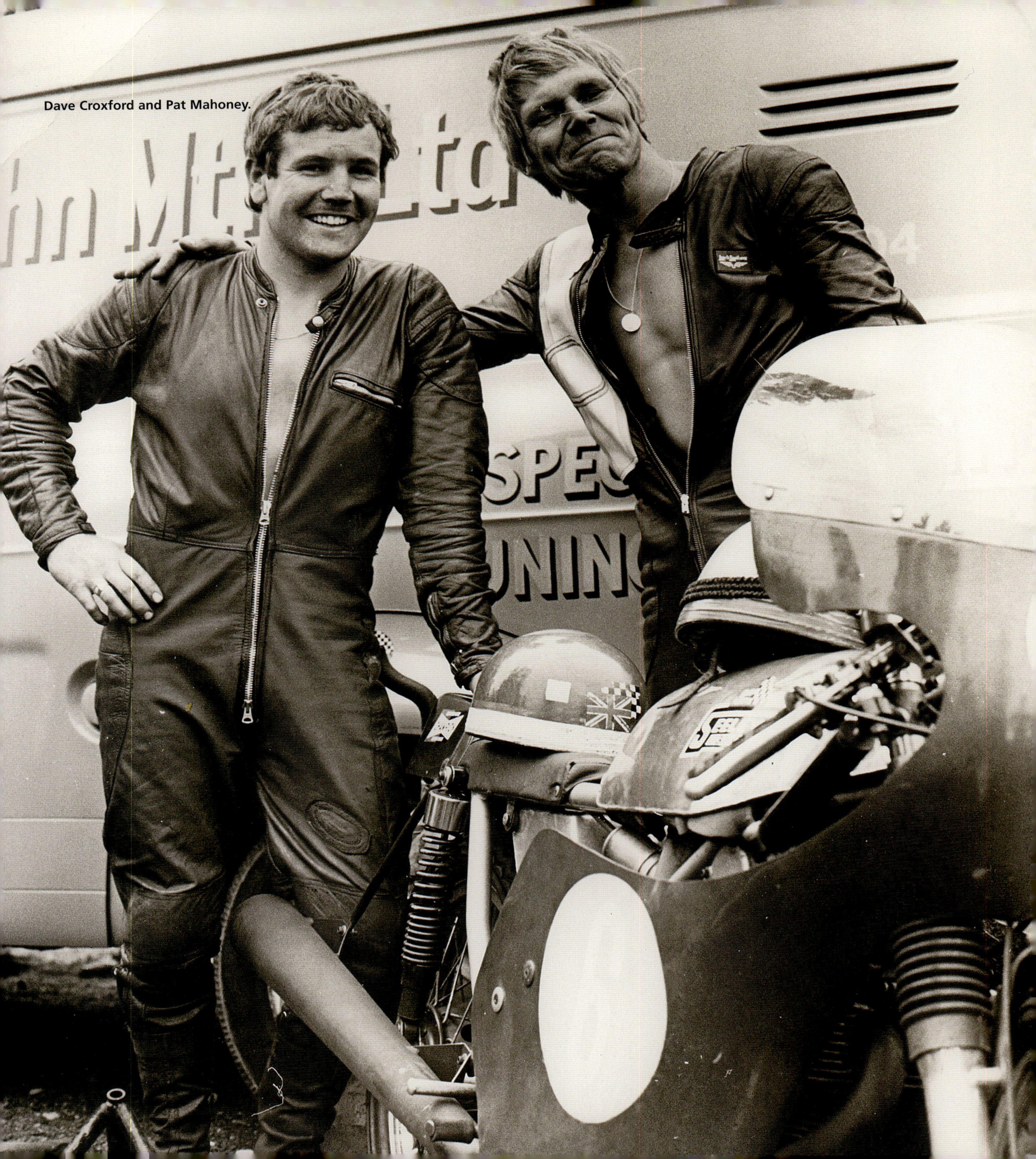

Dave Croxford and Pat Mahoney.

Gordon Pantall, Seeley, Manx Grand Prix 1969.

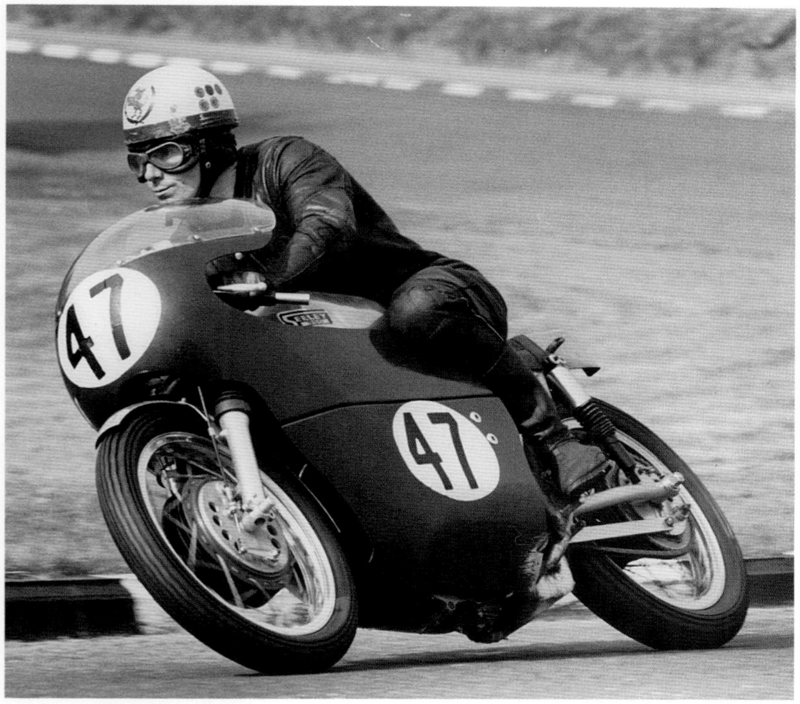

undoing. Silvio drifted off the track onto the rough verge then for a good distance fought for control of the Jawa before regaining the course. By then Read was not far behind, and within 2 laps was back in front again leaving the foolish Italian to take second place and a rocket from the Jawa Team for his stupidity.

Franta Stastny was out of the running when his Jawa went sick but worse was to come. Jack Findlay's Jawa four seized and threw Jack down the road at some 70mph. Unfortunately, the Jawa hit Findlay in his back causing severe bruising and a hospital visit. For Jack Findlay that was the last straw and it would be the parting of the ways between him and Jawa. It had been a difficult season for this likeable Aussie. Even to the last Grand Prix of the year, the Yugoslavian, the organisers refused to raise their start money stating that it would be more than Agostini was offered. Findlay then pointed out that rather than ride for the £100, Agostini had preferred to race in England.

Without Ago at the Italian Grand Prix, Alberto Pagani managed to bring his works Linto home in first place in the 36 lap race, a Grand Prix first for Pagani and for Linto. John Dodds was in third place and Marsovszky seventh, it was a great result for Linto. Perhaps they had finally overcome their reliability problems, which could be bad news for us! We were not out of the picture completely, Steenson and Chandler were fifth and sixth on their Seeleys and continental regular Campanelli was eighth.

It was astonishing how competitors crammed so much racing into such a short period. Brian Steenson for example had travelled from Northern Ireland on Saturday 30th August, raced at Snetterton next day, and gone up to Oulton Park that evening (not an easy journey), for Monday's International. He then made the long drive to Italy to be in time for practice and the Italian Grand Prix, making three major meetings within eight days and without today's motorways. That was dedication!

Back in the Isle of Man, first week of September it was the conclusion of the Manx Grand Prix events. In Tuesday's opening race, the 4 lap lightweight 250cc event, Alex George the 20 year old Scot from East Kilbride sprung a surprise. His built-from-spares Yamaha gave him endless bother and he hadn't figured on the practice leader-board. Yet on the day, Alex sped his Yamaha to a fine win, heading 57 finishers in all, with a record race speed of 90.63mph and record lap of 92.4mph. John Griffiths from Crewe took second place with Don Padgett making up the rostrum positions.

Next that afternoon the 6 lap Junior 350cc race was held in ideal conditions. 94 competitors came to the line. Starting in pairs with the usual 10 second intervals our own Micky Collins, who had been looked after by Wally Rawlings and our Manx racing service, was among the starters. It was Collins' first visit to the 'Magic Isle' and certainly he was under no pressure. Windsor tool-maker Robin Duffty, Aermacchi, after a huge struggle in the earlier laps with Bill Milne, also Aermacchi mounted, had only seconds between them. On lap 5, Milne's race ended, his bike grinding to a halt. Brian Warburton, Yamaha, and Gordon Pantall, Seeley, were tying for third place. Warburton got the better of Pantall only to retire, the Yamaha refused to start after refuelling. Then Pantall holding fourth place also clanked to a halt, a broken carburettor stub the cause. Robin Duffty won by a good margin from Andy Chapman, Padgett Yamaha, whose other role in racing was to drive the controversial ex-Greenwood Mini three-wheeler. Manxman Danny Shimmin who certainly seemed in line for a rostrum finish, missed a gear and threw his Aermacchi up the road at Brandywell Corner. But in an impressive effort scrambled back onto the machine, minus a windscreen, to complete the race, finishing in fourth, but with the consolation of the fastest lap at 93.71mph. Fastest man in practice, Clive Brown, Norton, suffered machine problems earlier on, but came home third. Peter Elmore, AJS, was fifth and to our delight Crayford's Micky Collins was on the leader-board, bringing his Seeley home in sixth place, only a fifth of a second down on Elmore. Once again 57 finishers! Not only would Micky Collins collect a Manx Grand Prix Replica, he was also presented with the Newcomers Award. Our team in the Island and those back at Belvedere were elated with this result, and pleased for this likeable young man from Kent.

After a day's rest, Thursday 4th September was Senior day. As 87 competitors lined up in the Glencrutchery Road, dark clouds swirled low over Snaefell. Rain was in the air but it would not stop two Welshmen who dominated an electrifying Senior Manx Grand Prix. It was be a dust-up between Gordon Daniels on the Ray Cowles entered Matchless and Gordon Pantall's Seeley. Daniels took the lead from the start with race favourite Clive Brown, Norton, in second place, but he retired at the end of the first lap with carburettor problems. Pantall then in second navigated the tight Governors Dip hairpin at the end of the second lap had a 'whoopsee'. Somehow the front brake cable hooked itself around the rev counter and Pantall crashed, no injury, but a bent footrest. Gordon restarted, but having lost vital time fell back to third place, Gerry Mateer, Norton, snatching second place by a split second.

Gordon Pantall, determined to make up for his disappointment in the Junior Race, got within 32 seconds of the flying Daniels. On the fifth lap, by Ramsey he was leading by two seconds. At the start of the last lap he was over 21 seconds in the lead having recorded a lap of 96.37mph, but Swansea's Gordon Daniels was not about to give in. The last time at Ramsey, Pantall's lead was down to 8 seconds. The mountain section would decide the outcome. Pantall with an early start number was first across the finish line raising his arm in triumph believing he had the race in the bag. As the seconds ticked away it was tense, but Daniels had been given the hurry up signals at Ramsey. Recording the fastest lap at 96.66mph he charged over the line, 7 seconds ahead of Pantall, a great race over 226.5 miles of the toughest course in the world. So with Red Dragon flags flying, it was Daniels, Pantall then Brian Warburton, Norton, making up the rostrum positions. There were 48 finishers, the last being Mick Grant, Velocette, at 70.17mph. Many competitors had received support from Seeley racing during the Manx Grand Prix, and it was very satisfying to have our machines on both race leader-boards.

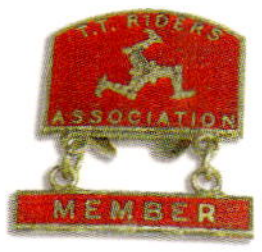

A total of 2,050 laps (nearly 78,000 miles), were covered by the Manx competitors that year of 1969. three riders had been killed in practice; Gordon Taylor, Mick Bennett and Iain Sidey, as well as many injured. Bank Holiday Monday at the Darley Moor Circuit saw the death of TT and Short Circuit competitor, 29 year old Roly Capper who crashed his Honda and hit a concrete-filled drum. four riders in one week was a high price to pay for participating in our sport. Speed and danger were part of the attraction or perhaps we are just lemmings and some of us get pushed over the edge. The truth is that we'll never know, even less understand!

On the bright side, at the end of August and into September, Colin Seeley Racing Developments, through its many riders had achieved nine rostrum positions and eight places between fourth and sixth, inclusive of the clean sweep by Ron Chandler at Crystal Palace, Dave Croxford claiming his second British Championship, Micky Collins sixth in the Junior Manx Grand Prix and Gordon Pantall second in the Senior, and finally Brian Steenson's fifth in the Italian Grand Prix with Ron Chandler sixth - tremendous encouragement for us!

During the first week of September, another of Britain's racing aces, 33 year old Don Godden from West Malling in Kent, was in Oslo for the finals of European Sandtrack Championship. Godden, runner-up in 1967 and 1968, aimed to make it third time lucky. The meeting held on the Wednesday evening under floodlights was contested by 18 of the best riders from West Germany, Denmark, Sweden, Czechoslovakia, Norway, Austria, Finland and Britain. Only nine riders could qualify for the 4 lap final held on a 1,000 metre circuit. Don Godden with one win and two second places topped the qualifying list. On his 500cc Hagon JAP, Godden came to the line hoping this would be his year. The 30,000 crowd watched him, initially away in fifth place, but he soon shot into the lead and raced away unopposed to a superb win, with Jan Odegard and Kurt Pedersen second and third, a great result for our man from Kent.

Following the Italian Grand Prix at Imola the circus sped off to Yugoslavia for the country's first Motorcycle Grand Prix at Opatija, the 3.7 mile Adriatic cliff side course. Motorcycle racing's answer to the Monaco Grand Prix had been completely resurfaced only days before, great in the sunshine, not so good in the damp. Unfortunately for the three main contestants in the 250cc World Championship - Herrero, Carruthers and Andersson, with only one championship point separating them - damp and drizzle greeted them at the start line for the 21 lap final. These three were evenly matched on very different machines; Carruthers Benelli four, Andersson's Yamaha twin and Herrero's amazing Ossa single cylinder. Apart from other lower points awarded for all three competitors to date, Herrero had achieved three wins, one second, two thirds; Carruthers two wins, two seconds, two thirds; Andersson the same, so It was very close. Herrero's left wrist was still in plaster from his Ulster crash. On the opening laps, frantic to win and clinch his first world Championship, he tried perhaps too hard, having some near misses in the tricky conditions. Finally, he lost the plot on a fast downhill double bend section on lap 7. Battered and bruised, Herrero's race and championship bid was over, but what a star. Kel Carruthers and team mate Gilberto Parlotti, brought into support Kel in his bid for honours, weren't far behind and were shocked to see Herrero spinning down the road just in front of them. They slowed their pace, letting Kent Andersson cut the Benelli's lead. For the last 7 laps the contest ebbed and flowed until the Scandinavian suffered a huge tank 'slapper' right in front of the Grandstand, a real fright for him, who in the last 2 laps could not regain the lead. Aussie Kel Carruthers brought his works Benelli under the chequered flag first, followed by Parlotti on the other Benelli, less than half a second behind, with Kent Andersson in third place, but second in the championship. In a different league, 18 other competitors finished this great race. For the likeable 31 year old Kel Carruthers from Sydney it was his first world title, and well-deserved. The hero for me in this epic was the Spaniard, Santiago Herrero on his remarkable single cylinder Ossa machine.

In the 350cc race Silvio Grassetti on the fragile works Jawa four should have been given a medal. Having been narrowly beaten by Phil Read at Imola the previous Sunday, he brought the Jawa home to its first ever victory, well ahead of Gilberto Milani, Aermacchi. Inevitably, I thought of Bill Ivy.

The 500cc race was without Agostini. He was at Lincolnshire's Cadwell Park for the WD & HO Wills sponsored international meeting. This allowed Londoner Godfrey Nash on his 8 year old Manx Norton to take pole position from a trio of Lintos, a couple of Patons, two works Aermacchis and a collection of Matchless and Nortons. With drizzle falling for the 29 lap race, Silvano Bertarelli and Gilberto Milani on the 382cc works Aermachis shot ahead. Godfrey Nash settled into third place moving up to second when Bertarelli was out with a misfire. On lap 7 Milani crashed on the same fast down hill section as Herrero, suffering a broken arm and leg. Because of the difficult nature of the course, Milani had to wait for a further 22 laps and the end of the race before receiving proper medical attention and an ambulance. Nowadays a red flag or a pace car would be there immediately. Godfrey Nash rode the conditions in fine style to achieve his first Grand Prix win. His consistent finish places during the season got him to a third place in the 500cc World Championship, only two points behind Gyula Marsovszky on the Linto in second.

Over at Cadwell Park, world champion Agostini on his first visit to the tricky 2.25 mile undulating circuit, also had poor weather. Persistent drizzle throughout the day made the track treacherous and provided miserable conditions for the 25,000 fans, hoping for some real fireworks between Ago, Phil Read and Rod Gould in particular. Gould still wasn't at his best after the Oulton Park crash. He won the 250cc race after Read retired with a loose gear lever, but troubled with his injured wrist he was then out of the running for the main event. In the 8 lap 350cc race Agostini and his MV leapt into the lead, but our champion, 'Speedy' Read, despite a mediocre start, fought to the front, recording his only win of the day. Ago, a true champion, kept Read in his sights and never gave up, finishing second with all the locals nibbling at his heels. Phil Read received the massive Tommy Wood Trophy and £40 for his efforts; Agostini £25, Ken Redfern, Aermacchi, £15 for his third place, and £3 for the Ruislip 'Rebel' in sixth place on his Kuhn-Seeley – just enough for a few pints of Guinness!

For the main event, 10 lap final of the WD & HO Wills Championship International Trophy Race the track was drying out. Ago on the 500 works MV rocketed straight into the lead with Dave Croxford, Kuhn-Seeley, following. Phil Read made another bad start but rushed through the field, thrashing the 350cc Yamaha through to third place before the two-stroke twin seized, his race over and a disappointment to the damp dejected spectators.

Ken Redfern, the 24 year old Yorkshireman, in a fine performance on a 750 Norton, finished second to the champion, receiving the biggest cheer of the day. Dave Croxford was

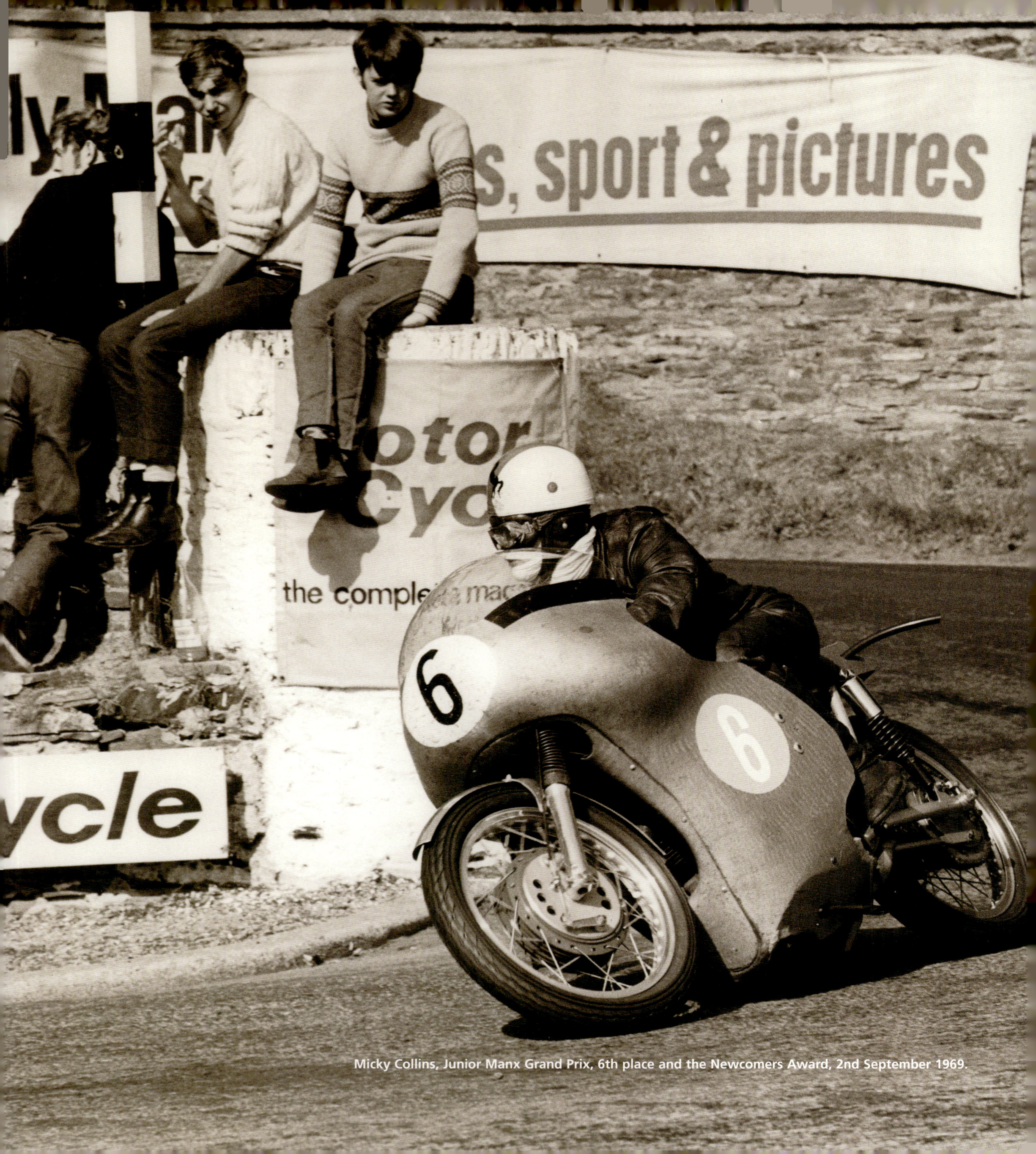

Micky Collins, Junior Manx Grand Prix, 6th place and the Newcomers Award, 2nd September 1969.

third, followed by Tony Jefferies, John Hedger then Paul Smart on his Seeley. £100 and the Trophy was presented to Agostini, £60 to Redfern, £40 meant more 'fags and Guinness' for Croxford and £6 for Smartie in sixth place and £2 for eighth place – such rewards!

Following the Manx Grand Prix, Maestro Mike phoned to confirm that he had reached agreement with Chris Lowe of Motor Circuit Developments to race at Mallory Park's Race of the Year, on 21st September. Could we still supply a Seeley 500 for the event? It would be Hailwood's first outing on a racing motorcycle since Riccione in March on the Honda 500 four. At that time we had no spare machines, only Mick Collins' 350cc Seeley, so with his co-operation the Seeley which had completed all those miles around the Manx TT course was stripped, rebuilt and fitted with a 500 G50 engine unit. As a back up, we borrowed Derek Woodman's Seeley. The original plan was to test at Brands on Thursday, but Mike had a bout of flu and had car racing commitments at Oulton Park on Saturday, the day before the Mallory Park event. So, the test had to be cancelled. Wally and I had considered it a tremendous accolade that the nine times World Motorcycle Champion and eleven times Isle of Man TT winner Mike Hailwood again wanted to race a Seeley. Mike must have been aware that he could not possibly win against the MV works machines of friend and rival Giacomo Agostini, or the likes of Phil Read and Rod Gould on their swift 350cc Yamaha machines. There were also big capacity machines of Percy Tait, Dave Croxford, Malcolm Uphill and Paul Smart just to name a few. It would have been a tall order unless it rained, which always levelled the playing field.

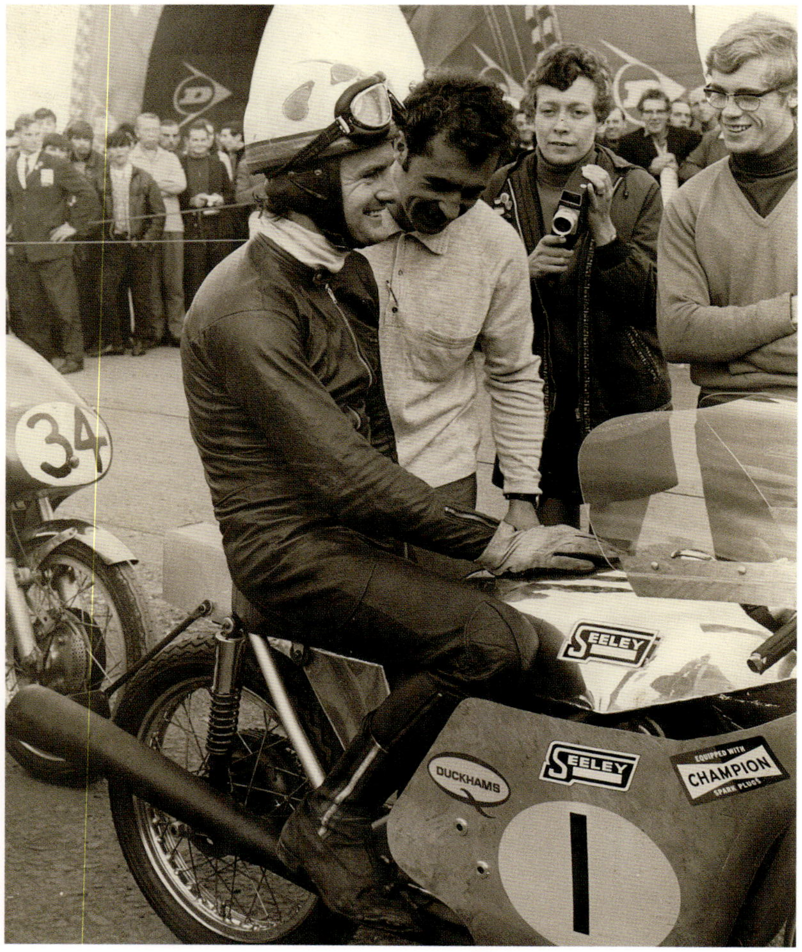

Mike Hailwood and me.

Under our Duckhams Oils contract, Ron Carnell, the company's competition manager, brought the Duckhams Oils' support caravan to Mallory Park early Sunday morning where few of us realised that nearly 60,000 fans crowded into the 1.35 mile Leicestershire circuit for the Carreras sponsored Thousand Guineas International Race of the Year. Mike the Bike decided to use the Duckhams' caravan as his base for the day and once the many enthusiasts found out where he was, they surrounded it, pushing programmes and bits of paper through the windows to obtain autographs. Such was the admiration of our champion, that at one point the caravan was rocking from side to side from the pushing and shoving. Dickie Davies, ITV sports presenter, could not believe it. What a fantastic atmosphere!

Eddy Dow took over the race commentary from the late Peter Arnold. Jack Walton was Secretary of the Meeting and Arthur Taylor Clerk of the Course, with Honda's Alf Briggs as Chief Scrutineer. After morning practice in which Mike managed a dozen laps, trying both Seeleys, finally deciding that Derek Woodman's bike with the short original megaphone suited him better than Collins' machine fitted with the Blair system. Racing started at 12.30pm with the Senior Race for machines 350cc – 1000cc, 62 competitors entered for two heats although there would be some non-starters. Mike Hailwood raised the first cheer of the day, bringing his Seeley home in the first heat ahead of the fast improving Ken Redfern on a 750cc Norton Domiracer, with our own Ron Chandler, Seeley, in third. Agostini easily won his 5 lap heat ahead of Dave Croxford on the 750cc Kuhn-Seeley Norton, with Brian Kemp 750 Curley-Norton third. Heat 1 of the sidecar event was next, then the 20 lap final of the Senior Race, where, as expected, the Italian Ace on the three cylinder MV was unchallenged. Hailwood made a superb start and was contesting second place with Croxford and Percy Tait riding a 700cc Rickman-Metisse. Suddenly Croxford was out with a broken primary chain leaving Tait just getting the better of Mike the Bike and taking the second spot. Malcolm Uphill on another of those 700 Rickman Metisse machines came in fourth followed by Chandler and Rex Butcher on their 500cc Seeleys fifth and sixth. For all this effort Hailwood received £3 for his heat win, Redfern £2 and Ron Chandler £1. For the final Agostini received £50, Percy Tait £30 and our own hero £20, £1 a lap! With a restart at 2.00pm, 10 more events were to follow.

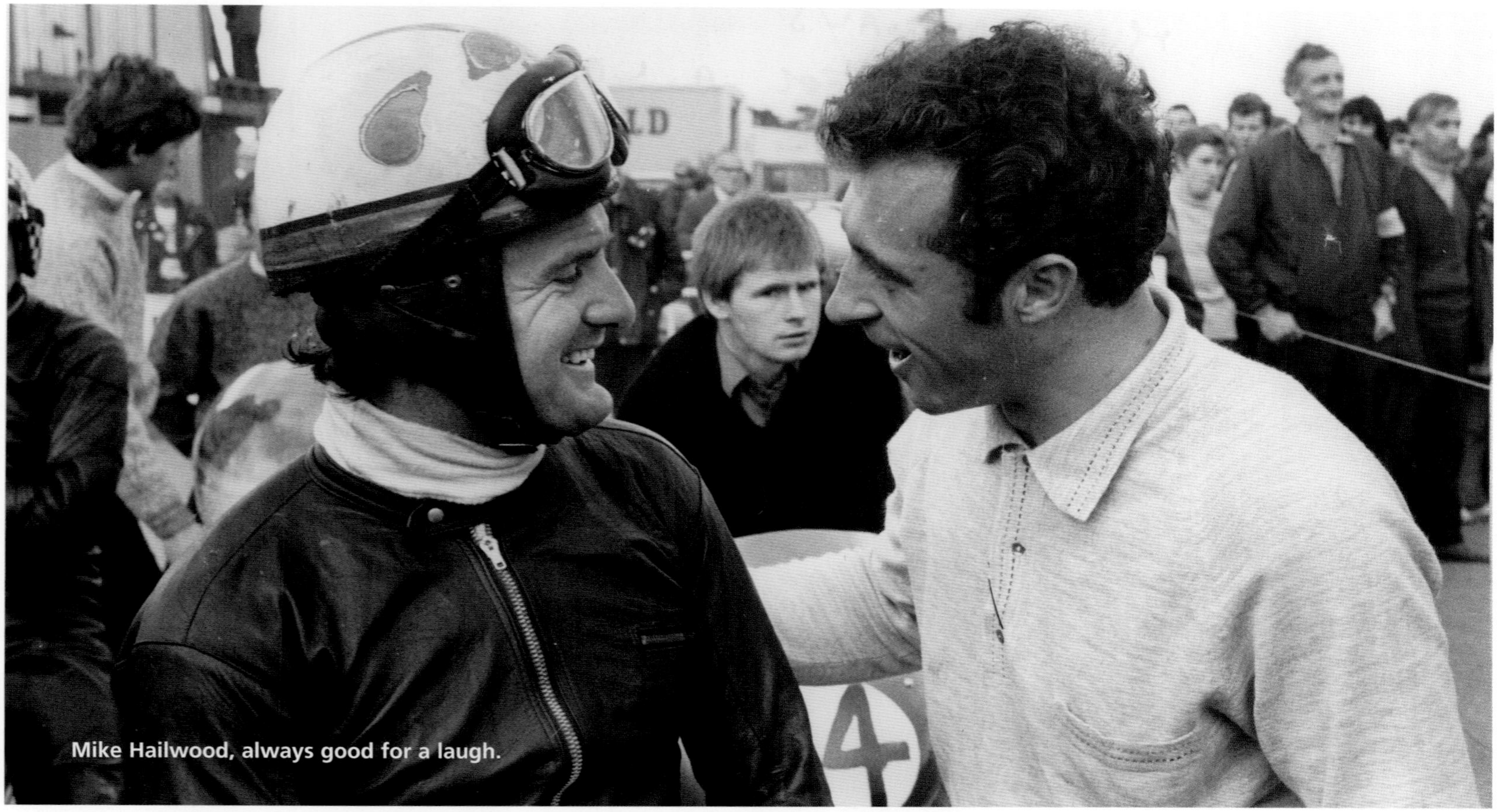
Mike Hailwood, always good for a laugh.

With Rod Gould and Phil Read both winning a heat of the 350cc Junior Race, Agostini may have been wondering about the 15 lap final. The stage was set for a thrilling race. The Italian ace was away first, with Speedy Read and Gould in hot pursuit. Read slipped by Ago at the Esses on the first lap and Rod Gould did the same next time round. Then Ago, lying third, began to get a feel for the slippery course. He sneaked by Gould then set his sights on Read, who to the delight of the fans seemed to have the race in the bag. Then one of the exhaust tail pipes fell off the Yamaha, taking the edge off the performance. Agostini and Gould came steaming by, with Gould keeping the Italian under pressure to the very end. Phil Read was now trailing in third position, ahead of Tony Rutter, Cliff Carr and Kel Carruthers making up the first six places. The fact that a four times World Champion and three times Isle of Man TT winner would risk his reputation at such a splash and dash circuit against the local aces was more than appreciated by the vast crowd. From that point Ago became and would always remain a favourite with British fans on and off the track.

The 250cc lightweight had 12 riders from each heat. Gould and Read won their own qualifying races and were the favourites for the 10 lap final. Read struggled to get his Yamaha to fire up so Rod Gould took the lead, but on lap 2 was forced to retire his Yamaha with engine trouble. Dave Browning, Paul Smart and Brian Kemp, all on Yamahas, fought a wheel to wheel battle for the first spot, Paul Smart getting the verdict by a close margin from Kemp with Browning third. Phil Read, having been half a lap down at the start, came fourth, winning £15. Winner Paul Smart was awarded the grand sum of £40.

The 125cc ultra-light race was a ding-dong between Stuart Graham on a works Suzuki and the new world 125cc champion, Dave Simmonds, Kawasaki, with Graham taking the honours. Competitors for the 30 lap Race of the Year sponsored by Carreras the cigarette people was by invitation only for machines between 100 -1000cc. 24 protagonists came to the line. With much more than the £40 first prize at stake, all the regular British stars were up for a dip into the 'pot of gold' but Agostini on the mighty three cylinder 500 MV got there first, scorching ahead with Rod Gould once more in hot pursuit. Phil Read didn't have much luck, his Yamaha refused to start and he was rammed by Brian Kemp on the Curley 750 Norton. This took some fizz out of the race. Then Gould, with pound signs glistening in his goggles, crashed in spectacular style at the Esses when the Yamaha seized. Gould who had been riding brilliantly, was thrown down the road, escaping with a wrenched knee. Those dammed two-strokes!

Meantime, our hero, Mike the Bike, certainly not on a start money special, was riding for all his worth, wringing the best out of the 500cc Seeley. Malcolm Uphill, 700 Rickman Metisse, Croxford, 750 Kuhn-Norton, Ken Redfern, 750 Norton Domiracer, and Percy Tait on the second 700 Metisse all contributed to a great scrap - one our champion was enjoying! Eventually, Percy Tait retired when the Rickman-Metisse starting misfiring, leaving the fast improving Ken Redfern to claim a clear and well-deserved second place with the 'Ruislip Rebel' Croxford on the Seeley-framed Kuhn-Norton clinching third spot by a couple of lengths from the Welshman, Uphill. Mike Hailwood brought his Seeley into a creditable fifth place, the first single cylinder machine home, ahead of Paul Smart on the 750 Francis-Norton. Agostini, although unchallenged, put on a faultless display, the sound of the multi-cylinder MV, which was music to the ears, came across the finish line to claim the £1,050 first prize. Redfern, the Yorkshireman collected £500, Croxford £250, Uphill £150 and Hailwood £100 with reducing payments back to ninth at £15 and the other finishers received £10. The whole Carreras prize fund amounted to around £2,315.

Chris Vincent continued his winning ways in the 10 lap sidecar event, bringing his famous 650 BSA kneeler over the line ahead of Pete Brown also 650 BSA and Brian Rust with his 650 Triumph. £50 for the 'Brummie' and £5 for Tony Wakefield, BMW, in sixth place or 10 shillings per lap was hardly enough to keep the BMW in spares!

Apart from the Carreras sponsored race of the year, a total of only £526 was allocated in prize money which covered 10 solo heats and finals. There was £142 for the sidecar competitors. With two heats and a final and at least 36 competitors, it did not add up to much for all that effort. Quite rightly the world champions were given appearance money as were some of the local aces. Total prize money of £668 offered was pretty hopeless at such a high profile meeting, bearing in mind that £25,000 might well have been taken at the gate. Good little earner for someone!

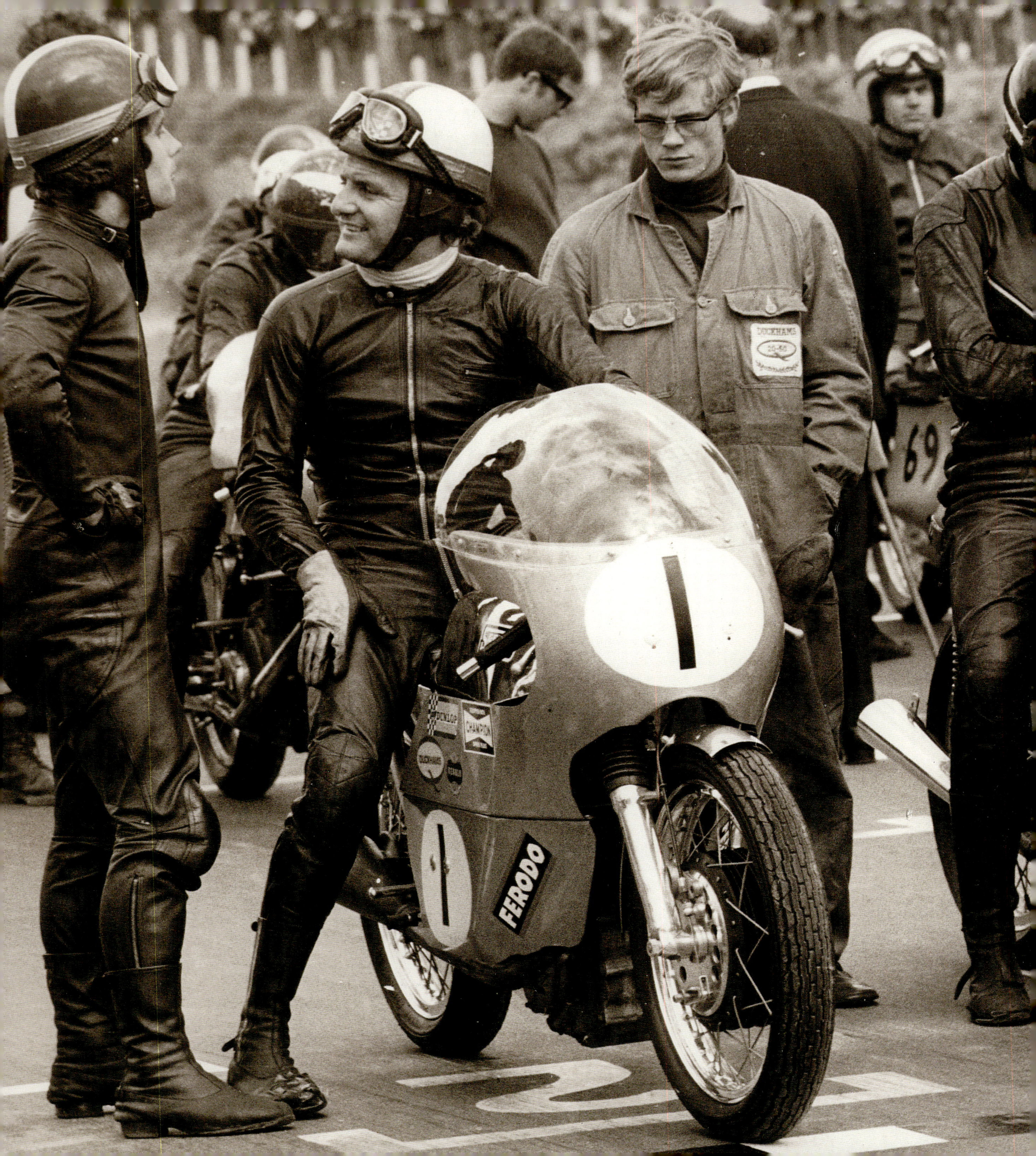
DUCKHAMS
DUNLOP
CHAMPION
FERODO

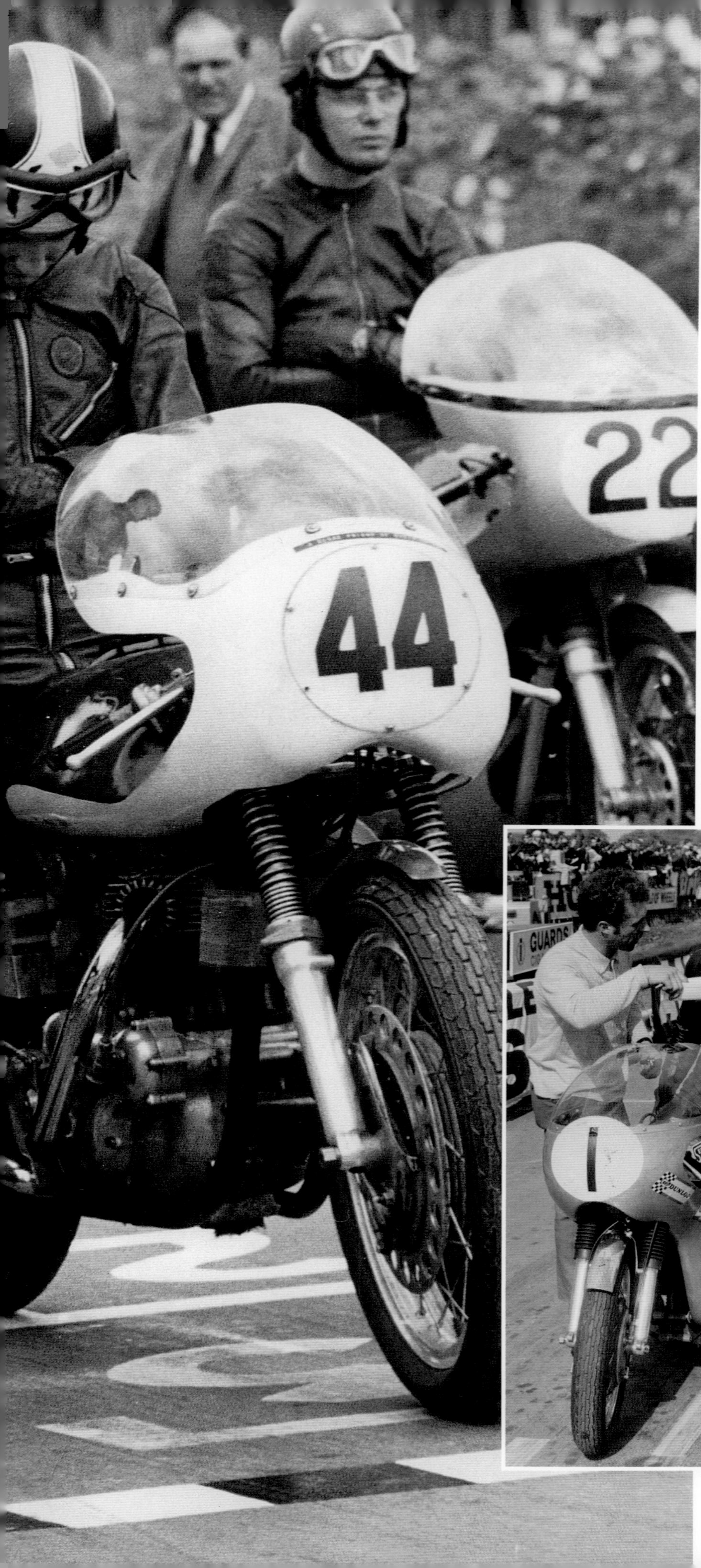

Giacomo Agostini chats to Mike Hailwood, 500cc Seeley, Mick Collins, acting as mechanic for the day, looks on. Ken Redfern, 745cc Domiracer is 44, and John Cooper 500cc Seeley is 22. Mallory Park, 21st September 1969.

The meeting itself was fantastic. Just being in the presence of the world champions Agostini, Read, Simmonds, Carruthers and of course 'Mike the Bike' was very special. For Seeley Racing it had been an excellent day, Duckhams' Ron Carnell was delighted to have been involved, at one of the high points in his long career in motorsport. Wally Rawlings, Micky Collins and myself had something to celebrate and we looked forward to reporting to our enthusiastic staff the next day.

On Tuesday 23rd September 1969 one of the most successful achievements in motorcycling history was celebrated, 21 years of business by Honda, the firm's founder Soichiro Honda having started his business in a shack back in 1948 was now the world's largest producer of motorcycles.

In 1961 Honda changed the world of Grand Prix motorcycle racing when Tom Phillis won their first ever Grand Prix, the 125cc Spanish, held at Monjuich Park, then going on to win that year's 125cc world championship. Hailwood gave Honda their first taste of victory at the IOM that year by winning the 125 and 250cc events. Redman, McIntyre, Takahashi and Taveri all played their part, giving Honda 18 Grand Prix wins that season. Mike Hailwood made it a double for Honda in 1961 by winning the 250cc world championship, his very first. In 1962 Hailwood moved on to MV Agusta so Jim Redman came to the fore at Honda, and with a total of 11 Grand Prix wins, took world titles in both the 250 and 350 events with the popular Swiss rider Luigi Taveri taking the 125cc title – a clean sweep for Honda. With a little help from their friends McIntyre, Minter, Takahashi, Robb and Tanaka, a total of 25 Grand Prix races were won by Honda in 1962, making it one of their most successful years. Jim Redman repeated his performance in 1963 winning both 250 and 350 world championships achieving ten Grand Prix first places and Taveri three. A total of 13 Grand Prix successes was well down on 1962, but of course still impressive. Redman snatched the 1964 350cc world title (three in a row) with eight wins, but with only three wins would have to give best in the 250cc class to Phil Read on the Yamaha. Taveri on the works 125 Honda won his second world title. Redman recorded 13 Grand Prix wins, Taveri five and Ralph Bryans three, 21 Grand Prix successes for Honda that year.

'Now listen, this is how you do it!'

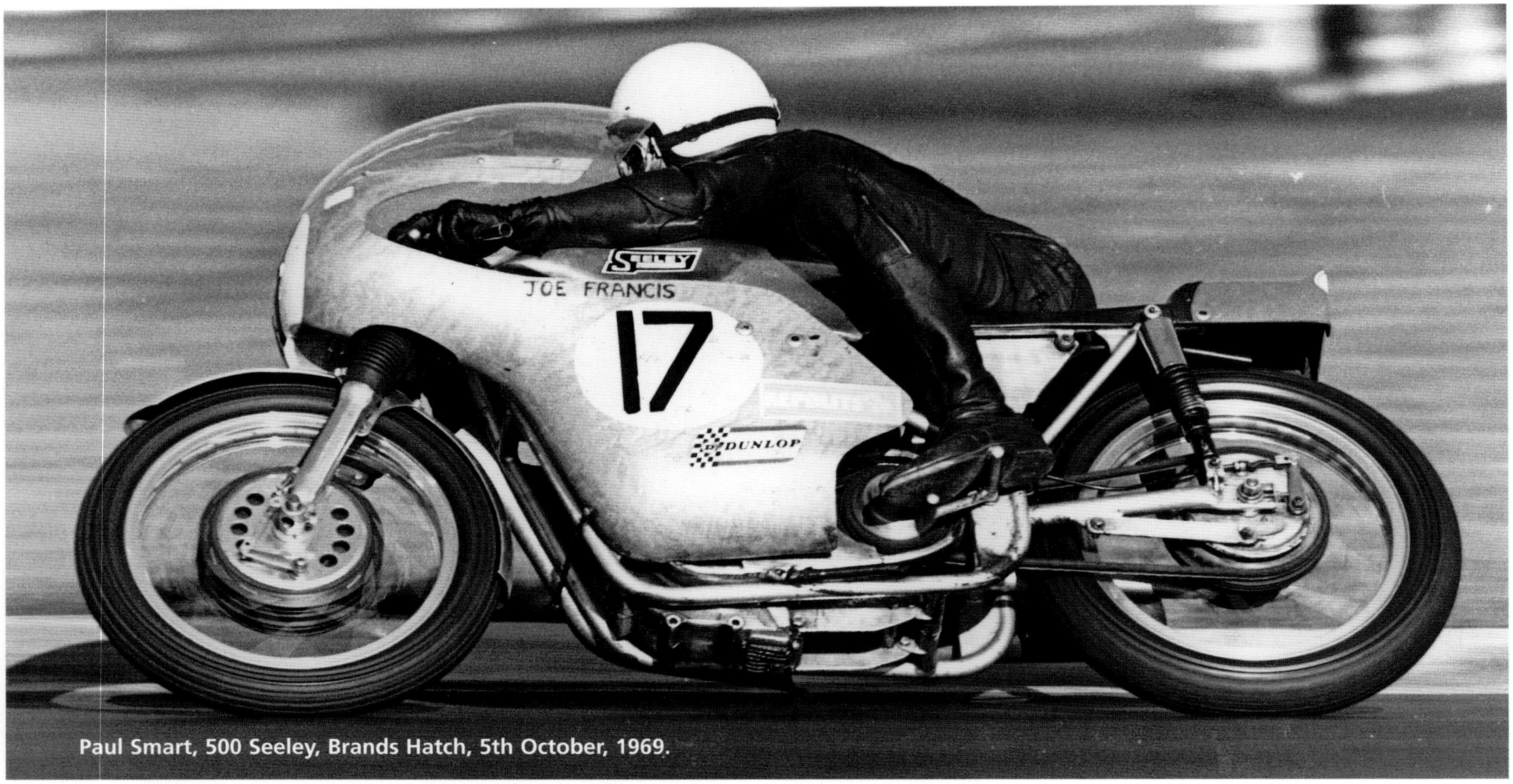

Paul Smart, 500 Seeley, Brands Hatch, 5th October, 1969.

Mike Hailwood, still at MV Agusta, in the period 1962-64 won three 500cc world championships for the Italians, but their 350 MV left the door open for Honda to keep winning this class. Redman for the fourth time won the 350cc World Championship in 1965, with Ralph Bryans giving Honda its first ever 50cc world title with Taveri in second. A total of 12 Grand Prix successes for the Honda riders was the lowest point thus far. Hailwood won his fourth 500cc world title for MV Agusta in 1965. Much thinking must have gone on at Honda at the end of that season, particularly as Phil Read had won the 250cc championship on a Yamaha for the second consecutive time, and sure enough, Mike Hailwood was back with Honda for 1966.

Hailwood did not disappoint, winning both 250 and 350 world titles and coming second to Agostini in the 500cc championship, the first season for Honda in that class. With a total of 19 Grand Prix victories for Hailwood and Honda in one season it was the best ever recorded at that time by an individual rider, (the next best was John Surtees in 1959 with 13 victories). Swiss ace Taveri won the 125cc championship making it a clean sweep for Honda, a repeat of the 1962 success. The 29 Grand Prix victories for Honda in 1966 would prove to be their best season to date.

1967 was the last year of the official Honda Racing Team in that time. Hailwood again took the 250 and 350 titles, leaving Phil Read and Giacomo Agostini once more in his wake. Then Hailwood so nearly gave Honda its first ever 500 title. By the end of the season against Agostini on the works MV, both riders had scored five Grand Prix victories, but Mike had one more race retirement than Ago. By the narrowest of margins, Agostini was awarded his second world title. This was a great disappointment for both Hailwood and Honda, but Mike had performed brilliantly, adding a further 16 Grand Prix victories to his tally. Combined with Ralph Bryans successes, this made a total of 19 Grand Prix wins in 1967, the third best result for Honda in that seven year period.

It was sad to see the official Honda Racing Team leave the scene, not to return for 16 years. In 1983 Freddie Spencer managed to win the first ever 500cc World Championship for Honda. Then in 1985 somewhat replicating Hailwood, Freddie Spencer won both the 250 and 500cc World Championships with Honda achieving a total of 14 Grand Prix victories, a fantastic achievement but still five short of Mike Hailwood's 1966 miracle total. Soichiro Honda must have been delighted with the success of his team. It had been a massive commitment as huge sponsorship deals just weren't around.

Perhaps there was some cash from the Castrol Oil Company, with a few gallons of oil, and tyres from Dunlop, but for Honda to achieve 138 Grand Prix victories and 16 world championships in seven seasons of racing was fantastic. Jim Redman headed Honda's table with 45 Grand Prix wins and six world championships, Mike Hailwood not far behind with 41 victories and five world titles. Next in line was Luigi Taveri with 26 victories and three world championships. 112 Grand Prix victories between these three was a serious achievement, not forgetting Tom Phillis 125cc world champion in 1961, and Ralph Bryans the 50cc class champion in 1965.

For Wally Rawlings and me it had been an unforgettable time, as we had competed often at world level in the same period as the impressive Honda Racing Team which to witness in action was so special. As a sidecar crew we had always presented ourselves in a professional manner. Our outfit was always immaculate and this caught the eye of many solo riders, including Mike Hailwood, who became interested in what we were trying to achieve with our Seeley racing machines, hence our involvement with him, who is still the greatest in my opinion.

In 1969, secret negotiations had been going on with the British Motorcycle Racing Club's (BEMSEE) secretary, Jim Swift and his American equivalent, for a proposed Match Race series between the top British and American riders. The idea was to run six relatively short races, three at Brands and three at Mallory Park, with teams of six riders from each country, as part of the Easter race weekend. Castrol Oil's sponsorship and the glamour of an American visit could certainly add some spice to the British racing scene. A fortnight after Mallory Park we all headed to Brands Hatch for the last British international meeting of the year, October 5th on the Grand Prix 2.65 mile circuit. Sponsored by the Evening News, the event attracted most of Britain's best plus Giacomo Agostini, six times world champion and winner of 51 Grand Prix events, all within 5 years. (He was to continue his Grand Prix career up to 1977 adding a further 71 Grand Prix successes, 122 Grand Prix victories in all, amounting to an awesome 15 world titles).

The half page advert in Motorcycle News the week before Brands, highlighted Agostini

Mike Hailwood on a 500 Seeley, Race of the Year, September 1969.

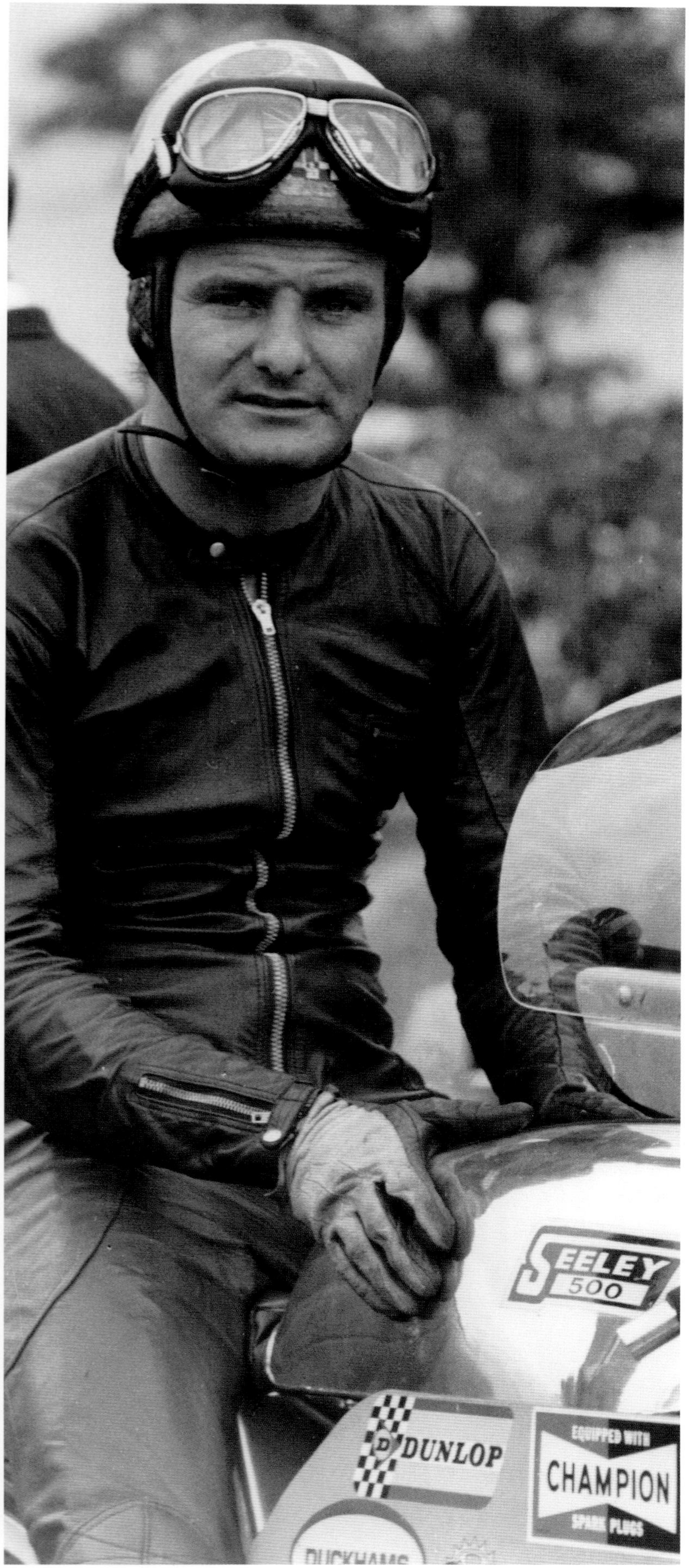

and Phil Read as the main attractions, then Stuart Graham was listed. He had won a couple of GPs back in 1967 but not a World Championship. He achieved little in 1969 but was listed as a star along with Peter Williams and Percy Tait, neither of whom had had the best of seasons. British Champion and local Brands hero Dave Croxford, along with rising stars Mick Andrew and Brian Steenson were never mentioned. Adding insult to injury, the advert mentioned big prize money. In fact the whole lot amounted to £1,154 shared out between seven events and two heats of the 1000cc sidecar event. £75 was the top prize.

On a sunny autumn day 18,000 spectators filed into Brands Hatch, at 12s 6d (62 pence) each, and children 5 shillings (25p). Stands were extra. Honours that day were shared between Ago and 'Speedy' Read. In the 10 lap Junior Race it was tight between the two champions with Read on his 350cc Yamaha taking an early lead. With the fastest lap he came home to win by a few seconds from Ago. 47 competitors were entered for the 10 lap 500cc race and the final of the Redex Trophy which Dave Croxford already had in the bag. Ago's big MV cleared off leaving Croxford, Butcher, Smart and Andrew jostling for second position. Then an inspired Paul Smart on his Joe Francis-Seeley pulled away to claim that rostrum position. Mick Andrew, more or less recovered from his recent injuries brought his Kuhn-Seeley home into third place. Croxford, after a couple of lurid slides due to oil on the rear tyre, finished fourth claiming £15 prize money. More importantly for the cigarette-smoking, Guinness-drinking, E-type Jaguar driver Dave Croxford, the Redex Trophy and the £100 that went with it were his.

This would be the last we would see of Croxford on a Seeley G50. His contract with the Gus Kuhn Racing Team was finished and Dave looked set to race a Yamaha in 1970. Our association with him over two years had been just brilliant,.Dave was a real trouper, and an entertainer on and off the track. He had achieved so much in two seasons, winning races, circuit titles and two British 500cc championships on his Seeleys. Croxford's contribution to the Seeley Racing Company was considerable. Both Wally and I had really enjoyed working with 'crazy horse', never a bad word and friends to this very day.

In the 20 lap Evening News' Race of the South, Agostini took no prisoners disappearing to the front. Phil Read, much to his surprise, had pretty well a race long duel with the young upstart Mick Andrew on the Kuhn 750 Seeley-Commando. Earlier that day Andrew had been presented by Ago with the Grovewood Award and £250 as the most improved racer in 1969. Now he was showing his form, and having caught 'Speedy' Read on the ninth lap entered into a thrust and counter-thrust with the ex-world champion. Finally with the extra power of the Norton, Mick Andrew took second spot and £60, leaving Read and his 350cc Yamaha in third place to pick up £40, not much for all that effort, but that's show business.

With business expanding fast we were bursting at the seams, every available space taken, with people and machinery everywhere. Our Old Forge Works would have been heated by the furnace when shoeing horses was the activity, but we had paraffin stoves in every nook and cranny - a real pain to keep filling, cleaning and trimming the wicks. Our forge with its one toilet was a bit of a throw-back. Manager Ken Burnside and I had been looking at other alternatives, even considering moving to the Isle of Man, where the Tourist Board supported our TT and Manx Grand Prix Race Service. Also Joe Francis, previous owner of Brands Hatch and boss of the well-known Joe Francis Motors,

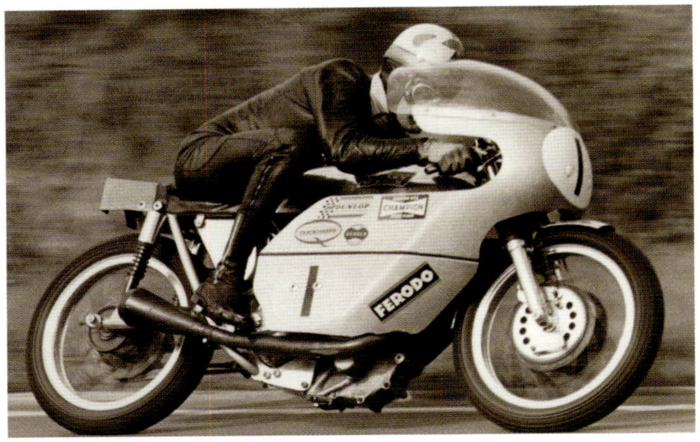

Mike Hailwood on the 500cc G50 Seeley.

distributors of AMC spares, had retired to the Isle of Man. Through his connections with the House of Keys, a meeting was arranged. For Colin Seeley Racing Developments Ltd to uproot and move to the 'Magic Isle' was tempting, but a huge undertaking. After visits and negotiations, a new factory unit was offered, initially rent free, near Ronaldsway Airport - a good location. Housing could be provided at low cost for our key workers and the Manx Government would cover the cost of the move, but in addition I requested a payment of at least £10,000 to make it all worth while. Disappointingly at the time, this was refused. I felt that our business could be good for the image of the Isle of Man with its long history of motorcycle racing. Perhaps it was a lucky escape, but it seemed like a good idea at the time!

Burnside and I also visited Brandon in Suffolk where I had lived as a child for a couple of years at the end of the war. The Borough Council were keen to encourage industry, offering new industrial units and some housing rent free for a good period of time, but no cash. Finally, and probably more sensibly, we talked to the Greater London Council about renting a new unit on the local Thamesmead Estate, only minutes away from our existing premises. We could then retain all our key people, and be under one roof. Our association with Dr. Gordon Blair and Queens University would be a key factor in future developments. We planned to install an engine test bed, grand designs as they say. However, the real rental cost and the length of lease commitment, combined with our lack of funds, meant we decided against it. Perhaps a mistake, but easy to say in retrospect.

Then came some good news. My old sidecar racing opponent John Tickle, maker of footrest kits, clip-ons and all sorts of bits and pieces, agreed to purchase the Manx-Norton package and manufacturing rights, existing stocks of spares, jigs, fixtures and drawings. A consortium of well-known tuners and entrants, all with good intentions pulled out when the financial strain to continue manufacturing Manx Nortons got too difficult. In this life there are talkers and doers. When I took on the commitment of the 7R and G50 engine units and components, many said we would not last more than a few weeks. After three years of hard work, we had enjoyed considerable racing success and had more than proved our critics wrong. 33 year old John Tickle was a good engineer and I hoped he would make a success of the Manx Norton project. The payment from him, although not vast, would provide some cash flow to help us through the difficult winter period.

Phil Read however, decided to drop the Weslake 500cc twin racer enterprise. He had

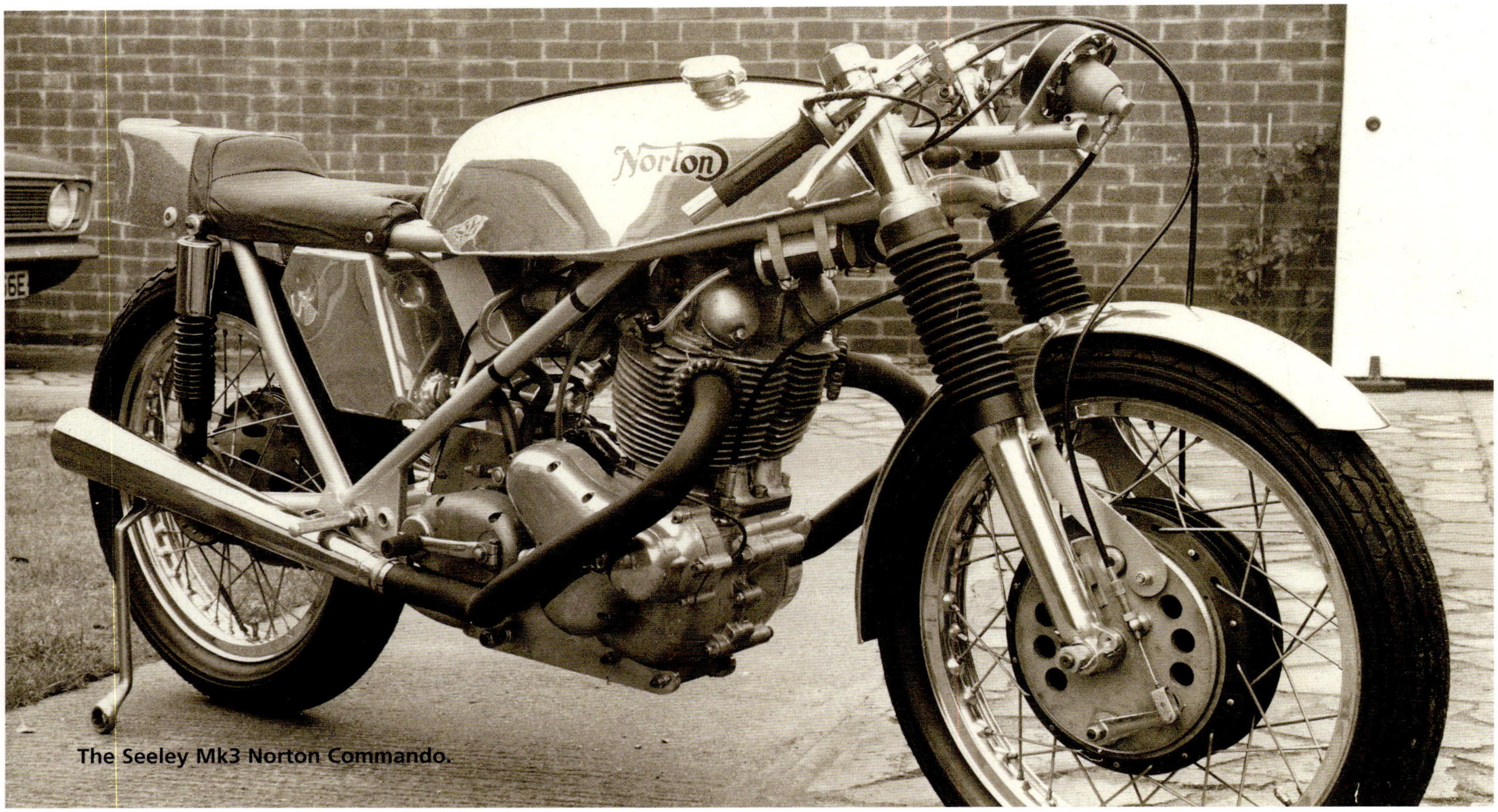

The Seeley Mk3 Norton Commando.

invested money in a plan to help develop and market complete machines to be available by June, priced around £1,200 (£849.15s for a Seeley). By November the project was in serious trouble. Back in May at the North West 200, its one appearance, it failed to complete a lap. The engine suffered lubrication problems and a lack of horsepower. Phil decided to abandon the venture, which had been too ambitious from the start.

John Tickle informed the press that the 1955 Manx Grand Prix double winner Geoff Tanner would be joining him, to be in charge of the Manx Norton engine building they planned to produce fifty Norton machines in 1970. Godfrey Nash, third in that year's 500cc world championship on his Norton was to be Tickle's works rider.

At the other end of the racing spectrum it was rumoured that Benelli was to offer Agostini a sum equivalent to £23,500 to race for them in 1970. Count Agusta on hearing this news quickly drew up a new contract for the Italian star, rushed it round to his home and had it signed before Ago knew anything of Benelli's possible approach – smart move by the MV Agusta factory boss.

Rod Gould who had ridden so brilliantly in 1969, suggested that the circuits should consider having clutch starts, to eliminate the potentially dangerous problem of engines failing to start on the line, a not uncommon occurrance, particularly with two strokes. This was an excellent idea, and one that would be tried out by Brands Hatch, Snetterton and Mallory Park in 1970.

Over in South Africa, Mike Hailwood on his way to Cape Town for a car race was driving his expensive Iso Griffo sports car, when he hit a cow straying across the road. The car was written off, which was a slap in the face for Mike, or was it a cow pat on the head!

October 25th the latest Seeley model arrived, my daughter Joanne, a second child for Joan and myself, to join Colin junior, could they, in time make a sidecar racing crew?

Back in Italy it was all happening. The Piaggio, manufacturers of the Vespa Scooter, bought the famous Gilera firm for £2 million seemed a huge sum of money at the time.

Once more, we were thankful the year was drawing to a close. It had been another fantastic and intriguing twelve months, much pain and anguish but also success for competitors on Seeley machines. We had achieved 148 top six placings including 39 firsts inclusive of 56 rostrum positions - and they were just the ones we knew about!

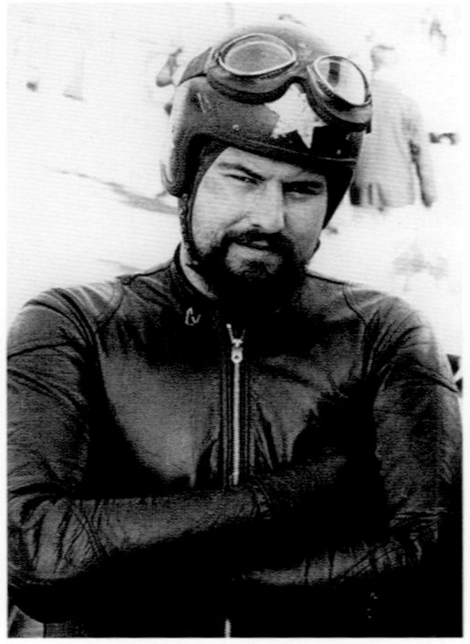

John Tickle.

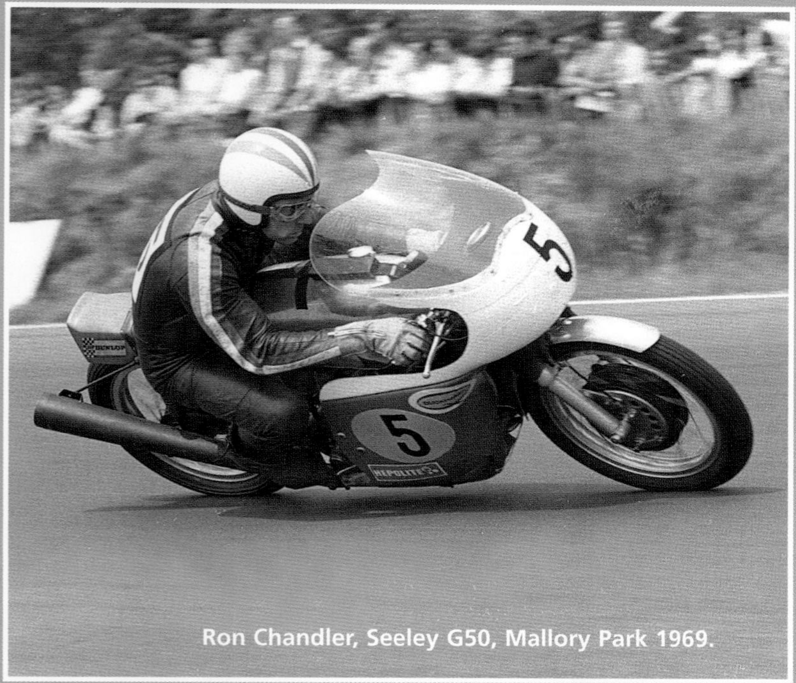

Ron Chandler, Seeley G50, Mallory Park 1969.

We were proud that John Blanchard had won Northern Ireland's North West 200, with Brian Steenson second and John Cooper fifth. In the Senior Isle of Man TT we had achieved third, fourth, sixth and seventh, and Tom Dickie was fourth in the Junior TT helping to win us the Manufacturers Team Prize. Brian Steenson came second in the 500 Ulster Grand Prix on his Seeley to winner Agostini, MV. In the Isle of Man Manx GP, a sixth for Micky Collins and the newcomer's award. A second place in the Senior Manx was Welshman, Gordon Pantall. Mike Hailwood's successes at the Mallory Park Race of the Year and Dave Croxford winning his second successive British 500 Championship with team-mate Mick Andrew third, and finally our own 'Mr. Regular' our friend and supporter Ron Chandler brought his Seeley into seventh place in the 500cc World Championship. A great conclusion to the year for all of us.

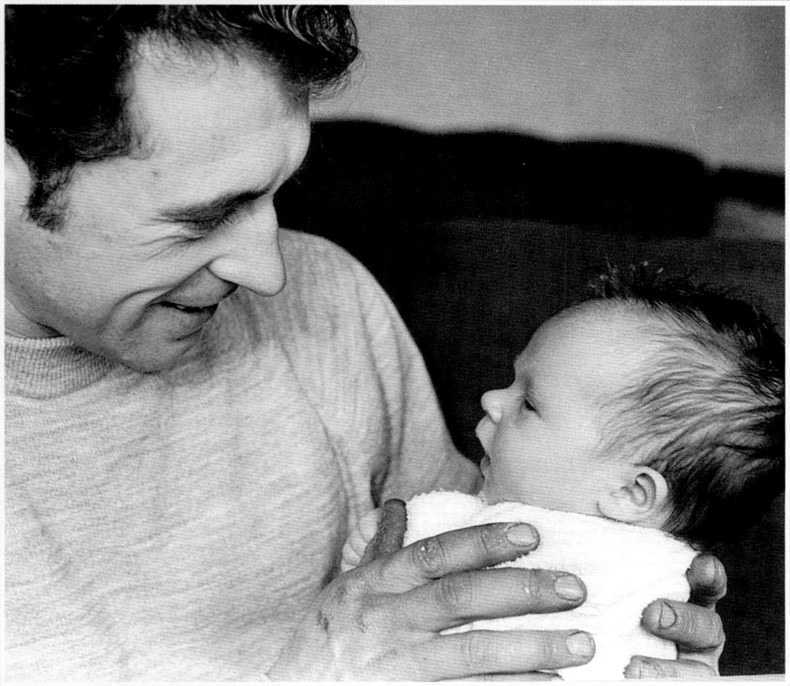

Joanne Seeley, new team member for 1970.

VOLUME

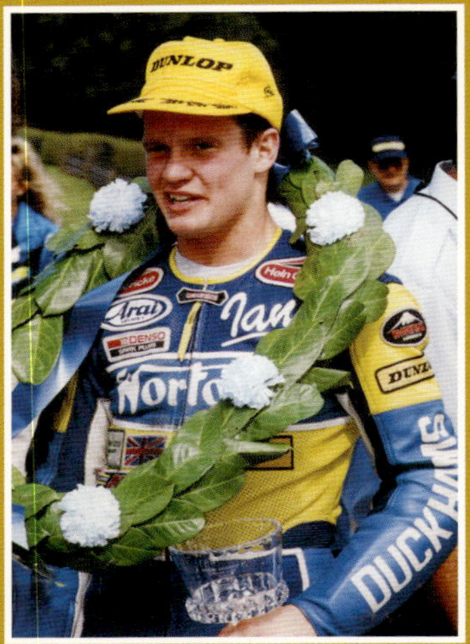

Ian Simpson, 1994.

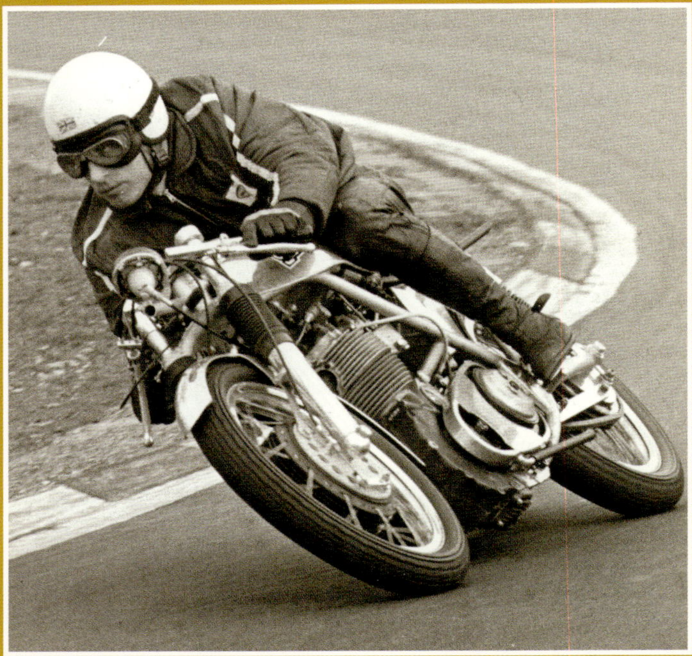

Me testing at Brands, 1970.

Crighton Norton launch, Brands 1992.

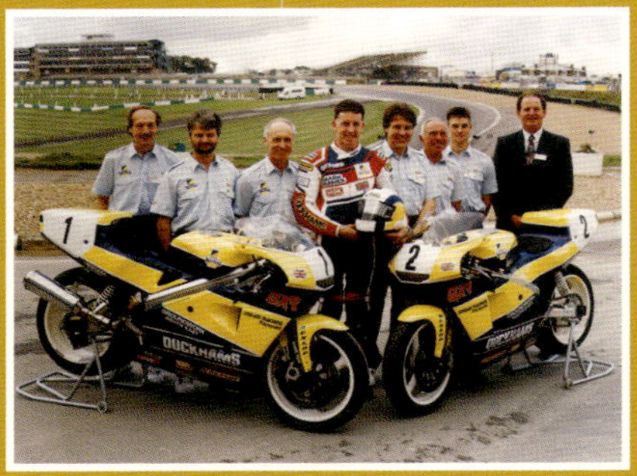

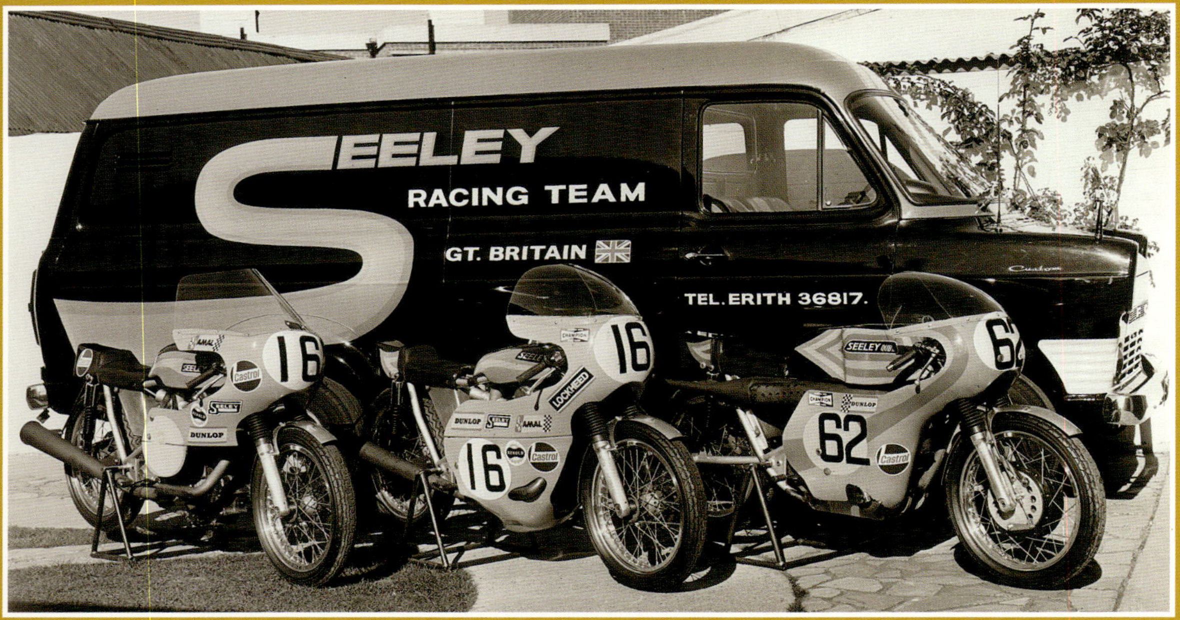

The Seeley Racing Team.

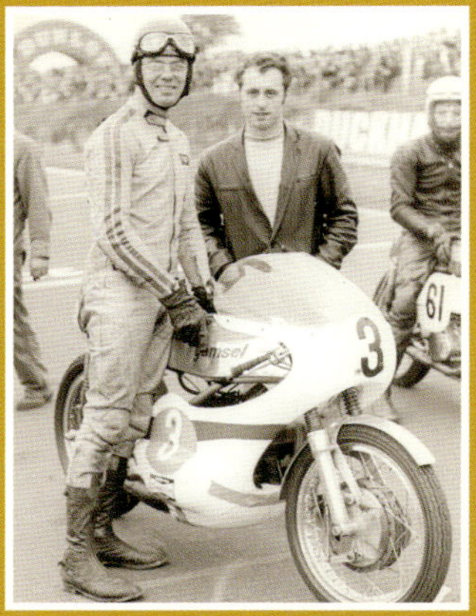

John Cooper and me.

TWO ...and the rest

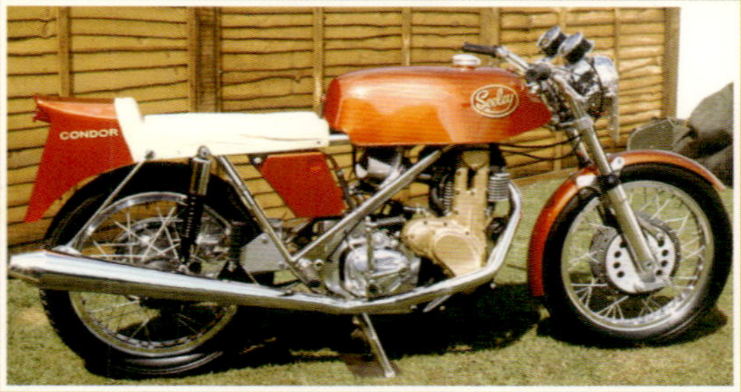

The Seeley Condor, 1971.

Still to come in Volume Two, Colin Seeley Racing Developments goes from strength to strength producing racing machines for the 'Best of British' John Cooper, Paul Smart, Dave Potter, Barry Sheene to name just a few. In addition, 1971, Colin joined Bernie Ecclestone as joint MD of Motor Racing Developments in charge of the Brabham Racing Car production.

In 1976 under the Colin Seeley International banner the 750cc Seeley Honda range of motorcycles were built, leading to an association with Honda UK and the production of the Phil Read Replica machines and the TL200 trials motorcycles.

In 1986 Colin became co-ordinator for the Brabham Formula One team. Returning in 1992 to his first love, motorcycles, Colin managed the Crighton-Norton Rotary Superbike Team. Colin recalls the tensions the disappointments and thrills of Superbike racing in the 1990s providing a first-hand insight into the politics and personalities on and off the track. His inimitable 'hands-on' approach and attention to detail led to his personal support of Jim Moodie, Ian Simpson, Phil Borley, Scott Smart and Australian Karl Muggeridge, resulting in major achievements for these riders.

Colin's passion for the sport is evident on every page and his personal perspective is fascinating. He gives an almost unbelievable behind the scenes account of the decline and the sorry demise of Norton Motors.

Now aged 70, Colin is a motorcycle consultant to Bonhams Auctioneers and events advisor to Mallory Park Circuit. His commitment to the sport and boundless energy continues to be respected and valued throughout the motorcycle fraternity.

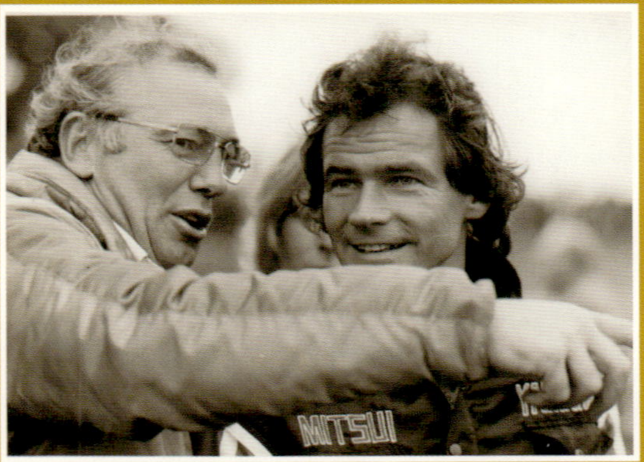

John Cooper and Barry Sheene.

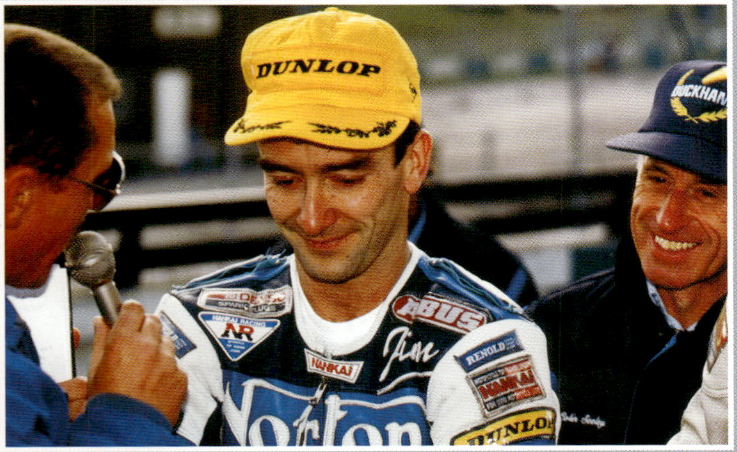

Jim Moodie, 1993.

Index